ALLIED ESCORT CARRIERS OF WORLD WAR TWO IN ACTION

Below: HMCS *Nabob*.

Allied Escort Carriers of World War Two in Action

Kenneth Poolman

Blandford Press
London New York Sydney

CONTENTS

First published in Great Britain in 1988 by Blandford Press, Artillery House, Artillery Row, London SW1P 1RT.

Distributed in the USA by Sterling Publishing Co. Inc., 2 Park Avenue, New York, NY 10016.

Distributed in Australia by Capricorn Link (Australia) Pty. Ltd., P.O. Box 665, Lane Cove, New South Wales 2066, Australia.

British Library Cataloguing in Publication Data:
Poolman, Kenneth
Allied escort carriers of World War Two in action.
1. World War 2. Naval operations by Allied navies. Escort ships
I. Title
940.54'5

ISBN 0-7137-1221-X

Jacket front illustration:
This painting by Geoff Shaw shows the escort carrier USS *Gambier Bay* (CVE-73) during the desperate fight off Samar Island in the Battle for Leyte Gulf in the Philippines, when a Japanese battle fleet trapped a group of the vulnerable ex-merchantmen protected only by their aircraft.

The illustrations in this book have been collected from many sources, and vary in quality owing to the variety of circumstances under which they were taken and preserved. As a result, certain of the illustrations are not of the standard to be expected from the best of today's equipment, materials and techniques. They are nevertheless included for their inherent information value, to provide an authentic visual coverage of the subject.

Edited and designed by DAG Publications Ltd. Designed by David Gibbons; edited by Michael Boxall; layout by Anthony A. Evans; cartography by Richard and Hazel Watson; typeset by Typesetters (Birmingham) Ltd, camerawork by M&E Reproductions, North Fambridge, Essex; printed and bound in Great Britain at The Bath Press, Avon

ACKNOWLEDGEMENTS

I wish to thank the members of the staff of the United States Naval Historical Center at the Washington, DC, Navy Yard for their very kind and expert help in guiding me through US Navy records, notably Dr Dean Allard, Mr Bernard Cavalcante and Mr Mike Walker of Operational Archives Branch; Mrs Margaret Wadsworth and Mrs Terri Schuster of Ships Historical Section; and Mr Chuck Havoline, Head of Photographic Department.

I am also grateful to David Brown, Head of HM Ministry of Defence Historical Branch (Navy), Mr Alan Francis, Mr Philip Wilton and Mr David Ashby of his staff; and to Commander G. I. Peterson, USN, Mrs Katherine Bradley, Librarian, Petty Officer Katherine Liuha and Petty Officer Gary Smith of the Public Affairs Office of the US Navy Forces in Europe.

Others who have helped me generously with information, photographs, drawings and encouragement are: Colonel Rhodes Arnold, US Air Force; Mr F. Bailey; Captain Nigel Bailey, OBE, RN; Lieutenant (A) Barclay, RNVR; Mr R. Bennett; Mr William J. Biggerstaff; Mr E. J. Bird; Mr John R. E. Booker; Mr Alan Bowers; Mr Jackson Brooks; Mr Martin Bryce; Mr Neville N. Bradpiece; Mr Ian R. Buckley; Mr Peter B. Buckley; Mr Donald Cash; Mr John R. Chipman; Mr Jack G. Cockburn; Mr Peter Cockrell; Mr Ted Condo; Mr Barry Cookson; Mr Stewart Crawford; Captain A. P. Culmer, DSC, RN (Rtd); Mr Maurice Daine; Mr W. V. Davis; Mr Joseph F. Dickerson; Mr K. Dixon; Mr Alan G. Dodgson; Mr F. A. Dowler; Mr John Eames; Mr A. T. Edwards; Mr Syd Eldridge; Mr C. Ellis; Lieutenant-Commander Leslie Ellis, RN (Rtd); Mr L. W. Ellis; Mr Peter Embleton; Mr C. W. Finch; Mr Jan Olav Flatmark; Mr R. Forbes; Mr E. G. Fuller; Mr Frank Garbutt; Ms Jean Greenwood; Lieutenant-Commander John V. Haddock, RN (Rtd); Mr Carl Hazen; Mr A. Henley; Commander W. E. Higham, RN (Rtd); Mr C. T. D. Hosegood; Dr John Hotchin; Mr Ken Illingworth; Mr L. Ingram Brown, of *Nautical Magazine*; Lieutenant-Commander R. H. Jeffery, RD, RNR (Rtd); Lieutenant-Commander Thomas Jobling, RNR; Mr D. R. Johnston; Mr D. G. Jupp; Mr K. Jones; Lieutenant-Commander Lawrence J. Kelly, DSC, RNVR; Mr Merleme Kelly; Mr P. C. Kelly; Lieutenant (A) J. D. Kelsall; Mrs Elizabeth Lay; Rear-Admiral H. Nelson Lay, RCN (Rtd); Captain W. W. P. Lucas, MN; Lieutenant Fred J. Mallgrave, USNR (Rtd); Major A. E. Marsh, RM (Rtd); Mr D. Mason; Mr W. A. Masson; Dr Dean Mawdsley; Commander B. A. McCaw, DSO, RNVR; Mr Alan A. McFarlane; Mr A. H. McGie; Mr Iain Anderson McKilligan; Lieutenant-Commander J. D. McRae, RCNVR; Mr J. Mees; Mr Lee Merriman; Mr J. Miller; Mr J. Morley; Mr Ken Morley; Lieutenant-Commander Paul Mullane, USN, of *Navy Aviation News* (USA); Mr Michael Oakey of *Aeroplane*; Mr Patrick O'Dowd; Mr D. V. Oliver; Mr C. R. Parkes; Mr Robert B. Parke of *Flying* (USA); Mr James Paterson; Mr Tony Patrick; Mr Alec Penstone; Dr Philip R. Phillips, MD; Mr Jeremy Poolman; Mr Anthony Potochniak; Commander Jeff Powell, DSC, RN (Rtd); Lieutenant (A) John Powell, RNVR; Mr E. W. Powell-Chandler; Mr Richard G. Ramsey; Mr J. E. Robson; Mr S. M. Royne; Lieutenant-Commander (A) W. N. Sailes, DSC, VRD, RNVR; Mr R. Selley; Mr R. J. Shaw; Mrs Anne Sherry; Mr E. M. Smith; Mr L. Smith; Mr Robert Soper; Commander J. H. Stenning, RN; Mr Frank Stone; Mr W. L. Stroud; Commander E. R. H. Swann, CBE, RNVR (Rtd); Mr D. F. Thomas; Mr Geoff Thomas; Ms Jeanne J. Thomas; Mr Tony Tickner; Mr C. E. Turner; Mr H. A. Vadnais; Mr Gordon A. Waddington; Ms Katherine H. Weick; Mr Morley F. Wheeler; Commander D. C. B. White, OBE, FRAeS, FMA, RN (Rtd), Director, Fleet Air Arm Museum; Mr Paul White of the National Archives of the USA; Mr G. R. S. Williams; Miss Jenny Woods of the Art Department, Imperial War Museum; Mr J. Woods; Mr William H. Wright-Buckley; Mr D. Young.

My thanks go also to: the Fleet Air Arm Officers' Association; The Fleet Air Arm Museum, RNAS Yeovilton, Somerset; the *Gambier Bay* Association; The Mercantile Marine Service Association; The RNVR Officers' Association; Still Picture Branch, National Archives of the USA; The Tacoma Boatbuilding Company; The Taubman Plan Service of Jersey City, New Jersey, USA, for plans of USS *Bogue, Sangamon, Casablanca* and *Commencement Bay*; Mr Satish Bhatt, Mr Dinesh Bhatt and The Letter Press, Twickenham, for their expert help in the preparation of typescripts and drawings; Todd Pacific Shipyards Corporation, and to the following magazines and periodicals:

Aeroplane Monthly; Aircraft Illustrated; All Hands (USA); *American Legion Magazine; Air Progress Magazine; Battle Picture Library; Flight International; Flight Magazine* (USA); *Flying* (USA); *The Hook* (USA); *Military Affairs* (USA); *Military Journal* (USA); *Nautical Magazine; Naval Aviation News* (USA); *Naval Reservist News* (USA); *Navy News; Navy Times* (USA); *Noncommissioned Officers' Association Magazine* (USA); *The Officer* (USA); *The Officer Personnel Newsletter* (USA); *The Retired Officer* (USA); *Sea Breezes; Sea Power* (USA); *Shift Colors* (USA); *Ships Monthly; VFW Magazine* (USA); *Wings of Gold* (USA).

For photographs I also wish to thank: The Crown; the Ministry of Defence (Navy); A. Duncan, Photographer; the Fleet Air Arm Museum, Yeovilton, Somerset; the Imperial War Museum; The Museum of Science and Technology, Chicago; The National Archives of the USA; The National Maritime Museum, Greenwich; Philipson, Photographers, Newcastle-upon-Tyne; The Royal Canadian Air Force; The Royal New Zealand Volunteer Reserve; The Shell Company; Swan Hunter Ltd; The United States Air Force; The United States Naval Historical Center, Washington, D.C.

Last but most of all, I want to thank my wife for converting my hieroglyphics into a readable script.

Kenneth Poolman

Below: HMS *Vindex*. (IWM)

PREFACE

WE left the Mersey on a sunny summer afternoon, the troopship *Volendam*, former Dutch luxury liner, stuffed with squaddies, erks and jack-my-hearties for the Med, with only a brief backward glance at the twin towers of the Liver building. We green ODs of the Naval Draft for Malta had the best accommodation (proper thing too), several decks above the sweaty pits of the Brylcreem Boys and the Brown Jobs. We made for the NAAFI canteen and spent the remains of Casuals grudgingly issued from a dirty pay office window back at Guz Barracks, on ticklers, nutty and the fraudulent Saltwater Soap which was supposed to give you a lather in the salt water used in the ship's showers. (It didn't.)

Then we were out of the North Channel into the splendid sea, shining emerald, movie-blue, and with smoke signing our autographs on the white-hot sky, formed up into a bobbing convoy of troopships, including the liner *Orion*, pregnant with WRENS, WAAFS and ATS, tank transports, freighters, 'Keep-away-from-me!' ammo ships, and the sloops, corvettes and destroyers of the escort. We sunbathed recklessly, to speed up a tropic tan. One man overdid it, and was humped into sick-bay, where he died.

After the sooty squalor of RNB it was a luxury cruise. I read Laurie Lee and Garcia Lorca by the rail ('How many boats in the port of Malaga . . .'), pink knees peeping out of George Sanders shorts, the deck a hotplate for frying feet, the mid-ocean sun scattering shards of hot light.

Then I was aware of the newcomer in our escort, seen as a thin black stick on the horizon. As I watched, a tiny black dot detached itself from the black stick, like a gnat airborne from a twig. The black dot rose and began to circle the convoy. As it neared our section it grew into a green-grey Grumman Wildcat fighter, one of the hundreds on loan from the USA, as was the black stick, our escort carrier, a converted merchant ship.

The small fighter dived, straightened out and roared along the convoy lane past us, at Plimsoll height over the shot-silk sea, its Pratt & Whitney revving loud, a tubby machine which looked, and was, of a ruggedness suited to the shocks of landing fast on a 400-ft flight deck, unlike our own beloved but delicately underpinned Seafire, the navalised version, with folding wings and deck hook, built with golden rivets, of Supermarine's immortal Spitfire. Under my excited eye the pilot sat, canopy open, in his straps and buckles all male and cavalier, lounging in his Yankee leather armchair. As it reached the end of the lines of dipping ships, the Wildcat climbed, an upside-down cross of De Gaulle in silhouette, became a black fly-speck and presently merged with the black stick on the horizon.

The sight of that dashing peelow in his potent war machine changed my life. How soon could I get a transfer?

It came two ships later, after US-built minesweeper *Antares*, which stupidly mined herself off Yugoslavia (only casualty the Chief Buffer, who bit his tongue, our only loss the NAAFI stores, which fell out of the hole in the bottom), and clapped-out ocean greyhound *Kimberley*, 'Cunningham's taxi', sister of Mountbatten's *Kelly*, which was to give me a best-seller. Fuel was added to my fire by the sight of Seafires wing-folded on the flight-deck of HMS *Attacker*, built in the Western Pipe and Steel yard in San Francisco. *Kimberley* returned to the UK, and I passed my selection board for pilot or observer at Lee on Solent, the last Fleet entry to do so before the dropping of The Bomb brought the end of the war and of all Fleet Air Arm courses. All US-built escort carriers were returned – and I have been writing about them ever since.

Kenneth Poolman,
West Humble, 1987.

INTRODUCTION

THE conversion of merchant ships to aircraft carriers, which produced the escort carriers of World War 2, had its precedents in World War 1.

Eugene Ely flew a Curtiss Boxkite off a forward ramp on the cruiser USS *Birmingham* in 1910, and later landed on a platform over the fantail of the battleship *Pennsylvania*, proving that land planes could operate from warships, but one or two planes per ship were not going to be enough for use in maritime war. Specialist 'aviation vessels' were needed. The holds of merchant ships could carry planes, and a British tramp steamer was converted on the stocks to HMS *Ark Royal*, to carry ten seaplanes, operated from the water. In 1914, with the *Ark* not finished, three small passenger/mail steamers, *Empress*, *Engadine* and *Riviera*, were given a quick fortnight's conversion to operate a few seaplanes, one of which made a pioneer sortie at Jutland, and others limited reconnaissance, bombardment spotting, and attacks on shore targets in home waters and the Mediterranean. Other similar packet boat conversions followed, and one, HMS *Ben-my-Chree*, launched the first aerial torpedo attack in history at Gallipoli, and supported the Army in Asia Minor.

Further progress was made with HMS *Campania*, an old liner fitted with a 'flying-off deck' for seaplanes on wheeled trolleys, HMS *Furious*, a redundant cruiser, which added a 'flying-on deck' and operated wheeled landplanes, and finally HMS *Argus*, built on a liner's frame, with the first stem-to-stern, fully-flush flight deck.

Convoys were protected from U-boats in British coastal waters by land-based airships and aeroplanes and the frail and comparatively short-range seaplanes and flying boats of the time. Deep sea air cover might have been possible with *Argus* and *Furious* (whose Camel fighter-bombers destroyed two Zeppelins in their sheds) but they were only used with the Fleet and were not tried in trade protection. On her way to the Mediterranean in August 1918 HMS *Riviera* accompanied a convoy from Southend to Devonport, where she coaled and watered, and picked up another convoy, which she accompanied for two days before breaking off for Gibraltar.

In 1922 the holds of the collier *Langley* were turned into hangars in her transformation into the US Navy's first carrier. With total tonnage restricted by the Washington (1922) and London (1930) treaties, Britain, the USA and Japan devoted their carrier building programmes exclusively to large carriers for Fleet work. In Britain and the USA there were proposals for 'flying deck cruisers' and 14,500-ton trade protection carriers with a dozen torpedo/spotter/reconnaissance machines, and in Britain for the adaptation of fast mail steamers on the outbreak of war and the fitting of flight decks to tankers and grain ships. The US Bureau of Construction and Repair studied plans to convert ten fast (20–21-kt) passenger liners 'for quick action when the war emergency required'. In March 1939 Captain John S. McCain, Captain of the Fleet carrier USS *Ranger*, urged the Secretary of the Navy to build 'pocket carriers' for use 'where the employment of the big carriers would be wasteful'. Five months later Britain went to war with virtually no air defence for her merchant fleet, so vital for her survival.

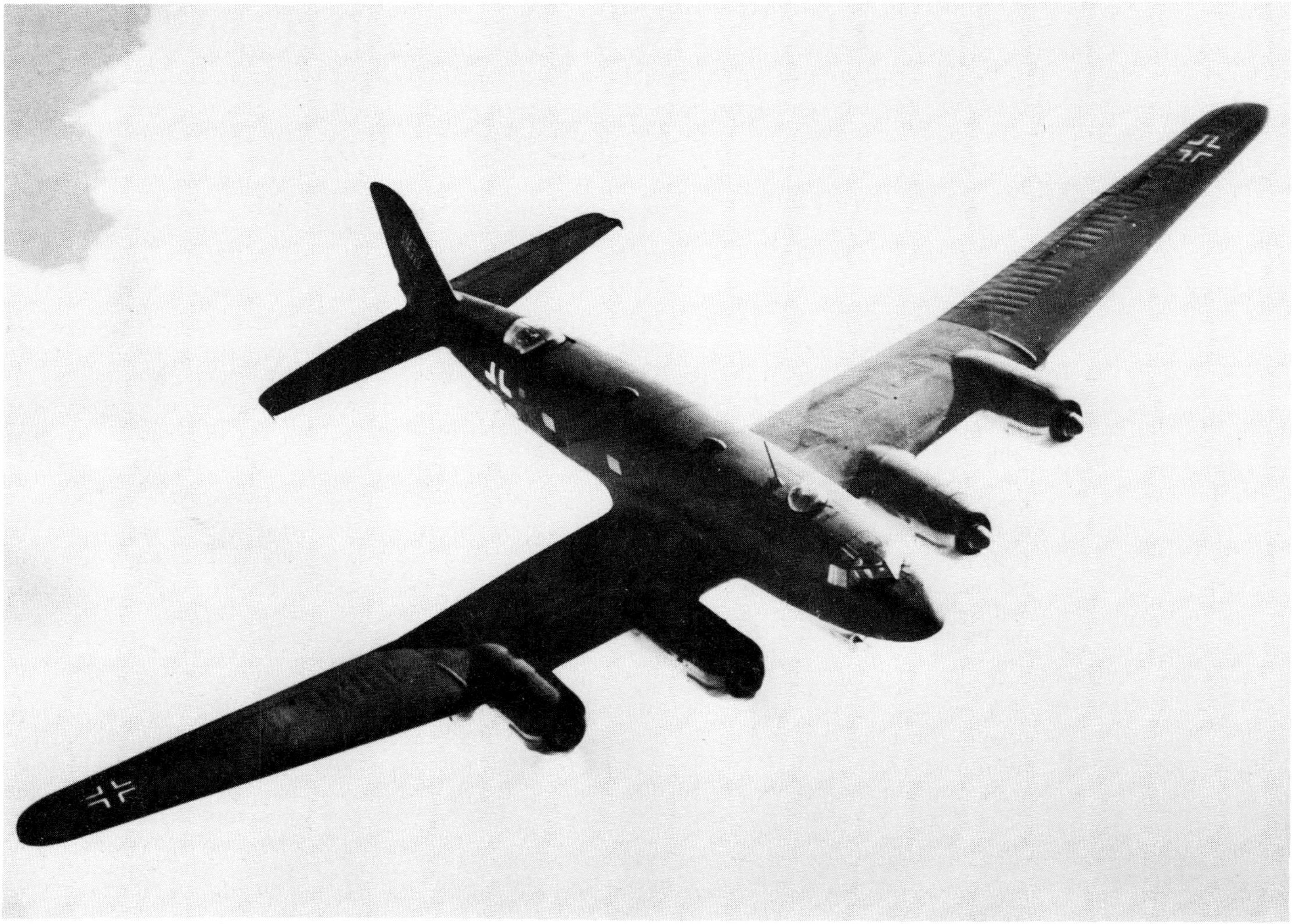

Above: 'The slender, sinister Condor' . . . Technical troubles with the new Heinkel He 177 Greif (Griffon) 'Ural bomber' led to the converting of the record-breaking Focke-Wulf FW 200 Condor airliner as a long-range maritime bomber/reconnaissance *Hilfskreuzer* (auxiliary cruiser). The military machine was officially named Kurier (Death Courier by the popular press), but these names did not stick. The Condor entered service with I *Staffel* of I *Gruppe* of the new *Kampfgeschwader* (bomber group) *40*, attacking Allied ships off Norway in April 1940, and before the fall of France from Bordeaux-Mérignac airfield, flying recce/bombing missions over the Atlantic. The Condor had some success bombing Allied shipping from masthead height with 551lb (250kg) bombs at a top speed of 200mph (322kmh), and guiding U-boats to the attack. But it was unstable on take-off, with a strong swing to port, its rear wing spar and slender after fuselage were too weak for combat stresses, its fuel lines located too close to the outer skin of the fuselage, and the menace of the 'Scourge of the Atlantic', as Churchill called it, declined as Allied shipping gained the protection of fighters, first in catapult ships, then in escort carriers. The version shown is the 200C-I, with a 7.9mm machine-gun firing from a fixed cupola, another facing aft, and a 20mm cannon and a third 7.9mm machine-gun in a belly position.

Below: The Fairey Fulmar. (J. M. Goulding)

1

AUDACITY

FOR the period of the 'Phoney War' the new Asdic submarine-detection weapon helped keep down Allied merchant ship sinkings by U-boat. But HMS *Courageous*, operating as part of the first 'hunter-killer' anti-submarine group, with four destroyers in company, was sunk by Otto Schuhart's *U-29* on 17 September 1939, only a fortnight after the beginning of war, and in the Norwegian campaign of April/May 1940 her sister *Glorious*, alone save for a screen of two destroyers, fell in with the battlecruisers *Scharnhorst* and *Gneisenau* and was peremptorily sunk when the Phoney War became real and blitzkrieg was overrunning Europe.

These losses left the RN four carriers, *Argus, Eagle, Furious* and *Hermes*, all dating back to World War 1, the modern *Ark Royal* and the brand-new *Illustrious*; few enough, and none to spare for convoy escort.

On 12 June, before the final collapse of France a *Staffel* of *Kampfgeschwader 40*'s Fw 200 Condor long-range maritime reconnaissance bombers moved into the airfield at Mérignac near Bordeaux and began to pick off single unescorted ships in the Atlantic, and alert U-boats to the presence of convoys. Their attacks increased when the German defeat in the Battle of Britain led to a concentration on the war at sea.

Right: Two very near-misses on a troopship, photographed from the low-flying Condor which has just attacked her, flying from bow to stern, and is now climbing to repeat the attack and/or report the position to its base for relaying to the U-boat Headquarters at Lorient – a cumbersome process which illustrated the lack of efficient communication between the Luftwaffe and the Kriegsmarine.

THE CONDOR MENACE

The slender, sinister Condors, adaptations of the successful pre-war airliner, became a serious menace, with their range of 3,200km (2,000 miles) and an average load of five 250kg (551lb) bombs delivered from masthead height. In August they sank 15 merchantmen totalling 53,283 tons, and increased the rate steadily, reaching a peak on 25 October when Oberleutnant Jope's aircraft bombed and burned out the 42,500-ton liner *Empress of Britain*, and alerted Hans Jenisch's *U-32*, which sank the gutted liner when she was under tow. In November the Condors sank 18 ships totalling 66,438 tons. They outranged and easily eluded the squadron of RAF Blenheim fighters sent to patrol the Atlantic from Northern Ireland. Ships were routed further north, merchantmen were given obsolete anti-aircraft guns, but, as the Chief of Air Staff, Air Marshal Sir Charles Portal, told the Chiefs of Staff Committee, 'The only method of protection likely to be effective is the ship-borne high-performance fighter.'

One step in this direction was taken immediately. No catapult-equipped cruiser could be spared from the Fleet, but the old World War 1 seaplane carrier HMS *Pegasus*, ex-*Ark Royal*, which trained Fleet seaplane crews and was already fitted with a catapult, was equipped with three naval Fulmar fighters, and on 3 December 1940 attached to Convoy OG47, outward-bound for Gibraltar.

STOPGAP MEASURES

Captain M. S. Slattery, RN, Director of Air Matériel, put forward a plan to fit 'the simplest possible flight deck and landing equipment' – arrestor wires and safety barrier but no hangar – 'to suitable merchant ships', to operate six Hurricane fighters. As stopgaps he wanted catapults fitted to some merchant ships, each to operate one

Right: HMS *Pegasus*, ('Peggy'), originally a tramp steamer hull converted to an early (seaplane) carrier *Ark Royal*, which first saw service at Gallipoli in 1915, a seaplane crew trainer between the wars, when her name was given to the new Fleet carrier and replaced by the more appropriate name *Pegasus*, the legendary winged horse, and a Fighter Catapult Ship, carrying three Fulmar fighters, in World War II. Originally the two steam cranes seen in the illustration lifted the seaplanes between the sea and the forward raised platform, but she was later fitted with an athwartships hydraulic catapult. (P. A. Vicary)

Hurricane, and he urged that 'the merchant ship carrier, a feature of which would be the continuance of its ability to carry its normal cargo, should be investigated at once'.

Hawker were already working on a modification of a Hurricane Mark I with spools and strengthening for catapult work, but there was a serious shortage of catapults. There was also a dearth of 'suitable merchant ships'. The Ministry of War Transport would not agree to the withdrawal of more merchantmen than they had already lost to naval service, and insisted that the Admiralty look at vessels already taken over as auxiliaries of some kind.

The Bank Line's *Springbank* was taken over as an Auxiliary Fighter Catapult Ship, to be fitted with the heavy cruiser *Kent*'s discarded cordite catapult. Four small refrigerated fruit/passenger liners were in the early stages of conversion to Ocean Boarding Vessels when the work was stopped. Three of these were Elder & Fyffe banana boats, *Ariguani, Erin* (renamed *Maplin*), and *Patia*, which were equipped with catapults and naval Fulmar fighters, later changed for Sea Hurricanes. The other vessel was the former German MV *Hannover*, captured in the West Indies in 1940 when she had tried to run for home with bananas through the British blockade. She was steamed to England by Royal Mail engineers in June 1940 and, with all the big yards full to capacity, was handed over to the small Blyth Drydock & Shipbuilding Company in Northumberland for conversion, first to an OBV, then to an Auxiliary Aircraft Carrier.

Meanwhile the Admiralty ordered catapult equipment for 50 merchantmen. These were to be called Catapult Aircraft Merchant (CAM) Ships, and, unlike the RN Fighter Catapult Ships (which were to operate independently as warships), would continue to carry their cargoes, in convoy, flying the Red Duster. Pilots would at first be drawn from the FAA but ultimately from the new Merchant Ship Fighter Unit of the RAF. The longer-term plan was for more auxiliary carriers, for some of which Britain would look to the USA.

At the age of 52 Rear-Admiral Bill 'Bull' Halsey, Commander Aircraft Battle Force, United States Navy, had won his gold wings to make him eligible for command of a carrier, and had strong views on the importance of naval aviation. He had watched the Royal Navy struggle through 12 months of war, and on 13 December 1940 he told the US Chief of Naval Operations, 'If the USA is drawn into this war, the Navy's six big carriers will have to go on active duty immediately, leaving no means of training carrier pilots or transporting planes. You must find some suitable merchantmen and convert them into auxiliary carriers.'

It was a significant echo of Slattery's memo, but about the same time the US Secretary of the Navy, Frank Knox, was telling the Chairman of the Maritime Commission, Admiral Emory Scott Land, that naval aircraft were now too fast and

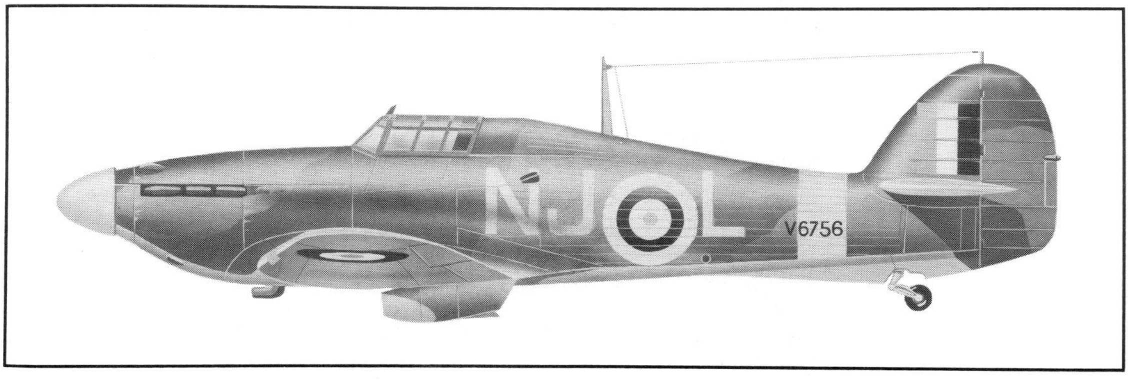

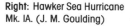

Right: Hawker Sea Hurricane Mk. IA. (J. M. Goulding)

Right: HMS *Ariguani*, Fighter Catapult Ship, ex-6,746-gross ton, 14-knot Elder & Fyffe banana/passenger boat, with Sea Hurricane on her rocket-powered catapult, and another one (later increased to two) in the hold. A Sea Hurricane from *Ariguani* was the first catapult ship fighter to destroy a Condor. (MoD(Navy))

Right: A CAM (Catapult Aircraft Merchant) ship *Empire Darwin* with Sea Hurricane fighter in position on the catapult for'ard. The aircraft was controlled from a position at the break of the foc'sle or in the bridge superstructure. (Royal Canadian Air Force)

heavy for converted merchantmen to handle. President Roosevelt, however, influenced by the other 'Naval Person', Winston Churchill, who wanted the USA to build auxiliary carriers and Lease-Lend some of them to Britain, 'recommended' to the Chief of Naval Operations the conversion of a 'merchant ship, 6,000 to 8,000 tons displacement, speed not less than 15 knots' to operate ten planes, either helicopter or fixed-wing, with low landing speed for convoy anti-submarine protection. Any ship selected should have a sister which could be similarly converted for the British.

THE FIRST ESCORT CARRIERS

Halsey was still riding his hobby-horse, complaining that his *Enterprise* and *Saratoga* were being misused to ferry 80 Army planes each to Hawaii, in which condition they were inoperable as fighting ships. Then, on 7 January 1941 the US Maritime Commission advised the Navy that the modern C3 (cargo ship 137–152m or 450–500ft in length) vessel *Mormacmail* of the M (diesel) type, and the C3P (turbine) *Mormacland* of the Moore-Macormick Line (9,000 tons gross, 150m or 492ft long overall, diesel-engined, with a maximum speed of 15 knots, which normally operated between the USA and Scandinavia carrying general cargo and 12 passengers), could be made available for conversion to carriers. Eighteen months was quoted for the job. The President cut it to three. The two ships were acquired for conversion on 6 March. The first was completed at Newport News in less than three months and commissioned as the USS *Long Island*, AVG-1 (A for a category of auxiliary vessel, V for heavier than air, G for aircraft carrier), on 2 June 1941, predating by a fortnight the hoisting of the White Ensign aboard the first British auxiliary carrier, ex-German *Hannover*, renamed *Empire Audacity* as an Ocean Boarding Vessel, then altered at some time during her second conversion to the simple HMS *Audacity*, which had a fighting ring to it. She was commissioned by Commander D. W. McKendrick, RN, a former Fleet Air Arm Swordfish pilot, on 17 June.

Right: The first AVG, USS *Long Island*, in succession AVG/ACV/CVE-I, ex-MV *Mormacmail*, the first escort carrier to be commissioned, 2 June 1941, with HMS *Audacity* following her a fortnight later. Here two Brewster Buffalo F24 fighters, unsuccessful rivals of the Grumman Wildcat for US Navy front-line service, but bought for training purposes (and sold to the Royal Air Force for combat), form a small deck park on the short flight deck, which was later lengthened as a result of trials. (US Navy)

HMS *AUDACITY*

The *Hannover*, a small, trim, almost new vessel of 5,537 gross tons (total cubic capacity of 100 cu ft/ton), built by Bremer Vulkan of Vegesack near Bremen for the Nordeutscher-Lloyd Line, had been launched on 29 March 1939. Of 144m (474ft) overall, beam 17m (56ft), draught 8.4m (27.5ft), she had been designed as a banana carrier, and her two 2,325bhp diesel engines gave her a service speed of 15 knots. On 22 January 1941 Blyth Drydock & Shipbuilding began her transformation, first into a boarding vessel, then into an Auxiliary Aircraft Carrier.

Masts, derricks, funnel, upper-bridge and other superstructure down to boat deck level were cut away, and a steel flight deck only 112m (368ft) long and 18m (60ft) wide laid down. A small box structure level with the flight deck on the starboard side for'ard, repeated on the port side, housed a combined bridge/flying control, while ducts under the flight deck aft replaced the funnel. She was given a petrol system; a gun armament of four 20mm Oerlikons, four 2-pdr pom-poms and one 4in gun; and simplified arrestor gear. As she was first completed there were only two arrestor wires, later increased to four hydraulically retarded wires aft for landing into, with one more last-ditch 'Jesus Christ!' wire up ahead, which had no hydraulic retardation and would hand out a short, sharp shock to plane and pilot, and a wire safety barrier beyond that.

There was no steam jet as in more modern carriers to indicate the direction of the wind for flying off. A man stood well forward on the flight deck with a pennant raised in his hand, and an officer plugged a voicepipe connected with either wheelhouse into a socket in the middle of the flight deck to con the ship. To compensate for the extra topweight of the flight deck, concrete ballast was carried in the bottom of the ship. Her former holds were filled with empty barrels to aid flotation if she was torpedoed. There were no catwalks round the edge of the flight deck and only rope safety nets.

HMS *Audacity* was 'to be used at the outset for carrying fighter aircraft as a counter to the Focke-Wulf. If and when this menace has been met and defeated . . . the *Empire Audacity* might well then be used to carry TSR aircraft and so provide a convoy with its own anti-submarine patrols'.

Wanting fighters with a chance of catching and destroying Condors the Admiralty pressed for Hurricanes, thought too fast to land on a carrier by the Air Ministry, whose pre-war neglect of the Fleet Air Arm of the RAF (which represented British naval aviation until restored to the Navy on 24 May 1939) had left the Navy without modern aircraft. On 7 and 8 June 1940 off Norway seven surviving Hurricanes of No 46 Squadron, RAF, with low pressure in the tyres but without arrestor hooks, landed easily aboard HMS *Glorious*, steaming at 26 knots into a 15-knot wind. The Navy got Hurricanes. Hawker had produced a Sea Hurricane 1A for catapult launch. Now hooked Hurricanes began to arrive at RNAS Yeovilton, Somerset, the Royal Navy Fighter School, designated Sea Hurricanes Mark IB. Most of the these, however, had a long list of defects after RAF service, but the Navy had prudently taken over a batch of 85 Grumman Wildcat G36As (the US Navy's F4 F-3) originally ordered by the French, and ten of these were allocated to No 802 Squadron, FAA, reserved for HMS *Audacity*. They were renamed Martlet I in British service, after the fast-flying bird which in heraldry is legless.

The makers claimed a top speed of 523km/h (325mph) at 4,725m (15,500ft), but FAA test pilots could get it no higher than 490km/h (305mph), and speed at sea level fell short of the 467km/h (290mph) claimed by some 8km/h (5mph). Landing speed was 107km/h (66.5mph), climb a modest 1,006m (3,300ft) per minute, maximum range 1,850km (1,150 miles), ceiling 8,534m (28,000ft), and armament four Browning 0.5in machine-guns. A general disadvantage was that these ex-French machines, like the USN's F4F-4s, lacked folding wings, though this was of less importance in *Audacity*, which had no hangar, but she later received some of a folding-wing version as Martlet IIs. The Martlet I had the nine-cylinder Wright Cyclone engine, but the Martlet II and Wildcats F4F-3 and -4 the 14-cylinder Pratt &

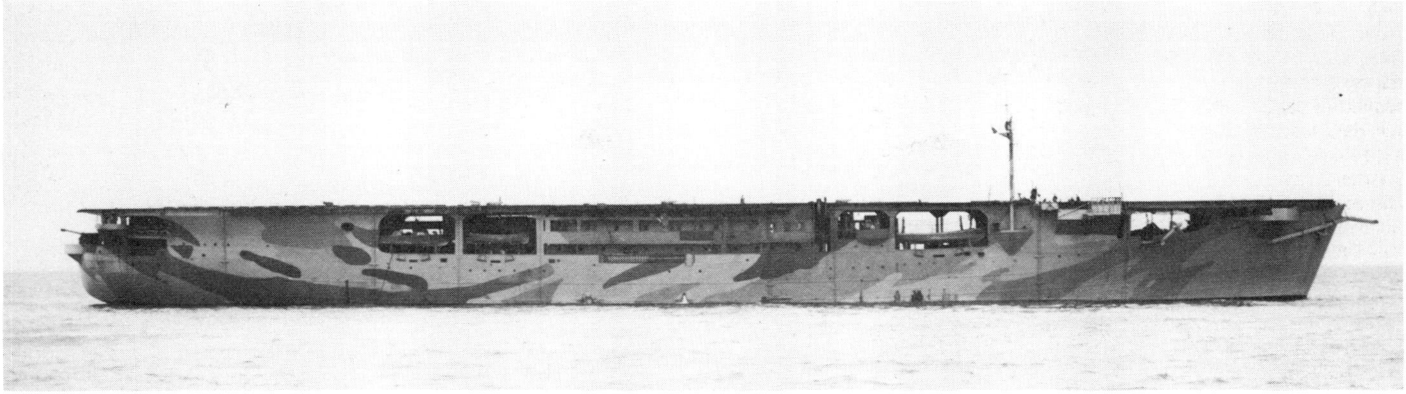

Above: HMS *Audacity*, first escort carrier to see action. Her small bridge/flying control position can be seen just forward of the mast, below the level of the flight deck; most of her original, passenger ship, officers' accommodation was retained, even to the comparatively luxurious cabin furniture and fittings, is conspicuous amidships. She has no radar here, and no hangar, and was a very basic conversion from the captured German MV *Hannover*. (IWM)

Whitney Twin Wasp, which gave more power at medium and high level but was a good 159kg (350lb) heavier than the Cyclone, and the *Audacity* pilots found their new Mk II Martlets generally faster than the Mk Is but slower in the climb and less efficient in take-off.

The squadron was mostly composed of young Volunteer Reserve pilots, among them a clerk, a public schoolboy, a Cambridge undergraduate, a teacher of German and a divinity student, with a sprinkling of regulars, including the CO, Lieutenant-Commander John Wintour, RN, who had spent some time before the war in civil aviation. They worked-up in Scotland in the spring of 1941. American pilots had found the Wildcat a good aircraft, but in unskilled hands an 'ass buster'. It had manually-operated landing gear. Pumping the handle to raise it on take-off with a usually overloaded plane was difficult at first, and it was easy to recognise a rooky pilot by the porpoising gait of his machine. To add to his problems, torque from the engine and propeller made the barrel-shaped fighter want to roll over, so the pilot had to stand on the rudder pedal and shove the stick over into the corner to counter this dangerous tendency. There was also a fierce swing on take-off, which the Royal Navy engineers cured by lengthening the tailwheel legs to bring the rudder into the slipstream in the three-point attitude. Although the undercarriage was purpose-built for heavy deck landings, the mid-wing design and large airscrew of the F4F demanded long main legs with retraction upwards into the belly of the fuselage and a narrow track.

Two Martlets and their pilots were lost in a snowstorm, one crashing into the top of Ben Lomond, the other into the loch. Two more were shanghaied to defend the old *Argus*, which was ferrying Hurricanes to Russia. The six remaining planes flew out to their carrier one mild autumn day in 1941 as she steamed south of Arran. She looked frighteningly small, especially to those pilots used to Fleet carriers, but each man made six landings safely and started to settle in.

There were two crashes during working-up in the Firth of Clyde. A Martlet, approaching too low, caught its hook on the edge of the round-down and tore it off. Another aircraft hit the mast with its starboard wing, pivoted 90 degrees and

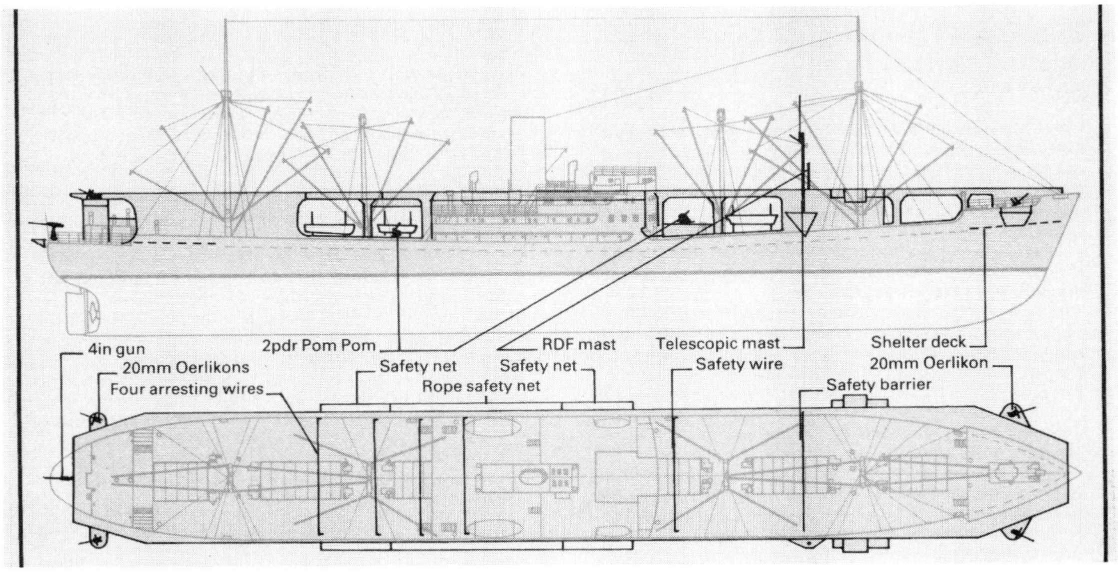

Right: Outline of HMS *Audacity* superimposed on that of MV *Hannover*, showing the basic modifications made.

Above: Some 802 Squadron members and one of *Audacity*'s Martlets. The pilots are (left to right): Sub-Lieutenant(A) 'Sheepy' Lamb, RN, a Colonial Scot and Flight Leader, who had served in the Fleet carrier *Glorious;* Sub-Lieutenant(A) Graham Fletcher, RNVR (capless); ex-St. Paul's public schoolboy; Sub-Lieutenant(A) Bertie Williams, formerly a Manchester clerk; and Sub-Lieutenant(A) 'Pat' Patterson, lover of classical music, in the cockpit. Patterson and 'Fletch' attacked a Condor, its heavy-calibre 0.50-inch bullets hit its weakly constructed rear fuselage, and its tail fell off. Fletcher was shot down and killed by a U-boat's cannon, Patterson was lost when *Audacity* was sunk by U-boat torpedo.

swung over the compass platform so low that it smashed the wood and glass screen. Glass showered on the prone figures of the shaken bridge occupants, and the Martlet spun into the sea.

Below decks it was almost possible to forget that this was a ship of war. The pilots occupied *Hannover*'s original passenger staterooms, each with a bathroom and two elegant, comfortable beds. Adjoining the cabins for'ard were the wardroom and the ante-room, which the young ex-civilian pilots persisted in calling the 'dining room' and the 'lounge', thus underlining the uniqueness of this small merchant ship reborn to defend merchant ships.

On 3 August 1941 the Fighter Catapult Ship HMS *Maplin* sighted a Focke-Wulf Condor as she was about to join a convoy. Lieutenant (A) R. W. H. Everett's Sea Hurricane IA was launched, overhauled the Condor, and shot it down. It was a very welcome 'first' for the catapult ships, which now included the CAM ships.

With U-boats now being built faster than they could be sunk, and KG40 at full three-*staffel gruppe* strength, Allied merchant ship losses were rising sharply. The Gibraltar and West Africa convoys were especially vulnerable, as they were within range of the Condors for much of the voyage. Convoy SL87 from West Africa started with 11 ships and four escorts, and lost four of the merchantmen. HG73 left Gibraltar for Britain with 25 ships and a strong escort of ten vessels, but off Cape St Vincent a Condor reported it and a wolf pack intercepted, sinking nine ships. It was to prevent losses like that that HMS *Audacity* sailed from the Clyde on 13 September 1941 to join the escort for Convoy OG74 to Gibraltar, with six Martlet Is and IIs ready for action out on her open flight deck.

They flew regular patrols in section pairs, the first pair taking off at dawn, the last, two hours before dusk. If a convoy was being shadowed, an extra patrol was flown off. On the afternoon of the 15th, two days out, the ship heard Sub-Lieutenant Lamb, Red Section Leader, shout, 'Submarine submerging on the starboard side!,' then the clatter of machine-guns. Against the U-boat's hull the 0.5s were harmless, but they forced the submarine below, where she could not keep up with the convoy. At dusk on the 17th a Martlet was fired on by a British freighter.

Audacity's shortcomings were showing themselves. Lack of a hangar meant that for a take-off all aircraft not flying had to be ranged as far aft as possible first, which left only about 90m (300ft) of deck. The air mechanics cursed her, working out on the open flight deck in the wild Atlantic weather and damp sea air, which jammed throttles, seized-up guns, earthed firing circuits, corroded gun wells, breech blocks and barrels, IFF switches, spark plugs and contact breakers. After dark they had to use torches masked by blue filters, screened by hand or jacket.

At 18:15 on the evening of 20 September Sub-Lieutenant Lamb, RN, and Sub-Lieutenant Eric 'Winkle' Brown, RNVR, on the dusk patrol sighted a U-boat diving. Lamb dropped a sea marker and the Martlets climbed above it so that *Audacity*'s RDF could get an accurate bearing and distance and pass them to the surface escorts. Two sloops depth-charged and damaged the U-boat, but two hours later two ships were torpedoed.

Next forenoon the rescue ship *Walmar Castle* was looking for survivors when she was bombed by a Condor. Sub-Lieutenants N. H. Patterson and G. R. P. Fletcher, RNVR, were scrambled at once from *Audacity*, and sighted a Condor at about 180m (600ft). They pressed home attacks to point-blank range, with cannon and machine-gun fire curving up at them. Patterson attacked from the quarter, slipped into position astern, then broke off to avoid collision. Fletcher got a full deflection shot from dead abeam, and had only fired 35 rounds from each gun when the whole tail unit of the big Focke-Wulf broke off. The rest of the aircraft spiralled into the sea, and the only thing recovered from it was a pair of white overalls. Fletcher's 0.5s had found one of the Condor's worst features. It was weak in the after part of its airliner's slender fuselage, and in the rear wing spar. These parts had been strengthened in the new 200C-3, but it was still vulnerable there. Three more ships were sunk that night by U-boats. McKendrick wished for some TSRs.

Audacity docked at Gibraltar on the 27th, and left again on 2 October to pick up the 70 ships of Convoy HG74 from the Mediterranean and Freetown for the United Kingdom. In savage winter weather, *Audacity* rode light and corkscrewed wildly, and flying from the small vessel was only possible on six days. RAF Coastal Command aircrews were not used to meeting friendly

Above: This Martlet (Wildcat) Mk I has just left *Audacity*'s flight deck for a patrol. Note the narrow-tracked undercarriage, which caused the aircraft to rock from side to side on deck when the ship rolled. It was raised by hand-cranking, which made the machine 'porpoise' in the hands of an inexperienced pilot.

fighters, particularly Grumman Martlets, over the Western Ocean. Too often they neglected to switch on their IFF (Identification Friend or Foe). Identification by Martlet probably meant yet another wearisome hauling of any machines parked for'ard (to enable any plane in the air to land on) to right aft for the search plane to take off, a process known commonly as 'musical fucking chairs'. 'Winkle' Brown was fired on by a four-engined machine and wounded in the mouth by splinters from his shattered side windscreen. He managed to return to the ship but was not strapped in tightly enough, hooked the 'Jesus Christ' wire and smashed his face against the gunsight. HG74 made the Clyde without loss.

Audacity joined OG76 on 31 October for Gibraltar. Again she met foul weather. Fletcher landed on a deck which was pitching 20m (65ft) and rolling 16 degrees. Just before noon on 8 November a Condor approached the rear of the convoy. Lieutenant-Commander Wintour made one attack from the quarter and one from the stern, setting the Fw on fire. Apparently thinking that its gunners had ceased firing, he ranged up alongside the burning bomber. One of its guns opened fire, Wintour banked away and took a 7.9mm shell right underneath the cockpit. Loudspeakers all over *Audacity* which had been wired to pick up the pilots' victory yells relayed his dying scream. His wingman, Sub-Lieutenant D. A. Hutchinson, RN, closed in and finished off the Condor.

About two hours later Lamb and Brown were returning to the carrier when they saw a Condor below them. They dived and Lamb called, 'I see another one! I'll take the high one and you take the low one!' Accidents, faults and battle damage had so reduced the number of airworthy aircraft that Brown was flying one with a bent airscrew, which vibrated and put an extra strain on the engine. He swept down on the Fw and with his second short burst set its starboard inner engine on fire. The German hid in cloud. Brown followed him in a dangerous game of hide and seek. Suddenly the cloud cleared revealing the Condor coming at him head-on about 457m (500yd) away. Brown put his thumb on the firing button and held on. The Condor's front windscreen shattered then Brown pulled up and just cleared his canopy. The big machine stalled and spun clumsily, hitting the sea with an impact which severed the port wing. Two men scrambled out of a hatch, and the Condor sank. OG76 reached Gibraltar unscathed, even though the *Stoerbrecker* wolfpack had been nearby at one stage.

When *Audacity* was at Gibraltar, the *Ark Royal* was reported sunk by a U-boat in the Mediterranean, and on 7 December came the astounding news that the Japanese Naval Air Arm had shattered the US Pacific Fleet in Pearl Harbor, Oahu. Four days later Germany declared war on the United States.

At home the Seafire programme was getting under way. Lieutenant-Commander Peter Bramwell flew Seafire *BL676*, one of the 48 original Spitfire VBs allocated to the FAA, in deck suitability tests with HMS *Illustrious* in the Clyde in Christmas Week 1941. With the for'ard part of the carrier's flight deck damaged in a mid-Atlantic collision and unusable, the trials went off well and gave the production programme the seal of approval.

Audacity left Gibraltar at 17:00 on 14 December with a new CO for her squadron, Lieutenant Donald Gibson, RN, and four patched-up Martlets, to join Commander F. J. Walker's crack 36th Escort Group as an extra escort in the defence of Convoy HG76. As there were only four aircraft available, and average wastage so far had been four aircraft per trip, anti-submarine patrols were restricted to occasions when there was a strong probability that U-boats were in the offing.

On the fourth day out Sub-Lieutenant Fletcher raced across the convoy to attack a U-boat (*U-131*), which started firing, and just as he was opening up with his Brownings a cannon shell hit his windscreen and killed him.

Next forenoon the sloops *Blankney* and *Stanley* sank *U-434*. *Audacity* was down to three serviceable Martlets, but one machine had to be flown above the thick cloud cover and another below, to apprehend Condors. Gibson's and Hutchinson's guns jammed when they attacked another Condor, but they drove it off. In the grey early hours of the morning *Stanley* was hit by a torpedo and blew up in a great sheet of flame. Walker's *Stork* drove her attacker to the surface and destroyed her. An hour later a torpedo passed very closely under *Audacity*'s stern, a merchant ship was hit and sunk, and at 11:30 two Condors were sighted shadowing the convoy. Red Flight scrambled. Brown took one Fw, Lamb the other. Brown deliberately used the head-on attack as the best tactic for coping with the well-armed Condor, which fell to his guns. Lamb damaged the other, then lost it in cloud. *Stork* sighted another in the forenoon and passed its position and bearing to the carrier, which directed Sub-Lieutenant J. W. Sleigh, RN, and Sub-Lieutenant H. E. Williams to an interception. Sleigh made several stern attacks with no result, then tried a head-on attack. His bullets hits the cockpit of the Condor and Sleigh held on so long that the Martlet's rear fuselage struck it a glancing blow. He returned to the carrier with part of the Condor's W/T aerial wrapped round his tailwheel and a hole in the fuselage further forward. The Condor was destroyed.

The inevitable shadower appeared with the dawn and again Lamb and Brown scrambled. They chased it for 88km (55 miles), as far as their fuel would allow. The afternoon patrol reported two U-boats lying in wait dead ahead of the convoy, which was able to alter course to avoid them. While these two machines circled the convoy no submarine dared show itself. It was almost dark when they returned to the ship, but deck lighting and the illuminated bats of the Deck Landing Control Officer (the 'batsman'), guided them safely aboard.

On dawn patrol next day, 21 December, Brown sighted two U-boats lying alongside each other astern of the convoy, a plank between them, one of the submarines with a hole in her hull. Brown got right above them where their cannon could not bear, dived and shot men off the plank. Walker hunted them and another reported by a Martlet, then sighted a third. The dark closed in, with *Audacity* rolling badly. Brown took two passes to get aboard off the dusk patrol. As soon as he was down, *Audacity* turned to leave the screen and begin her night zigzag to starboard of the convoy. This time no escort could be spared for her. The convoy made a big alteration of course to throw the U-boats off balance, and four escorts faked a battle astern with depth-charges and starshells to draw them off the convoy. The only ships fooled were some of the merchantmen, which fired snowflake and lit up the whole scene, including the iron ore ship *Annavore*, which was torpedoed and sank immediately, and the unmistakable silhouette of *Audacity*.

Below: The end of a Condor. Two of its crew have manned a small rubber raft, others are swimming towards it. (IWM)

Four minutes later a torpedo hit her aft, flooding the engine room. After settling down with the stern just awash, she remained steady. The flooding of the engine room cut off the electricity supply in two or three minutes, and in ten minutes stopped the engines. She floated like this for some twenty minutes, held up by her cargo of empty barrels. Boats with crews in them were lowered, attached by boat ropes, and Carley floats secured astern of them. The ship's company was ordered to Abandon Ship stations, except for the 4in gun's crew. Then there appeared in the darkness, about 180m (200yd) on her port beam, a U-boat weirdly glowing with St Elmo's Fire. An Able Seaman got off a few rounds at her from an Oerlikon, then the U-boat (*U-751*) fired two torpedoes which hit the carrier well for'ard. There was a tremendous explosion which blew off the whole fore part of the ship. The remainder reared steeply in the air. Martlets secured aft broke their lashings and careered down the tilting flight deck. Men threw themselves off the deck into the cold, dark sea. *Audacity* sank ten minutes later. Corvettes picked up some survivors, but Commander McKendrick was washed away just as he was being dragged into a whaler.

In the forenoon of the 22nd a Coastal Command Liberator escort joined the convoy and forced down two U-boats. The Germans then left HG76 alone, except for an unsuccessful bombing attack by one Ju 88 on Christmas Eve. On Christmas Day the escorts left the convoy and the merchantmen proceeded to their various ports of call.

The *Stoerbrecker* pack had been given specific orders to single out *Audacity* for attack. Admiral Dönitz reported, '. . . the worst feature was the presence of the aircraft carrier. Small, fast manoeuvrable aircraft circled the convoy continuously, so that when it was sighted the boats were repeatedly forced to submerge or withdraw. The presence of enemy aircraft also prevented any protracted shadowing or homing procedure by German aircraft. The sinking of the aircraft carrier is therefore of particular importance not only in this case but also in every future convoy action . . .'

2

SHAKEDOWN – THE BAVGS

IN the autumn of 1941, while the conversion of the second C-3 freighter, the *Mormacland*, for the British was nearing completion at Newport News, Virginia, four more practically new C3P & C-Ms, all sister ships of *Mormacmail* and *Mormacland* (all completed between 1939 and 1941), were acquired for conversion to an improved *Long Island* design for handing over to the Royal Navy. On 31 March the US Navy type codes AVG and BAVG were created for the new carriers. *Long Island* thus became AVG-I, the second ship B (for British) AVG.I.

AVG-I, USS *Long Island*, with her hangar, elevator, accelerator and more than three times the aircraft capacity, was a more sophisticated vessel than her British-built contemporary, HMS *Audacity*, and unlike the latter was not plunged into war on completion, but was available as an experimental vessel for more thorough tests and trials. Her 91m (300ft) flight deck of Oregon pine planks extended over the major part of the ship. Her 'half-hangar', open at the forward end, and repair shops were immediately underneath the flight deck in the after part of the ship. Immediately beneath the level of the forward round-down was a narrow bridge. (The BAVGs had a slightly longer hangar and longer flight deck.) After commissioning in mid-1941, she carried out tests to evaluate the operation of aircraft in AVGs, which proved the need for two elevators instead of one, for ease and speed of operations, a longer flight deck and a stronger anti-aircraft armament. In her original form she was fitted with arrestor wires stretched across the whole length of her flight deck, indicating that she was expected to cope with landings over the bow if necessary, in accordance with pre-war American carrier doctrine. These were reduced in number in a later refit.

After escorting the first US-Gibraltar convoy (USGI) she was transferred to the Pacific, and in August 1942 ferried 19 Marine Corps Wildcat F4Fs and 12 Dauntless SBDs to Guadalcanal, trained pilots, and transported planes to the Pacific task forces. That autumn her flight deck was extended forward, and she was fitted with a short radar mast and SG (surface search and SC (air search) sets the latter of which was replaced by SC-2 before the end of the war.

On 26 December 1941, in the wave of new building after Pearl Harbor, the American Secretary of the Navy signed contracts for the conver-

Below: HMS *Archer*, BAVG-I.

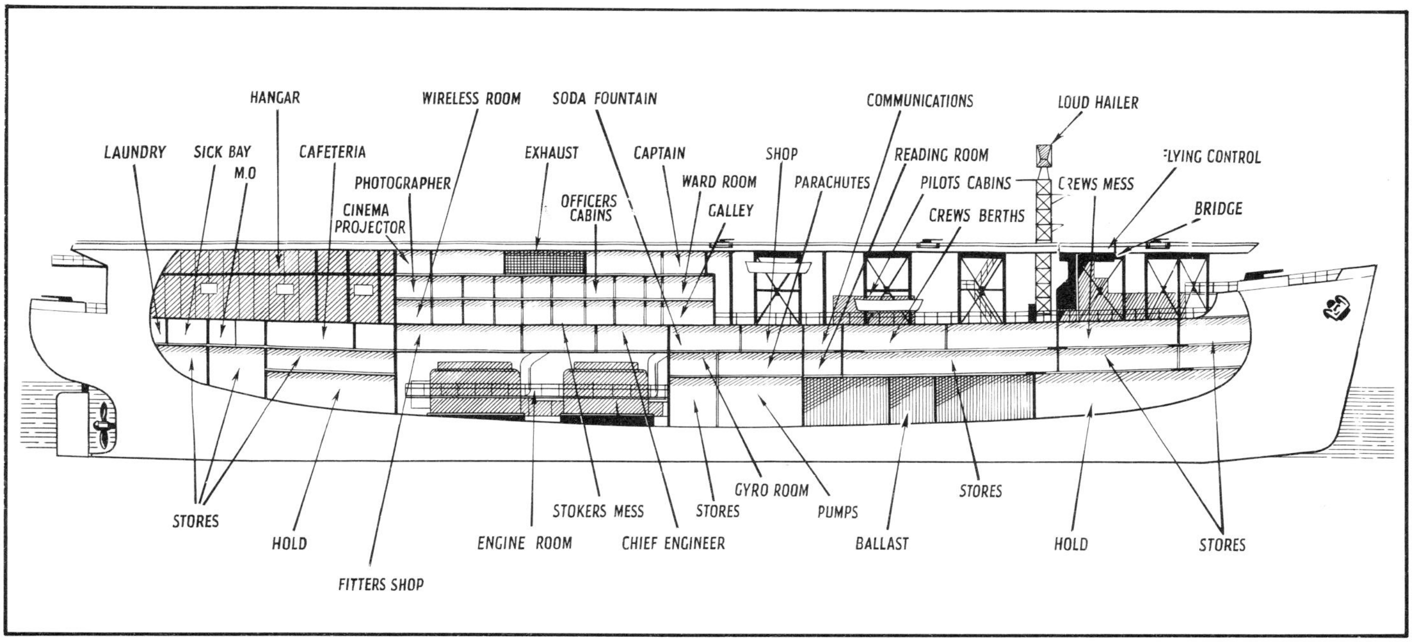

Above: Homemade instant bridge on *Archer*, set up in the centre of the flight deck when flying was not in progress. (Cdr. A. C. R. Duvall)

sion of 24 more merchantmen to AVGs. Only 20 of these C3-S-A1s were available for immediate conversion. Ten were allocated to the Royal Navy, ten to the US Navy. Some of these had not been launched when modifications for their new role began, and conversion measures could be carried out more rapidly on them than on the BAVGs. Meanwhile, to acquire some more escort carriers quickly, as the first of the C-3 conversions were not likely to be in commission before the winter of 1942, the US Auxiliary Vessels Board acquired four new tankers, already taken over and in service as naval oilers, for accelerated conversion to AVGs.

The first five BAVGs were larger than *Audacity*. BAVG-1 was of 9,000 tons displacement, BAVG-2 to -5 of 8,200 tons. The sister ships were 150m (492.5ft) in length and 18m (60ft) in the beam. Like *Long Island* their flight decks, 125m (410ft) long, 26.5m (87ft) wide, were planked with Oregon pine. Each ship incorporated a 'half-hangar', extending about a third of the ship's length under the flight deck, one elevator, and one accelerator at the forward end of the flight deck to port. BAVGs-1 and -2 had a small combined bridge/flying control platform flush with the flight deck and overhanging the sea to starboard, similar to *Audacity*'s, its weight balanced by a room-full of pig iron on the port side below decks. An 'instant bridge' composed of portable screens was set up in the middle of *Archer*'s flight deck when flying was not in progress. All the other BAVGs had a small, narrow bridge island tower to starboard, repeated in principle in all other auxiliary carrier bridges. Diesel engines gave a maximum speed of 16½–17 knots. Each ship was to carry a squadron of 15 aircraft. Gun armament consisted originally of three single 4in anti-aircraft guns and 15 20mm Oerlikons (four twin and seven single).

BAVG-I commissioned at Norfolk, Virginia, on 17 November 1941 as HMS *Archer*. Her Captain was J. I. 'Streamline' Robertson, who had been the new Fleet carrier HMS *Illustrious*' first Commander (Air). BAVG-2, ex-*Rio Hudson*, was due to complete on 2 March 1942, BAVG-3, ex-*Rio Parana*, on 1 May 1942, and BAVG-5, ex-*Rio de Janeiro*, on 1 July 1942.

Equipment and Machinery Failures

When *Audacity* was sunk on 22 December in the bitter battle for HG76, *Archer* was in Hampton Roads on her trials. The ship's original funnel had been removed and its exhausts split to emerge on either side of the flight deck amidships. It was soon found that when maximum speed was wanted for flying operations the ship's diesels produced volumes of black smoke which tended to engulf the flight deck, and aircraft often had to make several darts at the deck to land on because the pilot could see neither the batsman nor the deck. On Sunday the 23rd three US Navy Wildcats joined her for deck landing and accelerator trials. On the first launch the catapult misfired and the fighter was released prematurely, plunging into the sea and drowning its pilot, Lieutenant-Commander J. J. McRoberts, USN. Able Seaman Giddings dived over the side and made repeated plunges, but without success.

After repairs to the catapult and successful trials, *Archer* left Hampton Roads for Jamaica, where her squadron, No 834, was practising anti-submarine patrols with four Swordfish. First her gyro compass failed, then her Busche-Sultzer diesel broke down, partly under the strain of

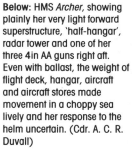

Below: HMS *Archer*, showing plainly her very light forward superstructure, 'half-hangar', radar tower and one of her three 4in AA guns right aft. Even with ballast, the weight of flight deck, hangar, aircraft and aircraft stores made movement in a choppy sea lively and her response to the helm uncertain. (Cdr. A. C. R. Duvall)

trying to squeeze another knot and a half out of it to help the Swordfish limp off the deck. Both were repaired at Norfolk, then the steering gear broke down and the gyro failed again. Both were repaired, then the radar gave up and *Archer* collided with the Peruvian steamer *Brazos* and was holed in the bows, being finally towed into Charleston.

Archer's new ship's company found her clean and spotless throughout, and she was fully supplied and victualled with American stores. As the *Mormacland* she had carried 12 passengers in some luxury, in addition to her general cargo, and her original staterooms were still more comfortable than the average warship's accommodation, each with a shower and a large bunk and supplied with new, soft, thick blankets. The ship's cook found a lavishly equipped galley, with a gleaming new set of American pots and pans. The china would have graced a five-star hotel, and the sugar bowls were full.

Germany had by now turned her main U-boat offensive on to the stream of shipping passing along the eastern coasts of the Americas, carrying petrol and oil from the Gulf of Mexico for the Allied war effort, aluminium ore from Brazil and the Guianas. This vital pipeline was severely damaged. In January 1942 U-boats sank 320,000 tons of Allied shipping, in February about 500,000 tons, most of it off the American coast or in the Caribbean.

The Atlantic convoys, temporarily spared heavy U-boat attack, were suffering more attacks by land-based aircraft. In February the Fw 200C-3 was superseded by the C-4, the best version of the Condor, with a potential range of 4,440km (2,760 miles) and an extra 13mm cannon.

The rate of production of the new Lease-Lend BAVGs was slower than expected, and the Admiralty turned to Captain Slattery's idea for a merchant ship aircraft carrier which could also carry normal cargo. Two 7–8,000 ton, 10½–12 knot grain ships, which were loaded through trunk hoses and could be fitted with flight decks, were selected to operate four Swordfish apiece. John Lamb, Marine Superintendent of the Anglo-Saxon

Right: 'I don't mind if I do'. HRH King George VI behind the wardroom bar on a tour of HMS *Archer* conducted by her Captain, former Swordfish pilot and Commander(F) of HMS *Illustrious*; Commander 'Streamline' Robertson (left).

Right: Swordfish about to leave *Archer*'s deck, taken from the rear cockpit of its predecessor. (Cdr. A. C. R. Duvall)

Above: A contemporary drawing by Roland Davies for the *Illustrated London News* of the idea for a Merchant Aircraft Carrier converted from a grain ship. Cargo was to be carried in eight large holds, filled through trunkways extending to the flight deck, where flush watertight hatch covers would be fitted. The cellular double bottom extended fore and aft and was arranged to carry water ballast, oil fuel and fresh water in their appropriate tanks. The space between the second and upper decks was principally allocated to stores. the hangar contained ample space for up to four wingfolded Swordfish and aircraft spares, including such large items as wings and tailplanes. A hangar hoist 42ft by 20t was specified to transport aircraft to and from the flight deck, for which a minimum length of 422ft and width of 62ft was required, with a minimum freeboard of 28ft 6in at the forward end above the load waterline when the ship was in service condition.

Below: Vertical view of HMS *Archer*. Note the arrester wires, forward barriers and the single lift well, through which all aircraft movement between hangar and flight deck had to be made – often with frustrating effects on operations.

Petroleum Company, heard about them and said at a meeting of the Petroleum Board, 'What about doing it with tankers?' The Board was enthusiastic. The Admiralty and Ministry of War Transport raised objections on grounds of possible fire risk but as shipping losses mounted, changed their minds, selected six Anglo Petroleum 12,000 ton (deadweight) tankers, and increased the grain ship conversions to six.

The quality of RAF Hurricanes selected for navalisation had improved from 'clapped-out' to 'serviceable', and it was hoped to send the first operational squadron on the next Russian convoy in *Avenger*, after they had been anglicised. *Avenger* was herself used to test the suitability for the small carriers. 'Winkle' Brown, who had won the DSC flying from *Audacity* and was currently testing all operational Fleet Air Arm machines aboard each jeep carrier before she went into service, found that with reasonable care a Sea Hurricane could be flown from a BAVG quite successfully. As a carrier-borne fighter it was a strongly-built machine, with a sturdy, wide-tracked undercarriage to absorb the shocks of deck-landing and make taxying easy though it was short on range, a harsh staller, and its various air scoops on the underside made it a bad ditcher. A Martlet's 'sting' type arrestor hook was in its tail, the best location for picking up a wire, but the Sea Hurricane IB's hook was attached half-way up the fuselage, making it necessary to approach the deck in a nose-up, three-point attitude which gave the pilot a poor view of the deck. A short turn on to the deck or a crabbing approach to give a view of the deck over the wing roots was not recommended, as a sharp use of rudder produced a tricky increase in nose heaviness, and straight-and-level approach, accepting the handicap of the bad view, was the drill. The right height and a gentle touch on the controls were essential, as the undercarriage had a lively bounce.

Archer, after repeated engine troubles, reached New York on 15 July and went into a small private yard in Hoboken, New Jersey, opposite Times Square. Some of her officers went over to nearby Brooklyn Navy Yard to lunch aboard BAVG 4, which had commissioned as HMS *Dasher* on 1 July. *Dasher*'s engines were Sun-Droxford diesels, about as trustworthy as *Archer*'s Busche-Sultzers. On trials in the Navy Yard they backfired frequently on starting up, with a shattering explosion, pieces flying out of their exhausts.

The Convoys' Need for Carriers

Convoys to Murmansk and Archangel in north Russia with war supplies, weapons and food, begun in the autumn of 1941, came under particularly heavy attack from spring 1942, by German ships and aircraft based in Norway, as Russian resistance grew. CAM-ship Sea Hurricanes had given occasional cover, but they were one against an air fleet. *Empire Morn* sailed with PQ15 but did not launch her fighter. Torpedo planes sank three merchantmen and the cruiser *Trinidad*, with the cruiser *Edinburgh* (and her gold) sank in the homeward convoy. Returning in May in QP12, *Empire Morn* launched Flying Officer J. B. Kendal, who destroyed a Ju 88 but was killed baling out. Pilot Officer Hay, catapulted from *Empire Lawrence* in the outgoing PQ16, shot down one Heinkel 111 and damaged another, but bombers singled out the CAM-ship and sank her.

The convoys to Russia, North America and Gibraltar all needed the air cover which only carriers could give. Allied shipping sunk by U-boats reached a horrifying total of some 700,000

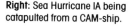

Right: Sea Hurricane IA being catapulted from a CAM-ship.

tons in June, most of this in American coastal waters, but the growing convoy system drove the sea wolves back to the Atlantic.

Avenger was refitting, *Biter* was fighting the Atlantic weather and duff diesels on passage to the UK, *Dasher* was farting metal in Brooklyn Navy Yard. PQ17 had to make do with two anti-aircraft ships and the CAM-ship *Empire Tide*. The operation was a notorious disaster. Assuming, on insufficient evidence, that the German battle fleet was about to fall on the convoy, the First Sea Lord in London ordered the ships to scatter, making it hopeless for Senior Officer Escort, Captain Broome, and his handful of destroyers to cover all his charges; he was, in any case, withdrawn to supplement the covering cruiser force for an attack by *Tirpitz, Scheer* and *Hipper* which never came. Fifth Air Fleet sank 14 and U-boats ten of the 35 merchantmen. *Empire Tide*'s Sea Hurricane was not launched.

The new, Spitfire-derived Seafire had the same handicap of a poor view as the Sea Hurricane, but parallel production of the Seafire IB, a transitional version with a minimum of naval modifications, and the IIC, built from scratch as a navalised Spitfire, was being rushed along. The Admiralty wanted the Seafire IIC for the carriers in Operation 'Torch', the invasion of North Africa. The first machines of both marks were received by the Navy on 15 June, in time for Torch.

Right: A Sea Hurricane being loaded from a lighter. Sea Hurricanes were delivered to the FAA after RAF Hurricanes had successfully landed on HMS *Glorious* in an emergency off Norway in 1940, but the first arrivals, Sea Hurricane IBs, fitted with arrester hooks, were RAF veterans with many defects, and American Martlets were substituted. Overhauled Sea Hurricanes performed well on Russian Convoy PQ18 with HMS *Avenger* and proved to be a reasonably sturdy deck-lander, though short on range, a harsh staller, a bad ditcher, with poor pilot forward view. Though superseded by the Seafire, Wildcat, Hellcat and Corsair, Sea Hurricanes gave valuable service in RN-manned escort carriers in the Arctic, Atlantic and Mediterranean. (IWM)

THE *AVENGER* CONVOY

After the bloody débâcle of PQ17 there were no more Arctic convoys for two months, until PQ18 went to Russia in early September. By that time the shrinking Arctic day gave them a few hours of darkness to hide in. To shorten the odds still further, HMS *Avenger*, with 12 Sea Hurricane IBs, and the anti-aircraft cruiser *Scylla* (known to her ship's company as 'The Toothless Terror') were added to a strong force of sloops, corvettes and minesweepers and a special 'fighting destroyer escort' of 16 Fleet destroyers.

The six Sea Hurricanes of *Audacity*'s old 802 Squadron, the only unit with experience of auxiliary carrier operations, joined *Avenger* in mid-summer together with six Sea Hurricanes of 883 Squadron. Six more spare Sea Hurricanes were stowed in the hangar with their wings detached and slung from the deckhead. *Avenger*'s Sea Hurricanes were all Mark IIBs, with eight 0.303in machine-guns. Some Mark IICs, adapted from RAF Hurricane IIAs with four-cannon wings, which Director of Naval Air Division wanted, would have been preferred to fight Condors, Ju 88s, Heinkels and the armoured Bv 138s. The Hurries were joined by three Swordfish and five three-man crews of 825 Squadron.

Before sailing, Admiral Burnett and *Avenger*'s captain, Commander Colthurst (like McKendrick of *Audacity* a former Swordfish pilot), established tactics for Operation 'EV'. Priority was to destroy shadowers, followed by a change of course, rather than wait for an attack. *Illustrious* and *Formidable* had been almost sunk by land-based aircraft. Now one small ex-merchant ship with a wooden flight deck and a handful of obsolescent fighters faced Fifth Air Fleet's 92 torpedo-bombers, 133 long-range and dive-bombers.

On 3 September *Avenger* left Scapa Flow for Iceland. It was cold and rough. Most of the air group were seasick, and one Sea Hurricane was lost over the side. Before they reached Iceland they were shadowed by a Condor, and at Seidisfjord on the 5th an Fw 200 tried to hit her with two bombs, which destroyed two houses ashore. 'We should have a nice trip', wrote a young Swordfish telegraphist/air-gunner, 'now that the Germans know we are here.'

Avenger and *Scylla* left Seidisfjord on the 8th with two destroyers, and had just gained the open sea when *Avenger* had to shut down both main engines, with sludge and sand in the oil fuel. For three hours she lay stopped, thankful for the cover of darkness. She had barely got under way when one of her escorts sighted a submarine, and later she steamed past a mine, which was sunk by gunfire. There was a second breakdown just north of Jan Mayen Island when the magnetic clutches shorted out. The ship was rolling badly and aircraft were breaking loose in the hangar. She finally joined the convoy, which had left Loch

Right: HMS *Avenger,* BAVG-2, in dazzle camouflage. She was similar to *Archer,* with the same type of bridge/flying control position forward below the edge of the flight deck, but her hangar extended further forward. (IWM)

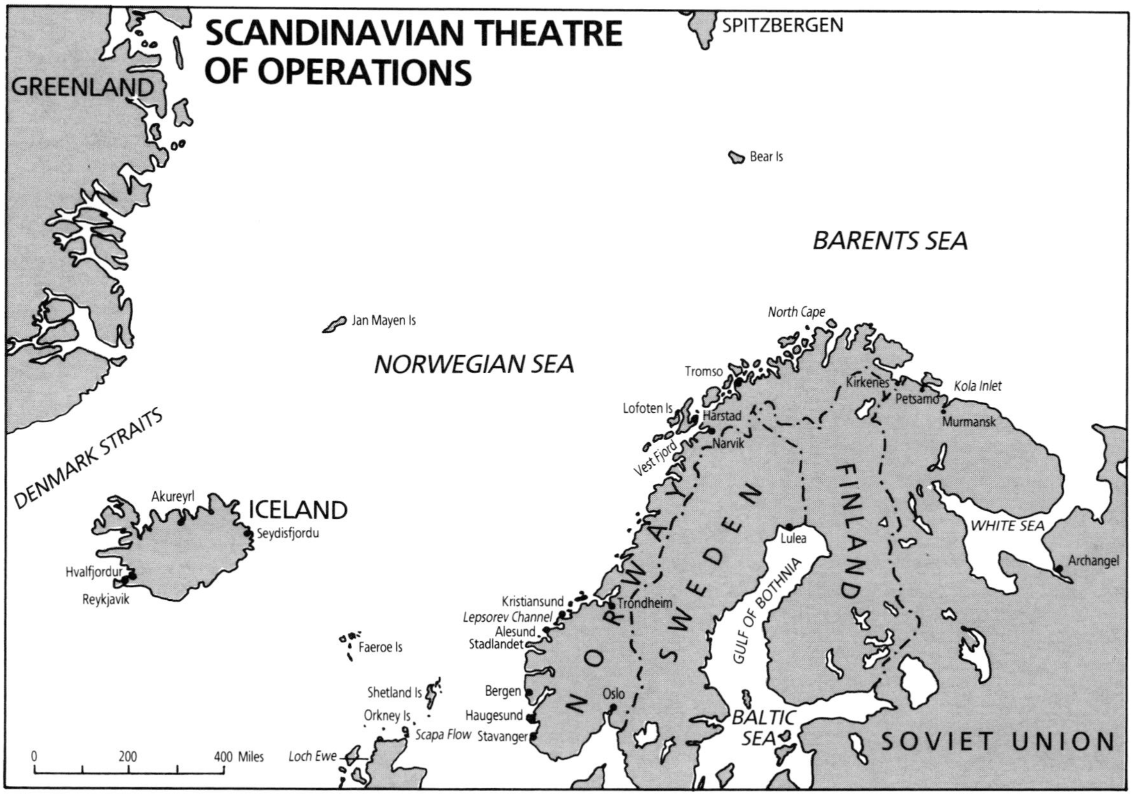

Right: Scotland and Iceland to North Russia.

Ewe in western Scotland on 2 September, under air cover from Iceland, and took station at the tail of Column 2.

On 12 September a Bv 138 shadower appeared. R/T and radar shut-down were at once relaxed and four Sea Hurricanes scrambled. They closed the German but he evaded them in the low cloud and mist. R/T was banned again, and when a shivering Swordfish crew sighted two U-boats they took no action and waited to return to the ship to report them, and hunting destroyers found no contact. On Sunday the 13th Lieutenant Bennett's dawn patrol Swordfish sighted a U-boat but had only small fragmentation bombs to drop on her, as the Stringbag could not lift depth-charges in the windless conditions prevailing, even from a lengthened flight deck. His successor on patrol, Sub-Lieutenant Evans, sighted two more submarines, which dived out of reach. Again the persistent Blohm & Voss appeared, and a section of Sea Hurricanes was scrambled. Again he evaded pursuit in cloud.

The weather cleared steadily. About 09:00 one Russian and one American merchantman were torpedoed and sunk outside the range of the escorts' asdics. The sky began to fill with aircraft round the horizon's rim. Sections of Sea Hurricanes sortied and chased them all forenoon, their 0.303s impotent against the armoured Bv 138s. Swordfish sighted numerous U-boats ringing the convoy. One crew saw a Blohm & Voss drop a mine right in the path of the convoy, which was warned in time to alter course. Some of the fighters also reported submarines.

About 15:00 six Ju 88s of KG 30 broke off from the circus which was now orbiting the convoy and flew across the ships at about 460m (1,500ft), dropping bombs through holes in the clouds. The attack was a diversion, and the Sea Hurricanes obliged. They attacked the 88s, and were caught hopelessly out of position for the attack by 40 torpedo-carrying Heinkel 111s of KG 26 and ten Ju 88s of KG 30 which came in over the water at about 15m (50ft) in line abreast and about 45m (150ft) apart, the 88s looking, Admiral Burnett thought, 'like giant nightmare locusts', too low for radar to have tracked them, most of them with two torpedoes slung under the belly. Major Werner Klumper, the formation leader, could not locate the carrier reported by the shadowers, and began to doubt whether it existed at all, as there was no sign of any fighters. In fact the Hurricanes were still away over the horizon chasing the decoy 88s, and Colthurst had taken *Avenger* some distance from the convoy to be in a better tactical position. The German aircraft flew into an intensive barrage of flak, which knocked five of them down and spoiled the aim of others. Some 96 torpedoes were dropped, eight freighters hit and sunk. *Avenger*'s fighters destroyed one Heinkel. The rest returned to base, six of them so badly shot up by flak that they were written off.

At 16:15 nine He 115 torpedo-bombers approached the starboard flank of the convoy. A fierce destroyer barrage made them drop their loads too far off to score. One Heinkel fell to the barrage, the rest got away. Once again the Sea Hurricanes were away chasing shadowers, and Lieutenant E. W. T. Taylour, Commanding Officer of the 802 Squadron Flight, was shot down in flames and killed in an attack on a Bv 138. About 18:40 12 Heinkel 111 torpedo-bombers loomed out of the dusk from the convoy's starboard quarter and attacked in small groups. This time barrage and Sea Hurricanes between them destroyed half the force.

As the short night fell, *Avenger* had little to show for her efforts – one Blohm & Voss damaged for the loss of Taylour. 'At the end of this unfortunate day', Colthurst confessed, 'I realised that my operation of the ship and her fighters had been wrong . . . I had not appreciated the hopelessness of sending even four Sea Hurricanes to attack the heavily armed enemy shadowers.' Ashore, Bv 138 crews re-affirmed the existence of a carrier with the convoy, and Major Klumper was ordered to seek her out and direct his main attack on her.

As light began to streak the sky towards the end of the graveyard watch on the 14th, a U-boat's torpedo hit and sank the big tanker *Atheltempler* in the rear of the convoy. At 09:40 a Swordfish crew sighted a U-boat. W/T silence had been relaxed, and Burnett sent the destroyer *Onslow*, which depth-charged and sank the submarine, *U-589*.

Ju 88s, He 111s and Bv 138s sniffed round the convoy all forenoon, but this time Colthurst held his Sea Hurricanes back. About 12:30 a group of 22 Ju 88s and Heinkel 111s came in low from dead ahead. *Avenger* got nine Sea Hurricanes away before they closed the ships. *Scylla* was leading Column 5, and Admiral Burnett had a ringside seat . . . 'It was a fine sight to see *Avenger* peeling off Hurricanes whilst streaking across the front of the convoy from starboard to port inside the screen with the destroyer escort blazing away . . .'

This time Klumper, leading 22 torpedo-carrying Heinkels of I Squadron, KG 26, sighted *Avenger* steaming to the north of the convoy. He had just ordered his formation to split up when the Sea Hurricanes dived on them and did the job for him. He shouted a warning over the R/T but it was too late. Chased by the fighters, the Heinkels swept over the convoy into a murderous curtain of flak. The Sea Hurricanes saw two bombers launch their torpedoes at the carrier and miss. They then flew along her side level with the bridge, and were shot down by her guns at almost point-blank range. In this attack I/KG 26 lost five aircraft, and of the remaining 17, nine reached base but were written off.

A wave of Ju 88s came in from astern, about 20 of them picking out *Avenger* and destroyers of the screen. The carrier was near-missed by 46m (50yd), as her pilots defended her . . . 'I found myself with my section mate – a Petty Officer – tackling 14 Ju 88s flying in diamond formation, a

Below: Anti-aircraft cruiser HMS *Scylla* (the 'Toothless Terror'), flagship of Admiral Burnett, accompanied *Avenger* and Convoy PQ18 to Russia, September 1942. (IWM)

Right: A Sea Hurricane Mk IB during refuelling. The arrester hook can be seen in its housing just forward of the tail wheel, the sturdy wide undercarriage, and the gaping air scoop under the fuselage which made the machine a bad ditcher.

pretty hard nut to crack, for if they can keep formation, their cross fire keeps every plane covered. However, I made a quarter attack on the leading plane, then swung away straight at one of the planes on the side of the diamond. At the last moment I flicked underneath him, he got the wind up and pulled the nose of his plane hard up, and the Petty Officer, flying just on my starboard wing, gave him a lovely burst which put paid to his account. The formation broke up, and there was a lovely scrap all over the sky.'

Dove-tailing into the end of this attack came another wave of 25 Heinkel 111 torpedo-bombers racing in from ahead, 17 of them making for *Avenger*. The Sea Hurricanes put some of them off their aim. Three Hurricanes went down through the barrage and were shot down, though their pilots were saved. Colthurst combed tracks skilfully, only to face another wave of 88s. A near miss started a fire in *Avenger*'s catapult room, but it was the last attack of the day, and the convoy took stock. The ships were intact. The enemy had lost 24 aircraft. *Avenger*'s Sea Hurricanes claimed five destroyed, three probables and 14 damaged, not to mention the ones scared off, made to miss or throw their bombs or torpedoes away.

Below: Blohm & Voss Bv 138 flying-boat. Its thick armour made a Sea Hurricane's 0.303in machine-guns ineffective. (IWM)

Fog closed in, turning back the Stringbag dawn patrol, persisted all forenoon, then began to clear, and *Avenger*'s radar revealed a large force of aircraft approaching. The carrier pulled out of line and peeled off ten Sea Hurricanes which climbed to intercept. The enemy dropped their bombs, then hid in the thick cloud. Those who ventured below were turned back by the Sea Hurricanes or the barrage, which laid a carpet of white-hot fire over the ships. The cloud broke up, and Burnett was about to order an emergency turn of 90 degrees to remain under its cover when ships' radio operators on the same frequency as the German bombers heard their commander report that his aircraft were at the end of their fuel endurance. By 4:45 *Avenger*'s radar screen was clear. PQ18 and the return convoy QP14 were now within range of the 13 Catalina flying boats and 23 Hampden bombers sent to Russia, and *Avenger* was needed for 'Torch'.

Next morning she, *Scylla* and the fighting destroyer escort left to join the homeward-bound convoy. When nine Heinkel 115 torpedo float-planes attacked PQ18 on the forenoon of 17 September the only aircraft with the convoy were one Catalina, which had taken over anti-submarine patrol from *Avenger*'s weary Swordfish, and the Sea Hurricane on *Empire Morn*'s catapult. Failure of the fighter's electrical system prevented launching, but she was ready for a second attack by 15 Heinkels an hour later. Flying Officer Burr had to swerve to miss the balloon cables of the merchantmen and jink smartly to avoid those which opened fire on him with Bofors and Oerlikons. Diving on the Heinkels he shot one down. All the other Heinkels missed with their torpedoes, and Burr calculated that the 265l (70 gal) remaining in his tanks should just get him to Keg Ostrov aerodrome near Archangel, 368km (240 miles) away. He arrived with only 19l (5 gal) left in his reserve tank.

PQ18 arrived in Archangel with ten merchantmen lost out of 39 in the period when the Sea Hurricanes had been operated incorrectly, but afterwards, in spite of their ineffectual .303 calibre guns, they had put the whole German effort off its stroke and shot down some eight bombers, damaging at least a dozen more, for the loss of four machines (three to their own barrage) and one pilot. A total of 41 German aircraft were lost in the operation. But more effective aircraft were needed. For months the Director of the RN Air Division had been trying to get Hurricane IICs, with 20mm cannon, for the auxiliary carriers. 'It is hoped', he said, 'that these aircraft will be available to protect the future PQ convoys. If not, Martlets (0.5 guns) must be used in lieu.' Radar to register very low flying aircraft was also needed.

Thick weather, fog, ice and bitter cold helped UK-bound QP14 until out of range of aircraft. One merchant ship was sunk by a U-boat, but immediately after *Avenger* had left the convoy on 20 September, hotfoot for Seidisfjord, Scapa Flow and her part in 'Torch', the destroyer *Somali* was torpedoed and sunk, and two days later the Fleet Auxiliary *Grey Ranger*.

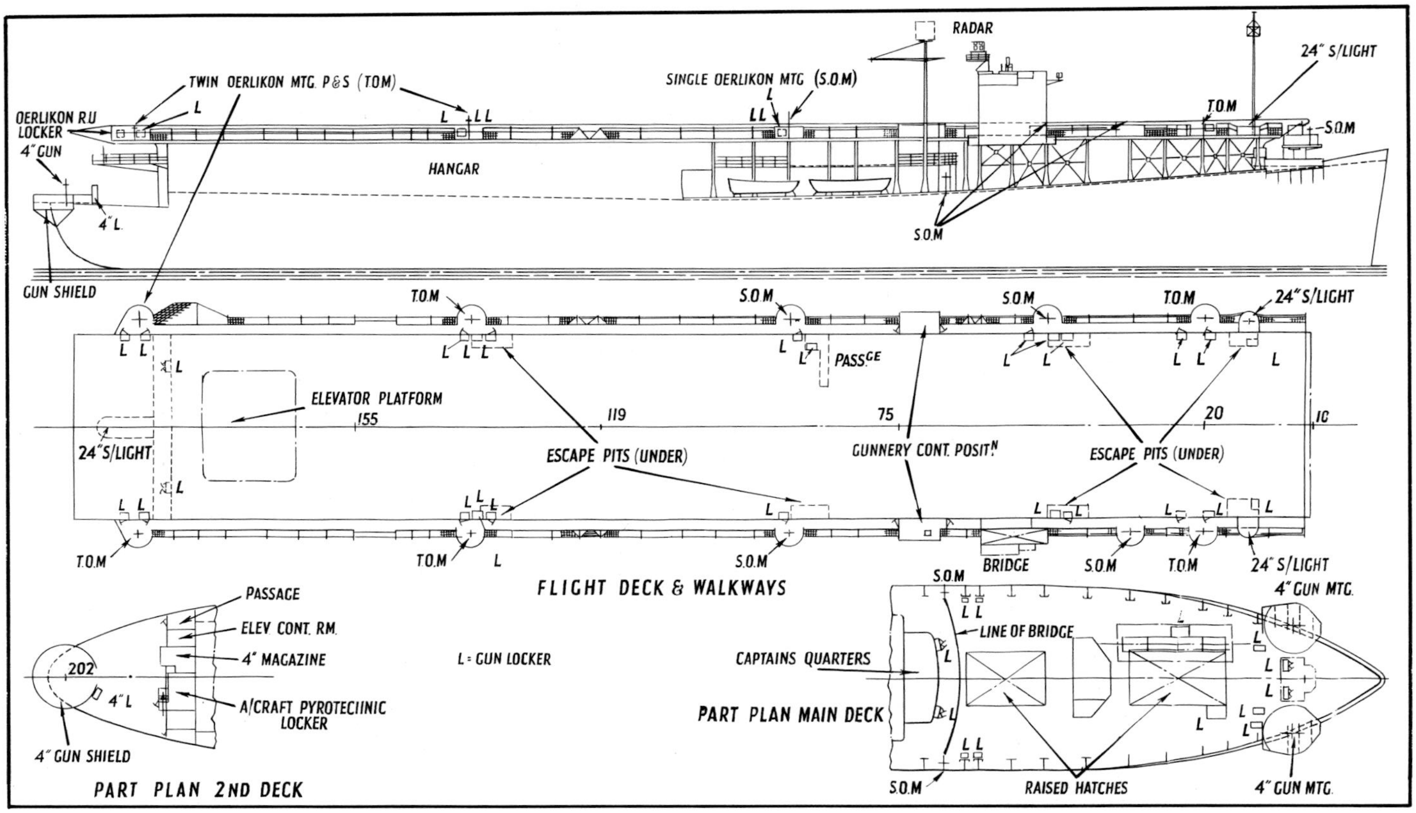

Above: HMS *Biter*. (MoD(Navy))

Right: HMS *Biter*, BAVG-3. Her bridge/flying control position in an 'island' was superior to those of USS *Long Island*, HMSS *Archer* and *Avenger*. Forward is the HF/DF 'Huff-Duff' aerial bearer, and *Biter* is carrying, typically of RN-manned escort carriers, a Type 279 air search/gunnery spotting radar set, with its aerial on the mainmast. (IWM)

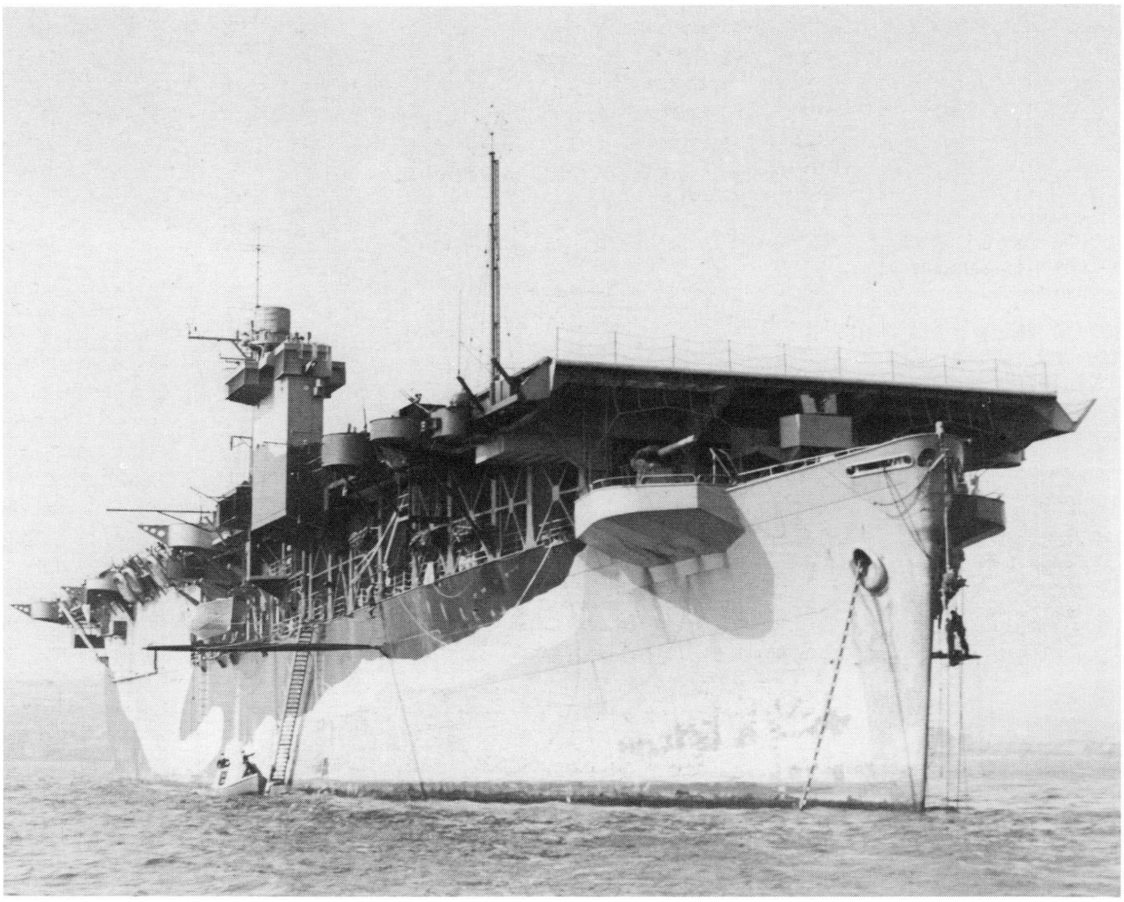

3

A Torch in Africa

TWICE before Allied carriers, British at Diego Suarez in May, American at Guadalcanal in August, had provided the sole air support for amphibious landings. Now they were to continue the experience together in Vichy-French North Africa, to support landings near Algiers and Oran on the Mediterranean coast and in French Morocco. The capture of Oran and Algiers would give the Allies Algeria and two good supply ports outside the range of the Axis air forces in Sardinia. The way would then be open for an advance eastwards by land coupled with a thrust from Egypt by General Montgomery's British Eighth Army.

The acquisition of North Africa would enable ships to take shorter routes to the Middle and Far East, furnish a launching base for a southern invasion of Europe, experience for the later thrust across the English Channel, and a boost for Allied morale. The Atlantic coast of Morocco would provide bases for air and sea operations in the Atlantic, the port of Casablanca a staging post for supplying the Mediterranean, and a back-up bridgehead if either or both of the Mediterranean landings should fail.

Right: The motto of HMS *Biter* was *Volo ut mordeam* (I fly that I may bite).

THE BUILD-UP

There was an urgent rush to get ships, troops and aircraft ready for Operation 'Torch'. The Royal Navy wanted their first three BAVGs for air protection and close support, a British responsibility, in the two Mediterranean operations, but *Biter* did not complete her anglicisation until the last day of August. On 3 September *Avenger* left Scapa Flow for a voyage into the unknown with PQ17, from which she might never return. If she did, it would not be much before the end of the month. *Dasher* was on her maiden voyage from the USA, and *Archer* was still there, completing repairs in her Hoboken yard, reluctant to relinquish the joys of an almost peacetime Big Apple. All four had histories of chronic engine trouble . . .

On the night of 9/10 August a strongly escorted convoy for Malta, including *Indomitable, Victorious* and *Eagle,* cleared Gibraltar (Operation 'Pedestal'). With it also was *Furious,* carrying another transfusion of Spitfires to be flown off to the cratered runways of Hal Far, Luqa and Takali. By the time she had steamed far enough to fly off her cargo, *Eagle,* cruisers *Manchester* and *Cairo* and a destroyer had been sunk by enemy aircraft, submarines or motor torpedo boats. Five of the 14 merchant ships reached Malta. Sea Hurricanes embarked in the carriers suffered heavily. Only one of *Eagle*'s 801 Squadron machines survived, only five of 880's and 885's combined total of 18.

Seven Royal Navy carriers were scheduled for 'Torch', *Formidable, Victorious, Argus* and *Furious,* and the auxiliary carriers *Avenger, Biter* and *Dasher*. The Sea Hurricane losses sustained in four Pedestal squadrons to be used in 'Torch' were made good with Seafires, IBs and IICs. Neither mark had folding wings, and the designers of the *Illustrious*-Class had not anticipated, in sizing the lifts, the embarking of non-folding aircraft of Seafire dimensions. Fleet carriers *Formidable* and *Victorious* carried just six Seafires apiece, two in deck parks, four on outriggers, to add to their main complement of Martlets (24 in *Formidable*, 15 in *Victorious,* which also carried six reconnaissance Fulmars), and their Albacore TSRs. *Argus* and *Furious,* with their large, old-fashioned lifts, could operate Seafires normally, and the slow old 'Flat Iron' embarked 18 IICs of 880 Squadron, *Furious* 801 Squadron, its decimated strength brought up to full establishment with Seafire IBs.

The elevators in the US-converted auxiliary carriers were large enough to accommodate the non-folding Seafires but they were allocated Sea Hurricanes. The Seafire had not actually been tested for suitability in the small ACVs. 'Winkle' Brown now did the job with the aid of *Biter*. It was a trickier proposition than the *Illustrious/Victorious* Seafire trials, with only half the length of flight deck.

He took off from Macrihanish and picked up the carrier in the Clyde . . . 'I flew round the ship, turned on to my approach path, and came in. As I closed the stern I swung the nose to starboard with the rudder, and counteracted the swing by putting on slight opposite bank. In this way I made the Seafire crab in sideways, so that I had a view of the deck over the leading edge of the wing.

'I sank towards the stern. I was over the round-down at a speed very close to the stall. Quickly I took off the bank and kicked off the rudder as she sank on the deck. She made a good three-point touch-down and caught a wire.'

The Seafire received its clearance for operations in ACVs, though it was too late to consider embarking them in the 'Torch' auxiliaries. *Avenger* retained her 12 Sea Hurricanes of 802 and 883 Squadrons, *Biter* embarked 800's 15 Sea Hurricane IIBs and IICs, *Dasher* carried six spare Seafires (for other carriers) as well as her own 12 Sea Hurricanes, six of 804 Squadron, six of 891.

There were to be two separate forces for the Mediterranean landings: the Eastern Task Force for the Algiers assault by the British First Army, with Vice-Admiral Burrough commanding *Argus* and *Avenger*, three cruisers and five destroyers; and Central Task Force for the Oran landings, with *Furious*, *Biter* and *Dasher*, the battleship *Rodney*, cruiser *Delhi* and nine destroyers, under the command of Commodore Troubridge.

ENTER THE '*SANGAMONS*'

The Western Task Force for the landings in Morocco by Major-General George S. Patton's troops was an all-American organisation, commanded by Vice-Admiral Henry K. Hewitt. Air cover and support were to be provided by the 14,500-ton pre-war carrier USS *Ranger* and the four newly-converted oilers, USS *Sangamon*, *Santee*, *Chenango* and *Suwannee*, acquired in a hurry in December 1941 to make up for the shortage of C-3 hulls for conversion. The five flat-tops carried a total of 97 fighters and 44 strike aircraft. The Royal Navy in the Mediterranean, facing far greater potential air attacks, had reversed the proportion, with 138 fighters to 39 Albacores.

Sangamon was the second US Navy vessel of that name, the first being one of John Ericsson's famous early armoured monitors, called after a river near the birthplace of Abraham Lincoln in Illinois, which in the Civil War of 1861–65 had supported the Union Army from the waterways of Virginia. Her unlikely descendant was to carry out not dissimilar duties for other US armies. One of 12 tankers built on a joint Navy-Maritime Commission design, she was laid down as the *Esso Trenton* (MC hull 7) on 13 March by the Federal Shipbuilding & Dry Dock Company of Kearney, New Jersey, launched on 4 November 1939, operated by the Standard Oil Company of New Jersey on runs from Gulf Coast ports to the east coast and acquired by the Navy on 22 October 1940. She was renamed *Sangamon* and designated a Fleet oiler, AO-28. After service off the west coast and in Hawaiian waters, *Sangamon* shifted to the Atlantic Fleet in the spring of 1941, and through the Neutrality Patrol period carried fuel from the Gulf Coast oil ports to bases on the east coast of the USA, in Canada and Iceland. On 7 December 1941, when the US entered World War 2, she was at Argentia, the convoy terminal port of Newfoundland, Canada, offloading her cargo. Within a week she started south again to renew her now more urgent schedule. But the provision of auxiliary carriers was urgent too, and with the New Year 1942 she was selected for conversion. On 11 February she arrived in Hampton Roads. Three days later she was re-classified AVG-26, and work was begun at the Norfolk Navy Yard.

During the spring and summer the need for auxiliary carriers increased. Work on *Sangamon*, three other *Cimarron*-Class oilers, and 20 C-3 merchant hulls was continued and speeded up. In August *Sangamon*, first of her class, was ready. Her conversion had added a flight deck 153m (502ft) long and 24.7m (81ft) wide, elevators, a hangar deck, a catapult, sonar gear, aircraft ordnance magazines, workshops and stowage space for spares. Her accommodation had been enlarged to house her increased complement and aviation personnel, and her armament increased to two 5in and 22 40mm guns. On 20 August she was redesignated ACV-26 (A for auxiliary, C for carrier, V for heavier than air) in accordance with the new code, and five days later she was re-commissioned by Captain Charles W. Wiever, USN. Shakedown in Chesapeake Bay followed a return to the yard for repair and improvements to her ventilation system.

During the shakedown it was convenient, and hopefully of mutual benefit, to use the new CVE for qualification tests of a new naval fighter, the Chance-Vought Corsair F4U-I, which promised to be an outstanding machine, with a maximum speed of 574km/h (357mph) at 762m (2,500ft) and 652km/h (405mph) at 5,944m (19,500ft), (being the first single-engined fighter to exceed 400mph), a ceiling of over 10,670m (35,000ft), a combat endurance of four and a half hours with a 537l (142-Imp gal) drop tank, a battery of six 0.5in machine-guns with 400 rounds each and 454kg (1,000lb) worth of external stores in place of a drop tank. The main self-sealing fuel tank, fitted just ahead of the pilot (unfortunately lengthening the nose and reducing the view forward), was armoured, as were the windscreen, seat and cockpit sides. For such a big, heavy (6-ton) machine, two tons heavier than the F4F-4, the Corsair had a remarkably tight turning circle, could match the supremely aerobatic A6M3 Zero in the first half of turn at the Japanese fighter's fighting speed, and turn inside a Seafire with ease. Although its Pratt & Whitney engine produced 2,250hp, with water injection, its weight made its rate of roll inferior to contemporary British and Japanese fighters, and its rate of climb poor at not much more than 914m (3,000ft) per minute. The Corsair was always easily identifiable by its inverted gull wing, which raised the fuselage so that the powerful engine had room to swing the big 3.96m (13ft) Hamilton propeller, and reduced drag considerably by its 90-degree interception with the fuselage, which was a short, light but sturdy affair with all the robustness necessary for carrier landings. Also incorporated was a hydraulic system by which the pilot could fold the wings, open and shut the engine cowlings and air cooler ventilators, operate the undercarriage and deck hook, and by which the guns could be loaded – though use of the system in the F4U-I required great care, as the controls were so arranged that it was possible, as some pilots found to their cost, to fold the wings instead of retracting the undercarriage. A Corsair and its pilot of No 1833 Squadron in HMS *Illustrious* were lost in this way when the Fleet carrier was in the Mediterranean on her way to the East Indies in 1944. To meet anticipated Navy/Marine needs, Goodyear and Brewster were also given contracts to produce Corsairs as the FG-I and F3U-I respectively, with Vought retaining overall design responsibility.

On 25 September Lieutenant-Commander S. Porter, USN, flew out to *Sangamon* in the seventh production F4U-I. Only four landings and take-offs were made, and by the end of those Porter had had enough of the 'bent-wing bastard' from Bethpage. The first problem he encountered was the blocking of his forward view by the long nose in the three-point attitude assumed over the round-down. Equally off-putting was the Corsair's performance on the deck. The compression of air and oil inside the oleo-pneumatic struts of the otherwise excellent undercarriage did not absorb the shock of a carrier landing sufficiently and bounced the machine clear of all the wires. The Corsair also tended to swing wildly on touchdown, and windscreen and cockpit became covered by oil escaping from the hydraulically operated cowl flaps and valve push-rod mechanism. The large wing area led to floating in the ground effect over the deck, with an unpredictable wing-drop at the stall. Porter departed and the prancing Corsair went back to the drawing board. *Sangamon* carried on with her shakedown, then returned to the yard for repair and improvements to her ventilation system.

The Santee is a river in Georgia USA and the name of a Sioux tribe – when most tribes collected scalps, the Santee collected heads. The frigate *Santee* was the scourge of Confederate blockade runners, and was in service until she sank at her moorings at Annapolis, where she had been a school ship, in 1912. USS *Santee*, the second of the *Cimmarron* quartet to be re-commissioned as an auxiliary aircraft carrier, was launched on 4 March 1939 as the *Esso Seakay* under a Maritime Commission contract (MC hull 3) by the Sun Shipbuilding & Dry Dock Company at Chester, Pennsylvania. Operated by Standard Oil of New Jersey, on the West Coast, she set several records for fast oil hauling, which impressed the US Bureau of Ships. Acquired by the Navy on 18 October 1940, and commissioned on 30 October as AO-29, she served in the Atlantic. When American neutrality ended on 7 December 1941 she was carrying oil for a secret aerodrome at Argentia. In the spring of 1942 her conversion to an auxiliary was begun at the Norfolk Navy Yard

Right: USS *Santee*, ACV-29, a converted US Navy oiler and one of the largest escort carriers, made her début off Casablanca in Operation 'Torch' and suffered heavy aircraft losses, though no aircrewman was killed. Radar details have been censored. (US National Airchives)

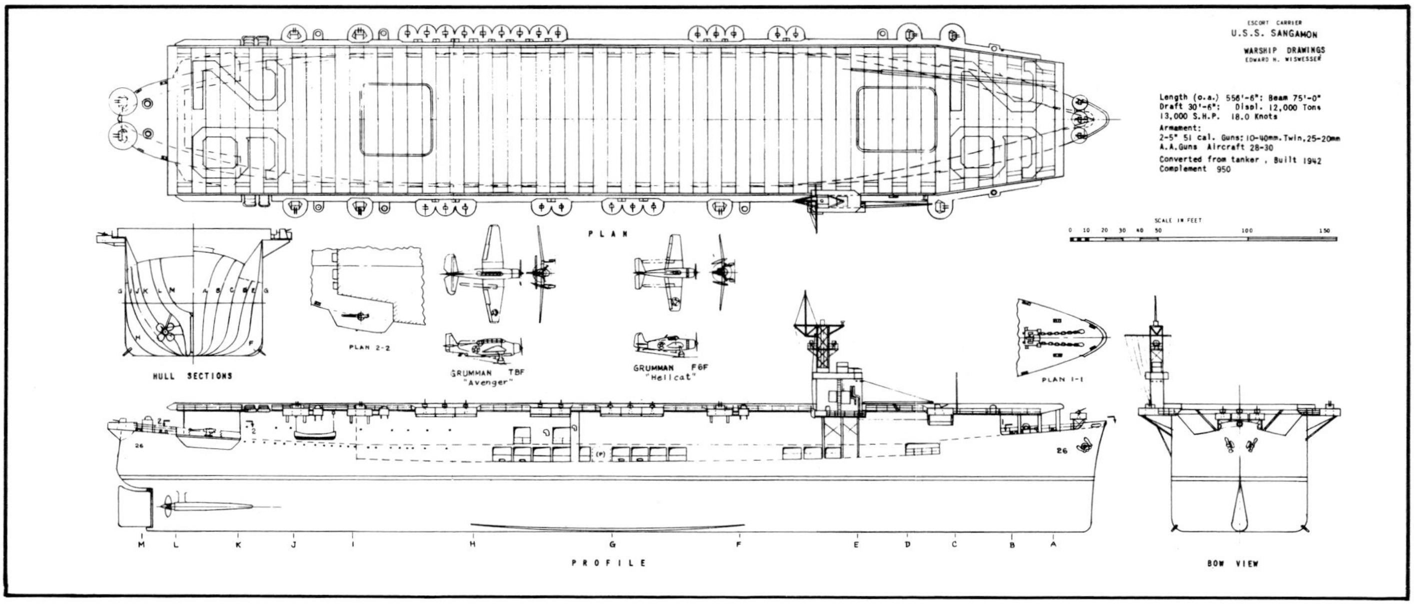

Above: USS *Sangamon*. (Taubman Plan Service)

and carried out at an urgent, cracking pace. Commissioned on 24 August by Captain William D. Sample, USN, ACV-29 was fitted out with equal haste, and although officially completed on 8 September, workmen from Norfolk were still on board when *Santee* carried out minimal trial runs between 21–23 September in Chesapeake Bay, and her decks were piled up with unsecured stores. Nevertheless the new carrier reported to Command Task Force 22 on the 24th and the first plane landed on her hastily cleared flight deck that day.

The *Chenango*, named for a river, town and county in New York State, taken from an Indian river name meaning Big Bull, also had a fighting history, the first of the name being a side-wheel steamer which blockaded the Confederacy. The second *Chenango*, ACV-28, was launched on 1 April 1939 as *Esso New Orleans* by Sun Shipbuilding, and later steamed many thousands of miles in two oceans, Hatteras to Honolulu, on tanker duty for the Naval Transportation Service. As ACV-28 she was recommissioned on 19 September 1942, and began loading Army P-40 fighters for a date off French Morocco.

Suwannee is Indian too, a river serenaded by Stephen Foster and Al Jolson, which rises in Ware County, Georgia, and flows southwest across Florida to freshen the Gulf of Mexico at Suwannee Sound, but, strangely, the first *Suwannee* was a Yankee vessel, an iron-hulled gunboat built in Pennsylvania in the Civil War to hunt Confederate commerce raiders. The oiler/flat-top was laid down on 3 June 1938 at Kearny, New Jersey, by the Federal Shipbuilding & Dry Dock Company under a Maritime Commission contract as the *Markay* (MC hull 5), launched on 4 March 1939, delivered to the Keystone Tankship Corporation and taken over by the Navy on 26 June 1941, renamed *Suwannee*, (AO-33). After six months as an oiler with the Atlantic Fleet *Suwannee* was redesignated ACV-27 on 14 February 1942 and decommissioned on 21 February at Newport News for conversion to a *Sangamon*-class escort carrier by Captain Joseph J. Clark, USN.

'Jock' or 'Jocko' Clark was something unique in the US Navy. He claimed to have Cherokee Indian blood and had risen from the lower deck to enter the Naval Academy at Annapolis, where he graduated with the Class of 1917. War service in the battleship *North Carolina* was followed by a spell in destroyers in the Near East. Various aviation posts on the West Coast of the USA, at sea, and in Washington followed, and he was Executive of the carrier *Yorktown* in Halsey's raids on the Gilberts and Marshalls, the first attack made on Japanese territory in the Pacific. Sent to Washington to await his next ship, he gave Admiral King, Chief of Naval Operations and Commander-in-Chief, United States Fleet (both titles he had created for himself) his views on how to win the war in the Pacific. Both were 'go-go' men, aggressive, impatient with fools, hard-driving. They had clashed at various points in Clark's career, and had a grudging respect for each other, as natural warriors pushed to the forefront in combat situations. 'When they get into a war,' King said sardonically of civilians, especially politicians, 'they send for the sons of bitches.' The Cherokee commander told the Chief of Naval Operations that another 150 carriers would be needed to win the naval war. To his surprise King agreed with him and sent him off round the country to propound his views. During the summer of 1942 he was ordered to Newport News, Virginia, to fit out and command the *Suwannee*.

The *Sangamons* retained their capacity as tankers, which not only gave them a considerably

Right: John 'Jocko' Clark USN, part-Cherokee Indian, Captain of USS *Suwannee* in Operation 'Torch'. (US National Archives)

Far right: Jocko Clark as a *Suwannee* cartoonist saw him.

wider range than all other auxiliary carrier classes except the later *Commencement Bays* (which were purpose-built copies of the *Sangamons*) so that they could stay at sea for 30 days or more, but which also enabled a *Sangamon* to keep four escorting destroyers and a light cruiser topped up for the same length of cruise. Later on, some of the tank space was of necessity taken over for larger crew's quarters and weapons and stores stowage without losing much of their fuelling capacity. They had the basic soundness of design and construction which had made them some of the finest tankers in the world. They were superior to both the *Archer* Class early C-3 conversions operated by the Royal Navy in 'Torch', and the newer class of ACV, the leadship of which, USS *Bogue*, was at this time on her trials off the west coast of the USA. The *Sangamons* were faster (18½ knots maximum) than the diesel BAVGs and had the more powerful and reliable steam-turbine engines driving twin screws, which made them more manoeuvrable. Length overall was 168.5m (553ft), and their flight decks (153 by 26m or 503 by 85ft) were longer by some 18m (60ft) than those of the BAVGs and the newer C-3 conversions. Much greater hangar space gave over twice the capacity for aircraft stowage as the BAVGs: HMS *Biter* carried 15 fighters in Torch, *Sangamon* 32 aircraft, comprising Lieutenant-Commander W. E. Ellis' VGF-26 Fighter Squadron of 14 Wildcats, Lieutenant-Commander J. S. Tracey's Bomber Squadron VGS-26 with eight Avenger TBFs and nine SBD-3 Dauntlesses, and *Suwannee* embarked 29 F4F-4s and nine TBFs. *Bogue* had embarked one of the new 'Composite' squadrons created for Trade Protection auxiliary carriers, in her case 12 Wildcat F4F-4s and 9 TBFs, which was about the average for a Compo. The much larger air component of a *Sangamon* was usually designated an Air Group, although the first air unit to join USS *Sangamon* was designated Composite Squadron (VC) 26. An ACV air group consisted initially of a fighter squadron (VF), operating Wildcats, and a bomber squadron (VC) with both Avenger TBF/TBMs and Dauntless SBD dive-bombers, both squadrons taking the same distinguishing number as their group. From mid-1943 Hellcat F6Fs replaced the Wildcats. In early 1944 the Dauntlesses were dropped from *Sangamon*-Class bomber units, which then operated only Avengers, their code letters being changed to VT.

Following the ship trials, the imminence of 'Torch' allowed the *Sangamons* only a few days to work-up with their new air groups. *Santee* began a bob-tailed shakedown with her VC 29 on 24 September, and finally embarked the group, comprising 14 Wildcat F4F-4s, eight Avenger TBFs and nine Douglas Dauntless SBD-3s, on 12 October. The F4F-4's Pratt & Whitney Double Wasp engine developed so much torque that in the hands of the rookies who made up the majority of the *Sangamon*'s pilots, the F4F-4 wanted to drift off to port when full power was applied for take-off. The Dauntless dive-bomber was a floater. It had so much wing area that when approaching the deck light on fuel after a mission and with a strong wind down the deck the SBD often continued to glide after the power was cut, missing all the wires and sometimes the barrier as well.

On 13 October Task Group 22.3, with Captain Sample as Senior Officer in *Santee*, and the destroyers *Rodman* (DD.456) and *Emmons* (DD.459) as screen, though far from combat readiness, 'shook loose', as Sample put it, from Norfolk Navy Yard for Bermuda. None of the ship's company knew where they were headed as the new carrier left Cape Henry behind. Many had a more immediate problem – seasickness, which started for some as *Santee* clared the Cape and began a gentle roll. Soon most of the greenhorns were greener still, unable to appreciate the fact which soon became clear to old shellbacks that this tanker turned flat-top was basically a very steady and smooth-riding ship, and in calm water it was difficult to know if she was under way when below decks. Even at sea she rolled and pitched very little compared with the smaller ACVs, but now the roll increased in momentum, and that night off Cape Hatteras she ran into a major storm. The wind howled, the rain beat through every opening, and the sea poured across the open well deck. The ship plunged and rolled, sometimes alternately, sometimes together, and a peak gust of 68 knots was registered. Both motor whale boats were smashed in their davits under the round-down of the flight deck aft. The greenhorns were convinced that the ship was going to sink, and did not really care. The mess hall was only sparsely patronised. But next day the winds gradually subsided, and on the third morning *Santee* anchored in a quiet Bermudan cove, where the shaken young matelots were given liberty. To walk on firm ground again in this lovely island was pure joy.

Santee was to pick up an SBD here. This aircraft, shiny and new, was brought alongside *Santee*, and the carrier's new crane was swung out, lifting the Dauntless to the level of the flight deck when the cable broke, dropping the brand-new machine more than 9m (30ft) back on to the lighter. *Santee* left for the wars one plane short.

TG.34.2, with the four carriers *Ranger, Sangamon, Santee* and *Suwannee*, cruiser *Cleveland* and the destroyers of Desron-10, were finally assembled, under the command of Rear-Admiral McWhorter, USN, at Bermuda, where they had formed up in an attempt to deceive any shadowing U-boats into thinking that this was simply a normal convoy or extra-large submarine hunting group bound for the South Atlantic.

TG.34.2 swung across from Bermuda to join the bulk of the invasion convoy, Western Task Force 34. The fourth of the *Sangamon* quartet, Captain Ben Wyatt's USS *Chenango*, was there, having steamed across with TG.34.8, carrying 78 P-40F Warhawks for the Army. More warships steamed down from Casco Bay, Maine, to escort the 28 personnel and vehicle transports carrying 37,000 troops. The carriers were deployed near the perimeter of the convoy and flew anti-submarine patrols during the daylight hours. Admiral Jean Darlan, Commander-in-Chief of the Vichy French forces in Morocco, was an opportunist quisling, and the Allies were uncertain how he and his men would behave. There were heavy warships at Casablanca, including the modern battleship *Jean Bart*. On 26 October the Western Task Force was joined by a warship squadron which included the US battleships *Massachusetts, New York* and *Texas*.

THE TORCH IS LIT

Between 22–27 October all the 'Torch' convoys left port, those for Oran and Algiers from the Clyde in Scotland. On the night of 23/24 October at El Alamein, 96km (60 miles) inside the Egyptian border, the British Eighth Army, heavily reinforced and resupplied via the Cape, began a new offensive. By nightfall on 3 November, with the 'Torch' armadas on the last legs of their advance, General Rommel's army was in full retreat westwards.

The convoys for the Mediterranean sailed as far to the west as possible, and avoided Condor reconnaissance from Bordeaux. U-boats which might have sighted them as they headed for the Straits of Gibraltar had been drawn off to attack a northbound convoy from Sierra Leone. The Western Task Force took a route well to the south of the Azores, remained undetected by the wolfpacks in the Central Atlantic, and as it approached the Moroccan coast split into its three attack task groups.

Serious opposition from the Vichy French warships at Casablanca had to be anticipated, and it was probable that high surf would make it difficult to land on the open beaches, so the occupation of some smaller harbours was thought wise, to ensure that enough troops were landed to take Casablanca. Accordingly there was to be a major landing at Fedala, 8km (5 miles) north of Casablanca, to be covered by Captain Robert Emmett's Centre Attack Group including the USS *Ranger* and *Suwanne*, with secondary landings at the port of Mehedia, 104km (65 miles) to the north, protected by *Sangamon* and Rear Admiral Munroe Kelly's Northern Attack Group, and at Safi, 200km (125 miles) to the south, which was *Santee*'s responsibility, with Rear-Admiral Lyal A. Davison's Southern Attack Group.

By the night of 7 November all of 'Torch's' three expeditions were lying off their landing beaches, and between 01:00 and 03:00 next morning landing craft were crunching ashore everywhere. Just before dawn Albacores lumbered off the old *Argus*. They were followed by swift-winging Seafires, and from *Avenger* shadowy, humped Sea Hurricanes rose and tucked in their wheels.

TARGET ALGERIA

It was reckoned that the French forces might find it easier to surrender to American troops than to the British, against whom many of them carried a bitter grudge for the previous attacks on their ships at Oran and Mers-el-Kebir, and Americans led the British assault force on to the beaches, one to the west, one to the east of Algiers. For the same reason Fleet Air Arm aircraft from the British carriers flew with American markings.

Right: Deck cargo. USAAF Warhawk P-40 fighters aboard HMS *Archer* en route for North Africa and Operation 'Torch'. The aircraft were flown ashore from a position just off the coast of Morocco. (Cdr. A. C. R. Duvall)

Right: Hangar cargo. USAAF P-40 Warhawks being ferried to Morocco for Operation 'Torch' by USS *Chenango*, the only one of the four new escort carriers of the *Sangamon* class not to see combat in the operation. Her P-40s were flown ashore to Port Lyautey airfield. (US National Archives)

The assault spearheads landed and advanced on the town with little opposition, but mounting surf held up the follow-on, and an early entry into Algiers itself from the sea was frustrated by forts dominating the harbour, but by noon Blida airfield, 42km (26 miles) inland from Algiers, had been taken. Spitfires from Gibraltar began flying in immediately, though as ground crews were yet to arrive *Argus* and *Avenger* maintained a patrol of four fighters, with four more at readiness on deck. Just after the last machine had landed at dusk the carrier group was attacked by Heinkel 111 torpedo-bombers. *Avenger*, near-missed by several torpedoes, contracted another case of engine trouble, blight of the BAVGs, but by the evening a truce had been signed, and next day, 10 November, she was moored to a buoy in Algiers harbour for repairs. Since the first take-off at dawn on 8 November she had launched 60 Sea Hurricane sorties.

In the Oran landings the Allies met much fiercer opposition from the French. Troops had been landed at three points, one to the east of the town, two to the west near the small port of Arzeu,

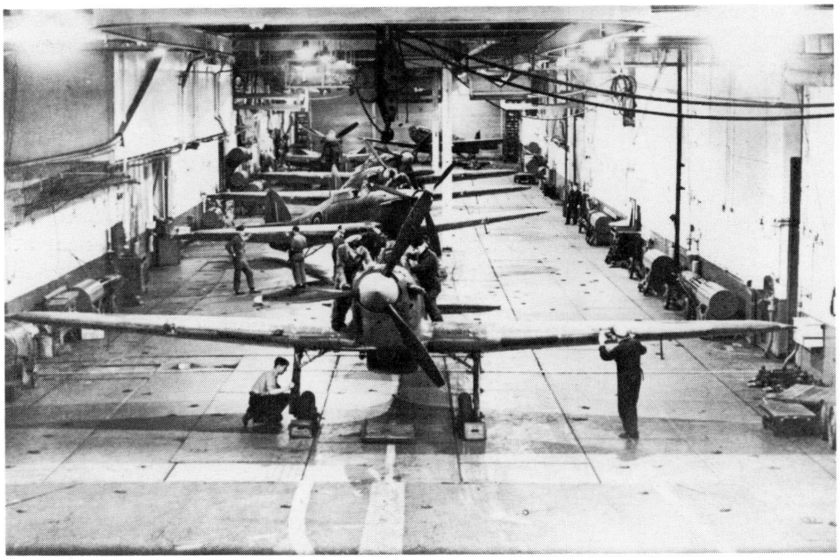

Top: Five Sea Hurricanes in the hangar, with a Seafire (background, right).

Above: Sea Hurricanes ranged on the flight deck (here on a fleet carrier). The flight leader is plugged into an electric starter. (IWM)

which was quickly taken. But attempts to open Oran harbour were repulsed, and there was a great potential threat from the three main airfields, La Senia, Maison Blanche and Tafaroui.

A thick haze badly reduced visibility all over the combat area, but by 06:00 on 8 November *Formidable, Furious, Biter* and *Dasher* had between them launched 42 aircraft against the three airfields. La Senia, the main Armée de l'Air base, was attacked by eight Albacores of 822 Squadron from *Furious*, escorted by six of 800 Squadron's Sea Hurricanes from *Biter*, six from *Dasher*'s 891. The Albacores were entering their dive when they were bounced by nine French Dewoitine D520 fighters. In the fight which followed the Albacores lost three aircraft, with two damaged and one shot down by flak, but managed to destroy five out of the six hangars on the airfield and 47 aircraft, while four of their close escort of six 800 Squadron Sea Hurricanes from *Biter* flown by Lieutenant K. M. Bruer, Sub-Lieutenant R. L. Thompson, Sub-Lieutenant R. M. Crosley (two) and Sub-Lieutenant B. L. Ritchie, shot down four Dewoitines and shared a fifth with an Albacore TAG. On returning to the carriers at 08:15 one of *Biter*'s aircraft crashed on the flight deck and temporarily blocked it, so *Dasher* received the remaining four 800 machines as well as three of her own from 891 Squadron, the fourth having been shot down by a Dewoitine. Another aircraft from an afternoon sortie crashed ashore, and by dusk that day *Dasher* had ten serviceable Sea Hurricanes on board, of mixed parentage. The six Sea Hurricanes of *Dasher*'s 804 Flight also flew close escort. After she had launched the Albacores *Furious* flew off ten Seafires of 807 Squadron, which strafed the Martin 167s of Flotille 4F at Tafaroui, while *Formidable*'s six Seafires reconnoitred Mers-el-Kebir harbour, where Sub-Lieutenant A. S. Long, RNZNVR, shot down a Martin 167.

The haze over land and sea destroyed more carrier fighters than the enemy, including six of *Furious*' Seafires, one in a deck landing crash, the other five in ditchings or crashes ashore, and five out of six Sea Hurricanes on a mission from *Dasher*, the sixth being shot down by a Dewoitine. *Dasher* had to play host to more wandering, temporarily homeless Sea Hurricanes when a deck crash had put their ship's flight deck out of action.

Six Seafires from *Furious* and six Sea Hurricanes from *Biter* made the final fighter sweep of D-Day, against Tafaroui, where air reinforcements were reported to be arriving. The Sea Hurricanes provided top cover for the Seafires, which strafed the field and hit a landing Leo 45, which blew up, its attacker being damaged by the blast and forced to ditch alongside *Furious*.

Fighting continued throughout the 9th. Force H stood by to fight off aircraft, surface ships or submarines, but only some sporadic Luftwaffe and Regia Aeronautica bombing or torpedo attacks materialised, all blunted by the combat air patrol Martlets. *Biter* flew off 20 sorties, *Dasher* only six. The latter returned two of the *Biter* guests which had been operating from her back to their own ship. With the RAF and USAAF beginning to operate from the captured airfields, the need for direct air support from the carriers shrank. After eight more tactical recces and four unblooded fighting escort sorties, at dusk *Furious, Biter*, and *Dasher* began a programmed withdrawal to Gibraltar. On the 10th the enemy surrendered. In an unrehearsed attack on the port of Bougie, 160km (100 miles) further east, a Ju 88 bomb hit *Argus* a glancing blow and destroyed four of her Seafires. With only seven fighters left operational, she borrowed four 802 Squadron Sea Hurricanes from *Avenger*, under repair in Algiers harbour, and the 11 machines coped with beach patrols until RAF fighters took over.

Above: It never rains. . . . A second Sea Hurricane crashes into KI F, which has already given the deck a hearty peck.

THE SANDS OF CASABLANCA

D-Day dawned warm and clear for the Western Task Force. Cal Durgin's aggressive *Ranger* anticipated the strike signal 'Play ball!' and launched planes at 06:15. First off the deck was Lieutenant-Commander John Raby, leading nine F4Fs of his Fighting Squadron 9. Racing the 120km (75 miles) to Rabat, the regional capital and French Air Force Headquarters, the Wildcats dived through heavy flak to strafe the local aerodrome and destroy seven grounded fighters and 14 bombers. Later that morning they shot down a French aircraft, and on their third sortie Raby's fliers blasted seven Dewoitines on the ground at Port Lyautey, 145km (90 miles) to the north in *Sangamon*'s parish. Wildcats in squadron strength from *Ranger* and *Suwannee* lost four planes in a dogfight with 16 French fighters but shot down eight of the enemy. Eighteen Dauntlesses dive-bombed submarine pens at Casablanca. The *Jean Bart*, unseaworthy but carrying a big punch in her 380mm (15in) battery, cruisers, destroyers and shore batteries opened fire on the American ships. The new battleship *Massachusetts* and two US cruisers returned the fire, planes from *Ranger* and *Suwannee* strafed and bombed them. The French cruiser *Primaguet*, two big flotilla leaders, five destroyers and a number of submarines sortied to give battle. The destroyers fired torpedo spreads at the USS *Massachusetts* and the cruiser *Tuscaloosa*. This bold squadron was shelled, dive-bombed, strafed, scattered and chased. The *Primaguet* was bombed into a burning hulk. Hit by warship fire, three destroyers were finished off by aircraft, the remaining French ships being driven ashore or forced back into harbour. The two carriers kept planes in the air all day fighting off French attempts to attack landing craft and transports at the beaches, then at 14:30 the French forces at Fedala surrendered, and General Patton's main assault troops began going ashore. SOC Seagulls from a cruiser and a battleship broke up French columns with impact-fuzed depth-charges.

The northern landing at Mehedia on the mouth of the Sebou River was also hotly opposed. *Sangamon* had lurked in the darkness well out over the horizon until it was time to play her part. As she waited there, a French coastal convoy of five lighted merchantmen, with the escort vessel *Lorraine*, blundered into the invasion transport area. *Lorraine* immediately informed the signal station at the Kasba fort of the presence of the American fleet, obviously intending to invade the area at dawn. Kasba signalled back 'Quels sont les bateaux?' just after midnight, and at 06:30 fighters and bombers from the Rabat-Salé airfield strafed and bombed the landing boats, and two Dewoitine fighters attacked the cruiser *Savannah*. At 07:30 air protection for the invasion force was requested and in just over 15 minutes 20 Wildcats from *Sangamon* and *Ranger* were in the area. By 09:00 they had shot down some nine aircraft and driven off the rest. They then transferred their attention to the Port Lyautey and Rabat-Salé airfields, after which the northern landing was free of air attacks.

At daybreak on 9 November the Third Armored Landing Team moved off up the Rabat road and was attacked by a column of tanks of the famous Chasseurs d'Afrique. *Sangamon*'s planes and *Savannah*'s guns destroyed four tanks, and the rest withdrew into the dubious shelter of an aromatic eucalyptus grove followed closely by Lieutenant R. Y. McElroy in his Avenger, flying so low that his wings smelled of eucalyptus oil afterwards, but he pinpointed the tanks and led an attack on them in which his TBF took 13 hits from AA guns. At 09:00 more French tanks appeared but were defeated in a mobile battle in

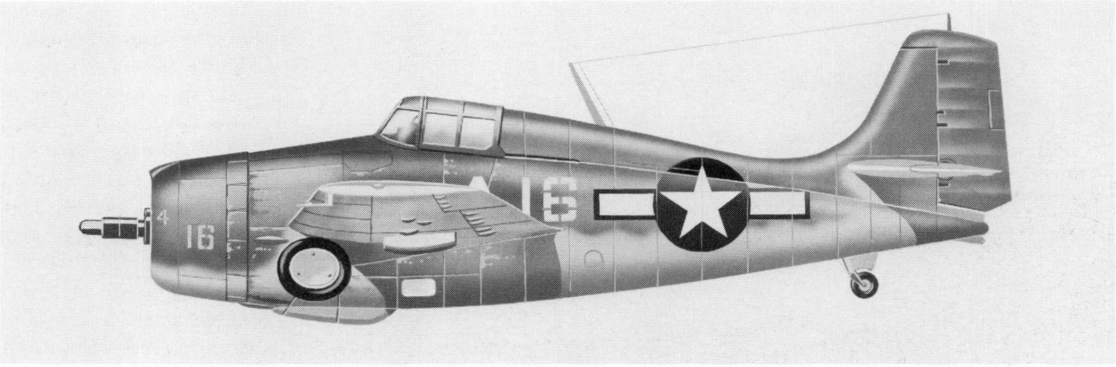

Right: Grumman F4F-4 Wildcat. (J. M. Goulding)

Opposite page top: A Sea Hurricane chews up the deck after losing its starboard undercarriage leg in an argument with the barrier (FAA Museum)

Opposite page, centre: Sea Hurricane in the Goofers. (FAA Museum)

Opposite page, bottom: A French Dewoitine fighter shot down during 'Torch'. (FAA Museum)

this good tank country. An urgent request for dive-bombers to destroy a road block was answered in 15 minutes by *Sangamon* SBDs. By 10:30 on 10 November P-40s from *Chenango* were using Port Lyautey airfield. Fort Kasba was the most troublesome source of opposition. Reminders of *Beau Geste* were banished four minutes after the first request for more SBDs, when they made such an accurate bombing attack on the fort that its garrison marched out with their hands up.

In the south at Safi, *Santee*, greenest of the green *Sangamon*s, was in support, with her 14 Wildcats, eight Avenger TBFs and nine Dauntless SBDs. The weather off Safi as at the other landing places, was fine and sunny on D-Day morning, but not perfect for the aviators. There was no wind, an absolute dead calm prevailed. *Santee*'s top speed was only a little over 18 knots, and she needed every extra knot of wind to get planes off the deck with any sort of worthwhile load. After the catapult malfunction during working up which had cost one Dauntless SBD, Captain Sample did not want to use it for this first important operational sortie, so the order was given to deck-launch. The ship was wound up to flank speed, almost 19 knots, and the first TBF 'Turkey' piloted by the air group commander, started its roll down the deck. It seemed to be hardly moving as it neared the bow. As it went over the edge of the flight deck the bulky Grumman fell towards the sea. The experienced pilot quickly converted this to a dive to gain more airspeed, pulling his wheels up at the same time. For a moment clouds of spray thrown up by his propeller lashed the water behind him. Then slowly he was clear and climbing. The next two pilots were not so experienced. Both splashed. The other TBF's bomb loads were cut, and they made it off the deck. The SBDs followed with one 227kg (500lb) bomb each, and finally seven Wildcats, to fly CAP protection for the transports and landing craft. Engine torque caused one Wildcat to take off over the side catwalk, and its tail hit the uptilted barrel of one of the 40mm quick-firing cannon, but the machine remained airborne and disappeared over the horizon with the others, heading for an attack on Marrakesh airfield.

For hours the *Santee* sailors sweated and sweltered in the sun-warmed, torpid air, squinting in the glitter off the steel-smooth sea, listening for the drone of aero engines, watching for the black dots, like flies, on the horizon, but there were only the ships of their escort to look at and in the east the dim outline of the African coast. There was a sudden crackle of static, and the distorted voice of an F4F pilot reporting his oil line cut – whether by enemy action or otherwise he did not specify – then the silence returned and he was not heard from again. Then quite suddenly they were there, regrouping round the ship for a landing. There was still no wind, but almost all the planes landed safely. There was one barrier crash when a TBF caught the last wire and entangled its propeller in the barrier cable. Finally all the aircraft were aboard, except the Wildcat that had hit the gun on take-off. In doing so it had damaged the tail hook housing, and when the pilot lowered the hook it did not extend fully, but he was signalled to come in. He made a perfect touch-down, catching the first wire, upon which the rest of the hook was pulled out with a wrench that broke the plane in two just behind the cockpit. The tail flew backwards over the fantail into the sea. The forward part of the plane careered on up the deck, with everyone on deck scattering wildly, its starboard wing caught the corner of the island and it bounced sideways into the barrier. The pilot climbed out shaken but unhurt. This spectacular incident added to the excitement on the flight deck. They had met the enemy. There was a bullet hole through the windscreen of one plane, and a wounded Dauntless rear gunner to prove it.

Later in the afternoon troops on the beach called for smoke cover. The one smoke tank aboard could only be fitted to an SBD and represented the maximum load the plane could carry under the best conditions. An SBD was ranged. The pilot was dubious, and argued with the Air Officer, but the latter won. The wind had picked up slightly, and the SBD, with the heavy tank under its belly was spotted as far back on the fantail as it could get. *Santee* turned into the slight wind, and the plane started down the deck. It reached the

forward round-down and the oleo struts had not even started to extend, meaning that the plane was still well below flying speed. It went over the bow and dropped like a stone into the water less than 90m (100yd) ahead of the ship. Fortunately the crew swam clear and were later picked up, wet and extremely displeased with the Air Officer. Another SBD came into land on at the end of its mission, the pilot cut his motor and, true to character, the Dauntless floated, missed all the wires, cleared the barrier and landed among the aircraft parked for'ard, damaging six other planes, three beyond repair.

The drama of Safi was not over for the *Santee*s. The fighters flew off on a strike – and did not return. Having spent too long over the target, they ran out of fuel before they could locate the carrier. Some landed on or near Mazzagan airfield and were taken prisoner, their planes lost to *Santee*. The Squadron Commander, Lieutenant-Commander Paul Blackburn, was listed as missing. The last adventure involved the TBFs. With the airfield in US Army hands, it was decided that *Santee*'s Avengers should make a token landing there. But the field was soft sand and had been used before only by light aircraft. The big TBFs got bogged down. They were towed to the road which bordered the field, with a fruit orchard on the other side, and tried to take off. The road was narrow, with the trees cramping a take-off run, and there was a cross-wind. All but one of the planes that tried it ended up in the ditch, and the excitement must have been too much for the pilot who made it into the air, as he went into the barrier on regaining *Santee*.

Her score now was: almost all her 14 fighters captured or at the bottom of the Atlantic; six out of eight TBFs lost ashore, with two damaged machines below in the hangar; two SBDs lost, with seven safe aboard; but all aircrews alive. Fortunately only one aircraft was requested immediately for reconnaissance ashore, and Lieutenant-Commander Joseph Aloysius Ruddy, USN, *Santee*'s Air Group Commander, flew the mission himself. He climbed into his cockpit with some difficulty, 'burdened like a porter on a long safari', as Captain Sample reported, with a murderous-looking knife, rifle, shotgun and handguns, a garrotte, a special knapsack crammed with various home comforts, including food, a pair of 7 by 50 binoculars and a camera.

Another of *Santee*'s aviators, strictly against orders, stirred up the dormant French at Marrakesh airfield. On a recce over the field he saw one plane landing and two starting up engines, dropped two bombs, which failed to detonate, and was fired on by AA guns. With the French there forced into reluctant action, Joe Ruddy led some of *Santee*'s surviving aircraft there, and on the way sighted a motorised column of troops heading for Safi from Marrakesh. Three planes

Above: Douglas Dauntless SBD-3 bombers aboard USS *Santee*. As the fore part of the flight deck is full, the Air Officer has ordered this aircraft to be struck below, and has just ordered the next SBD to go round again until the deck is clear. (US Navy)

Right: A Grumman Avenger TBF is brought up from an escort carrier's hangar for a mission, angled diagonally on the lift for clearance.

peeled off and claimed to have destroyed 12 of the 14 trucks. Another aircraft destroyed 20 grounded planes at Marrakesh, and attacked another convoy of 40 trucks on the way back to the ship.

In 'Torch' US Navy escort carriers were going into action for the first time, and there was a general lack of experience, a feeling too of rehearsal – for the hard battles to come in the future. However, *Santee*'s first and subsequent strikes had helped the landing gain a foothold in the harbour in the early hours of D-Day, with heavy fire from the battleship *Texas*, the cruiser *Philadelphia* and the destroyers close-in knocking out batteries. Before long, transports were unloading at the quays, and 6,000 men and 100 tanks were beginning their march northwards to Casablanca where the French were resisting fiercely, with the Navy in support off the coast. As the Army reached the *Santee* planes still bogged down, engineers laid steel mats to assist take-off. *Santee* launched aircraft and refuelled her consorts until Friday 13 November, when she sailed for Bermuda with her task group.

The fighting round Casablanca continued throughout the 9th, and the *Jean Bart* was hit twice by Dauntlesses, but her one remaining workable turret opened up again on an American cruiser. Dauntlesses armed with 907kg (1,999lb) bombs sank her in shallow water, and all her guns were at last silent. Later that day a French submarine narrowly missed *Ranger* with a salvo of four torpedoes. In the afternoon 'Jocko' Clark's *Suwannee* became the first US carrier to sink an enemy submarine in World War 2, when her planes found and destroyed what they thought was a German U-boat under a fog bank, but which turned out to be one of the three French boats which had sortied from Casablanca on the

Top left and left: An Avenger TBF, given a wave-off by the Landing Signals Officer ('Bats'), has hooked a wire, which slams it to the deck. The machine plunged over the side and hung precariously from the port catwalk. A rope was let down to the stranded crew, who climbed to safety. The Captain and Air Officer study the wreck grimly. (US Navy)

Above: This inexperienced pilot failed to counteract his Wildcat's built-in swing on take-off, veered to starboard and tried to demolish a 20mm AA gun and its crew, with inevitable results. A gunner's 'battle bowler' has been knocked off and flies through the air. (US Navy)

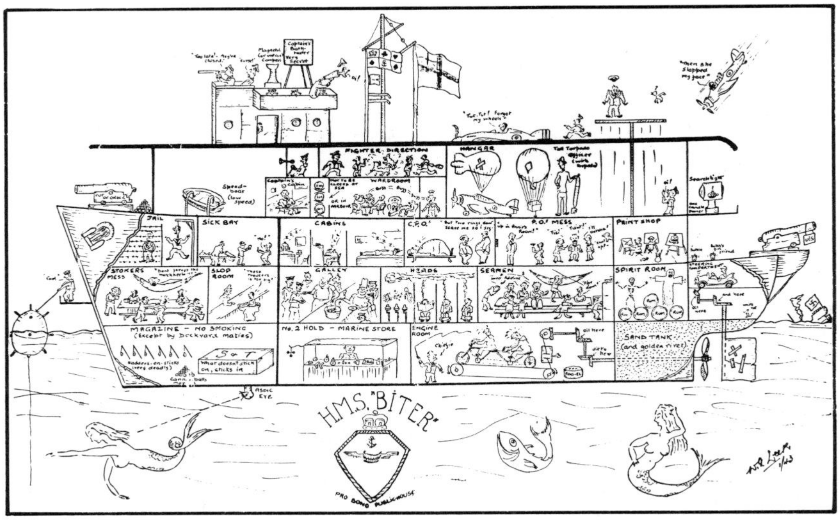

Above: Cartoon of HMS *Biter*, drawn by an unskilled but inventive member of her ship's company.

first day of the assault. They did not know it at the time but after the war it transpired that they had sunk three more French submarines in harbour.

In 'Torch', although less than a month after commissioning, *Suwannee* maintained constant combat air patrols, anti-submarine patrols and ground support. In four days of operations off the West Africa coast her 29 Wildcats and nine Avengers between them flew 255 sorties, losing five aircraft. On the forenoon of the 10th the power of the battleship *Texas*, the cruiser *Savannah* and a destroyer force finally subdued the stubborn defence of Mahedia to the north sufficiently for a destroyer to enter the river and carry a party of troops to capture the airfield at Port Lyautey, 14.5km (9 miles) upstream. *Chenango* began flying off her consignment of 78 Army P-40 fighters to the field, many of which were damaged on landing.

General Patton now had enough troops round Casablanca to plan a land assault on the town on the 11th, but by that time word had come through that Admiral Darlan had been accepted by General Eisenhower as the responsible authority in French North Africa, and had agreed to end all resistance and co-operate with the Allies.

HMS *Archer* also brought 35 Curtiss P-40F Warhawks for the USAAF. The fighters lined up in turn, had the strop attached, and the grim-faced young pilots forced their heads back against the head-rest ready for the thrust of the catapult, opened up to full revs, gave a thumbs-up and the catapult took control. The Warhawks squatted down as their hydraulic legs were compressed under the pull of the catapult, then leapt forward along the short length of deck and into the air, often disappearing from view over the bows before finally clawing into the air. One forgot to take his brakes off, and his Warhawk was dragged protestingly over the bows by the catapult, unused to such resistance. The pilot was half-way out of the cockpit before the machine hit the water. The strain was too much for the catapult, which failed just as the last Warhawk accelerated.

THE LOSS OF *AVENGER*

Biter and *Dasher* left Gibraltar in convoy for Britain on 12 November and reached Greenock safely on the 19th. *Chenango*, whose important but passive role had been the same as *Archer*'s, got her lumps on the passage home when she was one of the unlucky returning vessels to run into a hurricane. Wild seas washed away a gun director, two gun mounts, twisted and tore the superstructure and ripped the flight deck upward and aft like a sardine can.

On 14 November *Argus* and *Avenger*, her fractious engines turning again, left Gibraltar as escorts for Convoy MKFI of eight merchantmen for Britain. The ships were in four shallow columns, with *Avenger* the middle ship in the second column of three, *Argus* to starboard of her in the third column. At 02:55 in the blackness of the graveyard watch a depth-charge from a screening destroyer on the port beam was heard and felt by the other ships, which had begun a 45 degree emergency turn to starboard when a white rocket went up from the *Almaack*, lead ship on the port wing, to indicate that she was hit. Two minutes after this a torpedo from *U-155* hit *Avenger*'s thin, unarmoured merchantman's plates right abreast her bomb stowage room, port side, above her oil fuel tanks. Men in the *Macharda*, two cables astern of *Avenger*, saw a high column of water and heard an explosion, then a few seconds later there was a vivid red flash from a second and much greater explosion which blew a whole section of the ship right out. *Avenger* was enveloped in a soaring column of dull red flame as she broke in two and jacknifed upwards, bow section disappearing almost at once, stern section lingering briefly, aircraft breaking loose on deck, men jumping overboard or sliding down into the flames. The *Ulster Monarch* steamed over the carrier's former position three minutes after seeing the first flash and found nothing left of her except avgas gleaming and stinking on the sea and the smell of burning oil, with two small twinkling lights on the Mae West life jackets of survivors. They were two of the twelve men from the carrier picked up at dawn. For 802 Squadron this was the third carrier to sink under them, first *Glorious*, then *Audacity*, and now *Avenger*. Captain Marsh, RN, who, as a flight commander had re-formed the squadron after it had been wiped out in *Glorious* and before it went to *Audacity*, spoke to some of the survivors, who told him that the ship had sunk so quickly that the only men to escape had been in a rest room just below the flight deck, and even this was flooded before they all got out. Captain Coulthurst and Commander (F) Nigel Skene were both among the missing.

4

NEW BROOMS

WHILE the few available auxiliary carriers were occupied proving their worth in 'Torch', ambitious new carrier building programmes were under way in the USA which would produce 22 Fleet carriers, nine Light Carriers and no fewer than 99 auxiliaries. The first of the 20 conversions from C-3 merchant hulls ordered after Pearl Harbor were in commission. The lead ship, USS *Bogue*, was exercising with her new Composite Squadron off San Diego, while the first of the ten for the Royal Navy, HMS *Attacker*, was in British waters. In the summer of 1942 the US Navy had ordered 24 auxiliary carriers of the *Prince William* Class, an improved Long Island type also based on C-3 hulls. but the Allies needed more carriers than the shipyards could produce. Then 'Hurry Up Henry' stepped in.

'HURRY UP HENRY'S' FLEET

Henry J. Kaiser personified the American Dream. Born in upstate New York, he left school at 13 and applied dynamic energy and determination coupled with long-sighted practical vision to a career in industry. In 1909 he went into the gravel and cement business and in 1914 was building roads in Canada, Cuba and California for half the cost and in half the time other firms took. He gained Roosevelt's confidence when he built the great Boulder and Grand Coulee Dams. When war came in 1941 there was a great shortage of merchant shipping. 'Hurry Up Henry', as the Press called him, filled the gap. On the Pacific coast he built seven shipyards, a steel mill, an engine plant, and for his work force a whole community, Vanport City, second largest in the State, on swamp land between Portland and Vancouver, Oregon, with 10,400 housing units, a hospital, schools and shops. There was a dire shortage of skilled men, and Henry trained up an unskilled, largely female, work force to become experts at just one simple job.

Using new techniques like prefabrication and all-welding, they produced in great numbers the Liberty Ship, not a pretty vessel but with a kind of gaunt, functional beauty. At their peak of performance they could turn them out at the rate of one every eight days, the record being 7 days, 14 hours and 29 minutes for the 10,500-ton SS *Robert Peary*, a record in any shipyard. 'Wilma the Welder' worked three shifts 24 hours a day, with one

Below: 'Hurry Up Henry' Kaiser looks through a peephole in one of his blast furnaces where metals were mixed for his new escort carriers, 'Kaiser's Coffins'.

Below right: Admiral Earnest J. King, Commander-in-Chief, United States Fleet. (US Navy)

Right: Wilma the Welder worked eight hours a day in wartime US shipyards. She was no Helen of Troy but she launched 122 CVEs. (Todd Pacific Corporation)

shift's welders racing the next to see which could complete the highest footage of welding.

When Henry heard of the need for more 'jeep' carriers he talked briefly with his designers and, as some concession to established channels, hurried along to the Bureau of Ships with drawings of a very basic aircraft carrier prepared by naval architects Gibbs & Cox, based on one of his merchant hulls, and an offer to build 30 or more of them in six months, provided the Navy gave him a free hand in their design and construction. The BuShips bureaucrats turned him down. 'Stick to what you know' had been the gist of their reaction. Liberty Ships, wartime throwaways, were one thing, aircraft carriers quite another, more complex, subject to many more stresses – you could not build an ACV Kaiser's way. Conservative Navy and BuShips brasshats disliked Henry and suspected that profit was the name of his Hurry Up game. Opposition from established shipbuilders could, of course, be expected.

But Henry hurried straight along to the White House, showed his sketch and made his pitch to his old patron F.D.R., who looked briefly at the drawings, said, 'Done, old sport', shook his hand, and in spite of resistance by BuShips, Admiral Emory Land's Maritime Commission and fishheads in the Service, got a contract to build a maximum of 55 small carriers on Maritime Commission PL fast transport hulls, with BuShips and BuAer to supervise developments and construction. On Henry's assurance, four ships were scheduled for delivery in February 1943, the rest by the end of the year. George Sharp, Kaiser's design agent, went ahead with working drawings, hull lines were drawn with the help of BuShips' James Bates, and the Navy gave special advice on the design of the flight deck.

There was only one real problem – engines. With the number of US shipyards up from a prewar 12 to 300, all building some type of warship, there was fierce competition for all materials and equipment, and for once Kaiser was last in the queue. The *Bogue* Class had cornered all the available steam engines, the forthcoming BuShips-designed *Commencement Bay* Class, copies of the *Sangamons*, had been promised standard geared turbines. Kaiser was left without engines, but not for long. Henry found the Skinner Uniflow reciprocating steam engine, developed in 1912. The opposition smiled. He could have the Skinner, and welcome. The Skinner was hard to manage, expensive to operate, unable to maintain a proper supply of clear boiler feed water, and the expanding steam tended to carry lubricating oil into the condensate – no one in his right mind would choose the Skinner . . . 'Problems', said Henry, 'are opportunities in working clothes.' He built a plant to produce the rogue engines, and put his engineers to work righting the faults. They put loofah sponges in the hot wells, and diatomaceous earth filters in the condensate lines, and the Skinner became a working proposition, driving twin screws for greater safety and easier manoeuvring in the confined spaces of a crowded wartime harbour or when facing torpedoes.

A Winter's Tale

With this great promised fleet in build or on paper, there would still be no auxiliary carriers available before the spring of 1943, for the Battle of the Atlantic or Russian convoys, the latter suspended during 'Torch' for lack of escorts, and badly needed. In November U-boats sank 700,000 tons of Allied shipping, 500,000 of it in the Atlantic, but after 'Torch' *Archer* went into Alexandria Dock at Liverpool for her anglicization programme, and increases in her gun armament, *Biter* to Dundee for overhaul and *Dasher* to Liverpool for enlargements to her Air Direction Room. On flying exercises in the Clyde was a spartan, narrow-decked British-built small carrier, HMS *Activity*, converted by the Caledon Shipbuilding Company at Dundee and commissioned on 27 September. Her longer, 150m (492ft), flight deck did not compensate for her lack of a catapult. She could operate 15 aircraft but was scheduled for pilot training. The new *Bogue* Class HMS *Attacker*, with capacity for at least 18 aircraft and all American amenities, including an accelerator, was queuing up for her British modifications. Of 'Torch's' oiler/ACV quartet, *Sangamon, Suwannee* and *Chenango* were in the Pacific, *Santee* had been retained in the Atlantic but after repairs was to go south of the Equator to hunt blockade runners. The first four 'Kaiser coffins' were due for delivery in February but delays had crept into the new programme, due to a combination of teething troubles and official interference. In January contracts were signed for the first ships of a further ACV class (the *Commencement Bays*) of 23,000 tons and a maximum speed of 19 knots.

The huge demands of 'Torch' and the general wear and tear of a hard year's fighting at sea seriously reduced the number of convoy escorts available. The Allies were only sinking U-boats at about half the rate at which they were being built. Winter was a good escort on the Russian run, with its fierce gales and fog and the long Arctic nights. A few single unescorted merchantmen, two JW and two RA convoys got through. Light cruisers HMS *Sheffield* and *Jamaica* turned back the heavy cruiser *Hipper* and the pocket battleship *Lützow* (ex-*Deutschland*). But with February the gales decreased, daylight began to push back the Arctic darkness, Dönitz started a new offensive with 100 U-boats and Allied ship losses started to rise again. Four Allied auxiliary carriers were preparing to join the convoys. *Dasher* actually started for Russia with the 28 merchantmen of Convoy JW53, but a heavy gale arose; *Dasher* sprang several welds in her hull and turned back for repairs, then there were three.

BOGUE RUNS INTERFERENCE

HMS *Archer* and *Biter* were working up with Swordfish and Martlets in the Firth of Clyde, but the US Navy's *Bogue*, ACV-9, was ready first. Launched on 15 January 1942 at the Seattle-Tacoma Shipbuilding Corporation's Seattle, Washington, yard as the SS *Steel Advocate*, *Bogue* was commissioned eight months later by Captain Giles E. Short, USN, a regular Navy aviator of long experience, including service in the old *Langley*, in *Yorktown* as a squadron commander, and as Air Group Commander in *Enterprise* in 1939. *Bogue*'s vital statistics were much the same as *Long Island*'s. She displaced 7,800 tons, overall length was 138.9m (455ft 8in), beam 21m (69ft 6in), flight deck 34m (111ft 6in) wide (2.75m or 9ft more than *Long Island*'s), draft 7.9m (26ft), maximum speed 18 knots (two knots more), armament two 5in AA guns, ten twin 40mm and 27 single cannon, her engines geared turbines. The first three of the *Bogue* Class, *Bogue* herself, *Card* and *Core*, had two catapults at the fore end of the flight deck, but most others of the class only one.

Many of *Bogue*'s ship's company were survivors from the *Lexington*, sunk on 8 May in the Coral Sea battle, and found the small merchantman/carrier claustrophobic below decks. *Bogue* began trials on 26 October in Puget Sound, Washington. On 24 November she embarked the 12 tubby Wildcat F4F-4 fighters and nine deep-bellied Avenger TBF-Is of her Composite Squadron (VC) 9. For *Bogue* and her class, steam turbines had been preferred to diesels, and she was two or three knots faster than the *Archers*. Training cost the lives of an Avenger crew in a mid-air collision, but continued all the way to Panama, with operational anti-submarine patrols flown as *Bogue* crossed the Gulf of Mexico and steamed up the coasts of Florida, Georgia and the Carolinas to Norfolk, Virginia, for modifications, exercises in mid-ocean refuelling and more flying practice. An F4F crashed on deck and plunged overboard, killing the LSO and drowning its pilot. On 24 February *Bogue* sailed for Argentia, the Atlantic convoy base in Newfoundland, Canada.

ACV.9, typically of all her tribe, from AVG.I, *Long Island*, to CVE.117, USS *Saidor* (commissioned on 4 September 1945), was not a pretty ship, with her deep, blunt-stemmed merchant hull, topped off and top-heavy with the rectangular slab of the hangar deck, though to see her swing into wind and launch planes was to become aware of a certain beauty in motion. The open bridge on the small island tower, the shape of a cornflake box stuck vertically on the starboard side of the ship, well forward, was the Officer of the Deck's territory and the Captain's habitat in dangerous waters or when flying was in progress.

Below: USS *Bogue*, name ship of the post-*Long Island* class of US-built escort carriers, which pioneered their anti-submarine operations in the Atlantic, and was the first to sink a U-boat (*U-569*) with her aircraft, on 22 May 1943, followed very closely by HMS *Archer*, a Swordfish from which destroyed *U-572*, the first escort carrier to score a kill with the new rocket-projectiles (RPs). (US Navy)

It was only a few steps away from his emergency cabin just below, where he slept at sea to be in close touch with the action, a simple two-room suite, bedroom with bunk, chest of drawers, chair and chart table, and office/dining room. The Air Officer ruled the after part of the island, with his telephones and flags, and below in the Air Office used models of the flight deck and aircraft to plan deck spotting. Next door was the Air Plot for tracking the ship's planes in the air.

In harbour, with the squadron disembarked, the hangar was spacious enough for Bob Hope or Betty Grable and a full USO troupe to put on a show. There was also a fully equipped cinema projection room above the after end. A screen was lowered from the deckhead for'ard so that the men who fought the U-boats could watch John Wayne or Erroll Flynn winning the war. At sea the 'garage' was crammed with TBFs and fighters. *Bogue* could pack in 30 aircraft, but even with wings folded there was not much space for her current eight big Avengers, 12 Wildcats, torpedoes, depth charges, spare engines, propellers, wings, rudders, elevators and wheels. There was also a repair shop, and a badly damaged plane could be rebuilt faster than the Navy Yard could do it.

Below the hangar deck was the mess hall, a cafeteria where the enlisted men lined up for defrosted Hamburg Steak, French fries, beans, coffee and Mom's apple pie with ice cream, or a sirloin steak. Coffee, hot chocolate and sandwiches were available at all times, day and night.

Allied merchant ship losses rose in February 1943 to a disturbing total of 63 ships (359,328 tons) as SC121, first of four convoys to be sailed to Britain at short, staggered intervals, left Sydney, Cape Breton Island, with the eight surface escorts of US NAvy Group A3. *Bogue* arrived at Argentia on 1 March and on 5 March sailed with two old destroyers *Belknap* and *George E. Badger* as Task Unit 24.4, a Mid-Ocean Carrier Escort Group under Commander Task Force 24, to join the escort for HX228, the second convoy of the group.

Escort Group B3, comprising two British destroyers and a corvette, two Polish destroyers and three Free French sloops, joined the convoy in the forenoon of 6 March, the *Bogue* group in the afternoon. It was a big convoy of 61 merchantmen in 13 columns. On the 7th *Bogue* took station in a lane of her own, seven cables wide between the fifth and sixth columns, where she could launch planes by accelerator, and flew off TBF anti-submarine patrols, dawn to dusk. They sighted no U-boats, but ahead of them SC121, savaged and scattered by gales, with asdics knocked out, was running into heavy concentrations of them. HX228 turned to starboard into some wild, non-flying weather, but on the 10th HF/DF intercepted signals from a U-boat just 40km (25 miles) forward of their port beam.

It was Kapitänleutnant Hunger's *U-336*, southernmost boat of the 13-strong *Neuland* Group, stationed across the path of HX228. *Bogue*, on orders from Senior Officer Escort in the British destroyer *Harvester*, launched Lieutenant Alex McAuslan, who sighted Hunger in mist and rain. 'This is it!' he called to his crew, and dived. Hunger crash-dived. Twice McAuslan attacked, twice his DCs stuck in the racks. He alerted a destroyer, then shortage of fuel drove him back to *Bogue*. Lieutenant Roberts was returning off patrol when his turret gunner saw a U-boat crash-diving two miles from the carrier. Roberts hit the button. One DC fell, detonating late and feebly, a second charge stuck when low temperature affected the release mechanism. At dusk, with shore-based air cover promised at dawn, the *Bogue* group left for Argentia. Her TBFs had driven off one shadower, but his successor, Langfeld in *U-444*, watched the carrier leave, alerted the pack, and six merchantmen were torpedoed, three U-boats and HMS *Harvester* sunk. Behind them SC122 and HX229 were at sea. In the mid-Atlantic gap U-boats hit them and destroyed 21 ships totalling 140,842 tons. An RAF Liberator saved HX229 from further attacks and sank a U-boat.

Bogue returned to Argentia to investigate the depth charge faults, and ten days later joined SC123. At first the wind was too light to receive *Bogue*'s heavy aircraft, then it blew up and down the Beaufort Scale, the temperature fell, and the convoy threaded an icefield at night, the bergs looking like a ghost fleet of white-sailed Flying Dutchmen. It was certainly no weather for flying sailors. Daylight brought raging gales and snow storms. *Bogue*'s TBFs patrolled round the convoy whenever the fury moderated, but were often recalled to the small, gyrating deck and 40-knot winds, though none was lost. It was too rough for *Bogue* to refuel the thirsty destroyers, and when her screen reached their limit Short took them zigzagging home, sparing a TBF to cover ONSI from Britain until fog closed in and ice rimed the flight deck. As before, U-boats appeared when the carrier had gone. A destroyer's DCs damaged the wolfpack organiser, and SC123 reached port unscathed under cover of a Liberator from Iceland. SOE Escort, Commander Donald McIntyre, DSO, RN, reported himself 'pleasantly surprised by the heavy weather in which this small carrier was able to operate'.

U-boat commanders were also impressed. On 26 March, with the German offensive at its height, Kapitänleutnant Purkhold of *U-260* reported to Konteradmiral Eberhardt Gott, Dönitz's Chief of Operations in Berlin, that 'an aircraft carrier inside the screen of a westbound convoy' had prevented him from closing the convoy. The report revived Dönitz's disquiet over the discovery of *Audacity* with her first convoy, but the Germans, recorded the Admiralty, 'never came so near to disrupting communications between the New World and the Old as in the first twenty days of March 1943'. 'It appeared possible', wrote the Chief of Naval Staff, 'that we should not be able to continue convoy as an effective system of defence.' Total losses for the month were a horrifying 103 ships (627,377 tons), two thirds of these in convoy.

THE LOSS OF *DASHER*

Throughout the period of this slaughter HMS *Archer, Biter* and *Dasher* had been working-up with aircraft. On 27 March *Dasher* was in the Firth of Clyde with her aircraft being refuelled in the hangar when she was rent by a tremendous explosion, which blew the whole great slab of her lift out of its well, and the after 4in gun into the sea. The ship sank in some four minutes in about 128m (420ft) of water, and six or seven minutes later the carrier's avgas welled up on the surface and caught fire, trapping those men who had jumped over the starboard, lee side of the ship, and there were many casualties. The British Board of Enquiry attributed the disaster to the igniting of petrol fumes from a leaky valve in a petrol compartment, and blamed the American safety arrangements, 'by our standards practically non-existent', for stowing volatile high-octane fuel in ordinary tanks. The US Navy blamed British inexperience with the system, which was revised on British lines in every US-built RN-manned escort carrier, thus causing further delays in putting them into action, and raising Admiral King's blood pressure.

FIRST MAC-SHIP COMMISSIONED

On 14 April the first grainer Merchant Aircraft Carrier, owned by W. Thompson of Leith, *Empire MacAlpine,* was commissioned. Cargo in the grainer MACs was carried in eight large holds, filled through trunkways extending to the flight deck, where flush watertight hatch covers were fitted. The hangar contained space for four Swordfish with wings folded, the flight deck was 128.6m (422ft) long and 18.9m (62ft) in the beam. One 4in gun, four 20mm and two 40mm Oerlikons formed her gun armament. All Swordfish for the MAC-ships were drawn from No 836 Squadron of the Fleet Air Arm, formed originally by Lieutenant-Commander Ransford Slater, RN, and based first at Belfast, then at RNAS Maydown, near Londonderry, on Lough Foyle.

CONTRASTS IN ALLIED EQUIPMENT

On opposite sides of the steep Atlantic American-built auxiliary carriers with American aircraft

Below: MAC *Empire MacAlpine.* (MoD(Navy))

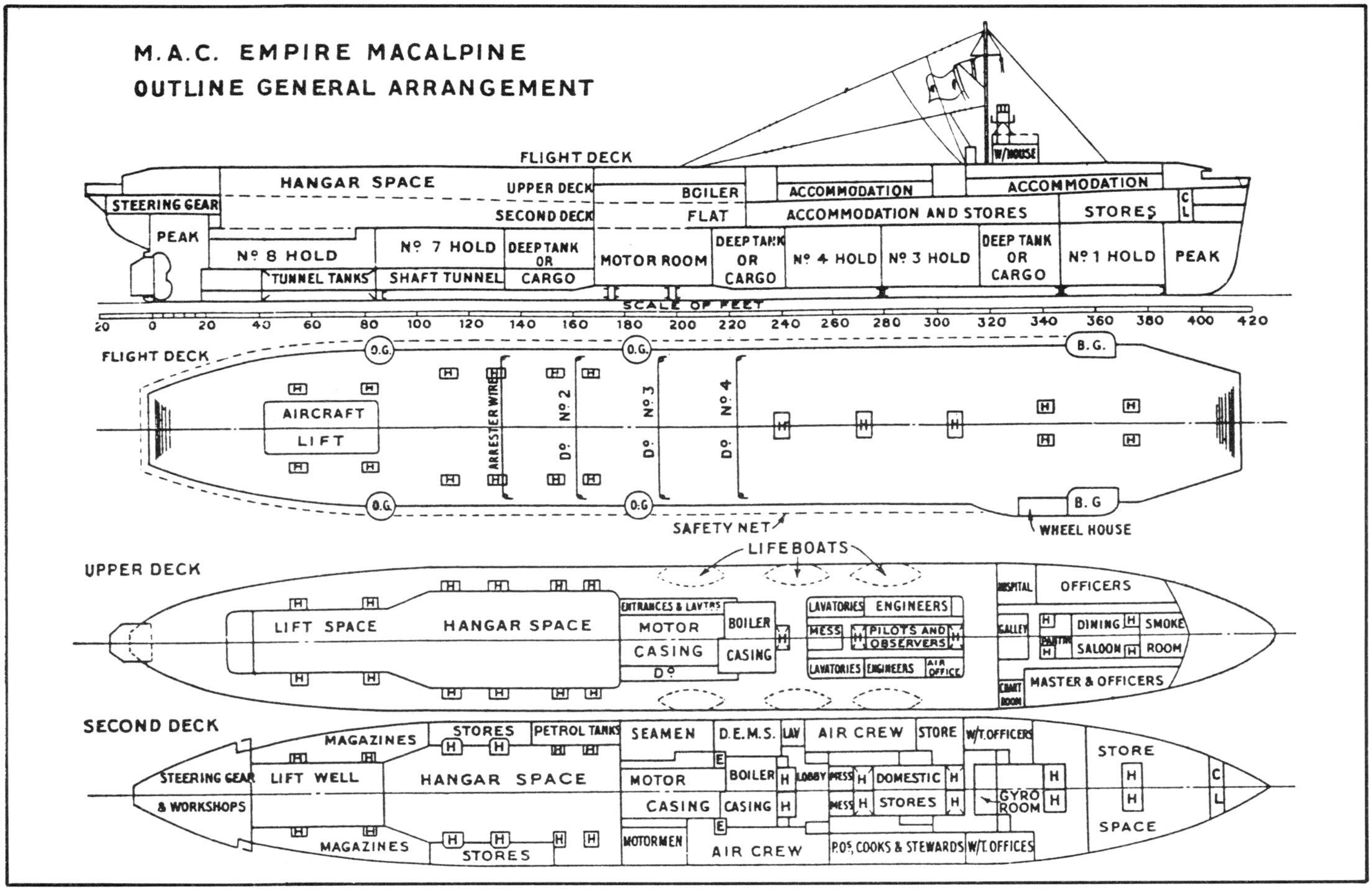

Above: The grainer/MAC ship *Empire MacAlpine*, with her aircraft.

Right: On 25 April 1943 the tenth, and last, *Bogue*-class escort carrier for the Royal Navy, HMS *Ravager*, ACV-34, was commissioned. She spent much of her career as a training carrier, and is seen here later in the war with a variety of aircraft in her hangar, including US Lease-Lend Hellcats, British Barracudas and a Fulmar.

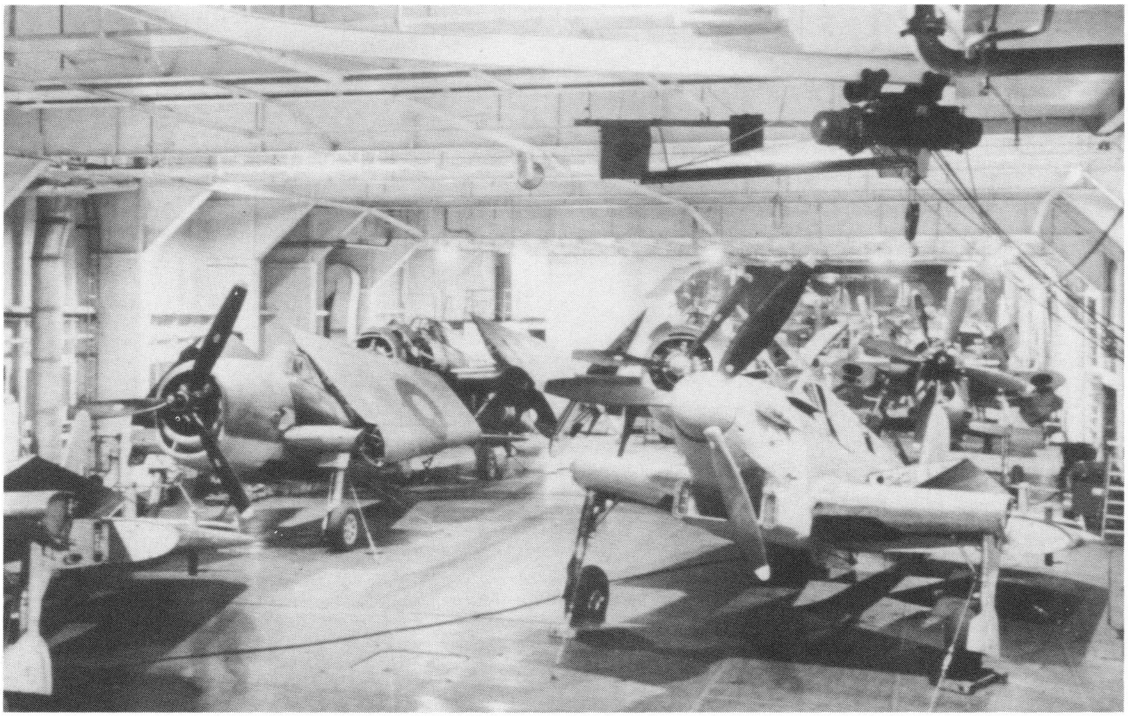

Left: The Swordfish has landed safely and is being spotted on the lift by the flight deck party, under the eyes of the pilot. Smaller birds still airborne await scraps from the gash buckets. (Public Archives of Canada)

Right: A Swordfish Mk II, photographed from its consort 'Stringbag'. Her 'Atlantic' colour scheme of white, with sea-grey upper surfaces, is well weathered.

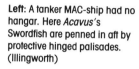

Left: A tanker MAC-ship had no hangar. Here *Acavus's* Swordfish are penned in aft by protective hinged palisades. (Illingworth)

prepared to join the US-UK convoys, *Bogue* for the third time, *Archer, Biter* and *Dasher* on their first operational trips on this run, though the latter pair had been in action before. As ships, *Bogue* was superior to the RN-manned BAVGs, in speed, engine performance and reliability, and aircraft capacity. Both carried basically similar Grumman fighters, the Royal Navy's Martlet II and the US Navy's Wildcat F4F-4. Both had folding wings.

Contrasts between the Avenger TBF-I and the Swordfish TSR II however were spectacular. The stately Stringbag biplane dated back to early 1933 and was obsolete before 1939. The Avenger was the most modern naval bomber in service, and had only got its name after Pearl Harbor. The Avenger, with a 14-cylinder, two-row 1,850hp Wright R-2600-8 Cyclone radial engine turning the immense 3.9m (13ft) Hamilton Standard propeller, had a top speed of 440km/h (274mph) at sea level, 417km/h (259mph) at 3,414m (11,200ft), and 275km/h (171mph) in cruise at 1,524m (5,000ft); a Swordfish with no warload might just manage 200km/h (125mph), 129km/h (80mph) in cruise. Range of a Swordfish on internal tank at economical cruising speed was 878km (546 miles), 1,239km (770 miles) with an extra 261l (69 gal) tank. A TBF could fly 1,778km (1,105 miles) on its basic tankage, 2,236km (1,390 miles) with two drop tanks. The pilot, radioman and turret gunner of a TBF had comfortable closed cockpits, a Stringbag driver sat in a windy open office with the observer and telegraphist/air-gunner in an open bathtub-shaped cockpit low down behind him. A Swordfish had a slow-firing 0.303in machine-gun in front of him, a 0.303 Lewis on a Scarff ring mounting aft. An Avenger pilot had only a 0.30in cowl gun, the radioman another in the belly, the gunner a big 0.5in in his turret. The Avenger was a rugged all-metal monoplane with a strong undercarriage; the Stringbag, although tough enough for its day, was put together with wood and fabric, and more prone to break a leg in a rough landing.

An Avenger was obviously the latest thing, the Swordfish looked like something from *Dawn Patrol.* Yet the TBF did not have all the advantages. The old machines were slow, but kind to hamfisted young pilots. They could be pulled off the deck and put straight into a climbing turn at 55 knots. They had a better view from their open cockpits and could often sight a U-boat sooner, though they were vulnerable in their leisurely dive on a well-defended target. The British trio's Stringbags had better ASV (Air-to-Surface Vessel)

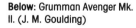

Below: Grumman Avenger Mk. II. (J. M. Goulding)

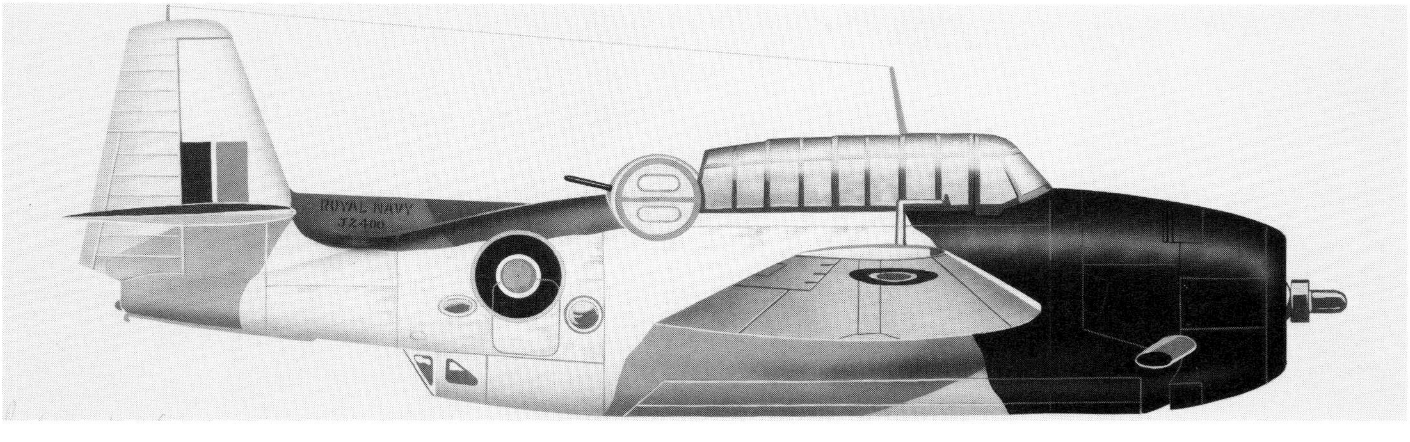

radar than the Avenger. The Avenger could lift four 227kg (500lb) bombs, the Swordfish one less, but some of Lieutenant-Commander O. A. G. Oxley's No 819 Squadron's machines in *Archer* had had their lower planes specially strengthened to operate the new rocket projectiles, with racks for eight fitted to each aircraft. It was a Stringbag which first tested RPs for the RN on 12 October 1942, and *Archer*'s Swordfish were the first naval aircraft to take them to sea. A Swordfish in a position to loose off eight rockets was quite as formidable in fire power as an 8in cruiser firing a broadside. Swordfish had crippled the Italian Fleet at Taranto, and flying from Malta had disrupted Rommel's supply convoys, but at sea with the BAVGs they could not use the American catapults, and would have to balance weight with wind over the deck very carefully.

BITER WITH ONS4

On 21 April HMS *Biter*, with No 811 Composite Anti-Submarine Squadron of nine Swordfish and three Martlet IIs, led by Lieutenant-Commander A. J. B. 'Fanny' Forde, left Hvalfjord, Iceland, to join the escort for Convoy ONS4, on passage to Argentia.

There had been no agreement between SOE Commander Donald MacIntyre and Captain Conolly Abel-Smith of *Biter* on the operating policy for the carrier. MacIntyre expected her to join the convoy on the 22nd but Abel-Smith intended to operate her and her screen as an independent unit covering her charge from a distance, with greater speed and flexibility to hunt down U-boats before they closed the convoy. Instead of joining ONS4, *Biter* shadowed it at a distance, maintaining strict radio silence. SOE's signal on the 22nd requesting the carrier's position was not answered. MacIntyre's HF/DF indicated a U-boat patrol line ahead. Did *Biter* know? The crew of a *Biter* Swordfish, freezing in their open cockpits as the slow biplane battled through snow, sighted a surfaced U-boat and drove it under. *Biter* gave MacIntyre a glimpse of her silhouette through the swirling snow, then hauled off again. MacIntyre took two escorts off down a Huff-Duff bearing, calling up *Biter* for assistance. Shortly after he had himself sunk the U-boat (*U-191*) with his DCs and new Hedgehog mortars, a Swordfish appeared, 'indifferently briefed', he complained, 'and too late'.

Below: Grumman Avenger TBFs above their carrier task unit. The pilot sits in a comfortable leather-covered armchair with a good forward/downward view, and his bomb-aimer/radioman's 'offices' are roomy, though the turret gunner is compressed into foetus shape when he mans the gun. (IWM)

BOGUE WITH HX235

Meanwhile *Bogue* and four destroyers of the new Task Group 92.3 were leaving Argentia for a rendezvous with HX235, which had been routed further south than her previous two convoys. Before this operation, six of her 12 under-employed Wildcat fighters had been removed, her nine Avenger TBFs increased to 12. With U-boats between her and the convoy, *Bogue* flew four Avengers ahead, which gave early cover, joined HX235 herself next day and, unlike *Biter*, once again tucked herself in between the sixth and seventh columns of the convoy. In mild weather the TBFs flew 80–95km (50 or 60 mile) patrols ahead of the ships and off each bow, and circular sweeps at visibility distance. *Bogue* refuelled her parched screen.

Further north in less friendly weather *Biter* was still holding aloof from ONS4, though flying patrols round the convoy. On Easter Day Swordfish 'L' sighted a surfaced U-boat 13km (8 miles) from *Biter* and dropped two calcium sea markers to guide the destroyer *Pathfinder* from *Biter*'s screen, which after five separate attacks sank *U-203*.

Bogue's few halcyon days were over. Wind dropped, a swell rose. The ship demonstrated just how susceptible were the auxiliary carriers, with their light merchant hulls and heavy superstructure, to pitch, especially after they had emptied their tanks into their escort brood. Then the sea subsided and in clear skies midway between Newfoundland and Ireland Lieutenant Roger Santee, USN, sighted a surfaced U-boat and attacked. His four DCs richocheted off the sea, and left no evidence of a hit, but SOE signalled to *Bogue*, 'Please thank pilot whose excellent attack certainly prevented interception of the convoy by this U-boat.'

Next night it looked as if the convoy would be crossing the tracks of U-boats on passage to or from patrol. Short asked SOE if, rather than remain passively inside the convoy, 'Shall I run interference?' SOE was not familiar with American football but got the drift and agreed. Short's TBFs searched for 80km (50 miles) ahead with his screen. No U-boats appeared, and at

Above: HMS *Biter*, from a Swordfish which has just taken off. Two Martlets are ranged aft, on standby, and the ships of the convoy plod on in the background. The carrier has left the convoy to find a wind for launching, and will return as soon as the outgoing patrol is airborne and the incoming one safely aboard. (Peter B. Buckley)

dawn *Bogue* returned to the convoy, first sending a patrol of four TBFs to cover it. Light winds and a heavy swell made landings dangerous, but they were now within range of shore-based German aircraft, and Wildcats flew combat air patrols. Short repeated his positive tactics on the night of the 30th, and carried on to Belfast to have HF/DF fitted and send his air squadron on a fortnight's course at the RAF Coastal Command Anti-Submarine School at Ballykelly.

The passage of these convoys without loss and with the destruction of two U-boats, one shared by a carrier-borne aircraft, reflected a turn for the better for the Allies. Changes in convoy routing, increased operations by escorts, including the first auxiliary carriers on the routes, and by land-based long-range aircraft reduced sinkings in April to 56 ships, totalling 327,943 tons, a little over half the figure for bloody March, and 18 U-boats had been sunk, almost matching the rate of production.

Nevertheless, by May Day 60 U-boats in four groups had gathered in the gap between land-based air coverage south of Cape Farewell. In early May *Archer* escorted ONS6 to Canada without attack, though Sub-Lieutenant (A) P. Martin was drowned when his Swordfish crashed over the side into the sea.

SWORDFISH VULNERABILITY

HMS *Biter* and the 5th Escort Group picked up homeward-bound HX237 in the forenoon of 7 May and once again held off to act independently. Visibility was bad. Two Martlet pilots, flown off to give the fighters something to do, with occasional runs down the convoy lanes 'to hearten the Masters and their crews', lost the convoy, ditched, and were rescued. On the 9th, 5th Escort and *Biter* were ordered by Commander-in-Chief, Western Approaches to join the convoy. *Biter* took up station in a lane all to herself. Weather was bad but on the 10th a Swordfish on patrol at visual distance round the ships sighted a U-boat, attacked her with two depth-charges, and was hit by 20mm shells. Another U-boat fought back on the 11th when a Swordfish left a heaving, rain-lashed flight deck on a Huff-Duff bearing, and there was a repeat next day. This time the Swordfish was shot down by the U-boat (*U-230*) and destroyed by her own DCs.

These losses resulted in new tactics for the vulnerable Stringbags. In future a single Swordfish on sighting a surfaced U-boat was not to attack alone without orders from the carrier, unless the quarry dived, but to hold off and shadow the target, hopefully undetected, until reinforcements arrived, which should include a fighter to silence the U-boat's guns before a TSR attack. Swordfish were to patrol in pairs whenever possible.

Signals from U-boats filled the ether. At noon a Swordfish attacked a diving U-boat (*U-89*), which was picked up and finished off by escorts *Broadway* and *Lagan*. A Very Long Range Liberator appeared and damaged *U-456* with Coastal Command's first use of a Fido homing torpedo, a job completed by a *Biter* Swordfish and the destroyer *Pathfinder*. Two more U-boats were sighted and attacked by Swordfish pairs. With HX237 now under the protection of Coastal Command, *Biter* and the 5th were sent 320km (200 miles) to the southward, where SC129 from New York was being threatened by a wolf-pack. On a practically windless day, the Swordfish were able to lift only two 18kg (40lb) bombs in their racks. Attacking a U-boat with these weapons, one aircraft was hit by gunfire and the observer wounded.

At 10:00 on 21 May *Archer* and 4th Escort joined eastbound HX239, 11 columns of merchantmen and B3 Escort Group. *Archer* took station as rear ship of the seventh column, from which, though a vulnerable position, it was easy to drop out of the convoy to find a wind. Wind and sea were dangerously high for flying, but the RCAF would be with them until the 22nd.

Just moving into the U-boat danger zone from Britain were the 38 ships of ON184 and the eight destroyers of their close escort. Also supporting this convoy, and acting independently as a U-boat hunting group, were *Bogue* and her four destroyers of Task Group 21.12. In his last report Captain Short had criticised the practice of tying a carrier to her convoy, and CINCLANT was giving him the freedom of action which Abel-Smith had wanted for the *Biter* group. After three sorties with no kills, *Bogue*'s aviators were frustrated.

THE FLEET WITHOUT SHIPS

Coincident with *Bogue* taking up her independent cover of ON184, on 20 May Admiral King created the Tenth Fleet. This organisation had no ships of its own, but from cramped and crowded quarters on the third floor of the Navy building in Washington, always buzzing with the urgency of a flagship in action, began to exercise, under the direct command of King himself, 'unity of control over US anti-submarine operations in that part of the Atlantic under US strategic control . . . to control allocation of anti-submarine forces to all commands in the Atlantic, including the Atlantic Fleet,' with Commander Tenth Fleet, 'in order to ensure quick and effective action . . . to be given control of all LR (long range) and VLR (very long range) aircraft, and certain groups of units of auxiliary carriers, escort ships and submarines which he will allocate to reinforce task forces which need help, or to employment as "killer groups" under his operational direction . . .'

As his Chief of Staff in immediate command of the new unit, King brought in Rear-Admiral Frank 'Frog' Low, the brain behind Jimmy Doolittle's raid on Tokyo with Army medium bombers from *Shangri La* (USS *Hornet*). Using F-2, the Combat Intelligence Division of COMINCH, Tenth Fleet had its Anti-Submarine Measures Division for research, material development and training, units for statistical and analytical work, and its Operations Division for moving ships into action, which was actually accomplished by 'recommending' a course of action to Admiral Ingersoll's Atlantic Fleet – with which CINCLANT was tacitly expected to comply. Frog Low was also in close contact with Rodger Winn's U-boat Tracking Room in the Admiralty in London, which maintained a very accurate U-boat plot, aided by the Naval Intelligence Division, and was served by a network of Huff-Duff monitors from

Right: HMS *Broadway*, the former USS *Hunt*, one of the 'four-stacker' destroyers transferred to the Royal Navy, which, with the frigate *Lagan*, finished off *U-89*, damaged by a Swordfish from HMS *Biter*, 11 May 1943. (IWM)

Right: Prang aboard *Archer*. Note the rocket rails under the wings.

the Shetlands to Land's End, and in Iceland, Greenland, Newfoundland and Jan Mayen Island in the Greenland Sea, linking up with Tenth Fleet's similar chain down the western shores of the Americas, so that practically the whole Atlantic was covered.

FRUSTRATED EFFORTS

On its very first day of operations Tenth Fleet learned from its Huff-Duff network that a school of U-boats, perhaps as many as 40, was manoeuvring between Cape Race, Newfoundland and Cape Farewell, Greenland. This urgent knowledge was passed on to CINCLANT, with the assumption that a wolf-pack was forming to attack ON184 and HX239. *Bogue* was ordered to run down the various bearings.

At 21:10 on 21 May Compo 9 CO Bill Drane's duck-egg-blue-and-grey TBF was flying the last patrol of the day in lovely summer weather 100km (62 miles) ahead of the convoy when Drane sighted and attacked a large U-boat, the first boat of a powerful *Rudel* formed by merging the *Donau* and *Mosel* packs. Tenth Fleet's Huff-Duff tuned in to *Donau-Mosel*, and located several U-boats in *Bogue*'s parish.

On the dawn patrol next day, 22 May, Lieutenant (jg) Roger Kuhn's TBF No 2 was cloud-hopping at 140 knots about 88km (55 miles) south-east of *Bogue* when he sighted a U-boat surfacing. He stalked the target while he made his report, then dived on her out of the cloud, and was met by a hail of 20mm shells. He fired his own 0.303 cowl gun and held on. At 180 knots, two seconds from release, his bullets hit the gun's crew, and at 45m (150ft) he let go three Mark 44 flat-nosed Torpex DCs and one Mark 17 TNT. Turret gunner Smith saw them all explode, one under the U-boat's stern, then turned his 50-calibre on men at the 20mm. The submarine circled, blew off a tall jet of compressed air, trailing a big bluish oil streak, finally stopped and sank slowly by the stern.

Lieutenant Dick Rogers in a Wildcat sighted the wake of Kapitänleutnant Rudolph Bahr's *U-305*, and dived out of cloud. Bahr crash-dived, stayed down until the fighter had disappeared, then coolly surfaced again and continued his pursuit of the convoy. He and the lead ships of ON184's screen closed one another head-on, and Ensign Stewart Doty in TBF No 6 sighted *U-305* through a rain squall, dived, reduced to 200 knots to guard against ricochet as the sub loomed under his nose, lowered his wheels briefly to slow down even more, pressed the bomb release, then the emergency release in case the DCs were still aboard. The four charges went off close on the U-boat's port quarter, her stern jerked to port, the whole boat lurched to starboard, she slowed and yawed in the waves and sank under a huge blue oil bubble.

To Doty it looked like a certain kill, but *U-305* was not dead, though a charge had ruptured the pressure hull. Bahr made temporary repairs, and surfaced again, still determined to overtake the convoy. But there were more *Bogue* planes in the air. He got to within 42km (26 miles) of the convoy's starboard quarter when Lieutenant R. L. Stearns in TBF 5, circling the ships at 460m (1,500ft), sighted him. Opening the throttle, Stearns dived. At 685m (750yd) he fired a burst from his cowl gun. The submarine replied with 20mm fire. Stearns held on and released his four DCs in salvo, set shallow, fired two more bursts and saw his DCs explode off the stern and port bow of the U-boat. Below, *U-303*'s crew struggled with leaks as Bahr eluded two destroyers, and eventually headed for Brest.

Right: An Avenger about to land aboard a US Navy escort carrier. The left arm of the Landing Signals Officer is extended horizontally, telling the pilot 'You're in the groove.' In a US-manned carrier the position of the LSO's 'paddles' indicated the actual configuration of the machine – too high, too low, port/starboard wing low/high, etc. – and it was left to the pilot to make the correction, but the same signal from an RN 'batsman' meant exactly the opposite, e.g., a raised left paddle meant 'Raise your starboard wing!' and was an *order*. This difference in operating procedure made any Allied interchange of airmen potentially dangerous.

Right: Lieutenant(jg) William F. Chamberlain, USNR from USS *Bogue*, attacks *U-118*, a 'Milch cow' tanker and general supply submarine. In the lower left of the picture a depth 'bomb' (depth-charge) can be clearly seen about to enter the water, while ahead of it a fountain of white water rises from a near-miss. These two DCs damaged the U-boat, she rose to surrender, and it was hoped to capture her, but her Engineer Officer scuttled her and went down with his ship. (US Navy)

THE FIRST TO SCORE

Frustration filled *Bogue*'s Ready Room, though Doty's U-boat had been celebrated as a 'probable', when at 17:23 Huff-Duff picked up a U-boat transmission 37km (23 miles) off the convoy's port quarter, and Lieutenant (jg) William F. Chamberlain, USNR, with James O. Stine as radioman and Donald L. Clark in the turret, was launched in Stewart Doty's re-armed and re-fuelled TBF 6, climbed into cloud at 460m (1,500ft) and headed down the bearing at 160 knots. Seven minutes after take-off Chamberlain sighted the wake of Kapitänleutnant Johannsen's *U-569*, dived and at 30m (100ft) released all four DCs. Jim Stine got pictures of surprised men in the conning tower. Don Clark shot them up with his 0.50s, and saw the four charges score a perfect straddle, two on each flank of the boat, 12m (40ft) apart. Chamberlain called up *Bogue*, and Howard Roberts was launched in TBF 7. Chamberlain flew back to *Bogue* and was over the ship when he heard Roberts' excited shout over his earphones . . .' 'The sub is coming up!'

The sea around the U-boat seemed on fire from the rays of the westering sun, and Roberts dived at a steep angle. At 180m (600ft) his four DCs fell in salvo. As he pulled out at 30m (100ft) and almost stalled, spray rose and formed an arch over the U-boat's hull. Johannsen had decided to surrender, and ordered a white flag to be got ready. But there was nothing white on board. Curtains, table cloths and sheets were all of oil-resistant green cloth. The U-boat rose, sank, rose again on her side, sank again, rose on an even keel, and men started jumping out of the conning tower hatch. Escort commanders had been briefed to capture a U-boat intact, for its signal manual, orders and code books, and especially its Enigma code machine and daily rotor settings. Roberts' and Chamberlain's turret gunners opened up to keep the crew inside the boat and be unwilling to open the sea cocks. No more heads appeared in the hatchway, but the exodus started again when the air gunners had to change ammunition cans, and some men waved a drab green table cloth. Out of bullets, the two TBFs circled, waiting for reinforcements, and the old ex-US Navy four-piper destroyer HMCS *St Laurent* came foaming up, boarding party at the ready. She was just too late. *U-569*'s Engineering Officer had remained aboard and when he saw *St Laurent*'s boat being lowered he rushed below, opened the sea cocks, and went down with the boat, which sank before the boarding party reached her. The destroyer rescued 24 men. Elation at sinking the first U-boat to be destroyed by an auxiliary carrier was only marred by the failure to capture her.

Back in Washington the new boys of Tenth Fleet were also celebrating this, the first U-boat kill in which they had had a hand, and so soon. To widen any crack in U-boat morale that Johannsen's surrender might portend, Commander Albrecht of Op-16-W, the US Navy's Special Warfare Branch dealing in psychological warfare, delivered in his fluent, perfect German one of the Branch's special broadcasts by the fictitious 'Norden' to the German Navy in which he outlined the best procedures for a surrendering U-boat, recommending that 'something white' should always be carried in a U-boat, as US Navy pilots could not be expected to pick out a green cloth against the colour of the sea. The broadcast was monitored in Germany by U-boat Headquarters, who forbade this precaution. One of those who had also heard it was the commander of *U-460*. When some weeks later he found himself in a hopeless position in an attack by aircraft he produced his white dress shirt, the only white article he had dared to smuggle on board.

Below: Swordfish 'B' of 819 Squadron, HMS *Archer*, sank *U-752* on 13 May 1943, the first naval aircraft to score with rocket-projectiles – from the painting by John Hamilton. (IWM)

Now the scene of action shifted south to HX239, *Archer*'s convoy. At 09:58 on the 23rd Swordfish 'B', armed with eight of the new rocket projectiles, pilot Sub-Lieutenant (A) Harry Horrocks, RNVR, who had distinguished himself flying an Albacore TSR from Malta against the Italian Fleet, observer Sub-Lieutenant (A) W. W. Noel Balkwill, RNVR, and telegraphist/air-gunner Leading Naval Airman John W. Wicks, was flown off *Archer* with orders to circle the port quarter of the convoy and await instructions. At 10:58 they were flying at 460m (1,500ft) when a U-boat was sighted about 16km (ten miles) off. It was Karl Shroeter's *U-752*, heading at 15 knots for the convoy.

Horrocks at once turned to port into cloud cover. Balkwill told him to steer 195 degrees, which should bring them into a good position for a surprise attack. The Swordfish flew on blind for four and a half minutes, then Balkwill called, 'Break cloud now, Harry. She ought to be dead ahead, range just over the mile.' They nosed out of the cumulus and at once saw the U-boat, fine on their port bow about a mile away, holding her original course and speed. Horrocks dived to the attack, target held firmly in the Stringbag's old ring-and-bead gunsight.

He achieved complete surprise. At 730m (800yd) he fired the first pair of RPs. They hit the sea about 140m (150yd) short. The U-boat's klaxon squawked and she upped in a crash dive. At 365m (400yd) the second pair left the rails and fell 27m (30yd) short of the conning tower. The third pair were closer, but still 3m (10ft) short. The U-boat was tilted steeply, her stern clear of the sea, when the fourth and last pair hit her. The two 11kg (25lb) solid heads, fired at 180m (200yd), smashed into the submarine's hull about 6m (20ft) ahead of the diving rudders. She continued to dive for several minutes, then returned to an even keel on the surface and began to circle to port, gushing oil. Men leaped out of the conning tower hatch and manned the 20mm gun. Swordfish 'B' opened the range and requested *Archer* for reinforcements. Nearby Martlet 'B' arrived, firing a long burst into the conning tower, killing Shroeter. The U-boat's crew fired a few rounds at the fighter, then retreated into the conning tower. The Martlet flew over to the destroyer *Escapade* and directed her towards the U-boat. At 10:50 men jumped into the sea as she sank beneath them. *Escapade* arrived and picked up 13 survivors, and ten more were rescued some hours later by *U-91*. As *Archer* left her station to recover aircraft, all ships hoisted 'Well done, aircraft', and the carrier was cheered through the convoy.

5

FIDO AND THE MILCH COWS

CHAMBERLAIN'S and Harry Horrocks' victories were part of a change in the pattern of the Battle of the Atlantic. In the month of May 45 merchant ships were sunk by U-boat – 11 fewer than in April – but most significant was the figure of 41 U-boats sunk, 35 by British hunters, six by the US Navy, in real terms more than balancing the number of their victims. It was a clear-cut victory. During the whole period February-May only two ships were sunk in convoy in the Atlantic while air escort was present. On 24 May Admiral Dönitz signalled to his U-boat captains, 'The situation in the North Atlantic now forces a temporary shift of operations to areas less endangered by aircraft.'

These areas were the Central and South Atlantic and Indian Oceans. The Central Atlantic was the US Navy's responsibility. Through it steamed big convoys of troopships, tankers and freighters from the Americas for Gibraltar, North Africa and Malta, swelling the build-up for the invasion of Sicily, and from West Africa to Britain. Negotiations between the Portuguese dictator Salazar and the British – he would not treat with the Americans – for the use of the Azores as a British air base were in progress, but the situation to the north now freed *Bogue* to come south and her new sister ship USS *Card*, commanded by brilliant naval aviator Captain Arnold Jay 'Buster' Isbell, USN, arrived on the scene in the escort for the 78 merchantmen and 12 tank landing craft of UGS8A for Gibraltar. Isbell's planes of Compo I flew extra patrols on moonlit nights, but saw no submarines with UGS8A or the return GUS8. It was frustrating for the American aircrews, their captains and for Admiral King. Out of a total of 189 U-boats destroyed in the eighteen months of their war, the US Navy had accounted for only 32. In the first five months of 1943, when 96 U-boats had been lost, 16 were down to the Americans. But the situation was about to change.

Right: Grossadmiral Karl Dönitz, a U-boat captain himself in World War I, lost a son in the U-boat Service which he commanded in World War II – before being promoted to head of the Kriegsmarine.

RUDEL TRUTZ

Dönitz had now been promoted Grossadmiral, in command of the entire *Kriegsmarine*, of which U-boat Command was the heart. On 26 May he herded 17 of his depleted U-boats into a north-south patrol line based on the 43rd line of longitude and thumbed his nose at the Allies by naming the new pack *Trutz*, meaning bold obstinacy or defiance. His first order was to deploy off the Azores and await instructions. German Abwehr spies in Spain reported the departure of a convoy from North Africa, and German B-Service Intelligence told U-boat command that this was GUS7A, routed between 37°17′ West and 30°36′ North. Dönitz ordered *Trutz* to form a barrier across its path. But Tenth Fleet had picked up full information on *Trutz*. *Bogue* and four destroyers forming Task Group 21.12 left Argentia on 30 May and headed south to provide 'offensive support' for Convoys GUS7A (westbound), UGS9 (eastbound) and Flight 10 (eastbound), and to seek out the thickest concentrations of U-boats in the area plotted by Tenth Fleet.

Fog and cloud prevented patrols at first, but by late on 1 June *Bogue* was in the western part of the *Trutz* area on a southerly course which would enable her by the 3rd to cover both GUS7A, which seemed in greatest danger, and the two eastbound

Top: The Grumman TBF Avenger first saw service with the US Navy at the battle of Midway, June 1942, and was used as the standard torpedo-bomber by the USN, and as a bomber and minelayer by the Royal Navy (first as the Tarpon, later by its original name) throughout the war. (NASM/Greenhoff)

Above: The Grumman F4F Wildcat was the US Navy's standard fighter at the beginning of World War II, and was also used by the Royal Navy as the Martlet and later under its original name.

convoys, which were 640km (400 miles) to the west. TBFs patrolled ahead and on the flanks, and *Bogue* refuelled her screen. At dawn on 3 June GUS7A appeared to be out of danger. Short sent a TBF to escort Flight 10 for a while, and that night altered course north-east towards what Frog Low's plotters had calculated was the centre of the *Trutz* barrier. Weather was good on the 4th. Flying started at 08:00 with patrols ahead and around the Group. Short reached the position where, according to Tenth Fleet, he could expect a confrontation, but the day wore on and nothing was sighted. At 18:15 five TBFs were launched in bright sunshine to search a wide sector from north to south. Half an hour later Lieutenant (jg) Harry Fryatt, flying wing on Lieutenant Biros' TBF, sighted a U-boat a mile on his starboard beam. Fryatt dived, Biros followed, and battle with *Trutz* began.

The Avengers roared low towards surprised, frightened faces, Fryatt dropped four DCs close to the U-boat, Biros put his in the splashes, debris flew, the sub put up her nose and sank quickly stern-first. At 19:15 Ensign Ted Hodgson overtook and surprised a U-boat gleaming in the sunlight 16km (ten miles) from Convoy Flight 10 and 80km (50 miles) from the task group. The TBF had time to level out and drop its four DCs before a brief gun battle flared up and the U-boat dived. Meanwhile, 40km (25 miles) from *Bogue*, two charges stuck in the bomb bay when Bill Fowler's TBF attacked *U-641* through a hot barrage. The others exploded off the starboard bow. Drane's Avenger dived out of the sun and raked the U-boat's disappearing stern with his charges.

Short knew from the plot that they had hit part of the *Trutz* line. By 08:00 next day five TBFs and a Wildcat were airborne. At 08:50 pilot McAuslan sighted a U-boat heading west at high speed and signalled Rogers' F4F to strafe her. Rogers bored in from her port quarter, duelling with the German gunners until his machine almost scraped the periscope. He made three runs, then McAuslan dived and dropped his DCs from 30m (100ft), straddling the enemy between bow and conning tower. Her bows tilted high in the air and she slid below. McAuslan circled for nearly an hour, watching the slow, inexorable spread of the huge blue oil slick marking the destruction of Korvettenkapitän Bruno Hausmann's *U-217*.

U-217 had been the southernmost boat of *Trutz*. Worried that USG9 might be heading into trouble from the southern part of the *Trutz* line, Short turned south and proved its port flank with his TBFs, concerned at least to keep the enemy down and prevent his concentrating for a pack attack. At 17:00 on the 8th Lieutenant Balliett's TBF found Manseck's *U-758* 16km (ten miles) south of the convoy and closed it fast. This big, well-armed boat fought back hard. Balliett got a straddle in the face of heavy flak, blowing men off the conning tower and lifting the U-boat's hull. The submarine did not dive, and when Fowler's TBF attacked ten minutes later it was hit in the engine, wings and tail, though shaking the U-boat's stern with its DCs. An F4F arrived to silence the flak, the enemy dived, and a third TBF bombed the swirl. The U-boat surfaced again, trailing oil, fired all her guns at the circling planes, then dived again emitting oil bubbles. Later the damaged U-boat *Manseck* dodged a destroyer hunt and crawled home.

At dawn on 12 June *Bogue*'s tired planes and pilots began another hunt. At 13:45 Stearns' TBF No 12 and Johnson's F4F were 32km (20 miles) out on the carrier's starboard quarter when Stearns sighted a U-boat lying stopped on the smooth sunlit sea about a mile ahead of them to starboard. It was Kapitänleutnant Czygan's big 1,600-ton *U-118*, a minelayer/supply boat. The first of these 'milch cows' had been commissioned in April 1942, big, clumsy boats with a cruising range of 19,300km (12,000 miles) and 720 tons of fuel, including enough to refuel – and sufficient stocks of food to re-victual – 12 medium-sized or five large attack U-boats, which increased their time on patrol, or their radius of action to the farthest reaches of the Caribbean or the Cape of Good Hope. The milch cow fleet was brought up to 19 by the addition of the 1,600-ton Type IX minelayers, and for a year the system worked very well. Between April 1942 and May 1943 the milch cows refuelled and re-victualled U-boats nearly 400 times.

When he became head of the Anti-submarine (Intelligence) Section in COMINCH, the USN's Commander Kenneth Knowles, who also served with Tenth Fleet, concentrated on the problem of the milch cows. From a log of U-boat transmissions picked up by Huff-Duff he identified certain regularly repeated signal patterns as arrangements for supply operations. From bearings of these signals, the refuelling areas, mostly near the Azores, could be worked out, and even advanced warning of a refuelling operation given. When the US Navy's ACVs moved into the Central Atlantic, one of their specific missions was to track down and sink milch cows, four of which were always kept on station in the Azores area.

Stearns made his report, other TBFs on patrol heard him and diverted to his aid. Meanwhile Johnson strafed the boat, now submerging, and Stearns got a perfect straddle. The U-boat submerged to a shallow depth, trailing oil and air bubbles. Fowler's TBF and Tennant's Wildcat arrived as the enemy surfaced again. One of Fowler's charges hit the deck, rolled off and exploded alongside. Men tried to activate the four machine-guns in the for'ard conning tower and the twin 20mm in a 'bandstand' aft of that, but the four aircraft strafed the boat into silence. Fryatt's TBF came up and got a straddle with two DCs. The U-boat listed to starboard and started to sink by the stern. Chamberlain joined in, and exploded two DCs right under the battered boat, lifting her out of the white frothing sea. As he dived again the milch cow fired at him and was peremptorily silenced by an F4F. His second pair also burst right under the hull, and one of them penetrated a mine compartment where some six to a dozen mines were lying. *U-118* blew up with a shattering explosion, tossing huge pieces of steel and debris into the air. Fryatt flew over the survivors and dropped his rubber boat. Some waved their thanks.

As far as Short knew, his victim had been a *Trutz* boat, and the 17 survivors could not or would not put him right. He sent his few overworked planes north, east and west, refuelled his destroyers, then steamed to the southward, throwing out air searches and patrols. But the hard-worked accelerator had developed faults and was unsafe. A fully loaded TBF could seldom rely on wind alone to get airborne, and without the accelerator the sort of coverage *Bogue* had been providing would be seriously reduced. His old screen destroyers also needed repairs, and supplies would run out in another four or five days. *Bogue* reported to CINCLANT and Ingersoll ordered her to Bermuda, which she reached on 20

Right: *Core*'s Lieutenant(jg) Steere crashed his TBF on take-off, and he and his crew were rescued smartly by the carrier.

Above: On 12 June 1943 four TBFs and two Wildcats combined to attack the milch cow *U-118*, which blew up when a mine compartment was penetrated after 28 minutes' combat. The U-boat lies helpless, smothered in foam from bomb bursts, the sea pocked by bullets. An Allied destroyer picked up 17 survivors. Lieutenant(jg) Fowler's TBF can be seen top right circling for another attack. (US Navy)

June, struggling to deck-launch patrols on the way in the light winds prevailing. Ingersoll signalled 'Well done'.

Dönitz moved *Trutz* further south to trap the USA-Gibraltar convoys, disposing the surviving 15 boats in three north-south patrol lines 32km (20 miles) apart with their centre 1,367km (850 miles) east of Bermuda, but Tenth Fleet discovered the new concentration, and routed east-bound USG-10 south to avoid it. *Santee*, which had been hunting blockade runners off Brazil with the cruiser *Savannah*, escorted eastbound USG10 round the southern end of *Trutz*, and the only ship lost was a Free French naval tanker sunk by Oberleutnant Gunther Kummetat's *U-572*, Antilles-bound and not a member of *Trutz*, homed in by a radio signal from one of the secret agents planted in the convoy, others of whom had also broken radio silence and/or shown lights to guide U-boats.

British forces had begun July well, sinking *U-126* in the North Atlantic and *U-628* off the Bay of Biscay on the 3rd, *U-535* in the Bay on the 5th. A US Army Liberator sank *U-951* west of Lisbon on 7 July, and next day another US Liberator, guided to *U-232* by its new microwave radar, hit the submarine with two bombs and literally split it in two, though itself badly damaged by the U-boat's accurate flak. Coastal Command of the RAF sank *U-514* in the Bay of Biscay and *U-535* west of Portugal.

But the US Navy was not idle. *Card, Core* and *Santee* and their hunting groups moved into the Central Atlantic, the executive branch of the Tenth Fleet, their Combat Intelligence Centres extensions of the Fleet's intelligence organisation. CINCLANT, Admiral Ingersoll, never quibbled when the Tenth's 'recommendations' reached him, and if any group commander objected Frog Low could always pull Admiral King's rank on him. Together the three CVEs mustered almost 100 Wildcats, Avengers and Dauntlesses, with a screen of 12 destroyers, most of them veterans of the Battle of the Atlantic.

On 15 July the code letters of the US Navy auxiliary carriers were changed, for the last time, from ACV to CVE (C for Aircraft Carrier, V for heavier than air, E for Escort), thus belatedly bestowing the status of Combatant Ship on the category. The familiar term 'Escort Carrier' was now officially used, though the old designation more accurately allowed for the various duties of these maids of all work in US Navy service, including amphibious assault, aircraft ferrying and refuelling at sea. The Royal Navy began to divide its CVEs, a label which it adopted, into the specialist categories Trade Protection, Fighter or Assault carrier.

Isbell's *Card* was supporting westbound GUS8 with orders to 'operate independently against any reported concentration within striking distance, as long as we could get back to the convoy before the concentration could reach it'. *Card* TBFs searched the *Trutz* area but Dönitz, infuriated by its total failure, had ordered it eastwards to re-form south of the Azores. *Santee* and her group left Casablanca on 7 July to support GUS9. On 11 July they were passing through the same area, some 1,125km (700 miles) south of the Azores, as USG11, which was being supported from visual distance by the new USS *Core* (Captain Marshall Greer) and her group, and the two carrier groups were switched, with *Core* taking over support of GUS9, and the experienced *Santee* group with more aircraft detached to hunt U-boats south of the Azores. The discredited *Trutz* group was broken up into three small packs and moved on to positions off the Portuguese coast and south of the Straits of Gibraltar, but there were now 16 independent boats south and east of the Azores, some on passage to or from South American waters, some refuelling from milch cows. Tenth Fleet's Huff-Duff picked up a transmission by Oberleutnant Konstantin Metz's milch cow *U-487* on the morning of 13 July, and fixed his position just north-west of the Cape Verdes. A *Core* TBF/F4F attack team caught it on the surface, with men sunbathing or trying to pull a floating bale of cotton aboard. The Wildcat was shot down and the pilot killed, but the TBF's depth-charges damaged the boat, and another *Core* plane sank her.

Next forenoon it was *Santee*'s turn. Lieutenant (jg) John Ballantine sighted a U-boat, which dived when his Wildcat team-mate strafed her, but the TBF was carrying one of the new acoustic torpedoes, known officially for security reasons as a Mark 24 mine but more familiarly as Fido or Wandering Annie by the US Navy, the B-Bomb and Oscar by the British. Armed with Torpex, Fido homed on the cavitation of a vessel's screws, via a hydrophone in its head, shielded so as not to

Right: The secret acoustic torpedo, designated Mk 24 mine for security reasons, and unofficially known as Fido, Wandering Annie, Oscar or the B-Bomb, in the bomb bay of an Avenger (foreground). (US National Archives)

home on its own propeller noise. When dropped, Fido dived, levelled out at a pre-set depth, and homed on prop noises within a range of 1,370m (1,500yd). If no sound was picked up the torpedo made an upward circular search, which it maintained for 15 minutes.

Ballantine's U-boat crash-dived, presenting him with perfect conditions for a Fido drop, which had to be made at slow speed from a low height. Ballantine released his at 76m (250ft), 180m (200yd) ahead and about 30m (100ft) to starboard of the swirl. As he circled to port he saw 'a pronounced shock in the water'. A ring of foam about 6m (20ft) in diameter arose, and a brown slick from the B-Bomb. It marked the end for *U-160* and her new captain, Oberleutnant Gerd von Pommer-Esche, and was the first kill with this new weapon by an aircraft from a CVE. Next morning, north-west of Madeira, *Santee*'s Lieutenant (jg) Claude Barton's Fido destroyed Kapitänleutnant Werner Witte's *U-509*. *Core*'s Bob Williams was carrying four DCs on dawn patrol, 15 July, when he sighted *U-67* 43km (27 miles) from GUS9. After 70 days at sea and a fruitless patrol between the Caribbean and Chesapeak Bay, Kapitänleutnant Gunther Muller-Stockheim was looking for a milch cow. Williams' attack produced a wide spread of oil, crates, planks and just three survivors floating in the blue holiday poster sea.

BATTLES IN THE BAY

Since the spring, aircraft of RAF Coastal Command and the US Army Air Force had been waging a new campaign against U-boats in the Biscay area, to catch them before they even reached their Atlantic patrol stations or as they neared their Brittany bases after an exhausting patrol. With 10cm radar and the Leigh Light, their successes against U-boats in transit on the surface by night mounted, whereupon the U-boats fitted more guns and fought it out on the surface in daylight, submerging at night, and evened the score. The demands of the bomber raids on Germany kept Coastal Command short of aircraft, and on 24 June Walker's crack RN 2nd Escort Group of sloops entered the Bay and sank two U-boats.

Following this success, the Admiralty sent *Archer*, with B5 Escort Group, into the area for Operation 'Seaslug', her Swordfish to hunt U-boats, and four Martlets to cover CAP and Stringbag support against the Luftwaffe along the Biscay coast. Thick weather, fog and haze inhibited air activity, which was probably just as well for BAVG-I and her small squadron. Martlets played hide and seek with a Condor in thick cloud and drove off Ju 88 snoopers. After two days of this pointless and dangerous game, with *Archer* breaking the rule that a CVE must never be exposed to heavy land-based attack, it was abandoned. Nearby, an RAF Wellington fought a stubborn duel with a milch cow, damaged her, was hit by cannon shells and crashed on top of her.

'Seaslug' was *Archer*'s last operation. The commission ended at Gareloch on 6 November, and with it her short but colourful career as a warship. Her engines could be relied upon no longer. In farewell, her ship's company sang:

There'll always be an Archer
With aircraft always there –
Providing all her engines work
She'll get them in the air.

There'll always be an Archer
As long as there's a berth,
A Lease-Lend gift from Heaven
But no bloody good on Earth.

She was still of use as a stores and accommodation ship, and as such she spent the rest of the war, first in the Clyde, then at Belfast. Her last commission as one of His Majesty's ships ended on 15 March 1945.

Bogue, now commanded by her former Executive Officer Joe Dunn, a submariner before putting up wings, was heading east from the USA with UGS12. Warned by Tenth Fleet of a concentration of U-boats ahead, on the 21st Dunn took four destroyers to break it up. He found nothing, swung south at night, but hurriedly reversed course when his Huff-Duff picked up a U-boat making a signal recognisable from its Enigma groupings as a sighting report near the convoy. At dawn, in bad flying weather, squally, dim and murky, with a choppy sea, he sent off a patrol. Three TBFs were escorted by three of the new Wildcat FM-Is, lighter versions of the F4F-4 developed especially for escort carriers, with two of the latter's six Browning 0.50s eliminated and a lower performance, in use by the Royal Navy as the Wildcat Mk V, built by the Eastern Aircraft Division of General Motors. Doty's Turkey found a surfaced boat 17km (11 miles) ahead of the carrier, also heading for the convoy. Donohoe's FM-1 strafed, Doty followed and put his DCs 46m (150ft) ahead of the U-boat's tilting screws. A gush of oil came up.

At 09:27, 312km (194 miles) south-west of Sao Miguel in the Azores, four-stacked *George E. Badger* got a ping 3,658m (4,000yd) on *Bogue*'s port bow. Leaving *Bogue* with only one escort, *Badger* pursued the erratic contact, pinging and fading, pinging and fading, as the U-boat twisted and turned below. Finally, after four attacks and 40 DCs, wreckage, clothing, mutilated and dismembered bodies began surfacing. From the sonar issued a strange loud howling noise then bubbling and hissing sounds . . . The last piece of evidence of the end of the *U-613* to be lifted out of the water was a German translation of Poe's *Murders In The Rue Morgue*. *Bogue* joined USG12 at noon, and at 14:00 Stearns' TBF surprised milch cow *U-648* refuelling *U-527* in the rain and fog. The supply sub dived to safety but four DCs sank *U-527* as she nosed into a fog bank.

Santee was supporting westbound GUS10 in hazy weather on 30 July when an attack team searching 240km (150 miles) away to starboard sighted two U-boats in company steering south towards the convoy. *U-43*, on a mission to mine Lagos Harbour, had the hose out to refuel *U-403* when Lieutenant (jg) Bob Richmond's TBF, with the new mix of two DCs and one Fido in his bomb bay, dived and splashed his DCs 12m (40ft) from *U-403*, then slowed and lost height to loose his dog on veteran Kapitänleutnant Hans-Joachim Schwandtke's *U-43*, en route to Lagos carrying mines on deck. The submarine crash-dived, the dog bit, the U-boat's own mines blew her to pieces. Dönitz warned his captains of the 'new, more dangerous bombs', and dispersed the concentration of U-boats west of the Azores, though there were still many sailing between Biscay, where RAF Coastal Command had been sinking them, and the American coasts, where 20 ships had been sunk in July, the Ivory Coast, the Durban-Mozambique area and the Indian Ocean.

In July 37 U-boats had been sunk, 25 of them by American forces, the first time in the war that the US Navy had beaten the RN in U-boat kills. Dönitz cancelled all operational cruises and ordered homeward-bound boats to return via the Piening route (so called after the U-boat captain who pioneered it) along the shores of Spain. The average number of boats at sea, which had already dropped from the peak number of 118 in May, to 84 in July, was reduced to 59 in August. In four months of the Allied counter-blitz, out of 347 U-boats at sea, 120 were destroyed – 34 per cent, and in August it was 50 per cent. 'Do not report too much bad news, so as not to depress the other boats,' signalled Dönitz to his submarines at sea, and suppressed the appalling casualty statistics, never once mentioning to anyone that he himself had lost a son in this naval armageddon.

An attack team from *Card*, in loose support of USG13 with her TG.21.14, found veteran Markworth's homeward-bound *U-66* 735km (457 miles) west-sou'-west of Flores. The F4F killed the officer of the deck and badly wounded Markworth but the boat survived DC and Fido attacks and next morning, 7 August, was lying alongside *U-117*. In just over three months, since they had begun moving into the Azores area, the US escort carrier groups had sunk eight milch cows. *U-117* was one of the only three left, with, according to U-boat Command's War Diary, 'no more reserve tankers available'.

U-66 and *U-117* were surprised by Lieutenant A. H. Sallenger's TBF, which attacked out of the sun. Two DCs damaged the milch cow so that she could not dive, *U-66* submerged and the TBF ran the gauntlet of heavy fire from *U-117* to drop its Fido. Two more TBFs attacked with DCs, their radiomen photographing results from the planes' bellies. The U-boat submerged, rose again, slipped back, and one TBF let Annie wander. A big shock wave, bubbles and a circle of pale water indicated the end of *U-117*.

Next morning Sallenger was on patrol with Ensign John Sprague's Wildcat, this time in squally, overcast weather, when they sighted another U-boat pair, *U-262* and Kapitänleutnant Adolf Graef's *U-664*. The two planes strafed, and Sallenger came in for a DC run. With some 914m (1,000yd) to go the TBF jolted, hit in the belly by the first of several shells which knocked out radio, intercoms and other electrics, and killed the radioman. Sallenger carried on and pressed the DC release, which did not work. As he reefed round for another try from the starboard quarter, engine cutting out intermittently, the plane sluggish, he got all the flak, as the F4F was busy with the other boat, and was hit again. Port fuel tank on fire, he pressed his manual DC release, saw two explosions close to the U-boat, flew on for about a mile, turned into wind and pancaked the bulky machine with a jarring crash. As Sallenger and his turret gunner Downes inflated their rubber boat in the water they saw Sprague shot down and killed by flak.

With no knowledge of the fate of either plane, Isbell took the *Card* group into the centre of their patrol area. Sallenger and Downes were rescued but that night the carrier, in happy ignorance, was missed by three torpedoes from *U-664*. It was an

Above: *U-664* under attack by *Card* aircraft, 9 August 1943. The German crew seems to have been taken by surprise, as the gun in the *Wintergarten* aft of the bridge has not been manned in time to fire on the aircraft making the attack. The happy dolphin on the conning tower was a logo for Atlantic U-boats.

expensive failure. The following afternoon the U-boat was sighted by Lieutenant (jg) G. G. Hogan, USNR. His TBF was part of a new formula thought up by Isbell and Compo I CO, Carl Jones – a mix of one TBF armed with two 227kg (500lb) instant-fuzed bombs, one with two DCs and a Fido, and one F4F. If a U-boat fought it out, the bombs went down first to destroy or cripple her or force her down. If she dived the other TBF used her DCs and Fido.

Hogan climbed to 610m (2,000ft), dived and released a bomb at 230m (750ft). The U-boat was submerging, with only her conning tower and stern visible. The bomb exploded off her port bow, the blast rocking Forney's TBF as he dropped his two DCs. The whole boat lifted, throwing men off their feet. Lighting failed, switchboards short-circuited. fuzes blew, and Graef brought her up. Men came on deck and started breaking out life rafts but were shot off the casing by Hodson's diving Wildcat, and the U-boat started to dive again. Hogan's second bomb exploded off her port quarter. Graef tried to go deep, but the leaks were bad, there was no main lighting, and cracked battery cells were filling with water. Forney looked at the flotsam and the men in the water, and witheld his Fido, then the U-boat rose again, bows up, and drifted round in a circle to port. Three more TBFs, with fighters, arrived from *Card*. Two 227kg (500lb) bombs from Lieutenant Hewitt brought a stream of men out of the hatches, and Ensign Carter's DCs, released accidentally, speeded up the process. *U-664* sank just after the last survivor had left the boat.

Signals showed that U-boats in transit were being re-routed north of the islands, and *Card* went to hunt there. On the fine but hazy afternoon of 11 August Ensign Jack Stewart's F4F and Hewitt's TBF surprised the 740-ton supply boat *U-525* 595km (370 miles) west-nor'-west of Corvo, and Hewitt's Fido destroyed her. By this time Dönitz had lost nine of his 12 Central Atlantic milch cows. On 23 August a *Core* TBF/F4F team was looking for U-boats reported ahead of USG15, south-west of Fayal, when it picked up *U-84*, urgently looking for a refueller after a blank patrol off Cuba. This boat survived their attack but next day Williams' TBF found *U-185*, another parched boat, and sank her with depth-charges. While the destroyer *Barker* was rescuing chlorine-choked survivors, *U-84* poked her grey bows out of a rain squall 16km (ten miles) away, and a covering Avenger destroyed her with a Fido. *Core*'s engines were now in urgent need of repair, and she returned home. *Card*, at Casablanca, took her place and while investigating a reported concentration of U-boats north-west of the Azores, Long's TBF sank the 740-ton milch cow *U-847* with its B-Bomb.

She was the 16th U-boat destroyed by US Navy CVEs since *Bogue* had moved south from Argentia on 30 May, with three planes destroyed by the enemy and only one ship lost from the convoys they had protected. In August American forces sank ten of the 25 U-boats destroyed, six of them victims of *Card*'s and *Core*'s groups.

Right: With zigzagging convoy and sunlit sea for a backdrop, an Avenger TBF roars off down the deck.

6

'WOOLWORTH' CARRIERS

BOGUES FOR BRITAIN

On 30 September 1942 the first of the ten new *Bogue* Class CVEs for Britain, HMS *Attacker*, built in the Western Pipe & Steel Corporation's yard in San Francisco, was handed over to the Royal Navy. Five more *Bogue*s were converted at Western Pipe, and delivered to the British in succession, HMS *Stalker* (commissioned 21 December 1942), *Fencer* (1 March 1943), *Ravager* (25 March 1943), *Searcher* (7 April 1943) and *Striker* (28 April 1943). The Ingalls Shipbuilding Corporation at the mouth of the Pascagoula River on the Gulf of Mexico, originally an off-shoot of the parent company of Robert Ingalls, Senior, a prominent ironmaster of Birmingham, Alabama, were turning out one merchant ship a month, using prefabrication and all-welding, when the Maritime Commission directed four uncompleted hulls to be converted to CVEs for the Royal Navy. These became the other four *Bogue*-Class boats for the RN, HMS *Battler* (commissioned 31 October 1942), *Hunter* (9 January 1943), *Chaser* (9 April 1943) and *Pursuer* (14 June 1943). HMS *Tracker*, the sixth, overdue BAVG, built by the Williamette yard on Puget Sound, Washington, was commissioned on 31 January 1943. On her early voyages she showed herself an unusually lively ship, even for a top-heavy BAVG, and gained the reputation of a ship which would 'roll on wet grass'. In her radar workshop a nut on a piece of string registered a greatest angle of roll of 45 degrees.

The *Bogue*s had a large hangar designed to accommodate 18+ aircraft, and two elevators, which greatly improved plane handling and spotting the deck. Gun armament of two 4in AA, four double Oerlikon 40mm AA and 15 single Oerlikon 20mm AA, was superior to HMS *Archer*'s two twin Bofors and ten Oerlikons.

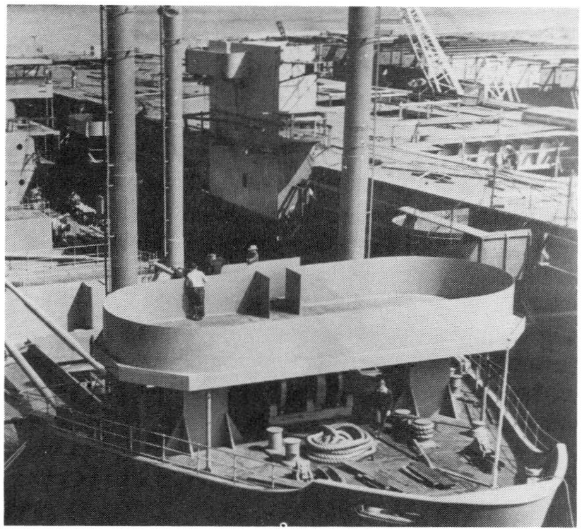

Right: Foreground in the Western Pipe and Steel outfitting dock, the C-3 conversion to the transport *Sea Bass* for the US Marine Corps, with ACV-14 (*Fencer*) next in line, the stark basic box of her bridge island in place, *Striker* next to her.

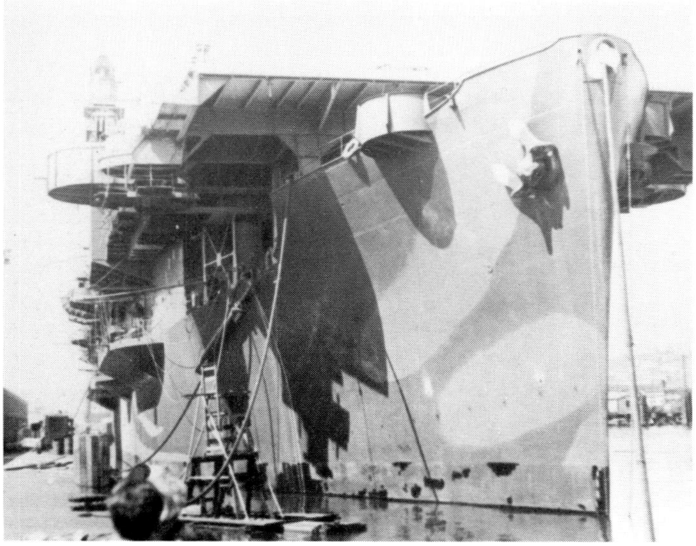

Below right and left: Bow and stern views of HMS *Attacker*, first of the *Bogue* class escort carriers to be handed over to the Royal Navy, illustrate her Captain's description of CVEs as 'an awful lot perched on very little'. Her merchant ship bows and the excrescences of her two after twin Oerlikon 20mm cannon can be clearly seen. (D. Mawdsley)

In all American-built carriers the food was steam-cooked and served cafeteria-style. HM American ACVs left the USA lavishly victualled. When *Chaser* departed Ingall's yard, every member of her ship's company was given a carton of 200 cigarettes on behalf of the builders. When the Yankee goodies ran out, however, the diet reverted to the usual British stodge, bulk-cooked and unappetising, and the soda fountain was removed.

There was a well-equipped barber's shop, and a modern laundry, but many of HM ships were too short-handed to make use of it, and the men had to return to dhobying RN-style in a bucket with Pusser's soap, and hot water from the boiler room. Traditional hammocks were replaced in the CVE by three-level bunks arranged very close together in units of six, and hinging upwards, though the ancient call of 'Wakey-wakey! Lash up and stow' was not abandoned. Hammocks would have given a better sleep in ACVs as they would have absorbed the heavy rolling for which these top-heavy ships were notorious. These quarters were deep in the ship, and conditions were unhealthy and claustrophobic. Men were afraid of being trapped down here if the ship was torpedoed. The noise of water hammer in the pipes each morning when the water was turned on always sounded like a torpedo hitting the hull. Telegraphist/air-gunners preferred to spend their off-duty hours in the comfortable chairs of the Ready Room immediately below the flight deck on the port side aft, where in *Battler* the blackboard bore permanently the approach speed of a Swordfish – '60 knots – not 59 or 61', as a reminder to new pilots.

The open hangar of a CVE was light and airy, with its numerous exits leading to sponsons on the ship's side, and in hot weather the after lift would be lowered to catch the breeze. There were film shows there once a week. Two large workshops were tooled up for wood and metal working, and *Battler*'s doctor described her sickbay equipment as 'most generous'. It included luxuries like a bacteriological research chest and an X-ray fluoroscope.

Battler's small Fighter Direction Room was packed with equipment. There were two plotting boards for large and small coverage, the Fighter Direction Officer's R/T for talking to aircraft, and autotelephone communication for ships. On the bulkhead opposite him was a board recording aircraft serviceability, crews, fuel and ammunition state, whether airborne and if so on what job employed, time of departure and estimated time of return. A smaller board recorded ships in company and their call signs.

'The general impression', wrote an *Aeroplane* columnist, 'left after visiting such great ships as the *Queen Elizabeth*, *King George V*, *Ark Royal*, *Illustrious*, etc, is one of cramp – cramming so much into so little. The *Battler* is roomy, from hangar to heads. American designers must be thanked.'

Below: Finally completed, ammunitioned, stored and more or less shipshape, HMS *Attacker* lies in the smooth, oily water of San Francisco Bay just before weighing for the UK.

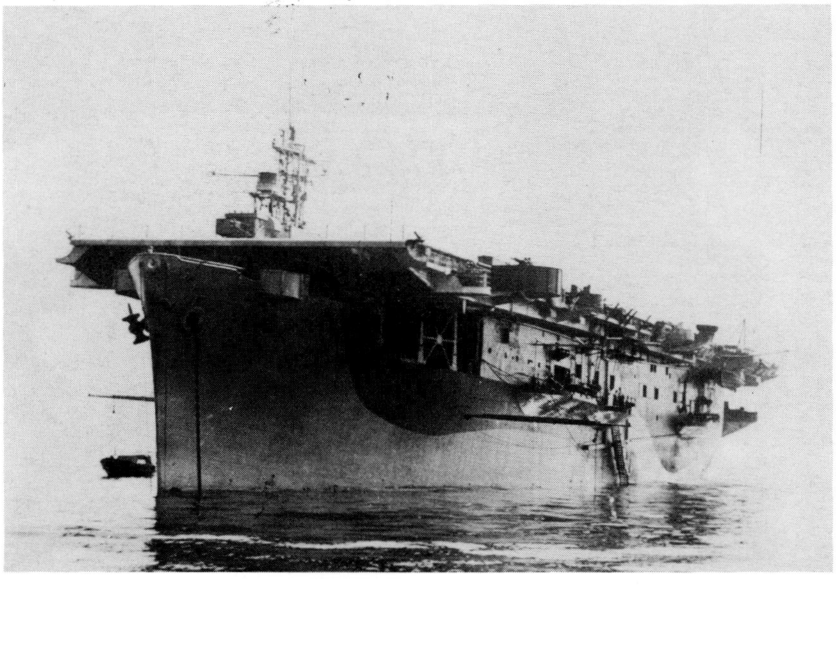

SEAFIRES FOR THE CVEs

Part of the delay in getting some of the American gift horses into service after a long voyage from the West Coast or the Gulf of Mexico was the modification to operate fighters only, with extra radar and other fighter direction equipment. These Fighter carriers received Seafire IICs and later the low-level LIICs. The basic Trade Protection carriers, as *Battler* was to remain, were allocated Composite Squadrons, mixtures of Swordfish and fighters. The Martlet, generally slower than the Seafire but more resistant to the rough and tumble of convoy work and U-boat hunting, and less likely to meet faster Axis fighters, was preferred for Trade Protection carriers but was in short supply. Two of the 14 Seafire squadrons formed were disbanded and their pilots distributed between four Composite Squadrons, allocated nine Swordfish and six Seafires each.

With 'Woolworth carriers' and MACs on hand or in the offing, on 8 June the RAF Merchant Ship Fighter Unit, which equipped the CAM-ships, was officially disbanded. There had been long periods when the 'Hurricats' had been the only deep-sea air defence available. The presence of one in a convoy was a deterrent to prowling Condors and U-boats. On the sunny evening of 28 July the two Sea Hurricanes from the last CAM-ships left in service, the *Empire Tide* and *Empire Darwin*, rounded off the history of this bizarre unit by shooting down two Condors.

Battler embarked six Swordfish of No 835 Squadron and four Seafires (three IICs and one of the new LIICs) of No 808 Squadron to form an *ad hoc* Composite unit. The Seafire had been intended as a medium- to high-level fighter. Fitted

Right: HMS *Battler* during her final fitting-out at the Ingalls Shipbuilding Company, Pascagoula, on the Gulf of Mexico.

Far right: HMS *Battler*'s crest. (Barry Cookson)

with the Merlin 45 engine a IB could achieve its respectable maximum speed of 571km/h (355mph) at 3,960m (13,000ft). The IIC was 32km/h (20mph) slower at this height, and took longer to reach it – 670m (2,200ft) per minute, 137m (450ft) per minute slower than the IB – but with the Merlin 46 could achieve 555km/h (345mph) at 5,790m (19,000ft), and match current Luftwaffe fighters. But Seafires had hardly ever been involved in combat at these heights. Most encounters had been below 3,050m (10,000ft) with long-range recce aircraft or Italian bombers and torpedo planes. In the first meetings between IBs, IICs and Ju 88s the IB had held on longer in the chase but could not overhaul the enemy. From early March the Merlin 32 was fitted to IIC airframes, a four-bladed propeller replaced the universal three-bladed one, to take full advantage of the big increase in power, a Coffman cartridge engine starter superseded external electrical power, and the result was the Seafire LIIC, an outstanding low-level fighter, faster than the IIC at all heights up to 7,620m (25,000ft), the LIIC's ceiling, with a considerably shorter take-off run than the IB and IIC, and a rate of climb of 1,005m (3,300ft) per minute up to 1,830m (6,000ft) – 1,097m (3,600ft) per minute with maximum emergency boost – faster than any other naval aircraft of World War 2.

No 807 Squadron, the first unit to be equipped with the IIC – as early as 23 June 1942 – was also the first to receive the LIIC, either converted IICs or direct from Westland's production line, and by mid-May 1943 had its full establishment of the mark. In some units the wingtips were cropped to increase rate of roll for combat and low-level speed by 8km/h (5mph), though ceiling was lowered to 6,096m (20,000ft) – not so important in a low-level fighter, take-off run and approach speed slightly increased, and the aircraft became heavier on the controls and more tiring to fly. In March also, as the LIIC began its career, the production of the IB ceased, when some 146 IBs and IICs had been delivered. 801 Squadron remained in *Furious* with their IBs until the old carrier retired in September 1944, and the mark saw carrier service just once more, in the ACV

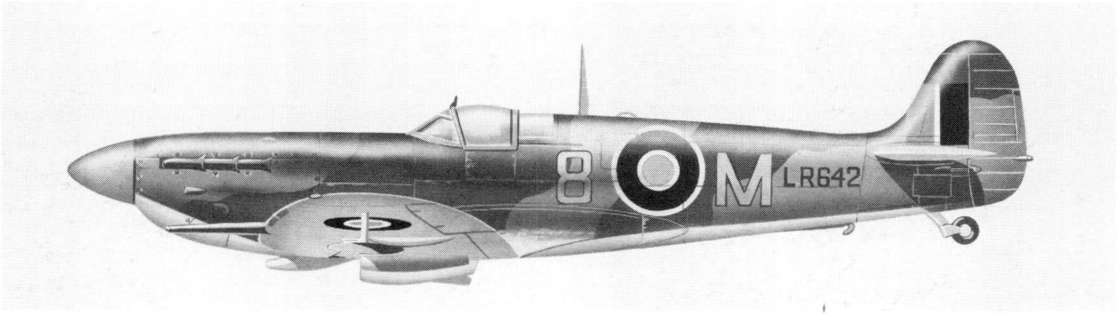

Right: Seafire Mk. IIC. (J. M. Goulding)

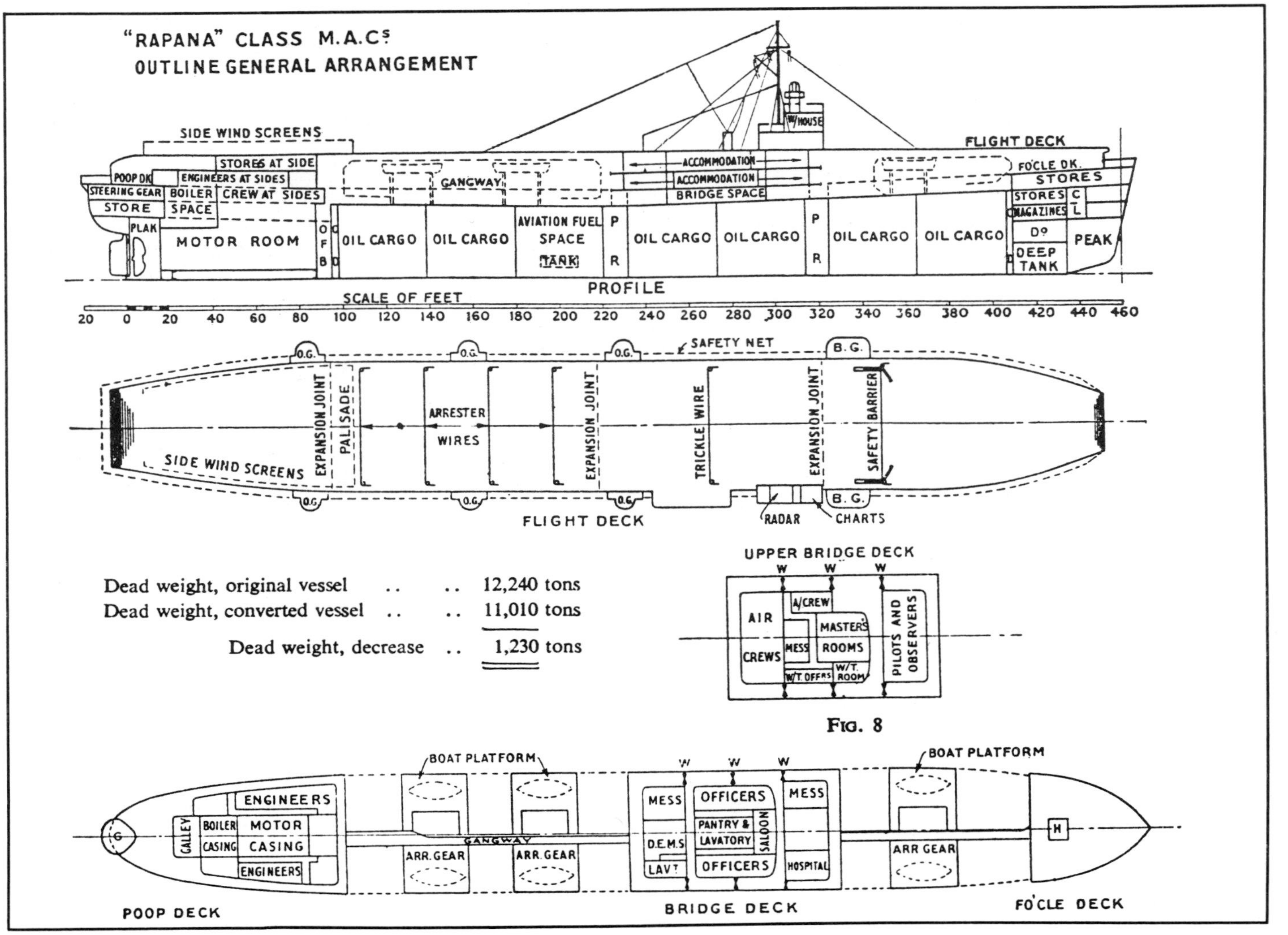

Fig. 8

Above: Tanker MAC *Rapana* of the Anglo-Saxon Petroleum Company. (Shell photograph)

Fencer's Composite Squadron later in the year. Production of the LIIC was stepped up to equip the Fleet carriers and ACVs which were to take part in 'Avalanche', the landings at Salerno in Italy, scheduled for September, with as many of the superior new mark as possible. In the autumn some LIICs were fitted with two F.24 cameras, one vertical, one oblique, to become the Seafire LRIIC fighter-reconnaissance aircraft.

On 4 June *Battler* left Belfast on her first convoy operation, to escort the combined slow convoys OS49/KMS16/XK9 to Gibraltar. She flew off the usual anti-submarine patrols at sea, and on 11 June scrambled two Seafires to investigate a suspected 'hostile' which turned out to a friendly RAF Coastal Command machine not displaying IFF, an all too frequent story. No enemy aircraft were sighted on the outward passage, but two of the Seafire IICs were disabled in an accident and had not been repaired or replaced when *Battler* left Gibraltar again with the two combined convoys MMS16 and SK9. This time genuine shadowers appeared after two days, and at 10:30 on 22 June *Battler* launched Lieutenant P. Constable, RN, the CO of 808A Flight, in the LIIC, *MB302*, and Sub-Lieutenant A. G. Penney, RNVR, in the serviceable IIC to attack an Fw 200 which was circling the convoy. The LIIC in the lead, both Seafires bored in to close range and opened fire with a combined battery of four 20mm cannon and eight 0.303in machine-guns. Two minutes later the Condor fell blazing into the sea.

THE MAC-SHIPS SAIL

Also on passage to the UK was Convoy HX245, with 91 ships the biggest convoy to attempt the crossing from Halifax to Britain since war began. In the convoy was *Empire MacAlpine*, making her first round trip as a MAC, and to port of her in the next column was the new CVE HMS *Chaser* with her 845 Squadron, only the second FAA unit to be equipped with the Avenger, which was given the name Tarpon in RN Service.

The Grumman Avenger torpedo-bomber had first appeared in 1941 and began to replace the US Navy's ineffectual Douglas Devastator TBD-1, though not soon enough for more than a few to take part in the battle of Midway, in which the

Douglases devastated only their own crews. Avenger *JT773* was tested in England, and deliveries of the Lease-Lend Tarpons began in early 1943, 401 of this version being handed over in all. The first front-line British squadron was No 232, actually allocated 15 USN TBF-1s, as their Tarpon Is were not ready; they operated them in the Pacific in the spring and summer of 1943 from HMS *Victorious*. No 845 Squadron received its first Tarpon Is at Quonset, USA, on 1 February, followed by 14 other FAA squadrons at monthly intervals, originally operating 12 machines apiece although in some cases this was later reduced to nine, with the addition of a sub-Flight (three aircraft) of Martlet fighters. Tarpon pilots received deck-landing training aboard USS *Charger*, the original BAVG-4 retained by the US Navy.

In US Navy TBFs a radioman sat behind the pilot in the 'glasshouse' and also operated the 0.50-calibre gun in the turret. A bomb-aimer sat in the belly aft of the bomb-bay and worked the 0.30-calibre gun in the ventral hatch. The FAA at first put the observer/navigator/radar operator, with all his charts and navigational gear, and the telegraphist/air-gunner together in the central position, but two proved to be a crowd and radio plus TAG were subsequently moved below. In January 1944 both the name 'Tarpon' and 'Martlet' were replaced by the original 'Avenger' and 'Wildcat'. In the same year TBM-1s and -1Cs, built by General Motors, entered RN service as Avenger IIS, followed by TBM-3s and -3Cs as Avenger IIIs.

The Tarpon could not use the British 45.7cm (18in) torpedo and the American 57cm (22.4in) type provided was short, fat, heavy, slow and unreliable. The Fleet Air Arm TBFs carried mostly 227kg (500lb) bombs, depth charges, mines or rocket projectiles, largely for use against land targets or coastal shipping, as in many attacks off Norway, land-based over the English Channel during 'Overlord' and in defence of Russian convoys. Many Avengers were operated by escort carriers, including HMSS *Fencer* (852 Squadron), *Premier* (846 and 856), *Queen* (853), *Trumpeter* (846 and 852) and *Searcher* (882). Others served aboard CVEs in the Indian Ocean and East Indies, notably HMSS *Ameer* (845 Squadron), *Begum* (832), *Shah* (851), *Empress* (845) and *Emperor* (845).

When *Chaser* and *Empire MacAlpine* came to fly off patrols, the lively motion on the ACV, which rode light on the water, sometimes grounded its Tarpons, whereas *MacAlpine*, with 10,000 tons of grain in her holds, was less boisterous, and her four antique Stringbags became the watchdogs over this huge convoy. Unfortunately, when the MAC was between Columns 6 and 8 in the evening, recovering aircraft off patrol, she collided with the merchantman *Empire Ibex*. For the rest of the trip she was down by the bows and leaking for'ard, capable of operating, but only in an emergency, which thankfully did not arise.

On 25 July 1943 the first Anglo-Saxon Company's Merchant Aircraft Carrier, the tanker *Rapana*, went into service, having only berthed at Smith's Dock in North Shields, Northumberland, for conversion on 2 February. The all-welded steel flight deck, 140m (460ft) long and 19m (62ft) wide, was 11.5m (38ft) longer than the grainer *MacAlpine*'s, but a tanker's layout made the fitting of a hangar impossible. The deck was constructed in sections with telescopic joints to allow it to

Right: HMS *Chaser*, built at Ingalls' yard on the Gulf of Mexico, was the second RN-manned escort carrier to embark American Grumman Tarpons (later discarded for its original name of Avenger), three of which can be seen parked on her flight deck in this picture, which has got past the censor, who would have whited-out the American SC air search radar antenna atop the short lattice mast and the British surface radar in its cabinet on the stump lattice structure below and forward of it.

Opposite page, top: The grainer MAC *Empire MacRae* in convoy.

Opposite page, centre: *Rapana.* A tanker's basic design, with the engines located aft, prevented the fitting of a hangar, which was possible in grain ships. (Shell photograph)

Opposite page, bottom: Tanker MAC *Rapana* after completion, with a simplified version of the CVE-type bridge island. As in escort carriers, a well-guyed mast for'ard carriers the Huff/Duff aerial, and a Type 271 (mainly surface search) radar is fitted in the cabinet above the compass platform. (Shell photograph)

expand and contract freely in temperature changes between the North Atlantic and the Caribbean and the flexing of the deck in a seaway. A CVE-type bridge/aircraft control island, a petrol system, a new electrical system, magazines, workshops, and extra accommodation for the FAA were added.

The MAC *Empire MacAndrew*, converted in Denny's yard, entered service in July 1943, followed by the grainer conversion *Empire MacRae*, completed at Lithgow's in September. The tanker MAC *Amastra*, another Smith's Dock job, began conversion on 22 April 1943 and completed in October. The tanker *Gadila* began her transformation on 5 August and completed on 18 February 1944. 'Winkle' Brown, official sampler of all types of aircraft in escort carriers, tested a Martlet aboard *Amastra*, but this was never followed up, largely because the Condor threat had dwindled, though a fighter operating in combined attack with a Swordfish or Avenger, as in ACVs, would have been valuable.

DELAYS IN DOCK

By the end of August 1943 the new Lease-Lend escort carriers *Attacker, Battler, Stalker, Hunter, Fencer, Chaser, Searcher, Striker* and *Ravager* had reached the UK from Western Pipe and Ingalls, but none was yet available for the convoys, and *Biter*, the only operational survivor of the BAVGs (*Charger*, BAVG-4, was retained by the US Navy for pilot training), accompanied Convoy SC137 to New York.

There was increasing criticism in the US Navy Staff of the six- to eight-month delay between the handing over of a Lease-Lend CVE to the Royal Navy and her going into service. Much of the delay was accounted for by the period between commissioning in the USA and arrival in Britain. Before sailing to the east coast, trials were necessary. In the case of the west coast ships, which had to make the long trip east through the Panama Canal, it was usually five or six weeks before they reached Norfolk, Virginia. On the east coast their hangars and flight decks were often crammed with new aircraft, and they joined a convoy to make their first trip across the Atlantic, sometimes by way of Casablanca with machines for the Allied forces in North Africa, and it was probably at least a month before they reached the UK.

It was difficult to reduce this overall period of two to three months, and once in a British port a new Lease-Lend carrier queued up to go into dockyard hands for various modifications. After the loss of *Dasher* this included drastic alterations to the American petrol system. The American conversions were also unstable. The Admiralty would not countenance the US Navy practice of pumping sea water into empty fuel tanks, and between 12,000 and 2,000 tons of extra ballast were added to each ship. This had some effect, but they were still very lively sea boats, which would 'roll in drydock'. American flight decks were lengthened to operate British aircraft, which could not use the American catapults. Another source of delay was the need for repairs, often to engines or to plating joints, which were the result of the building of the comparatively flimsy, often all-welded ships at tremendous speed in yards and by hands unused to this type of construction. One time-consuming modification which displeased the Americans was the Admiralty's decision to further adapt some of the Lease-Lend carriers to be 'fit for full fighter operation, and not merely for anti-submarine work'.

The American understanding was that the CVE gift horses were provided to sink U-boats. Their own escort carriers were thought of as all-purpose and fitted out and used as such, with new or extra gear sometimes fitted for a particular operation, eg, 'Dragoon'. On 27 August the Allied Anti-Submarine Board reported to Admiral King, US Navy Chief of Staff, that 'at the present stage of the war these delays are not considered acceptable', and suggested that five of the next batch of seven Lease-Lend CVEs should be retained by the US Navy. The Admiralty Lords in London pleaded congestion in dockyard construction and repair facilities in Britain, added to manning problems as responsible for much of the delay. Admiral King, persuaded partly by the consideration that the US Navy might have at least as much difficulty in manning five extra ships, suddenly added to the programme, urged the Admiralty to reduce the time taken to get them into service.

Delay caused by the congestion in British shipyards, which looked like becoming worse

Below: Study – MAC-ship with kitehawks. This is the grainer *Empire MacAndrew*, converted by Denny Brothers. She appears to be fitted with a Type 272 surface/air search RDF set, with its scanner cabinet on the stump trellis mast on the after part of the bridge island.

now that new CVEs for the Royal Navy were being completed on the west coast of the USA at an average of about one every three weeks, was reduced considerably when the Canadian Government offered to do the 'anglicizing' modifications and additions, of which the first assessment produced a list of 150 items, at their expense to CVEs built on the west coast, and placed the work with the Burrard Drydock Company of Vancouver. The work was done at Lapointe Pier in Vancouver harbour. Under the energetic lead of the company's President, Mr Wallace, and General Manager, Mr Wardle, a commercial wharf and goods shed were converted in two months to a dockyard staffed by a most miscellaneous horde of men and women, only two per cent of whom had previously done ship work. But the alterations specified were standardised, and each man or woman taught one job. They worked hard day and night, with mistakes getting fewer as each new ship was completed.

THE 'RULERS'

Burrard's first anglicizing job was HMS *Ameer*, originally commissioned as USS *Baffins*, ACV-35, one of 25 of the new 'Ruler' Class of escort carrier being converted for the Royal Navy in parallel with 50 Kaiser *Casablanca* Class (the original order had been reduced by five) on the west coast of the USA. A batch of the *Casablanca*s had originally been promised to the Royal Navy, but the US Navy, pleasantly surprised at the quality of the Kaiser 'assembly line' ships, after all the accusations of graft in the boardroom and gimcrackery in their all-welded construction, and aware of the advantages of wide standardisation in design, prefabricated parts and construction methods, equipment, repair and servicing (simpler than in other classes), and performance, decided to retain all 50 built for its own use, mainly in the Pacific. Allied naval bases from San Diego to Sydney would then have only two different classes of CVEs to maintain. The four larger *Sangamon* Class ex-oilers were now such highly-prized veterans of the Pacific war, with their big aircraft capacity and refuelling capability, that BuShips was building, from scratch, a new class of escort carrier, *Commencement Bay* (CVE-105) and her nine sisters, to the same formula.

In lieu of the *Casablanca*s promised, the US Navy lent all but the lead ship *Prince William* (CVE-31) of that type to the Royal Navy, which named most of them after rulers of various kinds (*Ameer, Emperor, Nabob*, etc) and some after subjects of aggressive or vigorous action (*Puncher, Reaper, Smiter*, etc) and they were designated the *Ruler* Class. A typical Ruler was 150m (492ft) long (overall), 21m (69.5ft) in the beam, with a flight deck of 33m (108.5ft), capable of 18 knots (maximum), operating 28 aircraft.

7

SEAFIRES OVER SALERNO

Opposite page, top: The shark's teeth markings, seen here on Major Al Wright's Seafire LIIC ascending from *Stalker*'s hangar during the work-up for 'Avalanche', were also used by the Royal Air Force in North Africa, and the American volunteer 'Flying Tigers' in Burma. (A. D. Brown)

Opposite page, bottom: HMS *Battler* seen from *Hunter* in an angry sea on passage to the Mediterranean for Operation 'Avalanche' at Salerno, Italy, *Hunter* having survived the traumatic destruction of aircraft in a hangar accident. Note the overhang of the sponsons from the flight deck catwalk (the goofers). (Barry Cookson)

BY early May 1943 the Allies had driven the Axis out of Africa, and speedily moved on to the next step in the invasion of Europe, Operation 'Husky', the taking of Sicily. More than 1,000 land-based fighter and tactical support aircraft were massed in Tunisia, Malta and Gozo, within easy reach of the invasion beaches, and there was no demand for carrier-borne aircraft.

'Husky' began on 10 July. General Patton's American army landed in the west and raced north; Montgomery's British army met stronger opposition in the south-east but fought its way up the coast. Force 'H' was stationed east of Sicily, with *Formidable* and *Indomitable* flying CAP over the Allied ships in the area. When a lone Ju 88 approached just after midnight on 16 July it was mistaken for an Albacore returning from patrol, and torpedoed *Indomitable*, which limped off to Malta. Her disablement once again demonstrated the vulnerability of carriers operating within range of land-based bombers, when a single aircraft could take out a modern armoured Fleet carrier.

The lightly-built escort carriers, with their unarmoured merchant hulls and low speed, were at far greater risk. Nevertheless, they were now to be employed in similar circumstances, in a role for which they seemed miscast. This was Operation 'Avalanche', the assault on Italy. A beach-head had been established in Calabria, on the toe of Italy, but 'Why crawl up the leg like a harvest bug from the ankle upwards?,' asked Winston Churchill, 'Let us strike at the knee.'

FORCE 'V'

The 'knee' was the Bay of Salerno, near the great port of Naples on the west coast of Italy. A simultaneous drive to the east could cut off Axis troops before they could retreat behind the natural defences of the rivers flowing down east and west from the Appenines to the sea.

The distance between Salerno and the Sicilian airfields was between 350 and 385km (220 and 240 miles). Spitfires and Mustang A-36As of the Tactical Air Force in Sicily could offer 20 minutes over the beach-head, P-38 Lightnings of the Strategic Air Force no more than 40. With carriers only 32 to 48km (20 to 30 miles) offshore, even the short-winded Seafires could linger for over an hour above the combat zone and could quickly reinforce standing patrols if the enemy attacked in force.

Escort carriers *Attacker, Battler, Hunter* and *Stalker* were to take a major part in 'Avalanche'. There was a false start by *Hunter* when a Seafire of the ferry cargo in her hangar burst its heavy-weather double-hemp lashings in a gale on passage to Gibraltar and started a chain of destruction which ended with ten Seafires of the ferry cargo and one from 834 Squadron written off and all the other machines in the hangar damaged, some badly. After returning to England to make good the losses, *Hunter* rejoined the other three CVEs at Gibraltar. While there the four carriers embarked the Seafire LIICs of three squadrons and two fighter flights. *Hunter* and *Stalker* disembarked the Swordfish of their 834 and 833 Squadrons. For 'Avalanche', *Hunter* added the 14 LIICs of 899 Squadron to the six LIICs of her own 834 Flight; *Stalker* increased the six LIICs of her 833 Composite unit temporarily by the addition of 14 LIICs of 880 Squadron.

Towards the end of the month the four CVEs exercised off Gibraltar with the maintenance and repair carrier HMS *Unicorn*, which had been co-opted into active service owing to the general shortage of carriers and was now bringing 30 Seafire LIICs to the battle. It was the only opportunity for the inexperienced Force 'V' pilots fresh from training to work-up with their carriers. Afterwards the five ships sailed for Malta via Oran.

Under the command of Rear-Admiral Sir Philip Vian, KCB, of *Altmark* fame, they formed Force 'V', the inshore squadron which would supply low- and medium-level air defence of the northern beach-head until the airfield of Montecorvino could be captured and made operational, hopefully by the end of D-Day. Force 'H', with the Fleet carriers *Formidable* and *Illustrious*, was to provide the heavy covering force for the assault, inshore support and reinforcement groups, and close air and anti-submarine protection for Force 'V'.

Just after six o'clock on the evening of 8 September came the welcome news of Italy's unconditional surrender. Twelve hours later, at 06:05, D-Day, 9 September, the carriers turned 195 degrees into the wind. Ten minutes later, a

quarter of an hour before first light, the first Seafires left the decks of Force 'V', four fighters per patrol from the CVEs and eight from the bigger *Unicorn*, which was to fly high-level patrols for an hour and a half after dawn and before dusk in the absence of land-based aircraft from Sicily, as well as support the escort carriers' low-level LIICs. These circled above Capri controlled by the Fighter Direction ship *Palomares*, to deal with attacks before they reached the beach-head, which was patrolled by USAAF ground-attack Mustangs.

GERMAN HIT-AND-RUN TACTICS

Losses in the Tunisian and Sicilian campaigns, and the prior claims of the Eastern and Home fronts plus the capitulation of Italy just before 'Avalanche', had seriously whittled down Axis air strength, but the Luftwaffe reacted swiftly with what they had, first with a night raid on Force 'H', then, shortly after the first Seafires had reached their patrol area, with a flight of six Ju 88s. As soon as they sighted the Seafire LIICs, the 88s jettisoned their bombs and fled, outdistancing the Seafires. One flight of LIICs was enough to turn back another attempted raid by more than a dozen 'Jabos' just after noon, but echoes off the high ground behind the beach-head and to the north swamped the radar screens of the directing ships, and pilots had to rely on their own eyes, which had trouble penetrating the thick haze prevailing. Nevertheless the Seafires continued to repel air attacks, most of which were hit-and-run raids carried out by fast, low-flying Fw 190s and Messerschmitt Bf 109s. Some attacks, however, were mounted by the Dornier Do 217s of Kampfgeschwader 100 carrying the new and highly effective electronically-steered Henschel Hs 293A 'glider' bombs. One of these sank the surrendering Italian battleship *Roma* on D-Day, and they were clearly a serious threat to the ships of the 'Avalanche' fleet. In the afternoon the low-level Seafires were switched from their station over Capri to a sector over the beach-head.

ATTRITION ON THE FLIGHT DECKS

If combat conditions were harsh and frustrating, with nothing tangible to show for each uncomfortable hour of sweat and strain, and pins and needles in the bottom, the air space above the beach-head was safer than the return to a small, unforgiving deck, blurred by the glitter of the glassy sea, with the wind asleep, reefing the long nose round out of the circuit into a Seafire's curving approach, keeping 'Bats' in sight between the wing stubs and the exhausts and hoping for the best, but pitching too fast into the wires and pecking the deck, scattering splinters of Oregon pine, writing off the prop, or landing like a brick, graunching the fragile oleos, with the plane screeching down the deck spewing sparks, scat-

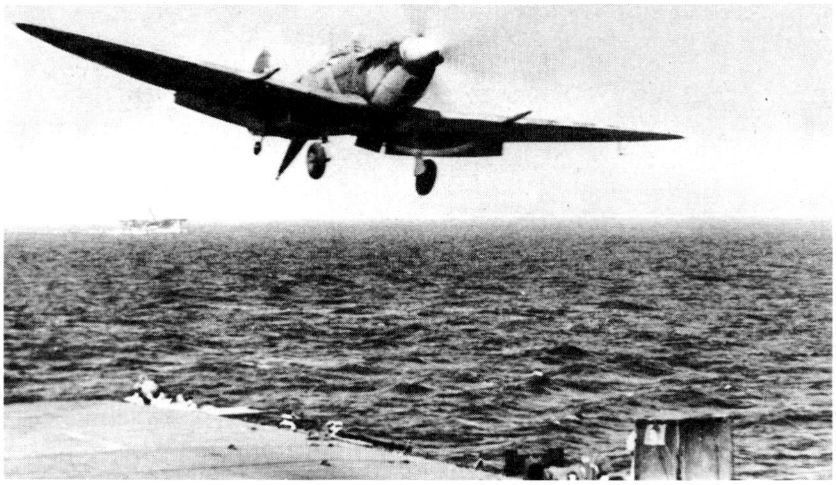

Above: A *Hunter* Seafire going round again after a wave-off during 'Avalanche'. Low wind speeds, sun dazzle off the calm sea, the Seafire's fragile undercarriage and general inexperience in this type of flying operation contributed to a high Seafire attrition rate in the Bay.

Above: Seafire LIIC MB301 8-D ends up messily in *Battler*'s barrier after its hook has failed to operate. (FAA Museum)

Below: This Seafire LIIC of *Hunter*'s 807 Squadron turned over after hitting the first barrier, though the pilot escaped serious injury. Note the fully retracted hook and the drop tank still in place. (Crown)

tering jagged shards of airscrew, airscoop, ailerons, tailwheel, slamming against the island, a write-off, plane and pilot, or bouncing over all the wires and ripping off the undercarriage on the barrier, to slam straight into the last machine to land.

Inexorably the accidents mounted, some catastrophic, the pilot killed or badly hurt or burned, shattered undercarriages – a Seafire's weakest point – wrinkled after fuselages, wings smashed, engines impacted, tanks burning, exploding, a heap of junk that was once a slender Seafire given the deep six. By dusk on D-Day 265 sorties, a record, had been flown by Force 'V's' Seafires, but at dawn on D-plus-One Montecorvino was still in enemy hands, and the Force was required for an unscheduled second day's duty.

It was all down to inexperience, beginning at the top. Vian was not an aviator, had not handled a carrier group in battle, did not know that carriers operating together must have more sea room. The five flat-tops were working with their circuits almost overlapping in a 'Box' far too close inshore, all too conducive to hasty, nervous landings, made more often than not with no wind over the deck, raising a plane's approach speed a good 10 to 15 knots higher than in the vigorous, steady blow down the narrow decks in the Clyde. It was no better for those who had been given a pierhead jump from *Indomitable* to a CVE, with flight decks 30 per cent smaller, and 15 knots slower than a big Fleet carrier.

The sortie rate was high, the schedule tight. A Seafire's endurance was 85 minutes, with 60 minutes spent over the beach-head. 'Patrol maintained all day – landing on and flying aircraft every hour,' *Stalker*'s log recorded for D-Day. On the rare occasions when a carrier found a wind, a Seafire, with its aerodynamic shape, might well float over all the wires when the batsman signalled the 'Cut', then it was into the barrier or over the side.

COMBAT FRUSTRATION

The Seafires slogged through another gruelling day. The enemy came on in greater strength, but invariably the tip-and-run 190s or 109s jettisoned their bombs on sighting the Spitfire lookalikes and fled, sprinting away from frustrated Navy pilots like Sub-Lieutenant (A) E. J. Davies, RNVR, of 833 Fighter Flight, who went to the help of some P-38s bounced by Bf 109s. As soon as Davies' Seafire burst through the haze a 109 ahead of him turned and ran. Davies managed to get off only two short bursts before the Messerschmitt left him behind, though a patrol from 897 Squadron had better luck in the early evening, when the Squadron CO, Lieutenant-Commander (A) W. C. Simpson, RNVR, sighted 12 Bfs in the westering sun at about 3,650m (12,000ft). With such odds they did not run, but the Seafires out-

Left and above: One of *Stalker*'s 880 Squadron LIICs crumpled its port wing on hitting a gun barrel in the catwalk, hit the sea upside down, and drowned its pilot. (A. D. Brown)

Below: Refuelling and rearming a Seafire LIIC aboard an escort carrier at Salerno. (IWM)

Right: A Liberator MR.6, with a range of 950 miles, had the largest radius of operation of any Allied maritime reconnaissance bomber. Used by the USAAF, RCAF and RAF Coastal Command.

turned and out-dived them. Simpson shot down two 109s, and his wingman damaged two more.

Although these were the only scores made by Force 'V' fighters on D-plus-One, they aborted 40 enemy sorties, and the small carriers racked up 232 sorties, only 12 fewer than on D-Day, with 40 per cent fewer operational aircraft. The attrition on the flight decks continued, and Montecorvino airfield, though in Allied hands, was still unusable owing to the hail of shells passing over it from both sides. During the night US Army Seebees began the job of levelling a 914m (1,000yd) airstrip on a tomato-growing estate near Paestum, aiming to have it ready for dry-weather operations by noon on the 12th.

A third day began with only 39 serviceable Seafires. These overworked machines and their tired pilots achieved a remarkable 160 sorties, 30 more than the planned limit, and a World War 2 record for carrier utilisation. The glider bomb-carrying Dorniers eluded high-level Spitfires and P-38s, and scored several hits on the vital inshore gunfire support ships. The Seafires were still destroying themselves on the flight decks of the CVEs. 'Seafire failed to land on and crashed into sea,' *Stalker*'s log recorded that forenoon.

The Martlets and Seafires of Force 'H' flew CAP, dawn to dusk. They had had only one combat, when four Martlets ganged up on one helpless Fiat RS14 floatplane on D-Day and shot it down. With guided missiles and U-boats in the area, the Fleet carriers left at dusk on the 11th in accordance with the original plan. The 'Woolworth carriers' were more expendable. After the last patrol of the day, eight of *Formidable*'s Martlets, two of her Seafire IICs and six of *Illustrious*' all landed aboard *Unicorn* for use in the protection of Force 'V', freeing the latter's fighters for the patrols over Salerno. Two of the IICs crashed and became

Right: An LIIC of 899 Squadron makes a near-perfect approach to HMS *Hunter*'s deck. (A. D. Brown)

Right: An 880 Squadron Seafire LIIC takes off from HMS *Stalker* on another patrol over the beach-head, looking weathered and battle-worn. The white port wingtip is possibly an identification marking felt necessary in the prevailing haze. (A. D. Brown)

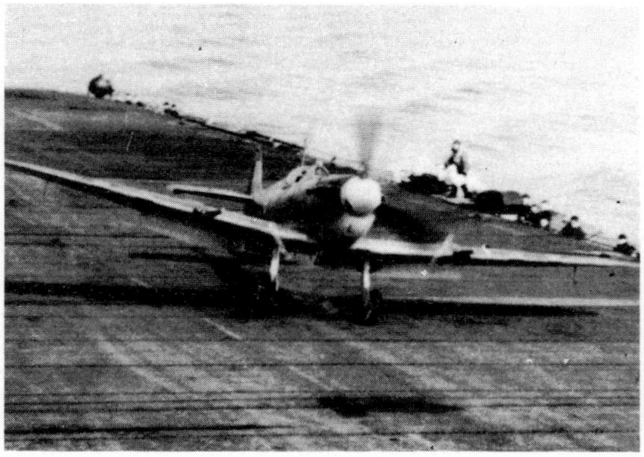

Right: This one made it, though it is leaning heavily on its port oleo leg.

unserviceable but next morning another nine Martlets from *Formidable* flew aboard *Unicorn*.

A notable exception to the attrition aboard the pine-planked flight decks of the CVEs was 834 Fighter Flight, which had been in *Hunter* since 7 July, giving its experienced leader, Lieutenant F. A. J. Pennington, RNZNVR, time to teach his pilots (all New Zealanders who had come from *Indomitable*), how to tackle landing aboard the flight decks of the small escort carriers. Deck landing accidents were reduced to four prop pecks, and all six aircraft were still serviceable. Pecking was reduced in *Hunter* by Captain McWilliam, who had 50mm (2in) trimmed off the 3m (10ft) diameter airscrews, with no drop in performance, and the 'mod' became standard.

THE PAESTUM STRIP

On 12 September dawn patrols took off on their fourth weary day of duty over the beach-head. 'Seafire landing on crashed into bridge island killing Stoker Ross,' HMS *Stalker* logged. 'Other aircraft directed to HMS *Battler*.' When the Paestum strip became available, the best of the remaining serviceable Seafires were selected, and at 13:52 Lieutenant-Commander J. C. Cockburn, RN, *Stalker*'s Lieutenant-Commander (Flying), led two LIICs from his own ship, four from *Attacker*, five each from *Battler* and *Hunter* and ten IICs from *Unicorn*, to Paestum. Brake failure wrote off one Seafire on the dusty strip, where the pilots found that they themselves had to maintain and refuel the aircraft, which was hard labour, using 19l (5gal) drums, 23 for each machine. None of the naval fighters was fitted with dust filters, unlike the Mediterranean Spitfires, which threatened a short life for the Merlin. They could only manage one mission that first day, a search for enemy tanks, and spent an uneasy night in tents, under a continuous bombardment, though they found flying there more relaxing with the anxiety of deck landing removed. At dawn 12 LIICs with four IICs as top cover were cruising through the thick haze when two Mustang A-36As bounced them, and topcover shot one of them down. The pilot baled out unhurt, and while the Seafire pilots were being debriefed an American Major sporting two pearl-handled revolvers on his thighs burst in demanding to know 'Which of you Limey sons of bitches shot down my goddam idiot Number Two?'

The noon patrol of 20 Seafires carried out an uneventful sweep and on returning found the USAAF 33rd Fighter Group in possession at Paestum. The strip was hopelessly congested with the 100 Curtiss Warhawks, and Force 'V's' 25 machines were moved on to Asa, where the Spitfires of the RAF's No 324 Wing were now established. Eight LIICs flew on dusk patrol, and the RAF Servicing Commando overhauled the dust-grimed naval fighters ready for further action. But dawn patrol by eight Seafires next day, 14 September, was the last mission, the 56th while ashore, for the tired Seafires and peelows of Force 'V', which was disbanded at Palermo on 20 September.

Below: HMS *Tracker*, BAVG-6, a lively sea boat, would 'roll on wet grass'. She began operations in the autumn of 1943, with a 'Composite' Squadron of Swordfish and Seafire IBs.

8

CARD CUTS LOOSE

OFFENSIVE 'GNAT'

Battler headed east for the Arabian Sea while *Attacker, Hunter* and *Stalker* covered the fast Gibraltar-UK convoy MKF24, which reached Britain at the beginning of Dönitz's new autumn offensive in the Atlantic. Twenty U-boats lay across the paths of the next convoys, but the three CVEs were put into dockyard hands for refit, repair and/or re-equipping.

British radar and Asdic had become very efficient in locating U-boats. Aircraft and surface escorts had been beating them with the new forward-throwing DC and bomb launchers, Hedgehog and Squid. The Germans had produced their own 'Gnat' acoustic torpedo, which was the heart of the new offensive. It was at its most efficient against ships steaming at medium speeds, and was mainly intended for attacking the convoy escorts.

There were seven escort carriers in dockyard hands in Britain and four more at the working-up stage, but none ready to accompany Convoys ONS18 and ON22 to Canada. The Admiralty's Submarine Tracking Room had plotted the build-up of U-boats, and the 9th Escort Group was switched from Biscay to reinforce the convoys' close escort of eight ships. Close air support was to be provided by the three Swordfish of the MAC-ship *Empire MacAlpine*.

In spite of thick fog a Coastal Command Liberator sank *U-341* but the wolf-pack's Gnats crippled the frigate *Lagan*, sank the Canadian destroyer *St Croix*, two merchantmen and the corvette *Polyanthus*. Another Liberator sank *U-338* and the destroyer HMS *Keppel* rammed and sank *U-229*. By the afternoon of 22 September the fog had gone, leaving good visibility but no wind. With the sky clear up to 6,100m (20,000ft), Sub-Lieutenant Barlow in *Empire MacAlpine*'s Swordfish 'B', armed with only two DCs (all they could lift off the deck), sighted a U-boat steering towards the convoy at a good 17 knots. Barlow reported to *MacAlpine* and was joined by Sub-Lieutenant Gifford's Swordfish 'C', with four RPs. Instead of combining, they attacked separately, and were lucky to escape damage from intense flak. A fighter might have made the difference.

Gnats sank the frigate *Itchin*, carrying survivors from the *St Croix* and *Polyanthus*, and another four merchantmen before the U-boats withdrew from the battle. To counter the Gnat the Admiralty produced the 'Foxer', which was towed behind a ship sounding off like a ship's propeller, to attract a Gnat fired at her and explode it clear of the ship. Unfortunately it interfered with an escort's Asdic, but modifications were made, and the only further victims were a Polish destroyer in October 1943 and two frigates and a corvette early in 1944.

Two more Trade Protection CVEs were ready to join battle. No 842 Composite Squadron, which had been assigned to HMS *Fencer* (Captain E. W. Anstice, RN), a new *Bogue* Class ship from Western Pipe, had received 12 Swordfish and a fighter flight of six Seafire LIICs in clipped-wing form in early July, and No 816 Composite, allocated to HMS *Tracker*, took delivery of its nine Swordfish and six Seafire IBs a few days later. Both squadrons spent a month at Macrihanish working-up with their new aircraft and joined their ships in mid-August. *Fencer*'s 842 Squadron lost its LIICs, which were needed for the forthcoming Operation 'Avalanche', and were replaced by the six Seafire IBs *NM921, NX822, NX911, NX985, PA100* and *PA121*, taken from the fighter training squadrons. *Fencer* was reserved for a special mission in October, *Tracker* escorted HX258 to Britain. The first tanker MAC-ship *Rapana* left Halifax with SC143 on 28 September, and claimed one U-boat damaged in the pack which sank two merchantmen and one destroyer for the loss of four boats.

OPERATION 'ALACRITY'

Meanwhile *Fencer* and 842 Composite were seven days into their special mission. In the area round the Azores U-boats lurked in the paths of American convoys sailing between New York and Gibraltar and on the flank of UK-Gibraltar/West Africa convoys. US Navy escort carriers had policed the area very efficiently, but it would obviously be more satisfactory if Very Long Range aircraft could be based in the Azores to augment them.

The Portuguese dictator/Prime Minister Dr Salazar had been approached but was stubborn. He refused absolutely to allow the Americans to participate in any such scheme as he feared their influence on Portuguese life, and worried that once they moved into the Azores it might be impossible to get them out. The British government had been trying to persuade him to allow them the use of the islands for a period of two years, but Salazar was also afraid of possible German reprisals and of the reaction of General Franco, and refused. A plan for occupation by force was prepared, but the British were reluctant to use this, and eventually won Salazar round. By the agreement of 18 August 1943 Britain was allowed the use of air bases on Fayal and Terceira Islands from 8 October.

The plans for Operation 'Alacrity' were activated, to install the necessary base facilities in Fayal and Terceira. An expedition, commanded by Commodore (Vice-Admiral, Retired) R. V. Holt, RN, sailed from Britain on 3 October 1943. *Fencer* weighed from the Clyde at 05:30, proceeded in company with the 8th Escort Group and rendezvoused with the troopship *Franconia* near Ailsa Craig. Off Rathlin Island *Fencer* began to pitch in the first surge of a big ocean swell. Centre piece of the little squadron was the grey liner *Franconia*, escorted by three destroyers, anti-submarine trawlers, and *Fencer*. On board the *Franconia* was Air-Vice Marshal Geoffrey Bromet, RAF, who had once flown Short and Wight seaplanes in support of the Dardanelles landings from HMS *Ark Royal*, renamed *Pegasus* when the Admiralty wanted her original name for the new Fleet carrier of 1936, and selected as the first of the Fighter Catapult Ships in World War 2. Bromet was to be Senior British Officer, Azores. With him Bromet brought ground crews for Numbers 206, 220 and 233 RAF Squadrons.

The weather from the start was bad, and it was much too rough to fly. 'Stringbags flew a bit,' wrote Fighter Leader Desmond Kelsall, 'but not enough wind for Seafs.' Captain Anstice mustered the ship's company and briefed them on the object of the expedition. 'Resistance by the inhabitants of the Azores is not expected but you should be on your guard, as German agents are known to be working in the Islands,' he cautioned. U-boats were also thought to be using the bays and creeks of the islands to make repairs, charge batteries and load fresh stores.

FUELLING PARTY

Coming up from Bermuda was Buster Isbell with USS *Card*, the old four-stacker destroyers *Borie*, *Barry* and *Goff*, and *Bogue*'s veteran Compo (VC) 9 (Lieutenant-Commander H. M. Avery) which, with their new Avenger TBF-1Cs, caught milch cow *U-460* about to cast off its hose from the smaller 740-ton *U-264*, into whose gaping gut she had just pumped 60 tons of diesel oil. She was preparing to launch balloons on which to float the hose across to the 1,600-ton *U-422*, waiting to port for her turn at the tit, while *U-455* stood by in the queue to starboard. Some 11 to 13km (seven or eight miles) ahead were several more shapes which could be another group.

Weigle's TBF, Heim's and Puckett's Wildcats and the three TBFs off the dawn patrol were on their way, but Stearns was not going to give this prize bag any more time to get away. Already the four submarines were shifting their formation. The two big 1,600-ton flankers pulled out wider, and the smaller *U-264* and the milch cow *U-460* fell in behind the port hand 1,600-tonner, with *U-264* pulling slightly ahead of the refueller. Stearns attacked alone into the combined fire of four U-boats. He aimed for the triangle formed by the small sub, the fueller and the port hand 1,600-tonner, but the blazing barrage put him off his stroke, and his 227kg (500lb) bomb fell between *U-264* and the fueller. The precious milch cows were under orders to dive if attacked but this one stayed put. The skipper of *U-264* shouted against the racket of his 20mms, 'Dive! Dive!'

Stearns still had a homing torpedo in his bomb bay but doctrine forbade letting Fido loose while there were still subs on the surface. Besides, to lay a Mark 24 meant releasing from 60m (200ft) and at 120 knots, and he would have been shot down long before he had reached release point. He circled out of range of the U-boat's guns, waiting

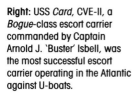

Right: USS *Card*, CVE-II, a *Bogue*-class escort carrier commanded by Captain Arnold J. 'Buster' Isbell, was the most successful escort carrier operating in the Atlantic against U-boats.

Right: USS *Card*. Note the rectangular antenna of the SK (air-search) radar which has replaced the shorter-ranged, less accurate SC. The small mast for'ard carries the HF/DF aerial.

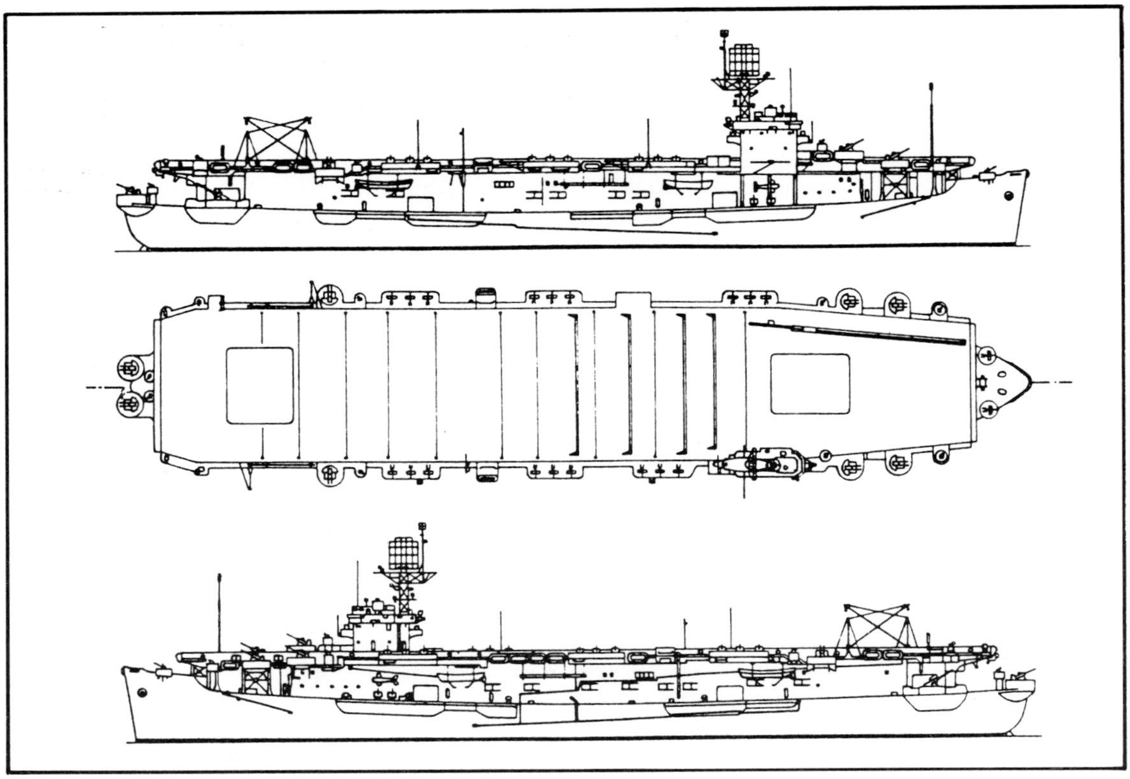

for the reinforcements. Meanwhile the submarines weaved about on radical zigzag courses, staying as close as they could together. At 11:30 Weigle's TBF arrived and while he circled to await the fighters he reported the situation to the ship. Isbell sent off every plane – five more TBFs and two F4Fs. Realising that the first TBF was being swiftly reinforced and that if they remained on the surface they would be overwhelmed, the U-boats began circling to cover each other's dives. At 11:34 *U-264* pulled out of the circle and began to dive. She was the smallest of the four, and Stearns and Weigle left her alone, waiting for the fighters.

About a minute later Heim and Puckett arrived. After exchanging signals with the TBF pilots, Heim's Wildcat, closely followed by Puckett's, dived on the 1,600-tonner which had been on the portside of the formation and was putting up the most lethal barrage. To silence her would leave them a better chance of sinking the fueller. Heim pushed over at 460m (1,500ft), Puckett behind him. They seemed to be flying through a solid curtain of fire 46m (150ft) high, some 90m (300ft) wide and 7–8m (25ft) thick, filled with black and white bursts of smoke. Heim passed over the U-boat's stern and pulled out 15m (50ft) from the water. Dave Puckett was following him down into the fire, his six 0.50s blazing away. Heim's guns did not seem to have cut down the barrage at all, and Puckett's Wildcat lurched several times as it was hit. Shrapnel struck the fuselage just below the cockpit, and another piece knocked its port outboard gun off its trunnion. Heim came in for another strafing run. At first the barrage seemed as hot and heavy as ever, but as the sub loomed large over his cowling its guns fell silent until there was only one gun firing at him. When he was about 150m (500ft) from the target this one stopped. This boat, *U-455*, then dived before Puckett could get in another run, so he joined up with Weigle, who was preparing a bombing run on what he thought was the fueller. As Puckett dived the fire from the two remaining surfaced U-boats flared up but had died down again to almost nothing when Weigle came in. He approached from astern, fine on the U-boat's starboard quarter. Strafing with his two 0.50-calibre cowl guns, he inadvertently pressed the bomb release button, and all his four DCs fell and exploded, the nearest a good 230m (750ft) short. He vented his anger by strafing the whole length of the boat, then just had time to make a second strafing run from the sub's starboard beam before she submerged, at 11:41, in a very steep crash-dive.

Now there were two U-boats, two TBFs with two torpedoes, two fighters. Stearns, seeing Weigle starting to attack, had manoeuvred so that he could drop his Fido on the diving submarine, but when he saw that the other boat was undamaged he reefed his plane round in a tight turn and started a run on this one, which was actually the refueller, *U-460*.

Heim strafed her from the starboard beam, Puckett from abaft the beam. Heim came in again from the starboard quarter. The sub was not

Opposite page, bottom: The Wildcat is launched, flaps down for flying speed, and sinks towards the ocean, always a traumatic moment for the Goofers on 'Flyco' (right of the picture), on the bridge and the catwalks, not to mention the aircrew of the machine. Most of the heavily loaded aircraft managed to reach climbing speed before hitting the water (some dunking their wheels or feathering the sea with their propellers), but some did not and took a deep six, the crews praying that they would be able to clear the aircraft in time to avoid being run down by the ship, which would have been put under hard starboard helm to avoid them. The turret gunner was most at risk, as TBF turrets often stuck.

fighting back. As Puckett dived on her again she started to submerge, making a violent turn to port. Stearns, out on her starboard side, lowered his wheels and prepared to make his run up the U-boat's track. The U-boat suddenly put on hard left rudder but Stearns turned with her and his Fido splashed 15m (50ft) in front of the point where she submerged. The torpedo ran a short distance straight ahead, turned sharply to port towards the quarry and exploded about 75m (250ft) further on. There was no plume of foam, but the water erupted in an unmistakable shock wave. A brown slick formed, and about a minute later a mass of debris began to rise to the surface in the middle of it, evidence that the target was breaking up.

This was all there was to see when the second killer group of five TBFs and two F4Fs arrived. They patrolled the area and mistakenly attacked four whales which happened to pass through this patch and broached at the wrong time. A second quartet which came up to breathe and sound in the afternoon was also strafed by *Card* planes, and when Stewart Holt in TBF '7' reported a surfaced sub 5km (three miles) from the scene of the earlier U-boat battle, Isbell was sceptical.

But this was the real thing. The cetacean patrol had found the damaged *U-422* of the refuelling party. Holt was at 1,220m (4,000ft) when he sighted her, with Ensign Horn in a Wildcat flying wing on him. He waggled his wings and pointed to the target, about 3km (two miles) ahead on their starboard bow. Horn saw it and broke away to strafe. Holt repeated the contact by radio, then Horn dived and beat up the sub, which crash-dived. Holt, coming in from astern, lowered his wheels and throttled back just as the sub's conning tower dipped beneath the sea. He dropped his Fido ahead of the swirl and slightly to starboard, pulled up his wheels and closed his bomb bay doors, while radioman Don Allen took pictures as the torpedo splashed. Frank Kuczinski was taking photographs too with his turret camera, and saw the shock wave as the Fido exploded. As they circled the spot they saw oil and debris and a dark coloured life raft come to the surface. An oily, scummy stationary slick mushroomed up and grew steadily in size. It was *Card*'s sixth kill.

On 8 October the 'Alacrity' group sighted Terceira Island far away and blue on the horizon. The sky cleared and the sun came out. The carrier flew off patrols all day. Young RNVR Subby Ken Morley flew his first anti-submarine patrol in 'his' Seafire IB, PA100, the machine allocated to him and which he most often flew (except when on standby, when pilots used whichever machines were warmed up on the flight-deck). The fighters always patrolled in pairs, and Morley flew as No 2 to Desmond Kelsall. In the warm, scented dusk they approached Angra do Heroismo, where two Walruses from *Fencer* flew RAF ground staff ashore and the carrier parted company with *Franconia*, which anchored off the town, its lights shimmering and flickering in the water. *Fencer* continued to fly off patrols throughout the 9th and most of the 10th, when the RAF Coastal Command Hudsons and Fortresses which were to operate from the islands were expected at Lagens airfield on Terceira. But the bad weather had delayed them, and it was decided to fly part of *Fencer*'s squadron ashore for temporary duty in their place. On the 10th, *Fencer* anchored off Angra to disembark stores. Next day the carrier put to sea and flew off nine of her Swordfish, one of which crashed in the sea, and Kelsall's and Morley's Seafire Red Section flew to Lagens. They landed amidst an army of monster flying grasshoppers.

Card continued to head north, flying off patrols, refuelling her short-winded old destroyers. Weather had improved, but by noon on 11 October it had worsened again, and all planes in the air were recalled to the ship. As *Card* pitched heavily, the single screw rose out of the water, and the vibration could be felt throughout the ship. It grew dark. Phosphorus broke round the bow and seemed to light up the whole ocean. Wind and sea had abated sufficiently by dawn on the 12th, Columbus Day, to fly again. Balliett, on a port

Below: Launch. A Grumman F4F Wildcat fighter positioned on the catapult of *Bogue*-class CVE USS *Core*, ready for launching. In the hydraulically operated American accelerator a shuttle moved along a slot running fore-and-aft in the fore end of the flight deck. The aircraft was taxied over the after end of the slot, its fuselage attached to the shuttle by a strop, or bridle, and its tail to a hook incorporating a breaking-ring designed to break at a certain pressure. The shuttle was tensioned until the aircraft strained at bridle and hold-back hook, engine revving. The pilot opened the throttle, the catapult was fired, and the aircraft shot forward. In this picture the strop temporarily connecting the aircraft's tail to the catapult can be seen.

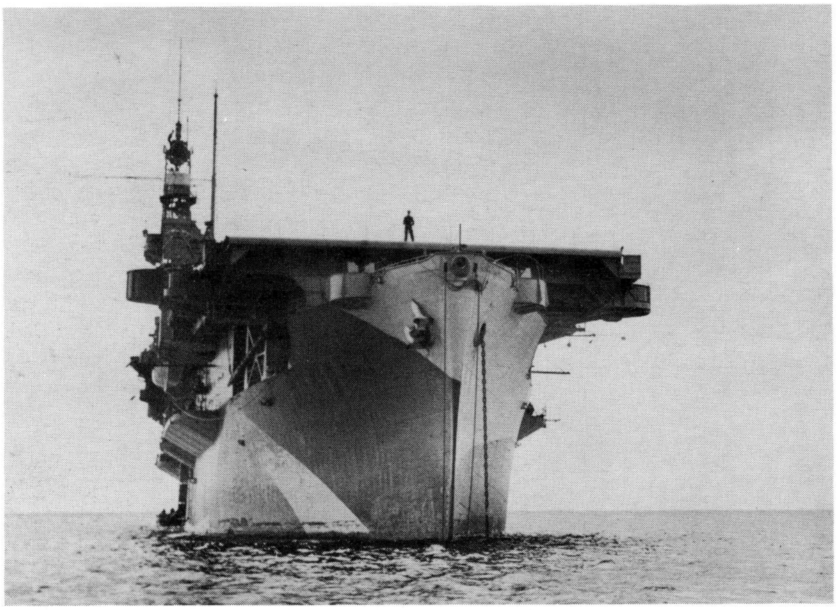

sector forward search in mid-ocean directly between Newfoundland and Ireland, sighted the milch cow *U-488* heading west-nor'-west to refuel boats of the *Rossbach* group, let his Fido loose and reported her destroyed. At 10:45 next forenoon Compo 9 CO Howard Avery's B-bomb sank *U-402*. For the rest of the morning and early afternoon Avery's crews combed the area of the earlier attacks and pushed further out to follow up contacts signalled to *Card* by COMINCH.

At 16:45 Harry Fryatt in Avenger 'T9' found *U-378* 70km (44 miles) from the ship. He dived, and the U-boat fought back with all her guns. 'T9' was hit several times. One shell struck the starboard landing gear, and shrapnel cut both the hydraulic lines for lowering the gear, as well as the manual emergency release cable. Fryatt dropped his 227kg (500lb) bomb, the sub began a crash-dive, and Fryatt followed up with Wandering Annie before the periscope had disappeared. *U-378* had been damaged, but survived.

Fryatt, heading back for the ship in rapidly worsening weather, with the high wind and heavy seas of a Force 10 gale blowing, knew the plane was hit, but did not know the extent of the damage. He arrived over *Card* to find the carrier pitching and rolling heavily in the darkness. As he flew downwind past the ship the batsman's Talker and Teller, binoculars levelled, could just make out detail on the TBF. 'Hook down,' he reported. 'Port wheel down . . . Starboard wheel retracted!' Fryatt tried to lower his undercarriage, but could not get his starboard wheel down. All efforts to dislodge it failed. By then four more TBFs were in the circuit. With darkness deepening rapidly and the weather getting worse all the time, Isbell acted decisively to save his young aviators. Having recovered the four undamaged aircraft, not without difficulty, he took a calculated risk, ordered the flight deck lights turned fully on, and signalled Fryatt to come in.

The TBF sank towards the round-down. Fryatt got his port undercarriage down, but the starboard wheel was uselessly jammed and because of

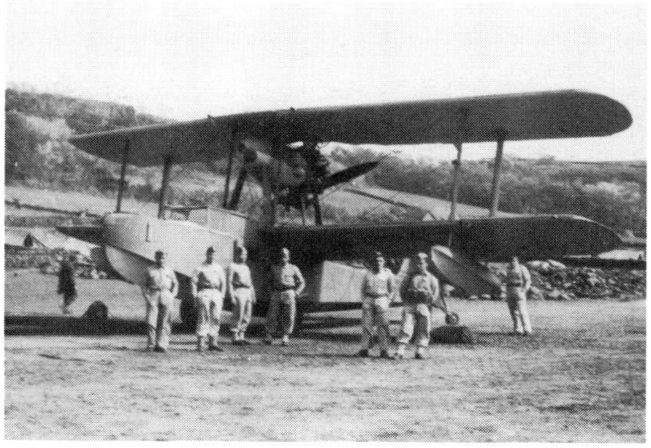

Right: *Fencer*'s two Walrus amphibians flew the RAF ground crews to the airfield at Lagens on Terceira Island, Azores, and became the first British aircraft to land there. the RAF accommodation tents can be seen in the background. *Fencer*'s aircrews lived in a cowshed. Here Lieutenant Winser's aircraft is seen with attendant Portuguese soldiers. (Ken Morley)

Right: Five of *Fencer*'s twelve Swordfish were landed at Lagens airfield, Azores, as well as her six Seafires, which flew regular patrols over the islands looking for U-boats. (Ken Morley)

Opposite page, top: HMS *Fencer* (Captain E. W. Anstice, RN). *Bogue*-class escort carrier built by the Western Pipe & Steel Company at San Francisco as CVE-14, joined Operation 'Alacrity', the establishment of an Allied air base in the Azores, in which the carrier's aircraft, particularly her Seafires, played an important part. (Ken Morley)

Opposite page, centre: *Fencer*'s batsman Bill Wilson – 'Get that starboard wing down!' The censor has whited out *Fencer*'s American radar and the YE homing beacon aerial but not the British 271 surface search scanner in its distinctive cabinet. (Ken Morley)

Opposite page, bottom: Sub-Lieutenant(A) Ken Morley, RNVR in one of *Fencer*'s 842 Squadron's six Seafire IBs, makes a near-perfect landing, August 1943, before Operation 'Alacrity'. This CVE and her squadron quickly established a reputation for efficiency and reliability. (Ken Morley)

the loss of hydraulic fluid he could not get his landing flaps to extend fully. He made a fair approach, slightly fast. Ahead of him the flight deck was clear, except for TBF '12', which had been pushed forward to the extreme starboard edge of the deck as there was no more room on the hangar deck.

The batsman whipped his paddle across his chest. Fryatt closed his throttle. Hook trailing, roaring through the darkness across the dim footlights of this floating stage, the big plane missed all the wires, ballooned over the barrier, hit the bridge island just above Flying Control with its starboard wing and lost a wingtip, careered on, smashed into the TBF parked for'ard, and screeched to rest 4.5m (15ft) from the edge of the flight deck. As it did so it swept pilot Roger Kuhn, who had been standing there, into the sea. Instinctively Kuhn kept a tight grip on the flashlight he was carrying. When he bobbed up in the water he switched it on. In a few minutes *Barry* came up out of the darkness and hauled him aboard, with nothing worse than a minor leg injury. Fryatt's plane, badly damaged, was repaired on board. Fryatt and his crew were shaken but unhurt.

Seafires on Terceira

As *Card* began to swing south-east, en route for Casablanca to support west-bound Convoy GUS18, away south-west in the Azores *Fencer*'s Seafires flew anti-submarine patrols round the islands, checking bays and inlets for U-boats, accompanied the Swordfish on dawn and dusk patrols, and provided close anti-submarine patrols over the Terceira anchorages. For eight days they swept Terceira, Graciosa, San Jorge, Pico and Fayal, and saw only fishing smacks, and tunny and sharks in the clear water. With some ancient oil lamps lining the flight path, they flew a few dusk patrols to try to catch conning towers rising, but had no better luck. Local folklore had it that on the south end of Terceira near Praia de Vitoria was the entrance to Atlantis, but they never found that either.

The Lagens detachment slept on camp beds in a cowshed, or in tents, with no toilet facilities, and lived on cold tinned food or ship's biscuit ferried in by Stringbag from *Fencer*, washed down by chlorinated tea, Azorean anis, and the occasional canned beer. The aircraft were maintained by RAF ground crews. Lagens field was long and dusty, and petrol and oil filters had to be checked daily. For refuelling, 4½-gallon tins of petrol were dragged on trolleys more than a quarter of a mile from the petrol dump to the airfield. Yet, in spite of the hardships, there was a spirit of adventure in the air, and morale was high. And, truth to tell, the Seafires seemed happier flying from terra firma. Kelsall appropriated a Portuguese squadron mascot of a mosquito in boxing gloves and the motto he found written on a wall, 'Chega-te e logo ves!' ('Up and at 'em!') for the side of his Seafire.

On the strip the constant grating of the crickets

Right: Seafire Leader Desmond Kelsall at Readiness in Seafire IB No. PA121, with air mechanics Jauncey and Browes. The Portuguese squadron mascot of a mosquito in boxing gloves and the motto *'Chega-te e logo ves!'* (Up and at 'em!) has been painted on the aircraft just below the windscreen. (D. Kelsall)

Right: The first aircraft to operate from the new Allied air base at Lagens on Terceira in the Azores, an RAF-manned B-17 Flying Fortress, comes in to land, to be turned round and sent out on patrol immediately. (Ken Morley)

was accompanied by a warbler who sang all day, and there were goldfinch, robins, quail, blackbirds, black caps and sinister buzzards. All around the airfield the land was chequered with peasants' small, cultivated holdings, backed by green, wooded hills and red volcanic cliffs. A local workman built them a fireplace out of lava blocks. On the 19th Yellow Section (Sub-Lieutenants Andrew Sachnovsky and New Zealander Ken Gilbert) relieved Kelsall and Morley, who hitched a lift back to *Fencer* in a landing craft.

As *Card* dropped her hook in Casablanca harbour on 18 October the first of the Azores-based aircraft, an RAF Flying Fortress, touched down at Lagens. From now on air protection would be available to Allied ships over the whole North Atlantic north of 30 degrees north, the latitude of the Canary Islands, with patrols from the Azores overlapping those from Newfoundland, Great Britain, Gibraltar and Morocco.

The Azorean B-17 flew on patrol the day after it had landed, allowing *Card*'s weary aviators a brief rest as they accompanied GUS18 home through U-boat infested waters. Eventually there were some 3,000 British and Commonwealth airmen in the Azores and a strong force of aircraft, including more B-17s and Royal Canadian Air Force Lancasters. Mitchell bombers provided a meteorological service, with one aircraft flying 800km (500 miles) to the south-west from Terceira, and another to the UK to deliver the weather forecast which helped the RAF choose the best nights for the 1,000 bomber raids on Germany.

REINFORCEMENTS

But land-based planes could not cover every square league of ocean. While *Card* was steaming west under the new Azorean umbrella, *Core* (Captain James R. Dudley, USN), with four-pipers *Greene, Belknap* and *Goldsborough*, filled her billet. On 19 October Charles Brewer, CO of *Core*'s Compo (VC) 13 Squadron, in a Wildcat, and Lieutenant R. W. Hayman in a TBF sighted *U-398*. This submarine's Gnats had just sunk the Polish destroyer *Orkan*, and on the U-boat's 'bandstands', which the German matelots called *wintergarten*, were the two single 20mm and quadruple 20mm cannon which had almost taken the young lives of Harry Fryatt and his crew on 13 December. Hayman was luckier than Fryatt, with the Boss in a fighter to block for him. Brewer braved the awesome flak, chased the gunners out of the *wintergarten*, and exploded ammunition in the conning tower, which was like a lethal Fourth of July for some wild moments. While everyone on the conning tower was diving for cover, Hayman dropped his bomb, which blew *398*'s pressure hull apart.

On 24 October HMS *Fencer* and her destroyer screen sailed from Angra in the golden afterlight of sunset, their part in 'Alacrity' completed. The carrier's Swordfish flew night patrols, their hooded exhausts masking the tell-tale flame – birds, fulmars and stormy petrels followed them all day. The Seafire Leader had time to contemplate 'carrier life in the informal way it goes in these escort carriers – which must surely be the best life of all in the FAA. No big ship complex with all its bullshit – much more like a destroyer atmosphere really.' The Americans had also begun night flying to counter the U-boats' practice of surfacing in the dark to re-charge batteries and radio base. *Croatan* had initiated this in home waters on 5 September, and the *Bogue*-Class USS *Block Island*, commissioned on 8 March, but hitherto used to transport Army fighters from New York to Belfast (the only places where airfields adjoined deepwater anchorages), was now hunting U-boats round the clock, particularly milch cows driven north by the patrols from the Azores. Her new 'Night Owl' Avengers had had guns and bomb racks removed to allow extra gasoline tanks to be fitted, giving them the stamina to stay airborne for as long as 14 hours. *U-220* had been sowing mines off St John's, Newfoundland, and was making for a rendezvous with a milch cow when the CVE's aircraft attacked and sank her.

At first light on 30 October *Card*, with faithful flush-deckers *Borie*, *Barry* and *Goff*, having seen GUS18 safely through the danger zone, was some 360km (225 miles) south of the point where *Block Island*'s planes had sunk *U-220*, making 15 knots, on a northerly course. Avenger 'T11' on the dawn patrol reported an oil slick 145km (90 miles) ahead of the ship. As the first patrol was returning to the ship, two TBFs were launched to cover the forward sectors. Both of these returned after two hours on patrol with engine trouble, a recurring malady in VC-9's hard-flown Grummans, along with persistent hydraulic leaks, gear box oil seal failures and other defects which brought machines in on deferred forced landings. After many heavy landings on a gyrating flight deck aircraft were being grounded by a lack of spare wheels. Scraping the barrel, Isbell's Air Officer found five TBFs to make another patrol, one of them, 'T11', to search the area of the oil slick. At 13:52 Harry Fryatt, who had the squadron record for sighting subs, found another one 92km (57 miles) from the ship. This boat followed Dönitz's new orders belaying the 'fight back' tactics, and dived as Fryatt approached and dropped his Fido. They saw no oil or debris, but photographs convinced Isbell that the sub had been sunk.

At 16:08 Bill Fowler in Turkey 'T7' sighted one U-boat refuelling another 43km (27 miles) astern of *Card*. Both opened fire on Fowler, with the suckling sub frantically casting off the hose and crash-diving. When Balliett's and McAuslan's TBFs arrived the milch cow submerged and was immediately attacked with Fidos by Fowler and Balliett. Two explosions were heard, and oil and debris came to the surface to mark the end of *U-584*. Isbell mistakenly thought he had killed the calf and lost the cow. It was too late for a further air search, but he sent the keen young Charles Hutchins in the old four-piper *Borie* to chase the escaping sub. A little after midnight Hutchins signalled Isbell 'Scratch one pig boat . . . Am searching for more!' Forty-five minutes later radar found him *U-405*.

After a night chase through 6m (20ft) waves, and a furious gun battle, *Borie* rammed the U-boat, temporarily locking them together, and a wild hand-to-hand fight developed, with rifles, revolvers, shotguns, Tommy guns, a Bowie knife, hot shell cases, even a coffee pot, all used as weapons. At last shells and depth-charges sank

Below: On the evening of 30 October 1943 USS *Card*'s patrolling TBF Turkeys sighted a milch cow U-boat refuelling another submarine. The Avenger sank the milch cow (*U-584*), and the suckling (*U-405*) was destroyed by the old four-piper destroyer USS *Borie* from *Card*'s screen, after a chase, a ramming, a boarding, and a hand-to-hand fight, though *Borrie* also received mortal damage. Here she is photographed abandoned and burning from the TBF which gave her the *coup de grâce*.

Right: North and Central Atlantic.

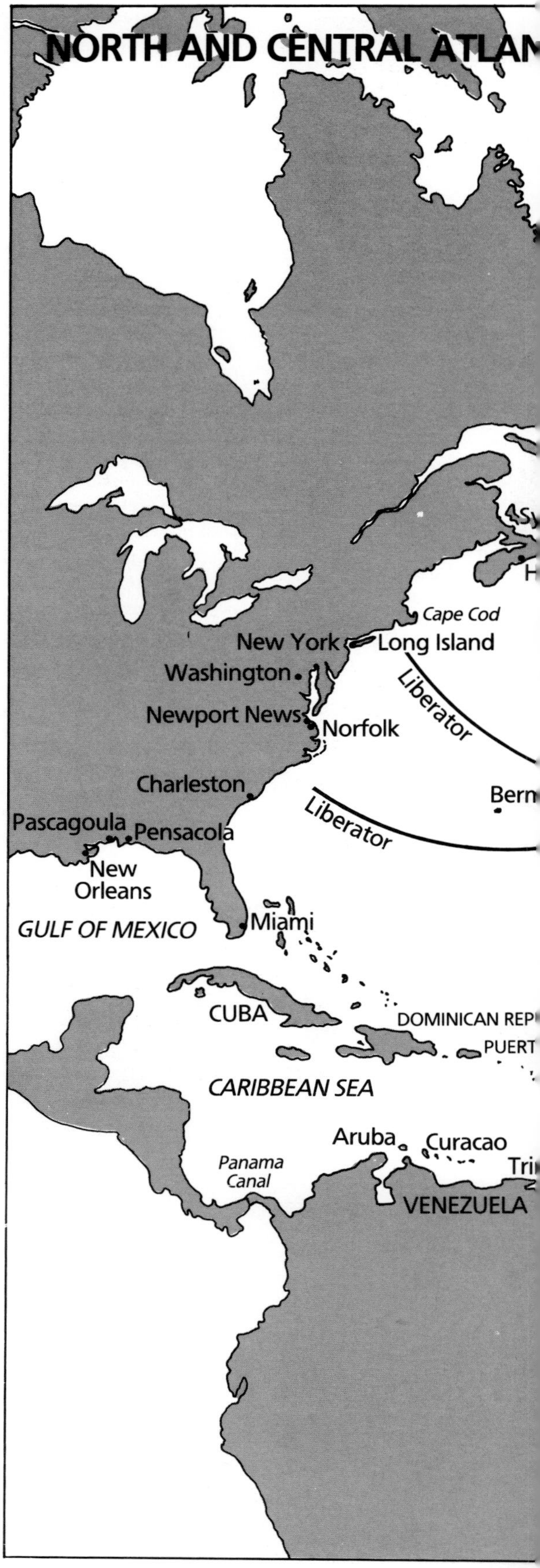

U-405, but *Borie* too was in a sinking condition, her worn-out plates stove in, and she was abandoned, with *Card* standing by. A TBF finished her off with depth charges, and *Card* turned for Norfolk. After 45 days and nights of storm and battle, she raised the Capes of Chesapeake, passed through Hampton Roads at dusk, and at half-past nine had her wires ashore in the Navy Yard, so that 2,000 men and three ships could get some rest.

HMS *Biter* and the 7th Support Group brought Convoy ON207 safely into Argentia on 3 November, and sailed again on the 7th to support HX265. Although there were two groups of U-boats about 1,125km (700 miles) east of Newfoundland, and *Biter*'s Stringbags made several sightings, the enemy was concentrating on SC146, the next UK-bound convoy to sail. Then in mid-Atlantic on 16 November one of *Biter*'s Swordfish carrying a homing torpedo made a crash-landing in the sea just astern of the ship. The shock of the crash released the torpedo, which homed on the carrier. The main explosive charge did not go off, and the torpedo merely detonated on the ship's rudder, demolishing its bottom after corner and damaging the structure of the rudder to the extent that the steering was slightly affected. Hull plating below the waterline at the stern suffered minor damage. 'A case of *Biter* bit?', signalled SO escort.

On 29 November *Bogue* joined the hunt once more. She was 620km (385 miles) east of Terceira when Lieutenant (jg) Bernard Volm, USNR, from St Louis, Missouri, in a TBF sighted a fully surfaced submarine. Three more TBFs were launched led by Lieutenant (jg) Harold Bradshaw, USN, a Wyoming man and university graduate who had quit the Standard Oil Company in 1934 to join the Navy as an apprentice seaman, and had had the *Wasp* sunk under him at Guadalcanal. Harry Bradshaw was 'all Navy'. He headed straight for the contact point, leading Ensign Bob McAshan from Houston, Texas, and New Yorker Lieutenant (jg) Elisha Gaylord, both USNR '90-day wonders'.

Bradshaw made the first attack run, McAshan and Gaylord close behind him, and two big explosions marked the end of *U-86*. At dusk next day, 30 November, Lieutenants (jg) James E. Ogle III, from Johnstown, Pennsylvania, in a TBF, and Carter E. Fetsch of Lakeview, Oregon, in a Wildcat badly damaged Oberleutnant Horst Hepp's *U-238*. The ten boats of the pack still intact, except for sprung plates, pipe leaks, broken glass and shattered nerves, were withdrawn.

Heading this way was HMS *Fencer* making her first escort run covering the combined OS60 for West Africa and KMS34 for Gibraltar. No 842, the Lagens Squadron, was still aboard, with four Martlet IVs, equivalent to the US Navy's Wright Cyclone-engined Wildcat F4F-4B (top speed 512km/h (318mph) at 5,913m (19,400ft), 442km/h (275mph) at sea level, 249km/h (155mph) in cruise,

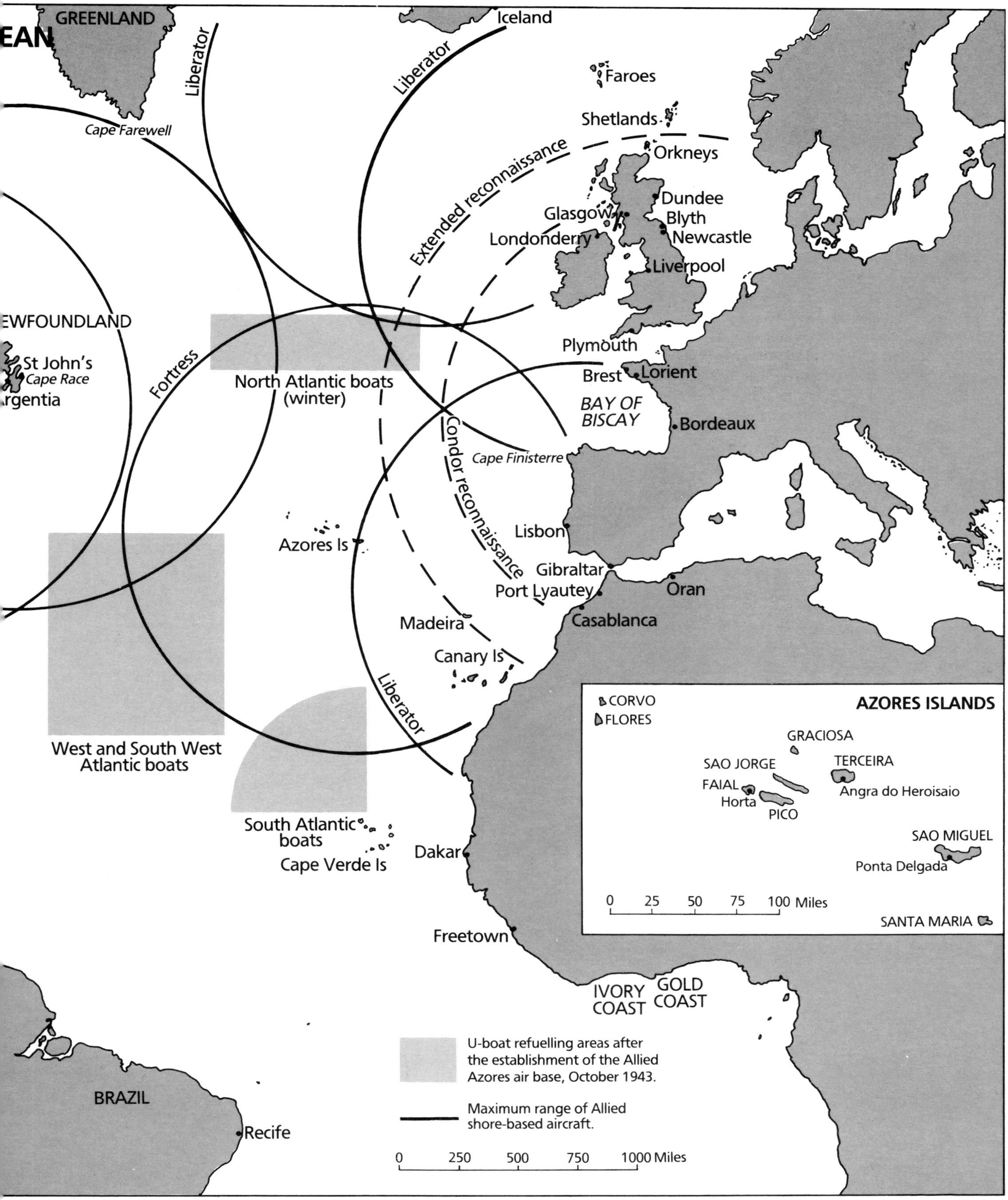

GREENLAND
EAN
Iceland
Liberator
Liberator
Faroes
Shetlands
Orkneys
Cape Farewell
Extended reconnaissance
Dundee
Glasgow
Blyth
Londonderry
Newcastle
Liverpool
EWFOUNDLAND
St John's
Cape Race
rgentia
Fortress
North Atlantic boats (winter)
Plymouth
Brest
Lorient
BAY OF BISCAY
Bordeaux
Condor reconnaissance
Cape Finisterre
Lisbon
Azores Is
Gibraltar
Port Lyautey
Oran
Casablanca
Madeira
Canary Is
Liberator
West and South West Atlantic boats
South Atlantic boats
Cape Verde Is
Dakar
Freetown
AZORES ISLANDS
CORVO
FLORES
GRACIOSA
SAO JORGE
TERCEIRA
FAIAL
Horta
PICO
Angra do Heroisaio
SAO MIGUEL
Ponta Delgada
0 25 50 75 100 Miles
SANTA MARIA
IVORY COAST
GOLD COAST
U-boat refuelling areas after the establishment of the Allied Azores air base, October 1943.
Maximum range of Allied shore-based aircraft.
BRAZIL
Recife
0 250 500 750 1000 Miles

125km/h (78mph) landing, climb 594m (1,950ft) per minute, range 1,770km (1,100 miles) maximum; ceiling 10,363m (34,000ft)) added to four of its Seafire IBs. The first Martlet to attempt a landing had crashed, ditched and taken its pilot down with it. On 1 December Lieutenant (A) Les Wort, RNVR, from Romsey, Hampshire, in Martlet *JV344*, and Sub-Lieutenant (A) Richard A. 'Flash' Fleischmann-Allen of Topsham, Devon, in Marlet *JV427*, were launched and in seven minutes had shot down an Fw 200. On her return run with MKS3 in December *Fencer* flew night anti-submarine patrols without mishap. Just after dawn on 11 December Sub-Lieutenant (A) Sakhnovsky, RNVR, was scrambled in Ken Morley's Seafire *PA100* to intercept a shadower, in heavy drizzle, a 150m (500ft) cloud base, and visibility in places as low as 15m (50ft). His radio failed owing to the lack of waterproofing round the IB's radio bay hatch, but he caught a blurred glimpse of the Condor and fired two short bursts before rain hid the Fw again. His radio still mute, Sakhnovsky managed to find *Fencer* again and land safely.

This was the Seafire's last combat during convoy protection. *Tracker*'s Seafires were disembarked for good, *Fencer* kept some of hers until they were exchanged for Martlets (now to revert to their American name of Wildcat) on 17 March 1944. Only in the Indian Ocean aboard *Battler* did the Seafire continue as the principal fighter in CVE Trade Protection. Her six IICs were exchanged on 21 March 1944 for Wildcat (previously Martlet) Vs, the British version of the low-level FM-1 from the Eastern Division of General Motors, specially redesigned and built for escort carriers when it was found that the earlier CVEs could not cope with the heavier, more powerful Hellcat F6F fighter. The FM-1 was of lighter construction, with improved R/T, more armour and a bigger stores capability, but 'sacrificed' two of the F4F-4's six guns to save weight, and gave a disappointingly poor performance, with a low-level top speed of no more than 450km/h (280mph), and a rate of climb of less than 762m (2,500ft) per minute.

Bogue sailed down to Casablanca, where she spent four days. With her screen, the three veteran Atlantic DDs, *Clempson, Osmond Ingram* and *George E. Badger*, plus *Dupont*, having refuelled, the group now headed south-west to escort Convoy GUS23 on its way past a concentration of U-boats which Tenth Fleet had indicated was gathering in one of the new, far-flung refuelling areas, in this case a rendezvous for South Atlantic-bound boats north-west of the Cape Verde Islands. In this area cruised the 1,600-ton milch cow *U-219*. One of the boats looking for refreshments from her was *U-176*, bound for the Indian Ocean.

On the clear, cloudless morning of 12 December, *Bogue* and her screen were steaming

Left: Sub-Lieutenant(A) Richard A. 'Flash' Fleischmann-Allen, RNVR and Lieutenant(A) Les Wort, RNVR after shooting down an Fw 200 Condor with their Wildcat IVs while *Fencer* was escorting combined Convoys OS60 to West Africa and KMS34 to Gibraltar, 1 December 1943. (Ken Morley)

Left: CVEs were lively ships. *Fencer* en route for Gibraltar with Convoy KMS34. (D. Kelsall)

some 1,045km (650 miles) west-by-south of the Canaries, towards the Cape Verde refuelling area, Claude Stewart's questing Avengers in their grey and white Atlantic camouflage scattered round the compass. At 08:22 Elisha Gaylord in TBF '13' was cruising about 60km (38 miles) south of the carrier when he saw a sub 6.5km (four miles) away, turned and started a DC run. Dunn sent off Carter Fetsch in Wildcat FM-1 'F2' and Texan Jack Murray in 'F7', followed by *Dupont, George E. Badger* and Harry Bradshaw's TBF. Meanwhile Gaylord had trouble. A broken line in the hydraulic system meant that his bomb bay doors would not open and he could not lower wheels or flaps to slow him down. He got his doors open by manual pump just in time to drop Fido as the U-boat submerged, and saw first oil, then a shock wave and a circular pattern of bubbles.

Next day the seemingly tireless Bradshaw, in spite of long hours aloft on the previous day, led the dawn patrol. About 08:00 he sighted a moving oil slick, and called in *Clemson* and *Osmond Ingram*. Coached by Bradshaw, *Clemson* made sonar contact and fired a nine-charge pattern, set deep. At 11:16 the bows of *U-176* broke surface. Leaking badly, she came up at a sharp angle, slid back, rose on an even keel, and men tumbled out of the conning tower hatch. Jim Ogle's TBF and two FM-1s strafed from abeam to drive the crew back into the boat and keep her afloat for capture, but three minutes after she had surfaced there was a heavy explosion and a sheet of flame from the conning tower. Smoking heavily, the submarine slowly submerged. A few minutes later there came the deep rumbling roar of an underwater explosion. A gusher of oil and debris surfaced, and *U-172* was no more. The destroyers rescued the captain and 45 men.

Bogue headed north-west towards another new refuelling zone in the Central Atlantic. At 13:05 on 20 December Lieutenant (jg) Wallace LaFleur of Lafayette, Louisiana, was on patrol in his TBF in cloudless weather 965km (600 miles) south-west of Fayal in the Azores and 273km (170 miles) from the carrier when he sighted *U-850* 9.5km (six miles) away. He made a DC run at once. *Bogue* launched Harry Bradshaw and Ensign Glendon Goodwin from Shawnee, Oklahoma, in TBFs '18' and '19', and Squadron Exec Kenneth Hance and Lieutenant (jg) Irving Cockroft of Oakland, California, in FM-1s. Hance was another regular Navy pilot, who had served pre-war in the prestigious Scouting Squadron 3 in *Saratoga*.

This group sighted the sub at 13:30, firing at the circling LaFleur. Ken Hance pitched straight in, strafing almost down to the deck, and Bradshaw dropped DCs. Cockroft hit the ammunition locker in the after part of the conning tower and it went up with a bright flash of flame. *U-850* started to crash-dive.

This was a job for Fido. Bradshaw and LaFleur opened bomb bay doors, lowered wheels and flaps and came in low. Bradshaw's homer splashed 60m (200ft) ahead of the swirl, LaFleur's in the same area just as the U-boat's bows emerged again. The two explosions merged into one great blast, which threw the U-boat's stern high in the air, scattering debris and scummy water 45m (150ft) above the surface. The whole after part disintegrated and the submarine sank instantly.

At debriefing some of the aircrewmen described a platform abaft the conning tower of the sub which was thought to be a launching pad for a 'Flying Dutchman', a cross between a kite and a helicopter which some U-boats were now carrying. This weird little aircraft came in three main parts, including the pilot's seat and a central column to carry a horizontally rotating three-bladed *Hubschraube* airscrew. When assembled, the machine was attached to 300m (985ft) of cable which was unreeled from a drum in the conning tower. The submarine went to maximum speed, and as the helicopter rose in the wind the pilot started the motor, which operated the airscrew. When aloft the pilot communicated with the boat by means of a sort of walky-talky. To return on board, the cable was reeled in, with the pilot steadying the machine, using the propeller, and there was a parachute attached to the rear of the central rotor column. If the boat was attacked while the Dutchman was flying, the cable would most likely be cast off and the pilot abandoned.

While *Bogue* was finishing off *U-850* east of Bermuda, the action was hotting up 1,600km (1,000 miles) to the north-east, on the St John's-Brest line.

BREAKING THE BORKUM LINE

Card, at sea again in support of GUS24 out of Gibraltar bound for the USA, was ordered north to hunt the *Borkum* Group of 13 new U-boats forming a patrol line west of Biscay, north of the Azores, near the new refuelling area for North Atlantic U-boats and right across the paths of combined KMS36/OS62 for Gibraltar and West Africa, and fast tanker convoy PU5 from Trinidad for Britain. With the escort for KMS36/OS62 was the new Lease-Lend CVE HMS *Striker*, another Western Pipe & Steel ship built in San Francisco, carrying No 824 Composite Squadron of nine Swordfish and six Sea Hurricanes.

To complicate matters, there was a blockade runner on the loose. The two ships *Pietro Orscolo* and *Orsorno* had reached these latitudes from Kobe, Japan, heading for Bordeaux with tin and rubber. Dönitz ordered his *Borkum* boats to look out for them and give them what protection they could, and a squadron of destroyers from Biscay ports to escort them in. On the 18th a Coastal Command aircraft sank the *Orsorno*, and the Luftwaffe searched for the surviving *Orscolo*. On the 22nd one of their aircraft sighted *Card*, heading for the *Borkum* line. On receipt of the sighting report U-boat Chief of Operations Gott told *Borkum* to forget about the *Orscolo* and hunt down the carrier.

Card, with her three 1919 four-stackers *Leary*, *Schenck* and *Decatur* getting low on fuel, was running before a wild north-westerly gale. *Borkum*'s other targets, KMS36B62 and PU5, were close together right on top of the subs. The Gib-West Africa convoys had the protection of HMS *Striker* and her Swordfish and Sea Hurricanes – whatever that was worth in the vicious weather – but on the 23rd two U-boats attacked the rich tanker target of PU5.

All the CVEs in the area, *Striker*, *Tracker* and *Card*, were fighting the gale and having difficulty operating aircraft. At daybreak *Card* tried to put up a patrol, but the flight deck was corkscrewing so wildly that the TBFs could not even be taxied forward to the catapult. Then a signal from Tenth Fleet reported the *Borkum* line 137km (85 miles) ahead of *Card*. Just after 10:00 it was possible to fly. A Wildcat pilot sighted a merchantman steaming north. She was flying the British Red Ensign, but did not answer the FM-1's challenge correctly. Isbell checked with Gibraltar and was told that he had found the *Orscolo*. Coastal Command Wellingtons, Halifaxes and Liberators were vectored towards her, and after a running battle she ran aground.

In the afternoon another German aircraft sighted *Card* and reported her position to the *Borkum* boats, which were still looking for her. At 21:20 *Card*'s Huff-Duff began intercepting U-boat signals, then her radar operator started reporting a maze of blips on the screen. At 22:30 he got a small clear echo 10.5km (6.5 miles) away and closing.

'The worst feature was the presence of the aircraft carrier . . .' Dönitz was out to get *Card*. As Isbell was ordering Logsdon in *Schenck* to attack the single echo, from just under 3km (two miles) astern *U-415* fired three torpedoes at her. The range was too long, and the German skipper was too keen. They all missed and raced off blindly into the night. On *Card*'s bridge the TBS squawked. 'Am engaging U-boat.' *Schenck* had dug out *U-305*. Isbell called Jim Keys in *Leary*. 'Join *Schenck* to assist,' then, to shake off the pursuing sub, 'Left full rudder. Flank speed.'

Schenck pounded *U-305*, then lost her. *Leary* chased one good echo, *Schenck* another. A lookout shouted 'U-boat diving!' *Schenck* swung round and a torpedo raced past her. Logsdon dropped a nine-charge pattern. A blip grew on *Schenck*'s screen where *U-645* was coming up. *Schenck* changed course, the sub dived. Radar handed over to sonar, which found her under a mile distant.

Kyes in *Leary* saw a white wake . . . 'Hard right rudder!', but it was too late. The torpedo, brushing aside the *Foxer*, hit *Leary* in the after engine room, another blew open the after hold. All power gone, the destroyer listed, the stern settled. Kyes ordered 'Abandon ship!' Watson, his Exec, last of his ship's company to leave, went over the side. Kyes paused for a second, with only the dead in the engine room for company, then a torpedo from another sub *U-382*, hit the ship in her for'ard engine room, and she went quickly. The survivors clung on to life in the rough seas. Commander Kyes, seeing a black messman trying to keep up with no life jacket, gave him his own, and was never seen again.

The men were floating near the crippled *U-645*, with *Schenck* closing in. As Logsdon passed the *Leary* survivors he lowered his gig, which saved a good number of men from the cold sea. Watson organised some order and discipline among the men, while himself supporting a dying sailor. A U-boat sank the British destroyer *Hurricane*, but *Schenck* finished off *U-645*. Aircraft from the Azores and from escort carriers swept the area, and the remaining U-boats went deep and called off the action. No-one remembered it was Christmas Eve. *Card*, zigzagging with only *Decatur* as screen, survived the hunt, and on Christmas Day the seas abated. *Card* refuelled her two parched destroyers, and took aboard survivors from *Leary*. On 2 January 1944 three ships came sailing into Hampton Roads, not one man aboard them unaware that they had once been four.

After this battle Dönitz abandoned the use of the wolf-pack, which had once been such a deadly menace. In the last three months of 1943 he had lost almost one U-boat for every merchantman sunk. (Total Allied merchant ship losses were 67 ships, U-boat losses 62.) In November-December 2,218 Allied merchantmen in 72 convoys sailed the North Atlantic without loss.

Below: The new Trade Protection escort carrier, HMS *Striker* (converted by Western Pipe & Steel Corpn. in San Francisco, accompanied her first convoy on the UK–Gibraltar run in December 1943, with her 824 (Composite) Squadron of nine Swordfish and six Sea Hurricanes. Weather was bad, with gales and heavy seas, and operating aircraft was often hazardous. The undercarriage of Sub-Lieutenant(A) Peter Aked's Swordfish LS245 collapsed in a hard landing. (Cdr. Stenning)

9

NIGHT OWLS

'I fly for enjoyment, I fly just for fun,
And I'm awfully anxious to shoot down a Hun,
But as for deck landings at night in the dark,
As I told Wings this morning, stuff that for a lark!'
– *My A25* (FAA song)

BY the end of 1943 an increasing flow of new escort carriers was coming from Allied constructors, at a prolific rate from American builders, more modestly from the fewer, smaller, British yards. The ten Lease-Lend *Bogue* Class were all in British hands and some had seen action. The ten ships, known from their names as the 'Ruler' Class, for Britain from the American *Prince William* Class (of which only the latter was retained in the US Navy), were coming through the pipeline. The Kaiser programme of 50 prefabricated carriers for the US Navy, after initial delays, had now got well into its stride, and 19 had been commissioned. HMS *Activity*, the first British conversion since *Audacity*, was completing a refit after more than a year stemming the tide in the Firth of Clyde as a Deck Landing Training Carrier, and three new Trade Protection carriers of British design and construction were almost ready for service.

NEW BRITISH CONVERSIONS

As early as February 1941, with the conversion of *Hannover* to HMS *Audacity* in its early stages, the Admiralty had asked for more merchant ships to be made available for conversion to auxiliary aircraft carriers. The Ministry of War Transport had refused to remove any merchantmen from trade to provide carriers for its protection, but they did agree to reserve several new merchant hulls for conversion. The first of these was *Activity*, which had been building as the 11,800-ton *Telemachus* in the yard of the Caledon Shipbuilding Company at Dundee since 1 February 1940. *Activity* was launched on 30 May 1942 and commissioned on 29 September 1942. She was larger than *Audacity*, with a hangar and capacity for 15 aircraft. On 4 October 1943 she went into Gladstone Dock at Liverpool for a refit in preparation for active service.

Meanwhile, three fast cargo liners under construction had been acquired by the Ministry of War Transport from the Port Line under the Defence (General) Regulations, 1939, and allocated for conversion to auxiliary aircraft carriers, of which one had been laid down in Belfast, 'a child of Harland & Wolff in the iron forest', on 12 August 1941; one at Swan Hunter's, Newcastle-upon-Tyne, on 1 July 1942, and one at John Brown's, Clydebank. They were to be as near as possible sister ships. The Admiralty sent the original plans to John Brown, who made copies and sent them to Swan Hunter and Harland. On 12 December 1942 Admiralty Job No 4698 at Swan's was allocated the name HMS *Vindex* after the early carrier of 1915, a converted merchantman. The John Brown ship, HMS *Nairana*, got her name from a similar packet boat conversion of 1917 and the third sister at Harland was named after HMS *Campania* of 1916, the conversion from

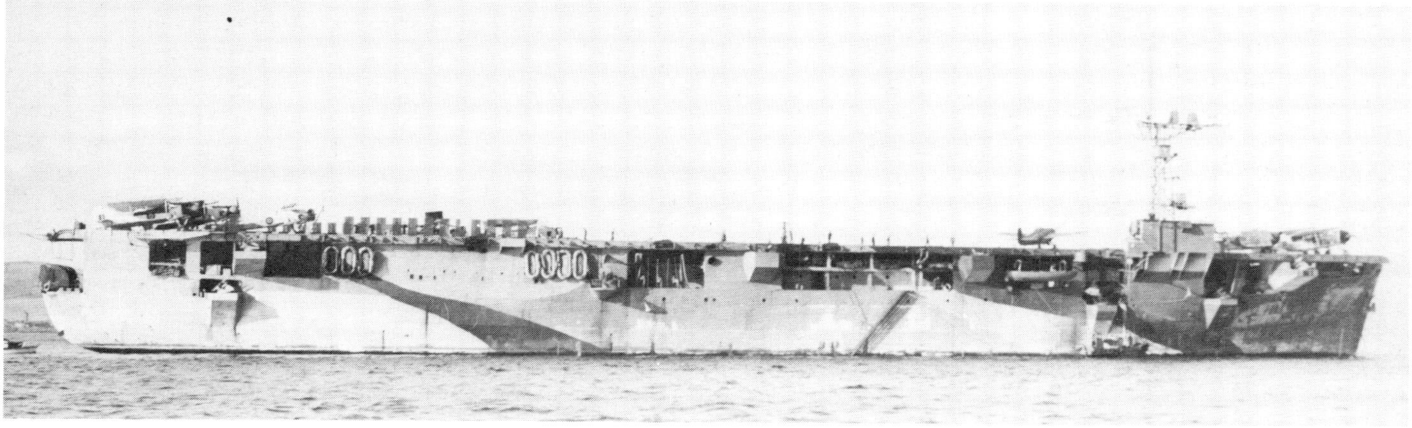

Below: HMS *Activity* was the second escort carrier to be designed and converted in a British yard since HMS *Audacity*, having been under construction as the 11,800-ton merchantman *Telemachus* at the Caledon Yard. (IWM)

Above: HMS *Nairana*

Below: HMS *Nairana*, converted by John Brown of Clydebank, builders of the Queen Mary. *Nairana* was the model ship for the three British sister escort carriers converted in the UK in 1942, the others being *Campania* (Harland & Woolff, Belfast), and *Vindex* (Swan, Hunter, Newcastle-on-Tyne). Compare her abbreviated bridge island structure with those of the USS *Bogue* and *Casablanca* classes. (National Maritime Museum)

the Cunard liner of the same name. The new *Vindex* was launched on 4 May 1943 and completed on 3 December; HMS *Nairana* was launched on 20 May and completed on 12 December, and HMS *Campania* was launched on 17 June 1943.

The three sisters were powered by diesels, Doxfords in *Vindex* and *Nairana*, Burmeister & Wain in *Campania*, driving twin screws, like the American Kaiser ships. But the British-built escorts were different from the American in many ways, cruder, if of sturdier construction, more resistant to the buffeting of the rude northern seas where they were to operate. Their hulls were riveted in the traditional way, considered by the Admiralty to be stronger than the new American all-welded construction.

The MAC-ships plodded on giving a feeling of safety to whatever convoys they sailed with, as U-boats seemed to avoid them. For their part most of the Royal Navy air parties in the MACs, after initial disappointment at their postings, began to feel a defiant pride in their role, and some crews painted out the letters 'RN' on their aircraft and substituted 'MN.' This glow of identification, however, began to die down as most of them made trip after barren trip without even sighting a U-boat, let alone sinking one.

The two Swordfish aircrews of the tanker MAC *Empire MacColl* sailed with grainer MAC *Empire MacCallum* and Convoy ONM243 for Canada on 4 July bearing a grudge. They had made four trips without a score and without leave, and one of the ship's three aircrews was removed just before weighing, suggesting to the other two that their job was not considered important, boosting a bitter frustration and an urge to take it out on somebody. At 11:25 on the 8th *MacCallum* flew off two of her Free Dutch crews on patrol, Swordfish 'T1' with RPs, 'T2' with DCs. At 12:52 T1's pilot, Lieutenant (A) Francoix Otterveanger, with a score yet to settle for the rape of his country by the Nazis, reported 'U-boat in sight'.

SOE Escort, Commander G. H. Stephen, DSC, OBE, RCNVR, had sent two signals to the convoy Commodore warning him of a Free French submarine in the area of their air patrols, with requests to pass it on to the carriers, but signal procedure was botched, and neither was received. Not until 13:58 did Stephen connect the Dutchmen's target with the French boat and repeat his signal with any urgency. This was received by the MACs, and *MacCallum*'s Air Staff Officer, with his aircraft about to attack, signalled them to look for friendly recognition signals from

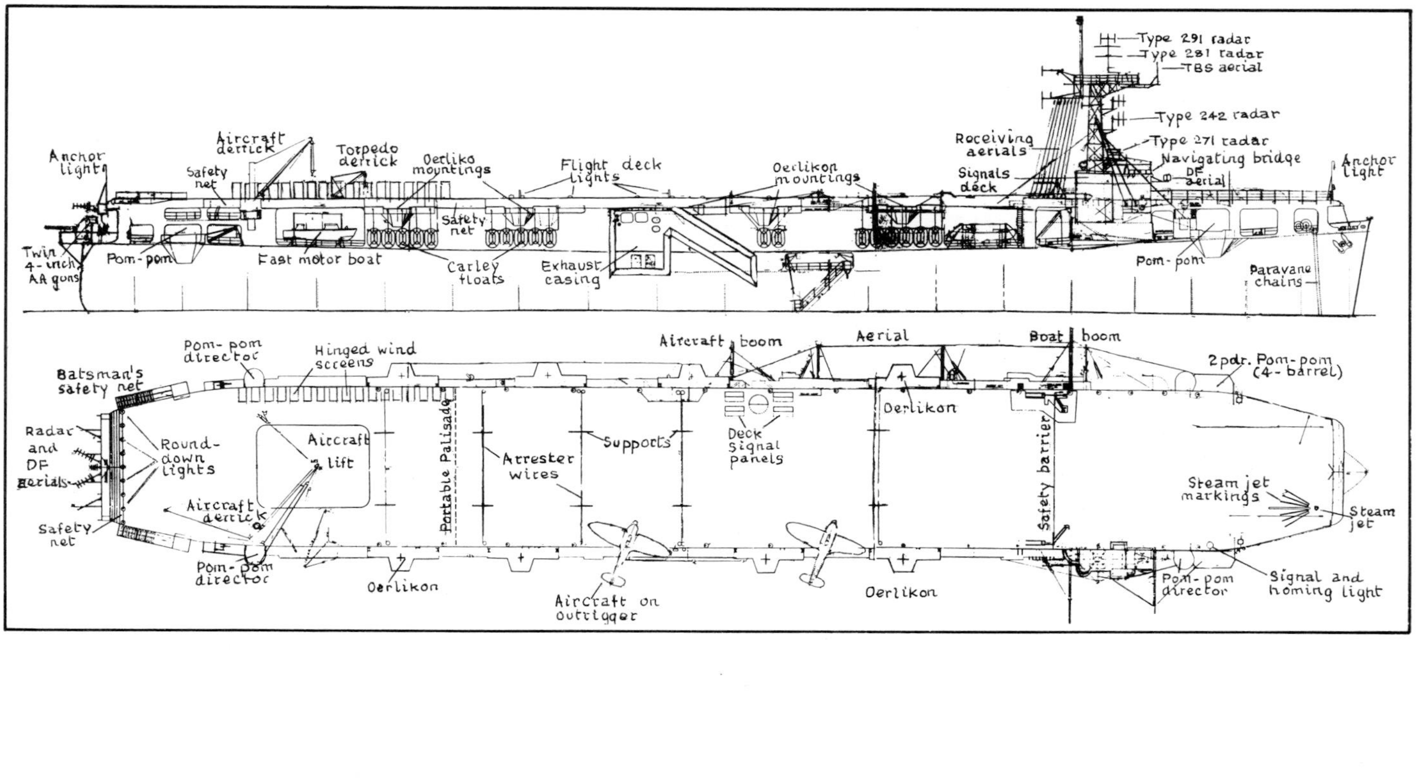

Above: HMS *Vindex* being fitted out at Swan, Hunter's yard. Her exhaust vents can be clearly seen in the projecting box structure amidships. (Crown)

Centre: It was often possible to include two MAC-ships in an Atlantic convoy. Here the duty MAC (astern) turns into wind to fly off a patrol. (C. W. Finch)

Bottom: Swordfish from the tanker MAC *Empire MacColl* were directly involved in the tragic error which caused the loss of the Free French submarine *La Perle*. Note the absence of a hangar, which could not be fitted in tanker MAC conversions, and the wind-breaker palisades raised aft on the flight deck to protect the aircraft, which has to remain in the open.

the submarine, but the signal was lost on the crowded channel.

When Otterveanger dived to attack he thought it slightly odd that the target was neither firing on him nor taking evasive action – nor diving – though that could be because of damage. Then the submarine started flashing, which Otterveanger apparently thought was gunfire, and even if the sub had been signalling, with the correct colour (red) and letter (L) of the day, it 'meant nothing' to him as this was 'one of the usual tricks of the Jerries'. In fact the submarine flashed 'L' repeatedly, and the pilot of Swordfish 'A2' from *MacColl* saw a 'reddish glare'. The two *MacColl* Swordfish and *MacCallum*'s four destroyed the submarine in about four minutes. Wreckage and personal belongings came to the surface. Floating shocked and stunned in the midst of it was Premier-Maitre (CPO) Mécanicien Cloarec Emile, the only survivor from FFS *La Perle*. Unknown to SOE, she had made a detour from her original course.

On the convoy's arrival at Halifax a naval intelligence officer boarded the MACs and threatened everyone with punishment under the War Emergency Powers if they revealed the truth of the sinking. To some it was the 'luck of the MACs', but in fact out of 217 convoys which included a MAC-ship only one was successfully attacked by U-boats. Later in the war some of them were also used to ferry aircraft.

Bogue had a 137m (450ft) flight deck, HMS *Activity*'s was 150m (492ft) in length, *Nairana*'s and *Vindex*'s 153m (503ft) long overall, with an effective length of 151m (495ft) between the tops of the round-downs forward and aft, but the width of *Bogue*'s flight deck was 31m (102ft) to *Activity*'s 20m (66ft) and *Vindex*'s 23.5m (77ft), giving the American CVEs a greater margin of pilot error. A Swordfish taking off from *Activity* seemed to fill the narrow deck. Another operational disadvantage of the British-built carriers was that they had only one lift, a massive 13.7 by 10.7m (45 by 35ft) steel slab aft. Any aircraft moved between hangar and flight deck had to go up or down through the one hole, which complicated operations, and there were other penalties, as *Vindex* was to find out. Overall, from stem to cruiser stern, *Vindex* and *Nairana* were 160m (524ft) long, 20.7m (68ft) in the beam at their widest point, underwater, with a draught of 7.5m (24ft 9in) for'ard, 7.8m (25ft 6in) aft, fully loaded. *Vindex* displaced 13,445 tons standard, 16,830 with full load, *Nairana* 13,825 tons standard, 17,210 deep load. *Vindex*'s hangar had a clear height of 5.3m (17ft 6in) and capacity for 18 aircraft. She was armed with one twin 4-in high angle quick-firing gun aft under the round-down, 16 2pdr pom-poms in four quadruple mountings, and eight twin 20mm Oerlikon quick-firing cannon in the catwalks round the flight deck.

Some time before completion key men appointed to the new ships began to arrive at the yards. HMS *Vindex*'s new Executive Officer, George McCombe, was one of those rarities, a Commander RNVR, and a world traveller and expert linguist with a loud voice which earned him the nickname of 'Boom'. 'Boom' McCombe was determined that *Vindex* should be the most efficient and best appointed ship of the three new British-built sister carriers. To accomplish this he had to circumvent the Admiralty Overseer and his rule book. With the connivance of the foreman carpenter he obtained many items not specified in the contract, such as notice boards, cupboards, shelves, and for the mail a replica of a British Post Office pillar box painted red, with a slot head, 'Mail Closes' and changeable ivorine tablets for every hour of the day. Captain E. W. Swann, OBE, RNVR, Chairman of Swann Hunter, presented *Vindex*'s wardroom with a grand piano.

Lieutenant-Commander 'Press On Percy' Gick, RN, *Vindex*'s Commander (Flying), a go-getter, a slasher of red tape and a technical innovator, was working in the Admiralty when he was appointed to *Vindex*, having served in *Ark Royal*, and flown with 815 Squadron when it had attacked and slowed down the mighty *Bismarck*. He was a passionate torch-bearer for the cause of night flying from carriers, having had great success in the Mediterranean in the use of flares from sea level to locate U-boats in the dark. He was quite determined – *Vindex* had to be a night-flying carrier. He roamed the Admiralty, lobbying. To Admiral Sir Dennis Boyd, former Captain of the *Illustrious*, and Chairman of the relevant committee, he said, 'Have you heard about my new job? Isn't it marvellous? *Vindex* – the first night flying anti-submarine carrier!' He checked the list of all those down to attend the next meeting, and made sure he met them, in their offices or clubs or in Admiralty corridors, and gave them the word. At the meeting the duties of all operational or near-operational carriers were reviewed. Up came the name *Vindex*. Dennis Boyd said, 'Oh yes, she's going to be the first night-flying carrier.' No-one said, 'No, ' and *Vindex*'s role was fixed.

Vindex's first commanding officer was Captain H. T. T. Bayliss, another rarity – an RN Captain with wings on his sleeve. He had followed a

Right: HMS *Vindex*. Two Swordfish and two Wildcats are ranged ready for take-off.

Right: Seafire Mk. III of 899 Squadron, HMS *Khedive*. (J. M. Goulding)

special RN-sponsored course at Cambridge after service in World War 1, reading English Literature and the Natural History of the Sea, and had later qualified as an observer in the Fleet Air Arm. As such he had served in the old seaplane carrier *Pegasus*, converted from a cross-Channel steamer, the pioneer carriers *Furious*, *Eagle* and *Argus*, had commanded the rogue escort carrier *Archer* on her day of glory when Harry Horrocks' Swordfish had become the first ship-borne aircraft to score with the new RPs, and later in her brief and abortive operations in the Bay of Biscay, where Bayliss had wished that his Swordfish had been equipped and trained to attack in the dark. Although only 43, he was heavy-set and solidly built, and looked older. He seemed at first rather grim and taciturn, but this was down to the problems of taking over a brand-new ship, and he was soon seen as a firm but fatherly figure, viewed with awe by all as the only man who could drink a pink gin and smoke a pipe at the same time.

Vindex was commissioned on 15 November 1943, and at 04:15 on the 23rd hoisted the White Ensign for the first time and put to sea, anchoring in the Clyde on 11 December. In the forenoon of 18 December, 13km (eight miles) off the Cumbrae Light, she landed on five Sea Hurricanes and 12 Swordfish of No 825 Composite Squadron, Percy Gick's old unit. Young Peter Cumberland, not long since a Merchant Taylors' schoolboy, slightly marred the event by making a heavy landing in his Swordfish and smashing its undercarriage.

To standardise operational methods and rationalise administration, in October 1943 Naval Fighter Wings were formed, each consisting of between two and four squadrons, operating from a single Fleet carrier or from up to four of those escort carriers which were to be used almost exclusively to support amphibious landings and would be re-designated Assault carriers. Assault carrier wings were given comprehensive training in strafing, fighter-bombing, air combat and tactical reconnaissance, based on the Seafire LRIIC, which would also be used for bombardment spotting for the Fleet when defence by modern fighters could be expected. By the end of 1943 every FAA Assault carrier squadron had eight pilots trained for bombardment spotting. The first Wings were Nos 3, 4 and 24. No 24 was a Fleet carrier wing, comprising 887 and 894 Squadrons, which received the first wing-folding FIII Seafires. Nos 3 and 4 were allocated to the *Bogue* Class CVEs *Attacker*, *Hunter* and *Stalker* and the new 'Ruler' Class *Khedive*. These four ships had originally been refitted as Fighter carriers, and retained their fighter direction facility, but briefing and operations room facilities were enlarged and more equipment for ship-to-shore and ship-to-ship communication added. Modification of the ships' magazines to carry mostly fighters' ammunition and gun spares meant that it would be difficult to switch to the operation of Tarpons (Avenger TBF/TBM) or Swordfish. Assault carriers were equipped with Seafires, Wildcats or the newer Grumman Hellcats, and the new cruiser HMS *Royalist* was modified as the Assault Squadron Command Ship. The two Assault Wings 3 and 4 embarked in HMS *Attacker*, *Hunter* and *Stalker* during December 1943 and January 1944 as the ships completed their refits, for training in the new organisation.

Of the Trade Protection escort carriers, British-built *Nairana* was commissioned on 12 December, and with *Vindex* went to Gourock for working-up. Six other Trade Protection ships were in dockyard hands, the veteran *Biter*, the CVEs *Fencer*, *Tracker*, *Striker* and *Pursuer*, and the British-built *Activity*. *Campania* was still fitting out in Belfast. This left the Trade Protection carrier *Striker* temporarily the only Royal Navy escort carrier operational in Western Approaches Command. She saw OS62/KMS36 safely on its way south, and carried on without a break. Five MACs went into service, however, the grain ships *Empire MacCallum*, converted by Lithgow, and *Empire MacKendrick*, a Burntisland conversion, the tankers *Empire MacMahon* (Swan Hunter), *Empire MacCabe* (Swan Hunter) and *Alexia* (Palmer's, Hebburn-on-Tyne, Northumberland). *Striker* escorted the next West Africa/Gibraltar-bound pair, OS63/KMS37, safely through the Azores danger zone, and returned with SLI44/MKS35. Reconnaissance Ju 290s spotted this convoy and guided the Azores U-boat group towards it. *Striker* scrambled her Sea Hurricanes, which drove the snoopers off, and the U-boats failed to make contact.

'CAN DO' IN THE ATLANTIC

On 5 January 1944 the US Navy put another new escort carrier into service in the Central Atlantic,

Above: 'Like a lean Bing Crosby with a strong dash of Bogart'. Captain Daniel V. Gallery of the USS *Guadalcanal.* (From Page 1 of 'The Story of The *U-505*') (Museum of Science And Technology, Chicago)

the USS *Guadalcanal*, CVE-60, the sixth of the Kaiser conversions to be completed. 'Hurry Up Henry' Kaiser had underestimated the time required in preparation before mass production of 50 complicated ships like carriers could begin, and it did not always help to have BuShips breathing down your neck all the time. With the first four 'assembly line' carriers due for delivery in February 1943, the first, USS *Casablanca*, CVE-55, was not actually handed over until 8 July. Production then began to pick up speed, and the whole contract was completed one year later.

Guadalcanal was launched on 5 June 1943, and soon afterwards her new captain-designate came to Vancouver on the Columbia river, Washington State, USA, to have a hand in her fitting out. Captain Daniel V. Gallery, USN, was a restless, clever, energetic sailorman, an Irish-American who looked like a lean Bing Crosby with a strong dash of Bogart. He had already read all the reports turned in by Atlantic carrier captains, and two years away from sea duty as commander of the US Fleet Air Base at Reykjavik, Iceland, made him that much keener to cast off. Dan Gallery was a deep water seaman, preferring the ocean wastes where all's blue to cabined, cribbed confinement ashore. Meanwhile he got on with the job in hand up under the midnight sun. The mission of his 12-plane squadron was to give cover to convoys up to a range of 800km (500 miles). To raise the sagging morale of men who had to fly long hours in fog, freezing cold, cloud and darkness, he built a new camp with proper streets hacked from the frozen ground, mock-ups of American fire hydrants made from practice bombs painted red and palm trees cut from metal pipes covered with burlap bearing painted softballs for coconuts. Kwitcherbelliakin, he called the place. He fretted as he listened to BBC accounts of the great battles of Coral Sea and Midway, in which carrier-borne air fleets fought each other for the first time. With 20 years as a professional sailor and naval aviator, 'I didn't want to sit out the greatest war in history on the beach. I wanted a ship.' In May 1943 he got his orders to report Stateside to take command of an escort carrier.

He was impressed with Kaiser's vast new yard hacked out of swamp land, and the way 'factories accustomed to building bridges, oil tanks and farm machinery built miscellaneous sections of ships', which 'poured into Vancouver, Washington, by rail, and were put on an assembly line as if they were car parts,' and how 'great chunks of ships were welded together in out-of-the-way parts of the yard . . . picked up by huge cranes, carted down to the building ways, and hoisted into place . . .'

Guadalcanal was commissioned at Astoria, Oregon, on 25 September 1943. Gallery got the men lined up on the flight deck in their best blues, read the orders, and had the commission pennant and colours hoisted. The ship's chaplain, Father Weldon, read a prayer, and the new Captain told his mostly raw crew that if the ship did not have the Presidential Citation flying from her foretruck within a year 'we will be unworthy custodians of the great name being entrusted to our care'. He also issued each man with a printed statement of his philosophy . . .' The motto of the *Guadalcanal* will be "Can Do", meaning that we will take any tough job that is handed to us and run away with it. The tougher the job the better we'll like it.' The ship departed on 15 November for the Panama Canal and Norfolk, Virginia, where she arrived on 3 December. One month later, 3 January 1944, *Core*'s old Composite Squadron (VC) 13, now commanded by Lieutenant-Commander Adrian H. Perry, USN, of Pasadena, California, embarked in the ship, with 30 officers, one civilian technician, 52 enlisted men, six Avenger TBF-1Cs, six TBM-1Cs and nine Wildcat FM-1s. Two days later, 5 January, *Guadalcanal* put to sea as flagship of Task Group 22.3, with four of the new 25-knot destroyer-escorts, built specifically for convoy escort, the USS *Chatelain, Pillsbury, Flaherty* and *Jenks,* forming her screen.

Guadalcanal was the first of 'Kaiser's coffins', which critics said were structurally shoddy and liable to break up in a seaway, to wet her stem in the steep Atlantic stream, and she was Gallery's first carrier command. Both were on trial. 'Operate against enemy submarines,' was Royal Ingersoll's simple directive. This gave Dan Gallery a roving commission, which suited his temperament. He knew that pickings would probably be lean, that the days of the big wolf-packs were gone, but he had one idea in mind, one score which no American skipper had yet made, which, if he pulled it off, would explain all that practise in towing their destroyer plane guard with the 38mm (1.5in) wire hawser.

Heading for Bermuda the group ran into very heavy weather. Two FM-1 fighters were so badly damaged that they had to be put ashore. *Guadalcanal* steered north-east for the U-boats' Central Atlantic refuelling area. On 10 January Lieutenant (jg) Jim Scoby's TBF crashed over the port side on attempting to land. His turret gunner was rescued but Scoby, who had won the Distinguished Flying Cross when with *Core* for his part in the sinking of the milch cow *U-487* on 13 July 1943, and his radioman Almon Martin were lost.

Just before sunset on 16 January a patrol of two TBFs, piloted by Ensigns B. J. Hudson of Coeur D'Alene, Florida, and W. M. McLane from Gainesville, Florida, flying about 480km (300 miles) west-by-north of Flores in the Azores and 64km (40 miles) from the ship, sighted the supply boat *U-544* refuelling a smaller U-boat. Hudson dived and made a run, firing rockets and dropping two DCs between the two boats. The smaller sank slowly by the stern, and some 40 men began to abandon

Above: At the end of January 1944 the new fighter escort carrier HMS *Searcher*, built by Western Pipe of San Francisco, was available to C-in-C, Western Approaches. Here she is with three of her Wildcats airborne. (G. Whyte)

the refueller. McLane then came in for a similar rocket and DC attack. The explosions blew men off the deck of the milch cow and she sank stern-first at a sharp angle. This sub was destroyed and the other badly damaged. The 'Can Do' carrier had scored, and on her first time out.

On 20 January the TBF piloted by Bert Beattie of Salmon Falls, Idaho, failed to return from patrol. Lost, with radio apparently out, the plane was last seen to go down off the north-west coast of Flores that evening, and three men were spotted struggling in the surf. An uninflated raft from Beattie's plane was picked up nearby and the body of his radioman Dale Wheaton was recovered. There was no trace of Beattie or his turret gunner Hugh Wilson.

When they returned to Norfolk on 16 February only three TBFs and three TBMs could be flown ashore to East Field, the remainder of VC 13's original 21 aircraft having been unloaded as unserviceable at Bermuda (two FMs), lost at sea (six TBFs), or out of commission on board ship (three TBFs and four FMs). With five aviators added to the list, it had been a costly maiden voyage, but Gallery expected to lose men and planes on a realistic shakedown, and 'Can Do' sailed proudly through Hampton Roads with one swastika painted on her bridge. Next time, he vowed, the 'Can Do's' aviators took off to hunt U-boats it would be as qualified night fliers.

THE NEED FOR NIGHT FLIERS

With few refuellers left to maintain U-boats on far-flung stations, Dönitz drew in his Atlantic boats round the British Isles, stationed singly, 48km (30 miles) apart, on a patrol line stretching from the Faroes round to Brest, about 400km (250 miles) west of Ireland, with a number within easy reach of the French coast in case of invasion. Whereas the Germans were using about the same number of submarines as at high tide in 1940, C-in-C Western Approaches now possessed a far larger number of escorts, organised in experienced groups.

At the end of January 1944 he also had nine escort carriers ready for action, veteran ex-BAVG HMSS *Biter* and *Tracker*, *Bogue* Class *Fencer*, *Striker*, *Searcher* and *Pursuer*, the latter two being Fighter carriers, and the British-built *Activity*, *Vindex* and *Nairana*. He had also been allocated the new 'Ruler' Class ships *Atheling* (Trade Protection) and Assault carriers *Ameer* and *Slinger*. *Tracker*'s Seafires had been replaced at the end of December by Martlets, now to be known by their original American name of Wildcats (with 'Avenger' replacing 'Tarpon' for the Grumman TBFs now in RN service). *Fencer* retained hers, the last Royal Navy Trade Protection escort carrier to do so, until 17 March, when she too made the switch. In January and February the addition of the tankers *Medula* and *Adula* to the MAC fleet brought its total to 16, which meant that at least one could normally be provided for each North Atlantic convoy, thus releasing escort carriers for work with the Escort Groups.

On 29 January *Activity* and *Nairana* left the Clyde in support of southbound OS66/KMS70 with Walker's veteran 2nd Escort Group to act as a separate 'hunter killer' group in the waters west of

Below: HMS *Searcher* with a convoy. (G. Whyte)

Ireland, where U-boats were now to be found once more.

Nairana had barely turned into wind to fly off her first-ever operational patrol when she received an urgent signal from Lieutenant-Commander Wemyss in the sloop *Wild Goose* warning Captain Taylor that his new ship was wide open to a torpedo attack by a U-boat which the sloop's Asdic had just picked up. *Nairana* at once took avoiding action, and *Wild Goose* and Walker's own *Starling* ran down the contact, destroying the U-boat, *U-592*, in a 'creeping attack'. Later the Group transferred its support to two Halifax-bound convoys, ON222 and ONS28. On the 4th and 5th *Activity* oiled *Kite, Starling, Woodpecker, Wren, Magpie* and *Wild Goose*. Both carriers took station inside the convoy for the night, Walker's sloops riding herd round the ships at distances of 9–16km (six to ten miles) from the convoy's centre, Asdics and radar combing the dark ocean. In the grey first watch, 434km (270 miles) west-sou'-west of Cape Clear, they got a ping and at the end of another creeping attack chalked up one more U-boat kill, their fourth in three days.

On the heels of these hunters came *Fencer* and *Striker* with the 16th Escort Group, supporting ON223. On 10 February a U-boat surfaced astern of *Fencer*. True to form this taut ship flew off a striking force of two Stringbags on the double. They were quickly over the U-boat, and Swordfish 'A', pilot Sub-Lieutenant (A) W. H. Thompson, observer Sub-Lieutenant (A) G. V. Pickard, TAG Leading Airman C. A. Bailey, sank it, *Fencer*'s first kill.

Two days after this, on 12 February, Captain H. R. Graham was taking the new Fighter carrier HMS *Pursuer* south with OS67/KMS41 for West Africa/Gibraltar. *Pursuer*, built by Ingall on the Gulf of Mexico, was carrying Canadian Lieutenant-Commander D. R. B. Cosh's 881 Squadron of ten Wildcats, and Australian Lieutenant-Commander L. A. Hordern's 896 Squadron. At 18:38, 560km (350 miles) west of Finisterre, the officer of the watch recorded sunset. At 18:44 the last patrol of the day was being struck below, when an Admiralty signal reached the bridge warning of an impending air attack. At 18:52 the carrier's radar screen was registering three-plus bandits. Five minutes later *Pursuer* scrambled the four Wildcats of Lieutenant-Commander Cosh, Lieutenant H. O. Wilson, RCNVR, Sub-Lieutenant (A) N. K. Turner and Sub-Lieutenant (A) T. L. M. Brander.

At 19:05 came the 'Tally-ho!' from two of the fighters as the Wildcats got amongst the attacking force of seven He 177s, carrying glider bombs, and Fw 200s. At 19:10 one enemy aircraft fell in flames five miles on the beam of the convoy, followed by a second on the port bow. *Pursuer*'s guns opened fire on the rest. At 19:30 the four Wildcats formed

Opposite page, top: A landing Seafire from HMS *Searcher* has missed all the arrester wires and hit a wire barrier forward.

Opposite page, centre: 'Flagship' Avenger 4A of Lieutenant-Commander(A) R. D. 'Bobby' Head, RN, CO of *Tracker*'s 846 Squadron, approaches Gibraltar on a convoy run.

Opposite page, bottom: Hunter-killer group. Lieutenant-Commander Wemyss' sloop *Wild Goose* of Captain Walker's crack anti-submarine 2nd Escort Group, photographed from *Nairana*, with one of the latter's Swordfish acting in support.

Top: A Heinkel He 177, failure as a long-range maritime bomber, was used as host to the Hs 293 radio-controlled 'glider' bomb, as seen in this picture from the camera of an attacking aircraft.

Above, left: The Henschel Hs 293 radio-controlled missile might have been hugely effective if it had gone into service earlier in the war, but it was only used sporadically from the summer of 1943, when Allied fighter cover was so strong that attacks could not be pressed home. (US Air Force)

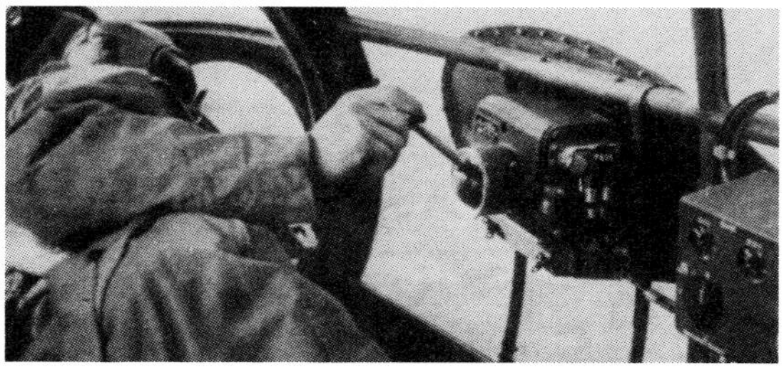

Above, right: The Hs 293 was guided to its target by a simple joystick control. (US Air Force)

up over the carrier in the dark to meet the next attack, but at 19:50 the enemy were seen to be retiring and Captain Graham guided the Wildcats down with his Aldis signalling lamps and 25cm (10in) searchlight. Turner and Brander both received the DSC for their hard night's work in destroying one He 177 and one Fw Condor. On 16 February, four days after the *Pursuer* quartet's evening battle, when *Biter* and *Tracker* and the 7th and 9th Escort Groups were supporting OS68/KMS42 and also keeping a watch on nearby ONS29, two of *Biter*'s New Zealanders, Lieutenants E. S. Erikson and W. C. Dimes, shot down a Ju 290 which had tried to hit one of the ships with a glider bomb.

In the Central Atlantic USS *Block Island* was on the loose again, with Lieutenant-Commander R. M. Payne's Composite (VC) 6 and its 12 TBFs and nine FM-2s. The latter was a version of the General Motors' disappointing FM-1, also with two guns eliminated, specially designed for the short decks of escort carriers. In the FM-2 (the RN's Wildcat Mk VI) the Wright Cyclone of the Martlets I and IV was adapted for US Navy use, replacing the Pratt & Whitney Twin Wasp of the Martlet II, F4F-3 and -4 and FM-1, thereby increasing take-off rating by 100hp and full throttle rating at 3,350m (11,000ft) by 190hp. The height of fin and rudder was increased to improve low speed directional control, and the result was a great improvement on the FM-1. Speed was still modest – 480hm/h (300mph) at low level, over 515km/h (320mph) at 3,960m (13,000ft), initial rate of climb slightly more than 914m (3,000ft) per minute, climb to 4,570m (15,000ft) recorded as one minute less than the FM-1, and a reduction in weight of some 227kg (500lb) improved handling and manoeuvrability, so that an FM-2, most numerous of all Wildcat marks, could be confidently flown against the A6M-3 Zero or the A6M-5 Zeke Japanese fighters. The group was supported by the destroyer *Corry* and the new destroyer-escorts *Thomas, Breeman, Bronstein* and *Bostwick*. On 26 February the carrier refuelled them off Fayal in the Azores, then headed north to support convoys under threat from submarines lurking north of the U-boat refuelling zone midway between Newfoundland and Ireland. Sheldon Kinney's *Bronstein* sank *U-603* as it was about to fire Gnats at *Block Island*.

The MAC-ships took over responsibility for the continuous air coverage of all North American ON and HX convoys, leaving the Western Approaches escort carriers to cover the Gibraltar/West Africa routes. In February 18 U-boats were destroyed, over half of them in the North Atlantic, for the loss of 18 Allied merchantmen, only eight of which were sunk outside the Indian Ocean.

As the surviving U-boats finished their patrols they were fitted with the new *Schnorkel* breathing tubes, which enabled a submarine to recharge its batteries and vent the boat from below the surface. Thus a U-boat could remain submerged in dangerous periods, provided the waves above were not too high for the breathing snout, though a U-boat's underwater speed would still handicap it greatly. The answer to this was the new Type 21 boat with a submerged speed of 17 knots, and better still the really revolutionary Walter boats, which would use hydrogen peroxide fuel to maintain a speed of 25 knots underwater for 12 hours. There was the Balkon hydrophone, which could detect an enemy at 80km (50 miles), and the S-gear, a supersonic underwater detector which could do this even better. How many of these could be produced, with Allied raids pounding German factories and shipyards, in time to have any decisive effect on the war was problematical.

Right: Lieutenant(A) E. S. Erikson, RNZNVR's Wildcat returns to HMS *Biter* after shooting down a Junkers Ju 290 glider bomb carrier, in co-operation with Lieutenant(A) W. C. Dimes, another New Zealander in the FAA. (Peter B. Buckley)

Patrols of necessity extended through dusk into darkness had made clear the need for night flying squadrons in escort carriers, as championed by *Vindex*'s Percy Gick and *Guadalcanal*'s Dan Gallery. Experience such as the pairing of *Activity* with *Nairana* in defence on Convoy OS69/KMS43 in February, and the combination of *Fencer* with *Pursuer* to support SL149 proved the feasibility of operating escort carriers in pairs, sharing an all-weather, round the clock facility on a rota system with, say, one carrier mainly responsible for daylight patrols, one for night operations. This could be especially valuable in the Russian convoy programme now being resumed on a large scale. It would have been preferable to standardise on the Wildcat, or its younger, more powerful brother the Hellcat, and the Avenger, all from the same firm, all able to use the American accelerators fitted in the Lease-Lend carriers, all superior to current British machines as carrier-borne aircraft.

The obsolete Swordfish often found difficulty in taking off with a full war load. In windless conditions and light airs, *something*, fuel and/or armaments, or the TAG, had to be left behind to enable a Swordfish Mark II to get off the deck, even with the advantage of the extra 12m (40ft) or so of flight deck which the British-built carriers had over the American. The weight of the ASV radar, essential for night operations, did not help the problem, and the new ASV Mk XI was even heavier. It was quite usual to have to de-fuel a Swordfish to carry two depth-charges and a full crew, though too drastic to dispense with the TAG in a Swordfish II, as the observer (who already had more than enough to do to operate the radar and navigate the aircraft), would have difficulty coping with the radio and, in rare circumstances the Lewis gun as well, and in any case a modification to cockpit fittings would then be necessary. There were delays in the fitting of RATOG (Rocket-Assisted Take-Off Gear) to Mk IIIs, in which the rear cockpit was redesigned to dispense with the TAG.

BLOCK ISLAND'S 'NIGHT OWLS'

The central Atlantic was fairly quiet when the 'Can Do' carrier put out from Norfolk again on 7 March, though there were U-boats bound for the Caribbean, South Atlantic and Indian Oceans passing through the Central and Cape Verde submarine refuelling areas. Night flying with *Guadalcanal*'s new squadron, Composite (VC) 58, started in full moonlight, and by the time the

Below: The Fairey Swordfish Mk. III dispensed with the telegraphist/air-gunner in order to be able to carry a full weapon load, new ASV Mk. XI radar, and RATOG (Rocket-assisted take-off Gear). (J. M. Goulding)

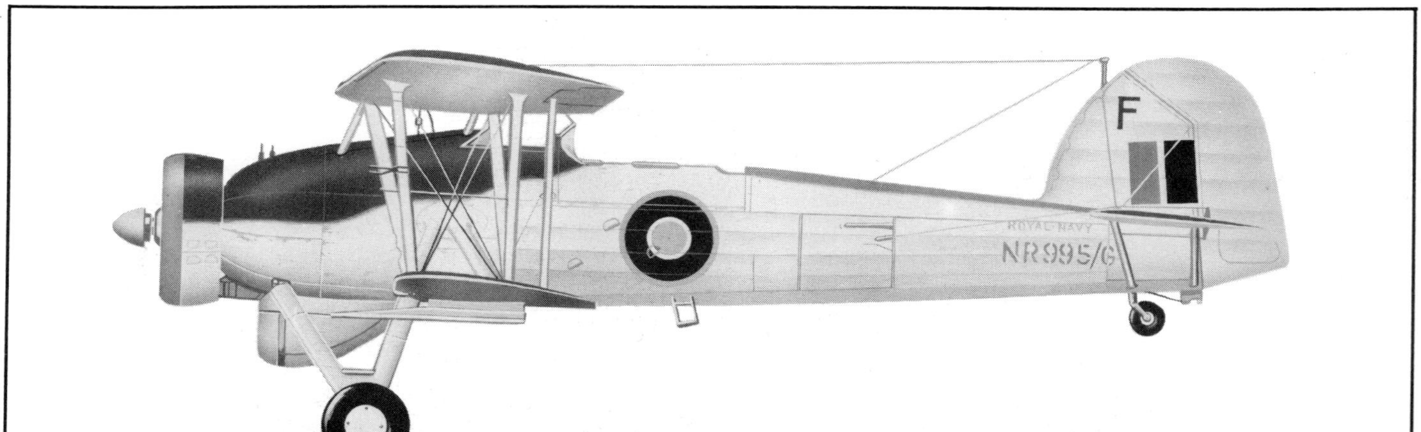

Right: Fighter pilot. Lieutenant(jg) Bill 'Tex' Cole of Composite Squadron (VC) 6 aboard USS *Block Island.*

moon had waned and the nights were black they knew their way down to the deck in the dark and were getting acquainted with the stars.

Block Island, with her 'Night Owl' Avengers and new CO Captain Francis M. Hughes, USN, left Casablanca on 11 March and headed south-west for the area off the Cape Verdes where U-boats for Brazilian waters and the Indian Ocean refuelled. Four days later and 480km (300 miles) west of San Antao, 'Can Do' got a blip on her radar. The group headed down the bearing but a thick haze of dust, like a sandstorm on the sea, blown from the Sahara, lay between them and the target, blanketing radar and clogging aircraft filters. Then, in the early evening of 16 March the U-boat surfaced and radioed U-boat HQ asking for a course to the nearest milch cow. *Block Island*'s Huff-Duff was listening, and Hughes sent *Corry* off down the bearing. The destroyer got a radar echo and tracked it down. As the sun began to shine through the gold dust on the sea the trackers came to the end of the trail, and found a balloon tied to a float bobbing in the water, with strips of tinfoil tossing their radar beam back at them. Aphrodite, as submariners called this device, had beguiled another sea hunter. Other underhand tricks which German scientists had invented for a U-boat in a tight corner were the *Alberich,* a rubber coating over the submarine's hull to prevent sonar detection, and the *Pillenwerfer,* which emitted *Bold,* a chemical cartridge producing bubbles reflecting the sonar wave like the hull of a U-boat.

For all her captain's cunning, *U-801* was not going to get away, though. *Block Island*'s dawn patrol found her in another part of the ocean, a TBF's 227kg (500lb) bomb started leaks in her engine room, and *Corry* and *Bronstein* finished her off with DCs.

When the sun rose on 19 March *U-1059* was taking it easy on the surface. Keep-fit fanatics were even enjoying a morning dip in the ocean, and the whole boat was refreshing itself with air and light, when Compo 6's dawn patrol sighted

Right: TBF crash in USS *Block Island* (I) by Lieutenant(jg) 'Curly' Cowles of VC-6 on top of an Oerlikon cannon position. Crashes like this one into the catwalk were the most difficult to clear away. (US Navy)

Above: Even COs can have an off-day. Lieutenant-Commander 'Rapid Robert' Payne, USN tangles with the barrier. (US Navy)

Right: Ensign 'Fitz' Fitzerald, USNR who escaped from the turret in Norman Dowty's TBF when it was shot down. Dowty's radioman, Edgar Burton, was also lost. Note the hunting knife and sidearm, carried by all USN aviators in the Pacific. (US Navy)

them and sent Bill Cole ahead in his FM-2. The swimmers raced back to the boat to man their cannon as the Wildcat bored in. Norman Dowty's TBF, diving on Cole's tail, caught the full broadside. He got his DCs away, two of which blew the sub's stern high in the air and sank her, then suddenly fell away into a sliding descent and crashed into the sea. Ensign Fitzgerald in Dowty's turret, climbed out. The front cockpit was empty and there was no trace of radioman Edgar Burton either. As the TBF sank Fitzgerald inflated the life raft, and found himself among the survivors from the U-boat. A badly bleeding man approached the raft. Fitzgerald pulled him aboard, applied a rough tourniquet to his wound, and pushed him back into the sea. Other Germans tried to get aboard, but Fitzgerald warned them off with his knife and 0.38 sidearm. The rescue boat picked him and seven Germans up, including the U-boat captain, but Dowty and Burton were lost. VC 6's flight surgeon, Lieutenant Simpson, removed a 0.50-calibre slug from the German captain's buttocks.

Guadalcanal reached Casablanca from the USA without making any contacts, but with the 'Can Do' night fliers getting in plenty of practise. There had been accidents. One TBF, approaching in the dark of a moonless night, came in too high, and the pilot opened the throttle to go round again. But he was further over to starboard than he thought. His wing hit the bridge, and the plane crashed in flames against the island, blocking the only exit door. The crew got clear of the burning wreck, miraculously unhurt, but smoke and flames enveloped the island, where seven men, including Captain Gallery, were trapped. In the plane's bomb bay were four live DCs which, according to the manual, had a life of three minutes in a petrol fire. The deck crew, led by asbestos-clad 'hot papas', got the fire out in two and a half minutes.

Gallery accepted the risks of night flying from carriers. The ship was in danger every time a night recovery was made, as planes could not land without some illumination. He figured that to show hooded lights in order to have planes in the air at night was a worthwhile trade-off.

THE ORDEAL OF *VINDEX*

Striker was to pair with *Vindex* to cover the 24-hour capability, but was shanghaied to escort the combined OS70/KMS44. *Vindex* left Lough Larne, Northern Ireland, at 06:15 on 9 March, with the Royal Canadian Navy's 6th Escort Group, destroyer *Qu'Appelle*, frigates *Waskesieu* and *Outremont*, corvettes *Prescott* and *Edmunston*.

They weaved across the angry ocean all day, breaking off zigzag only for the carrier to fly off Sea Hurricane patrols. A young Ordinary Seaman was washed overboard, an air mechanic was blown into the sea in a snowstorm by an aircraft's propwash and lost. The first of the nocturnal Swordfish took off into the surrounding gloom at 20:25. Two days later *Vindex* was topping up *Qu'Appelle* when Asdic got a bite off the port bow. The carrier cast off the hose to launch Peter Cumberland, observer Frank Jackson and young TAG John Stone in Swordfish *LS428*. Just north of Valentia Island Jackson got a U-boat echo on his ASV. They saw her, fully surfaced, and attacked. Up came the cannon shells. Cumberland dropped his DCs. There was a loud BANG, and a thump on the fuselage. Stone called out 'I think I've been hit, sir!' Cumberland dropped a marker flare and returned to *Vindex*. With difficulty Stone was lifted out of the blood-soaked cockpit. He was dead.

Homing on Cumberland's flare, Swordfish *LS430* attacked with two RDX-filled DCs. As they passed over the U-boat the observer saw sparks fly up but no explosion. Swordfish and Sea Hurricanes chased contacts next day. One tired pilot fired an RP along the flight deck. Stone's body was committed to the sea, and the patrols went on, round the clock, with one night blurring into the next. Sub-Lieutenant Webb slammed his Swordfish into the barrier. *Vindex*, refuelling *Qu'Appelle*, was near-missed by a torpedo. Watered petrol brought down Sub-Lieutenant Norman Sharrock's Swordfish in the sea, and *Outremont* rescued the crew. Then Sub-Lieutenant Couch got a U-boat echo on his ASV, fixed the spot with flares and sea markers, and the sloop *Starling* destroyed the U-boat with DCs. *Vindex* was credited with half a kill.

By now there was strong discontent and frustration amongst the aircrews. Keenness had been blunted by the continuing malfunction of depth-charges and the likelihood of ditching with water in the fuel. There were only eight crews for 12 Swordfish, and the strain of round-the-clock operations was beginning to tell. A special grudge was the lack of a good meal before they took off to face the bitter cold and darkness, the stresses of anti-submarine searches and the anxiety of navigation over the trackless ocean, and spokesman Paul House, Senior Observer, informed Commander (F) that if they were not properly fed they would not fly. Captain Bayliss saw to it that their victualling improved.

Right: In early March 1944 HMS *Striker* escorted combined convoys OS70/KMS44 to Gibraltar and West Africa. On the 13th, Sub-Lieutenant(A) Allen's Sea Hurricane JS282 bounced too hard on touch-down, floated into the barrier and smashed its nose. (Cdr Stenning)

Right: HMCS destroyer *Qu'Appelle*, a member of HMS *Vindex*'s hunter-killer group in a gruelling fortnight of round-the-clock U-boat hunting, comes alongside the carrier to refuel. She has exchanged her 4.7in 'B' gun for a forward-firing mortar.

Tests were made to find the fault in the new RDX-filled DCs. The buzz was that saboteurs had filled them with sawdust, but the fault was traced to the safety mechanism, one washer having been inserted at the factory in the wrong place. On several nights their radio frequency of 4,340 kilocycles was completely swamped by stock prices delivered in a fast, butch-female American voice from Miami, 4,800km (3,000 miles) away, and had to be changed.

Still the cause of water in the avgas had not been found. At 22:50 on Sunday the 19th the Swordfish of Mike Varley, Harry Burns and Basil Hall-Law crashed into the sea with fuel failure four cables off *Vindex*'s starboard beam. A Swordfish immediately flew off to find them, but turned back on hitting thick fog. *Waskesieu* and *Outremont* went looking for the Stringbag's dinghy in the wild black waste of sea. The fog cleared and Bennett's Swordfish 'K' and two others took off to search for Varley's crew. They found nothing. Burns had been a close friend of Peter Couch's. 'It was', he said, 'the most miserable flight of my life.' At 09:20 *Waskesieu* found the empty dinghy and a piece of wreckage from the crashed aircraft, but no crew.

Flying continued, with heavy rain squalls. An outbreak of radio and compass failures was aborting Sea Hurricane sorties. Moving these fixed-wing machines round the small hangar and getting them up on deck with only one lift was often a nightmare. Sometimes six or seven machines had to be extracted from the hangar and parked on deck to get at the aircraft needed for operation.

The weather had begun to reach gale strength and on the following afternoon all *Vindex*'s aircraft were struck down into the hangar, and the ship battened down. Just before midnight the port and starboard gyros and the steering gear failed, and *Vindex* began steering by main engines. The Lower Power Room and the after switchboard were flooded, and the sea was washing through messdecks and flats. Conditions had improved marginally by 09:00 next morning, and Sharrock's crew manned a Swordfish. They were given the green light when *Vindex* was at the top of a crest. By the time the Stringbag reached the end of the flight deck the ship was pointing down into the next trough, and Sharrock flew straight into a wall of water.

Bayliss' swift 'Stop starboard! Hard-a-starboard!' saved them from being run down by the ship, which answered her helm so quickly she seemed about to roll over. Nevertheless, when Sharrock and Observer Basil Jones came up they were both caught by the bow wave. TAG Chris Williams found himself against the side of the ship, with the sea booming against her plates. He struck out and away from the suction, looked back and found himself alone in the ocean, with the carrier's stern disappearing. Then a wave lifted him high and he spotted their M-type dinghy about 45m (50yd) away. He swam over to it and found that it was holed and only half inflated. He sighted Jones struggling to stay afloat, and towed him to the dinghy, then Sharrock appeared in his one-man dinghy. Eventually *Waskesieu* picked them up.

At 01:25 in the darkness of the middle watch next day, 24 March, New Zealander Doug Webb returned with *Vindex* pitching badly, cut his engine, missed all the wires and sailed on. The top wire of the barrier sliced off his undercarriage, the Swordfish pancaked heavily on the mercifully empty fore end of the flight deck and graunched to a stop 2.5m (8ft) from the round-down with two unused depth charges still on the racks. Avgas leaking from the carburetter was ignited and the aircraft started to burn. Webb and Observer McIlwraith tore off their harness, leaped out and ran aft. TAG Mears jumped out and was brought up sharply by his 'anti-cavorting' chain, which he unhooked frantically and tried again. One DC was visible, and the flight deck party played a hose on that. At 01:45 the darkness was lit up by an explosion from the burning wreck. Sharrock saw it from *Waskesieu* and thought *Vindex* had blown up or been torpedoed. A hole 2.5 by 1.2m (8 by 4ft) was blown in the flight deck and a smaller hole in the deck below that. On the next deck down Ordinary Seaman Hampton was killed by a sliver of metal from the DC.

Vindex was scheduled to keep the seas among the U-boats for three weeks, but after these pioneer 14 days and nights of round-the-clock operations under the strains of insufficient food and sleep, equipment failure and foul weather the squadron had had enough. They had lost three old friends, four Swordfish had gone to the bottom and there were several near write-offs in the hangar. Eddie Ward, one of the best pilots in the squadron, taking off in the dark in bad weather, had hit the bridge island and torn off 1.2m (4ft) from both his starboard wing tips. Only his flying skill got him back on the deck again.

The return for this attrition and effort was half a U-boat kill. In their round-the-clock fortnight the Swordfish of 825 had notched up 235 hours and 100 deck landings by night with 40 hours and 22 deck landings by day.

With aircrews sometimes flying three times a night, fatigue was a great problem. Gick and the doctors would look for those who were cracking up under the strain. If a pilot on landing did something a bit more eccentric than his normal personal style and repeated it two or three times, 'Wings' got worried. One of the MOs would always sit in the Ops Room when a crew returned, chatting and listening for signs of strain. A round-the-clock capability was simply too much to ask of one lone escort carrier and one composite

Above: Doug Webb's Swordfish after his crash of 24 March 1944 aboard *Vindex* and the explosion of one of his depth-charges, which blew a hole in the flight deck (left).

squadron, even if up to full strength, as 825 was not.

'THAR SHE BLOWS!'

Further south, *Guadalcanal* had reached Casablanca from the USA without action, but her night fliers had got in plenty of practise, unhampered by bad weather. On 30 March she and her group left in support of westbound GUS37. On 8 April, Gallery broke away to track down an HF/DF bearing.

Lieutenant-Commander Dick Gould, CO of Compo 58, caught *U-515* creaming along in the moonlight 96km (60 miles) from the carrier, the German lookouts relaxed after safely negotiating the dangerous waters of Biscay. Gould dived as low as he dared in the darkness and dropped DCs. They shattered a gauge or two and started a small leak, but were not close enough to cause any serious damage. Gallery put all available planes in the air and despatched DEs *Pope* and *Flaherty* on a hunt. Several times during the night the U-boat came up to breathe and re-charge. Each time she was depth-charged. The charge in her batteries got lower, the air in the boat grew fouler.

First light revealed an oil slick, and sonobuoys dropped by the dawn patrol also gave her away. At 06:45 a TBF straddled her with two DCs. Some of *U-515*'s men began to curse their ambitious commander. Kapitänleutnant Werner Henke was almost a carticature of the clean-cut, arrogant, ruthless Junker, who gloried in war. He had sunk some 150,000 tons of Allied shipping. When without warning he had sunk the liner *Ceramic*, steaming alone with women and children for Australia, 640km (400 miles) west of the Azores on 7 December 1942, he surfaced, picked up one survivor for information and propaganda purposes, and left the rest to drown. 700 lives were lost. When things went well his crew forgave, even boasted about the unnecessary risks he ran, the promotions he froze to keep a veteran crew together. But it was well known that, although eligible for shore duty, he had volunteered for this extra cruise. Some said that he was in love with war, others that he wanted to add Diamonds to the Oak Leaves with his Knight's Cross of the Iron Cross. Anyway, it began to look now as if this was one cruise too many.

At 10:30 *Pope*'s sonar registered contact 3km (two miles) from *Guadalcanal*. Hedgehogs and DCs damaged *U-515*'s pressure hull, but Henke took the boat down, trying to get below sonar's probing finger, but a close pattern shook the whole boat and started bad leaks. Henke ordered all tanks blown, hoping that the pumps could work faster than the cracks in the hull would open.

Commander Fred Hall in *Pope* said tersely into the TBS mike to all the DE captains, 'We want to get this baby before dark. *Don't miss any bets*!' At 02:14 Commander Jesse Johnson, 'Can Do's' Exec, shouted 'Thar she blows!' as *U-515*'s bow emerged from the sea between *Pope* and *Flaherty* just as two depth-charges from *Chatelain* exploded near her. Every gun in the group immediately opened fire, a TBF and two Wildcats strafed with RPs and machine-guns, as the submarine surfaced, streaming white water. Hatches were slammed open and the German seamen came jumping out into the barrage of shells and bullets of all calibres. Some fell, others leapt overboard, as the water poured in through cracks in the pressure hull, and she sank, stern-first 280km (175 miles) north-west of Funchal, Madeira.

Gallery rescued 44 of *U-515*'s men, including Henke, who angrily accused him of killing six of his men 'as they came up to surrender'. The Irish-American was not the man to listen to arrogant Prussians, and put him below in the brig, but the German's words made him think again about that scheme in the back of his mind . . . Henke, the fanatic, the U-boat ace, had come up to surrender, not to fight, although he had had three enemy destroyers within point-blank torpedo-range. For all they knew the U-boat might have been recoverable when she surfaced, and was destroyed unnecessarily by the barrage. Perhaps next time, if there *was* a next time . . .

Ingersoll signalled 'Well done!' The ships and planes of the group searched in a slowly expanding circle round the point where *U-515* had gone down, though the weather was bad for flying. Shortly after midnight another U-boat surfaced. TBFs attacked and forced her down.

She came up again at dawn, 480km (300 miles) from Horta and 80km (50 miles) from *Guadalcanal*. Three TBMs attacked her from the still dark western sector of the sky with RPs and depth-charges, and *U-68* sank, leaving just three survivors and oily debris scattered on the sea. The planes dropped life jackets, and when a destroyer arrived she found only one man left alive, a seaman named Kastrup, who, though badly wounded himself, was clinging on to a life jacket and supporting a dead shipmate.

With tongue in cheek, Gallery claimed 'probably damaged' for the second victim. '*Exceptionally* well done!' radioed Ingersoll.

10

ARCTIC ESCORT

NO aircraft carrier had accompanied a convoy to Russia since *Avenger* had sailed with PQ18 in September 1942. At the end of March 1943, with the Arctic day drawing out, with the new battleship *Tirpitz*, the battlecruiser *Scharnhorst* and the pocket battleship *Lützow* lurking in the creeks off Altenfjord, northern Norway, with no carrier available to fight a convoy through against air attack, and with the Atlantic battle claiming so many of the escorts, the risks were considered unjustifiable, and the convoys to Murmansk were temporarily suspended.

NEUTRALISING *TIRPITZ*

It was intended to re-start them in the autumn, provided something could be done to draw the enemy's fangs. The biggest threat was from the heavy warships, but they were outside the range of bombers from Britain, and there were no carriers available to bring a striking force within range. Conventional submarines could not hope to penetrate the anti-submarine defences protecting the ships, but on 11 and 12 September six submarines left Loch Cairbawm in northern Scotland, each towing one of the new X-craft or 'midget' submarines, which were to attempt to penetrate the mines and nets of Kaafjord, where *Tirpitz* and *Scharnhorst* lay, and Langefjord, which hid *Lützow*. On the 22nd two of the midgets got through to *Tirpitz* and planted their explosives beneath her. The explosion lifted the huge 50,000-ton battleship several feet out of the water and badly damaged her main turbines. The German Naval Staff estimated that she would be out of action until at least April 1944. On the following day *Lützow* left for the Baltic and a scheduled refit. Attempts to locate her by Avenger torpedo-bombers failed, but at least she would be immobilised for several months.

This left the *Scharnhorst*, which C-in-C Home Fleet, Admiral Fraser, felt was not sufficient of a menace to rule out the running of convoys, as long as strong escort and covering forces were provided. The Admiralty considered that the 40 ships a month which they were committed to send to Russia were too large and unwieldy a number to send all in one convoy, especially with the risk of winter gales scattering them and handing U-boats and bombers another PQ17. Each monthly quota was to be sent through in two parts, each with strong close escort, cruisers covering them south of Bear Island, and heavy units of the Home Fleet standing by further to the south-west.

Thirteen ships trapped in Archangel since March reached Britain safely, the two halves of JW54, followed by JW55A, reached Russia unmolested, then the enemy woke up. JW55A had been shadowed, and on 19 December Dönitz promised Hitler that *Scharnhorst* would attack the next convoy. On 20 December JW55B, with 19 merchantmen, left Loch Ewe, western Scotland, and on the 23rd the 22 ships of RA55A left Kola Inlet, each with a close escort of ten destroyers and three or four corvettes, both groups covered by Admiral Burnett's cruisers *Belfast, Sheffield* and *Norfolk*, with Fraser's battleship *Duke of York*, cruiser *Jamaica* and four destroyers in the outfield. JW55B was shadowed constantly from the 22nd and diverted further north. At 03:39 on Boxing Day the Admiralty signalled Fraser that *Scharnhorst* was probably at sea. At 08:15 she appeared on *Belfast*'s radar, only 48km (30 miles) from the convoy, and at 12:21 Burnett's cruisers engaged her. At 16:17 in the darkness of the Arctic afternoon she swam into *Duke of York*'s radar net and after taking heavy punishment sank at 19:45.

The threat of the German battle fleet was now temporarily removed, and the Admiralty planned to keep it that way by sending a carrier striking force against the temporarily immobilised *Tirpitz* as soon as the ships and aircraft could be mustered. Heavy covering forces for the convoys were no longer needed, and the Arctic weather would inhibit flying. A ferocious gale turned back JW56A in early January 1944, delaying it for ten days. U-boats sank three ships, then waited for JW56B, which was attacked by 15 U-boats under orders to make the escorts, particularly any escort carriers which might be with them, prime targets for their acoustic torpedoes. The destroyer *Hardy* was lost, *U-314* destroyed, the destroyer *Obdurate* damaged, and the merchantmen got through. The weather got worse, with snow and ice, heavy seas and biting cold. The combined escorts of the two JW56 half-convoys sailed on 3 February with RA56's 37 ships. Helped by a shadowing aircraft's mistaken report , which threw the U-boats out of position, the convoy reached Scotland safely.

CHASER WITH JW/RA57

After this, Admiral Fraser returned to the formula of the large convoy with a very strong escort. To protect the 43 ships of JW57 he borrowed escorts from C-in-C Western Approaches, and was able to muster a powerful close escort which included 17 destroyers and the Trade Protection escort carrier HMS *Chaser* (Captain H. V. P. McClintock), which had been 'arcticized' with steam heating at all gun mountings, flying stations and catapult machinery, and was now carrying the 11 Swordfish and 11 Wildcats of No 816 Composite Squadron, commanded by Lieutenant-Commander F. C. Nottingham, RNVR. The escort was commanded by Vice-Admiral (Destroyers) Vice-Admiral I. G. Glennie, in the light cruiser *Black Prince*, and deeper cover was provided by the cruisers *Berwick*, *Jamaica* and *Dragon*. It was an arrangement which recalled PQ18, 18 months earlier, with its escort carrier and 'fighting destroyer escort', though weapons on both sides had improved since then. *Chaser* carried more anti-submarine aircraft than had *Avenger*, and her rugged Wildcats with 0.50in machine-guns were better than Avenger's 0.303-armed Sea Hurricanes for engaging the heavily armed and armoured German shadowers.

The Germans stationed 14 U-boats in two patrol lines across the path of JW57. They relied heavily on radar-equipped shadowers, like the Condor which appeared on 24 February. *Chaser* scrambled a section of Wildcats. They engaged the Fw but had more of the trouble with gun stoppages which afflicted Brownings in the Arctic, and one of the Wildcats was badly damaged by return fire. Next day the first U-boat appeared, with the rough Arctic weather preventing patrols from *Chaser*. Only one Swordfish struggled off her heaving, spray-lashed deck that day, though the faithful Coastal Command Catalina, bucking through the gale towards her terminal point, sighted and sank *U-601*, and the destroyer *Keppel*, a veteran of PQ17, sank another U-boat. That night the destroyer *Mahratta* was torpedoed and sunk, and morning brought snow storms and severe icing. But U-boat contacts were increasing, and McClintock kept his Swordfish hunting all day. Frozen, fatigued crews returned to a dangerously rolling, pitching carrier, and the flight deck became strewn with disabled Stringbags. The Wildcats damaged a Jabo on the 27th but by noon there were only eight of them serviceable and the Swordfish were down to six, two of them with dangerously high oil temperature. *Chaser*'s arcticization broke down. Barrier machinery, arrestor wire sheaves and guns seized up, and a bursting steampipe put the main R/T set out of action. On the 28th the wind dropped, and was now too low for Swordfish to lift a full war load, but the convoy was within range of Russian fighters, which escorted it to Kola.

On 2 March *Chaser* joined the 31 ships of homeward-bound RA57, which detoured to the east to confuse the U-boats while Russian aircraft patrolled the approaches to Kola, where the enemy was thought to be heavily concentrated. For two days the ships sailed undetected, with blizzards and raging seas making flying impossible. On 4 March the U-boats found them, but the weather abated, and *Chaser*'s Swordfish 'B', pilot Sub-Lieutenant (A) P. J. Beresford, Observer Sub-Lieutenant (A) D. F. Lang, TAG Leading Airman J. Beach, found *U-472* 43km (27 miles) from the convoy, hit her with a salvo of RPs and so badly damaged her that it was an easy job for the destroyer *Onslaught* to finish her off with gunfire. The Swordfish hounded the U-boats while daylight lasted, and Swordfish 'B' damaged a second submarine and made a good attack on a third. The Wildcats sortied against shadowers by day but were again frustrated by gun failures, and *Chaser* could do nothing about the night snoopers tracking them by radar, as she had no night fighters. Though with limited success against one enemy, the tough Grummans were constantly beating the weather. Every landing on the gyrating carrier was a test of man and machine. 'The Wildcats', reported Captain McClintock, 'continued to take the most almighty clouts, and come up smiling. You apparently cannot ask too much of an

Below: The ships of convoy JW57 plod steadily on towards Russia, under a menacing winter sky.

Above, left: The White Cliffs of Kola, with a low ceiling of threatening cloud, seen from *Chaser*'s flight deck.

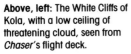

Above, right: A Swordfish from *Chaser* turns up on the sunlit path leading to a U-boat. During the return to the UK of Convoy RA57 from Russia, *U-472* was badly damaged by rockets from Sub-Lieutenant(A) Beresford's Swordfish B, and finished off by destroyer HMS *Onslaught*'s guns. In a successful rocket attack by an 816 Squadron Swordfish, Sub-Lieutenant(A) Mason sank *U-366* on 5 March, and next day Sub-Lieutenant(A) Bennett's Swordfish X destroyed *U-973* and damaged another U-boat.

American undercarriage beneath a good pilot.'

Chaser's Air Direction room kept a mainly anti-submarine plot, which did not help the fighters but which the aggressive Stringbags of 816 made the most of, even when the crashes on the heaving deck reduced them to four serviceable machines. On 5 March Sub-Lieutenant Mason's Swordfish 'F' crew sighted *U-366* 8km (five miles) away, stalked her cleverly from cloud cover, and sank her with a full salvo of eight RPs, four of which scored direct hits. The dawn patrol got six contacts before breakfast, Sub-Lieutenant Bennett's Swordfish 'X' sinking *U-973* with a six-rocket salvo, and damaging another U-boat at dusk.

This one small carrier had been asked to do too much. A second carrier was necessary, as in the Atlantic, to mount full-scale fighter and strike operations simultaneously, particularly as night flying was clearly required. Improved aircraft performance was also needed. The Wildcat was strong and tough but not fast enough, and its guns did not like the cold. The limitations of the old Swordfish had again shown themselves. It could not lift a full war load in low wind conditions, its speed of attack was poor, and its open cockpits exposed the crew to the full miseries of Arctic weather. Some of 816's crews were so numbed with cold after a patrol that they had to be lifted out of their cockpits.

ACTIVITY AND *TRACKER* WITH JW58

All these critcisms, and more, were aired in the Admiralty, and improvements put in hand. They could not all be made in time for the next convoy, JW58, which sailed on 27 March, with 48 merchantmen the biggest convoy so far sent to Russia, but a big effort was made. The convoy would have two CVEs, originally to be *Biter* and *Tracker*, but *Biter* was not ready in time, and *Activity* was hurriedly steamed up from Greenwich to Scapa to take her place. *Activity* was not arcticised, and her No 819 Squadron under Lieutenant-Commander O. A. G. Oxley had only three Swordfish and seven Wildcats. *Tracker* (Captain J. H. Huntley) was better equipped. Her No 846 Squadron (Lieutenant-Commander R. D. Head) had seven Wildcats and 12 Avengers, the first of the TBFs to join a Russian convoy, even though her aircrews had not flown for three weeks, neither squadron had had any experience in the Arctic, and there was no time for them to exercise together. Fraser also borrowed two escort groups from Western Approaches, the 8th and Captain Walker's famous U-boat killers of the 2nd. In command of the whole escort was Rear-Admiral F. Dalrymple-Hamilton in the cruiser *Diadem*. In all his force comprised, beside the two CVEs and the cruiser, 20 destroyers, Walker's five crack sloops, the four corvettes of 8EG, and the US cruiser *Milwaukee*, which was being lent to the Russians. Captain Willoughby in *Activity* was Senior Officer, Escort Carriers.

OPERATION 'TUNGSTEN'

A further contingency was the possibility that the *Tirpitz* had been made operative again. To prevent her taking action an attack by Barracuda bombers, Operation 'Tungsten', was to be carried out against her simultaneously with the passage of JW58. *Activity*, *Tracker* and *Diadem* joined the convoy on 29 March, the CVEs occupying two rear spaces in Column 7, the columns on either side of which had only two ships in them. If the wind direction forced a carrier to leave her station, she was to stay inside the escort screen, if possible. If she had to go outside, the two escorts nearest to her point of departure were to act as her close escort. *Activity* was to concentrate on dealing with shadowers, *Tracker* with U-boats, putting up one Avenger and one Wildcat as a basic striking force. *Activity*'s three Swordfish, the only aircraft armed with RPs, might also be useful.

The voyage started dramatically. On the very first day out, 29 March, Walker's *Starling*, leading 2nd Support Group, sank *U-961*, an unlucky transit boat heading for the Atlantic. Next afternoon the first shadowers appeared. At 15:10 *Activity* scrambled two Wildcats to intercept. This pair failed to locate the enemy, but the section which took off to relieve them at 17:07 shot down a Ju 88 eight minutes later.

During this early flurry of action, Force II, the *Tirpitz* attack group, left Scapa for Altenfjord under Rear-Admiral A. W. la T. Bisset in the cruiser *Royalist*. Later that evening Admiral Fraser left with Force I, which included the battleships *Duke of York* and *Anson*, the Fleet carrier *Victorious*, the cruiser *Belfast*, and six destroyers, his first task to cover the convoy to Russia, in case the *Tirpitz* should sortie against it before the air strike could be sent against her.

Away to the north shadowers were trying to maintain constant surveillance of JW58. At night, without opposition, they were bold, and used flares to illuminate the convoy. In daylight they rarely came closer than about 30km (20 miles) and kept below 300m (1,000ft), knowing that British Mk 79B radar was ineffective in these conditions. But the convoy escorts were eager and efficient. On 31 March aircraft from *Tracker* and the destroyer *Beagle* between them sank *U-355*. At 07:15 an Fw 200K was sighted, and *Activity* flew off two Wildcats. This time no guns jammed, and they shot him down. His successor eluded the fighters, but at 16:32 Wildcats from *Activity* shot down another Fw 200K. An hour later this Condor was replaced by another. Again *Activity* scrambled two fighters, and at 18:18 they shot him down.

By the morning of April Fool's Day Fraser felt reasonably certain that he had fooled the Germans. Neither Force I nor II had been sighted, *Tirpitz* was still in Kaafjord, JW58 was making good progress, and the weather was favourable. Leaving the convoy to look after itself, he advanced the time of attack by 24 hours. The two forces met 350km (220 miles) north-west of Altenfjord on the afternoon of 2 April and regrouped into a new Force 7 (battleship *Anson*, Fleet carriers *Victorious* and *Furious*, cruisers *Jamaica* and *Belfast* and six destroyers), and Force 8 (cruisers *Royalist* and *Sheffield*, six destroyers and four escort carriers, the new 'Ruler' Class Assault carrier *Emperor*, the Fighter carriers *Pursuer* and *Searcher*, and the Trade Protection carrier *Fencer*). Both groups shaped course for the flying-off position about 160km (100 miles) nearer Altenfjord, with the CVEs steaming at their common full speed of 17 knots, Vice-Admiral Moore in *Anson* in command, Fraser covering from the north in the battleship *Duke of York*. As the ships plunged through the darkness 42 Barracudas were bombed up, 65 fighters (Lease-Lend Corsairs, Hellcats and Wildcats, British Seafires) and nine Swordfish were fuelled and armed. Two strikes were planned, one hour apart, each with 21 Barracudas from *Victorious* and *Furious*, supported by 40 Corsairs, Hellcats and Wildcats from all the carriers, with 25 Seafires and

Below: The Fighter carrier HMS *Searcher* took part in Operation 'Tungsten', an attack by Barracudas on the German battleship *Tirpitz* mounted simultaneously with the running of Convoy JW58 to Russia. Her Wildcats, which can be seen here, joined Corsairs and Hellcats to provide fighter cover for the attacking bombers.

Above: Senior TAG of 846 Squadron, Petty Officer Barlow occupied the lower belly position. (Cdr Jeff Powell)

Top right: The CO of 846 Squadron, Lieutenant-Commander(A) 'Bobby' Head, RN climbs out of his 'Flagship', Avenger FN909, after a sortie. (Cdr J. Powell)

Above right: Senior Observer Lieutenant Jeff Powell, RN in the 'glass house'.

Wildcats and nine Swordfish from *Furious* and *Fencer* providing combat and anti-submarine patrols.

At 04:16 the ten Corsairs of 1834 Squadron began take-off from *Victorious*, followed by the first Barracuda, with the other fighter escorts taking off from *Emperor*, *Pursuer* and *Searcher*. The first CAP and A/S patrols of the day left *Furious*' and *Fencer*'s decks.

Tirpitz was about to weigh anchor for sea trials when she sighted the first aircraft at 05:28. Then the Hellcats and Wildcats were on her, spraying her upperworks with 0.50s, and the Barracudas began their bombing run, under a shield of Corsairs giving top cover. The strike returned to the carriers leaving *Tirpitz* erupting with smoke and flame from several direct hits. By this time the second strike was in the air. Eighteen Barracudas and 39 fighters got airborne in nine minutes and hit *Tirpitz* at 06:35, Hellcats strafing the flak defences thickly grouped round the battleship, low-flying Wildcats raking her decks, clearing the way for the Barracudas. Two Barracudas were shot down, one Hellcat ditched on the way back. Fourteen direct hits had been scored, putting the *Tirpitz* out of action for three months. The determined aggression of the force's fighters against heavy flak was typified by the conduct of Temporary Lieutenant Orbell Ray 'Titus' Oakes, Royal Marines, who, after this and subsequent attacks on targets off the Norwegian coast, was awarded the DSC 'For bravery, leadership, skill and devotion to duty while operating from HMS *Emperor* during successful strikes at enemy shipping . . .'

Meanwhile JW58 had steamed safely on its way. The escorts had got into their stride and the air crews of both carriers were showing outstanding determination. The Avengers found difficulty getting their DCs away, owing to inaccurate machining of the lugs on their crutches, but in the forenoon of 1 April a TBF from *Tracker* made a promising attack on a U-boat. On returning to the carrier it crashed right on the round-down and caught fire. The pilot, Sub-Lieutenant (A) A. E. Ballantyne, RNVR, struggled out of the cockpit and staggered for'ard with his clothes on fire. The flight deck Chief ran to him and tried to beat out the flames, but Ballantyne died a moment or two later from his burns. The observer and TAG were also badly burned but recovered. *Activity* had a Swordfish crash in the afternoon, which reduced her RP strike capability to two aircraft.

Right: Sub-Lieutenant Alan Ballantyne's Avenger after it has crashed on *Tracker*'s round-down. Ballantyne was fatally burned and died almost immediately, but his observer, Sub-Lieutenant(A) 'Cab' Calloway, RNVR and TAG, PO(Air) Gates, escaped with their lives. Calloway was very badly burned about the face, but recovered after plastic surgery. (Cdr J. Powell)

But the escorts kept up the pressure. On 2 April a Wildcat/Avenger team attacked a U-boat, leaving it diving steeply with its propellors in the air, bleeding oil, and at 16:45 two Wildcats from *Activity* shot down a Ju 88 shadower. The veteran destroyer *Keppel* sank Kapitänleutnant Becker's *U-360* in a Hedgehog attack. The carriers had no night fliers to make their capability total, but at 03:15 on the 3rd *Activity* flew off a Swordfish armed with eight RPs to patrol ahead of the convoy, and Captain Willoughby ordered *Tracker* to have a strike at readiness from 04:00. Thirty minutes later the Swordfish reported a suspicious object which dived without leaving a swirl, and dropped a marker. At 05:00 the pilot returned to the marker and sighted white water cascading off the casing of a U-boat surfacing about 9.5km (six miles) on his starboard beam. His report sent a *Tracker* Avenger/Wildcat strike team scrambling. The Swordfish hung on, dodging heavy fire from the U-boat, which had remained contemptuously on the surface. At 05:43 the strike arrived, the Wildcat dived and silenced the guns, the Swordfish attacked with RPs, the Avenger with depth-charges. One Swordfish was shot down but the U-boat, Oberleutnant Heger's *U-288*, blew up. The convoy reached Kola without loss on 4 April. Three U-boat groups, *Thor* (*U-278, U-312, U-313* and *U-674*), *Blitz* (*U-277, U-355, U-711* and *U-956*) and *Hammer* (*U-288, U-315, U-334* and *U968*) had been deployed against the convoy, as well as *U-716, U-739, U-360, U-361* and *U-990* on passage – a

Right: 'The Wildcat dived and silenced the guns . . .' First move in the destructrion of *U-288* on 3 April 1944 by aircraft from HMSS *Tracker* and *Activity* in Convoy JW58 to Russia.

total of 17 boats, four of which had been destroyed, together with six aircraft, by the Allied escorts, for the loss of only one aircraft.

The presence of two taut CVEs and their bold squadrons, even without night capability, had paid off handsomely. Three Fw 200s, two Ju 88s and one Blohm & Voss Bv 138 had been shot down by the fighters and all daytime shadowers severely harassed. The strike aircraft had sunk one U-boat and contributed to the destruction of another, and two more had been destroyed by the surface escorts. Of some 27 U-boats based in northern Norway, the Germans had used 18 and lost four. On the return trip with 36 merchantmen lack of wind kept all but two lightly loaded Swordfish from *Activity* on deck, and the Germans restricted reconnaissance to night radar searches, making only a few half-hearted and unsuccessful attacks, although two groups, *Donner* and *Keil* (ten boats in all) were used.

ACTIVITY AND *FENCER* WITH RA59

There were to be no more convoys to Russia until the autumn, but there were 45 empty merchant ships in Kola Inlet to be brought back to the UK, as well as the American crew of the USS *Milwaukee*, and 2,300 Russian sailors to bring over to man the old battleship *Royal Sovereign*, which was also being handed over to the Soviet Navy. *Activity* had been in Scapa Flow less than a week when she was ordered to sail with Rear-Admiral R. R. McGrigor's escort force to bring back RA59. All her experienced Swordfish crews had been taken out of the ship to fly in support of the landings in Normandy, scheduled for early June, and she was left with only three inexperienced pilots for her three Stringbags, and three experienced men among her seven Wildcat pilots, but to make up the complement five pilots from *Chaser*'s 816 Squadron, with experience in the February-March convoys, were given a pierhead jump, and with her this time was the veteran *Fencer* (Captain W. W. R. Bentinck, RN) with most of her seasoned 842 Squadron crews, though they had had no experience of Arctic operations.

On 19 April McGrigor in HMS *Diadem* led his two carriers, 16 destroyers and four frigates of the Canadian 6th Escort Group out of The Flow. *Fencer*'s squadron provided A/S patrols. One of her Swordfish crashed on deck but 842's efficient air mechanics quickly fitted a new engine and propellor, two new mainplanes and a new undercarriage. One of *Activity*'s green Swordfish crews came in too fast off the dawn patrol, tore the hook out, ditched, and was rescued by HMCS *Waskesieu*. The other Swordfish crashed on deck. Four and a half days in Vaenga Bay were spent repairing aircraft, with some limited shore leave. 'What a grey, barren, cheerless place we found,' wrote E. W. Tyler, Chief TAG in 842 Squadron. 'Very little help from the local authorities was

Opposite page, top: The first Avenger attack on *U-288*, taken by Observer Sub-Lieutenant(A) Rex Woodward, RNVR from the lower aft position in Lieutenant(A) John Toner's aircraft. The U-boat's 37mm gun is not manned, and the 20mm is the only gun in action.

Opposite page, centre: The second attack on *U-288*.

Opposite page, bottom: *U-288* from the bomb bay during the third attack, after which the U-boat blew up. (Cdr J. Powell)

Right: A Stringbag comes to grief in the Goofers. The behaviour of the matlow running flat-out *towards* the aircraft is, in view of the 250lb bomb still attached to the starboard lower mainplane, puzzling – unless he has seen that one or other of the aircrew is injured and needs help to leave the machine.

Below: Arctic escort. *Activity* in Kola Inlet, north Russia.

available, but we were allowed a short walk ashore. No drink, no eats, no fun, nothing, so back to the ship as soon as we could get the boat.'

RA59 weighed on 28 April, *Fencer* with the Soviet Admiral Levchenko, his staff and their body servants on board, while *Royal Sovereign*'s future Russian ship's company was distributed round various ships. The fair weather gave way to heavy seas, snowstorms and a following wind, but two *Activity* Wildcats damaged a Bv 138. That evening Huff-Duff U-boat bearings poured into *Activity*'s air plot. A merchantman carrying many of the Soviet sailors was torpedoed, broke in half and quickly sank. While *Fencer*'s Air Officer Operations, Lieutenant-Commander Glaser, was frantically busy briefing aircrews, Admiral Levchenko and his staff were continually crowding into the small office with enquiries about the number of Russian seamen rescued. At last, 'Bugger off!' said Glaser, 'I have more important things to do.'

The next day was May Day, and two Wildcats from *Activity* celebrated it by making a good attack on a Blohm & Voss shadower. Snow was falling heavily, and at one time both flight decks were 15cm (6in) thick with it. *Fencer* was arcticized and her steam jets quickly cleared a flight path, but *Activity* was faced with a long job using cold water from fire main hoses, brooms and shovels. It was her turn to fly off the midday patrol, but Captain Willoughby had to ask *Fencer* to take over.

There were examples of strike aircraft being caught with the wrong weapons. Since U-boats had started fighting back on the surface, RPs were preferred. If they submerged, depth-charges or a Fido were the appropriate weapons. It was not possible for a Swordfish to carry a selection to cover all situations, in fact in the light airs of the early part of this trip a Stringbag bearing two DCs was the most awesome display of power possible with which to challenge a U-boat floating battery. In that case the Swordfish would call in reinforcements, hopefully at least one RP machine and another with more DCs. In strong winds later on it was just possible to operate an RP aircraft, but the U-boat inevitably dived. From 2 May, the day when Catalina escorts arrived from the Shetlands, various formulae were tried, sometimes flying a pair of Swordfish, one with DCs, one with RPs, or two such pairs at the same time. Sometimes the usual patrolling aircraft were flown ahead and on both flanks of the convoy, and as soon as a contact was made, a striking force of three Swordfish, two with rockets, one with depth-charges, scrambled from the carrier.

Several good attacks were made, the last being on the 3rd, when a Swordfish/Wildcat team from *Fencer* engaged a U-boat. *Fencer* claimed in all one U-boat probably sunk, one certainly damaged, and three probably damaged. It was a modest claim, and the real score was later discovered to have included three U-boats sunk, *U-277*, *U-674* and *U-959*. For 72 hours her aircraft had kept up A/S patrols with only one short break, not to mention ad hoc strikes. Late on the 3rd *Fencer* and three escorts were sent on ahead, as they were needed for 'Overlord', the landings in Normandy. In his report Captain Willoughby, SO Escort Carriers, said of *Fencer*, 'A feature of the carrier operations with RA59 was the extremely high standard of *Fencer*'s deck landing operations.'

Right: You shouldn't have joined! *Fencer* with RA59 from Russia. *Fencer* was 'arcticized', with steam heating at the guns and other important positions, and took over much of the flying from *Activity*, which was not, though the efforts of brooms, squeegees and frostbitten hands were still needed.

11

'RIDE 'EM COWBOY!'

DÖNITZ now had most of his Atlantic boats on short leashes, but was still sending single submarines out to the coast of Brazil and the Indian Ocean. To top up these in the refuelling area west of the Cape Verdes cruised the 1,600-ton milch cow *U-488*. On the 16th and 17th of April she refuelled *U-129* and *U-537*, heading for the Indian Ocean. To close this route CINCLANT sent two hunter-killer groups to the area, one built round the new Kaiser carrier USS *Tripoli*, CVE-64, the other based on the older *Croatan*.

Croatan, the 'Old Crow', CVE-25, was a *Bogue* Class ship, launched on 3 August 1942, completed 28 April 1943. Operational since 2 July 1943, she made her maiden voyage on convoy escort to Casablanca, where she found the harbour littered with burned-out, rusting wrecks, relics of 'Torch'. Her TBFs depth-charged one U-boat, but another was not pursued because *Croatan*'s Composite Squadron (VC) 19 (12 TBFs, six FMs) was not qualified for night operations. After several 'milk runs', flight deck and hangar packed with planes, she resumed anti-submarine operations on 14 January 1944. Captain John Vest called for volunteer night fliers, and soon the whole group had qualified, the first CVE unit to do so. A Japanese submarine was reported lurking under the weed of the Sargasso Sea. Night owl Lieutenant Sallenger, with five U-boat kills already in his cruises with *Card*, found the enemy by radar in the dark and sank her with Fido by flarelight.

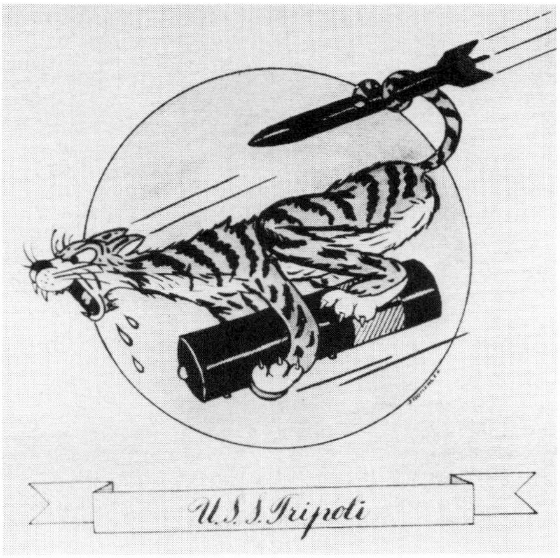

Right: Mascot of USS *Tripoli*, CVE-64, a Kaiser-built escort carrier, commissioned 31 October 1943, which began service as the nucleus of Escort Carrier Task Group (TG) 21.15 in the Atlantic, April 1944. (US Navy)

Tripoli (CVE 64), originally MC hull 1101, was laid down as *Didrickson Bay* on 1 February 1943, renamed on 3 April, and commissioned on 31 October 1943 at Astoria, Oregon, by Captain Wendell G. Switzer. She left Norfolk, Virginia, on 15 March as the hub of Escort Carrier Task Group (TG) 21.15, with Compo (VC) 13 and the five DEs of Escort Division (CortDiv) 7, for the Cape Verdes refuelling grounds. *U-543* was attacked on 19 April, but escaped. *U-66*, very low on fuel and provisions after a long patrol in the Gulf of Guinea, was looking for refueller *U-488* on the 26th when Avenger Night Owls (specially equipped night-fliers) from *Croatan* sighted the refueller by moonlight 1,125km (700 miles) west of Sao Antao Island, and in the forenoon she was destroyed by CortDiv 7's Hedgehogs. Oberleutnant Sechausen in *U-66* saw this hunt going on but did not know that his refueller was the target, and carried on the now desperate search, kept down by CVE aircraft. *Bogue*'s and *Block Island*'s groups were about to relieve *Croatan* and *Tripoli* when Tenth Fleet gave them *U-66*, now 885km (550 miles) west of Sao Antao.

By the evening of 5 May the submarine's batteries had almost run out of charge. Planes or no planes, she had to come up. *U-66* surfaced about 5km (three miles) from *Block Island*. The carrier picked her up on radar, sent Brent Abel's DE *Buckley* after her, and got out of harm's way. Sechausen eluded these hunters but early next morning Lieutenant Jimmie J. Sellars in a Night Owl got him on his ASV screen 32km (20 miles) due north of him, and alerted *Buckley*.

The DE got an echo and closed, with the enemy between him and the moon. Sechausen saw what he wanted to see, and thought the shadowy vessel heading for him was the milch cow. He even fired three red flares to guide her. Abel said, 'Thank you very much' and hit *U-66* near the conning tower with his first salvo. Then *Buckley* ran the sub down at flank speed, with Sellars up aloft spotting for his guns; she dodged a torpedo and laid her bows right across the U-boat's fo'c's'le.

Germans climbed up on to *Buckley*'s fo'c's'le, some with their hands up, some with guns. The *Buckley* men threw shell cases and coffee mugs at them, or used their fists. The Gunner's Mate threatened a group round the capstan with a hammer and they surrendered. One German ran into the wardroom and fled when a steward's mate threw a pot of hot coffee at him.

The *Buckley* went astern and scraped clear. Sechausen threw the helm over and hit the DE on her starboard side aft, his bows going under her keel so that a *Buckley* sailor was able to toss a hand grenade down through the open conning tower hatch to feed the fire he could see burning inside the U-boat. Pulling clear, the sub tried to get away, with men leaping out of her flame-filled hatchways, but sank in clouds of hissing steam, leaving 36 survivors.

VINDEX AND 'UNCLE WILLI'

HMS *Vindex* weighed from Moville, Northern Ireland, at 20:45 on 24 April, with some improved equipment on board. 'Wings' Percy Gick had attached a Swordfish RP rack to a Sea Hurricane wing and fired rockets. Then a fighter was fitted with racks for two RPs under each wing and tested successfully, whereupon five of *Vindex*'s Sea Hurricanes were fitted with the same gear, retaining their 20mm cannon as well. The sixth fighter had two of its cannon removed to make way for two marine markers for the rapid investigation of Huff-Duff U-boat bearings. Eight of 825's Swordfish were fitted with the new ASV Mk XI, but with 13 Swordfish crews and eight fighter

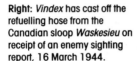

Right: *Vindex* has cast off the refuelling hose from the Canadian sloop *Waskesieu* on receipt of an enemy sighting report, 16 March 1944.

Right: An 825 Squadron Sea Hurricane aboard *Vindex*, showing off her very lethal-looking 20mm cannon and her RP armament created by the carrier's Commander(F), Lieutenant-Commander Percy Gick, RN.

Right: Atlantic winter. Clearing *Vindex*'s flight deck. New Zealand Sea Hurricane pilot Sub-Lieutenant(A) 'Al' Martin has fun with the 'Dodgem car' towing tractor, March 1944. These little battery-powered vehicles were originally acquired from the US Navy at Norfolk, Virginia, British carriers having previously lacked any type of flight deck tractor. Aircraft were usually towed tail-first for better directional control.

Right: *Vindex*'s seaboat approaches Sub-Lieutenant(A) Martin, who has ditched his Sea Hurricane with water-polluted avgas, 5 May 1944. Martin died very shortly after this picture was taken.

Below: Flight deck party spotting a Swordfish on *Vindex*. Wing bays on these old-type machines were folded manually.

pilots, the squadron was still undermanned for round-the-clock operations, especially as she was on her own again.

Patrols began an hour after weighing. One of Bayliss' objectives this time was the destruction of the U-boat known as 'Uncle Willi', which made regular, 12-hour weather reports. On 27 April Commander Donald MacIntyre's 5th Escort Group joined the carrier. The 5th was a new team, manned by men fresh from basic training, for whom this operation was a shakedown cruise, though in practice 'more of a "throw-up" than a shakedown for them,' observed MacIntyre.

Bayliss shaped course for the haunts of 'Uncle Willi' in bad weather, with high seas, blinding rain and poor visibility, plus a breakdown of his Type 281 radar. Watered avgas brought down a Swordfish in the sea. MacIntyre's, literally, green operators failed to pinpoint the evening U-boat weather report, but with Huff-Duff tip-offs from Tenth Fleet and Enigma information the met man's area of operations was narrowed down to a strip of ocean about 32km (20 miles) wide. At 16:50 on 5 May three Sea Hurricanes took off for a search, looking very lethal with their four cannon and four RPs apiece, but the engine of New Zealander Al Martin's aircraft seized, and he was drowned after ditching.

Just after six o'clock next morning the sloop *Bligh* threw the last of a 26-charge pattern, set for 152 and 261m (500 and 856ft), and as it exploded the 750-ton *U-765* broke surface roughly a kilometre (half a mile) astern.

825's CO, Lieutenant-Commander Freddie Sheffield, formerly an Oxford don, in Swordfish 'V' saw the U-boat come up about 1.5km (one mile) on their port beam, opened up to full throttle and turned towards her. At a range of 90m (100yd) he dived to attack through fire from the U-boat's ack-ack which damaged his centre section and starboard mainplane. Coming down at 120 knots on the submarine's port bow, he released his two DCs at 23m (75ft). TAG CPO Mick Dale saw them straddle the conning tower, sink, and explode. Some 30 seconds later the submarine broke in two, bow and stern both rising to 45 degrees, and the two halves sank, leaving a dozen survivors in the sea. Two of them waved to the Swordfish as Sheffield flew low over them. MacIntyre's *Bickerton* came up and rescued eight men. It was discovered from the prisoners that *U-765* had been one of a patrol of five *Schnorkel* boats set up in mid-Atlantic between Newfoundland and the Azores, each boat with a meteorologist on board to give the Kriegsmarine and the Luftwaffe accurate weather forecasts and to monitor the movements of Allied shipping for some forewarning of the invasion of Europe.

After this success a gale hit the group, and lashed the ships for 48 hours. This appeared to stir up water lying at the bottom of the avgas tanks, and after the next refuelling several pints of water were found in aircraft tanks. The slow, careful filtering of the fuel held up operations, on top of the savage weather. Despite winds gusting at 45 knots, and heavy hail showers, the Swordfish flew through the night of 6/7 May in search of the relief weather reporter. Only when seas were breaking over the forward end of the flight deck, and the carrier's stern was rising and falling 15–18m (50 or

Right: Sub-Lieutenant(A) Johnny Moore's Sea Hurricane has missed all the arrester cables on *Vindex*'s flight deck in bad weather and tangled with the barrier.

60ft), was flying cancelled. Next morning two fish were found entangled in the barrier.

Vindex's one all-important lift was located aft on the flight deck. The movement of the huge slab of the lift platform was controlled by a 220-volt electric motor in a compartment below the bottom of the lift well, assisted by a counterweight to balance the weight of the lift platform and any aircraft on it, located inside a sealed casing on one side of the well. By the forenoon of 9 May, with all the intensive use of this single lift for the round-the-clock movement of Swordfish and heavy Sea Hurricanes in and out of the hangar, the wires on which the counterweight was hung had become stretched. There came the fatal moment, at 09:45 that morning, when the counterweight reached the bottom of the lift well before the platform had reached flight deck level. The switch which normally tripped when both weight and lift reached the extreme of their travel, cutting off the motor, did not trip. All the wires of the motor windings burned out trying to push the lift up the last important foot or so, and the lift was stuck – with the morning patrols to fly off. It could be operated by hand cranking, but it took a whole hour to move it up or down. It was a Commander (F)'s nightmare.

The lift motor was beyond the resources of the ship to repair, and the only alternative means of power was the after capstan motor. Supervised by Chief Engineer Hector Weir, work began to move the motor from its bed on the quarterdeck, take it through the torpedo workshop and down into the lift motor space, for connection to the lift mechanism. This was an awesome chore, with the ship pitching and rolling. Very slowly the capstan motor was manhandled forward. This was a seaman's job, and was organised by Percy Gick.

Right: Return from the Faroes. HMS *Vindex* beds down her Swordfish. Note barrier details in the foreground.

Below: A Swordfish from *Empire MacMahon*. (J. M. Goulding)

Right: On 2 June 1944 Sub-Lieutenant(A) Hayes' Sea Hurricane Q of *Striker*'s 824 Squadron came to grief. With his services mercifully not needed, the 'Hot Papa', middle foreground, has discarded the top half of his hot and heavy asbestos suit. (J. Stenning)

Right: 7 June 1944. *Striker*'s Lieutenant Godden has missed all the arrester wires but has been wrenched to a halt by the safety barrier. (J. Stenning)

Right: Lieutenant Clarke's Sea Hurricane NF684 bounced, its hook hit the deck and it slammed into *Striker*'s barrier, writing off propeller and undercarriage and displacing the port outer cannon. Did he tell his girlfriend Sheila? (J. Stenning)

The engineers were responsible for the cutting of holes in bulkheads by oxy-acetylene torch, and for securing the motor to the bottom of the lift well.

Meanwhile flying had to go on. Using the agonisingly slow manual procedure, an aircraft which had crashed on deck was lowered into the hangar, replacement machines were inched up, and thereafter the ship was operated much like a tanker MAC-ship, which had no hangar, all aircraft being maintained on the flight deck. The capstan motor was lowered into place below the lift well, the engineers welded it to the deck, connected it to the driving drum of the lift motor, and Wings could range his aircraft properly again. The repair took 24 hours. While it was under way Senior Pilot Gordon Bennett landed on in Swordfish *LS416*, while the DE *Keats* refuelled astern.

With *Keats* topped up, Bayliss was not too worried when foul weather returned, with a Force 7 wind and a heavy sea and swell. At 03:30 on the 11th Doug Webb's Swordfish 'M' came in to land on. *Vindex* was in violent motion, rolling, bucking and yawing. Webb reached the deck just as the ship heaved upwards. Undercarriage and lower starboard mainplane smashed, the Swordfish skidded along trailing the damaged wing, snagged a wire, slewed to starboard, plunged over the side, and the three men were drowned. The whole air staff, especially the surviving air crews, had about reached their limits, physical and mental. Eight of the flying personnel had been killed, ten more were temporarily unfit for operational flying. The total wastage in air crews had been so great that after two round-the-clock missions only 35 per cent of the original Swordfish crews remained, proving conclusively that one escort carrier could not carry out continuous 24-hour operations. *Vindex* reached the Clyde on 15 May.

As soon as 'Stop engines' had been rung down, Chief Engineer Hector Weir turned his full attention to the urgent problem of the petrol contamination, which had not been solved by filtering. Night after night he had spent lying awake counting the aircraft landing on the flight deck above, wondering if any of the squadron's young men had ditched in the cold, dark ocean with a dead engine, blaming himself for the continuing unreliability of the fuel. Round and round went his thoughts. The water could not be in the petrol when it was piped into the ship . . . Something was happening *inside the storage tanks* . . . The answer came to him slowly . . . The petrol was pumped from the storage tanks to the aircraft refuelling points in the hangar by compressed air . . . When air is compressed it gets *warm* . . . The six interconnected storage tanks were surrounded by cold water, as a safety precaution . . . When the warm compressed air got inside the tank it was rapidly cooled, and condensed into *moisture* . . . It was this water which was adulterating the petrol . . . His solution was daringly simple – dispense with the surrounding water. Fill the whole petrol system with sea water, driving out all air. Pump the fuel aboard, simultaneously opening the outlet to the sea so that the sea water was forced out as the petrol came in. The light, high-octane aviation gas would not mix with the salt water, and the result would be a tank completely full with uncontaminated fuel. When it was required to refuel aircraft, pump sea water into the system again at one end. The sea water, because of its greater density, would displace the avgas, driving it back through the system and up to the refuelling points. Having convinced Bayliss, he was given permission by the Admiralty to convert *Vindex*'s petrol system to the new arrangement.

LULL IN THE NORTH ATLANTIC

It seemed a long time since North Atlantic convoys had been beset by wolf-packs. Huge convoys of as many as 100 ships were now sailing between North America and the United Kingdom without sight or sound of a U-boat, under the air protection of MAC-ships, of which there were now 18 in commission, so that it was possible to send two or three in each ON or HX convoy. On 26 May Lieutenant (A) S. A. Mears in *Nairana*'s Sea Hurricane *NF698* and Sub-Lieutenant (A) F. Wallis, RNVR, in Sea Hurricane *NF691* attacked two 290s, destroying one and probably the other too.

The U-boat effort in the Atlantic had been badly blunted, and most of the surviving boats as they returned from patrol were being reserved to attack future Russian convoys or the anticipated movement of assault forces across the English Channel. In May just five Allied merchant ships were sunk, 22 U-boats lost. The Germans withdrew the majority of their submarines remaining in the North Atlantic.

LOSS OF *BLOCK ISLAND*

CVEs *Block Island* and *Guadalcanal* were discharging the US Navy's responsibilities in the Central Atlantic south of the Azores. *Block Island* had left Casablanca on 23 May to relieve *Bogue* on patrol round Madeira and the Cape Verdes. On the 28th one of *Block Island*'s Night Owl Avengers sighted two U-boats. The carrier's strike aircraft attacked both submarines on that day and again on the 29th, with no apparent result. Captain Hughes was following the estimated track of one of the U-boats and was about 515km (320 miles) west-sou'-west of Funchal, Madeira, steaming in the pale light of a first-quarter moon on the evening of the 29th when at 20:13 a torpedo from his quarry, which had slipped inside the destroyer-escort screen undetected, struck the carrier, followed by a second. She immediately lost all way, power gone, rudder jammed. Hughes got all hands up from below, except the damage control parties. As they were assembling, a third torpedo shattered the thin unprotected plating of the CVE, and she started to settle swiftly by the stern. Lookouts in the DE *Eugene E. Elmore* sighted the enemy's periscope and attacked her. The aggressive U-boat fired an acoustic torpedo which smashed the stern of the escort *Barr*.

At 20:40 Captain Hughes ordered 'Abandon ship!' While the men were going over the stricken carrier's side another torpedo narrowly missed the *Elmore*, which chased the U-boat and lobbed three Hedgehog mortar bombs ahead of her. Seconds after the last charge had exploded, 'two short booms and one big wham' followed by 'another heavy, crawling explosion' were heard as *U-549* broke up. *Ahrens* and *Robert I. Paine* rescued 951 men from *Block Island*'s ship's company, then the dying carrier's bows rose until they were perpendicular and she slowly slid below. Some very efficient damage control saved *Barr* from sinking.

'CAN DO' JUNIOR

A report of the sinking reached *Guadalcanal*'s radio room. Gallery cleared lower deck and passed on the sad news, then Task Group 22.3 left the search area and headed north-east for Casablanca to refuel. Their course followed the U-boat route to the Bay of Biscay, and they got a report of a U-boat homeward bound on this path. She was calculated to be about 480km (300 miles) north of them and Gallery estimated that he would pass directly over her on 2 June, if the information was correct. In fact the U-boat was 1,095km (680 miles) away to the north-west of them, roughly half-way between the northern Cape Verde island of Sal and the coast of French West Africa, some 435km (270 miles) north-west of Dakar.

U-505, one of the large type IXC boats, was commissioned by Kapitänleutnant Loewe on 26 August 1941 in the Deutsche Werft yard in Hamburg, and made her first cruise off Freetown, where she sank three Allied freighters and a tanker. She next cruised the Caribbean, sinking two American freighters and a sailing ship. In October she was back in service under a new captain, Kapitänleutnant Cszhech. She sank a freighter off Trinidad on 7 November but was so badly damaged by an aircraft bomb that she barely made Lorient. In February 1943 she was bombed again off the mouth of the Orinoco River and again only just reached port. Three or four times she broke down on trials. 'The *U-505* had been very successful before the bomb hit it,' a crewman wrote, 'but now something like a curse lay over the boat.' They finally left Lorient again in June 1943, bound for the South Atlantic. A British destroyer depth-charged them off the Spanish coast, and they limped back to base trailing oil. Morale was now very low, and the captain was particularly depressed. In October *U-505* put out again, but off the Azores she was attacked, and six DCs shook them 'like peas in a can'. The hunter lost the scent, but Cszhech went into his cabin and shot himself. After more repairs she put to sea again with the inexperienced Oberleutnant Harald Lange in command.

Lange tried throughout the night of 29/30 May to surface and recharge batteries, but every time he came up his Naxos radar detector receiver screeched a warning of aircraft and he had to go down again. He turned east to avoid what he thought were planes from an Allied carrier group, but which were in fact transport aircraft on the south Atlantic run and bombers being ferried from America to West Africa. Still Naxos and his older Wanz receiver gave urgent warning of planes overhead, but late on 31 May he managed to get a good charge into the batteries and turned north again.

On the night of 2/3 June *Guadalcanal* ran over the U-boat's reported position. About 01:00 a loud-mouthed sonobuoy began to sound off, the carrier altered course for the position, and Lange heard her TBMs depth-charging 95km (60 miles) away. In 'Can Do' Commander Earl Trosino, Chief Engineer, reported to Gallery. 'Captain, we've got to quit fooling around here and get into Casablanca. I'm getting down near the safety limit of my fuel.' Both vessels headed north on converging courses. *U-505* surfaced at night to recharge again. A TBM flew within 10km (six miles) of her, and minutes after she had submerged again another TBM flew right over her. She settled down for a quiet, homeward-bound Sunday, 4 June.

Up above, sunrise brought a beautiful, clear day, but the frustrated Gallery, thinking that his one and only target on this cruise was now out of range astern, and worried about his fuel state, could not enjoy it. Then, abruptly, at 11:10, the bridge loudspeaker blared raucously. 'Frenchy to Bluejay! I have a possible sound contact!' 'Frenchy' was the DE *Chatelain*. 'Left full rudder,' ordered Gallery, 'Engines ahead, full speed.' He grabbed the TBS microphone. 'Bluejay to Dagwood. Take two DEs and assist Frenchy.' In *U-505* the hydrophones picked up propeller noise. Lange raised the asparagus and saw three ships bearing down on him, planes in the air, and a carrier in the distance. 'Take her down.' He jinked the boat to confuse sonar, then they heard the frightening rumble of engines as *Chatelain* steamed right over them. Her sonar sang out loud and clear, skipper Dudley Knox broadcast 'Contact evaluated as sub. Am starting attack.' *Chatelain* wheeled and tossed 20 Hedgehogs into the air ahead. The two Wildcats of Lieutenant Bill Roberts and Ensign Jack Cadle circled overhead, then suddenly dived and began shooting. Cadle yelled on his radio 'Sighted sub! Destroyers head for spot where we're shooting!' *Chatelain* steered for the bullet splashes and fired a spread of 12

272kg (600lb) DCs, set shallow. The charges splashed and sank.

Seconds later those above felt the sea quake, those below thought the whole ocean was exploding round them in a shattering, eat-splitting shock. Lights went out as the boat heeled over on her beam ends. Mess tables, messtraps, crockery and food struck the men as they were thrown off their feet. There was a shout of 'Water is coming in!' The rudder could not be moved. 'Blow all tanks. Abandon and scuttle!' Lange shouted. Above, the ship's bullhorns broadcast Cadle's voice, 'Sub is surfacing!'

At 11:21, 240km (150 miles) west of Cape Blanco, French West Africa, *U-505* broke surface, white water cascading off her rusty-grey conning tower. Gallery could not be sure if the enemy had come up to abandon ship or to fire a final spread and take at least one of her attackers with her. Then men started leaping out of open hatches. They met heavy fire. Lange was first out and was knocked unconscious by a 40mm shell. Two men picked him up and dragged him overboard. The rest jumped off as *U-505* with her jammed rudder circled to starboard, settling by the stern. Gallery broadcast to all ships, 'I want to capture that bastard if possible!' 'Can Do's' own boarding party, led by Lieutenant (jg) Albert L. David, was already in the motor whaleboat on its way across the water, helm angled to take it towards the circling U-boat. The first man of the boarding party leaped from the boat on to the slippery casing of the submarine, a coil of rope in his hand. Gallery, watching through binoculars, yelled into the TBS, 'Ride 'em, cowboy!'

Right: The capture of *U-505* (Museum of Science and Industry, Chicago)

Not knowing if they would be shot by men waiting below, or if the sub was about to sink or blow up, David scrambled down the conning tower ladder, leading the boarding party. In the radio room they found code books. A gushing sea-cock was sealed off again. Up above, the swell caught the whaleboat bringing over Earl Trosino and more engineers, and dumped it down on the sub's deck, breaking its back and spilling the men out on the casing. Trosino had never been in a submarine before, having spent most of his career in tankers, but he knew machinery, and soon found out which valves to open and which to close, while Gunner Barr rushed through the boat looking for the 14 TNT charges which he knew were normally set off to sink an abandoned U-boat, to find with relief that none of them had been activated. Meanwhile *Guadalcanal* came up and took *U-505* in tow. Someone mounted a Stars and Stripes over a swastika flag on a boathook and stuck it in a voicepipe on the U-boat's bridge. When Lange saw it he said, 'Herr Gott! I will be punished for this!'

From then on it was a battle of engineering skill and seamanship to haul the unwieldy, stern-heavy submarine to Bermuda. Once the tow parted, her rudder jammed, and she yawed off to starboard. Trosino set up hand steering gear. To raise electrical power to blow the after ballast tanks and lift the U-boat's stern, the speed of the tow was increased, and with the wire dangerously taut, 'Can Do' and the submarine, now christened 'Can Do Junior', made 12 knots. The submarine's propellers windmilled faster, turning the main shafts and the electric armatures, which acted as generators and recharged the batteries. On 6 June, at about the time the Allies were landing in Normandy, an oiler met the group and topped up their almost dry tanks; on 9 June a tug took over the tow, and ten days later *Guadalcanal* escorted the victorious procession into harbour at Bermuda, the traditional broom hoisted at her maintruck. It was the first time a ship of the US Navy had boarded and captured a foreign enemy's man-of-war in battle on the high seas since the USS *Peacock* had captured HMS *Nautilus* in 1815. The Royal Navy had captured the *U-570* earlier in this war and sent her back to sea as HMS *Graph*. but 'Can Do Junior' was the first submarine prize taken by United States forces. 'Can Do' had done it.

Of greater practical importance than the submarine herself were the current code books, the Enigma cypher machine, the hundreds of decoded despatches, and the acoustic torpedoes captured.

Bogue intercepted *U-802*, heading for Cabot Strait and the Gulf of St Lawrence on 15 August, but the Avenger of Lieutenant (jg) Wayne Dixon was lost, with him and his crew G. Scimio and C. G. Melton, and the U-boat reached its objective,

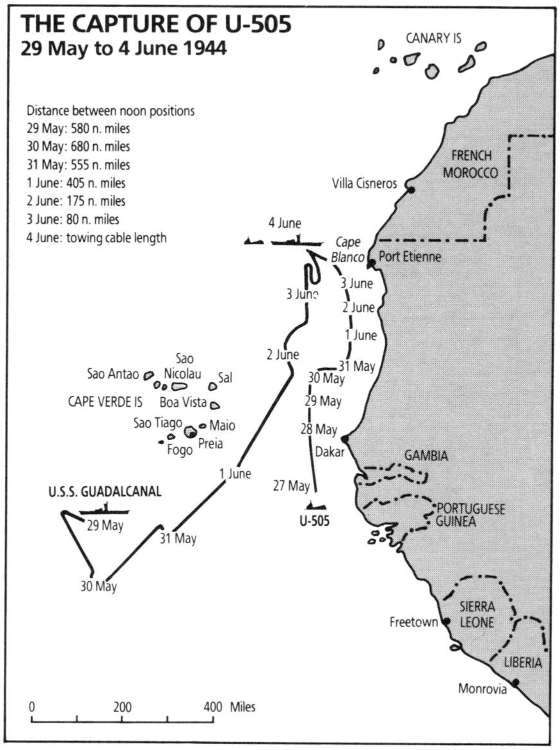

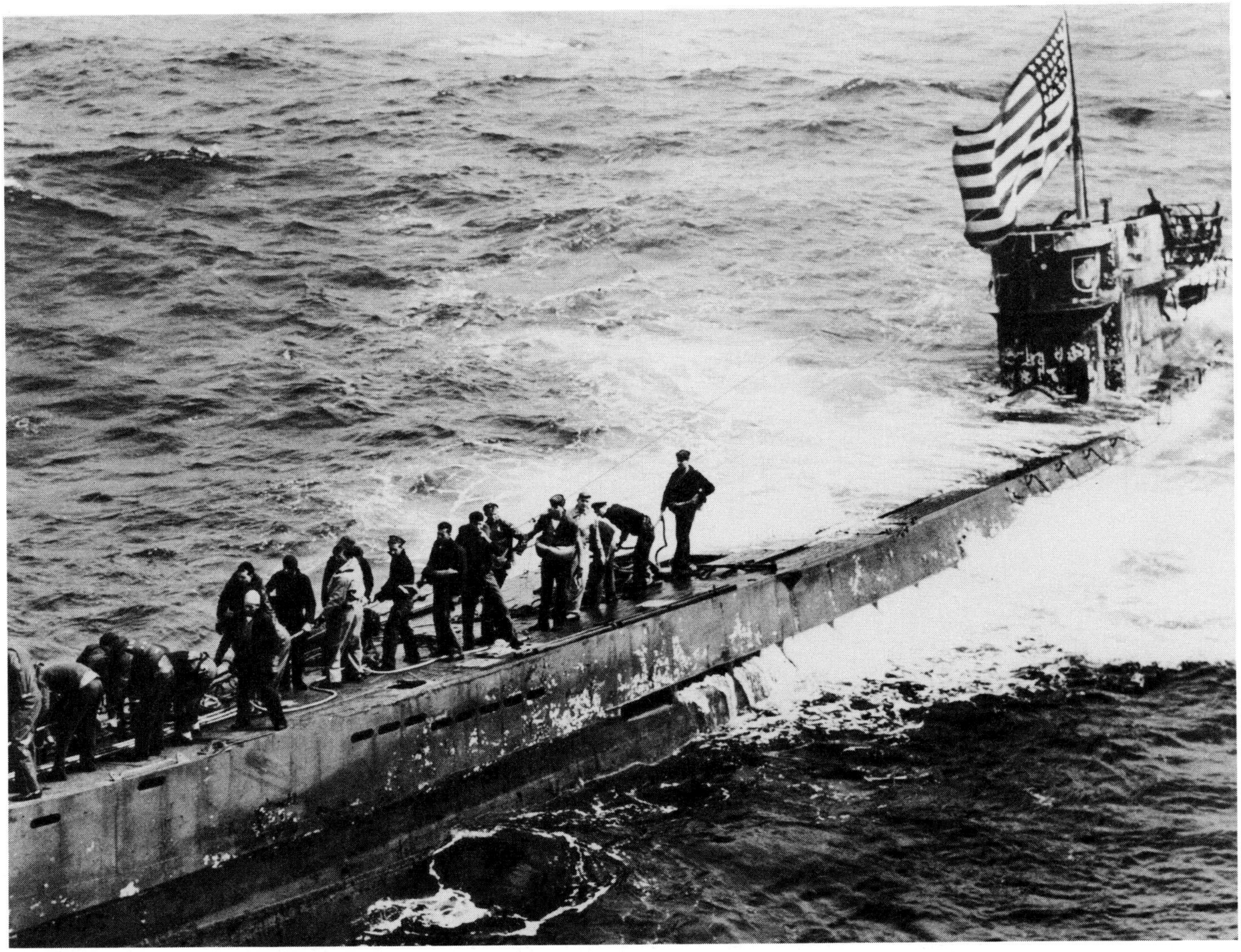

though failing to do any damage there. Then on the morning of 20 August Lieutenant (jg) A. X. Brokas in a TBM sighted Korvettenkapitän Armin Zinke's *schnorkel* boat *U-1229* about 480km (300 miles) south-by-east of Cape Race, Newfoundland. His attack badly damaged the submarine's batteries and she submerged to *schnorkel* depth to vent the choking, poisonous chlorine gas which filled the boat. This failed, and she was trapped, unable to dive or to re-charge her damaged batteries. The only way was up, to face the bombs and rockets of five TBMs, which sank her just after 13:00.

Tripoli, Captain Thayer T. Tucker, was in Recife, Brazil, on 18 September, with all hands resting after a tiring and unrewarding three weeks in the South Atlantic, when a Huff-Duff report of an impending rendezvous of two U-boats off the Cape Verdes sent her to sea again in a hurry. The 1,080-ton cargo submarine *U-1062*, en route from Penang, had been ordered to refuel the outward-bound *U-219* at a point 965km (600 miles) west-

Left: The capture of *U-505*. Men of *Guadalcanal* secure the towing hawser aboard *Can Do Junior*. (US Navy)

Left: The prize. Captain Gallery on the bridge of USS *Can Do Junior*, the first foreign man-of-war boarded and captured by the US Navy since the taking of HMS *Nautilus* by USS *Peacock* in 1815. (Museum of Science and Industry, Chicago)

sou'-west of Fogo. On 28 September Captain John R. Ruhsenberger's *Mission Bay*, CVE-59, joined *Tripoli* and, following the British example, the two Kaisers alternated in maintaining continuous air patrols. Shortly after the two groups had merged, Lieutenant W. R. Gillespie in a TBM of *Tripoli*'s VC 6 radioed, 'I've got him. He's shooting at me! I'm going in to make a run.' Those in *Tripoli* could see the TBM and one Wildcat attacking the U-boat. Gillespie had his microphone keyed open. Aboard the carrier they heard him cry out. It was the last anyone ever heard from him or his crew, radioman Ray Truss and Bob Hess, a reserve turret gunner and a relief for the regular crewman, who was sick. Hess, who was 36 and had grey hair, was called 'The Old Man' by the aircrews. *U-219*, still looking for the milch cow, had shot down Gillespie's aircraft, but the refueller herself, not far from the rendezvous, was picked up by an aircraft sonobuoy on the 30th and destroyed by Hedgehogs and DCs from *Mission Bay*'s screen. *U-219* reached Batavia on 12 December.

SECRET WEAPON

Among the 42 survivors from *U-1229*, destroyed by *Bogue*'s planes on 20 August, was a man named Oskar Mantel, former barman from Yorkville (a strongly German-American district of Manhattan), and member of the Nazi German/American Bund. With him he carried $2,000. After interrogation by the FBI, Director John Edgar Hoover reported to the Director of Naval Intelligence that Mantel was to have been put ashore by *U-1229* to act as a spy, and that, according to this recalcitrant and arrogant Nazi, Dönitz was planning an attack by a special force of U-boats armed with the flying 'buzz-bombs' which had been hitting London upon targets on or near the eastern US seaboard, possibly New York and Washington. Shortly afterwards Hoover reported the same story as overheard in the ramblings of a seaman in a Bowery bar. In Tenth Fleet Commander Knowles added this information to recently taken photographs of U-boats in their Norwegian bases showing structures mounted on the decks of several boats which British Intelligence had evaluated as launch platforms for buzz-bombs. Knowles' executive officer John Parsons considered these to be wooden tracks which the Germans used to load torpedoes, but Knowles already had intelligence of a special rocket under development for use by U-boats, and the whole idea had to be taken seriously.

Apprehension deepened when, on 27 November, two more would-be spies were captured and their stories backed up Mantel's boast. Put ashore at night at Hancock Point in Frenchman's Bay, Hancock County, Maine, very near a US Navy base, by dinghy from Oberleutnant Hans Hilbig's *U-1230*, were Erich Gimpel, *V-Mann No 146*, alias Edward G. Green, and American traitor and fervid, Jew-baiting pro-Nazi William C. Colepough from Old Black Point, Connecticut. They aroused the suspicions of 16-year-old Boy Scout Harvard Hodgkins when he passed them on Route 37 walking in heavy snow, dressed in very inappropriate light clothes, with no hats and struggling along with heavy suitcases. His Scout instincts activated, young Hodgkins back-tracked the footprints of the two strange men and ended up at the water's edge. That was enough for Harvard. He told the constable at Hancock, who called the FBI. The strangers were trailed to New York and arrested. Their suitcases contained German-made automatics, cameras, secret ink chemicals and the disassembled parts of a radio transmitter. Gimpel had on him $60,000 and $100,000 worth of diamonds. The money was in crisp new banknotes with *Deutsche Reichsbank* printed on the wrappers, and intended to finance acts of sabotage and the spreading of panic and confusion, to be co-ordinated, Gimpel confessed, with attacks on shore targets by U-boats 'being fitted out with a rocket-firing device for guided missiles, which would enable them to bomb the coast from positions well under the horizon'.

The idea of off-shore bombardment by V1s from submarines had occurred to Dönitz on 28 September 1942 when Hitler had told him of the 'secret weapons' under development at Peenemünde, and had promised to launch a programme to modify them for use by U-boats. German security being what it was, word of this began to get out via Allied agents in Germany and leaks by U-boat prisoners of war, some of whom actually named the new rocket as *Raketen Tauch-Geschoss* (RTG), a rocket-propelled underwater missile, 20 years before Polaris.

The detail which the two spies provided made it unlikely that this was defiant boasting, and the authorities dared not dismiss it as an attempt at spreading terror propaganda. On 7 November a joint Army-Navy press release warned the American public, who had never imagined suffering the same front-line bombardment as England, that 'robot bomb' attacks on the USA were possible.

If the buzz-bomb story had been designed as morale sabotage, Admiral Ingram put it to the test on 8 January 1945, when he told a press conference, 'Gentlemen, I have reason to assume that the Nazis are getting ready to launch a strategic attack on New York and Washington by robot bombs . . . and that the East Coast is likely to be buzz-bombed within the next 30 or 60 days . . .' The warning made headlines from coast to coast, but there was no widespread panic. The prevailing attitude was that of New York's Mayor Fiorello LaGuardia, who told his citizens, 'We've got to hustle and provide our forces with everything they need so they can end the menace as soon as possible.'

12

DRAGOON

ORIGINALLY, as proposed and tentatively agreed at the Quebec Conference in mid-1943, a landing in the south of France (Operation 'Anvil'), was to be synchronised with the invasion of Normandy (Operation 'Sledgehammer'), to divide German forces in France and enable the Allies to go all-out either for the heart of Germany with a two-pronged attack, or for the southern force to extend Eisenhower's right flank (with captured Marseilles a far better port than Cherbourg to supply it) and to evict the U-boats from their last Mediterranean bases at Marseilles and Toulon. Such a move would also be of great political and sentimental value to the Allies, especially if French troops were used to liberate central and southern France, *la douce Provence*, where the FFI were already very strong. American leaders, including President Roosevelt and General Eisenhower, supported this plan, as did de Gaulle's Free French, but Winston Churchill opposed 'Anvil'. His eyes were on the eastern Mediterranean and a drive up through the Aegean (close to his Gallipoli failure in 1916) and the Balkans into Hungary and Austria, perhaps bringing Turkey into the war on the Allied side.

Roosevelt, along with Eisenhower, thought this scheme absurdly impracticable, and told General Maitland Wilson, Supreme Allied Commander in the Mediterranean, that the British Prime Minister's pet scheme 'must be sidetracked'.

'Sledgehammer' went ahead, its name changed to 'Overlord', 'Anvil' was postponed owing to a shortage of landing craft, and its name changed to 'Dragoon' because, Churchill growled, he had been *Dragooned* into accepting it. On 'Overlord' D-day plus one, 7 June, in France, and three days after the fall of Rome had signalled some progress in the Italian offensive, General Wilson quoted 15 August as D-Day for 'Dragoon'. But now Churchill came up with a variation on his Aegean caper, this time, in view of the advance in Italy, to push the Germans out of the boot into Istria and on through Yugoslavia into the Hungarian Plains to Budapest ahead of the Russians, and on to Vienna, where he envisaged a second great Congress to end the war there and then. He talked forebodingly of the 'rugged nature' of the Rhône Valley, its 'great hazards, difficulties and delays'. Roosevelt pointed out how much worse were the hazards of the Balkan plan, with the route to Hungary far more difficult than the Rhône Valley. Eisenhower insisted that there must be a second landing in France by 30 August. On 5 August after the Allied breakout in Normandy, Churchill, supported by American General Bedell Smith, proposed landing the 'Dragoon' troops in Brittany to reinforce the breakout, though the 42,000 troops for the landing were already in beaching craft in the Mediterranean, and as late as 9 August, D-6, Churchill was asking for this switch of plan. Although he failed to get his way, the familiar cherubic face, monster cigar and V-sign were seen on the bridge of HM destroyer *Kimberley* off the beaches of Provence on D-Day and heartily cheered, though his request to be landed with the troops was flatly vetoed by C-in-C Mediterranean. At least, he said, he had 'done the civil to Dragoon'.

THE NEED FOR CARRIERS

Under General Wilson, the invasion was the task of the Allied Seventh Army under Major-General Alexander M. Patch, USA, with Free French troops under General de Lattre de Tassigny, supported by naval forces under Vice-Admiral Henry K. Hewitt, USN, and air forces under Brigadier-General Saville, USAAF. Admiral Hewitt had been ordered on 1 February to plan and prepare for this operation. From the start it was clear that the distances from the nearest Allied air bases in the Mediterranean were generally too great for land-based air support on D-Day, and until airfields ashore could be captured.

From the nearest airfields, in north-western Corsica, directly to the landing beaches was some 160km (100 miles), to Marseilles 250 (155), Toulouse 530 (330), making no allowances for following highways or railway tracks as on an armed recce, or for avoiding heavy flak areas. The advantages of carriers operating offshore were obvious. As at Salerno, a squadron of Allied escort carriers armed with fighters only would be used almost exclusively to support the Army, but unlike Salerno the majority of the fighters were to be used offensively, for armed reconnaissance, ground support on call for the army units, and ground strafing sweeps over the landing area and beyond, as well as bombardment-spotting for the battleships and cruisers. This time, there would be no Fleet carriers giving deep support to the inshore CVEs, with all US big carriers committed to the Pacific, and British Fleet carriers also preparing to go east. With Italy out of the war, there was no possibility of attacks by heavy warships, and there were enough surface escorts to take care of U-boats. Luftwaffe strength in the Mediterranean was not great, owing to the demands of other fronts. The frail CVEs were to do the whole job on their own.

THE ROUND-UP

While the FAA's No 3 Fighter Wing had been receiving their army co-operation training for a land-based role in 'Overlord', No 4 had worked up for carrier-based duties in 'Dragoon', which was at this time still scheduled to coincide with the Normandy landings.

For 'Dragoon' the four Fighter carriers *Attacker, Hunter, Khedive* and *Stalker* were modified to Assault carriers. The fighter direction capability was retained but facilities were expanded to cover co-operation with amphibious forces and the Army ashore. Additions included: new radar; an operational telephone system with over 100 telephones; new briefing room, army plot and cabins around the Aircraft Direction Room so that key officers could operate for days on end in the immediate vicinity of their jobs – briefing pilots, collecting intelligence – and keep in touch with events by W/T and R/T. Little villages grew up under the flight deck in which departments fought for store rooms to hold radio gear, aircraft war stores, pyrotechnics and smoke equipment. 140 extra bunks were fitted for the increase in personnel, with more air ventilation, racks, hooks and lockers.

In the last fortnight of April four Assault carriers, *Bogue* Class boats *Attacker, Hunter* and *Stalker*, and the newer 'Ruler' Class *Khedive* ('Key-dive' to her ship's company), all reserved for 'Dragoon', had exercised with British troops in Ulster, then *Khedive* went into Rosyth Dockyard for repairs and modifications. While she was in dock her new Seafire LIIIs made themselves useful flying dawn and dusk patrols off the east coast of Scotland, with the occasional scramble to intercept German weather recce aircraft.

CVEs, unlike the *Illustrious* Class of Fleet carrier, as built, had lifts large enough to take a non-folding-wing Seafire, but more folding versions could be accommodated in a carrier's hangar or deck park than either the Hellcat or Corsair. The latter two Lease-Lenders entered FAA squadron service in autumn 1943, but the inevitable delays anticipated, owing to the 4,830km (3,000-mile) supply line from the USA and competition from the US Navy and Marine Corps for delivery (plus the fact that *Indefatigable* and *Implacable* lacked clearance in their hangars for wing-folded F4Us) made the first wing-folding Seafire essential.

The folding was introduced swiftly, partly due to earlier studies, and demonstrations followed by Seafire *MA970* in early November 1942. The C-wing folded upwards just inboard of the inboard cannon and downward at the wingtip, with a loss of only ten per cent in 'stiffness', and locked level at front and rear spars. With no power-folding, unlike the Hellcat and Corsair, the outboard cannon bay deleted, and the smaller fairings needed to fit the new Martin-Baker ammunition belt-feed mechanism, the overall weight increase was only 57kg (125lb). A more efficient Merlin 55 engine was fitted, and there was a gain of 32km/h (20mph) at all heights and in rate of climb in comparison with the LIIC, above 3,050m (10,000ft), the FIII being a medium- to high-level fighter. Delivery of 103 machines started in September 1943, but the FIII was soon outclassed and outnumbered by the LIII, with a more powerful, low-level, lighter exhaust system and the smaller Vokes carburettor air filter, and a consequent increase in low-level speed to 576km/h (358mph) at 1,830m (6,000ft). The first 38 LIIIs were non-folding (to be modified later), and equipped the two squadrons of No 3 Fighter Wing at the end of February 1944 for their land-based operations during 'Overlord', and HMS *Khedive*, the first CVE to receive the mark. The last version of the LIII was the FRIII, fitted with cameras for photo-reconnaissance, which served in the East Indies and Pacific.

Attacker, Hunter and *Stalker* joined a convoy for the Mediterranean, where the Luftwaffe had begun a new offensive against shipping. Their squadrons (4 Wing's 807, 809 and 879) were still equipped with non-wing-folding LIICs and LRIICs. They picked up some LIIIs at Gibraltar, but were still understrength. The three Assault carriers spent seven weeks in June and July in trade protection, with a few Swordfish for anti-submarine patrols. There were no air or U-boat attacks on any of the convoys they escorted.

Some of their Seafires were disembarked to North African airfields, from which they flew patrols over coastal shipping and, with the LIIIs and most of the LRIICs left on board or at Blida airfield near Algiers, Lieutenant-Commander George Baldwin, DSC, RN, led eight LIICs and 20 pilots from *Hunter*, eight LIICs and 14 pilots from *Stalker*, 12 LIICs and 18 pilots from *Attacker* to operate in Italy as 'D' Naval Fighter Wing with Spitfires of the RAF in support of the Army in its attack on the Gothic Line. Dust was an enemy, obscuring vision and necessitating the big tropical filters, which reduced speed. Six Seafires were destroyed, five badly damaged – a quarter of the front-line reserve for 'Dragoon', only three weeks away. On the other hand, the sort of work the Seafires had been doing was valuable practice for that operation.

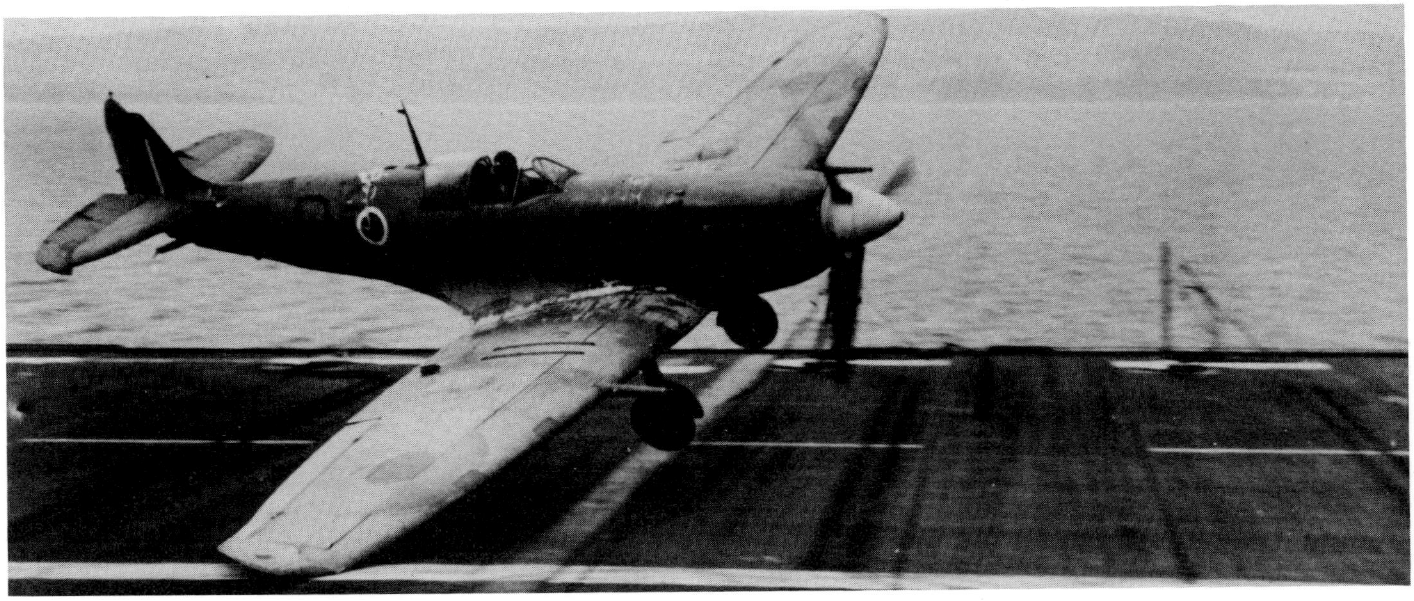

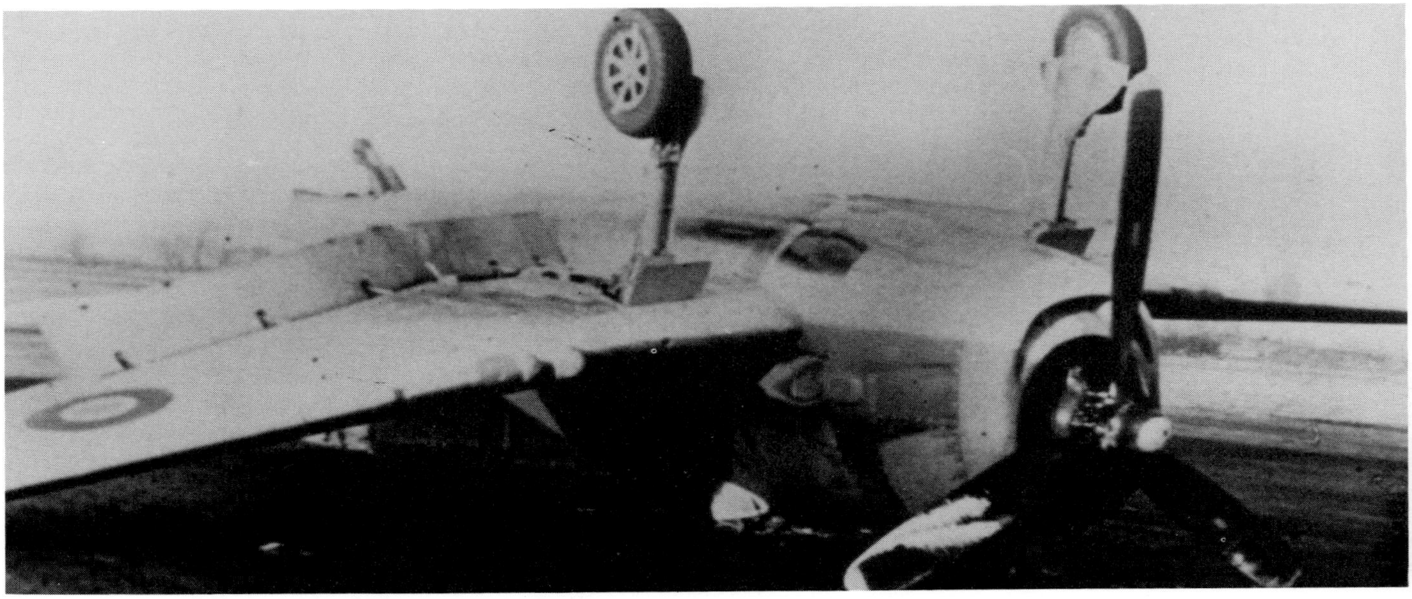

Right: Grumman F6F-3F of 800 Squadron, HMS *Emperor*. (J. M. Goulding)

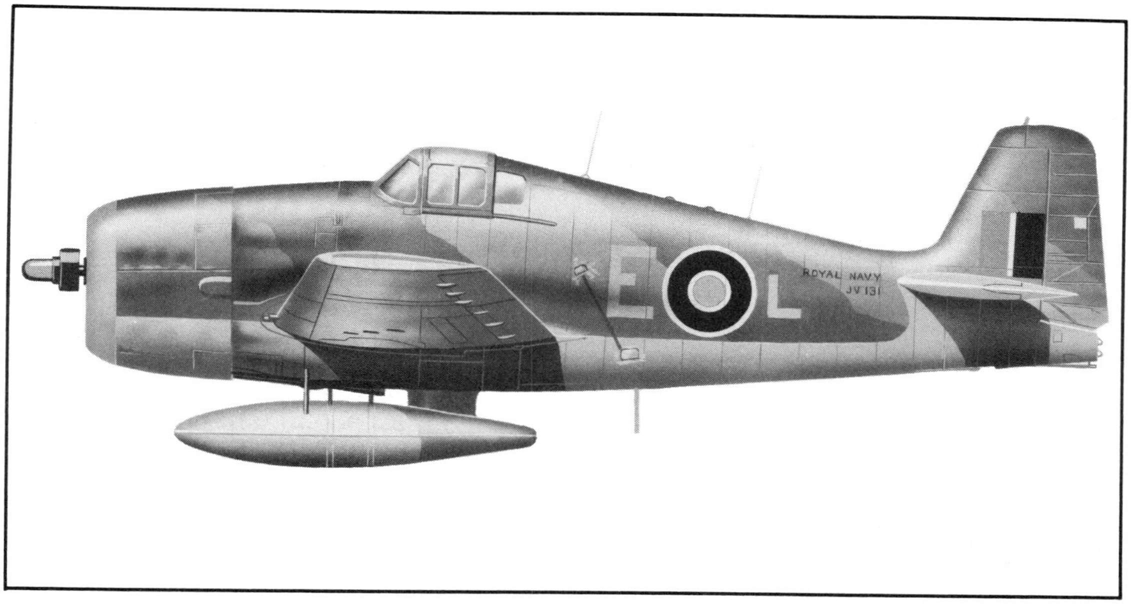

New Royal Navy Seafire and Hellcat pilots prepare for Operation 'Dragoon' with the training escort carrier in the Firth of Clyde. Here Seafire and Hellcat pilots learn the hard way aboard HMS *Ravager*, and another Hellcat just makes it, hook snagging the last arrester wire, prop chewing up the barrier. Other aircraft also used *Ravager*'s decks. A broken Corsair droops forlornly, and the future looks grim for one Avenger driver . . .

Assault carriers *Emperor* and *Khedive* and Fighter carriers *Pursuer* and *Searcher* left Home Waters on 15 July and reached Malta on the 25th. Meanwhile, Assault carriers *Attacker*, *Hunter* and *Stalker* gathered in the scattered units of their wandering 4 Wing. The land battle was to be a predominantly American operation, but the US Navy, with all its commitments in the Pacific, could contribute only two CVEs. On 2 May Rear-Admiral Calvin T. Durgin, USN, brought in USS *Tulagi* (CVE-72) and *Kasaan Bay* (CVE-69), and the Escort Carrier Squadron for 'Dragoon' was complete, with Admiral Troubridge flying his flag in the command cruiser HMC *Royalist*. Cal Durgin had been a naval aviator since 1920, and on his record were a Master's degree in aeronautical engineering and service in *Saratoga* and *Yorktown*. He had commanded USS *Ranger* off Casablanca in 'Torch', with the ex-oiler *Suwannee* attached to him, and had afterwards assessed the fighting value of the CVEs. Their low speed, he reported, lack of armour, and weak armament made it dangerous to use them where a confrontation with an enemy superior in these departments was likely, but with a more powerful group, or with adequate protection by their own air and naval forces, the 'Woolworth carriers' could do all that the Fleet carriers could do, and here he was with two of Henry Kaiser's assembly-line CVEs in a perfect situation in which to prove it. Both ships had been temporarily equipped with extra facilities for operating aircraft in support of troops ashore, but could not be thought of as equivalent to the more elaborately fitted-out specialist RN Assault carriers.

Right: Veteran, USN aviator, Rear-Admiral Calvin T. Durgin, in command of Task Group 88.2, composed of the Kaiser-built US *Tulagi* (CVE-72) and *Kasaan Bay* (CVE-69), and the Royal Navy's HMS *Hunter* and *Stalker*, for the Operation 'Dragoon' landings on the Riviera, South of France. Behind him are some of *Tulagi*'s TBFs and Hellcats. (US Naval Historical Center)

Rear-Admiral Sir Thomas Troubridge, another 'Torch' bearer, who had commanded *Furious*, *Indomitable* and the inshore CVEs off Oran, was in overall command of the 'Dragoon' squadron, Task Force 88, and in tactical control of the five CVEs forming Task Group 88.1, with Rear-Admiral Durgin commanding the four carriers of Task Group 88.2.

The two *Casablanca* Class US Navy CVEs had a two-knot advantage over the Lease-Lend Royal Navy carriers, a mixture of *Bogue* and 'Ruler' Classes, which made for less dramatic landings, and the Hellcats of both groups had twice the range (2,410km or 1,500 miles maximum) of the Seafires, plus greater durability. All the American Navy pilots had been fully trained in spotting and anti-submarine work but were short on co-operation with the Army. The two Wildcat squadrons (881 and 882) in the RN Fighter carriers *Pursuer* and *Searcher* each contained 12 pilots specially trained in spotting, to add to the 32 pilots of 4 Wing. The Observer/Fighter squadron in *Tulagi*, VOF-1, was the first carrier-based US Navy air unit to be given specialist training in bombardment spotting.

HMS *Emperor* had operated the Grumman Hellcat F6F in action from a Royal Navy escort carrier for the first time when her 800 Squadron had flown them in anti-shipping strikes off Norway in late 1943. In the USA 600 of these big brothers of the Wildcat were ordered straight off the drawing board in June 1941, and XF6F-1 flew shortly after the battle of Midway. After incorporating an improved 2,000hp Pratt & Whitney R-2800-10 Double Wasp engine in the design, stepping up fuel tankage, giving the pilot more armour protection, and making improvements in handling, the AF6F-3 was airborne a month later and the type was accepted immediately by the US Navy. In particularly great demand after the early failure of the Chance-Vought Corsair to pass its carrier qualification trials, the F6F was rushed through production, allocated to its first squadron in January 1943, and by the following September was the standard fighter in Mitscher's Fast Carrier Force.

The Hellcat was one of the finest all-round fighters of World War 2. The F6F-3 (and the Royal Navy's Hellcat I) had a top speed of 605km/h (376mph) at 5,270m (17,300ft), a range of 1,915km (1,190 miles) (normal) or 2,410km/h (1,500 miles) with drop tanks, an endurance of seven hours, a service ceiling of 11,580m (38,000ft), and was armed with six 0.50in Brownings, with racks for bombs and rockets. It was straightforward to handle, and its wide-tracked undercarriage gave it greater stability on the deck than the Wildcat. But it was two tons heavier, including its 22.7kg (50lb) of armour, 473l (125 gal) drop tank and standard

Right: USS *Kasaan Bay* from Rear-Admiral Durgin's flagship *Tulagi*, steaming for the Riviera. (US National Archives)

military stores, and needed 60m (200ft) more than the F4F to get airborne. The flight decks of the early escort carriers could not cope with it in low wind conditions and it was for them that the Goodyear FM Wildcats were designed. On 21 April 1944 production of the F6F-3 ended with the 4,403rd machine, of which the Royal Navy received 252 as the Hellcat I, as well as the improved F6F-5. The RN received 930 of these as the Hellcat II and 80 F6F-5N nightfighters, fitted with the excellent American AN/APS-6 radar.

THE LANDINGS

For ten days Task Force 88 exercised near Malta, to standardise US and RN carrier operating and tactical methods, and on 12 August sailed for the Riviera with its 224 fighters, plus one Swordfish in *Hunter* and a Walrus in *Emperor* for liaison and communication duties. At Casablanca and Solenzara in Corsica was a Royal Navy reserve of four Hellcats, eight Wildcats and 18 Seafires, reflecting the anticipated ratio of losses. Also at Casablanca were the seven US Navy F6F-3E night fighters of VF(N)-74 for night defence of the Task Force, and five Avenger TBM-1s of VC-74 to supply a communications and anti-submarine facility.

The invasion was preceded by a heavy four-day air bombardment of selected targets by XII Tactical Air Force. Before dawn on Love (Landing) Day, 15 August, there was a further massive bombardment by heavy bombers and by aircraft from Task Force 88. French Commandos and US

Right: Grumman F6F Hellcats aboard USS *Tulagi* en route for 'Dragoon'. USS *Kasaan Bay* is behind her, and a British-manned escort carrier leaves the convoy (left) presumably to operate aircraft for CAP (US National Archives)

Above: Seafire LIII activity aboard *Khedive* in 'Dragoon'. *Khedive, Hunter* and *Stalker* operated LIIIs, the first Seafire mark to encorporate folding wings. Here, all the wingtips are hinged downwards to reduce the overall area of the machines for hangar or deck parking, and one aircraft has been spotted diagonally on the lift for striking down into the hangar. Note 'K' (for *Khedive*) recognition letter painted on the lift – useful to prevent landing on the wrong carrier, which was not unknown, with many escort carriers so similar in appearance. (A. D. Brown)

Special Service battalions landed on the Hyères Islands and near Cape Negre to secure the western flank. Simultaneously, strong units of US, Free French and British paratroopers dropped 24km (15 miles) inland to block roads which might be used by the enemy for reinforcements. As in Normandy, there was at first light a heavy bombardment of coastal batteries and other fixed defences, by dive-bombers from TG.88.1 and gun and rocket fire from American Admiral Morton Deyo's battleship squadron. The landings, by 3rd, 30th and 45th Infantry Divisions of the US Seventh Army under General Patch and one Free French armoured combat command, went in at three beaches between Cap Benat, just east of Hyères, and St Raphael, just west of Cannes. Sea and sky conditions were perfect.

The two groups of Task Force 88 worked separately 48km (30 miles) offshore, usually within sight of one another. Flying operations began at 06:00. TG.88.1 operated over the beachheads, spotted for the naval guns and dive-bombed fixed defences. Low-level Seafires of *Attacker*'s 879 Squadron bombed enemy communications into the assault area near St Tropez, while *Khedive*'s 899 Squadron Seafire LIIIs flew CAP over the Group. Lieutenant-Commander F. M. 'Tiny' Fell, DSO,RN, led his No 7 Naval Fighter Wing of Hellcats and Wildcats from 800 (*Emperor*), 881 (*Pursuer*) and 882 (*Searcher*) Squadrons in dive-bombing and strafing, tactical recce, Force and beach cover. Visibility was generally poor but hits were made on forts and gun batteries. Because of the light wind, all aircraft carrying bombs had to be catapulted or 'Swanee ranged' and flown off using the full length of the flight deck, which meant hard work for the deck-handling party.

The Seafires of TG.88.2 from *Hunter* and *Stalker* flew mainly Combat Air Patrols over the carriers or the landing beaches, and at the end of D-Day had flown 86 sorties, Hellcats from *Tulagi* and *Kasaan Bay* flew fighter-bomber missions against targets near Frèjus, Cannes and Cap d'Antibes then beach cover from Cap Rous to St Maxime, and VOF-1's specially-trained Observer/Fighter Hellcats worked with *Nevada, Texas*, the US cruiser *Philadelphia* and the Free French *Montcalm* on spotting duties. One VOF pilot flew so low to observe the target that he hit a barrage balloon cable and had to make a water landing. Many aircraft on specific missions also struck targets of opportunity, and the railway was cut between Sisteron and Portuis, St Maxime and Aix, Arles and Miramas, and at several other points.

BREAKOUT

By the end of D-Day there had been only a feeble reaction by the enemy. Seventh Army was firmly established on the beachheads and probing

Right: Rear-Admiral Cal Durgin congratulates *Tulagi's* pilots for destroying a target beyond the reach of naval guns during the invasion of southern France, 16 August 1944 – photographed in the carrier's Ready Room. Note chalk board notice in the background: 'Be sure to charge guns on take-off'. (US National Archives)

inland, and on 16 August, D+1, armed recce with bombs and RPs was the order of the day. Aircraft which had been on CAP joined in strafing German troops and transport on the inland roads. Tiny Fell led an armed recce of eight fighter-bombers and hit a German Divisional Headquarters in a chateau. Hellcat fighter-bombers or long-range USAAF P-47 Thunderbolts bombed roads and railways, bridges, locomotives, freight cars and motor transport inland before flying CAP over the beaches. The CO of *Kasaan Bay*'s VF-74 skip-bombed the mouth of a railway tunnel, Seafires of *Stalker*'s 809 made three hits on a gun battery, and four Hellcats of *Tulagi*'s VOF-I were also reported to have put all their four 227kg (500lb) bombs inside the 15m (50ft) square surrounding a gun emplacement. An aggressive flight of 879's Seafires from *Attacker*, led by the Squadron CO, Lieutenant-Commander D. G. Carlisle, SANF(V), savaged a motor column near St Maxime. Coastal defences were again pounded by the guns of the Eighth Fleet, with the two Wildcat squadrons from *Pursuer* and *Searcher* and some of *Attacker*'s low-level Seafires spotting very effectively.

It was a bad day for accidents. Three of *Emperor*'s Hellcats, landing almost straight into the sun in a whisper of wind, hit the barrier, and a fourth was dumped into the port Goofers. Luckily all the pilots escaped injury. Two pilots flew Hellcats which could not carry bombs to Casablanca and brought back two better-equipped ones, and the ship's Walrus, wallowing in with two more Free Dutch pilots, racked up the carrier's 1,000th landing since her commissioning in December.

On the morning of the 17th, D+2, an armed recce aircraft sighted the enemy corvette *Uj 6081* off Toulon. Eight 88.2 Seafires strafed her, and she was sunk by destroyers. Some 85 troop and ammunition carriers were destroyed in attacks on columns of vehicles evacuating Brignols, Tourves and St Maxime, led by Springbok Carlisle's flight. In response to a call in the afternoon to knock out an aggressive battery still firing from the island of Port Cros, eight Seafire fighter-bombers from *Khedive*, four from *Attacker*, and Hellcats from *Emperor*, *Tulagi* and *Kasaan Bay* swamped it with direct hits. TG.88 aircraft continued to bomb roads and railways to slow down the rapidly retreating enemy and prevent reinforcements from reaching him.

There were fewer requests from Patch's thrusting GIs for specific strikes on the 18th, D+3, and with the chain of communication to the carriers via *Royalist* becoming more and more attenuated some planes arrived too late, but five armed recce missions hit rail and road transport east of the Rhône and as far north as Valence and Grenoble. *Stalker* Seafires attacked lighters off Cap

Right: Seafire LIII NM998 K-O of 899 Squadron lifts a 500lb bomb off *Khedive*'s deck for a 'Dragoon' strike.

Right: Its wheels still on the deck, a Seafire LIIC of *Attacker*'s 879 Squadron slams into the barrier, its carburettor air intake the first excrescence to be torn off. (R. C. Jonas)

Right: The starboard oleo leg of a *Khedive* Seafire LIII is collapsing, and the other one looks none too healthy. The Seafire's frail undercarriage was its weakest feature. (A. D. Brown)

Couronne, west of Marseilles, Hellcats of VOF-I and VF-74 hit trains near Carcassonne with RPs. *Searcher*'s Wildcats gave Force cover for ten hours.

GENERAL CHASE

Landings strips at Ramatuel and St Raphael were completed on the 19th, D+4. Let off the leash, the carriers swung west to a point 40km (25 miles) south-west of Marseilles and let loose more than 200 planes on the retreating enemy up the Rhône Valley. Low-level Seafires from *Attacker* were called in to dive-bomb a tank laager near Avignon, hit and brewed up a bunch of Tigers, and lost an LIII to flak, though the pilot, Sub-Lieutenant (A) A. I. R. Shaw, was captured uninjured, escaped, was recaptured, and escaped again.

Cal Durgin's deep-chested F6Fs from *Tulagi* and *Kasaan Bay* flew 320km (200 miles) west-nor'-west to bomb Toulouse Airport, the glider bomb base, where they hit buildings and destroyed five Dornier Do 217s, the missile-carriers. Near Avignon they sighted three Ju 52-3m transport planes and shot them down. It was the first day on which the carrier planes had met the Luftwaffe. In separate 190km (120 mile) sorties up to the Rhône Valley VF-74 Hellcats diverted 130km (80 miles) westward and destroyed two Ju 88s and a Do 217 near Issoire in the Auvergne 19km (12 miles) south-sou'-east of Clermont Ferrand, while VOF-I shot down three Heinkel He 111s and knocked out another on the ground.

PROFIT AND LOSS

Deck landing accidents had so far been far fewer than at Salerno, in spite of low winds and patchy visibility. Pilots this time were better trained, and the operation was conducted at a less frenetic pace. But the pilots needed rest, and ships replenishment. *Emperor, Attacker, Pursuer* and *Searcher* from TF.88.1 withdrew on the night of the 19th, D+4, for one day off at Maddelena, Sardinia. *Khedive*, with 18 of her original 26 aircraft still serviceable, only three combat losses and deck landing accidents suffered by her relatively inexperienced 899 Squadron, temporarily joined 88.2, in anticipation of increased spotting requirements. In this group *Hunter* and *Stalker* had hitherto suffered only minor deck-landing incidents, but now, with pilots growing very tired, a heavy swell began to rise, and there were some serious crashes, with four replacement aircraft also damaging themselves on arrival.

TF.88 was reduced by four carriers, but with Cal Durgin's 88.2 plus *Khedive*, flew an aggressive programme on the 20th, D+5, which more than made up for the reduced number of aircraft, but paid the price. The two American Hellcat squadrons spotted for the US battleship *Nevada* and the two cruisers USS *Augusta* and *Quincy* in a fierce bombardment of gun emplacements at San Mandrier and Cicie and west of Toulon, all of which were destroyed. One pilot was shot down by flak, but baled out safely north of Toulon into the hands of the Germans, who held him until the surrender of the port on 26 August. Meanwhile, the Seafire LIIIs of 807, 809 and 899 from *Hunter, Stalker* and *Khedive* flew all the combat air patrols and many of the 97 armed recce sorties which destroyed nine locomotives, ten rail cars and 118-plus motor vehicles west of Toulon, and immobilised ten barges in the harbour. Seafires of *Khedive*'s 899 and Hellcats from USS *Kasaan Bay*'s VF-74 dive-bombed a convoy of F-lighters in the Rhône delta, sinking four and driving six more aground, and a belligerent thrust up-river knocked out many road and rail targets.

In a search for more retreating motor transport Lieutenant-Commander H. Brink Bass, USN, CO of *Kasaan Bay*'s VF-74 and a veteran of the Battle of the Atlantic (where he had served as fighter leader of VF-29's 12 F4Fs in *Santee* and assisted in the sinking of *U-160* by John Ballantine's Fido on 14 July 1943), was hit by flak while leading a low-level attack near Chameler, north-west of Lyons, and his Hellcat was seen to crash and burn. His death was a particularly heavy blow to the squadron which he had so painstakingly trained. A damaged Seafire trying to land aboard *Hunter* after a hot and heavy armed recce crashed, killing the pilot (who, wounded, apparently lost consciousness as he touched down) and five ratings, and there was a similar accident aboard *Stalker*. Two Seafires were shot down, VF-74 lost four F6Fs, with three others damaged, while flak destroyed a VOF-1 Hellcat over Toulon.

Maximum effort was proving expensive, but there was no let-up. In a spectacular thrust late in the day westward across the Golfe du Lion and inland west of Carcassonne to a point 48km (30 miles) from the foothills of the Pyrenees, Hellcats destroyed 75 motorised vehicles in repeated hedge-hopping runs on three separate convoys. One plane was hit by flak but the pilot brought it down safely. He and a pilot from VF-74 shot down some 48km (30 miles) from the Spanish border were picked up by the Maquis, which was particularly active in this area, and passed down the river line back to the war through the Bordeaux area. These targets were the last motor convoy movements observed this far to the west. About the same time Toulon fell to the Maquis and Free French forces.

Khedive's 899 Squadron had escaped loss, and on the 21st took a day off at Maddelena to refuel and re-arm, as the main body of TG.88.1 returned and with *Hunter* and *Stalker* of 88.2 sent a tidal bore of over 100 fighter-bomber Seafires, Wildcats and Hellcats hunting up the Rhône Valley, destroying over 100 vehicles north of Avignon. Low cloud, industrial haze and the smoke from forest fires started by the Germans forced the

Right: A returning *Khedive* Seafire heads for the bridge island, its starboard wing cutting a swathe of destruction down the catwalk.

Right, centre and bottom: Seafire crashes aboard HMS *Khedive* in 'Dragoon', biting, rather than pecking, the flight deck. (Peter Embleton)

pathfinding TAC/R Seafires from *Attacker* to fly below 1,830m (6,000ft), the minimum safe height, and two of them were shot down, though the pilots survived. *Searcher*'s Sub-Lieutenant H. Wood did not return from an attack which destroyed a railway bridge and much of the track, and the Hellcat of *Emperor*'s Sub-Lieutenant Greve, one of an all-Dutch armed recce up the Rhône Valley, was shot down in flames but ditched in the river and the pilot was seen to swim ashore. His Dutch colleagues shot up a motor patrol boat heading for him. *Tulagi* and *Kasaan Bay* supported a heavy bombardment of Toulon and hit defences around Marseilles.

CLIMAX

The carrier planes reached the peak of their destructive effectiveness on this day, in pursuit of a fleeing enemy. Road bridges, rail junctions, trains, locomotives, many trucks and miles of track were destroyed. Retreating German columns, mostly in the Nimes-Remoulins-Uzes-Bagnols area north-west of the Rhône delta, were heavily attacked, many Germans killed in troop-laden trains and trucks, and over 225 motor vehicles destroyed or badly damaged. To the fore in this general chase were Tiny Fell and his hunting Grummans of RN 7th Naval Fighter Wing. Tiny found a road jammed for 65km (40 miles) with German transport and reckoned to have destroyed two-thirds of it before dusk came down. There was a bad crash in *Attacker* when New Zealander R. A. Gowan's Seafire LIIC caught a loose plate near the after lift with his hook, floated over wires and barrier and into the deck park, damaging four aircraft and breaking his leg. The guns of a wing-folded Wildcat in *Searcher*'s hangar were accidentally fired, wounding two ratings and penetrating three decks to hole a diesel oil tank, fracture a firemain and knock out the refrigerating machinery, and the ship herself was stopped twice with boiler trouble and steering motor failure. VOF-1 attacked barges in the Bouches du Rhône area near Arles, and south of the city two Hellcats already damaged by flak attacked three tri-motor Ju 52 transports flying in to evacuate key German personnel and, though further damaged by the Junkers' guns, shot them down into the salt marshes of the Camargue.

THE SEAFIRES' LAST FLING

With the Allied Army firmly in control, and the Germans everywhere in retreat, harried and slowed down by CVE and XII TAC fighter-bombers, the first, consolidating period of 'Dragoon' was over, and next day, 22 August, D+7, *Khedive* rejoined 88.1, and the redoubtable Durgin and his fighting 88.2 retired thankfully to Maddelena, dropped the hook in Arsacheva Bay, and the pilots rested or swam, while repair parties sweated over the aircraft in the baking hangars. *Tulagi* and *Kasaan Bay* had used up more bombs than *Hunter* and *Stalker*. They too were short on ordnance, but Captains Torlesse and Sinker felt generous. Boats and barges worked overtime transferring 227 and 113.5kg (500 and 250lb) bombs from the British to the American CVEs. But the latter were still short, and on the morning of the 23rd, D+8, with 88.2 due to relieve 88.1 in the combat area, *Tulagi* and *Kasaan Bay* got under way early to try to scrounge depth charges and more bombs from ships in Propriano Bay, but their stores were bare, and 88.2 finally sailed about 16:00 for the Côte d'Or.

Meanwhile, 88.1 had been having a last fierce fling at the enemy. On the 22nd a TAC/R flight from *Attacker*, unusually wide-ranging for the short-winded Seafires, reported a very big laager of enemy transport away to the west near the port of Narbonne on the coast of Corbières. There had been reports of a German armoured division there. Leaving *Searcher*'s Seafires to spot for the bombardment of Toulon, Troubridge steamed his other four carriers 190km (120 miles) to the south-west across the Golfe du Lion to a position 80km (50 miles) south of Narbonne, off Cap Bear, and flew off 84 fighter-bombers and 12 TAC/R aircraft to attack armoured cars, tank transporters, fuel bowsers, trains and rail track. At the end of a six-hour blitz 11 Panzer Division had lost over 50 irreplaceable heavy vehicles, several armoured vehicles and three locomotives. An all-Dutch flight shot up transport, and Tiny Fell and his Hellcats were in the thick of it as usual, bombing and strafing rolling stock and mechanised transport. Lieutenant (E) Rodgers, RN, dived into the ground while attacking a railway station and was killed. Pilots and flight deck parties were now very tired. In addition to Rodgers, *Emperor* alone lost three more Hellcats. One was badly damaged and ditched, Lieutenant Devitt, DSC, baled out when he could get only one wheel down, another pilot taxied over the side. There would have been more such incidents but for the patience and skill of batsmen like *Emperor*'s New Zealand DLCO Lieutenant Hill, MBE, and *Attacker*'s Lieutenant Longbottom. It was noticeable throughout the entire operation that the sleek and aerodynamic Seafires, though fragile deck-landers, could take off from the deck in light airs which forced the tubby Grummans, Wildcats and Hellcats to use the accelerators.

Khedive's 899 Squadron lost one Seafire, *Emperor* two Hellcats. On 23 August, D+8, the Wildcats of *Pursuer* and *Searcher*, took the spotting role off Toulon, while Seafires from *Attacker* and Hellcats from *Khedive* and *Emperor* flew offensive patrols. The carrier planes were beginning to run out of moving targets. They destroyed 60 lorries, staff cars and armoured cars in the Nimes-Bagnols area, and turned to the destruction of railway track, demolishing three bridges and cutting the

line in nine places. Aircraft losses continued. In *Emperor* one Hellcat flew into the barrier and was badly damaged, another taxied into a parked aircraft and chewed off its tail. When operations ceased the Squadron had lost 11 aircraft out of 27 in eight days' flying.

These were 88.1's last sorties in 'Dragoon'. At dusk on the 23rd the five carriers left for Maddelena and 88.2 took over once more. *Hunter* and *Stalker* had been unable to get either replacement aircraft or bombs at Maddelena and with 33 Seafires left out of an original 47, were restricted to strafing. Admiral Durgin's cautious retention of CAP further reduced the Group's offensive potential.

Toulon and Marseilles were now under heavy siege by the Allied Army. For two days, 24/25 August, the Seafires of *Hunter* and *Stalker* and the Hellcats of *Tulagi* and *Kasaan Bay* spotted for the ships bombarding Toulon and the Gulf of Foz area, Marseilles, the two islands Rattoneau and Pomegne west of the great port and Cap Croisette to the north-west. The CO of VOF-1 from *Tulagi* fell victim to the intense flak and was rescued from the sea by a destroyer. At the same time Seafire and Hellcat fighter-bombers hit the retreating enemy west of the Rhône under the direction of General Saville at XII TAC. Rhône bridges were prime targets. The bridge at Pont St Esprit was destroyed, and a big concentration of motorised and horse-drawn vehicles attacked to the south-west near Bagnols. More retreating transport was strafed and bombed further up the valley north of Montelimar, trains and lighters attacked. Two Seafires were lost, and one pilot taken prisoner. Other road and rail traffic trapped west of the Rhône was attacked, and two marshalling yards hit. A request to take out the bridge at Le Ponzin was answered promptly by dive-bombing VOF-1 and VF-74 Hellcats, which demolished it with one direct hit and several near misses and *Kasaan Bay* pilots blocked two other bridges.

THE HELLCATS TAKE THE WEIGHT

By this time most of the enemy had retreated beyond the Seafires' effective range. *Hunter*'s aircraft thrust up the Rhône for 190km (120 miles), their longest, and their last armed recce. A report of 'hundreds of M/T near Montelimar' resulted in the destruction of 41 motor vehicles and 15 rail cars. One *Stalker* pilot was shot down and killed on a low-level mission, and one *Tulagi* pilot took to the water. On 27 August, D+12, *Tulagi*'s hard-worked catapult broke down. The Army was fighting on the east bank of the Rhône to halt and destroy remnants of German forces trying to break out north. To the west targets were dwindling, and it was time for the Seafires to leave. At dusk on the 27th *Hunter* and *Stalker* were detached to CTF.88 at Maddelena.

Right: One of HMS *Searcher*'s Wildcats has written itself off on a gun sponson.

The two American Kaisers remained to fly any further missions needed. Their aircraft reconnoitred the Marseilles area at the request of USS *Augusta* and *Quincy*, made three last long-range strikes on M/T columns north of Montelimar, knocking out 45-plus vehicles and one locomotive, and blocked the bridge at Lavoulte minutes before the enemy could cross it. In their last fighter-bomber sortie Durgin's gung-ho Hellcats flew 300km (185 miles) up the Rhône Valley to within 16km (ten miles) of Lyons, but found only a few motor vehicles and one locomotive to attack. That day Marseilles fell, and 'Dragoon' was over.

The CVEs had exceeded all expectations. Only an auxiliary function in support of the advancing Army had been anticipated, with beach protection and CAP, but as the operation proceeded with little or no interference from the Luftwaffe it was soon obvious that the carrier planes were capable of offensive missions deep into enemy territory. The Hellcat for long-range work and the Seafire for short-range missions made such an effective team that the enemy was unable to prevent the consolidation of beach-heads, to regroup his forces for a stand further north, or to make an orderly withdrawal. The destruction of road and rail transport and coastal gun positions by the planes of TF.88 established a record.

The Grumman Hellcat was the star of the show. As spotter, fighter-bomber, RP platform in low-level tactical recce, or photo-recce missions, the big cat from The Iron Works was 'ace', a master of all trades frequently launched with a mix of bombs, belly tank and rockets to cover all demands in one armed recce sortie. Tanks, troops, trains, bridges, barges and planes were all the same to the F6F. Flak held no special terrors, air combat no fears. More returned shot-up than were shot down. In 'Dragoon' a daily average of 95 per cent availability was maintained aboard all Hellcat carriers. Cal Durgin was telling anyone who cared to listen that Hellcats with solid-head rockets replacing Avengers would save a lot of weight, crewmen and time to and over target. The US Navy accepted 12,275 F6Fs between January 1943 and September 1945. F6Fs shot down more than 5,100 enemy aircraft in World War 2 – 19 for every one of the 270 Hellcats lost in combat.

With the performance of *Tulagi* and *Kasaan Bay*, the welded, prefabricated, mass-produced Kaiser boats had once again proved themselves, against snide references to 'Woolworth carriers' and 'banana boats'. They could launch powerful new fighters like the Hellcat, even in zero wind. A *Casablanca* with 28 F6Fs or Corsair F4Us was a potent strike weapon, better than the C-3 conversions because they could park 16 Hellcats for'ard of the barrier, and with their simplified, prefabricated construction were far easier to maintain. Only *Tulagi*'s Flag communications facility could be improved, her Combat Information Center enlarged to control aircraft on offensive missions, all features which the British had fitted into Assault versions of the basic gift-horse American-built CVEs, like *Attacker*, *Hunter*, *Emperor* and *Khedive*, at the expense of some initial sea time and Admiral Ernie King's blood pressure.

13

THE MINING GAME

FOLLOWING the Allied invasion of France the war in the north flared up. Shipping routes down the Norwegian coast to Germany became more important to the Reich for the withdrawal of troops. With the loss of the French ports Bergen became the main U-boat base. With repairs to the damage done by Tungsten in April almost complete, *Tirpitz* would soon become a menace again, though the virtual end of the Battle of the Atlantic had released more carriers and Coastal Command squadrons for Norwegian and Russian waters. In fact the increase in attacks on Axis shipping had begun well before D-Day, 6 June.

Coastal Command strikes reached as far as the Kattegat. To the north, along the 640km (400 mile) stretch between Stadlandet and the mouth of Vestfjord, there were constant raids by aircraft from the new *Victorious*, the veteran *Furious* and CVEs *Emperor, Fencer, Pursuer, Premier, Searcher, Striker* and *Trumpeter*.

CANADIAN CARRIERS

On 10 August 25 Fighter Wing in *Indefatigable*, with its 887 and 894 Squadrons' Seafires, escorted the 'Ruler' Class Trade Protection escort carriers *Nabob* and *Trumpeter* on the minelaying Operation 'Offspring', a maiden strike for both CVEs. *Trumpeter*, laid down as ACV-37, USS *Bastian*, was launched on 15 December 1942 from the Commercial Iron Works, Portland, Oregon, and commissioned into the Royal Navy on 4 August 1943. *Nabob* was about a month behind her. Laid down on 20 October 1942 as ACV-41, USS *Edisto*, at the Seattle-Tacoma Shipbuilding Corporation yard, and launched on 9 March 1943, she was commissioned on 7 September of the same year. Because of the acute shortage of personnel in the Royal Navy, the Canadian government had agreed that the Royal Canadian Navy should man two escort carriers, HMSS *Nabob* and *Puncher*, with the RN supplying aircraft and air personnel. Captain Horatio Nelson Lay, RCN, a descendant of the man on the column, took command of *Nabob*. *Puncher*, laid down on 21 May, was still on the stocks.

By the end of December *Nabob* had 507 RCN men on board, 327 RN and nine RNZN, and resentment was growing on the lower deck among the RCN men because, with the ship under British Admiralty orders, they were given RN food, much inferior to RCN victuals, and in the RN contingent because the RCN ratings were receiving almost double their pay. Captain Lay put these grievances to his Admiral in Washington but got no reply. It was an inauspicious start to a commission.

Early in January 1944 *Nabob* embarked fuel, ammunition and stores and began working up. On the 25th she was in the Straits of Georgia, north-west of Vancouver, taking aboard the Avengers of No 805 Squadron, FAA, for their first deck landing. There was only about 9–10km (six miles) of water available for this, before the ship had to turn to avoid the sandbank at the mouth of the Fraser River and make another run into wind, and the landings went very slowly. When it came to the last Avenger in the circuit, the chart indicated that they had just enough room to take it aboard before they reached the sandbank. But the chart lied, and at 15:26, about two hours before high water, *Nabob* went aground. Another new CVE, HMS *Ranee*, tried in vain to tow her off, and finally, with the ship lightened by the discharge of 5,000 tons of oil fuel, avgas, ammunition and stores, two salvage tugs were called in to free her, luckily undamaged. After this she was called 'Canada Dry'. Arriving at the US Navy Almeda Air Base, San Francisco, on 7 February, *Nabob* embarked 13 Avengers of 852 Squadron by crane, and sailed again on the 15th with the USN Blimp *K115* as air escort, which caused much laughter until the first Avenger off the deck

Below: HMS *Trumpeter*, originally CVE-37, a Ruler-class escort carrier, ferries Mustang P-51B fighters from the USA to Britain. Almost all escort carriers performed this duty.

ditched ahead of the ship, and the blimp swooped down and dropped a dinghy so swiftly that all the pilot, who was alone in the aircraft, had to do was walk along the wing and get into the dinghy. But the crash was taken by some men as another bad omen.

The pay and messing grievance came to a head when some junior ratings locked themselves in their messdeck. When a patrolling Avenger reported a U-boat, 'Action Stations' brought the 'mutineers' rushing to their posts, but at Norfolk many men, most of them French Canadians, bloody-minded over the poor food and the discovery that they were leaving Canadian waters, deserted the ship. With some difficulty Lay got his gout-ridden admiral on the phone and explained the problem, serious enough to prevent the ship from sailing. Not only was the food greatly improved but the whole ship's company received RCN rates of pay, and went on their way rejoicing to Staten Island, where *Nabob* embarked a deckload of 45 P-51 Mustang fighters, and on 23 March sailed in US troop convoy UT-10 for the UK, to an empty Belfast Lough, with everyone gone to keep a date off Normandy.

Fog threw a blanket over *Nabob* one night, with all 12 TBFs airborne. Bats got them all down but one. Waved off once, the mist-veiled Grumman appeared again low off the bows, and hit the water with two fat 136kg (300lb) DCs in the belly set to 7.6m (25ft). At 7.6m they duly exploded. The pilot was blown up through the canopy and amazingly picked up alive by *Nabob*'s destroyer plane guard. Flag Officer Training came out from his lair at Larne to check the carrier out, and said, 'Lay, your ship is in reasonable condition but your Air Department is awful,' then departed. He took the ship's Commander (F) with him and next day sent out a relief, who had just two days to pick up the pieces and put them together, with *Nabob* due to join the Home Fleet at Scapa.

To Scapa they went, in company with *Trumpeter*, to join the First Cruiser Squadron under the orders of CS.I, Rear-Admiral R. R. McGrigor, CB, DSO, RN, but not before Paymaster Charlie Dillon had stolen the band from the RCN cruiser *Ontario*, some time off completion, so that the first Canadian carrier swung to her anchorage in The Flow to the tunes of 'O Canada' and 'The Maple Leaf Forever', which caused the sailors and men aboard the lonely Canuck destroyers *Sioux* and *Algonquin* to swell with pride.

OPERATION 'OFFSPRING'

It was decided to mine the Norwegian 'Leads', channels running between the coast and outlying islands, much used by German shipping. On 9 August CS.I, in the fleet carrier *Indefatigable*, with *Nabob*, *Trumpeter*, cruisers and destroyers, sailed for Norway to lay mines in the Leads north-east of Alesund, protected in the air by Hellcats, Seafires and some of the new Firefly two-seater fighters. The six Avengers of 852 Squadron were launched from *Nabob* and took station astern the 18 Avengers of *Trumpeter*'s 846 Squadron which, led by Lieutenant-Commander 'Bobby' Head in his Avenger *FN909*, Observer Lieutenant (A) Jeff Powell, RN and TAG PO G. Wells, RN, shaped course in the dull, grey afternoon towards Lepsörev Channel and Haarhams Fjord. Landfall was made on Storholmen Light, where the Avengers formed up in column of sub-flights of three and, ably protected by flak-suppression Fireflies and top-cover Seafires, flew in firm formation at 60m (200ft) through ragged flak, and simultaneously laid 23 standard Mk VIII mines, each with a different delay. Distant and top cover Seafires added an appropriate bonus by sinking the 90-ton German minesweeper *R-89*, as well as setting a radio station on fire and destroying six Messerschmitt Bf 110s on Gossen airfield. An exceptionally heavy barrage met a second minelaying strike and shot down one Avenger and a Firefly. The Avengers laid a total of 47 mines in the biggest carrier minelaying sortie of the war. The Avenger lost, *FN830*, took its crew with it,

Below: Strike. Avengers and Wildcats of *Trumpeter*'s 846 Squadron have been brought up from the hangar in preparation for a strike in Norwegian waters. (Cdr J. Powell)

Right: Strike. Avengers head for the Lepsorev Channel in Operation 'Offspring', the biggest carrier minelaying sortie of the war, led by Lieutenant-Commander Head's 'flagship' Avenger FN909. (Cdr J. Powell)

Right: Strike. Stornholm Light, one landfall for Avenger strikes in Norwegian waters. Aircrews and lighthouse keepers would wave to one another, and the airmen would throw down cigarettes and packets of chocolate. (Cdr J. Powell)

Below: Strike. Mine drop by Avengers of 846 (*Trumpeter*) and 852 (*Nabob*) Squadrons. (Cdr J. Powell)

Below right: Strike. Mine ricocheting off the water. (Cdr J. Powell)

Right: Swordfish Mark III, fitted with RATOG and new ASV XI radar (Note its aerial on the wing strut of the photographing aircraft) with its unmistakable bulbous scanner housing beneath the forward fuselage. To save weight, the TAG's position was eliminated from the rear cockpit.

pilot Sub-Lieutenant (A) Johnny Gaunt, TAG Petty Officer Airman Ashton, RN, and Observer Sub-Lieutenant (A) 'Alfie' Salisbury, who had been engaged to be married. In May 1986 his close squadron friend Morley Wheeler, who was to have been his best man, visited Alesund, and passed over the spot where Alfie and his crew lie, a personal mission fulfilled after many years.

'VICTUAL' TO RUSSIA

A repaired *Tirpitz* lurked in Kaafjord, new U-boats in Bergen harbour, but convoys to Russia could be delayed no longer, and events in France had released many of the Neptune escorts and aircraft. German forces everywhere were on the defensive, but Vice-Admiral Sir Frederick Dalrymple-Hamilton was given a strong force for Operation 'Victual', the passage of Convoy JW59 to Russia. His flagship, the cruiser *Jamaica*, and the 'arcticized' CVEs *Vindex* and *Striker* would form the Heavy Escort, with five destroyers and the 20th Escort Group.

'GOODWOOD' FOR *TIRPITZ*

It was essential to prevent *Tirpitz* from attacking the convoy, and Operation 'Goodwood', the largest Home Fleet sortie with aircraft ever planned, was mounted, in two Groups, Force 1 with *Indefatigable, Formidable* and *Furious*, three cruisers and six destroyers, and minelaying Force 2, *Nabob* and *Trumpeter* and five frigates, with three heavy cruisers, six destroyers and five frigates as a covering force. Admiral Dalrymple-Hamilton transferred his flag to *Vindex*, the better to keep in touch with flying operations, direct tactics and co-ordinate the actions of air and surface escorts. It was the first time a Royal Navy CVE had worn an Admiral's flag, a symbol of the proper status of the much maligned vessels.

Before sailing the five carriers of Force 1 rehearsed take-off, forming up in a single formation of about 150 aircraft below 90m (300ft), and carrying out dummy strikes on Loch Eriboll on the northern Scottish coast, which resembles Kaafjord from the air, with the additional help of scale models of the fjord and surrounding terrain, and good photographic coverage. Nearly 200 aircraft, the largest number yet operated together by a British fleet, were to be flown off these carriers. Barracudas were to dive-bomb *Tirpitz*, protected by Hellcats, Corsairs and the new Fireflies, while Seafire fighter-bombers would attack other shipping. Two Avenger squadrons, 853 in *Nabob* and 846 in *Trumpeter*, led by Lieutenant-Commanders 'Bobby' Bradshaw and 'Bobby' Head, RN, both veterans of strikes in the Mediterranean, were to synchronise mine drops, 853 alongside *Tirpitz*, with 12 mines set at various time delays, 846 across the narrow entrance to Kaafjord from a height of 15m (50ft).

VINDEX AND *STRIKER*

At 11:00 on 15 August *Vindex, Striker* and *Jamaica* sailed to catch up with the convoy: 28 freighters, 14 of them carrying explosives; two tankers; two escort oilers; a rescue ship; a special crane ship, and 12 MTBs for the Russian Navy.

The Heavy Escort rendezvoused with the ten columns of the convoy at 09:30 on 17 August and the two carriers took station in the box, four stations deep, aft of the four short centre columns. Missing from Column 5 was the battleship USSR *Arkhangelsk*, formerly HMS *Royal Sovereign*, now known in the RN as *The Royal Rouble*, due to join the convoy with eight old ex-US Navy four-piper destroyers latterly in RN service which had also been handed over to the Soviet Navy.

Striker's 824 Squadron flew off Swordfish anti-submarine patrols, but became completely hidden in fog, and the returning machines had to land aboard *Vindex*. At noon on 18 August the 'Goodwood' force left Scapa Flow for Norway and the

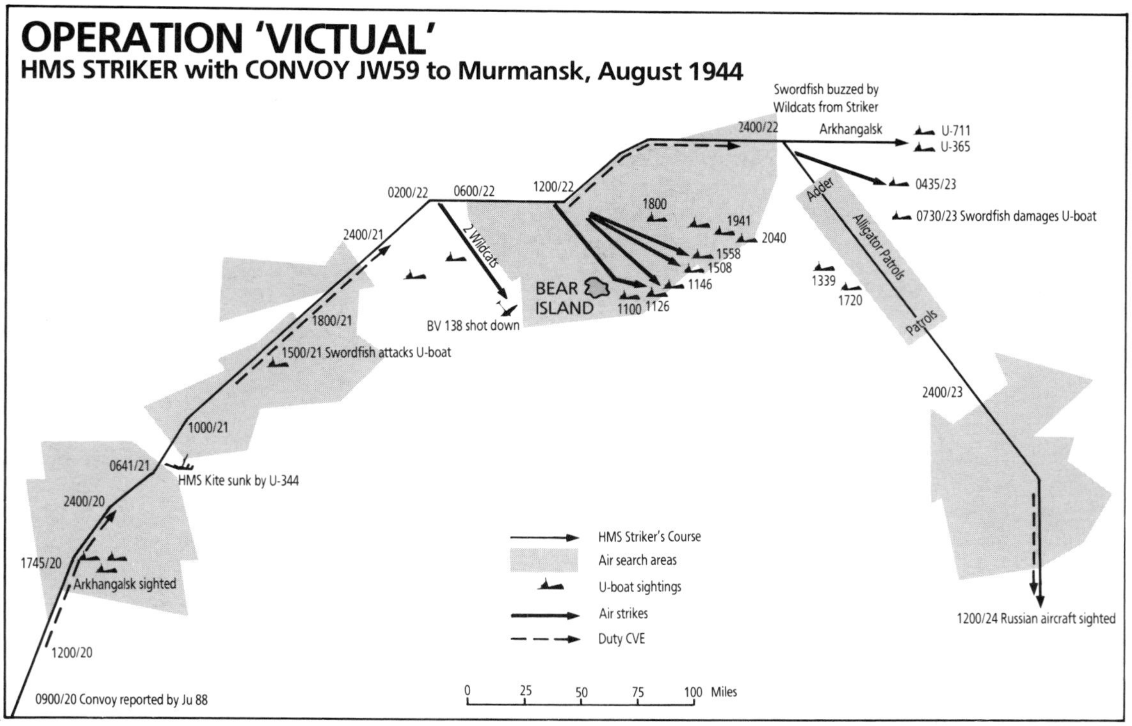

Right: HMSS *Striker* and *Vindex* escorted JW59 to Russia (Operation 'Victual') in August 1944. On the 22nd, Sub-Lieutenants J. D. Lacey and B. J. C. Dibben from *Striker* shot down a shadowing Blohm & Voss Br 138 flying-boat.

Right: Snowman, temporary addition to *Vindex*'s ship's company, in Operation 'Victual', with *Striker* astern.

Tirpitz, which lay at short notice for steam in Kaafjord, with *Vindex* flying off single Swordfish on Viper patrols. It was decided to divide the duty of Controlling CVE into 12-hour periods, with *Striker*'s aircraft flying the 'daylight' patrols, and *Vindex*'s Swordfish, with their new ASV Mark XI radar, making the 'night' flights, the two ships relieving each other at 10:00 and 22:00 daily. In reality the further north they steamed the longer grew the daylight hours, until the sun just kissed the horizon and rose again, even though it was two months past Midsummer's Day. At 17:45 on the 20th the high spotting top of the *Royal Rouble* was sighted from a *Vindex* Swordfish as the ponderous old battler wallowed along butting high seas and headwinds, and Admiral Levchenko joined up at 22:15.

FIRST LOSSES

Secret Ultra information from decoded U-boat signal traffic had indicated the likely positions of U-boats across the convoy's path, and at 06:44 the sloop *Kite* had slowed to clear her tangled foxers when she was hit by two Gnats from Kapitänleutnant Pietsch's *U-344*. The sloop heeled over, her stern broke off and she sank. The destroyer *Keppel* stopped and with great difficulty rescued just 14 men from the bog of thick, choking oil on the sea.

Vindex's plot showed three U-boats astern and closing, with another approaching from the east, and she sent Swordfish after them, four at a time through the night. Wildcats from *Striker* and Sea Hurricanes from *Vindex* hunted bogies, and at 03:10 on the 22nd New Zealanders Lucey and Dibben in a Wildcat pair chased a Bv 138 through cloud and shot it down in flames. At 08:30 Gordon Bennett and his observer Peter Couch were returning to *Vindex* in bright, slightly cloudy weather, with hailstorms, when they sighted a U-boat 5km (three miles) off to port. It was *U-344, Kite*'s destroyer. Bennett made his approach from astern, using his boost override to squeeze every knot he could out of the slow Stringbag, weaving in evasive action. From 15m (50ft) he dropped his stick of three Mk XII Torpex DCs, set for 6.7–7.3m (22–24ft). The first splashed alongside the sub's starboard quarter, the second amidships, while the third hit the fo'c's'le, rolled down the canting deck and lodged under the mine guard at the bows. Ten seconds later, with the U-boat's bows at about 7m (24ft), this charge went off, and *U-344*, propellers still turning, took another crew to their deaths in the depths of the Arctic Ocean.

In sunshine and clear skies at 11:00 *Striker*'s Mark II Swordish 'X', pilot Sub-Lieutenant (A) T. G. Hounslow, RNVR, with an Oscar on his racks, sighted a U-boat, armed his 'mine', and closed her. She opened fire on him, increased speed, zizagged then turned hard-a-starboard and dived. Hounslow followed her round and dropped his Oscar 180m (200yd) ahead of the swirl. There was no sign of a hit, but his markers were sighted by three Sea Hurricane pilots from *Vindex*, who attacked with RPs. The U-boat submerged, and Sub-Lieutenant Talbot in Striker's Swordfish 'B' dropped his Oscar. Five minutes later a big patch of fresh oil spread over the surface.

STHAMER STRIKES

Meanwhile the Goodwood aircraft were at least keeping *Tirpitz* bottled up in her fjord. *Nabob*, carrying four Wildcats and 14 Avengers, and *Trumpeter* were to have flown off a strike with mines, but low cloud over the target stopped the operation. At 17:16 the afternoon was still bright and sunny. *Nabob* had just finished recovering her aircraft, and was preparing to refuel her three frigate escorts as Force 2 withdrew to the west. Captain Lay was on the bridge watching men dragging the fuelling hoses along the flight deck. Below on the seamen's messdeck Able Seaman Tony Tickner, the mess' singalong pianist, was leading a singsong at the piano. 'You'll never know', sang Jack-my-Hearty, 'just how much I love you . . .' The ship had been closed up at action stations all day, and 'Up spirits!' had just been piped. Outside the Spirit Room down in the depths of the ship the mess rum bosuns with their mess kettles were waiting to draw the issue, supervised by Lieutenant J. B. Goad, RCNVR. At the periscope of *U-354* Kapitänleutnant Hans-Jurgen Sthamer took one last look at the sitting targets before his eyes . . . 'Fire!' A spread of torpedoes left his forward tubes.

In *Nabob* the song was coming to its end. 'You'll never *know* . . .' Tony's singer struck the G-minor chord, and Hans-Jurgen Sthamer came in on cue . . . BANG! Up on the bridge Captain Lay saw his motor boat disintegrate before his eyes, and thought he must be dreaming.

The torpedo hit the carrier on the starboard side well abaft the engine room bulkhead, and the ship took a 70 degree list. The explosion killed five men in the naval airmen's berthing space just under the hangar deck, and caused heavy flooding. The Spirit Room area was flooded almost immediately and everyone outside it was killed except Lieutenant Goad, who floated up as the water rose through three decks and ended up in the after elevator well, where someone saw him floating and fished him out. Another lucky man was a stoker who was washed out of the shaft tunnel and landed up unhurt on the quarterdeck. In the ship's galley the cooks were desperately trying to avoid the scalding steam from fractured pipes.

The ship continued to go ahead slowly but all electrical power had gone. The engine room fans stopped, and when the temperature there reached 65°C (150°F) it was evacuated. *Nabob* lacked the watertight bulkheads of a regular warship, and the ship rapidly sank from a draught of 7m (24ft) to 13m (42ft). The large 'tween-deck hatches not being watertight, flooding rose to the galley deck, where vents allowed the air to escape, preventing the hangar deck from collapsing.

Below: *Nabob* drags her tail as she struggles to reach home. (Cdr J. Powell)

At about this moment Sthamer struck again. A Gnat acoustic torpedo from *U-354* hit SO Escort's sloop *Bickerton* and blew the whole stern off, killing more than 40 men. Her siren jammed in the 'on' position, so that she seemed to be moaning piteously at her fate. She was eventually sunk by HMS *Vigilant*.

NABOB'S ORDEAL

In *Nabob* Engineer Lieutenant Forrester's damage control parties were shoring up bulkheads, none of which had given way so far. Strongest of all was the engine room bulkhead, which was some way from the explosion and as far as could be seen had not been weakened by it. HMS *Kempthorne* came alongside and took off the 214 Fleet Air Arm personnel, ten of them wounded. The auxiliary generators were started and soon the fans were running again in the overheated engine room. When the temperature there was back to normal the engine room staff were able to start raising steam again. Engineer Hinchcliffe told Captain Lay that they would be able to go ahead slowly. Although the propeller shaft tunnel was flooded, the shaft and screw and the engines appeared to be undamaged. Flooding was under control by 19:00, and cautiously they started to steam ahead at 4½ knots, later increased to 10, on course for Britain, escorted by *Trumpeter*, the mining strike having been finally abandoned. To lighten the stern the two 5in guns on the quarterdeck were cut up with acetylene torches and thrown overboard, while the aircraft and anything else movable were pushed right for'ard.

Below: Stores are jettisoned from *Nabob* to lighten ship. Foreground is the ship's HF/DF aerial mast, to the left two twin Oerlikon sponsons. (Donald Cash)

Bottom: Life-rafts on *Nabob*'s flight deck for emergency, with the stricken carrier in a sinking condition. (RCN)

Later that evening *Nabob*'s Huff-Duff intercepted a signal from a U-boat following her close astern. In spite of the heavy draft aft and the possibility that the catapult might have received some hidden damage, the Squadron CO, Lieutenant-Commander 'Bobby' Bradshaw, insisted on trying an assisted launch. With Senior 'O' Lieutenant R. E. Parkinson and TAG CPO 'Cab' Galloway, he got off safely in the dark, and *Nabob* boosted off another Avenger, piloted by Sub-Lieutenant Jupp. The two TBFs flew for four hours in the fog and darkness, then had to be brought aboard *Nabob*'s tilting deck.

Jupp's Avenger arrived first and made a good landing, but by the time Bradshaw approached, the ship was in a fog belt. He was almost out of fuel, and his landing had to be a first-timer. In the aircraft they could see *Nabob*'s masthead above the fog but could not make out her heading. Captain Lay switched on the ship's forward searchlight, which at least showed them where the bridge island was, and Bradshaw came in blind. He had got his bearings almost right. The heavy Avenger floated up the angled deck and crashed into the parked aircraft, wrecking two Avengers and damaging four other aircraft. The shock triggered off Bradshaw's guns, his DCs fell off and rolled about the deck, but an intrepid party of seamen managed to secure them at the cost of a few crushed fingers and toes. The wrecks were then cleared away smartly in case the sorties had to be repeated.

That evening a further 200 of the ship's company were transferred to the destroyer HMCS *Algonquin*, and all spare aircraft dinghies were inflated and together with several rafts were lashed down on the flight deck. At first Lay headed for the Faeroes, the nearest land, with *Trumpeter* in attendance, 'until *Nabob* sinks', as someone said, but as the distance shortened it was decided to try and make Scapa.

On the 23rd the weather turned windy and the sea rose. The hangar deck now bulged upwards some 60cm (2ft) for over half its length, and Forrester watched anxiously the dividing bulkheads below, which were all-welded. Morale was not improved by a ghostly moaning which echoed through the hangar as the ship pitched or rolled. The damage control parties reinforced the threatened bulkheads with more timber. With the ship's galley destroyed, food for everyone was prepared in the wardroom galley and served on the hangar deck, and the mainbrace was spliced regularly. Finally, after almost 1,770km (1,100 miles) of laboured steaming, they reached Scapa. C-in-C Home Fleet came aboard. 'I never thought she would survive,' he said. The ship was towed to Rosyth to go into drydock. There was a great hole 50 feet by 40 feet in her thin merchant hull and so much damage that the Admiralty paid off *Nabob* on 30 September. Other carriers started to 'borrow' various items from her to replace damaged equipment, and eventually she was thoroughly cannibalised.

Meanwhile, *Tirpitz* remained undamaged, and it was essential that another strike be mounted against her before she could attack the convoy, even with the Goodwood force in the offing. JW59's escorts had enough on their hands hunting the U-boats chasing them. Just after 15:00 *Striker*'s Swordfish 'B' sighted a U-boat trailing a big oil slick, which dived before the Stringbag could use its RPs. 'B' dropped its Oscar, with no noticeable results. Another U-boat, sighted by a Swordfish 50 minutes later, also got away. The convoy was getting too far off track for Kola, and swung back due east. U-boat transmissions filled the air in the south and south-east. Twice more Swordfish from *Striker* sighted U-boats, but could not reach them in time, though they were keeping the enemy submerged. At 09:30 on 22 August *Vindex* took over Controlling CVE for the night. Half an hour later Sub-Lieutenants Eric Johnson and Malcolm Piercy got a contact on their ASV to the south-east, flew down the bearing and found a surfaced U-boat, which dived before they could reach it. Just before midnight Peter Cumberland reported a U-boat 67km (42 miles) south-east of the convoy. This boat opened fire on them, and two Sea Hurricanes were scrambled from *Vindex*. The U-boat dived and disappeared, and Cumberland dropped his B-bomb in the swirl. A relieving Swordfish crew reported a big patch of oil, pieces of wood and large lumps of congealed diesel oil.

At 02:15 on the 23rd the convoy turned south for Kola, with three U-boats ahead of them. At 03:03 Bennett's Swordfish 'M' got an echo 14km (nine miles) on their port beam. In clear light they saw a U-boat, a long black shape. Bennett closed her. Puffs of smoke rose round her as she opened a hot fire with pom-pom and cannon. Shells burst near the fragile biplane. Bennett went down to 550m (1,800ft), and saw the U-boat submerging. He dropped three DCs which brought up thick oil and debris. At 16:35 a Swordfish had a brush with a 750-ton U-boat, steering for the convoy, and all its RPs failed. At 07:30 two Sea Hurricanes chased a bogey which turned out to be a Soviet-manned Catalina of the 118th Reconnaissance Regiment, the beginning of air cover from Russia. At 13:45 a *Striker* Swordfish duelled with a heavily armed U-boat, dropped DCs when it dived, and oil arose. At 02:35 Shaw's Swordfish from *Vindex* sighted a trimmed-down U-boat 87km (54 miles) north-west of the convoy. U-boats were now converging on JW59 from all points of the compass. Shaw attacked through thick flak with RPs and claimed two hits. He had found Hans-Jurgen Sthamer's *U-354*, *Nabob*'s attacker and *Bickerton*'s

Right: Crack Swordfish crew, Sub-Lieutenant(A) Eric Johnson, pilot, left, and Sub-Lieutenant(A) Malcolm Piercy, observer.

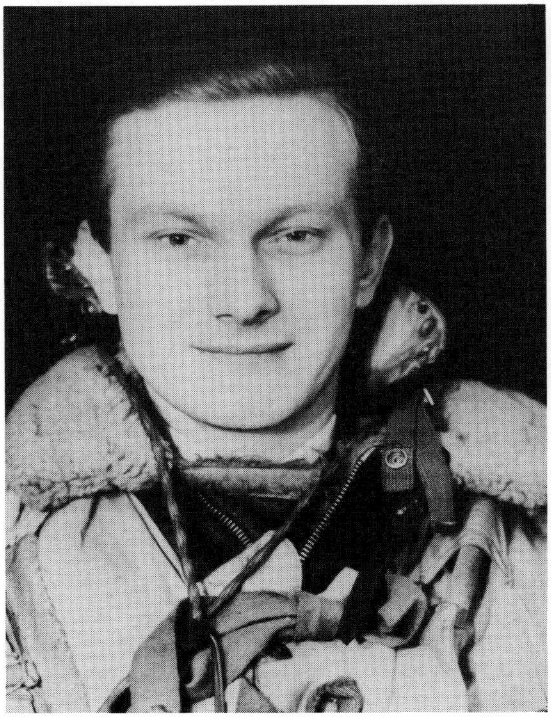

killer. A sloop appeared and a long hunt began with DCs, Squid and Hedgehog missiles. Oil surged up, and *U-354* never returned to port.

That afternoon the 'Goodwood' Barracudas, bombing blind through the smoke screen, hit *Tirpitz* with two bombs, while Seafire fighter-bombers attacked the U-boat anchorage at Hammerfest. Up in the Barents Sea the U-boats were dropping astern. *Vindex, Striker* and *Jamaica* shepherded 16 ships to Kola Inlet. The other 17 merchantmen sailed on a further 724km (450 miles) east to the White Sea and the ports of Arkhangelsk, Bakharitza, Ikonomia and Molotovsk.

Vindex, Striker and *Jamaica* sailed again on 28 August, overtaking UK-bound RA59A five hours later. As on the outward run there was little darkness on passage, but fog prevailed. Pilots made blind landings by the Morrison Method, and *Vindex* took on all routine searches until the weather cleared, while to the south Goodwood's Barracudas were bombing blind through the thick blanket of smoke and flak round *Tirpitz*, which remained virtually undamaged. A total of 116 bomber and fighter-bomber sorties had produced only two direct hits, one of them a dud. It took two squadrons of RAF Lancasters with 5,443kg (12,000lb) bomb to sink *Tirpitz*, on 12 November.

The aircraft and men of *Vindex* were showing signs of wear and tear. There were engine failures, duff DCs and RPs, erratic compasses, ASV black-outs, and good airmen grew tired. Eric Johnson's Stringbag, landing with failing oil pressure, bounced off the bridge island into the sea upside-

Right: On 1 September 1944 during the passage of Convoy RA59A from Russia to the UK, Sub-Lieutenant(A) J. C. H. Simpson's Swordfish LS231 missed the arrester wires, ran with some force into the wire safety barrier, and its Bristol Pegasus engine fell off. Thankfully, the 250lb depth-charge left on its starboard wing was not dislodged by the shock. (Cdr Stenning)

Right: *Vindex*, 4 September 1944, returning with Convoy RA59A from Russia. A Sea Hurricane has crashed into the deck park composed of another Sea Hurricane and two Swordfish, writing itself off and badly damaging the other aircraft.

Left: 'Begonia' targets. The MV *Deutsche Levant* is shrouded in smoke, three minesweepers and a flak ship can be seen. (Cdr J. Powell)

Left: The mining game. Mine-carrying Avenger of 846 and 856 Squadrons sow magnetic mines in the narrow Salhusstrommen Channel on 13 January 1945, supported by Hellcats. (MoD(Navy))

down and on fire, *Vindex*'s port whaler came to the rescue. New Zealander Johnny Moore was given the cut just as *Vindex*'s stern rose and batted the Sea Hurricane into the deck park, almost wrecking another fighter and two Swordfish. *U-394* was destroyed by escort vessels, the kill evidenced by thick oil, wreckage and human remains.

'*Campania*', wrote Peter Cockrell, one of the new carrier's divisional officers, 'was not beautiful, and quite difficult to handle with a stiff wind on the beam, but I grew to like the old lady.' Early in September, commanded by Captain K. A. Short, RN, she joined *Striker* for 'Rigmarole', the passage of JW60 and RA60, with the 12 Swordfish IIIs and four Wildcat VIs of 1813 Squadron and three experimental night-flying Fulmars.

To coincide with 'Rigmarole', Operation 'Begonia' was organised, a mine drop by 18 Avengers from *Trumpeter* (nine of her own 846 Squadron, nine from *Nabob*'s 852) in Aaramsund, 96km (60 miles) south-west of Molde. Nearly all the ex-*Nabob* aircraft had been damaged on disembarkation but their maintainance crews had not followed them, and the 846 Squadron mechanics worked all-out to have the 18 machines ready. *Trumpeter* was overcrowded with aircraft, so that those to the front of the range would have to be catapulted until there was deck space for the rest to make a free take-off. As there was no room for fighters, the old *Furious* was snatched from an honourable retirement, with 24 new wing-folding Seafire IIIs of 801 and 880 Squadrons as close escort and top cover respectively, with some aircraft as CAP. Her Barracuda squadron, Lieutenant-Commander (A) Bob Woolston RN's No 827, was to fly A/S patrols during the first strike, and follow up the mining with an anti-shipping strike. *Trumpeter* sailed from Scapa Flow in the late afternoon of 11 September, in company with *Furious* (Senior Officer), the heavy cruiser *Devonshire* and Captain D26 in *Myngs*, with *Maine, Vigilant, Algonquin* (RCN), *Musketeer* and *Verulam* making up the destroyer escort. The wind Force 3, and the barometer high.

The strike leader was Lieutenant-Commander (A) R. D. 'Bobby' Head, CO of 846 Squadron, a veteran of the night shipping strikes from Malta, and the 852 Squadron team was led by their CO Lieutenant-Commander (A) R. E. 'Bobby' Bradshaw, well known for his exploits in 826 Squadron in the Western Desert.

For security reasons the targets for these mine-laying strikes were not announced until the force was on the point of sailing from Scapa Flow, and with the short sea passage to Aaramsund the aircrews were hard-pressed in the time available to study and absorb the mass of Intelligence detail and local area photographs. The essence of a daylight low-level attack was surprise, with no delay over the target area. The Norwegian coast around Aaramsund was difficult to identify accurately and quickly at very low level, and strike leaders always chose a prominent lighthouse for their landfall, Storholmen Light for attacks in the Lepsörev-Haarham area, Svino Light for Aaramsund. The aircrews formed the habit of throwing out packs of cigarettes and chocolate over the land surrounding the lighthouses.

For Senior Observer Jeff Powell, RN, master-minding strike navigation from Head's Avenger, the final part of the run was always an anxious time, until he sighted and identified the landfall point, particularly in the more northerly latitudes, where the P8M remote reading compass tended to be unreliable. But the Avenger was a superb observer's aircraft, once he had been moved from the rear compartment, which had been crowded and had a very restricted view, to the centre cockpit with its almost all-round view, excellent chart table to work at and the ASV radar and aerial controls ideally sited. This modification had been developed in 846 Squadron in December 1943.

Svino Light came up exactly as expected. The message 'Out lights – Go!' was passed by R/T to the fighter cover, which climbed to 300m (1,000ft) and flew on ahead to attack their targets, and the minelaying aircraft were ordered into dropping formation. As they flew over the lighthouse the Norwegian crew came out to wave.

To their surprise, as they reached the channel in which they were to lay the mines they found it occupied by half a dozen vessels, and a heavy AA fire began from batteries ashore and various ships. But the minelayer Avengers steadily maintained their position through the flak until the order to drop was given. At the moment of dropping, each crew accurately fixed their position so that the dropping positions could later be plotted and reported. All the mines dropped correctly except that of strike leader Bobby Head. A hit by flak on the run-in nobbled all *FN909*'s hydraulics, including the bomb bay mechanism. The bomb bay doors swung to the half-closed position, and interlocks prevented weapon release until the doors had been re-opened manually. But Head continued to lead his minelayers in to the point of release, then jettisoned his mine on the run out near Svino Light.

The planned run-in was not easy, with the escorting Seafires weaving in and out of the Avenger formation as their cannon strafed the enemy shipping and radar and gun positions ashore. In addition to their planned attacks on shore targets, the Seafires shot up a large, lightly loaded motor vessel plus two smaller vessels, a powerful tug which had the large vessel under tow (no doubt to assist with awkward turns through the crooked Aaramsund), a small fishing drifter used as a flak ship, and three M Class minesweepers escorting the merchant ships. The large MV, later identified as the *Deutsche Levant* of the *Athen* Class (4,500 tons), was superficially damaged and set on fire, stopped and ringed by mines. One smaller MV of about 1,000 tons blew up, either from mine or canon attack. One of the M Class minesweepers, *VP5307*, blew up and sank, and the other two, *VP5105* and *VP5309*, were damaged and beached. As an additional weapon, Bobby Bradshaw lowered his landing hook before passing over a radar array and control hut on Flada Island, east of Vorkso, and flying only a few feet above the ground carried away all the W/T aerials located at that position.

Four Avengers and three Seafires were damaged by flak, and one Seafire shot down, with its pilot, Sub-Lieutenant (A) M. A. Glennie, lost. The follow-up shipping strike by *Furious'* Barracudas was cancelled, as the whole area had been so thoroughly alerted by the first operation, no other shipping targets had been seen and it was considered unwise to prejudice the chances of two 'protected' liners, MVs *Drottingholm* and *Arundel Castle*, which were in the area returning to the UK from Sweden with repatriated prisoners of war. In the event, the aircraft returning from Aaramsund were surprised to find themselves flying over the two liners, which signalled 'We are thrilled to see you. Thank you very much for your kind welcome,' but never knew that they came quite close to being attacked.

Lieutenant-Commander Head landed on *Trumpeter* last, at 13:15, because of his flak damage, with no flaps and only one wheel locked down. He heeled over to starboard as the damaged wheel gave way, but came to rest amidships with the Avenger right on the centreline of the ship, as perfect a landing as anyone could expect in the circumstances. It was his last operation in 846 Squadron, as he was leaving to take up a shore appointment on the staff of Flag Officer Flying Training. It was the very last combat for the finally time-expired old *Furious*, which, on 19 July 1918, had launched six naval Sopwith Camel 2F1 fighter-bombers on the first ever maritime air strike from the deck of a carrier, destroying two Zeppelins in their hangar.

Right: Hit by flak in Begonia, the 846 Squadron 'flagship' Avenger FN909, cannot lower its starboard wheel . . . (Cdr J. Powell)

Right: But Lieutenant-Commander Head gets them down safely. He and observer Sub-Lieutenant Jeff Powell RN climb out unhurt. (Cdr J. Powell)

14

'OUTING' TO ATHENS

THE Admiralty considered that the performance of No 4 Fighter Wing in 'Dragoon' had justified their faith in the specialist Fighter and Assault CVEs, the creation of the fighter wings and the Escort Carrier Squadron. There were enough Trade Protection CVEs and MAC-ships to cover North Atlantic and Russian convoys and shipping strikes. The Escort Carrier Squadron could now be used to hammer the Germans retreating from their Balkan fortress. Seven ships of the squadron were assembled in Malta and sailed in early September for Alexandria, where an air and sea offensive in Greek waters was being prepared, to prevent the fugitives and their equipment from being used in the West and, more urgently in the eyes of Prime Minister Churchill and President Roosevelt, to prevent Communist forces, battle-hardened in the Greek and Yugoslav resistance movements, from rushing in on the heels of the Germans and taking power. The first stage was the destruction or immobilising, by surface ships, submarines and aircraft of enemy sea and air transport in the Eastern Mediterranean, the Sea of Crete, the Aegean and coastal areas of mainland Greece, with British and Nationalist Greek troops following up and restoring the Greek and Yugoslav governments in exile.

The Germans withdrew beyond the range of Allied strike aircraft in North Africa, and the Escort Carrier Squadron was called in, though short of aircraft after 'Dragoon', with few available at RN Air Station at Dekheila, near Alexandria. When *Hunter* and *Khedive* sailed from Alexandria on 9 September they carried 20 Seafires apiece, *Hunter* with 15 LIIIs and five LRIICs, all LIIIs in *Khedive*. *Attacker* and *Stalker* left a few days later, *Attacker* with 15 LIICs and five LRIICs, *Stalker* with much the same as *Hunter*.

BREAKING THE CRETAN LINE

The first phase of the operation, jauntily called 'Outing', was the neutralising of the outer air defence ring Crete-Scarpanto-Rhodes, commencing with Rhodes, with its four airfields, all vessels in its harbours and coastal waters, all transport on its roads. For the first three days of operations the Seafires from *Hunter* and *Khedive*, and the Fighter carriers *Pursuer*'s and *Searcher*'s Wildcats provided combat air patrols during the daylight

Right: 16 Seafire LIIIs aboard a CVE of the Escort Carrier Squadron in Grand Harbour, Valletta, Malta, en route for Alexandria and Greek waters, early September 1944. (IWM)

Above: Area of Campaign by the Escort Carrier Squadron, September/October 1944.

hours for the Command Cruiser *Royalist* and her destroyers, which at night hit shipping in the Sea of Crete, and for a minesweeping force clearing a path for the occupation of Kithira Island, between the western end of Crete and the Peloponnese. On the 16th Seafire and Wildcat fighter-bombers from *Pursuer* and *Searcher* scourged vehicles on the roads of Crete and caiques in the harbours. Three Wildcats were gashed by flak but returned safely.

Next day *Khedive*'s and *Searcher*'s Seafires and Wildcats bombed and strafed motor transport on the western part of the island and ships off the rocky shores, but in the afternoon the *meltemia*, sinker of Ulysses' black ships, blew out of the Sea of Crete, and when two salt-rimed Supermarines returned from a recce to Rhodes they were very rudely buffetted before they made *Khedive*'s spray-lashed deck. It was still blowing hard next day but *Emperor* joined the squadron in the afternoon, and her tough Hellcats rode the wild wind to Suda Bay. There, not far from the rocks where the wreck of *York* rotted and rusted, 15 flying boats (Do 24s and Bv 222s) rolled uneasily. The recce planes called in four more Grummans, which punched holes in the targets before a strike of eight Seafires from *Attacker* and *Stalker* appeared with 227kg (500lb) MC bombs. Flak shielded the harbour, and the bombs near-missed, ripping the hulls here and there. Four LIIIs of *Khedive*'s 899 Squadron flew a barrier patrol across the mouth of the Bay, but the enemy waited until dark. The carriers had no night fighters with them, the Seafires flew back to their ship, and the transports got away. While the Seafires slept, silently dripping oil, in the darkened, gently rolling CVEs, *Royalist* and her destroyers roamed the gleaming Sea of Crete by the light of a half-moon, when the conning tower of *U-407*, one of the last three German submarines left in the Mediterranean surfaced, streaming white water, just beyond the carrier group's screen. A lookout in the nearest destroyer spotted her in the moonlight. All through the night the three destroyers of the screen hunted her, and sank her just before dawn. The squadron weigh-ed anchor and sailed for Rhodes, where Hellcat scouts had seen a harbour full of ships.

Just before noon on 19 September *Emperor, Khedive, Attacker* and *Pursuer* between them put up 22 Seafires, ten Hellcats and ten Wildcat fighter-bombers, humping 42 227kg (500lb) and 20 113kg (250lb) bombs. Ahead of them in Rhodes Harbour lay the transport *Pomezia*, three depot ships and some other auxiliary vessels, a KT (Kriegs-Transport) and various caiques and small craft. Roaring in over the outer harbour wall the strike took the drowsy mariners by surprise. Not until the attack was almost over was there some ragged flak from guns round the harbour, and by then 879 Squadron Seafires from *Attacker* had hit *Pomezia* and holed two depot ships with near-misses falling between the stone jetty and the ships' sides, while 899's LIIIs had hit another depot ship and severely damaged the KT-boat. All the squadron aircraft returned safely, with not one Seafire deck prang after over 160 sorties.

The very satisfactory result of Operation 'Outing' Part I was the destruction or disabling of most of the enemy's large and medium-sized transport ships, leaving many of his outlying garrisons bottled up, and the outer wall of his island defences smashed. The Germans tried to fly out key men in Junkers Ju 52/3m transport aircraft, but RAF Beaufighters, redundant in their allotted role as night CAP over the warships, were switched to these targets. Controlled by the Fighter Direction Ship *Ulster Queen*, they destroyed 20 of the transports and damaged 20 more. Long-range Beaufighters and USAAF Lightning P-38s destroyed others on the ground, including 25 on airfields near Athens.

Right: Twelve of 899 Squadron's Seafire LIIIs ranged aboard HMS *Khedive* ready for an armed reconnaissance to the north of Crete. (FAA Museum)

Right: HMSS *Attacker* and *Khedive*, seen from the bridge island of Fighter CVE HMS *Pursuer*, four of whose fighter-bomber Wildcat VIs can be seen parked and hooded, ready-ranged for operations in early September, 1944, heading for attacks on Rhodes Harbour. *Attacker*'s and *Khedive*'s Seafire IIIs can be seen on their flight decks. (FAA Museum)

Far left: Two of HMS *Pursuer*'s Wildcat VI fighter-bombers climb into the sun near the island of Rhodes, preparatory to an attack on Rhodes Harbour. (G. Whyte)

Left: 807 Squadron Seafires from *Hunter* have set a Siebel Ferry on fire north of Cape Cassandra, and a coaster takes evasive action, 9 October 1944. (FAA Museum)

Left: Bombing-up Wildcats on HMS *Pursuer* (IWM)

Bottom: HMS *Aurora*, named for the ancient Greek Goddess of the Dawn, sailed from Alexandria to relieve the light cruiser HMS *Black Prince* in the Greek islands, carrying out sweeps of the Aegean Sea and the Sea of Crete by night, handing over at first light to the fighter-bomber Seafires, Wildcats and Hellcats of the Escort Carrier Squadron. (IWM)

With Operation 'Outing' I completed, the Escort Carrier Squadron withdrew to Alexandria to take a brief breather to replenish and re-arm. King Farouk visited *Hunter* and was entertained by a display of carrier operations by 807 Squadron and the appropriately named *Khedive*'s Seafires of 899, topped off by a 24-aircraft flypast. Before he left the carrier at Alexandria the King presented a gold watch to every pilot in the two squadrons, and crates of oranges and Turkish Delight to the ships' companies.

With the German outer defence line neutralised and the Sea of Crete safe, the strike force could advance to its next task, the penetration and domination of the Aegean, requiring a partial repeat of 'Outing' I among the inner islands and the destruction of hostile shipping between the Greek and Turkish shores. Flanking the south-eastern gateways into the Aegean were the Dodecanese Islands annexed by Italy, which were to be reoccupied, and the Cyclades, the islands of the Attic archipelago, a scattering of barren, sun-baked rocks protecting Athens against seaborne attack from the south-east, but not from Seafire fighter-bombers. This bypassed trading kingdom amongst the white-washed cottages of fishermen and sponge divers was flung there, it was said, by the hand of Zeus, but had paid more tribute through the centuries to the sword of the god of war, piracy and plunder, most lately swung by a German hand after a century of brutal Ottoman rule. Twice in this war the British had entered Greece as allies, both times repulsed by the new barbarians. Now they were coming again, on wings. With every Seafire shot down, Icarus fell again from the sun.

The most direct route into the Aegean was up the Kinaros Channel between the two island groups, flanked by enemy garrisons, with the long, narrow island of Ikaria, from which attacks could be made over the whole Aegean and Sea of Crete, restricting its north-eastern exit. The Axis had sewn a large and sprawling minefield in the Channel, and on 26 September minesweepers got to work, under the protection of HMS *Stalker*'s Seafires, the light cruiser *Black Prince*, replacing *Royalist*, and two destroyers. The carrier's 809 Squadron flew CAP over the ships as well as strikes in the teeth of heavy flak, against shipping, airfields, barracks and radio stations on either hand. In an attack on the Axis naval base at Leros in the Dodecanese they destroyed a Ju 52/3m, and strafed ships and caiques in the harbour. On 28 September a *Stalker* fighter spotted for the bombardment of Lythis Island by the Free Greek destroyer *Calpe*, and otherwise unemployed CAP pilots beat up its radio station and sank a big naval barge.

On the 29th the sweepers were still at work, but the programme could not wait. The *Black Prince* group, reinforced by three more destroyers, followed them up Channel. One flight of four Seafires swept ahead, searching the channels, and dive-bombed a convoy of Siebel ferries, scored a direct hit and two near-misses, and called in destroyers. They completed the job, and rejoined *Black Prince*. The cruiser group then penetrated the outer ring of the Cyclades and, with four Seafire pairs spotting for them, bombarded the island of Syros, only 120km (75 miles) from Athens. This attack, coming after three years of enervating dolce vita in the sun, and followed by a Seafire strike which sank a tank landing craft and damaged a coaster and an E-boat, so shook the garrison commander that he destroyed all his secret files in anticipation of a landing, which never came.

As *Pursuer* and *Searcher* left Alexandria for the UK, *Stalker* and *Black Prince* came in for replenishment, and *Hunter* and the light cruiser *Aurora* sailed to take their places in the islands in company with *Attacker* and *Emperor*. On 1 October the three carriers put up Seafire and Hellcat patrols to check that Crete and Rhodes remained dormant. They met plenty of flak, but there was no movement on the roads or in the harbours. *Emperor* remained in the area, while *Attacker* and *Hunter* steamed up the Channel behind the sweepers and flew off a strike to hit the island of Levitha, which stuck out into the Channel on a spur of the Cyclades, in a perfect position for observing operations in the Channel. Eight *Attacker* Seafires strafed while eight from *Hunter* bombed the radio station. *Hunter* then continued up Kinaros with the cruiser *Aurora* and her destroyers to fly CAP over the sweepers, and *Attacker* turned south to rejoin *Emperor*. Radio Levitha was still providing the Germans with a running commentary on Allied movements in the southern Aegean, and on 5 October armed seamen from *Aurora* and the destroyer *Catterick*, with Seafires spotting for a bombardment by *Aurora*'s

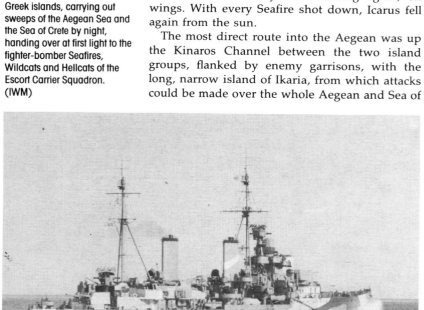

Right: Seafires from the *Bogue*-class fighter escort carrier, HMS *Hunter*, hit targets in the Sea of Crete, the Aegean Sea and on the Greek mainland. (D. Mawdsley)

6in guns, captured the island. On 6 October *Stalker* and *Black Prince* joined the force, the two carriers refuelled *Aurora* and the destroyers, the cruisers made a stealthy night sweep up and down the length of the Aegean as far as the Gulf of Salonika, and at dawn 'Outing' II commenced.

'OUTING' II

The operation got off to a bad start when a Seafire of 809 Squadron was shot down as it strafed lorries on Cos. In the afternoon four fighter-bombers from each carrier strafed and dive-bombed a convoy located by Tac/R. An 809 Seafire sank a 1,000-ton freighter, others forced a coaster aground. An 807 Seafire was shot down by flak, but the squadron got its revenge two hours later when two of its aircraft located the 1,000-ton freighter *Silva* 64km (40 miles) west of Leros. The sighting pair kept the air by leaning out their avgas, and shadowed the target until a fighter-bomber quartet arrived and sank the *Silva* in just over two minutes.

The CVEs kept up the pressure by day, with *Aurora* and *Black Prince* hunting by night. A recce Seafire from *Hunter* found a medium-sized transport off Khalkis, 160km (100 miles) from the ship, and eight fighter-bombers left her dead in the water. Seafires of 809 sank a *Dresden* Class tanker off Cape Cassandra with their bombs and cannon shells, and damaged an F-lighter, a caique and a heavily armed Siebel ferry, which put up a fierce and accurate barrage, and damaged two Seafires. One of them ditched half-way back to *Stalker*, its pilot being rescued by the destroyer *Tuscan*, and the other, hit in the oil tank by metal splinters, just managed to regain the carrier, with half a pint of oil left in the leaking tank. On the same day the Seafires began a series of attacks on the railway running up the east coast of mainland Greece, the main lifeline for the Germans, now in full retreat on Salonika. This first attack destroyed two locomotives and a score of trucks, a modest opening to a hard-hitting series. On the 9th the German torpedo boat *TA 38*, formerly the Italian *Spada*, was sighted running south out of the Gulf of Salonika, heading for the strike force. Two flak-suppression Seafires of 807 led eight 809 fighter-bombers, which bombed the TB in the Politi Channel. Hit or nearmissed, she stopped, then turned off to starboard and crawled off up the Gulf of Pagastikos to Volos, but the Seafires persisted, and she was scuttled. Others sank Siebel ferries off Cape Cassandra, and aircraft from both squadrons sank a 600-ton concrete barge off Mudros.

Then it was time for *Hunter* and *Stalker* to return to Alexandria. *Emperor* was their replacement. She steamed unobtrusively up the mid-Aegean, her Hellcats wing-folded and silent, while the other two CVEs drew attention to themselves and away from *Emperor* by flaunting their Seafires over the Cyclades in offensive Tac/Rs, strafing Syros in the northern islands and Thira on the edge of the Sea of Crete to the south.

Hunter and *Khedive* left the Mediterranean at the end of October, leaving the Escort Carrier Squadron with three carriers, *Attacker*, *Emperor* and *Stalker*, 40 Seafires (a mix of LIIIs, LIICs and LRIICs), *Emperor*'s 20 Hellcats, and one Walrus. On 11 October *Emperor* revealed its presence in

Above: Train-busting on the Larisa-Salonika railway on the Greek mainland. A Seafire of 879 Squadron from HMS *Attacker* has set fire to both ends of a train, 24 October 1944. (FAA Museum)

Above right: Lieutenant(A) D. S. Ogle of 809 Squadron from HMS *Stalker* in a Seafire LIIC has set the starboard wing of a Ju 88 on fire and having expended all his ammunition is taking photographs with his port-facing oblique F.24 camera. His last exposure showed the 88 burning in a field. (MoD(Navy))

Centre: Seafire somersault. The flight deck party is disentangling the barrier cable from the stricken machine, which has redeemed itself somewhat by obligingly coming to rest on the forward lift. (FAA Museum)

Bottom: The Escort Carrier Squadron. HM escort carriers *Khedive, Stalker, Emperor, Hunter, Searcher, Pursuer* in line-ahead, photographed from HMS *Attacker*. (IWM)

the Gulf of Salonika by sending out Hellcat fighter-bombers to neutralise Axis traffic on land and sea. They badly mauled three convoys at sea, and cut up the railway from Larisa up to Katerini on the Gulf of Salonika. During the night she quit the area as stealthily as she had arrived, and next day her Hellcats were beating up Rhodes to keep things quiet there while she was en route to Alexandria, which she reached just in time to top up and leave again with *Attacker, Stalker, Royalist* and six destroyers, the force for Operation 'Manna', landings on the mainland near Athens.

'MANNA' FOR GREECE

On 14 October *Emperor* detached from the force to resume shipping strikes in the Gulf of Salonika, while the 'Manna' carriers flew Tac/R sorties over the enemy island bases as a precaution against a stab in the back while they were busy in the Saronic Gulf. On the 15th landings began, with Seafires from *Attacker* and *Stalker* flying cover throughout the day. The assault met only token opposition, and the only enemy aircraft to appear was a cautious Ju 88. The pilots of a pair of LRIICs from *Stalker* cruising at 1,220m (4,000ft) in scat-

Above: A Seafire makes a good landing after a sortie.

tered white cloud saw it first, and Lieutenant (A) D. S. Ogle, RNVR, caught up with it about 40km (25 miles) north of Athens, his speedo reading 668km/h (415mph), and had fired his last cannon shell when the Jabo's starboard engine gushed flame. *Stalker* flew off one CAP on 16 October, then joined *Emperor* in the northern Aegean. Attacker remained off Sounion, mounting CAP until dusk, then threaded the Cyclades for the last time on passage back to Alexandria.

THE OLYMPUS STATION

Shipping targets in the Aegean were rare by now, and the two CVEs there hit marshalling yards, trains and track, bridges and tunnels on the mainland, and shot down one Dornier Do 24 flying boat in flames into Pagastikos Gulf. A *Stalker* Seafire was hit by flak, the pilot baled out and landed on Mount Olympus, home of the ancient gods, 32km (20 miles) north-east of Larisa. In the last sorties of the day Seafires attacked a convoy off Cape Stavros, damaged several ships, and sank an armed trawler. Meanwhile *Emperor* had left for Alexandria and home. *Stalker* herself had only one more day of operations in the Aegean. A rising wind and sea reduced it to a few hours, but the Seafires made it count. Three locomotives, a dozen large lorries and an armoured car were written off, and even as German repair gangs were working on the railway track previously cut, the fighter-bombers tore it up elsewhere. The squadron lost two more aircraft to some accurate flak, but the pilots baled out and landed like visiting gods amongst cheering Greeks. Next day, 20 October, *Stalker* left the attack area and anchored off Chios to refuel. Everyone got a good night's sleep and in the morning she heaved up her hook, and on her way to Alexandria four of her Seafires signed her off with a dive-bombing attack against coastal defences on Rhodes.

Attacker, steaming up the Kisaros Channel to take her place, flew off eight Seafires to bomb the airfield on Cos, then picked up speed to continue the bombing of the Larisa-Salonika line. She sighted the snow cap of Olympus, and on 23 October Seafires destroyed three trains, wrecked a goods yard, and tore up the track. In the forenoon of the 24th fighter-bombers crippled two trains and so savaged the coastal railway line that all traffic on it was stopped. No 879 Squadron said goodbye by bombing a marshalling yard near Salonika. As the last Seafire landed on, *Attacker* left the Olympus station for good, refuelled off Chios next day, and supported landings on Sappho's island of Lesbos and on Piscopi (Tilos) in the outer chain of the Dodecanese between Cos and Rhodes, their presence helping the garrison commanders make up their minds to surrender. This was the last operation by the Escort Carrier Squadron in the Mediterranean.

THE SEAFIRE REDEEMED

The joint cruiser/carrier offensive against shipping, and lines of communication in mainland Greece, isolated 20,000 German troops of the island garrisons and slowed down the German retreat to a crawl. A subsidiary cause for satisfaction in the Air Department at the Admiralty was the redemption of the Seafire. Five were lost to flak, with three pilots saved, and three damaged, a very low casualty rate for the time spent on operations, the more gratifying because of the small number of flight deck accidents, none of them ending in a write-off or serious casualty. These statistics almost restored the reputation which the naval twin to Mitchell's marvel had lost at Salerno.

15

THE U-BOATS SIGN OFF

THE LAST RUNS TO RUSSIA

JW61, which sailed for Russia on 20 October 1944, was a large convoy of 62 ships, protected by a strong close escort, two support groups and, for the first time in Russian convoys, three Trade Protection CVEs, *Tracker*, *Nairana* and *Vindex*. The latter's 811 Squadron, a re-formed unit, lost two Swordfish and their crews in icy seas, another drowned its Observer, and morale was so eroded that the squadron was disbanded shortly after returning to the UK.

Wildcats from *Nairana* and *Campania* in JW and RA62 (Operation 'Acumen') shot down two Ju 88s and one Blohm & Voss, and *U-835* was sunk, with one Wildcat pilot killed but no convoy losses. The new US-converted Trade Protection carrier *Premier*, laid down in October 1942 as a 'Ruler' Class carrier, ACV-42, joined the Home Fleet and began minelaying in Norwegian fjords and harbours and mounting strikes against coastal shipping.

Winter in the Norwegian and Barents Seas was a wild enemy. On one trip in very heavy weather, with no room below, one of *Trumpeter*'s Avengers had to be left ranged in the open, parked facing for'ard with wings spread and controls locked, bound to the deck with 16 12.5mm (½in) hemp and 16 flexible steel wire 30cwt lashings, firmly secured and very strong. The plane was humming loudly and vibrating, her restraining wires jerking and whipping with the kicks of the wind on her belly and wings, when the lashings parted and the whole machine leaped into the air. With windspeed better than 100 knots and the ship's speed

Right: *Vindex* by moonlight.

Right: Sunrise, HMS *Vindex*. 'Start up Wildcats!'

Above: Winter in the Barents Sea. HMS *Trumpeter* thinks she is a submarine. (Cdr J. Powell)

at dead slow ahead, the heavy Avenger flew along abreast of the carrier for a while. Then her nose fell and she swooped down as if by some miracle she was going to land on again. But her airspeed was maintained and up she rose again, keeping company with the ship. It could not last, of course. The gale turned her away from the eye of the wind, she flipped over on her back and in the darkness whitened by flying spray and spume hit the sea about four cables away.

The service to Russia ground relentlessly on. 'The convoys varied', wrote Peter Cockrell, a divisional officer in *Campania*, 'from the disagreeable to the perfectly horrible.' By the beginning of January 1945 most of the Home Fleet escort carriers had re-equipped with Avengers. HMS *Puncher*, now the only Canadian-manned escort carrier in service with the RN, which had joined the Home Fleet in November 1944, was the sole CVE to fly Barracuda torpedo-bombers. *Puncher* was another 'Ruler' Class carrier laid down at the Seattle-Tacoma Corporation's yard.

The Fairey Barracuda, a monoplane with an ugly shoulder wing, did some good work, but had a faulty exhaust system and a record of suddenly diving into the sea off a high-speed stall. Diving could strain the main wing spar to breaking point, the skin would wrinkle and rivets pop at the leading edge, and the machine was difficult to escape from in crashes, which were frequent. The Barra was also asked to perform in too many roles, a plane of all trades and master of none, though it had its defenders among pilots with the skill to master it. In a number of day and night anti-submarine patrols and minelaying sorties in the North Sea, Atlantic and Arctic, *Puncher*'s 821 Squadron lost four crews and a large number of aircraft. However, Lieutenant (A) John Powell, RNVR, whose aircraft was hit only once, by cannon fire, says 'The Barracuda has been unfairly criticised, I think, largely because it followed the Swordfish, which we all loved. It was excellent at deck landing but required RATOG when fully loaded for a squadron take-off.'

HOTBED IN THE ARCTIC

At dawn on 6 February 1945, *Campania* and *Nairana* joined Convoy JW64 for Operation 'Hotbed'. A bold Ju 88 from Bergen was the first enemy to appear, and was destroyed in the last glow of sunset by Lieutenant (A) Fleischmann-Allen, RNVR, late of HMS *Fencer* and the Azores caper, before severe icing stopped flying. On 22 February a violent storm of hurricane (Force 11) strength forced the carriers to leave the rapidly dispersing convoy and heave to. *Campania* had rolled 48 degrees and back again to 45 degrees, and was in some danger of capsizing. Peter Cockrell had the middle watch and was constantly using the ship's engines to keep her head into wind. By next morning the storm had eased off and the convoy slowly formed up again.

The weather softened, the sky lightened – and 30 torpedo-carrying 88s came in at sea level. Flak broke them up and brought down four, *Nairana*'s Wildcats another two. Her rudder jammed as she took violent evasive action, and she swung round in circles, narrowly escaping collision. More aircraft fell to the guns of escorts and merchantmen, including the Wildcats of New Zealander Sub-

Below: 'The Barracuda Two will be the death of you . . .' A Fairey Barracuda Mk II. (J. M. Goulding)

Right: *Campania*'s crest and motto.

Lieutenant (A) J. A. Quigg and his wingman P. J. W. Davies, both of whom ditched. Kiwi Al Burgham, *Nairana*'s most experienced pilot, dived through the barrage and shot down an 88. As the ships groped their way into Kola Inlet through blinding snow in the middle watch an escorting frigate was torpedoed.

When RA64 left Kola in bitter cold on 17 February, U-boats had gathered. The sloop *Lark* sank *U-425*, then was torpedoed herself, and a merchantman was hit, though not sunk. The red sun rose, cold mist began to form, the dreaded 'Arctic Smoke' – hopeless flying weather. There was a huge blinding flash and a terrible roar in the heart of the mist as the sloop *Bluebell* was hit and blew up in a mass of orange flame. *Campania* had on board some of the 500 men, women and children rescued with great dash and daring from the Norwegian island of Suroy off the town of Hammerfest in the approaches to the German naval anchorage in Altenfjord, home of *Tirpitz*, by four British destroyers in anticipation of their being taken as hostages for the sabotage activities of some of their men. Later, holidays of hard blue sky appeared, and there were no more attacks that day, but as they left the U-boats behind the other enemy rose up. Stringbags patrolling ahead of the convoy ran into knife-edged winds and scourging snow. The seas rose and threw the topheavy CVEs about like toy boats. Hit by a big cross-sea, *Nairana* flung two Swordfish overboard, and soon the ships were reeling before a full gale, with winds lashing them at 70 knots. The pounding continued for 24 hours, winds howling, the carriers wallowing and taking green seas over their flight decks, aircraft treble-lashed below.

When at last the gale began to let up and the escorts were herding the scattered merchantmen back into formation, torpedo bombers found them. *Nairana*'s tannoy blared, 'Range four Wildcats!' Fighting to keep a foothold on the slippery, canting deck the flight deck party shoved and pulled the fighters into position aft. One by one the Wright Cyclones roared, the tubby machines crabbed forward, gathered speed, sank over the bows, then strained upwards. The first pair, pilots O. K. Armitage, RNZNVR, and N. W. Sargent, RNVR, sent one 88 limping away, white smoke pouring from one engine; the second pair, Subbies Gordon and Blanco, shot down another, destroyers *Onslow* and *Zealous* one each, with one more shared by planes and escorts, and more damaged. Getting the fighters aboard again in a 70-knot wind with the after round-down rising and falling 15m (50ft) was even worse than flying them off, but batsman Bob Mathe guided them in, though Sargent's Wildcat took two wave-offs, bounced the third time, missed all the wires, slowed just short of the barrier, was caught by the wind and swept sideways back down the deck. A combination of quick throttle and grabbing hands

Below: HMS *Nairana* with a deck park of four Sea Hurricanes in Arctic white coats (Atlantic camouflage of white upper surfaces and sea-grey top decking and undersides. (R. P. Selley)

Above: Some did it backwards . . . Not a reversed negative but a Swordfish landing on *Nairana* over the bows – one way of beating a fickle wind.

stopped him just short of the round-down.

In the graveyard watch more signals from air shadowers and U-boats were picked up, but the weather was worsening again, and soon the convoy was being savaged by a gale even fiercer than the first, with headwinds of 80 knots. The RN considered 40 degrees of roll the safety limit for these ships, and when *Campania* started rolling 45 degrees she was hove to. Many ships rode out the gale, which did not begin to abate for 24 hours, when another shadower reported a widely scattered convoy. *Campania* joined up with a group of ships gathered round the Commodore, and by the first dog watch all but one ship, the *Henry Bacon*, were back in position. Nineteen hunting Ju 88s missed the main body but hit the straggler, and two Wildcats from *Nairana* found her in a sinking condition. Her survivors claimed that she had shot down two 88s. Early on 24 February Coastal Command Liberators arrived. When the two CVEs reached Scapa their Swordfish flew ashore to Hatston together. Watching from *Puncher*, young Canadian Jackson Brooks marvelled at the contrast between this Dad's Navy spectacle and the flypast of an RAF squadron of the new Meteor jet fighters which he had seen while on leave. The gale which had scattered RA64 hit The Flow two days later. In the buffetting *Puncher*'s mooring shackle parted and she drifted helplessly up against the anti-submarine/torpedo net. Lines passed to tugs snapped with the strain, and she stayed put until 00:15 on the 25th when the wind blew her over the net and she was able to drop her hook in a more secure anchorage.

Operation 'Hotbed' was the climax, as it transpired, of the convoys to Russia. Never before had fighters operated from carriers in so harsh a blizzard. The attrition among them made it obvious that more should be carried, though not at the expense of anti-submarine capability. *Campania*'s modern Air Direction Room had been invaluable in the direction of her own fighters and anti-submarine patrols, and in the supplying of vital information to *Nairana*'s ADR and to SOE and the escorts to keep them in touch with the air situation. The convoy had lost two escorts, two merchantmen and two fighters to enemy action, but the German air torpedo attack had been beaten, 15 enemy aircraft certainly and seven more probably destroyed, with one U-boat sunk.

In the period April 1944–May 1945 the CVEs *Campania, Emperor, Fencer, Nairana, Premier, Puncher, Pursuer, Queen, Searcher, Striker* and *Trumpeter* between them carried out a total of 45 offensive operations in Norwegian waters, including all the minelaying, in which *Premier*,

Above: Blame the met man. It took a full gale to pitch this Wildcat into the Goofers during Operation 'Hotbed'.

Puncher and *Trumpeter* were the specialists. These operations were in addition to raids by RAF Mosquitoes, Hudsons and Beaufighters.

In another airborne mining strike by aircraft from *Trumpeter* on 14 October 1944, Operation 'Lycidas', a new squadron CO made landfall 48km (30 miles) to the south-west of the intended spot, and mines were laid in the Aaramsund Channel again, but on the following day the correction was made by *Fencer* and *Trumpeter*, and mines sewn in Ramsoysund. On 24 October in Operation 'Hardy', Lepsorev and Haramsfjord were sown again, by *Campania* and *Trumpeter*.

There were no more FAA strikes on *Tirpitz*. In November RAF Lancasters caught her in clear weather without her smokescreen, hit her with six-ton 'blockbuster' bombs, and capsized her, some 1,000 of the ship's company being drowned or suffocated.

The narrow Salhüstrommen Channel near Haugersund in southern Norway was visited on 7 December in Operation 'Urbane' by 856 Squadron Avengers from the new Trade Protection escort carrier *Premier*, escorted by Lieutenant Vittle's fighter flight of Wildcat VIs, which flew on ahead to beat up shore batteries. The TBFs dropped their mines in strict formation amidst the surrounding miasma of acrid black smoke, with air-gunners swinging their turrets round and raking the shore with their 0.50s. Sadly, Lieutenant Vittle was lost on the operation.

Force I for Operation 'Selenium' I, HM cruisers *Norfolk* and *Dido* and three destroyers, left Scapa on the night of 10 February 1945 to patrol within gun range of the enemy shipping route between Bud and Kvithholm off the Norwegian coast, approaching from the north after dark next day. Force 2 comprised the heavy cruiser *Devonshire* and four destroyers escorting *Premier* with her seven minelaying Avengers and four Wildcats of 856 Squadron, and the new, Canadian-manned escort carrier *Puncher* with 14 Wildcats of 881 Squadron and four Barracudas of 821.

The 'Ruler' Class *Puncher* was the second, after *Nabob*, of the two escort carriers manned mainly by Canadians. As Canada was not a party to the Lend-Lease Agreement, the ships remained British, but *Puncher* carried 650 Canucks in her ship's company, her air groups being RN, as the RCN did not have an FAA of its own. On 21 July 1944 *Puncher* loaded 40 USAF P-47 Thunderbolts, P-51 Mustangs, and P-61 Black Widows, and on the 28th sailed for Casablanca in a fast (14-knot) convoy comprising 17 ships – troopers, oilers, the US Navy Kaiser-built escort carrier *Shamrock Bay* and the escort force of three destroyers and six destroyer-escorts, led by the US cruiser *Cincinatti*. On 7 August *Puncher* and *Shamrock Bay*, escorted by three Free French ships, arrived in Casablanca, still littered with wrecks from 'Torch', and off-loaded the aircraft cargo right away. Italian prisoners of war stripped off the protective tape, and the engines were run up while the planes were still on the jetty. Six days later the Black Widows were seen in action for the first time over the beach-heads of 'Dragoon'. *Nabob* was disabled on 22 August, and on the 30th *Puncher* loaded FAA Corsairs and Wildcats, together with No 1845 Squadron, and sailed for the UK on 5 September in Convoy CU38, first with a USN escort, which was replaced on the 14th by the RCN destroyers *Iroquois, Assiniboine* and *Qu'Appelle*. She sailed up the Irish Sea to Greenock, and left again for New York on 19 September in a convoy of 37 ships escorted by the USS *Clarke* and eight DEs, arriving there ten days later, to load 72 USAF machines. At Liverpool on 18 October *Puncher*'s role as ferry carrier was over.

She had a boiler clean ready for action, ammunitioned and stored ship for the operation of a torpedo bomber squadron, and on 6 November turned into wind to land on aircraft for the first time, a Barracuda and an Avenger to test arrestor wires and catapult. FOACT, Lumley-Lyster, inspected them and actually seemed pleased with their progress. Next day 821 Squadron's 12 Barracudas flew aboard. Most of the pilots were as new to carrier operations as the Canadian handlers, and five aircraft had barrier crashes in deck-landing trials, not a bad average. In fact 821 Squadron had not operated from a carrier before. Since formation in 1941 with Fairey Albacores the squadron had worked in support of the Eighth Army in North Africa and in the battle of Malta, with one DSO, 16 DSCs, two DSMs, one BEM and numerous Mentions in Despatches to show for it.

When the hated Barracudas carried mines or torpedoes they were too heavy for a free launch and relied on RATOG, or catapulting if there was insufficient wind down the deck. On 28 November a gear failure in the engine room brought the ship to a dead stop, but spares from *Nabob*, now decommissioned, put her right, and on New Year's Day 1945 she embarked four Barracudas and 14 Wildcats, and began intensive training and working-up, and some operational A/S patrols. The gruff Lumley-Lyster joined them again, and for the first time in ten days she had no prangs, though a 'seat in the Goofers was worth fifty quid'. On 15 January an 821 A/S patrol covered the torpedoed *Thane*, and on 1 February *Puncher* joined the Home Fleet at Scapa as an operational carrier.

At 07:00 on the 12th Force 2, zigzagging in warm sunny weather at 15 knots, joined Force I for a mine drop in Skateströmmen, abreast of Skaten Lighthouse, by seven Avengers from *Premier*, with 12 *Puncher* Wildcats as cover, and *Premier*'s four 856 Wildcats as close escort. Five mines were laid, one was dropped set to 'safe', and the seventh had to be jettisoned by an Avenger returning unserviceable to its carrier. A *Premier* Wildcat, with the sun in the pilot's eyes, ignored the DLCO's signals to gain height, hit the round-down, broke off its tailwheel and hook, bounced along the rolling, pitching deck, hit the barrier and, its guns not set to 'safe', accidentally opened fire, injuring 11 men on the flight deck and damaging the Wildcats and Barracudas in the deck park for'ard of the barrier. Next day there was another drop, 'Selenium' II, off Mjaaholm.

After a brief respite in harbour, with several trips to the firing range to practise 40mm and pom-pom shooting, *Puncher* landed on nine Barracudas and ten Wildcats and embarked a load of 46cm (18in) aircraft mines. At 08:00 on 21 February she slipped her moorings and with cruiser *Dido, Premier* and destroyers *Myngs, Cavalier* and *Scorpion* headed for the Norwegian coast again. This operation was in two parts, the first, code named 'Shred', a minesweeping run through a suspected German-mined area off Stavanger by six minesweepers of the 10th Flotilla. Heavy seas were running off this part of the Norwegian coast, and streaming the sweeping gear was a tricky feat of seamanship for the 10th. The sweep was accomplished, though no mines came to the surface.

At 11:30 the following forenoon *Puncher* turned into wind and nine mine-laden Barracuda IIIs used their RATOG to get off the deck for mine drop 'Groundsheet' in Salströmmen Channel, off Haugesund, again, with an escort of eight *Puncher* Wildcats, and eight more from *Premier* as top cover. Unfortunately landfall was made over Stavanger instead of Utsire, and the fighters lost contact with the minelaying Barracudas, which met very heavy flak and lost two aircraft. The remaining seven Barracudas laid their mines in Karmoy Channel, while the fighters destroyed a Dornier 24 flying boat at its moorings and shot up two silo-type buildings on the waterfront at Stavanger. The strike returned at 13:30, nearly all the Barracudas badly damaged, and firing red warning flares as they approached the fleet. Most badly damaged was the aircraft of 821's CO, Lieutenant (A) G. F. Cornish, RN, and he landed with just 7.5l (two gal) of fuel left. 'By 23:30 we were back in Scapa', recorded Jack Brooks aboard *Puncher*, 'and a sadness was felt throughout the ship, as 821 had become *our* squadron and these were our first casualties.'

There was a mine drop at Askevold anchorage, Granesund (Operation 'Cupola') by *Premier* and *Searcher* on 20 March, and *Puncher* sailed on 23 March when she went to sea to land on 12 Barracudas and four Wildcats for her next strike. During the period in harbour many of her ship's

Below, top: German SS *Alten* and two escorts under attack by CVE aircraft. (Cdr J. Powell)

Below, top right: Avengers and Wildcats from the escort carriers *Queen, Searcher* and *Trmpeter* attack a U-boat depot ship at Kilbotn, Norway, in the last FAA strike of the European war.

Bottom, left and right: Kilbotn. The atack on German shipping seen from the bomb bay of Lieutenant Sailes' Avenger from *Queen*. The main target, a U-boat depot ship, visible through the smoke was sunk. (W. Sailes)

company were put through commando training to prepare for a possible army support role in Norway, and seized the opportunity to gorge themselves on fresh eggs and milk from Scottish farms, which shipboard rationing did not include. The operation was 'Prefix', a combination of anti-shipping strikes and a mine drop, involving *Puncher, Searcher, Nairana* and *Queen*, cruisers *Bellona* and *Dido* and an escort of seven destroyers. The weather was hostile but in the forenoon of the 26th a strike was flown off by *Searcher* and *Queen* to attack shipping in Trondheim Leads and towards Kristiansand North. Nearer the coastline, which was approached at 90m (300ft), conditions were better, and two ships proceeding up Tustna/Stablen Fjord were strafed. In the middle of this, eight to ten Messerschmitt fighters were sighted and engaged by two flights of Wildcats, which shot down three and damaged two more. The Avengers were not so lucky. Finding no suitable targets, they had to jettison their bombs and return to the fleet. Operation 'Muscular', a night strike by *Nairana*'s aircraft, had to be cancelled because of the weather. The last part, Strike C, of 'Prefix' was a raid on enemy shipping at Aalesund by fighters. Two vessels alongside a jetty were attacked, and a radio station at Vikeroy Island shot up. *Puncher* lost one Barracuda, which did not return from A/S patrol.

On 6 April *Trumpeter, Queen, Puncher* and *Searcher*, escorted by the cruisers *Birmingham* and *Bellona* and eight destroyers, sailed from Scapa to attack the U-boat pens at Narvik. *Puncher* embarked the Barracudas and Wildcats of the illustrious 825, with battle honours from Eugene Esmonde's death-or-glory attack on *Scharnhorst* and *Gneisenau* to the grim night anti-submarine offensive in northern waters, in particular association with Temple Bayliss' bold *Vindex*. In company with *Trumpeter, Queen* and *Searcher*, cruisers

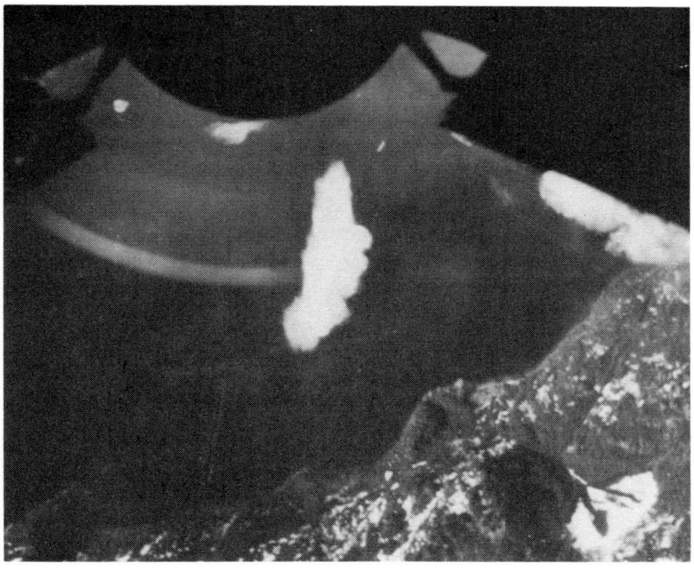

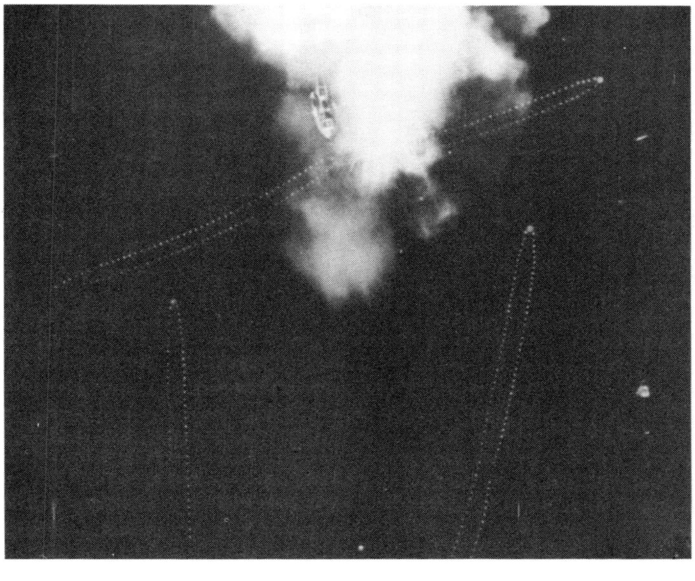

Above: The return. The flight deck of *Trumpeter* looks inviting to her Avengers returning from a strike. (Cdr J. Powell)

Birmingham and *Bellona*, escorted by destroyers *Carysfort, Offa, Onslow, Scorpion, Scourge, Zambesi, Zealous* and *Zest*, the force left Scapa at 06:00 on 6 April. They crossed the Arctic Circle on 7 April in mountainous seas, and the weather, the worst enemy, took charge of an operation planned by mere men. Damage was widespread throughout the squadron. The shock of waves striking from above and below the forward end of *Puncher*'s flight deck cracked the deck right across. Life floats were torn away and gun sponsons smashed. There were several near collisions with destroyers in drifting snow with visibility near zero, and the strike was cancelled.

On 4 May an attack on the U-boat depot ship at Kilbotn, near Harstad, Operation 'Judgement' was made by 44 Avengers and flak-suppression Wildcats from the 'Rulers *Queen*' (853 Squadron), *Searcher* (882) and *Trumpeter* (846). Flak was thick round the target, but the depot ship, *U-711* lying alongside her, and a merchantman were sunk. One Avenger and one Wildcat were lost. Later the CVEs dallied to put up anti-submarine and CAP for the re-occupation of Denmark.

The last active Russian convoy operation was 'Roundel', the running of JW/RA66. JW66 sailed on 17 April, with *Vindex*, 'Ruler' Class *Premier* and the 19th Escort Group. *Vindex* had borrowed *Campania*'s veteran 813 Squadron, which reversed the proportion of TBRs to fighters, with eight Swordfish and 12 Wildcats, balanced by *Premier*'s 12 Avengers of 856. The outward run was quiet but by the time RA66 sailed from Kola the enemy were waiting outside in some force. The frigate *Goodall* was sunk with heavy loss of life, only 44 of the crew being saved, but the loss was avenged on 29 April, when *U-307* and *U-256* were destroyed.

The following day 856's 'tartan' crew, pilot Sub-Lieutenant Stewart Murray from Edinburgh, observer Sub-Lieutenant Neil Muir from Paisley and telegraphist/air-gunner Leading Naval Airman Stewart Crawford from Glasgow, were returning to *Premier* after an anti-submarine patrol. The carrier was about 160km (100 miles) north of Murmansk, the patrol had been uneventful and they were still carrying their four depth charges. They found the ship and at 16:40 were making a normal approach to the deck when

suddenly the big Avenger stalled through icing on the wings. Stewart Murray, in a desperate attempt to go round again, drew in the undercarriage as the TBF reared over on its side, but they were too near the round-down and had no chance of making it. Stewart Crawford was up in the turret when there was a tremendous grinding of metal followed by a deathly silence. Crawford's first thought was to release the escape hatch on the turret, which was on its side, and dive into the water some 18m (60ft) below. Then he thought 'Don't be a bloody fool – you won't last long in that water. No-one will pick you up anyway.'

In his haste to reach the rear cockpit he forgot to unplug his helmet and nearly strangled himself. Then the lever on his Mae West got caught in the pistol grip turret control and immediately inflated like a balloon. By this time the engine was on fire. He managed to wriggle out of his flying gear, reach the rear cockpit and open the door. To his horror he realised that the plane was suspended in mid-air from the stern of the ship. Very cautiously he shuffled along the side of the fuselage as Captain Gardiner shouted over the loudspeaker 'Get that air-gunner out!' before reaching the safety of the flight deck, once or twice being nearly knocked over the side by the force of the water jets from the fire hoses which were now being played on the wreck.

In all escort carrier operations in Atlantic, Norwegian or Arctic waters throughout 1944 and 1945 until the end of hostilities in Europe, outstanding work had been done by roving quartets of HM Wildcats attached wherever the need arose to RN CVEs to form CAP, cover or close escort for bomber or minelayer Swordfish, Barracuda or Avenger squadrons. These flights were formed at Eglinton in Northern Ireland, a typical fighter four being E-Flight, which embarked in *Fencer* on 17 March 1944, when that happy and efficient ship made the necessary change from Seafires to Wildcats, more suited to the rough and tumble of escort carrier operations, and with other flights formed part of the Fleet umbrella in Operation 'Tungsten' while the Barracudas attacked *Tirpitz* in her Kaafjord lair, supported by Corsairs and Hellcats, disembarking to Hatston in the Orkneys on 11 April. There were several weeks in *Fencer*, the only ship these FAA gypsies could ever call theirs. In RA59 from Russia, 28 April–25 May 1944, they were part of the team which destroyed three U-boats. In Operation 'Wanderer', 20–25 June, they flew in the sweep from Scapa to Jan Mayen and back via the Norwegian coast, looking for trouble; they were with the 13 July convoy to Gibraltar, the mine drops 'Lycidas', 15 October, 'Hardy' on the 24th, JW61 to Russia later in the month, in *Vindex*, January 1945 . . . It was a peripatetic life, living largely out of Pusser's suitcases, but an important part of Fleet Air Arm operations.

THE 'SEEWOLF' SORTIE

The 60 days maximum time limit for an attack on New York and/or Washington by buzz-bombs or V2 rockets from U-boats forecast by Admiral Ingram on 8 January expired in the second week of March, and New York was still intact. In Washington, on the third floor of the Navy Building Ken Knowles and Jack Parsons had been piecing together scraps from their various sources of intelligence, and making sense. A submarine attack force *was* moving on US shores. Seven U-boats, with hand-picked crews and commanders, forming a special *Rudel*, were on their way across the Atlantic. Knowles soon knew that the operation was code-named *Seewolf*, that in the interests of secrecy the seven boats selected were basically ordinary Type VIIs, the standard 740-tonners used in the Atlantic throughout the war, cruising at 17 knots on the surface, and eight knots submerged, with the recent addition of the *Schnorkel*, and normally armed with 12 torpedoes and a 20mm twin AA gun. The seven boats had avoided making themselves conspicuous by sailing at staggered intervals and had formed two main groups of three on passage, with one, the reserve boat *U-881*, sailing alone behind the others.

Rear-Admiral Alan McCann, Frog Low's successor as Chief of Staff, Tenth Fleet, was able to give CINCLANT, Admiral Ingram, this breakdown of the boats of *Rudel Seewolf*, and their progress to date. This enabled the tough Ingram, former Navy football star, to run interference on them. In Operation 'Teardrop' he organised two 'Barrier Forces' to apprehend them.

The first Barrier Force put to sea at the end of March. One line of destroyers took station along the parallel of St John's, Newfoundland, with the Kaiser-built CVE USS *Mission Bay* cruising some 64km (40 miles) behind them in support. Another picket line composed of 20 destroyer-escorts steamed up and down a 190km (120 mile) stretch of the 30th meridian, passing between Fayal and Flores, with Ken Craig's *Croatan* and her screen of four escorts backing them up in the rear. The weather was very bad, with mountainous seas, and over a hundred men were injured in *Croatan* alone by crashing mess tables, benches and crockery, and accidents on deck. All ships were in position on the morning of 11 April, but when on the following day news came in of the death of President Roosevelt, the ferocity of the elements together with the urgency of the mission made it impossible to hold a memorial service for the Chief Executive who had always valued the Navy so highly and supported it so well.

Rough seas and fog prevented planes from flying, but when on the evening of the 15th *Seewolf*'s *U-1235* (Oberleutnant Franz Barsch), her *Schnorkel* useless in the heavy seas, came up to ventilate and re-charge, she surfaced on *Stanton*'s radar screen and the DE's searchlight illuminated

Right: HMS *Premier*'s 'Tartan crew', left to right Sub-Lieutenant(A) Neil Muir, RNVR (observer) from Paisley, near Glasgow; Sub-Lieutenant(A) Stewart Murray, RNVR (pilot) from Edinburgh; Leading Naval Airman Stewart Crawford, RN (telegraphist/air-gunner) from Glasgow, beneath their Avenger. (S. A. Crawford)

Right: Take-off. The Tartan TBF leaves *Premier* about 100 miles North of Murmansk on anti-submarine patrol. (S. A. Crawford)

Right: The return. The Muir/Murray/Crawford aircraft, burdened with ice on the wings, stalls just short of the round-down. (S. A. Crawford)

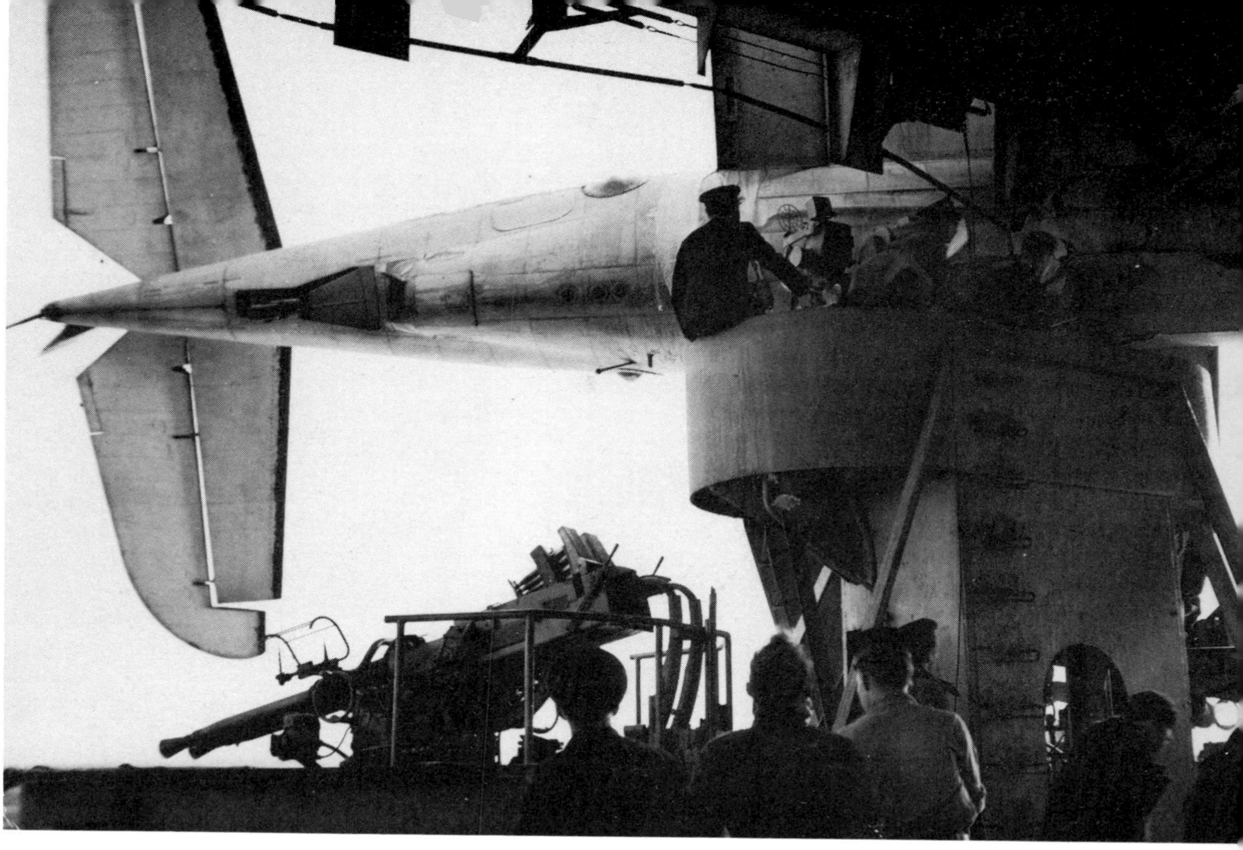

Right: Not a pretty sight. The crashed Tartan Avenger from below the round-down. The aircraft was jettisoned later. (S. A. Crawford)

Right: Murray's Avenger lodges on the stern. The picture was taken by Sub-Lieutenant(A) Drinkwater in Sub-Lieutenant(A) Rennie's Swordfish – which had itself yet to land-on . . . (S. A. Crawford)

Right: TAG Stewart Crawford climbs to safety from the stranded aircraft and is almost knocked over by the force of the hoses. (S. A. Crawford)

Above: Standby. Sub-Lieutenant(A) Dennis White of 850 Fighter Flight passing the time aboard HMS *Fencer* in some abnormally hot weather in the Atlantic. 850 Fighter Flight was a peripatetic unit which was switched from CVE to CVE according to need. Much of their sea-time was spent in the Arctic. (Cdr Dennis White)

her. *Stanton* and DE *Frost* sank her with Hedgehogs, producing a series of deep explosions like a thunder roll, the last of which smashed the remaining crockery in *Croatan*, 19km (12 miles) away. The same two ships sank Kapitänleutnant Gerhard Schoetzau's *Seewolf U-880* with Hedgehog next day 800km (500 miles) north of Flores after another searchlight hunt through thick fog. This time an even more violent explosion shook the Old Crow like a shack in an earthquake, and gave weight to the theory of *Seewolf* flying bombs or rocket missiles. Crafty veteran Richard Bernadelli in *U-805* got away from *Croatan*'s escorts in the wild weather, but the sinking of Oberleutnant Hans Offermann's *Seewolf U-518* by the DE *Carter*, bucking doggedly through huge seas, on 21 April was the writing on the sea for Dönitz. With only three Seawolves left in the pack, he disbanded it on 23 April.

Bogue brought her VC-19 and 10 DEs from Quonset, *Core* 12 more escorts up from Bermuda, and the two forces met in mid-ocean to take over from the weary First Barrier ships. Fourteen DEs formed a picket line at 8km (five mile) intervals along the 45th parallel, with *Core* 64km (40 miles) north of the left flank and *Bogue* the same distance south of the right. After dusk on 20 April the whole line headed west, with the carriers pushing out round-the-clock air patrols. At 06:45 on 23 April DE *Pillsbury* got a contact, and six DEs went after it. A *Core* Avenger pilot reported the feathery wake of a *Schnorkel*, made a bomb run and claimed a kill. Two DEs followed it up and found a dead whale. Early in the afternoon Bill South, CO of *Bogue*'s VC 19, sighted a U-boat surfacing near the centre of the DE line, 119km (74 miles) from *Bogue*. South attacked and the carrier's screen joined in. The hunted sub was Kapitänleutnant Paul Just's *U-546*. Hounded by the *Frederick C. Davis* to a range of only 595m (650yd), he fired his stern tube and blew the eager DE into a flaming wreck. 'Men died instantly in the molten vortex of that eruption,' runs the official account; 'others, trapped in a mangle of bulkheads and machinery, went down with the ship.' 'It was a matter of life and death,' Just said later, 'a question of me getting the *Davis* or the *Davis* getting me.' All that day the vengeful DEs hunted the *Seewolf*. At last, battered by DCs and Hedgehog, the stubborn boat surfaced dramatically to surrender. All ships with a clear range opened fire. Men fought their way out of the U-boat's hatches. With her bridge smashed to pieces and her Schnorkel severed, *U-546* sank. Just was rescued and professed to know nothing about any V1s or V2s. From Washington Tenth Fleet's McCann signalled 'Four down, three to go!' Of the seven Seawolves only *U-805*, *U-858* and the relief boat *U-881* were left.

At dawn on 6 May the DE *Farquhar* destroyed Oberleutnant Heinz Frischke's *U-881* with depth-charges just as she was about to torpedo the CVE *Mission Bay*. Next day Grossadmiral Dönitz surrendered all German forces to the Allies. Bernadelli in *U-805* and Kapitänleutnant Theo Bode in *U-858* had slipped through Joss Ingram's barriers. At Schnorkel depth they made for their patrol stations off the east coast of the USA. On 9 May when he was off Cape Race Bernadelli found out that the war was over. The morning air smelled sweet as he climbed out on to the bridge. He looked round the watery landscape. 'Verdamnter Atlantik!,' he said, then signalled CINCLANT for surrendering procedure. Off the Delaware Capes, Bode hoisted two olive-green blankets.

The only missile developed for use by a submerged submarine was the RTG, a 38cm (15in) rocket, launched at 35m/sec (115fps), then breathing air to increase its speed to 100m/sec (328fps), with a range of only 4,000m (4,376yd). It was in fact designed as an AA missile, to enable U-boats to fight aircraft while submerged. Operation *Seewolf* was merely a last-ditch act of defiance by Dönitz, at the expense of the lives of some 200 young men, to try to give Germany a little more collateral in a surrender settlement.

TIMELESS VOYAGE

Bad weather damage to *Puncher* in the aborted Narvik attack had necessitated a spell in dock. Men returning to her on 7 May could see huge bonfires being prepared on hilltops along the way. Next day was VE-Day, and Glasgow went wild. The *Puncher* men's only regret was *Queen* with two destroyers dashed to Copenhagen to accept the surrender of the entire German forces in Denmark, arriving there three days before the

Allied armies – a role originally earmarked for *Puncher*.

Although hostilities in Europe formally ceased at midnight on 8 May, and with them in theory all hostile naval operations in European waters, the Admiralty was suspicious of the attitude of individual U-boat commanders. Peter Cockrell from *Campania*, after celebrating rather too well on VE-Night, found himself with a boarding party of one Petty Officer and six well-armed men rushing aboard surrendering U-boats to prevent scuttling . . . 'This was rather fun. I had never even seen a U-boat – great black beasts covered with barnacles. All went well. Any arguments by their Commanding Officers – rabid Nazis – were settled by the menacing waving of my Webley revolver!'

The two convoys JW/RA67 were run to and from Russia later in May, with surface escorts and the CVE HMS *Queen* (Captain K. J. D'Arcy), with 853 Squadron's eight Avenger IIs and eight Wildcat VIs. But there was no trouble. The round voyage was code-named 'Timeless', which was strangely appropriate. It was a unique and heady experience to sail through Arctic seas empty of periscopes, with asdic and radio silent, and to patrol skies void of the hovering shadows which had come to seem as much a feature of the Arctic heavens as the Aurora Borealis.

Right: The flight deck of HMS *Queen*, 'Ruler' Class CVE-49, is bare, and men standing idly about, on Operation 'Timeless', the last convoy run to Russia in World War II, May 1945, by which time the war in Europe was over.

16

'RULERS' IN THE INDIES

'They say that the Fleet came to Trincomalee
Early in 'forty-four,
Heavily laden with sailors and men
Bound for the Japanese war.
There's *Ameer* and *Atheling*, *Battler* as well,
and *Begum* just came for the ride –
You get no promotion in the Indian Ocean,
We'd rather be back in the Clyde.'

IN April 1942 Admiral Chuici Nagumo erupted into the Bay of Bengal with the crack First Air Fleet and five of the six carriers with which he had attacked the US Pacific Fleet in Pearl Harbor, four fast battleships, two cruisers and a screen of destroyers, capturing or sinking 100,000 tons of Allied shipping, striking at Ceylon and the east coast of India, destroying the carrier HMS *Hermes* and the heavy cruisers HMSS *Cornwall* and *Dorsetshire*, but unable to find the rest of the British Eastern Fleet. Admiral Somerville, with *Illustrious* and *Indomitable* and six old battleships, did not shirk a confrontation with Nagumo but the low endurance of his fleet compelled him to put in to Addu Atoll before the Japanese could be brought to action. After that, however, operations in the Pacific had absorbed too many Japanese ships to enable them to do more than operate submarines west of Singapore. But this threat grew worse when, after the U-boat defeat in the North Atlantic in the spring of 1943, Dönitz spread his boats further afield, some to the Indian Ocean to join the Japanese submarines working there.

To prevent Axis submarines from using the Vichy French-held island of Madagascar, Allied troops, protected by aircraft from HMS *Illustrious* and *Indomitable*, occupied the island. But the Axis submarines were not relying on fixed bases. In June seven U-boats refuelled from the tanker *Charlotte Schliemann* at a rendezvous off Madagascar, then attacked the vital traffic which, with the Mediterranean closed off by the Luftwaffe, sailed round the Cape of Good Hope for Ceylon or India, and through the Mozambique Channel with supplies and reinforcements for the Middle East. In June Axis submarines sank ten ships, and the German armed raider *Michel* another two, a total of 67,929 tons.

In six months the Japanese had occupied the whole of their 'Greater South-East Asia Co-Prosperity Sphere', stretching from New Guinea to the Gates of India. Somerville's carriers left him, *Indomitable* for the Malta relief convoy 'Pedestal', *Formidable* for the 'Torch' landings in North Africa, and in January 1943 *Illustrious* went home for a refit. In that month 17 Allied ships totalling 97,214 tons were lost. Ships sailing on the important routes from Durban/Bombay-Aden, Bombay/Calcutta-Colombo, were organised in convoys, though there were not enough escorts. Losses fell to seven ships (46,401 tons) in August, and *U-197* was sunk by RAF aircraft. Early in September five more U-boats fuelled from the 10,000-ton tanker *Brake* south of Madagascar, and spread out north. In September six Allied ships (39,471 tons) were sunk, most of them by Japanese submarines, eight of which were patrolling the Indian Ocean. In October another six ships (25,833 tons) were lost, but *U-533* was sunk in the Gulf of Oman.

For some time Somerville's understrength force had consisted of nine cruisers, five of them old, and even those virtually immobilised because his small force of 13 destroyers had to be used as convoy escorts in lieu of the sloops, corvettes and carriers he lacked to hunt U-boats. Only one submarine, the Free Netherlands *O.24* was operational. But now the surrender of the Italian Fleet and the immobilisation of the *Tirpitz* allowed the release of ships for other duties. Seven submarines and a depot ship arrived in September/October.

BATTLER GOES EAST

Battler had embarked the Swordfish of 834 Squadron, formerly in *Hunter*, at Gibraltar on 22 September, collected Pennington's 834 Seafire LIIC fighter flight from *Hunter* at Bizerta, and steamed through the Mediterranean and the Red Sea to fly off the squadron to Khormaksar, Aden, on 4 October while she went for a boiler clean. From there 834 flew along the coast of the Aden Protectorate (South Yemen) to an airstrip between Mukalla and Riyan, which looked across 320km (200 miles) of water border between the Gulf of Aden and the golden haze of the Arabian Sea to the Horn of Africa, with Socotra Island a scrap of desert 240km (150 miles) further east, its pointed headland of Ras Darish sign-posting Calicut and

Right: No. 834 Squadron crest (Motto: '*Volo ut Mordeam*' – I Fly that I may Bite)

scented Malabar. But Riyan was no jewel of Arabia, just a fortnight of sleepless days slapping sand flies at the edge of a scorching runway bordering the desolate sand sea of Rub al Khali, the Empty Quarter, where the wandering Bedu anchored their black tents. There were shivering night A/S patrols, sometimes in silver moonlight. The white-flanked Swordfish watched over the Aden-Bombay convoys and the flocks of ships steaming up from the Equator.

Battler's Swordfish humped rockets, depth charges or 113kg (250lb) bombs around in the heat, but the only enemies seemed to be the bugs and cockroaches which infested the ship. When he sighted a surfaced submarine, New Zealand pilot Percy Craig wasted no time in loosing off a full salvo of eight RPs, but they all missed. A little later *Battler* received a message from HM submarine *Trident* warning the carrier's ship's company never to set foot in Aden when *Trident* men were ashore there.

Battler escorted a convoy on her way to Bombay, where she docked on 25 October. On 4 November she was out on Indian Ocean convoy work, then on 13 November the British submarine *Taurus* sank the Japanese *I-34* off Penang, Malaya, five

Right: 'A certain beauty in motion'. HMS *Battler* in the Indian Ocean. (Barry Cookson)

Top: Lieutenant-Commander Brooks Walford, RN, formerly Swordfish observer in strikes against Axis shipping from Malta, lectures officers of No. 834 Composite Squadron in *Battler* east of Suez, 1942. Front row, Lieutenant(A) Alex 'Sandy' Brunt, DSC, RNZNVR.

Above: *Battler*'s hangar. Bringing up a Swordfish. (Barry Cookson)

Below: Fitting solid-head RPs on one of *Battler*'s Swordfish. A 40lb practice bomb lies on the deck.

more Allied submarines arrived, and Allied shipping losses for November/December fell. Convoy was suspended on some routes, then reinstated in February 1944 after six individually routed ships were sunk in January. On 27 January Vice-Admiral Sir Arthur John Power arrived at Trincomalee as Second-in-Command Eastern Fleet, with the battleships *Queen Elizabeth* and *Valiant*, battlecruiser *Renown*, carrier *Illustrious* and the repair carrier *Unicorn*, which was used operationally for a time, and the Fleet concentrated on destroying enemy tankers supplying the U-boats.

In February the *Charlotte Schliemann* was sighted by a Catalina from Mauritius and ultimately sunk by the destroyer *Relentless*. On 12 March a *Battler* Swordfish sighted the tanker *Brake* south of Mauritius after a tip-off by British Intelligence, while refuelling two U-boats. In an attempt, almost certainly too late, to conceal the carrier's presence from the enemy, the aircraft followed orders not to attack, but guided the destroyer *Roebuck* to the target, which was sunk by gunfire. The two U-boats were within easy range of *Battler*'s Seafires, but only two Swordfish were scrambled, without fighter escort, and the submarines got away. Later the same night a submarine was detected shadowing the carrier. It was attacked by 834's CO, Lieutenant-Commander Eric Dixon-Child in a Swordfish, and no further trace of her was found. On 21 March *Battler* arrived at Durban for a refit. Here 'Faj' Pennington's Seafires of 834's idle Fighter Flight were flown ashore, and a flight of Wildcats took their place.

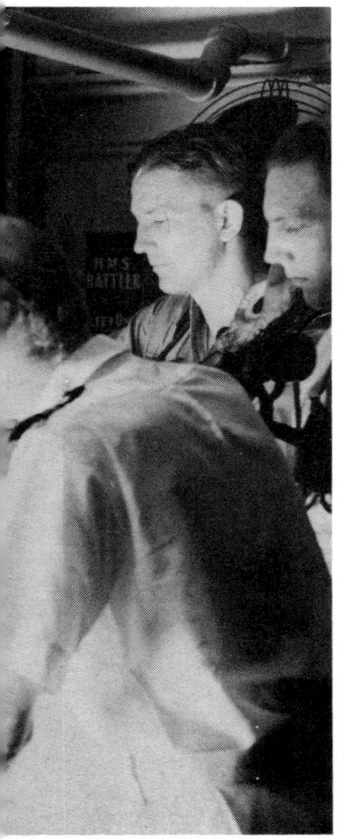

Left: 'We are *here* . . .' Lieutenant Rouse, *Battler*'s Fighter Controller, briefs the carrier's fighter pilots. From left to right: Lieutenant(A) F. A. J. 'Faj' Pennington, DSC, RNZNVR, the Fighter Leader; next to him Sub-Lieutenant(A) James Edmundson, RNZNVR; fourth from left Sub-Lieutenant(A) Alistair McCleod, RNZNVR; fifth from left Sub-Lieutenant(A) Doug Alexander, RNZNVR. There was a very high percentage of New Zealanders in the FAA, almost all of them of first-class leadership material. Lieutenant, later Lieutenant-Commander, Pennington was one of the most outstanding fighter leaders of World War II. Thanks largely to his example and instruction, his 834 Fighter Flight manned entirely by New Zealanders, emerged from the Salerno attrition with a record of only four deck pecks, no injuries and all six aircraft still serviceable. Later, tragically, he was killed in a mid-air collision. (Barry Cookson)

Top: Ready for the green. A patrol of one Swordfish and two Seafires ranged for take-off from HMS *Battler*. This is one of the many photographs taken aboard *Battler* by Ron 'Twinkle' Stilling, commissioned official Royal Navy photographer, later a distinguished member of the *Evening News* staff. (Royal Navy)

Above left: A Stilling photograph of a *Hunter*'s Swordfish awaiting the signal for take-off. (Royal Navy)

Above right: Five of *Battler*'s fighter pilots in front of one of their Seafires. Left to right: Al McCleod, 'Faj' Pennington, Jim Edmundson, and far right Doug Alexander. Stilling always asked his human subjects and some thought his mechanical ones as well, for a 'twinkle' before clicking the shutter.

Below: Composite patrol. One of *Battler*'s Seafires flies between two of her Swordfish somewhere in the Indian Ocean. the Stringbags are finding it difficult to keep up. (Barry Cookson)

Left: 'All serene?' was a favourite expression of Major Burch, HMS *Battler*'s Commander(F), one of the many distinguished Royal Marine officers in the Fleet Air Arm (left). To his right is Lieutenant-Commander(A) Eric Dixon-Child, RNVR, CO of 834 Squadron. Here Major Burch is about to drop his flag for take-off. He bears a striking resemblance to the late Errol Flynn. (Barry Cookson)

Left: Even COs have prangs. Lieutenant-Commander Dixon Child's broken-backed Swordfish after a heavy landing on *Battler*. (Barry Cookson)

Below: Stilling photograph of a Swordfish returning to *Battler* after sighting the U-boat refuelling tanker *Brake* in the Indian Ocean, 12 March 1943. (Barry Cookson)

Right: The Deep Six. 'Twinkle' Stilling view of a crashed Swordfish from *Battler*. The aircraft's rubber raft has been released from its stowage in the upper port wing and inflated itself, pushing aside its retaining panel. (Barry Cookson)

Below: A Seafire takes-off.

Above: A Seafire ready for take-off from HMS *Hunter* in the Indian Ocean. A 'Twinkle' Stilling picture. (Barry Cookson)

Below: HMS *Atheling*, Ruler-class Trade Protection escort carrier, left Greenock, Scotland, for the Indian Ocean in bad weather. Here, snow lies thick on a Corsair. *Atheling* joined the British Eastern Fleet in March 1944. (Robert Forbes)

THE 'RULERS' ARRIVE

Meanwhile, the Eastern Fleet was further reinforced by three Lease-Lend escort carriers of the 'Ruler' Class, the Fighter carrier HMS *Atheling* and the two Trade Protection carriers *Begum* (Captain C. L. Howe, CBE) and *Shah* (Captain W. J. Yendell, RN), the Free French battleship *Richelieu*, and more destroyers. *Atheling* was supposed to be an 'unlucky' ship. Laid down as ACV-33, USS *Glacier*, at Seattle-Tacoma Shipbuilding, completed at Puget Sound Navy Yard and commissioned into the RN on 3 July 1943, some of her men were hurt when an overloaded gangway collapsed. She then had engine trouble twice in the Caribbean, lost a stoker to the toxic fumes of leaking avgas in the Mediterranean, and two more men in the Indian Ocean in an accident with a paravane. HMS *Begum* (ACV-36) was commissioned first as US *Bolinas*, then transferred to the Royal Navy on 4 August 1943. HMS *Shah*, ex-USS *Jamaica*, ACV-43, was handed over to Britain a month later, 27 September 1943. Some 'Ruler' Class ships were equipped to cover close support duties as well as anti-submarine, among them *Shah*, *Begum* and the later arrival *Rajah*, and were then known as General Purpose carriers.

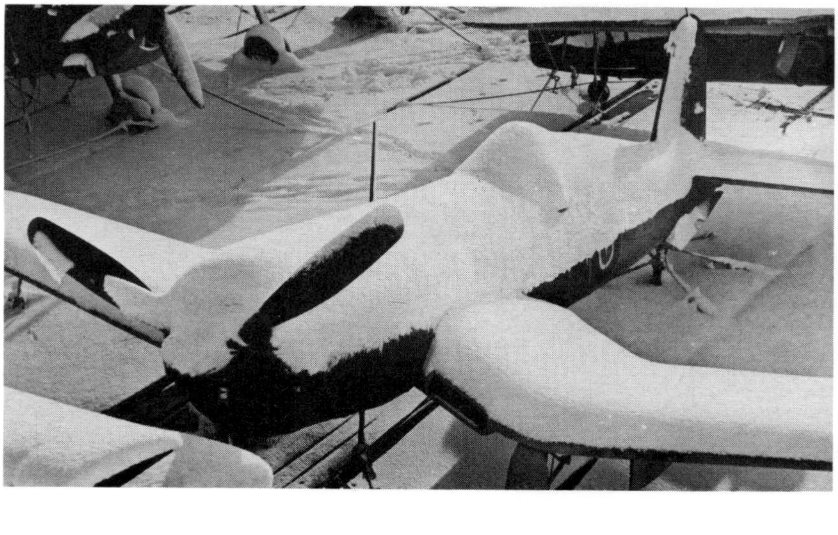

Squadrons were formed from reserve aircraft and personnel, No 889 with Seafire IICs, and FIIIs from the first production batch, the earliest of the Mark to serve outside the United Kingdom; and 890 with Wildcat Vs. Commanding Officer of 889 was Lieutenant-Commander F. A. J. Pennington, the New Zealander who brought with him into the squadron some of the pilots of 834 Fighter Flight, who had left *Battler* with him when she had exchanged her Seafires for Wildcats at Durban, and whom he had trained so well for 'Avalanche' at Salerno. The two units began working-up with *Atheling*.

Also working up with their squadrons in April were General Purpose escort carriers *Shah* and *Begum*, preparing for convoy escort in the Indian Ocean. *Shah*'s 851 Squadron had formed as a TBR squadron at Squantum, Boston, Massachusetts, on

1 October 1943, with 12 Avengers, 13 pilots, 13 observers and some 100 other personnel, including telegraphist/air-gunners, under Lieutenant-Commander A. M. Tuke, RN, the only regular officer. After familiarisation with their new and comparatively sophisticated aircraft (the TAGs had not handled a turret before) the squadron flew down to Norfolk, Virginia, in December to qualify in deck-landing aboard USS *Charger*, CVE-30 (formerly BAVG-4).

On 19 April USS *Saratoga* and HMS *Illustrious* hit oil tanks, the airfield, tankers, supply ships and submarines in the harbour, and the radar and power stations at Sabang on Weh Island just off the northern tip of Sumatra. This was the first of a series of dual-purpose strikes to deprive the enemy of vital fuel supplies and to divert his attention from the major combat areas in the Pacific. A month later, on 17 May, the big Japanese avgas dump at Surabaya and the oil refinery at Wonokrono were hit, then *Saratoga* sailed for the USA.

'RULERS' IN TRADE PROTECTION

On 13 May Compo 851 re-embarked in *Shah* with its 12 Avengers and four Wildcat Vs. 889's Seafire FIIIs and 890's Wildcat Vs completed their short deck landing training. Sadly, Lieutenant-Commander Pennington and his wingman were killed in a mid-air collision.

On 22 August Admiral Somerville was relieved by Admiral Sir Bruce Fraser, C-in-C Designate of the Pacific Fleet, which was to be formed with the most modern of the ships assembled at Ceylon, with Admiral Power to command the East Indies Fleet, comprising the ships remaining in the Indian Ocean.

AMEER SUPPORTS THE ARMY

With preparations for the recapture of the Philippines in the final stage, Admiral Fraser was asked for more diversionary strikes, and obliged by attacking enemy bases on Car Nicobar and Nancowry Islands, and on Belawan Deli and Pangkalanberandan in Sumatra. Following this, on 16 January 1945 the British Pacific Fleet itself, comprising *Illustrious, Indomitable, Victorious* and *Indefatigable*, battleship *King George V*, four cruisers and ten destroyers, sailed from Ceylon for Australia and duty with the US Fifth Fleet.

After severe losses in Pacific battles, the main operational unit of the Imperial Japanese Fleet was the Second Diversionary Attack Force at Singapore, comprising the two battleship/carriers *Ise* and *Hyuga*, the two heavy cruisers *Ashigara* and *Haguro*, destroyer *Kamikaze* and smaller units. All were part of the new 10th Area Fleet under Vice-Admiral Shigeru Fukudome, covering the East Indies and Indian Ocean, with the beached 13th Air Fleet's 55 fighters, and 17 torpedo planes – the remnants of six air groups. Also at Singapore were the disabled heavy cruisers *Takao* and *Myoko*, damaged in the Philippines.

To oppose Fukudome, should he interfere with Allied landings planned to assist the advance of the British Army in Burma or support the landing of Japanese reinforcements, Admiral Power had at his disposal in the East Indies Fleet: the Third Battle Squadron (*Queen Elizabeth* and *Renown*) under Vice-Admiral Walker, nine cruisers of the 5th Cruiser Squadron (Rear-Admiral W. R. Patterson), and four escort carriers of the Escort Carrier Squadron under Rear-Admiral Clement Moody (Fighter carrier *Ameer*, Trade Protection carrier *Begum*, Assault carrier *Empress*, General Purpose carrier *Shah*, with the older *Battler* as an aircraft ferry) plus some 20 destroyers.

As General Slim's 14th Army troops drove the Japanese south through the Arakan region of Burma towards the capital, Rangoon, they captured Akyab, the only good port in the Arakan, and the useful airfield on Arakan Island. Then South-East Asia Command, under Lord Louis Mountbatten, mounted a series of amphibious landings further ahead to cut off the retreating enemy. Early in January 1945 the forces for Operation 'Matador', a landing on Ramree Island to capture the port and airfield of Kyaukpyu, and Operation 'Sankey', to take nearby Cheduba Island, were assembling.

In the support and covering force was HMS *Ameer*, commanded by Captain P. D. H. R. Pelly, DSO, RN, with Major Bill Aston, who had served in *Furious, Courageous* and *Glorious*, as CO of 833 Squadron in the Western Desert and in 'Torch', as her Commander (Air), one of many Royal Marine aviators in the FAA. *Ameer* had been Burrard's first customer for anglicization, completed on 18 October 1943, and should have joined the Eastern Fleet in the early spring of 1944, after conversion to a Fighter carrier by the Caledonian Shipbuilding Company at Dundee. Unfortunately one of her main boilers blew up, and she swung round the buoy at Greenock for two months while a replace-

Below: Hellcats of 804 Squadron, ready for operations, leaving HMS *Ameer* for Trincomalee, 20 December 1944. Note the plane guard escort vessel in attendance to rescue any pilot forced to ditch. (G. Thomas)

Right: HMS *Ameer* on Operation 'Matador' with destroyer HMS *Raider.*

Opposite page, top: 'The Barracuda Two will be the death of you . . .' The Barra's grotesque shoulder wing undercarriage has let her down in training aboard HMS *Rajah.*

Opposite page, centre: HMS *Rajah.* Ruler-class *Rajah* brought a batch of replenishment Hellcats for the Eastern Fleet, which she joined in early 1945. (Tony Patrick)

Opposite page, bottom: Left to right, battleship HMS *Queen Elizabeth,* Fighter escort carrier HMS *Emperor* and FFS battleship *Richelieu* in Operation 'Sunfish' in the East Indies, a programme of air strkes, with *Emperor's* specially equipped Hellcats of 888 Squadron carrying out photo-reconnaissance of future targets in Malaya. Seen from HMS *Khedive.* (Peter Embleton)

ment boiler was found and fitted. Repairs complete, the flight deck was filled, the hangar stuffed full with new replacement Corsairs, Hellcats and Avengers, spare parts and engines, all of which were disembarked at Cochin, southern India, at the end of May.

Ameer left Trincomalee for 'Matador' on 18 January to give support and air protection over the invasion beach at Kyaukpyu, north Ramree. Troops landed on 21 January, the Japanese were taken by surprise, and by dusk the airfield was in Allied hands. Royal Marines embarked in the cruisers *Newcastle, Kenya* and *Nigeria* (Rock Force) sailed for Cheduba on the 23rd and met *Ameer,* the light cruiser *Phoebe,* destroyers *Norman* and *Raider* and sloops *Spey* and *Teviot* at sea. *Ameer's* Hellcats flew air cover over the landing, which was unopposed.

By this time the Japanese Co-Prosperity Sphere was shrinking, with garrisons being withdrawn from bases on its outer barrier, the Lesser Sunda Islands, Timor, the outer Moluccas, scattered islands in the Banda Sea and Arafura Sea north of Australia. Java, Borneo and Sumatra were to be held as long as possible, with a final stand in Malaya and Indo-China, which meant moving troops from the Andamans and Nicobars and 5,000 men from Timor to Singapore, from which Indo-China could be reinforced. The Secondary Diversionary Attack Force at Singapore was to cover these movements, though *Isa* and *Hyuga* left on 10 February with avgas for Japan. It would be part of East Indies Fleet's duties to interfere with any such movements.

Next to the retaking of Burma was the capture of Malaya. For landings planned at Port Swettenham and Port Dickson on the Malayan coast of the Malacca Strait, and for the advance southward to Singapore (Operation 'Zipper') photographic information was needed on Japanese defences, especially Phuket Island at the northern entrance to the Malacca Strait, which would make a good forward base for the advance on Singapore. This was largely beyond the range of shore-based photo-recce planes, and on 22 February *Ameer,* with the photo-recce Hellcats of 888 Squadron, and Captain J. S. R. Brown's *Empress,* escorted by a cruiser, destroyers and frigates, sailed on Operation 'Stacey'.

Fighting camera failure, no wind and a temperamental catapult, and with the ship sweltering in the heat, the Hellcats took their pictures of Phuket, then overflew the Malayan Peninsula to the Kra Isthmus, which the Hellcats photographed and over which one Avenger dropped 40,000 propaganda leaflets. Though lit by the spotlight of a full moon, the 'Stacey' force went undetected until 1 March. Just after the start of the morning watch, aircraft of the Rising Sun attacked the ships. CAP Hellcats of *Ameer's* 808 Squadron destroyed a 'Dinah' (twin-engined Mitsubishi Army recce-bomber), the first Japanese aircraft to be shot down by aircraft from a British escort carrier, and two hours later a flight of four 804 Squadron Hellcats from *Empress,* led by Lieutenant John Myerscough, RNVR, shot down an 'Oscar' (single-engined Nakajima Army fighter). Hellcats from *Ameer* rounded off the day by shooting down another Oscar after dinner.

21st ACS

The Escort Carrier Squadron was to be re-formed with the new designation of 21st Aircraft Carrier Squadron, under a new commander, Commodore G. N. Oliver, RN, as part of the East Indies Fleet. In February *Khedive* (Captain D. H. Magnay, RN) and *Emperor* (Captain Sir Charles Madden, Bart, RN) joined *Ameer, Shah* and *Empress* with the Fleet,

bringing with them the Hellcats of No 3 Naval Fighter Wing, led by Lieutenant-Commander R. H. P. Carver, RN. In March *Hunter* and *Stalker* arrived at Ceylon with the 807 and 809 Squadron Seafires of No 4 Naval Fighter Wing, and began working-up with Hellcats of 3 Wing.

A number of very experienced Royal Marine pilots were now ably filling the Commander (Flying)'s job in escort carriers. In *Khedive* was Major Alan 'Minnie' Marsh, RM, who, although awarded two engineering scholarships to Manchester University, had enlisted in the Royal Marines straight from school in November 1930 and was the first Marine officer to apply for transfer to the FAA while still under training as a 2nd Lieutenant, and afterwards served in *Courageous*. In 1940 he flew with 804 Squadron in the defence of Scapa Flow, in *Furious* for fighter cover over Norway, and as Flight Commander when the squadron was supplying the Fighter Catapult Ships with aircraft and pilots. After commanding the squadron he was in the thick of the air fighting in Malta convoys 'Bellows' and 'Pedestal', and became Commander (F) of the CVE *Rajah*, which was carrying out deck-landing training and convoy work across the Atlantic and to India and Ceylon. When *Rajah* began ferrying aircraft Marsh took over as Wings of *Khedive*. 'To say I got a shock when I arrived on board at Sheerness on New Year's Eve 1944/45 would be an understatement. The ship had been in action in the landings in the South of France and in the eastern Med and had just come out of a refit at Tilbury. It was in an appalling state. Broken gear everywhere, firefighting gear untested, no racks for the long range fuel tanks or rocket rails and just a general unprepared shambles. No-one seemed to realise that the Squadron (808) was equipped with Hellcats or that there was much difference between these and the Seafires which they had been operating – the Hellcat is in fact twice the weight of the Seafire. Even the batsman had never controlled a Hellcat. The Captain was new and had never served in a carrier, he was a gunnery officer, and this was to prove very awkward indeed. Finally the Air Staff at Colombo refused to let us have more than a nominal four days for deck landing training and work up – a recipe for disaster.'

OPERATION 'SUNFISH

On the afternoon of 8 April Vice-Admiral 'Hookey' Walker sailed from Trincomalee with Force 63 on Operation 'Sunfish', a more ambitious version of Stacey comprising air strikes, anti-shipping sweeps, bombardments, large-scale photo-reconnaissance over beaches, airfields and ports, and small-scale over a wide area in the Kuala Lumpur, Port Swettenham, Port Dickson and Malacca areas, with the Force divided into two groups: Group I, *Queen Elizabeth* (Flag), the Free French battleship *Richelieu*, the heavy cruiser

London and destroyers *Saumarez*, *Verulam* and *Vigilant*; and Group 2, CVEs *Emperor* (flag of Rear-Admiral Patterson) and *Khedive*, heavy cruiser *Cumberland*, with destroyers *Venus* and *Virago*.

AIRCRAFT LOSSES

No 808 Squadron (CO Lieutenant-Commander 'Lash' Rankin, DSC), previously equipped with Seafire IICs, had flown from *Battler* and from the Paestum strip at Salerno but as presently constituted most of its pilots were new to the East Indies and still learning to operate their powerful American Hellcats. The brief four days permitted them at Colombo for deck landing training and work-up had not been sufficient, and in Wings' Minnie Marsh's view this was responsible for a number of very bad crashes. Of 808's 24 Hellcats, seven had been disembarked at China Bay, Trincomalee. Four of these under Lieutenant S. J. K. Edwards, RNR, were detached to *Empress*, the other three flying back to *Khedive*. One of these was flown by Chief Petty Officer (Air) C. E. Gregory. 'In the case of Gregory, his aircraft was fitted with rocket rails under the wings which none of the pilots liked as it raised the stalling speed. Gregory was making a rather high approach and appeared to stall, as the aircraft lost height rapidly and he was hurriedly waved off by the batsman. Gregory opened his throttle too late, the aircraft began a right turn in a stalled condition and crashed on to the flight deck emergency steering position, bursting into flames. The aircraft fell over the side and all that remained was a pillar of smoke in the sea where the Hellcat had sunk.' This left 19 Hellcats and 22 pilots.

In *Emperor*'s air group were six specially fitted photo-reconnaissance Hellcats of 888 Squadron, the four Hellcats of *Khedive*'s 808 and Avengers of 851 Squadron. On 11 April Lieutenant (A) R. J. Foxley, RNZNVR, engaged seven Oscars 16km (ten miles) north-west of Sabang heading for the big ships of Force 63 as they withdrew. Neither side scored but as Foxley was returning to the ship he saw one Oscar following him. He eluded it, and when it turned away followed it with the clever tactical use of cloud and shot it down. Later in the day another section, led by Lieutenant (A) R. B. Mancus, RNVR, a former Fighter Catapult Ship pilot, plus two aircraft from *Emperor*, were vectored on to a bogey which they intercepted at 16:20 and discovered to be a Dinah twin-engined Mitsubishi Army recce bomber, which was shot down by Sub-Lieutenant S. C. Richardson after a stern chase.

On the 12th Force 63 refuelled from the Royal Fleet Auxiliary tanker *Echodale*, and closed the coast of Sumatra. On the 14th the Force entered the Pulo Nias Channel to fly off PR aircraft from *Emperor*. Returning to *Khedive*, 808 Hellcat *JW865* piloted by Sub-Lieutenant (A) I. Walker, RNVR, missed all the arrestor wires, smashed through the barrier and overturned, caught fire and plunged overboard, taking unmanned Hellcat *JX760* with it and killing its own pilot, a Petty Officer and two air mechanics on the flight deck.

The weather was still bad on the 15th, but the urgent photo-recces were repeated. The Force steamed down the western coast of Sumatra, and the PR Hellcats took off from *Emperor* in a position west of Padang, climbed over the high Pegunungan Barisan, crossed the breadth of the island and the Malacca Strait, and in poor, murky visibility took their pictures. Sub-Lieutenant (A) J. W. Tomlinson, a very experienced PR pilot, was drowned when he ditched in the sea 16km (ten miles) off Port Swettenham. The photographs, thanks to the weather, were of poor quality, and there was a repeat performance next day. Japanese aircraft appeared but remained above 9,100m (30,000ft). With the Pratt & Whitneys gulping fuel and the pilots oxygen, the covering Hellcats of Sub-Lieutenant (A) A. Bedding and J. West-Taylor, RNVR, climbed stubbornly to intercept a 'Lily' bomber escorted by two Oscars and shot one Oscar down.

On the 16th the first two CAP aircraft reconnoitred the coast from Airbangis to Natal for shipping targets for the destroyers to vent their frustration on. At the same time eight Avengers, escorted by four Hellcats from *Emperor*, attacked shipping in Emmahaven harbour. Two Hellcats strafed the airfield at Padang, damaging several Dinahs and destroying an Oscar. Immediately after the attack the section leader, Sub-Lieutenant (A) Jimmy McNee, RNVR, was himself attacked by an Oscar apparently flown by an ace pilot, as it made attack after attack in an amazing series of aerobatics, mostly upside-down. McNee violently defended himself but his aircraft was badly damaged. Eventually the ace broke off, leaving

Below: A Hellcat PR.I of No. 888 Squadron FAA before take-off on what the long-range tank indicates was to be an extended photo-recce.

Right: No. 888 Squadron crest and motto '*Nullo Missio*' ('No respite'). (J. Paterson)

Below: Three of 888's PR Hellcats on a mission over East Indian jungle. (Cdr B. A. McCaw)

Bottom: Lieutenant(A) Dickson of 888 Squadron's PR Unit, in his Hellcat. The camera symbols below the cockpit represent PR missions flown. (J. Paterson)

another Oscar on the scene, which McNee destroyed with a deflection shot on the turn from a range of several hundred metres. McNee returned to *Khedive* and landed his Hellcat successfully with no hydraulics and a badly battered machine, a tribute to the way they built aircraft back at The Ironworks.

OPERATION 'DRACULA'

In the long months of the Japanese occupation of Burma, South-East Asia Command had planned 'Dracula', an amphibious assault on the port and Burmese capital of Rangoon, which lies on the broad peninsula where the great Irrawaddy River, 1,600km (1,000 miles) from its source in the high Patkai, flows into the Andaman Sea through its many mouths. Always other theatres, other landings, took priority. 'Torch', 'Avalanche', 'Overlord', 'Dragoon', all in turn appropriated the ships and landing craft, men and machines of a limited supply. Now Slim's 'forgotten army' was threatening the capital from landward. Supremo Mountbatten began to think he could leave Burma to the Army, with the Eastern Fleet in support. The 14th Army would take Rangoon, leaving him free to concentrate all his forces on taking Malaya before the monsoon came – first the capture of Phuket (Operation 'Roger') in June, then the Port Swettenham and Port Dickson landings ('Zipper') in October, finally the assault on Singapore ('Mailfist') in December. But the Army slowed down, Chiang Kai Shek demanded the return of his Chinese contingent, and the Americans warned that almost half their transport aircraft supplying the 14th Army would be switched to the aid of the Nationalist Chinese from 1 June. If the Army did not reach Rangoon by then it risked being bogged down by the monsoon. Mountbatten postponed the drive on Singapore and reinstated 'Dracula', which he thought stood a better chance of taking Rangoon before the rains came.

CAP over the assault convoys would be supplied by four Assault carriers of the 21st Aircraft Carrier Squadron, newcomers *Hunter* (Captain A. D. Torlesse, RN) and *Stalker* (Captain L. C. Sinker, RN) with the Seafires of No 4 Naval Fighter Wing, *Khedive* and *Emperor* with the Hellcats of No 3 Wing, and the fighter direction cruiser *Phoebe*, plus four destroyers, the whole commanded by Commodore Oliver in the command cruiser *Royalist*. The remainder of the East Indies Fleet, as Force 63, was to carry out a covering operation ('Bishop') in the Andaman Sea to oppose any enemy interference with the landings. For this job 'Hookey' Walker commanded the *QE*, *Richelieu*, cruisers *Cumberland*, *Suffolk*, *Ceylon* and *Tromp* (Free Dutch), Assault carrier *Empress*, with 20 Hellcats of 804 Squadron, General Purpose carrier *Shah*, with ten Avengers of 851 Squadron and four Hellcats of 804, and five destroyers. In addition, three submarines patrolled the southern end of the Malacca Strait, with two more in the Eastern Bay of Bengal.

Force 63 sailed from Trincomalee on 27 April. On the 28th the first of the four main assault force convoys sailed north-west through the Andamans from captured Kyaukpyu, Ramree Island, for Rangoon, the other three following at 24-hour intervals. At dawn on the 30th Force 63 bombarded the two airfields on Car Nicobar, following this up with a Hellcat strike, and moved on to Port Blair, South Andaman Island, leaving its airfield runways cratered. *Emperor, Khedive, Hunter* and *Stalker*, with 44 Hellcats and 54 Seafires (LIIIs and FRIIIs), sailed for Rangoon from Akyab. Low-level CAP was flown, and on 1 May, D minus 1, an experienced pilot touched down too fast, bounced over arrestor wires and barrier into the deck park, writing off his own machine, pushing another into the sea, and damaging a third so badly it was given the deep six.

THE 'DRACULA DEPRESSION'

The weather was everywhere bad, the 'Dracula Depression' lay heavy over sea and ships. Heavy black clouds, thunderstorms and sudden squalls

Right: An impressive view of HMS *Begum*, Ruler-class escort carrier commissioned as ACV-36, USS *Bolinas*, transferred to the Royal Navy 4 August 1943, fifth of her class to be 'anglicized' at Burrard's yard in Vancouver, Canada, later converted to a General Purpose carrier. Here she carries out a leisurely unmooring, starboard anchor almost home, with the foc's'le officer signalling the state of play to the bridge. (IWM)

Right: Commissioned 11 August 1943, ex-CVE-32, HMS *Slinger*, Ruler class, with *Striker* and *Speaker* was one of the first ships of the RN 30th Aircraft Carrier Squadron to serve with the British Pacific Fleet, her main job the ferrying of replacement aircraft to the Fleet carriers. Here she turns into wind to launch the two Seafires ranged aft, attended by her 'crash boat', ready to pick up any ditching pilots.

Above: My turn next . . . HMS *Khedive's* Hellcats line up for the catapault off Car Nicobar Island. (Maj Alan Marsh)

signalled the early approach of the monsoon, the times of tides dictated the arrival of the assault force off Rangoon in darkness and restricted landing craft movements to certain times, but by the end of May Day the assault force ships had assembled on time and in the right place, with only a few leaks and breakdowns. At dawn the Indian assault troops found a city almost empty of the enemy, and there was very little fighting. Ghurkha parachute troops were dropped over Elephant Point, which they captured after a brief struggle. The dockyard was almost unusable, with wreckage blocking the berths and mines in the harbour. Cranes had been toppled or sabotaged, sheds looted and burned. There was no power, water or sanitation. Useless Japanese banknotes swirled fitfully in deserted streets like dead leaves. And then the monsoon broke.

A heavy sea arose, and the carriers pitched drunkenly, with a film of rain blurring windshields, and two more Seafires of 807 Squadron were totalled in crashes. Seafire pilot Sub-Lieutenant (A) C. de G. Vyner, RNVR, from *Hunter* was lost when his machine hit the sea in a fierce rain squall. To the south-east, 3 Wing Hellcats from *Ameer* and *Shah* of Force 63 bombed coasters off northern Arakan and strafed airfields at Victoria Point. Redundant at Rangoon, *Emperor, Khedive, Hunter* and *Stalker* turned south. At dawn on 6 May Seafires from *Stalker* escorted a Hellcat strike on Port Victoria, and strafed the airfields. Hellcats from *Shah* and *Empress* attacked Port Blair harbour. Sub-Lieutenant J. A. Scott, RNVR, tried to fly his damaged machine back to his carrier, but crashed into the sea within sight of her, and was lost. Then, at 17:20 that afternoon, the destroyer *Venus* in 21st ACS' screen intercepted enemy radio transmissions dead astern using the call sign of the *Haguro*.

The ten Avengers of No 851 Squadron in *Shah* were the only aircraft available for an attack on heavy warships, but they could not carry British torpedoes. With no American tinfish, 227kg (500lb) bombs would have to do. Then the transmissions stopped.

Next day, 7 May, *Empress* and *Shah* launched the last sorties of 'Dracula', Hellcat strikes on Car Nicobar, and on the 8th came the news that the war in Europe was over. The ships reached Ceylon next day and had spliced the mainbrace when a signal flew round for steam and a departure at 06:00. Ultra intercepts of Japanese signals had revealed that a heavy cruiser of the *Myoko* Class, *Ashigara* or *Haguro*, or possibly *Taiho*, if she had been repaired, was due to arrive at Port Blair, South Andaman, before nightfall on 12 May, and leave again before daylight.

THE *HAGURO* HUNT

Ships' companies worked all night ammunitioning, and at 06:00 on 10 May Group II of a new Force 61, 21st ACS with *Hunter* (21 Seafires and an air/sea rescue Walrus), *Emperor* and *Khedive* (a total of 38 Hellcats and a Walrus), and *Shah* (nine Avengers of 851 Squadron and four Hellcats), destroyers *Rotherham, Nubian* and *Penn*, all under Commodore Oliver in *Royalist*, left harbour. Group I, *Queen Elizabeth* (Flag), *Tromp* and *Tartar*, followed, and Group III (Rear-Admiral Patterson), *Richelieu, Cumberland* (Flag) and Captain Manley Power's 26th Destroyer Flotilla, brought up the rear.

The weather for Operation 'Diadem' was fine, calm and sunny, a great change from the 'Dracula Depression', as Force 61 steamed east, carriers in the van. At 22:30 Lieutenant-Commander Andrews' submarine *Subtle* reported a *Myoko* Class cruiser painted pink and green coming up Malacca Strait with a destroyer and two other escorts. It was *Haguro* (Captain Kahu Sugiura) in exotic camouflage, with destroyer *Kamikaze* (Lieutenant-Commander Kinichi Kasuga), two submarine chasers and an air escort of three Jake (Aichi 13A) floatplanes from Sabang, heading for the Andamans to evacuate the garrisons and do as much damage as she could.

Haguro was a heavy cruiser of the *Myoko* Class designed by Vice-Admiral Yuzura Hiraga to conform to the 10,000-ton limit of the Washington Naval Treaty, and was completed on 25 April 1929 by Mitsubishi. She carried ten 8in guns of an improved model fitted in 1939, new anti-torpedo bulges and thick 127mm (5in) side armour, a heavy wartime AA armament of four triple, eight twin and 24 single 25mm guns, two quadruple torpedo tubes firing the powerful and reliable 49-knot Long Lance Type 93 torpedo, and reasonably up to date air warning and gunnery control radar. Although overdue for docking after three years of battle, she could still steam as fast as 'Hookey' Walker's destroyers.

Subtle got into a good attacking position and was about to fire a spread of torpedoes when *Haguro* turned sharply to starboard and steamed north-east away from her. 'Hookey' Walker headed for Ten Degree Channel, between the Andamans and Nicobars, to intercept the cruiser. At dawn on the 11th fuel contamination in *Shah* reduced her to six knots and she dropped behind, with *Nubian* screening her. In very light winds the force lost time manoeuvring to launch aircraft for CAP, and at 12:30 swung south-east for Six Degree (Great) Channel. A bogey appeared on the *QE*'s radar screen 130km (80 miles) to the north. Two Seafires from *Hunter*'s CAP flew down the bearing, but saw nothing. The aircraft did not sight Force 61, but another from Car Nicobar did. Following orders, Sugiura turned back.

In Colombo Chief of Staff Commodore Searle, with Admiral Power away in Rangoon, monitored Ultra intercepts and signalled to Walker 'You have been sighted. Your target returning to base. Assume you will return to area of Position Q and await news.' Walker headed for Position Q 320km (200 miles) south-west of Achin Head, the northernmost point of Sumatra, and flew off strikes and searches. Fighter-bomber Hellcats from *Emperor* hit Car Nicobar airfields, while others chased a bogey and were diverted to *Shah* for recovery while their ship was busy flying off. One tore his hook out and damaged Hellcats in the deck park. Four *Khedive* CAP Hellcats hit a monsoon rain squall and barely made the deck.

In the trailing *Shah*, 851's Avengers were standing by, armed and fuelled, for a strike, when her catapult was found to be faulty. To get them off the deck the TBFs were de-bombed and de-fuelled down to 300l (80 gal), and exchanged with *Emperor* for some of her Hellcats. *Emperor*, an Assault carrier, with facilities mainly for directing fighter-bomber sorties, was not equipped to operate light bomber strikes, but the Avenger crews were briefed at 21:00 for an anti-shipping strike, then stood down.

OPERATION 'MITRE'

In heavy squalls and torrential rain Walker refuelled on the 13th, his carriers topping up the destroyers with difficulty, *Virago* colliding with *Emperor*. By 04:00 on 14 May he was in Six Degree Channel, but there was no word of the enemy, and he returned to the refuelling area. Sugiura was actually waiting off the lighthouse west of Pulo Burnet for signs and portents. When he heard that the transport *Kurishoyo Maru No 2* and her escort the subchaser *SC57* had safely reached Car Nicobar, he decided to follow. Ultra monitors picked up mutilated signals suggesting that a cruiser would be in Macassar Strait on 16 May. Colombo repeated this to Walker as 'Another *Myoko* sortie expected soon', and reported the departure of an 'auxiliary vessel and escort' (*Kurishoyo Maru No 2*) from Car Nicobar with troops for Singapore. At 02:45 on the 15th Walker ordered Manley Power's destroyers, screening a detachment of Force 61 in Six Degree Channel, to chase the transport and her escort (Operation 'Mitre'), but warned that if contact with an enemy cruiser seemed likely 'Mitre' might be cancelled.

EMPEROR ATTACKS

It was Sub-Lieutenant Burns' Avenger 'B', one of a quartet of *Emperor*'s borrowed Avengers, which sighted the *Maru* first, at 09:37, reported her, but was hit as it attacked, and ditched. A second strike of three Avengers ('G', 'J' and 'K') from *Emperor* was already in the air, led by Lieutenant-Commander Fuller, who now headed for the position given by Burns' ditched 'B' to look for both the enemy ships and the Avenger's crew. At 10:38 they overtook five ships in circular formation on the same course as themselves, and reported them as the enemy. They were in fact Manley Power's destroyers, the presence of which had not been properly indicated at the *Emperor* briefing. Fuller realised the mistake and cancelled the signal.

Meanwhile the staff at Colombo, still without Admiral Power, were regretting their signal forecasting 'Another *Myoko* sortie'. It was meant to warn, but knowing Hookey Walker it would probably only encourage him to give 'Diadem' another try. The submarines in Macassar Strait had surely warned off the enemy cruiser from a possible relief run to the Andamans or Nicobars and/or a sortie into the Andaman Sea. Any further attempt to cut her out must fail and might drive her into Penang at the northern mouth of the Strait on the Malayan side, where she could become an even bigger embarrassment to the East Indies Fleet. If she was in the Strait a penetration to attack her there would be dangerous and probably only serve to turn her back to Singapore, to fight another day or play the 'fleet in being' game. Walker's and Manley Power's present involvement with small fry might well suck them into a trap.

At 10:41 Power's destroyers were still on course at 27 knots when leader *Saumarez* received the signal 'Cancel "Mitre",' from Colombo. Power noticed that the time of origin of the signal showed that it had been sent before Avenger 'B' had made the original report of the auxiliary vessel and escort. Reducing to 15 knots but maintaining his course, at 10:56 he sent an emergency signal to Walker and to C-in-C requesting confirmation of the cancellation 'in view of aircraft Duty Baker's report.' Three times, on three different frequencies in the next hour and a half he repeated the signal, with no reply, but kept on course rather than abandon a chance of attacking the enemy.

Meanwhile Fuller in Avenger 'G' was on his own. Avenger 'K' had wasted too much fuel stalking Manley Power's ships to continue, while 'J' had abandoned the search to guide Avenger 'C' of the first strike, blown off course by a wind stronger than had been indicated at the *Emperor* briefing. 'J' escorted 'C' to within 48km (30 miles) of the carrier, then 'C' finally ran out of fuel and ditched. Its last signal was picked up in the destroyer *Virago*, passed to Walker, and the crew was rescued with difficulty from a rough sea by Lieutenant Weaver's Walrus from *Hunter*. Fuller flew at 30m (100ft) through the Great Channel between Great Nicobar and Sumatra to get below the beam of the radar on Weh Island. Landsdell, his Observer, warned him that if he continued to hold on to his full bomb load they would only have time for 20 minutes in the search area, and Fuller jettisoned his bombs. Shortly afterwards he passed within 365m (400yd) of Burns and his 'B' crew in their dinghy, but did not see them.

HAGURO SIGHTED

In *Emperor*'s operations room they had worked out a more accurate fix on Burns' position. This was signalled to Fuller but the monsoon gobbled it up. At 10:44 he sighted two ships steering 180 degrees at about ten knots, three minutes after Manley Power had received the 'Cancel "Mitre"' signal. Descending from the clag into the clear he flew across them, dodging a light but accurate ack-ack and machine-gun fire from the smaller vessel, and identified them as the 'Mitre' targets. At 10:45 he sent out a short sighting report and was continuing to shadow when he sighted two more ships heading towards the *Maru* 24km (15 miles) to the south. Circling them out of gun range he identified them as a *Myoko* Class cruiser and a *Minekaze* Class destroyer. It was *Haguro*, 'very large and very black', Fuller reported, 'against a very dark monsoon cloud,' and her faithful *Kamikaze*.

As the Avenger approached, *Haguro* and *Kamikaze* turned to starboard on a course parallel with *Kurishoyo Maru* and opened fire on the bulky Grumman with close-range and AA guns. Fuller climbed to 914m (3,000ft) to a shadowing position midway between the two Japanese forces, transmitting details of the enemy.

Virago picked up his transmissions and immediately signalled '. . . from aircraft Duty George "One cruiser one destroyer bearing 310°"'. Just after 12:00 Manley Power read the decoded signal and became 'the most relieved man in the Indian Ocean'. Exultantly he increased speed back up to 27 knots. A few minutes later came an answer from Admiral Patterson in *Cumberland* to his last emergency signal requesting confirmation of Colombo's 'Cancel "Mitre"'. 'You should sink enemy ships before returning,' ordered Patterson. The Admiral had not received Fuller's enemy sighting report and was referring to the *Kurishoyo* pair, but Power, with a Nelsonian blind eye, read what he wanted to read.

By 12:50 Avenger 'G' had been airborne for three hours and fuel was low. For his last signals Fuller climbed directly over *Haguro* to give Force 61's direction-finders the chance of an exact fix, then left the scene. At 14:55 they switched their IFF to DISTRESS. They were given a course to steer, and two of *Hunter*'s Seafires to escort them to the home of *Emperor*'s borrowed deck, which they reached at 15:15 after five hours and 11 minutes aloft.

THIRD STRIKE FROM *EMPEROR*

Meanwhile, at 13:38, from a position 177km (110 miles) due west of Sabang *Emperor* launched three Avengers, 'P', 'Q' and 'R', to find, fix and strike *Haguro* and her *Kamikaze*. The TBFs passed over Power's destroyers, bow waves curling, wakes foaming. Reaching the last reported position of *Haguro* the Avengers began a square search, 140 degrees for 24km (15 miles), 230 degrees for another 24km, 320 degrees for another 24km. They were almost at the end of the third leg at 15:41 when the leader, Sub-Lieutenant (A) Crompton, sighted *Haguro* and *Kamikaze* about 19km (12 miles) on his starboard bow, steering due east at between 15 and 20 knots.

The three Avengers transmitted sighting reports as they climbed into the sun, turned at 3,050m (10,000ft) and dived out of a cloudless sky, weaving and jinking as they passed through *Haguro*'s barrage, which nicked 'P' and 'Q' as they released their bombs at 914m (3,000ft). The bombs dropped all round the cruiser, and the TBFs left the scene at full speed, 290 knots, chased by the flak and lethal columns of hard white water thrown up by 8in shells from *Haguro*, and all returned to *Emperor* by 18:30. Fuller was expecting to fly another strike against *Haguro*, but Commodore Oliver considered the range too great and cancelled a scheduled strike by *Emperor*'s own 800 Squadron Hellcats.

Right: The Japanese heavy cruiser *Haguro*, seen here in more peaceful days.

THE DESTROYERS ATTACK

Crompton's had been the last sortie from the carriers against the enemy, and had caused *Haguro* to turn to the east and lose vital minutes. Now it was Power's and the 16th Flotilla's turn. *Haguro* was 120km (75 miles) north-east of the destroyers. As darkness came down on them the destroyers spread out in line abreast and began to patrol across the Strait of Malacca between Penang and the Sumatran shore to trap *Haguro* and *Kamikaze* as they came down from the north-east. It was night, and the Strait was 210km (130 miles) wide at this point. The enemy might still slip through. But at 22:45 *Venus*, nearest to *Haguro*, picked her up on radar. At 00:15 in the graveyard watch, 16 May, with *Haguro* 21km (13 miles) off, the flotilla took positions for a 'star' attack from different points of the compass. *Haguro* turned and ran to the north, then turned to port right across the bows of *Venus*, which missed her with a salvo of torpedoes. *Haguro* turned away. *Kamikaze* shaved *Saumarez*'s bows and scraped down her port side under heavy fire. *Saumarez* engaged *Haguro* and was hit in one boiler room, where two stokers were scalded to death. *Saumarez* and *Verulam* fired torpedoes and made three hits. *Venus* and *Virago* scored hits, then *Vigilant*, and *Haguro* lay stopped. *Venus* finished her off with two torpedoes, and *Haguro* sank at 02:05, about 72km (45 miles) south-west of Penang.

LAST STRIKES IN THE INDIES

The big fish had gone, the minnow remained. At 07:00 *Emperor* launched four Hellcats with eight 27kg (60lb) RPs apiece to find *Kurishoyo Maru No 2*, but she had in fact already berthed at Penang. Fuller, disgusted at the refusal to launch another strike against *Haguro*, was also angry at what he considered the meagre efforts made to find Burns' crew, and requested permission to use all his available Avengers to make a thorough search. This was turned down, but Sub-Lieutenant Fletcher, a close friend of Burns, was ordered to fly one more search, to look for the enemy and for Burns' dinghy. Launched at 10:30, he made a box search in the mouth of the Malacca Strait, but returned just after 18:00, tired and dejected after a fruitless search on both counts.

Just after 16:00 two Oscars dived on Force 61 through the ack-ack barrage, but the CAP Seafires, which had flown this boring duty with only one aircraft lost in 60 sorties, were on them before they could select targets, and they jettisoned their bombs and fled for Sumatra. As dusk began to fall, and the last CAP had landed on, *Virago*, down to only 18 tons of oil fuel and with her boiler room pumps losing suction, was just closing *Hunter*'s stern to refuel when an Oscar made a dead set at the carrier, and dropped a fragmentation bomb which near-missed *Virago*, but steel splinters killed and injured men in the destroyer's after damage control station.

The sinking of the *Haguro* effectively ended the Japanese naval effort in the East Indies and Indian Ocean. During 'Dracula' *Attacker*, after delays in her refit at Taranto, had reached Ceylon with her 879 Seafire Squadron, and she and *Hunter* were used to bring replacement aircraft from India and South Africa. Seafires and Hellcats supported the final attacks in Malaya. *Ameer* shot down a 'Val' dive-bomber, but another bomber dived into the minesweeper *Vestal* off Phuket Island, killing 15 men and putting the ship in a sinking condition. This was the first and only attack on the East Indies Fleet by the special Kamikaze attack force of suicide pilots, of which Walker had been warned. *Ashigara* was sunk by the British submarine *Trenchant* in the Banka Strait on 8 June, *Kurishoyo Maru No 2* and *SC 57* were sunk by destroyers *Eskimo* and *Nubian* off Sabang on the 12th and *Myoko* was torpedoed by the US submarine *Bergol* on the 13th.

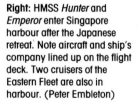

Right: HMSS *Hunter* and *Emperor* enter Singapore harbour after the Japanese retreat. Note aircraft and ship's company lined up on the flight deck. Two cruisers of the Eastern Fleet are also in harbour. (Peter Embleton)

17

HANGING ON IN THE PACIFIC

'Once in his life a man should know when to throw himself from the temple of Kiyomizu'.
General Tojo Prime Minister of Japan.

WITH the surrender of Casablanca to General Patton on 11 November 1942 all Vichy-French resistance in North Africa ceased. Now Allied armies could drive east along the Mediterranean coast to link up with General Montgomery's British Eighth Army, which was tumbling the Africa Korps westwards through the Duce's former colonies. The job of the three naval task forces was done, and most of their ships returned to their bases. Too late to interfere significantly with the landings, Dönitz disposed his U-boats to ambush the returning vessels. Five American transports were sunk, and on 14 November *U-155* destroyed *Avenger* west of Gibraltar.

Of the American oiler/carrier quartet, the first US Navy ACVs to see action, *Sangamon, Santee* and *Suwannee* left Casablanca in mid-November, Captain Bill Sample ruefully counting the cost in hardware of *Santee*'s sorties to Safi – seven serviceable aircraft left of VG-29's original 32, with all his fighters, six TBFs and two SBDs lost. But the US Navy's first escort carrier squadron had done enough to demonstrate some of the skills which an ACV could offer. Though with little opposition, their potential for offshore strikes was clear, while *Chenango* had ferried a big cargo of aircraft to the front and afterwards refuelled 21 destroyers.

It was this milch cow act which delayed her departure from West Africa, so that she caught the full force of a hurricane in the Atlantic on her passage west. Water poured in through the ventilators. All the bows back to the forward elevator was soon a no-go area. Waves broke over the flight deck. First her life rafts, then the motor whaleboat, two 1.1 gun directors, two entire 20mm mounts, and her catwalks began to go. Her entire forward structure was twisted and rent, her flight deck rolled backwards. Heavy repairs were necessary before she returned to service.

All four ACVs made a short stop at Bermuda, before carrying on to Norfolk, then, on 5 December, *Sangamon, Suwannee,* and later *Chenango*, left for the Pacific. *Santee* was remaining in the Atlantic to join the cruiser *Savannah* in a search for blockade runners in the South Atlantic, then to assist new *Bogue* Class ships and the British BAVGs in convoy protection further north. The other three *Sangamon*s sailed south for the Panama Canal. They passed through on 11–12 December without incident (and without liberty) and the only sign that the locks and channels were a tight fit for the tanker carriers was a tangle between *Suwannee*'s signal yard and the Canal control tower. The ship's Construction and Repair Department turned to, and the yard was removed amid much confusion about midnight under the close supervision of the First Lieutenant, who perched precariously on the roof of the control tower. In a few hours after that she steamed out into the broad Pacific, just a few days before the new *Bogue*, lead ship of her class and first to see action, transited in the opposite direction on her way to hunt U-boats in the Battle of the Atlantic.

In the 12 months since the Japanese carrier-borne attack on the US Pacific Fleet in Pearl Harbor, the bloody drama which had opened there had continued its impetus, with the Japanese expanding dynamically through the great arc stretching from China, down through Burma and Malaya, oil-rich Sumatra, Timor and the Arafura Sea, which washes the capes of northern Australia, New Guinea, the Solomon Islands and the South Pacific, and north across the Equator through the Gilberts to point the sword at Honolulu once again, absorbing as they went Wake Island, the Mariana and Marshall Islands, the Philippines, Guam and the Micronesian chain.

This eruption of power swept aside what naval strength the Allies could scrape together. On Wake a gritty resistance by US Marines was crushed. On 8 December Admiral Tom Phillips with the battleship HMS *Prince of Wales* and the battlecruiser *Repulse* left Singapore to attack Japanese landings on the north-east coast of Malaya. A carrier was to have sailed with him, but the *Ark Royal* had just been sunk, *Illustrious* and *Formidable* were making good their Mediterranean damage in the USA, *Furious* was adjudged too old and worn, *Eagle* and *Hermes* too slow and with too few aircraft, *Indomitable* was commissioning. *Victorious* was the only carrier in service suitable

Right: Strategic Points In The Pacific.

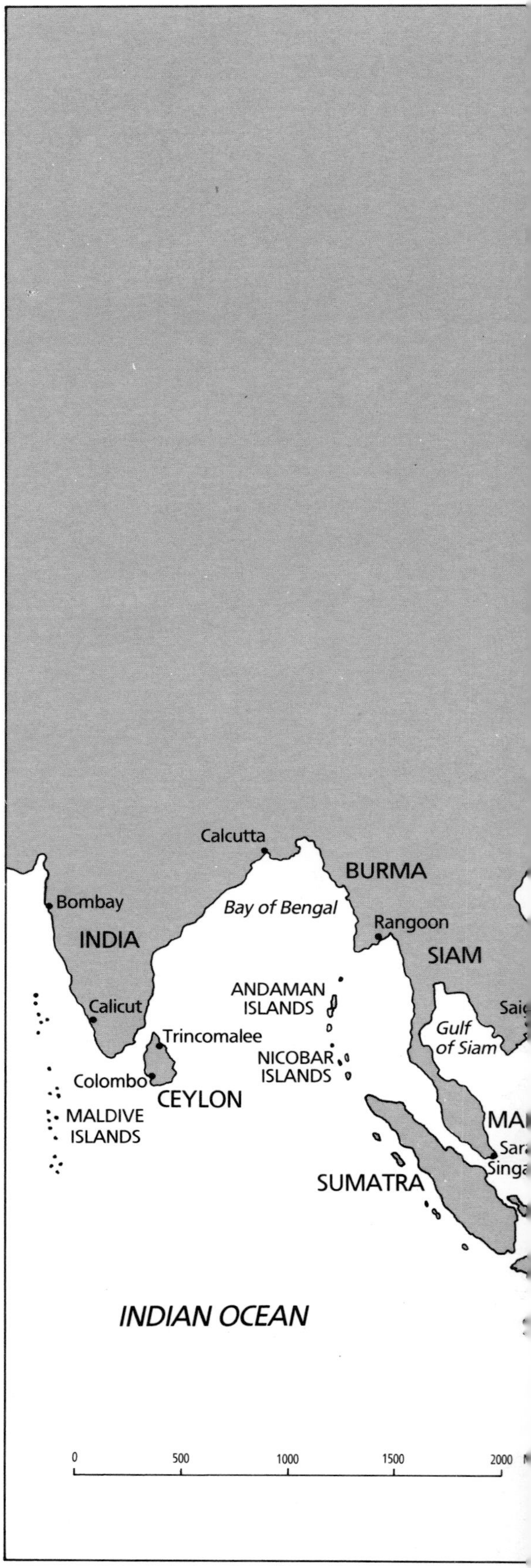

for the job, but with *Tirpitz* almost ready for action, home waters had priority. Admiral Phillips sailed without air cover and went down with his ships beneath the bombs and torpedoes of Japanese aircraft from Indo-China. Of an Allied force of five cruisers and nine destroyers which met a similar Japanese force in the Java Sea, only four American destroyers survived. Resistance by a few RAF Hurricanes and Brewster Buffalo fighters in Malaya was overwhelmed.

'HOLD WHAT YOU'VE GOT . . .'

Throughout this dark period the Allies maintained a necessarily defensive stance, striking defiant blows at the Japanese whenever and wherever possible. 'Hold what you've got and hit them when you can,' were COMINCH Admiral King's orders to Admiral Chester Nimitz, who took over CINCPAC on 31 December 1941. What Nimitz had were the remnants of the United States Navy left after Nagumo had struck at Pearl, but things could easily have been worse.

Only two of the battleships in harbour, the *Arizona* and *Oklahoma*, were irreparable, though it would be more than a year before the rest were ready for service. The Japanese had chosen 7 December for the attack because they thought that on an American Sunday morning all the big ships of the Pacific Fleet would be in harbour. In fact none of its three carriers, *Lexington, Saratoga* and *Enterprise* was there. *Saratoga* was refitting at San Diego, the other two had been doing the humdrum job which so angered their CINC Bull Halsey. *Lexington* was at Midway, the westernmost island in the Hawaiian chain, over 1,930km (1,200 miles) away, completing delivery of a squadron of obsolete Vought-Sikorsky SB2U Vindicator dive-bombers to Marine Bomber Squadron VMSB-241. Halsey in *Enterprise* had completed delivery of Marine aircraft to Midway and the 12 Wildcats of Marine Fighting Squadron VMF-211 to Wake, 2,090km (1,300 miles) southwest of Midway, and was less than 320km (200 miles), 24 hours, steaming, from Pearl. In fact *Enterprise*'s air group was expected over Pearl that morning, and the approaching squadrons aroused no surprise below on the islands or in Ensign Manoel Gonzales, on patrol from *Enterprise*, who fell to his death thinking he had been shot down by friends. Halsey knew that something was wrong when the carrier picked up Gonzales' last horrified 'Don't shoot, I'm American!'

It was too far for The Big E to launch a strike, which might in any case have tipped off Nagumo to her presence. The Japanese Admiral now knew the disturbing fact that he had missed the US carriers at Pearl. The pilots who shot down Gonzales did not identify his machine as carrier-borne, but the cautious Nagumo ignored his Staff's pleas for a third strike on Oahu. Ironically, the absence of Halsey's main force on his hated

FAR EAST THEATRE OF OPERATIONS
Kodiak
ALEUTIAN ISLANDS
KOMANDORSKI ISLANDS
Attu
Kiska
Adak
Umnak
KURIL ISLANDS
Sea of Japan
HOKKAIDO
KOREA
HONSHU
SHIKOKU
KYUSHU
PACIFIC OCEAN
East China Sea
RYUKU ISLANDS
Okinawa
Chichi Jima
BONIN ISLANDS
SAKISHIMA ISLANDS
VOLCANO ISLANDS
Iwo Jima
FORMOSA
Kong
Midway
HAWAIIAN ISLANDS
Oahu
Wake
Pagan
Saipan
MARIANA ISLANDS
Tinian
Rota
Guam
Luzon
PHILIPPINE ISLANDS
Samar
Eniwetok
Bikini
MARSHALL ISLANDS
Wotje
Kwajalein
Majuro
Mili
Jaluit
Yap
CAROLINE ISLANDS
Palaus
Woleai
Truk
Ponape
Tarakan
Talauds
Morotai
CELEBES
Halmahera
NEW GUINEA
Manus
Makin
Tarawa
GILBERT ISLANDS
Nauru
Ocean
Hollandia
Wewak
Ceram
Banda Sea
Salamaua
Port Moresby
Arafura Sea
Timor Sea
Nahamed
ELLICE ISLANDS
Nukufetau
Funafuti
SOLOMAN ISLANDS
Vanikoro
NEW HEBRIDES
Espiritu Santo
SAMOAN ISLANDS
Coral Sea
Efate
FIJI ISLANDS
AUSTRALIA
New Caledonia
Noumea

ferrying missions had saved the USA from immediate disaster.

When Japan made her do-or-die leap from 'the temple of Kiyomizu' – a sacred shrine on a mountain top – the Imperial Navy included ten carriers (the six heavy Fleet carriers *Akagi, Kaga, Soryu, Hiryu, Shokaku* ('Flying Dragon') and *Zuikaku* ('Lucky Stork'), two light Fleet carriers *Hosho* and *Ryuyo*, and two light conversions from Fleet fast submarine tenders, *Zuiyo* and *Shoho*, with five big new carriers under construction (*Taiho, Shinano, Unryu, Katsuragi* and *Amagi*) and two large passenger ships (*Hitaka* and *Hayakaka*) being converted to carriers *Hiyo* and *Junyo*. The US Navy had the five heavyweights – *Lexington* and *Saratoga, Enterprise, Yorktown* and *Hornet* (commissioned in December 1940) – and the two light carriers *Ranger* and *Wasp*. The disparity was even greater in that the US Navy had to divide its lesser number of carriers between two oceans, and *Yorktown, Wasp* and *Ranger* were stationed in the Atlantic.

The first US auxiliary carrier *Long Island*, AVG-1, ex-*Mormacmail* of the Moore-McCormack Line, had been commissioned on 2 June 1941 and retained on the east coast for evaluation and experiment with this new type. After Pearl Harbor, orders for the 20 *Bogue* Class AVGs, ten of them for Britain, were placed on the west coast, and the four *Sangamon*s were taken over for accelerated conversion at Norfolk on the east coast so as to be ready for the invasion of North Africa in November 1942.

Just after New Year's Day, 1942, *Yorktown* steamed post haste up from Panama to join the Pacific Fleet, and was sent off immediately with *Enterprise* to escort a troop convoy to Samoa in the South Pacific, but on the 11th the balance swung back again when *Saratoga* was badly damaged by a submarine torpedo 800km (500 miles) south-east of Pearl, and she limped east to the Navy Yard at Bremerton on Puget Sound, where building had begun on the first *Bogue* Class AVGs.

Between 20–23 January 1942 the Japanese took a further step in the isolation of Australia by occupying the islands of New Britain and New Ireland, just east of New Guinea, covered by Nagumo's carriers and First Air Fleet, the Pearl Harbor assassins, and set up a powerful air/sea base at Rabaul in New Britain, from which to launch the invasion of New Guinea, with Australia to follow.

'. . . HIT THEM WHEN YOU CAN!'

Nimitz, to press Kings 'Hold what you've got and hit them when you can!', now had enough carriers to lead three attack forces and on 1 February he sent two of them into action, with Halsey's *Enterprise* and Task Force 8 raiding Kwajalein Atoll in the western Marshall Islands, from which the Japanese had mounted the assault on Wake, while that tough and canny old sailorman Rear-Admiral Frank Jack Fletcher, who had transferred from *Saratoga*, took *Yorktown* and TF.17 to let the Japanese in the Gilbert Islands further south know that the US Navy was alive and punching. The strike, with more of the same to come in the next few months, was basically a morale-building exercise for the Navy and the public after the trauma of Pearl, while the rapidly growing giant of American industry, fuelled by a righteous anger and huge government contracts, began to turn out the ships, planes and weapons which would overwhelm the Axis.

The Allies were still taking heavy blows from the advancing Japanese. On 18 February 135 Japanese aircraft and four of Nagumo's carriers hit Darwin in northern Australia from Timor and the Timor Sea, sinking five ships and smashing port installations. Two days later *Lexington* and TF.11 raided Rabaul but were put off their stroke by heavy bombing attacks. On the 14th *Enterprise* and TF.8 hit Wake, but on the 27th the US Navy suffered a painful blow when the old *Langley*, once CV-1, now ferrying crated P-40s to Java, with her flight deck partially cut away, was sunk by shore-based bombers off Tjilatjap, Java, while Admiral Doorman's Allied cruiser squadron was being destroyed in the Java Sea. On 4 March Halsey raided Marcus Island, 5,790km (3,600 miles) west of Pearl, the deepest penetration so far of the Japanese-held central Pacific. On 7 March the Japanese made the short hop south-west from Rabaul and took Lae and Salamaua, both with airfields, in the Huon Gulf on the north-east coast of New Guinea. On the 10th 100 planes from *Lexington* and *Yorktown* in the Coral Sea flew overland to surprise and attack them there. On 18 April 16 North American B-25 Mitchell bombers led by the famous airman Lieutenant-Colonel Jimmy Doolittle left the decks of the new *Hornet*, commanded by veteran naval aviator Captain Marc Mitscher, just 800km (500 miles) east of Tokyo to raid the Japanese capital, Kobe, Hagoya and Osaka.

Over-confident after their dynamic successes, the Japanese High Command was intent on continuing the rapid expansion through the Pacific by capturing New Guinea and the Isles of Melanesia, thus cutting off the USA from Australia, which would then fall into their hands. Only Admiral Isoroku Yamamoto, Commander-in-Chief Combined Fleet and an early prophet of the carrier war, had reservations about this overweeningly ambitious plan. He knew that he must waste no more time in pinning down and defeating the still potent and growing US Pacific Fleet, before it could restore and weigh down the pre-Pearl balance of strength. His plan, code-named MI, was to mount, with the full might of the Combined Fleet, the capture of Midway Island, a threat which Admiral Nimitz would not be able to ignore, and lure the US Fleet of carriers and cruisers into a hopeless battle.

The outrage of Doolittle's raid caused instant acceptance of MI, but the assault on New Guinea, Operation MO, was not abandoned. Between 5–9 April Nagumo with four of his carriers ranged the Indian Ocean in a raid which was also intended as a diversion, but the Navy Combat Intelligence Unit at Pearl convinced Nimitz that Nagumo's foray did not imply a Japanese assault on India but that the next enemy move would be an attempt to take Port Moresby, in south-eastern New Guinea across the Gulf of Papua from Australia, with a seaborne expedition from Rabaul through the Coral Sea.

THE FIRST CARRIER BATTLE

On 3 May reports came in of the Japanese capture of Tulagi Harbour at Florida Island in the Solomons which could be the establishment of a toehold in the Solomons for immediate follow-up. Next forenoon Frank Jack Fletcher with *Yorktown*, three heavy cruisers and six destroyers, hit shipping in the harbour and sank a destroyer. Decoded Japanese signals indicated a strong force east of the Solomons and the departure of a large convoy and escort from Rabaul. US Intelligence had been right. This was the Port Moresby assault force. *Shokaku, Zuikaku*, two heavy cruisers and seven destroyers were steaming south-east of the Solomons to fall on the American carrier force now known to be in the area should it interfere with the Moresby invasion convoy. Knowing these dispositions, Fletcher sent a cruiser force to await the convoy south of the Huon Gulf in the Coral Sea, and took his carrier force south-east to find the Japanese main carrier squadron. A dawn search on 7 May found *Shoho* and the four cruisers of a convoy-covering force, but missed *Shokaku* and *Zuikaku*, which were in range but hidden in a patch of murky weather. Fletcher's whole strike force overwhelmed and sank the small carrier. Next morning both main carrier forces found each other and flew off strikes. *Shokaku* was badly damaged, *Lexington* destroyed. By then the Moresby convoy had turned back.

VICTORY AT MIDWAY

Meanwhile decoded signals had indicated that Japan's next move would be against Midway Island. *Yorktown* was hastily repaired and joined *Hornet* and *Enterprise*, just back from the Doolittle raid, under Fletcher, and steamed fast for Midway, as did the might of the Japanese Combined Fleet, Nagumo with carriers *Kaga, Akagi, Hiryu* and *Soryu*, two battleships, cruisers and destroyers, Yamamoto with seven battleships and outrunners. At dawn on 4 June Nagumo's carriers hit Midway and return strikes by Midway planes were almost annihilated. At 08:00 *Enterprise* and *Hornet* flew off a strike of 100 planes, and the vital battle had begun. The carrier air fleets hammered each other's ships and suffered severe losses. The Americans lost *Yorktown*, but destroyed all four of Nagumo's carriers and their irreplaceable veteran air groups.

THE ZERO-SEN

It was at Midway that American pilots began to encounter in any numbers the Japanese aircraft that was to be their most formidable opponent in the air – the legendary A6M Type O 'Zero' fighter. The Imperial Japanese Navy had issued a specification for a new monoplane fighter at the beginning of the war with China in 1937, demanding: a maximum speed of 500km/h (311mph) at 3,960m (13,000ft), a sustained rate of climb of 850m (2,800ft) per minute up to 3,050m (10,000ft), a maximum endurance (with external fuel tankage if necessary) of six to eight hours, and an armament of two 20mm cannon and two large calibre 7.7mm machine-guns, a heavy battery for its time. Total all-up weight should not exceed 2,495kg (5,500lb) (less than the empty weight of an F4F-2). Mitsubishi followed these parameters and improved on them. Quantity production was ordered in July 1940 and by the time of the Pearl attack most carrier-based *Sentai* (squadrons) were flying it.

With a maximum speed of 523km/h (325mph) at 4,877m (16,000ft), which could be reached in five minutes, faster than the Spitfire or Messerschmitt Bf 109E, and its famous manoeuvrability, the

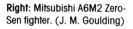

Right: Mitsubishi A6M2 Zero-Sen fighter. (J. M. Goulding)

Above: Japanese fighter pilot in front of his Mitsubishi 'Zero' fighter (Allied code name Zeke), the most formidable opponent of Allied carrier pilots in the Pacific. Very effective at first, in the hands of experienced pilots, it sacrificed structural strength and pilot-fuel tank protection for manoeuvrability and heavy armament, and its performance fell off as pilot losses grew.

Zero-Sen ('Zeke' in Allied code) could out-turn any contemporary fighter, and in the hands of a skilled pilot was superior to any other naval fighter, except in its basic structure, which was of lightweight construction, and its lack of protection for pilot or fuel tanks, both sacrificed in the interest of performance. In a dogfight with the far more rugged F4F, F6F or F4U a Zero pilot had to be able to dictate tactics and outfly his opponent. With the expert, experienced aircrews of the early part of the war this was possible, but as they were killed off in increasing numbers, beginning with Midway, a Zero in the hands of their skimpily trained, green replacements would either burst into flames when hit or crumple like a bamboo tea house. In retirement, Captain David McCampbell, Congressional Medal of Honor, the US Navy's leading fighter ace in World War 2, who shot down 34 Japanese aircraft, including nine in one combat when he and his wingman Ensign Roy Ruching attacked a formation of 40 enemy fighters, recalled 'The Zero was a good aircraft, so you had to take advantage of every opportunity. The best way was to get on his tail and let him have it. The only thing we really learned early in the war was not to shoot at the pilot or the engine but fire at the wing root. That was where the gasoline was. Most of the Japanese planes we shot down, including the Zero, blew up right in front of us when we hit them in the wing root.'

THE FIGHT FOR THE SOLOMONS

Rebuffed and frustrated in the central Pacific, the Japanese threw their energies into strengthening their Solomons bastion to the south, in which the key was the island of Guadalcanal, where they began building an airfield. In great haste the Americans planned and actioned an invasion of the island before the airfield could be finished and used against them. *Saratoga, Enterprise* and *Wasp* covered the landing by Marines, which began five months of a brutal blood-letting campaign, including battles in the seas round the island so brutal that 'The Slot', the waterway which threaded the islands, seemed in the reflected glare of shellfire and burning ships to run with blood. In a night of action off Savo Island the US cruisers *Quincy, Vincennes* and *Astoria* were sunk and their crews incinerated; the Australian *Canberra* was also sunk and USS *Chicago* disabled. American warships from the Fleet anchorage at Espiritu Santo in the New Hebrides just south-east of the Solomons slugged it out with Japanese squadrons coming down from Guam, Truk and Rabaul.

LONG ISLAND LEADS THE WAY

Having escorted the first US-Gibraltar convoy, USG-I, *Long Island*, ACV-I, went to the Pacific and in August ferried a load of 19 Wildcat F4Fs and 12 Dauntless SBDs to the Marines on Guadalcanal, becoming the first escort carrier to serve in the Pacific. Afterwards she returned to the west coast to qualify pilots in deck landing and continued to transport replacement planes to the Pacific carriers, including escort carriers in the front line. Some of these aircraft were flown in the night battle off the eastern Solomons on the 24th when *Saratoga*'s planes sank the carrier *Ryujo* and turned back the landing force she was escorting.

In a final battle off Tassafaronga on the northern shore of Guadalcanal a force of Japanese destroyers, some of them carrying troops, engaged five American cruisers with destroyers and torpedoes, damaged the *Minneapolis, New Orleans* and *Pensacola*, and sunk the *Northampton*, but it was their final fling in the campaign. Their reinforcement became a trickle and the Americans consolidated their hold on the island.

The Japanese may have temporarily lost Guadalcanal, but they were not giving up the Solomons. They strengthened their positions at their airfields at Munda Point on the west coast of

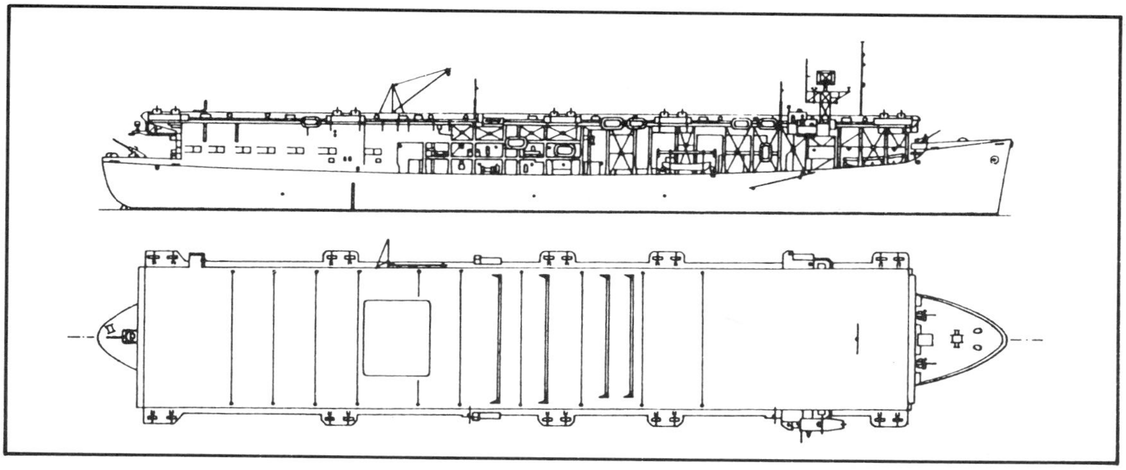

Right: The USS *Long Island*, AVG/ACV/CVE-I, the first escort carrier to be commissioned, was also the first to work in the Pacific theatre of war when she ferried Marine aircraft to Guadalcanal in August 1942. In the autumn of 1942 her flight deck was extended forward and a short lattice mainmast fitted to carry SC air-search radar and a topmast for the YE homing beacon aerial.

New Georgia and Vila on Kolombangara. The Americans began nightly bombardments of both airfields by cruisers and destroyers, made preparations for full-scale invasion, and began construction of an airfield in the Russell Islands between New Georgia and Guadalcanal, where they built up the airfield and beat off the nightly tit-for-tat raids by Japanese aircraft.

NEW CARRIER CONSTRUCTION

The establishment of the airfields on Guadalcanal and in the Russells greatly extended the range and scope of American air power in the South Pacific at a time when Halsey's Third Fleet, backed up for a few months by the loan of HMS *Victorious*, was desperately short of carriers and waiting impatiently for the CVs, CVLs and ACVs of the new building programme. As early as one month after Midway there were 131 aircraft carriers of all types in various stages of construction, conversion or on order, comprising: one Large Carrier (CVB), 22 Fleet Carriers (CV), nine Light Carriers (CVL) and 99 Escort Carriers (ACV, later CVE). The US carrier-building programme was bigger and more successful than that of the Japanese. The USA could herself produce most of the raw materials necessary, while the Japanese relied on a very vulnerable overseas pipeline. US shipyards were also immune from attack. The US Navy's aircrew training and aircraft replacement programmes kept pace with the carrier construction and replacement programmes, but there would be almost a whole year more after Midway with essentially the same major vessels that existed after the battle.

THE *BOGUES* GO TO WAR

In the summer of 1942 the Navy had ordered 74 additional escort carriers. Of the 24 steam turbine C3 type led by the USS *Prince William* (ACV-31), only the latter remained in US Navy service, serving as a willing workhorse throughout the war, ferrying aircraft to forward areas, including New Caledonia, Samoa, and Espiritu Santo (returning to San Diego with worn aircraft engines and parts), Townsville in Australia, Casablanca in the Atlantic, and Port Everglades in Florida, on the Gulf of Mexico, with two periods training and qualifying pilots out of San Diego and Key West, Florida. The remaining 23 ships were to go to the Royal Navy in 1943 and 44 as the 'Ruler' Class. The 'Hurry Up Henry' Kaiser programme was falling behind its schedule. The lead ship *Casablanca* was supposed to have been delivered in February, but would not make the target by several months.

The delivery of the 20 *Bogue* Class ACVs (ten for the USN, ten for the Royal Navy) began on 15 June 1942 with the commissioning of the USS *Copahee*, ACV-12, on that day. Begun as the SS *Steel Architect*, *Copahee* had been partially converted and launched by the Todd Corporation and completed in the Navy Yard at Bremerton, opposite Seattle on Puget Sound, Washington, and in September also began the job for which Bull Halsey had wanted 'jeep carriers', and which she would continue to do throughout the war, the transportation of aircraft to the ships and bases of the US Pacific Fleet, beginning with the long trek to Guadalcanal to replenish the Marine Corps air groups there. Second *Bogue* to commission, on 20 August 1942, for the US Navy was ACV-16, USS *Nassau*, named for a sound on the coast of Florida. She had been laid down on 27 November 1941 by the Seattle-Tacoma Shipbuilding Corporation as Maritime Commission Hull No 234 of the C3-S-A1 merchant type (C3 – Cargo vessel, 131m (429ft) in length; S – steam turbine-powered, with one propellor; A1 – in its original shelter-deck design, the whole indicating a type of merchantman converted to escort carrier). Launched on 4 April 1942, she was acquired by the Navy on May Day, towed to the Navy Yard for conversion to an ACV, and entrusted to the command of Captain Austin K. Doyle, USN. A typical *Bogue*, *Nassau* was 151m (495ft 8in) long, 34m (111ft 9in) in beam, with a draft of 8m (26ft), a displacement of 9,800 tons, a flank speed of 18 knots, a complement of 890,

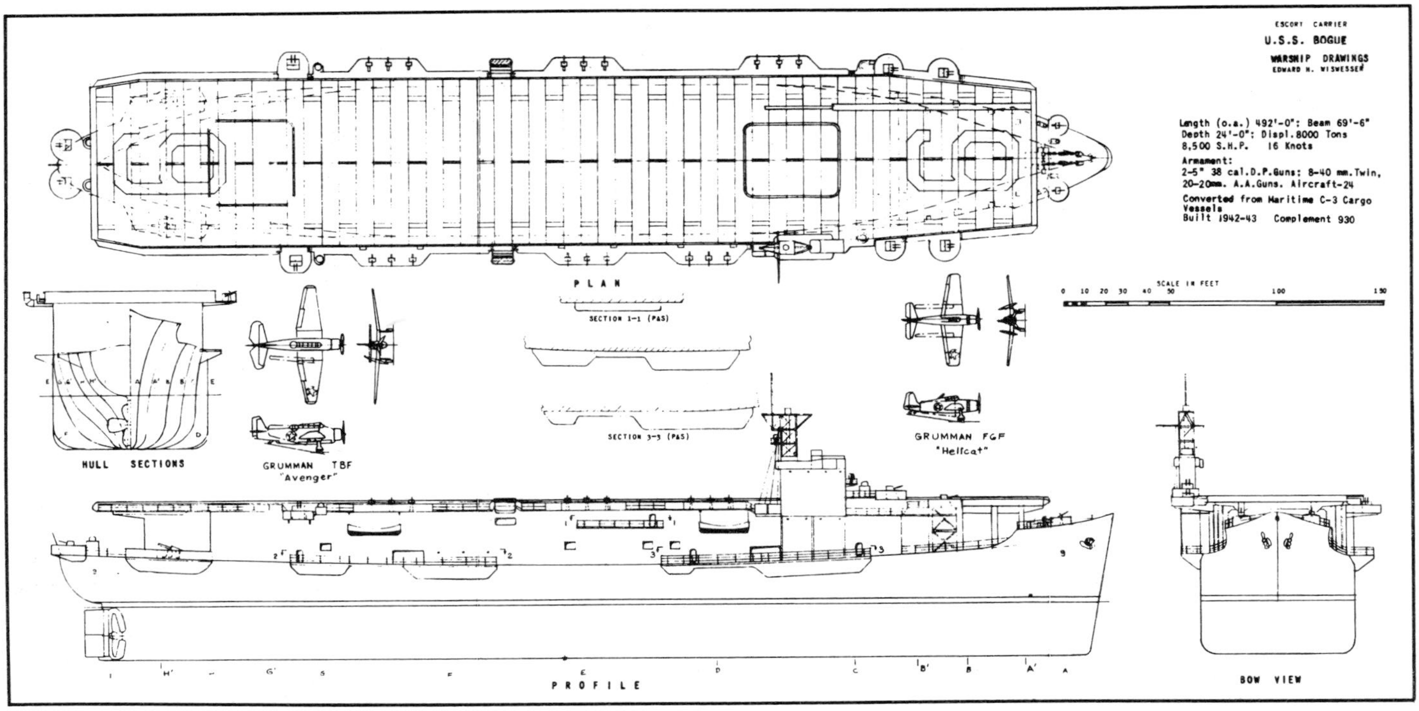

Top: USS *Bogue*.

Above: Captain F. W. McMahon's *Suwannee*, ACV/CVE-27, one of the converted oiler quartette. Planes from her and her sister *Chenango*, ACV/CVE-28, contributed to the final capture of Guadalcanal Island in the Solomons by supporting landings there in late January 1943, and destroyed 11 of the 12 Japanese planes which sank the cruiser USS *Chicago*. Note her SC radar.

armed with two 5in guns and 20 40mm cannon, and with capacity for 21 aircraft (operational) or some 90 (ferry). On 10 October 1942 she put in to the Naval Air Station at Alameda, California, embarked a ferry load of aircraft and four days later sailed for Pearl, thence to the Palmyra Islands for four months of ferrying donkey work in the area Palmyra-Noumea-Espiritu Santo.

Third *Bogue* to commission, was the USS *Altamaha* (ACV-18), the name of a sound in Georgia which was given originally to the conversion at Ingalls which was eventually launched at HMS *Battler*. Launched on 25 May 1942 at Seattle-Tacoma Shipbuilding, *Altamaha* was completed at the Navy Yard and commissioned on 15 September 1942 by Captain J. R. Tate, USN, and served as an aircraft transport between the west coast and the Pacific islands until March 1944, when her normal job was briefly interrupted by a few weeks of glamour as a submarine hunter with Composite Squadron 66. *Bogue* was the fourth of her class to be commissioned, and went to the Atlantic. Next of the family to see duty in the Pacific was USS *Barnes*, built by Western Pipe & Steel at San Francisco; she became HMS *Attacker*. The one and true *Barnes* was another Seattle-Tacoma ship, launched 22 May 1942, commissioned 20 February 1943 by Captain C. D. Glover, USN, and set to work transporting planes and aircrew from Stateside to the forward areas, interspersed with periods of aircrew combat training.

THE *SANGAMONS* STRIKE

With their combat experience in 'Torch', much greater aircraft operational capacity and great value as refuellers, the *Sangamons* were to continue an active role. After reporting to Commander South Pacific at Espiritu Santo, *Suwannee* steamed south down the New Hebrides chain to Havannah Harbour, Efate, where she arrived on 17 January 1943, moored to Buoy 14, and prepared for operations with the South Pacific forces, along with *Sangamon*. *Chenango* arrived at Noumea, New Caledonia on the 18th, to make up a trio of sisters which would be serving as Carrier Division 22 (Car Div 22) to give air cover to convoys and assault forces in the Solomons and damaged vessels leaving the combat areas. On 21 January

Captain F. W. McMahon, USN, took over the ship from 'Jocko' Clark, who was returning Stateside to assume command of the *Yorktown*. With *Enterprise* and *Saratoga*, the three *Sangamon*s made the only five combat carriers in the Pacific.

With her new skipper at the helm *Suwannee* steamed out of Havannah on 27 January 1943 in company with Admiral Giffen's cruiser force for a rendezvous with Guadalcanal-bound troop transports to supply air cover on passage and at the disembarkation. Just after dusk a large force of Japanese torpedo bombers made an attack on the convoy with flares and float lights – the first night attack by enemy planes. A number of the Japanese planes were destroyed but the cruiser *Chicago*, recently repaired after her mauling at Savo Island on 9 August, was once again crippled. Darkness stopped the action, and at dawn a mass of khaki swarmed down the cargo nets on the troopships into amphibious landing craft, while battleships, cruisers and destroyers pounded away at enemy gun positions commanding the beachhead. The enemy counter-fire dwindled, the landing craft streaked for the beach, and the troops waded ashore, with *Suwannee*'s planes hovering over them, bombing, bombardment spotting and strafing on request.

At sea the *Chicago* was under tow, with a screen of five destroyers, when 13 torpedo bombers flown down from Munda attacked her. Despite a heavy ack-ack barrage from the destroyers and a desperate attack by aircraft from *Suwannee*, *Chenango* and *Enterprise* which destroyed 12 of the 13 Japanese planes, the cruiser was fatally hit and sank. Most of her survivors had been rescued when another group of 15 Japanese bombers was sighted. In need of a pause for recuperation after their strenuous efforts, *Suwannee* and *Chenango* avoided attack by dodging into a weather front. The *Sangamon*s continued to provide air cover for the convoys pouring men and supplies into Guadalcanal. They sortied from Espiritu Santo, each carrier taking it in turn to patrol 130 to 145km (80 or 90 miles) south-east of Guadalcanal for ten to 12 days while her air group fought off the Japanese bombers attacking Henderson Field by day and night.

In the meantime Vice-Admiral Leary's flagship was alerted by the signal 'Jap Fleet is at sea and will try to reinforce Guadalcanal.' Cardiv 22,

Below: Launching a TBF from USS *Suwannee* in the South Pacific. (US National Archives)

Above: USN Landing Signals Officer (batsman) in bright red and yellow sweater gives a pilot the 'Cut'. Royal Navy batsmen (Deck Landing Control Officers) mostly wore normal gear, sometimes, in the Pacific, white flying suits. (US Navy)

Sangamon, Suwannee and *Chenango*, four battleships, four cruisers and destroyers steamed for Vanikoro Island to block the north-eastern approaches to the Solomons. All the CarDiv's TBF 'Turkeys' were on deck in condition II, loaded with torpedoes. At 02:00 Leary flashed 'I expect to contact the enemy at dawn,' but at dawn the enemy was not there. Withdrawing their reinforcement convoy, 20 destroyers closed the island at nightfall and evacuated the troops. Shortly afterwards the capture of Guadalcanal was announced as complete.

After the retirement of the Tokyo Express, Leary's force successfully covered the occupation of the Russell Islands, between Guadalcanal and New Georgia, in late February. *Suwannee* detached the 11 F4Fs and nine TBFs of her Air Group 27, *Chenango* part of her Air Group 28, to Henderson Field on Guadalcanal for mopping-up operations, in which they amassed impressive combat records for themselves. At the end of February a convoy of six Japanese troopships, two supply ships and eight destroyers left Rabaul for Lae on New Guinea. From 1 March it came under attack by 150 aircraft of General Kenney's Fifth US Army Air Force, and only two destroyers were left to make Lae. In April came the welcome news that as a result of a decoded signal the aircraft carrying Admiral Yamamoto had been shot down and the Commander-in-Chief Combined Fleet killed.

STRATEGIES – MACARTHUR V. NIMITZ

So far in the Pacific war the major thrust by the Japanese through the Central Pacific via Midway had been decisively beaten back, and ensuing action had been the result of Japanese attempts to extend their domination of the South Pacific by capturing the Solomons and New Guinea, and Allied attempts to stop them. American victory in the Solomons, with only Bougainville and its off-lying islands in the north-west still occupied by the Japanese, denied them the use of the islands both as a defensive barrier and as stepping stones to the conquest of the whole great sprawl of islands south of the equator from New Caledonia to the Tuamotus, and the consistent Allied repulse of attempts to take New Guinea protected Australia, while success in both quarters gave the backing for a two-pronged advance to encircle and neutralise Rabaul, advance via New Guinea to the Philippines and on through the Ryukus to Japan itself.

At first it was assumed that this move on its own was the best line of advance. It was certainly the strategy of General MacArthur, commanding the South Pacific area. He had promised as he stepped aboard the PT Boat which had snatched him from Corregidor 'I shall return', and this was an article of faith, if not an obsession. To MacArthur, the soldier, this was the only way – solid reoccupation of the enemy's stolen territories, with the Navy protecting his flanks as he marched – one massive concentration of power.

But there was another way. There would be difficulty in deploying the whole massive strength of American arms in the southern theatre, with its lack of good harbours and its roundabout supply routes from the USA. An advance through the central Pacific, making maximum use of carrier-borne aircraft, though starting further from the Philippines, by 'island hopping', knocking out or capturing only the enemy's key bases, might well bring American forces, particularly land-based bombers, more quickly within range of Japan itself than the plod through New Guinea, even with the latter enjoying powerful support from the sea. This was the view held by Admiral Nimitz, Commander-in-Chief of the Pacific Fleet and Supreme Commander Pacific Ocean areas, and the choice most likely to appeal to the 'Naval Person' Franklyn Roosevelt. In the end it was decided by the Combined Chiefs of Staff to use the advantages of both strategies – mutually supporting advances north (through the Mariana and Palau Islands) and south (via New Guinea and the Philippines) of the Equator.

ALEUTIAN SIDESHOW

Although Attu and Kiska in the Aleutian Islands, occupied by the Japanese on 7 June 1942, with their impenetrable weather and their distance from the hub of action in the central Pacific, were of little conceivable use to either side, there would always be a doubt in Allied minds, and American and Canadian forces constantly attacked communications between the islands and Japan, with destructive air raids being mounted from the American base at Dutch Harbour, Unalaska Island in the Aleutians further east. On 27 March an American force of two cruisers and four destroyers fired on a small Japanese convoy off the Komandorski Islands 240km (150 miles) west-north-west of Attu, and ran into an escort of four cruisers and five destroyers. After a three-hour battle, with *Salt Lake City* badly damaged, both forces withdrew. After this encounter an assault was planned to evict the Japanese, and on 10 May American forces landed on Attu, the least well-defended of the Japanese-held islands. Its capture would put the Allies in a more comfortable position between Kiska and the Kuriles Island chain stretching north-east from the tip of Hokkaido. Rear-Admiral R. W. Rockwell was to command the amphibious forces under the general direction of Vice Admiral Kinkaid, commanding the North Pacific Fleet.

Below: *Bogue*-class escort carrier USS *Nassau*, ACV/CVE-16, supporting the capture of Attu Island in the Aleutians in May 1943. Wildcats take off from a wet flight deck in typically foul Aleutian weather. (US National Archives)

The main landing at Massacre Bay and a diversionary landing at Holz Bay on 11 May, were preceded by bombardment from the invasion fleet, which included three battleships, cruisers, destroyers, and the escort carrier USS *Nassau*, CVE-16. After a ferrying stint Compo (VC) 21, formed for escort carrier anti-submarine work in the Atlantic, was temporarily split up. The torpedo element was not needed for the forthcoming operation. The fighter flight was expanded to 24 F4F-4 fighters and 30 pilots, commanded by Lieutenant-Commander L. K. Greenamyer of Corpus Christi, Texas, and joined *Nassau* for refresher and qualification landings and take-offs, then ten days' invasion support training over the Channel Islands off the coast of southern California. Bad luck seemed to shadow CVE-16. A plane handler was killed, a pilot badly hurt in barrier crashes, and a pilot killed in a forced landing on San Clemente Island. On 23 April *Nassau* joined Task Group 51.1 and departed for the foggy, freezing Aleutians.

She began preliminary operations on 4 May with the Task Force. The initial landings on 11 May were only weakly opposed. Two eight-plane flights of F4F-4s from *Nassau* strafed ahead of the troops and two F4F-4s and two F4F-3(P)s spotted for the guns. Marine pilots were to have flown the spotter missions, but they failed to qualify in carrier operations, and Skipper Artie Doyle substituted VC-21 pilots. The first plane back hit the barrier, Ensign Paul Beaumont ran out of gas just short of the flight deck, and Ensign Kostrzewsky ditched in the afternoon.

As the troops probed inland they met a desperate and effective defence from concealed gun emplacements in the slopes leading up from the shore, which Wildcats attacked with 45kg (100lb) bombs. Lieutenant Ted Condo, later awarded an Air Medal for his work, duelled with a flak battery at Holz Bay, but with the cloud ceiling at only 460m (1,500ft) was hit by a 40mm shell behind the cockpit and lost his tailwheel. For two days Attu was fogged in the forenoon, preventing flying. The bad luck of *Nassau* returned on the 14th when an F4F quartet flew off and never returned. One pilot was rescued but two others had crashed on high ground. On the 16th Marine Sergeant W. P. Breeden splashed and was lost, Lieutenant (jg) Frank Register of Bismarck, North Dakota, went down to flak at Holz Bay. The foul weather closed in on the 17th/18th. Fog and rain and a heaving flight deck smashed undercarriages and made work for the barrier. Attu was secured on 31 May, and Kiska found deserted. VC-21 lost eight aircraft and five pilots at Attu. Back at San Diego the temporary fighter members were detached, and the bomber element, which now included SBD dive-bombers, rejoined. The squadron was sent to the South Pacific, where they were land-based for the Solomons/Rabaul campaign.

18

THE ROAD TO TOKYO

THE Allied amphibious offensive in New Guinea opened at the end of June concurrently with the attack on New Georgia in the Central Solomons. These were two prongs of a thrust to encircle the powerful Jap base of Rabaul, by General MacArthur, commanding the South-West Pacific Force, and Admiral Halsey's South Pacific Force, which included the Third Fleet and its core, Marc Mitscher's Fast Carrier Task Force. To ensure full co-ordination between them, Halsey was temporarily put under the control of MacArthur. The Army supremo also had a naval force under his direct command, the Seventh Fleet, at this stage comprising an amphibious force, the cruisers and destroyers of an Australian squadron, eight American destroyers, often one or two American cruisers, and some submarines, and it was the Seventh Fleet Amphibious Force which kicked off the campaign by capturing the islands of Kiriwina and Woodlark off the south-eastern coast of New Guinea, from which fighters had range enough to escort bombers to Rabaul, and positions at Nassau Bay, near Salamaua further north-west on the New Guinea mainland, to link up with Australian troops fighting in the interior.

Meanwhile Halsey moved to capture the Solomons airfields at Munda, New Georgia, and Vila on Kolombangara. As at Guadalcanal, the Japanese used destroyers to reinforce and supply their garrisons by night, via Kula Gulf.

On 15 July ACV, the code for an escort carrier, became CVE (C=Carrier, V=heavier than air, E=Escort), thus belatedly bestowing on this fighting breed the status of Combatant Ships.

MacArthur's troops, landing in New Guinea on 4 September, had had a head start over Nimitz's Central Pacific offensive, but now, reinforced, the Fifth (ex-Third) Fleet, under Vice-Admiral Ray Spruance, was ready to step out boldly now on the road to Tokyo. Added to its strength were the new CVs *Essex*, *Bunker Hill*, *Lexington* and *Yorktown*, and five of the new light carriers (LCVs), built on cruiser hulls, *Independence*, *Princeton*, *Belleau Wood*, *Cowpens* and *Monterey*, all six new battleships of the *Washington* Class and the larger *Iowa* and *New Jersey*.

Also available to Admiral Spruance were six escort carriers. On 5 November the oiler trio of McFall's CarDiv 22 steamed into Espiritu Santo lagoon. On 16 October *Suwannee* had steamed down to San Diego to embark a new squadron, Air Group 60, under Lieutenant-Commander Allan C. 'Ace' Edmands, comprising Squadrons VF (Fighting) 60 (12 F6F Grumman Hellcats) and VC (Bomber) 60. *Chenango* had acted as training

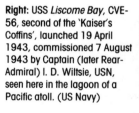

Right: USS *Liscome Bay*, CVE-56, second of the 'Kaiser's Coffins', launched 19 April 1943, commissioned 7 August 1943 by Captain (later Rear-Admiral) I. D. Wiltsie, USN, seen here in the lagoon of a Pacific atoll. (US Navy)

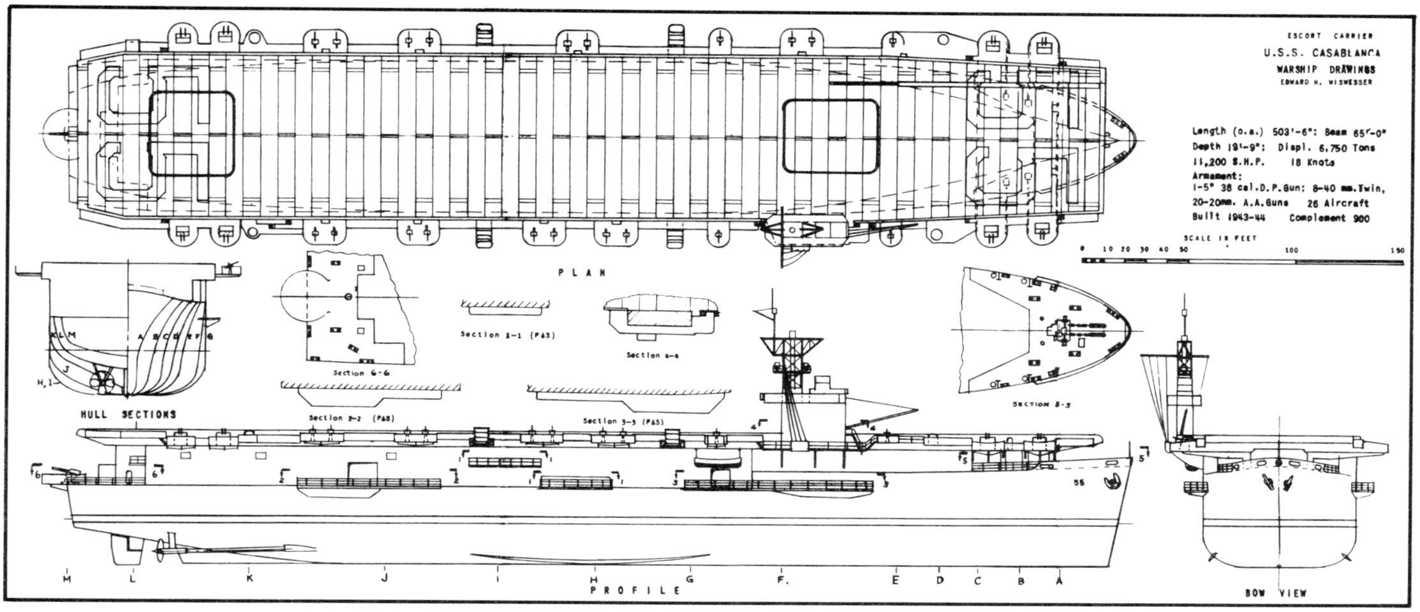

Above: USS *Casablanca*, name ship of the class of Kaiser-built CVEs. Note the two exhaust stacks on either side of the flight deck, and the few openings in the hangar – in contrast to the *Sangamons* – and the twin screws. (Taubman Plan Service)

carrier for new air groups until 19 October, when she, *Suwannee* and *Sangamon*, which had had an Action Information Center installed, left for the New Hebrides, *Sangamon* with Composite Squadron VC-26 (12 F6Fs, nine SBDs, nine TBFs), *Chenango* with air Group CVEG-35, comprising Fighting Squadron VF-35 (22 F6Fs) and Bomber Squadron VC-35 (nine SBDs, nine TBF/TBMs).

'KAISER'S COFFINS'

Also with the Fifth Fleet were the first of the *Casablanca* Class CVEs to go into action in the Pacific. *Casablanca* herself, CVE-55, launched on 5 April 1945 from the Kaiser yard, commissioned on 8 July by Commander W. W. Galloway, USN, was serving as a training ship for escort carrier crews in the Straits of Juan de Fuca, between Puget Sound and the Pacific. The second of the Kaiser 50, USS *Liscombe Bay*, CVE-56, launched on 19 April, was commissioned on 7 August by Captain I. D. Wiltsie, USN, and trained with Composite Squadron VC-39 until 21 October, when she left San Diego for Pearl Harbor, arriving there a week later. The third Kaiser, USS *Coral Sea*, CVE-57, (later renamed *Anzio*), launched on May Day, followed much the same programme, working out with Composite Squadron VC-33 and its six FMs, one SBD and 12 TBFs before sailing for Pearl. CVE-58 USS *Corregidor*, launched on 12 May, commissioned on 31 August by Captain R. L. Bowman, USN, left San Diego for Pearl with Compo VC-41 (11 F4Fs and six TBFs) on 26 October. At Pearl the three Kaisers were designated CarDiv 24 under Rear-Admiral Mullinix, who had just left command of the *Saratoga*, for attachment to Task Force 52, Northern Attack Force, under Rear-Admiral Richard K. Trover for the first step in the invasion of the Gilbert Islands – the seizure of Tarawa and Makin Islands by Operation 'Galvanic'.

These islands were chosen as the first objectives in the central Pacific thrust because they were the only ones within effective bombing range of American-held airfields. At this time carrier-borne aircraft were not considered sufficient to carry out effectively the prolonged pre-landing bombardment considered essential in an amphibious operation, and aircraft of the Seventh Air Force were stationed in the Ellice Islands, 1,125km (700 miles) away from the Gilberts to the south-east ready to supply the days, or even weeks of bombing thought necessary. It was hoped that the airstrips crammed into the small islands on the reefs of coral atolls could be pounded to pieces, allowing troops easy landings from the smooth water of the lagoons. If the theory was wrong, a frontal assault would be bloody, as there could be no tactical surprise.

The Fifth Fleet forces were divided into two sections, the Northern Attack Force, to which the three virgin *Casablancas* of CarDiv 24 were attached, for Makin, known to be poorly defended, and the Southern Attack Force, including the three *Sangamons* of CarDiv 22, for Tarawa, 160km (100 miles) further south, which had a much larger garrison. Also attached to the Tarawa force were the CVEs *Nassau* and *Barnes* with 44 Hellcats to be flown ashore when the island was captured. The Makin *Casablancas* were on trial, the first of the breed to go into action. 'Kaiser's coffins' they were often called, and said to be shoddy goods which would break up at their welds in heavy weather, sink at once in the blast of a near-miss. Before the battle, scheduled for 21 November (eastern hemisphere time), *Liscome Bay* and *Corregidor* changed their understrength squadrons, and all three Kaisers went into action with 16 of the improved FM Wildcats from General Motors and 12 TBFs, the larger *Sangamons*

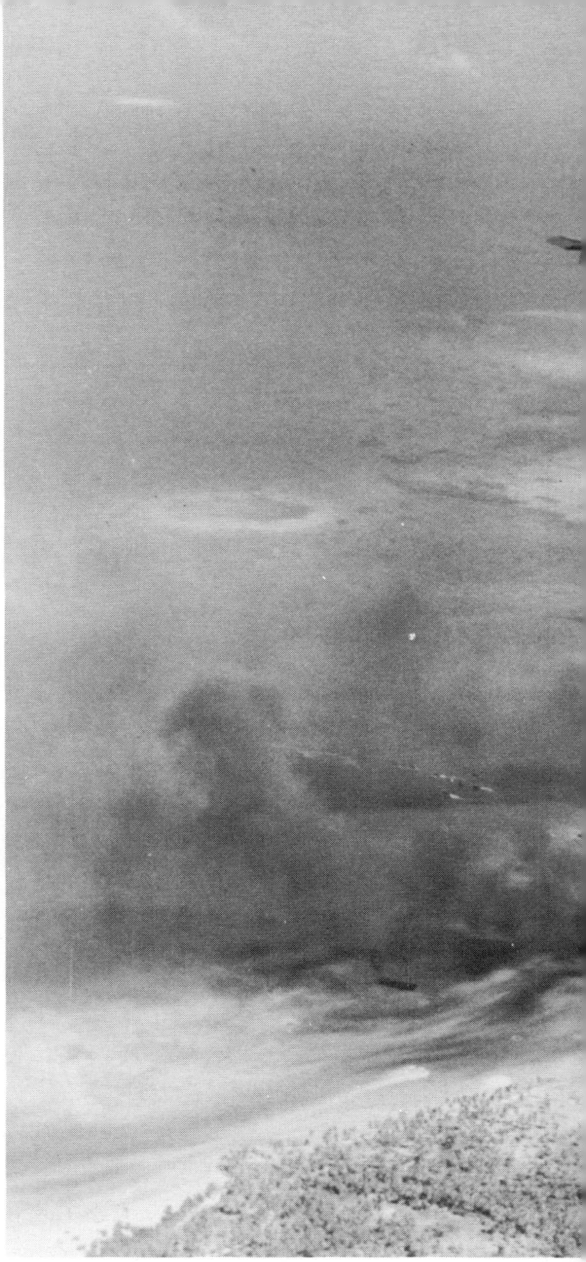

Above: An FM-1 Wildcat fighter from the USS *Corregidor* over Butaritari Island, Makin Atoll, during the pre-invasion bombardment, 20 November 1943. The photograph looks to the east, with Flink Point lower centre and 'Beach Red' lower right. Heavy smoke is from oil fires in the vicinity of Kings Wharfe. The aircraft is piloted by Lt. G. V. Knudson, USNR.

with 12 F6F Hellcats, nine TBFs and nine SBDs apiece. Between them the six CVEs added nearly 200 aircraft to the 700 put up by the 11 CVs and CVLs of Mitscher's Fast Carrier Force. They covered the advance of the transports and warships.

The assaulting Marines took to their landing craft at dawn on 21 November, under a fighter umbrella. At Makin the fighting went much as expected. The resistance came chiefly after the landing. The hammer of 6,500 Marines cracked the nut of 350 Japanese soldiers, all of whom were killed, for a loss of 65 men, with 121 wounded. For the three Kaiser boats the operation was not much more than a realistic shakedown, with the island a shooting range for their squadrons.

*SANGAMON*S AT TARAWA

Tarawa was another matter. On the main island of Betio in the atoll – just over 3km long by 800m wide (two miles by half a mile) and hardly 3m (10ft) above sea level at any point, the Japanese had lavished their energies in defence, constructing half-buried bomb shelters, gun emplacements, and some 500 pillboxes of coconut logs and reinforced concrete, which could only be demolished by a direct hit. About half of the garrison's 3,500 men may have been killed by the preliminary bombardment but the rest gave the US Marines one of the bloodiest battles in their history. The stranding of the landing craft on an unmapped reef 360 to 640m (400 to 700yd) from the beach did not help, with the men having to wade ashore under a lethal hail of machine-gun fire or be ferried in the all too few amphibious tanks and boats. Reinforcements were put ashore on D+1 and gradually and painfully the defenders were pushed back and eliminated. The escort carriers bombed and strafed the beaches ahead of the troops, attacked the Japanese beyond the

Above: Four USS *Coral Sea* Avengers fly over Butaritari Island, Makin Atoll, 20 November 1943.

beaches, and protected the convoys offshore from 20 November to 8 December. By D+4 Betio was declared 'secure'.

After previous raids on Japanese bases, including the attacks on Rabaul and in associated sea battles, Japanese air strength had been so decimated that there were at this time fewer than 50 planes in the whole Gilberts and Marshalls area. On the evening of D-Day 16 surviving torpedo planes from the Marshalls made a concentrated attack on Rear-Admiral Montgomery's three-carrier force off Tarawa, three aimed at *Essex* and *Bunker Hill*, the rest at the light carrier *Independence*, which shot down five attackers but took one bad hit and steamed slowly away for repairs. This was the only air attack made on the ships.

For the next three days there was a lull for the carrier task groups, as the Marines fought their grim battle ashore. On the evening of 23 November four FMs from *Liscome Bay* lost the ship in a squall and made to land on *Yorktown*. Three of them made it, but the fourth pilot had never made a night landing before, forgot to lower his hook, gunned his engine instead of cutting it when he touched down, bounced over the barrier into the deck park, killed five plane handlers and wrote off six aircraft in the ensuing fires, while he himself was thrown clear and escaped with minor injuries. Japanese submarines had also done their best to interfere with the landings, and several contacts had been reported.

CarDiv 24 was part of TG.52.13, with battleships *New Mexico* and *Mississippi*, cruiser *Baltimore*, destroyers *Hall, Franks, Hughes, Morris, Maury, Gridley* and *Hull*. At 05:00 on 24 November the group was steaming in the circular Cruising Disposition 73, *Liscome Bay* was acting as guide at the centre, with *New Mexico, Mississippi, Baltimore, Coral Sea* and *Corregidor* forming the first circle round the CVE, and the destroyers a larger circle beyond them, though there was a gap on the formation's starboard quarter which had been left by *Hull* when she departed at 04:00.

Death of a Kaiser

A black, moonless night was suffused with rose on the horizon as dawn approached. When three bells struck in the morning watch bugles rang out as the carriers were summoned to flight quarters. Deep in the ships dopey gobs and grunts fell out of their bunks, middle watch keepers swore and turned over, their dream of Betty Grable shattered by the bullhorn, new watchkeepers topsides shivered in morose silence. *Liscome Bay* had been scheduled to fly off a dawn patrol, and there were 13 armed and fuelled aircraft spotted on the flight deck. In the hangar planes, kept degassed during the night by standing order, were being fuelled. At 05:10 *Liscome Bay*, as guide, began to make a 60 degree turn to starboard to face east in anticipation of daybreak, and the formation followed. At 05:13 the talker of a gun's crew in the starboard gallery just for'ard of *Liscome Bay*'s bridge island shouted into his phone mouthpiece that he could see a torpedo wake off the starboard bow, heading for the ship. The commander of the Imperial Japanese Fleet's submarine *I-175* had set himself up for a good shot through the gap left by *Hull* in the American formation when it began to turn towards him and he fired while the carrier was still in his sights.

There was no way *Liscome Bay* could avoid the torpedo. It struck her starboard side between the forward and after engine rooms. Both elevators were blown upwards, breaking the power system, and both fell back into the hangar deck. Racing along the open fuel lines where the volatile avgas surged at pressure, fire ran through fractured points and swiftly swept through the entire hangar. Part of the bridge island was destroyed and the forward part of the ship caught fire, which

Above: Pilots of *Suwannee*'s Fighting Sixty Squadron read while awaiting the call 'Pilots man your planes!' in the Ready Room. 'Cess' (short for Cesspool) is Lieutenant(jg) Givens, C. Wilson, pilot and Safety Officer, a product of the Marine 'cowboy boot school' in Texas; 'Rabbi' is Lieutenant(jg) John D. Shea Junior, pilot and Engineering Officer, from Butte, Montana, pastmaster at nursing sick Hellcats. (Dr Philip Phillips)

was soon raging throughout the whole hull. *Liscome Bay* lay stopped, all communications lost, with a list to starboard, when there was a second and cataclysmic explosion further aft than the first, apparently originating from within the ship, where at least nine 907kg (2,000lb), 78 454kg (1,000lb), 96 227kg (500lb) bombs and a large number of torpedo warheads were stored. Some 30m (100ft) of the after flight deck was blown off, and the whole side of the ship opened up along the starboard gun gallery fore and aft. 'The entire ship seemed to explode', reported Ensign D. D. Creech of *Coral Sea*, 'and the interior of the ship glowed with flame like a furnace.' 'Abandon ship!' was passed by the Navigator and Gunnery Officer, but there was a widening spread of oil on the water, ignited by a Wildcat which was blown off the bows, burning and exploding, and a strong wind from the port side made it impossible for men to swim clear of the rapidly drifting wreck.

From the destroyer *Hughes* which passed close abeam *Liscome Bay* on her port side, her Captain reported, 'Men were seen jumping off the flight deck into the water, one group of about five men jumping with a rubber boat which tumbled after them. This group appeared to land directly into flaming oil which seemed to cover the area all along the starboard side and around the bow. At this time the entire after half of the ship was blazing furiously and smoke and flame poured out of the hangar deck from all directions . . . Halfway between the island and the stern there appeared to be a huge hole from flight deck to at least one deck below the hangar deck.' It is impossible to even guess at the horrors being enacted below decks in the burning carrier. Admiral Mullinix, Captain Wiltsie and the Executive Officer were last seen leaving the ship by a rope line to the water's edge. *Liscome Bay* sank on an almost even trim, with a 30 degree list to starboard, at 05:35, leaving 204 survivors from a crew of 846, 41 of them badly burned stretcher cases. Captain Crommelin, Chief of Staff of CarDiv 4, and *Liscome Bay*'s Air Officer were among the survivors.

Liscome Bay was the fourth escort carrier to be destroyed by internal explosion associated with the igniting of fuel and ammunition, in three cases (*Audacity*, *Avenger* and *Liscome Bay*) initiated by torpedo hits, and it revived all the criticism of the category in respect of structure and speed, by the Royal Navy with regard to the American CVE fuel system, and in general by uninformed laymen, who got hold of the censored news and once again chuntered of 'Woolworth carriers,' 'banana boats' and 'cut-price carriers'. Shellbacks in the CVE fleet talked gloomily of 'death-traps', but a draft to one of 'Kaiser's coffins' brought with it a cachet of notoriety, the special glamour of the doomed.

Undoubtedly the thinness of the CVE's unarmoured sides and insufficient internal bulkheads had contributed to the losses, but the months of dangerous combat to come were to throw up examples of US Fleet carriers being destroyed in the same way, partly through faults common to all American-built flat-tops. Putting aside the loss of one jeep carrier, however, the object of 'Galvanic' was soon achieved. Before long the bombers of the Seventh Army Air Force were established at the captured airfields on these islands and on Apamama, 130km (80 miles) south of Tarawa, which had been seized without opposition, in preparation for the next step in the Central Pacific campaign, the attack on the Marshall Islands.

ADVANCE TO THE MARSHALLS

For the advance into the Marshalls Nimitz proposed to ignore the Japanese-held atolls of the eastern chain (Wotje, Maloelap, Mille and Jaluit), which were within almost point-blank range of the western Ralik Chain, and take the strong Japanese base on the large Kwajalein Atoll dominating the latter and the whole of the Marshalls, with defended islands at its northern and southern ends (Roi-Namur and Kwajalein Island), 65km (40 miles) apart. At the same time he planned to secure the unoccupied atoll of Majuro 400km (250 miles) south-east of Kwajalein which had a particularly good anchorage for a Fleet and room for airstrips, while Japanese airfields on other atolls were neutralised by air attack. The Seventh AAF would take out Mili, Jaluit and other islands to the south, working from their new bases in the Gilberts; Wake Island, 965km (600 miles) north of Kwajalein, would be hit by aircraft from Hawaii, via Midway; the middle islands, Wotje, Maloelap and later Eniwetok Atoll, were the responsibility of the carrier force, which would also bombard Kwajalein before the amphibious assault.

The carrier force included CarDivs 22 and 24 in TG-52 of the Fifth Fleet. The heavyweight CVEs *Sangamon*, *Chenango* and *Suwannee* formed CarDiv 22 as in 'Galvanic'. All three CVEs returned to San Diego after 'Galvanic' for further

Below: For the invasion of the Marshall Islands CarDiv 24 included the two new *Casablanca*-class escort carriers *Manila Bay*, CVE-61, and *Natoma Bay*, CVE-62, to replace *Liscome Bay*, sunk by the Japanese submarine *I-75* at Makin. Here CarDiv 24 practises division formation and manoeuvring exercises in Hawaiian waters on 13 January 1944, photographed from *Manila Bay*, with *Coral Sea*, *Corregidor*, *Natoma Bay* and *Nassau* in that order astern. (US National Archives)

training and enjoyed Christmas at home, *Sangamon* to work-up with a new air group, CVEG-37 (VF-37 with 12 F6Fs, VC-37 with ten TBF/TBMs), *Chenango* with her new CVEG-35 (12 F6Fs, nine TBF/TBMs, nine SBDs), *Suwannee* her CVEG-60, now commanded by Lieutenant-Commander Harvey O. Feilbach, USNR, who had succeeded 'Ace' Edmands in December. On 13 January the three veterans sailed for the Marshalls via Honolulu, to form part of Northern Attack Force.

CarDiv 24 had two new members. In place of *Liscome Bay* were two more Kaisers, *Manila Bay*, CVE-61, and *Natoma Bay*, CVE-62. *Manila Bay*, launched on 10 July 1943, was commissioned on 5 October at Astoria by Captain Boyntun L. Braun. After shakedown she sailed to pick up a load of damaged planes at Pearl for San Diego. After training with Composite Squadron VC-7 (16 FMs, 12 TBFs) she left again for Hawaii, picked up Rear-Admiral Ralph Davison and became flagship for CarDiv 24. Launched on 20 July 1943, sponsored by Lady Halifax, wife of Lord Halifax, British Ambassador to the USA, *Natoma Bay*, CVE-62, was commissioned on 14 October by Captain Harold L. Meadow, USN. After shakedown she too ferried aircraft and personnel between San Diego and Hawaii for Commander, Fleet Air, West Coast until 3 January, when she embarked Compo VC-63 and sailed for Hawaii, reported to ComCarDiv 24, Fifth Amphibious Force, and sortied with TG-51.2 for the Marshalls.

KWAJALEIN

The CVEs of CarDivs 22 and 24 left Pearl for Kwajalein between 20 and 22 January. At 16:51 on the 25th, during routine flight operations, a returning *Sangamon* Hellcat failed to hook a wire on landing, broke through the barriers and crashed into parked planes for'ard. Its belly tank, torn loose, skidded forward spewing flaming fuel. Fire soon spread among the planes and raged along the flight deck, with flames beating up over the bridge, making ship handling very difficult. Captain Wieber turned the ship out of wind so that the fire could be fought, and by 16:59 it was under control. Seven of the ship's company died in those desperate eight minutes, seven others were badly burned, and of 15 who jumped overboard to escape the flames, 13 were picked up, two lost. Temporary repairs were made at sea, and on 1 February the two parts into which the force had been divided arrived on their stations off Roi and Kwajalein Island for the preliminary bombardment.

This time, learning from Tarawa, the ships, which included eight 16in battleships, and the TBFs, TBMs and dive-bombing SBDs, unloaded twice the weight of missiles far more effectively than at Tarawa, and killed some half of the garrison before the Marines went in, carried ashore by many more amphibious tanks and armoured troop carriers. The seven CVEs launched CAP and anti-submarine patrols as well as bombing, strafing and beating up enemy ammunition dumps and ground installations, and steamed so close inshore in daytime that the ship's company could see their pilots bombing the beaches, and at night flames shooting up from blazing fuel dumps and planes destroyed on the ground. Casualties to the assault forces at both islands were light. Roi was secured on the day of

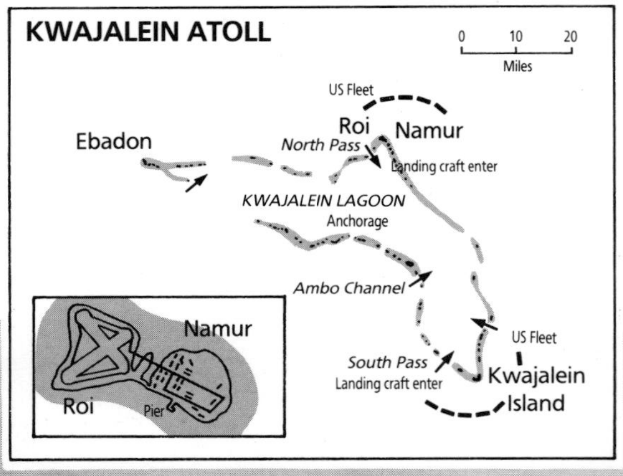

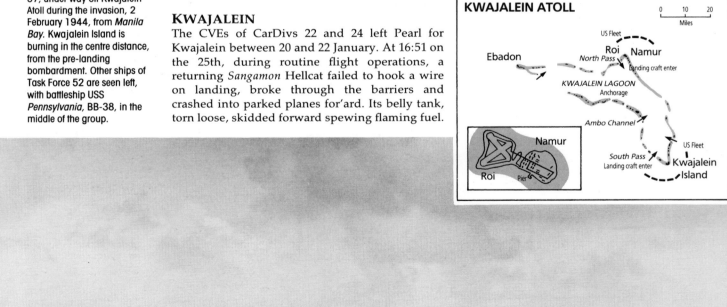

Below: USS *Coral Sea*, CVE-57, under way off Kwajalein Atoll during the invasion, 2 February 1944, from *Manila Bay*. Kwajalein Island is burning in the centre distance, from the pre-landing bombardment. Other ships of Task Force 52 are seen left, with battleship USS *Pennsylvania*, BB-38, in the middle of the group.

Above: Kwajalein Island, Kwajalein Atoll, 4 February 1944, the last day of major fighting for possession of the island, which has been given a severe 'Nimitz haircut', seen from a *Manila Bay* TBM, looking west, with landing beaches in the upper left distance surrounded by landing craft. Several LVTs are on the beach in the foreground, moving towards the front lines, off the view to the right. The blockhouse/barracks area is right-centre, with some buildings still burning. The seven CVEs in the action flew CAP and anti-submarine patrols as well as strafing and beating up ammunition dumps and ground installations from close inshore. (US National Archives)

assault, Kwajalein by 5 February, and the airstrips on both were soon in operation. With Majuro also in American hands, and another airstrip being rapidly constructed there by the Seebees, the whole eastern chain of Japanese-held islands was dominated, and was never more than a minor nuisance afterwards.

So successful had been the Kwajalein operations that it was decided to capture Eniwetok, the most north-western of the Marshall atolls, to round off the position in preparation for the next major thrust – either to Truk, 1,050km (650 miles) west-sou'-west of Eniwetok, or to the Marianas 1,600km (1,000 miles) west, forming the eastern boundary of the Philippine Sea). Whichever objective it was to be, an immediate bombardment of Truk by the Fast Carrier Force (six large and five light carriers, eight fast battleships, six or eight cruisers and 30 or 40 destroyers) was indicated – to cover the Eniwetok assault and hopefully throw a heavy punch at the Combined Fleet, in harbour or at sea.

CVEs at Eniwetok

Admiral Spruance took three of the four Fast Carrier groups with him to Truk, leaving the fourth group and the two CVE divisions to cover the taking of Eniwetok. Admiral Koga had withdrawn the Combined Fleet a week previously, but Mitscher's planes destroyed more than 100 defending fighters and whatever there was left in Truk harbour, including a light cruiser and three destroyers. That night a few remaining planes hit the light carrier *Intrepid* with a torpedo, which put her temporarily out of control, and next morning another Japanese destroyer was sunk.

Birth of the Fleet Train

Up until this point in the Pacific war the supplying of the great number of Allied ships engaged in operations had been met by fuelling at sea from a fleet of tankers moving round from one pre-arranged mid-ocean rendezvous to another, with any further supplying and all repairing done at Pearl Harbor, but with the next leap to the west, return trips to the main base would prevent rapid progress. A great and growing fleet of transport, fuelling, repair, salvage, hospital and cargo ships was built up, in all some 35 types of auxiliary on the Navy list. These cut the fighting fleet loose from its home bases, gave it freedom of movement, and facilitated the quick establishment of new repair and supply stations in far distant islands and atolls. One of these was now set up on Majuro. There it could meet any demands made by ships returning from combat, including replacement aircraft for the carriers, and from there it could despatch the ships needed as a train for supplying the Fleet at sea – tankers, ammunition ships, escort carriers with replacement aircraft and pilots, and store carriers.

From Truk, after refuelling in mid-ocean, the Fast Carrier Force headed for the Marianas, 965km (600 miles) to the north-west on the eastern edge of the Philippine Sea, to probe the defences of Saipan, Tinian and Guam. Japanese planes attacked the Force at night and were dealt with by gunfire from the screening force, as Mitscher could not afford to make repeated runs into the wind, a north-east trade. An enemy attack by day lost most of its planes, and at Saipan and Tinian the strike force destroyed many more, for the loss of six Hellcats, sank shipping, and photographed defences on all three islands.

While this raid was in progress Marines and infantry captured Parry Island, the main island on Eniwetok atoll, mopping up the other islands round the lagoon in a few days. The seven escort carriers of CarDivs 22 and 24 covered this operation, continuing their anti-submarine and combat air patrols and bombing and strafing attacks, destroying ammunition dumps and gun emplacements. Work was started at once to develop an advanced base here for the next major assault, which was to be on the Marianas, concentrating on Saipan, from which AAF bombers could strike at the Philippines and Japan itself.

As a preliminary step to the Saipan and Tinian assaults, the Fast Carrier Force left Majuro in late March to strike at the Palau Islands, 3,540km (2,200 miles) to the westward, where strong Japanese naval forces were stationed. On the evening before the strike an air attack was beaten off and many of the aircraft destroyed. Next day, 30 March, Mitscher's planes hit the Palaus in the southern waters of the Philippine Sea, Yap and Ulithi to the north-east, and Wolea in the western Carolines. Thirty-eight ships were sunk, 157 Jap aircraft destroyed, for the loss of 25 US planes. For two weeks CarDiv 22 flew CAP and anti-sub-

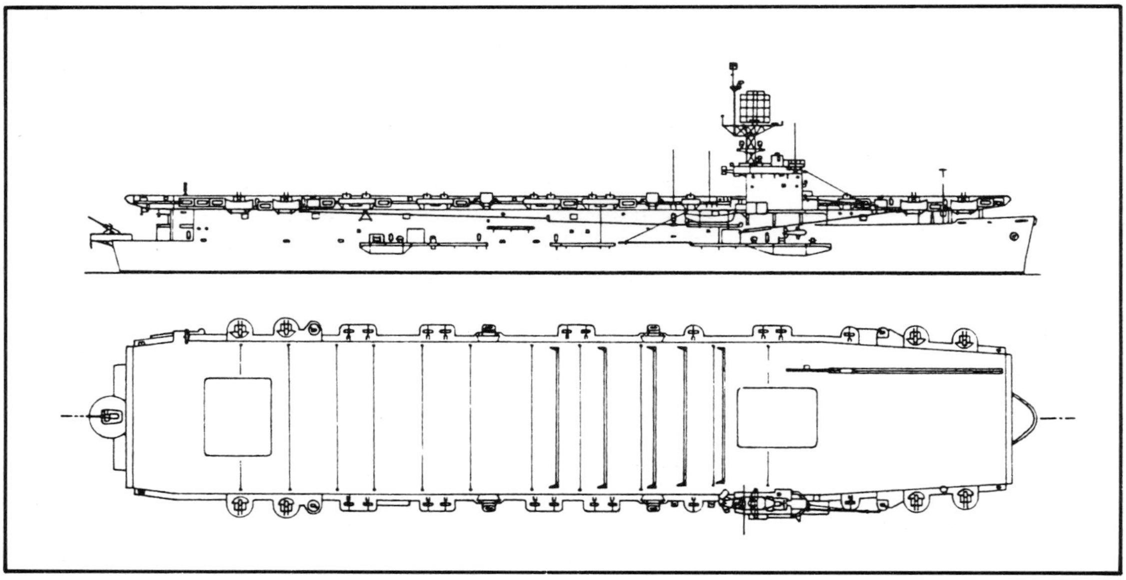

Right: USS *White Plains.* The USS *White Plains,* CVE-66, was one of the new *Casablancas* to join Carrier Support Group 5 for the invasion of the Marianas, others being *Kalinin Bay,* CVE-68, *Fanshaw Bay,* CVE-70, *Kitkun Bay,* CVE-71, *Gambier Bay,* CVE-973, *Hoggatt Bay,* CVE-75, and *Midway,* CVE-63, later renamed *St. Lo.*

marine patrols over the oilers, ammunition ships and supply vessels of the Fleet train assembled to replenish Task Force 58. *Chenango* refuelled the carriers *Langley* and *Princeton.* These attacks convinced Admiral Koga, who was in the Palaus and saw some of them for himself, that the next American move would be a thrust from New Guinea against Mindanao, the southern and largest island in the Philippines, and ordered the Combined Fleet to concentrate in southern Philippines waters and prepare for a decisive battle there. He himself then flew off for Mindanao but was never seen again, and was succeeded by Admiral Toyoda.

SANTEE JOINS THE ACTION

Waiting for Mitscher's parched carriers between the Carolines and the Admiralties was Task Group 50.15, their support group, protected by the *Sangamons* of CarDiv 22, now their original four in number with the addition of the wandering *Santee.*

For the Mariana landings Admiral Richmond Kelly Turner's amphibious force carried nearly six divisions under Marine Lieutenant-General H. M. 'Howling Mad' Smith, covered by the whole weight of the Fifth Fleet under Spruance, which included many old battleships, some of them salvaged from Pearl Harbor, and escort carriers in addition to the ships of the Fast Carrier Force, which would comprise seven big carriers, eight light carriers, seven fast battleships and many cruisers and destroyers, with a Mobile Service Squadron of the Fleet train moving up behind them.

NEW KAISERS

The escort carrier force had also increased by new ships from Kaiser's yards. In addition to *Coral Sea* and *Corregidor,* which with three *Sangamons* were to form the Carrier Support Group 5, were the new *White Plains* (CVE-66), with Composite Squadron VC-68, *Kalinin Bay* (CVE-68), with Compo VC-3, *Fanshaw Bay* (CVE-70), with Compo

Below: *Santee* joins the Pacific war. (US National Archives)

VC-8, *Kitkun Bay* (CVE-71) with Compo VC-5, *Gambier Bay* (CVE-73), with Compo VC-10, *Nehenta Bay* (CVE-74), with Compo VC-11, *Hoggatt Bay* and *Midway*. Each of these ships carried a standard Composite Squadron of 28 aircraft, made up of 12–16 FM-2s and 9–12 TBM Avengers. *Manila Bay* and *Natoma Bay* were to stand by to fly cargoes of P-47 Thunderbolt Army fighters ashore to airfields on Saipan as soon as they were captured. From 12 May to 2 June *Santee* flew her own air group CVEG-26 off to Manus and embarked the 66 Corsairs, 15 Hellcats and personnel of Marine Air Group 21, and headed north.

On 11 June 58 Hellcats left the decks of Mitscher's fast carriers and flew 320km (200 miles) to raid Guam and its small neighbour Rota, destroying Japanese fighters, and for the next two days F6Fs and TBMs struck airfields on Saipan, Tinian, Rota and Panan islands and at shipping in the harbours, with the task force's fast battleships bombarding defences on the west coasts of Saipan and Tinian. At the same time General MacArthur's Fifth and Thirteenth Army Air Forces working from New Guinea started a series of heavy attacks on Yap and the Palaus to prevent Japanese reinforcements being moved in from the south.

Below: In the assaults on the Marianas Islands, CVEs *Manila Bay* and *Natoma Bay* carried Army P-47 Thunderbolt fighters and their pilots to be flown ashore to airfields on Saipan Island as soon as they were captured. Here, pilots of the 73rd Fighter Squadron, 7th US Army Air Force, are briefed on the flight deck of *Manila Bay*, with the unmistakeable nose of a P-47 peering over their shoulders.

Gambier Bay's FM-2s shot down a Jap snooper, and on 13 June a TBM 'Turkey' reported a periscope, and destroyers attacked, producing an oil slick, while a *Kitkun Bay* fighter destroyed a Betty (Mitsubishi G4M1/G4M3 Navy Attack Bomber). During the night *Gambier Bay* and *Kitkun Bay* left the task group to join *Coral Sea* and *Corregidor* and the bombardment forces off Saipan. A small echo appeared on *Gambier Bay*'s surface radar. Destroyers investigated, and sank the enemy submarine *RO-114*, then *RO-111*.

Next morning, the 14th, two of Mitscher's four task groups, 58.1 and 58.3, were sent to attack Iwo Jima in the Volcano Islands and Chichi Jima in the Bonins, about half-way between the Marianas and Japan, with good airfields which the enemy might use for staging aircraft reinforcements from the north. Meanwhile the rest of Task Force 58 took up positions just west of Saipan, while the advanced elements of Admiral Turner's amphibious force, old battleships, escort carriers and minesweepers, were clearing the way for the landing. Heavy bombardment all day was followed by a further pounding at daylight on the 15th, under cover of which the first landings went in, on the southern part of Saipan's west coast.

TARGET SAIPAN

At 08:00 *Gambier Bay*'s first strike was in the air. Jap flak was light but Fighter Leader Stewart's Wildcat was hit in the engine, ditched, and Stewart was rescued by a destroyer. VC-10 flew support all day, while the other CVEs were flying CAP. On his second sortie 'Polack' Hank Pyzdrowski passed over Marpi Point at the extreme northern end of the island and saw men, women and children holding hands and leaping from the 275m (900ft) cliff to certain death, and later saw hundreds of bodies in the surf. The grunts were having a tough fight below and called on VC-10 for help. TBMs hit the enemy with 45kg (100lb) fragmentation bombs. That evening *GB* pilots listened to Tokyo Rose on the radio. They were laughing at her threat to send the mighty Combined Fleet against them when the General Alarm sounded. CAP from another CVE shot down four prowling Bettys. Everyone feared an air attack. 'I must admit I'm scared,' wrote Ensign Lischer to his parents, 'as I think everyone is.' Padre Carlsen noticed that the ship was unusually quiet that night, with men whom he had not seen in chapel abnormally respectful to him.

The quiet was shattered at 03:00 (16th), Clang! Clang! Clang! General Quarters sounded, the

Right: Admiral Jisaburo Ozawa, Commander-in-Chief, Combined Fleet.

bugle called all troubled dreamers to battle. The strike left to assist the Marines on the bloody beaches. Tanks repulsed a screaming banzai charge. Padre Carlsen passed on pilots' commentary over the ship's loudspeakers . . . 'One tank . . . Scratch one tank!' Below, the cane fields were burning. *GB* launched TBMs to silence enemy artillery pounding the Marines as they moved towards Aslito airfield, Pyzdrowski's radioman Jerry Faulds sighted a gun battery to the east of the field, and three TBMs took it out with 227kg (500lb) bombs. Ack-ack was fierce but sporadic, as the fleet's big guns kept it down.

SPRUANCE STANDS FIRM

Mitscher's 58.1 and 58.3 planes were blasting Guam and Tinian to cut off retaliating aircraft and destroy the runways, while his main force waited for news of the Japanese Fleet. That morning, the 16th, it came. US submarines had seen a Japanese fleet streaming out of San Bernardino Strait, north of Leyte in the Philippines, into the Philippine Sea between the Philippines and Saipan. The report mentioned 12 carriers heading for Saipan and the Fifth Fleet. This was Jisaburo Ozawa's Combined Fleet, with nine carriers, six battleships (including the *Yamato* and *Mushashi*), 13 cruisers and 30 destroyers. Ozawa had hoped to fight Spruance south of the Marianas, but when news of the attack on Saipan came in he was

Below: FM-2s, a lighter version of the Wildcat designed specially for escort carriers, fly CAP from *White Plains* in the Marianas operations. Note long-range wing tank. (US National Archives)

forced to sail straight for the landings, hoping that his 450 aircraft plus some 600 on the Marianas airfields, which Mitscher's 58.1 and 58.3 were even then battering, would hit Task Force 58, and his surface ships destroy Turner's invasion force. If battle was joined near the Marianas his aircraft could attack at long range, then land on Guam or Rota to refuel and re-arm and attack again. With the eastern trade wind blowing, his carriers had the weather gauge and could launch aircraft as they advanced, whereas to attack him Spruance's carriers would have to double back each time they flew off planes. Even so, if the American commander had known of Ozawa's simple plan, relying as it did on land-based planes, many of which were now burning wrecks on Aslito field, he might have steamed flat-out west to hit Ozawa as far from the landing beaches as possible. But he did not know and was getting no further long-range reports, as recce flying boats found it almost impossible to operate from the open Saipan anchorages. At Coral Sea and Midway the Japanese had approached in two widely separated bodies from different directions, and Spruance believed this to be standard Japanese doctrine. His job was to protect the landings, and to leave them unprotected to chase one fleet while another got in behind him and destroyed Turner's force was unthinkable. He therefore recalled Groups 58.1 and 58.3, reinforced Task Force 58 with some of Turner's cruisers and destroyers, sent all unwanted shipping east of the Marianas, and on the evening of the 18th retired eastward for the night out of range of the enemy.

Sallada's Navy

The CVEs carried on with the job of supporting the Marines ashore and giving air protection to the amphibious landing forces, Sallada's Kaiser boats (CarDiv 26) lying off the south-western invasion beaches, the *Sangamons* steaming with Task Force 53, the back-up for TF 52, to the east of the island, *Santee* with her load of Thunderbolts waiting for the capture of the airfields.

Captain Goodwin had told his ship's company on the 17th that the Jap Fleet was out and that Admiral Spruance had told the fast carriers and battleships to 'Go get 'em!' Things had been too easy for the CVEs. The whole of Sallada's Navy had lost only six planes, and with Stewart's rescue *Gambier Bay* not a single man. At dusk on the 17th she flew off the five small OY-I Marine observation planes she had been carrying.

At dusk *GB*'s combat information centre (CIC, popularly known as 'Christ I'm Confused') reported a Jap formation 96km (60 miles) away, and the ship went to General Quarters. She had just recovered her CAP, and the flight deck was cluttered – the sort of target the Jap pilots loved. More bogeys were coming in at 200km (126 miles) and the first group was closing fast . . . The relief CAP shot down several of them but another group closed them . . . A damaged fighter was raided for gear then pushed overboard to clear the deck just as the ship's guns started chattering. A black shape hurtled down, a bomb burst and the ship shuddered. Another plane came in on the bow. Captain Goodwin watched it, then . . . 'Hard-a-starboard!' That bomb missed, but there were others. Each time the Captain anticipated the bomb, and swung the ship in time, then a gun's talker shouted 'We got him!' The plane hit the sea and exploded in flame. Strapped in his Wildcat on the catapult drenched with spray, Lieutenant Roby felt naked. When the combat ended it was dark. 'Bats' McClendon got out his irridescent suit to match his paddles and brought in every plane but one, which had been hit by the celebrated flak gunners of Tinian and dumped in the wet. A bomb penetrated *Fanshaw Bay*'s after elevator and exploded in mid-air above the hangar deck, killing 14 and wounding 23. Fires broke out, and the fire main was ruptured, flooding compartments aft, but in just under an hour the damage was brought under control. Listing 3 degrees to port and nearly 2m (6ft) down by the stern, she limped off to Pearl for repairs.

Next day, 18 June, started with the ship's CAP shooting down a Betty, and continued fierce and hot. Jess Holleman's TBM was set on fire by flak. He was over enemy territory and did not know what his crew would do, so stayed put, scorched by flames, ditched in Tanapag harbour and was rescued, but never saw his crewmen again. McClendon landed planes in a hurry. There were no accidents, no wave-offs. Six Jap torpedo planes came in out of the rising sun. *GB*'s cannon hit the lead plane and it flew down the flight deck like a blazing meteorite. Other planes attacked, were

Below: A Marine OY-I observation plane takes off from USS *White Plains,* 18 June 1944. (US National Archives)

hit, their non-self-sealing tanks exploded and blew them into burning ruin. Around them *Kitkun Bay*, *Coral Sea* and *Corregidor* were pumping shells at torpedo planes snaking between them. *GB*'s Ensigns Charlie Dugan and Joe McGraw flew straight into the barrage. Dugan's Wildcat lost part of a wing but still flew, a 20mm shell tore away McGraw's canopy, Gene Seitz shot up a bomber with his wheels and flaps still down. *GB*'s gunners splashed another Jap which flew over the flight deck below the bridge. Darkness drew on with carrier planes still in the air, one of them McGraw's FM with some 50 shell holes, no radio, no flaps, with Roby's machine also damaged. Both were told to wait until last. By then *GB*'s flight deck was blocked by Dugan's crashed plane, and they were told to land on *Kitkun Bay*. Roby made it, McGraw took three wave offs, then flew back to *Gambier Bay*, now uncluttered. By now it was completely dark. Captain Goodwin turned on all the lights, McClendon picked up his fairy wands, and McGraw, who had never made a night landing before, approached, flapless, at 20 knots too fast, the wind scourging his uncanopied head, hit the deck hard, bounced into the barrier, and walked away. 'Luck of the Irish' said Flight Deck Chief Montgomery. With all planes safely down, 'Mr Daring' Dugan described in rich Irish-American accents how he had disposed of a Jap with his last bullet, and the Captain made him repeat it over the intercom.

All through that long night of 18/19 June the two fleet commanders marked time, Ozawa so as to be out of range of Spruance's planes when the Japanese strike was launched in the morning, the American Admiral burdened with his duty to the landing force. At first light Spruance ordered a search for the enemy, and 640km (400 miles) to the west Ozawa sent off his strike. At 480km (300 miles) Mitscher's aviators looked in vain for the Combined Fleet. Then the submarine service did some of his work for him. At 09:00 the *Albacore* torpedoed the new carrier *Taiho*, Ozawa's flagship, forcing him to shift his flag, and at noon *Cavalla* hit and sank *Shokaku* with three torpedoes.

'The Marianas Turkey Shoot'

Off the coasts of the Marianas the situation was reversed when CAP TBMs from the CVE *Suwannee* destroyed the Emperor's submarine *I-184*. About 10:00 the first Japanese striking forces began to appear on Spruance's radar screens, including a large force of planes coming up from Yap and a reduced force of aircraft, actually some 250, from Ozawa's carriers. They were met by an air fleet of Hellcats, and the great 'Marianas Turkey Shoot', or Battle of the Philippine Sea, began. Most of the Japanese aircraft were shot down before they could reach the Fleet, while Hellcats and Avengers attacked

Left: A twin-engined Japanese aircraft is shot down while attacking CVEs in the Marianas, photographed from *Kitkun Bay*, 18 June 1944. (US National Archives)

Left: A Japanese bomber is destroyed in an attack on CVEs of TG.52.II in the Marianas, 18 June 1944. (US National Archives)

the Guam airfields, curtailed the sorties of the few planes based there and the handful which had survived the carrier plane battle and landed for gas. At noon the submarine *Cavalla* sank the *Shokaku* and the planes on board her. This left Ozawa with the *Zuikaku*, the two converted liners *Hiyo* and *Junyo*, and four smaller carriers.

THE FIRST KAMIKAZES

All this was unknown to the CVEs, which carried on flying CAP over the landing area and striking at facilities in the Marianas, all except *Kalinin Bay*, which sailed to ferry planes to and from Eniwetok until 24 June. Tinian's airfields were neutralised. *Gambier Bay*'s Rich Roby shot down a Kate bomber over Ushi airfield, while back on the ship Lieutenant Harden stood in the Goofers and watched his close friend Dean Gilliatt take off for a patrol, flip over into the sea and drown. Gilliatt had been looking forward to seeing his new baby on the next liberty. Remorselessly the bullhorn called for a replacement. The Japanese were by this time so desperate that they began trying to crash their aircraft into the ships, a disturbing trend. The battleship *Indiana* was slightly damaged in this way. By this time the carrier men were worn out after five consecutive days and nights of battle. They did not know that the CV and CVL aviators had shot down 400 Japanese planes out of some 545 engaged, carrier-borne and land-based, with many more destroyed in *Taiho* and *Shokaku*. In the whole Japanese Combined Fleet only 60 aircraft remained, 40 of them in *Zuikaku*, while the US Fleet had lost in action only 17 fighters out of nearly 300 engaged.

SPRUANCE STRIKES

Constant turning into the easterly wind had prevented Spruance closing the enemy during the day, and at nightfall, leaving one carrier group to cover Saipan, he headed west, but Ozawa, without totally abandoning the idea of returning to the attack, had retired north-westward to replenish from his fleet train, and it was not until 15:20 on the 20th that American searches discovered him 480km (300 miles) to the northward. Though fuel was low, the hour was late and the distance only just within their reach. Mitscher at once emptied all his flight decks, and his massed aircraft reached the Japanese Fleet just before sunset, brushed aside a thin fighter defence, sank *Hiyo*, and badly damaged *Junyo* and many other ships. Toyoda ordered Ozawa to withdraw. Only 20 American planes were lost in the attack, but they had to pay the price of operating at extreme range. Mitscher turned on all his lights, but many aircraft were damaged on landing, and 80 ditched in the sea, many of their crews being rescued by destroyers. The cautious Spruance decided not to send his fast battleships in pursuit of the enemy while this was in progress. Not knowing that *Taiho* and *Shokaku* had been sunk, he preferred to keep his fleet concentrated in the hope of hitting Ozawa again next day, but recce flying boats reported the Japanese some 560km (350 miles) away at dawn, and many of his ships were very short of fuel. He sent the two groups with the most fuel after Ozawa, but they could not catch him and abandoned the chase.

CHENANGO'S WAR

There was no further interference with the taking of Saipan, and the other islands in the group could now be dealt with. On 21 June a low-flying enemy bomber was shot down by a fighter division from *Chenango*, and on the following day she sent aircraft on a photo-reconnaissance of Guam in preparation for landings there, and mounted a one-ship offensive against Pagan Island, 320km (200 miles) north of Saipan, which the enemy were using to stage aircraft down from the north to attack American shipping off the landing beaches. All alone she steamed off the island, launched her entire air group of 32 planes on a strike which severely crippled the airfield and shot up gun positions, sank four supply ships, damaged several others, and shot down a Betty which tried to follow them back to the ship. At 10:00 on the 22nd CVE *Natoma Bay* catapulted off 24 Army P-47D Thunderbolts to captured Aslito airfield on Saipan, 12 more next day, with *Manila Bay* boosting off four that day and her remaining 33 on the 24th. Task Force 58 planes followed up *Chenango*'s attack, bombarding Pagan (24–25 June), Iwo Jima (24 June and 4 July), and Chichi Jima, 240km (150 miles) north of Iwo Jima (4 July).

Making use of the photographs taken by *Chenango*'s aircraft on 22 June, the invasion troops under Major-General Geiger landed from Rear-Admiral Conolly's amphibious force on 21 July for nine days of bloody fighting. The CVEs' planes were on constant call. By the end of this period *Chenango* pilots had flown 364 sorties against the enemy on Guam. Strafing, bombing, and ground support used up every pilot and aircrewman and earned them 32 medals and commendations. They dropped 74 tons of bombs, destroyed many gun emplacements, troop concentrations, bridges, tank and truck convoys and at least one desperately needed enemy ammunition dump which exploded with spectacular violence, and the ship's four photographers won commendations for their fast and excellent work in delivering to the flagship clear shots of the beachhead. At 16:00 on 30 July *Chenango*'s Lieutenant (jg) Terrar was ordered to attempt a landing at Oroto airfield, which had been reported taken. He completed his mission successfully, reporting that the field was operational for all but very heavily loaded planes, and thus became the first man ever to land on the first United States' ground in the Pacific to be recaptured, after it was re-taken.

KAISERS AT TINIAN

Meanwhile, Tinian had been invaded on 24 July by the Marine divisions that had conquered Saipan, with CarDiv 26 of Sallada's Task Unit 52.4 providing cover and support against the tough Colonel Kiyochi Ogato, who had gained his reputation as an iron man with the famous Kwantung Army in Manchuria and had obviously inspired his 9,000 men on Tinian. With the island only 8km (five miles) from Saipan, much of the preliminary bombardment was carried out from there, but on 23 July, D-1, *Gambier Bay* and *Kitkun Bay* began the CVE effort with 50 TBM sorties carrying 45kg (100lb) bombs, rockets and incendiaries to set fire to canefields and a village on the north end of the island. *GB*'s planes were weary after Saipan, and her ensuing effort was much reduced, while Chiefs Montgomery and Flanders did their best to revive the tired veterans. But the operation turned out to be their smoothest yet. By 1 August Tinian was secure, and CarDiv 26, minus *Corregidor* which had left on 28 July for an overhaul at San Diego, sailed down to Guam, where the Japanese were still resisting. *Gambier Bay* put up combat air patrols over the invasion force. On 2 August *Kalinin Bay* rejoined from her ferrying duties. Two days later the three *Sangamons* left for Eniwetok and a month's rest and replenishment, *Santee* arrived and flew off the 81 aircraft of Marine Air Group 21, which became the first air unit to operate from the island.

Below: TBMs from *White Plains* bomb an island airfield in the Marianas, seen from one of her aircraft. (US National Archives)

On the 11th *Gambier Bay, Kitkun Bay* and *White Plains*, with four destroyers, sailed for Espiritu Santo. On the 13th they crossed the Equator, and in *Gambier Bay* Neptune's Courtiers gruesomely updated the traditional ceremony by administering electric shocks to the Pollywogs via a replica of the electric chair, and some pilots reported 'unfit for flight operations' from bruised buttocks sustained in running the gauntlet. At Espiritu Santo Admiral Sallada was promoted to command of CarDiv F-6 and took Captain Goodwin as his Chief of Staff. For their part, most of *Gambier Bay*'s officers had thought Goodwin too dictatorial, and Assistant Air Officer Waring called him 'Sir Hugh'. The ship's Executive Officer, Dick Ballenger, took over command until the arrival of their new Captain. Pyz Pyzdrowski was standing guard over six new replacement TBMs ashore when a large, tall Captain climbed up and sat in one of their comfortable pilot's seats. Nervously the ensign said, 'Sir, these planes are set aside for VC-10 of the *Gambier Bay*. If you want to check out in one of them I will have to have an order from the Captain.' The tall man grinned. 'Consider it issued. I'm Bowser Vieweg, new Captain of the *Gambier Bay*. And you can check me out right now.'

Captain W. V. R. Vieweg had been an aviator almost since graduating from Annapolis, class of '24, and he had just come from *Hornet*, where he had had the daunting experience of serving as Chief of Staff to the larger than life 'Jocko' Clark, ex-*Suwannee* and *Yorktown*, the first Cherokee Indian to reach flag rank in the US Navy, commander of Task Group 58.1. Vieweg had flown most Navy planes, except a TBM, but after an hour's instruction he was complete master of it. Back in the ship he called all pilots to the Ready Room and told them, 'Gentlemen, I just want to tell you that as far as I'm concerned this ship has one primary mission; to get you safely to the point where you can accomplish yours.' The pilots of *Gambier Bay* felt better than they had for a long time.

THE ROAD TO THE PHILIPPINES

On 26 July MacArthur had turned President Roosevelt against any continuation of Nimitz's plan to drive to Formosa and on to Japan via the Ryukyu Islands. The grand plan was that the Sixth Army would advance from New Guinea to Mindanao in the Philippines via the islands of Morotai and Talaud, whence to Leyte and the northern Philippines, with Nimitz's ships and planes protecting MacArthur's right flank, capturing or neutralising the Palau and Yap Islands and Ulithi Atoll, beginning with an assault on Peleliu Island in the Palaus to coincide with MacArthur's

Right: Grumman F6F-5 Hellcat, USS *Santee*, CVE-29. (J. M. Goulding)

seizure of Morotai, planned for 15 September. On completion of the Marianas campaign Admiral Spruance and his amphibious commander Vice-Admiral Turner withdrew to Pearl Harbor to plan the operations that were to follow the re-conquest of the Philippines, while Admiral Halsey and Vice-Admiral Wilkinson, who had been planning the assault on the western Carolines at Pearl since 15 June, took their places, with the Fifth Fleet re-designated the Third Fleet while Halsey commanded it.

On 31 August Mitscher's Task Force 38 began widespread preliminary air strikes, against Iwo Jima and Chichi Jima, Yap and Mindanao – the first attack on the Philippines – off which his cruisers and destroyers destroyed a convoy of 32 small cargo ships. With surprisingly little air opposition here he switched his attacks north to the central Philippines (12–14 September) while softening up the Palaus, Talaud and, in co-operation with the Far East Air Force, airfields in the Celebes.

Kaisers in the Palaus

Only two of the Palaus were to be captured, Peleliu and Angaur in the extreme south of the chain, Peleliu having the only airfield in the group, Angaur a good site for another. Halsey actually thought this assault a waste of time, which made it a waste of lives. With *Gambier Bay, Kalinin Bay, Kitkun Bay* and *White Plains* bombing and strafing, the First Marines landed on Peleliu at dawn on 15 September, after three days of bombardment. They got a footing and by the evening of the second day the airfield had been taken. But fighting was hard. Inland the Japanese had placed guns in pillboxes, which needed the help of the carrier aircraft to knock out. VC-10's commander Ed Huxtable, who had been co-ordinating the attacks of a strike group from *Gambier Bay, Kitkun Bay* and *White Plains*, saw tanks heading along a road near a position the marines had called Bloody Ridge for the airfield and the beachhead, and called out 'Everybody go!' There was a free-for-all, with a mêlée of planes strafing and rocketing the tanks, which never reached the beach. On the 16th the wind died. 'The trouble with Mister Kaiser's coffins', said LSO McClendon, 'is that they're 15-knot ships in a 25-knot war.' 'Hux' himself just made the deck, tank-destroyer Bassett put his machine in the catwalk. On the 17th *Gambier Bay* fighters flew to help the marines in the rough gulley country, and there were strikes from all the carriers, which also diverted to support the assault on Angaur, where the grunts had the same trouble with pillboxes and blockhouses. *Gambier Bay* sent eight FMs with 113kg (250lb) bombs as her contribution. Angaur was secured in three days, and the same force was sent to take Ulithi Atoll, 480km (300 miles) to the north-east.

The Mobile Service Squadron was brought forward, and Ulithi, 1,370km (850 miles) east of Leyte, became the principal forward base until forces could be established in the Philippines. Jack Stewart led his *Gambier Bay* fighters on the long 480km (300 mile) flight to Yap, each with a 113kg (250lb) bomb, pilots hoping they would not meet any Jap planes on the way, and burn up gas, but the only enemy aircraft they saw were some burned-out wrecks on Yap. While they were in the area Captain Vieweg thought they should take a look at Ulithi Atoll, which Nimitz wanted as a staging base. Huxtable flew there and saw no trace of a military presence, and the assault force confirmed it when they landed. Admiral Ofstie took CarDiv 26 into the wide lagoon and anchored briefly. Ashore marines were already building Duffy's Tavern.

The parallel assault on Morotai by the Seventh Amphibious Force of MacArthur's Navy, with support from CarDiv 22 (*Sangamon, Suwannee, Chenango* and *Santee*, with repaired *Fanshaw Bay* and *Midway*) met with no opposition from the enemy, after a neutralisation of airfields on Ceram, Halmahera, by General Kenney's Air Force bombers and Marc Mitscher's strikes on the northern Celebes and the Philippines.

19

APPOINTMENT AT SAMAR

'And dawn gleaming bright
In exultation will find us
At the temple of Yasukui'
– Lieutenant Yokoyama, Imperial Japanese Navy

THE SHO PLAN

At 10:00 on 20 October, after a furious bombardment by Kinkaid's guns and CVE planes, four divisions of US troops landed in Leyte Gulf. Kurita left Brunei to penetrate the Philippines and break out into the Philippine Sea for Leyte Gulf. Later he detached a smaller force under Vice-Admiral Nishimura to reach the Gulf from the south via the Surigao Straits in concert with another force under Vice-Admiral Shima sent from Japan. Ozawa sailed south with his carriers hoping to occupy Halsey while Kurita fell on the invasion fleet. This was the Japanese SHO victory plan, and it looked like giving Toyoda and Nimitz the showdown they both wanted. US submarines *Darter* and *Dace* sighted and reported Kurita in the South China Sea, damaged a cruiser and sank two more, including the Flagship *Atago*. Kurita had to swim for his life, and transferred, via a destroyer, to *Yamato*. From the Philippine Sea Halsey's task group, less the refuelling 38.1, fanned out to cover the eastern gaps in the Philippines, with the Flagship *New Jersey* in the centre group facing San Bernardino Straits.

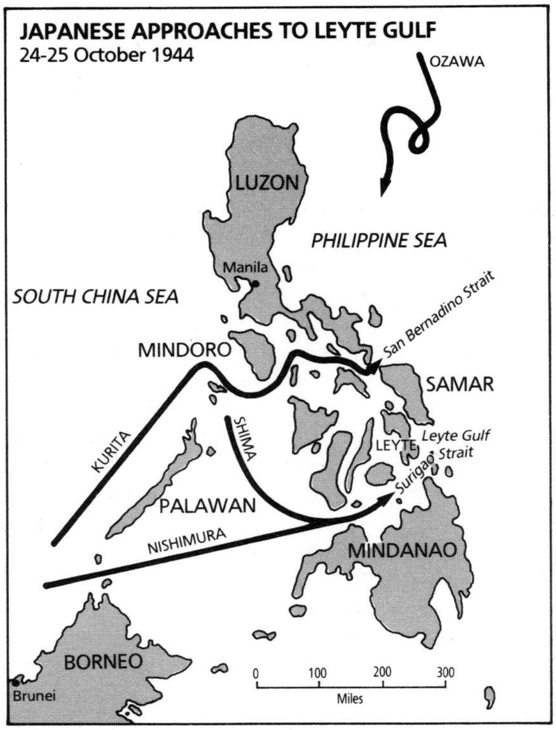

SPRAGUE'S SIXTEEN

Tommy Sprague's TG.77.4 of CVEs moved to a position 65km (40 miles) to seaward of Leyte Gulf and its 16 ships in three groups formed a line along the coast of Samar, the large island immediately to the north-east of Leyte. To the south was Taffy One, commanded by the group commander himself, comprising: CarDiv 22 (*Sangamon*, *Suwannee*, and *Santee*, with *Chenango* away at Morotai collecting new planes), and Rear-Admiral G. R. Henderson's CarDiv 28 (*Petrof Bay*, with *Saginaw Bay* also absent at Morotai). Next in order to the north was Taffy Two, commanded by Rear-Admiral Felix Stump, with his own CarDiv 24 (*Manila Bay* and *Natoma Bay*), and Rear-Admiral W. D. Sample's CarDiv 27 (*Kadashan Bay*, *Marcus Island*, *Ommaney Bay* and *Savo Island*). Furthest north, 190km (120 miles) from Taffy One, was the Taffy Three of Rear-Admiral Clifton A. F. Sprague, usually known as 'the other Sprague' or by his Annapolis tag of 'Ziggy' to distinguish him from his group commander. He flew his flag in the 'lucky' *Fanshaw Bay* of CarDiv 25 (*Fanshaw Bay*, *Kalinin Bay*, *Saint Lo*, *White Plains*), with Rear-Admiral Ralph Ofstie's CarDiv 26 (*Gambier Bay* and *Kitkun Bay*). With the exception of the veteran *Sangamons* of CarDiv 22, all the carriers were Kaisers, the standard Pacific CVEs, each with a Composite Squadron of 11–18 Wildcat FM-2s or Hellcat F6F fighters and 11–12 Avenger TBM-1Cs. The *Sangamons'* air groups contained more aircraft in a different mix, with 17–26 Hellcat F6F-3s or -5s and six to nine TBM-1Cs or TBF-1s.

Tommy Sprague's 16 CVEs supported the landings by bombing and strafing. Jack Stewart, Fighter Leader of *Gambier Bay*'s Compo (VC) 10, was ordered to take eight FM-2s to attack the southern end of Samar which abuts Leyte Gulf, where the Japanese had brought up artillery to overlook the Gulf, and a force of troops which

Above: Vice-Admiral Takeo Kurita.

might well be moved to Leyte. The fighters were to strafe, and to bomb with a new weapon – napalm, gasoline thickened with the aluminium soap of naphthenic and palmitric acids into a sticky gel that burned more slowly than gasoline but at a much higher temperature (982°C or 1,800°F). The results were awesome. An explosive charge scattered the sticky goo, which stuck to what it hit until burned out.

Other aircraft flew support missions for ground forces in action on Leyte, provided fighter sweeps against the western Visayan Islands and northern Mindanao, and launched strikes against enemy airfields in those areas, including Del Monte, Tacloban, Cebu, Opon, Medellin, Alicante, Fabrica Bacalod, Carolina and others. Anti-shipping sweeps sank coasters, luggers and enemy PT-boats. Enemy troops and installations were destroyed.

HALSEY TAKES THE BAIT

At dawn on 24 October Halsey's planes sighted Kurita's Central Force and the combined Shima/Nishimura Southern Force. Leaving Kinkaid to deal with attacks in the south, two of his groups struck Kurita in the Sibuyan Sea and sank the *Mushashi*, but not before decimating a fierce air attack from Luzon which mortally wounded the LCV *Princeton*. The Taffy CVEs put up more than 100 planes, including eight-plane CAPs to protect Kinkaid's ships and the troops ashore. Halsey's earlier strikes had reduced Jap air strength in the islands to about 30 fighters and 50 bombers, but the Second Air Force on Formosa reinforced them with 350 aircraft, and 250 planes were sent to attack Kinkaid. Roby and Courtney from *Gambier Bay*'s VC-10 each scratched a Sally (Mitsubishi Ki-21 Army heavy bomber). Seitz shot the wings off another, Dugan got two kills near Tacloban airfield on Leyte (now in American hands), McGraw flamed two Lily bombers and returned to *Gambier Bay* with 30l (eight gal) left in his tank. Hit by bombs, and his force apparently crippled, Kurita turned back.

Halsey was reasonably satisfied that he had nobbled Kurita's Central Force, and thought that the Shima/Nishimura Southern Force was another part of a three-pronged concerted attack on the US forces in Leyte Gulf. The truth could only be known when the Japanese carriers were located. He felt sure they would show up, but from which direction was uncertain. Marc Mitscher thought from the China Sea, but Halsey agreed with his Staff, who all favoured Empire waters, and ordered a thorough search to the northwards. In *New Jersey* his Flag Secretary Doug Moulton kept thumping the chart, and asking 'Where the hell *are* they, those goddam carriers?'

Then came a hot signal from Sherman's TG.36.1, as a result of an air search. 'Three carriers × two light cruisers × three destroyers 18° 32′ North 125° 28′ East × course 270° × speed 15.'

This was part of the Northern Force, steaming some 320km (200 miles) east of Cape Engano, the north-eastern tip of Luzon, 305km (190 miles) to the nor'-nor'-east of Third Fleet, out of range of the majority of Halsey's ships, even if dusk had not begun to fall. The slow common speed of all the Japanese forces, never more than 15 knots, reinforced Halsey's view of a concerted Japanese action, with a common focus in time and space, supported again when the Central Force was seen to have reversed course for San Bernardino Strait. 'The crippled Central Force's dogged second approach to San Bernardino', wrote Halsey, 'and the weak Southern Force's simultaneous approach to Surigao against overwhelming strength, were comprehensible only if they were under adamant orders to rendezvous with the carriers – the Northern Force – off Samar next day, the twenty-fifth, for a combined attack on the transports at Leyte . . .'

Halsey's mind computed Third Fleet's best move. The Shima/Nishimura Southern Force he could ignore. Kinkaid could easily deal with that. 'The Central Force, according to our pilots, had suffered so much torpedo damage, especially to its gun and fire-control equipment, that it could not win a decision; it, too, could be left to Kinkaid.'

This was hasty reasoning. Kinkaid had enough on his plate in the south. And Halsey, at this point thinking as the late and therefore more likely to be biased convert to airmanship, had over-estimated the damage done to Kurita's Central Force by his pilots. 'The pilots' reports', he wrote later, 'proved dangerously optimistic, but we had no reason to discredit them at the time.' On such a fateful occasion there was every reason to treat the pilots' overlapping reports with caution. This estimate left the Northern Force fresh and undamaged, its carriers giving it a scope hundreds of kilometres wider than the others. If Third Fleet could destroy these carriers, 'our future operations need fear no threat from the sea'.

There were three battles Halsey could fight. He could wait off San Bernardino for the Northern Force to come to him, yielding Ozawa the initiative with his carrier planes and those on the Luzon airfields; leave TF.34's battleships to guard Bernardino while he hit the Northern Force with his carriers (which, he thought, would mean dangerously dividing his fleet); or leave the Straits unguarded, thus taking up, he thought, the initiative and surprising the Northern Force. In fact Ozawa had already taken the initiative, in his move to decoy Halsey away from the Gulf, and it was the US Third Fleet Commander who would be surprised, but this was the option he chose. As for Kurita's Central Force, even if it cleared San Bernardino, 'It could hope only to harry the landing operations . . . It could merely hit and run.' Halsey failed to define the degree of 'harrying' and 'hitting' the Central Force could still manage. It was a decision which the prudent, unimpetuous Ray Spruance would not have made.

Writing off Kurita, Halsey headed north with three of his Fast Carrier groups, ordering McCain's refuelling TG.38.1 to steer in the same direction as soon as possible, and made a vaguely worded signal meant to convey his intention to detach his battleships and some cruisers sometime later, but which both Kinkaid and Nimitz assumed to mean that he was detaching the ships immediately to cover the San Bernardino Straits, in case the force (Kurita's) previously attacked should double back. Reassured, Kinkaid then completed his own plans for attacking the large enemy force heading for Leyte from the south.

At midnight on 24/25 October 20 PT-boats attacked Nishimura in the Surigao Straits, followed by a devastating fire from Oldendorff's destroyers, eight cruisers and six battleships. By 04:00 the flagship *Yamashiro*, the other battlewagon *Fuso* and two destroyers had been sunk or were sinking, leaving only the crippled and blazing cruiser *Mogami* and two destroyers. Shima now approached from the south with two heavy cruisers and the light cruiser *Abukama*, which ran into a PT torpedo. *Nachi* rammed the burning *Mogami*, and Shima retired. A few hours later a CVE strike finished off *Mogami*.

Halsey had taken the bait, and was steaming at flank speed for Ozawa's half-trained ragbag force, which had been squawking loudly in plain language to make sure that Halsey could not overlook the squadron, which comprised: one large carrier (*Zuikaku*) and three light carriers, their total of only 120 aircraft, almost all expended in attacks on Sherman's group, two battleships with launching platforms but no aircraft, three light cruisers and ten destroyers. A few hours later one of Mitscher's night shadowers reported a strong enemy force steaming at 20 knots for San Bernardino Straits. Halsey dismissed this as the hara-kiri Central Force group emasculated by 'torpedo hits, bomb hits, topside damage, fires and casualties', and remained on course. The force was indeed Kurita's Second Fleet, minus *Musashi* but otherwise only superficially damaged and very far from being a spent force, with four battleships, six heavy cruisers, two light cruisers and eleven destroyers. At dawn, having passed through the San Bernardino Straits at midnight, it was steaming down the eastern coast of Samar at 20 knots. Jack Stewart and a double CAP of eight FM-2s which had been up over the force for an hour and a half were returning to *Gambier Bay* with nothing to report.

Lieutenant Lynch, watch officer in *Gambier Bay*, observed sunrise at 06:24. At 06:38 a signal from *Fanshaw Bay* authorised Taffy Three to secure from General Quarters. At 06:43 Lynch received word from the Air Plot that one of *St Lo*'s anti-submarine patrol planes had reported a Japanese task force 32km (20 miles) on Taffy Three's starboard beam as the CVEs headed westwards. Right on top of this came an order from *Fanshaw Bay* to change course south-east to 130 degrees. Lynch looked at his radar PPI repeater and saw the force referred to bearing 269 degrees from them. The General Quarters alarm at 06:47 coincided with an excited report from Ensign Jensen on A/S patrol from *Kadashan Bay* of 'Four Jap battleships and eight cruisers with destroyers . . .' 'Check identification!' said Ziggy Sprague. At this point geysers of foam coloured red, green and yellow began to rise among the CVEs. Only the Japanese, their radar crude and unreliable, used this old-fashioned method of checking the fall of shot from individual ships, and Ziggy had his answer. Then, dim but unquestionable through the mist and drizzle, tripod masts heaved above the horizon astern. 'Kee-rist!' said Ensign Leo Zeola, 'look at those pagodas!'

MOMENT OF TRUTH

There were ten fighters on deck and seven TBMs with empty bomb bays. 'Pilots man your planes,'

Right: Rear-Admiral Felix B. Stump, USN, classmate of 'Ziggy' Sprague at Annapolis and his staunch supporters at Samar. (From Page 11, *The Escort Carriers in Action*)

ordered Vieweg, to clear them away. Zeola and Tetz ran to the Ready Room, grabbed their parachute harness and made for the flight deck. All fighters but one had engines running, pilots aboard. Zeola ran for the empty one, began to hoist himself up, and was confronted with the grinning Irish face of Joe Dennis McGraw. Gellhorn rang down for more revs. 'Are you making all possible speed?' 'Affirmative,' said Lieutenant Fred Mallgrave. 'Enemy ships are closing,' said Gellhorn. 'Permission requested to light off smoke screen burners,' asked Mallgrave. 'Granted.' Smoke poured from *Gambier Bay*'s vents, and from all the other ships of Taffy Three, and Sprague signalled Taffy One and Taffy Two for help.

This was it, the moment all CVE men dreaded, when the worst had happened, when the bad dream had come frighteningly true, when you were trapped, in a steel eggshell hull bursting its welds at 18 knots running from an enemy that could do 30 and blow you to pieces, with nowhere to go but down. CVE – Combustible, Vulnerable, Expendable. Kaiser's coffins. Woolworth carriers. Banana boats. Remember the *Liscome Bay*?

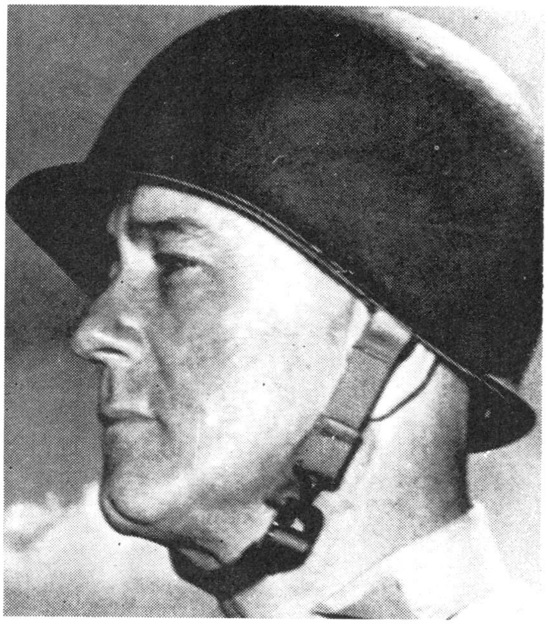

THE OTHER SPRAGUE

To the south in USS *Manila Bay*, Rear-Admiral Felix Stump, commander, Taffy Two, stocky, bluff, solid, as his name suggested, former CO of Scoron 2 in *Saratoga*, navigator of *Lexington*, commander of the old *Langley* (the ship that had taught his generation of US naval aviators how to fly from carriers), was worrying about Taffy Three and his friend 'Ziggy' Sprague. Knowing 'Ziggy' well from Annapolis days, both class of '18, he had always thought of the scholar-athlete from Boston's élite Roxbury Latin School as brilliant but highly strung, and had developed a brotherly, almost fatherly protective attitude towards the 'other Sprague', while admiring the brilliance, to which he himself did not aspire. 'Ziggy' Sprague had stood by the new battleship *Tennessee*, and later the legendary *Yorktown*, and invented the flight deck arrestor gear system which had saved the lives of many aviators. 'Ziggy' Sprague had always been in front. Even at Pearl on that terrible

Below: USS *Gambier Bay*, CVE-73, first victim of the Samar battle. (US National Archives)

day 'Ziggy' Sprague's little *Tangier* had (of course) to be the first ship to open fire on the Japs, and he had earned his command of the second *Wasp* in the great 'Turkey shoot'. But there was always, though he would never have aired the thought, that small element of doubt in Stump's mind. How would it be, how would 'Ziggy' show in a really tough spot, when he was cast adrift in a sea of troubles – like now, when he was looking down the 17.9in barrels of the *Yamato*, with the weight of 34 ships and the lives of nearly 20,000 men on his back? Well, Taffy Two would do what it could for 'Ziggy', though it had so many of its planes out on other duties.

At 01:55 in the black, wet graveyard watch, Kinkaid had ordered group commander Tommy Sprague to fly three daylight missions. Tommy, with his own commitments, had passed the buck to him, and he had ordered Young's *Ommaney Bay* to do it with Smith's Compo 75. He hoped that Tom Kinkaid would appreciate what it meant to re-spot the deck in the dark, on a slippery, rain-lashed flight deck, and to get planes off with men not trained in night flying.

Young had only completed launching at 06:58. And there were other planes out. Greber had launched a ten-plane replenishment mission from *Marcus Island* at 05:45 with 3,330l (880 gal) of water and 1,200 K rations for the 96th Division isolated on Leyte, and she had only two TBMs left to mount a torpedo strike right away. The search planes would have to be recalled, be re-armed with torpedoes or 227kg (500lb) bombs. But Stump was determined to send as many planes to 'Ziggy's' help as he could. Impulsively he called up *Fanshaw Bay*. 'Don't be alarmed, "Ziggy",' he said, 'Remember – we're in back of you. Don't get excited, don't do anything rash.' Sprague was glad to hear the familiar reassuring voice, and to know that Taffy Two was just over the horizon, but he knew exactly what he must do, and intended to do it. His screen and his planes must take the weight, with Taffy Two and Taffy One flying in help as soon as it was available. Taffy One, in its regular day operating area about 65km (40 miles) off Surigao Island, south-by-east of Leyte Gulf and the other side of Dinagat Island from Surigao Strait, some 210km (130 miles) south of Taffy Three, had launched a strike of 11 TBMs and 17 Hellcats to join in the chase of Nishimura's and Shima's defeated ships about an hour before Kurita's first salvo landed in the wake of Taffy Three, and these aircraft were helping to finish off the sinking *Mogami*. Steering 090 degrees, with the wind coming from 070 degrees, he could run and launch at the same time, and throw everything he had in his magazines at the Japs, relying on smoke to hide him – which would be blowing in the right direction too – and the destroyers and DEs to win him time. That way too he could hope to draw the Japanese into the central blue of the Philippine Sea and away from Kinkaid in the Gulf.

Below: The weight of command. Rear-Admiral Clifton 'Ziggy' Sprague, commanding Taffy Three, at a desperate moment in the fight of the CVEs off Samar. (US National Archives)

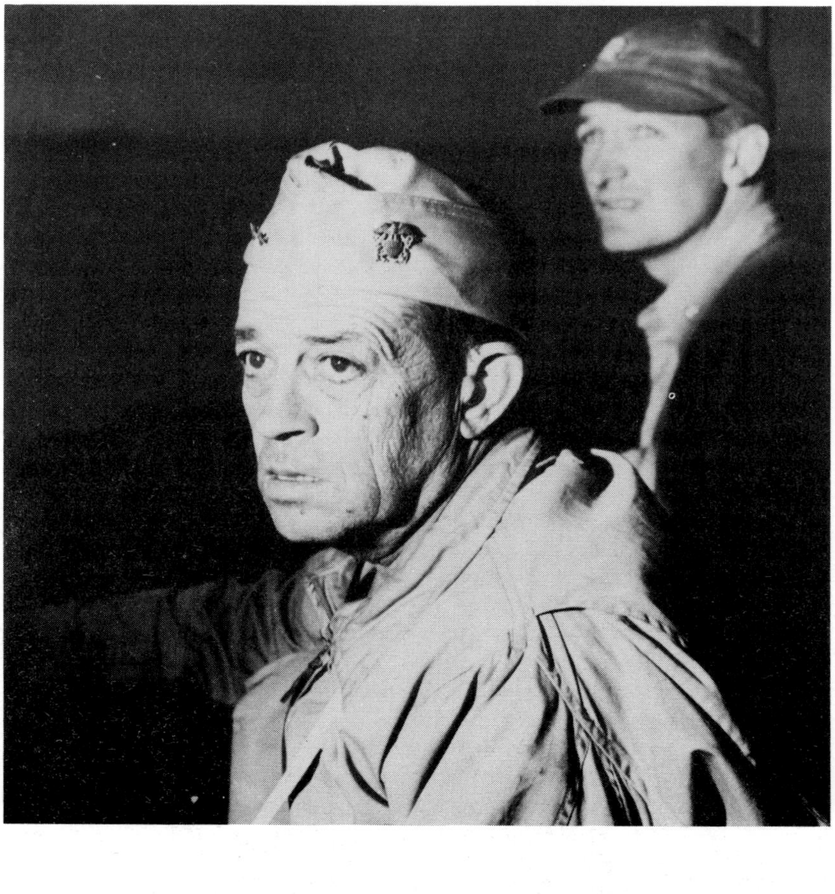

HEAVEN-SENT CVES

'By Heaven-sent opportunity', signalled Kurita to Toyodo, 'we are dashing to attack the enemy carriers,' convinced that the assault force commander would never station his escort carriers so far from the beaches and unprotected by big guns. They must be outrunners of Halsey's fleet. The Second Fleet was deployed in four columns with the lead ships in a 60–240 line of bearing, steering 170 degrees at 20 knots. The easternmost column was a destroyer screen, then came CruDiv 7 (heavy cruisers *Kumano, Suzuya, Chikuma* and *Tone*). Next westwards steamed CruDiv 5 (heavy cruisers *Haguro* and *Chokai*), then another destroyer line. Five kilometres (three miles) behind CruDiv 5, steamed BatDiv I (*Yamato* with her nine 17.9in guns and the 16in *Nagato*). At the same distance behind CruDiv 7 was BatDiv 3, 14in battleships *Kongo* and *Haruna*. LCs *Noshiro* and *Yahagi* and two destroyer squadrons were in the van. Sprague's six carriers were steaming in a rough circle 2,286m (2,500yd) in diameter, and the DD screen patrolled sectors of an outer circle 5,486m (6,000yd) from its centre. Soon the two Japanese cruiser columns were creaming forward from their port quarter and closing, with the four battleships right up their fantails. 'A perfect set-up to polish off this unit,' thought Captain

Sullivan in *White Plains*. *White Plains* and *Fanshaw Bay* on the exposed flank of the force, were surrounded by red, blue, green and yellow fountains. 'They're shootin' in Technicolour!' said his signalman. He was immediately thrown off his feet as a high-calibre shell pitched alongside the ship, which twisted violently, the movement opening the general circuit breaker, all electrical power and steering control being momentarily lost. 'This salvo measured the carriers as calipers,' reported Sullivan, 'diagonally from the port quarter to the starboard bow, four shells dropping microscopically close forward and two aft.'

Fanshaw Bay, in spite of her exposed position, had got her remaining fighters and 11 TBMs into the air even before the first salvo had arrived from Kurita. For a while *Gambier Bay* seemed to be escaping unnoticed. Vieweg was too busy getting his planes clear to land others to worry about that. To launch they had to turn to port and head into the east wind, away from Leyte, with Halsey somewhere to the north. Ed Huxtable climbed into an empty TBM. 'What's she armed with?' 'Nothing,' the plane captain said. He looked up at the bridge. The Captain was waving his arm forward in sweeping motions. There was a sound like a rifle shot. He turned and saw a tower of water falling on *White Plains*. Once in the air he called Sprague for orders. 'Attack immediately!' came the reply. Gallagher came up on the lift in a TBM carrying a one-ton torpedo, and taxied towards the accelerator. Behind him the plane captain ran, yelling 'Gas! It's got no gas!' Gallagher went off with 170l (45 gal), five minutes' flying, and made for the first big ship he saw. Bob Weatherall's TBM came up, full of gas and torpedo, taxied forward, and was boosted. A third plane came up. Hank Pyzdrowski shook hands with his gunner and radioman, and they got aboard.

At about 07:15 a heavy rain squall got briefly between Taffy Three and the enemy. Tommy Sprague called Kinkaid 'Permission to run for cover of battleships?' 'Denied,' said Kinkaid. Sprague knew then that his ships were expendable. If all 16 must be sacrificed to save the assault, that was the way it was going to be. They could move east and they could move west but they must not go south for safety. They probably wouldn't have made it anyway. *Yamato* had a flank speed almost twice that of a Kaiser carrier, and every yard gained to the south would have brought the enemy closer to Kinkaid's ships in Leyte Gulf. With a heavy heart he saw the rainbow fountains rise again around his ships. Kinkaid ordered Oldendorff to organise a striking force of three battleships, five cruisers and two destroyer squadrons to rendezvous and hasten to the aid of Ziggy Sprague, and Oldendorff began to replenish his bunkers and magazines on the double.

Pyzdrowski's TBM was still on the accelerator. He got the 'cut'. Switching off the engine, he ran towards the bridge. 'What's the matter? The cat's charged. We can go off without wind!' (The TBMs had been fitted with new, more efficient carburetters.) Commander Borries raised a clenched fist. *Hold*. Pyzdrowski turned, just in time to see the TBM being fired off, crewless. It took off beautifully, climbed, banked over to port and hit the water. The last plane had left the *Gambier Bay*.

TAFFY THREE HITS BACK

The DDs and DEs were fighting their stubborn fight. Under heavy fire they pressed home their attack with torpedoes. The heavy cruiser *Kumano* was hit and turned for home, *Yamato* and *Nagato* were hit and also had to turn away for a time, and the Japanese line, already spread out as the cruisers raced to outflank the American carriers,

Below: Getting closer. Splashes from Japanese shells near *White Plains* during Kurita's attack on CarDiv 25.

Above: 'Hot papas' waiting for business in position near the bridge island, where crashes often occurred. (US National Archives)

became somewhat disorganised. The USSS *Johnston, Hoel* and *Samuel B. Roberts* harassed the Japanese and defended their CVEs until they were sunk.

Meanwhile, the planes of Taffy Three were getting between the enemy and their carriers. As their role was mainly ground support, the CVEs carried few armour-piercing bombs, or torpedoes, but the TBMs, Hellcats and Wildcats threw GPs and depth-charges at the enemy, then their bullets, and when they were gone made dummy runs to keep the gunners busy. Ensign Shroyer followed 12 strafing FM-2s, dropped two 227kg (500lb) bombs and hit the fantail of a cruiser. Half an hour later he saw her lying dead in the water. Gallagher, low on gas, aimed his torpedo at a cruiser, was hit, ditched and was never seen again. Rich Roby drifted from group to group, strafing until his guns were empty then made dry runs on several cruisers. Ensign Ostercorn dropped his two bombs on a cruiser. Seitz made several runs on battleships and cruisers and saw a cruiser and two destroyers lying disabled. Light cruiser *Yahagi* and four destroyers from the Japanese vanguard made the only organised torpedo attack by Second Fleet in the battle, and Lieutenant Leonard Waldrop, USNR, achieved the extraordinary feat of exploding a torpedo from *Yahagi* by strafing it as it was porpoising towards the end of its run, while a second 'long lance' was deflected from its target by a shell from *St Lo*'s 5in gun. Sprague ordered all airborne planes to concentrate on the four most menacing cruisers (*Haguro, Chokai, Chikuma* and *Tone*), swung the force round to 200 degrees (SSW), then back to 170 degree (south by east) at 07:32, and ordered the carriers to 'Open fire with the pea-shooters when the range is clear.' A few minutes later he altered course again to due south, in an attempt to keep the inside track towards Leyte Gulf, and hopefully find help en route, though in fact he had no choice – with enemy cruisers to port, destroyers coming in on his starboard quarter and cruisers and battleships astern and overhauling him. To maintain an easterly course now would mean a Balaclava charge down the muzzles of 32 8in guns.

At *Gambier Bay*'s 'pea-shooter' Lynch saw the dyed splashes walking closer to the ship, and knew it would be only a matter of time before they were hit. At 07:45 Gunnery Control ordered him to open fire on the Japanese cruisers bearing 200 degrees from them, about 13km (eight miles) distant. He fired his first shot at 15,550m (17,000yd), all the time conscious of the red/purple, green and yellow geysers erupting from the fire of three different ships close aboard on either hand. With his sixth round he scored a hit on one of the cruisers firing at them, and a few rounds later hit another cruiser, but was then ordered to cease firing in the belief that it simply drew attention to them. With the CVE force now heading in a south-westerly direction, *Kalinin Bay* was in the most exposed position on the formation's port flank, and at 07:50 she was hit by the first of several accurate 14 and 16in shells from the battleships and 13 from the 8in heavy cruisers. Badly damaged and flooding, she managed to keep her station and steamed on, her pea-shooter firing defiantly. That there had not been far more hits on these easy targets was down to the poor Japanese gunnery.

GAMBIER BAY IS HIT

At about 08:15 *Gambier Bay* was hit on the after end of the flight deck, which was pierced and fires started. The 5in crew broke out two hoses and put out the fire. Lynch felt the ship slow down. Control ordered him to flood his magazine. About five minutes later they were ordered to open fire again, but there was no power on the gun and they could not hand-train either as it had been jammed by the blast from a near-miss. More men came out on the fantail from below decks, one with a badly mutilated arm, which Lynch bandaged from a first aid box.

The attacking cruisers had closed now to 9,100m (10,000yd). Their shells were falling all round *Kalinin Bay, Kitkun Bay, St Lo, White Plains* and *Fanshaw Bay*, all of which were being damaged by near-misses. The Japanese, convinced that they were faced with Halsey's big ones, were firing

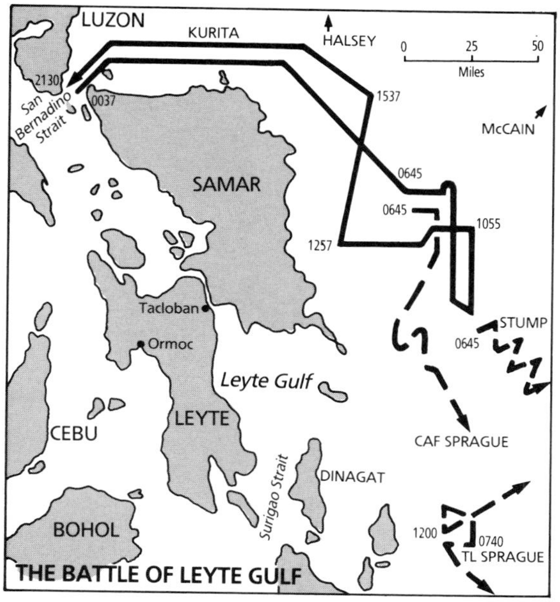

THE BATTLE OF LEYTE GULF

armour-piercing shell, one of which passed right through the flagship. *St Lo* was lucky in that her smoke hung low on the sea like a pall, obscuring her from the Japanese.

Halsey, of course, was many miles away to the northward, chasing the coat that Ozawa, the crafty veteran, was trailing off Cape Engano. The Northern Force had swum within range, and a 186-strong Third Fleet air strike waiting in the wings off Engano, 80km (50 miles) in advance of Halsey's battlewagons, was unleashed on it. The Third Fleet Commander was relishing the thought of the final battle to be fought when he had caught up with his aviators, the opportunity he had craved since cadet days, of destroying the enemy in a great battleship action, when at 08:22 he received the signal, delayed somewhat en route, from Kinkaid: 'Enemy BBs and cruiser reported firing on TU.77.4.3 from 15 miles [24km] astern.'

In his autobiography Halsey attempts to shift some of the blame on to Kinkaid – 'I wondered how Kinkaid had let "Ziggy" Spague get caught like this, and why "Ziggy's" planes had not given him some warning, but I was still not alarmed. I figured that the 18 little carriers had enough planes to protect themselves until Oldendorff could bring up his heavy ships.' He was asking too much – of Kinkaid, who, with his mind of necessity now on the situation in and near the Gulf, had had no reason to believe that San Bernardino was not covered, of Jesse Oldendorf, who was busy fighting the Shima/Nishimura Southern Force, and of 'Ziggy' Sprague and his aviators, who were, as Halsey should have realised, heavily involved in support of the landings, and in no way expecting an enemy battle fleet to hit them in the flank.

At 08:30 another signal reached *New Jersey*'s bridge. 'Urgently need Fast BBs Leyte Gulf at once.' 'That surprised me,' recorded Halsey. 'It was not my job to protect the Seventh Fleet. My job was offensive, to strike with the Third Fleet, and we were even then rushing to intercept a force which gravely threatened [as he had no evidence to doubt at the time] not only Kinkaid and myself, but the whole Pacific strategy.'

However, he ordered McCain, the same McCain who in 1930, as Captain of the USS *Ranger*, had urged the Navy to build 'pocket carriers', to 'Strike enemy vicinity 11° 20′ North 127° 00′ East at best possible speed,' and repeated it to Kinkaid. McCain cast off the refuelling hoses and at 09:40 set course for Samar at 30 knots. At 10:30 he ordered a strike, and inside 15 minutes *Hancock Hornet* and *Wasp* flew off 46 fighters, 33 dive-bombers (Helldivers) and 19 TBMs, a 98-plane strike, lightly loaded, which meant no torpeckers, as the distance was 340 nautical miles, 'extreme range and then some', as McCain put it, and there had been no time to fit disposable wing tanks. A safe return was problematical.

Off Samar, *Gambier Bay* was taking the heaviest punishment now. Hank Pyzkowski stared frustratedly into the elevator well. Down there was the ship's last TBM, fully gased and a torpecker in its belly. As he watched, it caught fire and began to burn. He ran for the bridge tower to see what was happening there. In the Air Plot he saw some men slumped against the bulkhead. One of them had no head. Another salvo burst close aboard the ship, smashing a hole in the thin plating, and he returned to the flight deck, just in time to see the *Yamato* fire a full broadside, an awesome sight. The carrier was slowing down fast, the battle ensign was drooping at the masthead.

THE BATTLE OFF SAMAR

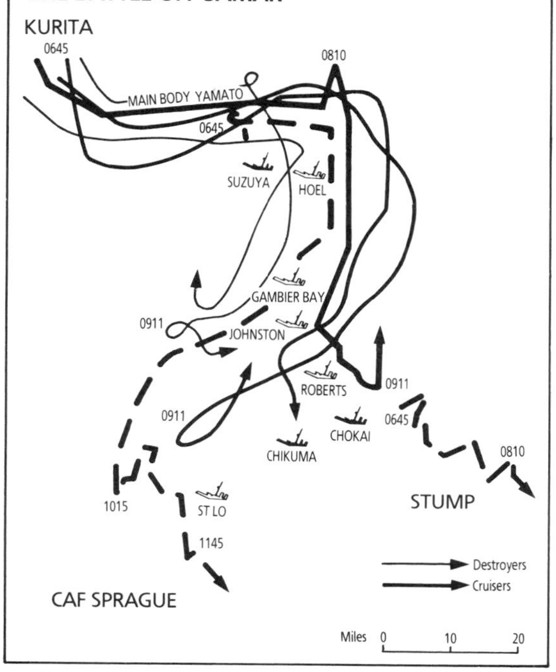

The ship was in extremis, listing to port, taking hit after hit. With her last defiant action the destroyer *Johnstone* fired on the cruiser hitting *Gambier Bay*, to draw her attention. From 10,970m (12,000yd) Hathaway's *Heerman* opened fire on *Chickuma*, which did not appear to notice but carried on pouring salvoes into the stricken carrier. When *Haguro*, *Chokai* and *Noshiro* joined in, CVE-73's life could be measured in minutes.

In the ship a bulkhead gave way and the Philippine Sea burst through. The APs were piercing the ship everywhere. Seaman Heinl was in the starboard magazine swapping experiences with Seaman Klotkowski and Mike Williams, who did not know that his two elder brothers in the ship were already dead, when the carrier shook from another shell hit and the lights went out. When the emergency lights came on Mike was dead too, and Klotkowski, his left arm severed, died within minutes. Heinl rushed to the catwalk to find a Corpsman. On the flight deck bodies strewed the deck, which ran with blood, among them that of the surgeon, Doc Stewart. A shell blew the motor whaleboat to splinters. At every hit the frail hull whipped, the decks undulated like a wave. On the catwalk Seaman Gilman, one of the fire rescue team, was slumped against the bulkhead, trying to hold his intestines in. A lookout said casually into his chest microphone '*Tone* Class cruiser bearing 060 degrees now 3,000 yards . . .' Yeoman Hammond, the bridge talker, took the message and was about to pass it on when there was a tremendous explosion behind him which blew the pilothouse to bits. Hit in one foot by splinters, Quartermaster Birger Dahlstrom struggled with the wheel. The power had failed several times, and they were in hand steering. 'Have you any control?,' asked the Captain. 'No, sir, everything is dead.'

In the after steering compartment Quartermaster Haggerty was waist-deep in water, welling up from the leaking hatch to the 5in magazine flooded earlier by Lynch. A shell burst deafeningly somewhere amidships, the loudspeakers squawked once and fell silent, as if the voice of the ship had died. The stench of burning diesel oil and cordite was everywhere, the ship had almost stopped, racked with shell hits. The ship was dying, the sudden knowledge came with the engulfing stink of burning diesel oil and avgas, cordite and hot steel, and in the midst of this floating inferno that had once been a ship, with the corruption of the flesh all about them, they thought the unthinkable, that they could die too. In his mouth Chief Montgomery tasted futility as he moved round the shambles of the flight deck from shell hole to shell hole, playing a hose on the fires. Chief Flanders rushed up with another hose. 'It's no good,' Montgomery said, 'She's going,' and heard his own voice echo strangely amidst the cries of 'Corpsman! Corpsman!' Men were wandering about aimlessly, stunned and shell-shocked. Another shellburst. The nightmare continued. McClendon was fighting fires on his own patch, the flight deck, men crying out and falling all around him, the resinous, burnt-sugar smell of smouldering Oregon pine in his nostrils. He would bat no more in *Gambier Bay*. In the after engine-room Commander Saunders, Lieutenant Mallgrave, Chief Walter Kalbe, Fireman Person and Oiler Joe Lemirande were waist-deep in water. 'Let's get to hell out of here!,' shouted Saunders. Securing the boilers so that they would not blow up, they went up the ladder.

On deck, Pyzdrowski was watching the enemy cruisers grow bigger and bigger, like phantoms in the smoke, and planes from all three Taffies diving at them. He still had his revolver strapped

Below: The battle off Samar, 25 October 1944. Ships of CarDiv 25 under attack by Admiral Takao Kurita's Second Fleet, taken from USS *White Plains* herself under fire. (US National Archives)

to his waist. Numbly he took it out, wondering whether they would be boarded, as in the days of wooden ships and iron men, like Broke leading the Shannons aboard the beaten *Chesapeake*, with Lawrence dying down below . . . *Don't give up the ship*! Bowser Vieweg would never surrender. From the ruin of the bridge the Captain surveyed the burning wreck of his first command. Only a matter of time. And time had become a Jap cruiser, closing to point-blank range. Already they were less than a mile off, destroyers at their flanks, the black pagodas behind them . . . 'C for combustible, V for vulnerable . . . E for expendable . . .' There was only one thing left to do. He picked up the hand microphone, but it was dead. He passed the word. 'Abandon ship!' It was 08:50, they had fought for two hours. Where was Bull Halsey?

Most men left the ship over the port side, which was nearer the water. Mallgrave cut loose a cargo net and climbed down that. McClendon followed Pyzkowski down a rope, was dislodged by the man behind him and knocked Pyzkowski off the rope as well. Shells were pitching amongst the swimmers. One man was caught in mid-air by an ascending waterspout, was tossed 12m (40ft) into the air and came down red with dye; many were killed by blast or shrapnel. Plucking up the courage to jump from the bows, Leo Zeola remembered at the last minute that he still had his helmet and gunbelt on, tore them off and jumped. Right aft the 5in crew threw the floater nets clear of the side and they, the magazine crew and various men who had collected there, jumped into them or off the side.

When Lynch had helped the injured man into the water he went over to the port side to see if there was anyone else about, and returned to the starboard side just as another shell hit the fantail to port and pierced the deck. There Lynch found Lieutenant (jg) Edmundson prone on the deck, his right leg practically torn off by shrapnel. Lynch bound it up with a bandage and he and a seaman who had appeared lifted Edmundson and threw him over the side. Lynch looked into the hangar but could see nothing for thick smoke. He was stuffing his pockets with more first aid dressings when another salvo almost lifted the fantail out of the water and threw him half overboard, and he dropped into the sea.

At 09:07 *Gambier Bay* rolled over and sank into the Cape Johnson Deep, 3,500 fathoms down (6,400m), after the last shell to hit her had knocked her threshing starboard propeller off. An enemy destroyer came up but stopped only to take photographs of the survivors. Nearby was what was thought to be a Japanese battleship dead in the water, but which was in fact a damaged cruiser. She moved off again but sank later. After that all they had to fear was not being rescued before the sharks got to them.

Some 740km (460 miles) to the north Halsey was still under fire from Kinkaid's increasingly desperate signals, including, at 09:00, 'Our CVEs being attacked by 4 BBs × 8 cruisers plus others × Request Lee cover Leyte at top speed × Request Fast Carriers make immediate strike.' Halsey fumed . . .' I had already sent McCain. There was nothing else I could do, except become angrier.'

At 09:19 he altered course to due north to close Ozawa's battered squadron. At 09:22 another signal from Seventh Fleet begged for an 'early air strike and support by heavy ships as my BBs are low on ammunition'. Halsey was astonished . . . 'Low on ammunition! Why hasn't Kinkaid let me know before?' Then he looked at the time of origin of the signal and realised that it had been delayed nearly an hour in reaching him. He replied huffily, 'I am still engaging enemy carrier × McCain with 5 carriers 4 heavy cruisers has been ordered to assist you immediately.' But Kinkaid could think only of Sprague, facing far worse odds than Custer at the Little Big Horn . . . 'Where is Lee? Send Lee!,' he signalled. Halsey had just read this message when he was handed another.

This one was from CINCPAC himself. 'The whole world', it ran, 'wants to know where is Task Force 34.'

'I was stunned', recalled Halsey, 'as if I had been struck in the face. The paper rattled in my hands. I snatched off my cap, threw it to the deck, and shouted something that I am ashamed to remember.' The apparent insult was not of Chester Nimitz's doing. To fool the enemy, coded signals were often padded out with gobbledygook, which the decoding officer normally spotted and deleted, but a drowsy, drunk or smart-ass encoder at CINCPAC had added 'The whole world wants to know' to the original message, which sounded plausible enough for the New Jersey's decoder to leave it untouched.

At 11:15, rage having given way to depression, Halsey reversed course to 180 degrees, to take six of his fast battleships, two heavy cruisers and 18 destroyers of TF.34 and Bogan's carriers of 38.2 south to the desperate battleground off Samar at flank speed, hoping now to intercept Kurita in lieu of Ozawa before he had finished with Tommy Sprague. The big battlewagons wheeled in the turn, with Ozawa, his last two remaining carriers crippled and dead in the water, 'exactly 42 miles [67.5km] from the muzzles of my 16-inch guns'. It was a hard decision to make, and Halsey's heart was heavy as he steamed south on what was later called 'The Battle of Bull's Run', the white water curling crisply from *New Jersey*'s bow, leaving Sherman's Task Group 38.3 and Davison's 38.4 to continue the attack on Ozawa's remnant.

CHOKAI DESTROYED

To the southward the battle raged. *White Plains*, for a time the focus of the action, led a charmed life. Exchanging shells with *Chokai*, her 5in fantail gun hit the cruiser at least twice, knocked out a forward turret and damaged her engines. 'Hold on a little longer, boys,' said Chief Gunner Jenkins, 'we're suckin' 'em in to 40 millimetre range.' At that point Commander R. D. Fowler's five planes from *Kitkun Bay* got into the act. First circling to find some cloud cover he attacked out of the sun, scoring hits amidships on and round the stack, and on the bows, with two near-misses off the stern, one of which damaged the rudder, sending the cruiser into a turn to starboard. She steamed on for some 460m (500yd), then blew up and sank within five minutes. The *Kumano* had been hit by a torpedo for'ard early in the action, and *Sazuya, Tone, Chickuma, Chokai* and *Haguro* had all been damaged to varying extent by aircraft and/or destroyers.

FELIX STUMP WEIGHS IN

As the *Gambier Bay* was sinking, the presence of a group of enemy 'Fleet carriers' was reported to Kurita. This was actually Taffy Two, on one of the few occasions when Stump actually caught sight of the enemy. He had launched all serviceable (and some unserviceable) planes left in the force soon after 'Ziggy' Sprague's Mayday, and armed and boosted off the others when they returned from their various missions. By the time the ration runners had returned to *Marcus Island* from feeding the Army, there were no torpedoes left, Taffy Three planes having landed and taken them all. Tom Murray's TBMs of Compo 21 bombed up and took off northwards with barely time to catch their breaths, Stump's orders not to make selective strikes but to 'cripple as many as you can' ringing in their ears. Heading NNE to launch, Stump then swung round to ESE to open the range, then back into wind to fly off CAP, both for Taffy Two and the Gulf ships. By 08:30 he had mounted three strikes totalling 36 fighters and 43 TBMs, which strafed, bombed and rocketed Kurita's scattered ships. At 08:33 T.2 found the wind again to launch another eight fighters and 16 TBMs and to take aboard six TBMs lost from T.3. The enemy lead ships were then 27km (17 miles) astern, and Stump caught a glimpse of Kurita's pagodas, 14in shells from which straddled his rearguard destroyers at 08:41. A quarter of an hour later Stump despatched two more strikes to hit the cruisers and battleships which, mistaking Taffy Two for some of Mitscher's big carriers, had taken off at flank speed after them, led by *Haruna*, in hopes of a coup which would gain their captains immortality. The Taffy Two planes claimed hits on two cruisers (one probably *Chickuma*).

KAMIKAZES HIT TAFFY ONE

In Taffy One Tommy Sprague was recovering the 28 planes sent on missions to Surigao, some with the welcome news that they had finished off the burning *Mogami*, re-arming them and packing them off again to hit the force which was carving up 'Ziggy' Sprague's ships. The turn-round was on its way at 07:40 when Taffy One was jumped by nine enemy planes. They were in fact units of a new Japanese secret weapon. Vice-Admiral Onishi, commander of First Air Fleet in the defence of the Philippines, desperate to find a substitute for the massive, well-nigh irreplaceable losses suffered by the aircraft available to him, and alarmed by the news from Surigao, activated the first of the new Shikishima *Kamikaze* units, which embodied *Nison Seishin*, the spirit of Japan, to ensure that she would always prevail over any foe. Kamikaze ('Divine Wind' or 'Tempest') was the name traditionally given to the typhoon of August 1281 (others say a similar heavy puff in 1577), sent, according to Japanese mythology, by Divine Providence, which destroyed two fleets sent by Kubla Khan, from Korea and South China, to conquer Japan. Most of the invading army was drowned and those already ashore were exterminated or enslaved by the Japanese at their leisure. The name had now been applied to the new tactic for the destruction of enemy warships by young pilots eager to sacrifice themselves in this glorious act, though by sacred Shinto law they owed a debt to the Emperor which even their deaths could not repay. It is interesting to note here the words of one of Kubla Khan's wise Confucian advisers, who told him 'I have heard that one may conquer an empire on horseback, but one cannot govern from the saddle.' The first Kamikaze attack on an American carrier had been carried out on 15 October off Luzon when TG.38.4 was attacking Japanese airfields in preparation for the Leyte landings, and was flown by Rear-Admiral Arima, commander of the 26th Air Flotilla, who dived his Judy (Yokosuka D4Y Navy Carrier Bomber Suisei) and one 227kg (500lb) bomb into the flight deck of the Fleet carrier *Franklyn*, killing three men and wounding 12, but causing only superficial damage to the ship.

After the ritual drinking of saki, wearing their Divinely inscribed white headbands, ceremonial swords at their waists, five young knights of the samurai climbed into their machines on the airfield at Mabalacat on Luzon and took off for the American Fleet under attack by the Imperial Fleet off Samar, escorted by four ordinary mortals in Zeros. Blick's *Santee* had just finished launching five of Bennett's Avengers and eight FM-2s of Funk's VF-26 for Taffy Three relief when an enemy plane dived on them out of cloud and so near that there was no time to bring guns to bear on it. Coming in strafing, it crashed the flight deck on the port side for'ard and bored through to the hangar deck where it exploded, blowing a huge hole and starting fires immediately next to a pile of eight 454kg (1,000lb) bombs. Only *Santee*'s luck prevented these from detonating, and the fires

Top: *Kamikaze* pilots drink the ceremonial glass of saki before taking-off on their suicide missions.

Above: Sayonara. *Kamikaze* pilot just before take-off to attack the US Fleet.

were under control by 07:51, but the CVE sustained 32 casualties, 16 of them fatal.

A second *Kamikaze* A6M was circling *Suwannee* from astern, under heavy fire from the carrier. Hit by one shell it spun, recovered and rolled over in a dive, heading straight for *Sangamon*. It was about 150m (500ft) from her when another shell from *Suwannee* deflected it and it splashed at a safe distance. At the same time *Petrof Bay* was narrowly missed by a third Zero suicider which was knocked down by flak. Five minutes after the fires had been extinguished in *Santee* she was hit on the starboard side between frames 58 and 60 by a torpedo from the submarine *I-56*. Thanks to the sturdy basic construction of the ex-tanker she survived the blow, which would probably have been fatal to a Kaiser. With a slight list from flooding, *CVE-27* was making 16.5 knots by noon. Meanwhile, *Suwannee*'s gunners were keeping their eyes on another Zeke circling in and out of cloud at about 2,400m (8,000ft). Sure enough, it peeled off and dived. The CVE's cannon pumped away. The Zeke was hit, rolled over smoking, straightened out and dived for *Suwannee*'s starboard side, hitting her flight deck 12m (40ft) forward of the after elevator, making a 3m (10ft) hole, and her bomb exploded between flight deck and hangar deck, blowing a hole 7.5m (25ft) in diameter, and causing many casualties. The fire started on the hangar deck was quickly suppressed but the after elevator was inoperative for two hours, when flying was resumed.

This initial gambit by the Kamikazes was well organised. By flying many diversionary sorties, with aircraft zig-zagging and constantly changing height and speed, other Japanese planes drew out the CAPs to investigate them, which also clogged up the radar displays and R/T channels – the enemy knew that the Americans used only two interception frequencies – and the real attackers, in small groups or even singly, were able to make undetected approaches. For a Kamikaze pilot the almost vertical high-level plunge in the radar's overhead blind spot was the most difficult, as the high terminal velocity gave him less time to make last-minute corrections to allow for evasive action by the target ship. Alternatives were either a climb to 3,050m (10,000ft) and a steep dive or to less than 150m (500ft) for a shallow-angle attack. The latter was generally preferred, as a steep dive needed good weather and high skill, whereas even a green pilot could make corrections in a slower attack at an angle which could be steepened or flattened easily. Aiming point was the carrier's flight deck abreast the island, with other ships the base of the bridge structures. The four Zekes which had attacked *Santee*, *Suwannee* and *Petrof Bay* had not been detected by radar, and struck out of a clear sky. Their families could now look for the shades of the pilots 'gleaming bright in expectation' in the heroes' holy temple of Yakasumi.

'FIGHTING SIXTY' SCORES

Before and after the Kamikaze episode, planes from Taffy One's air groups operated a shuttle service to the battle line, notably Harvey Feilbach's CVEG-60 planes from *Suwannee*. Quinn La Farge from DeWitt, Arkansaw, led six Hellcats down on a heavy cruiser, probably *Tone*, whose shells were straddling a CVE. Two direct bomb hits and several near misses slowed her down. Two other Hellcat pilots, Group Executive Officer Don Knapp from Santa Barbara and big, red-haired Paul Linskog from Minneapolis, flew through thick flak to cover a torpedo attack on a battleship by six Avengers under Lieutenant-Commander Warren Vincent, CO of VT-60, from Coronado, California, and helped them to score four hits. VT-60's Exec Bob Chase from Palo Alto faced flak from 15–20 Japanese warships to hit a battleship. 'Fighting Sixty' also destroyed 30 planes in the air, without loss to themselves, Ken Montgomery from Philadelphia being credited with five, Royce Singleton from Oklahoma City with five, Quinn La Farge with three in the air and six on the ground later.

EMERGENCY LANDING

On reaching their fuel limits some planes returned to their carriers to refuel and re-arm, others flew ashore to replenish. Jack Stewart's FM-2s from *Gambier Bay* had carried out their dawn mission strafing, bombing and rocketing the enemy for MacArthur's troops on Leyte. About 07:30, with their fuel low, Stewart called their air controller before returning to the ship, to be told to his dismay that the Japanese had come down from San Bernardino like wolves on the fold, and the carriers could not receive planes. An alternative was captured Tacloban on Leyte. When he arrived the sky was full of planes. Some 100 planes from all 16 CVEs, and some from TF.38, were orbiting the field, which the rains had turned to mud. The first machine in the pattern went in to land, its landing gear stuck in the mud and it nosed over, blocking the runway. With four fingers of fuel in his tank, the second pilot *had* to land – or go out to sea and ditch – and in his desperation put down in the sand on the seaward side of the runway. He bounced hard and strained his oleos but he made it, and soon planes were landing, on sand or swamp, every few seconds, some tipping up and pecking the ground, some smashing their landing gear, some crashing and catching fire, with parties of MacArthur's fusiliers dragging planes off the landing strips to clear the space again. When Ed Huxtable joined the stack the field was so full that the Controller, Commander Whitehead, was accepting only emergency cases. Hux circled for an hour and shortly after 11:00 was diverted to Dulag Field.

KURITA BREAKS OFF

When the grey, rain-pocked waters of the Philippine Sea closed over *Gambier Bay*, Kurita's ships dominated the field, but with the cruisers making heavy work of a job that should have been like shooting fish in a barrel and *Haruna* leading a *banzai* charge upon what his staff were identifying as *Essex* Class Fleet carriers. They were dangerously spread out if, as the tired and confused Admiral assumed from intercepted American signals in plain language, a strong carrier force was forming on Kinkaid's orders over the horizon to the south. Rationalising the situation, he persuaded himself that the American army had been long enough ashore to be beyond his power to stop or destroy, and talked vaguely of looking for the main American force to the north. He knew no more of Ozawa's whereabouts than Nimitz or Kinkaid did of Halsey's. Both fleets seemed to have vanished into the rain. Two recce seaplanes launched from *Yamato* had been promptly shot down by American fighters. Kurita took counsel of his fears, sitting stone-faced and inscrutable on his bridge chair high above the huge rifles of *Yamato*, once thought unsinkable – until this morning in the Surigao Straits. And all the time in scattered bunches the enemy's Avengers, Wildcats and Hellcats, as if in endless supply from the sheltered cornucopia of American industry, were attacking him. Yamamoto was right. They had awakened a sleeping tiger. Another cruiser, the *Suzuya*, was dead in the water and had to be sunk. He intercepted a message in plain language instructing some of the enemy's planes to land on the newly won airstrips of Leyte. This was an emergency measure, but Kurita imagined whole fleets of shore-based aircraft rising to attack him if he ventured any further south. At 08:11 he signalled all his scattered units, 'Cease action. Come north with me, 20 knots.' As the cruiser *Tone* passed close to a raft full of *Gambier Bay* survivors, Admiral Ugaki, Kurita's Chief of Staff, ordered his men to salute the Americans.

Kurita's order surprised and frustrated the captains of his free-riding advanced units, but they assumed that it was a case of *reculer pour mieux sauter* and hauled their plunging vessels round to the northward. To the south on the bridge of *Fanshaw Bay* 'Ziggy' Sprague's mind was concentrated on dodging torpedoes. He did not know how much longer they could last. *Gambier Bay* was gone. His own 'Fanny Bee' was under fire from two cruisers and several destroyers. *Kitkun Bay* had just been damaged and shaken up by a near-miss, *Kalinin Bay* was holding together by blind faith and good damage control, her flight deck so torn up that she could no longer land planes, *St Lo* was badly holed, but her flight deck still usable – for how long? He thought of Felix Stump, whose masts he could see from time to time just over the southern horizon. Felix was all Navy. He would never run. And beyond him was Tommy with the big *Sangamon*s. At least there would be no-one to muddle their names again – unless it was Davy Jones. And beyond them lay the open Gulf, rich with Kelly Turner's ships . . . There was always Jesse Oldendorff and his old Pearl retreads. *There* was a stubborn old sundowner . . . But where was he? And where, oh where was Halsey?

In the office of Admiral King, Chief of Naval Operations and Commander-in-Chief of the United States Navy, Washington, the atmosphere reflected the blistering heat of the great battles being fought over 11,250km (7,000 miles) away across the wide Pacific. 'Jocko' Clark, after over three and a half years at sea, had been ordered to take leave but he was spending some of it in Washington, and happened to be in King's office on that traumatic morning when the red-hot signals from Kinkaid hit the Chief's desk like exploding shells. Then King exploded too, berating Halsey for taking his battleships away from San Bernardino Straits, leaving the way open for the Japanese Central Force to strike Kinkaid's transports in the Gulf. Clark was torn between the longing of a true fighter to be out there in the ring and the excitement of realising that he had a ringside seat to history in the making. 'Many times I had seen King angry but this topped everything I had seen before.' Disaster seemed imminent. Kinkaid's only other defensive force, Oldendorff's old battleships, were away pursuing Nishimura's damaged ships westwards in Surigao Straits. There seemed to be nothing to prevent Kurita from annihilating MacArthur's transports. Then, just as Clark was about to leave, a despatch was brought to the Commander-in-Chief reporting that Kurita had withdrawn the Central Force back into San Bernardino Straits . . .

. . . On the bridge of *Fanshaw Bay*, 'Ziggy' Sprague had wrenched his thoughts away from the self-indulgence of despair. What did the British say? *You shouldn't have joined if you can't take a joke*. Suddenly he was aware of someone shouting, and turned to register the next disaster. One of his signalmen was shouting, 'Goddam it, boys, they're getting away!'

He rushed from one side of the bridge to the other, and looked round from beam to beam. 'I could not believe my eyes, but it looked as if the whole Japanese Fleet was indeed retiring. However, it took a whole series of reports from circling planes to convince me. And still I could not get the fact to soak into my battle-numbed brain. At best, I had expected to be swimming by this time.' For two and a half hours six escort carriers and their seven DD/DE escorts had engaged nine capital ships, including the largest and most powerful battleship in the world, with only one carrier lost, though at the cost of two destroyers and one destroyer-escort. If they had not been alone responsible for turning Kurita back, they had provided the deciding factor. Sprague, of course, had no means of telling whether the Japanese Admiral was not merely regrouping for a more concentrated attack, but 'for such relief much thanks' was the prevailing mood of Taffy Three when the fact of the enemy's retirement had sunk in. Sprague thought that their smokescreen was one of the biggest factors in the survival of his main force.

In fact Kurita had at first merely intended to re-form, re-group and carry on for Leyte and the landing force, right through the battered carrier squadron, but changed his mind, as he later revealed, because he thought Sprague's slow-coaches were actually making 30 knots and could not be brushed aside. When Felix Stump read this extraordinary statement he commented, 'I knew you were scared, "Ziggy", but I didn't know you were *that* scared.' Because of the smoke the Japanese lookouts had suffered from optical illusions, and saw the carriers as *Independence*, *Ranger* or *Essex* Class CVs, the *Fletcher* Class destroyers as *Baltimore* Class cruisers, with a *Pennsylvania* Class battleship hiding amongst the carriers, and when Stump's Taffy Two was sighted from *Yamato*'s towering masthead it was reported as another of Mitscher's Fast Carrier groups. At 12:35 a recce seaplane from *Nagato* reported that there were 35 transports in Leyte Gulf but Kurita figured that by the time he had reached the Gulf most of them would be gone. He abandoned the fight and shaped course for San Bernardino.

The attacks by the TF.77.4 aircraft continued. Torpedoes had proved very successful both for Taffy Three and Two, especially considering that the CVE pilots were not trained for the job. The attacks were mostly ad hoc, but some were organised. Stump had launched his fifth strike at 09:35 (11 TBMs with four semi-armour-piercing 227kg (500lb) bombs each, one with a torpedo, and eight FM-2s) and had hit the cruisers again. Air attack finished off *Chokai* and *Chikuma*.

'KAMIKAZE' – THE SECOND ATTACK

With the light-headedness of euphoria the Taffy Three sailors and airmen watched the enemy ships shrink to mastheads on the northern horizon. Unable to use his own *Kalinin Bay*'s ravaged flight deck, Lieutenant Jim Murphy, very short of gas, alighted on *St Lo*. He had only just gone below decks when some five or six Shikishima suiciders jumped the force, having approached very low, beneath the radar beams, climbed into cloud near the target and dived on the ships before the CAP could stop them, while most of the carriers were recovering aircraft. *Kitkun Bay*, flagship and sole representative of Ralph Ofstie's CarDiv 26, took the first blow. The Zeke crossed her bows from port to starboard, climbed, rolled and dived towards the bridge, strafing. Ofstie ducked, and its dark shadow passed over them, released its bomb, swerved into the port catwalk and cannoned off into the sea. The ship's damage control party rushed in to quench the ensuing fires. Two *Kamikazes* made passes at Sprague's *Fanshaw Bay* but the luck of the 'Fanny Bee' prevailed, and both were shot down.

Two more aimed for *White Plains*, dived through a dense 40mm barrage, and pulled out. Captain Sullivan applied hard right rudder. A plane came in weaving under the fire of all the after guns, shuddering as it was hit over and over again by cannon shells. Just aft of the round-down it rolled over, dived, and narrowly missed the port catwalk, to explode just before hitting the sea. The carrier's flight deck was bombarded with sharp shards of steel and remains of the Japanese pilot, and 11 men were hurt.

Lieutenant Yuko Sehi's plane, also hit in the dive, diverted towards the *St Lo*. Smoking, it smashed through the flight deck and burst into flames in the hangar, its two bombs exploding simultaneously, bombs and torpedoes in the hangar also going up. Further devastating explosions sent the elevator, huge sections of the flight deck, and entire planes as high as 230m (750ft) into the air, and scattered a storm of pine splinters. In minutes the entire ship was ablaze, and at 11:25 the unluckily renamed *St Lo* (ex-*Midway*) sank in a huge pyre of hissing steam and thick smoke, penetrated by towering flames which were dowsed as she took the deep six, taking 100 men with her.

Meanwhile Captain Whitney in *Kitkun Bay* had sighted 15 Judys (Navy Yokasuka single-engined dive-bomber/recce aircraft) approaching from astern. Three FM-2s were hurriedly launched but one of the bombers passed between them and made for *Kitkun Bay*'s flight deck. Its wings were shot off as it closed the round-down, its bomb hit the water 23m (25yd) off the ship's starboard bow, adding to her underwater damage, and the fuselage struck the fo'c's'le like a big rocket, causing serious damage and fires – which were put out in less than five minutes. Two more aircraft hit *Kalinin Bay* adding more damage to her 15 shell holes, but she was able to continue steaming. Again the *Fanshaw Bay*, the 'Lucky Lady', was unharmed. Two FM-2s from *Kitkun Bay*'s Compo (VCS) 5 shot down one of the escorting Zeros.

The Hunt for Second Fleet

Planes from all the Taffies were despatched to the north-west to hunt Kurita, including the homeless aviators of *Gambier Bay*. Jack Stewart found gas and ammunition at Tacloban and kept four of his FM-2s airborne for most of the 25th. Ensign Turner's fighter was forced down in the sea. Burnett and McGraw landed aboard Captain Fitzhugh-Lee's *Manila Bay*, and at 11:15 joined her fighters and ten TBMs in a search for the Japanese Second Fleet. Bennett, another *Gambier Bay* orphan, joined up with them for an attack on a cruiser and scored one near-miss. Crewmen reported two hits on the stern of one cruiser. They returned and landed on *Fanshaw Bay*. Later McGraw joined a group led by Commander Fowler, commander of *Kitkun Bay*'s VC-5. McGraw dived and strafed a battleship, and saw Fowler's bombs hit amidships. McGraw then expended his remaining ammunition strafing a cruiser and a destroyer. Returning to the carriers he saw the *Chokai* as he flew right over her but missed the *Gambier Bay* survivors nearby. Reaching the *Manila Bay* at 14:15, he was in the air again at 15:00 as section leader of an eight-plane CAP. The Japanese were now moving more aircraft into the Leyte area. McGraw sighted 18 Vals (Aichi D3A Navy Type 99 Carrier Bombers) with an escort of 12 Zeros. He shot down one fighter and his wingman another, then ran into a flight of six Zeros, and prudently retired to the tenuous sanctuary of *Manila Bay*, his foster home. At 17:00 Taffy One launched all remaining planes to attack Kurita, then continued her north-easterly course to join up with Taffy Three.

Stump Strikes off Ormoc

That evening, as the sun sank out of the sky, a Japanese submarine narrowly missed the *Petrof Bay*, herself the temporary refuge of other wandering pilots who had made dusk landings aboard her. Other pilots back from various strikes made weary landings at Tacloban or one of the other Leyte fields. Felix Stump's Taffy Two still held the ring. Under cover of darkness four Japanese transports from Mindanao escorted by the light cruiser *Kinu* and the destroyer *Uranami*, which had joined them from Manila, had landed 20,000 troops at Ormoc Bay, on the west coast of Leyte, to reinforce the defenders, but they were slow in departing, and in the morning the ships were sighted by Stump's search aircraft as they steamed north up the inner channel between Leyte and Cebu Islands. Stump scraped the hangar for any remotely serviceable aircraft and the magazines for anything lethal to throw at them. The unit was fresh out of torpedoes and heavy bombs but two of the transports, and the destroyer, heavily holed by small bombs and rockets, sank in the afternoon, and the *Kinu*, already damaged by Mitscher's planes on the 24th in Manila harbour, went down with the sun.

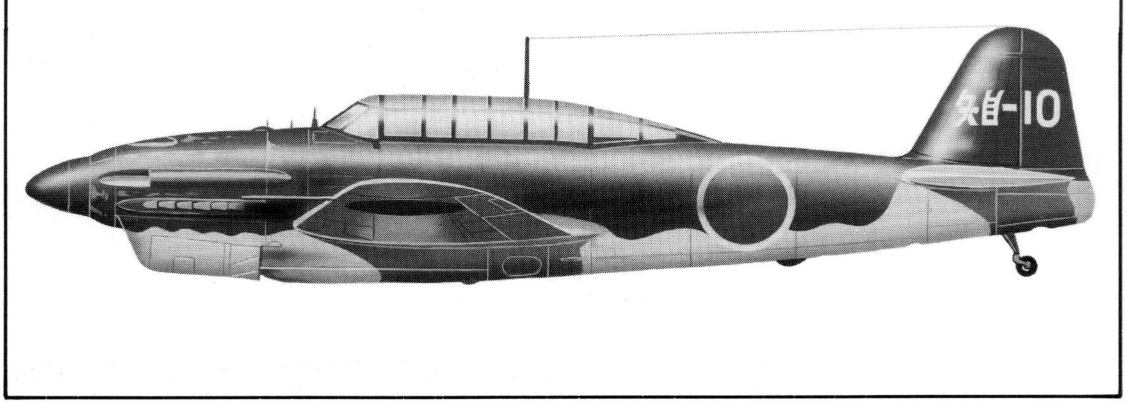

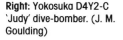

Right: Yokosuka D4Y2-C 'Judy' dive-bomber. (J. M. Goulding)

SUWANNEE'S LUCK

Twenty-four hours later came TG.77.4's last action. Early in the afternoon a *Kamikaze* strike of a Judy with four A6M5s as escort found Taffy One as the three *Sangamons* and *Petrof Bay* approached the Admiralties en route south-east for Espiritu Santo. CAP planes shot down about 12 of the enemy, who narrowly missed *Santee, Sangamon* and *Petrof Bay*, but one Zeke crashed into a manned TBF on the *Suwannee*'s forward elevator, damaged by a *Kamikaze* on the previous day, killing the Avenger crew and its own pilot. Both planes exploded, and seconds later another Japanese pilot, with less flare for the heroic, dropped a 227kg (500lb) bomb from a safe height right in the midst of nine planes parked for'ard, wrecking them all and starting fires which raged for several hours, though *Suwannee*, another 'lucky' ship, could well have been destroyed if they had spread to the lower decks, or if her damage control had not been so notably efficient. When the ship's roll was called the casualty list comprised 143 dead and 102 wounded, some of whom died later, out of a ship's company of 1,100.

Distinguished already by a tradition of ingenuity and initiative, this taut ship added another feather to her war bonnet when her First Lieutenant was immediately despatched by plane right across the Pacific to the Puget Sound Navy Yard, Washington, with photographs of the

Right: *Suwannee* burns after a *Kamikaze* attack.

gaping holes in the flight deck, shrapnel-torn superstructure, and the tangles of wreckage that had once been the forward elevator and the catapult. In the Yard Navy marine engineers, architects and technicians studied Lieutenant Dobson's photographs and reports, and, instigating a policy which was to set a precedent thereafter for ultra-expediency in ship repairing, prepared blueprints for repair in advance of *Suwannee*'s arrival. Shipfitters, under the direction of the Master Shipfitter, started construction of a new flight deck elevator. Welders began the prefabrication of large stretches of deck plating to be cut to accurate size as soon as measurements arrived. Studying the photographed mass of twisted steel in the carrier's catapult room, machinists began construction of a new turkey shooter while the boilermakers assembled repair materials against the CVE's arrival.

McCAIN STRIKES

After a three hour flight for McCain's tired flyers, Stump gave the strike leader the position of the enemy, and they attacked Kurita at 13:10, through some of the fiercest flak of the war and opposition by Japanese fighters, though the Zekes were driven off by the McCain fighters. Three bombers were lost and others damaged, adding little to the damage already inflicted by CVE planes. On the return to McCain the pilots fought the dropping needles on their fuel gauges. Of the 12 *Hancock* Helldivers, only three returned to the ship before dark. One was shot down by flak, two ran out of fuel 55 and 72km (34 and 45 miles) short of their carriers, four found a home aboard Stump's CVEs, two landed at Tacloban, one of them crashing. Nine planes landed on rough strips on Leyte, and 11 planes were reported missing. A second, 53-plane strike was launched from *Hornet* and *Hancock* at 12:45, two hours closer to the targets, but was unco-ordinated and achieved little. In all, four hits on *Yamato* were claimed, nine on other battlers, one on *Nagato*, and others on cruisers and destroyers. Takeo Kurita had fought his last battle. Some historians have found it easy to criticise him for his conduct off Samar, but 'Those who have

Below left: Casualties. A pharmacist's mate dresses a badly burned shipmate aboard *Suwannee*. (Dr P. Phillips)

Bottom left: Casualties. *Suwannee*'s wardroom becomes an emergency station during the Samar battle. (Dr P. Phillips)

Below, top right: Casualties. The bodies of *Suwannee* men killed in the Samar battle are collected in the wardroom for burial at sea. (Dr P. Phillips)

Bottom right: Casualties. Night burial at sea, USS *Suwannee*. (Dr P. Phillips)

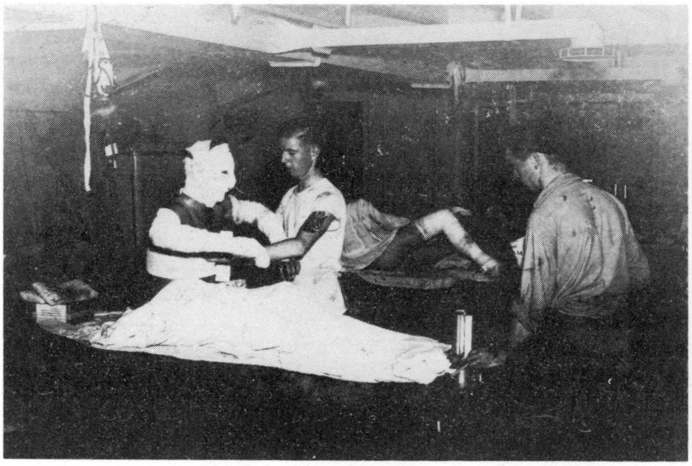

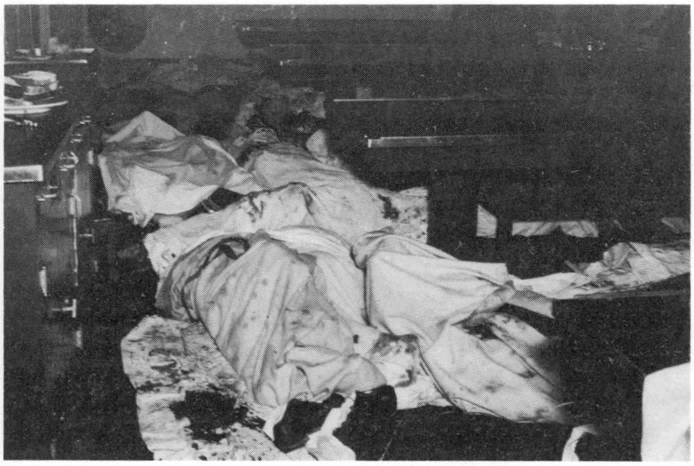

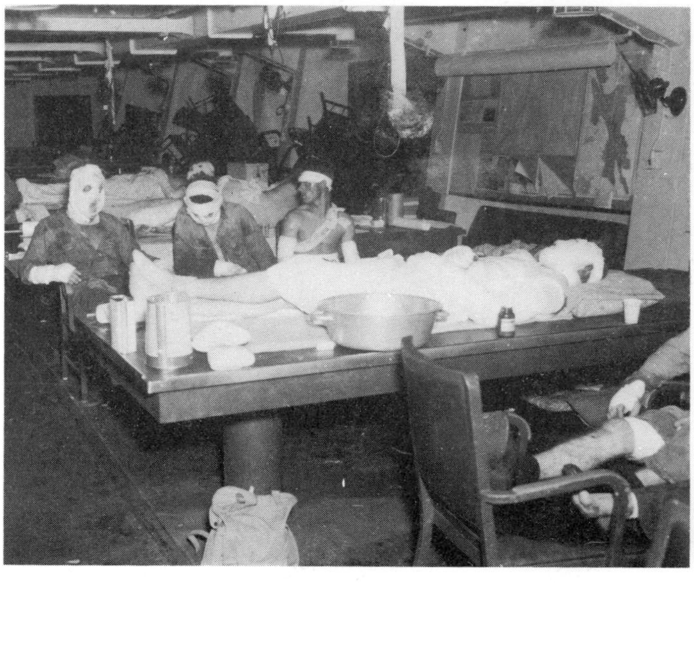

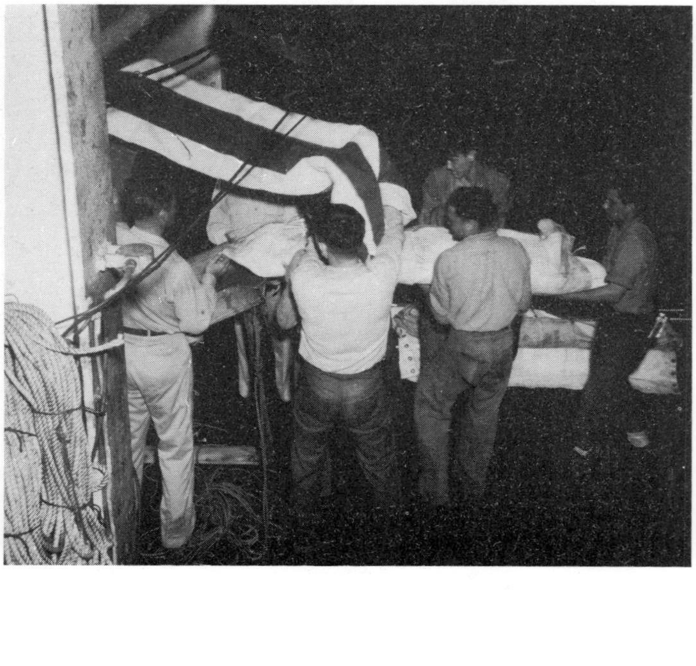

Above: Fire destroyed many aircraft in deck crashes. Here a quartet of CVE Hellcats are ablaze.

endured a similar ordeal may judge him,' growls Winston Churchill from the pages of his *History of the Second World War*.

More Maydays came in from Kinkaid but Sherman's and Davidson's carriers continued to batter Ozawa, making heavy weather of it. The carrier *Chitose*, which sank later, and *Chiyoda* were crippled, *Zuiho* damaged and a destroyer sunk, while the light cruiser *Tama* and Ozawa's flagship, his one big carrier *Zuikaku*, were sent crawling home by torpedo attack. To the south Halsey missed Kurita by three hours at San Bernardino. Belatedly he sent air strikes from TG.38.1 and TG.38.2 after Kurita but succeeded in sinking only the light cruiser *Noshiro*, while Kurita managed to reach Brunei with *Yamato*, *Kongo* and *Nagato*. (The Japanese gave most of the credit for sinking the *Gambier Bay* to the battleship *Kongo*, which became known as 'the ship that sank a carrier'.) After some effort by a massive strike of 200 aircraft, the carriers of TGs 38.3 and 38.4 sank *Zuikaku* and *Zuiho*, and *Chiyoda* was finished off by Halsey's cruisers.

To give longer warning of *Kamikaze* attacks in future, a number of destroyers were to be fitted with appropriate radar, to be stationed as pickets up to 96km (60 miles) from the carriers in the direction of the most likely threats, and 'Tomcat Pickets' were to be used as 'delousing stations', past which all aircraft returning from a mission were to pass to make sure there were no Japs on their tails, with attached CAP to deal with any. 'Jack Patrols' of fighters at low level, controlled by screen destroyers, would provide fast-reaction last-ditch defence of the big ships. Group Fighter Direction Officers in the HQ ships were ordered to hand over control to any ships likely to be in a better position to handle the fighters, which were to be increased in numbers at the expense of dive-bomber SB2Cs.

20

DIVINE WIND

ON 16 December, Halsey's carriers rendezvoused with their Support Group. The three replenishment units TU 30.8.2, 30.8.3 and 30.8.4 took station ten miles apart, each comprising four oilers, one destroyer and two destroyer-escorts. Kaiser-built CVEs *Cape Esperance, Kwajalein, Nehenta Bay* and *Rudyerd Bay* and *Bogue* Class *Altamaha,* CVE-18, accompanied them as components of Task Units 30.8.12 (two CVEs and two destroyer-escorts), organised as replenishment aircraft units, assigned to operate independently, conducting such flight operations as necessary for fly-aboard delivery of replacement aircraft for the big attack carriers. TG.30.7 (one CVE, three destroyers and two destroyer-escorts) was designated an anti-submarine group to provide surveillance for the entire Third Fleet during the replenishment operations, stationed in an operating area about ten miles to the east of TG.30.8, where it was least likely to interfere with the manoeuvring of other units.

The 97 ships of Task Force 38 approached the Logistics Support Group. As the ships separated into the groupings tailored to the replenishment process, there was a total of 132 vessels of all types, steaming in close proximity to each other, an awesome sight and a very congested mass of shipping. Around them the weather was deteriorating fast, a restless south-westerly was sweeping across the Philippine Sea. In *New Jersey* it had reached 25 knots, not enough to worry a battleship, but on her bridge Halsey, who in nearly 50 years in the Service had experienced most kinds of weather, did not like the look or feel of this one. This was something special. He worried for his tossing tin cans and light-ballasted CVEs.

The LCVs and CVEs reported heavy rolling and extensive damage to their parked aircraft. About 09:40 CVEs *Cape Esperance* and *Kwajalein* reported trouble with their steering gear. Ten minutes later Captain Bockius took *Cape Esperance* out of the formation in a wind of 80 to 90 knots with gusts up to 115, mountainous, tangled seas and visibility zero. *Cape Esperance* began to lose aircraft from the flight deck, rolling constantly to 40 degrees. One by one, in spite of the rope and wire lashings, they tore loose and took other aircraft of the densely packed deck-load with them over-

Right: The other enemy. USS *Anzio,* CVE-57, rolls 45° in the early stages of the great typhoon encountered east of the Philippines, 17 December 1944. A TBM and an FM-2 look far from secure, though heavily lashed to the flight deck.

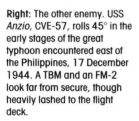

Top: 'One . . . two . . . six . . . Heavy!' The flight deck party heaves the remains of what had once been a Hellcat towards the side for dumping from USS *Altamaha* after the December 1944 typhoon. (US National Archives)

Above: USS *Scrapyard*. Hellcat remains aboard USS *Altamaha* are searched for anything salvageable (and for souvenirs) after the typhoon.

board. Captain Olney's *Altamaha*, operating with the southernmost oiler units, was also getting her lumps, beginning when following seas broke over the fantail with a force of some 17 tons per square yard and surged through the hangar deck curtains, flooding the after elevator well. Extreme rolls caused a 6-ton aircraft crane to uproot itself, demolish three planes, added to the mass of shifting debris threatening to rupture the sides of the hangar. At 10:09 the planes on the flight deck started to break loose. The first one fell into the forward elevator well, which had been opened to lower the ship's centre of gravity and allow the escape of avgas fumes from the hangar deck. The elevator then remained jammed in the lowered position. A second plane fell down the well on top of the first.

Planes burst their stout lashings and started a chain of crashes, with many aircraft sliding off the flight deck into the churning waters of the Philippine Sea, carrying away life rafts, and nets, rails and radio antennae, badly damaging all the 20 and 40mm guns on the starboard catwalk. Water from a broken fire main, swollen by the following seas, soon filled the after lift well to a depth of over 1m (4ft). Thwarted by the clogging of submersible pumps with debris, Captain Olney had to resort to hand buckets. It would be a long and dangerous job, with the mass of debris shifting about the hangar, and anyone who fell into the lift well ran a serious risk of severe injury, even death. Up on deck Olney 'frequently saw the wings and tail surfaces of planes ripped bodily free from their fittings and blown over the sides', and at one point, with the ship heading into the wind, the propellors of four new aircraft parked right above the bow began windmilling at about 200rpm. A little later 'these planes were torn from their moorings and flung like chips over the side'.

FIRE IN *CAPE ESPERANCE*

At 11:49 Halsey directed Mitscher's TF.38 to take 'the most comfortable course, with the wind on the port quarter'. The LCV *Langley* reported heavy rolling. At 12:28 Captain Bockius reported a fire on *Cape Esperance*'s flight deck. A rampaging plane had stuck on the top of the starboard for'ard stack and burst into flames, which rose to bridge level. Bockius ordered everyone clear of the area except those needed to conn the ship, and continued his efforts to bring *Cape Esperance* to a more comfortable heading, but she continued to roll wildly and pound into the vicious cross-seas, first her bows, then her spinning propellers lifted into the air by giant waves, often hogging on a mountainous crest, bow and stern both airborne, imposing maximum strain on the ship's lightly built, welded hull. That was the time for a Kaiser carrier to break her back, as Henry's critics had forecast, but the buffetted *Cape Esperance* did not, groan and creek though she might. In these few hours in the Philippine Sea she was exposed to the worst that the great ocean could do to a ship, then, as if she had acquitted herself with sufficient honour, the sea gave her a break. First, heavy spray put out the fire, then wind and sea rose to a climactic crescendo, hurling the aircraft one by one into the sea. As more and more were swept away the deck load lightened, the centre of gravity sank, and the berserk fury of the typhoon decreased. By the time 32 planes had been lost from her deck load of 39, *Cape Esperance* was riding reasonably safely.

The same freak of fate possibly saved the *Altamaha*, though she was one of the few *Bogue* Class carriers to serve in the Pacific and more sturdily built. Had the bulk of her deck cargo not been lost she might well have met the same terrible end that overcame the three *Farragut* Class destroyers *Aylwin*, *Hull* and *Monaghan*, which capsized. Totally exhausted, *Altamaha*'s bucket brigade scooped the last pail of scummy sea water from the after lift well by 16:30. To three war correspondents sailing with *Cape Esperance* the typhoon was far worse than any battle 'because you couldn't heave anything at anybody, but just had to wait and take it'. They confided to Captain Bockius that they 'had not expected to see Christmas again'. Perhaps the December Typhoon of 1944, with the more exact precedent of the Great Blow of 1281, might have been more appropriately named a Divine Wind than the *Kamikazes*, which in fact originated from man alone. There were to be repetitions of both.

LINGAYEN GULF

The next step in the drive on Tokyo was the capture of Luzon, the large island at the north end of the Philippines. Avoiding the heavily defended mouth of Manila Bay, the assault force was to land in Lingayen Gulf, 177km (110 miles) north of Manila, where the Japanese had landed three years before. On 3 January 1945 TF.38 struck at airfields in the Ryuku Islands and Formosa, on 6 January at Luzon, when Jesse Oldendorff's battleships, cruisers and destroyers began a three-day bombardment, pounding the beaches and giving cover to a minesweeping force.

Covering the force on passage to and at the Lingayen beaches, also covering and supporting the preliminary bombardment, the landings and initial breakout were the 18 escort carriers of Task Group 77.4 under Rear-Admiral Durgin, Captain of *Ranger* off Casablanca in 'Torch', later of Task Group 88.2 off the South of France. He commanded four groups of carriers, his own Lingayen Carrier Group comprising *Bismarck Sea, Hoggatt Bay, Lunga Point, Makin Island* (Group Flag) and *Salamau*; the Close Covering Group (Rear-Admiral G. R. Henderson), with *Kadashan Bay, Marcus Island, Petrof Bay* and *Saginaw Bay* and the Lingayen Protective Group (Rear-Admiral R. A. Ofstie), with *Kitkun Bay* and *Shamrock Bay*. The fourth group, to support landings at San Fabian further along the coast was Felix Stump's Taffy Two Squadron, with *Natoma Bay, Manila Bay, Ommaney Bay* and *Savo Island*, with the addition of *Steamer Bay* and *Wake Island*. This was an all-Kaiser show, with the *Sangamon*s all in dockyard hands in the USA for overhaul, and in the case of *Suwannee* and *Santee* for more permanent combat damage repairs than had been possible at Manus, but there were some replacements in the squadron for the *Sangamon*s. *Hoggatt Bay* had been cruising these waters south and west of the Marianas in support operations for two months, and an escort of her group had sunk the submarine *I-77*. *Shamrock Bay*, CVE-84, at first intended for the Atlantic, had delivered VCs-42 and -93 to Hawaii from San Diego, and embarked VC-94 for duty, with an unusual complement of 12 TBMs and 20 FM-2s. *Steamer Bay*, CVE-87, commissioned on 4 April 1944, had flown Marine Air Group 61 to Espiritu Santo, carried another 72 aircraft and 298 Marines to the Marshalls, brought 72 replacement aircraft for the Third Fleet in the Palaus and Philippines before being given a taste of action off Luzon. Off the Gulf in the South China Sea was TF.38's replenishment group under Captain J. J. Acuff, including six oilers and the CVEs *Nehenta Bay* and *Rudyerd Bay* with the Second Service Group of eight tankers, and storm-battered replenishment escorts *Altamaha* and *Cape Esperance*. Also under Durgin's command was his old *Tulagi* from 'Dragoon'. Since then she had served in the Pacific in a special anti-submarine task group which carried out sweeps as it steamed from Pearl Harbor via the Marshalls and Ulithi for Saipan. Throughout December 1944 she con-

Below: USS *Wake Island*, CVE-65, on her way to the Lingayen. She carries the usual mix of SG (surface search), SK (air search) radar, with the YE homing beacon aerial crowning the topmast, and the Huff-Duff aerial at the truck of the small foremast. (US National Archives)

tinued anti-submarine work in the Palaus and the southern Marianas.

THE KAMIKAZES BREAK THROUGH

The whole invasion force made rendezvous off the Palaus on 3 January 1945 and headed for Lingayen Gulf via the Surigao Strait, Mindanao Sea, Sulu and South China Seas. On the 4th a series of constant air attacks on the force began, featuring the *Kamikaze* corps. In the afternoon in the Sulu Sea off Panay Gulf the Group was assailed by *Kamikazes.* The American radar was partially blanked off by nearby land masses, and two got through the screeen and the Jack patrols. One was shot down and crashed 460m (500yd) from Durgin's flagship *Makin Island*; the second, under fire from a battleship, dived on *Ommaney Bay*, nicked the carrier's island and crashed into the starboard side of her flight deck, releasing its two bombs. One bomb went through the deck and exploded in the hangar, setting off a series of explosions among the fully gassed planes on the for'ard third of the flight deck. The second bomb went through the hangar deck, ruptured the fire main on the second deck and penetrated to the engine room, where it exploded and started oil fires. All power and bridge communications were cut off, and fires soon spread out of control everywhere. Men struggling with a fiery holocaust on the flight deck soon had to abandon it because of the heavy black smoke and fierce flames from the burning planes and the richochets from exploding 0.50in ammunition in them. The escorts could not lend their power to the fight because of these and the intense heat from the fires. By 17:50 the entire topsides area had become untenable, and the stored torpedo warheads threatened to go

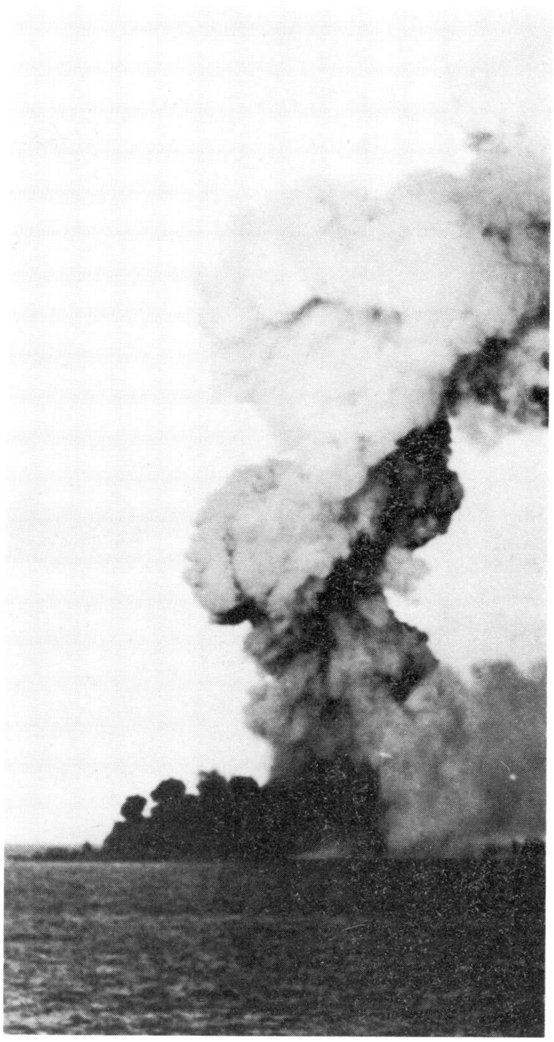

Right: The end of the *Ommaney Bay*, CVE-79. The Kaiser explodes after a *Kamikaze* attack in the Sulu Sea off Luxon in the Philippines during the assault at Lingayen Gulf. (US National Archives)

Below: The Kaiser USS *Shipley Bay*, CVE-85, joins the Pacific war, two TBMs on her deck.

Above: *Block Island II.*

off, which they did a few minutes later, showering nearby ships with debris. The 'Abandon Ship!' was given. At 19:45 the ship was sunk by a torpedo from the destroyer *Burns.* Casualties were 93 men dead or missing, and 65 injured. Seven survivors picked up by other ships were later killed by another *Kamikaze* attack.

On the 5th the air attacks intensified. One *Kamikaze* grazed *Savo Island.* Combat air patrol FM-2 fighters 24-strong broke up morning and early afternoon strikes, and shot down 12 A6Ms and Val Aichi D3A bombers. At 16:50 a third attack sent all hands to General Quarters again. Vectored by the carriers, their fighters destroyed several enemy planes, and ack-ack fire splashed several more, but three planes got through to the cruisers USS *Louisville* and HMAS *Australia,* and the destroyer *Stafford.* Just before 17:50, two *Kamikazes* dived at *Manila Bay* from the port side. The first plane hit the flight deck to starboard abaft the bridge, starting fires on the flight and hangar decks, destroying radar installations and wiping out all communications. The second suicider aimed for the bridge, missed the island close aboard to starboard and splashed off the fantail. Firefighting parties quickly brought the fires under control, including those on board two fuelled and burning TBMs in the hangar. *Manila Bay* was resuming limited air operations within 24 hours, when the limitations of CVE and HQ ship radar, the swamping of their displays by the myriad echoes from the many ships and land masses close by, the inexperience of FDOs and the poor performance of the FM-2 Wildcat against the A6M5s of the suiciders and their escorts, allowed 11 of the 28 aircraft to score hits. Most repairs to her damaged electrical and communications circuits were completed by 9 January, when the landings began. Casualties were 14 men killed and 52 wounded. On the 14th she resumed full duty, flying 104 sorties against targets in western Luzon, and effective close support for ground troops at Lingayen and San Fabian, and bombed, rocketed and strafed gun emplacements, buildings and troop concentrations from Lingayen to Baguio.

There were more air attacks as the ships neared Lingayen Gulf, and when they began the preliminary bombardment and minesweeping. Three minesweepers were sunk. On the 8th the sky was spotted with dogfights. In the forenoon a bomb-carrying Japanese Army fighter dived on *Kadashan Bay.* Her gunners hit it, it nosed over at the last minute, and hit the ship just below the bridge, tearing a hole in the thin plates of the CVE, rupturing the avgas system, and starting fires. Some smart damage control brought these under control and saved the ship. Down some 1.5m (5ft) at the bow, *Kadashan Bay* left the area as soon as possible with only three seamen hurt.

On the evening of this busy day the last of the assault ships arrived in the Gulf, screened by CVEs *Kitkun Bay* and *Shamrock Bay.* The latter had taken aboard planes from the damaged *Kadashan Bay;* now an Oscar suicider from a group of six *Kamikazes* trying to hit her was struck by her fire and rammed *Kitkun Bay* instead. *Shamrock Bay* took her planes aboard as well, while *Kitkum Bay* fought the fires and flooding caused by the Oscar, which had crashed into her port side amidships at the waterline, blowing a large hole. Fire and flood were brought under control, but she had sustained 16 dead and 37 wounded. FM-2s of CAP shot down four of the *Kamikazes.* Next day, with a 13 degree list and only one engine operating, she withdrew and proceeded by stages to Leyte, Manus, Pearl and San Pedro, California. Stump's six CVEs provided direct air support ahead of the amphibious troops after the assault in the San Fabian area. Between the 12th and the 17th planes damaged and destroyed bridges, fuel and ammunition dumps, barracks, roads and vehicles. After replenishment at Mindoro, the squadron cruised west of the island until the 29th, then moved into position to support amphibious landings on the west coast of Zambales Province and at Subic Bay.

Meanwhile Japanese air attacks on all the units of TG.77.4 had continued. Just before 09:00 on the 13th a *Kamikaze* carrying two 250kg (550lb) bombs crashed *Salamaua*'s flight deck. In minutes the flight deck, hangar deck and spaces below that blazed with scattered fires which soon threatened

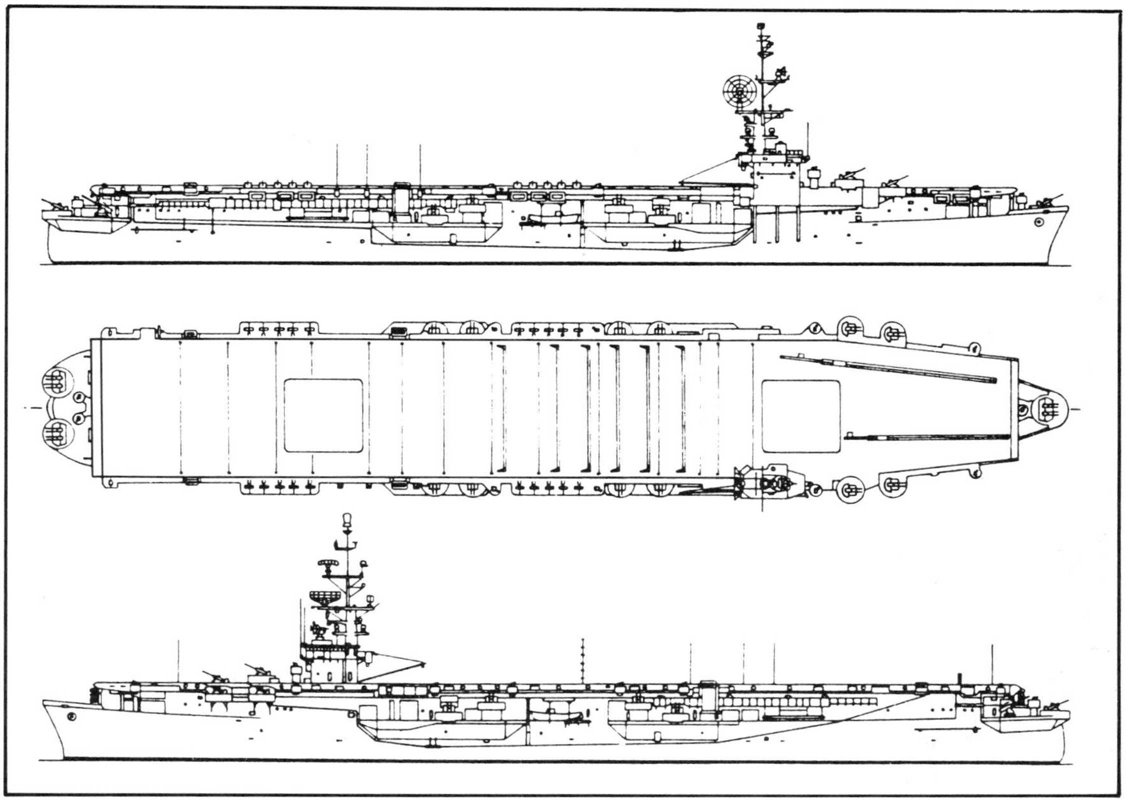

Right: *Commencement Bay*, CVE-105. (Taubman Plan Service). Two CVEs of the new *Commencement Bay* class of escort carriers, *Block Island* (II), CVE-106, and *Gilbert Islands*, CVE-107, joined *Suwannee*, CVE-27, of the fighting *Sangamons* (on which the *Commencement Bays* were based), to fly CAP and strikes at Balikpapan, Borneo, in lieu of planes of the land-based Far East Air Force. All ships of the *Commencement Bay* class were purpose-built by the Todd Pacific Corporation of Tacoma, Washington State. (Taubman Plan Service)

to merge into one giant conflagration. This was all caused by one bomb. The other did not explode but punched a hole through the starboard side of the ship near the waterline, and sporadic flooding began. Power and communications all failed, water reached one of the engine rooms and the starboard engine quit. *Salamaua*'s gunners splashed two other by-blows of the Divine Wind, but 15 men lost their lives and over 80 were injured. Temporary repairs got the ship to San Francisco, where rapid repairs were begun at once. Between Love-Day and the 13th the Kamikazes had hit 11 more of Kinkaid's ships. In spite of their limitations, the FM-2s claimed over 60 enemy planes destroyed around the assault force, though this probably included aircraft which subsequently crashed into ships or in the sea after an attack.

While MacArthur's GIs were fighting in Luzon and marching on Manila, Halsey took TF.38 on a Jeb Stuart raid into the South China Sea. On 12 January his planes struck at shipping in Saigon harbour and Camranh Bay, Indochina, and sailed north-east along the shipping route to Japan, along which vital oil from the Indies passed, hitting two convoys hard and annihilating a third. Keeping the Japanese guessing, on 15 February the Fast Carriers made attacks on Formosa, then swung back west to hit Hong Kong, Canton and Hainan on the 16th, before returning to the Pacific, raiding Formosa again on the way. Here they came under Kamikaze attack, which damaged the CV *Ticonderoga* and a destroyer. On the 22nd the force sailed NNE to give the Okinawan defences a taste of what was to come, then returned to Ulithi.

CVES AT BALIKPAPAN

On Luzon MacArthur's troops fought stubbornly to reach Manila, with air support from the Far East Air Force and further amphibious landings. After a fierce battle in the outskirts of the city on 4 February and more hard fighting to take the Bataan Peninsula and the fortress island of Corregidor at the mouth of Manila Bay, they entered the city and found it in ruins. In March the Sixth Army landed on Mindanao, Panay and Cebu Islands, and there were 12 smaller landings. Finally, with its job in the Philippines done, the Seventh Amphibious Force supported Australian troops in the capture of bypassed Borneo. For their landings at Tarakan (1 May) and Brunei (10 June) they were covered by the Far East Air Force but for Balikpapan (1 July) weather and Japanese interference made support from seaward necessary. The CVEs *Suwannee* and the two new *Commencement Bay* ships *Block Island* (II) and *Gilbert Islands*, with six escort vessels, steamed down from Okinawa to take their place, under Rear-Admiral Sample, flying effective CAP over the landing areas and strikes against Japanese positions. With the success of this assault the Japanese occupation of the Borneo oilfields was over.

21

ICEBERG IN APRIL

'It is better to die with honour
than to live without honour'
– Lieutenant Yuko Sehi, IJN, *Kamikaze* pilot

AT this point in the Pacific war it was thought by the American High Command that only a landing on Honshu, the biggest island of Japan itself, where her capital, largest cities and heaviest industry lay, could guarantee her surrender, but there were several more major steps to be taken, more bloody landings to be made, to ease the effort and reduce the butcher's bill of such a giant undertaking. One more large base, from which aircraft and ships could stop all Japanese imports and hit her home defences really effectively before and during an assault on Honshu, was needed, as close to the homeland as possible.

Okinawa, with its good airfields, only 800km (500 miles) from the nearest point of Kyushu, 2,010km (1,250 miles) from Tokyo, was the answer, but first – Iwo Jima. With ships and aircraft working from the Philippines as well as the Marianas, essential oil and avgas supplies from the Co-Prosperity Sphere (now a gong with a very hollow ring), had to run the gauntlet both of aircraft, as in Halsey's strikes, and of the remarkably effective American submarines, but too much was still getting through. The Super-Fortresses in the Marianas could bomb Japanese industry in the home islands, but because of the distance – 2,010km (1,250 miles) Saipan to Osaka – could take no escorting fighters and only small bombs. The island of Iwo Jima in the Volcano Islands was small (8 by 3km or five miles by two), but had two good airfields, and its capture as a refuelling point would allow Mustang fighters to accompany the B-29s all the way to Honshu and back. The bombers could thus bomb more accurately, with much bigger bombs, and did so in the pre-invasion bombardment of Okinawa, the taking of which would block all shipping to the homeland, move the Super-Fortresses even closer to it – and perhaps even make an invasion of it unnecessary.

KAISERS AT IWO JIMA

At the end of January Admiral Spruance, having planned the next moves in Hawaii, relieved Admiral Halsey, which made the Third Fleet once again the Fifth Fleet, with Marc Mitscher replacing McCain, who had taken over command of the Fast Carrier Force (now Task Force 58), under Halsey, and Vice-Admiral Turner in charge of the Joint Expeditionary Force (approximating to the

Right: The USS *Bismarck Sea*, CVE-95, one of the last of the *Casablanca*-class carriers from the Kaiser yard to see action in World War II, loads Dauntless SBD bombers from a lighter. The bulk spread and topweight of a CVE's flight deck is well illustrated in this picture. (US Naval Historical Center)

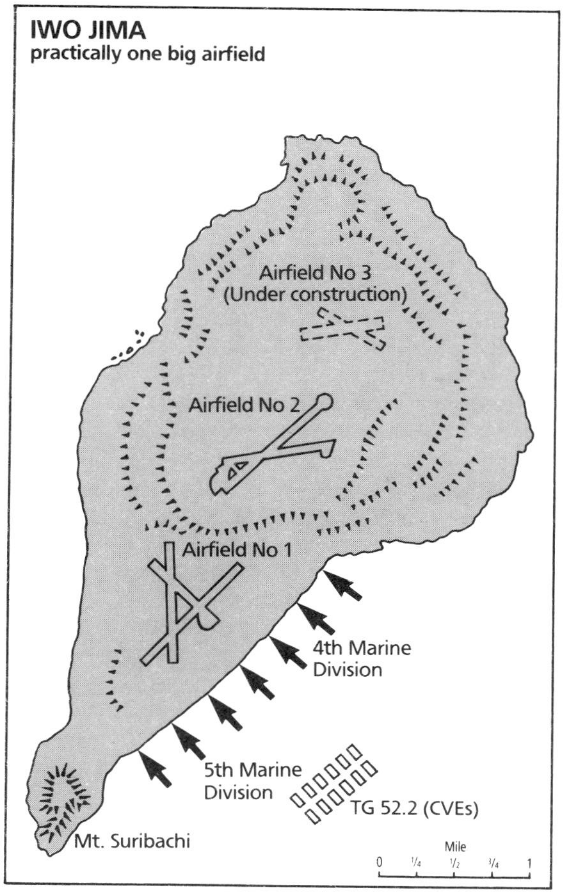

two Amphibious Force commands of the Philippines campaign). Most of the old battleships, escort carriers, cruisers and destroyers of the Seventh Fleet were also transferred to the Fifth Fleet and were formed into an Amphibious Support Force under Rear-Admiral Blandy. The CVE force (Task Group 52.2) was under Rear-Admiral Durgin and comprised: *Anzio* (ex-*Coral Sea*), *Bismarck Sea*, *Makin Island*, *Natoma Bay*, *Lunga Point*, *Petrof Bay*, *Rudyerd Bay*, *Sargent Bay*, *Saginaw Bay*, *Steamer Bay*, *Tulagi* and *Wake Island*.

D-Day was to be 19 February 1945, when two divisions of US Marines under 'Howling Mad' Smith were to be landed on the south-east coast of Iwo Jima. TF.58 opened the campaign on 16, 17 and 18 February by hitting airfields and aircraft factories in the Tokyo area, to supplement the B-29 attacks and help prevent interference with the Iwo Jima operations.

LOSS OF THE *BISMARCK SEA*

The main attack started on 16 February with a three-day aerial and gunnery bombardment by Blandy's ships (six old battleships, four heavy cruisers, one light cruiser, the CVEs, destroyers, and small gunboats) and by Army aircraft. The weather was bad, with rain and mist, which camouflaged the heavy fortifications, dampened the fiery ardour of napalm and made many of Cal Durgin's wing tank bombs fizzle out, while rocket attacks, though accurate, were ineffective against the concrete bunkers, gun emplacements and concealed defences which 74 consecutive days of bombing by B-24s from the Marianas had not knocked out.

Great importance was placed on combat air patrols, as attacks by Kamikazes from Formosa and the Ryuku Islands were anticipated, and the CVEs, all Kaisers, carried an average Composite Squadron of a dozen TBMs and 16–20 FM-2s, except for *Wake Island*, which carried the 28 FM-3 Wildcats of Observation Fighting Squadron 1. For two days after D-Day on 19 February there was little in the way of aerial opposition, but on the 21st *Saratoga* was hit by no fewer than five suiciders, badly damaged but able to steam back

Right: FM-2 fighter No. N27 coming in for a landing aboard *Bismarck Sea*, either missed the arrester wires or broke its deck hook, and smashed its way through another FM-2 and two Avengers in the deck park, damaging them and hurtling over the bows, 19 December 1944. Notice pilot, Ensign Woods, USNR, of TFM P33, lying on the deck. (US Naval Historical Center)

Stateside for repairs. Things went harder for the *Bismarck Sea*, hit at 06:45 by a bomb-carrying G4M3 Betty on the after elevator, after shooting down a plane which was heading for the *Lunga Point*. The explosion first cut the elevator cable, and the great metal slab crashed down on the hangar deck, ruptured the fire main, cutting off nearly all the water supply, and dislodged torpedoes from their racks. Electric light and towering flames roaring up from the lift well provided a beacon for a second Kamikaze which made a vertical dive, with two bombs, straight into the well at the same spot. The hangar deck, crammed with fully-gassed planes was soon a mass of flame, as ammunition, avgas tanks and war stores round the hangar exploded. It became obviously only a matter of time before this ghastly inferno engulfed the whole ship, and with flames licking at the torpedoes and bombs 'Abandon Ship!' was called. The Captain, Exec and Navigator left the ship last, just after 07:00, minutes before a cataclysmic explosion as the torpedoes went up and blew the ship wide open. She continued to burn and explode until she rolled over and sank about 09:15, taking with her 218 men out of a ship's company of 943, 19 FM-2s, 15 TBMs (including three from another ship), and two OY light observation planes. Two more G4M3s aimed torpedoes at *Lunga Point*. Both torpedoes missed, but the second plane hit the CVE's island, starting a fire, then skidding into the sea. The fire was soon put out, and a fourth attacker was shot down.

ENTERPRISE BAY TAKES THE STRAIN

With the withdrawal of *Saratoga*, whose F6F-5Ns of VF (N)-53 had protected the CVEs at night, *Enterprise*, the only other night-flying carrier available, took her place. The 'Big E', the fabled 'Fighting Lady', was unaccustomed to cruising with the small CVEs, which had peculiar names like *Saginaw Bay*, *Petrof Bay*, *Natoma Bay*, *Steamer Bay*, etc. *Enterprise*'s duty radio operator reported her arrival to the CVE Flagship, and *Suwannee*'s operator asked him to repeat the name of the ship. Again he was asked to repeat, and the CV's operator tapped out 'Just call me *Enterprise Bay*'.

Left: Iwo Jima Island during the pre-invasion bombardment, 17 February 1945, looking north, with the extinct Volcano of Mount Surabachi, stormed by the US Marines in an epic attack, in the foreground. Photographed from a *Makin Island* aircraft.

Left: USS *Bismarck Sea*, CVE-95, explodes after being hit by two Kamikazes off Iwo Jima, 21 February 1945, photographed from USS *Saginaw Bay*, CVE-82.

Left: Invasion shipping off Iwo Jima, 28 February 1945, seen from a *Makin Island* plane. (US National Archives)

Left: Mitsubishi G4M 'Betty', one of which hit and destroyed the CVE *Bismarck Sea*, 21 February 1945. (J. M. Goulding)

Early on the 22nd the 'Big E' flew off search planes to look for *Saratoga* pilots who had ditched on the previous day, and two of these TBMs were shot down by their own fleet, their crews lost. On 25 February Mitscher's planes again began attacking airfields and aircraft factories near Tokyo, in co-ordination with more than 200 Super-Fortresses, then moved south-west for a strike at the Okinawa airfields on 1 March to keep the Kamikazes down, finally returning to Ulithi for replenishment, though the need to return to a fixed base for restocking was less and less urgent as the Mobile Service Squadrons constantly increased their scope, and items such as the very biggest bombs became available. Ashore on Iwo Jima the fighting after the easy landing and the capture of the main airfield on the second day, had become bitter, bloody and slow, with the Japanese under the tough and able Lieutenant General Kuribayashi resisting from a maze of pillboxes and blockhouses, concealed gun positions and caves, interconnected by tunnels, and a reserve division tossing queasily in their transports offshore, was thrown in. A Super-Fortress returning from Tokyo on 3 March made a forced landing, and work on each airfield as it was captured was rushed through. The CVEs left on 8 March to prepare for Okinawa, the Marines raised the flag on Mount Surabachi, and fighting finally ceased on 16 March. *Enterprise* remained with Durgin until 10 March, her F6F-5Ns having shot down six enemy aircraft, and the lack of night-fighters in the CVEs was partly made good by the deployment of VF(N)-33 aboard *Sangamon*, with eight F6F-5Ns.

The next step would be the crunch of the first leather-neck's boot on the sands of Okinawa in Operation 'Iceberg', but Admiral Spruance knew that its big garrison would defend this vitally important prize, so close to the homeland, to the death. The great combined strength of Fifth Fleet carriers and the Far East Air Force could not hope to knock out Japanese air power in the home islands by bombardment. Air attacks on the Okinawa invasion fleet from the north, which would certainly include a strong contingent of *Kamikazes*, would have to be defeated in the air.

ENTER THE BPF

From the south-west, air reinforcements would doubtless be staged in via the Sakishima Gunto islands, particularly Ishigaki and Miyako, and Formosa, where Kamikazes were also stationed. These could be kept largely in check by continuous bombing from carriers. Selected for this duty was the newly arrived British Pacific Fleet, under Admiral Sir Bruce Fraser, with Admiral Sir Bernard Rawlings as commander of the Fleet at sea, and Vice-Admiral Sir Philip Vian leading four Fleet carriers, *Illustrious, Indomitable, Indefatigable* and *Victorious*, the fighting nucleus of the BPF, which also included battleships *Howe* (Fraser's flagship), and *King George V*, five cruisers and ten destroyers. On its way to Sydney, which was to be the home base of the BPF, the Fleet made two heavy strikes on oil refineries at Palembang in southern Sumatra, Japan's main source of avgas, thereby making the air battles to come that much easier for the Allies, and was now at Ulithi fuelling for its first operation in the Pacific. General MacArthur had wanted the BPF to cover his Borneo assaults, but Nimitz and Spruance had thought that its four Fleet carriers would be wasted on what they considered only a glorified sideshow, and claimed it for Okinawa.

At this early stage US Navy tankers provided the fuel, but in future a British Fleet Train on the very successful American model would replenish the BPF. From an advanced base, Logistic Support Group would sail to replenish the Fleet at intervals when it was operating in the forward areas. Without the resources of the Americans, the British Fleet Train had taken and would continue to take, a long time to create. For the early replenishment operations there was a shortage of supply ships, and tankers carried extra stores, from fresh vegetables to depth-charges. The equally important supply of replacement aircraft (and the removal of damaged duds) was provided by escort carriers of the 30th Aircraft Carrier Squadron, at first comprising only *Bogue* Class *Striker* and 'Rulers' *Slinger* and *Speaker*, with *Striker*'s erstwhile commander Captain R. P. Carne promoted Commodore of the Squadron, and *Speaker* (the only escort carrier to be completely 'RN-manned', with no men under T124 articles) flying CAP over the replenishment area. The BPF was to become one of the four Task Groups of the Fast Carrier Force, designated TF.113, and later, as part of the Fifth Fleet, TF.57, with the first Logistic Support group 112.2.1.

NEW JEEPS FOR 'ICEBERG'

Facing what was certain to be as hard a task as the capture of the Philippines, Spruance was commanding a force of equal strength and similar components, all gathered in the vast lagoon of hot and humid Manus. No fewer than 26 CVEs were present. For close support and CAP Cal Durgin was commanding a group (TG.52.1) of 14 CVEs, comprising three squadrons, Unit One (TU.52.1.1) under 'Ziggy' Sprague, and Unit Two (TU.52.1.2) commanded by Felix Stump (a pairing of close friends calculated to produce the best results, as the two men complemented each other), and Unit Three (TU.52.1.3). This comprised Sample's *Suwannee, Santee, Chenango* and *Steamer Bay*, the latter the odd ship out among the repaired and rejuvenated veteran ex-oilers, and *Sangamon*, which had added night fighters to her 18 F6F-5s, the stranger among Sprague' *Anzio, Fanshaw Bay, Lunga Point, Natoma Bay* and *Savo Island*. Stump

Above, top and bottom: HMS *Atheling* delivers a deck cargo of Corsairs to the US Navy at Guam, and Corsairs and Wildcats to the British Pacific Fleet.

Above right: More a bite than a peck. Graunched Seafire on *Atheling*. (Robert Forbes)

commanded seven Kaisers, *Marcus Island, Petrof Bay, Saginaw Bay, Rudyerd Bay, Sargent Bay, Tulagi* and *Wake Island*. Eight Kaisers operated the standard Composite Squadron of 16–20 FM-2s and 12 TBM-3s, while *Fanshaw Bay* and *Wake Island* had embarked two Fighting/Observation Squadrons, each with six TBMs and 24–26 Wildcats respectively. Also attached to TF.58 were the four Kaisers *Breton, Hollandia, Sitkoh Bay* and *White Plains*, all loaded with Marine fighters for landing on Okinawa, two CVEs supporting the Fleet's logistics group (*Makassar Strait* and *Shamrock Bay*) and four with replacement aircraft for TF.58 (*Amiralty Islands, Attu, Bougainville,* and *Windham Bay*, all Kaisers). CVEs added to Mitscher's CVs and CVLs made a grand total of 28 US Navy and four British carriers in 'Iceberg', carrying between them over 1,300 fighters (580 day Hellcats, 92 night-fighting Hellcats, including 16 now in *Sangamon*, 380 Corsairs, 280 Wildcats, 40 Seafires and 12 Fireflies).

DEATH OF BUSTER ISBELL

The Fast Carriers led off by hitting airfields on Kyushu and Japanese warships in Kure on 18/19 March. On the 19th the Japanese started as they meant to carry on when the CV *Franklin* was bombed as she was launching aircraft and reduced to an almost burned-out hulk. In the holocaust died Captain 'Buster' Isbell, great sailor, aviator, captain and leader, whose taut ship *Card*, CVE-11, had so distinguished herself in the bloody waters of the central Atlantic, and who had seemed destined for the highest rank. Mitscher retaliated throughout the 20th and 21st, left the Japanese air defence much subdued, topped up from his Fleet Train tankers, and took up position for repelling air attacks from the north.

In Ulithi lagoon lay the great fleet, including Task Force 57, which was fuelled from American tankers and sailed on 23 March, its own tanker replenishment group preceding it by 24 hours; on the 26th, on station 160km (100 miles) south of the Sakishima Gunto, it began a series of strikes against airfields there and occasionally against those on Formosa, which were to continue for the next month (and again later, in 'Iceberg' II), with periodic withdrawals to a replenishment area to take on fuel, food, bombs, bullets and replacement aircraft from its Logistic Support Group.

When *Speaker*, with Lieutenant-Commander Barry Nation's 1840 Squadron of 16 rocket-firing

Mk III Hellcats, left Manus, Captain James revealed to his ship's company that the ship's job would be to fly CAP over the Fleet's replenishment area in the invasion of Okinawa. Practise flying was started on passage to the area, but a heavy swell made it pointlessly risky to continue. In the waters around Okinawa minesweeping had already started on 24 March under cover of a bombardment by Admiral Lee's battleships of the Fast Carrier Force, and on the 26th landings were made on the small island of Kerama Retto just 32km (20 miles) west of southern Okinawa, where there was a good anchorage at which to set up an advanced base, with CVEs, including *Sangamon, Natoma Bay, Marcus Island, Savo Island* and *Petrof Bay* giving cover and support. The minesweeping continued and two hours before sunrise on 1 April, after the usual bombardment from carrier planes and big guns, 'Iceberg' I, the first phase of the operation, began with leathernecks landing on the west coast of the southern end of Okinawa. By that evening 50,000 men were ashore and two airfields had been captured. Two days later the troops were firmly astride the island, cutting the enemy force in two. The lighter forces in the north were quickly dealt with, but against the strong southern army a long and bloody struggle began.

THE INVASION OF OKINAWA

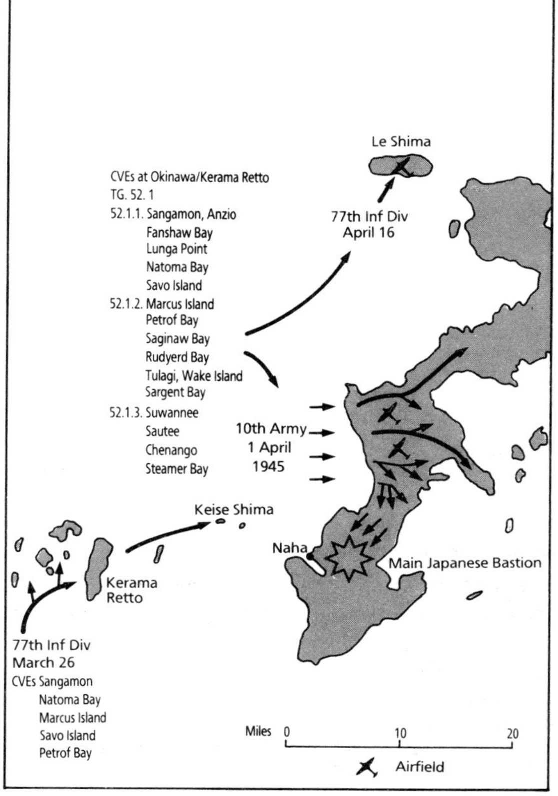

KAMIKAZE – THE LAST FLING

Meanwhile the Japanese threw everything they could scrape from the barrel at the Allied besieging forces. The Corsairs and Avengers of the British TF.57 flew dogged and dangerous sorties to beat up aircraft and churn up the runways on Ishigaki and Miyako, relieved at replenishment periods by a squadron of US CVEs, but the airstrips were surfaced with crushed stones and were repaired overnight, and on D-Day the enemy in the Sakishimas and Formosa retaliated with the first of many *Kamikaze* attacks. One suicider hit HMS *Indefatigable* but, unlike the American carriers with their flammable pine flight decks, the steel-decked British carriers suffered little, and the plunging banzai planes got the worst of the encounters. This made up for the intolerable heat inside the British 'closed' hangars in the coming summer months of attrition.

There was a strong element of the heroic, self-sacrificing *Kamikaze* in all operations during this, the last dying phase of the war. On 1 April Captain Ariga of *Yamato* cleared lower deck. From 'A' turret, above its three huge rifles, he said, 'My friends, the enemy is at our doors. Already he is trampling the sacred soil of Okinawa, but these guns are going to hurl destruction upon him. Remember the words of our ancestors: "Shikishima no Yamatogokoro o hito tawaba Asahi ni niou Yamazakura bana!" ["If you are asked what is the heart of *Yamato*, reply that it is the scent of the wild cherry tree in the Rising Sun."] On the 4th the crew were given hot saki with the salty biscuits called *sembes*, and drank to victory or a glorious death. On 6 April, with death sweet in their nostrils, they left the Inland Sea in company with the light cruiser *Yahagi* and eight destroyers, with orders to attack shipping off Okinawa. Their fuel tanks were not full, and there was a definite understanding that they were not to return. They were sighted that evening, and the Fast Carriers steamed north to meet them. Next day in the East China Sea about 480km (300 miles) north of Okinawa, *Yamato, Yahagi* and one destroyer were sunk, and with them effectively died the Imperial Japanese Fleet, but in Japanese air attacks a *Kamikaze* hit the CV *Hancock* and caused serious damage. From now on until the end of May, while bitter fighting continued ashore, *Kamikazes* attacked the Fifth Fleet almost continuously, with occasional lulls of a day or two. From time to time groups from TF.58 sailed north for attacks on Kyushu airfields to reduce the number of Japanese aircraft left for attack, but most of the time the Fast Carriers and the CVEs of Durgin's Support Force had their hands full trying to beat off the suiciders.

During this period about 900 Kamikaze aircraft of various types, Army and Navy, attacked the Fleet, including 18 Yokosuka (Navy Yard) MXY-7 and -8 Navy Special (*Kamikaze*) Attack Ohka (Cherry Blossom) manned rocket bombs, each carried to the vicinity of the targets by a G4M2E

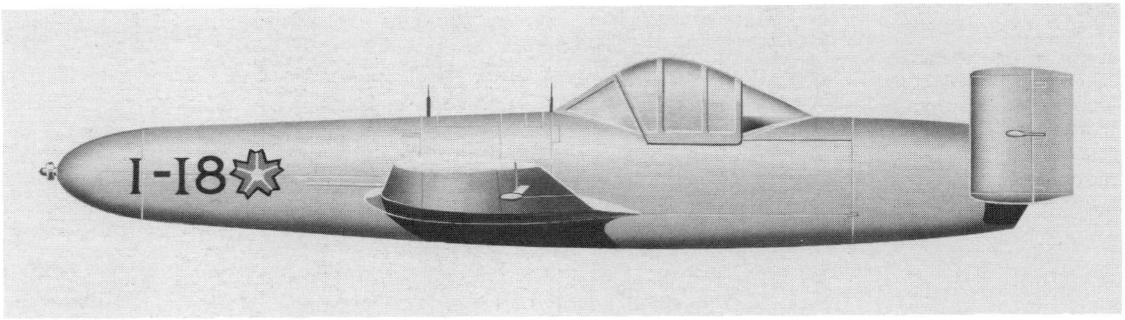

Right: Yokosuka 'Ohka'. (J. M. Goulding)

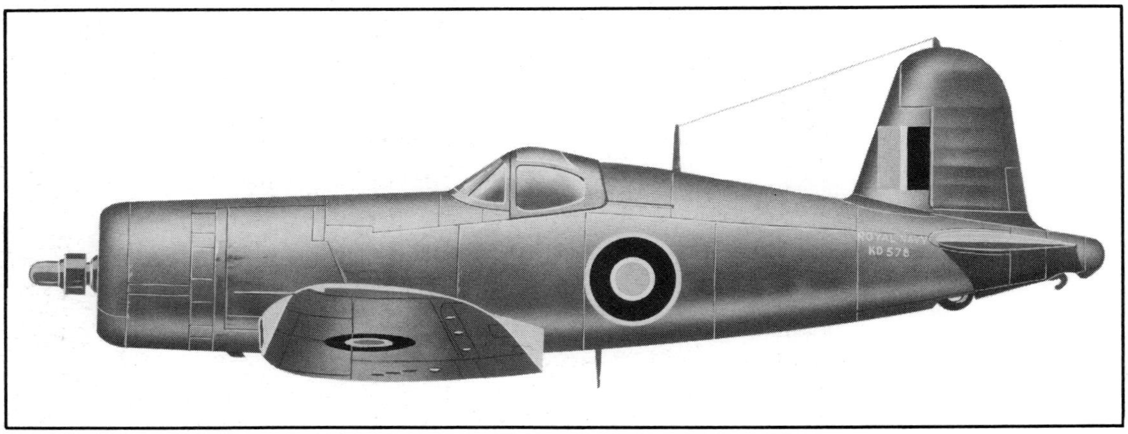

Right: Corsair IV. (J. M. Goulding)

Betty bomber. Hellcats gave meaning to the Allied nickname of Baka (Foolish) bomb of the MXYs by shooting down all 18 Bettys and their unlaunched Bakas. Some 200 suiciders hit and damaged their targets, which included the big carriers of TF.58 and TF.57, as well as smaller craft. The outriding destroyer fighter-direction pickets suffered badly. On 16 April the CV *Intrepid* was badly damaged, on 4 May HMS *Formidable* was hit off the Sakishimas, followed by *Indomitable*, and on the 9th *Victorious*, and *Formidable* again. None of the tough British carriers was out of action for more than a few hours, but they lost aircraft and sometimes speed of handling was reduced. On 11 May Mitscher's flagship *Bunker Hill* was struck by two planes practically simultaneously and almost burned out, with 400 men dead. Three days later the *Enterprise* was hit. On the night of 11–12 March 24 Francis PIY Navy *Ginga* (Milky Way) bombers made a 2,250km (1,400 mile) one-way trip from Kanoya. Twelve got through to the Ulithi anchorage. One hit an islet in mistake for a carrier, one hit the carrier *Randolph* while she was ammunitioning, and the others were destroyed.

SANGAMON TAKES THE HEAT

Having contributed to CAP cover and support of the landing on Kerama Retto, *Sangamon* returned to TU.52.1.3 and throughout 8 April launched supporting strikes and patrols over the Hagushi beaches of Okinawa from an area some 80km (50 miles) south of the island. On the 9th she moved with her unit into an area 112km (70 miles) east of Sakishima Gunto and relieved the British TF.57, raiding the airfields on Ishigaki and Miyako while the British group sailed for replenishment area Cootie for two days of refuelling, storing and shipping replacement aircraft from *Striker*. As CAP carrier, *Speaker* had to have four aircraft in the air, and one spare on the deck, from dawn to dusk in two-hour sorties when replenishment was taking place.

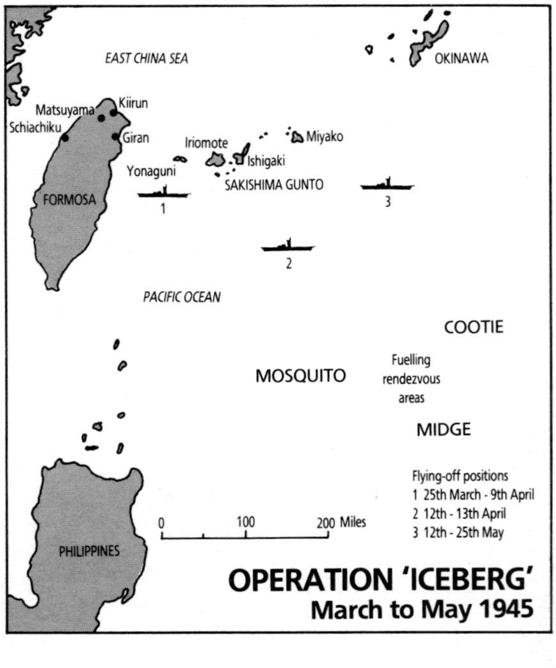

OPERATION 'ICEBERG'
March to May 1945

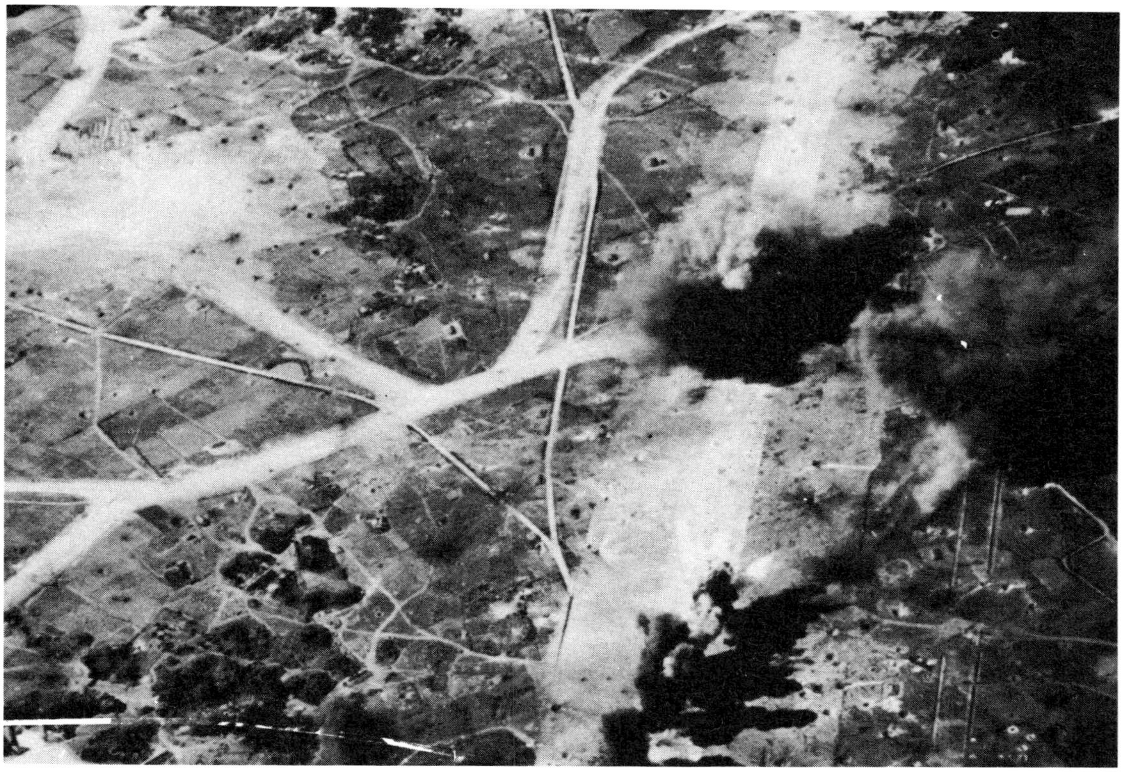

Right: CVEs of the US Fleet alternated with the Fleet carriers of the British Pacific Fleet in bombing and strafing airfields in the Ryukus and Formosa, south-west of the Japanese home islands. Here Nobara Field on the island of Myako is cratered once again.

TF.57 returned, and on the 10th and 11th 'Ziggy' Sprague's six Kaisers raided Schinchiku and Matsuyama airfields on Formosa. On the 12th, they returned to provide air support for the embattled marines on Okinawa, then covered the occupation of Ie Shima, and on the 18th relieved TF.57 once more off the Sakishimas. Dawn and dusk strikes were launched daily, and *Sangamon*'s Hellcat F6F-5Ns made 'heckler' flights over the fields at night. On the 22nd eight fighters and four bombers of a dusk strike caught 25 to 30 enemy planes warming up on Nobara field, central Myako. Seven Oscars tried to intercept *Sangamon*'s planes, but the attack was pressed home. While the bombers returned to the carrier, the Hellcats engaged the Oscars and shot down five. The ship's night fighters were called in and intercepted four more Oscars, shooting down two.

After a month of duty, 14 out of *Speaker*'s original 16 Hellcats were still serviceable. One of them, the CO's personal aircraft, consisted of the engine of one damaged plane buttoned on to the undamaged fuselage of another. 1840's Hellcats had performed consistently well, and towards the end of April were all transfered, with pilots, to *Indomitable* to replace losses, while *Speaker* was switched to replenishment duties, loaded up with Avengers, Hellcats, Corsairs, Seafires and Fireflies, and the newly arrived 'Ruler' became CAP carrier, for which she retained 16 of her less experienced pilots for working up before transfer to the Fleet carriers.

Until the end of the month *Sangamon* continued to take her place neutralising Japanese airfields. On 4 May 'Iceberg' II, the second phase of the Okinawa offensive, began. *Sangamon* put in

Below: *Suwannee* clocks up her 6,000th deck landing of the war with a smooth Hellcat alightment. (Dr P. Phillips)

to the new base on Kerama Retto to re-arm. Loading, frequently interrupted by bogeys, was not completed until evening. At 18:30 the CVE got under way. Enemy aircraft were reported some 48km (30 miles) away. Land-based fighters were vectored on to them and shot down nine, but one got through, and at about 19:00 began circling towards a position on *Sangamon*'s port quarter. The CVE went into a hard turn to port to avoid the enemy and to manoeuvre into launching position, opening fire on the suicider, joined by her escorts. The plane crashed into the water 7.5m (25ft) off the starboard beam.

Other bogeys followed the first. At 19:25 another broke through the interceptor screen, ran into clouds to avoid ack-ack fire, emerged, and increasing speed headed for the *Sangamon*. At 19:33 he dropped his bomb and hit the centre of the flight deck. The bomb, and parts of the plane, burst through into the hangar and exploded, hurling flames and shrapnel in all directions. Fires broke out on the flight deck, the hangar deck and the fuel deck, communications with the bridge were lost and the ship was soon out of control. With *Sangamon* swinging in the wind the fires spread, but by 20:15 steering control had been regained and brought the ship back on to a course which helped the crew fight the myriad fires scattered all over the ship. With the fire main ruptured and water pressure low, CO_2 bottles were brought into action, and nearby ships came alongside to assist. By 22:30 all fires were under control, and communications with other units had been regained by using a VHF channel in the sole remaining undamaged plane. At 23:20 *Sangamon*, with 11 dead, 25 missing and 21 seriously wounded, got under way to return to Kerama Retto for temporary repairs. From there she sailed for Pearl Harbor and Norfolk, Virginia, for thorough repairs. It was to be her last voyage on active service. The name ship of the oiler/carrier class, she has never attracted the attention given to her three sisters, but her war had been every bit as combative as theirs. 'When she was sailing,' one of her ship's company said, 'she was *flying*.'

Below: A Japanese Kamikaze plummets into the sea, narrowly missing *Sangamon*'s flight deck. This was probably the first of several Kamikazes that attacked the carrier off Kerama Retto in the early evening of 4 May 1945. Note the smoke from 20mm guns firing directly at the plane. (US National Archives)

FLYING LEATHERNECKS

On 10 May the new *Commencement Bay* Class escort carrier *Block Island*, CVE-106, second of the category to bear the name, entered the battle with MCVG-1, first all-Marine air group to serve in the jeeps. Equipped with the eight F4U-6 Corsairs (some of the first to fly aboard CVEs), eight F6F-SN night-fighting Hellcats and two F6F-5 photographic Hellcats of Squadron VMF-511, plus the 12 TBM Avengers of VMTB-233, *Block Island* II was the first escort carrier to operate properly equipped night fighters. At monthly intervals more new leatherneck air groups embarked in the new *Commencement Bay* ships, (which had been based on the *Sangamon* Class), *Gilbert Islands* (CVE-107), *Cape Gloucester* (CVE-109) and *Vella Gulf* (CVE-111). *Gilbert Islands* joined 'Iceberg' on 21 May and carried out bomb and rocket intruder sorties over Okinawa, five Marine pilots being killed in action. The two others were too late for Okinawa, and were not used as intended, to give support to Marine infantry in amphibious operations, but took part in more general air operations. *Cape Gloucester*'s MCVG-4 VMF-351 with FG-1s (Corsairs manufactured by Goodyear), and F6Fs, and VMTB-132 with TBMS, fought off *Kamikazes*.

LAST STRIKES

Meanwhile the 'cast-iron carriers' of TF.57 carried on digging holes in the Ryuku runways and the Japanese kept filling them in. There were excursions, first an uncomfortable one to Leyte, known as 'Heat Rash Bay', from 23 April to 1 May, and after that to one or other of the replenishment areas Cootie, Midge or Mosquito on the 10th, 14th, 18th and 22 May, with *Striker, Speaker, Arbiter* and *Chaser* supplying, two at a time, replacement aircraft and crew, who also had the chance while aboard the carriers to brush up their carrier operating procedures. *Ruler* remained CAP carrier.

Arbiter, formerly USS *St Simon* AVE-51, whose motto 'Jus a caelo' (Justice from the skies) spoke for all the CVEs fighting in this just war, had come out from the Clyde with a squadron of Corsairs.

Right, top and centre: Exit *Sangamon*. A Kamikaze hit USS *Sangamon* on 4 May 1945 while she was on her way to bomb the Ryuku Islands and did great damage to her flight deck. By the time she reached Norfolk, Virginia for repairs the war was over. Her after lift was hurled skywards and fell back into the lift well, and the Kamikaze's exploding bombs wrecked the hangar. (US Navy)

Right: A hole blown in *Natoma Bay*'s flight deck was quickly repaired. (US Navy)

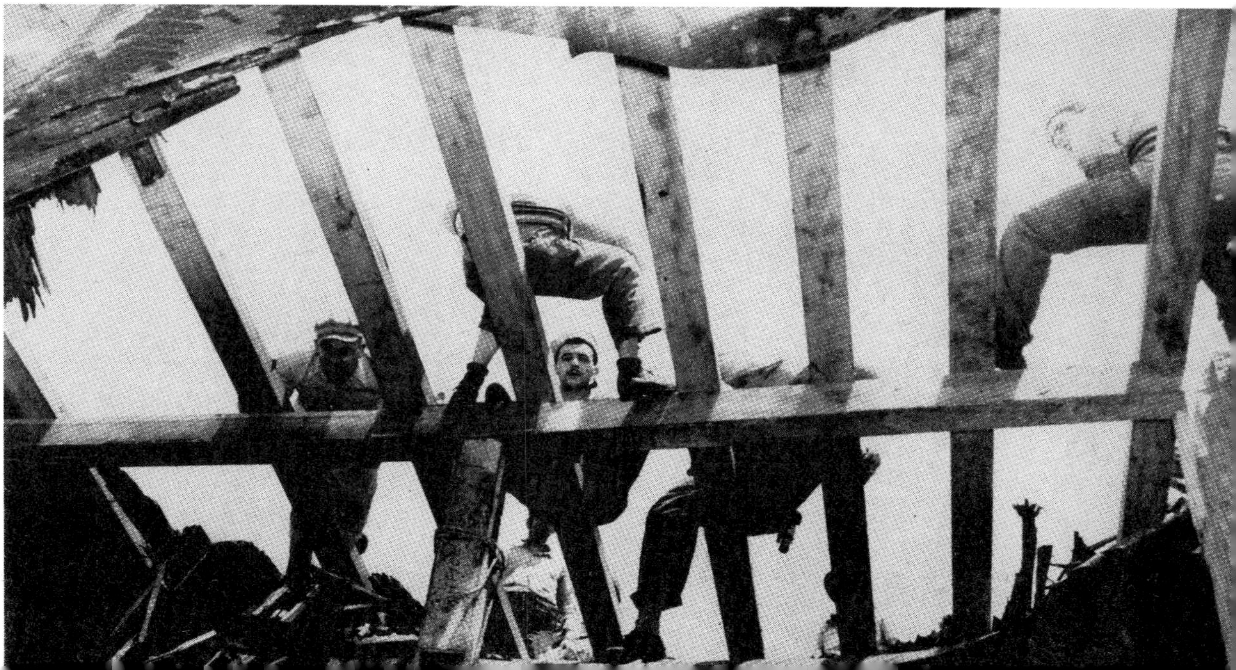

The sound of F4Us starting up aft on the flight deck was impressive, something like the sudden racket of Formula One cars bursting into song in the paddock before a race, but *Arbiter*'s squadron had some spectacular prangs on passage. For some time after the failure of the Vought Corsair F4U-1 in its carrier qualification trials with the *Sangamon* in September 1942, the 'U-bird' with its bent wing and cyranoic nose was allocated only to the US Marines for shore duty, and to the Royal Navy, which received 95 Corsair F4U-1s as Corsair Is. Their first deck landings, aboard HMS *Illustrious*, were traumatic. The CO of 1830 Squadron skidded over the side to his death, and many more of 1830 and 1833, the second Corsair squadron, finished pranged and prostrate. Modifications were made by Vought's Emergency Programme Dog and were all incorporated after the 688th machine, but the Corsair did not fly from US carriers until 1944.

PREPARING FOR 'OLYMPIC'

Meanwhile the anticipated climax of the Pacific war was approaching – the invasion of Japan. For the landings on Kyushu (Operation 'Olympic') and the invasion of Honshu which was to follow in 1946, the command structure was rationalised, with all Army forces to be under General MacArthur, all Air Force planes under Spaatz, all naval units to be commanded by Admiral Nimitz, and for the first time Admirals Halsey and Spruance were to be in active command simultaneously, Spruance to be responsible for the direct support of all amphibious operations, and Bull Halsey to wield the magnificent weapon of the Fast Carrier Force, in conjunction with the Twentieth Air Force, to bomb the heart out of Japan, with principal attention given to the air force and aircraft industry in Honshu.

After three weeks in Leyte Gulf, the Fast Carriers, with Halsey flying his flag in the battleship *Missouri*, put to sea in early July, his men and ships replenished, repaired, refitted and ready for the last campaign of this savage ocean war. By 10 July they were on station off the Honshu coast, only about 270km (170 miles) south-east of Tokyo, and the full flying strength of TF.38, approximately 1,200 aircraft, was launched against air-

Right and far right: The 'bent-wing bastard' Corsair was hard to handle for fledgling pilots on the small flight deck of a replenishment CVE, with 20 feet of nose obscuring his view, and an undercarriage which, even after modifications to the hydraulically operated legs, still had a built-in bounce which frequently caused trouble.

fields surrounding and north of the capital, following closely on heavy raids by as many as 500 Super-Fortresses at a time on these targets and on main industrial cities. The Japanese were unable to oppose these massive strikes with more than token resistance in the air, and there were no attacks on the carriers. It was supposed that the Japanese had hoarded a remaining 10,500 aircraft in the home islands, sending many of these further north to be out of harm's way for a last banzai, but strikes at northern Honshu and southern Hokkaido on 14 and 15 July were unopposed, and battleships could now bombard steel mills and oil installations in coastal towns in the area.

THE BRITISH FLEET TRAIN

By 17 July Halsey was back off Tokyo, and was joined there by Admiral Rawlings and the BPF, which now assumed its proper relationship to its parent Task Force 38 as a task group, bringing four Fleet carriers to add to the American 16 as well as three battleships and the cruisers and destroyers. There had been a big increase in the size and in variety of supplies offered by the British Fleet Train, ships of all nationalities within the British Commonwealth. There were tankers and colliers; ammunition and aircraft replenishment ships (escort carriers); repair and maintenance ships for escorts, aircraft (the carrier *Unicorn*) and armaments, torpedoes, mines, hulls, radar and aero-engines; a floating dock; victualling ships, with much frozen meat and fruit from Australia and New Zealand, water-distilling and accommodation ships. The Americans, who had created the Fleet Train feature of modern naval war, were amazed at the variety of goods and services on offer by this jewel of logistics, which would not, however, have been possible without their earlier, and continued, generosity. One flaw in this array was the slowness of the British tankers, but when the BPF got into difficulties of supply, the US Navy never said 'No' to requests for help, provided they were made realistically through sympathetic channels – which meant well outside the orbit of Admiral King. In this way Charles Evans, Commander (Air) of *Implacable*, obtained six new Avengers from American stores (having only asked for three) – for a bottle of Scotch.

Another feature of the British Fleet Train was the hospital ship, which had not originally been specified, but perhaps the most outstanding vessel of the Train was the exclusively British Amenities Ship, the converted Blue Funnel Liner *Menestheus*, which contained a 400-seat combined theatre/cinema, where its own *Pacific Showboat* revue was staged; canteen, NAAFI shop and restaurant; library, reading/writing rooms; tailor's, barber's and boot repair shops; ice cream parlour, soda fountain and, most welcome of all to thirsty matelots, a brewery with a production capacity of 6,810l (1,800 gal) a day. Unfortunately the *Menestheus* did not reach a Logistics Support Group before the war ended, but immediately afterwards she made a cruise comprising five days in Yokohama, ten in Kure, six in Shanghai, and three weeks in Hong Kong, entertaining 40,000 men, before urgent demands by the Blue Funnel Line forced her return to England and peacetime service, though she visited Allied Servicemen at Singapore, Trincomalee, Aden and Malta en route. She astounded the Americans, who tried to buy her in vain. A part-completed sister ship *Agamemnon* was never finished. At its peak the Train (TF.112) comprised 125 ships (712,000 tons) and 26,200 men. It was often said that there was only one creature comfort not available in the Train – and there was plenty of that in Sydney.

At the British base on Manus, a derelict airstrip became a busy airport, with satellite strips at Lorengan, Moberang and Pityilu. Later the Mobile Operational Naval Air Base (MONAB) *Nabaron*, one of seven such establishments, was set up, six of them in Australia, with an eighth at Hong Kong after the war, for the assembly and flight testing of replacement aircraft, which mostly arrived in crates, before they were loaded aboard replenishment escort carriers.

TANKER TROUBLE

Here, too, a problem developed. The aircraft replacement cycle Fleet-Manus-Fleet – carried out by a CVE making an average speed of 14 knots took about three weeks, and sometimes the right aircraft were not at the replenishment area when wanted, especially with TF.57's aircraft losses so high in 'Iceberg' (a disproportionate 98 lost to 57 enemy planes destroyed, which rises to a staggering 301 if the 203 aircraft rendered non-operational and requiring replacement are added, a reversal of statistics for comparable US Navy operations). In fact the British assault on the Sakishima Gunto, if confined to these statistics, looks very much like a Pyrrhic victory, as the destruction of only 57 enemy aircraft cannot be considered a sizeable contribution to the victory at Okinawa. Between them, HMS *Slinger* and *Striker* ferried 56 aircraft to the replenishment area, 43 of them to Fleet carriers, in three replacement trips, returning to Leyte with 19 'flyable duds'. 'Non-flyable duds' had their engines removed and were ditched over the side. Admiral Fraser thought it 'a pity to reduce such fine fighting ships to the role of mere ferries'.

JAPANESE SUNSET

The BPF/TF.37 had left Sydney on 28 June and rendezvoused with its Logistic Supply Group early on 20 July. Rawlings' ships were required by Halsey to refuel in one day. The BPF found this almost impossible, with its comparatively few, small, slow tankers, and by the end of the day was 9,460l (2,500 gal) short. Rawlings had to ask Halsey for help, and was topped up by the US Logistics Group, TG.30.8. The arrival of a typhoon helped out, as Halsey was forced to postpone the date of action, but the situation would almost certainly arise again.

American and British battleships bombarded coastal positions, and there were further air strikes in the Tokyo area, particularly against the remnants of the Japanese Fleet. Immobilised in Yokosuka without fuel, *Nagato* was damaged beyond repair, the attack was shifted to the Inland Sea and in the days 24–28 July the remaining two Japanese big carriers were knocked out of action and the last three battleships sunk in the main naval base at Kure. TF.37 was not allowed to take part in this act of retribution for Pearl Harbor, and was given subsidiary targets of airfields in north-east Shikoku, ships in the Inland Sea and at Osaka. The escort carrier *Kaiyo* in Shido Wan Bay was sunk.

A sudden change in the schedule of operations put the next refuelling point 1,125km (700 miles) beyond the original. Admiral Fisher's BPF Logistics Group just got there in time. The oiling problem had got so acute for the British that the CVES *Arbiter* and *Ruler* had been converted to Auxiliary Oilers, but the difficulty was not resolved, and again the US oiling group supplied the deficit. Refuelling took place on 31 July and was made more difficult by a typhoon swell which made the tankers as they emptied roll and pitch more and more violently, the replete warships ride more comfortably. *Chaser* and *Speaker* transferred replacement aircraft, *Ruler* flew CAP. Rawlings just completed fuelling in time, on 2 August, but felt sure that next time he would have to miss a day's strike. Then, mysteriously, Halsey was ordered to withdraw for a 'Special Operation'. The Fleet was then struck by another typhoon but was refuelling again on 6/7 August. Just as the British tankers ran dry, with many bunkers still half-full, the force was told via the BBC and Sydney Radio of the dropping of the atomic bomb on Hiroshima. On the 9th the second bomb was dropped on Nagasaki, and the Japanese began negotiations for surrender. The savage duel the Japanese had called 'Taiheiyo-no-Pacific' ('Cancer of the Pacific') was over.

Right: HMS *Atheling* appears at first to be two vessels, thanks to her camouflage. (Robert Forbes)

22

SWORDS AND PLOUGHSHARES

AFTER the end of hostilities the greater majority of US-manned CVEs were used in Operation 'Magic Carpet', the repatriation of American veterans and prisoners of war. Three exceptions were *Sangamon, Suwannee* and *Gilbert Islands. Sangamon*, CVE-26, was in reserve until delivered to the Hillcone Steamship Company at Norfolk, Virginia, on 11 February 1948. *Suwannee*, CVE-27, was in reserve at Boston until 1955, when she was redesignated Helicopter carrier CVHE-27. Struck from the Navy List in March 1959, she was scrapped at Bilbao, Spain, in 1962. *Gilbert Islands*, CVE-107, was in reserve until she was recommissioned for the Korean War in 1951. She ferried jet fighters to Japan, and was the first of the class used for jet touch-and-go practice. She became an AKV (cargo ship and plane ferry) in 1959, and in June 1963 was reclassified AGMR-I and renamed *Annapolis* as the US Navy's first major communications relay ship, on which duties she served in Vietnamese waters from 1965.

All the CVEs were eventually sold for scrap. First to go were USS *Roi*, CVE-103, which in the latter part of World War 2 had transported planes to the Fast Carrier Force, and *Solomons*, CVE-67. They were sold in 1946. *Casablanca*, CVE-55, *Admiralty Islands*, CVE-99, *Bougainville*, CVE-100, *Attu*, CVE-102, *Cape Gloucester*, CVE-109, and *Vella Gulf*, CVE-111, followed in 1947 and *Kalinin Bay*, CVE-68, Samar veteran, in 1957.

There was a big sale of old stock for scrap in 1959/60, after many of the 23 CVEs disposed of had spent several useful post-war years as Helicopter carriers (CVHE), 'Utility' carriers (CVU) or as cargo ships/aircraft transports (AKV), comprising: *Santee*, CVE-29 (CVHE), *Chenango*, CVE-28 (CVHE), *Manila Bay*, CVE-61 (CVU), *Natoma Bay*, CVE-62 (CVE), *Marcus Island*, CVE-77 (CVHE and AKV), *Savo Island*, CVE-78 (CVHE and AKV), *Petrof Bay*, CVE-80 (CVU), *Saginaw Bay*, CVE-82 (CVHE), *Shamrock Bay*, CVE-84 (CVU), *Kasaan Bay*, CVE-69, *Fanshaw Bay*, CVE-70, *Kitkun Bay*, CVE-71, *Nehenta Bay*, CVE-74, *Hoggatt Bay*, CVE-75, *Kadashan Bay*, CVE-76, *Rudyerd Bay*, CVE-81, *Sargent Bay*, CVE-83, *Shipley Bay*, CVE-85, *Steamer Bay*, CVE-87, *Takanis Bay*, CVE-89 (CVU), *Hollandia*, CVE-97, *Kwajalein*, CVE-98, *Munda*, CVE-104 and *Puget Sound*, CVE-113 (CVHE and AKV) were sold in 1962. Of these veteran shooting ships, the 'lucky' *Chenango*, which had survived nearly four years of savage sea warfare, though damaged by rough weather, almost lost another battle with high winds in Long Island Sound after she had been sold for $351,547.28 from the mothball fleet at Boston and was being shifted to New York and the scrap yard. An unwieldy, dead tow, the carrier was driven by 96km/h (60mph) gales against a sand shoal off Horton Beach at Southold at 06:00. A mile to the east the Sound's shoreline and bottom are covered with huge boulders. While a Coastguard cutter stood by, two tugs pulled the

Right: Ruler-class HMS *Trouncer*, seen here with a deck of replenishment aircraft during the last weeks of World War II, took part in RAPWI (Repatriation of Allied Prisoners of War and Internees)

ship free nearly six hours later, and took her across the Sound into the lee of the Connecticut shoreline.

WAR IN THE YELLOW SEA

Ten CVEs saw service in the Korean War, before they were sold for scrap. For six years World War 2 veteran *Tripoli*, CVE-64, served as a transport and plane ferry between the USA and European and Mediterranean ports, Hawaii and the Far East, and in August 1952 loaded F-84 Thunderjets for Korea via Yokosuka, Japan, the first of several such voyages. Reclassified as a Utility carrier in 1955, she was broken up in 1959/60. *Sitkoh Bay*, CVE-86, transported planes to Japan for Korea, and in 1951 carried a consignment of Grumman Bearcat F8Fs to the French in Indo-China. She was reclassified CVU and AKV before being scrapped in 1960. *Cape Esperance*, CVE-88, typhoon survivor, also ferried planes for Korea, attended the atomic bomb tests at Eniwetok, evacuated Chinese Nationalists from Hong Kong, transported aircraft to Italy, France, Portugal, and Pakistan, and was sold in 1959.

Several CVEs which had been commissioned too late to see service in World War 2 were also involved in the Korean War, including *Commencement Bay* Class USS *Siboney*, CVE-112, which transported planes to Turkey, to Japan for Korea, made vertical landing tests with Marine helicopters, was modernised in 1953, joined a hunter-killer anti-submarine group in the Atlantic, and flew in supplies to Tampico after the hurricane of 1955, before being sold in 1971. *Corregidor*, CVE-58, also ferried planes to the United Nations forces in Korea, and was scrapped in 1959. Three other *Commencement Bay* Class CVEs, all commissioned after the end of World War 2, supported the United Nations in Korean waters. *Badoeng Strait*, CVE-116, served as a training carrier before operating as part of the blockade and escort force off Korea, and gave invaluable close support on the Pusan Perimeter, as did *Sicily*, CVE-116, commanded by Captain John Thatch, a veteran fighter pilot who had invented the 'Thatch Weave' combat maneouvre, and which also maintained the blockade of the enemy in the Yellow Sea with Marine Squadron VMF-214 and their demothballed Corsairs alternating with a British Light Fleet carrier. A young Marine aviator in *Sicily*, asked by Captain Thatch for his opinion of his U-bird, said, 'The F4U was good enough for my old man, so it's good enough for me.' *Rendova*, CVE-114, reactivated from the reserve, relieved *Sicily* with the F4Us of VMF-212, and later HMS *Glory*, in Operating Area NAN in the Yellow Sea, to give close support off the west coast. Commander of the US Seventh Fleet in Korean waters was Admiral 'Jocko' Clark. *Rendova* took part in the Operation 'Ivy' atomic bomb test series, on 1 July 1946, when a US Air Force bomber took off from Eniwetok Atoll and dropped a bomb which exploded amongst target ships anchored in the vast 200km (125 mile) long lagoon of Bikini (the pre-World War 2 Escholz) Atoll, aboard which were thousands of scientific instruments and live animals. There was a second test on 25 July, when a bomb was exploded underwater, with some 25 warships used as targets, all of which were drenched with radioactive water, leaving them coated with an invisible radioactive film that defied all attempts at decontamination and they were either scuttled or sunk by gunfire in manoeuvres in 1948. *Rendova* cruised in a hunter-killer group in the Pacific, and served as AKV-59 before being decommissioned and placed in reserve.

FIRE AND FLOOD

Other CVEs had useful and interesting lives before succumbing to the hammer and the blowtorch. In May 1955 the *Thetis Bay*, CVE-90, was converted in the Puget Sound Navy Yard to the Navy's first Assault Helicopter carrier, CVHA-1. In August 1959 her 21 large troop-carrying helicopters carried 726,005kg (1,600,540lb) of supplies to the Chinese destitute after the Taiwan floods, and airlifted some 850 people; then in September 1963 she performed much the same service for the victims of Hurricane 'Flora' in Haiti. CVHA-1 lay off Port-au-Prince while her choppers flew medical aid and food ashore. She was scrapped in 1964 at Portsmouth, Virginia. *Matanikau*, CVE-101, saw little combat in World War 2, serving as a transport, and in the last six months of hostilities trained or qualified 1,332 pilots in deck-landing, with a short period of operations off the northern coast of Honshu. In January 1946 she landed US Marines at Taku, China, to support Chinese Nationalists against the Communists in the struggle for control of China. USS *Point Cruz*, CVE-119, was one of nine CVEs which were laid down during the war but were too late to see service in it. *Point Cruz* served in Korean waters. *Mindoro*, CVE-120, was completed by the Commercial Iron Works but was never commissioned.

CVE SAMARITAN

In RAPWI (Repatriation of Allied Prisoners of War and Internees) a similar operation to 'Magic Carpet', escort carriers in British service were used for the repatriation of time-expired Servicemen and prisoners of war. HMS *Trouncer* was nearing Port Said on her way to the Far East on 29 September 1945 when she received an urgent message giving the position of the troopship *Empire Patrol*, which was on fire in the Red Sea. Captain Rotherham immediately swung round and steamed at full speed to her assistance. A sight reminiscent of wartime greeted them. The trooper was well ablaze, and in panic many of the

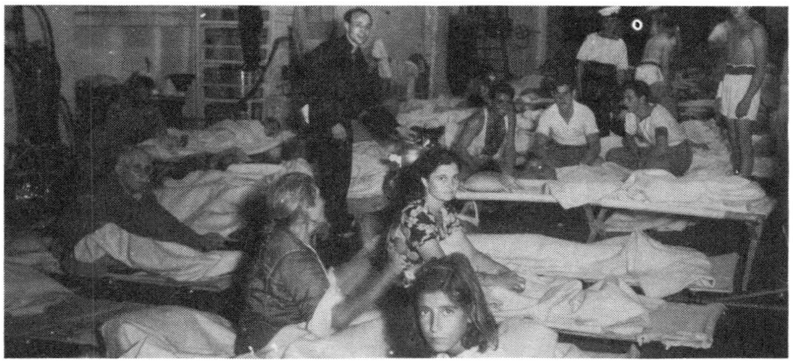

Right: HMS *Trouncer* goes to the help of the burning troopship *Empire Patrol*, carrying Greek women and children being repatriated. *Trouncer*'s men helped the exhausted survivors up the ladder and *Trouncer*'s hangar was untilized as a makeshift dormitory. (L. Ellis)

Below: Sword into ploughshare. MV *Rapana* as wartime tanker MAC, and peacetime tanker, after her reconversion. (Shell photograph)

passengers, most of them Greek women and children refugees being repatriated, with some Greek soldiers and UNRRA officials, had jumped overboard, hoping to be picked up by their boats, but many of them had drowned. *Trouncer* lowered all her boats and picked up survivors, and began the job of getting the remainder off the ship, which by now had been almost consumed by fire, with the hospital section an inferno. The flames had reached the engine room and stopped the pumps. *Trouncer* men struggled through a mass of screaming refugees and got the emergency pumps going but ran out of fuel, and their hoses made little impression on the fire. They had to use force to get some of the women and children off, holding them while they struggled and screamed, tying ropes round them and lowering them into *Trouncer*'s boats. By 20:00 that night they had saved 420 out of 500 refugees and 37 out of 49 crew members. The survivors were bedded down in the empty hangar, which looked like a huge hospital ward, and were cared for by the carrier's sick bay staff.

Most of the Lease-Lend escort carriers, 36 of which survived out of the 38 delivered (*Avenger* and *Dasher* being the only losses), were returned to the United States, where they were generally reconverted to merchantmen or scrapped. The *Archer* became in turn the *Empire Logan* (1946), *Anna Salem* (1949) and *Tasmania* (1955) until, as the *Union Reliance*, she was scrapped at New Orleans in 1962. HMS *Attacker* became the *Castel Forte*, *Chaser* the *Aagtekerk*, *Fencer* the *Sydney*, *Stalker* the *Rionw*. *Pursuer* and *Striker* were scrapped in 1946. *Biter* was handed over to the French Navy early in 1946 to become the carrier *Dixmude*, which operated American SBD-5s against the Viet-Minh in Indo-China, though unsuitable for sub-tropical operations. The Canadian-manned *Nabob*, which had been returned to the US Navy on 16 March 1945, was sold in March 1947 to a Netherlands firm for scrap, but when she arrived at Rotterdam the flight deck was stripped off and other parts of her carrier's structure removed, her damaged hull repaired, and she was sold to the Roland Linie Schiffart, Bremen, Germany, a subsidiary company of the Nordeutscher-Lloyd Line, and completed as the dry cargo ship SS *Nabob*. The first voyage was to Montreal in 1952 for a cargo of grain. In 1963 she was sailing on the Australian run and was also the training ship of the Line, carrying 18 probationary officers. In 1967 she changed hands again, was renamed *Glory*, and *Glory* she remained for the last unspectacular years of her life.

Of the four ships surviving from the five converted in British yards (*Audacity* having been lost), *Activity* was reconverted to the merchantman *Breconshire* in 1946. *Campania*, still in aircraft carrier form, became the Festival of Britain ship, and toured a mini-festival round the major ports of Britain and Europe in 1951. *Nairana* and *Vindex* had both originally been ordered by the Port Line as refrigerated cargo liners, intended for the Australia and New Zealand service. After the war they were bought back by the Port Line at a cost of £50,000 each, converted to the ships they should have been, at a cost of £1,000,000 apiece, and put on the Australasian run. Port Line ships all normally incorporated the name of an Australian or New Zealand port in their names, and *Nairana* was given the name *Port Victor*, which had been the original intention, but *Vindex*, as a special concession to her war record, was named *Port Vindex*. For 22 years she sailed between British and Australasian ports, carrying general cargo outwards, which included machinery, manufactured goods, heavy lifts, power station components, and car parts for assembly in Australian factories, and returned to the United Kingdom with wool, canned goods, frozen lamb and dairy products, mainly butter and cheese, from New Zealand. She was broken up at Kaohsiung, Taiwan, in the summer of 1971.

Right and Centre: Ugly duckling into swan. HMS *Vindex* becomes MV *Port Vindex*. (Philipson, Newcastle)

Right: The first MAC-ship *Empire MacAlpine* was transformed into MV *Suva Breeze*. (A. Duncan)

APPENDICES

1. US NAVY ESCORT CARRIER CATEGORY CODES, 31 March 1941 to 15 August 1945

AVG Aircraft Escort Vessel, 31 March 1941–20 August 1942: **A** – a category of auxiliary vessel; **V** – heavier than air; **G** – aircraft carrier.
BAVG British Aircraft Escort Vessel (on loan to Royal Navy).
ACV Auxiliary Aircraft Carrier, 20 August 1942–15 July 1943: **A** – auxiliary; **C** – carrier; **V** – heavier than air.
CVE Escort Aircraft Carrier, 15 July 1943–15 August 1945 (bestowed status of combatant ship): **C** – carrier; **V** – heavier than air; **E** – escort.

2. LIST OF ESCORT CARRIERS

(L-L = Lend-Lease)

Name	No	Commissioned	Remarks
BRITISH-BUILT			
Audacity		20 June 1941	RN (sunk)
Activity		29 Sept 1942	RN
***Nairana* Class:**			
Nairana		12 Dec 1943	RN
Vindex		3 Dec 1943	RN
Campania			RN
US-BUILT			
Long Island	CVE-1	2 June 1941	USN
***Archer* Class:**			
Archer	BAVG-1	17 Nov 1941	RN (loan)
Avenger	BAVG-2	2 March 1942	RN (loan)
Biter	BAVG-3	6 May 1942	RN (loan)
Dasher	BAVG-5	1 July 1942	RN (loan)
Tracker	BAVG-6	31 Jan 1943	RN L-L)
***Bogue* Class:**			
Battler	CVE-6	31 Oct 1942	RN (L-L)
Attacker	CVE-7	30 Sept 1942	RN (L-L)
Hunter	CVE-8	9 Jan 1943	RN (L-L)
Bogue	CVE-9	26 Sept 1942	USN
Chaser	CVE-10	9 April 1943	RN (L-L)
Card	CVE-11	8 Nov 1942	USN
Copahee	CVE-12	15 June 1942	USN
Core	CVE-13	10 Dec 1942	USN
Fencer	CVE-14	1 March 1943	RN (L-L)
Stalker	CVE-15	21 Dec 1942	RN (L-L)
Nassau	CVE-16	20 August 1942	USN
Pursuer	CVE-17	4 April 1943	RN (L-L)
Altamaha	CVE-18	15 Sept 1942	USN
Striker	CVE-19	28 April 1943	RN (L-L)
Barnes	CVE-20	20 Feb 1943	USN
Block Island	CVE-21	8 March 1943	USN
Searcher	CVE-22	7 April 1943	RN (L-L)
Breton	CVE-23	12 April 1943	USN
Ravager	CVE-34	25 April 1943	RN (L-L)
Croatan	CVE-25	28 April 1943	USN
***Sangamon* Class:**			
Sangamon	CVE-26	25 August 1942	USN (ex-AO 28)
Suwannee	CVE-27	24 Sept 1942	USN (ex-AO 33)
Chenango	CVE-28	19 Sept 1942	USN (ex-AO 31)
Santee	CVE-29	24 August 1942	USN (ex-AO 29)
***Archer* Class:**			
Charger	CVE-30	3 March 1942	USN (ex-BAVG-4)
'Ruler' Class:			
Prince William	CVE-31	9 April 1943	USN
Slinger	CVE-32	11 August 1943	RN (L-L)
Atheling	CVE-33	31 July 1943	RN (L-L)
Emperor	CVE-34	6 August 1943	RN (L-L)
Ameer	CVE-35	19 July 1943	RN (L-L)
Begum	CVE-36	2 August 1943	RN (L-L)
Trumpeter	CVE-37	4 August 1943	RN (L-L)
Empress	CVE-38	13 August 1943	RN (L-L)
Khedive	CVE-39	25 August 1943	RN (L-L)
Speaker	CVE-40	20 Nov 1943	RN (L-L)
Nabob	CVE-41	7 Sept 1943	RN (L-L)
Premier	CVE-42	3 Nov 1943	RN (L-L)
Shah	CVE-43	27 Nov 1943	RN (L-L)
Patroller	CVE-44	22 Oct 1943	RN (L-L)
Rajah	CVE-45	17 Jan 1944	RN (L-L)
Ranee	CVE-46	8 Nov 1943	RN (L-L)
Trouncer	CVE-47	31 Jan 1944	RN (L-L)
Thane	CVE-48	19 Nov 1943	RN (L-L)
Queen	CVE-49	7 Dec 1943	RN (L-L)
Ruler	CVE-50	22 Dec 1943	RN (L-L)
Arbiter	CVE-51	31 Dec 1943	RN (L-L)
Smiter	CVE-52	20 Jan 1944	RN (L-L)
Puncher	CVE-53	5 Feb 1944	RN (L-L)
Reaper	CVE-54	18 Feb 1944	RN (L-L)
***Casablanca* Class:**			
Casablanca	CVE-55	8 July 1943	USN
Liscome Bay	CVE-56	7 August 1943	USN
Anzio	CVE-57	27 August 1943	USN
Corregidor	CVE-58	31 August 1943	USN
Mission Bay	CVE-59	13 Sept 1943	USN

Name	No	Commissioned	Remarks
Guadalcanal	CVE-60	25 Sept 1943	USN
Manila Bay	CVE-61	5 Oct 1943	USN
Natoma Bay	CVE-62	14 Oct 1943	USN
St Lo	CVE-63	23 Oct 1943	USN (sunk)
Tripoli	CVE-64	31 Oct 1943	USN
Wake Island	CVE-65	7 Nov 1943	USN
White Plains	CVE-66	15 Nov 1943	USN
Solomons	CVE-67	21 Nov 1943	USN
Kalinin Bay	CVE-68	27 Nov 1943	USN
Kasaan Bay	CVE-69	4 Dec 1943	USN
Fanshaw Bay	CVE-70	9 Dec 1943	USN
Kitkun Bay	CVE-71	15 Dec 1943	USN
Tulagi	CVE-72	21 Dec 1943	USN
Gambier Bay	CVE-73	28 Dec 1943	USN (sunk)
Nehenta Bay	CVE-74	3 Jan 1944	USN
Hoggatt Bay	CVE-75	11 Jan 1944	USN
Kadashan Bay	CVE-76	18 Jan 1944	USN
Marcus Island	CVE-77	26 Jan 1944	USN
Savo Island	CVE-78	3 Feb 1944	USN
Ommaney Bay	CVE-79	11 Feb 1944	USN (sunk)
Petrof Bay	CVE-80	18 Feb 1944	USN
Rudyerd Bay	CVE-81	25 Feb 1944	USN
Saginaw Bay	CVE-82	2 March 1944	USN
Sargent Bay	CVE-83	9 March 1944	USN
Shamrock Bay	CVE-84	15 March 1944	USN
Shipley Bay	CVE-85	21 March 1944	USN
Sitkoh Bay	CVE-86	28 March 1944	USN
Steamer Bay	CVE-87	4 April 1944	USN
Cape Esperance	CVE-88	9 April 1944	USN
Takanis Bay	CVE-89	15 April 1944	USN
Thetis Bay	CVE-90	21 April 1944	USN
Makassar Strait	CVE-91	27 April 1944	USN
Windham Bay	CVE-92	3 May 1944	USN
Makin Island	CVE-93	9 May 1944	USN
Lunga Point	CVE-94	14 May 1944	USN
Bismarck Sea	CVE-95	20 May 1944	USN (sunk)
Salamaua	CVE-96	26 May 1944	USN
Hollandia	CVE-97	1 June 1944	USN
Kwajalein	CVE-98	7 June 1944	USN
Admiralty Islands	CVE-99	13 June 1944	USN
Bougainville	CVE-100	18 June 1944	USN
Matanikan	CVE-101	24 June 1944	USN
Attu	CVE-102	30 June 1944	USN
Roi	CVE-103	6 July 1944	USN
Munda	CVE-104	8 July 1944	USN
***Commencement Bay* Class:**			
Commencement Bay	CVE-105	27 Nov 1944	USN
Block Island II	CVE-106	30 Dec 1944	USN
Gilbert Islands	CVE-107	5 Feb 1945	USN
Kula Gulf	CVE-108	12 May 1945	USN
Cape Gloucester	CVE-109	5 March 1945	USN
Salerno Bay	CVE-110	19 May 1945	USN
Vella Gulf	CVE-111	9 April 1945	USN
Siboney	CVE-112	14 May 1945	USN
Puget Sound	CVE-113	18 June 1945	USN
Rendova	CVE-114		USN
Bairoko	CVE-115	16 July 1945	USN
Badoeng Strait	CVE-116		USN
Saidor	CVE-117	4 Sept 1945	USN
Sicily	CVE-118	27 Feb 1946	USN
Port Cruz	CVE-119	16 Oct 1945	
Mindoro	CVE-120	4 Dec 1945	
Rabaul	CVE-121	30 Aug 1946	
Palau	CVE-122	completed after the end of hostilities	
Tinian	CVE-123		
Bastogne	CVE-124		
Eniwetok	CVE-125		
Lingayen	CVE-126		
Okinawa	CVE-127		

3. ORIGINS OF ESCORT CARRIER NAMES

As a captured merchant ship under repair, HMS *Audacity* was at first called the *Empire Audacity*, '*Empire*' being the prefix for all British new merchant ship construction. As first an Ocean Boarding Vessel, then an Auxiliary Aircraft Carrier, 'HMS' was merely added to the name. Finally, when it became clear that the new vessel was not an armed merchantman but a fully-fledged warship, '*Empire*' was dropped, and HMS *Audacity* became the first in the run of RN escort carriers named after martial qualities or figures of action, from BAVG-1, HMS *Acher*, to the original ACV-24, HMS *Ravager*, all on loan from the USA.

The 23 *Prince William* Class US-built ships transferred to the Royal Navy under Lease-Lend were mostly rechristened with types or names of rulers (*Ruler, Ameer, Empress, Rajah, Atheling*, etc) and were known collectively in the RN as the 'Ruler' Class, but some had the older action man names (*Trouncer, Arbiter, Reaper*, etc).

Of the four other merchantmen converted in Britain, HMS *Activity* followed the action tradition, but the sisters *Campania, Nairana* and *Vindex* were all named after pioneer aircraft-carrying passenger steamer conversions of World War 1.

The first US Navy escort carrier *Long Island* was followed by the *Bogue* Class of AVG/ACV/CVEs, all named after North American (mainly southern USA) islands or minor waterways. Bogue Inlet lies on Onslow Bay, north-east of Cape Fear, near Wilmington, North Carolina; Card Sound is a continuation of Biscayne Bay, south of Miami, Core the name of a sound off the North Carolina coast.

The four ex-oiler escort carriers were named after former ships of the United States Navy which had pioneered a US waterways classification. The first *Sangamon*, named after a river in Illinois near the birthplace of Abraham Lincoln, was a Federal monitor in the American Civil War which had operated against Lee's army from Hampton Roads and the Virginia rivers. *Suwannee*, CVE-27, followed the iron-hulled, side-wheel gunboat *Suwanee*, a strangely inappropriate name for a hunter of Confederate commerce raiders. The name was modified by adding a second 'n' but the origin was the same southern stream, rising in Ware County, Georgia, and flowing south-west across Florida to the Gulf of Mexico at Suwannee Sound, which Stephen Foster and Al Jolson wrote and sang about.

Chenango, CVE-28, had a Civil War precursor too, the sidewheel armed Union steamer which Commander Tom Fillebrown, USN, commissioned on 22 February 1864, but she was properly Yankee-named, after a county, town and river in New York State. Some called her 'Unlucky *Chenango*' after she blew a boiler on her maiden voyage and scalded 33 men to death, though she later captured the Rebel blockade runner *Elvira*, laden with cotton and tobacco for Britain, and fought a Confederate battalion on the Big Black River, and her modern counterpart had the very opposite reputation.

'Naval Person' President Roosevelt, with his great love of the Navy, became personally interested in warship naming, and it was he who suggested that the names of battles and famous actions might be more inspirational than obscure waterways in Dixie, and a new policy began conveniently with the completion of the first Kaiser carrier *Casablanca*. Some were named for heroic fighting retreats (*Corregidor*, CVE-58, *Wake Island*, CVE-65), others after bloody defeats to be avenged (*Savo Island*, CVE-78, *Makassar Strait*, CVE-91), many after some of the stubborn victories of this war (*Guadalcanal*, CVE-60, *Solomons*, CVE-67, *Tulagi*, CVE-72, *Marcus Island*, CVE-77, *Cape Esperance*, CVE-88, *Makin Island*, CVE-93, *Salamaua*, CVE-96, *Kwajalein* (CVE-98), and a few after illustrious achievements of the past (*Tripoli*, CVE-64, *Manila Bay*, CVE-61, scene of a great victory against Spain). A large number still continued the publicising of minor waterways, except that these ships, instead of celebrating the Deep South, put the newest state of Alaska on the map (the ill-fated *Liscome Bay* and *Ommaney Bay*, *Natoma*, *Gambier*, *Petrof*, *Shamrock*, *Sitkoh*, *Kadashan*, *Rudyerd* and *Fanshaw Bays*), and other inlets in islands in the northern Pacific (*Kalinin*, *Kasaan*, *Kitkun*, *Saginaw*, *Hoggatt*, *Sargent*, *Shipley*, *Steamer*, *Takanis* and *Thetis Bays*). The later *Commencement Bay* Class carried on the famous victory line of CVEs (*Gilbert Islands*, *Salerno Bay*, *Vella Gulf*) with the exception of *Puget Sound*, which saluted the stretch of water in Washington State where so many escort carriers carried out their trials.

4. US MARITIME ADMINISTRATION CLASSIFICATION OF SHIPS, 1944

The US Maritime Administration adapted a system of classifying ship designs in 1944, using letters and numerals in a three-group code to outline the broad general characteristics of a ship and to specify the individual design. The first group consisted of a letter signifying the general ship type, with a number indicating specific length (measured at the load waterline in feet). The second group indicated the machinery type, the number of propellers and whether the ship carried more than 12 passengers. The third group represented the specific original design of the ship, indicating whether it followed the original design or a modification of it.

Example: the designation C3-S-A1 would indicate a cargo ship between 450 and 500ft [137–152m] in length, carrying fewer than 100 passengers (C3), and in conjunction with the other two groups of letters and numbers specifically of 492ft [150m] in length; steam turbine-powered, with one propellor (S); a conversion to a World War 2 CVE (A), of a basic design (1).

5. TASK FORCE 88 AIRCRAFT STRENGTH FOR OPERATION 'DRAGOON'

Ship	Unit[1]	Aircraft
Task Group 88.1		
HMS *Emperor*	800 Squadron	23 Hellcat I
HMS *Pursuer*	881 Squadron	24 Wildcat VIA
HMS *Searcher*	882 Squadron	28 Wildcat V
HMS *Attacker*	879 Squadron	24 Seafire LIII, LIIC, LRIIC
HMS *Khedive*	899 Squadron	26 Seafire LIII
HMS *Royalist* (Flag), command cruiser		
HMS *Delhi*, AA cruiser		
HMSS *Troubridge*, *Tuscan*, *Tyrian*, *Teazer*, *Tumult*, *Tenacious*, *Navarinou*, destroyers		
Task Group 88.2		
USS *Tulagi*[2]	VOF I	24 F6F-5, F6F-3
USS *Kasaan Bay*	VF 74	24 F6F-5
HMS *Hunter*	807 Squadron	22 Seafire LIII 2 Seafire LRIIC
HMS *Stalker*	809 Squadron	10 Seafire LIII 13 Seafire LIIC, LRIIC
HMSS *Colombo*, *Caledon*, AA cruisers		
USSS *Butler* (Flag), *Gherardi*, *Herndon*, *Shubrick*, *Murphy*, *Jeffers*, destroyers		

[1]800, 881 and 882 Squadrons constituted No 7 Naval Fighter Wing; 879, 899, 807 and 809 Squadrons constituted No 4 Naval Fighting Wing. [2]Rear-Admiral Durgin.

6. ROYAL NAVY AIRCRAFT STRENGTH, OPERATION 'AVALANCHE', 9–14 SEPTEMBER 1943

Ship	Unit	Aircraft
Force 'H' (Rear-Admiral, Aircraft Carriers: Rear-Admiral C. Moody)		
Illustrious	894 Squadron	28 Marlet + 10 Seafire IIC + 12 Barracuda
Formidable	885 Squadron	5 Seafire IIC + 32 Martlet + 12 Albacore
Force 'V' (Rear-Admiral P. Vian in AA cruiser *Euryalus*)		
Unicorn	809 Squadron	10 Seafire LIIC
	887 Squadron	10 Seafire LIIC
	897 Squadron	10 Seafire LIIC
Attacker	879 Squadron	10 Seafire LIIC
	886 Squadron	9 Seafire LIIC
Battler	807 Squadron	9 Seafire LIIC
	808 Squadron	8 Seafire LIIC
Hunter	899 Squadron	14 Seafire LIIC
	834 Flight	6 Seafire LIIC
Stalker	899 Squadron	14 Seafire LIIC
	833 Squadron	6 Seafire LIIC

7. THE SINKING OF *AUDACITY*: A GERMAN ACCOUNT

(Translation of a German account of the sinking of HMS *Audacity* broadcast at 18:15 on 30 December 1941 from Frankfurt Radio Station.)

Reporter: 'The U-boat, commanded by Senior Lieutenant Bigalk, which last week torpedoed an English aircraft carrier, has now returned to base.'

Senior Lieutenant Bigalk: 'I had only been at sea for a few days when I had to crash-dive one afternoon because of an English plane. In the hydrophone I heard screw noises under water and took them to be coming from a convoy. I told myself that I should get to the surface as soon as possible to see what was actually going on, so I came up quickly and only a few minutes later saw clouds of smoke, and a few minutes after that the outlines of some destroyers. There is the convoy! We were very glad to have found one just a few days after departure. First of all I approached the convoy to weigh up the situation. I saw a number of destroyers zigzagging wildly, and on their left, near them, I saw a long shadow, surrounded by more zigzagging destroyers. Suddenly a wild display of tracer bullets started up in the east. My other U-boat colleagues, who were also going for this convoy, had probably opened their attack. The destroyers headed for the tracers. The long shadow, which I first took to be a tanker, zigzagged first eastwards, then northward, presumably to get away from the convoy. I made for the big shadow immediately, to attack it. Suddenly the shadow turned away sharply and at the same moment there was a great illumination by rockets from the convoy. Other U-boats were attacking. Ten or 15 rockets hung over the U-boat as though transfixed. Destroyers nearby started firing tracer, and suddenly I saw in the light of the tracers and rockets a large aircraft-carrier lying in front of us. What an opportunity! A U-boat captain is not handed a chance like that every day. Everyone on the bridge was excited.

'I was in a favourable position for attack. I *had* to fire. I fired several torpedoes, then came the terrible tension of waiting to hear if one of them had hit its mark. Then there was a fiery detonation aft. A hit astern! The ship circled to port, then stopped, unable to maneouvre. My torpedo must have smashed her screws. I turned away briefly to reload. The for'ard compartment was loaded with provisions for the voyage and extra gear, but my torpedo mate and his crew worked frantically, while we on the bridge watched the carrier intently, worried that a destroyer might approach and spoil our chances. But the destroyers must have been furiously occupied elsewhere, as far out on the horizon there were loud explosions and detonations.

'The torpedo tubes were reported cleared for action, thank God. I made another attack, approaching the target at a crawling pace so she could not possibly hear me. The water was phosphorescing like mad, and I could only move slowly. I came nearer and nearer. I didn't care any more. I had to get so close that no torpedo could possibly miss. The gigantic shadow grew bigger and bigger all the time. I had got so close that the tinfish could not miss. I gave the order to fire. The torpedoes left their tubes. Seconds of great tension. *There*, a hit for'ard, 20 metres [114ft] aft of the stem. A great detonation, with a gigantic sheet of flame. Shortly after, another detonation, amidships. Again, a great column of fire. Hardly had this subsided when a powerful detonation was seen for'ard – probably ammunition or fuel going up. I presumed that petrol tanks or something like that had been blown up. As I turned away I took a last look at the carrier. The fore part was already flooded and the deck was canting upwards. At that moment destroyers were reported to starboard. They were racing at top speed towards the carrier, which was firing wild distress signals – great stars bursting in the air. I managed to elude the pursuit. I got a rain of depth charges, but they did not help the English, and I escaped.'

Reporter: 'And you arrived back here safely today. We are happy and proud to welcome you. You know from the communiqué that on that night when a convoy sailing from Gibraltar to England was attacked, many, many more tons were sent to the bottom of the Atlantic by your comrades, besides the aircraft carrier which you sank.'

8. GALE DAMAGE IN HMS *HUNTER*, AUGUST 1943

In March 1943 the Swordfish of No 834 Squadron flew from RAF Exeter, where they had been based for anti-E-boat patrols over the English Channel, to Macrihanish in Scotland. Here they acquired a flight of six Seafire LIICs and became a Composite squadron. On 6 July the squadron embarked in HMS *Hunter* for its role in Operation 'Avalanche', the landing at Salerno. Early in August *Hunter* sailed in company with *Battler*, the battleship *Ramillies* and a convoy for Gibraltar. The two escort carriers were crammed with aircraft, stowed in every possible place, some lashed to the deckhead in the hangar. *Hunter* had some 40 aboard, including her own Compo 834 machines, and it was almost impossible to walk through the hangar. *Hunter* was the starboard wing ship of the force, five cables on the starboard beam of *Ramillies*.

In the first afternoon watch a storm warning was received. Sure enough the wind freshened and the weather in general deteriorated. Orders were given to double-lash all aircraft. This was apparently done, though the buzz went round that the Air Branch had insufficient hemp rope to do the job properly, and that a request at Ship's Stores for some more had been turned down by the ship's Commander, who had previously served in the 'stone frigate' HMS *Royal Arthur*, a former Butlin's Holiday Camp at Skegness. What was certain was that no-one could find the special securing wires which had arrived on board just before sailing. The Chief Buffer was going round with that 'I *know* I put them *somewhere*' look. Not that anyone was particularly worried, as there had been a later forecast of 'improvement after midnight' which, in view of what was to happen, was not entirely accurate.

By about 20:00 a full gale was blowing out of the south-west, and the speed of the force was reduced to revolutions for 12 knots. All CVEs were top-heavy with flight deck, not to mention the weight of aircraft, and even with the many tons of counteracting ballast aboard were commonly known to 'roll on wet grass' or 'in drydock,' and when hangar rounds were made at 22:00 the ship was rolling a gentle 3 degrees but pitching heavily. After Commander (F)'s Rounds at 22:45 the hangar was darkened and work there ceased for the night, or so everyone thought, with two Petty Officers and three men left on watch there. At 23:56 *Hunter* went to action stations for ten minutes after the warning of an aircraft approaching. The hangar was visited again before 01:30 by Commander (F), Lieutenant-Commander G. A. L. Woods, DSO, RN, the CO and Senior Pilot of 834, and the Squadron Duty Officer. By that time the wind had increased to Force 11 and the ship was rolling 5–6 degrees. The night was very dark, and she was relying on her 272 radar to keep station on *Ramillies*. The old battlewagon had been pushing on stolidly through the storm with only moderate motion on her.

The motion on *Hunter* increased. At 02:30 a hatch cover broke loose and damaged a Seafire's wing. Five minutes later Commander (F) came to check the damage, and noticed Seafire 'X', parked aft, sliding on the wet deck and straining at its lashings. The other machines seemed secure but Woods went up to the bridge to ask Captain McWilliam to turn the ship to reduce the motion while the loose Seafire was re-lashed, and extra lashings put on all the other aircraft. The aircraft handling party was piped, but before they could reach the hangar the gale had found the Seafire's weakest point. The undercarriage of Seafire 'X' had collapsed and this machine had broken free from its lashings and rammed Seafire 'Y', the aftermost aircraft in the hangar, which had broken away and fallen into the lift well, and in doing so perforated a drum of chlorosulphonic acid, the fumes from which were added to the smoke and flame from a small fire which had started there. The Air Engineer Officer and a few ratings, including TAGs from 834 Squadron, tried to shift Seafire 'X', the original trouble-maker, back to its position, a forlorn hope in view of its weight.

At that point, about 02:44, the Force was ordered to turn 40 degrees to starboard to head the sea. There was some delay in putting the helm over. Captain McWilliam saw the crest of a huge wave on the starboard bow level with the flight deck. He ordered the wheel put to starboard but it was too late. The wave hit the ship with a thunderous crash and threw her over 50 degrees to port, so far that she seemed likely to go over on her beam ends. After three more very heavy rolls she settled on her new course, and began this time to pitch very heavily.

When the first wave struck, Seafire 'X' in the hangar slid across the deck carrying the handlers on the leading edge of its wing like tics on a bird of prey, its sharp wing-tips cut loose two other aircraft and in very little time half a dozen Seafires were loose in the hangar, and the 60 men desperately looking out for themselves. As the ship continued its frightening rolls Seafire 'X' retreated again into the elevator well where it remained half-in, half-out. Captain McWilliam reduced to seven knots, but the wind was now roaring at Force 12 from dead ahead, and this was not enough to keep *Hunter*'s blunt head to wind. Another two knots was just enough to give steerage way, and the motion was preferable to rolling.

Down below, 834's Swordfish 'F' had broken loose at the fore end of the hangar, and slid into Swordfish 'A'. Seafire '1' and '2's' undercarriages collapsed, they broke loose and lurched into Martlet '3', one of a few aircraft secured with wire lashings but which broke away immediately, seriously damaging Swordfish 'J'. The heavy rolling had caused water to flow from the sprayer pipes and the deck was made even more slippery by Glycol coolant dripping from smashed Seafire Merlins, not to mention the dense fumes of chlorosulphonic acid filling the after end of the hangar, where a handling party was still trying desperately to re-lash the first two Seafires to break loose but which, on another roll of the ship, slid down the sheer of the deck and broke loose all the other aircraft in the after end. The fire there was still burning, and a Seafire with a smashed undercarriage had split open its belly fuel tank, depositing gallons of avgas on the metal deck, and was sliding along in a shower of sparks, which ignited the petrol. Further up the deck was an uncombed hatch leading down to the fuel control room and thousands of gallons of avgas . . . At that point the sprinkler system came on and ran with foam. It became impossible to stand on the gyrating, treacherous deck, and men struggled to get clear of the aircraft, all of which now seemed to be loose, thundering and crashing about the hangar on errands of destruction. After colliding at high speed with a Seafire, TAG Neville Bradpiece dazedly swarmed up the nearest ladder, finding himself in competition with his CO.

Captain McWilliam saw the fumes rising from the for'ard lift well and ordered the after lift lowered to ventilate the hangar. The Duty Officer did not know of the Seafire in the lift well, and the great slab of the lift descended and crushed it. The descent of the lift automatically doused the lights, the fire increased, and the hangar was a place of nightmare, with burning avgas flowing down the deck like a scorching lava stream, the fire-fighting foam drenching men and machines, which were running amok, destroying themselves and running down the handlers, like a running of the bulls. Bradpiece's life jacket was covered with blood, and he dared not feel to find out what damage had been done. In fact it was only a bloody nose. A seman put out his hand to steady himself against the edge of a watertight door, the door swung shut, and he lost his fingers. Engines in crates had fallen and been smashed, torpedoes were rolling about the deck, a complete rack of depth-charges had torn loose from its welding, crated cannon had pierced the ship's side, leaving circular holes in the 12.5mm (½in) steel plates.

McWilliam saw heavy clouds of smoke rising from the after lift well and, receiving a report of fire in the hangars, called for help from the escorts. *Ramillies* closed *Hunter* and ordered *Stalker*, the port wing ship, to take charge of the convoy. McWilliam hove to, to minimise the risk of further damage, and the rest of the convoy followed suit. Commander (F) and his party struggled to clean up the shambles in the hangar.

At daybreak it was seen that the gale had snapped *Hunter*'s main W/T mast, which hung down dangerously, its yard and aerials swinging about. The port hangar side was pierced in several places. All the aircraft in the hangar had been damaged, many were write-offs, three of the tough Martlets were dented and holed. The convoy was only 30 hours from the UK, and it was thought best for *Hunter* to return for replacement aircraft and repairs to the elevator. Miraculously no-one had been killed in the mêlée but three officers and 13 men had been injured. Ten new Seafire airframes had been lost from the ferry cargo, and among 834's machines, of seven Seafires one fuselage was a complete write-off and two others were ruined aft of the cockpit; of six Swordfish one was unserviceable, and the rest had varying degrees of mainplane damage. *Hunter* had used lashings (a minimum of double 63mm (2½in) hemp) recommended in the Admiralty Pamphlet Securing Gear for Naval Aircraft, but some of these had parted. In future they would be additional to wire lashings, and Seafire undercarriages were strengthened to withstand side loads, with new arrangements for lashing down. As for freak waves, only a mod by God could work, with prompter reactions by ships' captains to dangerous weather. *Hunter* reached Liverpool on 6 August and sailed once more for Gibraltar on the 16th, flying anti-submarine patrols all the way without further incident, after one of the most bizarre episodes in naval aviation history. On 26 August 834's Swordfish, but not its Seafires, flew off to RNAS North Front, Gibraltar and *Hunter* docked later to off-load her cargo of new machines.

9. THE MORRISON BLIND APPROACH SYSTEM

At 10:00 on 4 July 1944 HMS *Vindex* anchored off Greenock after fourteen days of fog, fatigue and technical failure in the North Atlantic, hunting U-boats unsuccessfully, though the new ASV sets had improved in the latter part of the operation, with only nine failures in 84 sorties between 7 and 13 July. For night fliers like 825 Squadron the summer nights had been short, land often within range, the sea calm, making rescue easier, but the benefit of these factors had largely been counteracted by persistent low cloud and fog.

The ship sailed again at 07:45 on 4 August for two days of flying exercises in the Clyde exercise area and was off Ardrossan at 01:00 next morning when she was abruptly ordered on a U-boat hunt. Air searches began at 07:15 on 6 August with three Swordfish. By the time the Stringbags returned to the carrier at 09:45 thick fog had come down, with visibility 150 yards and cloud base at 200 feet.

These aircraft were brought aboard safely by a combination of flame floats, searchlights and a new experimental method of controlled landing in thick weather.

Tired of the anxiety of watching young pilots groping for the flight deck in nil visibility, the ship's Navigator, Lieutenant-Commander Geoffrey Milner, RNR had remarked to 'Wings', 'Press on Percy' Gick, 'Why don't we use an ASV set in the ship to bring them in?' Wings, always ready to try anything which might improve the performance of his aircraft, passed on the idea to *Vindex*'s Air Radio Officer, Temporary Sub-Lieutenant (A) John Mackenzie Morrison, RNVR, who modified a Mark XI unit and set it up outboard on the starboard side aft.

The basis of the unit was an inverted scanner which could rotate continuously in a horizontal plane. A tubular feeder and all control leads were taken down to the other part of the installation in the ASV workshop immediately below. The success of the system depended on a much modified Indicator Unit Type 97. Aircraft orbiting the ship anywhere within eight miles radius were picked up on this set and could be tracked in to 100 yards from the round-down, and bearing accuracy could be maintained to within a few degrees. Presentation was on a small PPI as used in an aircraft, but instead of a centre spot being the start of range markings, a 2-inch circle represented the zero. An aircraft was controlled from the blip on this screen, right up the approach path until it disappeared inside 100 yards. If an aircraft had to go round again, the blip reappeared soon after it had passed the bows of the ship, and the aircraft was under control virtually throughout, whereas an aircraft's set was ineffective for the last few hundred yards of an approach.

Sub-Lieutenant (A) Eddie Ward, RNVR of 825 Squadron was the first pilot to be brought in by the Morrison Method. His Stringbag was brought back to within five miles of the ship by Sub-Lieutenant Keith Brading in the Air Direction Room and handed over to Jock Morrison, as Control Officer, who passed the pilot the ship's course, and Ward began his run-in from about three miles astern, while Control was given his holding positions on each beam.

The pilot was ordered 'Over to Control', and from then on flew in the correct attitude for landing, at 75 on his radio altimeter, steering the ship's course, with the Control Officer following him on his own special PPI and ordering any necessary change of course . . .

'Charlie, Port Ten'.

'Port ten'.

'Charlie, steady'.

'Steady'.

In this way the pilot was talked down to within some 100 or 150 yards of the ship. The batsman, wearing headset and throat microphone (called a laryngua-phone), had been listening to all these orders, and on sighting the aircraft shouted 'Bats!' The pilot immediately kicked on right rudder and looked over his port side for the special illuminated bats. A last 'Skid port!' and 'Come down!' from Bats, and the Stringbag was dropping to the deck, her undercart struts straining, her hook snagging a wire and pulling it out like a startled boa-constrictor.

Ward was one of the best pilots in the Squadron, but with practise any pilot was able to make the Morrison Blind Approach System work for him, and it was adopted in *Vindex* for all bad weather landings in lieu of the Type 257 radar of the BABS system. Any type of aircraft fitted with R/T only, and preferably a radio altimeter, could be controlled in this way.

10. JAPANESE MERCHANTMEN/AIRCRAFT CARRIERS

Chuyo, Taiyo* and *Unyo

The Japanese NYK (Nippon Yusea Kaisya) Line introduced the new 17,000-ton luxury liners *Nitta Maru* and *Yawata* into their European service early in 1940. A third, the *Kasuga Maru*, was due for launching later in the year but by then the Line was running empty ships to Europe. Other services were well covered by the flourishing Japanese Merchant Marine, and with a need for more aircraft carriers implicit in the Imperial General Staff's plans for bringing the war to the east, the Navy took over the three liners for conversion, with their diesel engines replaced by turbines for greater speed. *Kasuga Maru*, redesigned by the Navy Department, was launched at Mitsubishi's Nagasaki yard on 19 September 1940, towed to the Sasebo Navy Yard, completed there in September 1941, and named *Taiyo*, a 27-plane, flush-decked carrier with one hangar and two lifts. Her two sisters were converted on similar lines at the Kure Navy Yard, and named *Chuyo* and *Unyo*, each with capacity for 30 aircraft.

The early proposals of the Royal Navy to convert large liners to carriers were dropped, and *Chuyo, Taiyo* and *Unyo* were superior to the small Allied conversions, except that, curiously, they were not fitted with arrestor gear or catapults. They were designed for use with the Combined Fleet rather than as convoy escorts, but proved inadequate and were confined to training carrier pilots and ferrying aircraft to island bases.

Hiyo* and *Junyo

In 1939 the keels of two larger, 27,000-ton luxury liners *Idzumo Maru* and *Kashiwara Maru*, for the Nippon Yusen Kaisya Line were laid down by Kawasaki and Mitsubishi, but as it became clear that they would be redundant as passenger ships, their design was altered so that they could be completed as aircraft carriers when Japanese plans for a Pacific war were activated, with double keels, extra height between decks, more fuel tankage, and provision for two hangars and two lifts. They were launched in June 1941 and though rather slow, with poor protection for their fuel tanks, joined the Fleet in the summer of 1942 to compensate for the big losses at Midway. *Hiyo* was sunk by Mitscher's planes in the battle of the Philippine Sea on 20 June 1944, *Junyo* damaged, repaired and refitted at Kure, all combustible materials being removed, tanks protected with concrete, and AA armament greatly increased, to include 168 0.50in rocket launchers and more 25mm quick-firing cannon. *Junyo* survived the war as a damaged hulk at Sasebo, where she was later broken up.

Shinyo

In the rush to replace the four Fleet carriers lost at Midway, the German liner *Scharnhorst*, blockade-bound in Kobe, was bought by the Japanese Government, renamed *Shinyo*, and shifted to the dock at Kure just vacated by the completed *Chuyo*, which served as a model for her own conversion, with extra bulges for stability, and electric turbines, using materials from the partially built and ultimately discarded hull of the intended fourth monster battleship of the *Yamato* class (with the third, *Shinano*, in a similar state). Commissioned on 15 December 1943, *Shinyo*'s armament of 50 massed 25mm cannon could not protect her against the US submarine *Spadefish*, which sank her in November 1944.

Kaiyo

The smallest of Japan's merchantmen/carriers was converted from the OSK Line's luxury liner *Argentina Maru* in early 1943 in the Nagasaki yard of Mitsubishi on similar lines to all the other Japanese carrier conversions, as an escort carrier, with one hangar and a flush flight deck, her diesels replaced by two sets of destroyer turbines for greater speed and reliability. As completed, she was 166.4m (546ft 3in) long overall, with a 159.7 by 23m (524 by 75.5ft) flight deck, and displaced 13,600 tons. At first used to transport aircraft to their bases, after the 'Marianas turkey shoot' *Kaiyo* trained new carrier pilots in an attempt to replace those lost in great numbers in the Philippine Sea. During an air attack on Beppu Bay, Kyushu, in July 1945 she was bombed, and turned over on her side in shallow water, where she was scrapped after the war.

JAPMACs

With the destruction of the Japanese Merchant Marine by US Navy submarines, the Japanese Navy chartered the 14,500-ton (20,469 tons full load) oil tanker *Shimane Maru* and late in autumn 1944 commandeered four ITL war design tankers under construction by Kawasaki for conversion to merchant aircraft carriers on the lines of the British MACs, with 160m (526ft) hull and main engines unchanged, well decks built into hangar spaces for 12 aircraft, covered by a 149 by 22.9m (489 by 75ft) flight deck. Exhaust vents from two boilers were trunked into a single funnel projecting horizontally outwards on the starboard side near the stern.

With the oil crisis, there were plans to convert the JAPMACs to coal burners. When her conversion was almost complete it was decided to convert *Shimane Maru* back to a pure tanker but she was sunk in an air raid. Work on the second ship, *Otakisan Maru*, was also stopped in February 1945 for a reconversion to burn coal, but she broke her moorings in a gale and sank when she drifted onto a mine. Work on the other two conversions, tankers Nos 14 and 16, was stopped in March 1945.

AMACS: *Chigusa Maru* and *Yamashio Maru*

Having decided that the Navy could not be relied upon to protect troop and supply convoys properly, the Imperial Army converted two 2TL/type tankers under construction at Yokohama on similar lines to the Navy's *Shimano Maru*, with a shorter flight deck, the well decks converted to hangar spaces, and Army artillery. While they were under construction in February 1945 it was planned to turn them also into coal burners. Only *Yamashio Maru* was completed as a carrier, and work on *Chigusa Maru* was stopped in January 1945 when, with the Army in retreat, she became redundant, and she was completed as a cargo ship to play her part in the great Japanese mercantile revival.

The two liners *Akitsu Maru* and *Nigitsu Maru* were also requisitioned by the Army for conversion, able to carry either or both aircraft and landing craft. A flight deck extended for about two-thirds of the ship, their funnel and bridge were retained but shifted to starboard, and an elevator was fitted aft but was not part of the flight deck. A total of 30 planes could be carried and flown off – eight if landing craft filled the hangar/hold. *Akitsu Maru* displaced 11,000 tons, *Nigitsu Maru* 11,800. Both were fitted with a 123 by 22.5m (403ft 6in by 73ft 9in) flight deck on a hull 149m (488ft 6in) long.

Towards the end of the war the Army took over the standard M-type cargo ship *Kumano Maru* on the stocks for an *Akitsu Maru*-type conversion but fitted a full-length flight deck. Her hangar could take 37 planes or 25 landing craft, with extra stowage on the flight deck. Landing craft were launched down ramps and through hinged doors in the stern.

11. THE PRESERVATION OF *U-505*

After the German surrender an American crew took *U-505*, captured by Captain Dan Gallery's CVE *Guadalcanal* on 4 June 1944, cruising on her own power on a War Bond tour of the Atlantic and Gulf coasts of the USA. At the end of the war with Japan she was berthed in the Navy Yard at Portsmouth, New Hampshire.

When two years had elapsed from the end of hostilities, *U-505* would have been scrapped or sunk at sea, following the terms of the Four Power Agreement covering U-boats, but Gallery, by then a Rear-Admiral, argued that this ruling applied only to U-boats surrendered after the war, and urged that *U-505* be preserved, as she belonged to the USA. The parish of Gallery's brother, Father John Ireland Gallery (a former Navy Reserve chaplain with Patrol Wing 7, which had hunted U-boats in the Bay of Biscay), was near the Chicago Museum of Science and Industry, and he thought the U-boat would make a crowd-pulling exhibit there. The Curator, Major Lenox Lohr, was keen to have it, as the museum had been asking the Navy for 24 years for an obsolete submarine. There was just the little matter of moving the U-boat to Chicago.

With the backing of Colonel McCormick's *Chicago Tribune* and other powerful institutions, Captain Gallery got the scrapping of *U-505* stopped, but it took two years for a bill to pass through Congress to permit the Navy to hand it over to the museum. The government offered no help, and the museum had to take possession of the boat at Portsmouth. Early in 1953 Chicago's Mayor Kennelly set up a committee to raise the $250,000 estimated as necessary to cover the move. In 18 months, helped by media coverage, $125,000 cash was raised and the equivalent of the remainder pledged in the form of free services by civic corporations and various professional bodies, such as the Great Lakes Dredging and Dock Corporation, which offered the use of its floating dock.

On 14 May 1954 *U-505* started her journey to Chicago via the Atlantic, the St Lawrence River, the Welland Canal and Lakes Ontario, Erie, Huron and Michigan, towed by the tug *Pauline L. Moran*, and arrived off the Chicago waterfront on Lake Michigan to a civic welcome and salutations by fireboat hoses and hundreds of yachts and pleasure boats, and a reception by the Mayor. After six weeks at Calumet Harbor preparing for beaching, *U-505* was placed in the American Shipbuilding Corporation's 244m (800ft) graving dock for the removal of 96 tons of pig iron ballast from the keel, and 30,000 of fuel oil left in her tanks, then she was moved to the Great Lakes Dredging's floating dock.

The 850-ton submarine normally drew 2.74m (9ft) of water, but to beach her near her museum site she had to be raised 1.2m (4ft) above the level of the lake. A special cradle of steel, timber and cement was constructed, hydraulic jacks boosted it under the hull, then lifted the whole parcel high enough to insert several hundred 50mm (2in) steel rollers between the cradle and railway tracks laid along the bottom of the dock. On the other side of the lake a special pier, strong enough to bear 1,000 tons, and with four rail tracks with heavy timber along the top, was built 15m (50ft) out into the lake from the shore line near the museum, which was conveniently close to the water.

A feature of the Lake's weather is the *seiche*, a sudden heavy surge of water raised by violent thunder storms. There was a *seiche* on the day *U-505* arrived at Chicago which drowned seven men fishing from a pier in Lincoln Park. If a bad *seiche* hit *U-505* during the tow, it could be disastrous. On Friday 13 August two tugs hauled floating dock and submarine from Calumet City, nudged her up the dredged channel and against the pier. A small *seiche* caught the dock, lifting it out of position, but subsided again, and *U-505* was finally beached soon after dark. In the forenoon she was raised

Below: 'Drive carefully – Submarine crossing.' *U-505* waiting to cross Chicago's Outer Drive to her final berth outside the Museum of Science and Industry, Chicago. (Museum of Science and Industry, Chicago)

Bottom: *U-505* in the American Shipbuilding Corporation's graving dock in Calumet Harbour, after her last voyage from Portsmouth, New Hampshire, to Lake Michigan. (Museum of Science and Industry, Chicago)

on 42 mechanical jacks to lift her the 1.3m (4ft 4in) necessary before she could cross the Outer Drive, Chicago's busiest highway.

On the night of 3 September the Outer Drive was closed to traffic at 19:00, rails were laid across the road, and the U-boat dragged across the Drive at the rate of 20cm (8in) per minute. The unique notice 'DRIVE CAREFULLY – SUBMARINE CROSSING' was put up to leave no doubts in the minds of the 15,000 people who stayed up until 04:00 to watch the U-boat's progress. The Drive was open again in time for the morning rush. Just 274m (300yd) more and a 67 degree turn, and *U-505* reached her final berth on a foundation of three concrete cradles outside the museum.

She was anchored to the midships cradle but sat in the bow and stern cradles on 20 pairs of 203mm (8in) steel rollers to allow for temperature variations between winter and summer, which caused the length of the boat to vary by as much as 75mm (3in), and would have cracked the concrete foundations if she had been rigidly secured from stem to stern.

On 25 September 1954 this German submarine was dedicated as a memorial to 55,000 American sailors who had lost their lives at sea in two world wars, by Fleet Admiral William Halsey, whose words of warning in 1940 had helped start the process resulting in the creation of the 128 US-built CVEs of which *U-505*'s conqueror had been one. It seemed a pity that the 'Can Do' herself, or the brave *Bogue* or *Card, Core, Suwannee* or *Santee, Tulagi* or *Tripoli, Cape Gloucester* or *Gilbert Islands*, could not somehow have been set down beside her.

BIBLIOGRAPHY

ANONYMOUS, *HMS Speaker*, Pinnacle Press, Australia, 1946.

BAKER, R., HOLT, W. J., LENAGHAN, J., SIMS, A. J. and WATSON, A. W., *British Warship Design in World War II*, Conway Maritime Press, Greenwich, England, 1983.

BEAVER, Paul, *The British Aircraft Carrier*, Patrick Stephens, Cambridge, England, 1982.

BROWN, David, *The Seafire*, Ian Allan, Shepperton, England, 1973.

– *Carrier Fighters*, Macdonald Jane's, London, England, 1975.

CALHOUN, Captain C. Raymond, USN (Retd.), *Typhoon: The Other Enemy*, Naval Institute Press, Annapolis, USA, 1982.

CHESENAU, Roger, *Aircraft Carriers of the World 1914 to the Present*, Arms and Armour Press, London, England, and Naval Institute Press, Annapolis, USA, 1984.

DRESSER, James, *Escort Carriers and their Markings during World War II in the Pacific*, Ames, Iowa, USA.

FRANCILLON, R. J., *Japanese Aircraft in the Pacific War*, Putnam, London, England, 1970.

FRIEDMAN, Norman, *Carrier Air Power*, Conway Maritime Press, Greenwich, England, 1981.

GILBERT, Commander Price, Jr., USNR, *The Escort Carriers in Action*, Ruralist Press, Atlanta, USA, 1945.

HEINL, Lieutenant-Colonel Robert D., Jr, USMC, *The Marshalls: Increasing The Tempo*, Historical Branch, G-3 Division, Headquarters, US Marine Corps, Washington DC, USA.

HOYT, Edwin P., *How They Won the War in the Pacific*, Weybridge and Talley, New York, USA, 1970; *The Men of the Gambier Bay*, Paul S. Ericson, Middleburg, USA, 1979.

HUMBLE, Richard, *United States Fleet Carriers In Action*, Blandford Press, Poole, England, 1984.

HURREN, B. J., *Perchance*, Nicholson and Watson, London, England, 1949.

JACKSON, Robert, *Strike From The Sea*, Arthur Barker, London, England, 1970.

JENSEN, Lieutenant Oliver, USNR, *Carrier War*, Simon & Schuster, New York, USA, 1943.

JONES, H. A., *The War in the Air*, Clarendon Press, Oxford, England, 1931.

MACINTYRE, Captain Donald, RN, *Wings of Neptune*, Peter Davies, London, England, 1963.

MARSH, Major A., RM (Retd.), *Flying Marines*, Royal Marines Museum, Portsmouth, 1980.

MORISON, Professor Rear-Admiral Samuel Eliot, USNR, *History of United States Naval Operations in World War II*, Little, Brown, Boston, USA, 1947.

MUNSON, Kenneth, *Aircraft of World War Two*, Ian Allan, Shepperton, England, 1962.

POLMAR, Norman, *Aircraft Carriers*, Macdonald, London, England, 1969.

POPHAM, Hugh, *Into Wind: A History of British Naval Flying*, Hamish Hamilton, London, England, 1969.

ROSCOE, Theodore, *On The Seas And In The Skies*, Hawthorne Books, New York, USA, 1970.

SOCIETY OF NAVAL ARCHITECTS OF JAPAN, *Plans of Ships of the Imperial Japanese Navy*, Hara Shoto Co., Tokyo, Japan, 1980.

TERZIBASCHITSCH, Stefan, *Escort Carriers and Aviation Support Ships of the US Navy*, Conway Maritime Press, Greenwich, England, 1981.

THETFORD, Owen, *British Naval Aircraft Since 1912*, Putnam, London, England, 1962.

WATTS, Anthony J., *Japanese Warships of World War II*, Ian Allan, Shepperton, England, 1966.

– and GORDON, B. G., *The Imperial Japanese Navy*, Macdonald, London, England, 1976.

WINTON, John, *The Forgotten Fleet*, Michael Joseph, London, England, 1969.

– *Sink The Haguro*, Seeley Service, London, England, 1979.

– *Convoy*, Michael Joseph, London, England, 1983.

GLOSSARY

Abwehr: German *Wehrmacht* (High Command) Intelligence Service.
Ante-room: Bar adjoining the Wardroom (*see*) in a British warship.
Aniz: Portuguese liqueur made from anise seeds, similar to the French anisette.
'Anti-cavorting chain': Chain clipped on by a Swordfish observer to fasten himself to the cockpit floor.
'Asparagus': German nickname for a periscope, originating before World War I.
ASDIC: Anti-Submarine Detection Investigation Committee, set up by Britain and France in 1918 which gave its name to the very successful apparatus for locating a submerged submarine with a sound wave and calculating its range and bearing. (American 'sonar').
Atoll: A coral reef enclosing a lagoon.
ATS: Auxiliary Territorial Service, the British women's army organization in World War II.
Avgas: Aviation gas (USA), or petrol (GB).
Ballast tanks: Submarine tanks, exterior in most Fleet submarines, which expel or admit sea water for rising or submerging, respectively.
Banana boat: Popular name for the refrigerated fruit-carrying/passenger ships plying between the West Indies or West Africa and Britain. Also applied to CVEs, some of which were converted from such vessels.
'Bandits': Allied R/T (*see*) Procedure term for enemy aircraft.
'Banzai': Literally 'Long, long live!' Japanese cheer, usually repeated three times, and battle-cry. Many charges commenced with the cry 'Banzai dai Nippon!'
'Bandstand': Platform for AA guns aft of the conning tower on U-boats, called *'Wintergarten'* by U-boat men.
Barrier: Two-stranded wire arrester device across the flight deck forward for stopping a landing aircraft which has missed all the arrester wires.
'Bats': Slang for the hand-held indicators used by a carrier's DLCO (Deck Landing Control Officer – RN), or 'batsman', and for the batsman himself (Landing Signals Officer – US Navy).
'Battle of Bull's Run': Pun linking American Admiral William 'Bull' Halsey's final belated dash south to the aid of the escort carriers in the battle for Leyte Gulf with the two battles of Bull Run (or Manassas Junction), both won by the Confederates from the Federal Government of President Abraham Lincoln in the American Civil War of 1861–64.
Battler: British slang for a battleship.
Beau Geste: Famous novel by P. C. Wren about the adventures of the three British Geste brothers in the French Foreign Legion.
bhp: Brake horsepower.
Blackcap: Small bird of the Warbler group, the male with a glossy black crown, body greyish-brown, female red-brown, its song a very rich warbling, which changes to an emphatic 'tac, tac' when alarmed, and a harsh churring.
Blenheim: An RAF light bomber built by Bristol Aircraft, pressed into service as a stop-gap fighter at the time of aircraft shortages in the early air war, 1939–40.
Blimp: Airship.
Bofors: Anti-aircraft quick-firing cannon.
'Bogey': R/T Procedure term for an unidentified aircraft.
Bomb, The: The atomic bomb dropped on the Japanese city of Hiroshima on 6 August 1945 which effectively brought World War II to an end.
Boulder Dam: Built in Black Rock Canyon on the Colorado River at the Arizona-Nevada border between 1930 and 1936, one of the projects initiated by President Roosevelt to provide work during the great Depression of the 1930s.
Bowie knife: Lethal weapon based on the type reputedly carried by the great American frontier scout, Jim Bowie, killed at the siege of the Alamo.
Brake horsepower: The rate at which an engine does work, measured by the resistance of a brake.
Brown jobs: Pejorative RN/RAF slang for soldiers.
Brylcreem Boys: Popular slang for RAF men, conveying the image of a 'spiv', 'smoothie' or 'lounge lizard', leading a soft, easy life free from the hardships of 'real' fighting, particularly that of the footslogger squaddy's (*see*) world of mud, sweat and blood – Brylcreem being a popular hair cream producing a glossy, smoothed-back hair style.
Bullhorn: USN equivalent of the British Tannoy loudspeaker.
Burlap: Coarse canvas for bags and furnishing.
BuShips: US Bureau of Shipping.
Butch: Applied to a woman with a masculine personality.
'Buzz bomb': The V1 missile, built round a small jet engine, launched against London from sites in German-occupied Europe.
Bv: Blohm & Voss, German aircraft manufacturer.
Cable: Maritime unit of distance equal to 100 fathoms, or 600 feet.
Caique: Small Greek sailing vessel.
Camel, Sopwith: Small single-seat British fighter-bomber of World War I. Tricky to fly, the close con-figuration of engine, fuel tank and pilot in a 'hump' (hence its name) made for instability, which caused many fatal crashes, but this factor in the hands of a skilled pilot could be turned to advantage, and the Camel was very successful with the Royal Flying Corps, the Royal Naval Air Service and later the Royal Air Force. A Mk 2FI 'navalized' Camel is on display at the Imperial War Museum, London, and an RFC version at the RAF Museum, Hendon, England.
CAP: Combat Air Patrol, flown by carrier fighters to defend their ships or fleet from enemy air attack.
Capstan: Revolving barrel winch for hauling in anchors and cable.
Casual, A: Small, standardized payment for a sailor whose papers have not yet caught up with him – often the case in the rapid re-drafting of wartime.
CarDiv: Carrier Division (USN).
Carvel-built: In a carvel-built boat the inside thickness of planking is laid at 45° to the keel, the upper ends lying aft, the outside thickness fore-and-aft, with the edges of all planks worked flush. Usually used for gigs (*see*) and power boats.
Casing: Low, usually self-flooding superstructure on a submarine, bearing a narrow deck (of wood in later USN boats) and gun positions, with stowage space inside.
Chasseurs d'Afrique: Famous regiment of French coloured colonial African troops, with white officers.
Chief Buffer: Chief Boatswain's Mate, in charge of a ship's seaman's branch in the Royal Navy. Familiarly known as 'Buffs'.
Chlorine: Yellowish-green poison gas, used in trench warfare in World War I by the Germans, emitted by damaged submarine batteries.
CINCLANT: Commander-in-Chief, Atlantic (USN).
CINCPAC: US Commander-in-Chief, Pacific.
Clinker-built: A method of boat construction in which planks run fore-and-aft, with the lower edge of one plank lapping over the upper edge of the next below, used for smaller pulling boats in the RN, whalers, dinghies, skiffs and some sizes of cutters.
COMINCH: Commander-in-Chief (American).
Commander(F): Commander (Flying), head of a British carrier's flying component.
Corvette: Small escort vessel, many named after flowers, used in large numbers by the RN in the protection of convoys. Would 'roll in drydock/on wet grass'. (*see* HMS *Compass Rose* in Nicholas Monsarrat's epic *The Cruel Sea*).
Creeping attack: Method of attacking a U-boat by the ships of a 'hunter-killer' group, in which an attacking

ship 'crept' silently up on a quarry, guided by another ship using her ASDIC (sonar).
C-wing: A mainplane of the RAF Spitfire VC, used in the Seafire IIC, each wing carrying one 20mm Hispano cannon and two 0.303-in Browning machine-guns. It had been hoped to add an extra pair of cannon to the IIC, but the weight penalty was too great.
Dauntless: Excellent Douglas-built US Navy dive-bomber, operational throughout World War II, outshining its intended replacement, the Curtiss Helldiver, which was put into action prematurely, before some important basic flaws had been removed. Sometimes difficult to land in a strong breeze, because the Dauntless was a 'floater', i.e., its large wing area which made it very stable in the air.
Deadweight (dwt.): The weight in tons of cargo, stores and fuel carried by a merchant ship when down to her loading marks (*see* Plimsoll Line), and equal to a warship's loaded displacement (total weight of ship and contents based on the volume of water displaced, less the weight of the ship, the latter being the lightweight tonnage). The deadweight of a ship is a good indication of her cargo-carrying and earning capacity.
Deckhead: A ceiling aboard ship.
Deflection shot: Burst of machine-gun or cannon fire aimed at the target from an angle, i.e., anywhere but dead ahead or astern.
Depth-charge (DC): Anti-submarine explosive charge set to explode at the quarry's calculated depth, indicated by the ship's ASDICs
DesRon: Destroyer squadron (USN).
Dhobeying: RN term for washing clothes, from the Hindustani, usually done in a bucket with shavings of 'Pusser's' (*see*) soap and scalding water begged from the boiler room or exchanged for 'sippers' of the daily tot of rum.
Dipping lug: A boat's, usually a gig's (*see*) rig, consisting of lug sails (four-cornered sails bent on an unequally slung yard) which can be dipped, i.e., the tack (forward lower corner of a sail) is unhooked and the luff (forward edge of the sail) and yard dipped, for the process of tacking.
Displacement: Displacement tonnage, the total weight of a ship and everything aboard her, derived from the volume of water displaced. Always used in connection with warships, never with merchantmen. Since 1920 Standard Displacement has been used, i.e., the full displacement less the weight of fuel and reserve feed water.
Dolce vita: The 'sweet life' of pleasure (Ital.)
Don: University lecturer.
Drop the hook: To anchor.
Duff: Slang for faulty.
Echo: Reflection of a target on a radar screen, commonly known as a 'blip'.
Enigma: German secret Naval code, intercepted by Allied listening posts and passed to the cryptanalysts of the British Government Code and Cypher School at Bletchley Park in Buckinghamshire, England, for breaking down, in which they had outstanding success. The resultant information was known as Ultra.
Erk: RAF slang for an aircraftsman.
Fairey Albacore: Intended replacement for the Swordfish, but slower.
Fairey Fulmar: British naval fighter named after the fulmar petrel pelagic bird, in front-line service with the carriers and Fighter Catapult Ships in the early years of World War II. Heavily armed with eight forward machine-guns but slowed down disastrously by the unnecessary observer's/air-gunner's cockpit, which also lacked a rear-firing gun. Thompson sub-machine guns, effective on the streets of Chicago, were issued to Fulmar gunners in the Mediterranean but were useless there as their muzzle velocity was too low.
Fantail: Stern (USN).
FDO: Fighter Direction Officer (RN), controlling fighters in the air by reference to his radar plot (*see*) in the ship.
FDR: Franklyn Delano Roosevelt, President of the United States throughout the greater part of World War II.
FFS: Free French Ship.
First Sea Lord: Operations head of the British Admiralty, always a naval officer, in contrast to the First Lord of the Admiralty, a political appointment.
'Fish-head': British naval aviators' name for members of the non-flying Navy, especially backward-looking 'big-gun' senior officers. The less offensive US Navy fliers' equivalent was 'black shoes', there being a tradition that the independent-minded mavericks of Naval Aviation wore brown shoes with their uniforms.
Fixed-wing: (1) Of conventional aircraft as distinct from helicopters.
(2) Of conventional aircraft with non-folding wings.
Flank speed: American for full speed.
'Flat-iron': The nickname for the old British carrier *Argus*, from her general shape, with a flat, flush flight deck (first of its kind in naval aviation) with no obstructions, curving to a point forward.
'Fleet-in-being': The theory that the retaining of a strong battle fleet in harbour ties down so many enemy ships as to make a hostile sortie in strength an unacceptable risk, a policy adopted by the German Navy in both World Wars after early losses at sea.
Flight Convoy: A military convoy of comparatively small operational craft, e.g., Landing Craft (Tank).
F-lighter: The German *Fahrprahm* (sometimes *Marinefahrprahm*), naval general purpose (personnel, stores, arms, etc.) ferry.
'Flat-top': Ugly name for an aircraft carrier.
Four-piper: (Four-stacker) Four-funnelled ship (US), e.g., the 50 old USN destroyers lent to Britain in return for the temporary use of naval bases in waters adjacent to the USA.
Freeboard: The height of a ship's side from the water.
Garotte: Cord used for strangulation.
'General quarters!': USN equivalent of the RN's 'Action stations!' calling all men in a ship to man their positions for battle.
Gig: A 30-foot, carvel-built (*see*) boat with two mahogany skins, fitted with a drop keel. Two masts with dipping lug sails, rather like an Arab how, made it the fastest Service boat under sail, and a spare mast hole in the centre of the boat enabled another mast to be stepped there, e.g., if one mast carried away in rough weather, when wash-strakes (washboards) could also be fitted to give more freeboard (*see*).
Giro compass: The older compass, activated by magnets, points to the earth's magnetic pole, but a giro compass, which is electrically driven, indicates the true North Pole, relying on a spinning wheel which maintains its axis and plane of rotation relative to space.
'Glider bomb': Misleading name given unofficially to the Henschel Hs 293 radio-controlled missile.
Grand Coulee Dam: On the Columbia River in the state of Washington. Another of the projects initiated by President Roosevelt to give work to some of the huge number of unemployed during the 1930s economic depression.
'Grunt': US Service slang for a US Marine.
Graveyard watch: The Middle Watch, midnight to 0400.
Grossadmiral: German equivalent of Fleet Admiral (USN).
Gross register (gt): The total cubic capacity of all enclosed space in a ship at 100cu.ft/ton. Used for general purposes and in general maritime registers.
Gruppe: German equivalent of a Wing establishment (RAF and FAA).
Guz: Sailors' slang for Devonport Barracks, near Plymouth. Officially HMS *Drake*.
Heads: RN term for lavatory, from sailing ship days, when men relieved themselves from positions outboard near the bows, and shouted 'Heads!' in warning.
Hedgehog: Type of Allied anti-submarine missile fired from a launcher on the foc's'le of a hunting surface warship ahead of the bows, enabling the attacking ship to maintain ASDIC contact with the target, whereas depth-charges were dropped from amidships or astern, and the attacker then lost sound contact as she steamed over the submarine's position. However, Hedgehog missiles only exploded on hitting the target, and the precision of attack required was difficult to achieve at any speed.
Heinkel He 111: Slow, poorly armed, and obsolescent German medium bomber. The He 111 lost heavily in combat with RAF Spitfires and Hurricanes in the Battle of Britain, and against Sea Hurricanes and Martlets (Wildcats) in Russian convoys.
Henschel Hs 293: Electronic missile carried by Condors, Heinkel He 177s or Junkers Ju 290As, and guided from them to the target by radio.
HF/DF: High Frequency Direction Finding, the interception of U-boat radio signals, the object being to find the submarine's position by the plotting of two intersecting bearings from separate interceptions. Known familiarly as Huff-Duff.
Holiday: Gap in the clouds.
'Homer': Homing torpedo.
Hot papas: Ratings wearing asbestos suits for rescue work in aircraft fires on the flight deck.
'Huff-Duff': *see* HF/DF.
Hydrophone: Hearing aid for picking up underwater noises.
Icarus: In ancient Greek myth, son of the great inventor Daedalus, who made him a pair of wings secured with wax. Warned not to soar too high into the sun, the rash young aviator defied instructions on his first solo, the wax melted and he fell to his death in the Sea of Crete.
IFF: Identification Friend or Foe. A small transmitter fitted in Allied aircraft sent out a signal which could be picked up on the radar screens of

friendly aircraft or warships to establish its allegiance. RAF Coastal Command aircraft often neglected to switch it on, causing many wild-goose chases by FAA machines.
Imperial Gallon: English cubic measure of capacity containing 277¼ cubic inches.
'Iron Works, The': Name given to the Grumman Aircraft Factory at Bethpage, Long Island, USA.
'Jabo': Junkers Ju 88 (*see*).
Jeb Stuart: Charismatic Confederate cavalry leader in the American Civil War, famous for his daring raids behind Federal lines.
'Jeep carriers': Another nickname for escort carriers, from their small size and utility design.
(jg): Junior grade. A US Navy lieutenant(jg) is the equivalent of a Royal Navy sub-lieutenant.
Junkers Ju 88: Fast German light bomber, used very effectively by maritime units of the Luftwaffe in Norway against Allied convoys sailing to and from Russia, in particular against the ill-fated Convoy PQ17.
Kapitänleutnant: A German senior naval lieutenant.
KG (Kampfgeschwader): Luftwaffe bomber group.
Kimberley, HMS: Destroyer of the 'K' class, sister ship of Earl Mountbatten's famous *Kelly*. *Kimberley* served in the Atlantic and Mediterranean, and was known as 'Cunningham's taxi' from the number of times she transported Admiral Andrew Cunningham, C-in-C, Mediterranean Fleet. She also took Prime Minister Winston Churchill to view the Allied landings in the South of France, Operation "Dragoon".
Knight's Cross: A division of the German Iron Cross.
Knot: A speed of one nautical mile (6,080 feet) per hour.
Konteradmiral: German equivalent of Rear-Admiral in USN and RN.
Korvettenkapitän: German equivalent of lieutenant-commander in USN and RN.
Kriegsmarine: 'War Marine', the German Navy.
KT: *Kriegstransport*, German war transport.
Kubla Khan: 1215–94. Grandson of Genghis Khan, and great Mongol ruler of China, founder of the Ywan Dynasty, patron of pioneer commercial traveller Venetian Marco Polo.
Laager: Park for armoured vehicles, from Boer word for camp.
'Lash up and stow!': Old Royal Navy order to vacate hammocks and lash them and their blankets into a tightly bound sausage for stowage in the space provided.
Laurie Lee: English poet famous for his writings on Spain (*A Rose For Winter*), and autobiographical books (*Cider With Rosie, As I Walked Out One May Morning*, the latter chronicling a walk through Spain just before the Civil War, with the poet earning his bread by playing the violin).
Lead ship: First ship of a new class to go into production.
Lease-Lend: Agreement between Britain and the USA, leasing overseas bases to the USA in return for valuable war equipment and supplies.
'Leatherneck': A US Marine.
Lee-on-Solent: Small Hampshire, England, seaside town, location of the Royal Naval Air Station HMS *Daedalus*, Headquarters of the Fleet Air Arm of the Royal Navy.
Leigh Light: Large airborne searchlight used by anti-U-boat aircraft of RAF Coastal Command to pick out a quarry.
Liberty ship: Type of utility World War II freighter built in large numbers very rapidly by US shipyards, using new all-welding and prefabrication techniques.
Light off: US Navy terminology for British 'light', e.g., 'Light off smoke-screen burners!'
Logistics: The science of moving and supplying fleets or armies.
Lorca: Federico Garcia Lorca, the great Spanish poet famous for his lyrical, often sombre verse based on gypsy themes and folklore, murdered by the Spanish Fascist Falange in the Civil War.
Lugger: Small craft with four-cornered lug sails set fore-and-aft.
Lug sail: Four-cornered sail bent on an unequally slung yard.
'Mae West': Life-jacket with a shape, when inflated, remiscent of the monumental bosom of the actress.
Maquis: French underground resistance.
Marine marker: Device dropped from an aircraft used in daylight or dark to release coloured dye on the water and a flare in the sky.
Marshalling yard: Assembly yard for goods trains.
Messerschmitt Bf 110: Twin-engined German fighter.
Messdeck: Place where the members of a ratings mess live, eat and sleep when off duty.
Messtraps: Cutlery, crockery and kitchen utensils belonging to a mess.
'Milk run': Well-established, regularly-run trip free of surprises.
Mitchell bomber: Standard USAAF Martin Mitchell twin-engined medium bomber.
Monsoon: Strong seasonal wind prevailing in South-East Asia, blowing from the south-west in summer, from the north-east in winter.
Mothball fleet: Warships preserved with plastic coating over all important equipment, for possible future use.
M-type dinghy: Inflatable two-man aircraft raft (RN) for use by observer and telegraphist/air-gunner in, e.g., a Swordfish.
NAAFI: Navy, Army and Air Force Institutes. Included canteens ashore and stores aboard ship supplying consumer goods.
Net register tonnage: Measured in the same way as gross tonnage (the total capacity of all enclosed spaces in a ship), the net register tonnage is the capacity of these spaces less those of the engine room and boiler rooms, crew accommodation, stores, and all spaces necessary for the working of the ship, i.e., the cubic capacity of all *earning* space. Most harbour dues and other charges are calculated on this figure.
OD: Ordinary Seaman (RN).
Oiler: American term for tanker (Brit.).
'Old Ironsides': The famous sailing frigate USS *Constitution*, which distinguished herself against the Royal Navy in the War of 1812, preserved in Boston Harbour and open to the public, the USA's equivalent of Britain's HMS *Victory*, preserved in Portsmouth, except that the US frigate is afloat, and the British line-of-battle ship is not.
Ordinary Seaman: Lowest adult rank in the Seaman Branch of the Royal Navy, above Boy and below Able Seaman.
Oscar: The new acoustic homing torpedo, known for security reasons as the Mark 24 mine, and unofficially as Fido or Wandering Annie, mostly by the Americans, as the B-bomb or Oscar by the British.
Outriggers: Booms extending outboard from a carrier's flight deck to accommodate aircraft for which there was no room elsewhere in the ship, and to keep the flight deck clear for operations.
P-38: Lockheed Lightning twin-tail-boom fighter of the USAAF.
Packet boat: Mail/passenger steamer.
Pancake: Bringing an aircraft down flat on the sea.
Pathfinders: Aircraft preceding an attack to fix the route, find the target and mark its position.
'Pecking': An aircraft making a poor landing and 'pecking' the flight deck with the tip of a propeller blade.
'Peelow': Onomatopoeic version of the French word for pilot, with vulgar double-meaning.
'Pig-boat': US sailors' slang for a submarine.
Pillbox: Small concrete-protected machine-gun position on land.
Plane: Port or starboard, main or upper wing of an aircraft.
Plane handler: Rating assigned to move aircraft on flight or hangar decks.
Plimsoll Line: White line within a circle painted on a merchant ship's side to indicate, when level with the sea, when the ship is legally fully loaded.
Plot: Map recording the general situation in an air/sea battle from radar information, and used to control aircraft.
Poe, Edgar Allen: 19th-Century American writer of powerfully macabre stories which have become classics of literature.
Pollywogs: Greenhorn victims of Father Neptune and his gang in the Crossing the Line ceremony.
Pom-pom: Multi-barrelled long-range Maxim automatic quick-firing anti-aircraft gun.
PPI: Plan Position Indicator. Map-type radar screen covering the whole area round a revolving scanner, which turns through 360°. Became the universal type of radar presentation.
Pressure hull: In terms of basic structure there are four types of submarine: single-hull, double-hull, partial double-hull, and saddle-tank. Early, short-leash submarines like the *Hollands* were single-hulled, which remained suitable for small coastal types, and satisfied the Royal Navy, concerned with operating in the North Sea and German coastal waters. But Germany, the USA and Japan faced long transits to and long patrols in likely operating areas, and copied the French 'submersible', building submarine hulls encased in an outer hull resembling a torpedo-boat, for good surface sea-keeping and to carry deck guns for defence, with diesel engines for fast surface speed, the underwater performance with the less powerful electric motor important only in presence of a target, the inner hull being designed to resist the pressure of the sea and hostile explosions when submerged, and therefore called the *pressure hull*. Between it and the outer hull were located buoyancy tanks and, when welded seams were introduced, oil fuel tanks. Most US Navy submarines of World War II were of partial-double type, double-hulled for two-thirds of their length, amidships. The Royal Navy experimented briefly with the

double hull, but adopted a compromise in which buoyancy tanks were slung athwart the pressure hull like saddlebags.

PT Boat: US Navy equivalent of the British MTB (Motor Torpedo-Boat).

'Pusser': A degenerate form of Purser, in charge of a ship's domestic supplies, hence 'Pusser's soap', etc.

Quarter attack: Also called 'High Side' or 'Beam' attack. A standard fighter tactic for attacking a bomber. From a position 'on the perch' some 500 feet higher than the target, and about 400 yards on the bomber's beam, the fighter pilot turned in towards the target, diving, and reversed the turn to put him on the bomber's tail, giving the latter's gunners problems of height and course deflection shooting all the way in.

RDF: Radio Direction Finding, the early British name for radar.

RDX: Explosive mixture containing TNT (Trinitrotoluine).

Reculer pour mieux sauter: Loosely, 'Withdraw to attack better'.

Regia Aeronautica: The Italian Air Force.

RNB: Royal Naval Barracks.

'Robot bomb': American name for German V1 and V2 guided missiles.

Rolling stock: Railway wagons.

Rotor settings: The German naval Enigma coding machine incorporated three, later four, rotors, each linking a letter of the alphabet to its code equivalent letter for the day, from a list covering six months. Each day the rotors, plus an outer setting ring and a plugboard setting, were altered. British cryptanalysts decoded Enigma signals, and were often able to pass on foreknowledge of U-boat movements.

Round-down: The after end of a carrier's flight deck was curved downwards to prevent a landing aircraft fouling the edge with wheels or arrester hook.

R/T: Radio Telephony. Radio telephonic voice communication between ship and ship, ship and aircraft.

Saki: Japanese rice wine.

Samurai: Old Japanese order of knighthood.

SANF: South African Naval Forces.

Sanders, George: Smooth-mannered British film actor, who incidentally publicized he knee-length 'shorts' worn by Englishmen in the Tropics by appearing in these roles in several films.

Sappho: Early Greek poetess who lived in the island of Lesbos, and was sexually orientated towards women, hence the term 'Lesbian'.

SBD: US Navy code for a scout/dive-bomber, e.g., the Douglas Dauntless.

Scuppers: Drain running round the edge of the deck to divert water overboard.

Scuttle: To sink a ship from inboard, by opening the sea cocks, exploding charges, etc.

Sea cocks: Valves for admitting sea water to a ship for scuttling.

Section: Operational fighter unit of two aircraft.

Seebees: US Navy construction engineers who followed closely the advance of Allied forces, clearing sites, constructing airfields, camps, etc, sometimes finding themelves in combat.

Self-sealing fuel tanks: Gas tanks lined with two layers of sorbo rubber of different consistencies, which close over a bullet hole.

Shakedown (cruise): Period allotted for a ship's company or air party to become acquainted with a new ship and their duties.

Shinto: 'The Way of the Gods'. Indigenous religion of Japan. According to its founding myths, the Great Sky Father sired from the Earth Mother the sacred rocks of the Japanese Archipelago as well as a multitude of lesser, pantheistic gods and goddesses representing all the components of nature: trees, rocks rivers, mountains, flowers, etc, and including the great Sun Goddess Omikami, the 'Heavenly Shining Great Deity', who sent her grandson to earth to take possession of the islands which became Japan. From him descended the family of the Emperors of Japan, who presided over their subjects with absolute divine right. The Emperor was the keystone of a rigidly paternalistic, formalized society and a harsh moral code of absolute obedience to superiors, including the family elders, whose lordship extended beyond the grave in a form of ancestor worship stimulated by contact with Buddhism. Exotic and elaborate ceremonies helped the perpetuation of the faith.

Short seaplanes: Mainstay bombers of the Royal Naval Air Service, later the Fleet Air Arm of the Royal Air Force, in World War I. Short S.27 Biplane No. 38, fitted with flotation bags, made the first British and second world aircraft launch from a ship in 1909, which was followed by the production of the S.41, the first wing-folding naval aircraft. Shorts made the first seaborne attack on a shore target (Cuxhaven, Christmas Day, 1914), and one of the best Short types, the 184, made the first successful anti-shipping torpedo strike by sinking a Turkish supply ship in the Dardanelles.

Siebel ferry: German general-purpose supply boat.

Slick: Tell-tale trail of oil upon the sea.

SOC Seagull: US Navy Curtiss-built single-float seaplane.

SOE: Senior Officer, Escort (RN).

Splicing the mainbrace: Allocation of a second, extra, tot of rum to celebrate some special event, e.g., VE-Day.

Spotting the deck: Arranging aircraft on the flight deck in the most practical way with reference to operations.

Squaddies: Services slang for soldiers.

Squeegee: Straight-edged rubber mop for pushing water into the scuppers.

Squid: Allied ship-borne anti-submarine missile, launched from the foc's'le, like Hedgehog (*see*), but superior to the latter in being set to explode at the target's depth, provided by special depth-finding ASDIC.

Staffel: Squadron (Ger.).

Standard Displacement: *see* 'Displacement'.

Starshell: Shell fired at a high elevation with a fuze timed to burst its casing and release a flare on a parachute to illuminate an enemy ship or fleet at night.

Stateside: The USA.

Static: Radio atmospheric interference caused by electrical discharges in the atmosphere.

St. Elmo's Fire: Incandescent electrical discharge occasionally seen on the upperworks of a ship in bad weather, also called corposant (from Spanish/Italian *corpo santo*, 'holy body').

Stream (verb): Put into the water, e.g., minesweeping gear.

Sundowner: A sunset drinker.

Swanny (Suwannee) range: Arrangement of aircraft, e.g., the Seafire in its fighter-bomber form, needing as long a take-off run from the flight deck as possible, with the aircraft lining the sides, pointing aft, and each taking off using the full length of the deck as it reached the round-down, as distinct from a mass take-off with the machines ranged in ranks, pointing forward. Pronounced 'Swanny' by RN aviators, but thought to have been invented aboard the US Navy oiler-CVE *Suwannee*, perhaps by the great 'Jocko' Clark himself, her Captain in Operation "Torch".

T124 Articles: Articles signed by British Merchant Navy officers joining the Royal Naval Reserve, by which they retained certain privileges of the MN.

Tac-R: Tactical reconnaissance.

Talker: Communications number in a gun's crew.

Talker and Teller (US Navy): Rating whose duty it was to report the state of preparedness 'Wheels down, hook down!', etc., of an aircraft preparing to land aboard a carrier to his Landing Signals Officer (RN 'batsman').

Thach Weave: Fighter formation pair manoeuvre invented by Lieutenant John S. Thach, USN to give the Wildcat F4F-3 a better chance against the superior speed and manoeuvrability of the Zero. Tested in combat by Thach and his wingman, US Navy fighter ace, Lieutenant Edward 'Butch' O'Hare, famous for destroying five Japanese aircraft in one engagement. Called the 'Scissors' by the RN. The two fighters of the section pair made successive turns to port and starboard in a 'scissoring' pattern across each other's flight path, which improved the lookout fields of both pilots and put each in a good position to protect the other's tail and go to his help at any point in the manoeuvre if he were attacked. The Weave became a standard defensive/offensive tactic in enemy air space. Pilots would begin 'scissoring' at the start of a patrol 'and just go on doing it', said one US Navy Corsair pilot.

Three-point landing: Landing in which the two main undercarriage wheels and the tail (or nose) wheel touch the deck at the same time – the sign of a good pilot.

Tidal bore: Tidal wave of exceptional height rushing up an estuary.

'Tinfish': RN slang for torpedo.

'Torpecker': USN slang for a torpedo, from the use of the high explosive Torpex (*see*) in many warheads.

Torpex: The most powerful of all non-atomic military explosives in World War II, a cast mixture of RDX (a mixture containing TNT), TNT and aluminium. Used in torpedo warheads.

Trimmed-down: A submarine ballasted so that only the conning tower is above water.

Trunnion: Projection on each side of a gun barrel enabling it to rest on and work in the carriage.

TSR: Torpedo/spotter/reconnaissance, a pre-World War II Fleet Arm aircraft formula, which produced, among other types, the Fairey Swordfish.

'Turkey': USN slang for a torpedo-bomber, particularly the Avenger.

'Turkey Shoot': The great 'Marianas Turkey Shoot' during the battle of the Philippine Sea, 19–20 June 1944, when aircraft of the US 5th Fleet under Admiral Ray Spruance destroyed 402 out of 545 Japanese aircraft for a loss of 17 of their own.

'Tween decks: Below.

'U-bird': US Vought Corsair naval fighter, from the shape of its inverted gull wing.

Ultra: *see* Enigma.

UNRRA: United Nations Repatriation and Rehabilitation Agency.

VC: US Navy code. (1) An average escort carrier's 'Composite Squadron', a mixture of fighter and bomber flights. The larger *Sangamon* class of converted oilers operated an air *group*, comprising three squadrons, fighter, torpedo-bomber and dive-bomber, the latter being dropped in early 1944. (2) A bomber squadron in a USN Fleet carrier.

VF: US Navy code for a fighter squadron.

VG: US Navy code for the air group of one of the larger *Sangamon* and *Commencement Bay* class escort carriers (comprising ultimately a squadron of fighters and one of bombers, VF and VC (*see*).

VHF: Very High Frequency (radio).

Waafs: Members of the WAAF (Women's Auxiliary Air Force).

Warbler: Any of several small songbirds, with a slender bill and sleek plumage.

Wardroom: The officers' mess in a warship of the RN and USN, traditionally located in the after part of the ship, but in some World War II ships, e.g., American or Canadian-built Fleet minesweepers, in the forward part.

Warhead: The nose of a torpedo, carrying high-explosives.

Wellington: Twin-engined Vickers Wellington bomber of unorthodox geodetic construction (a lattice type fuselage instead of the orthodox combination of frames and stringers, which enabled 'Wimpeys' to survive heavy damage). Also used against U-boats by RAF Coastal Command, and as torpedo-bombers in the Mediterranean. Designed by the famous Dr. Barnes Wallis, who later invented the spherical 'skip' bomb which breached the Eider and Mohne Dams in Germany, and the 'swing-wing' aircraft, which Britain neglected and the US developed into the F1-11 bomber.

Wight Seaplane: Early World War I British seaplane specially designed at Cowes on the Isle of Wight, Hampshire, by J. Samuel White as a torpedo-bomber for the RNAS, with big 5-bay, 63-foot wings, which folded in the production version. The prototype was displayed in the exhibition at Olympia, London, in February 1913, and saw service in the Mediterranean.

Wingman: Second pilot in a Section Pair formation.

Whaler/whaleboat: A 25-foot or 27-foot yawl-rigged pulling or sailing boat fitted with a drop keel, clinker-built (*see*), constructed of Wych or Sand Elm in England or mahogany in Malta (RN).

Wrens: Members of the WRNS (British Women's Royal Naval Service).

W/T: Wireless Telegraphy, i.e., signalling in Morse Code.

Yawl rig: Two-masted arrangement in a vessel, in which the mainmast, forward, carries a stay sail and a standing lug mainsail, the small after (mizzen) mast a small leg-of-mutton sail fitted with a boom.

Zeus: King of the Gods in the ancient Greek pantheon.

Right: Major Alan Marsh, Royal Marines (Retired) alongside the Wildcat Mk I AL246 in which he flew with 802 Squadron FAA, preserved in the Fleet Air Arm Museum, Yeovilton, England. (Maj A. Marsh)

INDEX

GENERAL

ALL THE KAISER'S MEN

Deutschland

Und wenn uns nichts mehr übrig blieb
So blieb uns doch ein Schwert,
Das zorngemut mit scharfem Hieb
Dem Trotz des Fremdlings wehrt.

So blieb die Schlacht als letzt Gericht
Auf Leben und auf Tod,
Und wenn die Not nicht Eisen* bricht,
Das Eisen bricht die Not.

Emanuel Geibel

Germany

And if nothing else to us be left,
There still remains the sword,
Which boldly wielded with fierce cleft
Defies the enemy horde.

Thus combat unto death we make,
Last arbiter indeed,
For if need will not iron* break,
Then iron shall break the need.

* *Eisen*/iron = sword

Quoted in Sven Hedin, *With the German Armies in the West* (John Lane, the Bodley Head, London, 1915), p. 79.

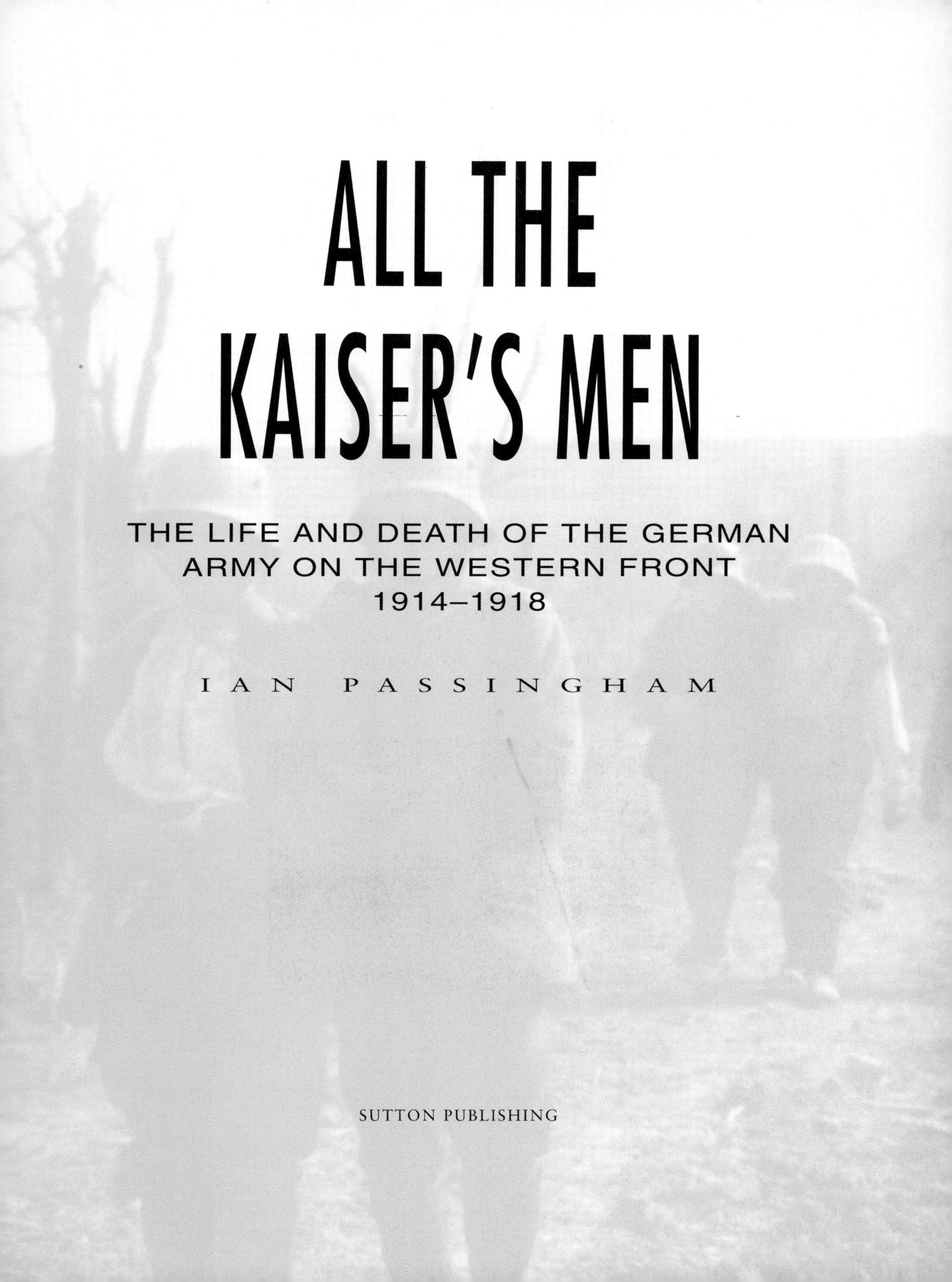

ALL THE KAISER'S MEN

THE LIFE AND DEATH OF THE GERMAN ARMY ON THE WESTERN FRONT 1914–1918

IAN PASSINGHAM

SUTTON PUBLISHING

First published in 2003 by
Sutton Publishing Limited · Phoenix Mill
Thrupp · Stroud · Gloucestershire · GL5 2BU

British Library Cataloguing in Publication Data
A catalogue record for this book is available from the British Library.

ISBN 0-7509-2881-6

Typeset in 11/14pt Sabon.
Typesetting and origination by
Sutton Publishing Limited.
Printed and bound in England by
J.H. Haynes & Co. Ltd, Sparkford.

CONTENTS

To

John Terraine

for whom truth, context and balance
are the most effective items
in a military historian's kitbag;

and to

All the Kaiser's Men –

who lived, loved and died
in the same way as their enemies,
but whose courage, endurance and sacrifice
were betrayed by Germany's
first great catastrophe.

To Germany (Autumn 1914)

You are blind like us. Your hurt no man designed,
And no man claimed the conquest of your land.
But gropers both through fields of thought confined
We stumble and we do not understand.
You only saw your future greatly planned,
And we, the tapering paths of our own mind,
And in each other's dearest ways we stand,
And hiss and hate. And the blind fight the blind.

When it is peace, then we may view again
With new-won eyes each other's truer form
And wonder. Grown more loving-kind and warm
We'll grasp firm hands and laugh at the old pain,
When it is peace. But until peace, the storm,
The darkness and the thunder and the rain.

Charles Hamilton Sorley

ILLUSTRATIONS AND MAPS

MAPS

ACKNOWLEDGEMENTS

My interest in the First World War did not begin formally at school, where the Tudor, Stuart and Georgian eras more occupied my history, but with a play, *Journey's End*, by R.C. Sherriff. What captured my imagination more than any other part of this remarkable drama was that it was set on the eve of the great German offensive of 1918. My curiosity led me to read Erich Maria Remarque's *All Quiet on the Western Front* and after that, the history books. Since then, I have been fortunate enough to serve in the Army myself and to understand that little bit more about the experience of military life in peace and war. Half of my career was spent in Germany/Berlin within the British Army on the Rhine (BAOR) as part of NATO, and in Berlin as a liaison officer to the former Soviet forces stationed in the German Democratic Republic (GDR). From these roots has grown an abiding interest in German history, culture and the German people, who have a great deal more in common with the British than we often acknowledge.

The First World War turned so many 'certainties' on their heads, not least of which was the dramatic reversal of alliances, especially those between Great Britain and France (traditional enemies), and that of Great Britain with Prussia/Germany as traditional allies. All this has led me to wonder precisely what the true experience of the German soldier was like between 1914 and 1918, and at the other end of the scale, whether German leadership was genuinely superior to that of the Allies during the First World War.

I have been privileged to carry out research on this book in places far and wide and, as usual, sources range from individual testament or memory of loved ones through a considerable wealth of primary and secondary sources, many of which have been translated from the 'notorious' German Gothic script, and other excellent studies of all aspects of the battles, campaigns, strategy, doctrine, leadership and tactics of the First World War on the Western Front in particular. While every effort has been made to acknowledge copyright holders of the references and illustrative material used in *All the Kaiser's Men*, should any copyright holders inadvertently have been omitted, I would urge them to contact the publishers directly.

I have received particular help from the Bundesarchiv, Imperial War Museum, Public Record Office, the Liddle Collection at the University of Leeds, Australian War Memorial and the German Historical Institute and hope that their advice, assistance and genuine interest in my efforts to realise my aim will be rewarded. The Imperial War Museum has provided continual support through its Department of Printed Books, Documents and Mapping Department, Photographic and Sound Archives, as well as the Reading Room and Library. Thanks to all the staff, I have been able to read and use extracts especially of captured letters, diaries, individual memoirs, and German regimental and other unit histories. My thanks go also to Renate and Oliver Farley, for their poignant family history of Renate's father, Robert and his brothers Karl and Alois, as well as that of Valentine Kühns.

As ever, I am immensely grateful for the support and encouragement of members of the Western Front Association (WFA), British Commission for Military History (BCMH) and the many travellers with Holts' Battlefields and History Tours who have shown a real desire to have a German version of the events of the First World War that they so diligently study and on which they spend time travelling to 'see the ground'. Of a large cast of fellow enthusiasts, whose knowledge and passion for the subject will always continue across social as well as working hours I wish to acknowledge the help of Peter Simkins, Michael Orr, Stuart Sampson, Kathy Stevenson, Jules Lyne, Bill Philpott, Isabel Swan, John Lee, Leslie Graham and Tony Cowan, among others. I would particularly acknowledge the assiduous and excellent efforts of Joy Thomas in bringing the British Official History to new life with extracts of the detailed German information held therein and so often missed or ignored. My special thanks go to Giles Allen for access to his outstanding collection of First World War memorabilia.

In general terms, studies of this great conflict have paid lip-service to the actual conditions for the troops on the other side of no-man's-land while acknowledging the 'mud, blood and horror' of life for the Tommy or the *Poilu* (French soldier). This is by no means the full picture, for tremendous strides have been made in considering Germany and the Central Powers as part of the equation and excellent studies are now available.

What I believe is still missing is a narrative account of all the Kaiser's men, particularly in the main theatre of war between 1914 and 1918 – the Western Front. Though not claiming to be in any way a definitive academic analysis of the German Army in the First World War, I trust that *All the Kaiser's Men* will give a wider readership an insight into the life and death of the German Army at that time to set against their knowledge of the British, Dominion or French experience.

Dr Correlli Barnett and John Terraine have been particular inspirations to me across the years, not least because of their outstanding contribution to the BBC's 'Great War' television series and their unwavering determination to inject objectivity into such an emotive subject as the First World War.

My thanks go also to Sutton Publishing for taking me on for a second time and to Jonathan Falconer, Nick Reynolds *et al.* for helping to take the manuscript, photographs, maps and diagrams and magically produce the book, a process that still fascinates me at every turn.

Last, but by no means least, I could not have even contemplated this work without the extraordinary forbearance and understanding of Sally, JJ and Eleanor. I hope that they will consider it worthwhile also.

PREFACE

Anyone who has ever looked into the glazed eyes of a soldier dying on the battlefield will think hard before starting a war.

Count Otto von Bismarck
(Speech to the Reichstag, Berlin, 1867)

The Great War, or First World War, gained such titles from the unprecedented scale on which it was fought from the outset. There had never been so great a concentration of armed force in world history as that which formed the respective blocs ranged against each other in August 1914. Each of the major continental armies, namely those of Germany, France, Austro-Hungary and Russia, had over one million men in the field and millions in reserve.

The only exception, as a key player on the Western Front, was Great Britain, with an Army of less than 500,000 and a mere 120,000 assigned to the British Expeditionary Force, or BEF. But Great Britain was not a continental, but a world power, with an empire that covered over a third of the globe. As an island-nation with imperial interests, its military strength relied on the then unchallenged supremacy of the Royal Navy, rather than a large standing Army.

Although Wellington and Napoleon and their generals had developed strategies and tactics based on the use of thousands of men almost a century before, in 1914 commanders such as Joffre and von Moltke were dealing daily with millions. Furthermore, these were millions armed with weapons more accurate, quick-firing and deadly than ever before. If the strategy and tactics were difficult enough, the logistical implications were a nightmare. But by 1914, the movement of men and *matériel* had also changed beyond all recognition since the last great European conflict of the Napoleonic era.

The sheer scale of the conflict determined the nature of the war itself. Plans drawn up by Germany, France and Russia prior to the hostilities envisaged rapid victory through swift mobilisation and then the prompt despatch of the vast armies to the forward battle zone via train. In short, the nation's rolling stock and railway timetables held the key to success. Once the armies were in place, it was believed that the offensive spirit, eloquently labelled by the French as *l'attaque à l'outrance*, would win the campaign – and the war – in weeks, rather than months or years.

The British provided the only coherent voice of reason at this stage, despite the popular enthusiasm for war that had gripped the people of all the nations that were then tumbling headlong towards Armageddon. Lord Kitchener, Secretary of State for War, warned his Cabinet colleagues that this would be no swift, victorious campaign. Rather, it would more likely stretch across a minimum of three years and with concomitant serious loss of life on both sides.

More poignantly, as war was officially announced in Great Britain and the crowds amassed in London and sang 'God Save the King', delighted at the great adventure on which they were about to embark, Foreign Secretary Sir Edward Grey had already seen the true apparition of the war about to unfold. Standing in a Foreign Office window with a colleague as the lamps were lit across St James's Park, he remarked sorrowfully: 'The lamps are going out all over Europe; we shall not see them lit again in our lifetime.'

On the other side, where we shall dwell in this book, the enthusiasm and arrogance of a nation that was more certain than any other of its destiny in this war, attitudes were very, very different. On 4 August, when Germany had declared war on Belgium and immediately violated her borders, Britain, under the terms of the Treaty of London of April 1839, ordered general mobilisation and issued an ultimatum. In Berlin, the British Ambassador, Sir Edward Groschen, presented the ultimatum papers to Chancellor Theobald von Bethman-Hollweg. The German Chancellor was incandescent over what he regarded was hypocritical harping on Belgium, which in his opinion was not the reason for Britain's decision to go to war. He stated that:

> England is doing an unthinkable thing in making war on a kindred nation . . . it was like striking a man from behind while he was fighting for his life against two assailants and as a result of this terrible step, England would be responsible for the dreadful events that might follow . . . [and this would be] all from just a word, 'neutrality'. Just for a scrap of paper Great Britain is going to make war on a kindred nation!

The ultimatum was rejected and Britain and Germany were at war.

But this time, the historical precedent of English and Prussian alliance against France had been turned on its head. The spirit of Wellington and Blücher was forgotten and Britain and Germany were enemies that were by now politically polarised. By the end of August their young men, many of whom had family and friends in the other country and whose cultural heritages were so closely tied, would be fighting each other in the land that had been so often the land of their mutual enemy, France.

It was ironic that in his invective against 'England', Bethmann-Hollweg had unwittingly used the phrase, 'like striking a man from behind while he was fighting for his life'. Four years later, German agitators would attempt to explain away Germany's defeat by accusing Socialist and Jewish politicians of 'stabbing Germany in the back' when she was fighting for her life. Neither accusation was true, of course, but each had a palliative effect for those who were leading Germany into a dark and bloody place.

By 5 August, Britain was transformed into Germany's most hated enemy. '*Gott strafe England*' ('God strike England') was on the lips of almost every German soldier, woman and child, convinced that they had been betrayed by an old friend. Crowds pelted the British Embassy in Berlin with stones and enraged Berliners described this betrayal as '*Rassen verrat*', or 'racial treason'. Many Germans sincerely believed that they were about to fight a 'defensive' war, believing that they were surrounded by hostile neighbours, all with evil intent.

Now even Britain had joined in the conspiracy as far as they were concerned. Many had not conceived of such a thing, having witnessed a Britain in decline on their visits to friends and family there in recent years. They had believed that social unrest was rife, authority diminished and that with a small, though professional army, Britain would have no stomach for a fight against Germany as the great new military and industrial power in Europe. They were to be proved so wrong.

But as the drama over Britain's entry into war and the reaction to it was played out, the Kaiser was predicting triumph, and quickly, to the delirious crowds in Berlin. Confident that his divine destiny was to lead Germany to the promised land of European – and then global – supremacy, he exhorted his troops as they departed for the front in early August with the imperial prophecy that:

> You will be home before the [autumn] leaves have fallen . . . The only countries that have made progress and become great were warring nations; those which have not been ambitious and gone to war have amounted to nothing.

However, the only German troops to return home before the leaves fell across Germany in the autumn of 1914 would be the thousands of wounded men who had become the first few of millions who would suffer the same fate – crippled, blinded or mentally afflicted by the horrors of a war that Germany had been so confident of winning at the outset.

As to being a successful warring nation, Germany would need two wars to finally come to terms with the fact that the noble Prussian military tradition on which she was founded as a nation state in 1871 was, for all its strengths, the very architect of its nemesis in 1918 and 1945.

Let there be no further illusions about the whys and the wherefores, the point, pointlessness, or apparent futility of the First World War between 1914 and 1918. The why, the point and the justification for the conflict were, and remain, rooted in containing the over-weaning ambition of a militaristic Germany.

The nation state of Germany was the prize for crushing the French in the Franco-Prussian War of 1870–71. Otto von Bismarck, the 'Iron Chancellor', brilliantly, but all too briefly, guided this fledgling nation. But goodwill and good intentions were blatantly tossed aside under the misguided leadership of Kaiser Wilhelm II. Germany, the 'new kid on the block' in Europe, rapidly became the 'new bully on the block'.

In August 1914, the US Ambassador to the Court of St James in London, Walter Hines Page, wrote: 'German militarism, which is the crime of the last fifty years, has been working towards [war] for twenty-five years. It is the logical result of their spirit and enterprise and doctrine. It had to come.'

Page had summed it up perfectly; the First World War was the inevitable result of German economic and industrial progress, coupled with an avowed militarism, from the outset.

It is no coincidence that the German term for the period 1914 to 1918 was always *Weltkrieg*, or 'World War', whereas in Britain it was principally known as the Great War, rather than the First World War or World War One and in France, *La Grande Guerre* was preferred to *La Première Guerre Mondiale*.

When Bismarck was forced out of office in 1890, his steady hand on the tiller was lost and the military, enthusiastically encouraged by the ambitious Kaiser, gradually, inexorably, tore the fabric of democracy apart. Ultimately, the Kaiser saw the military as the one and only true symbol of Germany's rise to European and global influence.

Coupled with this psychological export of Germany's symbolic power via the 'Prussian military tradition' between 1871 and 1914, Germany's industrial and technological progress in the same period was astonishing. Naturally, it suited the Kaiser and his generals that this progress was hitched strongly to the burgeoning power of the armed forces.

But with rapid industrial and technological advances came equally swift social change. An overwhelmingly rural population was transformed into an increasingly urban one, as well as a population that had expanded from 11 million in 1871 to almost 40 million by 1914.

Sweeping educational reforms, which emphasised higher and technical education, led to Germany's claim on some of the most prominent and brilliant chemists, engineers and pioneers in the electrical and communications industries, as well as the 'third dimension' of aviation, in which Count Graf von Zeppelin led the world.

The rapid increase in the strength of the German Navy was more than matched by that of merchant shipping and German trade, which was becoming truly global by the turn of the century. Industrial expansion was underlined by the truly astounding increase in coal and steel production – the very foundation of the modern state at that time.

All in all, Germany had come from nowhere as a nation and impressed the world. But this collective achievement in only four decades between 1871 and 1914 had sinister undertones. In the minds of the Kaiser and the military hierarchy, Germany's social, industrial and economic evolution was not only proof-positive that Germany was becoming a great nation, but also that she now possessed the infrastructure, manpower and resources for war.

Lord Haldane, statesman and British Minister for War between 1906 and 1911, knew Germany well – and understood the origin of the First World War more clearly than most. He wrote:

> The reason [for war] appears to have been at some period in 1913 the German Government finally lost the reins on the necks of men whom up to then it had held in restraint. The decision appears to have been allowed at this point to pass from civilians to soldiers . . . It is not their business to have the last word in deciding between peace and war.

Germany was unquestionably at the heart of the bloody conflicts that marked the first half of the twentieth century. Therefore, Germany must be the place to go to fully understand the context, rather than the myth, of the First World War.

It is a journey worth taking.

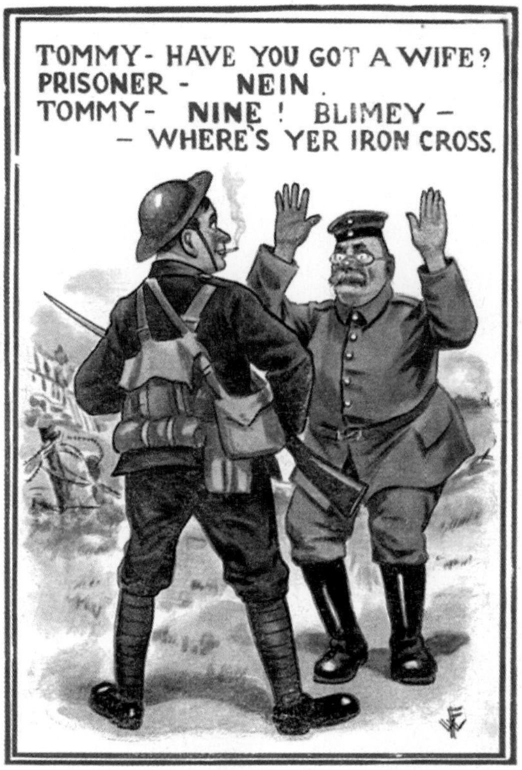
TOMMY- HAVE YOU GOT A WIFE?
PRISONER - NEIN.
TOMMY- NINE ! BLIMEY -
- WHERE'S YER IRON CROSS.

INTRODUCTION

The reader will appreciate that *All the Kaiser's Men* is a title that is not accurate for the 'purist', as the book deliberately concentrates on the German experience of the First World War on the Western front, the main theatre of war throughout the momentous events of 1914 to 1918. Nevertheless, with the collapse of Russia in 1917, the transfer of a million-or-so German troops from that theatre to the west and the German offensive/defensive campaigns on the Western front throughout 1918, the vast majority of the troops of the German Army were fated to serve on the Western front at one stage or another of the war. I hope that the book will be read with this in mind and that the narrative will be both accessible and fascinating.

References and research sources from German archives can be a mixed blessing, as much that was published from 1933 onwards would have had the dead hand of the National Socialist regime's propaganda ministry scrawled across it if it did not conform to the myths and blatant untruths that were peddled about the origins and conduct of the First World War. Nevertheless, providing the reader is reasonably well-versed in the history of that era and is prepared to keep an open mind, the sources dating from 1933 can, and should, still be regarded as important documents.

I have attempted to ensure that all abbreviations are used in full initially throughout the text and include most where appropriate in the glossary also. Where relevant, I have included translations of phrases and all of the poetry included in the book, and of many of the principal documents referred to either in the end notes or the bibliography.

Place names corrupted by soldiers on both sides, such as 'Wipers' for the Belgian town of Ypres, are included in their original and 'corrupted' manner and where German place names differ from either the French or Belgian original, e.g. *Ypern* for Ieper or Ypres, they are shown in italics.

The study has drawn heavily on both the German official history *Weltkrieg* (with the 'Government Health Warning' given in these notes), *Ypern 1914* and the extraordinary alternative *Weltkrieg* by Rudolf Stratz, as well as diaries and memoirs that range widely from those of personalities such as Ludendorff, Hindenburg and Crown Prince Rupprecht of Bavaria to those of prominent soldiers like Ernst Jünger and ordinary men such as Edwin Valentine Kühns, Alois and Albert Mühmelt and Herbert Sulzbach. These have been an endless source of revelation and fascination in my research. I would also recommend the *British Official History*, which has a wealth of translated information on German actions, attitudes and leadership issues in its voluminous footnotes and special sections on the German experience of a particular battle or campaign throughout, much of which has not been tapped by readers hitherto. Naturally, many other primary and secondary sources were used, as the text and bibliography will reflect. Where possible, maps are of German origin.

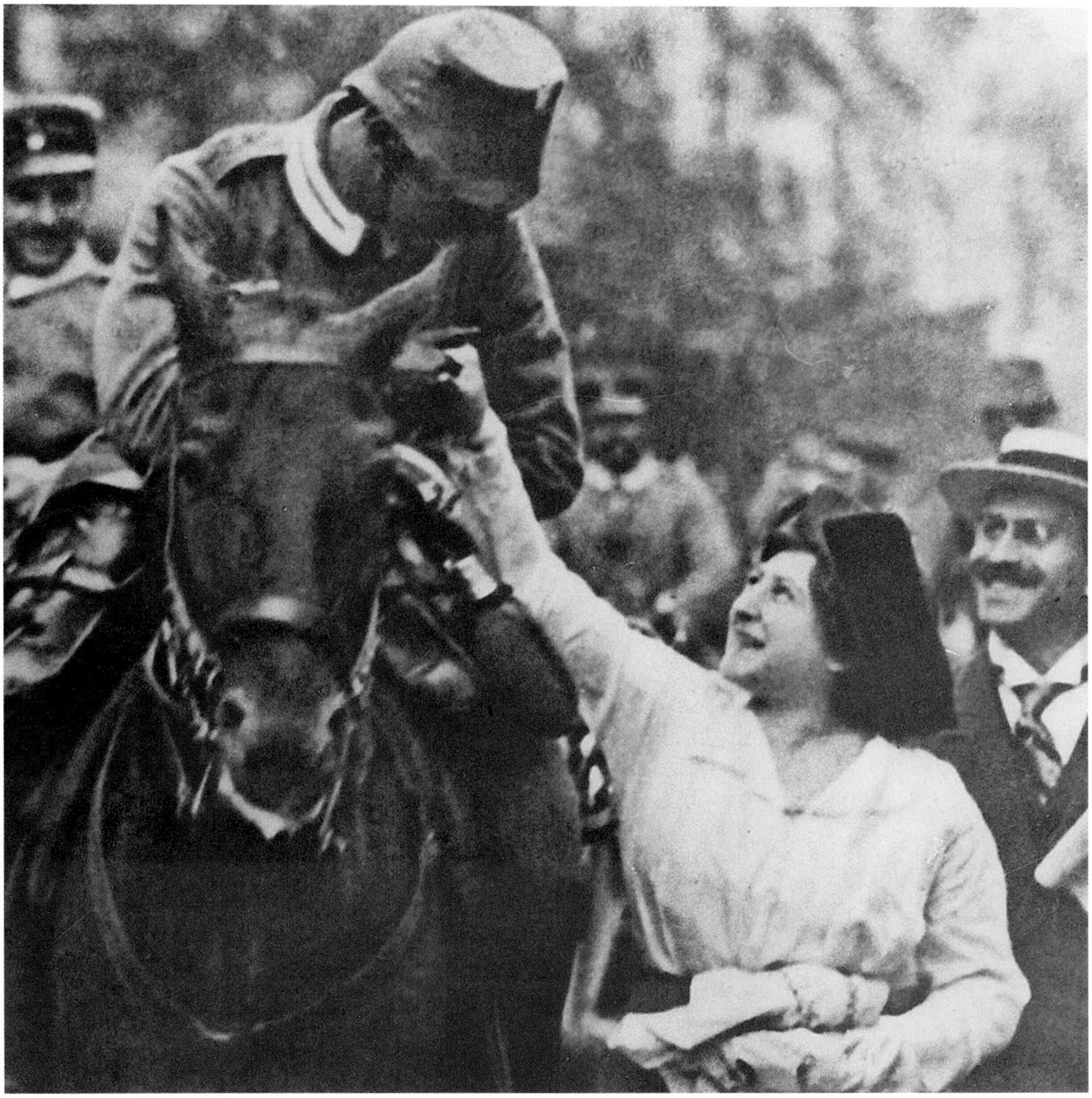

Kaiser Wilhelm II.
(Bundesarchiv)

Chancellor Otto von Bismarck.
(Camera Press, London)

CHAPTER 1

ROOTS OF CONFLICT: 1871–1914

'Where the army marches, all Germany marches too.'

In 1887, as Friedrich Engels predicted, less than two decades after the pivotal German victory in the Franco-Prussian war, that the next conflict, namely the First World War, would be fought on a scale and in conditions without precedent. It would lead to nothing less than the destruction of empires, monarchies and the notion of divine right for hereditary rulers:

> . . . [This fledgling state] – Prussia-Germany – can no longer fight any war but a world war; and a world war of hitherto unknown dimensions and ferocity. Eight to ten million soldiers will strangle each other and in the process decimate Europe . . . The ravages of the Thirty Years War telescoped into three or four years and extended to the entire European continent. It will lead to famine, pestilence and the general barbarization of both the armies and peoples of the competing nations. It will end in general bankruptcy and the collapse of the old state and traditional statecraft . . .[1]

But despite the huge political and social upheavals, as well as the enormous sacrifice for most of the nations embroiled in the First World War, the nature of the war's end and of the Treaty of Versailles would sow the seeds of another even greater worldwide conflict a mere generation later.

For Germany, with almost two million dead and approximately seven and a half million wounded, maimed, crippled and destitute soldiers returning to a country half-starved by the Allied blockade and woeful military and political mismanagement between 1914 and 1918, it looked as if it would be impossible for the German people to contemplate another major conflict.

And it seemed to be unthinkable that Germany would use military force again once it entered an era of democracy – the Weimar Republic – and despite the serious economic difficulties that were to beset it and the rest of the world in the 1920s and early 1930s.

But the impossible and the unthinkable happened. The real tragedy was that its roots were firmly embedded in Germany's experience of the First World War and a national psyche that accepted authority and believed the idea that Germany was destined for greatness and ultimately the leading role on the world stage.

Germany's fate throughout the first half of the twentieth century was fixed by her evolution as a nation state following the Franco-Prussian War of 1870–71. The fulcrum was the First World War – where German plans for European and global dominance, combined with military arrogance, dictatorship and a flawed strategy led only to political and military collapse in the summer and autumn of 1918. Sadly, the German Army was not forced to surrender unconditionally and the hard-won Allied military victory was undermined by the subsequent political failure of the Versailles Treaty.

In 1872 the German socialist Wilhelm Liebknecht had explained to a baffled British visitor: '[To understand] Germany, you must first grasp the fact that this new nation is like an inverted pyramid. Its apex, firmly embedded in the ground, is the spike on the top of the Prussian soldier's helmet. Everything rests on that.'

The Army, principally represented and led by Prussian influence, was unencumbered by constitutional restraints. The Chancellor and mentor of a unified Germany and the 'Second Reich' was Count Otto von Bismarck, the Iron Chancellor. He set about making the newly ascendant and confident Germany the strongest economic power in Europe, granting generous concessions to industry and creating a stable currency.

For the years after 1871, Bismarck enjoyed the support of a compliant Kaiser, namely Wilhelm I. When he died in March 1888, he was succeeded by his 57-year-old son Friedrich III, the husband of Queen Victoria's eldest and favourite daughter 'Vicky'.

Friedrich was a great admirer of British parliamentary institutions and envisioned a democratic Germany. Indeed, during the Franco-Prussian War, he had noted in his diary:

> I maintain even today that Germany could have conquered morally, without 'blood and iron' [in Bismarck's phrase] . . . It will be our noble but immensely difficult task in the future to free the dear German Fatherland from the unfounded suspicions with which the World looks upon it today. We must show that our newly-acquired power is not a danger, but a boon to humanity.

But it was not to be. Friedrich was Kaiser for a mere 99 days and died of throat cancer on 15 June 1888.

His 29-year-old son became Kaiser Wilhelm II. The difference between 'Kaiser Bill' and his predecessors could not have been more stark, for he immediately set about dashing any hope of a benign democracy within Germany. He hated constitutionalism and the power of political parties and he despised his father's liberal thinking.

Above all, he resented Bismarck's well-established authority and the personal respect that he enjoyed throughout Germany. Wilhelm refused to subordinate himself to the aging chancellor. Bismarck, on the other hand, remarked that: 'The new Kaiser is like a balloon. If you don't keep hold of the string, you will never know where he will be off to.' It was the beginning of a stormy, brief and ultimately fatal power struggle between Bismarck and the Kaiser.

Matters came to a head in 1890 when Bismarck unearthed an old decree, signed by Wilhelm IV in 1852, obliging Prussian ministers to consult with the prime minister before approaching the king. The chancellor, in attempting to limit the younger Wilhelm's exposure to the ideas of others, infuriated him. The Kaiser ordered Bismarck to repeal the decree or resign. Bismarck, embittered and totally frustrated by Wilhelm's hubris, chose to resign.

Unfettered by this political control, the Kaiser swiftly shifted the focus of foreign policy and set course for confrontation rather than mediation with other nation states that would have dire consequences for the Hohenzollern dynasty and Germany. Not content with becoming a dominant force on the European continent, Wilhelm was determined to transform Germany into a global power with a colonial empire and a powerful Navy that would more than match that of Britain in particular.

In fact, this new emphasis did suit the muscle-flexing mood of the day. Germany was enjoying an era of unprecedented growth, and most Germans saw in the Kaiser's *Weltpolitik*, or global policy, an outlet for their energy and desire to ensure Germany's greatness as the 'new kid on the block' on the world stage. Coupled with the public support for the Kaiser's initiative was the resurgence of a virulent form of racist nationalism, epitomised by the *Alldeutsche Verband*, or Pan-German League.

Founded in 1890, the league embraced the notion that pure-blooded Teutons were the creators and bearers of civilisation and thus responsible for all worldly progress. Jews and 'socialists', on the other hand, were a corrupting, negative force – a dogma popularised by Houston Stewart-Chamberlain, the Anglo-German author and son-in-law of the composer Richard Wagner. Beyond this extreme simplification of European affairs, the Pan-German League's professed goal was to gather all the countries considered to be 'German' in origin, such as the Netherlands, Belgium, Luxembourg, Switzerland, Austro-Hungary, Poland, Rumania and Serbia. From this enlarged Reich, the pan-Germans intended nothing less than to rule the world.

This notion was fuelled by this diabolical theory and by the outpourings of such writers as Heinrich von Trietschke, who popularised the glorification of war as a means to achieve greatness, and predicted that a new German empire would replace the old British empire and utterly subjugate the Slavs of central Europe. Buoyed by these ideas, the Kaiser drove a wedge between moderation and extremist views in the Fatherland.

The conflict that was to actually erupt in 1914 was preordained. It is my view that the touch paper for a European conflagration had been lit in the 1890s. Trietschke, greatly admired by Wilhelm II, wrote in 1892: 'Those who propose a foolish notion of peace show their ignorance of the international life of the Aryan race.' Democracies were dismissed as corrupt and, beneath the surface, ripe for domination by the emergent militaristic nation of Germany with the Kaiser at its head.

By the turn of the century, Wilhelm's penchant for bombast and the radical views coming from Germany sharpened a growing worldwide fear of a policy that appeared to advocate German military aggression. The Kaiser peppered his speeches with phrases such as 'a place in the sun', Germany's 'mailed fist' and a 'glistening coat of [chain] mail', to make this policy plain to all who cared to listen. When Herbert Asquith engaged Wilhelm in a discussion on the balance of power in Europe, he retorted: 'There is no balance of power but me; me and my 25 [Army] Corps.'

Worse, the ship-building programme masterminded by Admiral Alfred von Tirpitz was designed to match the Royal Navy ship for ship – a red rag to the British bulldog. It engendered a rivalry that became a principal factor in Britain's decision to seek an entente with her traditional enemy, France.

As a continental power, Germany's great strength lay with its army. But circumstances and ambitions beyond the continent arguably weakened that might as a result of Wilhelm II's desire for global influence and Tirpitz's ambition to rule the waves in place of the Royal Navy. Tirpitz had unequivocal faith in sea power and was equally convinced that Britain was determined to prevent Germany from striving to become the world influence that he believed was her destiny. In 1897, he affirmed in a secret memorandum that England was Germany's most dangerous naval enemy; and in that 'enemy's' mind, the Tirpitz factor was one of profound menace too:

> Sea-power played no part in the making of modern Germany, and that was irrelevant to Germany's home defence. It was sought deliberately as an engine of conquest and as the only effective weapon with which Germany could win power abroad and above all dispute British supremacy.[2]

In 1898, Tirpitz introduced the Navy Law, which was explicit in confirming such British fears. The Imperial German Navy was to expand dramatically and become an instrument of challenge and coercion, rather than directly confront the Royal Navy, at least for a number of years. In 1900 Tirpitz put forward the infamous 'Risk Theory', a policy by which Germany could build a modern maritime force to match the Royal Navy and threaten Britain's fleets protecting the empire abroad.

What's more, the public demonstration of Germany's naval expansion led to patriotic fervour and convinced the Kaiser that the Fatherland's future lay 'on the water'. By 1912, Chancellor Bethmann-Hollweg declared that: 'The fleet was the favourite child of Germany.'[3]

Tirpitz's aggressive policy led to inevitable reaction, not least by Britain. The First Sea Lord, Admiral Sir John Fisher, introduced the naval reforms as a direct response. Germany was careering towards isolation and enmity from the world's greatest sea power in addition to the opposition she had already brought upon herself from Russia and France. By 1907, the three nations had formed the Triple Entente. Germany had brought this upon herself, primarily because of Tirpitz, whose 'Risk Theory' had begun to turn towards a dark reality for Germany's future.

One by one, Germany had forfeited friendships and old alliances. In 1909, German Chancellor Bethman-Hollweg summed up the Kaiser's policy when he wrote: 'Challenge everybody, get in everyone's way and, in the course of it all, weaken nobody.'

The Bismarckian balance of power, based on firm government and a pragmatic foreign policy, was now a long-abandoned dream, for first Wilhelm II and then the military in Germany had torn it to shreds, strip by strip. Tirpitz and Count Alfred von Schlieffen had become the architects of Germany's destiny. Schlieffen, as Chief of the Army General Staff, had drawn up a plan of 'preventative war' to pre-empt any growing threat of attacks by France on one side and Russia on the other. The threats were tenuous, but the perception in Germany held sway.

By 1914 the German Army's thirst for war had gathered widespread support. By then, the control of economic and foreign policy had all but passed to the military General Staff.

After the assassination of Austrian Archduke Ferdinand and his wife Sophie in Sarajevo on 28 June, Germany became engaged in a race that was wholly driven by the military hierarchy in order to conform with the Schlieffen Plan. When the Russians began to mobilise on 29 July and the French followed suit on 1 August, the pressure on the Kaiser to kowtow to the Army was overwhelming. Simply, if he failed to order general mobilisation, the Schlieffen Plan would be jeopardised. He had little choice but to acquiesce.

The very size of the German Army forced a decision: from some 250,000 men in 1870 it had grown to over two million strong – almost one million of whom had to be moved by a strict timetable immediately. Any delay was intolerable and could be fatal, according to the General Staff. The chickens were now flocking home to roost – the Kaiser's arrogance and bombast since his accession had led Germany to the brink of war and he was now forced to make a decision by those to whom he had originally sought to give power without losing supreme control himself.

As the conflagration in Europe was about to ignite he realised too late that he had unwittingly handed over the reins of power – the conduct of the war and Germany's leadership – to a military High Command that would ultimately bring Germany to ruin and the Kaiser to exile.

During the Franco-Prussian War of 1870–1 Prussia, allied with Bavaria and other German states, defeated the French. In January 1871 the North German Federation was dissolved, giving way to the German Empire or *Reich*, with King Wilhelm the First of Prussia as its first emperor.

The father of the new army was Helmuth von Moltke the Elder (1800–91). An avid student of the theories of Clausewitz and Gneisenau, he devoted himself to the formation, instruction, and evolution of the German General Staff and the Army, both of which were to become renowned for their skill and professionalism in the art of modern warfare.

When war came in August 1914, the German Army was under the command of General Helmuth von Moltke the Younger. His officers and the troops that they led were confident that the great German Army would sweep any opposition off the battlefield in the west before turning its attention in force to the Eastern front. After all, they were about to implement the indomitable Schlieffen Plan.

This strategic initiative, conceived by Moltke the Elder, and subsequently developed by Count Alfred von Schlieffen when he succeeded Moltke as Chief of the German General Staff, envisaged a war on two fronts. But it would still win a war within months, not years. He declared that, 'In a two-front war, the whole of Germany must throw itself upon one enemy; the strongest, most powerful, most dangerous enemy and that can only be France.'[4]

Count Alfred von Schlieffen. *(IWM: HU 1777)*

The main German force was to attack France, striking through Belgium, move quickly into the department of Champagne, smash the French in one great battle, isolate Paris, then roll the remains of the French Army up to the Swiss border. Schlieffen was adamant that the right wing of this vast sweeping movement must be strong and seamless, reaching as far west as Lille to make the envelopment of the French Army complete. Schlieffen wanted 'the last man on the right of the right wing to brush the Channel with his sleeve' when the Kaiser's men marched stridently in to violate and conquer French territory.

Behind this massive advance by first-rate Active Army Corps through Belgium, reserve formations would rush to the Channel ports to cut off any British reinforcement of the French Army. This would leave one army, the Eighth, to secure East Prussia so as to contain any initial Russian advance and to cooperate with the Austrians, who were to attack Russian forces through Poland. Austria was to withdraw some troops from her front with Serbia to develop a strike at Russia through Galicia.

This was the plan, and it was accepted by the Kaiser, the government and the German High Command, as well as the General Staff. The power and influence of the German General Staff were so strong that the plan was endorsed without any debate on its moral or political implications. The violation of Belgian neutrality was hardly a major factor to most, for few influential German politicians or military men believed in its neutrality anyway. More dangerous, however, was the hubris and unquestioned authority of the General Staff and its head, Count Alfred von Schlieffen. The German foreign ministry was informed that:

> If the Chief of the General Staff, particularly such a pre-eminent strategical authority as Schlieffen, considers such a measure [violating Belgium] is necessary, then it is the duty of diplomacy to concur in it and to facilitate it in every possible manner.[5]

The Schlieffen Plan apparently provided the template for guaranteed success. When the test came, its architect was already in Valhalla and his successor, Helmuth von Moltke, was not cut of the same cloth as either his mentor or his renowned uncle. Moltke was a pessimist, who lacked Schlieffen's drive and zeal for the concept of concentrating his forces and most of his strength in one bold manoeuvre. If Schlieffen's motto was 'Be bold, be bold', then Moltke's was 'but not too bold.'

He worried constantly about the weakness of his left wing, rather than the strength of his right wing, in the west; and he had nagging doubts about the capability of his Eighth Army in East Prussia to contain any Russian aggression. Schlieffen had estimated that the vast army that was known as the 'Russian steamroller', largely because of the sheer weight of its numbers, would be slow to mobilise and therefore the Eighth Army's role would be merely to screen and contain the Eastern Front alongside its Austro-Hungarian allies while the war in the West was swiftly settled. Then, the concentration of force would be entirely at the East's disposal.

General Helmuth von Moltke ('the Younger'), Chief of the German General Staff until his failure on the Marne in September 1914.

(Rudolph Stratz, Weltkrieg)

But what if the momentum of the western offensive was stalled; and what if the 'Russian steamroller' lumbered forward more quickly than Schlieffen had predicted? Moltke wrestled with such 'worst case scenarios' and he made a few adjustments along the way, a little tinkering here and there, and hoped for the best. The test of Germany's master strategy and the man who was fated to bear the responsibility for implementing it was looming. It would be quite a test.

Owing to the efficient system of universal conscription, Germany was able to field a large professionally-trained army within days of war being declared in July/August 1914. In peacetime, every German male from the age of seventeen to forty-five was liable for some form of military service.

Although not eligible for service in the Standing Army until his twentieth birthday, every man on reaching seventeen became automatically liable to serve with the *Landsturm*, or Home Guard. On his twentieth birthday, he began to serve a two-year period, or three years in the case of cavalry or artillery, with the Standing Army, followed by successive periods of seven years with reserve forces – the *Landwehr* – and then back to the *Landsturm* for the final seven years of service. This system meant that each year saw a constant entry from one form of service to another up to age forty-five. This was the principal reason for the large pool of manpower at the onset of hostilities. In wartime men could be called up and sent to the front before reaching the age of twenty and were not automatically released from further service until their forty-fifth birthday.

There were three more categories: the *Restanten Liste* (reserved occupations, but eligible for military service in extremis), the *Einjahrige Freiwilligen* (one-year volunteers) and the *Kriegsfreiwilligen* (War Volunteers). The latter were men between 17 and 20 who were allowed to volunteer for active service before their official call-up date. Thousands of young men opted for this option in the heady days of July and August 1914.

Not surprisingly, the Reserve and *Landsturm* were practically all absorbed into the expansion of the Army in 1914. The *Landsturm* in particular was extensively drawn on to make up the huge losses of the autumn and winter campaigns of that year. The end of 1915 had exhausted most of these reinforcements. As a result, men training within the normal categories were called to the front earlier than planned.

Significantly, the situation became so dire by the beginning of 1917 that training drafts that expected to have been called to the colours in 1919 were drafted into service on the Eastern front two years early. This was to allow seasoned and experienced men to be transferred to the Western Front to replace the enormous losses there. It was abundantly clear from Germany's manpower situation alone that by the beginning of 1917 her Army was on the 'back foot' on the Western Front. The roots of this crisis were firmly embedded in the twin German catastrophes at Verdun and especially on the Somme in the previous year, as we shall see.

Between 1914 and 1918, the German Army was to prove time and time again that it had the capacity to remain standing after what appeared to have been knockout blows. This endurance against extraordinary odds came from the resourcefulness and courage of the ordinary '*Fritzie Schmidt*' (an allusion to 'Tommy Atkins' as the archetypal British soldier) and the leadership of junior officers and the stalwart senior and junior NCOs. On the face of it, these were similar characteristics of the Western allies. But there were marked differences, so often neglected by studies of the First World War.

Inevitably, the officer corps was modelled on Prussia, the dominant state prior to and after unification in 1871. Though only 30 per cent of the officers in the German Army of 1914 were aristocrats, they held most of the important command roles and staff appointments. This imbalance did not reflect German society, where the inspiration and drive of modernisation had been largely with the middle classes. This was demonstrated by the fact that in the more technical corps, such as the artillery and engineers, middle-class officers predominated. But few progressed to the higher levels of command.

Therefore, as *materialschlacht*, or the 'war of material' dependent on modern technology, evolved between 1914 and 1918, the German High Command struggled to handle it. It was an inherent weakness, obvious not at regimental level and in the trenches where the day-to-day fighting went on, but at the senior levels where the fate of the

German Army rested. It would lead to dogmatic, rather than pragmatic, doctrine and become a source of failure in 1918.

Halfway through the First World War, as the Somme campaign erupted, this weakness was explicitly identified by the Germans themselves. On 4 July 1916, Admiral Georg Müller, a senior aide to the Kaiser, discussed the state of German military leadership with General Ludwig von Lauter, the largely unheralded but crucially important Ordnance General for Heavy Artillery at OHL, the German Supreme HQ. Lauter was responsible for the logistical provision of this vital asset and understood the nature of modern warfare and the reality of *materialschlacht*. Georg Müller recorded Lauter's uncomplimentary comments about the German military leadership in his diary:

'Fräulein Feldgrau', the German soldier's pin-up in 1914. *(Allen Collection)*

> It was a war, he said, 'of young leaders and junior officers on the General Staff and in the field, a war that was dangerously undermining the authority of the Army commanders . . . ' Lauter warned the Staff [on this] emphatically in December before the Verdun offensive. When he expressed his opinion to von Falkenhayn later, the latter replied: 'Well, the French are being bled white, too. Moreover, if things go badly, we can break off and say that we only intended taking the forward [French] positions.' When I [Müller] asked von Lauter whether General Falkenhayn enjoyed great respect in the Army, he replied: 'Certainly not, and if the war ever ends there will be some interesting literature on the subject of the [German] war leadership.'[6]

After Falkenhayn's dismissal in August 1916, the 'duumvirate' leadership of Field Marshal Paul von Hindenburg and General Erich Ludendorff agreed that in the west they had succeeded to 'an evil inheritance.' In the context of the dreadful events unfolding for the German troops at Verdun and on the Somme, this view was entirely apposite. But it could just as easily have described the insidious inheritance that Germany had now chained herself to with a military dictatorship that was soon to become absolute. The worst part was that from August 1916 Hindenburg, the 'Hero of Tannenberg' and a military legend of the Franco-Prussian War to boot, gave

Deutschland, Deutschland über Alles: Germans were convinced that their much vaunted Army would win a swift and glorious victory – 1914 postcard.
(Allen Collection)

Ludendorff a legitimacy and status that would prove fatal for the Fatherland. Within months, the Kaiser became a political and military irrelevance and Ludendorff had a free reign to lead the charge to Germany's first twentieth-century nemesis.

The real strength of the German Army lay at the tactical level and rested on the shoulders of junior officers and the NCOs. The popular myth and tales of 'Lions led by Donkeys' in the British Army during the First World War could be more accurately applied to the German Army. German junior officers and NCOs were given more responsibility in their rank than their Allied equivalents, so that an *Oberleutnant* might well command an infantry company of 150 men and a sergeant or *Feldwebel* a platoon of around 40.

Germany's modernisation since 1871, which included universal education and a high proportion of well-educated men and women, worked to her advantage in war. Senior and junior NCOs were generally better educated than their Allied equivalents and they were trusted to use their initiative and play more important roles at the tactical level. These '100,000 men' were truly the backbone of the German Army, maintaining the highest standards of training and discipline, as well as inspiring their men to acts of courage and endurance that were the hallmark of the Kaiser's men throughout this war and would be when their sons went to war twenty-one years later.

The German Army in 1914 had an active strength of eight armies, with one, the Eighth, in East Prussia. Within these armies were a total of 25 Corps, with 50 infantry and 11 cavalry divisions. Behind these came 32 Reserve divisions, 7 *Ersatz* (supplementary Reserve) divisions and 16 *Landwehr* Brigades. The field Army was around 850,000 and the High Command was determined to use maximum and concentrated force in the West.[7]

The railways were soon sending the vast majority of these men and their weapons and other *matériel* towards the West for death or glory, while the remainder headed for the borders of East Prussia.[8]

CHAPTER 2

THE SCENT OF VICTORY, DISASTER ON THE MARNE

AUGUST–SEPTEMBER 1914

Aßschied

Vorm Sterben mache ich noch mein Gedicht.
Still, Kameraden, stört mich nicht.
Wir ziehn zum Krieg. Der Tod ist unser Kitt.
O, heulte mir doch die Geliebte nit.
Was liegt an mir? Ich gehe gerne ein.
Meine Mutter weint; Man muß aus Eisen sein.
Die Sonne fällt zum Horizont hinab.
Bald wirft man mich ins milde Massengrab.
Am Himmel brennt das brave Abendrot;
Vielleicht bin ich in dreizehn Tage tot.

Alfred Lichtenstein, 1889–1914
(Killed in action at Vermandovillers, Somme, September 1914)

Leaving for the Front

Before dying I must write my poem.
Quiet, comrades, don't disturb me.
We are off to war [and] death is our bond.
Oh, if only my girlfriend would stop howling!
What do I matter? I am happy to go.
My mother's crying; one needs to be made of iron.
The sun falls to the horizon;
Soon they'll be throwing me into a nice mass-grave.
In the sky the good old sun is glowing red;
[And] in thirteen days I shall probably be dead.

At the beginning of August 1914 there was an unmistakable mood of optimism across Europe. Throughout the continent, peace gave way to an explosion of patriotic enthusiasm for war. The tensions within each country – unrest and fear of civil disobedience, civil war and social upheaval brought on by poverty and the sheer drabness of most people's lives – were blown away like a cobweb on a fresh wind. The fresh wind was 'the cause' – a singular belief in each country of duty, honour, glory – and victory in the name of the Kaiser, King, Tsar or Emperor.

Within weeks of Archduke Ferdinand's assassination it was utterly irrelevant that it was Austria's *casus belli*, for it was, in irredeemable fact, Germany's war. The German Army attacked first – principally to knock out France in the west.

At 5 a.m. on 4 August, the German vanguard crossed the Belgian frontier. On the same day, the Kaiser, already more certain of victory than any other European leader at that time, addressed a packed Reichstag: 'I have no longer any knowledge of [Political] Party or creed . . . I know only Germans and in token thereof, I ask all of you to give me your hands.'

It was a stirring and convincing speech, which re-ignited the flames of nationalism and the inculcated belief in Germany's destiny to be the principal actor on first the European and then the world stage. All seemed possible in this Berlin theatre of dreams on that day. To underscore the Kaiser's rhetoric, Imperial Chancellor Theobald von Bethmann-Hollweg stepped forward next to ask the Reichstag assembly to endorse his request for a staggering war credit of £265 million. It was granted, unanimously.

By the end of that momentous day – with the Kaiser now at war with Great Britain and her imperial forces as well as France and Belgium in the west – Germany was inextricably on course for 'death or glory'. Her appetite for glorious war and sweeping victory grew by the hour – and Belgium was to be the *hors d'oeuvre*.

Belgium was the springboard for the much-vaunted Schlieffen Plan, as she provided the best route for the German Army to strike at the heart of France without having to bludgeon its way through the line of French frontier fortresses that ran from Verdun in the north to Belfort in the south.

The Great Adventure Begins I: Off to the Front.
(Allen Collection)

The Western Front 1914–1918.

The Great Adventure Begins II:
Tea for the troops.
(Allen Collection)

The Great Adventure Begins III:
Friends cheer a German cavalryman off to war.
(Bundesarchiv)

The Schlieffen Plan was brilliant in its simplicity. While the German Eighth Army contained any Russian threat on the Eastern Front, five armies would smash through Belgium and, once Brussels fell, swing west and south into France via Lille and then, with its right wing brushing the Channel, cut through the Somme region and Amiens and pass round behind Paris before taking the mass of bewildered French *poilus* and their commanders from behind. The consequence? A stunning victory that would surpass even the brilliant achievement of 1871. But this time it would take a mere forty days from start to finish.

The reality, however, was as predictable as the failure of plans drawn up by Staff Officers predicting 'sweeping success' by using 'big hands on small maps', in military parlance. On paper, using 'staff tables' to calculate the rate of advance, rate of fire, casualty rates and logistical requirements to sustain such offensives, and on the 'campaign map', the plan appeared sound.

But the campaign map and staff tables used to devise the Schlieffen Plan made one overriding assumption as its vital ingredient: speed was of the essence. Nothing was to hinder the German juggernaut's progress through Belgium, France and then the victory parade along the Champs Elysées. Belgium was simply a corridor through which the German forces would pass. Little resistance was expected, for her army was weak and ill-trained when compared with the might of its adversary. Or so the Germans thought.

The first real blow would fall on Liège, where fortresses acted as sentinels over the River Meuse and all routes to Brussels and then into France. Its garrison, led by the

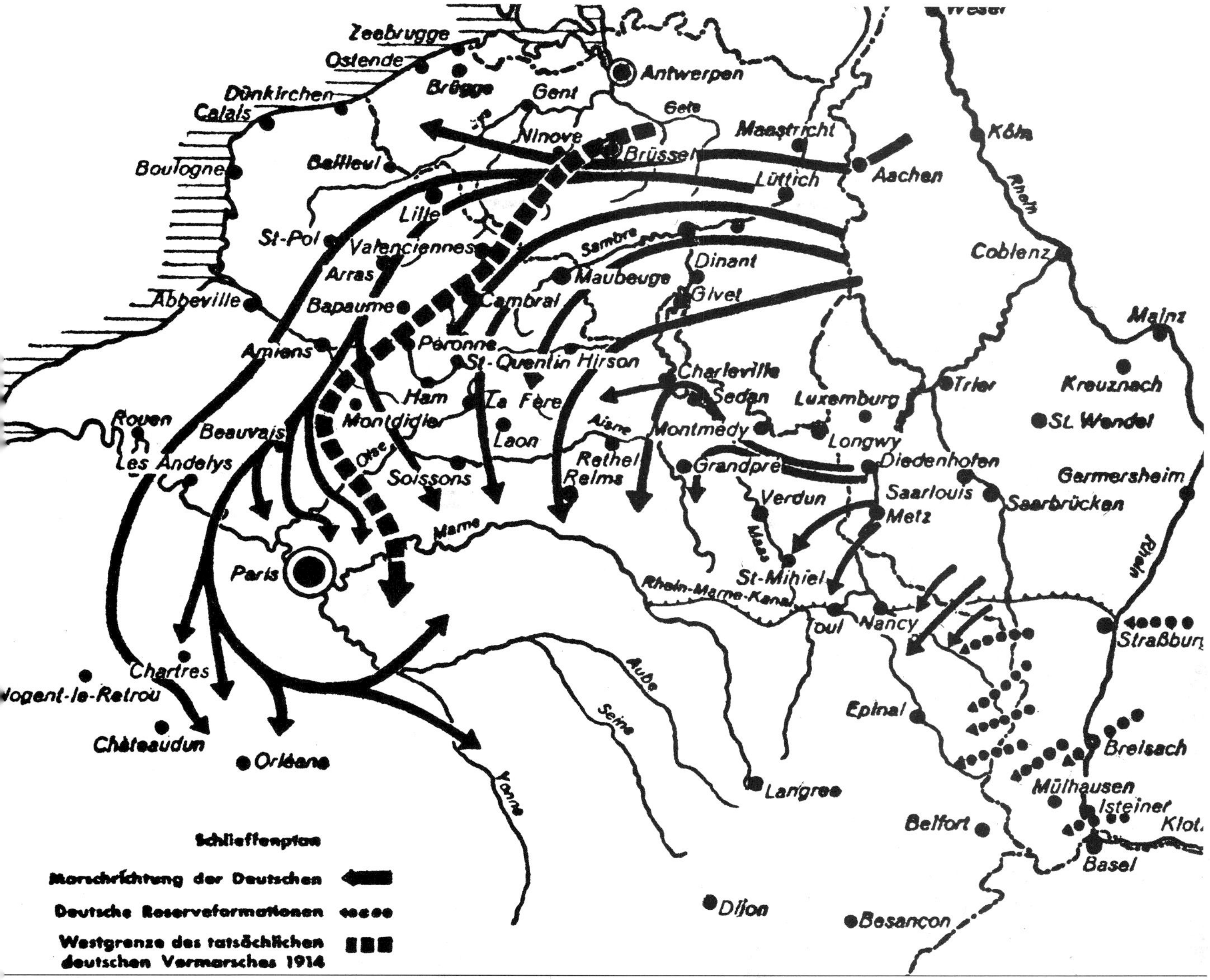

The Schlieffen Plan: Theory and Reality. The map shows the planned advance of the German armies (bold lines) and the western flank of the actual German advance to the Marne, August to September 1914.

(Rudolph Stratz, Weltkrieg)

redoubtable General Gérard Leman, was expected to capitulate after only a token struggle.

As the leading German divisions closed on Liège, most expected that the defenders would be simply swept aside and barely check their stride. They had good reason to think that at the beginning of August 1914. In theory the German war machine was overwhelming and unstoppable. It was commonly believed that

> Wer Unglück will im Kriege han,
> Der binde mit dem Deutschen an.
>
> ('If anyone wants a disastrous war,
> then let him pick a quarrel with a German.')[1]

The Belgian Army faced the most powerful, well-trained and well-equipped armed forces the world had ever seen. They were the mirror to the world of the image of the new Germany: a young, expanding, industrialised and confident nation with expansive ambitions for European and global leadership. The soldier was Germany and Germany's sons served her with pride, and were admired by her people. Where the Army marched, all Germany marched too.

With a peacetime conscripted army of almost 900,000 men and four million trained reserves, Germany had the potential to more than double that combined total to ten million. The backbone was the infantry, comprising 78 divisions, and at the centre of the German army's excellence was its 110,000 superbly trained junior officers and non-commissioned officers, or NCOs. Their status was firmly established elsewhere. Lt James L. Jack of the 1st Cameronians wrote in his diary on 12 August 1914:

> Of our Adversaries: The Austrians are gentlemen rather than soldiers. Germany, however, is very highly organised for a European war. Her armies have a tremendous reputation, and have smashed all enemies quite easily in the past fifty years . . . A Staff College friend . . . told me quite recently that the German infantry must be considered equal to ours notwithstanding their short service . . . compared with our long-service men, many of whom have seen a campaign . . . Perhaps we are a little better at musketry.[2]

The cavalry comprised a little over 100,000 men, its elite status reflected by the Kaiser's special patronage and the fact that his son, Crown Prince Wilhelm, elected to

German infantry 'Advance to Contact' in France, August 1914.
(IWM: Q53446)

join the Death's Head (*Totenkopf*) Hussars. Alongside the Hussars were the Dragoons, Cuirassiers and Uhlans, among others, all with characteristically flamboyant dress and styles. Before the growing influence of German aces of the air war such as Max Immelmann, Oswald Boelke and Manfred von Richthofen, the Red Baron, the cavalry were the most revered of the Kaiser's warriors.

Less glamorous, though infinitely more deadly, the German artillery was about to pitch this conflict into a new era of man's diabolical ingenuity and war's more distant slaughter.

In August 1914 the German field artillery was poor in comparison with the British 18-pounder and especially the outstanding French 75mm, '*soixante-quinze*'. But the 3,000-plus medium and heavy guns were awesome in both range and destructive power. From the outset, Germany had guns and mortars with calibres of 150mm, 210mm, 305mm, even 420mm, which were efficiently supplied with excellent ammunition and primed to rip both the men and the soil of France and Belgium apart.

With all these resources behind them and with an arrogant spring in their step, the first waves of assaulting German infantry swept towards the Liège defences. They were repulsed at great cost. At first, the apparently irresistible force of German military power crashed uselessly against the immovable object of Liège's forts and the plucky Belgian garrison within.

Even the capture of the citadel by the then little-known Major General Erich Ludendorff did not unhinge the fortress defences, so ably controlled by General Gérard Leman. This heroic defiance not only briefly shocked and checked the swaggering advance of the Kaiser's men, but also inspired the world to stop the German tidal wave. The phrase 'gallant little Belgium' was born and a myriad of cartoons appeared depicting caricatures of Belgium bullied but unbowed by Germany.

Inevitably, courageous and determined resistance would have to bow to the flexing muscle of German military power – the guns and mortars. Leman's men were brought to their knees by the 'heavies', including the Krupp 420mm and the Austrian-supplied Skoda 305mm pieces. The Liège forts were mercilessly pounded and crushed by the weight and concentration of such monstrous guns. The gallant General Leman was buried under the debris, but lived alongside many of his men to be captured by admiring and incredulous German troops.

But with the fall of Liège, the way became clear for the Schlieffen Plan to unfold rapidly once more. Brussels and the French border were the next items on the menu – and the Belgian Army had not the slightest hope of checking its pace again. That task had now to fall to Belgium's allies in France and Great Britain.

The French Army had mobilised and rushed to defend its borders in a tidy fashion while the rape of Belgium proceeded. France, like Germany, had drawn up a scheme to outflank its enemy and win a swift victory: Plan XVII, which would also conveniently reclaim Alsace-Lorraine, lost to Germany as a result of the Franco-Prussian War, and a constant thorn in the side since.

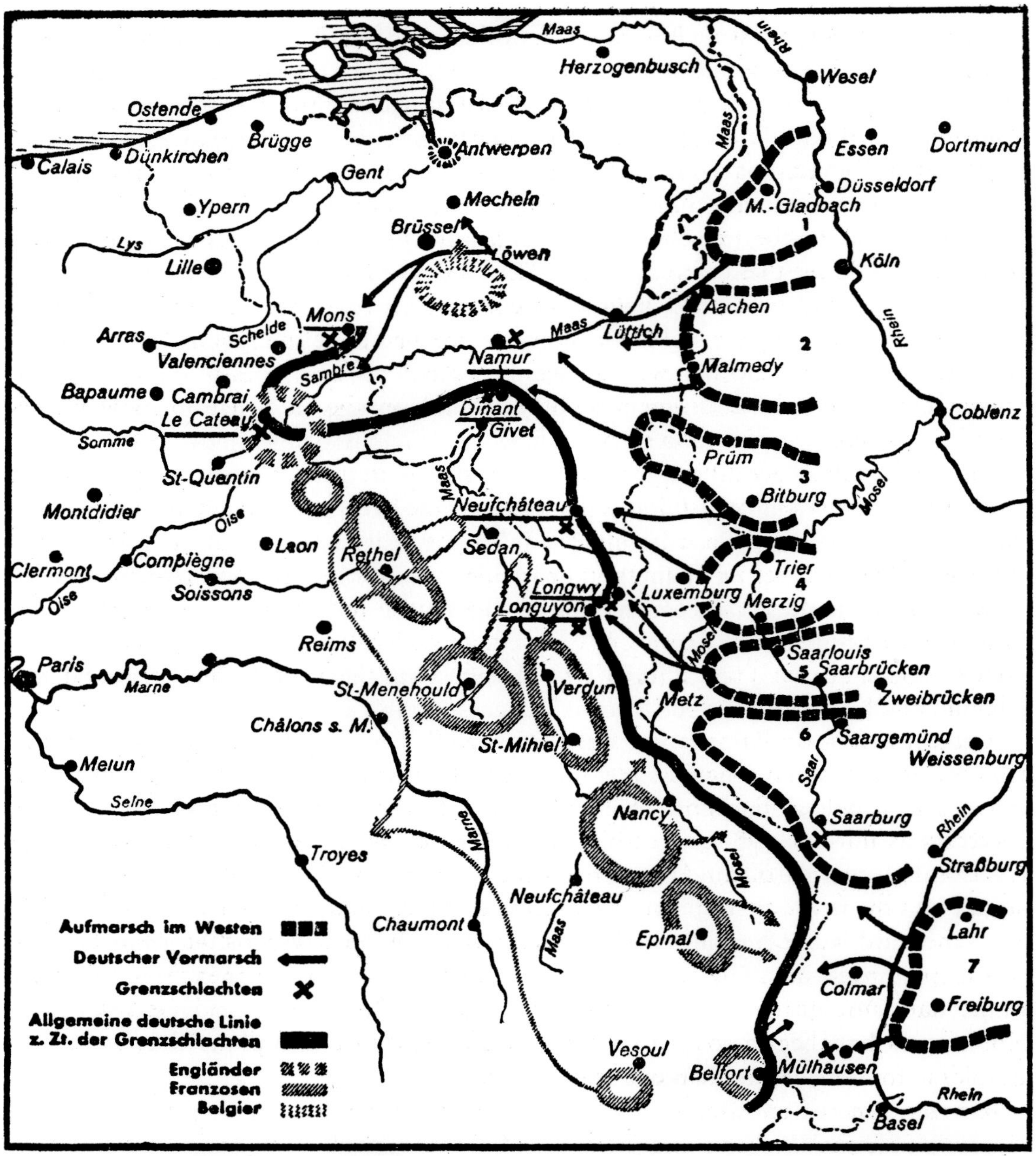

The German advance in the West: The 'Vormarsch' through Belgium and the 'Clash on the Frontiers', showing the German front line at the time of the border battles, August 1914.

(Rudolph Stratz, Weltkrieg)

Plan XVII was more straightforward than the Schlieffen Plan. The problem was that Plan XVII was less based on staff tables and campaign maps than it was on the firm, though naïve belief that French élan and the spirit of the offensive – *l'attaque à l'outrance* – would be enough to turn the German tide. The operational order for Plan XVII stated: 'Whatever the circumstances, it is the Commander-in-Chiefs' intention to advance, all forces united, to the attack of the German armies.'

So the *poilus* of the French Army headed into the breach entirely convinced that their élan would see them through. As in Germany, the French people had total faith in their Army; it had been their pride and constant in more recent troubled political times. Moreover, France had been itching for revenge after the ignominy of 1871. It was her eternal flame, which would re-ignite French passion to fulfil her destiny and make Germany pay for that previous humiliation. Now the moment had come and the flames of passion were burning high.

Yet the French Army differed from its German counterpart in two fundamental and almost fatal ways in August 1914. It was equipped for colonial or, in many cases, Napoleonic warfare, in stark contrast to its foe. Cuirassiers rode to war as if to Waterloo 100 years before and infantry divisions wore blue tunics and red trousers.

Many French officers regarded it as unfashionable not to wear white gloves and brandish a sword rather than an oily and inconvenient revolver when going into an attack. Above all, the French Army lacked then what their enemy had in abundance: medium and heavy artillery.

The crunch soon came and tested Plan XVII, and both élan and the French Cuirassiers' breastplates against *Herr* Krupp's abundant hot steel. As Liège was being reduced to rubble in the north, the French struck in the south towards Alsace. Early success was illusory and soon ruthlessly reversed by German counter-attacks and the devastating use of artillery. Whole regiments of infantry and cavalry vanished in the smoke and the fire, only to re-emerge as lines of dead and dying men and horses.

By the third week in August 1914, despite uplifting 'morale-boosting' reports in the newspapers back home, it had become clear that the respective French and German plans had 'not quite lived up to expectations'. The French and German High Commands had begun to live with the stark reality of war plans that were now unfolding for real, rather than in a staff exercise.

It was a time of uncertainty and a time for steady nerves at the very top on both sides. Not for the first time in this 'Great War' when steady nerves were needed at the very top, Germany was at a disadvantage.

The Army's Commander-in-Chief, General Helmuth von Moltke 'the younger', was an honourable and conscientious man, but a very pale shadow of his heroic and illustrious uncle. Above all he was a man of unsteady nerve and uncertain authority. Cowed by the forceful personalities of his leading Army commanders such as Crown Prince Rupprecht of Bavaria (Sixth Army) and Colonel-Generals Alexander von Klück (First Army) and Karl von Bülow (Second Army), he vacillated and became daily more distant from the action in hand. Moltke's weakness was to have awful consequences.

Ironically, it seemed that Germany had least to fear at this stage. During this hot and bloody August, it had become apparent that French tactics owed more to the days of Napoleon than the here and now. Peacetime French Directives stated that success in battle depended only on knowing where the enemy were and then deciding what to do. What the enemy intended to do was of no importance.

In Alsace-Lorraine, the French Second Army commander General Edouard de Castelnau had exhorted his men to pursue the Germans, who were apparently retiring on his front, 'with the utmost vigour and rapidity'. This they did – and met Crown Prince Rupprecht's Sixth Army head-on as they, in turn, were counter-attacking rather than retiring.

Suddenly it was desperately important for the French troops to know what the enemy intended to do. But it was already too late. The results were catastrophic, as the attacking lines of French infantry and cavalry had no time to even waver before being stopped dead in their tracks by German artillery and machine guns.

A French officer recalled later that they were shot down like rabbits because for the Germans they were such easy targets in their blue tunics and red trousers. Those who were not cut down immediately had no chance to do anything other than fall back.

German infantry assault an enemy position, August 1914.

(Allen Collection)

The remnants of the French Second Army were forced to withdraw in what was a near rout. Crown Prince Rupprecht may well have recalled Lord Wellington's comment almost a century before that the French 'came on in the same old way and we stopped them, in the same old way'.

The French High Command began to grasp the message that élan and breastplates had become obsolete; but not before the 'Clash of the Frontiers' had claimed almost 300,000 French casualties.

On 20 August, General von Klück's First Army entered Brussels. It was an almost endless stream of swaggering field-grey topped by *Pickelhaubes*, horse-drawn supply wagons and heavy calibre guns.

Klück was back on course, and the Schlieffen plan was now rolling through the Belgian capital while General von Bülow's Second Army to the south was giving Namur the same destructive treatment with the heavy artillery. The unstoppable force was on the move once more – the scythe-like thrust of the German armies began to swing left towards the French frontier as planned.

At last, after a series of terrible hammerings, the scales were falling from French eyes. The fantasy of easy victory with élan leading the charge was giving way to nothing less than the nightmare that this was a grim and bloody struggle against a terrifyingly well-equipped, well-led and deadly enemy.

The deadly enemy were also showing signs of a more bestial intent – that of atrocity against the hapless Belgian population. A German soldier recalled that his infantry company had stopped in a village for their evening meal when they came under fire from the surrounding houses, 'but when we stormed the buildings from where the firing started, we found only innocent-looking Belgian civilians at first – and then infantry rifles still hot from the firing'.[3]

The German solution to the problem of these '*francs tireurs*' – snipers, guerrillas, or innocent bystanders – was to root them out and carry out instant retribution. One of the worst examples of this German ruthlessness was at Dinant, where over 600 men, women and children, were rounded up and gunned down. Those German officers and men who protested or questioned how such atrocities could possibly be explained – and many did – were told that such incidents would be forgotten when Germany, as the victors, wrote its 'official' history.

At the time, the moral argument was an ambivalent one. After all, as Erich von Ludendorff wrote:

> It is true that innocent persons may have had to suffer, but the stories of 'Belgian Atrocities' are nothing but clever, elaborate and widely-advertised legends and the Belgian Government can alone be held responsible. For my part, I had taken to the field with chivalrous and humane conceptions of war. This guerrilla war was bound to disgust any decent soldier. My soldierly spirit suffered bitter disillusion.[4]

'Satisfaction: Peace Begins at Dinant' – a contemporary postcard recalls German atrocities. *(Allen Collection)*

The ordinary soldiers insisted also that the atrocities were committed on both sides. One captured soldier, Hugo Lagershausen, 1st *Ersatz* Company of a Reserve Infantry Division, interviewed during the official investigation, declared:

> About noon on 6th August I came to a dressing station set up on a farm . . . In the house I found about fifteen severely wounded German soldiers, of whom four or five had been horribly mutilated . . . their eyes had been gouged out and some had had several fingers cut off . . . The men were still living and groaning . . .

Another, *Landwehrmann* Alwin Chaton, of 78th Reserve Infantry Regiment, added that:

> In the course of the street fighting in Charleroi . . . I saw . . . a German Dragoon lying in the street about fifty or sixty paces in front of me. Three civilians were near him, of whom one was bending over the soldier, who still kicked with his legs. I shot among them . . . one fell [and] the others fled. When I approached I saw the shot civilian had a knife, covered with blood, in his hand. The right eye of the German Dragoon was gouged out.[5]

Naturally, Allied investigators suggested that these troops were merely trying to save their own skins, perhaps, despite reasonable treatment as prisoners of war. The truth almost certainly lies

The massacre at Dinant.
(Contemporary Postcard, Allen Collection)

somewhere in between, although there is no doubt that the scale of atrocity weighed heavily on the side of the advancing German armies in the west.

To the cultured German mind, the worst atrocity admitted at the time was the desecration of the fifteenth-century library in the ancient university city of Louvain on 25 August. Two hundred and thirty thousand volumes, including irreplaceable medieval manuscripts and some of the earliest books ever printed, were burned to a cinder in an act of wanton, insane destruction. Similar things would happen in Germany herself only two decades later.[6]

Still the inexorable drive of the German war machine continued and only the French Fifth Army under General Charles Lanrezac and a newly despatched British Expeditionary Force, or BEF, would stand in its way.

The BEF had begun to form up in France on 7 August. As a small, though superbly trained and led volunteer force with wide experience of recent colonial wars, its men expected to play a significant role in pushing the marauding Germans back. Its commander, the irascible Field Marshal Sir John French, would first have to deal with the prickly Lanrezac in the spirit of Anglo-French cooperation. Sir John was more Francophobe than Francophile and it soon showed. It did not bode well for the 'entente cordiale'.

By 22 August the Germans were swarming towards Mons, while Field Marshal French had resolved to advance north towards Brussels. Lanrezac had other ideas. In his opinion, the German threat was now so great that the only course open was to withdraw. On 23 August the BEF was ordered to 'dig in' and hold a line between Maubeuge and Valenciennes, its tip just south of Mons.

It did so, waited for the advancing German infantry and then meted out a terrible punishment. Klück's First Army was checked, its leading units devastated by the accuracy, speed and steadiness of the British fire that ripped into them. Then, reluctantly, the BEF skilfully withdrew under fire. One German officer who witnessed the events wrote: 'Up to all the tricks of the trade from their experience of small wars, the English veterans brilliantly understood how to slip off at the last moment.'[7]

The retreat from Mons had begun. The BEF, scarcely in the war, appeared to be in imminent danger of losing it. The Entente Cordiale was perilously close to unravelling within days of the BEF's arrival and all the advantages were now with Germany. The Schlieffen Plan was apparently going like clockwork.

In the last week of August the French were everywhere in confusion and falling back against the irrepressible German advance. The three armies of the German right wing, over half-a-million strong, were swinging towards Paris. With 'Schlieffen' on course in the west, news reached the advancing German troops on the Western Front that the plan had already stood the test in the east. The Russian First and Second Armies had been crushed at Tannenberg and the threat to Germany's eastern borders was over. Now the real test had to be proved in France.

A German motorised convoy wrecked by artillery fire (Villers-Cotterets Forest). *(Postcard, 1914, Allen Collection)*

As the French and reluctant British withdrew towards the River Marne, the Allied commander, General Georges 'Papa' Joffre, decided to strengthen his left wing, where Klück's First Army threatened to outflank the BEF and French Fourth and Fifth Armies. The British 2nd Corps under Gen Sir Horace Smith-Dorrien was already holding the line tenaciously at Le Cateau and buying time for Joffre's plan to bear fruit.

The allied withdrawal continued and both French and British troops were dog-tired by now under the relentless German pursuit. But the men of the German armies heading towards Paris and on the trail of the retreating Allies were as weary as their enemy. They were unwittingly demonstrating that Schlieffen's plan had failed to take into account the fact that even the most robust soldier needed rest, as well as food, water and ammunition, to remain effective. They had been on the go since Liège and were footsore and desperate for respite.

Their commanders and staffs were tired too, and fatigue invites error. A monumental error was about to lay its dead hand on the German Army. A gap had appeared between Klück and Bülow's armies, exploited by a French counter move around Guise and St Quentin.

Bülow was alarmed by the gap that had appeared and signalled Klück that he needed help. In turn, Klück halted his advance to the southwest between Amiens and St Quentin and turned inwards towards Paris and the River Marne. Paris may have now appeared threatened but Klück's action was the first major twist of the knife into the body of the Schlieffen Plan.

The soldiers were becoming disillusioned and bitter. They advanced on and on, staggering forward and marching at times as if sleepwalking in unison to the beat of the drum and the rhythm of the martial music:

> Zehn tausend Mann, die zogen ins Manöver . . .
> (Ten thousand men,
> Went off on manoeuvres. . .)

Only the thought of imminent victory and just reward for their achievement kept them going:

> Der Bauer hat
> eine wunderschönes Tochter. . .
> (The farmer had
> a beautiful daughter. . .)

In the first fateful week of September it seemed that everyone was on the move, including thousands of refugees, and everyone appeared to be heading in the same direction: towards Paris. In so many ways it was now the Allies' darkest hour. Moltke's armies were still on course to fulfil the Schlieffen prophecy that within forty days France would fall and Britain would lose an Army.

But the Allies' darkest hour was to herald hope and a deadly false dawn for Moltke and the Kaiser's men. By now Klück's First Army had not only changed its thrust from southwest to south, but also begun to swing virtually southeast between Clermont (to the west) and Compiègne (east) towards Bülow's Second Army and the River Marne. This manoeuvre now exposed the men of Klück's right flank like ducks in a shooting gallery to General Maunory's newly formed Sixth Army's front line.

Worse, Klück's actions had been carried out without reference to his commander-in-chief Moltke. When Klück did inform Moltke of his *fait accompli* and that the First Army was now passing east, not west, of Paris, Moltke meekly acquiesced. The German 'supremo' was by now hopelessly out of touch with events and losing any grip on his Army commanders.

The situation was not lost on the Staff Officers, signallers and clerks of GHQ. By the end of the first week of September, it was noted:

> Watching him closely, some of his colleagues are beginning to notice a change in von Moltke. The man's vitality seems impaired; his moral fibre snapped, or at least impaired . . . [After midnight] on September 8th . . . von Moltke . . . is still seated at his table, beginning a letter to his wife, to whom he writes almost daily. To picture Moltke's state of mind, we need only look over his shoulder as he sits alone in his office, writing . . . 'I cannot find words to describe the crushing

Above: General-Oberst Alexander von Klück, commanding German First Army 1914.
Below: General-Oberst Karl von Bülow, commanding German Second Army 1914.
(Rudolph Stratz, Weltkrieg)

> burden of responsibility that . . . weighs upon me today. The appalling difficulties of our present situation hang before me like a dark curtain through which I can see nothing. The whole world is in league against us; it would seem that every country is bent on destroying Germany, once and for all.'[8]

In such a state of mind, Moltke was not only losing control of his commanders, but also trusting to the judgement of subordinates. Here and now, the curse of the German General Staff was about to rear its ugly head. Moltke passed much of his command responsibility to *Oberst Leutnant* Richard Hentsch and he was despatched to 'clarify' the situation concerning the movements of Klück's First and Bülow's Second Armies. Within days Hentsch, as Moltke's representative, would single-handedly change the course of history.

On the other hand, as Klück turned to the east of Paris and the Schlieffen Plan began to unravel before Moltke's transfixed eyes, the French commander saw opportunity knock. Defeat could, at this late hour, be turned into victory. It was as though Joffre could suddenly see the light. Lt Edward Spears, BEF liaison officer at the French GHQ, witnessed the extraordinary events of Papa Joffre's reaction:

> I actually saw him on the afternoon that he decided on the Battle of the Marne . . . Very few people have ever seen anyone with such a burden

> placed on his shoulders with nobody to help . . . Just weighing the pros and cons of this movement and that movement, what orders to issue . . . It lasted perhaps a couple of hours. But when he got up, his decision was taken and the orders went out that night.[9]

In one of those curious moments of juxtaposition in life, when Joffre had pondered, then decided that the Marne was to be a decisive battlefield, the armies on either side of Joffre's front line, whether in retreat or apparently heading for swaggering success, had paused. Too exhausted to be either pursued or continue with that pursuit, friend and foe took a brief time out from battle.

For Joffre, the moment of decision had been reached; now that decision was translated into action and Klück and Bülow's troops would be afflicted by one of the most dramatic and decisive operations of the entire war. By 8 September, Paris was a mere 20 miles away, perhaps a little closer for some. The Kaiser's men thought that this well-earned respite was merely an opportunity to rest, regroup, replenish and prepare for the final sweep into the French capital. Joffre and Field Marshal Sir John French, commanding the BEF, had other ideas. After a fortnight in retreat, this lull for the French and British soldiers was to provide time to prepare once again for the offensive: *à l'outrance* at last.

The British in particular, so frustrated by the continuous order to fall back when they were more inclined to fight back as at Mons and Le Cateau, were to be given the chance to do just that. On the other side, Klück's left wheel to the south, which put the German right wing to the east of Paris and not, as Schlieffen had planned, to the west, gave Joffre a golden opportunity. It was one that he had no intention of missing. He noted that: 'The situation was impressive. Our front formed the arc of a vast circle encircling the enemy.'

With this picture in mind, he planned to hold his right flank firm to contain the German left wing while attacking Klück's First Army with his Sixth. Simultaneously, he would push the BEF and French Fifth Army through the yawning gap that now existed between Klück and Bülow. Field Marshal French, moved by Joffre's plea for British help, had no hesitation in providing it. Over the next twenty-four hours, the French and the BEF regrouped, issued fresh orders to turn about and advance once more and were on the move.

The first counter-punch would be thrown on 6 September. Joffre issued an order of the day; an order that could not have been more clear:

> The moment has passed for looking to the rear. All our efforts must be directed towards attacking and driving back the enemy. Troops who can advance no further must, at any price, hold onto the ground that they have conquered rather than give way. Under the circumstances which face us, no act of weakness can be tolerated.[10]

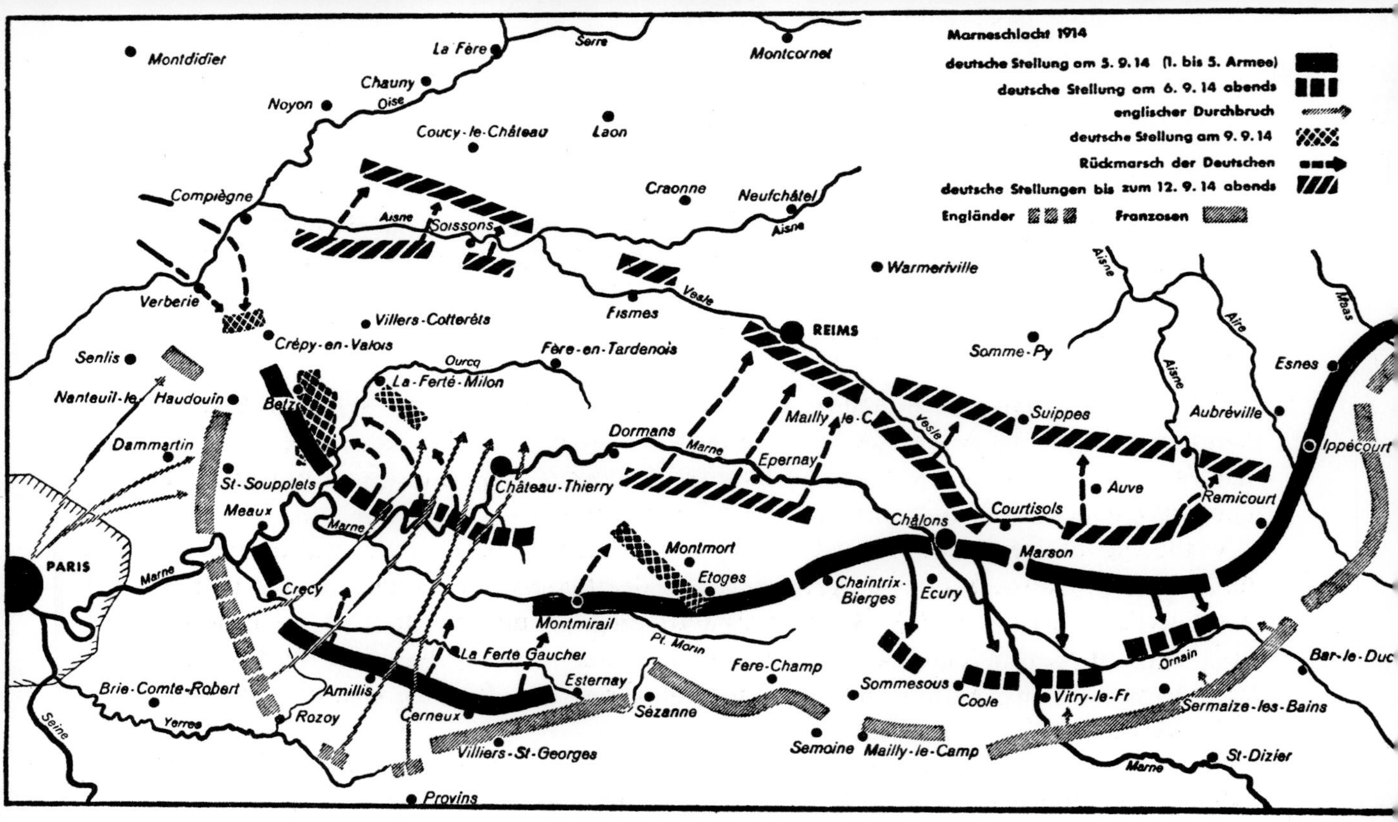

Marneschlacht (the Battle of the Marne) September 1914: the German positions on 5 September (First to Fifth Armies); British (and French) breakthrough; German positions on the 9th and withdrawal; German positions on 12 September.
(Rudolph Stratz, Weltkrieg)

But on this first day the French Sixth Army was checked by dogged German resistance and General Gallieni responded with an extraordinary expedient: he reinforced the hard-pressed attackers with a legion of Parisian taxis that careered out of the city crammed with troops and drove straight into the fight. In the centre, a weaker German opposition was swept aside by the French Fifth Army and the BEF, who cut a swathe across the Marne and severed any chance of further collaboration between Klück and Bülow.[11]

Between 6 and 11 September a miracle unfolded for one side, while a numbing disaster inflicted the other. By 11 September, the German First and Second Armies had fallen back and Moltke's tenure at the head of all the Kaiser's men would be dramatically cut short. Germany's scent of victory now resembled the foul odour of defeat.

The Marne demonstrated a feature of apparently uncharacteristic German indiscipline that was to occur again most prominently during the spring 1918 offensives, as described by a British officer:

> The Germans made themselves very comfortable – perhaps even drunk – at the villages occupied by them. The ground in their neighbourhood is often literally covered with wine bottles, besides equipment, abandoned wagons, carts and

> exhausted horses. The [locals] are furious at the wanton damage done to their property by their late 'guests', described heatedly as 'Huns', 'Bosches', 'barbarians', . . . The woods on the routes of the BEF are full of bewildered German stragglers [and] our captures of prisoners and transport are . . . very large.[12]

A vital factor in the German Army's disintegration was the authority vested in *Oberst Leutnant* Hentsch by Moltke. On 9 September, as a worried Bülow ordered Second Army's withdrawal, Hentsch met Klück's chief of staff Hermann von Kuhl at First Army HQ. Klück, the Army commander, was not present.

By the end of the meeting, in which Hentsch effectively ordered the withdrawal of the First Army also, Kuhl was preparing the draft reply for Klück to send to the beleaguered Moltke at GHQ. When it arrived, allegedly underwritten by the head of First Army, it was endorsed by Moltke. Hentsch had won the day, but the German Army were about to lose not only the battle on the Marne, but any chance of victory in the west in 1914.

By dawn on 12 September it was evident that the Schlieffen master plan had disintegrated; and there was no 'Plan B'. The Kaiser's men in the West were exhausted, wasted shadows of those who had so recently imagined beating a triumphant path to Paris 'before the leaves fell', as their Kaiser had promised. Now they had been thrown back from Paris and the Marne, stunned by their first defeat and left with the growing fear that victory had slipped from their grasp, perhaps forever.

For a brief period it seemed as though the German Army was on the verge of a humiliating retreat worse even than the Allied trek between Mons and the Marne. It

10 Bataille de la Marne
6 au 12 Septembre 1914
Maurupt (Marne)
Champ de bataille à l'est du chemin
de Pargny-sur-Saulx

German dead await mass burial, Marne, 1914.
(Postcard, Allen Collection)

Feldgraue begeben sich zur Arbeit im Schützengraben

Troops set to work on their trench: postcard sent by a soldier of 6th Bavarian Infantry Division to his fiancée.
(Allen Collection)

was possible that its troops could be standing with their backs against the River Rhine and facing invasion themselves. There was a general mood in the Allied camp that a complete victory was within their sights, providing there was a due sense of urgency. For a moment, winning the war by Christmas was a tantalising thought.

But now a pattern of events began to unfold that would become depressingly familiar on the Western Front. Pursuit of the demoralised German armies was slow, over-cautious, and curbed by bridge demolitions and gutsy delaying actions by German rearguards.

On 13 September Gen Douglas Haig's British Ist Corps reached the River Aisne, overlooked by the 'Chemin des Dames' ridge. The German *Korps* had beaten the British to it, but only after a forced march of 40 miles in 24 hours. The German units took up positions on the Chemin des Dames and began to dig in. From rudimentary trenches they were able to hold off any British attempt to dislodge them. Then the British men dug in too.

Thereafter, both German and Allied attempts to outflank each other moved inexorably and bloodily north from the River Aisne to the River Somme, towards Arras, the Douai plain and beyond. Each manoeuvre ended with deadlock, further digging-in and a no-man's-land between the respective trench lines.

This period became known as the 'Race to the Sea'; a misnomer, in fact, as it was neither a race nor an attempt to reach the Channel ports. Rather, the ensuing clashes were little more than a series of slow-motion dances of death northwards as the Germans and Western Allies instinctively edged right or left respectively to open or close fleeting outflanking opportunities.

CHAPTER 3

DANCE OF DEATH, FIRST YPRES AND A WINTER OF DISCONTENT

SEPTEMBER–DECEMBER 1914

The 'dance of death' had reached Flanders by 8 October 1914. As the Allied pursuit began, General von Falkenhayn took stock. Having succeeded the exhausted and utterly dispirited Moltke, he knew full well that he had a daunting task ahead of him.

Falkenhayn was fifty-three years old and was Prussian Minister of War when the war erupted. For a time he would retain this office as well as that of Chief of the General Staff. A firm favourite of the Kaiser, Falkenhayn was ruthless, enigmatic and deeply unpopular with most of the senior German military figures. Though this clash of personalities would have dire consequences later, Falkenhayn did have the nerve and authority that Moltke lacked.

The Allied success may have ended in a grim slogging match, but it not only stemmed the flow of the German haemorrhage across the majority of Belgium and much of France, but also left German plans for any really coherent further advance in tatters.

On 1 October, as the BEF began to redeploy orders from the Aisne to Flanders to protect their vital line of communication and resupply, the German war machine on both the Eastern and the Western Front was geared up one more time in an attempt to deal a knockout blow. It was another dreadfully uneasy time for the Allied commanders and their hard-pressed, dog-tired men.

In the East, Field Marshal Hindenburg and General Ludendorff, who had crushed the Russian armies at Tannenberg a little over a month before, launched a sweeping advance towards Warsaw. But the Russians evaded the net cast wide to trap them near Warsaw and outflanked the Germans.

General Erich von Falkenhayn, Chief of the German General Staff, September 1914 to August 1916.
(Rudolph Stratz, Weltkrieg)

Simultaneously, on the Western Front, Antwerp was pummelled by the giant howitzers that bombarded Namur and Liège. The French along the Aisne under General Edouard de Curière de Castelnau faced mounting pressure from renewed German assaults, and the progress of each corps of the BEF into Flanders was hampered by an increasingly strong German presence. De Castelnau held on and the BEF pressed on to Ypres so that each corps managed to arrive in the Ypres area just in time to meet the new German onslaught.

Falkenhayn acknowledged that this would be the final throw of the dice for 1914 and only now emphasised that a breakthrough in Flanders, and against the British in particular, would not only threaten their continued will to resist, but also physically cut them off from the Channel ports and therefore any hope of resupply and reinforcement.

German prisoners in the autumn of 1914.
(Postcard, Allen Collection)

18. A NEUFMONTIER
près de Meaux
Prisonniers Allemands
de la Croix-Rouge
sur la place de l'Église

'The Great European War' – a German gun and limber wrecked by a French 'soixante-quinze' 75mm quick-firing field gun, September 1914. *(Postcard, Allen Collection)*

He declared:

> The Allied threat to the German right wing must be eliminated. If this is not done, then the drastic action against England and her sea traffic with U-boats, aircraft and zeppelins, which was being prepared in reply to England's war of starvation [the Allied Naval blockade against Germany], was impossible. It was also questionable whether the occupied territory in northern France and Western Belgium could be held . . . The prize is worth the stake.[1]

The stake at Ypres and in Flanders was practically everything that both sides could spare. This, then, was the stage for the final theatre of dreams of German victory in 1914 for the Kaiser, Falkenhayn and those exhausted German soldiers who had so far fought and survived the opening months of the war in the West.

By the beginning of October, the Belgians had established a front line along the River Yser from Nieuport on the coast to Bixschoote. To the south, the French had extended their line as far as Armentières. French territorial infantry divisions, a cavalry corps and the BEF now moved into the gap between the Belgian and French lines in Flanders. Their mission was to find and then turn Falkenhayn's right flank.

Simultaneously, the huge German Fourth Army under Duke Albrecht of Württemburg was heading for the gap and the Channel ports. The first encounter came on 10 October just west of the town of La Bassée when II Corps halted a

Herzog (Duke) Albrecht of Württemberg, commanding the German Fourth Army at Ypres, October–November 1914.
(Rudolph Stratz, Weltkrieg)

German drive towards it. Despite heavy losses, III Corps reached Armentières, securing the bridges over the River Lys in that area. General Edmund 'Bull' Allenby's Cavalry Corps advanced on their left to support the proposed flanking attack to turn the German force. At this stage, the Germans in their path rapidly established blocking positions while Albrecht's Fourth Army struck out towards the Belgian line in the north.

Albrecht's plans were thwarted on 21 October when the Belgian High Command made the painful but vital decision to open the Yser flood barriers, inundating a vast area from the Nieuport to Dixmude. The Fourth Army therefore turned south and from 22 October its full weight was thrown against the rump of unoccupied Belgium.

Herbert Sulzbach, a gunner from Frankfurt-am-Main who had volunteered for military service as war was declared, was now about to witness the conflict at first hand as the Fourth and Sixth Armies geared up for the onslaught on Ypres. On 20 October at Lille, his unit, the 77th Field Artillery Regiment, received its warning order to move north into the cauldron that was to be the First Battle of Ypres. On 21 October, he wrote:

> Change of position. We pull forward, get our first glimpse of this battlefield, and have to get used to the terrible scenes and impressions: corpses, corpses and more corpses, rubble and the remains of a [captured] village . . . Trenches hastily dug by the British are full of bodies. We get driven out of this position . . . by infantry and artillery fire. We stand beside the guns with the horses [and] a dreadful night comes down on us. We have seen too many horrible things all at once . . . [they] make a very strong impression on us, barely twenty years old as we are, but these things also harden us up for what is going to come.[2]

While this German drive was under way, French and Belgian units either side of the BEF were driven back and General Haig's British I Corps found itself exposed in a salient around Ypres. French General de Mitry's Cavalry Corps and the French IX Corps took over the defence of the northern sector of the salient between 22 and 24 October as heavy assaults were launched by elements of both Albrecht's Fourth

Army and Crown Prince Rupprecht of Bavaria's Sixth Army from north and south respectively.

From 24 October, the battle for this 'Ypres salient' was a bloody, continuous and desperate contest. The sustained intensity of the fight, by day and night, was matched by the horrendous conditions of mud and bitter wintry weather.

While the battles in Flanders raged, rumours abounded in Germany as well as England about the enemy's atrocities. In many cases they were hysterically inaccurate and both macabre and unbelievable to the more discerning observer. In October, popular myths came thick and fast:

> The Germans declare that not only are black troops being sent against them (elements of the Indian Corps at Wytschaete), but also that English convicts are being set loose on them, that they recognise them by the 'blue convict band' on their arms. If I tell them that the English do not brand their convicts and these are only

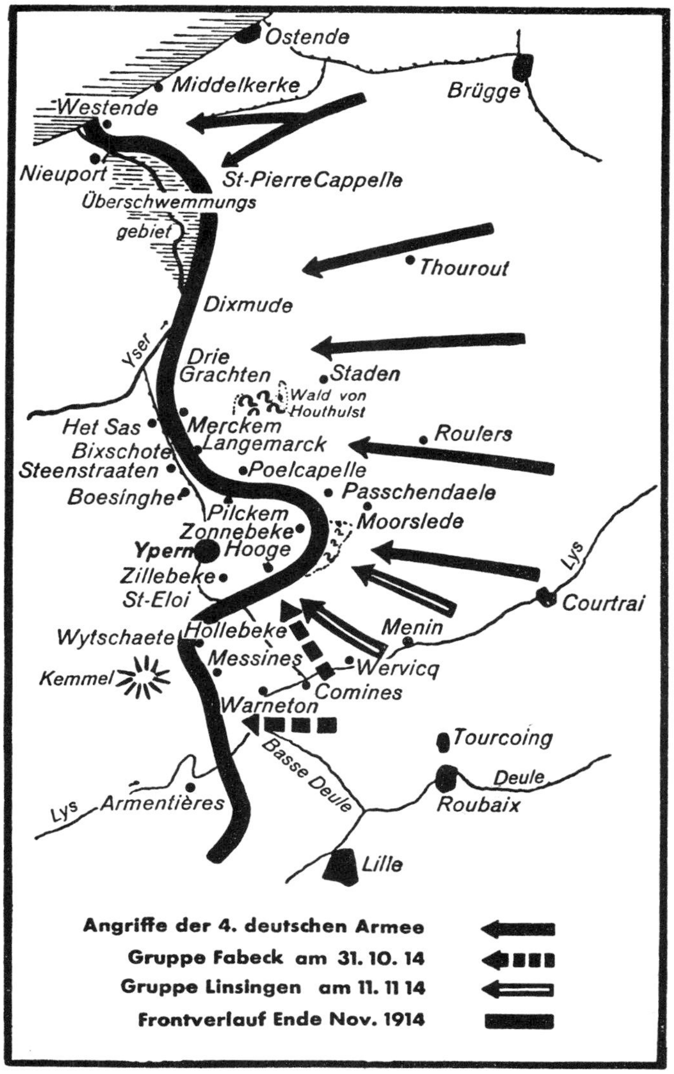

Ypern 1914 (First Ypres): the attack of the German Fourth Army. Gruppe Fabeck on 31 October and Gruppe Linsingen on 11 November highlighted.

(Rudolph Stratz, Weltkrieg)

A 'goulash cannon' and crew an hour before departing for the front, somewhere in France, 1915.

(Postcard, Allen Collection)

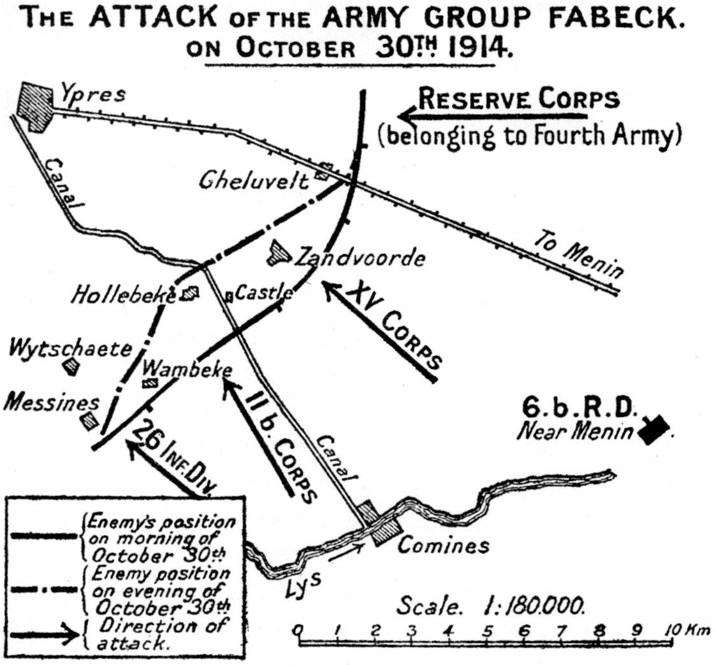

The attack of Army Group/Gruppe Fabeck on 30 October 1914.
(*German General Staff, Ypern 1914*)

tattoo marks, they won't believe me. Also, they assert that many of the British soldiers carry knives with a special twist in them, meant to scoop out the eyes of the wounded Germans.[3]

The reality of war was, of course, somewhat different. Bloody hard fighting it was, but that was all. There was little time or inclination for atrocity; the mounting losses on both sides were enough. Flanders fields were now the killing fields.

From 27 to 31 October, six fresh German divisions formed a new 'Army Group Fabeck' commanded by General von Fabeck, whose Chief of Staff was the redoubtable Lt Col (later General) Fritz von Lossberg. 'Army Group Fabeck' comprised XIII, XV and II Bavarian Corps. The XXIV Reserve Corps was also attached to 'Army Group Fabeck', but formed a *Kampfgruppe*, or Battle Group 'Gerok', which had I & II Cavalry Corps (four cavalry divisions), as well as a Bavarian cavalry division.

Army Group Fabeck then deployed into the gap that had existed between Fourth Army in the north and Sixth Army in the south and became the spearhead of Falkenhayn's renewed offensive from 30 October to 4 November. Supported by the usual concentration of heavy artillery, it was thrown against the British line between Ploegsteert Wood and the Menin Road, with its main effort centred on the capture of the southern high ground of the Ypres salient: the Messines-Wytschaete ridge:

> We now come to the most vital point of the battle, which was who was to be the victor in the fight for the Wytschaete-Messines Ridge.
>
> (Official German monograph, *Ypern 1914*)

On 30 October the 6th Bavarian Reserve Division worked its way forward towards Wytschaete during the day, but checked by the ferocity of enemy artillery fire. Nevertheless, it was ordered to capture the village on the night of 31 October. The plan was now for the 17th Reserve Infantry Regiment to attack from the east, while the 21st Reserve Infantry Regiment would simultaneously assault Wytschaete from the south.

Preparations were thorough, despite the lack of time prior to the attack. All assaulting troops wore white armbands to distinguish them from the enemy during any close-quarter fighting in the darkness; water bottles and bayonet scabbards were packed away in haversacks, rifles checked and bayonets fixed.

The assault would rely on surprise. However, that night there was strong moonlight and this, combined with the constant stream of star shells fired by the defenders of the ridge, made it impossible to advance close to the enemy positions without being seen.

However, at 2 a.m. on 1 November the Bavarian assault began, against stiff enemy artillery and rifle fire, the general direction of the onrush being the remains of the Wytschaete windmill, which was prominently silhouetted as the Bavarians attacked. In the north, the 17th Reserve Infantry Regiment, under the command of Colonel Fritz Hofmann, swept up the ridge and pressed home the attack, rapidly dislodging the defenders and taking this northern sector swiftly.

Surprise had been achieved because of the speed of Hofmann's advance and the excellent use of dead ground by men of the leading waves of the assault. Some of the enemy held out in isolated pockets of resistance in buildings or makeshift strongpoints, until they were overrun and killed or taken prisoner. It had been a short, sharp battle, but the Bavarians had triumphed.

At 6 a.m. Hofmann decided to withdraw his forces into a tighter local defence of the captured sector of Wytschaete as his troops had been continually shelled since taking this part of the village. A few minutes later, as Hofmann's reorganisation phase was under way, the leading troops of the 21st Regiment began to emerge from the southern part of the village, their advance having been delayed by heavy enfilade fire from the south-west. As the approaching men of 21st Regiment moved forward they saw troops in the dim light of early dawn scurrying through the ruins to their north and opened fire. It was a tragic mistake, as their targets were Hofmann's men and dozens were either killed or wounded as a result. After his personal intervention, the 'friendly fire' ceased and both regiments set to the task of improving their defences, expecting the inevitable counter-attack. They did not have to wait long.

At around 9 a.m. Wytschaete was heavily shelled and then assaulted by French regiments that had been rushed to the Flanders area as reinforcements. The remnants of both Hofmann's 17th and the 21st Bavarian Reserve Infantry Regiments were eventually forced to withdraw from the high ground.

To the south of Wytschaete, at Messines, an equally severe and bloody drama had unfolded during Halloween. On 30 October, the 26th (Württemburg) Infantry Division under Duke Wilhelm of Urach had already pushed reconnaissance patrols as far as the edge of the village – and these patrols provided valuable information on the state of the 'English' defences. As a result, it was decided to attack only after thorough artillery preparation, especially on enemy positions on the ridgeline north of Messines.

The plan was for 122nd Fusilier Regiment to attack the ridgeline north of Messines and provide the right-flank protection for the 125th Infantry Regiment while it attempted to assault and capture Messines itself. At the same time, 119th Grenadier

Regiment would attack the enemy defences south of the village and also provide vital left-flank protection for the 125th Regiment.

At 6 a.m. on 31 October, the German howitzers, medium and field artillery batteries began a heavy bombardment of the Messines defence lines. Two hours later the artillery preparation was strengthened by trench mortar fire. Zero Hour was at 10.30 a.m. and as the artillery bombardment fell, the assaulting Württemburg troops of 122nd Fusilier, 125th Infantry and 119th Grenadier Regiments moved into their jump-off positions.

At Zero Hour, the leading assault waves rose to begin the onslaught on Messines. But this was no attack by lines of field-grey uniformed men standing shoulder-to-shoulder and inviting wholesale slaughter by British rifle fire. They attacked in small groups, using short rushes, protected by the covering fire of other troops in the assault. They also utilised the natural contours and cover ('dead ground') of the slopes of Messines ridge to infiltrate the enemy defences.

By 11 a.m. the Stuttgarters of 125th Regiment had taken the north-east corner of Messines, but elsewhere the assault on the village itself rapidly devolved into a grim struggle for every barricade and building. German *Pionere* (Sappers) supported the assault by 125th Regiment. Their task was to destroy the smaller strongpoints established by the English defenders from the 4th and 5th Dragoon Guards and later the King's Own Scottish Borderers.

But most of the houses in Messines remained intact and the defenders caused the German advance to grind to a gory halt in the centre of the village. The greatest obstacle was the convent, protected as it was by walls a yard thick and strong towers from which the English defenders were firing rifles and machine guns and directing their artillery. It was a bloody struggle; reminiscent of the desperate attacks against La Haye Sainte or Hougomont during the Battle of Waterloo.

But this time the attackers prevailed. *Hauptmann* Heinrich's Württemburg battery of the 65th Field Artillery Regiment was brought forward, the men dragging the guns and lugging the ammunition through the debris of the village, and bombarded the convent. Soon after, the convent was in flames and many of its defenders were entombed beneath its ruins.

Leutnant Mösner and men of his company from the 125th Regiment managed to find a narrow footpath out of sight of the enemy, which led to the village centre and he was the first to enter the market-square at around midday.

After an abortive attempt to storm the square, he withdrew to a large house on the eastern edge of the square and decided to hold onto this foothold before reinforcement. The battle for the square became an epic. Mösner and his ever-dwindling group of infantry and engineers defended his strongpoint until evening against all the odds.

The position was reinforced and held by fresh troops of 125th Regiment and further fighting for the square ensued as darkness fell, but the bloody battle continued overnight and it had cost the German attackers dear – over 50 per cent casualties since the attack had begun.

To the north, 122nd Regiment had assaulted the ridgeline between Messines and Wytschaete and its left flank battalion had been ordered into the struggle for Messines itself because of the increasingly desperate and costly street fighting that Mösner and 125th Regiment were engaged in.

North of the village the left wing of 122nd Regiment established itself on the Wytschaete to Messines road after considerable resistance from the enemy – in particular the London Scottish Regiment. But the right wing of the 122nd was forced to go to ground short of the ridgeline itself. Once again, sporadic fighting continued throughout the night and casualties mounted without any further progress.

On the left flank, the 119th Grenadier Regiment were severely mauled by a determined and ferocious enemy. With casualties again in excess of 50 per cent, the remnants of the assaulting units had to dig in and continue the fight to simply secure the left flank of the German assault.

On the morning of 1 November, the German attackers, reinforced by units from the 3rd Division, had an unexpected respite, as a thick mist enshrouded the battlefield. By mid-morning, the mist had cleared and the attack was renewed across a 12-mile front.

The German attacks were pressed home, but the struggle for the Messines ridge continued for a total of four days. Wytschaete was won, lost, then won again by Fabeck's battalions in some of the most chaotic and bloody actions of the whole 'Ypern 1914' campaign. Eventually, Fabeck's men prevailed against a determined enemy. Allenby's cavalry, British infantry and the French 32nd Division (part of French XIV Corps) were forced to give way under the incessant pressure of Fabeck's infantry and the grinding attrition of the German guns.

By the end of 4 November, Army Group Fabeck held the ridge, but still faced a dented, though virtually unbroken Allied defence line. The French 32nd Division had been rushed in to support the beleaguered but resolute British defenders and Army Group Fabeck had failed to take its principal objective of Mount Kemmel.

As the Messines ridge was battered, the centre of the Ypres salient was also under heavy and sustained attack by Group Linsingen, which was hell-bent on taking the important high ground along the Menin Road centred on the village of Gheluvelt. The battle raged either side of the Menin Road and on the afternoon of 31 October, it appeared that the German troops had taken the high ground.

But after an attack comes the inevitable reorganisation and tired men expect some respite. This crucial factor gave General Haig's troops the opportunity to steal back the newly won territory from under the enemy's nose. The Germans were ousted by a truly spectacular counter-attack by just one BEF battalion, the 2nd Worcesters. Gheluvelt became a place of legend for the British but a scene of lost opportunity for the German army.

Meanwhile, the Fourth Army had been ordered to crush Allied resistance in the northern part of the salient and then sweep through to take Ypres. Albrecht flung in not only his well-trained divisions, but also those units of the inexperienced Reserve,

Landsturm and Freiwillige (Volunteer) on the basis that quantity had a quality all of its own. Against the now battle-hardened Regulars of the BEF, quantity merely meant a larger massed target. Falkenhayn was prepared to sacrifice thousands of the best of German youth, the Student Volunteers, who were wildly patriotic, enthusiastic and unswerving in their loyalty, but who were barely trained.

Around Langemarck in late October they were cut down by the steady, accurate fire of the British infantrymen before most could utter their cries of 'Vorwärts zum Sieg'. Wave after wave rose to begin their assaults singing *Wacht am Rhein*. It was a magnificent sight, but a most pitiful slaughter. Soldier-writer *Leutnant* Rudolf Binding wrote at the end of October that:

> . . . these young fellows we have, only just trained, are too helpless, particularly when their officers are killed. Our light infantry battalion, almost all Marburg students . . . have suffered terribly from shellfire. In the next division, just such young souls, the intellectual flower of Germany, went singing into an attack on Langemarck, just as vain and just as costly.[4]

The bodies were piled high after each assault ended under the withering British fire. One platoon alone of the Gordon Highlanders in this area counted 240 German dead in front of their position. It was a common sight at First Ypres and here it had been nothing less than the *Kindermord von Ypern*: the Massacre of the Innocents at Ypres. The German Fourth Army had been ordered by Falkenhayn to do nothing more than win the war. As it happened, thousands did nothing more than die. The Fourth Army had divisions that consisted of middle- and upper-class students and professional men all determined to help fulfil Falkenhayn's wishes, but:

> They had little power of manoeuvre because their training had been so scanty, but they were absolutely determined to win or fall. For the most part they fell.[5]

The German trauma around what was rapidly becoming this notorious Ypres salient was not confined to the student lambs to the slaughter. 'Veteran' units went the same way, the élite Prussian Guard Divisions among them. Falkenhayn's last throw of the dice had begun with abortive attacks against the French lines around Dixmude in the north on 10 November. But the final act came on 11 November. A renewed attack against the British line around Gheluvelt and the Menin Road by Group Linsingen was spearheaded by General Winkler's 4th Guards Division. A major victory suddenly appeared possible as the Prussian Guardsmen broke through the wafer-thin defensive line.

But defeat was snatched from the jaws of victory by a combination of confusion and uncertainty about what to do next. The situation was recorded in the Regimental histories:

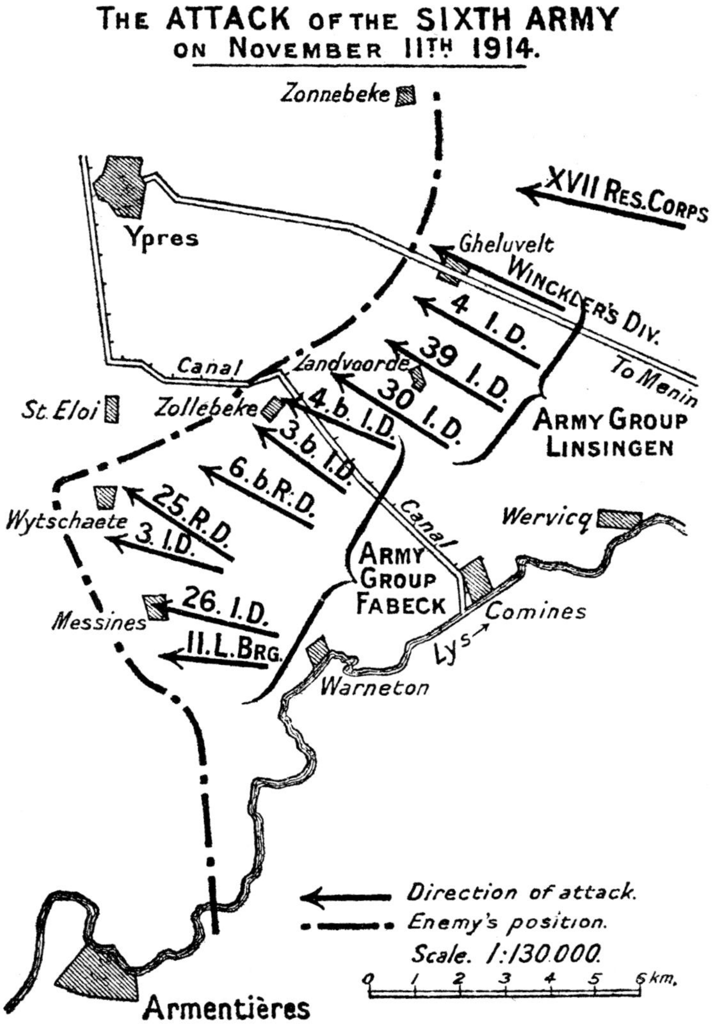

The attack of the Sixth Army.

(*German General Staff, Ypern, 1914*)

> Among the garden enclosures the leaderless lines abandoned the forward movement and drifted to the right . . . As no reinforcements could be got forward to the attackers, the assault came to a standstill at the third of the British lines.[6]

There was no third British line. By now there was barely a first line of defence in certain parts of the Allied front around Ypres. Only when it was too late, and the Prussians had been thrown back by a determined counter-attack, did the magnitude of their failure appear. A captured German officer on that day asked where the British reserves were deployed. The answer given was a tired wave by his captor towards the British guns rattling away against enemy targets at almost point-blank range. 'What is there behind?' he enquired. 'Divisional Headquarters', came the reply. 'God Almighty!' he exclaimed.[7]

The day ended with further British counter-attacks to restore and consolidate the line. Falkenhayn and every type of German unit from Freiwillige to Prussian Guard had failed to break the line and soul of the Allied defence of Ypres. 'They had little else except heavy casualties to show for their final and desperate attempt to break through', as the *British Official History* states.

First Ypres was over, with over 130,000 German casualties, 60,000 British and around 45,000 French. Out of it came the German acceptance that Allied actions were both aggressive and deadly.

The danger had been averted, but for a high price, and Germany faced a bleak winter of discontent, as did the Allies, on the Western Front. In the wider context, the numerically superior French Army to the south had frustrated all German attempts to break through their line, but their own attacks had also failed.

Deadlock had become the norm across the whole of the Western Front. Rudolf Binding wrote that:

> The war has got stuck into a gigantic siege on both sides. The whole front is one endless fortified trench. Neither side has the force to make a decisive push . . . Everyone seems settled on a winter campaign, [but] as far as I can judge; there is no possibility of an early finish . . . We are still stuck here for perfectly good reasons; one might as well say for perfectly bad reasons . . . This business may last for a long time.[8]

The official German account of the battle, *Ypern, 1914*, noted:

> As the November storms passed and frost and icy winds heralded to the mild climate of Flanders the approach of winter, the unbroken defensive lines on both sides were being slowly strengthened. The effect of artillery fire compelled them to make cover in good trenches and behind thick breast works . . . [We] had only been trained in the principles of attack . . . [But] the high sense of duty in each [German soldier] was of assistance and the methods of defensive warfare were quickly learnt.[9]

Trench warfare, no matter how 'quickly learnt', was often a foul experience, even as it began and even in the German trenches. One observer noted in November 1914 that:

> The dangers of trench life may be realised when I say that [often] neither the dead nor wounded can be removed. If you put up as much as a little finger above the edge of the trench, the bullets come whizzing round immediately. The dead bodies must therefore be allowed to remain in the trench; that is to say, the dead man is got rid of by digging a grave for him in the floor of the trench. A few days ago . . . a soldier was so badly hit by a shell that he was cut in two . . . [His shattered body] could not be removed without risk to the survivors and was therefore allowed to remain. But presently he gave rise to a horrible stench and whatever they did the men could not get away from the mutilated, blackened features. Sometimes arms and legs torn away from the body are allowed to lie about the bottom of the trench until somebody can [bury] them. One gets hardened in time . . .[10]

Defensive lines were protected in no-man's-land by ever thickening belts of barbed wire, and the space between German and British or French units varied from a few yards (normally just beyond grenade-throwing range), to almost half a mile. At first, the lines were haphazard, as trenches were dug where the encounter battle had ended. But these lines were adjusted to suit a position that was to the German's advantage. The reason for this benefit was simple enough: the German Army adapted to the conditions of trench warfare more quickly than the Western Allies because necessity has always been the mother of invention.

'Flanders' – German troops in the front line near Warneton, wearing gas masks, which would become indispensable after spring 1915. A placard on the trench wall declares: 'Gott Strafe England' ('God Strike England').
(Allen Collection)

By the end of 1914, Falkenhayn's armies held most of Belgium and a good proportion of northern France; and they had the luxury of choosing the best defensive ground, digging in and obliging the French and British to winkle them out. Therefore, the Germans could afford to consolidate their defences, while the Allies were under different pressures. As the French C-in-C General Joffre wrote at the time:

> The best and largest portions of the German army was on our soil and with its line of battle jutting out a mere five day's march from the heart of France. This situation made it clear to every Frenchman that our task consisted in defeating the enemy, and driving him out of our country.[11]

More locally, First Ypres had begun a four-year period of agonising restlessness and sacrifice on both sides in the macabre theatre that was the 'Ypres salient' and Flanders. By November 1918, no less than five major battles would have been fought here and 'the Salient' would hold a combination of notorious memory and compelling fascination for British, French and German soldiers alike. To the German soldier:

> Flanders! The word is heard by everyone in the German Fatherland with a silent shudder, but also with just and intense pride. It was here that the British were made to realise that German heroism was not to be vanquished . . . Let us only hold the hope that the seeds of [German] blood sown in Flanders will bring forth rich and splendid fruit for the German Fatherland.[12]

On 20 December, units of the BEF's Indian Corps deployed in the Givenchy sector south of Ypres were attacked in a new and horrific way. At precisely 9.00 a.m. the peace was shattered when the Germans blew ten small mines beneath the Allied trenches: the simultaneous explosions killed many Indian troops instantly. German infantry then swarmed across no-man's-land and quickly overwhelmed the stunned survivors, bombing their way to La Quinque Rue. Within hours, the Germans had captured trenches either side of Givenchy and made a 300-yard pocket east of Festubert. Although the German success was short-lived and they were driven back, the attack had signalled the beginning of a new type of conflict – the war underground.

As in many cases throughout the First World War, the German Army introduced a novel tactic or method, e.g. mining and tunnelling, gas, and flame warfare, only for the British and French to adopt and become very much more proficient at it. The prospect of being blown sky-high by explosives placed directly below the trenches was terrifyingly real in notorious locations such as Vauqouis, Vimy Ridge, Hill 60, Hooge, St-Elooi and the like for much of the remainder of the war.

By Christmas 1914, from Nieuport to Belfort the 'Dance of Death' had ended in stalemate. On the Eastern Front it was the same story. At home it was already abundantly clear that this was the first of more than one bitter winter at war. Soldiers on both sides of no-man's-land were issued with extra cigarettes, pipe tobacco, chocolate – and much-needed Christmas presents and mail from home. But it seemed that the 'killing fields' would remain open for business across the traditional Christmas season. In most places they did. But in Flanders, something quite remarkable happened.

Christmas Eve was a grim one indeed. Trenches and dugouts were so waterlogged that they became known as the 'waterworks'; communication trenches were glutinous and mud-filled, snow had fallen and it was bitterly, bitterly cold. In one place the BEF had 19th Infantry Brigade facing the 19th Saxon Corps. That night, the dam of a local stream burst, washing out men in both sets of trenches. By next morning, all either side could hope to do until major repairs could be done, was to crouch, half-frozen on the remains of the parapet behind makeshift barricades of empty ammunition boxes and sandbags.

At dawn it seemed that it could only be a matter of time before the sniping and shelling started. Nothing happened. Then, realising that this was Christmas Day, the Saxon troops began singing carols, the British responded in kind and for some hours peace broke out to mark the day.

Near Messines, a British artillery officer recorded on Christmas Eve that the Germans in their trenches began singing carols, at which many of the British troops cheered and sang along when they could. Someone in the German 'choir' called: 'You English, why don't you come out?' The response, bearing in mind that many Germans had worked as bar staff in England before the war, was predictable: 'Waiter!' But, as the carolling continued, one or two, then three or four, soldiers on either side put their heads above the trench. Soon there were fires and candles burning brightly along the parapets. Of course, in Germany now, as then, the main Christmas celebrations would normally take place on Christmas Eve, with family gathered around the traditional *Tannenbaum*, or Christmas tree. So for those British troops involved in this historic event, Christmas came a little earlier than planned.

On Christmas Day, sentries were posted, breastworks consolidated and German and British working parties shared tools to shore up respective defences against the ever-present threat of flooding. Gifts and souvenirs were exchanged, gossip flourished about home and family life in Germany or Great Britain, and both German and

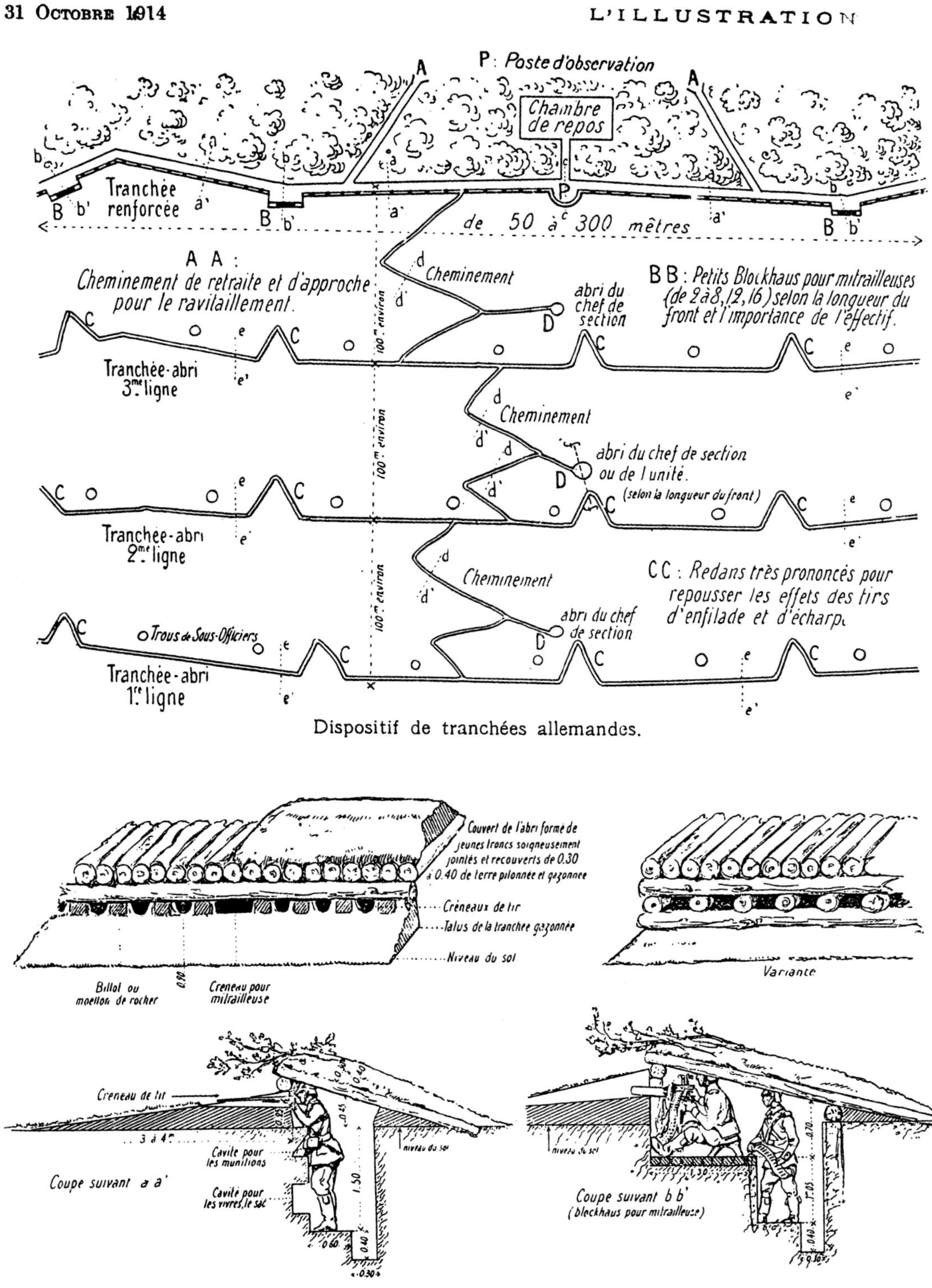

A French drawing showing German trench building, dated 31 October 1914.

(French Military Manual 1914)

British soldiers posed for informal photographs. Above all, most wondered why the hell they were fighting each other when they had so much in common.

The common bond and enjoyment of the occasion was tempered by the fact that this informal truce allowed both sides also to collect and bury their dead. The British chaplain in the sector read prayers for the dead in both English and German. A German officer took the opportunity of the truce to pass over a message and personal effects of a British officer mortally wounded in a previous raid. The German explained that he had found him badly wounded and groping for something in his pocket. He bent down to assist him and discovered a note and photograph of his wife. He held the photograph before the dying officer's eyes. The German officer explained: 'Communion with her portrait was his last sacrament. Tell her he died like that.' The chaplain promised that he would do so.

Crown Prince Rupprecht of Bavaria who was highly regarded by friend and foe, commanded Sixth Army in 1914 and 1915, then his own Group of Armies until the end of the war.
(Rudolph Stratz, Weltkrieg)

On a lighter note, there was the odd game of football also. In one, Scots associated with Clydebank and Partick Thistle played against Saxons who had played for a Leipzig team that had played in Glasgow in spring 1914. It is said that the final score was 3–2 to the Saxons.

It is no coincidence that Saxon troops played the most prominent role in the Christmas truce. Saxon troops had a strong empathy with their historical allies and friends across the wire and in many sectors where Saxon divisions held the line a situation of 'live and let live' prevailed. Little love was lost between the Saxons and their 'comrades-in-arms', the Prussians.

On the subject of Prussians, soldiers on both sides were witness to Saxon humour. Boards were apparently raised declaring: 'Do not fire on us – we are Saxons; wait until we are relieved by the Prussians.' Later, as the war correspondent Philip Gibbs

French prisoners of war on display to a curious public in Germany, late 1914.
(Allen Collection)

reported, a German unit facing a British battalion produced a board on which was painted: 'The English are fools.' It was shot to pieces by rifle fire. Soon afterwards, another board appeared, which read: 'The French are fools.' Once again it was immediately cut to ribbons with a volley of fire. Finally, a third board appeared: 'We are all fools. Let's all go home.'[13]

The war had to be prosecuted, but there were ways, and ways, of doing so. Throughout both world wars it was acknowledged that the Germans had excellent snipers. But 'live and let live' sometimes affected the practice of such men. Captain Ian Hay, an infantry officer of the 9th (Scottish) Division, was astonished to witness such an incident when a working party went out into no-man's-land one evening. He observed:

> No one was hit, which was remarkable, when you consider what an artist a German sniper is . . . Possibly, there is some truth in the general rumour that the Saxons, who hold this part of the line . . . conduct their offensive operations with a tactful blend of constant firing and bad shooting, which, while it satisfies the Prussians, causes no serious inconvenience to Thomas Atkins.[14]

Herbert Sulzbach, who had been in the thick of the action since the beginning of First Ypres, still held the German soldiers' common views that God was indeed on their side and that theirs was a just war. In October, he had noted in his diary that: 'We certainly did not want this war! We were only defending ourselves and our Germany against a world of enemies who have banded together against us.'[15] Furthermore, he had more reason than many to celebrate Christmas: 'The Regiment gave me a most splendid Christmas present: I was promoted to *Gefreiter*, lance-bombardier, and it did me good to be picked out like this after so short a time.'[16]

It was all rather too good to be true for those who wished for the informal truce to be extended. German and British troops could not fraternise like this. After all, according to the senior commanders on either side, it would be bad for morale. After the Christmas sojourn, German Army Order of the Day on 29 December declared that any further fraternising would be punished as a treasonable offence.

British reactions were similarly harsh, as commanding officers and units involved in the Christmas events were made examples of, being sacked, moved to more demanding sectors of the line, or disciplined in some other punitive way. The BEF also issued an Army Routine Order, which made it abundantly clear that British soldiers 'were in France [and Belgium] to fight and not to fraternize with the enemy.'[17]

Other informal arrangements would be made at times along the front lines of the Western Front, but never in the manner of Christmas 1914. The last vestiges of the innocence and sense of adventure that had infected the soldiers of every nation in August were finally snuffed out with the candles when Christmas Day 1914 passed and the nightmare of war returned.

Straight away, misunderstanding over the informal arrangements made to end the truce was typical of the dark auguries for the future. In one sector, a British sergeant was sent across no-man's-land with a note to the effect that the truce would end at 10 a.m. the next day. As the hour approached, warnings were shouted to German troops to take cover, but they did not. Soon after 10 a.m., a British subaltern was ordered to lob a jam-pot bomb near a German working party, just to scare them.

Unfortunately, the subaltern's throw was too accurate and the explosion wounded one of them in the leg. The poor wretch went down and writhed in agony as the others scuttled for cover. A single shot from the German lines hit the subaltern in the head, killing him outright, and moments later, machine gun and rifle fire erupted from both trench lines. All hell broke loose, and it was 'business as usual' once more.[18]

Lichtwirkung des die große französ. Offensive vorbereitenden
siebzigstündigen Artillerie-Trommelfeuers u. der Leuchtgranaten,
Ende September 1915.
A 379
E.P. & Co. A.-G., L.

An example of artillery 'Drumfire' and illuminating flare bombardment at night: landscape on a contemporary postcard, Western Front, 1915. *(Allen Collection)*

By the end of 1914, Falkenhayn had reluctantly conceded that the demands of the Eastern Front would compel him to take a defensive stance in the West. But at this time, despite the fact that vital manpower and resources, particularly artillery, had been diverted to the second front, he was convinced that the West was where the war was to be won. But both the Kaiser and Bethmann-Hollweg, the German Chancellor, deferred to the victors of Tannenberg, Hindenburg and Ludendorff, who urged that the Eastern Front should be given the priority in 1915.

It was a costly error. Rather than concentrate his available strength to exploit the exhaustion and weakness of the French and British in the West, Falkenhayn inadvertently gave them desperately needed time to regroup, reinforce and train new troops for the coming year. Worse, the respite gave more time for the hitherto tenuous trench systems on either side of no-man's-land to become more solid, especially on the German side, making it more difficult to crack the problem of deadlock.

For the Allies, Joffre was eager to at least straighten the line before the new year and thus launched offensives in December against the German defences in the Artois and Champagne regions. The Artois assaults by the Tenth Army began on 17 December against the high ground of Vimy Ridge and Notre Dame de Lorette (Loretto to the

Germans) just north of Arras. The French effort was bloodily stalled by a lethal combination of poor artillery support, thick fog, freezing rain and impassable, slippery mud for the infantry to attack across. Within a fortnight the French had lost 18,000 men for negligible gains. In Champagne, the French Fourth Army's onslaught began on 20 December, but was frustrated in much the same way. Joffre, undeterred, decided to try again a month or so later.

Ironically, the French offensives had merely served to strengthen the German defences still more. The consequences would be dire for Joffre's renewed attempts to crack the German defensive nut with both French and British offensives throughout 1915.

At first, social distinctions and antagonisms in Germany were obliterated as aristocrats, the middle class and workers joined ranks in the face of the common enemy. But as we have seen, the 1914 German Army on the Western Front was plunged into near-destruction at the Marne and beyond. The aristocratic, middle-class and working-class soldiers of that Army soon found that enemy artillery, machine guns and rifle fire obliterated social distinctions more effectively than any patriotic fervour could do; but literally.

As a result, by the end of 1914 German casualties included almost 120,000 dead (i.e. four times the number of fatalities for the whole of the Franco-Prussian War) and a further 400,000 wounded or prisoners of war. By Christmas the glorious adventure was over and the Western Front had frozen into the stalemate that was to endure in the main until 1918.

Despite the frustration of the early months of the war, however, the German people were encouraged to hold out against the increasing hardship of their own war on the Home Front in the successive years with the promise of ultimate victory.

In 1915, the German High Command's claim was that victory would come on the Eastern Front.

CHAPTER 4

1915: DEADLOCK, FALSE HOPES AND PROMISES

By January 1915, the rapid victory imagined by not only Germany and her allies, but also the Western Allies and Russia was but a distant and hazy dream. In the West, a linear siege warfare had begun, a virtually unbroken line of trenches either side of no-man's-land, running for almost 400 miles from the Channel ports to the Swiss border. On the Eastern Front, deadlock was rather more temporary and both Germany/Austria and Russia would look to 'finishing the job' within the next twelve months.

At sea, the German High Seas Fleet remained strong but largely impotent, as it had no intention of drawing the Royal Navy into a major maritime clash at this stage. Germany had another ace in the hole, however – U-boats – and fully intended to use them.

The quiescent nature of Germany's surface fleet did not deter Falkenhayn from seeking an alternative approach. He sought an end to the deadlock indirectly via a blockade of the British Isles, with the U-boat as his main weapon.

The plan was to starve Britain by cutting her off from her overseas trade, forcing a withdrawal from France and Belgium and leaving both countries to their inevitable fate without British support. It was estimated that 200 U-boats would do the job, in a role that was far removed from that employed until 1915, principally as auxiliary vessels for the surface fleet.

Unfortunately, two major problems diminished the proposed strategy. First, there were nowhere near 200 U-boats; only 28 were in service in August 1914, and their limited range, coupled with the Royal Navy's complete control of the Dover Straits, made the strategy impractical for 1915 at least.

The second obstacle was one that would have profound implications later in the war and help to bring the United States to the Allies' aid on mainland Europe. U-boat warfare was a clandestine affair, so Allied vessels would be sunk with little or no warning. Successful U-boat attacks gave considerable support to the Allied propaganda image of German barbarism. The loss of the SS *Lusitania* in May 1915, which caused American fury, and the limited effect of U-boat attempts to blockade Britain, led to a temporary halt in U-boat operations by the summer.

The prospects for Germany as 1915 dawned were not healthy. The great Schlieffen punch, designed to knock out France and the BEF with one blow, had failed. Subsequent assaults during the 'Dance of Death', Antwerp and especially First Ypres, simply guaranteed stalemate, but at huge cost on both sides. On the second front in the East, limited German forces still faced an enemy with a bottomless manpower barrel and, despite the terrible experience of Tannenberg a mere three weeks into the war, an extraordinary ability to endure and come back for more. Within weeks, Russia would threaten East Prussia and Galicia once more.

Furthermore, the German troops in the East knew that they were also propping up a sick and ailing Austro-Hungarian Army. Germany was, in the words of an infuriated staff officer in autumn 1914, 'shackled to [the Austrian] corpse'. The only bright spot was Turkey's entry into the war at the end of 1914 on the Kaiser's side, which meant that British, French and Russian resources could be stretched in southern Europe at little material cost to Germany.

Falkenhayn had redrawn the strategic map. Germany would consolidate in the West and concentrate her offensive resources and those of Austria-Hungary for a decisive blow against Russia. He reasoned that such a strategy would not only relieve the hard-pressed Austrian armies, but also deter Italy and the neutral Balkan states from siding with the Entente. Of course, he hoped that 'success [in the East] would be big enough to check the enemy for a long time', and still privately dreamed of resuming the main offensive in the West.[1] It was to remain a source of great resentment and frustration among the German commanders in the East, most notably Hindenburg and Ludendorff. Falkenhayn's dream would raise a spectre that would come back to haunt him in 1916.

The strategy in the Allied camp for 1915 was that centred on the great debate between the 'Westerners' and the 'Easterners'. For the 'Westerners', Field Marshal Georges Joffre and the French High Command, as well as British commanders such as General Douglas Haig of the British First Army, believed that a decisive victory could only come on the Western Front against Germany, the main theatre of war and the main enemy. The 'Easterners', who included Lord Kitchener, Winston Churchill and David Lloyd George, argued that Germany could be beaten without the enormous concomitant loss of life already characteristic of the Western Front by knocking Turkey out of the war. Germany's 'prop' in the region would cause the edifice to crumble and she would be defeated through the 'back door', or via this 'soft underbelly' of Europe.

Theory and practice often drift apart and this debate could only have one outcome, although it would take a very painful lesson to prove the point – at Gallipoli. The fundamental problem from the outset was that the 'Easterners' had flawed ideas, not the least of which was the notion that Turkey was 'propping up' Germany. Not only did Germany provide the backbone to Turkey's feeble military leadership, she also 'propped up' the other Central Powers, including Austria-Hungary.

Gallipoli, the great Dardanelles adventure, was to become a legend of notorious and costly failure on one hand, but extraordinary courage and sacrifice on the other. Ironically, the Allied withdrawal, arguably the most difficult operation of war, was brilliantly executed under the noses of the Turkish defenders without a single casualty in December 1915.

Joffre continued to focus on the Western Front and a series of offensives was planned throughout the year. Italy did join the Allied cause, fought four battles of the Isonzo and marked the end of the year with stalemate as rock-hard as that on the Western Front and almost 175,000 casualties.

The East–West debate widened the war to the Caucasus, the Middle East, Mesopotamia and Salonika, as well as Italy and the Dardanelles, while Germany remained as strong in the West as ever by the end of 1915.

In August 1914, the German people had accepted that unemployment – which reached 21 per cent that autumn – was a necessary side effect of mobilisation. Patriotic fervour and the sense of *gemeinschaft*, or unity, within the nation were enough to steel them for temporary discomfort. Besides, food supplies had been abundant after a bumper harvest that summer and industries were given free rein to produce the tools of war. Finances were ignored because the German leadership believed that they would foot the bill through reparations against their vanquished enemies.

It seemed to most German people that even if the war had not been won within weeks as the Kaiser had predicted, Germany would easily overcome potential deficiencies because she was self-sufficient. But the myths, deceptions and lies of war had already begun. For example, the Government stressed in autumn 1914 that German farmers produced 90 per cent of the nation's food supplies. But it omitted to point out that they did so only with the help of over two million tons of imported phosphate and nitrogenous fertilisers, six million tons of hard fodder, such as barley, corn and oats, and with the labour of over one million foreign seasonal workers. Without these, domestic production soon fell by over 20 per cent.[2]

The first food shortages appeared at home as 1914 drew to a close. But the German Army continued to procure what it needed without regard for civilian requirements and food prices soared as supplies dwindled. The government quickly imposed maximum prices on a host of food items, especially potatoes and sugar.

Berlin took steps to ward off labour unrest by nationalising wheat, and rationed bread at 5lb per person per week in January 1915, and then established maximum prices and production quotas on butter, fish, milk, pork, fruit and vegetables by November of that year.[3]

The Allied naval blockade was by no means the only reason for the poor conditions for the citizens of Germany. Their Government and military were exacerbating the problem. It was a problem that would only become worse.

Millions of words have been printed and spoken on television, radio and film about the virtually impregnable defences built by the German Army in the First World War. It is true that German engineering skills and ingenuity, together with abundant defensive stores in the early years of the war, provided the Kaiser's men on the Western Front with a formidable defensive capability. Falkenhayn's strategy for 1915 meant that Germany would have a clear advantage in this technique of warfare by year's end. This advantage would be severely tested in the summer of 1916 and beyond, but for most of 1915, trench warfare would favour the German Army in the West.

German units were well drilled in defensive tactics, and their 'sappers' strengthened the trench lines, communication trenches and dugouts. It was not long before the infantry and artillery units were relatively comfortable in their semi-permanent 'homes', despite the harsh winter of 1914/1915. In that period, field-artilleryman Herbert Sulzbach was able to record that:

> The snow . . . has turned the plains of Flanders into a winter landscape. [But] . . . mail arrives in the evening, and among other things, I get a parcel as a present from my old school. Then we read the newspapers out loud to each other. At the battery meanwhile they have made themselves much more cosy. The dugouts have tables and stoves and one even has a piano in it . . . Now we have been [two] months in this position. We exchange greetings with the British every day in the shape of shells; everything is gradually becoming a habit . . . We are preparing more and more for a static campaign. The infantry positions have been surrounded with strong barbed-wire entanglements.[4]

'Sanitäts-Unterstand': medical dugout, France, 1915.
(Allen Collection)

German trench system in the Champagne/Chemin des Dames sector, 1915.
(Allen Collection)

So it had come to this: the most enduring symbol of the First World War. Trench warfare was soon the fact of life on the Western Front, and most soldiers on each side of no-man's-land learned to deal with it, aware that their lot as infantrymen was roughly equal. For the majority of the war, that lot would be admirably summed up by the French writer Marie-Paul Rimbault who declared that:

> There's nothing so like a German soldier in his trench than a French (or British) soldier in his. They are both poor sods and that's all there is to it.[5]

The trench systems (*Schutzengräben*) that now took shape on either side of the wire began to reflect the nature of the Allied or German cause. There were fundamental similarities in their general structure, such as a front line supported by second line and reserve trenches, all of which were connected by communication trenches. Each front line trench system had a parapet (*Brustwehr*) and fire-step (*Schützenauftritt*) on the enemy side facing no-man's-land (*Niemandsland*) and a parados (*Rückenwehr*) to the rear, where spoil from the digging was deposited and which gave added protection from shellfire. The trench was reinforced with sandbags, timber, wattle, pickets, wire, and corrugated iron and, in many German positions, reinforced concrete.

'In the Trenches – Soldiers' Quarters in a Dugout', postcard dated 3 July 1915.
(Allen Collection)

German 21cm (210mm) gun in a well-protected shelter, 1915.
(Allen Collection)

Unless dug immediately before an attack, trench lines soon lost their purely linear appearance in favour of the more familiar 'zig-zag' or 'dog's tooth' appearance. This added further protection from the blast effect of shells, mortar bombs or grenades and prevented an enemy from devastating the trench with flanking fire. The straight section facing the enemy was known as the fire bay (*Schützenbank*) and each of the links left and right to the next fire bays was a traverse (*Quergang*).

A series of sentry posts were established by day and night within the fire bays and 'saps' were dug to extend cover from direct fire out into no-man's-land for listening and observation posts (OPs), as well as specific operations, such as trench raids. In front of the forward positions lay belts of barbed wire (*Drahtverhau*), which became the curse of assaulting troops on both sides. Held in place by iron pickets, it was rapidly laid and provided an obstacle that could be 100 yards deep. The trenches were further protected by machine gun positions, which provided interlocking arcs of fire across the defended sector into no-man's-land.

Despite the popular perception of German soldiers living in comparative luxury, dugouts (*Schützenhöhlen*) were more commonly used for officers and senior NCOs, forward HQs and medical posts. Most junior NCOs and men lived, fed and slept in the trench for the few days that they were assigned to front line duty, protected by rain capes and small hollows dug into the parados side of their trenches.

Nevertheless, the defensive stance of the Kaiser's men on the Western Front for much of the war did give them the luxury of concentrating their engineering effort in improving the sectors where time and terrain allowed. Larger shelters were built for the protection of the infantry in the line and especially the counter-attack (*Eingreif*) units that were crucial to German defensive tactics.

German troops at rest in the trenches, summer 1915.
(Contemporary sketch on postcard, Allen Collection)

The landscape dictated the methods used by the German Army. As a result, labyrinthine redoubts, which were essentially underground strongholds, fortified villages and concreted machine gun and field artillery positions emerged on the chalk land regions of the Somme, Artois/Arras and Champagne, where dugouts could be as much as forty feet deep. It is true that here many German troops had the comforts of electric lighting, piped water supplies and excellent air ventilation systems.

Plundered French household items also gave German officers and SNCOs the opportunity to furnish their dugouts with 'home comforts' such as timber wall panelling, tables and chairs, *objets d'art* and even carpeted floors. But, the idea that this wall-to-wall luxury for German officers and men was universal and remained throughout the war is a deeply flawed one. For example, although these deep defences were often virtually untouched by enemy artillery fire in the early stages of the Somme campaign in 1916, as the campaign evolved they became as much death traps for the troops inside as they had been safe havens.

On the other hand, in Flanders, 'the flooded plain', the wet conditions, low-lying land and clay subsoil made it impossible to dig deep trenches and dugouts. Consequently, both sides more commonly built trenches raised 6 feet or so above ground consisting of breastworks of sandbags, wood and corrugated iron. From mid-1915 onwards the German defences were strengthened considerably with the construction of reinforced concrete bunkers, strongpoints and fortified villages in depth running the length of the Ypres salient between Pilckem and Messines within an elaborate defensive network: the *Flandern Linie*, or Flanders Line. However, as on the Somme, the Battle of Messines and the 'Passchendaele' campaign in 1917 would prove that these apparently impregnable defences could also be neutralised and that in the mud and blood of Flanders, the Kaiser's men would suffer even more than their British and Dominion opponents.

In common with their adversaries, German infantry units were kept busy, even when in a 'quiet' sector, with the usual operational and administrative tasks that were part and parcel of daily life in the trenches. Top of the list were mail from home and the vital ration run, when hot food and drinks were brought up for the men in the front line. With regular artillery and mortar exchanges, such apparently mundane duties became deadly serious for the front line soldiers. Its arrival was, like the mail, good for morale. If it was lost when a ration party was blown to smithereens, morale dropped drastically; and principally because of the missing food, rather than the casualties among the ration party.

Schütze Max Heinz, after serving for a month or two opposite the French in Artois, summed up this phenomenon, so universal among the armies of the Western Front, and almost as relevant for an infantryman today:

> I also [now] understand the importance given to food, which had seemed such a petty thing to me at first. Food is the only thing [that] the soldier receives in return for his hard service. And the fresh air makes one hungry, as I soon discovered.[6]

Despite the popular myths surrounding the First World War, German troops, in common with their British and French opponents, did not spend four straight years in the trenches, but moved in and out of the front line according to the battalion and regimental duty rosters.

Consequently, there was time to visit the local town and enjoy the bars and cafés, as well as more exotic entertainments. A soldier's typical experience was on an excursion to the French town of Lille:

> I get leave to spend a day in Lille with two friends. Can you people at home imagine how we felt to get out of the mud of battle into a town actually inhabited by civilians and looking almost like peacetime? Shops, restaurants, cafés, civilians and military personnel in clean clothes . . . On the way back, we also sat in a bar at Lomme, where we met several comrades from the 107th Infantry Regiment. They sang patriotic . . . and sentimental songs. Tomorrow they have to go back to lie in a trench: here they forget the situation and also the fact that tomorrow they may be dead.[7]

It had not taken long for most of the patriotic young men who had joined up so willingly to help win the war for the Fatherland by the end of 1914 to feel rather short-changed by the turn of the year. The wild enthusiasm was replaced by the overriding need to do one's duty and a camaraderie based on a common fate. The average German soldier still had to believe that the great German Army would eventually prevail, although it had become increasingly difficult to see how.

The certainties of easy victory, assured by no less than the Kaiser himself as they marched to war, were already ancient history to the dwindling numbers of those who had been involved from the beginning. But a common bond helped the German servicemen to cope and to preserve each other's sanity. It was a familiar experience for Tommy Atkins and the *Poilu*. One German soldier typically wrote:

> The behaviour of the other men towards me underwent a great change after the [trench] raid. Only now . . . had I become a full-fledged [sic] soldier worthy of being treated as a human being. Closer contact with them and my own experiences of this monotonous trench warfare, with its terrible strain on body and mind, gradually brought me to a better understanding of their characteristics and habits. Most of that which had shocked me in the beginning [was] now quite natural . . . For instance, there was the eternal arguing and cursing about every possible thing, especially the officers. I was soon just as good at it as [anyone] . . . I also understood now the complete absence of enthusiasm for the war. It comes with the first drop of rain on a cold night, or on a forced march, or on during a battle when the soldiers hear the shrapnel singing about their ears.[8]

On 27 January, all the Kaiser's men were given the opportunity to mark and celebrate their Emperor's birthday. It cheered some, but the indulgence was a stark reminder that this was his first birthday since the war began and it was unlikely to be the last. Most wondered if they would live to mark their Kaiser's birthday in January 1916. They did not have long to ponder the question, for the Allies were about to test their mettle once more.

The next phase of the French Champagne offensive began on 16 February, but, not surprisingly, the German defences were more solid than ever and the 'French were expected'.

The first attacks showed some promise and the German line was penetrated in places thanks to the terrific 'drum fire' of medium field guns in support and especially the 75mm 'soixante-quinze'. *Gefreiter* Herbert Sulzbach, recently despatched to the Champagne area from Flanders with his artillery unit, was in the van of the German resistance against the waves of French infantry attempting to break through his lines. On 15 February he had noted in his diary that the French assault was imminent. On 18 February, he wrote hastily that:

> On Shrove Tuesday a fearsome enemy artillery fire . . . is laid on our trenches and gun positions: thundering and boiling and banging away . . . The French have

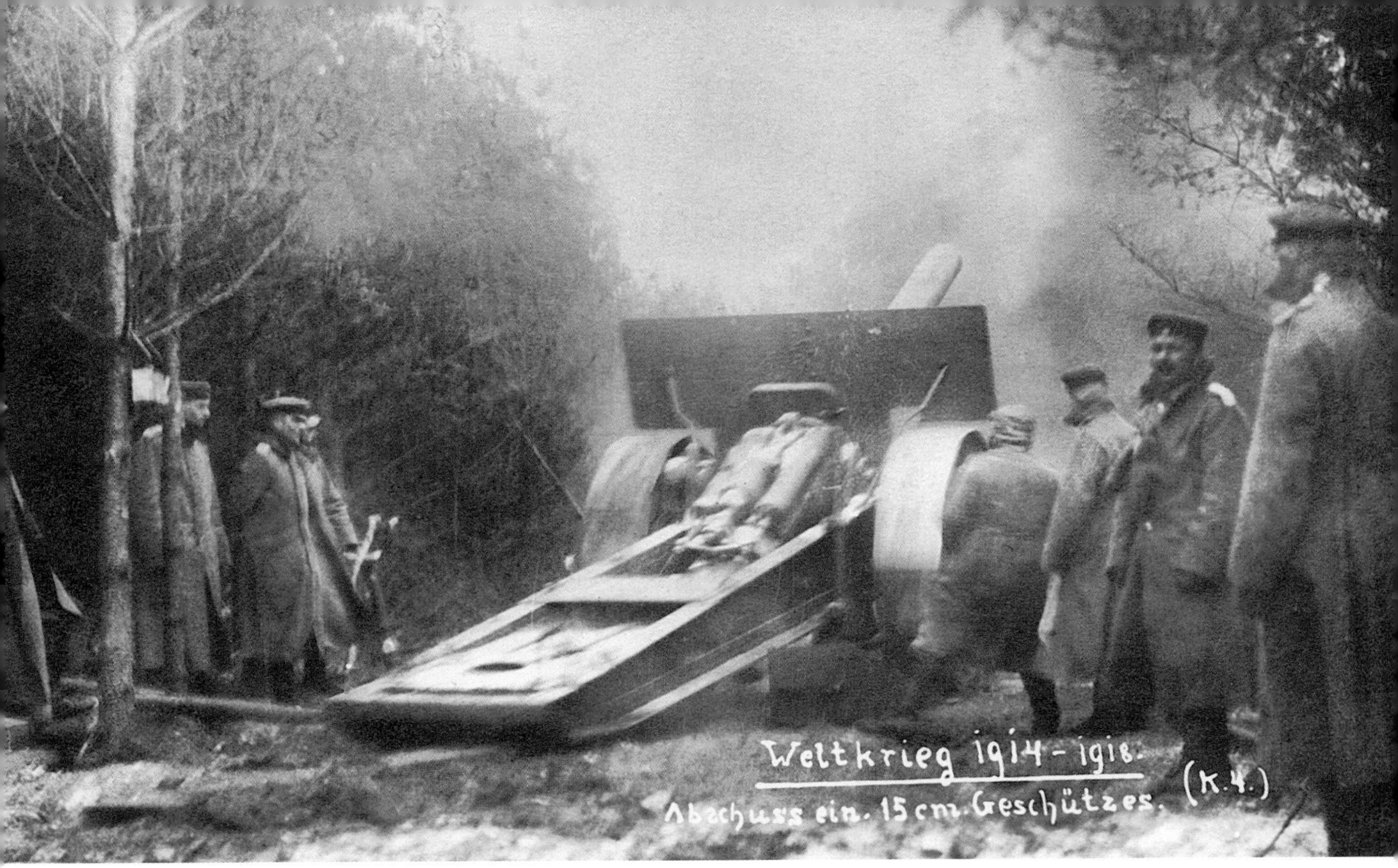

A German 15cm gun fires on French positions, Artois sector, 1915.

(Allen Collection)

> forced their way into our front trenches . . . [Now] the French have taken our main position . . . There is a good deal of confusion, [but] we hold on and quite early on the 17th of February the first of many French who have been taken prisoner come past us. Most of them are severely wounded and cannot hide the pain. Losses have been very high on both sides . . . After the French had forced their way into our main position, we counter-attacked and threw the beggars out again . . . Our infantry . . . are not afraid of anything, [but] though we gunners do get exposed to fire all the time, the infantry have a much worse time of it . . . The fighting continues . . .[9]

The fighting did continue; until 17 March in the main, and for another fortnight in rather more limited attacks. But, despite the early promise, the French offensive was snuffed out by the strength of the German defences and the ever-improving defensive tactics used by the Kaiser's men. The month long battle had cost the French an estimated 240,000 killed, missing, wounded and prisoners; a little less than half that number on the German side.

Further French attacks in the Aisne sector around Soissons, Meuse-Argonne, and a vicious tussle between mountain-trained French *Chasseurs Alpins* and German *Gebirgsjäger* troops in the Vosges on the southern flank, led to further failure for 'Papa' Joffre.

The German defences held firm virtually everywhere. Where local French success was achieved, German counter-attacks and overwhelming artillery support had thrown the hapless *poilus* back to their start points. The French winter offensives had been a manifest and bloody failure. The only possible 'plus' point on the Allied side was that Joffre had finally realised that the élan and courage of the French infantryman was utterly useless against heavily defended German trenches, strongpoints and well-drilled machine gunners and artillerymen.

The typical German infantryman was reliable and units had a strong 'regimental' *esprit de corps*, which gave each man confidence that if wounded, he would at least return to his own battalion when he was fighting fit once more. But the idea that *Fritzie Schmidt* was an unquestioning, resolutely obedient automaton was far from the truth even during the early months of the war. Most recognised that: 'Germany needs brave soldiers. Nothing else will do. We have to go through with it, however much we condemn the war itself.'[10]

German infantry 'march off to meet the enemy', postcard dated 7 August 1915.

(Allen Collection)

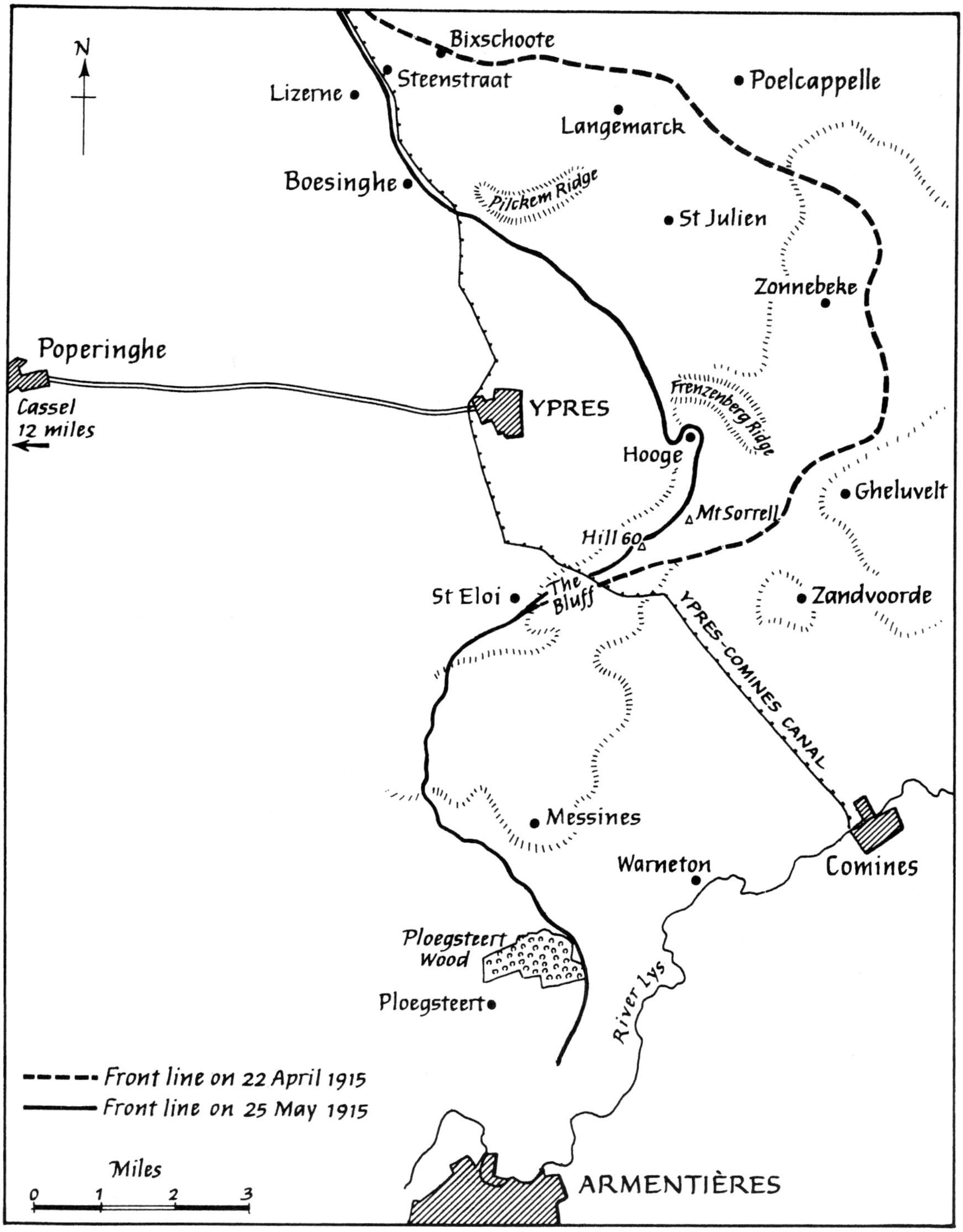

'Second Ypres'. Summary of the German offensive between 22 April and 25 May 1915, and scene of first major use of poisonous gas.

(Harington, C.H., Plumer of Messines)

The 'brave soldiers' were knocking the Allied offensives flat. Something had to change, and, as the BEF would soon discover to their cost, the vital ingredient was to be the war of the guns – artillery of all calibres – which the Germans had in plentiful supply already.

Falkenhayn's decision to go onto the defensive in the West had given the BEF the chance to make good the 90,000 or so casualties of 1914, most of whom were experienced and professional soldiers of the pre-1914 British Army.

But the BEF could do little to support the French attacks until spring 1915. Field Marshal Sir John French knew that the BEF was under pressure to take action on the Western Front from the French and because of the British political debate about operations elsewhere, such as the Dardanelles, which would divert vital *matériel* and manpower from the BEF.

The decision was made to attack the German line at Neuve Chapelle, capture the dominant feature of Aubers Ridge and thus threaten the important German road and rail junction at Lille.

The assault was to be by General Douglas Haig's First Army and preparations were meticulously made. Accurate and updated trench maps of the German positions were produced with the aid of photographic air reconnaissance by the RFC, the assault units rehearsed their attacks in detail and precise artillery timetables were produced for the first time. The British plan was to use surprise to catch the German garrison defending Neuve Chapelle off guard.

At 7.30 a.m. on 10 March the Germans were stunned by a 'hurricane' bombardment that fell on their front line defences for a mere 35 minutes before lifting the barrage to their second and support lines. As the artillery moved forward, the British and Indian assault troops rushed forward and swept into the German front line.

Within a few hours, and despite increasing German resistance once the defenders had recovered from the initial shock of the short, sharp bombardment, Haig's men had overrun 4,000 yards of the German front line and advanced to a depth of over 1,000 yards of the German defences. They had captured Neuve Chapelle into the bargain. However, German counter-attacks and the lack of British resources to exploit the situation led to a fraught, see-saw contest around Neuve Chapelle for the next three days. On 12 March, the British consolidated their gains and the battle drew to a close.

It was not long before the news reached the Home Fronts. In Germany, a wife wrote:

> Someone just returned from Neuve Chapelle says that the battle there was one of the most ghastly of the whole year . . . [The German] losses during the fight were appalling: 18,000; and the British were 12,000. (In fact, 12,500 German and 13,000 British casualties) . . . [A friend who was there] witnessed a sad sight . . . A man in the trenches had to watch his son dying by inches a few . . . yards away from him (between the trenches) and was powerless to help or reach him. He was his only son, and he saw him fall wounded and then die slowly, with many other wounded, lying there in the open ground.[11]

Although limited in its aims, the British assault on Neuve Chapelle was a jolt to the German belief that their defences were impregnable. But it also set a pattern of British (and French) offensives and German response that was to be so characteristic of Allied and German experience of the Western Front.

With methodical preparation and heavy artillery support, it was generally possible to break into the German first and perhaps second lines. But it became increasingly difficult to sustain an assault if fresh units and field artillery were not brought up quickly to consolidate the gains and limit the German response.

On the German side, the Kaiser's men became more and more adept at dealing with the penetration of their defences through the rapid use of counter-attacks and artillery fire to disrupt British or French attempts to press on.

But the next act of the Western Front drama in 1915 was about to turn such general rules on their head for two reasons. Falkenhayn had decided to go onto the offensive in Flanders once more and he planned to use a new, foul and insidious weapon when he did. Warfare would never be the same again.

Before the Allies could launch their next round of offensives in May 1915, the Germans struck unexpectedly in the Ypres salient. Falkenhayn had wanted to use his strategic reserves to support a great offensive aimed at Flanders, where he had come so close to victory at the end of 1914. But, his decision had been altered on the insistence of the Kaiser and the commanders of the Eastern theatre of war, Hindenburg and Ludendorff.

Nevertheless, he had a cunning but vile plan that he thought might just have the effect of increasing his war fighting capability on the Western Front also: gas. At first, this chemical weapon would consist of chlorine, but mustard and phosgene gases would follow. All were frightful harbingers of more ruthless methods of using technology to foul ends. Chlorine is a heavy gas, a powerful irritant to nose, throat and lungs once inhaled, and a high concentration will either severely and permanently damage the lungs or kill through asphyxiation.

At the beginning of 1915 Duke Albrecht of Württemberg's Fourth Army already had 6,000 chlorine-filled cylinders stockpiled opposite the British, French and Dominion forces defending the Ypres sector. For most of April, they were useless, for the release of the gas from cylinders was a crude method and entirely dependent on wind direction. The wind stubbornly refused to favour the Germans in the first three weeks of April. Even then, there was little enthusiasm on their part to use it. The official history later recorded that:

> Almost throughout our forces engaged, both commanders and troops, regarded with mistrust the still untried attacking method, if they were not wholly inclined against it.[12]

Then the wind changed and Fourth Army prepared to attack the northern sector of the Ypres salient with the new weapon on 22 April. The offensive was preceded by a sudden and vicious artillery bombardment that had the salient as its target and Ypres as its bull's eye. The medieval town, already damaged by desultory fire since October 1914, was now subjected to systematic destruction.

At 5 p.m. on that day, the bombardment grew, its violence drowning the sound of the hissing of cylinders releasing the chlorine gas towards the British and French front lines. The gas attack was witnessed as:

> . . . two curious greenish-yellow clouds on the ground on either side of Langemarck in front of the German line. These clouds spread laterally, joined up, and moving before a light wind, became a bluish-white mist, such as is seen over water meadows on a frosty night.[13]

The new and deadly vapour swirled slowly towards French colonial troops of the 45th Algerian Division and the French 78th Territorial Division. This time the trenches offered no protection from the enemy weapon heading towards them. The trenches gave some haven from artillery, mortar and machine gun fire but the gas crept into the trenches, hugging the contours of parapet, fire step and trench floor. Then it wafted unhindered into the dugouts. The putrid cloud, seen with curiosity at first as it headed towards the French, led to terror and agony as the first of numerous casualties tore at their throats coughing and barely able to breath.

The German assault troops, who had been packed in their forward trenches waiting for the order to attack all day, were staggered to see the chaos of panicking and fleeing French troops running blindly away from their trenches. When the assault units of the 46th, 51st and 52nd Reserve Divisions of Duke Albrecht of Württemberg's Fourth Army went over the top, the gas had moved on and was already dispersing, but the damage was done. They advanced against virtually no opposition and filled the breach left by the frightened, dead and dying French defenders.

In a short time, a four-mile gap had appeared in the Allied line between the left flank of the British Second Army and the right flank of the Belgian Army to the north. By nightfall the amazed and euphoric German attackers were in an excellent position to exploit their success thanks to this new terror weapon. The assault divisions were then reinforced to consolidate their gains that night. At first, it seemed that Ypres was at their mercy and that the salient would be pinched out as easily as the attack had been launched. But this brilliant opportunity was to be wasted for three reasons: the response of the British Second Army and the 1st Canadian Division in particular, the inaction of the assaulting German divisions, and the lack of German reserves to guarantee German success.

The response to the German attack was pretty swift, given the pandemonium caused at 5 p.m. on 22 April. By daylight on the 23rd, the Canadians had managed to push a number of hard-pressed battalions into the gap facing the German assault troops. The defence line was by no means continuous, but at least it plugged the hole with something and left the enemy with a new problem. The Canadians counter-attacked, were then hit by another gas attack on 24 April and were finally relieved in the first week of May after losses of over 6,000 officers and men.[14]

The inaction of the assaulting German divisions after their initial success on 22 April was due to the fact that they had no specific orders to do more than dig in on their objectives. As with the first use of tanks by the British in September 1916, no special tactics for the new gas weapon had been thought of, or at least no instructions appeared in the XXVI Korps, which had the principal role, or in its subordinate divisional orders, for this attack.[15]

Even if a concerted attempt to take the salient had ensued in the first crucial days of the offensive, the German supremo Falkenhayn would not have provided sufficient reserves. His main aim at Ypres and on the Western Front at this time was 'to cloak the transportation of troops to 'Galicia' [on the Eastern Front] for the next major offensive'.[16]

From 25 April, 'Second Ypres' became another murderous campaign for even less purpose on the German side than their enemy. Unwittingly, they were to die or be wounded for the sake of an experiment with the new gas weapon and to provide a deception for an offensive in the East. By early May, they had lost 860 officers and 34,073 other ranks, although these 'official' figures would not have accounted for lightly wounded men, an addition of at least 20 per cent on top, so around 42,000 all told. But British losses amounted to 59,000 officers and men.

Perhaps this was the only macabre gain that Falkenhayn could claim after Second Ypres. His new lambs to the slaughter had imposed more British casualties than they had had to endure themselves.

It would not end there, of course. After violent Allied protest about the use of gas as an abominable weapon, they manufactured and used it too. All manner of gas masks, or respirators, were hastily manufactured and introduced on both sides and war became even more uncomfortable than before. Later, its distribution would depend less on wind direction than the range and accuracy of artillery shells.

Chlorine became the first of the few – lachrymatory gas in June 1915; phosgene in December of that year, which had similar effects to chlorine but was more insidious as it was almost invisible; and mustard gas in 1917, a liquid that caused blistering, dreadful pain in the eyes, nose and lungs, but was rarely fatal. By November 1918, no less than 63 different types of poison gas had been used, but the few listed here are those that have epitomised the horrors of this alternative warfare ever since.[17]

April, and then May 1915, proved to be a 'wake-up call' for the British Home Front too. Modern technology brought the fight home by land, sea and air. For the first time in hundreds of years Britain lost her immunity from foreign violation when she was attacked again: from the air. In April, a Zeppelin dropped bombs on East Anglia, which signalled the beginning of an air offensive that would culminate in two attacks on London in September, killing 38 and wounding 124.

U-boats roamed at sea as the game of death grew more dreadful daily on the land of France and Flanders. Though the underwater threat in 1915 had not become as explicit an attempt as it would in 1917 to 'win the war for Germany', it was a distinct problem for Britain and her Allies nevertheless. On 7 May, the civilian liner SS *Lusitania* was sunk by a German U-boat just off the coast of Ireland with the loss of over 1,000 lives.

The fact that the *Lusitania* sailed with a cargo of ammunition, and passengers were specifically warned in US newspapers not to travel on this liner, was of no consequence once the deed was done. The successful detonation of a torpedo caused a huge explosion of anti-German hatred in Britain and America. The reaction was predictable, with shops and family households of those bearing even tenuous German names being attacked and the shops looted by angry crowds.

It led to an equally chilling wind for the Kaiser and within Germany itself. At the Kaiser's court in Pless, a personal aide noted:

> Will [the sinking of the *Lusitania*] mean war with America? Will it endanger the efforts of the Pope to preserve America's neutrality? . . . Discussion with His Majesty on the assurance demanded by Chancellor Bethmann-Hollweg to spare neutral shipping in the U-boat war. His Majesty has not the slightest idea of the seriousness of the situation . . .[18]

On the Home Front it was greeted as a portent of worse times to come. Disturbing the sleeping giant across the Atlantic was not a good move, as the Americans living in Germany made abundantly clear:

> May the 8th, 1915 will live vividly in my memory for the shock that we received by the sinking of the *Lusitania*. [Apparently] a great loss of life had been the just punishment, for [it] was carrying munitions to the enemy of Germany. Neutral America was providing these munitions . . . and what sacrifice could be too great for revenging that?! . . . The Americans here . . . had always . . . been cordial and friendly towards the Germans they met . . . But a sudden change now took place. The Americans openly avoided the Germans, almost cutting off their friends of only the day before.[19]

Despite these shocks to British and American immunities at home, the moment passed. It would take a while before transatlantic emotions were so stirred again. Meanwhile, the war, and the killing, went on.

Attacks, counter-attacks and stubborn unwillingness to give an inch of ground for political reasons, such as the Allies at Ypres and the German defenders everywhere, had led to yet more high casualty bills as the Second Ypres campaign rumbled on in early May. On 9 May, the French, with General Ferdinand Foch imbuing his *poilus*

Flammenwerfer. German tactics included the use of flame, as well as gas and explosive mining, in the Ypres salient in 1915.
(Allen Collection)

with the traditional offensive spirit, were on the attack again in Artois, supported by a British assault on Aubers Ridge to the north.

Foch attacked with 18 divisions and almost 300 heavy guns against a German defence of less than half the men, but with a marked superiority in guns of all calibres, trench mortars and the ubiquitous machine gun emplacements. The Artois offensive had the dominating high ground of Vimy Ridge and Notre Dame de Lorette just north of Arras at its centre.

Accordingly, the French XXXIII Corps at the centre of Tenth Army's offensive, led by General Henri Philippe Pétain, stormed Vimy Ridge at great cost and the *poilus* managed to claw their way up to the crest of the ridge in places. The speed and success of the first wave of Pétain's attacks had exceeded expectations, but, as a dreadful augur of what was later to come with the BEF at Loos, the French reserve divisions were not prepared or close enough to exploit this opportunity: the nearest reserve infantry division was over 7 miles away.

The German defenders of Crown Prince Rupprecht's Sixth Army were given desperately needed time to recover and then launch fierce counter-attacks and pummel the beleaguered French troops with all manner of artillery so that they were forced to withdraw from the ground so brilliantly won earlier.

Pétain's success had been fleeting and illusory, for by the time the French offensive had been exhausted in early June, a further 100,000 men had fallen for *la Patrie* and very little else. The German garrison in Artois had also suffered another 60,000 casualties, but their line had not budged.

At Aubers Ridge, the British were confident of success, as they had been boosted by their initial gains at Neuve Chapelle in March. The British commanders of the corps within First Army that were to assault Aubers were certain that they had 'got the measure' of German defensive tactics and could overcome them. They had not reckoned with the German response, which was a thorough review and application of 'lessons learned' from the battles fought earlier in 1915.

In the line between Festubert on the attacking British right flank and Bois Grenier on the left were the 13th, 14th and 6th Bavarian Reserve Divisions of VII Korps. The garrison had been increased from two to three divisions and, as the Bavarians had taken over part of the sector, this released men from the other divisions to strengthen the defences dramatically in the few weeks after Neuve Chapelle.

New dugouts, machine-gun and mortar emplacements were built and conformed with the fact that because of the high water table in this sector, trenches were improved with thick breastwork parapets and parados supported by sandbags and large-mesh wire. The barbed-wire belt in front of the positions was thickened and covered by interlocking, or cross-fire from an increased number of machine guns.

The attack on Aubers Ridge failed, with 11,600 British casualties against half that figure for those in its defence. The German situation reports on the evening of 9 May made little mention of it, as HQ Sixth Army was concentrating on containing the French offensive. It was clear that it was designed to support the French, but it did achieve surprise initially, as the bombardment was short, as at Neuve Chapelle.

However, when the assault began, the German defenders of Aubers Ridge, secure behind their strengthened and intact defences, reacted quickly once the barrage lifted and caused havoc. Against breastworks 12–20ft thick and 7ft high, the British bombardment was wholly inadequate and gave the subsequent attack no chance. The Germans were astonished and critical of the poor British artillery preparation for this attack and another later at Festubert.[20]

The continued French offensive meant that Rupprecht's Sixth Army expected further British attacks in the Aubers/Bois Grenier sector. They were not disappointed. On 15 May, another assault was launched against Festubert, just north of the La Bassée Canal. This time, the preparatory British bombardment lasted sixty hours on a more concentrated stretch of the German line. It was the first use of artillery designed to break down the enemy defences in a deliberate, systematic manner by attrition. The BEF was attempting to wear down the enemy 'by exhaustion and loss until his defence collapses', according to GHQ.

The battle for Festubert lasted for 12 days and resulted in the Germans giving up almost a mile of ground across a 3,000yd front. But once again, they had inflicted much higher casualties than they had sustained. The British losses were 16,000 officers and men killed, wounded or PoWs compared with 5,000 German.

The failed Allied attempts to break the German line in the spring offensive was much to do with their comparative lack of heavy artillery pieces, insufficient ammunition, and faulty tactics against a strong German defence.

As the war progressed it became primarily an artillery war and in the first two years, Germany had the lead in this deadly game. From the early months, it was the medium guns and 'heavies' that caused the real damage and guns such as the 150mm howitzer were respected and feared by French and British troops alike. With typical ironic humour, the Tommies called it a 'coal box', or 'Jack Johnson', after the contemporary Negro heavyweight boxing champion, a hero of his time. British soldiers were equally scathing of 'armchair generals' who had reported back home that the German guns were poor by comparison with Allied artillery:

> People who say that the German artillery fire is no good simply doesn't know what they are talking about. I can only figure it out as being something worse than the mouth of Hell.[21]

The establishment of the British Army was increasing as new troops arrived in France in their thousands, but new regimental and staff officers were scarce and ill-trained. There were similar problems in the French Army too.

For the German part, lessons were rapidly learnt as a result of the Allied attacks on ways to improve their defences, and to apply the tactics most suited to fighting a defensive battle, which they coined *Abwehrschlacht*.

The German General Staff produced an important solution to the growing manpower problem too. German casualties were high, but they made up their deficiencies by their policy of using a cadre of 25 per cent 'veteran' soldiers in each new division. Falkenhayn commented:

> The moral and technical superiority of the German soldier over his opponents [in 1915], which was daily becoming more evident, also offered a way out of this [manpower] difficulty. It turned out to be so great that it was possible to entertain the suggestion of *Oberst* von Wrisberg, to reduce by about 25 per cent the strength of the fighting units, the divisions, without doing any harm to their effectiveness.[22]

Throughout 1915, these methods gave the Kaiser's men a comparative edge against the French and British on the Western Front. Another phase of Allied offensives during the autumn and early winter of 1915 in Artois, Champagne and at Loos would prove the point.

German Defences I: German trench and OP, Champagne sector, which kept the French attacks in 1915 at bay.
(Allen Collection)

The fighting on the Western Front had continued in places throughout the rest of June and into July, the month in which another 'terror' weapon was brought into deadly play at Hooge in the Ypres salient – liquid fire in the form of the German *flammenwerfer*, the flame thrower. The Germans kept the Western Allies on their toes to mask their main effort on the Eastern Front, where the German and Austrian offensives were rolling back the Russian Army like a steamroller, an ironic analogy given the Russian Army's label in 1914.

But the battles in the West during the summer were dwarfed by the next offensives against Artois, Loos and Champagne, which began in September. French supremo, Papa Joffre, planned an assault on the same scale as that which had turned the German tide on the Marne twelve months before. In the event, after massive preparations throughout August and early September, the offensive was launched on 25 September. In Champagne, 35 French divisions were hurled against solid German defences with the advantage of dominating high ground from which the defenders had excellent fields of fire. In Artois, 18 French divisions attacked alongside 12 British divisions, whose objective was centred on the town of Loos.

There was some confidence that this time the German defence would be breached, for the whole offensive would be preceded by unprecedented artillery bombardments from a total of 2,000 heavy and 3,000 field guns. Joffre exhorted his troops two days before the attacks began by declaring that:

German Defences II: Fortified accommodation for the German defenders of the Chemin des Dames, 1915.
(Allen Collection)

> You will carry all before you. In one bound you will break through the enemy's defences and reach his artillery. Give him neither rest nor pause until victory is gained.[23]

But once again, the preparations, the artillery concentration and the élan and bravery of both French and British infantrymen alike were ultimately to no avail. Initial successes and stunned German defenders yielding ground were soon replaced by furious German counter-attacks against assault troops who were bereft of reserves to reinforce and replace them, and the casualties on both sides mounted horribly as the battle went on.

In Champagne, the French gained 3,000 yards and then discovered to their dismay that the main German defensive positions were in the heavily strengthened and manned second line. Between 25 September and 6 October, Joffre's men suffered another 143,567 casualties compared with 85,000 German losses. They had grasped some of their precious land from the enemy, but the cost was damningly high.

In Artois, the French attacks were a total disaster, for whereas in the previous battle their reserves were too far back, this time they were so close that German heavy and medium artillery ripped them apart before they could do a thing. The butcher's bill for absolutely no definable gain was almost 50,000 men, against German losses of around 30,000.

At Loos, the Germans faced the BEF's First Army under General Haig. The British plan for the attack included less heavyweight support from artillery than the French in Artois and Champagne, but this time, 5,000 cylinders of chlorine poison gas were to be used to augment the effects of the artillery bombardment and to gain much needed surprise. Haig imagined that the assault would provide an opportunity to break through the German lines and then capture the ground in the enemy rear as far as the Haute Deule canal. Six divisions of I and IV Corps were ordered to attack, and XI Corps were to be held in reserve on the understanding that its divisions would be rushed forward when the time came. Their availability was crucial, but in an attempt to minimise casualties, Field Marshal French was eager to keep them well back.

The German defences around Loos were held by the 117th and 14th Divisions from IV and VII Korps respectively. Three regiments of the 117th Division and one regiment of the 47th Division formed the main defensive line and each regiment had one battalion forward, one in support, 500 to 1,000 yards behind and the third in rest billets up to five miles behind the front.[24] Although a French deserter in August had disclosed that a great offensive was to take place in September, German commanders in the Loos area were informed by Sixth Army HQ that any British attack would be only 'partial or as a diversion,' to mask the main thrust by the French.

Nevertheless, reserve divisions were stood by to counter any British breakthrough and the infantry defending the Loos sector were well supported by artillery of all calibres. Although the BEF had almost three times the number of artillery pieces, most of it was concentrated on neutralising the front and second German lines rather than heavy counter-battery work. Even so, the German artillery batteries were very well camouflaged.[25]

The preparatory British bombardment began on 21 September and lasted for four days. Then, at 5.15 a.m. on the 25th, the gas attack began; the first use of gas by the BEF in the war, followed by the infantry assault at 5.50 a.m. The gas was more of a hindrance to the infantry attacking on the left and in the centre and in some places it drifted back towards the British lines.

But the 9th Scottish Division captured the heavily defended Hohenzollern Redoubt, Fosse 8 and the feature known as the Dump, sending the German survivors reeling back to the second line. Part of this was also taken by the 'Devils in skirts,' as the Germans nicknamed the Scottish troops. On the right, the 15th Scottish Division took Loos village.

Across the wire, the effects of the gas attack varied wildly. One thing was for certain: the gas took the garrison completely by surprise, much as it had done so devastatingly when first used by the Germans at Ypres the previous April. Infantrymen of the 22nd Reserve Regiment on the German right admitted after their capture that, although they had watched the gas cloud swirling towards their trenches, they did not realise what it was until it hit them. Most were not wearing gas masks and the gas caused the same effects as in April. Surviving company officers and NCOs found it impossible at first to control the general panic among their men.

At Hohenzollern Redoubt, it had a devastating effect, drifting right through the position and into its dugouts. Most of the defenders of the 157th Regiment abandoned the Redoubt before the main British assault began, because of the gas and also the damage caused by the British 9.2in howitzers. Many were killed by the continuing bombardment as they ran back towards the second line.

An officer of the 26th Regiment in the southernmost sector of the line facing the British later wrote:

> Gas Attack! A yellow white smoke welled from the British trenches at intervals of 15 metres. I ordered: Gas masks on and man the trench . . . The British trenches could no longer be seen . . . In ten minutes it reached the first wire entanglement and was fifteen metres high . . . At 6.25 a.m.,(5.25 a.m. for Allied time) . . . I gave the order to 'Fire' and everyone shot into the cloud. The machine guns clattered. All around us was white mist. Breathing was difficult . . . In front of the first platoon the British clambered out of their trenches. Our fire compelled them to return . . . At 7.10 a.m. the cloud lifted and went northwards.[26]

The British assault made good progress in most places and this caused considerable anxiety in the German command in the first few hours of the attack. The troops holding the forward defences had given ground so rapidly in places that serious plans were made to abandon the sector where the gap had appeared between Loos and Auchy. As far back as IV Korps headquarters at Douai by mid-afternoon, 'there were endless convoys of wagons formed up in double lines ready to march away, and the wagons of the Korps HQ were also awaiting the order to move off. It was a sad picture of retreat.'[27]

But as the day wore on, the situation was gradually restored. The dogged German resistance in the centre at Bois Carré and Lone Tree in particular, broke the initial impetus of the British advance. All local reserves were soon brought into the battle and other reserve units were ordered into action in the afternoon and evening. The only external troops available to reinforce this sector came from Sixth Army reserve, namely 8th Division and 2nd Guards Reserve Division, and they were ordered to fill the gap that had appeared between Loos and Auchy.

Even so, the situation remained critical and there was a serious danger that if the BEF's assault divisions were rapidly reinforced then the German position may indeed have become untenable. Once again, as with the French problems of having their reserve divisions either too close, as at the Artois offensive in September, or too far away, which had happened in Artois in the May offensive, the Germans were assisted by their enemy in their defence.

After the initial attacks, General Haig had signalled Field Marshal French that the reserves should be brought forward at 8.45 a.m. The 21st and 24th Divisions were warned about the task by 9.30 a.m., but the dissemination of orders and then great congestion on the approach roads delayed their arrival until late afternoon.

Thereafter, these divisions were compelled to advance at night across a battleground entirely unfamiliar to them and then attack the largely intact German second line positions at 11 a.m. the next morning. Exhausted from their route marches and without sleep, they attacked with wholly inadequate artillery support and into thick, uncut belts of barbed wire in front of the German positions and against heavy machine-gun and artillery fire. By lunchtime on 26 September, most of the battalions that had been dropped into this cauldron ceased to exist as effective units.

Hill 70 Redoubt was the scene of bitter fighting on 26 September, but even the British Guards Division failed to take it after bitter fighting. The British advance had been stalled by a combination of inexperience and exhaustion, the latter because of the distance that the reserve divisions had been forced to cover before attacking an immensely strong German second line.

German counter-attacks now became the main feature of the remaining battles around Loos, and most of the original British gains were recaptured, including the Hohenzollern Redoubt.

A German corporal (*obergefreiter*) involved in one of the fierce counter-attacks survived to recall:

> The mad attack begins. No one heeds the bullets, which rain upon us like hell. The enemy hesitates. He sees the frightful terrifying fence of shining bayonets, hears the wild shouts of our fast approaching line . . . Then they [flee] . . . We fire loud volleys into the flying mass. Frightful screams can be heard, drowned by the boisterous cheers of the German soldiers. The ground is covered with dead bodies, the wounded in blood . . . Not [one] enemy escapes the bloodbath.[28]

When the battle was over, the British had lost 50,000 men. The German casualties were almost 26,000 at Loos and 56,000 across the Artois/Loos and Champagne fronts. The autumn battles were now all but over, and the German Army remained as firmly fixed in their defence of conquered French and Belgian soil as ever. Though the madness went on at the Front, loved ones in Germany were receiving the news of the war with heavier and heavier hearts. For some, it had been too much already:

> A poor woman the other day in the train was holding up her hand and counting the fingers on it slowly – one, two, three, four, five, over and over again. The passengers gradually began to smile at her, until at last the man sitting next to her said simply, 'Don't laugh at my wife, ladies and gentlemen. I am taking her to the asylum. Her wits are gone. She has lost her five sons – all killed in action.'[29]

Even though the bloody events of 1914 and 1915 had seen little significant change in offensive and defensive doctrine, they had led to some innovation at tactical level on both sides of the wire. Under the inspiration of *Hauptmann* Rohr, the German Army was organising and training specially selected troops into assault detachments, *stoss truppen*, or 'storm troops'. The detachments were formed from section-sized squads that were taught to advance independently across no-man's-land and deal with enemy HQs, strongpoints and machine-gun posts through the use of 'infiltration' tactics, rather than attacking in the usual infantry platoon or company waves.

Lightly equipped, though heavily armed, the squads had specialist weapons, including flamethrowers, light trench mortars and carbines, rather than the standard-issue Gewehr rifle. They also carried extra grenades in sandbag 'pouches' slung over each shoulder. Later, they would be issued with the light version of the Maxim machine gun MG 08. The storm troops would come into their own in the opening moves of the Verdun offensive in February 1916, and special units were also used for counter-attack operations on the Somme later that year. Infiltration tactics were successfully employed during the German counter-offensive at Cambrai in November/December 1917. But it would be in the German offensives of 1918 that storm troops would become an enduring image and generate extraordinary myths about their elite status and their true impact on Germany's fate in that catalytic period on the Western Front.

For the Allies, French tactics were influenced in a similar manner to the German innovation through the ideas of a front line infantry officer, Captain André Laffargue, the author of *The Attack in Trench Warfare*. Though the BEF was rebuilding an army almost from scratch after the loss of most of its professional forces of 1914 and novel tactics were still to come, the British were at least introducing more effective infantry weapons such as the Stokes mortar and Mills grenade, as well as increasing their integral firepower with machine guns. By the end of 1915, each infantry battalion of around 1,000 men had and establishment of up to sixteen Lewis light machine guns and in October of that year, the British Army established the Machine Gun Corps, which concentrated the heavier Vickers machine guns into more effective tactical units.

One irksome and deadly method used by both sides from the onset of war was sniping. In one fortnight of trench warfare in December 1915, British troops sustained a total of 3,285 wounds of which almost 25 per cent were to the head or neck. Similar statistics would almost certainly be available from German and French casualty returns, and a fair number of those wounded in the head or neck would have been a result of sniper activity.

The *Scharfschütze*, or sniper, was not as terrifying as the constant threat of artillery or mortar bombardments, but he kept troops on edge and often became singularly responsible for lowering an enemy unit's morale. As a typical example, in the Vermelles sector in September 1916 one officer of the West Yorkshire Regiment put his head above the parapet for a brief look and was hit twice by two different snipers.[30]

As with many of the innovations of trench warfare, the Germans were the first to use snipers in a systematic manner. Soldiers awarded 'marksman' as a result of the routine personal weapons tests common to all infantry units regardless of nationality, were earmarked for special sniper training. German snipers earned the coveted 'oak-leaf' badge, additional pay and privileged status. Many, most prominently *Gefreiter* Walter Schmidt who had over two hundred kills to his name, were regarded by their comrades as 'aces' with the same esteem as air aces such as von Richthofen, Immelmann and Boelcke.

German snipers worked as units, remaining in the same sector for months along with their regiment and were stood down from normal trench duties and fatigues. (It was normal for German units holding the line to remain in the same sector for lengthier periods than their British and French opponents). This way, each sniper acquired an intimate knowledge of the terrain and most likely target areas, such as an exposed trench junction point or vulnerable sap.

Wearing camouflage capes and fresh foliage to break up their outline, snipers usually crept into no-man's-land shortly before dawn and remained there throughout the daylight hours. Snipers were constantly on the move, as he could fire no more than two or three shots from one position before being compromised. Snipers on both sides also used elaborately camouflaged static positions, such as dummy trees, although most were happier taking their chances on the ground in their chosen part of no-man's-land.

In December, the German industrialist Walter Rathenau declared that:

> When . . . England declared war, our country became a beleaguered fortress. Cut off by land and sea, it was made wholly self-dependent. After one year of conflict, we are facing a war the duration, cost, danger and sacrifices of which no one could have foreseen.[31]

The Allied blockade had become a major factor in the deterioration of the German Home Front. But it was by no means the only cause, for the military was an all-consuming beast and only the black market profiteers, industrialists and certain farming communities had benefited. For the ordinary German citizen, life was already tough by Christmas 1915. The lavish food parcels of 1914 were noticeably absent even at the fighting fronts. The only luxury in the trenches was at best a barrel of beer donated by a Commanding Officer or purloined by a wily Quartermaster. But even the soldiers who managed to take home leave were not much better off.

Traditional Christmas fare such as the Christmas tree, cake and fruitcakes were rare or often banned in the cities. Even the stalls of the renowned Christmas market, or *Weinachtsmarkt*, were devoid of the normal fare such as sausages, gingerbread, and chocolates. When the holiday passed, there was only time for universal reflection:

> Well, Christmas is over . . . For weeks past, the city seems to have been enveloped in an impenetrable veil of sadness, grey in grey . . . and which forms a fit setting for the white-faced, black-robed women who glide so sadly through the streets, some bearing their sorrow proudly as a crown to their lives, others bent and broken under a burden too heavy to be borne.[32]

Despite the unrest, shortages, anger and mourning at home, Germany's military balance by the end of 1915 looked better than that of the Allies. Falkenhayn's strategy of defence in the West and offensive operations in the East had frustrated all French and British attempts at a breakthrough on the one hand, and near catastrophe for Russia on the other, while Serbia was effectively marginalised.

But one vital factor had been overlooked. It would come back to haunt Falkenhayn and the German Army in the West. In December 1915 the BEF strength reached one million. Coupled with a change of C-in-C, as General Douglas Haig succeeded Field Marshal Sir John French, it was a clear indication that the British and Dominion contribution to the war on the Western Front was set to become ever greater. Falkenhayn had missed a golden opportunity in 1915, and an opportunity that would not come round again. A decade or so later, the eminent military writer General von Moser noted:

> There is no doubt as to what the proper course should have been in the spring of 1915 . . . The British Army should have been so defeated that it could never have developed into an efficient 'million [man] army'. It should have been like a newly sown field struck by a heavy hailstorm, which never recovers to bear a full crop; the result would have been certain if such storms of hail and battle had been repeated several times in 1915, when their fury would have been intensified by the hatred of the British which justly filled every German heart.[33]

By New Year's Eve 1915, total German losses since August 1914 had reached a staggering 2, 597, 052; no less than 601,751 were dead and a further 242,347 missing, presumed killed.[34] It was a very high price to pay for failure in 1914 and an almost wholly defensive posture on the Western Front throughout 1915. But the New Year promised new opportunities to reverse those fortunes, as German strategy shifted towards an offensive in the West and an attempt to sever the link between the French and British armies by knocking one of them out of the war. The place for the offensive was to be the historic fortress town of Verdun.

Regardless of the costly and indecisive offensives in Artois, with British support, and Champagne in 1917, French C-in-C Marshal Georges Joffre was encouraged by the increasing size of the BEF, and the fact that General Sir Douglas Haig had replaced Field Marshal Sir John French. Joffre convened an Inter-Allied Military Conference at his HQ in Chantilly from 6–8 December 1915 to seek a more unified Allied strategy.

Concrete emplacement in the Champagne sector, 1915.
(Allen Collection)

Germany had been able to react effectively to events in the West and other theatres because of her excellent rail/internal lines of communication. The main decision of the Allied conference was to reduce Germany's flexibility to switch her forces quickly from one theatre to another by launching simultaneous offensives on the Western, Eastern and Italian fronts. In late December, Joffre wrote to Haig suggesting a main Anglo-French offensive astride the River Somme, where the two Allied armies met. He added in January 1916 that the BEF should be involved in a number of smaller actions, designed to 'wear out' the enemy prior to the major offensive.

Haig, whose preference was a main effort in Flanders, deferred to Joffre in the interests of Allied unity and agreed that the main assault would be in the Somme sector, beginning in July, though the 'smaller actions' would be put on hold. The meeting between Joffre and Haig to confirm the details of the Allied offensives for 1916 took place at Chantilly on 14 February 1916. One week later, Joffre's *poilus* would be fighting for their lives in the defence of Verdun.

Chapter 5

'We Shall Bleed the French White at Verdun'

January–June 1916

An den Tod
Mich aber schone, Tod,
Mir dampft noch Jugend blutstromrot, –
Noch hab ich nicht mein Werk erfüllt,
Noch ist die Zukunft dunstverhüllt –
Drum schone mich, Tod.

Wenn später einst, Tod,
Mein Leben verlebt ist, verloht
Ins Werk – wenn das müde Herz sich neigt,
Wenn die Welt mir schweigt, –
Dann trage mich fort, Tod.'

Gerrit Engelke (1890–12 October 1918)[1]

To Death
But spare me, Death;
I am still in the first flush of youth,
My life's work as yet unfulfilled,
The future remains a mystery, –
So spare me, Death.

Sometime later, Death,
When I've had a full life, when it has burned away
Into my work – [and] when the tired ticker is waning,
When the world has nothing more to say to me,
Then [you can] carry me off, Death.

The German war poet Gerrit Engelke spoke for every German soldier, and probably every French and British one too, with his thoughts in 'An den Tod' ('To Death'). For 1916 was to be the year that remains in popular perception as that most associated with the slaughter and futility of the First World War. On the Western Front, the Germans opened their account with an offensive in February at Verdun, and in July, a combined Anglo-French offensive began on the Somme. Both campaigns would become notorious for certain reasons, but both campaigns would also lead to a dramatic change in Germany's fortunes. The military balance would not favour her by the end of the year.

During 1915 the French and British offensives had ground to a halt every time through lack of reserves and artillery resources to match the German guns, including the notorious 'heavies'. Joffre had dreamt of a real breakthrough, especially before the autumn battles. But they were only dreams and 1915 had ended in a desperate stalemate.

General von Falkenhayn was confident that the strength of the German defences would hold any major Allied attack. But he realised that the Western Front was the decisive theatre of the war, and that a purely defensive strategy would not win that war. The prospects of a breakthrough on the Western Front seemed bleak. First and foremost, he regarded the British as 'the arch-enemy', with France as Britain's 'best sword' on the continent. He needed a method to knock that sword out of Britain's hand.

Falkenhayn saw a way to succeed and put France out of the war without having to attempt a breakthrough, for he believed that the French were close to moral and military collapse. By the beginning of 1916, he concluded that:

> . . . the strain on France has almost reached breaking point, though it is certainly borne with the most remarkable devotion. If we succeeded in opening the eyes of her people to the fact that in a military sense they have nothing more to hope for, that breaking point would be reached and England's best sword knocked out of her hand.[2]

In January he told the Kaiser that he had noticed: 'the ever dwindling power of the resistance and limited ability of the French people to hold out', and that a massive 'breakthrough' offensive would not be necessary. He added:

> We can probably do enough for our purposes with limited resources. Within our reach behind the French sector of the Western Front, there are objectives for the retention of which, the French . . . would be compelled to throw in every man they have. If they do so the forces of France will bleed to death – as there can be no question of a voluntary withdrawal – whether we reach our goal or not.[3]

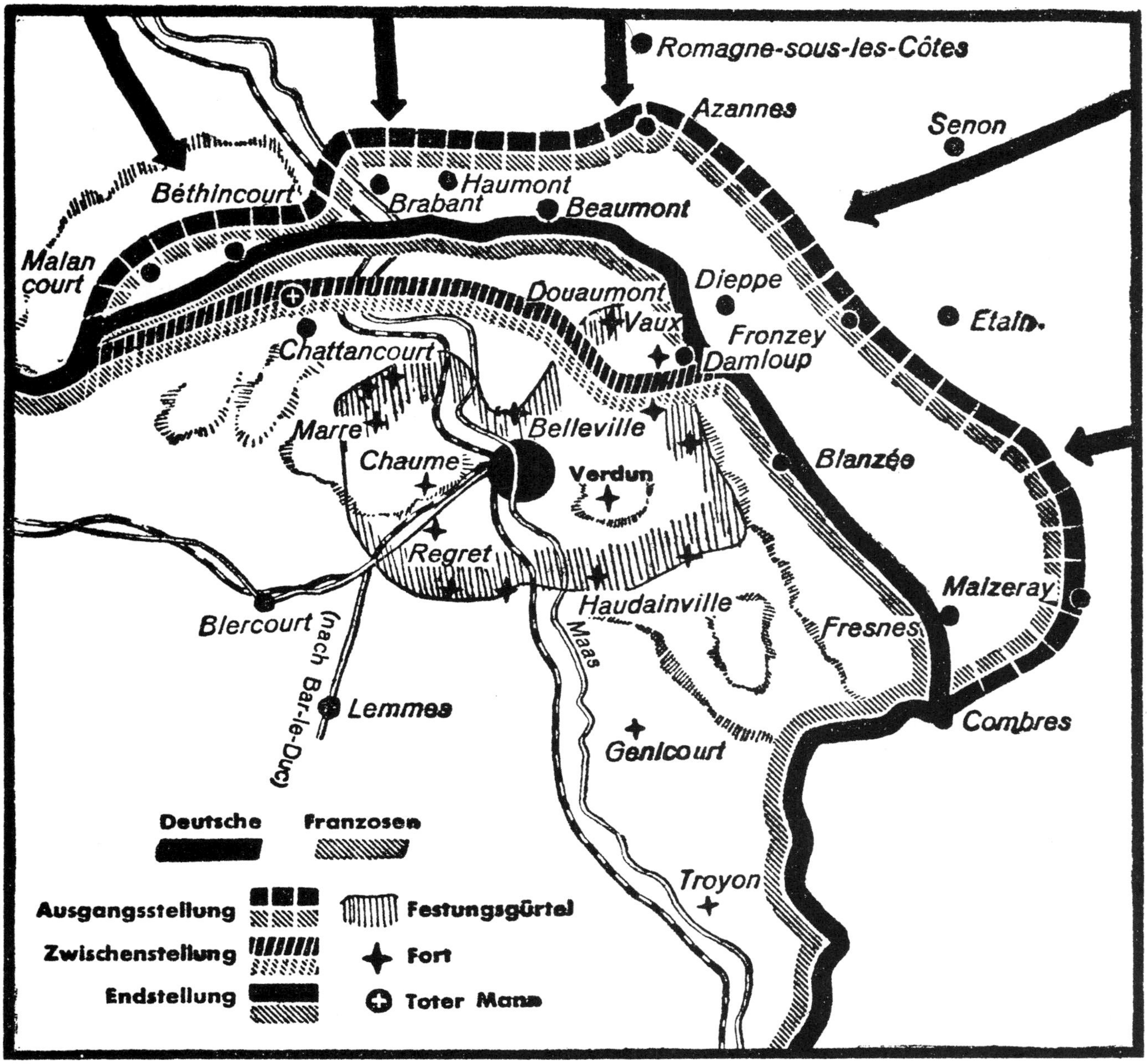

Verdun 1916: German and French front lines at the beginning of the German offensive on 21 February 1916; mid-campaign (August) and at the end of the campaign in December. The map also shows the *Festungsgürtel* or ring of forts; the forts and *Toter Mann*, or *Mort Homme*.

(Rudolph Stratz, Weltkrieg)

Verdun was such a place. Moreover, Falkenhayn's codeword for the Verdun campaign, Operation *Gericht* had sinister overtones.[4]

A traditional fortress-city, Verdun lies astride the River Meuse, and has long symbolised French national courage and pride. Built under the guidance of King Louis XIV's famous architect Vauban, it had for over 200 years withstood invasion, including a vain German attempt in 1914. Closely protected by outlying forts, Verdun had, since the autumn of 1914, been a relatively quiet sector of the Front. Now it was to be Falkenhayn's 'killing ground', where he would force the French to defend at all costs. Verdun, the heart of France, as the Germans described it, would be squeezed until the French could resist no more.

The Kaiser's son, Crown Prince Wilhelm, and his Fifth Army would carry out the attack. But there was friction from the outset between him, his tough Chief-of-Staff General Knobelsdorf, and Falkenhayn. The Crown Prince saw his main objective as the capture of Verdun itself. He pressed for simultaneous attacks against the weakened French defences on both sides of the River Meuse. Falkenhayn overrode the Crown Prince, insisting on limiting the offensive to the right bank only, a frontage of less than ten miles.

He had a different agenda, which stopped short of a breakthrough strategy but expected to inflict massive French casualties. But he was certain that that this would inevitably result in heavy German casualties also and was reluctant to make this clear to his battlefield commanders. So the German Fifth Army prepared for battle. Troops, ammunition, and guns of every calibre were brought up the line in great secrecy. Zero Day was set for 12 February, although poor weather would eventually delay the opening of the attack until 21 February.

Verdun was surrounded by hills and ridges that provided superb defensive positions. On the heights themselves, three concentric rings of forts were built, their guns placed so as to dislodge all but the strongest of infantry attacks. The forts were considered to be the crowning glory of the French defensive layout.

The strongest of these was Fort Douaumont, which had been designed to resist the heaviest shells. An elaborate telephone system controlled the fort's guns. These were mounted in turrets and consisted of one 155mm, one 75mm and three heavy machine guns. The fort could accommodate a full battalion of one thousand infantrymen. A series of underground passages linked each gun emplacement.

Each of the Verdun forts was designed to hold out for weeks at a time. They lay between five and ten miles from Verdun itself. They were covered by a protective network of trenches, redoubts, and thick belts of barbed wire.

But, since the autumn of 1914, these defences had been badly neglected and many guns removed for use in other more active sectors. The relative inactivity on both sides of the wire had lulled the French garrison into a false sense of security. Many of the forts, including Douaumont, were also undermanned. Overall, the French troops had been allowed to become slack.

Lieutenant Colonel Émile Driant, an infanty regiment commander, was unhappy about the situation. Throughout 1915 he had witnessed the decline in standards of the garrison. He was concerned that Verdun would be defenceless against any sustained German attack and pestered influential friends until the French Defence Ministry took action. They sent a Commission to inspect Verdun, which recommended that urgent steps were taken to improve the defences. But even then, the urgency of those steps was suspect.

By the end of January 1916, the French realised that a German attack was likely, and that Verdun was the main objective. Almost too late, Joffre ordered two French infantry divisions to reinforce the Verdun sector and the defenders of Verdun struggled frantically to improve their positions in a desperate race against time.

Unfortunately, the *poilus* were never great advocates of digging-in. Trained to attack whenever possible, they were even less happy with building elaborate trench and dugout systems around the forts that made up Verdun's defences. Early 1916 was cold and wet and made the life of the French soldiers in the front line at Verdun miserable.

As January 1916 passed into February, the French troops were at last spurred into action, thanks to the warnings of Colonel Driant and the undeniable sign of German preparations for an attack. The reinforcements that Joffre had at last released for Verdun were rushed into the line.

German storm troops practise the use of the flamethrower for the Verdun offensive.
(Allen Collection)

In the meantime, the *poilus* steeled themselves for the inevitable attack. One *poilu* wrote: 'We all pray to God that we are not too late with our preparations to meet the enemy . . . the German storm will soon break.'

But apathy, a universal problem for the French defenders of Verdun, was to have dire consequences. The trenches in the forward zone of the defence were poorly sited and prepared, and most would not withstand a heavy bombardment.

In contrast, the German front line itself curved round Verdun on either side of the River Meuse. Sited on high ground, it overlooked the city and its forts. With customary thoroughness, the German defences were both well-sited and formidable. Falkenhayn's men had reinforced concrete bunkers and bomb-proof underground shelters for headquarters, communication centres, medical facilities, ammunition stores, and accommodation for the men. Behind the front line, Falkenhayn arranged for narrow gauge railways to help in the movement of the extra ammunition and supplies needed for the attack.

Poised to assault Verdun, the men of Crown Prince Wilhelm's Fifth Army had faith in their commander, but deep suspicion and hostility towards Falkenhayn and his staff. One of Falkenhayn's aides even jeered at soldiers shivering in the wintry conditions. It was a sad reflection on Falkenhayn's relationship with his men and the remoteness of his staff from the troops on the ground.

Hauptmann Oswald Boelcke, German air ace and pioneer of air tactics.
(Rudolph Stratz, Weltkrieg)

Rittmeister Manfred Freiherr von Richthofen, the top-scoring air ace of the First World War.
(Rudolph Stratz, Weltkrieg)

A German soldier expressed the feelings of most of the men as he wrote:

> Courage has nothing to do with it. The fear of death surpasses all other feelings and terrible compulsion alone drives the soldier forward. We are motivated to fight on by this damned discipline of the Prussian Army . . . and the simple feeling that the terrible must be done.[5]

The wild enthusiasm for war had long since passed. There was a strange sense of foreboding about the forthcoming battle that this German soldier and thousands like him were about to experience. For the *poilu* it must have seemed a good deal worse than foreboding. Many would probably have agreed with the feeling: 'Nous sommes dans un pot de chambre et nous y serons emmerdés.'[6]

The evolution of air warfare took a giant stride forward in 1916 at Verdun and on the Somme. It was a momentous year for the German Air Service and one in which, as on the ground, the innate German sense of superiority over her enemies was eroded by the year's end.

The onset of trench warfare soon negated the traditional reconnaissance (recce) role of the cavalryman. Consequently, commanders on both sides of no-man's-land increasingly relied on the 'eyes and ears' of their evolving air forces. Reconnaissance was the *raison d'être* and aerial photography was the vital asset, as it gave accurate and up-to-date information on enemy positions, rear areas and troop concentrations. Pilots and their observers also identified enemy artillery batteries and other high-value targets and sent back crucial data to their own gun lines on the 'fall of shot' – the pattern and accuracy of the artillery barrage laid down on an enemy target.

The role was soon so important that other aircraft were designated to protect the recce flights and aerial combat – the war in the air – was born. Between 1915 and November 1918, the Western Front more than any other theatre of war witnessed a constant struggle for air superiority above the trenches, incessant attempts to use technology to provide 'unbeatable' fighter aircraft and ever more advanced tactics. With the designs of Anthony Fokker, the Germans developed a synchronising gear to allow machine guns to be fired through the propeller and this helped Fokker monoplanes to dominate the skies over no-man's-land until the Allies brought in new tactics and improved aircraft during 1916. The experience of Verdun and the Somme led to the formation of the German *Jagdstaffeln*, or specialist fighter squadrons, with single-seater aircraft such as the Albatross DIII. By mid-1917 they would form the first *Jagdgeschwader*, or fighter wing, led by the 'Red Baron' *Rittmeister* Manfred Freiherr von Richthofen. The unit became known as the 'flying circus' because of its colourful planes and its flamboyant reputation in action above the trenches.

German pilots such as Oswald Boelcke, Richthofen and Max Immelmann developed tactics in the early years of the war. Above all, Boelcke was both a brilliant pilot and tactician, inspired his fellow airmen and was widely respected by his enemies. After notching up 40 victories he was killed in an air collision with one of his own pilots. Of all the 'Aces' of the skies in the air war, Manfred von Richthofen was the top marksman, with 80 victories. Richthofen became an inspiration not only for other pilots, but also the German soldiers in the trenches and the German people. His successes and the reputation of his 'flying circus' were a real boost to German morale and to many he appeared both invincible and immortal.

The struggle above the battlefield of Verdun would soon become as savage and bitterly contested as that which was about to unfold on the ground.

The dawn of Monday 21 February 1916 brought fog to the French sector around Verdun. The stillness was suddenly shattered by a murderous bombardment of 1,220 German guns along a frontage of barely eight miles. It was the greatest artillery concentration thus far on the Western Front and it signalled the opening of the most prolonged and agonising struggle of the First World War. After a year on the defensive in the West, the German Army was once again on the attack.

For a while, it would seem as though the future of France, and the war, hung in the balance. Though the German commander General von Falkenhayn planned to wage a limited offensive, it would devour almost a million men, friend and foe. Verdun was to become one of the most notorious battles in history.

For nine terrifying hours, the German guns kept up a relentless barrage, obliterating the poorly prepared French front line trenches and burying hundreds of men alive. This storm of steel fell most heavily on Colonel Driant's regiment in a part of the front line hidden by a wood. Driant had been the man who had first alerted the French authorities over Verdun's vulnerability. Even though his defences were stronger than other French regiments in the line, his men still suffered.

At 4 p.m., the first waves of German infantry attacked. As the assault was pressed home, the French line was in danger of buckling. A massive infantry follow-up assault on this first day would have certainly broken the French line. But this was not what Falkenhayn had in mind.

He did not want the French to withdraw, but to pour their troops into Verdun so that he could destroy them. By the end of the first day, the German attack had penetrated the French defences to a depth of two miles in places.

After another furious bombardment, the Germans attacked again on the morning of 22 February. A terrifying and deadly new terror weapon came with the forward lines of German assault troops – the *flammenwerfer* or flamethrower. They were used with devastating effect on the most stubborn French resistance, torching the brave French soldiers where they stood.

Under this renewed attack, the French line began to give way. In danger of being entirely cut off, Colonel Driant decided that the remnants of his regiment should withdraw before they were slaughtered. As they retreated, Driant was mortally wounded.

By now, whole French infantry battalions were disappearing under the weight of the German assault. Falkenhayn's plan to destroy the French Army at Verdun seemed to be working. Worse, French troops were being killed by their own artillery and German machine guns broke up many French counter-attacks almost before they began. Communications broke down and desperate French commanders were forced to use runners, many of whom were killed before they could reach another position with their messages. Those that did get through brought messages of hopelessness in the face of the German assaults. One said:

> Lieutenant Commanding 3rd Bn/60th Regiment to 143 Bde. The CO and all my company commanders have been killed. My Bn is reduced to . . . 180 men. I have neither ammunition or food. What am I to do?[7]

By the end of the fourth day of the offensive the Germans were closing in on the forts that protected Verdun itself. The supposedly impregnable Fort Douaumont now

German infantry repel a French counter-attack at Verdun.
(Verdun Collection)

An exhausted German soldier at Verdun.
(Verdun Collection)

became the centre of German attention. German assault engineer Sergeant Kunze was the unlikely hero of what happened next.

On the morning of 25 February, under cover of a barrage, Kunze led his assault group from the elite Brandenburg Regiment onto the top of Fort Douaumont, but was blown off it by a stray shell into a ditch below. Miraculously unharmed, he looked around for an opening and found one just above him, so he ordered his men to form a human pyramid and then broke into the fort. Entirely alone, he began to wander through this vast concrete labyrinth.

He heard the muffled bangs of Fort Douaumont's 155mm gun. Guided by these, he made his way nervously to the turret. The French gun crew were oblivious of his presence until challenged by him and made prisoner.

Kunze then continued through the corridors, armed only with a pistol, and began to realise that Fort Douaumont was virtually unmanned. Its garrison had, in fact, been recently reduced to a mere 56 elderly French artillerymen. Scarcely believing his continued good fortune, he eventually found the remainder of the garrison in the main dormitory, many still in their beds. He simply locked them in the room, then called his own men into the fort. Sergeant Kunze had single-handedly captured Verdun's most prestigious bastion.

When the news of Douaumont's fall reached Germany, there was wild rejoicing. Church bells were rung and services of thanksgiving held as the German people were given assurance that Verdun, and therefore France – was about to capitulate.

In France, Fort Douaumont's surrender was greeted with dismay and disbelief. In Verdun itself, French troops streamed through the streets shouting: *'Sauve qui peut!'*

('Save yourselves!'). After five days of battle Verdun appeared to be on the verge of collapse and France was facing its most critical point of the war.

At this crisis point, Joffre, the French commander-in-chief, realised that only one man could save Verdun and perhaps France: General Henri Philippe Pétain. On the evening of 25 February 1916, Joffre ordered Pétain to take over the Verdun garrison.

On arrival, Pétain's first task was to reassure his men that their desperate situation would soon be brought under control. Thereafter, he worked tirelessly to contain and then defeat the German assault. His first orders were that Verdun was to be held whatever the cost and that the existing defences and artillery strength must be improved. As result, reinforcements were immediately diverted to defend Verdun.

Pétain was certain that deliverance could only be achieved by the sustained use of artillery and he began to deploy an increasing number of guns. Yet Petain's mere presence was his most powerful weapon. His encouraging phrase, 'They shall not pass', became immortal. Morale was revived almost overnight and there was new steel in the *poilus'* resolve to hold Verdun.

Meanwhile, along the only route into Verdun free from German shellfire, French trucks began to bring a steady and endless stream of supplies and reinforcements. This vital lifeline soon became known as 'la Voie Sacrée', or 'the Sacred Road'. During the first week of March, 190,000 men trudged along it on their way to the front line. Transport passed down the road at a rate of one truck every fourteen seconds.

Falkenhayn appeared to be achieving his aim of drawing the whole French Army into this slaughterhouse, but Pétain put his doctrine of 'firepower conquers all' into effect.

Increasingly heavy artillery bombardments caused the German assault to falter and Falkenhayn reluctantly to change his mind. He finally granted Crown Prince Wilhelm his wish to extend the attack to the western side of the River Meuse. By 8 March, the Germans had carved out a holding position across the river and another titanic struggle began.

The French casualties mounted again, as Falkenhayn had intended. But Pétain was inflicting severe losses on the Germans too.

By April 1916, French counter-attacks were better planned, fierce, and frequent. The Germans were beginning to be pushed back from the gates of Verdun. The thunder of the guns never ceased. To both French and German infantrymen, gunners and engineers engaged in or close to the ever-shifting, barely definable front lines, the artillery was a screaming, mind-numbing harbinger of death and mutilation.

Henri Barbusse explained that:

> A diabolical uproar surrounds us. We are conscious of a sustained crescendo, an incessant multiplication of the universal frenzy; a hurricane of hoarse and hollow

A German prisoner acts as a stretcher-bearer for a wounded comrade.
(Postcard, Allen Collection)

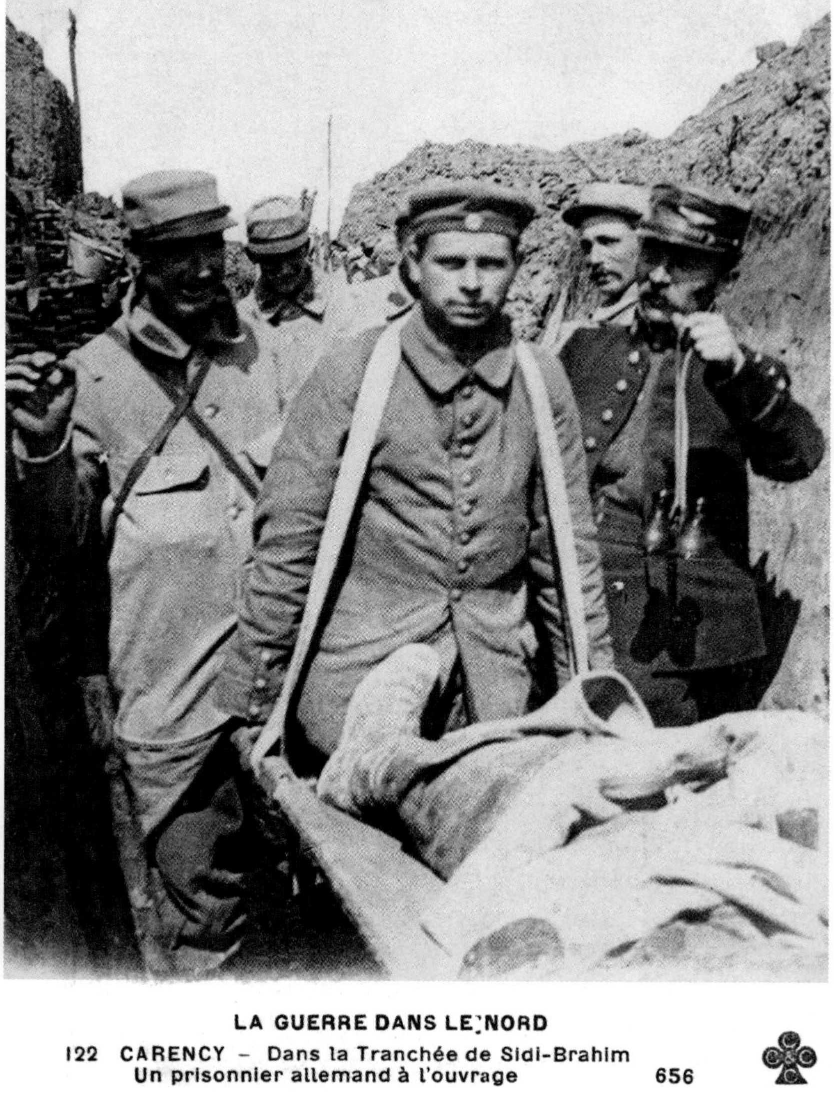
LA GUERRE DANS LE NORD
122 CARENCY – Dans la Tranchée de Sidi-Brahim
Un prisonnier allemand à l'ouvrage
656

banging, of raging clamour, of piercing and beast-like screams, fastens furiously with tatters of smoke upon the earth where we are buried up to our necks, and the wind of the shells seems to set it heaving and pitching.[8]

By May, the Verdun landscape had become a scene of surreal and nauseating horror. The battlefield had been pulverised by the massed artillery of both sides. A French pilot, flying above this livid, lunar landscape, compared it to: 'the humid skin of a monstrous toad'.

On the ground, soldier and writer Jacques Meyer described the real frightfulness when he noted: 'Everywhere there were distended bodies that your feet sank into. The stench of death hung over the jumble of decaying corpses like some hellish perfume.' When the Germans captured Côte 304 in May, one of the first demands of the assault troops was for a double ration of tobacco to mask the overwhelming reek of the corpses rotting around them. Like Jacques Meyer, a fellow French soldier wrote at this time that:

> We all had on us the stench of dead bodies. The bread we ate, the stagnant water we drank, everything we touched had a rotten smell, owing to the fact that the earth around us was literally stuffed with corpses.[9]

At last, the French artillery and infantry were beginning to gain the upper hand over Falkenhayn. One reason for this was that, unlike the Germans, the French were continually relieving their battle-weary units with fresh troops. Conversely, German morale dipped dramatically as the increasing number of German prisoners, exhausted from prolonged combat, testified.

Pétain's inspiration had saved Verdun, but the strain of dealing with continual crises and maintaining the fighting spirit of his men eventually exhausted him. In May 1916 he was promoted to make way for two more thrusting and ruthless men: Generals Robert Nivelle and Charles Mangin, the latter of whom was already known by the *poilus* as 'the Butcher'.

But the battle was far from over. It raged on, putting pressure on the British Army to attack earlier than planned on the Somme. By mid-July, the French had retaken some of the forts lost to the Germans at the beginning of the battle and the tide was turning in favour of the French. Furthermore, despite the horrific cost of the opening day on 1 July, the massive British offensive on the Somme successfully diverted Falkenhayn's attention from Verdun. On 11 July he would be forced to go completely over to the defensive. He could not simultaneously attack the French and resist the British and French pressure on the Somme.

Not only had Falkenhayn's policy of destroying the French Army failed, it had also dangerously sapped the German Army's strength. With the Brusilov offensive under way on the Eastern Front and also putting Germany under the cosh at the time, the pressure on Falkenhayn became almost unbearable. His days as the German military supremo were numbered.

Once the German Army was forced to go on the defensive at Verdun, the French were able to draw breath and prepare for the great counter-offensive that would drive the German Fifth Army back to its original start line by December 1916.

The price of Falkenhayn's failure and French endurance was prohibitive. The German casualties alone would amount to over 330,000 by December 1916. The French would suffer 377,000 casualties, of whom 40 per cent were listed as dead or missing. The sacrifice of both sides was horrific, as is still seen today by the graves and ossuary, which are permanent memorials to those who fell on both sides of the wire at Verdun.

The writer Guillaume Apollinaire, who was to die two days before the Armistice, wrote an ironic poem that could have summed up the mutually awful experience of German and French soldiers alike at Verdun:

> Ah Dieu! Que la guerre est jolie
> Avec ses chants, ses longs loisirs . . .
> Adieu! Voiçi le boute-selle.
> Il disparu dans un tournant
> Et meurt là-bas tandis qu'elle
> Riait au destin suprenant.[10]

'I had a Comrade.'
(Verdun Collection)

(Oh God! What a lovely war
With its songs, its long leisure hours . . .
Farewell! The trumpet call is sounding.
He disappeared down the winding road
And died far away while she
Laughed at fate's surprises.)

In the main defensive phase, Pétain's army had frustrated German efforts and rescued Verdun and the nation from the jaws of defeat. The later counter-offensive would make Robert Nivelle a 'Hero of Verdun' too, although his celebrity status and later promotion to replace Joffre as the French C-in-C would have rapid and dire consequences in 1917.

Above and overleaf: Verdun – Cause and Effect. Aerial photographs of Fleury/Verdun in 1914, 1916 and 1918. *(Allen Collection)*

The most tragic and long-term legacy for France was a deeply psychological one. During 1916, more than three-quarters of France's soldiers had passed along the 'Voie Sacrée'. Their experience would shape the character of the French Army for years to come. Haunted by the horror, Pétain wrote that 'the constant vision of death had penetrated the French soldier with a resignation that bordered on fatalism'.

The French writer, Paul Valéry, described the Verdun campaign as 'a kind of duel before the universe, a singular and symbolic journey'. There is no doubt that it was a supreme test of willpower for the Kaiser's men as much as for the *poilus* – not one man who fought at Verdun would ever quite recover from the eternal awfulness of simply being there. But for the French, the dreadful mental strain that inflicted them at Verdun would leave a wound that that would be torn open once more in spring 1917 and lead to mutiny.

Years later, General Frido von Senger und Etterlin would recall the price of Verdun at Notre Dame de Lorette, where he had fought prior to Operation *Gericht*. The results had been depressingly familiar. The inscription read:

> Piles of bones, once animated by the proud breath of life, now merely scattered limbs, nameless remains, human chaos, sacred agglomeration of countless relics – God shall recognise you, the dust of heroes.[11]

Falkenhayn had been determined to see Verdun become a symbol of hopeless French sacrifice. But the ordinary French *poilu*, led by Pétain, Nivelle or Mangin, would not

yield. The grim, prolonged and costly duel was to become a permanent scar on the French psyche; and it would have desperate consequences in April and May 1917.

For the Kaiser's men on the Western Front, it was to leave an indelible scar too. But an even greater agony was to unfold for them in the summer and autumn of 1916: the defence of the Somme.

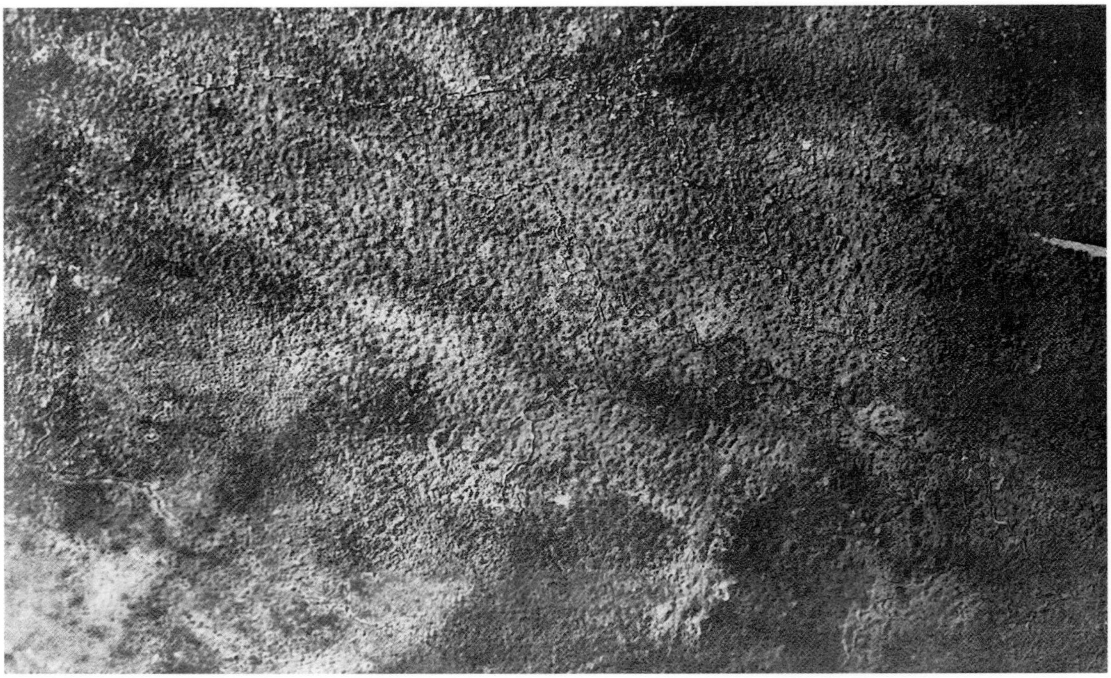

Fleury/Verdun 1918.

CHAPTER 6

MATERIALSCHLACHT – THE GERMAN AGONY ON THE SOMME

JULY–NOVEMBER 1916

A Dead Boche (Summer 1916)
To you who read my songs of War
And only hear of blood and fame,
I'll say (you've heard it said before)
'War's Hell!' – and if you doubt the same,
To-day I found in Mametz Wood
A certain cure for lust for blood:

Where, propped up against a shattered trunk,
In a great mess of things unclean,
Sat a dead Boche; he scowled and stunk
With clothes and face a sodden green,
Big-bellied, spectacled, crop-haired,
Dribbling black blood from nose and beard.
Robert von Ranke Graves (Somme, 1916)

The German Army's part in what many have described as the 'Slaughter on the Somme' was profoundly different from that perceived by most because the slaughter has been seen as a rather one-sided affair. The reality was very different.

Certainly from today's perspective it is difficult for many to comprehend a four-month military campaign in which a total of just over one million men became casualties. But to put this into perspective, it is worth remembering that in the 16 days of the main events of the Battle of Kursk on the Eastern Front in July 1943, regarded even today as a great Soviet victory, over 250,000 Red Army soldiers were killed, and

German machine gun crew: the scourge of unwary enemy infantry.
(IWM: Q23709)

a further 650,000 wounded or taken prisoner. Coupled with the German toll of around 300,000 casualties, of which over 100,000 were killed, the notion of a pure slaughter on the Somme is somewhat distorted.

It is true that the German Army on the Western Front by early 1916 was more skilled and better equipped for trench warfare than either the British or the French. This is not too surprising, as the BEF had only just expanded its Army from around 250,000 in 1914 to just over a million largely inexperienced men and the French had always been uncomfortable with the notion of defensive operations, rather than the 'offensive spirit'.

Many of the German veterans of the inconclusive, though bitter fighting at Ypres, Neuve Chapelle, Artois/Champagne and Loos in 1915 had survived and stiffened an army that had been well-led at the sharp end and remained resolute against Allied efforts in the West. It had come close to beating the Russian armies on the Eastern Front in that year also. In short, as John Terraine has noted: 'It must never be forgotten that the German Army of that period was very good indeed.'[1]

One of its undoubted strengths was in defence and the Somme sector was an excellent example. Strengthened after failed French assaults there in 1915, the trench systems bristled with barbed wire, strongpoints, deep and spacious dugouts and fortified villages. It provided an awesome array of defensive measures to counter any British or French offensive.

German machine gun crew in the anti-aircraft role.
(IWM: HU90289)

The impressive defences were augmented by the intimate knowledge of the German soldiers of their sector and the tactics that they would use to repel any attacks. Many of the German divisions were assigned to a specific sector of the Front and stayed put so that the junior commanders and HQ staffs were very familiar with the terrain and detailed plans to defend their area. Typically, each man would:

> March [again and again] up the same road from the trenches which for weeks we had been covering. Again and again we looked upon the same scene. We knew every house and every tree; at every turn of the way we knew just how far we were from our goal . . . We knew exactly what portions of the road came under enemy fire and we would pass them hastily, mechanically falling back into the ordinary marching tempo as soon as the bad spots were passed. Usually we were silent on the march.[2]

Apart from French attacks in early 1915, the German garrison on the Somme had enjoyed a relatively quiet time of it before the Allied offensive began. Equally, many of the British sent to the Somme sector had come from the Ypres salient and the Somme had given respite from the dreadful experience of daily life in the line in Flanders.

On both sides, once the routine was fixed and a reasonable pattern of front line, reserve and then rest in billets behind the lines was set, there was time for reflection and thoughts of home. Personal correspondence was typically mundane, but with a few matter-of-fact details

German 77mm field gun in action.

(IWM: Q.56487)

German crew manhandle a 75mm light trench mortar on the Somme, 1916.

(IWM: Q. 23. 816)

about the war thrown in. *Schütze* Alois Mühmelt was part of a front line battalion near Achiet-le-Petit, in the north of the Somme sector. In December 1915, he wrote:

Schütze Albert Mühmelt, one of three brothers who fought on the Somme in 1916. His eldest brother, Alois, was killed near Serre on 1 July. His other brother Robert was killed by artillery fire on 17 September and his body was never found. Albert survived the war. *(Farley Family Collection)*

Dear Parents!
First of all, congratulations to dear father on his birthday. May the dear Lord keep him in good health for a long time to come and be a comfort to his children. Here we have terrible rain day after day. The mud in the trench reaches above the knees. If only the war was over soon! Please send me some foot wrappings [large cotton squares used as socks with jackboots] and a few pairs of [proper] socks . . . Have you received the money? [This was a sum of 15 Marks from his pay sent home]. [My brothers] Robert and Karl have not written for some time.

Here artillery and machine gun fire goes on nearly all day on both sides. It is really a miracle that one doesn't get hit. One man of the 8th Company was killed by shrapnel yesterday. He was about to get his food from our field kitchen in a wood 800 metres behind the trench when suddenly two artillery shells landed among it. Our Company was in the same position for 10 days and we were shelled continuously, but lost no one. He was out of the front line and was hit by chance. No one is safe for one moment. Here at our quarters (billets) several enemy aircraft bombarded our battalion offices and the orderly room . . . We shot one aircraft down . . . The parish priest has written to me, but otherwise there is nothing to report.

Warmest greetings to you all, your son,
Alois.

P.S. Please write again soon. Is Hedwig [a sister married in Berlin] staying with you? I will soon have a watch sent from Berlin. It doesn't cost me anything. I will receive a hundred picture postcards for 7 Marks, which I shall sell. Then you get the watch gratis. They are said to be good.[3]

Alois was a typical German soldier 'doing his bit' along with his brothers Robert and Albert. He was to be killed on 1 July 1916. Robert was wounded during the Flers-Courcelette battle and died of his wounds. Albert fought on to the last days of the war, having been wounded, and then earned the Iron Cross for his valour during the Passchendaele campaign. He was to be taken prisoner by the British in October 1918. The brothers had joined up to serve God, the Emperor and their Fatherland and their beliefs and fates were typical of millions on both sides of the wire.

The German soldiers knew their trade and were formidable in defence. They knew the ground and intended to stay there. The real problem lay at the top. The German Army's most fundamental weakness throughout the war was rooted in its military leadership and now it was the turn of Erich von Falkenhayn, Chief of the German General Staff. Falkenhayn was a complex and enigmatic figure. A favourite of the Kaiser, he had been elevated to his supreme position as a result of Moltke's failure during the Battle of the Marne in September 1914.

Since then, he had single-handedly incurred contempt towards him from the best senior commanders in the German Army at that time, such as Ludendorff, Hindenburg and no lesser characters than the Kaiser's sons Crown Prince Wilhelm and Crown Prince Rupprecht of Bavaria.

Opportunities to at least reach for a resounding German victory in the East in 1915 had been spurned by Falkenhayn, but towards the end of 1915 he had conceived the diabolical plan to split the Allies in the West asunder by 'bleeding the French white' at Verdun. The German Verdun offensive, which began on 21 February 1916, did seriously threaten both the French Army's integrity as a fighting force and, more importantly as it was to turn out, its morale.

However, what Falkenhayn had failed to consider was that the extraordinary French resistance in front of Verdun would lead to a significant 'bleeding white' of the German Army too.

The impact for Allied planning soon became obvious. First, the French defence of Verdun was on the brink of failure almost daily for weeks and it was clear that something had to be done to relieve the pressure on the beleaguered *poilus*.

Second, Douglas Haig was obliged to conduct a combined Anglo-French offensive earlier than originally intended and on ground that was not of his choosing – centred on the River Somme.

Moreover, the French had been active in this sector in 1915 before handing the northern part over to the BEF, which had led the German First and Second Armies deployed across the Somme sector to greatly improve their defences in the interim. Last, but by no means least, this was to be the British Army's first major offensive since its expansion in manpower to over one million men by early 1916.

In late April 1916, as the charnel house of Verdun continued to work overtime, Falkenhayn wondered why there were no obvious signs of an Allied relief operation elsewhere. Rightly, he was convinced that one would come. Naturally, he was anxious to know where and when the Allied 'counter-offensive' would fall.

In May, General Fritz von Below, commanding the German Second Army between Noyon on the River Oise in the south to Gommecourt in the north, began to feel that the offensive might be directed against his front. It was held by only three Korps, some 150,000 men in all, and only two of these, General von Stein's XIV Reserve Korps and General von Pannewitz's XVII Korps, would be heavily involved at the outset of the allied 'push'. Below explained his reservations to Falkenhayn, especially as the Second Army had virtually nothing in reserve.

Falkenhayn, too occupied with the increasing bloodbath at Verdun, sent him labour corps personnel to assist in constructing third line defences and a detachment of 8in howitzers that had been captured from the Russians, with little ammunition to fire from them.

There were other concerns too. At sea, the Imperial German and Royal Navies clashed on 31 May at Jutland. Both sides claimed to have won, though neither did. However, British overall command of the sea was unaffected and the Naval Blockade of Germany continued unabated.

The German situation continued to deteriorate on land also. In early June, Russian General Alexei Brusilov launched a bold offensive on the Eastern Front, forcing Falkenhayn to divert five divisions there from the West.

As if things could not be much worse for the German troops manning the front lines of Verdun, the Somme and the wavering line in the East, their concerns were also drawn towards families and friends inside Germany. The war was beginning to really bite, causing unrest, a thriving black market and extraordinary resourcefulness by the women at home. Evelyn Blücher wrote in her diary:

> The unexpected duration of the war has led to unforeseen complications in the economic administration . . . [and the black market] has reached such a climax, that it almost seemed as if revolution . . . were threatening in Berlin . . . Long processions of women waiting for hours before the butchers', grocers' and bakers' shops were to be seen everywhere, and gave rise to the name of the 'butter-polonaise'. These women often got up in the middle of the night, to be first on the scene, and took campstools with them . . .[4]

By mid-1916, daily rations had been set at half-a-pound of sugar and meat or lard, one pound of potatoes, and 100 grams of butter per head per week. Eggs were almost impossible to buy, unless people were able to pay exorbitant prices. The population as a whole was undernourished and illness was on the rise.

Back on the Western Front, Below's fears of a major Allied offensive falling on his sector were being corroborated by a mass of evidence. But Falkenhayn was by now convinced that any Allied offensive effort would be directed around the River Scarpe; nearer Arras and the Vimy Ridge, rather than on the Rivers Somme and Ancre.

There was the infamous comment by British Government Minister, Arthur Henderson, that munitions factory workers were postponing holidays until the end of June and when asked why, merely said: 'The fact should speak volumes.'[5] This was issued as part of the general press release on his visit to the factory workers and was soon public knowledge throughout Europe.

Crown Prince Rupprecht wrote in his diary on 10 June: 'This fact should speak volumes. It certainly does so speak, for it contains the surest proof that there will be a great British offensive in a few weeks.'[6]

Espionage also corroborated the suspected imminence of the great offensive. On 14 June Rupprecht noted that: 'According to a report of an agent in The Hague, the British Attaché there has said that the offensive in the West will begin next week.'[7]

By 23 June Crown Prince Rupprecht was convinced through reliable intelligence reports that the offensive would be by both the British and French north and south of the Somme, but his views and those of OHL intelligence section were dismissed by Falkenhayn, who remained convinced that the full weight of the Allied attack would fall on Rupprecht's Sixth Army.[8]

Then, on the night of 23/24 June, a raiding party of the 91st Reserve Regiment in the Gommecourt sector captured a soldier of the British 46th Division, who stated that a 5-day bombardment would begin on 26 June and an attack on a 30-mile (sic) front would follow.[9]

Between 24 and 26 June, Rupprecht recorded that some of the French newspapers were reporting openly about an impending British offensive in which, at last, the great British Army, the work of Kitchener, would make a decisive attack and show what it could do. In Britain, the 'Great Push' was discussed in pubs and on the streets of town and country, and, to cap it all, Rupprecht noted confidently on 27 June that: 'Reports of the German Military Attaché in Madrid and an agent agree that the enemy offensive will begin on the 1st of July.'[10]

With four days to go, a soldier of the British 29th Division facing Beaumont Hamel was captured by troops of the German 119th Regiment, part of 26th Reserve Division. He also convinced them that an attack was soon to take place. At La Boisselle, the German 180th (26th Reserve Division) and 110th Reserve Regiment (28th Reserve Division) were given prior warning of the planned British assault by an intercepted British Fourth Army HQ message wishing all ranks good luck for the attack the following morning! Y Sap and Lochnagar positions were at least partially evacuated before the mines were blown either side of La Boisselle village.

Any chance of tactical surprise for the British between Fricourt in the south and Gommecourt in the north was lost before Zero Hour on 1 July because of the German

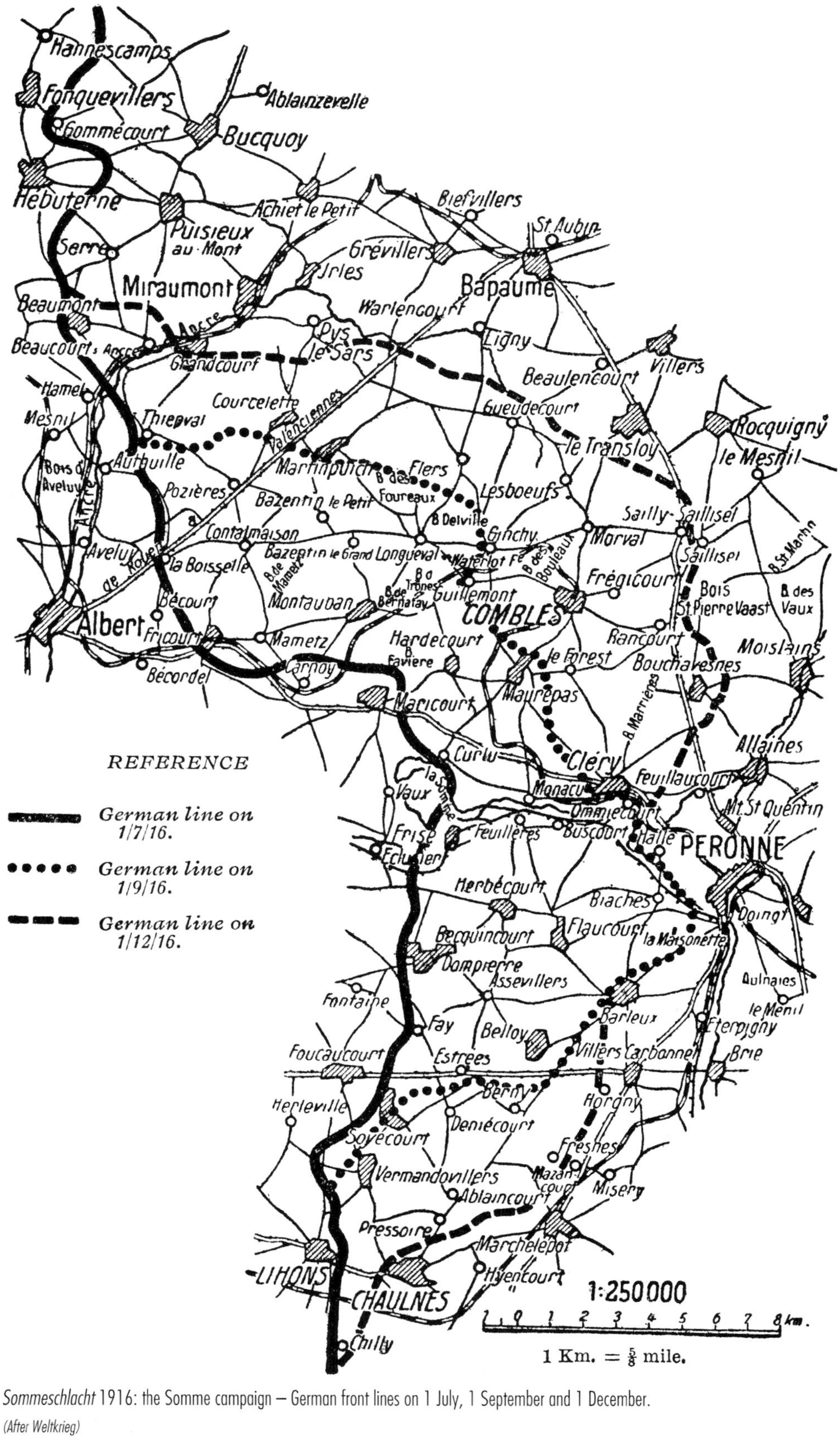

Sommeschlacht 1916: the Somme campaign – German front lines on 1 July, 1 September and 1 December.

(After Weltkrieg)

phone tap at La Boisselle and the premature explosion of the 40,000lb mine at Hawthorn redoubt near Beaumont Hamel, were imminent.

In the south, these remarkable revelations prior to the attack on 1 July were not passed on to the majority of the German troops. Second Army intelligence reports led to the conclusion that an attack against the Fricourt and Gommecourt salients and possibly local attacks in between, perhaps at La Boisselle, Thiepval and Beaumont Hamel. What had not been foreseen, except in part by Rupprecht's HQ, was the assault towards Mametz, Montauban and across the French Sixth Army sector.[11]

The British preliminary bombardment duly began as planned, with the Somme sector as its centre of gravity. Falkenhayn, despite the wealth of evidence, maintained

The effects of British artillery on the Somme in summer and autumn 1916.
(IWM: Q65442)

that the main threat lay against the Sixth Army and therefore left no more than three infantry divisions behind the Second Army as its immediate reserve.

Even so, regardless of the advantage of deep dugouts and labyrinthine redoubts, the German troops manning the front suffered considerably from the Allied preliminary bombardment. A twenty-year-old junior corporal of the 99th Reserve Infantry Regiment (German 52nd Reserve Brigade) near the village of Thiepval described the effects of it on 29 June: 'They were at it day and night. Shall I live until morning?' On 30 June, he continued the theme – but now it was worse still:

> One's head is like a madman's. The tongue sticks to the mouth in terror. Continual bombardment and nothing to eat or drink and little sleep for five days and nights. How much longer can this go on?

He was killed on 1 July.

The early morning of Saturday 1 July promised a fine day. It had rained for much of the week of the Allied preliminary bombardment and the German troops on the Somme had experienced very uncomfortable conditions because of the inclement weather as well as the downpour of artillery shells on their positions. But most knew that their ordeal was about to end. Most were desperately keen to at least escape their 'rat trap' dugouts (the shallow *Unterstände* and deep, mined *Stollen*) to fight the enemy on their own terms. Under the 'monstrous anger of the guns' they felt utterly helpless and vulnerable. When the seemingly endless barrage finally lifted, they knew that their reaction would be crucial – a matter of life and death.

The experience, tactical skill and courage of the German troops under the artillery cosh for so many days were about to pay off in a manner unforeseen by the commanders and men on both sides of no-man's-land. Every army has its good, bad and average units, formations and HQs, but on the Somme most of the German regiments in the line were good, knew the ground that they were defending intimately and had rehearsed their tactics time and again before the British and French attacks were launched. Both 26th and 28th Reserve Divisions, deployed between Redan Ridge in the north and Fricourt in the south had practised continually to improve their response times for rushing out of their dugouts, setting up machine-gun positions and artillery OPs and manning the parapet once the barrage lifted. Experience taught them that speed was the key. Experience had told them that they had to win that vital 'race to the parapet'.

Against this, the majority of the 100,000-plus British infantrymen that were about to go over the top, many for the very first time, were anticipating more of a mopping-up operation in clearing what they were led to believe were destroyed German front-line defences, rather than having to take on stiff resistance. Because of their relative inexperience, (some, like 4th and 29th Divisions were exceptions), the assault was begun at a walking pace for most and with 'full kit,' including rolls of barbed wire and pickets, digging tools, boxes of grenades, machine-gun and mortar ammunition all needed for 'consolidation' after the smashed German front-line positions were occupied, rather than taken. In other places, such as at Thiepval Wood, where the 36th (Ulster) Division faced the Schwaben Redoubt, considered the toughest nut to crack, and in the south where 18th and 30th Divisions were about to assault between Carnoy and Montauban, the leading waves had already crept into no-man's-land and were ready to race across it to catch the German troops with their defensive trousers down.

At 7.20 a.m., the drum roll of artillery fire was rudely and abruptly broken by an explosion beneath the Hawthorn Redoubt near Beaumont Hamel village. The sight, captured on film by the British, was spectacular. But the decision to blow this mine earlier than the planned Zero Hour was disastrous.

It trumpeted the imminent attack across the front and, as a result, set the tone for the ensuing British tragedy. In this sector, the troops of 119th Reserve, 121st Reserve (26th Reserve Division) and 169th Regiment (52nd Division) facing the British 29th, 4th and 31st Divisions respectively reacted quickly and were fully prepared for the assaults when they began ten minutes later. Crucially, 119th Reserve Regiment had special sections trained as a quick reaction force and they were able to win the firefight against the assaulting British troops attempting to occupy the lip of the crater blown by the Hawthorn mine between 7.20 and 7.30 a.m. The regimental history is a testament to the first minutes of triumph and tragedy on that day:

Battle of the Somme, 1916. German infantry with captured British Lewis light machine guns.
(IWM: Q.55482)

> During the intense bombardment there was a terrible explosion which for the moment completely drowned the thunder of the artillery . . . More than three sections of No. 9 Company were blown into the air, and the neighbouring dugouts were broken in or blocked . . . The ground all round was white with the debris of chalk, as if it had been snowing, and a gigantic crater . . . gaped like an open wound in the side of the hill. This explosion was a signal for the infantry attack, and everyone got ready and stood on the lower steps of the dugouts, rifles and machine guns in hand, waiting for the bombardment to lift. In a few minutes the shelling ceased, and we rushed up the steps . . . Ahead of us, wave after wave of British troops were crawling out of their trenches, and coming forwards towards us at a walk, their bayonets glistening in the sun.[12]

The fate of 29th Division at Beaumont Hamel and that of the Regular 4th Division assaulting Redan Ridge and the 'Pals' battalions of the 31st Division at Serre were now emphatically sealed. Though the German positions had been severely damaged by the artillery bombardment, with trench lines and dugouts destroyed, the deeper *Stollen* were relatively unharmed and it was from these that the German 'race for the parapet' began and was, in most cases, won. In 119th Reserve Regiment's sector, strongly built shelters around the fortified village of Beaumont Hamel were augmented by those in 'Y-Ravine' (*Leiling Schlucht*), and the Leiling and Bismarck Stollen to the south of the village.

As the day progressed, the scale of the British catastrophe and German success in this sector became gruesomely clear. Nowhere does any reference appear in the German divisional or regimental accounts of British penetration of the German line except for the brief battles for Hawthorn crater and the *Heidenkopf* or 'Quadrilateral' Redoubt position overlooking Serre and Redan Ridge. Two platoons of 119th Reserve Regiment trained for counter-assault operations repulsed British troops from Hawthorn crater using fire and manoeuvre tactics by moving from shell hole to shell hole and grenade fighting. Heidenkopf Redoubt was cleared after bitter fighting on the evening of 1 July and two companies of 169th Regiment counter-attacked the remnants of the British 31st Division who had occupied the German front line, successfully driving them back, and took 34 prisoners.[13]

At the end of the day, the three German regiments facing 29th, 4th and 31st Divisions recorded a total of 1,214 casualties of a total of just over 8,000 across the Somme front facing the British sector. The British divisions of VIII Corps had suffered a staggering 14,000 killed, wounded, missing and prisoners of war; a ratio of almost 7:1.[14] With the exception of the German 12th Division, which was unceremoniously driven out of its defences by the British 18th and 30th Divisions around Montauban, the dreadful events that unfolded for the British between Serre and Beaumont Hamel formed the template for 1 July.

Four front-line German divisions had taken on twelve British divisions between Gommecourt in the north and Montauban in the south and won the day. But, though the day was won, the battle was far from over, and the tables would turn as the campaign developed, although painfully and with tremendous sacrifice on both sides. Tactics would play their part, but *materialschlacht*, best demonstrated by the power of artillery, would decide the outcome.

There is no doubt that the Somme campaign was, like Verdun, a sustained and increasingly lethal artillery battle. The weight of the guns and the sheer number of calibres and stocks of ammunition largely dictated both the form and limitations of the campaign. The first day of July has always distorted the true picture of that campaign as a whole. Indeed, as a result of this narrow, blinkered perception, the widely held view remains that the German defences were always rock-solid, bristling with machine guns and utterly impregnable.

Few, if any, battles have been more scrutinised, more emotively discussed and more misunderstood than the 'Battle of the Somme' in 1916. That 1 July was a terrible day for the British Army cannot be disputed, but one day of a campaign of more than 140 days cannot begin to paint the full picture that historical perspectives should do. John Terraine underlined this point in a brief but apposite paper in which he noted:

> The reason for the disaster, unfortunately for mythology, is not to be found in any single, simple fact – such as an imprecise order (as at Balaclava), running out of ammunition at a critical moment (Isandlhwana) . . . or stupid generalship (popular myth). It is, as in most large affairs, rather in a complex of causes that we may find the key to this tragedy. The first of these deserving consideration is one that British insularity and a certain unconscious but unpleasant arrogance have obscured and often neglected entirely: the quality of the German Army.[15]

The difference on 1 July was that of the inculcated discipline and training that gave the German defenders the edge on that day. Despite the effects of the British eight-day preliminary bombardment of 1,732,873 shells and the real damage done by it, when the barrage lifted the German troops' discipline and courage enabled them to emerge from their dugouts and win that all-important 'race for the parapet.' Coupled with this fact on that fateful day was the overall inexperience of the commanders, staffs and soldiers of the British Fourth Army.

But, contrary to popular belief, the British would learn rapidly to adapt, change and match the apparently overwhelmingly superior German soldier man for man as the Somme offensive progressed. As the subaltern Charles Carrington wrote at the end of the campaign: 'Though enthusiastic amateurs when the fighting began, the British were soldiers at the end.'[16]

What is generally not acknowledged is that by 1 July, much of the German front line and second line positions had been demolished and that their defenders had sustained a minimum of 10,000 casualties before the fateful first day of the Anglo-French Somme offensive. The preliminary bombardment had had a significant physical and psychological effect, rendering much of the defensive sector untenable.

In most places it was only the uncut wire and the plodding nature of the British advance that provided the opportunity and time for the German machine gunners to recover from their ordeal and thereafter wreak havoc among their enemy.

But if the German soldiers now engaged in the Somme battle thought that their 8,000 casualties on 1 July compared with 57,470 British losses (of which over 19,000 were killed) was a sign of an easy campaign to come, they were very soon disillusioned.

Even at the failed attack against Ovillers by 8th Division and against La Boisselle by the 34th (Tyneside Irish and Scottish) Division on the 1st of July, the German defenders of the 180th Infantry Regiment and 110th Regiment were staggered by the resilience and courage of the British assault troops against ever increasing odds. A German eyewitness wrote immediately after the attacks:

> Looking towards the British trenches through long trench periscopes . . . there could be seen a mass of steel helmets above the parapet showing that the storm-troops (sic) were ready for the attack. At 7.30 a.m. the hurricane of shells ceased as soon as it had begun. Our men at once clambered up the steep shafts leading from the dugouts to daylight and ran singly or in groups to the nearest shell craters. The machine guns were pulled out of the dugouts and hurriedly placed in position . . . [Then] a series of extended lines of British infantry were seen moving forward . . . the first wave [of which] appeared to continue without end right and left. It was quickly followed by a second line, then a third and fourth. They came on at a steady easy pace as if expecting to find nothing alive in our front trenches . . .

As the advance developed and the German defenders took stock of the incredible scene before them, the barked orders of battle-hardened NCOs woke their men from inaction sparked by the surreal picture of thousands of British troops heading towards them as if on parade:

> The [leading wave] was now half-way across no-man's-land. 'Get ready!' was passed along our front . . . and heads appeared over each shell crater edge as final positions were taken up for the best view and machine guns mounted firmly in place. A few moments later, when the first British line was within a hundred yards, the rattle of machine gun and rifle fire broke out along [our] whole line of shell holes, [followed soon after by deadly accurate shellfire] . . . The advance rapidly crumpled under this hail of shell and bullets. All along the line men could be seen throwing up their arms and collapsing, never to move again . . . The extended lines, though badly shaken and with many gaps, now came on all the faster. Instead of a leisurely walk they covered the ground in short rushes at the double [and] within a few minutes the leading troops had advanced to within a

> stone's throw of our front trench . . . Again and again the extended lines of British infantry broke against the German defence like waves against a cliff, only to be beaten back. It was an amazing spectacle of unexampled gallantry, courage and bull-dog determination on both sides.[17]

The same eyewitness referred to another quality of British and Dominion character that was to prove decisive in the months and years of the war to be still played out when he noted that 'The British soldier, however, has no lack of courage and once his hand is set to the plough, he is not easily turned from his purpose.'[18]

The German defensive doctrine hitherto had been to conduct 'positional defence', where the front line was the main line of resistance, packed with troops, and any Allied penetration of this line was to be negated by infantry counter-attacks with supporting field artillery, and medium guns where necessary.

The preliminary bombardment on the Somme and, ironically, the weight of fire poured into the Verdun cauldron in the opening days of the German offensive in February, should have given Falkenhayn every reason to modify his defensive tactics after the events of 1 July. They did not; and the action that he did take proved to be a fatal error.

More vexing was the realisation that the BEF and French armies had launched a joint offensive, which had achieved most of its objectives on the British right flank and French sector by the evening of day one. Falkenhayn, OHL and the troops facing this attack were surprised and dismayed by the fact that the French, still heavily engaged at Verdun, had the capacity to mount such a strong, coordinated attack with heavy artillery support. The scale of the Anglo-French attacks and their implications for the future defence of the Somme, rather than any idea of success against these attacks on 1 July, were the matters that most taxed the German High Command. On 1 and 2 July, OHL summed up the situation as:

> *1st July:* Disastrous news from the Péronne sector this afternoon. Successful attacks by the English and French on our forward positions on a 10 km [sic] front have given them command of both banks of the Somme. [Geographically, this was entirely accurate and reflected the British success in the south between Fricourt and Montauban.]
> *2nd July:* A marvellous evening, but the mood was one of depression. Further bad news from the Somme . . .[19]

Heavy German casualties and loss of ground on 2 July in the French sector and thereafter in both French and British areas of responsibility were also attributed to the effects of concentrated artillery fire. On the same day, Below demanded immediate reinforcement by infantry divisions and especially artillery of all calibres. On 1 July he had lost over 109 guns north of the Somme and all of 121st Division's artillery batteries south of the river.[20] OHL assured him that three divisions, sixteen heavy batteries and three

Eingreif (counter-attack) troops wait to go over the top to reinforce troops already assaulting across no-man's-land. *(IWM: Q.23.753)*

flights of combat/reconnaissance aircraft were en route already. As a mark of just how serious the German High Command took the opening days of the Somme campaign, they rushed fifteen heavy batteries from the Verdun sector to boost Below's defence.

The success of the German counter-attacks on 1 July was varied, and in some places, such as against the junction between the BEF and French near Montauban that night, had failed. Major counter-moves by *eingreif* divisions were out of the question for the first few days, as the units assigned to such tasks still had to arrive and receive orders. Local counter-attacks, such as those against the French sector and those mounted to throw back the 36th (Ulster) Division at Thiepval and also at Fricourt, Mametz and Montauban, were costly efforts.

Tactical commonsense was also costly for the German commanders who chose to use their discretion in the opening days of the Somme battle. General von Pannewitz, commanding XVII Korps south of the Somme, withdrew on 2 July after receiving permission to do so by HQ Second Army. He had held the line near Herbécourt where the French had broken through and the retirement, providing a more solid defensive sector, was tactically sound. When Falkenhayn heard of this he immediately drove to Below's HQ at St Quentin and demanded to know how such a voluntary abandonment of territory could possibly be sanctioned.[21] As a result, Falkenhayn then infamously decreed that:

> [All units are reminded that] . . . the first principle of position warfare must be to yield not one foot of ground, and if it is to be lost, to retake it by immediate counter-attack, even to the use of the last man.[22]

General von Below's COS, General Grünert was held responsible for allowing von Pannewitz's withdrawal and was removed from his position to make way for *Oberst* Fritz von Lossberg, whose skills as a defensive expert were already acknowledged throughout the German Army.[23] Grünert's 'failure' was to have done his job rather too efficiently, for not only had he anticipated the Anglo-French attack against the Second Army, as his commander Below and Crown Prince Rupprecht had done, but he also asked firmly for reinforcements, which Falkenhayn and OHL had refused, because they had wrongly expected the main offensive elsewhere.

Falkenhayn's new edict of not one step back, regardless of tactical necessity, was soon proved to be obsolete and doomed thousands of his most experienced troops to be killed or mutilated, needlessly sacrificed for ever-more desperate attempts to retake ground of little tactical importance.

This policy was underscored by General Fritz von Below, who also unwittingly described the true nature of *materialschlacht* with his special order of the day on 3 July that:

> The decisive issue of the war depends on the victory of the [German] Second Army on the Somme. We must win this battle in spite of the enemy's temporary superiority in artillery and infantry . . . For the present, the important thing is to hold our current positions at any cost and to improve them by local counter-attacks. I forbid the evacuation of trenches. The will to stand firm must be impressed on every man in the Army. I hold Commanding Officers responsible for this. The enemy should have to carve his way over heaps of corpses.[24]

The shaken Second Army took stock on 3 July and reinforcements, including a desperately needed thirty-eight heavy artillery batteries and infantry to fully man the second line defences opposite the British successes between Fricourt and Montauban, were in place. Another four fresh infantry divisions were en route and would slot into the defence to plug the gaps on 5 July. It was a day on which the British, and particularly General Sir Henry Rawlinson, finally realised the magnitude of their losses on 1 July.

From the depths of near despair, at least the officers of Supreme HQ renewed their confidence when they received the latest situation report on the Somme fighting on the evening of 3 July: 'The evening news from all fronts was good. The Anglo-French offensive has been halted on the Somme and in places repulsed.'[25]

It was a wet, cold, dismal day on 4 July and this seemed to prophesy the gloom that overhung the Somme sector. Trenches and the steps into dugouts and redoubts became slippery, damaged trenches caved in. It was foul for both sides and the German defences offered little more protection from the weather than the British, for the latter were at least in billets if they were not already in the line.

The week or so that followed gave Below the respite needed, and with Lossberg as his new COS, he did not waste time directing the vital improvements needed for his defence of the Somme. Further heavy and medium artillery batteries were sent forward from Rupprecht's Sixth Army and Verdun; infantry divisions were resupplied with machine guns to full establishment and reserve infantry units were trained for the specialist counter-attack (*eingreif*) role. Three flights of German aircraft were transferred to Below, providing some defence against British air superiority and limited reconnaissance of the forward British positions.

By the time Rawlinson's Fourth Army was ready to attack in force once more, the German Second Army had been reinforced with a further 40 new or reinforced battalions, though they too would face fresh British and Dominion divisions from the First and Second Army.

By 7 July, the German defences in the second line were receiving the type of regular pummelling from British artillery that soon became the daily, dreadful curse of almost every ill-fated German soldier that served on the Somme. Where time had not allowed dugouts to be sunk deep enough, the effects of continual artillery attention were devastating. Infantry battalions in the line were losing one third of their strength from artillery fire alone. The third battalion of 122nd Reserve Regiment in the Bazentin-Pozières sector lost five officers and 238 men, the first battalion of the Lehr Regiment at Contalmaison a staggering 618 officers and men in this manner, and communications became all but impossible as the British guns cut even deep-laid telephone cables. As a result of continued British attacks, artillery fire and the disruption of communications, large-scale counter-attack operations were difficult to coordinate and even the relief of one infantry division by another in the line was a fraught and often costly manoeuvre.

The period 7 to 12 July saw further reinforcement in these difficult circumstances of the German 7th and 8th Divisions from Sixth Army and 77th Reserve Regiment of 2nd Guards Reserve Division from the Gommecourt sector into the main battlefield area. The infantry 'battle casualty replacements' were augmented by the provision of a further sixty-five gun and howitzer heavy artillery batteries and three artillery observation flights, two reconnaissance and one bombing flight.

On 11 July, Falkenhayn tacitly acknowledged that the Somme campaign was already hurting the German effort on the Western front by ordering a change of emphasis at Verdun. That afternoon, as the German Fifth Army's assault on Fort Belleville, a mere mile from the city, petered out, Falkenhayn arrived at Crown Prince Wilhelm's HQ and immediately ordered a 'strict defensive' at Verdun because of the serious situation developing on the Somme. On the 132nd day of the horrific struggle that had begun in February, German artillery units were ordered north, and infantry divisions would soon follow. The principal Allied objective of taking pressure off the

French defence of Verdun was realised, and it was to have further consequences for both Falkenhayn and the German troops who were now being fed into the 'mill on the Somme'.[26]

On the 13th, the Second Army braced itself for a further set of British attacks and Below carried out a reorganisation of his resources into *Kampfgruppen*, or battle groups, which were normally based on a particular commander and a minimum of two or three divisions. The *Kampfgruppen* were ad hoc groupings of units belonging to other formations, as there was little time to reinforce or reorganise after some of those units involved had sustained heavy casualties. Hence *Gruppe Stein*, with three divisions, faced the British line between Monchy au Bois and the River Ancre; *Gruppe Armin*, with two divisions, was deployed between St Pierre Divion/Thiepval and Longueval and *Gruppe Gossler*, with one fresh and two depleted divisions, was to hold the line between Delville Wood and the River Somme.

The long hard slogging match was already under way and on the British side, Haig anticipated a 'wearing down' rather than 'breakthrough' battle and the focus of the continued British efforts was on the sector between the Albert-Bapaume road and the right flank of the Fourth Army where it had its boundary with the French just north of the River Somme.

Ironically, what Haig had doubted and what the German commanders had not bargained for and has been so often ignored in the past, was the innovation and imaginative tactics that the British would use a mere two weeks after the first day on the Somme. General Rawlinson planned a night attack against Bazentin in the centre of the German second line between Pozières and Longueval. The French commanders too doubted that it could be done so soon after the failure of 1 July. But Rawlinson put into practice what he had originally considered doing on 1 July by attacking shortly before dawn and with his leading assault waves well into no-man's-land before the barrage lifted. Furthermore, the 'barrage', or preliminary bombardment, was

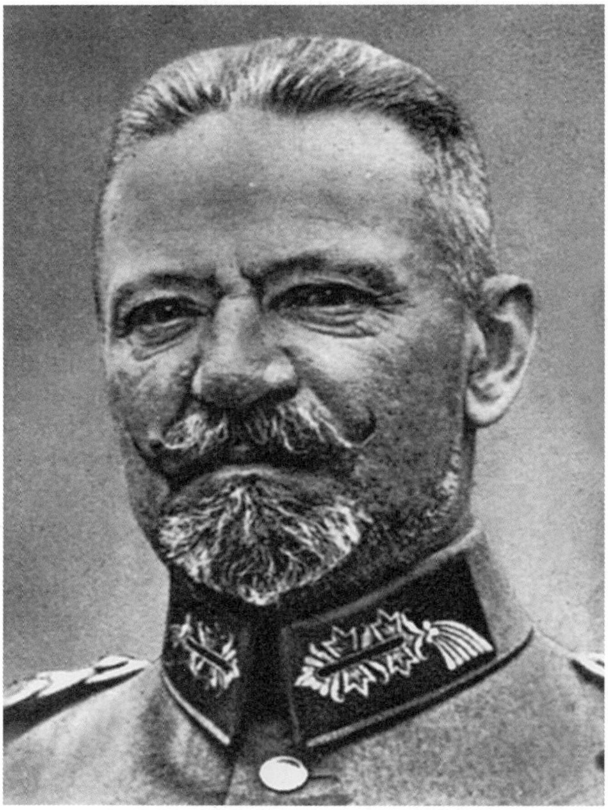

General Max von Gallwitz, GOC Army Gallwitz and a key commander at Verdun and the Somme in 1916; and also at Meuse Argonne against the American AEF in 1918.
(Rudolph Stratz, Weltkrieg)

short; so short that it took the German troops tucked away in their dugouts completely by surprise.

The assault was a resounding success and 6,000 yards of the German second line was taken between Bazentin-le-Petit and Longueval. Mametz, Bernafay and Trônes Woods had all fallen and success at Longueval gave promise of the capture of another German stronghold in Delville Wood. Even the dominating ground on which the German defences of High Wood stood was within the British assault troop's grasp. But this fleeting opportunity was let slip because of problems of communication and the lack of reserves to exploit it on the British side, and German recovery after the stunning setback that morning on the other.

July and August were the summer months of grim harvest on either side. Infamous names such as Delville and High Woods, Pozières, Mouquet Farm, Guillemont and Ginchy were scored into the very fabric of a German or British soldier's existence as the battles for each tree-splintered wasteland, or pile of rubble that was once a thriving rural village, ebbed and flowed by assault and counter-attack.

Throughout July and August, the Falkenhayn doctrine, which had in effect ordered his best troops to 'lose your life but not a foot of ground', became the bloody German testament of unbelievable courage and sacrifice, but sacrifice at a much greater cost to the German Army on the Somme than the damage it was doing in return.

Weltkrieg and unit or personal records demonstrate a consensus that by mid-August, with over 250,000 casualties to add to the 8,000 of 1 July, even the hardiest units were giving ground or surrenderring rather than take another massive pounding for virtually no purpose. Divisional strengths and the robustness of so-called 'fresh' divisions thrown into the line were diminishing in an alarming way. The commanders most involved on the ground, Generals Fritz von Below and Max von Gallwitz, were frustrated by the lack of time that infantry regiments withdrawn from the line after a battering at the hands of the British or French had to rest, regroup and train before being pitched back into the fray. Fresh divisions brought in from other sectors and new soldiers arriving as reinforcements for units that had already lost so many men in earlier Somme battles were quickly disillusioned and disheartened by the sheer weight of the Allied superiority in artillery, air power and other *matériel*.

So by the end of August, the 'mill' was grinding down the core of German morale as well. Its 125th Regiment summed this depressing situation up even with the benefit of hindsight: 'The days on the Somme were the worst in the war.' But if July and August were bad, the autumn months of the Somme campaign would mark a grave turning point for the German Army that had existed since 1914.

It is worth recalling here that in addition to the 'Rohr' and 'Laffargue' tactical innovations in 1915, the OHL had, in spring 1915, sanctioned the raising of special engineer, artillery and infantry units for 'special operations' in offensive or counter-offensive actions. Initially, the assault engineer detachment provided two companies of engineers as specialist *minenwerfer* (trench mortar) and *flammenwerfer* (flamethrower) teams; and an artillery *Abteilung* (unit) of twelve 3.7cm guns. These were in addition to locally established counter-attack infantry and field artillery (77mm gun) *Gruppen*, or sub-units, of between company and battalion strength.

From these roots grew the first *Sturmabteilung* and *Sturmbattailon*. By April 1916, OHL had formalised the establishment of one *Sturmbattailon* per army. Though all of these 'Storm battalions' were all Army troops, they were put under operational command of infantry divisions as the situation demanded. The standard order of battle (ORBAT) of a *Sturmbattailon* at this time was two or three infantry companies, a machine gun company, a *minenwerfer* company, an 'infantry gun' battery of four 3.7cm guns and a *flammenwerfer* section; a total of between 450 and 650 men. Battle casualty replacements came from special 'high-level ersatz' training units in Germany.

As the Somme campaign developed, infantry divisions warned off for the battle organised their own storm companies or battalions, although they were not officially authorised as Army establishments. Many fought with distinction during the campaign, but most were ultimately annihilated, ironically mainly because of their special training and discipline. Their relative success as *eingreif* (counter-attack) units compared with the ad hoc use of troops in the line for local counter-attacks meant that they were used again and again, rather than when their increasingly precious skills were most needed.

The Somme campaign was characterised by attack, counter-attack and attack, followed by yet more counter-attacks. It was this pattern, and that of the incessant crump of artillery fire, that turned this part of the Western front into a 'mill' as effective as that turning the screw at Verdun. By the end of July, the German Second and First Army resisting the Anglo-French onslaughts had carried out no less than sixty-seven counter-attacks. Each one was costly, and the more specialised troops were generally those whose loss was most difficult to replace. But one of the inherent problems of the German Army's doctrine that was to have fatal consequences in 1918 was its desire to use elites for the most difficult tasks to the detriment of the Army as a whole. Crown Prince Rupprecht of Bavaria was concerned about such implications because much of the most desperate fighting was constantly allotted to these special units. To him, it was a worrying shortcoming as the 'ordinary' infantry of the line were increasingly leaving such tasks alone: 'as instructors for the infantry [and developing tactics] they were excellent; but the view must not be allowed to arise that one cannot attack without them.'[27]

Although no elite units of this type existed in the British or French armies in the First World War, their advantage was that every battalion and every division would train and fight under a single tactical ethos and with weapons that would later provide the 'ordinary' infantry units the ability and flexibility to fight in a more cohesive way than the 'ordinary' German infantry battalion.

The British learned how predictable German defensive tactics were and used artillery with increasingly deadly effect to snuff out counter-attacks and continually blast the German defences. Regimental histories bear testament to the conditions to which the

German Army on the Somme was reduced by the incessant battering that it received throughout the offensive. Diaries and memoirs recall the 'Hell of the Somme' and the dreadful human experience of the *materialschlacht*, or the 'attritional battle'.

The elite, specially trained *eingreif*, or counter-attack units, which provided the 'main punch' with the artillery in attempting to throw back any British penetration of the German defences, were often annihilated by the sheer weight and accuracy of the British artillery ranged against them.

'The New Team': Chief of the General Staff Field Marshal Paul von Hindenburg (left) and General Erich Ludendorff, Quartermaster General, who were appointed to these posts to succeed General Erich von Falkenhayn on 29 August 1916. *(Rudolph Stratz, Weltkrieg)*

British artillery was increasingly supported from the air, as the Royal Flying Corps (RFC) held sway over the German airmen and provided vital information to the guns. It was cursed by the German soldier on the ground and by the High Command. General von Below, who defended the Somme sector during the campaign, wrote a memorandum for OHL in January 1917 which attested to this:

> The enemy's aeroplanes enjoyed complete freedom in carrying out distant reconnaissance . . . With [this] the hostile artillery neutralised our guns, and was able to range with the utmost accuracy on the trenches occupied by our infantry; the required data for this being provided by undisturbed [aerial] trench reconnaissance and photography . . . [With] bombing and machine gun attacks from a low height against our infantry, battery positions and marching columns, the enemy's aircraft [left] our troops with a feeling of defencelessness against the enemy's mastery of the air.[28]

The Allied casualties may have been comparatively high, but they were learning and applying the lessons of both Verdun and the early phase of the Somme campaign, whereas most German commanders continued to expect rigid discipline and self-sacrifice despite using already outdated tactics.

Changes had to occur in the German High Command and they did between 28 and 29 August. At Supreme HQ in Pless, daily routine was interrupted by a growing rumour that Falkenhayn was to be replaced by Field Marshal Paul von Hindenburg (and, by implication, General Ludendorff). On 29 August, a senior aide noted:

> Hindenburg and Ludendorff arrived . . . Hindenburg (today is the anniversary of Tannenberg) was appointed Chief of the General Staff and Ludendorff First Quartermaster-General, with promotion to Infantry General. Falkenhayn left unobtrusively for Berlin . . . At 6.00 p.m., I walked with the Chancellor . . . who told me incidentally that Falkenhayn had left because he refused to hear the Kaiser asking Hindenburg's advice on the conduct of the war. There was only one adviser to the Kaiser and that was the Chief of the General Staff. If the Kaiser insisted upon receiving Hindenburg he – Falkenhayn – must go! The [Kaiser's] reply was: 'As you wish.'[29]

Falkenhayn was gone, removed for, among other things, his profligate use of manpower. With his departure, fundamental changes were soon planned in both the defences of the Somme and German tactical methods, or doctrine, for the future. Most of the excessive loss of life and limb on the German part at Verdun and on the Somme until now could be put down to Falkenhayn's inflexibility. But greater threats to Germany soon appeared once he quit the stage.

Within months, General Ludendorff was to become nothing less than the military dictator of Germany, brushing the Kaiser's already diminished responsibility aside. Despite the 'legitimacy' afforded him by the ever present Hindenburg, loved by the people until the end as the 'Hero of Tannenberg' and trusted beyond that, Ludendorff became answerable to no one, unlike Haig or his French counterparts who had a full bag of British and French military and political issues to resolve before any plans could be laid.

It was with this political change, as well as the military disaster that was unfolding on the Somme, that the seeds of Germany's ultimate destruction in the First World War were sown. By the end of August the situation was described by the *Weltkrieg* as being 'the most serious crisis of the War'. The German agony was at least ameliorated by Falkenhayn's sacking and the new regime in the minds of most of the men at the front and those at home:

> Although the battle on the Somme has proved to be of much longer duration than anyone expected, no decisive action has taken place up to now. Bloodier and more costly as it has proved to be than any other phase of this murderous war, Germany remains determined not to be crushed by the Allies . . . Hindenburg's (and Ludendorff's) promotion as C-in-C in place of Falkenhayn (29 August) was a very popular step . . . It is said that Hindenburg made it a condition of his accepting the post that no further actions against Verdun should be attempted.[30]

As the Somme battles raged, Ludendorff and Hindenburg had to contend with an emerging conflict in Romania, and the Brusilov offensive on the Eastern Front. Desperately needed reinforcements, weapons and equipment were diverted there rather than to the Somme.

As a measure of the vital importance of the German defence of the Somme, an order was issued on 2 September to cease all offensive action at Verdun. Four infantry divisions and eighteen heavy artillery batteries were rushed to the Somme sector.

On 8 September, an emergency planning conference was held at Cambrai to review the situation. It was a grim meeting. It was soon apparent that the men of the First and Second Army defending the Somme sector were in dire straits.

Divisions could not be kept in the battle for more than fourteen days. The implication was that in effect a 'fresh' division had to replace an exhausted or virtually destroyed one every day. Consequently, each division had to complete at least three tours in the front line, without sufficient time for rest, reinforcement and training before being hurled back into the cauldron.

Worse still, as the British inexorably pushed the German line back, many of the defences were more rudimentary. German soldiers were more likely to fight from a loose trench line of shell-holes than from deep dugouts, which were now becoming death-traps as the British and Dominion troops became more adept at storming defensive positions.

September was to bring the heaviest German losses of the whole battle: over 220,000 were added to the lists of killed or missing, wounded or prisoners of war, by the month's end. Crown Prince Rupprecht was to mark the appalling state of affairs by noting that the battle casualty replacements covered a mere 10 per cent of the required total. Those battle-weary and bloodied troops that remained had to hang on – and hang on – in the hope of some relief from the daily artillery bombardments and bitter, bloody, morale-sapping British assaults.

'Tanks!' German troops surrender on encountering their first tanks on the Somme, 15 September 1916.
(Allen Collection)

Major counter-attacks were planned against Delville Wood, Pozières Ridge, Ginchy and Guillemont with no realistic chance that the manpower and resources would be available. All were cancelled.

In the first week in September, Hindenburg had noted that he 'had succeeded to an evil inheritance'[31] and acknowledged that no reserves existed at that time for offensive action. He demanded an immediate review of the tactics used, as well as a future strategy to ameliorate the desperate position that Germany was now in on the Western Front. The review led to the decision to prepare a much stronger and shorter defensive sector some 15–20 miles behind the then current Arras and Somme front lines – which was to become known as the *Siegfried Stellung*, or the Hindenburg Line – and to adopt new flexible, or elastic, deep defence.

But much of this almost became academic. Unknown to the German Army and its Central Power allies, the 'wearing down' battles that raged across the Verdun and Somme sectors of the Western Front between July and early September had been necessary parts of a wider Allied plan to go on to the offensive. It was unique: the only time in the whole war when the full power of the Entente was turned simultaneously on Germany. The Brusilov offensive in June, which had so shocked Falkenhayn, was followed up on 12 September by a combined Russian and Romanian assault in Transylvania. On the same day, the French Sixth Army renewed its offensive in the southern sector of the Somme. On 15 September, the Italians launched the seventh battle of the Isonzo river; and the British 'Flers-Courcelette battle' began.

The British attack at Flers-Courcelette was an indicator at least of the shape of things to come, as well as proving just how far the BEF had come since 1 July. The assault included the historic use of tanks for the first time, novel infantry tactics and a new artillery technique; the creeping barrage, which provided a good deal more protection for the infantry from German machine gun and artillery fire as they advanced. Much was achieved on this one day and stubborn German stains on the Somme landscape, such as High Wood, Flers and Courcelette villages were finally removed.

Once again, so many views have been expressed over the years since the event that purport to analyse the failure of a British opportunity, a failure of command and the poor individual and tactical performance of the tanks on this day. Most totally miss the point that 'Flers-Courcelette' was part of this Entente-wide effort to force the German war machine to overheat and grind to a halt by hitting it from as many angles as possible. So many also miss the heart of the matter: what did the attack, and the use of the tanks do to the enemy?

The answer lies not at the tactical level, but elsewhere. Although a breakthrough did not take place, the psychological effect on the already frayed nerves of the German defenders was almost unbearable. General von Below described 15 September as 'A very heavy day, with serious losses, even by Somme standards.'

Weltkrieg acknowledged later that the German defence of the Flers-Courcelette sector was 'as good as completely broken by the end of the day.'[32] But the forty or so

Mark I tanks that were involved on 15 September did not succeed tactically partly because they had not been tested in battle before. But the new weapon had to be tested in battle somewhere where they could at least potentially make a difference.

One thing that the German Army proved to be extraordinarily adept at in both world wars was to recover from almost fatal blows if the enemy gave them the opportunity to do so. It had no choice but to use this ability on the Somme. In 1917 there would be many occasions, such as at Arras, Messines/Third Ypres and Cambrai, when it would do it again.

However, the arrival of the tank was a serious blow to German morale. Casualties on 15 September were enormous. The 210th Reserve Regiment of 45th Reserve Division facing the Canadians around Courcelette lost nearly 70 per cent of its strength; and the 6th Bavarian Division, opposing part of the British XV Corps, lost over 50 per cent of its establishment. Regardless of loss, the counter-attacks kept coming, despite Hindenburg and Ludendorff's succession and the failures along the line in the Flers-Courcelette battle. The German strength ebbed, its 'motor' running down as the fuel provided by its most experienced troops was drained by the mounting casualties.

The battles continued and gradually refocused on the defences either firmly held or lost and then retaken on 1 July. One by one, Thiepval, Mouquet Farm, Schwaben Redoubt, the depth positions of Regina and Zig-Zag Trench, and then finally Beaumont Hamel, fell. Other defences along the Transloy Ridge to the south of the Albert-Bapaume road were pushed back as far as the impregnable Butte de Warlencourt. After 15 September, rain, and with it the foul mud which had cursed the first week of the campaign, came back with a vengeance and made the fighting all the more difficult for both sides. When 180th (Württemberg) Regiment was finally driven from Thiepval by the British 18th Division on 27 September, a black mood fell across those who had held off the enemy attacks since 1 July and come through it all so far. The setback was 'absolutely crushing. [To me] every German soldier from the highest general to the most lowly private had the feeling that now Germany had lost the first great battle.'[33]

The year was growing ever more horrendous for the men at the Front, but in the Fatherland itself, even the bad times before 1916 were almost a pleasant memory by comparison. The Government had no hope of concealing the images of broken men, broken lives and broken promises of a German victory, the latter promise so illusory that it might have been amusing, if it was not so deadly serious. Wives and daughters, mothers and sons saw the results of German ambition in the now overflowing hospitals throughout the nation:

> The unprecedented English artillery fire on the Somme is filling the hospitals more than ever, all those on the Rhine being over-filled, so that the wounded are being transported straight from the Western Front to the Tempelhofer Hospital in Berlin . . . Only yesterday I spoke to an official who told me that within the last week

'The Horror of the Somme.' The remains of a German officer found in the defences of Beaumont Hamel, 13 November 1916.
(IWM: Sutton Ref)

both of his sons had been sent home insane, having gone out of their minds at the awful things they had witnessed.[34]

After further losses at Morval and the fall of Thiepval, the die was cast on the decision to withdraw to a more defensible line. Work began in earnest as orders were issued after 15 September for a strict defensive attitude to be adopted on all fronts.

Between 23 September 1916 and 1 March 1917, the Hindenburg Line grew out of the French countryside from Arras via St Quentin to the River Aisne, shortening the Front by some 50 kilometres and releasing a vitally needed sixteen divisions from front line duty as a strategic reserve. Meanwhile November's foul weather finally drew the curtain on the bloody drama on the Somme in 1916.

Falkenhayn's edict that 'not one foot of ground should be lost' had dealt the German Army a bitter and near-fatal blow. Against all the historical tide of opinion that has portrayed the German military leaders and their men almost as supermen, the facts lead to the undeniable conclusion that the Somme proved to be the graveyard for most of the German 'old guard' of 1914/1915.

In 1928, the German *Reichsarchiv* produced a summary of the Somme campaign. It passed this verdict:

> It would be a mistake to measure the results of the Battle of the Somme by mere local gains of ground . . . The British and the French pursued a plan of exhausting the power of the defenders by the employment of ever-greater masses of artillery in constantly repeated attacks . . . [Our] grave loss of blood [in the battle] affected Germany very much more heavily than the Entente . . . The *materialschlacht* gnawed

terribly into the entrails of the defenders. The enormous tension on all fronts forced the [German] Supreme Command to leave troops in the line until they had expended the last atom of their energy, and to send divisions time after time into the same battle . . . Still more serious was that, as the demand for self-sacrifice greatly surpassed what could be expected of the average man, the fighting largely fell on the shoulders of the best, most experienced troops, and not least the [junior] officer. The consequence . . . was a frightful death-roll of the finest and most highly trained soldiers, whose replacement became impossible. It was in this that the root of the tragedy of the battle lies.[35]

'The Cost of the Somme.' Renate Farley lays a wreath at the grave of her uncle, Alois Mühmelt, who was killed in action on 1 July 1916 near Serre. He is buried at the German Military Cemetery at Achiet-le-Petit. *(Farley Private Family Collection)*

Even as the battle was being fought, this erosion of the fighting quality of the German Army was noted by, among others, Crown Prince Rupprecht of Bavaria, who recorded in his diary that the old experienced officers and men had decreased steadily in numbers, and the reinforcements had not had the same quality of soldierly instruction and training and were physically mostly inferior.

Charles Carrington concluded that the Somme was:

. . . where the British Army fought it out with the German Army, and established their superiority, inflicting casualties which Germany could ill-afford. The result is patent. In August the German Government dismissed von Falkenhayn, their Chief-of-Staff, who had failed in attack at Verdun and failed in defence on the Somme . . . In September, their worst month for casualties, their new leaders, Ludendorff and von Hindenburg, conceded defeat by planning a strategic withdrawal, though, with their usual tenacity they clung to their positions until the winter gave them a short respite before retreating. The German Army was never to fight so well again, but the British Army went on to fight better.[36]

The Battle of the Somme lasted for 141 days, or four and a half months. The struggle, endurance and courage on both sides were astonishing, and the cost is staggering to us today. Officially, the total casualties amounted to 419,654 British/

Dominion, 204,253 French and between 650,000 and 680,000 German men killed or missing, wounded or prisoners of war.[37]

In cold, statistical terms it could be seen as a slogging match that finished pretty much all square. In more pragmatic terms, it was a bruising, uncompromising contest between an excellent German army that was inexorably worn down and a new, though amateur, British army that learned quickly and became both stronger and more confident by the end of the campaign.

'Winter Vigil, 1916.'
(Allen Collection)

Germany was hurt more by the Somme than either the BEF or the French and the legacy was profound. The pressure applied by both Haig's BEF and the French on the Somme was undoubtedly a vital part of the process of weakening the German Army, the process of 'destroying its arms' and 'breaking its will'. German archives underscore the point:

> The Somme was the muddy grave of the German field army, and of the faith in the infallibility of German leadership.[38]

Though it would take two more agonising years for Allied victory to be complete, the German Army was gravely weakened on the Somme and at Verdun in 1916. As winter set in it became abundantly clear to Ludendorff and Hindenburg that the odds on *materialschlacht* would not favour Germany.

All the Kaiser's men now prepared for the restless hibernation of friend and foe alike as temperatures plummeted and 'real fighting' had to be put on hold. In Germany, the agony had only just begun. It was going to be a long, cold 'Turnip Winter'. At the Front, the curtains on the year were drawn with a:

> Good night, the old year creeps towards the grave:
> There are the young, and almost all the brave.[39]

CHAPTER 7

A TERRIBLE TURNIP WINTER: THE GERMAN HOME FRONT IN 1916

The majority of the German people were reduced in 1916 to a meagre and monotonous diet of black bread, fatless sausage and 3 pounds of potatoes per week, an egg per fortnight – and turnips. But very few understood the numerous reasons for their predicament. Much of it had to do with the increasingly dictatorial military leadership that nominally served under the Kaiser.

In the first place, the German Army consumed mountains of food, fodder and other important resources. As a whole, it demolished 60 million pounds of bread, 131 million pounds of potatoes and 17 million pounds of meat per week.[1] No one in government, let alone the German General Staff, had given a moment's thought to the implications of such massive needs in a protracted war. The consequence was that the people suffered from shortages even before the men at the front.

Second, the highly decentralised nature of the Bismarckian State militated against tight controls over the nation's food supply. The special interests of the many state governments often clashed with those of the Reich and this led to corruption, divisive economic and distribution policies, and eventual chaos nationwide.

Third, soldiers and statesmen followed separate strategies on labour, so that economic and social distinctions were magnified. The sense of *gemeinschaft* (national unity) had disappeared by 1916.

Fourth, mismanagement and lack of pre-war planning for anything other than a certain, swift victory, and an ingrained inability or reluctance to adapt to the new conditions of a protracted war, contributed greatly to the chaos of national food distribution. This scandalous failure was reflected in part by a three-way war at home among farmers, consumers and the Government.

When farmers refused to abide by the Government's injunctions against using grain and potatoes for animal feeds, Berlin ordered the wholesale slaughter of pigs in 1915. Some 9 million pigs, 35 per cent of Germany's total, were killed in what the public dubbed *Schweinemord* or 'the pig massacre'.[2] Prices soared overnight, farmers withheld pigs from the market and ration cards had to be issued. Panic set in and the national mood turned ugly, culminating in food riots in Berlin, and then other major cities in the Reich. It was a portent for future public unrest.

The Allies' naval blockade was a crucial and crippling factor of the situation in Germany. Introduced soon after the onset of war in August 1914, it was to have a profound effect on the German people. Known as the 'Hunger Blockade', it led to less than 30 per cent of the German merchant fleet operating at all by 1916. By early 1917 the blockade had a virtual stranglehold on Germany; a grip that would endure until after the Armistice. The Blockade forced German domestic production to take up the slack, but demand inevitably soon outstripped production. This in turn led to two appalling developments: the *ersatz*, or 'substitute', economy; and a rampant black market.

Ersatz products were found across the country, first in the industrial, and then in the agricultural and retail sectors. Cereals and potato harvests had dropped by over 50 per cent by early 1916. Bread became known as 'K-Brot', which stood for *Krieg-*, or war-bread, and was made from a combination of oat and rice meals, ground beans, peas and corn meal. Butter was replaced by a concoction of curdled milk, sugar and food colouring; cooking oil by a mixture of red beets, carrots, turnips and spices. Ground European beetles (cockchafers) and linden wood replaced fats. Worst of all, sausage – a German staple – was produced from an unsavoury recipe of water, plant fibres and animal scraps.

On the other hand, the black market thrived for those able to barter currency, clothing, coal and jewellery for food. Farmers were simultaneously reviled and prized for their decision to ignore government-imposed price ceilings for their own ends. By the end of 1916 almost half of all egg, meat and fruit production, one-third of dairy product output and a quarter of the grain, flour and potato supplies were sold on the black market at prices almost one thousand per cent above pre-war levels.

Government ineptitude and failure to suppress the black market demoralised millions of otherwise loyal German people and led to widespread unrest. It also spawned a new national pastime – smuggling. More than half of all food reached consumers illegally. Hoarding, bartering, smuggling and black-marketeering not only undermined the national economy, but also corrupted the moral order as Germany's civilian population inexorably split into two camps.

First, there were those who had nothing to exchange for food and other essential items, who suffered terribly throughout the war. Second, there were the 'chancers' who were able to gamble on the black market and smuggle the essential and luxury contraband, and who often made fortunes out of the misfortune of others on the Home Front, as well as from the men who were fighting and dying in the front line.

Huge numbers of urban dwellers went on weekend excursions to the countryside on what became known as *Hamster Reisen*, or 'Hamster Tours'. They left their towns and cities on a Friday evening with only a change of clothing, but a great deal of baggage, and returned on a Sunday with fully-laden suitcases and knapsacks carrying the spoils of weekends spent haggling with local farmers. Draconian government measures to stop this practice, enforced by an army of police, alienated the German people. This was made worse by the issue of ration cards for every conceivable foodstuff, item of clothing and even soap.

By the final months of 1916, the situation at home was truly dire. People were becoming gaunt and bony and their thoughts turned more towards what their next meal would be than to the war. Faces were like masks, blue with cold and drawn with hunger. Ordinary Germans had already seen enough of the war. They regarded it as a surreal, desperate carnage in which the High Command and politicians still indulged themselves, promising victory at the beginning of each year and remaining aloof from the sacrifice of both the troops and the people. Most Germans no longer wanted war, victory or no victory. What they wanted was peace and bread and work.

Verdun and the Somme had given the people plenty of reason to mourn, but the war on the Home Front was striking deeply too. Food queues were endless and women were forced to spend many a cold night, ration cards in hand, lining up for bread, meat and other basic items. Britain and France did not ration bread and sugar until mid-1918.

Could it get worse? It could; and it did.

By November 1916, coal shortages forced stores, restaurants and theatres to close early. Then, the winter of 1916/17 was the coldest for years and temperatures plummeted to –30°C in many parts of Germany.

Food, heat and mere survival became the only topics of conversation. A total of 1,016,000 men had died at the Front and the million-plus German casualties on the Western Front alone in 1916 added to the misery of those at home.

To cap it all, the dismal harvest of autumn 1916 ushered in the so-called 'Turnip Winter'. Heavy rains, an early frost and a shortage of field workers reduced the potato harvest by almost two-thirds. Turnips, whether boiled, baked, fried or raw, became the national staple instead. But the turnip, or *Kohlrübbe*, was a stringy, coarse root crop – tasteless and bland at the best of times. The German people were reduced to an unsavoury diet of turnip and gruel-like soup, known laconically as *Drahtverhau*, or 'barbed-wire'.[3]

The writer Ernst Glaeser noted that:

> The Turnip Winter really brought the War home. Hunger destroyed our solidarity; the children stole each other's rations . . . Soon, the women who stood in pallid queues before shops spoke more about their children's hunger than about the death of their husbands at the Front.[4]

The foul weather, horrendous shortages and deteriorating situation at home and on the Western Front especially were dreadful portents for 1917. The dreadful state of affairs called for something to lift the gloom, and irreverence was one. A German writer suggested a new creed:

> I believe in the Turnip, the Holy Provider of the German people, and in jam, its begotten son . . . I believe in the Holy War, the universal society of black marketeers, the community of foragers, the resurrection of taxes, the reduction of meat rations, and the eternal existence of the ration card.[5]

In the new year, the German High Command would turn its attention to winning the war at sea, and perhaps in the East, while defending its possessions in the West. But military strategy would do nothing to relieve the burgeoning pain and suffering of the very people for which this war was apparently being fought. It looked certain too that 1917 would be another bloody year at home and abroad.

CHAPTER 8

NEW PLANS FOR OLD – *ALBERICH* AND A CUNNING PLAN

JANUARY–MARCH 1917

Germany had endured unprecedented pain and suffering at home and at the Front by the turn of the year. Desperate measures at home during the 'Turnip Winter' were now matched by political divisions and drastic action by the German military leaders, Hindenburg and Ludendorff. Chancellor Theobald Bethmann-Hollweg, with a different view of the war's progress than his military rivals, believed that the prospects of concluding a reasonable negotiated peace were good at the beginning of 1917. Both the Central Powers and the Allies had sounded out the other side on possible peace terms at the turn of the year, but to no avail.

Ludendorff and Hindenburg would not hear of such a thing. They were totally committed to their belief that the opportunity for military victory still lay firmly in their grasp. 'Field Marshal Hubris' now took centre stage and guaranteed imperial Germany's decline and fall. On the Western Front, Britain and France were in a similar position. The military and civilian populations on either side of the conflict's divide would not entertain the idea that the huge sacrifices to date would be in vain. Germany' influence on the remainder of the Central Powers was all-encompassing and Germany demanded nothing less than outright victory. There would be no compromise.

From the sidelines, this obdurate German attitude would appear to have evolved because of Germany's confidence and strength against the Entente at the beginning of 1917. Far from it. The prospects for Germany at the beginning of 1917 were gloomy indeed.

The Allied naval blockade and 'Turnip Winter' were biting hard and the Home Front was another battlefield altogether for ordinary German people. Ludendorff and Hindenburg knew also that they were losing the *materialschlacht* – the war of manpower and *matériel* – and that the opportunity for victory on land in 1917 was

'Und Ihr? – zeichnet Kriegsanleihe' ('And You? – Subscribe to the War Fund'). Popular poster in Germany, 1916. *(Allen Collection)*

virtually non-existent. In the previous year, over one million German servicemen had become casualties and both the Somme and Verdun had punished the German Army so badly that it had no choice but to stand on the defensive in the West throughout the coming year.

Ludendorff therefore devised, and Germany embarked on, a high-risk strategy for 1917, as Falkenhayn had done to his cost in 1916. But Ludendorff's strategy marked him out as the chancer, the opportunist and it was a significant flaw in his temperament. Without a chance of offensive action on the Western Front and some doubt about progress in the East for much of the year, he fixed on strangling Britain's resources and starving her out of the conflict through unrestricted submarine warfare.

The inherent, huge risk was not so much that of provoking a dreadful British reaction at land and sea, but the very real danger of bringing America into the war. She had been sorely tested by the U-boat campaigns of 1915 and 1916; and memories of the *Lusitania* and other German excesses at sea remained very fresh in American and British minds. However, the Kaiser and German High Command endorsed Ludendorff's recommendations. But at Supreme Headquarters, there were those who already saw the writing on the wall once this decision was irrevocably made. Admiral Georg Müller, one of the Kaiser's senior aides, wrote in his diary on 9 January that:

From heroic pose to reality: An exhausted *Eingreif* soldier. (*Bundesarchiv*)

> Six o'clock audience [with the Kaiser] given to Chancellor Bethmann-Hollweg, Hindenburg, Ludendorff, Admiral Henning von Holtzendorff (Chief of the Admiralty Staff) and three Cabinet Chiefs . . . The crux of the Chancellor's speech was that in view of the opinion of the General Staff and the Admiralty he (the Chancellor) could not oppose unrestricted submarine warfare. It was not so much approval as an acceptance of the facts. Holtzendorff then spoke very enthusiastically on the subject, and was followed by [Hindenburg] who stated that the soldier in the trenches was waiting for the U-boat war, that the Army . . . had troops ready to go over to the offensive within a few months . . .
>
> Then His Majesty replied . . . very much in favour of unrestricted U-boat warfare, and upon this signed the decree that was laid before him. He remarked in passing that he expected a declaration of war by America. If it came . . . so much the better . . . [Later] the Chancellor told me that [now] the Kaiser had done untold harm to himself and to the Hohenzollern dynasty . . .[1]

The power behind the Kaiser's throne was now almost absolute. An ever-more frustrated and weakened Bethmann-Hollweg was destined to resign in July, to be followed by two Chancellors who would prove weaker still against the stultifying but total control of General Erich Ludendorff.

In the meantime, as in a tense and fragile marriage, Germany was hitched to Ludendorff and Hindenburg's decision for better or worse. Ludendorff calculated that unrestricted submarine warfare would reward Germany with victory before the United States was in any position to bring her full military weight to bear in Europe. The new offensive would begin, beneath the waves, on 1 February. By land, he and Hindenburg had a major surprise up their sleeves for the Allies on the Western Front. But if the German strategy for 1917 was to prevail, the military would have to increasingly rely on the support of the Fatherland when it was already enfeebled by war.

In the Fatherland the desperate 'Turnip Winter' bore down on the German people, and 1917 began almost unnoticed. Few were in the mood to look forward with any optimism. 1916 had been a disastrous year on the Western Front for Germany. But her heartland had also become unequivocally the New Front: a Home Front where war was as 'total' as the bloody struggles in the West or East. The Home Front battles were fought by legions of women against an army of police. Ernst Glaeser wrote: 'Soon, a looted ham thrilled us more than the fall of Bucharest or some apparent success elsewhere.'[2]

Hunger, anger at the shortages, and the mounting death rate fuelled riots, strikes and violence on the Home Front. Industrial unrest, which began at important factories such as Krupps and Siemens in 1916, increased dramatically in 1917. The situation became so critical by that autumn that the Army was called in to restore order by subjecting most of the factories to 'militarisation'. Workers' leaders were swiftly drafted and sent to the hardest sectors of the Western Front.

The architect of the Hindenburg Programme, who gave Ludendorff a legitimacy that he scarce deserved.
(Postcard, Allen Collection)

On 16 December 1916 the German Government introduced the Patriotic Auxiliary Service Law. Under this legislation, all men between 17 and 60 years of age became liable for work in the war production industry regardless of previous or current employment. The German military hand, in the shape of Hindenburg and Ludendorff, was at the tiller, and was demanding nothing less than 'total war production' across the Fatherland. Hindenburg became the Patriotic Auxiliary Service Law's patron: the law became known simply as the 'Hindenburg Programme'.

It was to be a full mobilisation of the Home Front and its aim was to dramatically increase Germany's military production. The bloody events on the Western and Eastern Fronts in 1916 had stretched the German Army's manpower and the nation's industrial capacity to wage war. Hindenburg and Ludendorff knew that without a general mobilisation of the civilian population in Germany, they could not hope to compete with the Western Allies in the deadly game of *materialschlacht*. The German High Command insisted that Germany was turned into 'one vast munitions factory'.

The Hindenburg Programme began in earnest in January 1917. Production targets were increased and were very ambitious. Artillery shell, mortar ammunition and machine gun output was to double, aircraft quotas tripled and coal and steel output would have to increase in line with the new programme. The implications for the adult population were profound; and deeply unpopular. For the working class and many of the skilled middle classes, it was nothing less than an end to flexible working practices and an imposition of government law to control all sectors of German industry. Protest followed and the Government attempted to find a formula that would make the Hindenburg Programme more palatable to the labour unions and to the very people on which it entirely depended.

With a good deal of compromise, the wheels of this new industrial engine conceived to oil the German war machine began to turn. There was a nationwide appeal for volunteers to enter war work. Nationalists hailed the Hindenburg Programme as an ideal focus for a renewed war spirit within Germany and the German High Command saw it as a means to dramatically increase arms production. It was another illusion.

Hindenburg, still regarded with respect by many German people as the hero of Tannenberg and Germany's saviour in the East in the first months of the war, called on them to unite in a supreme effort to strengthen the sinews of war. But the effort was beyond them in a country beset by the 'Hunger Blockade' and already severely ravaged by war. As the months passed in 1917, the national effort was usurped by a rush for profits by a corrupt and untouchable few and precious little evidence of an increase in production.

The German armed forces needed 12,000 tons of gunpowder per month, but were fortunate to receive 8,000 tons in April and a marginal increase to 9,200 tons in July. Steel production actually dropped by 225,000 tons in February and March 1917. There would be no major boost until after Russia's capitulation and the German preparations for the offensive in the first two months of 1918.[3]

Introduced to mobilise and streamline the means of production, the Hindenburg Programme actually created further barriers against such aims and led to a chaotic system born out of a constantly shifting workforce. Its provisions allowed workers to move from one job to another if they could find suitable improved working conditions and pay. The captains of industry, always bent on profit from their patronage of the war effort, offered ever-higher salaries to entice skilled workers to their factories.

The skilled workers quickly took advantage of this opportunity and the job-changing merry-go-round began. At the end of 1917, the management of the Siemens works in Berlin calculated that the composition of the labour force changed almost three times in that year. Inevitably, this disruption led to a serious drop in efficiency and production.

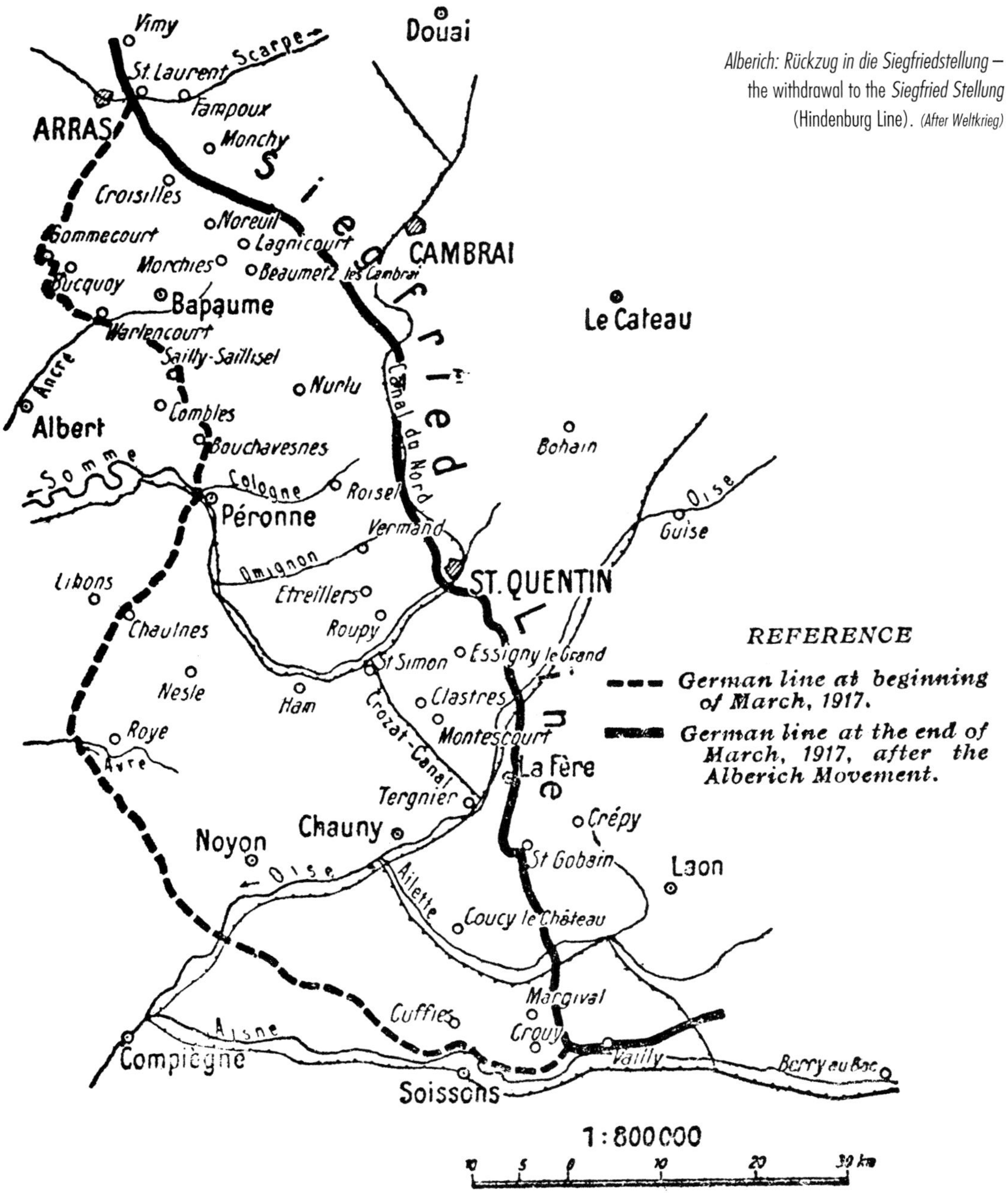

Alberich: Rückzug in die Siegfriedstellung – the withdrawal to the *Siegfried Stellung* (Hindenburg Line). *(After Weltkrieg)*

Even worse, of 25,000 German miners who had been released from military service to return to the coalface, over 3,000 left for higher pay elsewhere within a year.[4]

The Hindenburg Programme also put the much-vaunted railway network under terrific strain. Domestic rail freight was tied up for days, especially as it was a distant second priority behind the insatiable needs of the German Army in the field. Consequently, vital resources such as coal and foodstuffs were poorly distributed across the Fatherland and the ordinary population suffered more than ever.

As the wartime economy lurched from one crisis to another, women plugged the growing gap in the industrial and rural labour force. Throughout Germany, the war brought almost one and a half million new female employees into the labour market. But in rural or urban environments women had poor working conditions, lack of equal pay and depressingly long hours. Almost 85 per cent of female factory workers put in 65–75 hours per week and night work doubled from 1916 onwards.

Despite the best efforts of an almost fully mobilised nation, the Home Front could not hope to win its own war against want, privation and then famine. Overall, malnutrition in general and lack of foodstuffs high in protein and carbohydrates in particular exacted a terrible toll on the German people. The average diet provided a mere 1,000 calories per day by the end of 1917, reduced from a daily average of 3,500 in 1914. Meat consumption dropped from 1100 grams per person per week to a pitiful 135 grams.[5]

The German withdrawal to the *Siegfried Stellung*, or Hindenburg Line, under the codename *Alberich* (the evil dwarf featured in Wagner's *Niebelung* tale), in March 1917 was a clear admission of the failure of Germany's strategy in 1916. Verdun and the Somme campaigns had had the opposite outcome of that envisaged at Verdun, in particular by Falkenhayn, and bled the German Army white.

Throughout the winter of 1916/17 German engineers built the formidable defence lines of the *Siegfried Stellung*. Although kept secret from the Allies, it was sold to the German public as an impregnable bastion that would secure Germany's borders; a striking example of forward defence if ever there was one! For public consumption, it was described as 'an iron wall that no human power can overcome'.[6] Operation *Alberich*, the construction of the *Siegfried Stellung* (Hindenburg Line to the Allies) and the withdrawal to it was a most impressive feat of military engineering, deception and discipline.

Authorisation to withdraw was issued by Ludendorff, after some hesitation due to his fears of the potential harm to German morale, on 4 February 1917. When the main withdrawal was under way over the four days of 16 to 20 March, it took the Allies over a week to detect *Alberich*, much too late to counter it. Although the withdrawal was an acknowledgement of both the massive German sacrifice made in the charnel houses of Verdun and the Somme, and of the increasing strength and confidence of the Anglo-French Alliance, it gave the German Army in the West some advantage by improving a now shorter defensive line.

Erich Ludendorff: strident, and dictator in all but name between January 1917 and the last weeks of the war.
(Bundesarchiv)

Ludendorff agreed with Hindenburg, soon after taking command of the German Army, that powerful rear positions should be built. Ludendorff wrote later: 'Whether we should retire to them, and how the positions would be used, was not of course decided in September 1916; the important thing then was to get them built.'[7]

Built they were, and with truly awesome efficiency. The Hindenburg Line was a collective name for much more than a single fortified strip of occupied France. The powerful rear positions envisaged by Hindenburg and Ludendorff were divided into sections, each with its own codename.

The first was the *Siegfriedstellung*, which was sited to run from Arras to St Quentin and then continue down to Laon and the Aisne and so snip off the huge salient that was 'voluntarily' abandoned. It was extended north by the *Wotanstellung*, running from Quéant to Drocourt/Lille, and finally continued to the coast as the *Flandernstellung*, or 'Flanders Line'. Later, the *Brunhild Stellung* appeared in the Champagne and the *Kriemhilde Stellung* in the Meuse-Argonne sector. *Siegfried* was the strongest, most elaborate and, like the Wagnerian characters that each of the lines owed their names to, the stuff of legend. It was protected by anything up to nine thick belts of barbed wire in front of concreted machine-gun posts, trench complexes, reinforced-concrete shelters and deep, expansive dugouts.

The Hindenburg Line system was the 'ideal' model for the German Army's new defensive doctrine of flexible, or elastic, defence in depth, and provided a belt of defensive zones, rather than one continuous line of heavily defended strongpoints. Each stretch of the line had a forward 'outpost zone,' some 600 yards deep with observation and machine gun posts, plus some concrete dugouts for local counter-attack troops, or *stosstruppen*. Behind this lay the 'main battle zone,' across 2,500 yards, which included the first and second main trench/strongpoint lines and a thick network of concrete machine-gun emplacements, which provided interlocking arcs of fire criss-crossing no-man's-land, and some field artillery pits for mobile gunner units. The latter would really come into their own as anti-tank gun emplacements when the Allies used tanks en masse towards the end of 1917. The trench lines were protected by formidable belts of barbed wire, over 100 yards across in places, covered by machine gun, mortar and artillery fire.

Behind the trench systems were further concrete bunkers and dug outs for HQs, medical staffs and the crucially important *eingreif*, or counter-attack infantry units. As 1917 unfolded, third and fourth lines of resistance were added in several places, giving a total depth of much of the *Siegfried Stellung* or Hindenburg Line of between 5,000 and 9,000 yards.

The extraordinary construction and professional, disciplined conduct of the German withdrawal was marred by the deeply controversial 'scorched earth' policy ordered by Ludendorff. To the senior commander responsible for this whole sector, Crown Prince Rupprecht, it was a foul and wholly unnecessary act of war. He vehemently opposed it and even threatened to resign in protest, but was overruled by Ludendorff.

When the initial phase of the *Alberich* plan went into effect, the vast majority of the newly vacant land was left uninhabitable. Roads and railways, bridges and communication lines such as telegraph poles and cables were destroyed, wells were poisoned, town infrastructures damaged, whole villages razed to the ground, orchards and woodland felled and livestock slaughtered if it was deemed of no use to the withdrawing German troops. Worst of all, French women, children and the elderly were left behind, along with thousands of weapons, items of equipment and buildings booby-trapped to kill or maim unwary British and Dominion soldiers as they advanced through this man-made wasteland.

It was a policy that would come back to haunt Ludendorff, as Rupprecht predicted it would, by creating massive logistical problems for maintenance and resupply of the spring offensives in 1918. But Ludendorff never thought that far ahead. The wanton devastation of the countryside in 1917 was to be a major headache in 1918, and all of his own making.

Alberich's most insidious legacy was the thousands of nasty, and often deadly, surprises left to slow down the British pursuit. An English officer's diary recorded:

> March 14th: A busy day. It is reported that the German line appears to be held in the usual strength . . . March 15th: From a captured German [operation] order it appears that our patrols entered the hostile trenches only one hour after they had been vacated; pretty sharp work . . . The German trenches we have taken over are deep, well-constructed, and surprisingly dry . . . Masses of beer bottles (unfortunately empty) are strewn about, and guncotton, attached to shell cases and grenades, has been left ready to explode when picked up or accidentally kicked. We have had five casualties in this way . . .[8]

On the defensive in the West. A German sentry wearing body armour (early 1917).
(IWM: Q55484)

The Allied pursuit was slow and faltering partly for these reasons, and partly because of the problems that had been thrown up for the planning of the Allied spring offensives, especially the French Nivelle operation.

The Hindenburg Line was a masterpiece of the siege war on the Western Font and *Oberst* Fritz von Lossberg was the mastermind who inspired it. Lossberg was Chief-of-Staff (CoS) Second Army under General Fritz von Below. He had served as a Corps COS in 1914 and deputy chief of operations in OHL (*Oberst Heeresleitung*, German Supreme HQ) the following year, before becoming CoS to the Third Army and then to the Second Army on the Somme.

He represented the more positive side of the German General Staff system, as his undoubted defensive planning skills were respected at the highest level. He was of a

A German bunker and gun emplacement in the Zandvoorde sector of the Ypres salient in the winter of 1916.
(IWM: Q.45.589)

Der Meldehund an der Front.
Der Meldehund bringt während eines Gasangriffes den dahinterliegenden Truppen Nachricht.

Der Meldehund an der Front – Dogs used as messengers during an enemy gas attack. Dogs were used successfully by the German Army for message carrying and to bring up food, water and medical supplies in specially adapted containers when it was too hazardous for troops to do the same.
(Allen Collection)

rare breed in the higher echelons of the German officer corps as he was pragmatic, technically skilled and innovative.

But the German High Command did at least have the flexibility to encourage officers like von Lossberg, who masterminded the siting and strengthening of the defences on the Somme in 1916, to use their talents and allow them real influence if they were good enough, regardless of rank. Ludendorff and Hindenburg recognised that talent in Lossberg and employed him in OHL to devise the new designs for the defensive front and the new tactics to go with them.

He provided the practical advice for the siting and construction of the *Siegfried Stellung* (Hindenburg Line), and would personally intervene to expedite a rapid stabilisation of the weak German defences in the Arras sector in April, and then shore up the German defences in Flanders after the debacle at Messines in June and July prior to the British Third Ypres/Passchendaele offensive.

The most important principle of the new German defensive policy, or doctrine, was that of flexible, or 'elastic' defence in depth. It replaced that of static positional defence, so disastrously used by the German infantry under the weight of the Allied guns at Verdun and the Somme.

The layout was based on deep defence, i.e. well-spaced zones, to avoid total inundation by heavy and wide-ranging enemy artillery bombardments and so that each defensive line had to be taken by the attacking force. The infantry selected for the outpost (forward) zone were trained to observe and report enemy strengths and approaches, shifting constantly from one position to another to improve their chances of surviving enemy bombardments. They would dash from one shell hole or local dugout to another and not rely on a single, static trench line. Then, their role was to fight a brief delaying battle and inflict casualties on the enemy infantry as the advance began, before the surviving defenders withdrew to the next defensive area. This would buy valuable warning time for the main defensive garrison. If the situation demanded it, local counter-attack detachments (*stosstruppen*) would be thrown in, but this would be the exception – and in direct contrast to the policy pursued in positional defence, where costly counter-attacks were ordered to retake every foot of ground lost.

The main battle zone, up to some two kilometres deep, was sited on a reverse slope, contained the first and second main defensive trench lines manned by the 'front line' infantry battalions, and had thick belts of barbed wire covered by well-protected machine-gun emplacements. Directly behind were artillery observers, with *eingreif* battalions, field artillery and the tactical HQs, medical and communications centres. With a reverse slope position, machine-gun, rifle and mortar fire could sweep the crest of the high ground as the enemy were exposed crossing it. Pillboxes and reinforced concrete bunkers protected the defending troops throughout the main position. The deeper that the enemy infantry assault penetrated, the weaker it became, but the stronger the German defence became. Thus the enemy would eventually exhaust his efforts and inevitably withdraw or face annihilation or capture.

If the enemy managed to continue their advance, they would be absorbed by the reserve infantry counter-attack units, heavy machine guns and heavier artillery and mortar barrages in the rear battle zone.

In a nutshell, the new flexible defensive system bent back, allowing some penetration, then resisted in increasing strength as the enemy assault weakened and finally snapped back like an elastic band to eject the enemy from the defended area.

Though the winter of 1916/1917 was a bitterly cold one, Allied commanders fuelled hopes of a hot reception for the weakened German Army on the Western Front in spring 1917. The Allied conference at Chantilly in November 1916 affirmed that the West would remain the focus of unhinging Germany and the Central Powers, but political and military changes at the top in Britain and France in December threw such plans briefly into a spin.

On 7 December, David Lloyd George succeeded Herbert Asquith as Prime Minister and immediately set about the task of shifting the main effort away from the Western Front. He was openly critical of Haig and was keen to remove him from command, as well as wanting to look to other theatres of war to seek decisive success against

Germany and her allies, as he had done since 1915 first as Minister for Munitions and then as Secretary of State for War.

In the same month, the French C-in-C General Papa Joffre became another victim of the war when French Prime Minister Aristide Briand removed him for his lack of urgency in meeting the threat at Verdun and the continued high casualties of the French *poilus*. General Robert Nivelle, whose reputation had been enhanced by his exploits in the latter months of the Verdun campaign, replaced Joffre. Nivelle was a persuasive and hugely confident commander and he was certain that he had found a winning formula for 1917, which would hinge on a bold offensive on a wide front and overwhelming artillery support.

Nivelle was a charmer, a man of flamboyant gesture and plausibility, who convinced the Allied commanders and politicians that his offensive was the one to break the deadlock of the Western Front and finally 'knock the Germans for six,' as the new British Prime Minister wished. Even Lloyd George, ever the 'Easterner', was seduced by Nivelle's plan. The British and French politicians were anxious about the casualties in 1916 and saw no end to attrition until Nivelle convinced them otherwise. In short, his strategy was to achieve a stunning and rapid breakthrough.

Two diversionary attacks, by the BEF and the French between Arras and the River Scarpe in the north and the River Oise respectively, would fix German attention and reserves in this sector and mask final preparations for the main offensive against the Chemin des Dames in Champagne. Nivelle described this main blow as a strike with a 'mass of manoeuvre' – no less than twenty-seven divisions to exploit the break in the German line. According to the new French C-in-C, the breakthrough would come within 48 hours. His self-assurance and the 'certainty' of the spring offensive were echoed by Nivelle's fellow commander in the latter stages of the Verdun campaign, General Charles Mangin, who had declared in December that: 'We know the method and we have the Chief (Nivelle). Success is certain.'[9]

Nivelle seemed to have thought of everything; everything, that is, except the enemy's likely actions in early spring 1917. *Alberich* surprised him and the British, but it did not deter him from his plan. General Franchet d'Esperay, whose French Northern Group of Armies was ordered to carry out the diversionary assault in the Oise sector, suggested an immediate attack to catch the withdrawing German units off guard. Nivelle rejected this audacious request. He would not change his plan for d'Esperay or even to acknowledge the shift in German deployments. His inflexibility would cost him and the French dear in the months to come.

At the Calais Conference on 26–27 February 1917, the difference between Allied relationships and the more straightforward German High Command responsibilities were borne out by the intrigue regarding the role of Haig and the BEF as part of the Allied effort. Lloyd George, who had already made it plain that he would remove Haig if an opportunity arose, conspired with the French to subordinate the BEF to Nivelle's supreme command. This led to a strong protest from King George V and the War

Cabinet, so Haig and the BEF were spared. But the fallout was acute. The compromise left a feeling of greater mistrust between Lloyd George, Haig and other senior officers, and did little to promote Anglo-French relations only a few weeks before a major Allied offensive.

On the other side, Hindenburg and Ludendorff had few of these problems to contend with. Though they deferred to the Kaiser and Chancellor Bethmann-Hollweg, they held both the military and political reins of power. But the Germans would soon have another problem to tackle: the prospect of a new and powerful enemy.

CHAPTER 9

AMERIKA, ARRAS AND *L'AFFAIRE NIVELLE*

APRIL–JUNE 1917

Ludendorff had assured his troops and the German people that the war could be won in 1917 by strangling Britain's war effort at sea, while remaining on the defensive in the West and seeking a decision on the Eastern Front. But his assurances rang very hollow indeed in early April.

The United States of America declared war on Germany on 6 April in response to Germany's strategy of unrestricted submarine warfare and attempts to foment trouble in Mexico. US President Woodrow Wilson assured the American people that they now had an historic task of 'keeping the world safe for democracy'. Although the first American troops were despatched to Europe soon after the US commitment to the war, it would be a long time before America was ready for action. She lacked trained soldiers and the military infrastructure to provide the manpower and equipment needed on such a large scale.

General John Joseph 'Black Jack' Pershing, one of America's most experienced soldiers, was appointed to command the American Expeditionary Force (AEF). He arrived in France in June 1917 and quickly made it clear to his Allied counterparts that his army would ultimately fight only as a cohesive all-American force. He was not prepared to commit it to battle until its strength and equipment had been built up. It would take a year for the AEF to field over one million men on the Western Front, and although they would play an important part in the latter stages of the German offensives in early 1918, it would take until September of that year for the AEF to play a full part.

The immediate and deeply damaging blow of America's entry into the war for Ludendorff and Germany was a psychological one. The German High Command knew full well from the outset that the United States would provide two precious assets that the Central Powers would conversely find increasingly difficult to match as the war dragged on: manpower and an untouchable, insatiable industrial appetite. Although it would take time for the full impact to be felt, the promise of an overwhelming force to

Sketch 23.

Sketch 23.

The British Arras Offensive, 9 April to the end of May 1917.
(After Weltkrieg)

ARRAS, 1917
The End of the Battle.

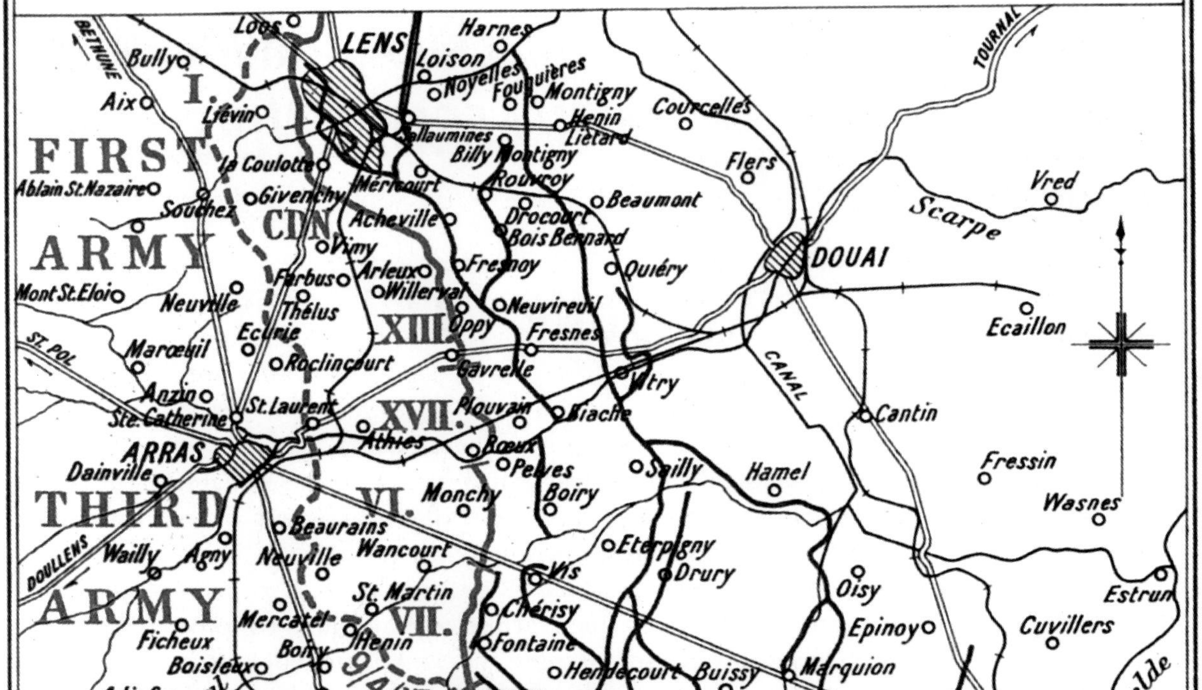

British Front at the End of the Battle. ——

German Lines, constructed and under construction } *Green.*

SCALE OF MILES.

5 4 3 2 1 0 5 10 15

Compiled in the Historical Section (Military Branch).

Ordnance Survey 1939.

take up the torch in support of the Western Allies against Germany was a constant thorn in Ludendorff's side from April 1917 on. It would affect his judgement and his decision on Germany's final attempt to tip the balance in Germany's favour in 1918.

Three days after America entered the war, the prelude to *l'Affaire Nivelle* began with the combined British and French offensives against Arras and the Oise. Nivelle's strategy remained as it had done before the German withdrawal and so the British Third Army (plus the First Army's Canadian Corps), comprising fifteen divisions and commanded by General Sir Edmund Allenby, launched its attacks on the snow-swept morning of Monday 9 April.

Although the French drive to the south under General d'Esperay had been truncated because of the withdrawal to the Hindenburg Line, the British assault against a total of ten German divisions was a great success at first. Nearly 3,000 guns blasted the German positions for four days and, when the assault went in 48 tanks were available to support it. The main objective was to punch a hole in the right flank of the *Siegfried Stellung* (Hindenburg Line) and old German (OG) defences in the centre before capturing parts of the German line from the rear. Further operations were to then threaten the German-held sector around Cambrai. To Allenby's north, the Canadian Corps was given the formidable task of taking Vimy Ridge.

General-Oberst von Falkenhausen was GOC Sixth Army that faced Allenby's Third. His grasp of the concept of the new 'elastic defence in-depth' was not as firm as that of commanders of other German armies on the Western Front and as a result, the Sixth Army was rather caught 'in transition' between positional and flexible defensive methods.

The main problems on the ground were that the forward zones remained crammed with troops, instead of lightly manned, and the important *eingreif* (counter-attack) divisions were kept too far to the rear to provide any rapid reaction forces against the British penetration of the German positions.

The Sixth Army's failure to change its modus operandi does not detract from the British Third Army's achievement over the first two or three days of the Arras offensive. British preparations were thorough and recent innovations were put into practice on a large scale for the first time. Falkenhausen's positions were severely damaged by accurate, heavy artillery bombardment and many of the extensive barbed-wire obstacles cut by shells using the '106' instantaneous fuse. The crucial 'race to the parapet', which had failed so badly on the Somme in early July 1916, was won more by the British and Canadian assault troops than by German machine gunners. The artillery were provided with excellent air OPs by the RFC which updated the Royal Artillery with timely intelligence on German gun-battery locations using new methods such as 'flash spotting' and 'sound ranging', despite the weather and increasingly hostile skies.

On 9 April former German bastions such as Neuville Vitasse, the northern segment of the *Siegfried Stellung* and, most famously, Vimy Ridge, fell like ninepins. The

German defences crumbled so completely in places that British progress threatened a limited breakout; and Falkenhausen had neither sufficient artillery, nor any *eingreif* units to stem the flow of some British assaults. Allenby's VI Corps advanced an average of two miles and captured German field guns and their crews caught out by the sheer speed of the attack and the British XVII Corps managed to do even better by rolling back Falkenhausen's bewildered troops over three and a half miles in one day. At that time it was the lengthiest advance since trench warfare had begun.

If these failures were bad enough, the loss of Vimy Ridge was the lowest point of German resistance in the initial events of the British Arras offensive. The Germans had held it since 1914 and considered it invulnerable. Once again, it was largely British innovation and ingenuity as well as meticulous rehearsal and preparation that won the day. The Canadian Corps had the benefit of approaching the German front line underground through a series of deeply dug tunnels that traversed much of no-man's-land. Not only did the Germans not see them coming, but also they were overwhelmed when the Canadians emerged and attacked as the barrage lifted. It was a stunning success for the Canadian Corps, but nothing less than an abject failure for the German garrison thrown off Vimy Ridge. One or two particularly stubborn rear guard actions were fought out on Hill 145 and 'the pimple' but by the end of the first day the Canadians held the ridge, which dominated the area around it.[1]

Arras, 9 April 1917: German prisoners are sent back from positions on Vimy Ridge, brilliantly captured by the Canadian Corps.
(IWM: CO 1155)

Old friendships, like old habits, die hard. There were still enough British and German servicemen on either side of the wire who had family or pre-war connections from 'the other country'. During the fighting at Arras, *Leutnant Graf* (Count) von Schaffgotsch saw a wounded English officer in difficulties near the German wire, so dashed forward to recover him in a rare lull in the battle. When he reached him he recognised a friend of his from his Oxford University days just before the war. The count tended to his English friend and ensured that he was despatched to the German field hospital before resuming his own duties in the front line. He escorted him to hospital.[2]

Between 9 and 11 April, the German Sixth Army suffered over 15,000 casualties and 7,000 prisoners and lost 112 guns and 350 machine guns. The British Third and First Army personnel involved in the assault around Arras and in the capture of Vimy Ridge took a remarkably low 8,238 casualties by comparison – and for tangible, important territorial gains. The German failure was attributable to the lack of preparedness of their new defensive tasks against the enemy assault, but compounded by the novel British tactics and also a greater confidence that they could take on German units and win.[3]

Arras had so far gone well and appeared to augur well for the wider Allied offensive. But at Bullecourt the German withdrawal had affected the original British planning so that the GOC of Fifth Army, General Sir Hubert Gough, could only attack the *Siegfried Stellung* around the village of Bullecourt and close to the junction of the *Wotan Stellung* line of the Hindenburg system. The assault against Bullecourt went in early on 11 April after a 'buckshee battle' the day before that had heralded the intentions of the 4th Australian Division's attack.[4]

Though supported by tanks (which the Aussies cursed anyway), the battle was a disaster, despite the extraordinary efforts of the assaulting Australian troops. It was a lesson in poor planning, but a tribute to stout and dogged defence by the regiments of the experienced and well-drilled German 27th (Royal Württemberg) Division. By the close of that day, the Australians had lost nearly 3,500 men, including 40 officers and 1,142 men captured. On the other side of the wire, it had dawned on the Württembergers of 27th Division that they had 'accomplished something extra-ordinary and had achieved a success that was rare for a division in defence'.[5] In contrast to the Australian casualties, 27th Division had lost 138 killed and 531 wounded, with no prisoners.

It was the only real success anywhere in the German line over the first three days of the Arras offensive and therefore General Moser, the commander of the defending XIVth Reserve Korps (*Gruppe Quéant*) and Major-General von Mauer, GOC 27th Division, were given appropriate accolades and medals.[6]

The Sixth Army commander Falkenhausen was not so blessed as the defenders of Bullecourt, for everywhere else his Army had lost significant ground. He was replaced by General Otto von Below on 23 April. Thereafter, Falkenhausen carried out more

'Horch (minen) graben', German mining listening gallery in early 1917.
(Postcard, Allen Collection)

mundane duties than those of command as Governor-General of Belgium. The immediate priority was to make good crumbling defences and for that task there was only one candidate: *Oberst* Fritz von Lossberg.

Lossberg was appointed COS Sixth Army and he set to his task of shoring up the German line straight away. His appointment coincided with a gradual turning of the tables as the British momentum began to slow. On 11 April the German bulwark at Monchy le Preux fell to a combined infantry and cavalry assault, and General Allenby stressed that 'risks must be freely taken in pursuing a defeated enemy', but within 24 hours, the mood had changed. British Third Army was encountering stiffer resistance as German reinforcements arrived to fill the gaps and the *eingreif* divisions became more active.

A pattern was emerging once more as another Allied offensive stalled. German discipline and courage had prevented a breakthrough; British preparations and the assaults were improving, but the momentum of an offensive could not be maintained through lack of reserves. Then German resistance stiffened and another uneasy stalemate ensued. This time, the logical thing for the BEF to do was to consolidate its gains and wait for the Nivelle offensive across the Chemin des Dames. But logic was the very last thing on Nivelle's mind in mid-April 1917.

The German withdrawal had virtually negated the French diversionary attack on the Oise and Nivelle was under pressure to modify his grand plan. Ironically, the Briand government that had put Nivelle in fell on 20 March and the new French Prime Minister Ribot forced a Council of War on 6 April, the day that America entered the war, and discussion even centred on cancelling any major offensives until the 'Yankees' arrived. The consensus was that *l'Affaire Nivelle* should be cancelled immediately if it

German blockhouse in the Champagne sector at Moronvilliers, 1917.
(Postcard, Allen Collection)

did not realise the promise of a swift and decisive victory. The chorus of disapproval was stopped by an ultimatum from Nivelle, which was nothing less than 'Back me or sack me'. Sadly, despite the obvious and widespread doubts about Nivelle's strategy, he called the doubters' bluff and they assured him of their total support. It was a bad, bad mistake.

Two days before the conference, a German raid on the French positions south of the Aisne managed to pick up the entire operation order for the Nivelle offensive. What's more, Nivelle was made aware of this desperately dangerous compromise, but did nothing. His whole plan depended on surprise, speed and the weight of artillery, but without surprise, now utterly gone, speed might be a problem for Nivelle's assaulting divisions as the Germans now knew where and when the French were coming. Nivelle now knew that only the brute force of artillery and the élan of his *poilus* would give him any chance of success. It did not augur well.

The great offensive was launched on a 25-mile front on Monday 16 April after a crashing 14-day bombardment by almost 4,000 guns and *poilus* of the French Fifth and Sixth Armies went forward confident that Nivelle's 'mass of manoeuvre' doctrine

Nivelle Offensive: German sentries in the forward zone ready to throw grenades.
(IWM: Q55005/G.O. 2393)

would be enough to overwhelm the German defences. But the assault was across some of the most difficult terrain on the Western Front and against German positions up to six miles deep and protected by the heights of the Chemin des Dames[7] where steep wooded gorges or marshy valley approaches would slow French progress. Worse, the German defences were solid, recently organised under the 'elastic defence in depth' doctrine and with the main obstacles tucked away on the reverse slope.[8]

Nivelle's superiority in numbers and artillery made little difference once the offensive was under way. Initial French confidence was rapidly lost as the leading assault troops discovered that they had overrun the lightly held enemy forward zone only to be cut down by a mass of machine-gun and artillery fire from the relatively undamaged German second line.

The next three days saw some German withdrawal after fierce resistance and by 20 April the French had advanced some four miles in places and taken key heights. With 20,000 German prisoners and 147 guns 'in the bag' the advance appeared to have made reasonable progress.

The reality was different. Most importantly, the promised rupture of the German line and subsequent decisive breakthrough had not materialised and any gains made by 20 April had been at great cost. In just four days French losses were 30,000 killed, 100,000 wounded or PoWs and almost 5,000 missing.[9] Although it would continue until early June and the total casualties stack up as 163,000 German and 185,000 on the French side, the damage to the French Army and to Nivelle's reputation was already done within the first four days.[10]

By 21 April, Nivelle's grip was already loosening and the 'grand plan' was reduced to the seizure of more limited objectives, rather than the capture of the whole of the Chemin des Dames ridge and decisive breakthrough. Further attacks did achieve some notable success, but it was not enough to salvage Nivelle's battered authority; General Pétain replaced him, but not before the French *poilus*' disillusion had turned to anger and then mutiny.

Regardless of the German success against the ill-fated Nivelle offensive, there were worrying signs of longer-term problems in the structure of the German Army that were becoming evident, not the least of which was dealing with the increasing vigour and skill of the BEF. Staff officer *Hauptmann* Rudolf Binding's comments at this time were prophetic:

> *17th April:* [On our logistics] I have no notion how to get our horses to move our infantry transport, our gun ammunition, ourselves, our guns . . . The Army order that all horses which are returned to veterinary depots on account of mange remain 'on the strength' of their units leads to the most deceptive statistics (I think that in some respects Ludendorff is the best liar on the earth), but does not help one forward . . .

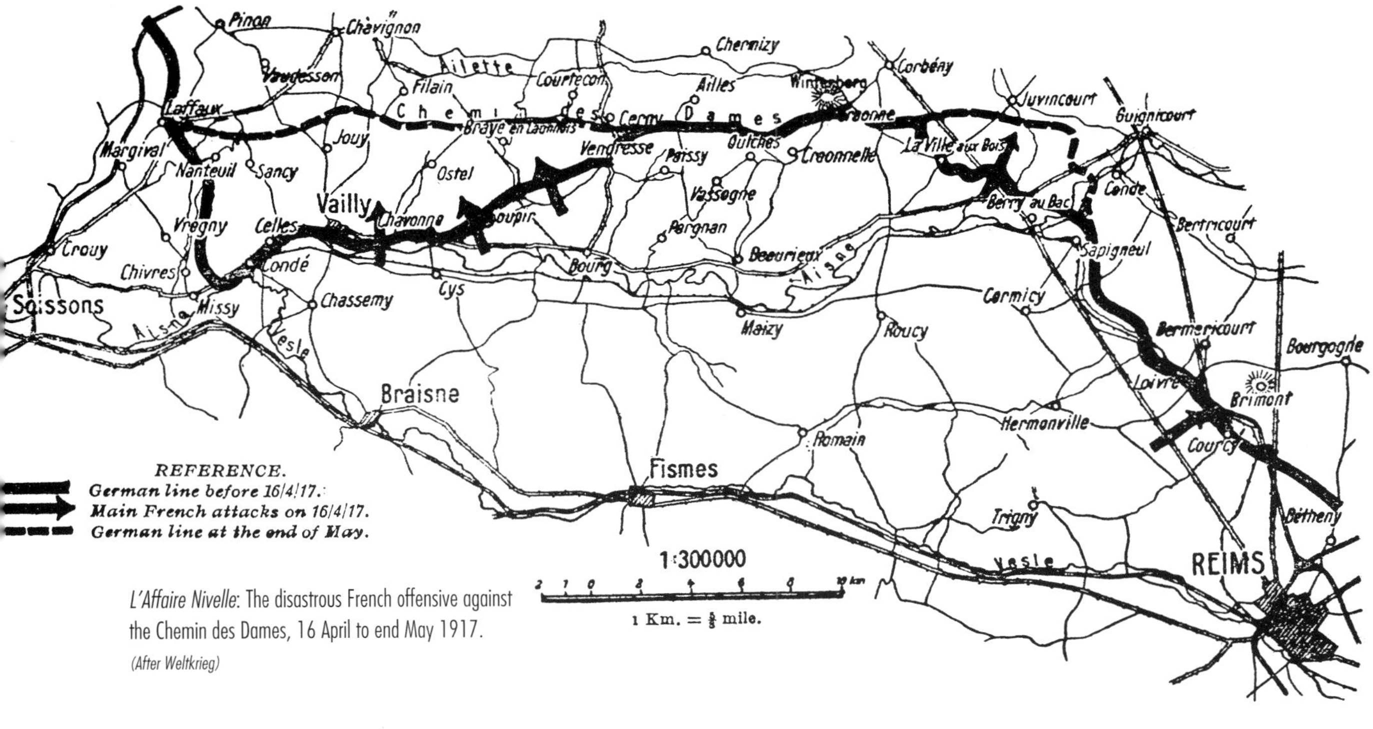

L'Affaire Nivelle: The disastrous French offensive against the Chemin des Dames, 16 April to end May 1917.

(After Weltkrieg)

German gunners use the 77mm field gun in the anti-tank role (Panzer Abwehr Kanone, or PAK) in 1917.
(Contemporary Watercolour, Allen Collection)

18th April: What a mess we are in! . . . We have to stand fast and meet every [enemy] thrust, even where it hurts us. Ludendorff christens this 'The Defensive Battle.' . . . The enemy's strategy is quite clear. He attacks hard at Arras [then] he attacks somewhere else in superior strength . . . From now on he will keep us constantly on the run. There will be no end to it until we have had our fill. On the whole I should not be surprised if the English (BEF, including Dominion forces), backed by a [largely] unused American Army, came out on top at the last. We economize . . . because we have to, whereas the enemy has enough to spare . . . What is the good of our people doing their utmost in the face of these odds?[11]

By the beginning of May, as the battle ebbed, German spirits lifted. The line was stabilised and it was abundantly clear that the Nivelle offensive had ground to a bloody halt. At Supreme HQ the staff heard encouraging, though sobering news, even though the Kaiser obviously saw it differently:

1st May: In bitter fighting out troops at Arras have withstood the attacks of the English, who are believed to have suffered very heavy losses. The same applies to the {French] battle in Champagne. But at today's audience our losses were also stressed, particularly our loss of commissioned ranks. His Majesty is in a jubilant mood. He insists that if the English now came forward with peace proposals he would reject them out of hand. [He said] They must be made to grovel.[12]

In spite of the losses in 1916, Ludendorff and Hindenburg had increased the German Army by 53 divisions to its highest ever total of 238 divisions by the beginning of 1917. Nevertheless, the manpower barrel was already running low and cosmetic changes had to made to maintain the hard-pressed German armies on the Western Front in particular. To this end, as part of Ludendorff's 'general muster' in the winter of 1916/1917, 4,500 officers were pulled out of administrative posts and sent for front-line duty alongside 124,000 other ranks fit for service but previously employed in training and staff and administration duties in Germany. Almost 33 per cent of the 250,000 men required on a monthly basis were returning wounded.[13]

In addition, almost 310,000 recruits from the class of 1899 were called forward early to make good some of the shortfall in the military establishment as a result of the huge casualties in 1916. Many recruits were undernourished and inadequately trained and there was a marked deterioration in discipline in places. Desertions were to become a constant problem in 1917 and 1918.[14] Yet the need for men at the Front was balanced by an ever-greater requirement for skilled workers at home and over 300,000 such men were withdrawn from front-line duty under the terms of the Hindenburg Programme. Defence in the West was difficult, but until June 1917 it seemed to be working, despite the best efforts of the British and French offensives.

As General Nivelle's star plummeted to earth and his grand plans were ground to dust along the Chemin des Dames, the BEF was obliged to continue the offensive at Arras. By the time of the next major strike here, *Oberst* Fritz von Lossberg had already made good many of the faults in the German Sixth Army's defences that had existed under General von Falkenhausen before the launch of the first offensive on 9 April. British efforts on 23 April and beyond therefore failed to achieve any of the spectacular successes of the first few days of the initial assaults.

The German troops now grasped flexible defence-in-depth tactics and their artillery was a good deal less vulnerable than it had been before to British counter-battery (CB) fire. Conversely, most of the British attacks did not have the consistently heavy artillery support that they had enjoyed earlier. The result was another bitterly contested series of assault – counter-attack and close-quarter fighting, where bastions of the German defence such as Rouex, the chemical factory and Fresnoy were lost, won and lost again. Bullecourt was the scene of another battle between the Australians and the stalwart German 27th (Royal Württemberg) Division, as well as the British 62nd, 7th and 58th Divisions and the German 3rd Guards Division over a bloody fortnight between 3 and 17 May.[15]

Overall, the British and Dominion forces suffered 160,000 casualties by 17 May against a German total of around 130,000. Arras came to a standstill and another bloody draw.

There was, at least, good news for Germany on other fronts as 1917 progressed. After collusion between Ludendorff and Russian Bolshevik Vladimir Ilyich Lenin in early 1917, the seeds of Tsar Nicholas II and the Romanov's destruction were sown, with Ludendorff having a major role in the export of revolution.[16] A final desperate fling by the imperial Russian forces in the 'Kerensky' offensive in July was to lead to catastrophe and a guarantee of Russian revolution.

On the Italian front, the Tenth Isonzo offensive was launched in association with the attacks on the Western Front, but on 12 May, and it raged for almost a month, with a disastrous result for the Italian allies. The pattern for 1917 was set firmly by the Tenth Isonzo offensive, for a renewed assault in August would have a similar outcome and the 'Twelfth' offensive, more readily known as 'Caporetto', in late October would be so devastating that an Anglo-French force of no less than ten divisions would be sent from the Western Front to stabilise the line and save the Italian Army from total humiliation.

The story on the Western Front was fated to be oh so different in the second half of 1917. It would witness German defeat on an explosive scale and then a battle that remains more notorious in British and Dominion nations' minds than those of subsequent generations of German people.

CHAPTER 10

CATASTROPHE AND 'THE GREATEST MARTYRDOM OF THE WAR'

JUNE–NOVEMBER 1917

Though the Allies had entered the New Year confident of victory and sure of Germany's weakness, the promise of spring 1917 had so far proved illusory. They were caught out by *Alberich* and were too cautious to exploit this sudden German withdrawal to the *Siegfried Stellung*, or 'Hindenburg Line'. Following the disastrous Nivelle offensive against the Chemin des Dames between 16 and 25 April and the slowing down of the initially successful British attacks around Arras, the newly-appointed French C-in-C, Henri Philippe Pétain, resolved to remain on the defensive until his shattered forces were reinvigorated and American troops could make their mark.

For the French Army, weakened by the titanic struggle at Verdun in 1916, the bloody repulse at the Chemin des Dames was the last straw. Thousands mutinied and sparked a real crisis. Pétain was regarded above all other French officers as the man who saved Verdun and cared deeply about the fate of his men.

Petain's view that the Allies should go on the defensive appeared sound enough, but with Germany almost fatally weakened and forced to withdraw to the Hindenburg Line in the West after the Verdun and Somme campaigns and entirely on the defensive there throughout 1917, such a strategy was out of the question. Above all, the British C-in-C Field Marshal Sir Douglas Haig now saw the chance to implement his preferred plan for an offensive in Flanders to break out of the infamous Ypres Salient, split the German Army in the north and secure the Channel ports against possible U-boat activity.

An essential preliminary operation was an attack on Messines Ridge, one of the most strongly held sectors of the Salient, to the south of Ypres. If this 'handle of

MESSINES - JUNE 1917
OUTLINE PLAN FOR 7th JUNE

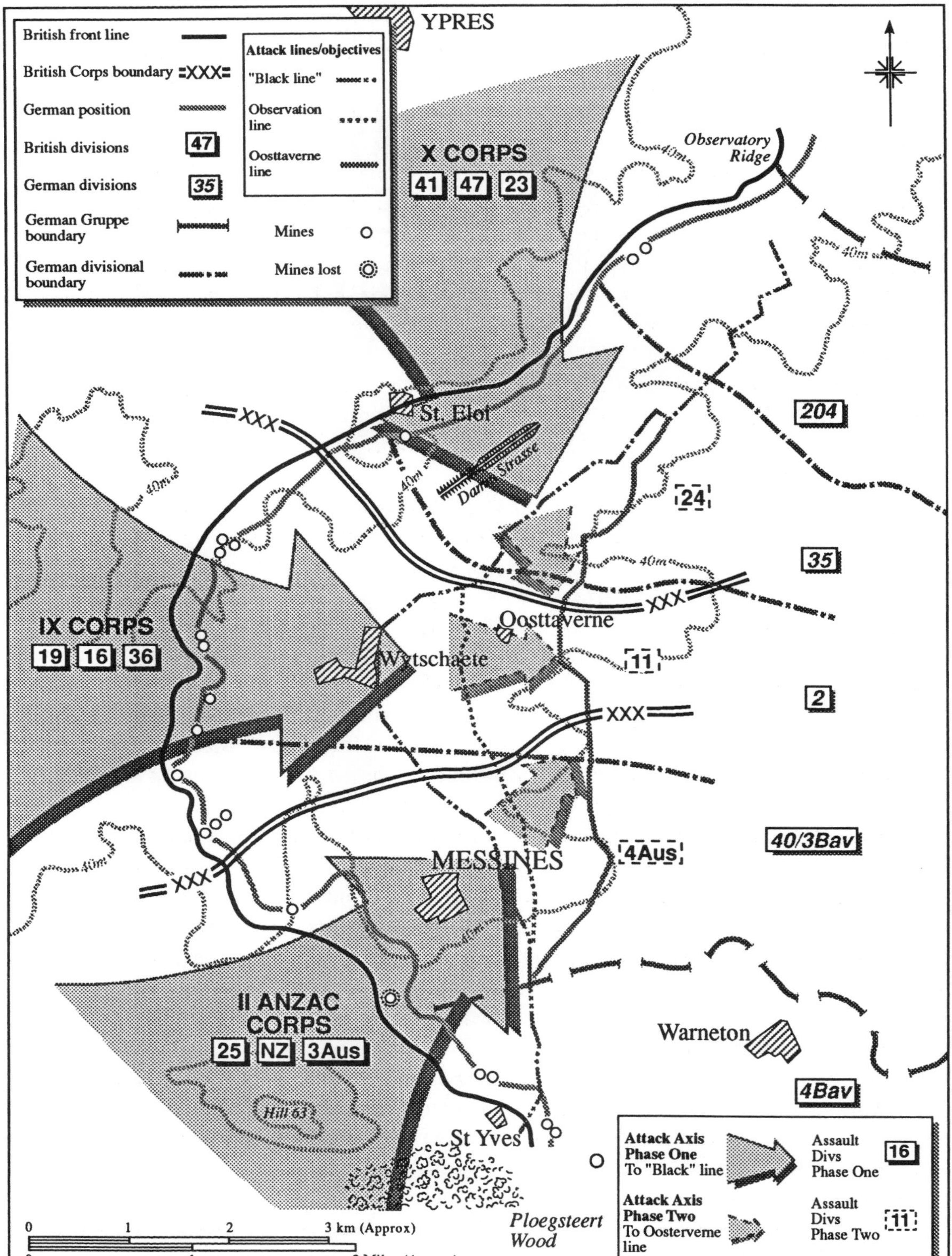

Messines: The plan (and events) of the British Second Army leading to the German debacle on 7 June 1917.

(I. Passingham, 1998)

the sickle' (the sickle being the geographical shape of the salient from north to south) could be grasped, it would facilitate the launching of the main offensive along the Menin Road and to the north towards the Passchendaele and Pilckem ridges and beyond.

The assault on Messines Ridge was entrusted by Haig to General Sir Herbert Plumer – commander of the Second Army. Preparations for the attack on the German defences of the *Wytschaete Bogen* (Messines-Wytschaete Ridge) had begun much earlier than 1917, for the Germans had held and fortified the ridge since Halloween 1914. Such formidable defences required a novel method of attack, but one ironically that would be a classic of siege warfare – the ancient technique of mining, or 'sapping' the fortifications.

Twenty-four mines had been planned and tunnels dug for each one, although one was lost at Petit Douve in June 1916 when the German tunnellers under command of *Oberst-Leutnant* Füsslein blew a counter-mine (*camouflet*) and destroyed the British tunnelling activity here.[1]

By 7 June 1917, 23 mines were laid and primed ready for action that morning. In the tunnels lay almost one million pounds, or 454,000 kilograms, of explosive over a ten-mile front. Unlike on the Somme on 1 July 1916, each mine would blow simultaneously and the average size of each charge – in excess of 40,000 pounds – was larger than any of the individual mines laid for the 'first day on the Somme'.

Furthermore, each of the Messines mines was placed in a precise pattern between Hill 60 and the Caterpillar in the north, to Trench 122/Factory Farm and the Birdcage in the south, to cause maximum disruption across the German defensive front and to destroy most of the toughest defences. British, Australian and Canadian Tunnelling Companies were employed to 'do the business' – the tunnels ranging from 200 to 2,000 feet in length and dug to a depth of between 50 and 90–100 feet.

On the other side of the wire, the story was quite different. Although the German *Gruppe Wytschaete*, defending the Messines Ridge with five divisions was well-entrenched, its commander, General von Laffaert, was convinced that his Korps would easily hold its positions and, despite evidence to the contrary, dismissed any major threat from British mines, or a determined assault by Plumer's men. Flexible defence had not been fully embraced by Laffaert, who felt that his defences were impregnable as they stood. His hubris was a fatal flaw and would condemn all of his men to a terrifying ordeal and thousands to gruesome deaths.

The preliminary bombardment of the Messines positions began in earnest on 25 May – and it was relentless. By the end of the month it was so intense that dogs had to be sent into the German lines to deliver some of the rations, water, medical supplies and ammunition needed by the beleaguered German troops cowering in even the most heavily fortified bunkers across the ridge line.

The meticulous British preparations for the battle involved improvements to roads and railways, frequent patrolling and air surveillance to confirm enemy strengths and the provision of the overwhelming artillery support by 2,266 guns of all calibres and an awesome array of aircraft from the RFC. Each corps and assault division rehearsed their roles for the impending attack to the last detail, so that every man knew precisely what his task would be in the heat of battle.

Nine infantry divisions were allocated for the main assault to capture the ridge itself, plus three to exploit this success by advancing later to seize the German rear positions based on the Oosttaverne Line, or *Sehnen Stellung*, by the end of the day.

At 3.10 a.m. precisely the 19 designated mines were detonated almost simultaneously – a mere 28 seconds separated the first from the last explosion – and the German front line across Messines ridge was engulfed by flame. Major Walter Kranz witnessed the event from the second German line and described the explosions as:

> . . . nineteen gigantic roses with carmine petals, or as enormous mushrooms, which rose up slowly and majestically out of the ground and then split into pieces with a mighty roar, sending up multi-coloured columns of flame mixed with a mass of earth and splinters high into the sky.[2]

The craters torn by the upward thrust of these convulsions were enormous: at the Caterpillar by Hill 60 it measured 260 feet wide at ground level, with a circle of complete obliteration 380 feet across; at Spanbroekmolen, a 250-foot crater and a diameter of obliteration of 450 feet, to name but two. Some of the German trench garrisons disappeared completely – vaporised by the intense heat and blast effects. Plumer's Chief-of-Staff Major General Tim Harington inspected some of the damage the next day:

> On entering a concrete dugout I found four German officers sitting at a table – all dead, killed by the shock. They might have been playing bridge. It was an uncanny sight – not a mark on any of them. I can see their ghastly white faces as I write.[3]

As these explosions erupted, all 2,266 guns and howitzers, 438 trench mortars and 454 Vickers machine guns raked the German front line and rear positions.

Then, behind the thumping screen of this barrage 80,000 infantrymen advanced as one to seize their objectives and within a few minutes the whole of the German front line had been secured by the first assault waves. Such was the ferocity and completeness of the effect of the mines and subsequent barrage that many of the German troops who had survived were dazed, confused and only too willing to surrender.

'Whitesheets' fell to the Irish without any major opposition, but the New Zealand Division had to fight hard to wrest Messines from the remainder of a punch drunk but resolute 3rd Bavarian Division. Nevertheless, Messines was fully subdued by 9 a.m.

By mid-morning, the whole of the ridgeline was in British hands and the three reserve divisions were on their way forward to exploit the unbelievable success so far achieved. Guns were quickly brought forward to continue the bombardment of the German depth positions based on the *Sehnen Stellung*, or Oosttaverne Line.

Almost 7,500 German prisoners were taken. Also, 150 guns and mortars, as well as 300 machine guns were captured. Ten thousand German troops were to be posted as 'missing' – the vast majority killed by the preliminary bombardment, effects of the mines and subsequent hurricane of shot and shell as the early hours of the battle passed.

During the early afternoon Mark IV tanks were brought into action to support the subsequent assault of the three reserve divisions, which was launched at 3.10 p.m., precisely 12 hours after the battle had begun. By the evening of 7 June, the entire ridge was securely held and all objectives, with the exception of a small disputed sector of the Oosttaverne Line, taken. By the end of the first day, Plumer had achieved an unqualified success at the cost of 11,000 casualties, and of those, only 10 per cent had been killed.

Laffaert's Gruppe Wytschaete had suffered in excess of 20,000 casualties of which between 30–40 per cent had been killed on the day, together with the 7,000 or so prisoners.

Messines: The pathetic, upside-down remains of the German concrete bunkers at Factory Farm, where one of 19 British mines blew the German garrison to kingdom come. *(IWM: E(Aus) 1269)*

Wounded German prisoners during the Messines battle.
(N.Z. H.59)

Though the battle would officially continue until 14 June, the British Second Army had inflicted fatal damage on the German defenders and their High Command's confidence on day one. The victory provided a much needed tonic to the Allied cause after the ultimate disappointment of Arras and the disaster of the Nivelle offensive.

For the German High Command it was a psychological and potentially disastrous military failure. Crown Prince Rupprecht, the commander of the Group of Armies facing the British in Belgium and north-east France, was convinced that the BEF's success at Messines would be followed up by further attacks designed on the same principle and throughout June planned to abandon the low-lying ground to the west of the River Lys. He feared a rapid British exploitation at the very least onto the vital area of the Gheluvelt plateau astride the Menin Road.

General Plumer had indeed envisaged such an operation, but Haig, who at the time preferred the younger General Sir Hubert Gough to theoretically exploit Plumer's success with a wider Flanders campaign, ultimately abandoned the proposal.

Militarily, Messines provided a basic lesson: that surprise, the use of all arms as a veritable orchestra of war, and assaults against limited, attainable objectives that could be held against the inevitable German response in the form of counter-attacks, should be the tactical aim – the essence of the 'Bite and Hold' doctrine. It was to prove a war-winning concept for the Western Allies in 1918.

The Germans identified five main reasons for the German debacle at Messines: the enemy's overwhelming concentration of effort and superiority in infantry, artillery, air power and tanks; the devastating and surprise effect of the 19 mines; the unfavourable position of the German front line on a forward slope; the cramped defensive area, where troops were deployed too far forward, artillery was vulnerable to enemy air activity and artillery fire and two divisions (40th (Saxon) and 3rd Bavarian Division) were caught in the middle of a relief in place when the British struck; and the failure of the 7th and 1st Guards Reserve counter-attack (*eingreif*) divisions. At first, it seemed that Messines was about to transform the nature of the fighting on the Western Front. Many Germans began to face the real prospect of defeat. Opinion was reflected by comments such as:

> How quickly the English (British) are advancing! I wonder if this latest victory will prove a turning point in the war . . . Here the military authorities . . . characterize every Allied advance as an elastic bend in the German line; or if it is reluctantly admitted that the first German line has been broken through, the attack must always waver and fail on the ever-renewed defence of the German reserves.[4]

German troops heard about the reverse and were well aware that their situation was growing weaker as the British piled on the pressure. It was reported from the Home front that:

> A soldier . . . just returned (wounded) from the Front, spoke about the hardships they had to endure. He had no bitterness for the enemy and the English were fine men to fight against . . . 'We all do our best for our [respective] countries and if we meet as prisoners or otherwise, we are perfectly friendly; but . . . there must be something wrong somewhere to make us [Germans] so hated by all other nations, as well as by our own allies.' . . . He went on to say that the [British] Army is in splendid condition, and always being reinforced by fresh and perfectly equipped troops, whilst the Germans have only a tired and worn-out Army . . .[5]

The stunning setback at Messines was a simultaneously gut-wrenching blow to German morale and the High Command's belief in its ability to contain continued Allied offensive action on the Western Front.

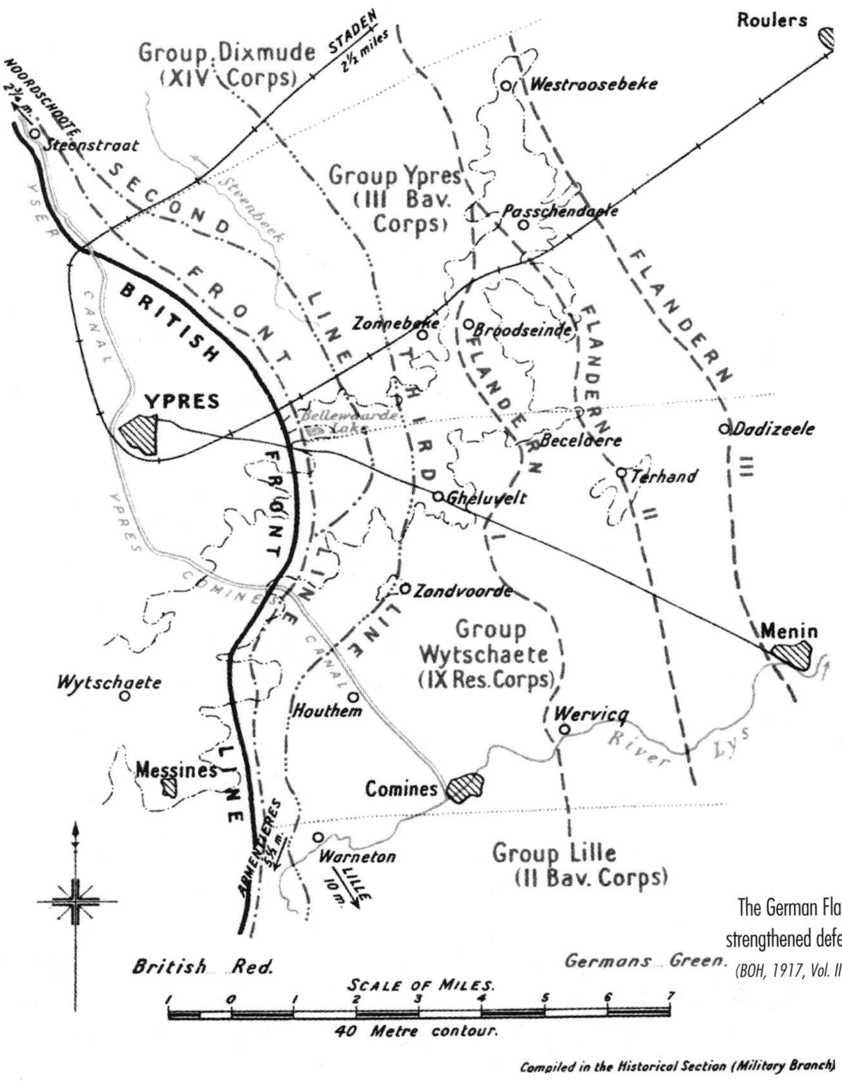

The German Flanders positions and strengthened defences in July 1917. *(BOH, 1917, Vol. II and by kind permission of the IWM)*

During the second half of June 1917 it was clear to the Germans that a major British offensive was planned for the Flanders sector and that Messines had been a necessary preliminary for the operation. The surprise to the German commanders most involved in the defence of the Ypres sector, namely Crown Prince Rupprecht, directing the Northern Group of Armies, and General Sixt von Armin, GOC of the German Fourth Army holding the Salient itself, was that the British had not attempted to exploit their victory at Messines by securing the southern half of the Salient up to and including the vital ground of the Gheluvelt plateau.

Partly because of this, the German forces were almost certain where the British blow would fall and worked day and night to improve the defences of the Flanders Line under the direction of their defensive mastermind, *Oberst* Fritz von Lossberg. What German intelligence could not fathom was the date of the impending assault by the BEF.

Crown Prince Rupprecht had every reason to be concerned about the general situation in the northern sector of the Western Front by the beginning of July. By now, despite the absence of the expected attack against the Gheluvelt Plateau, the signs of a massive British build-up to an offensive centered on the Ypres line were beyond doubt: railways were extended, artillery batteries increased across the front and the movement of British troops and their logistic back-up was incessant. Worse, there were dangerous indications that major diversionary attacks would take place simultaneously in the Arras, St Quentin and Artois sectors to the south. According to General Hermann von Kuhl, Rupprecht's Chief-of-Staff:

> During the battles of the Somme in the previous year it had been possible to contain the offensive – just – by weakening, to an absolutely dangerous degree, the other fronts – and put the forces collected into one major battle area. Even a light enemy attack against any other part of the front than the Somme and Verdun would have been a most serious danger. But such secondary attacks were more greatly feared at the outset in the summer of 1917 following the transfer [by the Army Group] of all dispensable men and materials to the Fourth Army in Flanders for the great defensive battle.[6]

However, Rupprecht was not fazed by a diversionary British reinforcement in the Arras region and stuck to the task of preparing the troops under his command as thoroughly as possible for the onslaught that was about to follow in Flanders.

The question of a voluntary withdrawal, as had been suggested at first to prevent the huge German casualties that were actually incurred at Messines but rejected before the battle, also became an issue in Rupprecht's conferences with Kuhl and Armin in late June. But all knew that the loss of the Salient and other Belgian territory was out of the question politically.

Despite a morale-boosting German attack against the British at Nieuport on the Belgian coast on 10 July, the average German soldier facing the BEF in Flanders prepared for the British assault with increasing concern at its possible consequences.

One of the German soldier's great strengths was his ability to stand and fight when others might quit the field or surrender more readily against poor odds. This quality of courage and discipline was imbued by the Prussian military tradition, but it could be a double-edged weapon at times:

> The Germans are such a patient and long-suffering race that they do not as yet realise their own power, and the Prussian precept, *Es ist verboten*, has been so drummed into them that they accept all regulations and orders without any further demur. I do believe that if they were bidden to go out and eat grass, they would obey in herds, without any further question.[7]

Grenadier Albert Mühmelt, who had survived the Somme the previous year, now prepared for the British offensive to begin in the Salient. He and his comrades were working day and night to make good their defences. Most doubted that it would be enough to save their skins.

General von Kuhl confirmed such fears at the time when he later wrote:

> In the last ten days of July the enemy's artillery fire rose to a bombardment of planned destruction . . . At times, the [British guns put down terrifying] drum fire . . . The big struggle for Flanders was imminent – the new 'Death of Ypres' was being proclaimed.

One thing was certain: despite the retrospective criticism of General Gough and Field Marshal Haig for the failure of the first weeks of the Third Ypres campaign, the week-long preliminary bombardment of the German positions across the Flanders defensive line brought heavy and mounting losses – and was both physically destructive and a great strain on German morale. At least four shattered German divisions had to be withdrawn before the British assault began on 31 July.

The Official Bavarian History of the Great War records that:

> For a long time now the riflemen had cowered in the shell holes which covered the whole area – the deepest of which were full of ground water. Low-flying aircraft and reconnaissance patrols of the British infantry kept the men in the battle area at full stretch at all times . . . [The full effects of the enemy artillery, hostile air and infantry patrol activity were profound] . . . It is no wonder then that in both officers and men nervous energy was consumed and fighting strength quickly diminished.[8]

Early on the morning of 31 July 1917 a storm of fire erupted which dwarfed the continual effort that had been made over the previous week or so. The German Fourth Guards Division recorded that:

> The storm of fire was . . . drum fire no longer: it was as if Hell itself had opened . . . It was as if the enemy wanted to announce to the whole world 'We are coming – and we shall overcome.'

After some success on the first day, the main Allied offensive in Flanders petered out as a result of dreadful weather from 31 July onwards and came to a grinding halt after the failure of the renewed attacks on 16 August – one of the worst days for the Allies of the entire Third Ypres campaign. But the breakdown of the British offensive was due mainly to the weather and the extraordinary resilience of the German units that were – to a man – fighting for their lives every day that the Allied assaults, incessant artillery bombardments and air harassment continued. This was no cakewalk for the German defenders.

'The Greatest Martyrdom of the War.' The dreadful effects of British artillery on German defences at Ypres: *Flandern 1917*.
(IWM: Q3117)

Leutnant Georg Bucher, who commanded an infantry platoon facing the onslaught before and during the British attacks on 31 July, wrote of his experience soon after his capture later in the battle:

> The English bombardment was in full swing but I went into my shelter and lay down fully dressed on my waterproof sheet . . . [The noise] wouldn't let me sleep. A fierce bombardment was raging over Flanders – over the sector where we lay. . . Sonderbeck, the duty NCO, burst in [to my dugout] . . . 'The big offensive has started', he panted, his eyes rolling . . . 'Already three men have been blown to bits,' he gasped – and hastily gulped a mouthful of rum . . . In a moment I was ready and hurried up the steps with him. There was an absolute downpour of earth and shell-splinters – on every side the night was lit up by explosions . . . There was a terrific explosion from the dugout from which we had just come . . . in a moment the dugout and four men in it ceased to exist: a 15-inch shell had blown the former heavily protected shelter to Kingdom come . . . The third night [of the bombardment] came.[9]

Soon about 50 per cent of Bucher's company were either dead, wounded or driven crazy by the English gunfire. Finally, Zero Hour loomed on 31 July and the heavy bombardment stopped. Bucher and his fellow survivors knew what that meant, and the last thing they wanted now was to be caught like rats in a trap inside the bunkers and dugouts in which they had sheltered for days. They manned the parapets, or the shell holes where the trench had been before the British artillery had blown it apart, and waited for the inevitable attack. At first, the Tommies advanced in groups, and got to within a hundred yards of Bucher's position before he and and the forty men who had survived a company of 160 opened fire. Then 'the English soldiers immediately began rushing at us in smaller groups . . . We had to fall back against this determined onrush.'[10]

According to the troops who, like Georg Bucher, had survived the horror of the bombardments and the first weeks of the struggle for the Ypres sector, the ordeal was almost unbearable because of the extraordinary courage and endurance of their British opponents in attacking through such dire weather conditions. General Hermann von Kuhl, Rupprecht's chief-of-staff, noted that:

> The first phase of the great struggle ended on about the 25th of August . . . But the fighting strength of the numerous German divisions had been used up; and it was already proving difficult within the entire area of Crown Prince Rupprecht's Group of Armies to replace them promptly with fresh divisions.[11]

Naturally, as the failed initiatives of General Gough were replaced by the more careful and experienced approach of General Plumer and the Second Army on the British side at this time, the German Fourth Army licked its wounds and prepared for the next major enemy assault.

Contrary to one of the most long-standing legends of the Third Ypres campaign, even the Germans acknowledged that the weather throughout September was warm, dry and, most importantly, that the tide had obviously gone out on the endless 'sea of mud' of popular myth.

For many German soldiers who had come through the Somme and perhaps Arras before Third Ypres, only a personal sense of duty and courage among their brothers-in-arms spurred them on. The Home Front offered nothing to compare with the comradeship of the combat zone in the battalion, your company or platoon, despite the inherent danger. *Schütze* Johannes Philippsen wrote in his diary in July 1917 of even the battle-hardened, experienced soldier's constant efforts to overcome his fear for the benefit of the pitifully naive new soldiers:

> We, who have seen the dark side, must substitute for that enthusiasm [of the new recruit] a deep-seated determination to stand by the Fatherland whatever happens as long as it has need of us. We know that death is not the worst thing that we have to

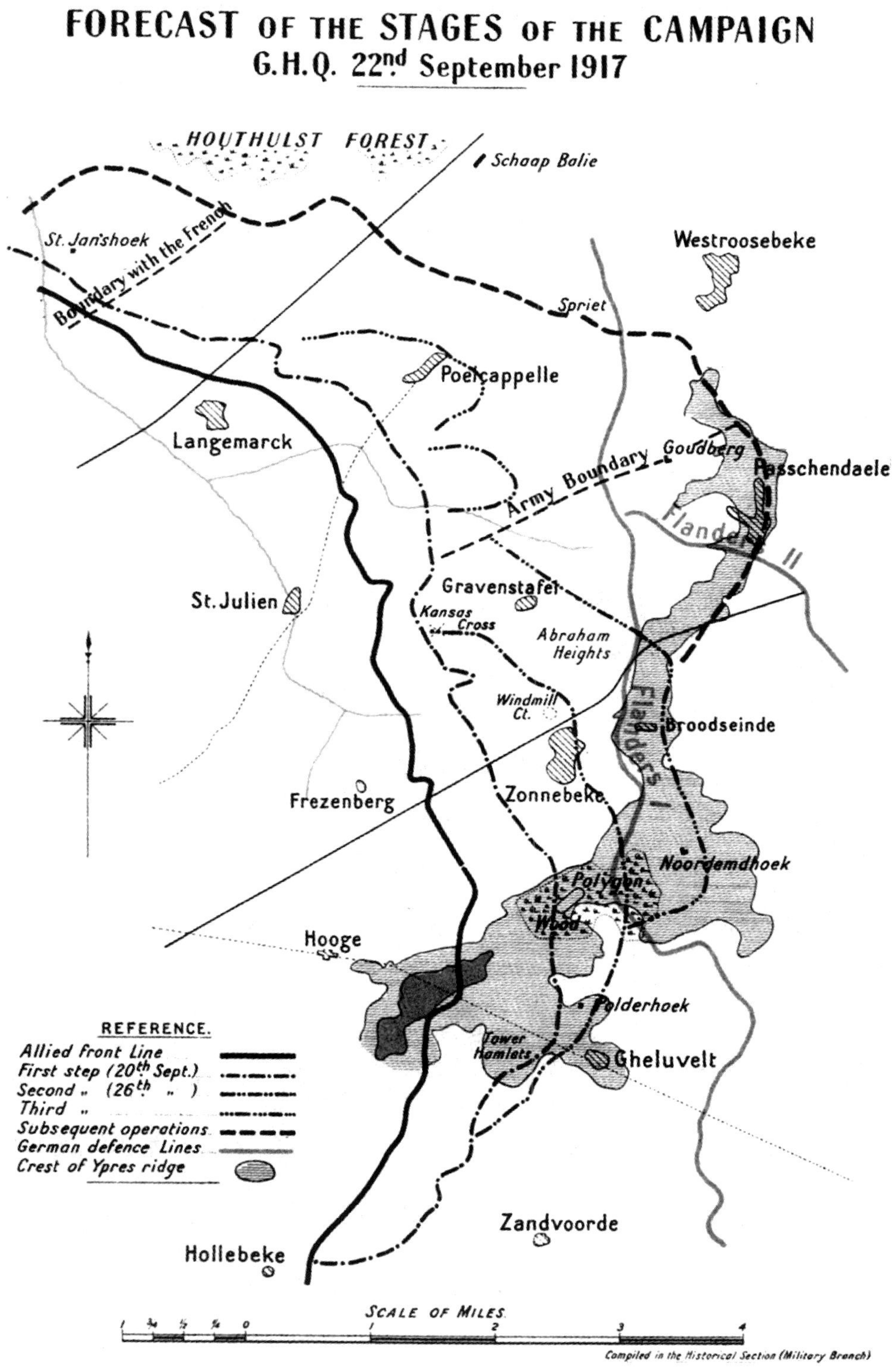

Flandern 1917 – Third Ypres/Passchendaele: BEF forecast of the stages of the campaign and German defensive lines in the Northern Sector of the Ypres salient, 22 September after the Battle of the Menin Road (20th) and prior to Polygon Wood (26th), Broodseinde (4 October) and the final German defence of Passchendaele Ridge (October to 10 November).

(BOH, 1917, Vol. II; by kind permission of the IWM)

The ruined town of Ypres, September 1917.
(IWM: E(Aus) 1171)

face. Thoroughly to realise everything and yet to go back, not under compulsion, but willingly, is not easy. To try and deceive oneself by working up a state of excitement is, I hold, unworthy. Only genuine self-command is any use to me.[12]

The next blows against the German line – namely, the battles of the Menin Road on 20 September, Polygon Wood on 26 September and Broodseinde on 4 October, were to push the German defenders to the edge of darkness and despair. These methodical, step-by-step advances boosted British morale while simultaneously hammering the morale of the German troops holding on. It came tantalisingly close to breaking the increasingly brittle crust on the German defensive pie in Flanders.

The success of these attacks has often been ignored by the maudlin majority of recent generations who enthusiastically latch on to the 'We died in Hell, they called it Passchendaele' theory, of both poets and Haig-baiters. But it was not ignored or diminished by German soldiers and commanders both at the time and in subsequent years.

Surely, this is where we should have been looking for the past decades for some balanced comment and historical perspective on the full story of Third Ypres, or 'Passchendaele'. We should have been asking not only, what it was really like for Tommy Atkins and his brothers-in-arms, but also how bloody and truly dreadful was it for *Fritzie Schmidt* by comparison? We know that the problem is not so much one of access to German archives and histories, many of which have been translated into English, or are accurately used in the British official history.

Instead many historians, writers and commentators have conveniently brushed aside the evidence of frightful conditions on the other side of the wire so as not to spoil the template of 'Passchendaele' being unremittingly horrific for the British, Canadians, Aussies, Kiwis *et al.* of the BEF crawling heroically, but futilely to their deaths through the mud-bath and blood-bath of Passchendaele Ridge.

When the storm broke again on 20 September, the German defenders were bewildered and often simply overwhelmed by the new tactics of the British Second Army: new, that is, to the vast majority of German troops who had not experienced such tactics at Arras and Messines. General Sixt von Armin, commanding the German Fourth Army, conceded later that he had overestimated the strength of his defences and fewer counter-attack units were available than were needed.

Flandern 1917. Third Ypres, 1917: foul conditions for both sides.
(IWM: E(Aus) 1200)

However, many of the counter-attack troops that were available and sent into the battle were literally blown away before they reached the hastily prepared defensive line of the attacking British infantry. 'Bite and Hold' tactics demanded limited attacks with overwhelming firepower, consolidation of the gains made and then the destruction of any German counter-attack: the inevitable and entirely predictable enemy response.

Against the British 'Bite and Hold' tactics, even the elastic defence-in-depth was often found wanting. Worst of all, the specially selected *eingreiftruppen* were still frequently sacrificed on the altar of German command hubris. When an attempt was made to alter the tactics on 4 October and carry out a pre-emptive counter-stroke near Broodseinde, the assaulting troops went over the top at precisely the same time as the British and Australian attackers and were rapidly cut down by machine gun and shellfire.

But then came the rains again; on 11 October Crown Prince Rupprecht commented that the rain had become Germany's greatest ally on the Western Front. Nevertheless, through the deteriorating weather following the battering of the German line around Broodseinde on 4 October, the subsequent assaults on the 9th and 12th of that month did push the hard-pressed German defences back a further 2 kilometres across a 6-kilometre front and threatened Passchendaele ridge for the first time. It also produced a crisis in the German High Command that was more acute than that simultaneously facing Haig and his commanders.

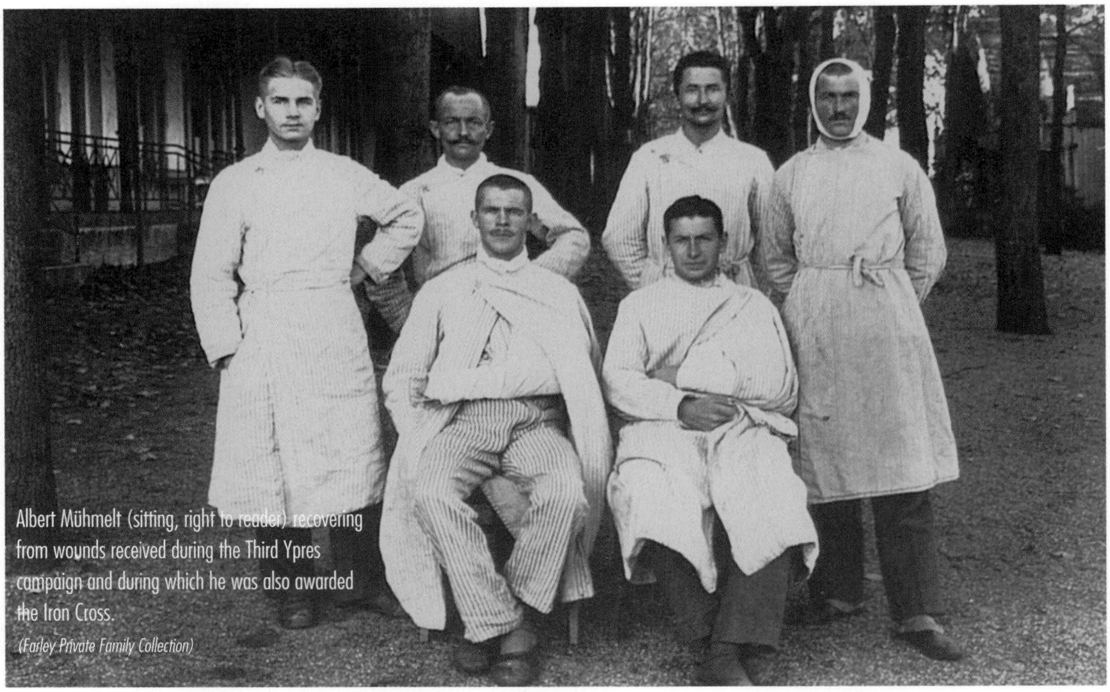
Albert Mühmelt (sitting, right to reader) recovering from wounds received during the Third Ypres campaign and during which he was also awarded the Iron Cross.
(Farley Private Family Collection)

By mid-October, Sixt von Armin's Fourth Army had suffered between 175,000 and 200,000 casualties. But it was not just the troop losses but also the impact that the desperate fighting was having on German morale. The German Official History later admitted that Flanders was having a traumatic effect: 'a deep mental shock' on both the soldiers who had survived so far but endured an increasingly desperate situation, and the men of the fresher divisions that were destined to go through the experience of Passchendaele.

Sixt von Arnim suggested that only a large-scale counter-offensive would restore the shredded morale of his troops defending 'Flanders Fields', but it was not an option. Every man was required already to take his turn in the line simply to contain the British attacks. Almost every man must have sensed similar anguish to that written in a letter, found on an unknown German officer whose battered corpse was found during the battle, which stated:

> After crawling through the bleeding remnants of my comrades, and through the smoke and debris, wandering and running in the midst of the raging gunfire in search of refuge, I am now awaiting death at any moment. You do not know what Flanders means. Flanders means endless human endurance. Flanders means blood and scraps of human bodies. Flanders means heroic courage and faithfulness even unto death.[13]

In the middle of October there was a pause once again as the BEF replaced their worn out divisions with fresh ones, most notably the Canadians, and brought their bigger guns forward. But despite this respite in the daily fighting, the British guns continued to harass the German defenders and it became increasingly difficult to find the reserves to shore up the Flanders Line.

The final agony was the bloody fortnight of the last week of October and first week of November. On 6 November, the mud-matted and blood-soaked rubble that was Passchendaele village fell to the Canadians.

By 10 November, the Third Ypres campaign was over – and the defence of the eternal salient had cost the Germans between 250,000 and 300,000 men. The British casualties were comparable, around 240,000. Though the significance of 1917, with Third Ypres at its core, was how it affected both sides.

It saw the British soldier at his lowest ebb; and for good reason. The promise of 1917 had been dashed by a number of factors, not least of which were the weather and the enemy's dogged resistance against ever-lengthening odds.

For the Germans in the line, all the necessary platitudes passed out by the German High Command about the victory in Flanders against the British offensive since July fooled no one in the foul, freezing trenches.

The dull, cold and wet weather that plagued August, October and November 1917 in Flanders actually burdened the defender more than the attacker. Contrary to the general belief, most German troops existed in a loose line of trenches made from adjoining shell holes and the bunkers were principally to shelter the troops and not designed to fight from. One account of thousands later encapsulated the experience:

> Our trenches have now for some time been shot to pieces . . . When attack and counter-attack have waged backwards and forwards there remains a broken line and a bitter struggle from crater to crater . . . The fight is carried on from clusters of shell-holes.[14]

Like the Somme in 1916, the Flanders campaign, according to one German officer who had lived through it, 'suffocated in swamp and blood'.[15] The British had failed to break through, but had at least gained the high ground in the northern part of the Ypres sector that allowed them to observe German artillery positions in the plains beyond Passchendaele.

Though the German Fourth Army had endured and refused to crack under the incessant pressure, it took no less than 73 infantry divisions and the grave losses to accomplish the stalemate that was to follow after 10 November. A German soldier, who had already fought here in 1914 and 1915, had written home on the eve of the campaign that: 'I have always had a horror of the name "Flanders"' – and this association was deep-rooted.

The artist Otto Dix, who experienced the Third Ypres campaign as an artillery officer, produced a work entitled *Langemarck*, and noted in his diary during the battle that Ypres was nothing but 'Lice, rats, wire entanglement, corpses, blood, schnapps, gas, guns and rubbish – This is the true nature of war.'[16]

Amazingly, even this depiction of the German experience was short of the true reality. Countless letters from front line soldiers were testament to the fact that as Flanders had been above all a battle between the guns – the sheer murderous quality of artillery – the individual soldier felt helpless and a victim of the 'great Flemish human mill'.[17]

Werner Beumelberg, who had also fought there, commented that:

> For half an hour on a day in a major battle it was possible to fight – the rest [was in a state of near-] unconsciousness, lying in puddles of mud, occasionally endeavouring to crawl into areas that were less fired upon; the constant terror of being mutilated or killed.[18]

The myth surrounding palatial concrete bunkers was most notably blown away by the memoirs of *Leutnant* Felix Lubinski, a Company Commander in the 74th Infantry Regiment:

> Life in the concrete bunkers is hell . . . Officers and other ranks share the same lousy plank beds . . . The plague of flies, grown fat on the corpses that surround

us, is terrible . . . The old military discipline was gradually slackening . . . The unexpected prolongation of the War, constant shortage of reserves, poor food conditions and the inexperience of the younger officers and NCOs – all added to the discernible deterioration of morale.[19]

Even worse, the concrete bunkers, far from sheltering the men inside, often became their mausoleums. Captain Kalepky of the 86th Infantry Regiment recalled:

The bunkers were reasonably strong and could withstand even direct hits from some of the heavy enemy shells, but owing to the ground conditions in the Flanders area they could not be erected over a strong foundation. When a couple of heavy shells opened up a crater close to them, they would lean over, sometimes with the entrance down, with the soldiers trapped inside. There was no way of rescuing them, of course, and we suffered a rather heavy number of fatalities in this way – and the thought of the painfully slow death of those entombed haunted us all.[20]

Despite the heroic efforts to hang on in Flanders, German discipline and morale were at an all-time low by the end of the battle. Non-combat casualties had risen rapidly because of the combined effects of exhaustion and the foul conditions in which the troops fought.

Unlike the British units, which withdrew to the relative comfort of billets behind the lines after each action, most of German units were compelled to remain in the line until they were ineffective as a fighting force.

The psychological effect of having to fight on until their company or battalion was ripped apart led to a 'grey desperation' among the German troops. *Flandern 1917* meant something more than Verdun or the Somme as it was, in every sense, a collective trauma for those at the Front and those at home who read about the frightfulness and saw the mounting casualty lists with equal despair.

The author Carl Zuckmeyer, a gunner during the Third Ypres battles, wrote later:

We were stigmatised, marked, either to die or live with the burden of a scarcely bearable, non-communicable memory that plumbed the darkest depths of our tortured souls.[21]

General Hermann von Kuhl's report, *Flandern 1917*, written in December of that year, concluded:

The sufferings, privation and exertions which the soldiers had to bear were indescribable. Terrible was the spiritual burden on the lonely man in a shell hole or trench, and terrible the strain on the nerves during the British bombardment,

> which continued day and night . . . The hell of Verdun and the Somme was exceeded by Flanders. The battle to hold Flanders has been the greatest martyrdom of the war . . . and looking back, it seems that what was borne here was superhuman, but perhaps it may still prove to be too great a courageous sacrifice.[22]

The last desperate battle for Passchendaele Ridge in the period following Broodseinde was an horrendous experience for both sides.

> I hear that the [BEF] is daily gaining ground . . . and see that the English view of operations in the West is that the Germans have been on the defensive or retiring for a whole year [since] Verdun . . . For us civilians looking on, the whole campaign seems to be more or less a useless slaughter.[23]

But the horror had been much more protracted for the German defenders and the psychological scars ran deep. The German infantryman remained a soldier who was courageous, dogged, well-drilled and loyal to his comrades. But he had come to fear one thing above all since the Somme campaign in 1916: the power, accuracy and deadly effects of the British artillery. Of the thousands who had to go through it, letters and diaries were excellent testament of the experience:

> Flanders: 20/9/17 . . . up to now I have never been in anything like it. Before Arras it was very bad. You may not believe me, but here it is the devil let loose . . . This is the seventh day that I have been in the open fields. I must stop, for the enemy is bombarding our position vigorously and I must seek shelter.[24]

The German soldier's endurance and survival against incessant bombardment were greatly admired, but it was by no means eternal.

For those in the Ypres salient, Passchendaele was the final act before winter and the promise of another false dawn and illusion of victory. Further south, men that had been spared this ordeal in Flanders, as well as many who had been moved south after their experience here, were about to face another British onslaught, but of a very different nature.

If they thought that artillery could draw heavily on their account of courage, the sight, sound and effects of massed ranks of British tanks supported simultaneously in the offensive by artillery, infantry and aircraft, would cause widespread panic on the first days of the Battle of Cambrai.

But between Passchendaele and Cambrai a meeting took place that would have fatal consequences. Ludendorff decreed that it was to be held at Mons, on 11 November 1917.

CHAPTER 11

MONS, CAMBRAI AND NEWS FROM THE EAST

NOVEMBER–DECEMBER 1917

The generals and their principal staff officers met at Mons on 11 November, one year to the day before Armistice would end this rotten affair. Ludendorff considered the situation. Russia was out of the war, so he could concentrate his resources in the West, although he knew that an offensive there would have to be swift and decisive. What he could not afford to do would be to wait, or become embroiled in a protracted campaign, for his resources, especially manpower, were finite; those of the Western Allies were almost infinite.

With this in mind, Ludendorff reasoned that:

> The Army had come victoriously through 1917 [on the Eastern Front]; but it had become apparent that the holding of the Western Front purely by a defensive could no longer be counted on, in view of the enormous [resources] which the Entente now had at its disposal . . . Against the weight of the enemy's material [our] troops no longer displayed their old stubbornness; they thought with horror of fresh defensive battles and longed for the war of movement . . .[1]

The collapse of Russia and victory on the Eastern Front gave Ludendorff the opportunity to reinforce his depleted troops in the West and provide them with the necessary superiority to overwhelm the Western Allies. To the German supremo's mind the timing was an essential factor. The Western Allies appeared to be exhausted.

Triggered by heavy casualties, the French Army had suffered widespread mutinies earlier in the year and the British Army had hit a low point in the autumn of 1917 as it struggled at great cost to capture Passchendaele. Furthermore, Field Marshal Sir Douglas Haig, as British C-in-C, was losing the confidence of the British government. Prime Minister David Lloyd George decided to restrict the flow of reinforcements needed to strengthen Haig's armies. This meant that the British troops in France were forced to go on the defensive.

Ludendorff now knew that Germany had but one chance to win the war. The main issue was whether to launch a major attack against the British or the French. He reasoned that France was becoming increasingly dependent on her ally and that if he could eradicate the British Army, France would be certain to sue for peace. He believed that he would gather sufficient troops in the West to attack and drive Haig's armies out of France. His plan was to destroy the British Army in France and Belgium while simultaneously cutting off the French to prevent their reinforcement of the BEF.

Ludendorff's definition of strategy was one that most would be hard pressed to find in a military manual, and it was to prove a fatal flaw. To him:

> Tactics had to be considered before purely strategical objects, which it is futile to pursue unless tactical success is possible. A strategic plan, which ignores the tactical factor, is foredoomed to failure . . .[2]

If wiser heads than his suggested that this view was generally contrary to accepted military thinking, they were given short shrift. When battle commenced in March 1918, Crown Prince Rupprecht asked for clarification on the German Army's strategic objective; Ludendorff retorted 'I forbid myself to use the word "strategy". We chop a hole. The rest follows. We did it that way in Russia.'[3]

The very real problem was that the terrain of the Western Front and the quality of men and *matériel* available to both the British and French armies were all in a different league to that of the events on the Eastern Front.

Above all, Ludendorff believed that he would be strong enough by February or March 1918 to destroy the British. The three conditions that he laid down were first, that the strength of the two sides was more or less equal; there were only sufficient troops for one offensive and the idea of carrying out an alternative offensive, even as a diversion, was impossible on any reasonable scale. The second condition was that the main blow must fall against the British 'at the earliest possible moment'. The third was as simply stated as it would be difficult to achieve. Thirdly, Ludendorff declared, 'we must beat the British'.[4]

But his principal strategic operations officer, *Oberst-Leutnant* Georg Wetzell, warned him that 'any prospect of success in the West depends upon other principles than those which hold good for the East or against Italy', and subsequently produced a more practical plan for an attack in the West.[5]

Wetzell warned Ludendorff that the successful modus operandi of military operations against the Russian Army in particular were not likely to guarantee victory against the French and British and that a breakthrough was almost impossible to envisage as a result of a single assault on one sector of either the French or British line.

This would facilitate the Allied defence, for they could bring their resources to bear to foil the German thrust.

Wetzell recommended a strategy that would cause maximum disruption to the British or French response: attacks in two or three sectors to confuse the enemy and deceive him into the premature use of his reserves. In the first phase, the British reserves would be drawn to the St Quentin sector, where the offensive would be carried only as far as a line from Bapaume to La Fère, north to south. The second phase would mask the movement of the 'great battering train' of heavy guns, mortars and aircraft of the High Command's strategic reserve alongside a massive concentration of infantry divisions to smash through the British defences on the Flanders front. The decisive phase would be an overwhelming onslaught through Flanders and the seizure of the critical town of Hazebrouck.[6]

OHL chose to back Ludendorff's view that one massive offensive across the Somme sector would offer the best opportunity for a devastating, swift victory. It depended entirely on surprise and the subsequent paralysis of the British defenders as the offensive rolled forward. If it failed to achieve the promised breakthrough, the options for victory would be greatly diminished and could never again be on the scale of this first onslaught. It was a huge gamble – a first and last throw of the dice – and the responsibility would now lie entirely at the feet of Ludendorff.

The greatest harm that the United States would inflict on Germany was a punch that had already been thrown on 6 April 1917; and it was a deeply damaging psychological blow for Germany. The mere fact that America had entered the war formally on that day was enough to upset the bloody, but delicate equilibrium that existed between the Allies and the Central Powers. The pressure of the growing number of American troops in France meant that the German Army must strike quickly. The United States had been contributing to their military-industrial output for much of the war, and since April 1917, men, and millions of them were available to make good the French and British losses.

Ludendorff knew that the American troops would be fit, well-nourished and keen as mustard to 'get at the Boche'. The contrast with his men could have not been more obvious. The unrest, poverty and hunger back home in Germany affected men's morale, which was hardly boosted anyway by the fact that they were not exactly well-fed at the Front. It was a bad time for most German troops, our *Fritzie Schmidt*, by the final months of 1917. Combat fatigue was not the only thing that gnawed away at their very fibre:

> We [ordinary German soldiers] are emaciated and starved. Our food is bad and mixed up with so much substitute (*ersatz*) stuff that it makes us ill. The factory owners in Germany have grown wealthy, [but here] dysentery dissolves our bowels . . . The people at home should see these grey . . . miserable, wasted faces . . . lips trembling and distorted with pain . . .[7]

Battle of Cambrai: 'G' Battalion Mark IV tanks operating with the British 40th Division passing captured German field guns at Graincourt, on their way to attack Bourlan Wood, 23 November 1917.
(IWM: Q.6337)

However, the promised American troops had so far failed to materialise in great numbers; only four US divisions were deployed in France by the end of 1917, and only one was 'in the line'. Ludendorff saw this as a golden opportunity to exploit in early spring 1918. But he knew that the German offensive in the West would have to be an overwhelming and swift victory or suffer the consequences of an irresistible American build up and before they could become overwhelmingly effective on the Western Front.

Just over one week later the German High Command and the soldiers of General von der Marwitz's Second Army defending the Cambrai sector were caught off guard and nearly suffered the same humiliation as the German defenders at Arras and Messines some months before.

The Cambrai sector was on the left of Crown Prince Rupprecht's group of Armies, was part of the Hindenburg Line and was manned by *Gruppe Caudry*, (XIII Korps) under General Freiherr von Watter, comprising the 20th Landwehr Division between the Bapaume-Cambrai road and Havrincourt, the 54th Division between Havrincourt and Vacquerie and 9th Reserve Division, with elements of the 183rd Division to the south. The 20th *Landwehr* Division had recently relieved 204th Division and was relatively fresh, although as a *Landwehr* unit it was of relatively poor quality. The 54th Division had arrived at the end of August after a battering in the Ypres salient and was in the line because the Cambrai sector was a relatively quiet part of the Front. It had assumed the nickname of the 'Flanders Sanatorium', where units like the 54th Division were sent to recuperate from the rigours and incessant unpleasantness of life in Flanders. Although German artillery and mortar ammunition was short in this sector, the defences were considered strong enough to withstand the expected enemy preliminary artillery bombardment and any infantry assault.

By chance, the 20th *Landwehr* Division was due to be relieved by a battle-hardened and tough infantry division, the 107th, on 25 November, and it began to arrive in Cambrai from the East on 19 November, twenty-four hours before the British offensive began. A further infantry regiment (from a neighbouring division) and five field artillery batteries arrived on the same day to bolster the German defences.

From 10 November the Cambrai sector was covered in fog and rain, making German aerial reconnaissance all but impossible. It was bitterly cold and it chilled the very marrow of the German troops holding the line. Partly because of the lack of air cover and because no other intelligence sources suggested otherwise, von der Marwitz confidently reported to his superior Rupprecht on 16 November that: 'Hostile attacks on a large scale against the [Second] Army front are not to be expected in the near future'.[8]

Coupled with von der Marwitz's assessment, there was a general feeling at OHL (German Supreme HQ) that with the closing down of the Passchendaele campaign almost a week before (on 10 November) and with events in the East and in Italy hardly in the Allies' favour, the main fighting on the Western Front was about to draw a dark shroud over 1917.

But as often happens, the confidence was a little premature. After inconclusive trench raids on both the British 55th and 20th Divisions facing *Gruppe Caudry*, some prisoners taken from a raid on the 36th (Ulster) Division on the night of 18/19 November revealed that an attack was being prepared in the Havrincourt sector against 54th Division at least. No date was gleaned for this probable operation, but the information did conform with the situation report from Crown Prince Rupprecht's HQ to OHL on 18 that: 'The British have failed in Flanders, [therefore] partial attacks may be expected on other parts of the front'.[9]

On 19 November parts of the Cambrai sector were 'buzzed' by British aircraft and a scrap of a telephone message suggesting movement south of Flanders was picked up by a German signals listening station in the same sector.

That evening, *Gruppe Arras* on the right (north) of *Gruppe Caudry* reacted to the intelligence passed on concerning the possible attack on the Havrincourt area by issuing a warning order to its divisions to expect some enemy attacks on the 20th after a 'relatively short' bombardment and that some tanks may be used to support an infantry assault 'here and there'. Finally, at 11.59 p.m. on 19 November, General von Watter sent out his own warning order to *Gruppe Caudry*, but it did not have quite the same 'punch' as that for *Gruppe Arras*. It merely stated: 'All units are to note that in the event of the anticipated [limited] attack on the Havrincourt sector, some tanks might be used.'[10]

'Some tanks.' Well, General von Watter would get it half-right.

At 6.10 a.m. on 20 November, the silence of a misty morning in the Cambrai sector was broken by the sound of tanks moving forward and the drone of British aircraft flying low over the German lines. At 6.20 a.m., the tanks and assaulting infantry crossed the 'Start Line' and began to loom in front of the German front line. Any German resistance was immediately broken by the thunder of a massive, sudden bombardment by over 1,000 guns, which ranged over the German defensive lines, artillery batteries and HQ positions in the rear zones. The German defenders were caught entirely off guard.

Aerial photograph of the German defences at Cambrai, November 1917. Note the three formidable belts of barbed wire forward of the main German defensive positions.
(Allen Collection)

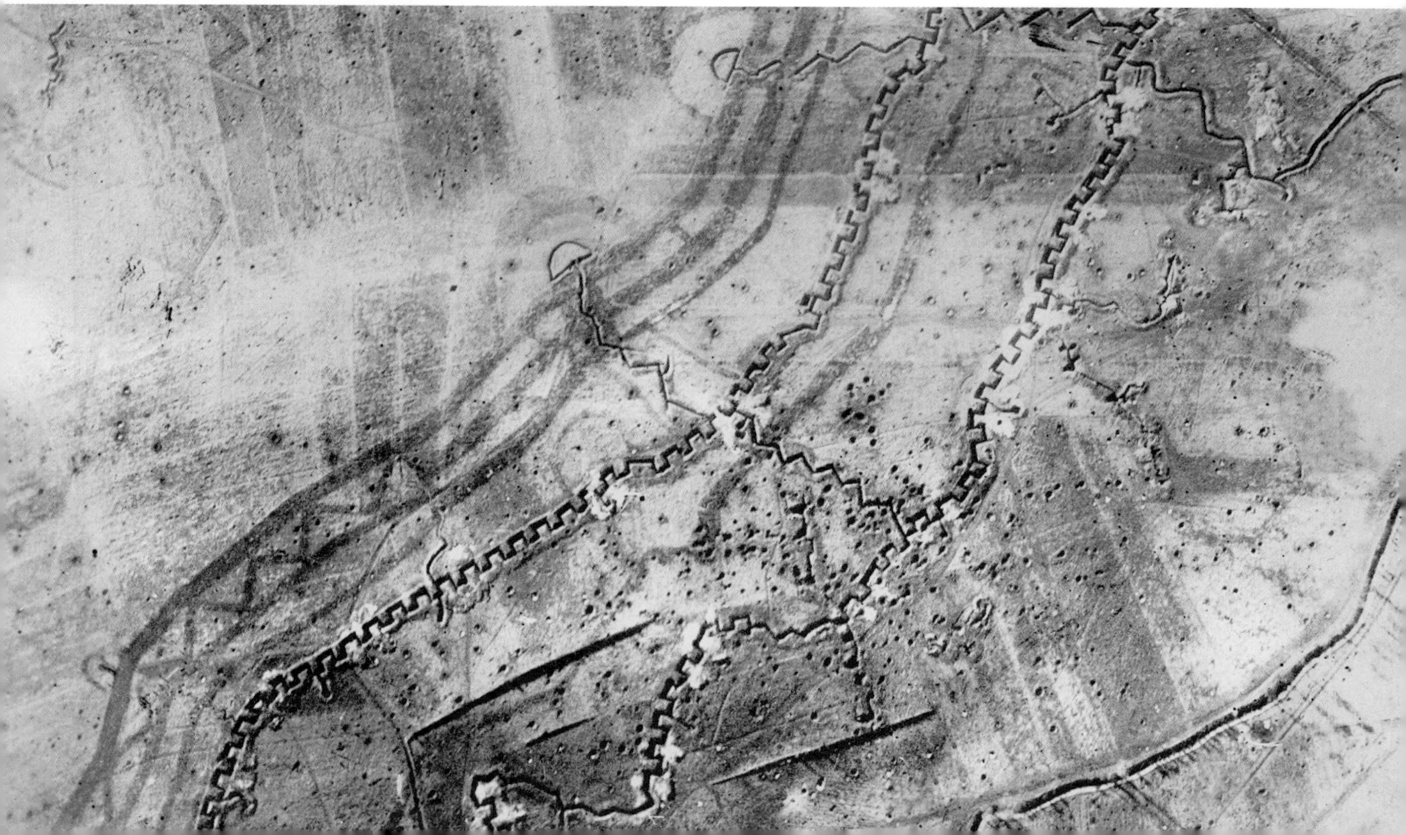

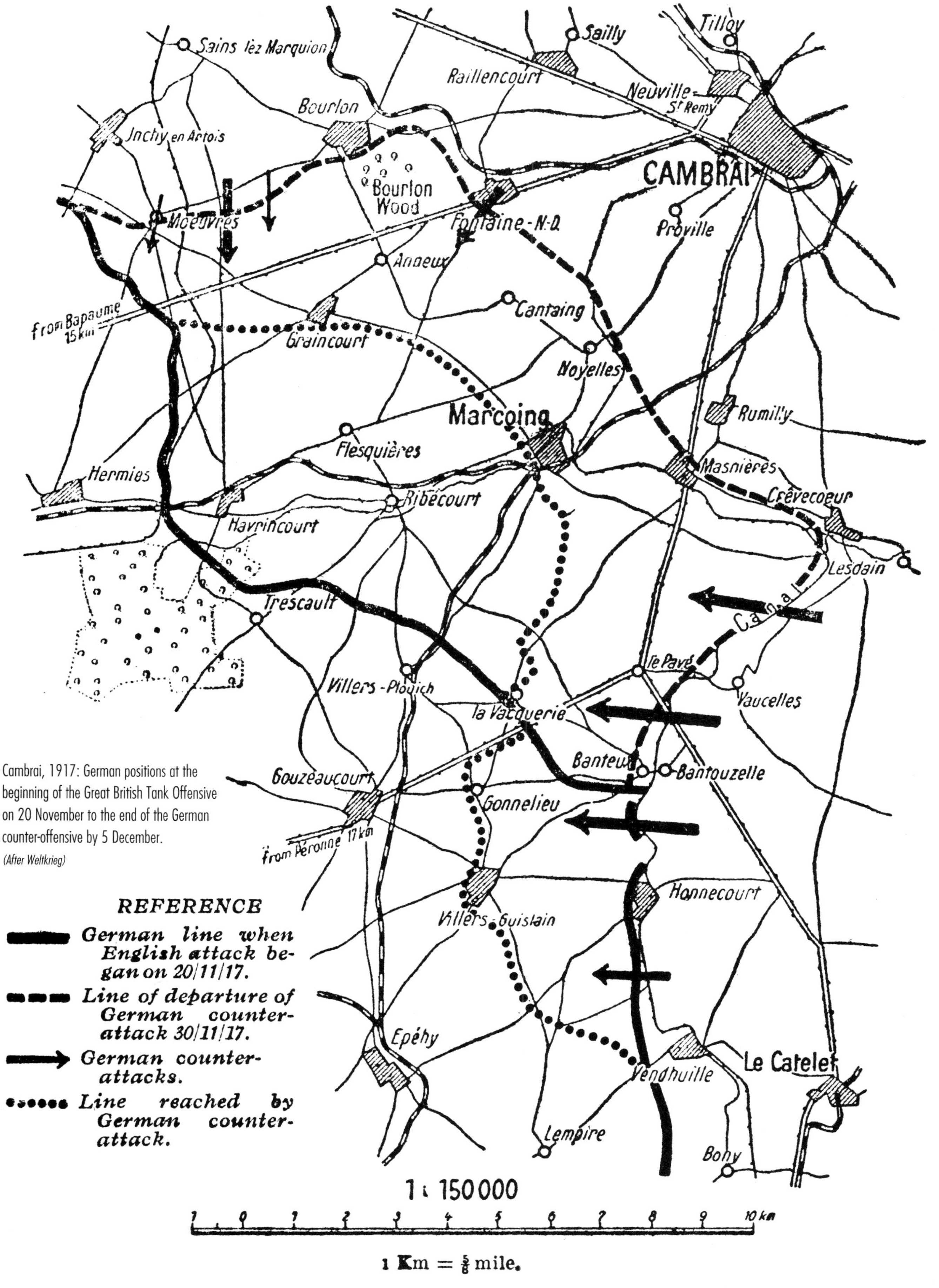

Cambrai, 1917: German positions at the beginning of the Great British Tank Offensive on 20 November to the end of the German counter-offensive by 5 December.

(After Weltkrieg)

Supported by six infantry assault divisions on a six-mile front, 378 Mark IV tanks burst into the *Gruppe Caudry* sector, and even in the Havrincourt area where the attack had been expected in part, the battalion and company commanders and their men were stunned by the sheer scale of the British armoured/infantry assault and the sudden, devastating 'predicted' artillery fire. At first, though some successful and fearless German resistance was put up, most of the survivors in the outpost zone either surrendered or fled the onslaught. One *Obergefreiter* recorded later that:

> There had not been any hint whatever of any preparation of an attack; . . . nothing extraordinary on a seemingly thin, quiet front . . . [Then] only after the attack started did we realise what was going to happen. The British forces, strengthened by hundreds of tanks, could move freely and overthrew our thin defences (They were actually attacking a sector of the Hindenburg Line) . . .[11]

In an almost futile gesture some German artillery units responded with weak counter-battery fire, but the British advance was so swift that most of the German shells fell behind the tanks and assaulting infantry.

Inevitably, once the forward positions of the Hindenburg Line were reached by the leading waves of British tanks and infantry, German resistance stiffened and some attacking infantry battalions were

British Mark IV tank captured by Germans and converted for their service.

(Postcard, Allen Collection)

held up by machine gun, trench mortar and rifle fire. But the massed tanks pushed on, crushing the thick belts of barbed wire and a number of German machine gun crews in their wake.

Funker (Signaller) Edwin 'Valentine' Kühns was serving near Bourlon Wood. When the British bombardment suddenly erupted, Kühns and his telephone section comrades were also taken completely by surprise. They were immediately shelled and throughout the first morning it seemed that confusion was turning to an overwhelming sense of chaos and the imminent collapse of German resistance. For the first 48 hours of the British advance, Kühns was heavily involved in managing the huge volume of telephone and messenger traffic. He noted that:

> All the time there were carrier-pigeon messages from Infantry Regiment Paczenski, sent 1 p.m. arrived 1.30 p.m. (sic). [Message read:] 'Last news, English infantry surrounding sugar factory, withdrawing . . . Tanks rolling back and forth along the road from Bourlon Wood.' Or 'Enemy attacking. Marching with heavy forces. Reinforcements needed urgently.'[12]

The one fully active German fighter unit, less than a squadron strong, reacted to the opening moves of the British Third Army's assault by scrambling all of its aircraft, regardless of the thick mist around them. At 6.30 a.m., as each plane taxied before taking off to meet the threat, the pilots and ground crews were staggered to see a number of British aircraft loom out of the gloom.[13] For most of the German flyers it was their last sight of anything as the RFC strafed the German airfield and ripped the grounded enemy planes to shreds. By 6.45 a.m., the RFC had complete control of the skies and exploited every opportunity to disrupt the German defences from the air and augment the great progress made on the ground.

The British offensive had started well; very well indeed. However, German helplessness inevitably turned to stubbornness, and then increasing resistance. In the 54th Divisional area near the village of Flesquières, the 51st Highland Division and their assault tanks were unfortunate enough to run into major difficulties against batteries of 108th Field Artillery Regiment, assigned to 54th Division. In the course of the fighting that followed, several tanks were knocked out as they attempted to advance on to the high ground close to the village.

The actions that day have become the stuff of battlefield legend, but the facts were that a number of 77mm field guns were manhandled out of their gun pits and fired directly at the tanks over open sights. At one stage, *Unteroffizier* Kruger manned one gun alone, as all the other crew-members were wounded or killed, and single-handedly knocked out a number of tanks.[14] The gunners of 54th Division's field artillery batteries had another important card up their sleeves: they were specially trained in anti-tank gunnery and had fought off French tanks during the Nivelle offensive the previous April.

Despite these heroics, as the day wore on it became clear that *Gruppe Caudry* was in deep trouble and that something had to be done urgently. General von der Marwitz, Crown Prince Rupprecht and Ludendorff all immediately acknowledged that the scale of the tank attack and the novel tactics used had the desired effect from the enemy's point of view: the German Second Army had been taken completely by surprise, its forward troops bewildered and helpless against such a mass of armoured vehicles and under an artillery bombardment that struck so heavily without any prior warning.[15]

Gruppe Caudry was deployed across part of the formidable Hindenburg Line, but it was hampered not only by the terrific surprise element of the British assault, but also by a heavy mist and the difficulty of coordinating a cohesive defensive response (as would happen on a much larger scale in reverse on 21 March 1918 on the Somme).

To cap it all, the Cambrai sector line was thinly held by second line combat units such as the 20th *Landwehr* Division, or units like the 54th Division deployed here to recuperate after a hammering at Ypres. It was a lethal combination, so that von der Marwitz and Rupprecht were very concerned about the deep penetration of their position and the speed of the British assault on the first day.

Ludendorff underlined the extent of the German surprise when he noted that:

> In the West the crisis caused by the Battle of Flanders, the Battle of the Laffaux salient [in the French sector] and their after-effects, passed away. We were expecting a continuation of the attacks in Flanders and on the French front, when on the 20th of November we were surprised by a fresh blow at Cambrai.[16]

By the afternoon of 20 November, Ludendorff and Rupprecht had agreed that the desperate situation must be restored by a deliberately planned counter-stroke. But that would take time and reinforcements that were not available to punch their way out of the corner that *Gruppe Caudry* found itself in. The crisis grew as each hour passed. The 54th Division and its artillery lost most of its fighting strength and its defences were almost non-existent by the end of the day. There were 5,785 officers and men killed or missing and a further 5,000 men wounded or taken as PoWs on 20 November. The 84th Regiment had its Regimental commander and the COs of all three battalions killed and its strength reduced to around 30 per cent of its original strength in this one day. The other front line divisions suffered almost as badly as the 54th, which had borne the brunt of the British thrust.

The situation became so grim that serious plans were made for a general withdrawal and the demolition of the canal bridges in front of Cambrai. The camp commandant of 54th Divisional HQ was sent with an ad hoc platoon of three officers and thirty men to defend the canal crossings at Marcoing and Masnières and for several hours in the afternoon of the first day there was a totally undefended one-mile gap in the Masnières-Beaurevoir defence line between Masnières and Crèvecoeur.

By pure chance, the British failed to identify this potentially fatal weakness before the gap was plugged and the attack began to lose some of its steam as the day drew to a close. But 20 November was deemed a British triumph and church bells rang throughout Great Britain to celebrate a great victory. The celebrations were a little premature.

By midnight on that same day, *Gruppe Caudry* was strengthened by the 107th Division and regiments pulled from both *Gruppe Arras* to *Gruppe Caudry*'s north, the Lens sector and *Gruppe St Quentin* to *Gruppe Caudry*'s immediate south. Three more divisions (119th of Fourth Army, 30th of Seventh Army and 214th of Sixth Army) were rushed towards the Cambrai sector and all would arrive within 48 hours.

The very real possibility of utter disaster had been averted; just. But the situation remained perilous for some days. Desperate messages came in thick and fast to divisional and regimental HQs from the sorely pressed front line units by telephone, runner or pigeon:

> Infantry Regiment 50: 'English have broken through [in our sector] with tanks and infantry, immediate back-up needed', then: Infantry Regiment 50: 'Enemy breakthrough Bourlon Wood with tanks. Some troops in retreat,' but 'Infantry Regiment 175 occupies railway embankment.'[17]

As the days passed after 20 November, the German defences were reinforced and resistance hardened as the British 'punch' lost its hitting power. Rupprecht and von der Marwitz now set about planning an equally stunning counter-blow as the day-to-day fighting continued in the guts of the Cambrai defence.

As the remnants of *Gruppe Caudry's* front line divisions and their reinforcements slugged it out against the remaining British tanks and infantry assaults, a new command, *Gruppe Bussigny* (based on XXIII Korps), was formed, commanded by a tough GOC, General von Kathen. On 24 November, preliminary orders were issued by Rupprecht's Chief-of-Staff General Hermann von Kuhl that a counter-offensive was to be launched 'at an early date'. *Gruppe Bussigny, Caudry* and *Arras* were all detailed for the offensive. Rupprecht discussed the proposed plan with Ludendorff and von der Marwitz at HQ Second Army (le Cateau) and then issued orders for the counter-offensive to the Second Army on the evening of 27 November. The attack was to be launched on 30 November. *Gruppe Bussigny*, supported by *Gruppe Caudry*, would attack from the south-east into the British flank and rear and recapture Flesquières and Havrincourt. *Gruppe Arras* was to then launch a heavy attack from the Bourlon Wood area towards the south.

The plan of attack for the German counter-offensive at Cambrai was straightforward enough. But new tactics were tested to infiltrate and overwhelm the hastily prepared British defences. A short but intensive artillery bombardment using both gas and high explosive shells was to be followed by an infantry assault in which the lightly equipped but heavily armed leading waves were ordered to bypass villages and strongpoints, infiltrating the British positions and pressing on to capture or destroy HQs and British artillery batteries. The spearhead of the attack would be led by troops with bags full of grenades and armed with light machine guns, light mortars and flamethrowers The assaults were to be accompanied by 77mm field artillery batteries moving forward as rapidly as possible to provide anti-tank fire and close support for the attacking infantry.

The vital ingredient for the success of these new tactics would be the same as that for the British on 20 November: surprise.

Until the evening of 29 November, General von der Marwitz and Rupprecht doubted that surprise could possibly be achieved. Both were convinced that the British must have been aware of increased German movements in the last few days and expected British trench raids and strong hostile air activity, but they failed to materialise. The night of 29/30 November was unusually quiet and the final German infantry moves into forward assembly and then jumping-off positions were made without any enemy interference.

At 6 a.m. on 30 November, the German guns opened up on the British 55th Division and the bombardment gradually spread across the southern sector of the Cambrai front. Within half an hour, it reached a crescendo of withering gas, high explosive and mortar fire, which caused havoc in many forward defences and cut all rear communications.

Zero Hour came at 7 a.m. and the German infantry swarmed across no-man's-land under cover of the artillery barrage, a thick mist and scant daylight. At daybreak,[18] German aircraft filled the sky and sought their revenge for the humiliation of being caught on the ground on 20 November, bombing rear positions and strafing British troops wherever possible. It was to be a day of mayhem across the Cambrai front as the German assaults were pressed home against some stiff resistance once the surviving British defenders recovered from the initial shock of the offensive against them.

Leutnant Ernst Jünger of 73rd Hanoverian Fusilier Regiment went into the initial assault and reflected the German and British experiences of that day:

> At 7 [a.m.] sharp we advanced in single file [and found] Dragon Alley unoccupied . . . We then entered the trench on the right. It was full of arms and equipment and English dead. It was the Siegfried line . . . Going further we met with resolute resistance . . . and we were driven back . . . Then we took part in another assault . . . The English resisted valiantly. Every traverse was contested. Mills bombs and stick grenades crossed and recrossed. Behind each we found dead or still quivering bodies. We killed each other out of sight . . .[19]

In the afternoon, attacking German troops were subjected to determined counter-attacks and heavy artillery fire. But the attack was pressed home and by the evening the British had been severely mauled.

Aus dem Westen.
Ein besonders konstruiertes Gewehr zur Bekämpfung der Tanks.

German anti-tank rifle on the Western Front, 1917.
(Allen Collection)

Losses were heavy on both sides, with *Leutnant* Ernst Jünger among the badly wounded, and the German infiltration methods often led to a loss of control, as troops assigned to this specialist role had not received sufficient training. Ludendorff also later suggested that: 'The success was all the more remarkable because it was in the main achieved by half-tired troops who had not been specially trained for attack.'[20]

At the other end of the scale, *Obergefreiter* Franz Benöhr, who had recovered from the shock of the first day of the British onslaught, noted later that:

> [Many of the tanks] moved so quickly at the beginning that they got lost and were then destroyed by our guns . . . Having arrived on the outskirts of Cambrai they had to stop for a day or two for reorganisation, replenishment and the like. Then it was too late for them to move on: Strong German reinforcements arrived and stopped the British attack.[21]

The battle raged on for a further four days, although much of the most intensive fighting took place on the first two days. By 5 December, both sides were well and truly exhausted; and the line was almost the same as it had been until the early hours of 20 November.

Between 20 November and 5 December 1917, Crown Prince Rupprecht had to use 20 infantry divisions against British Third Army's 15 infantry and 4 cavalry divisions in addition to the 386 Mark IV tanks involved on day one of the offensive.

The part played by the RFC in the British attacks and the German air arm during the German counter-offensive was of immense value to the ground troops that they supported, but losses were high on both sides.

Overall, the German Second Army lost around 45,000 killed, missing, wounded and PoWs (of which about 15,000 were suffered during the counter-stroke battles) and the British just over 44,000 men at Cambrai. As usual in war, statistics hide the bitter truth and tragedy of the casualties that they represent. If Ernst Jünger was one of the many casualties on the ground, Captain (later *General*) Frido von Senger und Etterlin's brother was a victim of the air war. Frido experienced the agony of battle when he heard of his brother's death and went to claim his body the next day:

> On the 1st of December . . . I disinterred my brother's body from a mass grave. As a fighter pilot he had been shot down on the previous day . . . In the clear winter sunshine I had spent a long time searching for the exact spot . . . With a couple of helpers I dug for hours in the mass grave while the German counter-attack swept past us . . . The English artillery fired on the advancing infantry and we had to seek shelter in the grave. On one occasion, we were buried up to the thighs. We managed to free [my brother's] body, which lay in the lowest of three layers of corpses. But the stretcher-bearers rightly refused to carry it back through that intense artillery fire. So I seized the legs of the body under my arms and dragged it towards my car, finally propping it up in the seat next to mine.[22]

Cambrai was a grim end to a gruesome year. Those that had survived it on the Western Front, whether German, British or French, saw only a dark horizon for 1918. Now there was a brief time to reflect and try to recall the days of the Christmases before the war.

Edwin Kühns spent Christmas and the coming of the New Year in the Cambrai sector, where he had survived the terrific British tank onslaught and German counter-attacks a few weeks before. Despite the cold, the hunger and the gloom of a frustrating 1917 on both sides of the wire, Kühns, his comrades and many other German troops at the Front were determined to make the most of the *Weinachtsfest*. He wrote that:

> The celebration was a very simple wartime effort. A Christmas tree with eleven candles . . . [and comrade] Gunther opened the proceedings with a short address and then distributed four Iron Crosses 2nd Class and one Württemburg Medal (Regional gallantry and service award).[23]

Germany had suffered, but survived 1917, just. The only ray of light was victory in the East, but it hardly cheered most of a German population now on the brink of starvation and suffering more than most from the insidious effects of disease brought on by malnourishment and poor medical facilities. It was yet another desperate year of mourning for lost sons, fathers, brothers and other loved ones who had 'fallen for the Fatherland'. By 31 December 1917 the German tally was 1,297,750 killed or missing, presumed dead; and well over half a million were destined to die in the battles of 1918.

The Hindenburg Programme had offered much and did little to fulfil that promise; far from it. After the horrible experience of the 'Turnip Winter' hopes had been raised by the promise of a decisive victory through submarine warfare. But this promise proved more hollow than those of 1914, 1915 and 1916 and, most depressing of all, provoked the American reaction that had been feared since the sinking of the *Lusitania* in May 1915 – war against Germany.

Throughout 1917, the dire reality of life in Germany had grown further and further apart from the images that politicians and military leaders peddled. The rewards for their deception were discontent, restlessness, civil disobedience and a burgeoning desire to end the war among the people. *Burgfrieden*, the pact of civil peace in wartime, was a notion now dead in the water. It had all gone horribly wrong and, with the exception of the profiteers and a healthy black market, Germans were existing in a surreal, *ersatz* life:

> People are devoured with anxiety as to the food resources for the coming winter, whilst the Government has to cope with . . . the increasing shortage of raw stuff and material for ammunition . . . As coffee and tea have entirely run out, all sorts of berries and leaves are being used as a surrogate . . . The difficulty of getting butter is increasing daily . . . no one will sell their butter even for very high prices.[24]

At every turn, shortages, ill-health and dark thoughts of a seemingly endless war were enough to leave Germany in a very black public mood on New Year's Eve 1917.

CHAPTER 12

WAR AT HOME AND *KAISERSCHLACHT* AT THE FRONT

JANUARY–MARCH 1918

On 1 January 1918, most German people felt numbed by the cold and numbed by the war, despite the end of the conflict on the Eastern Front. Every day was a day closer to the end of the war, but no one knew how many days, weeks or months that would take. There was a surreal atmosphere in the country and everyone went through the motions of 'normal life', but felt that they had left the gloom of the old year only to enter the darkness of the new one.

Ludendorff and Hindenburg would soon roll out the 1918 version of the ritual New Year promise of victory, but few would believe it unless it was tied to a firmer undertaking to win the war on the Home Front too. The German people steeled themselves for another massive military effort and another year of civilian deprivation, ill-health and yet more belt-tightening to see them through to an inevitable end, glorious or otherwise. To many it was undoubtedly the most dangerous and uncertain adventure of the whole war. On behalf of the Fatherland and in the name of the Kaiser, Ludendorff was about to throw down the gauntlet to fate and against an enemy who, if not crushed quickly, would destroy Germany.

By January 1918 public loyalty and respect towards the Kaiser was diminishing rapidly. Unrest was rife across Germany as conditions continued to deteriorate and the politicians and Ludendorff alike were increasingly criticised. But the Kaiser cut the saddest figure. Utterly devoid of any real authority, he found that the same people who greeted him so warmly a short time ago as a latter-day Caesar were now distributing leaflets in the back streets of Berlin proclaiming 'Down with the Kaiser, down with the Government'. The police were more likely to look the other way than arrest anyone carrying out such petty acts of treason.

It was not all doom and gloom for the German Army. At the end of 1917, Germany's one ray of hope lay on the Eastern Front, for after three years of costly

Entwicklung eines Kavallerie-Schützen-Regiments zum Gegenstoß.

German dismounted cavalry prepare to advance, machine gun on the flank, 1918.
(Postcard, Allen Collection)

defeats the Russian Army had collapsed and the nation had been thrown into turmoil by revolution. Revolution led swiftly to capitulation, the new regime suing for peace. By the beginning of March 1918, Ludendorff had three and a half million men, or 194 divisions, on the Western Front. Of these, 67 were concentrated between Arras and Quentin, outnumbering the British by nearly three to one.

But Ludendorff knew that such numerical advantages had not borne success in the past. Previous offensives had relied on massive, protracted artillery bombardments, designed to destroy enemy defences and thus enemy resistance. They had all failed. He realised that only novel attack methods would enable Germany to achieve victory.

He believed that the answer lay in the use of specially trained soldiers known as storm troops. Preceded by short but concentrated artillery barrages to the very depth of the enemy defences, the storm troops would attack the enemy trench lines. They aimed to bypass centres of resistance, and break through into the enemy rear areas. Here they would destroy headquarters, communications sites, and neutralise the enemy artillery.

Ludendorff's storm troop detachments were supported by specially selected and trained field artillery units. The storm troops were to be followed by 'assault units' consisting of infantry, machine gunners, trench mortar teams, engineers, sections of field artillery, and ammunition carriers. As well as being trained to help exploit the success of the storm troop units, they were practised in attacking strongly defended positions. They would also repel enemy counter-attacks. No obstacle should hold them up for long. Speed was paramount.

By exploiting success in this way, Ludendorff believed that the German offensive would develop an irresistible tide and achieve the elusive breakthrough.

On the other side of no-man's-land, Haig and his generals faced 1918 with little of Ludendorff's optimism. Given the exhaustion of their troops, he and the Allies knew that there was little choice but to hang on until the Americans could make a decisive difference to the course of the war. To repulse a likely German offensive, Haig realised that he needed to develop a new defensive system based on depth. He planned to adopt the German system that had so frustrated his troops at Passchendaele. The defences would be made up of a 'forward zone', or 'blue line', lightly manned, but with various strongpoints to blunt the initial attack; the 'battle zone', or 'red line', where the main fighting would take place; and finally the 'rear zone', or 'brown line'. British artillery, heavy machine guns and infantry counter-attacks on the 'brown line' would ultimately halt any German attack that got this far.

But Lloyd George's brake on British reinforcements being sent to France meant that Haig had fewer men than a year earlier. It made it very difficult for him to put his plan into practice. Worse still, the British had been forced to take over an additional 15 miles of the Allied Front from the French. Not only did this increase the pressure under which Haig was labouring, but it also placed him in a dilemma. He had to decide if he could risk weakening the line at any point to compensate for the extra frontage he had to defend.

The British sector was held by four armies; the Second in the North, then the First, Third, and finally the Fifth Army in the region of the River Somme. General Gough's Fifth Army was to take over the extension of the British front. But Haig decided that

General Erich von Ludendorff (on the right) prepares to 'punch a hole' in the British line in 1918. Ludendorff consults with the Kaiser (centre) and Field Marshal Paul von Hindenburg on the options for the Great Offensive in the West. *(IWM: Q23746)*

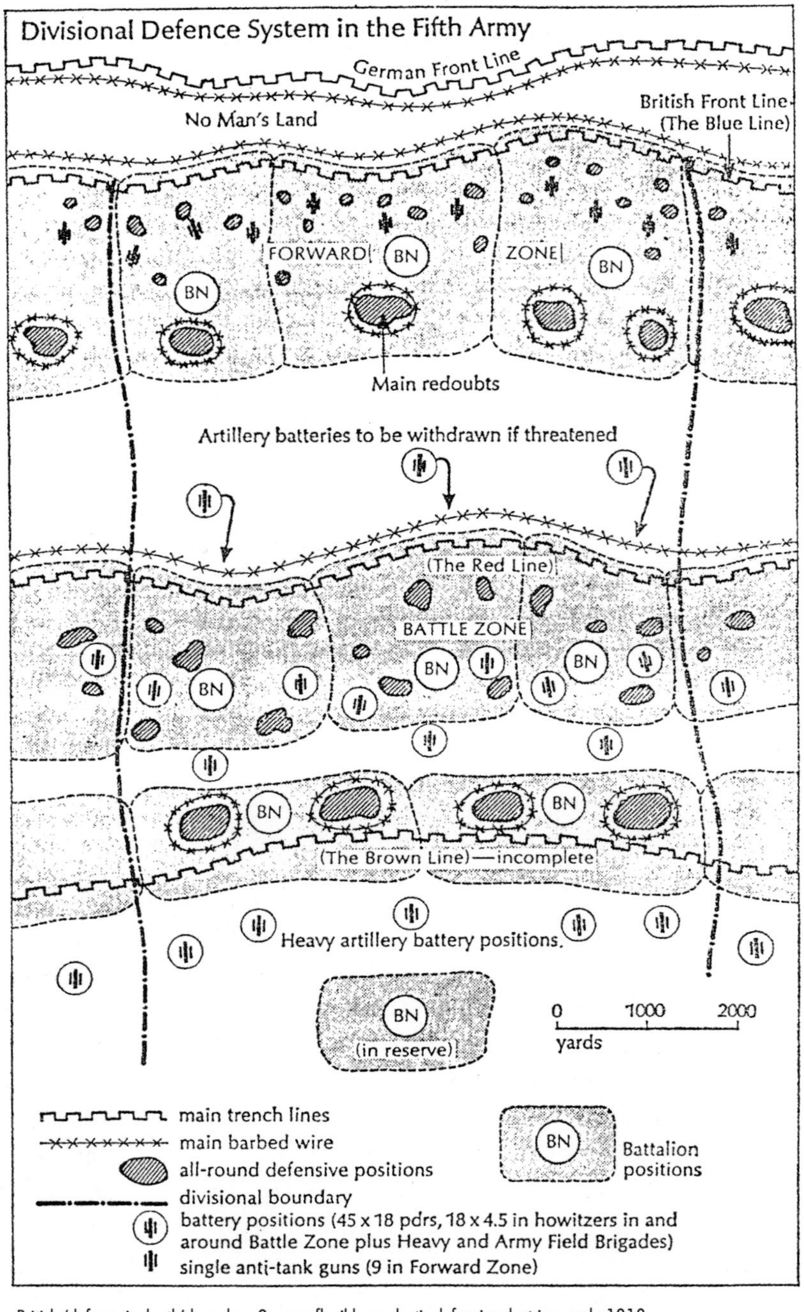

British 'defence-in-depth' based on German flexible or elastic defensive doctrine, early 1918.
(G.G. Wynne, If Germany Attacks)

he could not afford to reinforce Gough by much. The Fifth Army was therefore left to do its best to build its new defences in a desperate race against time.

The German troops began their final training for the March 1918 offensive in the West. They were certain that the deadlock would soon be over. One man wrote: 'Every German soldier on the Western Front felt that the decision of war and peace was at hand.'

The preparations for the offensive had been intense. Training centres were established in each army area. All infantry divisions, including those being transferred from the East to the Western Front, were given special instruction in infiltration techniques. Units already in the line were combed for the youngest, fittest and most battle-hardened men. These would become the backbone of the special storm troop detachments. Surprise and speed were the storm troops' principal tactics.

Many storm troops were issued with the 9mm Bergmann sub-machine gun, a novel weapon that was designed for close-quarter battle (CQB) and most of the company and platoon officers carried revolvers. However, the vast majority of the storm troopers still carried the 7.92mm Gewehr common to the German Army. The ubiquitous stick-grenade, or 'potato-masher' as it was known by the British soldiers, was one of the assault units' main weapons, held in special shoulder-slung pouches. This was characteristic of the *eingreif* troops used in defensive tactics prior to the great offensive.

Specially trained storm troop squads also used the flame-thrower, machine guns and trench mortars. German artillerymen were trained to shoot accurate artillery bombardments using maps rather than actual gunfire to register the guns on their targets, a method that had been used with such effect by the British prior to the opening phase of the Battle of Cambrai in November 1917.

Ludendorff's plan convinced his men that they were on the threshold of a great German victory. Trust in their commander at this time was total.

If ever a treaty made it abundantly clear why a nation should fight on against an ascendant enemy, Brest-Litovsk was the touchstone. On the Eastern Front a formal end to hostilities was reached on 3 March 1918 at Brest-Litovsk. The final treaty here between Germany and what was by then Communist Russia demonstrated precisely what peace on Germany's and, in particular, Ludendorff's terms would mean.

Under its conditions, Russia was forced to give up one third of her population, 50 per cent of her industry and 90 per cent of her coal production. Brest-Litovsk was punitive, over-reaching and evil in its intent. Anyone who has put hand on heart since and said that the First World War on the Western Front was futile is unlikely to have realised the significance of Brest-Litovsk. If Ludendorff's 'Grand Plan' for 1918 had succeeded, a similar 'Treaty of Paris', or, dare one suggest, 'Versailles Treaty' would have formally stripped France and Belgium at the very least of their assets.

Most important of all, as far as Ludendorff and Hindenburg were concerned, the elimination of Russia and operations across the Eastern Front, tacitly on the agenda since the armistice at Brest-Litovsk in November 1917, released precious assets that were expected to make the difference between losing and winning.

Back on the Western Front, the BEF in particular was recovering from the disappointments of 1917, with Passchendaele and the reverses at Cambrai after such spectacular beginnings still fresh in their minds. The experience of 1917 had changed the British soldier to some extent. Perhaps there was a greater fatalism; the old camaraderie had gone. One man remarked: 'There was still comradeship, but not the homely comradeship of the past.'

Those who were part of the desperately overstretched Fifth Army found the French defences they took over to be in poor condition, which placed an almost intolerable burden on them. General Gough's defences were the least developed in the British line.

Snatching the brief periods of rest they were allowed while out of line, the British troops hoped that when the German attack came they would not be in the trenches. Conversely, those manning the front line hoped that they would be at rest. Nevertheless, they did have a faith now in their ability to match the German soldier. There was an innate belief that they were gaining the upper hand against the Kaiser's men and that, despite the sacrifice, they would ultimately beat them in the field. The discouraging factor was when? To many the war seemed to be timeless, eternal; and now they knew that they would have to endure a German onslaught and further sacrifice if they were to bring the German war machine to a halt.

Haig, facing the awful responsibility of repulsing what he knew would be a massive German offensive when it came, put his faith firmly in his God and in his men. He believed firmly that their traditional patience, endurance, and fortitude would see them through what was set to be the sternest test of the war.

As March wore on there was an eerie sense of inevitability; the troops on both sides of the wire knew that the storm was about to break. Edwin Kühns, stationed near

German officers 'stock up' at the Gulaschkanone at the beginning of the 'Great Offensive in the West'. *(IWM: Q.55245)*

Cambrai, was fully aware that the planned onslaught would be a make-or-break effort. He had never before seen so many troops, guns and supply areas in his sector:

> The big offensive is now ready. All the villages near the Front are full of troops. Troop movement is on a massive scale . . . Everywhere, one sees that things are going to happen in the next few days. Yesterday we were issued with steel helmets. On the 15th of March four of us . . . took 20 minutes to get through the straggling village of Laurcourt to take over the Telephone Station. This is in a dugout . . . With so many soldiers here, they have to sleep outside. Absolutely everywhere is crammed with troops.[1]

Most of these troops were infantrymen who had trained for the forthcoming battle and now moved to their forward assembly areas a few days before the onslaught began. *Feldwebel* (Sergeant-Major) Max Schulz of 46th Infantry Regiment noted in his diary that:

> The whole regiment was paraded in Cambrai and our commander addressed us. He told us that we were going to take part in a great attack, that this would be the last big battle and that it would be decisive. We trusted our generals then and believed what he said. Our morale was very high. I thought of my parents and I prayed that God would bring me safely through it.[2]

Then, on the evening of 20 March, more than 6,000 guns and over 3,000 mortars were slotted into place just behind the 40-mile front and the assaulting infantry made their final move forward into their jumping off positions. It seemed to most German troops involved that this time they really would prevail. The planning, the training and the self-assurance that all had been considered down to the last detail gave them faith in their commanders and their own comrades with whom they were about to go over the top. In cramped dugouts and trenches, as the final hours, then minutes, ticked away there was time for reflection and for thoughts of home, or more simple pleasures:

> I didn't sleep much: too many things on my mind. I wasn't the only one. We thought of our next-of-kin, parents, wife or fiancée . . . [But] I hadn't even a sweetheart I was only twenty and I hadn't ever been with a woman. I wanted to survive to have that experience.[3]

Thousands of men were about to go over the top for the first time. Typically, they thought of whether they would meet the challenge and hoped above all not to let their *Kameraden* ('mates') down. Most wondered if they would survive, or be mown down by machine-gun fire soon after they had gone over the top. Either way, they were ready to do their bit and trusted in God and luck to see them through.

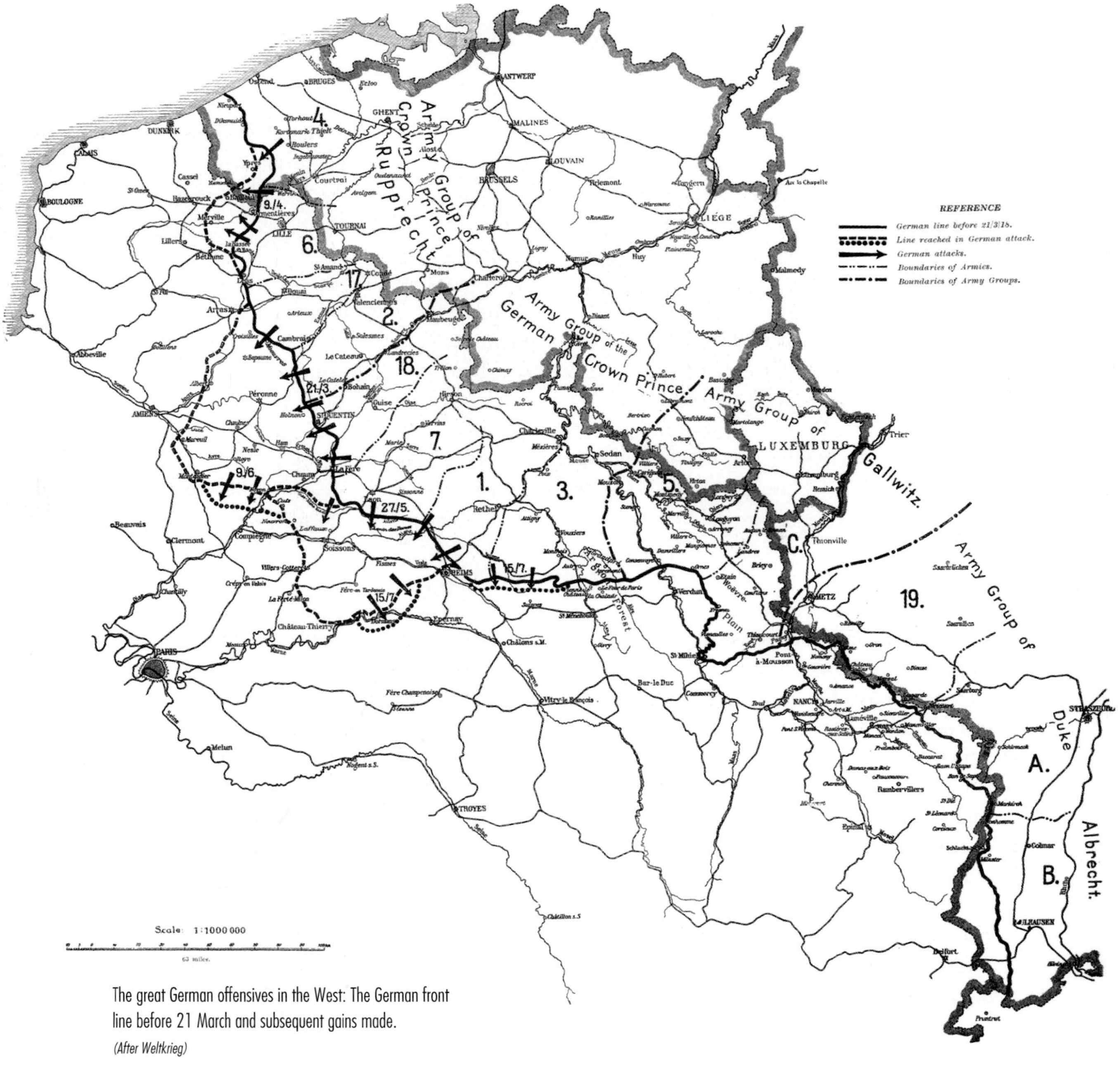

The great German offensives in the West: The German front line before 21 March and subsequent gains made.
(After Weltkrieg)

As the infantrymen wrestled with these final thoughts, the crews of the field guns, the 'heavies' and the thousands of mortars deployed across the whole attack front loaded their first shells and waited for the order to fire. The tension became unbearable.

At precisely 4.40 a.m. on 21 March 1918, Ludendorff struck: 6,423 guns and 3,532 mortars opened fire on the British defences. The barrage fell over a 40-mile front between the Sensée and Oise rivers. The effect was to inundate the entire length of the selected British sector between the forward positions and the battle zone.

Kaiserschlacht begins, 21 March 1918. German storm troops move forward near St Quentin. *(IWM: Q.55483)*

The British defenders were at first dazed by the sudden ferocity of the German bombardment. Then thousands of men began choking on the insidious poisoned gas mixed with the German high explosive shells. Desperately they reached for their gasmasks and tried to peer across no-man's-land through the impenetrable cloud that engulfed them. As the bombardment continued, Ludendorff's *sturmtruppen* had opened up the gaps in their own barbed wire defences in final preparation for the attack.

At last the waiting was over. At precisely 8.40 a.m. the first wave rose to their feet and crashed forward. Other waves soon followed. *Leutnant* Ernst Jünger recalled in his memoirs:

> The great moment had come. The fire lifted over the first trenches. We advanced . . . The turmoil of our feelings was called forth by rage, alcohol and the thirst for blood as we stepped out, heavily and yet irresistibly for the enemy lines.[4]

At first, it seemed that nothing would resist this human tidal wave as it began to storm through Haig's defensive lines. The German barrage moved 100 yards forward every two to three minutes, protecting the advancing men. Some British strongpoints, bypassed by the storm troops, continued to fight on until they were overwhelmed. The British guns also fought back until they were overrun or forced to withdraw by the speed of the German advance.

But the bitter, desperate fighting during the German assault was not without incidents of compassion on either side. Jünger, fired up by this long-felt desire to sweep away the enemy, pressed on ahead of his unit and suddenly discovered that he was on his own. Then,

> I caught my first sight of the enemy. A figure crouched, wounded apparently . . . in the middle of the pounded hollow of the road. I saw him start at the sight of me and stare . . . with wide-open eyes as I walked slowly up to him holding out my revolver . . . Grinding my teeth, I pressed the muzzle to the temple of this wretch, whom terror now crippled, and with my other hand, gripped hold of his tunic. With a beseeching cry, he snatched a photograph from his pocket and held it before my eyes . . . himself, surrounded by numerous family . . . I forced down my mad rage and walked past.[5]

Through the thick fog and preceded by the leading storm troop units, forty-three German assault divisions of the Second and Eighteenth Armies had risen up and attacked the British Fifth Army sector and a further nineteen divisions of the Seventeenth Army assaulted the British Third Army sector.

The British defenders were outnumbered and severely hampered by the impenetrable fog and deep-ranging heavy artillery fire. Many of the British artillery batteries were destroyed by German counter-battery fire or their gun crews were neutralised by the debilitating effects of gas shells. The British forward zone of defence quickly fell apart in places.

The short, but massive bombardment and the extensive use of gas shells within the *Bruchmüller* artillery fire plan left the ground relatively uncratered and assisted the initial German attacks and especially the infiltration tactics of the storm troops. The heavy mist, choking gas and breakdown in communications, as HQs were hit and telephone cables destroyed, added to British confusion.

The conditions masked the German advance as planned and the fog made it virtually impossible for many of the British strongpoints in the battle zone to support each other with interlocking machine-gun fire and vital artillery shoots into the mass of German assault troops. The situation looked most promising for General Oskar von Hutier's Eighteenth Army in the south where Fifth Army was weakest, and where its units had only just taken the line over from the French. Within hours, the German drive had slipped beyond the battle zone and threatened a break through in the British III Corps area. The right flank of General Gough's Fifth Army was forced back and then withdrew under fire to the Crozat canal.

The excellent progress of the Eighteenth Army masked the frustration of both Second and Seventeenth Armies in the centre and north of the attack sector. In the Cambrai sector, the plan to cut out the strong defences of the Flesquières salient by flanking attacks failed, leaving subsequent German units exposed to enfilade fire. The leading assault units of von der Marwitz's Second Army were unable to break through the British battle zones and Below's Seventeenth Army was held up by the well-prepared and immensely stronger defences of General Byng's British Third Army.

Nevertheless, by the end of the day, almost fifty German divisions had engaged in one of the most dramatic days of the whole war. The dazed but courageous men of General Gough's weakened Fifth Army had been thrown back by the sheer magnitude and shock effect of the German storm that had blasted them since dawn.

The early morning fog across the battlefront was a major ally for the German assault troops and blinded the British machine gunners, artillery observers and battalions manning the forward battle zones. There is little doubt, as events would prove a week later when Operation *Mars* was launched near Arras, that a clear day would have had a disastrous effect on the German offensive on 21 March. Martin Middlebrook's excellent study of the first day of *Kaiserschlacht* emphasises that without the fog that morning:

> . . . German infantry casualties . . . would have greatly exceeded the 40,000 men actually killed and wounded . . . and the German advance would have been halted in most places in front of the Battle Zone . . . The second phase of the battle would then have started under conditions much more favourable to the British . . .[6]

In the event, and despite numerous tales of heroic last stands and derring-do, 21 March was a disastrous day for Haig's BEF. It was the bloodiest day of the First World War. There were over 78,000 casualties, almost 40,000 on each side.[7] Though the *sturmtruppen* had advanced in one or two places up to ten miles by the end of the day in the south, overall, 21 March was a day of great sacrifice and confusion.

Most vexing for the German High Command would be the fact that although the total casualty figures were around 40,000 each, the British included no less than 21,000 prisoners (PoWs) and the remainder comprised 7,512 killed and 10,000 wounded, a sub-total of just over 17,500. This compares with a mere 300 German prisoners, but a massive 10,000-plus dead and 28,778 wounded, a sub-total of almost 39,000 killed or wounded.[8] It was a haemorrhage of manpower that Ludendorff could not possibly sustain.

Added to this, after the events of 21 March unfolded, Ludendorff had to contend with the reality and frustration of only partial success. Less than a quarter of the first day's objectives had been achieved, and at great cost. Furthermore, the unexpected achievement by Hutier's Eighteenth Army in the south led Ludendorff down a fatal 'garden path'. Ever the opportunist, and never the strategist, he would reinforce the southern thrust and send it bowling across the Somme countryside on a one-way ticket to nowhere of any tactical, operational or strategic consequence. The subsequent events of the spring offensives would dramatically prove the point that 'German strategy, both in peace and war, has always been opportunist, and concerned with looking for weak places rather than with formal objectives'.[9]

The fact that *Kaiserschlacht*, the Kaiser's battle, had begun without the stunning success expected was reflected at Supreme headquarters by Admiral Georg Müller, one of the Kaiser's chief advisers, who noted in his diary:

> *21st March:* . . . After lunch we drove in the direction of St Quentin to the 1st Guards Division in billets at the village of Essigny. Lightly wounded men were on their way down the line . . . Back in the train at 7 p.m. . . . The results of the offensive are not

> very satisfactory for the first day. [We were told] after supper that the British had taken a terrific pasting. Actually, the day's objectives were not reached.
> *22nd March:* The mood at breakfast was low. We must reckon with the possibility that the offensive might come to a standstill. The High Command were blamed for their undue optimism . . .[10]

Either way, the die was cast. Germany's 'Great gamble in the West' was under way and her fate now rested squarely on the shoulders of General Ludendorff.

The German tide continued to break across the British defences and further storm troop units and attack divisions were thrown into battle. Operation *Michael* seemed unstoppable, especially in the Fifth Army's sector, and British defences continued to crumble. By 24 March, they had driven the British back some fifteen miles. Some 50,000 prisoners had fallen into German hands, together with hundreds of artillery guns. By now, the Seventeenth, Second and Eighteenth Armies had all enjoyed success to some degree.

Hutier's Eighteenth Army was now opening a serious gap in the British line and the mood at Supreme HQ was somewhat different to that of the first 24 hours of the offensive. Admiral Müller noted ironically that on the evening of 23 March:

> His Majesty returned from Avesnes (Ludendorff and Hindenburg's forward HQ) bursting with news of our success. To the guard on the platform he shouted as the train pulled in: 'The battle is won, the English have been utterly defeated.' There was champagne for dinner. The communiqué was read telling of our great victory under the personal leadership of His Majesty the Emperor, a well-meaning lie by the Hindenburg-Ludendorff firm, which the German people will not believe for one moment.[11]

The generous accolade by Hindenburg and Ludendorff may well have been prompted by the ecstatic Kaiser's gesture in decorating Ludendorff with the Iron Cross with Golden Rays for the victory that he believed was at hand. It was, incidentally, the first time that it had been awarded for more than a century.[12]

But though the British Fifth Army had been sorely pressed and the Seventeenth and Eighteenth Armies had scored notable successes, the decisive breakthrough still eluded them. Despite the Kaiser's great optimism, *Kaiserschlacht* was by no means at an end, let alone won.

The ambivalent attitude of doubt then optimism among the German leadership as the *Kaiserschlacht* tide swept on was not shared by the British and French High Command. Both Haig and Pétain knew that the British were in trouble, and Haig was already rushing reinforcements from the northern sector of his front to plug the gaps in his defences. Though the British withdrawal continued in places as other sectors held firm, the BEF commander became increasingly concerned about the important road and rail centre at Amiens and the lines of communication to the ports beyond it.

Haig believed that only French assistance could guarantee that the desperate, though determined efforts of his men to prevent a German breakthrough would succeed. Contrary to the tales of many historians who suggest otherwise, Haig recommended that a 'battle conference' was held to consider and agree on a joint Anglo-French response to the German onslaught. He duly met his French counterparts on 26 March at Doullens. As a result, Marshal Ferdinand Foch was appointed as the Allied Generalissimo. Although Foch's authority was limited, his appointment did at least end the dangerous independence of the national commanders, ensuring closer cooperation between them, which undoubtedly strengthened British and French resolve.

By the next day, it appeared to the Kaiser, Hindenburg, Ludendorff and OHL that *Kaiserschlacht* was poised to at last achieve the desired breakthrough. On the face of it, the achievement, so oft quoted by those who imagine the German spring offensives of 1918 as the whisker away from victory, was extraordinary. In less than a week, Operation *Michael*, part one of the *Kaiserschlacht* proper, had punched a hole up to 40 miles deep into British territory.

But this great leap forward, the like of which had not been seen since 1914, was illusory. The successes had been most evident in the south and this was where Ludendorff had reinforced to exploit it.

There is no question that the front-runners in the 'Hindenburg Stakes' had advanced up to 40 miles beyond the front line that existed until the early hours of 21 March. Yet they were the front-runners and did not represent a general advance to anything like that depth. In most places north of Hutier's most successful penetration of the British line, the assault had gained fifteen miles at most, and achieved much less in the northern sector of the Somme region. Furthermore, the 40 miles gained were in the wrong place, for the direction taken was to the south west and not the sweeping wheel northwest, which was Ludendorff's original intention.

In the real world, Ludendorff could not hope to sustain this advance anyway because of the poor logistic tail that had struggled since the first day to sustain the ravenous demands of the German infantry and artillery as it pressed forward. The storm troop units had no integral logistic back up and relied on ammunition, food and water from the resupply of the attack divisions behind them. Logistic support across 40 miles of devastated countryside was a virtually impossible task for the German 'Q' branches and unit quartermasters without plentiful motorised and horse-drawn transport and huge engineer support in laying new road-track ways, railways and providing light railway rolling stock. Many of the transport columns that were organised and despatched towards the forward battle areas constantly ran the gauntlet of bombing and strafing by British aircraft.

On top of the massive logistical problems that existed, Ludendorff now had another fundamental flaw in the plan to contend with: how to exploit tactical success. He could not do it with either cavalry or tanks. Only nine tanks were used on 21 March – and five of those were captured British Mk IVs. Only seventeen of the lumbering

German A7V tank variant were built and their size (33 tons), crew of no less than 18 men and 'cross country' speed of around 2mph rendered them virtually useless anyway. The cavalry divisions were mainly on duty in Russia. As a result, the giant cracks in Ludendorff's assertion that strategy would take care of itself if the tactics worked were being exposed. It was noted that:

> As the year would show, the days of cavalry as an arm of exploitation on a modern battlefield were over; yet, feeble as it was, the cavalry was the only exploiting arm that existed. [For the Germans] to launch an offensive intended to win the war with none at all was not just foolish: it was criminal.[13]

Although it was not yet apparent, the tide was turning against Ludendorff. By the fourth week of March 1918, the British had been severely battered by the German offensive. But Ludendorff had not yet achieved his declared aim: complete breakthrough and the destruction of the British resolve to fight on.

On 27 March, the French Reserve Army under General Fayolle, to the south of the continued thrust into the guts of General Gough's Fifth Army, faced thirteen divisions of General von Hutier's Eighteenth Army. Hutier's attacking force had four rested divisions and was well supported by field and medium artillery. Fayolle had ten divisions, of which two were cavalry. Despite fierce resistance along the line throughout the day, Fayolle was forced back so that the German 206th Division managed to enter the road and rail centre of Montdidier.

On that same day in the BEF sector, the Fifth Army had a mere nine weak divisions against fifteen German divisions drawn from III Korps of Hutier's Eighteenth Army and XIV Korps of General Marwitz's Second Army to the north. Only six of the divisions had been first-line units on the opening day of Operation *Michael*.

The events of 27 March were a clear indicator of the problems of British doggedness in defence and breakdown in command and control that Ludendorff's plans had failed to take full account of, or had ignored. Such lack of foresight, based largely on a characteristically dogmatic approach, was costing the soldiers under the German High Command very dear. In an epic encounter at Rosières, south-east of Amiens, *General-Leutnant* Lüttwitz's III Korps planned to smash through the British defensive line held by *General-Leutnant* Watts' XIX Corps. By now, the British had learned and applied the hard lessons of the beginning of Operation *Michael* and the German attacks were more predictable than they had expected.

Consequently, from strong dug-in positions, field gun batteries continued to fire and hold their ground, and well-sited machine guns held their fire until the first German attacking waves were within a few hundred yards, then hit them with devastating fire. In front of Rosières, the British defenders refused to give ground, despite wave after wave of desperate German attacks. Even the elite 4th Guards Division was held up for over four hours by a 16th Irish Division, which was already weakened by 50 per cent casualties.

Lüttwitz's men must have been demoralised by such tenacity. But the troops of 208th Division, assaulting Harbonnières just south of the St Quentin to Amiens road, were incredulous when their attack was stopped by the 'death or glory' ride in a counter-attack by Brigadier-General Riddell, leading the remnants of his Brigade on a 'borrowed' artillery horse. By nightfall, though some German penetration had occurred, the British line had either been restored, or a new line had been consolidated against further attacks. Over 1,000 German prisoners were taken, with at least the same number dead and missing; rather more than the British losses in this sector on that day.

The German losses were as high as those suffered by the British, but many of the German troops killed were Ludendorff's irreplaceable storm troops. Those that were designated to take their place further weakened many of the infantry divisions that followed them into battle, were not fully trained for the role and thus inexperienced by comparison.

This stripping of 'ordinary' units to reinforce the depleted storm troop formations caused ever more resentment from commanders and the rank and file who remained in those units. Many complained that specialists, such as signallers, medics and transport personnel, were being transferred to front-line infantry units to make good the shortfall caused by those infantry battalions having to provide still more of the under thirty-fives for storm troop duties.[14]

Ludendorff's surviving troops were becoming exhausted by the intensity and unrestrained stress of battle. Also, they were running out of essential supplies such as food, water and ammunition. The shortages were already apparent even among units in the rear and HQ staffs. Edwin Kühns noted in his diary in the final week of March that:

> At this time, the food got worse. [Then] on Easter Sunday, we had nothing except half a loaf of bread per man . . . Everyone was miserable, as they were so hungry. A comrade brought a joint of horsemeat from a horse that had been killed, which we had to roast, but everyone had only about a quarter of a pound. That was the first horsemeat that I had knowingly eaten. It was very tough, but it tasted good.[15]

Still determined to achieve outright victory, Ludendorff launched Operation *Mars* on 28 March to trap the northern British armies by striking northwest from Arras. *Mars* was to be the crowning glory of the first week of the great offensive and it was designed to pull the hinges off the British defensive door, preparing the way for the German breakout and sweep towards the channel ports.

The normally cautious Rupprecht had great hopes for Operation *Mars*, and was moved to note in his diary: 'We stand immediately before the success of the final breakthrough.'[16]

But Ludendorff's plans had already begun to unravel. The storm troops were being lost against an increasingly tenacious British defence. The British and Dominion troops of the Fifth and Third Armies continued to fight and to hold on. When the German bombardment lifted on the morning of 28 March and Operation *Mars* was launched, there was no thick, swirling mist to cover the German advance, the preparatory bombardment was not as concentrated as on 21 March and the infantry tactics were less sophisticated.

A total of 29 assault divisions were assigned, with 16 in reserve, on a 33-mile front, but 12 divisions attacked between Lens in the north and Hendecourt in the south, towards Arras. By this time Haig's troops knew what to expect and mowed down the German troops as they came forward.

> [When] the smoke cleared . . . 200 yards in front [of our trench] were the enemy in full view bearing down on us in a compact and huddled mass . . . I counted five lines, each . . . five deep . . . In an instant the rattle of rapid fire, a fire sustained almost continuously for an hour till rifles were red hot . . .[17]

With the exception of some progress on the right flank, the assault was an abject failure and some ground was actually lost to the 3rd Australian Division. Almost two years on, it could have been a re-run of 1 July 1916, but with a German massacre before the wire and under the deadly machine guns and artillery of the British defenders. Eyewitnesses described the fruitless German attacks:

> The Germans came on time after time with the greatest bravery, sometimes almost shoulder to shoulder, each time assured that it required but one more effort to break the British front, only to be held and then repulsed by the combined force of guns, machine guns and rifles.[18]

The assault divisions took massive casualties for little territorial gain and thousands more were taken prisoner. A follow-on assault, Operation *Valkyrie*, which was planned as an exploitation phase after a *Mars* success, was quickly cancelled. The God of War had changed sides and meted out terrible destruction on the hapless German infantry. It is significant that both the German and British official histories have little to say except to underline the slaughter, for slaughter it was.

The disastrous results of Operation *Mars* were matched by the stench of deception that began to waft across the battlefield. The German assault troops now realised to their horror, as they overran British supply depots, that their resources were poor by comparison. Drained by continual battle, but euphoric in their achievements to date, they began to lose much of their renowned self-discipline. On the same day that their comrades were being slaughtered near Arras, many who had attacked across the former Somme battlefield of 1916 reached Albert. The results were rather odd:

> Today the advance of our infantry suddenly stopped near Albert. Nobody could understand why . . . Our way seemed entirely clear [and] . . . our division was right in

front of the advance, and could not possibly be tired out . . . As soon as I got near the town I began to see strange figures, which looked very little like soldiers, and certainly showed no sign of advancing, were making their way back out of town. There were men driving cows before them on a line . . . Men carrying a bottle of wine under one arm and another one open in their hand . . . Men dressed up in comic disguise. Men with top hats on their heads. Men staggering. Men who could hardly walk . . . When I got into the town the streets were running with wine.[19]

Exhaustion led to indiscipline, albeit briefly, as the troops at Albert were soon ordered forward once more. But Operations *Michael* and *Mars* had failed to find the formula for the promised breakthrough. Amiens remained an elusive prize and the

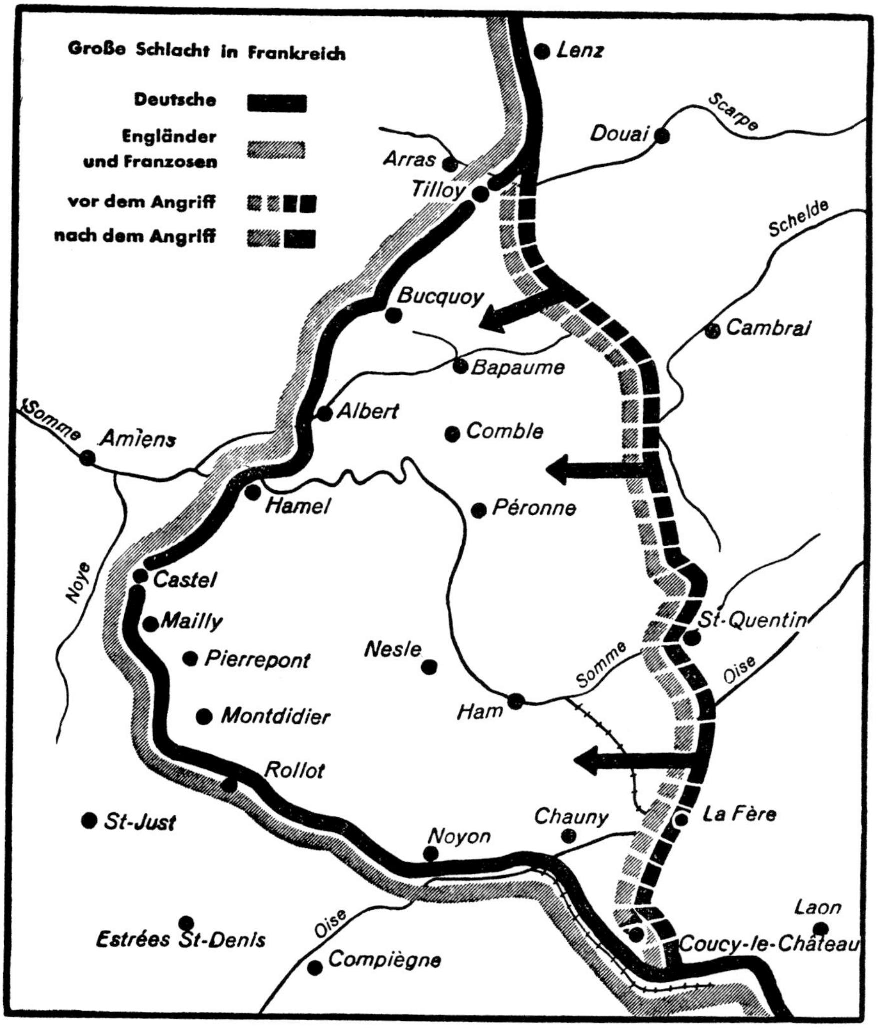

Kaiserschlacht: Die Michael Schlacht im März – Operation *Michael* and German gains made between 21 March and 5 April 1918.
(Rudolph Stratz, Weltkrieg)

great advance had swung towards the south-west, rather than the north-west, capturing little more than the land devastated by the Somme battles in 1916 and the ground ravaged by the Germans themselves in their withdrawal to the *Siegfried Stellung*, or Hindenburg Line, twelve months before.

Fatigue, the psychological blow of the huge losses sustained and disillusion had all taken their toll by the end of March. By then, most units could go no further and they were forced to go on the defensive. It had been an extraordinary week; but the British, supported by the French, had held. The first crisis was over for the Allies at least.

For all the Kaiser's men, the end of March brought a depressing realisation that the promised swift victory, like that promised four years earlier, was one that may go begging. The momentum of each assault, and that needed to sustain the offensive were dependent on manpower and horsepower respectively. The lack of motorised

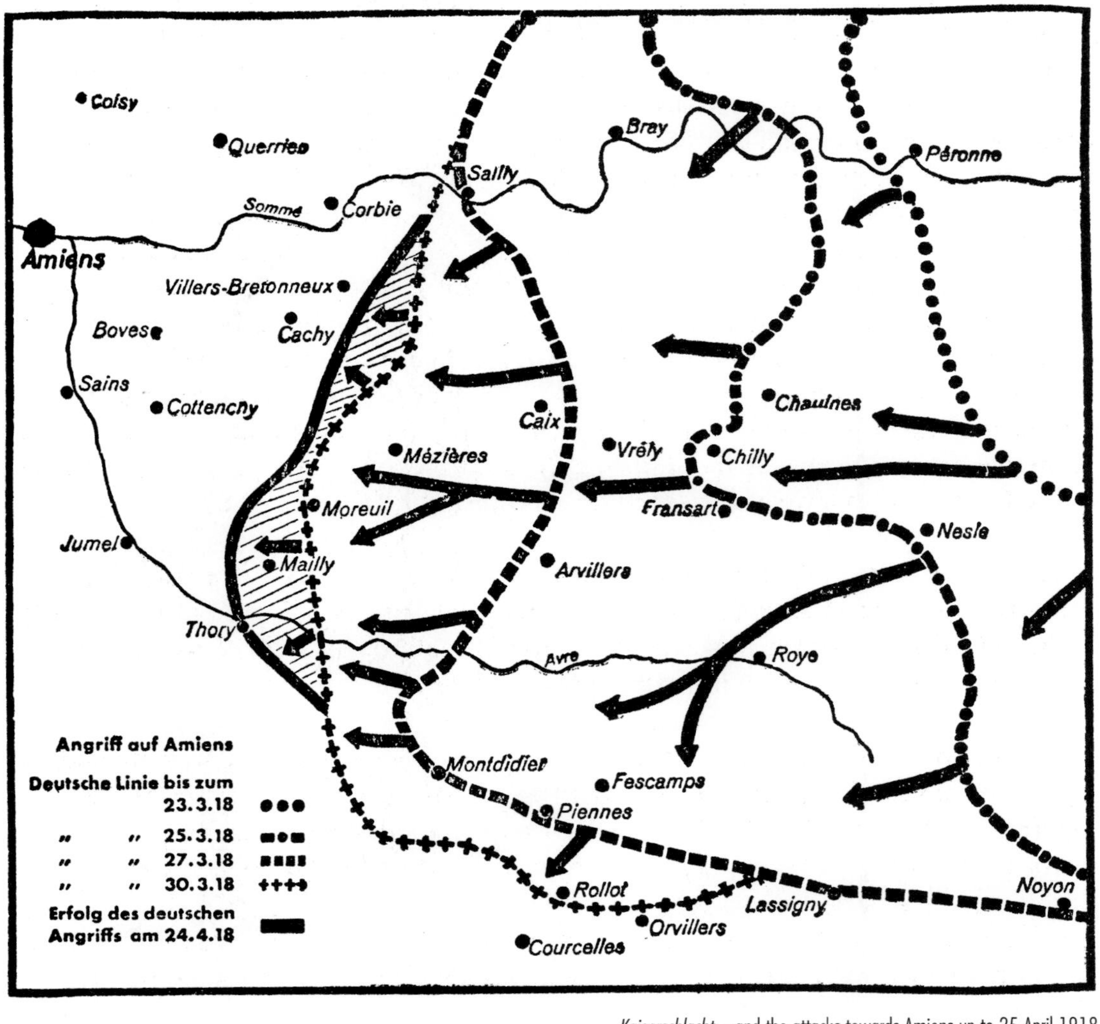

Kaiserschlacht – and the attacks towards Amiens up to 25 April 1918.
(Rudolph Stratz, Weltkrieg)

transport made the movement of troops, weapons, ammunition (especially artillery ammunition), and other supplies more difficult to move between the railheads and forward positions. Even the horse-drawn transport was nowhere near as plentiful as it should have been to sustain an offensive on this scale.

The problem became progressively worse once the offensives were shifted from Picardy and the Somme to Flanders, then the French sectors. In short, German logistics support was an immensely complex problem at the beginning of *Kaiserschlacht*. Within a week it had become a monstrous and ever-present nightmare.

Ludendorff's most precious and finite commodity, the German soldier, was the motor and dictated the mobility of the German Army throughout the offensive. The pace of the advance was thus entirely dependent on stamina and the speed of the advance on foot. Ludendorff had precious few tanks, no armoured cars and negligible cavalry, and so relied heavily on his storm troops and attack divisions to develop and maintain the momentum of each assault. The horrendous casualties among the storm troops in particular merely highlighted the differences between the elite assault units and the other divisions.

Although the *Michael* offensive had forced huge gaps in the British Fifth Army line and advanced up to 40 miles in places, it was at great cost and for little, if any, strategic advantage. General Gough had been a most prominent British casualty when relieved of his command, but his battered divisions had not broken. Within a week, Ludendorff had lost in excess of 250,000 men in an offensive that had promised so much on the first day, but was doomed once it became clear that the British refused to crack.

British casualties in the same period were 178,000, but almost half were prisoners of war, and the French had lost around 77,000. But the German casualties were excessively high. Such losses would be unsustainable if the rate continued.

Losses were one thing, but failure to crack the British defences open had led to a fateful downturn in morale. On 30 March, attacks on the left flank by the Second Army were as ineffective as those during the abortive Operation *Mars*. One Regiment of the German 18th Division involved on 30 March recorded:

> There was little time for preparation, poor artillery support and the English machine guns were so well hidden that they could not be knocked out. [Overall] the power of the attack was exhausted. Spirits sank to zero. The division suffered a reverse the like of which it had not yet experienced.[20]

Ludendorff needed to consolidate and maximise the strength that remained. But logic and cool thinking were not qualities that he had in abundance after the failure of Operation *Michael*. Despite fixing on another major offensive in the Lys/Flanders sector to the north, as March turned into April, he attempted to revive the offensive on the Somme by seizing Amiens.

Officially, Ludendorff sought to exploit his southern flank and sweep into Amiens before the British or French could consolidate their defences in front of the city. The

Seventh, Eighteenth and Seventeenth Armies would hold on to their gains and stand fast until the Second Army had pushed on to Amiens.

The Second Army's attempt failed: its leading assault wave, including the 9th Bavarian Reserve and Guards *Ersatz* Division, was blocked and then driven back in front of Villers-Bretonneux, some 10 miles short of Amiens, by the Australian 9th Brigade and British 14th and 18th Divisions. German accounts reported that:

> The Bavarian Division was forced to withdraw in the face of strong counter-attacks . . . [and] the Guards Ersatz Division, on its left, had reached Cachy (just south of Villers-Bretonneux), but also lost the ground that it had gained that afternoon.[21]

Crown Prince Rupprecht noted on the evening of 5 April:

> Orders were issued on the evening of the 4th [of April] to continue the attack on the 5th, but it was then discovered that the Allies had offered 'a particularly obstinate resistance' . . . and it was no longer possible to throw the enemy back . . .[22]

German operations on 5 April led the Kaiser's generals to ponder on another costly disappointment. Rupprecht was forced to concede that:

> The final result of the day is the unpleasant fact that our offensive has come to a complete stop, and its continuation without careful preparation promises no success.[23]

Ludendorff had admitted by this time that, by the end of 4 April, 'The enemy's resistance was beyond our strength,' and, bizarrely, given the butcher's bill in German casualties, that: 'We must not get drawn into a battle of attrition [as this] would not suit our strategic or tactical situation.'[24]

Rupprecht's impressive Chief-of-Staff, General Hermann von Kuhl, summed up the opening fortnight of the German spring offensive by stating that:

> Strategic success was illusory with 'Operation *Michael*' [and *Mars*] . . . the great tactical success had cost heavy sacrifices, some ninety divisions in all having to be engaged. The conclusion of the fighting left our troops . . . in very unfavourable positions, which led to extraordinary wastage.[25]

But Ludendorff called it a 'brilliant feat', which had cost much of the cream of his specially trained storm troops and first-line divisions. It had cost him personal loss also, as his youngest son Erich was shot down on 23 March and he had personally identified the body.[26]

The next throw of the dice would be where perhaps *Kaiserschlacht* should have been launched in the first place: Flanders and the Lys valley.

Chapter 13

Friedenssturm – The Greatest Myth of the War

April–July 1918

With the bloody debacle of Operation *Mars*, *Kaiserschlacht* was effectively finished in the Somme and Scarpe sectors. In spite of this catastrophe, Ludendorff was still convinced that the British must remain the main target. He hurriedly prepared to mount yet another offensive, this time in the area of the River Lys and around Ypres in the north of the British sector. Ludendorff's sense of humour was still intact, for the March offensive that had seen the failure of the main element of *Kaiserschlacht* now had an overarching name for the following offensives, *Friedenssturm*, or the peace offensive. *Friedenssturm* would lead to peace; but not quite the way Ludendorff had planned.

Preceded by Operation *Archangel* as a diversionary attack in the French Aisne sector on 6 April, Operation *Georgette* was to take place in Flanders, and aimed to capture the vital railhead at Hazebrouck and then cut off the BEF from its supply routes and rear areas as far as the coast. The operation was renamed *Georgette* rather than George, its original codename: plans had to be scaled down, as the German losses in March had been so heavy. *Georgette* was to be launched on 9 April, Ludendorff's 53rd birthday.

The German Sixth Army, under General Ferdinand von Quast, was ordered to attack between Armentières and Givenchy to tear the British defences apart and advance north-west to the important road and rail junction at Hazebrouck. On 10 April, General Sixt von Armin's Fourth Army was to assault the Ypres salient sector, and wrest the Messines ridge from British hands. Armin was determined to finally pinch out the 'Salient' where his Fourth Army had suffered so badly during the Messines and Third Ypres/Passchendaele campaign the previous year.

The German plan appeared sound, but the British defences were stronger here than had been the case on 21 March and not surprisingly many of the German divisions

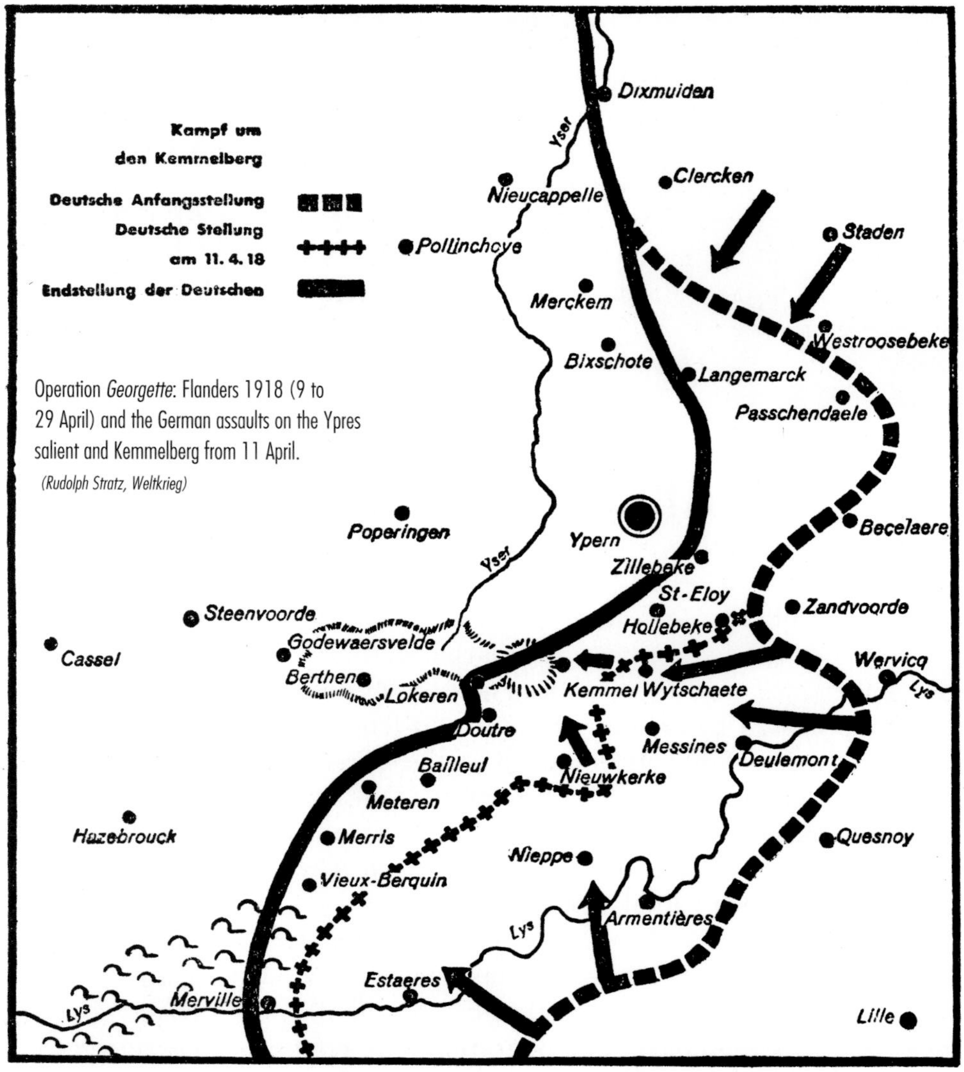

Operation *Georgette*: Flanders 1918 (9 to 29 April) and the German assaults on the Ypres salient and Kemmelberg from 11 April.
(Rudolph Stratz, Weltkrieg)

were inferior to those used in Operation *Michael*. Fifty per cent of the assault units tasked for Georgette were hastily trained, but second echelon 'trench' as opposed to 'attack' divisions. The one German advantage was that the BEF in this sector was desperately short of reserves to plug any gaps that may be forced in the British line.

Von Quast had eight attack divisions in the first assault wave and six in the second against four British divisions – from north to south the 34th, 40th, 2nd Portuguese and 55th – defending the sector between Armentières and Bethune. None of the fourteen German divisions had taken part in the March offensives and were brought into action after retraining for the assault from a period at rest out of the line. The 43rd Reserve Division, which faced 55th Division in the south of the attack sector, had come from Russia.[1]

The offensive was mounted on 9 April as planned and opened with the typical *Durch-Bruchmüller* bombardment. A familiar pattern soon emerged. As with Operation *Michael*, the attack was made through thick fog and, with the damage and further obscuration caused by the massive bombardment, the German offensive began with some excellent progress, which included brushing the dispirited 2nd Portuguese Division aside and advancing up to three and a half miles towards Hazebrouck by the end of the first day. The 1st Bavarian Reserve Regiment of the 1st Bavarian Reserve Division attacking in the Portuguese sector recorded in its war diary that: 'The trench garrisons surrendered after only feeble resistance.' The 141st Regiment of the 35th Division reported:

> First system taken without resistance. In the second our first prisoners were taken. 9.45 a.m., stiff resistance at strongpoint V captured and 70 Portuguese taken [prisoner].

The 42nd Division, assaulting the line on the left flank of the Portuguese defence and the right-hand units of the 40th Division, broke through all the hostile positions

Operation *Georgette*, launched on 9 April 1918. Assault troops pass through British defences in Flanders under cover of the smoke and fog of war. *(IWM: Q.55481)*

and cut an uninterrupted swathe to Estaires and Bac St Maur on the River Lys. By the afternoon, the leading units were across the river and preparing to advance still further. Its progress, and that of the 1st and 8th Bavarian Reserve Divisions to its left, depended on equal success by the German attacks to their south.

The hapless Portuguese were unwittingly providing Ludendorff with an early birthday present, but elsewhere the promise of breakthrough was left cruelly unfulfilled. As the German 42nd Division swept all before it, the German assault was about to be stopped in its tracks by the bloody-minded determination of one British division near Givenchy.

The British 55th Division was deployed on the extreme right of the British sector facing the German onslaught, its troops dug in and up against the German IV Korps, with three divisions, the 18th Reserve, 43rd Reserve and 4th *Ersatz* Divisions, in the leading assault waves.[2] The divisions attacked under the impression that they were facing a 'tired British division . . . only fit for holding a quiet sector of the line'.[3] They were soon put to rights. The 55th Division was fully prepared to meet any attack and, in stark contrast to their Portuguese neighbours, every man was aware of his responsibilities in resisting the German thrust. As the battle developed to their left, the men of the 55th Division formed a defensive flank to shore up their own defences against a German breakthrough from the Portuguese sector.

At 9 a.m., large groups of assault troops from the 18th Reserve Division appeared close to the newly established defensive flank on 55th Division's left. As soon as they could be seen plainly through the mist, the advancing Germans were cut down and the survivors driven back to seek shelter in the former Portuguese positions. When the main German attack against 55th Division was launched at 8.45 a.m. the German troops were well protected by the fog and a most effective creeping barrage.

The leading assault wave was on top of the forward defences before the British defenders could react. But once the barrage lifted, the momentum of the attack was lost almost immediately as the groups that had penetrated the British defences were killed or captured and the following waves were chopped up by machine-gun, rifle, artillery and mortar fire.

Despite this setback, the attackers of the 43rd Reserve and 4th *Ersatz* Divisions were determined to break the back of 55th Division's defence. By 10 a.m. they had worked their way forward to Givenchy church and were close to the canal on the Cuinchy road. They appeared to be on the threshold of success, but the pendulum swung once again over the next two hours as the British strongpoints held out and counter-attacks drove back the desperate German efforts to hold on to their gains.

By midday the British defenders had largely restored the situation. Further attacks continued in the afternoon and some German troops managed to infiltrate beyond the main defences and close in on field artillery in action, only to be killed or driven back by the guns firing point-blank at them. The German assaults were beaten back time after time, and when the fog began to clear, the disastrous nature of the attack on the

55th Division became apparent as the wire in front of their defences was seen festooned with dead and dying German troops. The final act came with the capture of no less than 640 Germans trapped within the network of British barbed wire and left with no choice but to surrender. Two German battalion commanders and their tactical staff groups, over a hundred machine guns and automatic rifles and over 620 officers and men, including a band with its instruments, were taken.[4]

This motley crew of German troops and two COs from battalions of the 4th Ersatz Division was the last 'main event' within the 55th Division's area. Operation *Georgette* had mixed results by the end of its first day, but in the south, it had been stopped in its tracks by a well-trained, disciplined and stubborn defence. German accounts acknowledged their failure against 55th Division, although not always accurately. Rupprecht noted on the evening of 9 April:

> In Givenchy, the 55th Division, a particularly good Scottish [*sic*] division, offered obstinate resistance.[5]

The last word on this day and this German 'difficulty' had to go to Ludendorff himself, who wrote that:

> In the evening [in the north] we were advancing towards Armentières, had reached the Lys and we were approaching the Lawe. In the direction of Béthune we made little progress. On the left, at Givenchy and Festubert, we were held up. The result was not satisfactory.[6]

The 55th Division had spoiled Ludendorff's birthday as surely as it had been spoiled in 1917 on the opening day of the British Arras offensive.[7]

On the 10th, General von Armin's Fourth Army launched its assault against the blood-soaked Messines ridge, where the British had blown the formerly 'impregnable' German defences of Wytschaete Bogen apart in June the previous year. It was defended by IX British Corps, and Messines by 25th Division, which had taken part in the British offensive here in 1917. The Fourth Army attacked with two Korps, XVIII. Reserve in the north and X Reserve in the south, each with two divisions in the first assault waves.

The preliminary bombardment began at 2.45 a.m. and the main assault was launched promptly at 5.15 a.m. through thick mist and over previously laid pontoon bridges across the Lys. The 17th Reserve Division, of XVIII Korps, captured Messines and then some of the ridge as they advanced beyond the village, but the leading battalions were rapidly stopped near Wulverghem by stiff British resistance and then counter-attacks. Units of the 49th Reserve Division (of Fourth Army reserve) were sent in to support the 17th Reserve Division and held a defensive line against the British counter-moves between Hill 63 and the southern end of Messines across the Douve valley for the rest of the day.

To their south, X Korps had attacked with the 31st and 214th Divisions in the van and pushed forward to take Ploegsteert Wood, Ploegsteert village and the northern part of the Armentières sector. Parties of German assault troops from the 31st Division infiltrated through the forward British positions in Ploegsteert Wood, but a rock-solid defence soon repulsed the main attacks. The 214th Division captured Ploegsteert village and then resolutely held on to its gains despite several fierce British counter-attacks.

General von Quast's Sixth Army resumed its attacks after 9 April at 6.00 a.m. on 10 April. North to south, II, Bavarian Korps, XIX, and LV Korps pushed on between Nieppe/Steenwerck and Givenchy/Festubert after regrouping and replenishment overnight. All along the front, the Sixth Army advance was stalled by determined counter-attacks and losses mounted drastically. Both OHL and Rupprecht's Group of Armies HQ made every effort to rush in reinforcements, mainly from Seventeenth Army, to press home the attacks. With these new units expected overnight, orders were issued to the Sixth Army on the evening of 10 April to take the high ground around Meteren and Bailleul on the Franco-Belgian border and to capture the crossings over the La Bassée canal on the following day.

Captured, but defiant. British prisoners during Operation *Georgette*.
(IWM: 55254)

Ludendorff achieved one major result from the German efforts on 10 April – the British evacuation of Armentières, which lay between the converging attacks of Sixt von Armin's Fourth and von Quast's Sixth Armies. Although British resistance had already been fierce and a number of Operation *Georgette*'s aims had been frustrated, Ludendorff still believed that the 'English' would crack under the continued pressure. He would have been greatly encouraged by Field Marshal Haig's appeals for French assistance in the face of the German onslaught, which appeared to go unheeded. The fact remained that by early on 11 April, the forward units of Sixth Army were less than five miles from the vital town of Hazebrouck and both British and French chiefs had every reason to be most concerned about the implications of its loss. On 11 April, Field Marshal Haig issued a special order of the day in which he emphasised that:

> There is no other course open to us but to fight it out. Every position must be held to the last man: there must be no retirement. With our backs to the wall and believing in the justice of our cause each one of us must fight on to the end . . .[8]

Haig's stirring appeal was of little use to the troops fighting on that day, but it did later add further steel to the resolve of the British and Dominion troops fighting tooth and nail to prevent a German breakthrough. The 11th of April was a significant day, for the British defences were bolstered by the arrival of the British 5th, 33rd and the 1st Australian Divisions just as the momentum of *Georgette* began to ebb and agreement was reached between Haig and Marshal Foch on French support at this crucial time. By 14 April, Foch had been elevated to Generalissimo of the Allied Armies and introduced a *roulement* of fresh and battle-weary divisions so that by 19 April, French infantry had taken over a nine-mile stretch in the centre of the British Second Army's sector in Flanders.

On the other hand, Ludendorff had already lost that luxury and, as with Operation *Michael*, his troops were becoming exhausted and heartily disillusioned. He decided to appeal to their honour and courage one more time by promising the prize of Ypres and the pinching out of the 'Salient' in which so many thousands of German soldiers had been lost alongside the British, French,

The Red Baron's death on 21 April 1918 was a massive blow to German morale.

(Ian Passingham: photograph from Bundesarchiv Luftwaffe Museum, Berlin)

Dominion and Belgian dead since 1914. But they were frustrated once again when the British reluctantly, though wisely withdrew from Passchendaele to a tighter defensive perimeter around Ypres and smashed all German assaults against the town.

By the final week in April, Operation *Georgette* was looking perilously close to failure and Ludendorff's frustrations were manifest. He was still obsessed by his desire to beat the British, but once again, they had proved that they could tough it out against his best efforts to dislodge and destroy them. Now the French were making their mark in support of their ally as his forces were becoming exhausted and severely depleted. However, he had one or two more cards up his sleeve; the time had come to play them.

While the ebb and flow of the Lys offensive reached the final stages, the Somme provided the headlines on 21 April. Baron Manfred von Richthofen, Germany's greatest ace, knight of the air and commander of the famous 'Flying Circus', was finally shot down and fatally wounded.

His death sent shock waves through the German Army and air arm alike, for he was a great inspiration to those serving at the front and to the German people. Although he had been wounded previously, his fellow pilots and the soldiers on the ground imagined him immortal, and he was a true hero of the Fatherland.

The manner of his death was controversial, as his 'kill' was claimed both by Captain Albert Brown of 209 Squadron RAF and Australian Lewis machine gunners. The ground fire was most probably Richthofen's *coup de grâce*, and when his body was

The monstrous German A7V tank with some of its eighteen crew in April 1918. *(IWM: Q. 37. 343)*

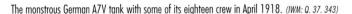

recovered he was buried with full military honours at Bertangles British military cemetery accompanied by an Australian Honour Guard.

A frustrated Ludendorff renewed his efforts in the south. By 24 April his troops had reached the village of Villers-Bretonneux, 'Villers-Bret' to its British and Australian defenders), less than ten miles from Amiens. 'Villers-Bret' had been the scene of a failed assault on 4 and 5 April immediately before *Georgette*.

The German attack on Villers-Bretonneux included the very first tank versus tank engagement in the history of warfare, featuring British Mk IV tanks and one of the few German A7Vs.

The A7V had a crew of eighteen, was armed with one 57mm gun and six machine guns. It had a top speed of a mere 3mph. In comparison, the ubiquitous British Mk IV had a similar speed, a crew of eight, and came in two versions: the 'male', armed with two 6-pounder naval guns and two machine guns, and the 'female', armed with just four machine guns.

On the edge of the wood of Bois l'Abbé, one and a half miles south-west of Villers-Brettoneux, was a section of British Mk IV tanks, a 'male' and two 'females', that were deployed to support the dug-in infantry. Suddenly an A7V lurched into view and the British tanks moved forward to engage it.

The British section commander, Lieutenant Frank Mitchell, in the 'male' Mk IV, fired at the German A7V, but missed and the German tank kept on coming. The A7V then halted and opened fire, hitting both 'female' tanks, which were forced to withdraw. But Mitchell's tank continued to advance. After a brief but hot exchange of fire the A7V was hit and the damaged German monster then withdrew.

The abortive tank attacks were part of Ludendorff's increasingly desperate attempt to find a way through the British defences. As battle raged in Flanders, German resources had been diverted for another thrust towards Amiens. German assault units occupied much of Villers-Bretonneux on 24 April. But the main German attack on Villers-Bretonneux was then decisively crushed by British and Australian troops in a brilliant counterattack. Villers-Bretonneux and Amiens would not be threatened again. On 8 August, it would be the scene of Ludendorff's nemesis: his 'Black Day'.

Back in Flanders, the final bloody days of Operation *Georgette* were played out and yet again, the German effort came to nought, for the main objective of Hazebrouck lay out of reach.

A major turning point in the war was reached on 29 April, before the Allied offensives and even prior to Ludendorff's next major effort on the offensive against the French. For it was on 29 April that he tacitly acknowledged that he had failed to achieve his principal aim: to destroy the British Army in France and Belgium. Legends, half-truths and myths have grown out of the German attempts to crush the BEF before knocking France out of the war, not least of which is the false observation that Ludendorff's main aim was to split the British and French armies, rather than seek principally to annihilate the BEF's fighting capability.[9]

Hindenburg (far left), the Kaiser and Ludendorff (right) at Avesnes, German forward HQ for the offensives against the British, in April 1918.
(IWM: Q.45.326)

Ludendorff had made fundamental mistakes, not least of which was to suggest that his strategy would take care of itself as long as he had the tactics right. Though successful to a degree, the storm troop tactics were largely self-defeating once the British learned to deal with the increasingly predictable German infiltration methods and the subsequent main advance by the attack divisions.

Ludendorff failed to learn another critically important lesson from his predecessor. In 1916 Falkenhayn concluded not only that the Western Front was the main theatre of the war, but also that Britain was the arch-enemy and the 'soul' of Allied resistance against the Central Powers. Most importantly, he was already certain that the German Army was not strong enough to defeat the British and force their withdrawal to the Channel ports while simultaneously pinning the French to the south of the River Somme. This was a major reason for Falkenhayn's decision to attack the French at Verdun rather than the British in another sector of the Western Front in early 1916. The events of 1916 bore out Falkenhayn's views, for the British Army proved a formidable counter to the German Army, after a bad start, on the Somme.

With the exception of Liège in August 1914, Ludendorff's experience of the offensive and open warfare had come only from the Eastern Front. However, with the temporary advantage of transferring a million men from that theatre of war in early 1918, he decided to ignore the lessons of 1916 and 1917 and was conceited enough to believe that he could destroy the British Army in place and that French capitulation would follow like night follows day. The success of *Kaiserschlacht* hinged on surprise and overwhelming penetration of the British sector on a limited front to tear the defences apart and trigger paralysis of command and resistance from the British. It was a pipe dream, and like the Schlieffen Plan in 1914, it took little account of the quality of the enemy facing the German onslaught.

When the Somme and Lys offensives failed, some German commanders in the field and influential people back home lay the blame at the feet of the troops. This was later encapsulated in an article that asked why the great spring offensive had petered out after a few days after showing so much promise at the outset. It suggested that:

> The key to the riddle must be sought principally in the psychological and physical condition of the troops. The best of the old German Army lay dead on the battlefields of Verdun and the Somme . . . As time passed, the picture gradually changed for the worse . . . the number of peace-time officers in a unit grew smaller and . . . they were replaced by young fellows of the very best will, but often without sufficient knowledge. At the same time, the old corps of NCOs rapidly disappeared, so that finally the difference between NCO and private soldier vanished, very much to the detriment of discipline.[10]

This analysis does not ring true, for if the loss of experienced officers and NCOs was the only criterion for an Army's failure, the British and French would have been fatally weakened as well. The root of the problem was not so much the German soldier as the tactics imposed and the leadership at the highest level.

The fundamental responsibility for the failure of *Michael*, *Mars* and *Georgette* was the impossible mission given to the German troops by Ludendorff. His original plan was, like the Schlieffen Plan, too ambitious and took too little account of the enemy. Ludendorff, a gambler who believed that strategy would fall naturally out of successful tactics, seemed to choose the most unimaginative and dogmatic approaches to his stated aim of breaking through British lines and then destroying the BEF.

Rather than seeking the weakest points of the British sector, he launched attacks against Arras (*Mars*) and Ypres (*Georgette*), which met fierce, well-organised and highly effective defences and cost the German assault troops dear. Though battered, the British were unbowed and had emerged from the opening German offensives confident that they could match the best that the German Army could offer in the future.

After *Georgette* there was an inevitable lull as both Ludendorff and the Allied commanders took stock. By the end of April, the German offensives against the British sector on the Somme, around Arras and in Flanders had resulted in almost 350,000 casualties.[11] The BEF had taken 240,000 casualties, of which around half had become PoWs, and the French 92,000 killed, missing, wounded and PoWs.

But the 'parity' between enemies hid the fact that the Germans had lost most of their first line storm troops and specially trained attack division personnel. They were irreplaceable: their slaughter and the failure of the breakthrough tactics against the increasingly stubborn British and Dominion forces left Ludendorff on the horns of a dilemma. Worse, the German manpower crisis was hardly matched by a similar prospect for the Allies. The Americans were coming: and they would soon be coming in an ever-rising tide. By 1 May 1918, the American Expeditionary Force (AEF) had

430,000 men in France and US divisions were around 28,000 strong; almost twice the establishment of British, French or German divisions at this stage of the war. By the end of May, the total rose dramatically to 650,000.

Coupled with this unpalatable fact, Ludendorff recognised that over the past weeks of the offensive there was a significant contrast between the dogged British spirit in adversity and the rapidly deteriorating quality and discipline of his assault troops. The failure of *Michael* and *Mars* had lowered general morale and led to some divisions attacking only after some serious coercion during Operation *Georgette*. The widespread examples of looting and drunkenness among the units that captured British supply dumps and houses in French villages with well-stocked wine cellars during Operation *Michael* underlined the problem of morale.

These breaches of the 'Prussian tradition' to carry out orders without question and the legacy of the huge casualty bill since 21 March were worrying signs, and serious concerns were put to Ludendorff by his commanders and staffs. Crown Prince Rupprecht and General Fritz von Lossberg, chief-of-staff of Fourth Army, stated that there might be little value in persisting with further offensives, and although Ludendorff disagreed, he did concede that dwindling manpower and *matériel* made it impossible to carry out two simultaneous large-scale offensives. Delay between one offensive and another were not only logical but also crucial to allow time for the redeployment of the 'battering train' and concentration of the forces required.

With these considerations in mind, Ludendorff fixed his attention next to a hastily conceived 'Plan B' for defeating the BEF on the Flanders plain. The concept was one of

Operation *Blücher* is launched on 27 May 1918.
(IWM: Q.23.767)

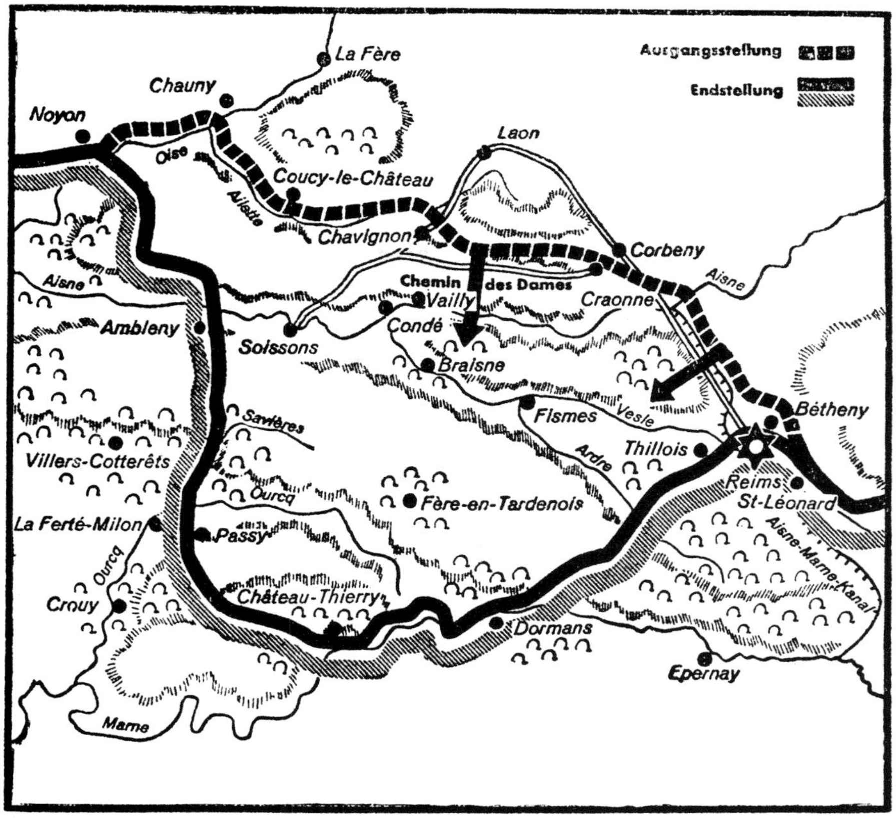

Blücher – Ludendorff's first throw of the dice against the French sector, Chemin des Dames/Champagne, 27 May to 3 June 1918.
(Rudolph Stratz, Weltkrieg)

the 'indirect method'. He aimed to draw the French south in a series of smaller scale attacks and separate them from the BEF. The British would be isolated and vulnerable, with their backs to the sea, as well as the wall. The German offensives would now turn on the French and Ludendorff chose to invoke the talisman of Wellington's victory against the French at Waterloo, Marshal Blücher, to open *L'Affaire Française*.

Operation *Blücher* was launched against the Chemin des Dames, where the French Nivelle offensive had come to grief almost a year before. With a month's gap between *Georgette* and *Blücher*, OHL had studied and applied many of the lessons learned from *Michael*, *Mars* and *Georgette*. The key was revision of the artillery's role, especially in the effectiveness of the creeping barrage to protect the assaulting infantry. Infiltration tactics made it very difficult to apply flexible fire plans, so one practical change was to allocate an artillery battery to each infantry regiment, making it 'under command' and committed to providing timely indirect fire for that regiment. Much effort had gone into specialist training for fresh troops who were incorporated into the assault divisions and storm troop tactics were modified for the different terrain and French defensive layout.[12]

General von Boehn's Seventh Army faced the French Sixth Army under General Duchêne, augmented by five divisions of the British IX Corps, sent to this sector to recuperate after fighting in both the March and April offensives. With the evil irony that besets some in war, three of these divisions were in the front-line when the offensive crashed into the forward positions on 27 May.

Zensiert
Paul Hoffmann & Co.
Berlin-Schöneberg.
Zu den Kämpfen in der Champagne.
Minenwerfer wird in Stellung gebracht.

German trench mortar (minenwerfer) brought into action during Operation *Blücher*. *(Allen Collection)*

Ludendorff's choice of the Chemin des Dames was sound, for the layout of the French defences here invited catastrophe. General Duchêne committed what by 1918 was cardinal sin, by packing his forward positions with troops, although the Allied doctrine had changed to flexible, or elastic, defensive tactics. If the German attack was preceded by a heavy artillery bombardment, Duchêne's front line units would be smashed before the assaulting German infantry went over the top. It was; and many French and British defenders were annihilated as feared.

The reason? Boehn was given all the assistance for Blücher that had been noticeably absent during the April offensive in Flanders. Thus, the Seventh Army's assault divisions had the benefit of a preliminary 160-minute hurricane bombardment of 4,000 guns; another classic orchestration by Colonel Georg Bruchmüller, or *Durchbruchmüller* ('Breakthrough-Müller') as he was now known by the German troops. The German barrage began at 1 a.m. (2 a.m. German time) on 27 May and 'was of a violence and accuracy that in the opinion of the most seasoned soldiers far outdid any other barrage that they had experienced'.[13]

The concentration of fire was even greater than that on 21 March and the initial bombardment was a mix of gas and high explosive (HE) at maximum rate of fire. The next phase targeted front-line trenches and belts of barbed wire alongside counter-battery (CB) work, and then rear area targets such as railheads, troop billets and HQ/communication centres were hit with heavy and medium barrages. Finally, the French and British defenders were rocked by drumfire from virtually all the guns as Zero Hour approached.[14]

At 3.40 a.m. seventeen German attack divisions, with the storm troop units in the van and protected by creeping barrages and heavy machine gun fire, rushed forward to assault the Chemin des Dames. The troops of Duchêne's Sixth Army were taken completely by surprise and then stunned by the violence of the whirlwind artillery bombardment.

It was a day of extraordinary success for Boehn and almost unmitigated disaster for Duchêne. The French defences were rolled back to the River Aisne by mid-morning and by the afternoon a huge gap had appeared where the best part of eight French and British divisions had held the line a few hours before. The Aisne bridges behind the forward defence had not been demolished and by evening, the Germans were across the river, had swarmed across the next ridge and reached the River Vesle.

Boehn's leading assault units advanced a staggering 10 to 12 miles by the end of the first day. Compared with the qualified success of the opening day of Operation *Michael*, *Blücher* was an unequivocal triumph.[15] By the end of the next day, Soissons was in German hands and by 3 June, Ludendorff's leading divisions had reached the Marne – the scene of so much heartbreak for German ambitions in 1914. Now it seemed that retribution was in the offing, for the Kaiser's men were only 50 or so miles from Paris and their offensive appeared unstoppable once again.

Operation *Blücher*'s achievement was beyond even Ludendorff's expectations. He was convinced once again that the war was there to be won and decided to reinforce this success, rather than stick with the plan to simply draw French reserves away from the British sector in the north before then launching his decisive blow in Flanders. Plan A (*Kaiserschlacht*) had become Plan B (*Blücher* and other planned French diversionary attacks to mask a decisive offensive in Flanders) and was now in danger of becoming

Operation *Gneisenau*: machine-gun crews brought into action. *(Postcard, Allen Collection)*

Plan C (smashing the French Army and marching on Paris). Ludendorff's increasingly ambivalent nature was there for all to see. It was not a pretty sight. Plan C was about to run into a new obstacle – and a new enemy.

Operation *Blücher* raised Ludendorff's hopes, but the momentum of the offensive was stopped around Chateau Thierry, where the American 2nd and 3rd Divisions supported the French counter-attacks. On 6 June, the 2nd US Division cut the German advance back at Belleau Wood. Though not major actions in the whole scheme of things, the Germans had been served notice: the Americans were not only coming, but they were spoiling for a fight.

Operation *Blücher* had been a spectacular effort and General von Boehn had achieved a brilliant advance. But, as during Operation *Michael* in March, the Germans had boxed themselves into a bag: a deep salient. It was a logistic nightmare, as the bulge in the line across damaged roads and rail links made it more and more difficult to resupply and reinforce the troops at the tip of the German thrust into the French guts. A British officer serving in the sector had traced the advance by the changing line of German observation balloons:

> The great sweeping semi-circle in the sky marked out the German position and suggested its dangers in an extraordinarily clear and graphic manner. The possibilities of a counter-offensive, thrusting at either angle of the bulge, was inevitably brought to mind.[16]

Ludendorff had little choice after 6 June other than to call a halt to *Blücher* and, in an attempt to expand the salient, consolidate the line and divert more French reserves, he brought in General von Hutier, who had provided the illusion of success with the 40-mile penetration of the British defences in March, to launch a new offensive.

The next blow, Operation *Gneisenau*, was to fall in the French sector towards the Matz between Montdidier and Noyon on 9 June. Hutier's Eighteenth Army assaulted on a 21-mile front against the French Third Army, whose commander General Humbert had not quite grasped the in-depth defence methods and made the same mistake of having too many troops forward. Once again, early results looked promising for Hutier and Ludendorff as the first day ended with an advance of 6 miles, and 8,000 French prisoners. But the momentum slowed more quickly this time than in Operation *Blücher* and the French High Command anticipated and dealt with the now all-too-familiar German tactics. On 11 June five French divisions, backed by terrific artillery and low-flying aircraft strafing sorties, carried out the inevitable counter-attack and the German offensive ground to a halt once more.

Operation *Blücher* had sorely pressed the Allies, for the amazing success in its first days had put the German Army once more within a Big Bertha's range of Paris.[17] But they had come through it, and now with increasing American support, whereas Ludendorff's vision of a decisive breakthrough had faded into a distant horizon.

Battle of the Marne: German medics attend to a wounded soldier, July 1918.
(IWM: Q.55374)

With *Gneisenau* and *Blücher* spent, Ludendorff was faced with a further bill of another 130,000-plus casualties, again many of the best of the rest of his forces, and even the achievement of 60,000 Allied prisoners and 850 guns could not soften the blow. After all, as the British had proved in March and April, guns, ammunition and other lost *matériel* could be swiftly replaced. Manpower could now be made good with the lifeblood of American troops pouring into Europe. But Ludendorff was finding it increasingly problematic to replace his lost weapons and *matériel* – and virtually impossible to make good the loss of men.

Most worryingly, as the whole German offensive effort was systematically torn apart, Ludendorff's nerve was unravelling too. The apparition of Helmuth von Moltke (who had died in 1916) and the Marne debacle in September 1914 appeared to stalk Ludendorff. The parallels of the promise of victory dashed by poor strategy and unexpected, fierce enemy resistance then and now, almost four years later, haunted him. His 'Grand Plan', a massive gamble from the outset, was crumbling before his very eyes.

Somehow, he continued to believe that a success in the French sector would set up his forces for a final crack at the British in Flanders, but now even pipedreams were looking dodgy. Nevertheless, like Don Quixote he determined to finish the business in the south with another tip at the French windmill. The ironic twist in the tale came when he fixed on an offensive in the Marne sector. To prepare for a major assault by no less than 43 infantry divisions either side of Reims, 5,000 guns under the baton of another *Bruchmüller* symphony inundated the French defences and the assault troops moved up to their jumping off positions for this 'final blow'.

The Second Battle of the Marne (*Reims-Marneschutz*) began at 12.10 a.m. on 15 July, but this time there was no glorious early success; rather it started badly and went rapidly downhill thereafter. The French Fourth Army, under General Gouraud, knew of the German plans and carried out a pre-emptive artillery counter-barrage onto the trenches packed with German assault troops before they had a chance to move. When they did attack, they were caught left and right and the offensive was almost over before it began. Any brief success was illusory once more, and one German officer who had come through the last four years was moved to write on this day that:

> I have lived through the most disheartening day of the whole war . . . Our guns bombarded empty French trenches . . . in little folds of the ground . . . lay their machine gun posts, like lice in the seams and folds of a garment, to give our attacking force a warm reception . . .[18]

The game was up. The German offensive soon became desperate defence when the French launched a massive counter-offensive on the Marne on 18 July. The ghosts of 1914 had decided to pay Ludendorff and all the Kaiser's men a final, fatal visit.

CHAPTER 14

COURAGE, ENDURANCE, DEFEAT

AUGUST–NOVEMBER 1918

By the end of July 1918, with his final offensive repulsed, and his own men being relentlessly mauled, Ludendorff finally realised that the war was no longer winnable. Haig, Foch, and the Allies took to the offensive. In August, the British, French and American armies mounted a series of rolling attacks that ruptured the German defensive line. The most stunning blow came at Amiens on 8 August. It would be Ludendorff's 'Black Day' for the German Army, and after this even he realised that there was no way back. The war would have to be ended, at Germany's cost. The British, Australian and Canadian assault on the German Second Army near Amiens on 8 August was a model of deception, surprise and combined arms operational excellence.

Signals (radio) deception duped the German defenders before the battle and 'predicted' artillery fire guaranteed that there would be no warning of the attack to come. An accurate, devastating bombardment crashed down on the unsuspecting enemy to open the onslaught at 4.20 a.m., and simultaneously the infantry, tanks and air force were launched against the Second Army's positions. A total of 372 Mark V and 72 'whippet' tanks, 800 aircraft (of which 376 were fighters) were in the van and worked brilliantly alongside the advancing infantry. By lunchtime, the Allied success was virtually complete.

The true nature of Ludendorff's 'Black Day' was affirmed by the official German account, which noted that:

> As the sun set on 8 August on the battlefield the greatest defeat since the beginning of the was was an accomplished fact . . . The total loss of the formations employed in the Second Army is estimated at 650 to 700 officers and 26,000 to 27,000 other ranks. More than 400 guns, besides a huge number of

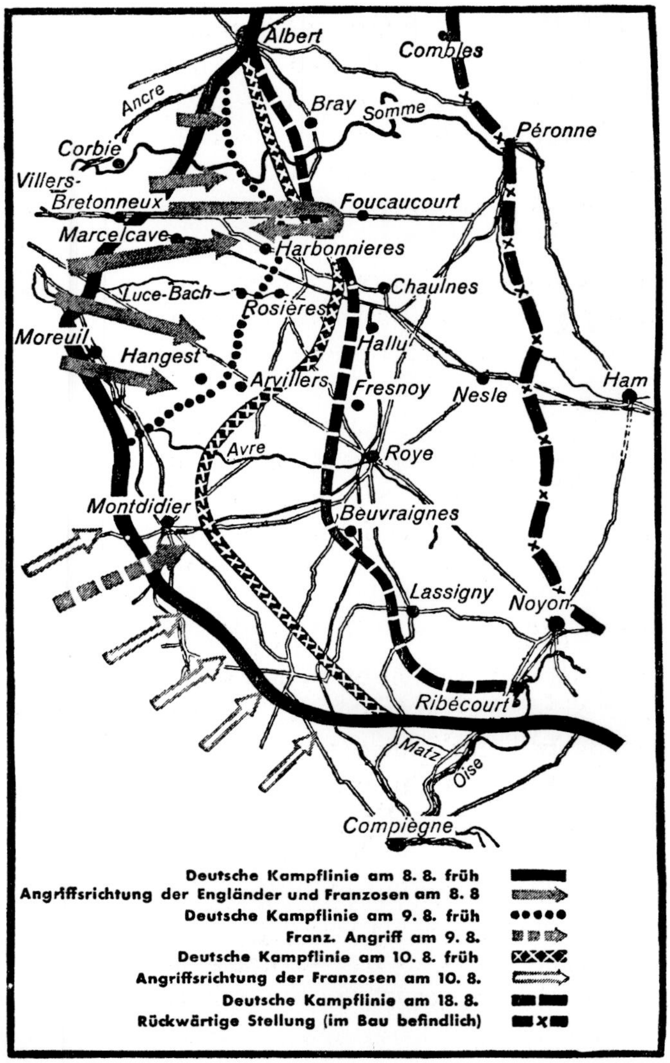

Amiens, 8 August 1918: The 'Black Day' for the German Army and notice to Ludendorff and Hindenburg that the war would be lost.
(Rudolph Stratz, Weltkrieg, p. 361)

machine guns, trench mortars and other war material had been lost . . . More than two-thirds of the total loss had surrendered as prisoners.[1]

By September three Allied Army Groups stood poised to strike: the British in the north, the French in the centre and south and the Americans facing the St Mihiel salient and the Argonne. The American Army Group's first task as a unified force was to eradicate the German Salient, or bulge in the line, at St Mihiel, which they did on 12 September. As one offensive lost its momentum, another would open, giving the Germans no time to reorganise between each Allied assault. The Allied supremo Ferdinand Foch, ordered 'Everyone to the fight', inspiring the Allies to press on to victory.

Most of the Kaiser's men were now utterly resigned to the prospect of defeat and despair. That they fought on in places with such tenacity and in such good order never ceases to impress and amaze many that either witnessed it then or consider it today. But it was a truly awful experience. Soldiers bemoaned their plight:

> Our artillery is fired out . . . We have too few horses. Our fresh troops are anaemic boys in need of rest, who cannot carry a pack, but merely know how to die. By thousands. They understand nothing about warfare, they simply go and let themselves be shot down . . . The summer of 1918 [has been] the most bloody and the most terrible . . . Every man here knows that we are losing the war . . . Still the campaign goes on – the dying goes on.[2]

Ludendorff, Hindenburg and an ever weaker Kaiser held on to the reins of power and the German Army simply held on – just.

Pershing's First Army carried out its initial independent action on 12 September, when it successfully pinched out the salient at St Mihiel and then planned to seize the Meuse-Argonne sector on 26 September 1918. His task was to assault the strong German defences, break through and thrust then towards Sedan. This entailed overcoming the Hindenburg Line. The terrain here was steep, thickly wooded and formidable. It favoured the defence and Pershing was left with no option but to make a frontal attack.

At Meuse-Argonne, 600,000 American and French troops in two armies would attack side-by-side, supported by 2,700 guns of all calibres, over 500 tanks, principally the Renault light tank, and 1,000 American and French aircraft to augment the offensive.

General Max von Gallwitz planned to exploit the Germans' defensive skills to the full and ensured that the Meuse-Argonne defences, with their well-positioned trench systems, concrete bunkers and deep dugouts, were developed to present a major obstacle to any Allied offensive. By late September 1918, four lines of prepared positions, fourteen miles deep, faced the Americans at Meuse-Argonne and the most daunting was the Kriemhild Line in the rear.

At midnight on Thursday 26 September 1918, Pershing's 2,700 guns fired the first salvo of a massive artillery bombardment. It lasted for four hours, stunning the German defenders of the Meuse-Argonne sector. Shortly after dawn, the American infantry stormed across no-man's-land, supported by incessant artillery fire.

Most of the German defenders had survived the American barrage and they now rose out from their deep dugouts to meet the onslaught. However, Gallwitz was at first

German retreat during the Allied '100-days' campaign. 21cm Howitzer battery in action, October 1918. *(IWM: Q.23.813)*

concerned that the American attack might be only a diversion. The weight that Pershing threw behind his assault soon made Gallwitz change his mind. He ordered his troops to counter-attack, which they swiftly did. The German resistance then hardened as their defence tactics began to come into their own. German machine guns were brought out from the dugouts and started to cause havoc among the 'doughboys'. Tank and infantry cooperation was becoming impossible, and as the tanks attacked German bunkers and trenches, they became more vulnerable to the German artillery.

Pershing's army also began to suffer severe resupply problems, caused in part by the difficult landscape and muddy conditions. In many places, the US troops were forced to go into hasty defence to protect themselves against increasingly heavy German artillery fire.

At the beginning of October Pershing desperately regrouped his forces in an effort to break the stalemate at Meuse-Argonne. When the Americans attacked again on 4 October, they did so without a preliminary bombardment. Pershing's men clawed their way forward, despite heavy casualties and by 12 October they were tantalisingly close to assaulting the last bastion of Gallwitz's defence, the Kriemhild Line.

The final assault on the Kriemhild Line began on 14 October. For three days and nights, the gruesome struggle between the gallant 'doughboys' and the still resolute German defenders continued. With the advantages of increasing fire support, the Americans began to make headway and the German defences started to buckle.

The 'doughboys' were finally beginning to clear the Kriemhild Line. On 16 October Brigadier-General Douglas MacArthur, commanding 83rd Brigade of the US 42nd 'Rainbow' Division, led his men from the front to capture one of the last German redoubts. The Germans began to surrender in droves.

The Kriemhild Line was at last in American hands. Pershing had finally reached the line that he had planned to capture almost a month before, and had advanced on towards Sedan. All that there remained to do was final mopping-up operations.

The titanic struggle had cost Gallwitz's Army Group 80,000 casualties, killed, wounded and prisoners. But the American success had been wrought at a high price too. During the Meuse-Argonne offensive, the Americans had suffered 117,000 casualties; almost 40 per cent of the total American losses for the war.

By early October the relentless Allied assaults had broken through the Hindenburg Line and forced the Germans back over 50 miles. As the advance continued, German morale dropped to a dangerous level across much of the Front. German troops facing the 28th Infantry Brigade/9th Scottish Division decided that they had had enough before the next phase of the offensive continued in the Ypres sector on 20 September. It was recorded that a number of Germans had surrendered to the sentry posts that night and that more would have crossed no-man's-land had their NCOs not prevented them from doing so. Commenting on this incident, the Brigade Commander noted that: 'The enemy's morale must have dipped; one has rarely heard of such a thing happening before an action . . .'[3]

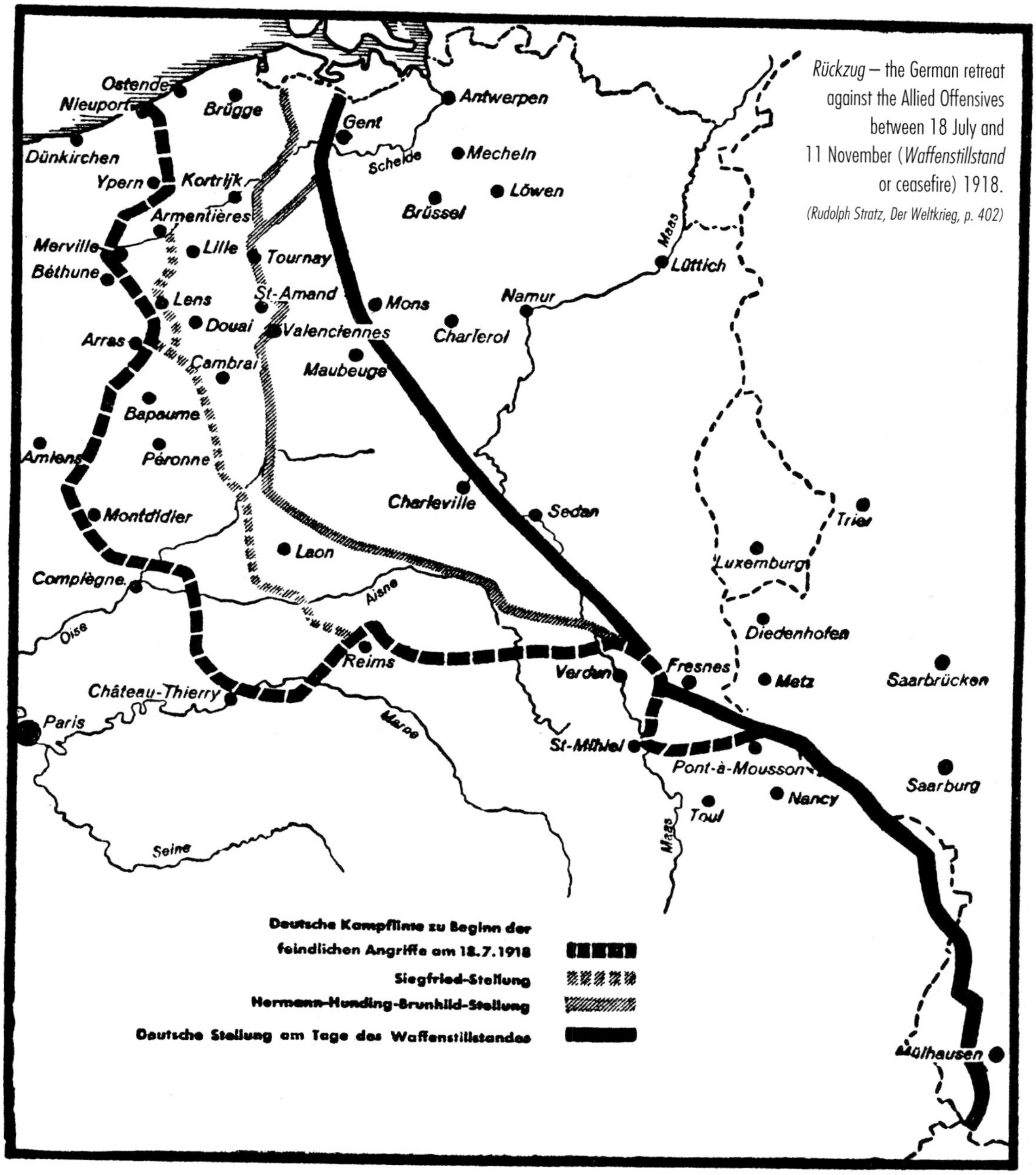

Rückzug – the German retreat against the Allied Offensives between 18 July and 11 November (*Waffenstillstand* or ceasefire) 1918.
(Rudolph Stratz, Der Weltkrieg, p. 402)

It was true, then. Despite their determined efforts, the Kaiser's men were exhausted and could no longer sustain a coherent defence. By now, almost one million Germans had been killed, wounded or captured. It was evident to every one of the Kaiser's men that the pendulum had swung dramatically against them. Edwin Kühns recorded in his diary on 7 October:

TOMMY - HAVE YOU GOT A WIFE?
PRISONER - NEIN.
TOMMY - NINE! BLIMEY -
- WHERE'S YER IRON CROSS.

Morale-boosting postcard, October 1918.
(Allen Collection)

> On 7 October our days were up. We were in retreat. We had to take over three [telephone exchange] stations [between Valenciennes and Maubeuge] . . . We were just days here when one formation after another arrived until, in the end, the village was overflowing. As well as these [troops] there were refugees . . . the market square was full of them and they had to remain for the night . . . Many died.[4]

The Allied offensives continued throughout October and, although some pockets of resistance remained, the German Army was effectively finished. With her armies crumbling and with unrest at home, Germany sued for peace and the Kaiser abdicated. Ludendorff, a broken and bitter man, had no choice but to resign in the late October.

The nightmare of the First World War had finally ended.

Between March and July 1918 Haig and Foch passed their sternest test. By the end of the first fortnight of the German onslaught, both knew that the Allies could hold on and this they had done with cool heads, supported by the extraordinary courage, skill and adaptability of the men under their command.

Some of the 400,000 German prisoners taken after 18 July 1918. *(IWM: Q2281)*

In contrast Ludendorff, having initially failed to make a decisive breakthrough, saw no other option but to continue his attacks. Thereafter, each renewed offensive set a desperate, costly pattern of fleeting initial success, containment and then bloody failure. Though some apparently enormous gains were made, their importance was illusory. Not one town or city was captured of tactical or strategic importance and no breakthrough had been achieved.

The cost, on the other hand, was enormous. In the final nine months of the war, the German Army had lost over one million men. Almost 400,000 were taken prisoner by the Allied armies in the period of the sustained advance since 18 July 1918, the offensive known popularly as the '100 Days': 188,700 by the BEF and a further 139,000 by the French, with the balance captured by U.S. (43,300) and Belgian (14,500) armies; a grand total of 385,500.[5]

In that period in the BEF sector alone, the Germans had faced no less than nine separate, but continuous battles, which served to keep them on the back foot and make it impossible to ever really regroup as they had successfully done after Allied attacks in the past.[6] The Allies had suffered heavily too. For example, the BEF sustained around 375,000 casualties in total between August and November. But the Allies had both the resources and the manpower to be able to turn the tide, which they had done in a comprehensive manner.

Ludendorff, Haig and Foch had been tested to breaking point in 1918. It was Ludendorff, not the C-in-C of the BEF and French supremo who had failed that test. His deception at the beginning of the year, which led his men to believe that they were capable of sustaining an all-out offensive against the Western Allies, who were overwhelmingly better equipped for sustained operations, and his nervous breakdown after Amiens guaranteed Germany's failure.

At the end, all the Kaiser's men had been out-fought and inexorably ground down by a combination of the courage, determination and bloody-mindedness of the Allied soldiers, well-coordinated, planned and executed all-arms offensives, and an overwhelming superiority in logistic support and *matériel*. *Materialschlacht* had brought them to their knees.

Regardless of the *Dolchstoss*, or 'stab-in-the-back', theory in Germany after the war and both historical myth and emotive perception in more recent years, the irrefutable fact is that the First World War was a military defeat for the main enemy in the main theatre of war – Germany.

But military victory has seldom guaranteed lasting peace. So it would be in the aftermath of Armistice.

Chapter 15
Dolchstoss: Versailles and the Diabolical Legacy

Reconciliation (November 1918)
When you are standing at your hero's grave,
Or near some homeless village where he died,
Remember, through your heart's rekindling pride,
The German soldiers who were loyal and brave.

Men fought like brutes; and hideous things were done
And you have nourished hatred harsh and blind.
But in that Golgotha perhaps you'll find
The mothers of the men who killed your son.
Siegfried Sassoon

In 1914 the Schlieffen Plan had proved to be a paper tiger. Any chance of success was wiped out by poor control at the highest level of German Army command, the unexpected gallantry of the Belgians, the suicidal élan of the French Army and the professional doggedness of the BEF. Simultaneously, unexpectedly swift mobilisation by the 'Russian steamroller' in the East and an offensive towards East Prussia led to General von Moltke's decision to despatch two additional German Army Corps from the Western to the Eastern Front. All combined to slow, then stall the German war machine rolling through Belgium, then France.

The depleted German force fighting the Belgian and Anglo-French forces no longer had the necessary impetus to achieve its original objectives. The Allies fought them to a standstill between 6 and 10 September during the 'Miracle on the Marne'. Moltke was sacked for his dilatory, indecisive conduct of the war in its first weeks and replaced by General von Falkenhayn.

The Marne was followed by the series of attempted outflanking manoeuvres (popularly but inaccurately known as the 'Race for the Sea') and, by the winter of 1914, to static, principally defensive trench warfare, the antithesis to German, or Prussian, military tradition.

'The curse of the Marne' would come back to haunt each of the commanders of the German Army who were to follow the unfortunate Moltke. 'The curse of the Marne' encompasses the inherent pattern of indecisiveness and then loss of command authority that were characteristic of Moltke in September 1914 on the Marne, Falkenhayn in his conduct of the Verdun and early phases of the Somme campaign in 1916, and finally Ludendorff with the *Kaiserschlacht*, the German spring offensives of 1918.

The German Army fought with great skill and tenacity throughout the war on the Western Front. Its soldiers certainly had the professional potential, doggedness and motivation to achieve victory in the West, just as they did in the East. But Germany not only lost the war, but was also humiliated and ruined as a result. So why did the highly regarded, generally competent and resolute German Army fail in the main theatre of war, the Western Front, in the First World War? The reasons are fundamental and diametrically opposite to widely held perceptions.

The first factor was that of command. On the Western Front, the German Army was committed to five major offensives between August 1914 and July 1918. These were the German invasion of France and Belgium under the Schlieffen Plan; the first battle of Ypres in 1914; the 2nd Ypres offensive in April and May 1915; the Verdun offensive between February and July 1916; and finally the series of German 'Peace' or *Friedenssturm* offensives between March and July 1918. Ultimately, each one of these offensives failed to achieve their stated objectives, but added further enormous cost to the ever-dwindling pool of German manpower – the reality, not the myth.

Despite the almost overwhelming tide of popular perception that 1916 was a year of senseless slaughter on the Allied side, the combined effects of the German Army's experience of the 'Mill on the Meuse' at Verdun and the desperate defence of the Somme throughout 1916 forced Ludendorff and Hindenburg to voluntarily withdraw up to 20 miles in places under Operation *Alberich* in March 1917 to occupy the *Siegfried Stellung* or Hindenburg Line. This policy rather diminished Ludendorff's own view that: 'The offensive is the most effective means of war: it alone is decisive.'

In fact, if 1916 saw the loss of most of the battle-hardened veterans of the old 1914 German Army, 1917 was perhaps the real turning point of the war, as vital cogs in the First World War machine clicked into place, forcing a fateful decision on Ludendorff by the year's end. These were the psychological effect of America's declaration of war on 6 April the gathering pace of revolution and finally military capitulation in Russia. On the Western Front, Ludendorff was encouraged by mutinies in the French Army presaged by the debacle of the Nivelle offensive in April/May; but simultaneously the German Army had to endure the grinding and costly defence against the British at Arras, Vimy Ridge, Messines, 3rd Ypres and the opening phase of Cambrai.

By the end of 1917, however, Russia was out of the war, French military resolve remained questionable and America lacked significant strength in Europe. Ludendorff realised that this combination of events had left him with a diabolical choice. The fateful decision was made, ironically, at Mons on 11 November 1917. He planned for a major offensive in the early months of 1918. The main aim was to crush the British Army, and then encourage an isolated French Army to sue for peace, before the Americans could deploy its vast manpower reserve to the Western Front. Ludendorff admitted that the offensive strategy was a high-risk gamble, a final card to play in the dreadful game of this war. If the gamble failed, Germany would lose the war . . . The gamble was doomed to fail.

The fact remains that Britain and France forced the German Army on to the back foot for the majority of the war on the Western Front. Its strong defences bore ample witness to their desire to stay put, conducting a defensive strategy rather than seeking a more offensive stance.

Overall, the German High Command had obviously paid little heed to the maxim that:

> . . . An army which thinks mainly in defensive terms is doomed. It yields initiative and advantage in time and space to an enemy – even an enemy inferior in numbers. It loses the sense of the hunter – the opportunist.[1]

In short, when their stated aims were frustrated by unexpected British and French resistance in 1914, 1915, 1916 and 1918, each of Germany's supreme commanders vacillated, panicked, or found it impossible to adapt to the changing situation. This, in turn, diluted the power of the German army. The soldiers were betrayed by their leaders and sacrificed on the altar of vanity and hubris.

The change of Commanders-in-Chief from Joffre, to Nivelle, to Pétain and finally Foch had a deleterious effect on the French Army, and also on the relationship between the French and the British, including Field Marshal French. But the British stood firm with Haig as C-in-C for the majority of the war.

The Allied military commanders always had to answer to their political masters, whereas from 1916 onwards, the German *duumvirate* of Ludendorff and Hindenburg were the heads of a military dictatorship in Germany. The Kaiser was marginalized and then virtually ignored by the military leadership. From early 1917 Ludendorff had virtually free rein to conduct the war as he wished and became de facto leader and dictator.

The second factor is that of the much-vaunted General Staff. Unlike the British Army, the German General Staff system allowed more junior officers authority, unthinkable in the Allied Forces. In some cases it proved to be brilliantly successful, for example in the case of *Oberst* (and later General) Fritz von Lossberg, who became Germany's military defensive expert. But even in this case, the fact that he became known as 'Ludendorff's fireman' proved that German tactical doctrine was not working at the operational and tactical level.

On the other hand, there were notable and highly significant failures – most notable of which was *Oberst-Leutnant* Richard Hentsch, who was given full authority to order General von Bülow's Second and General von Klück's First armies to retreat during the Battle of the Marne. It was a directive confirmed by Moltke on 11 September 1914, and it presaged the first major defeat of the German army in the war.

The significance of this interference, coupled with Moltke's obvious loss of authority and his command in mid-September 1914, cannot be overstated. The German campaign of 1914 was founded on the concept of a swift and decisive victory in the West by the 40th day of mobilisation. When the plan was altered and the strategy shifted by Moltke, Germany's first great gamble of the war failed.

The Schlieffen Plan was the only German recipe for success. Once it failed there was no 'Plan B'. As Holger Herwig noted:

> . . . the Battle of the Marne revealed the shortcomings of the Prussian General Staff system. Moltke . . . chose simply to issue general directives and to leave the actual campaigns with his army commanders. Neither Bülow nor Klück was up to the task . . . And that a mere Lieutenant-Colonel from Staff Headquarters could redirect the entire operations of the two most senior commanders in the German army, both in the rank of Colonel-General, speaks volumes for the critical over-dominance of the 'demi-gods' of the General Staff.[2]

The third factor is one of crucial importance – that of logistics. As the war ground on, the German army was increasingly limited by its inability to provide its troops with the resources that were vital to the war–winning strategy.

Much of this was due to the effectiveness of the Allied naval blockade of Germany, which presaged great hardship of the Home Front and helped to ensure that any serious thought of equipping the German army with massed tank formations and especially masses of motorised transport, was at best fanciful.

In March 1918, these logistic limitations, imposed on the German army attempting to press home its advantage during the vitally important early days of the offensive in the West, were obvious. Unlike the British, and to some extent the French, the German Army relied more and more on its dwindling reserves of manpower. Furthermore, when German troops overran the Allied supply dumps and hitherto untouched French and Belgian population centres, they found food, wine and other supplies denied to them for months, if not years.

Such discoveries led to serious breakdowns in both discipline and morale, although it is vital to underline here that, contrary to the view of some, this was not the major factor in the ultimate collapse of the German offensives in 1918. Rather, this was an indicator that the soldiers of the German Army had been deliberately misinformed about the apparently parlous logistical state of the Allied forces as well as their own.

When turning to the offensive it had always failed because of fatal flaws in the planning and conduct of each campaign.

German soldiers might well have felt as through they had been 'stabbed in the back' when the end came in November 1918. But the dagger had been thrust there by their own military masters and not by the politicians who were to become the 'November criminals' on which the *Dolchstoss Theorie* would thrive. *Dolchstoss* was by no means a universally accepted notion. Most ordinary officers and men who had fought and come through the dreadful experience of this war were determined to put the prospect of future violence aside.

But Germany was a place of violence in the months immediately after Armistice. After months of recuperation from serious wounds, a German officer was almost a victim of the chaos of this 'revolution'. Home with his parents after leaving hospital, he was jeered by Communist agitators for wearing his Army uniform. Suddenly, the mob shouted, 'Kill the dog, Officer scum, bloodhound!' He was chased, but managed to find a place of refuge as the crowd stormed by. He later wrote:

> I stood here for some time, deep in thought. I was not angry with the goaded people . . . just boundlessly sorrowful . . . 'So this is the gratitude of my native country for those four terrible years.' . . . Since that hour, I have never worn the uniform.[3]

Men like Albert Mühmelt, who had survived but lost two brothers during the

Ein unbekannter Deutscher Soldat – an unknown German soldier.
(Ian Passingham)

war, were just relieved to have seen it through. He would carve out a new life for himself and his family after the war – and bitterly oppose the revival of German militarism under the Nazi régime.

The First World War affected the German Home Front in ways unimaginable before 1914. Hunger became the main factor for the majority of the population and food shortages had appeared as early as autumn 1914. They became critical in late 1915, but the 'Turnip Winter' of 1916/17 was a dreadful experience from which Germany could never recover.

Food riots became as commonplace as the interminable queues, which became the centres of rumours, distrust and suspicion. Horsemeat replaced beef and pork and a plethora of *ersatz* products threatened to poison consumers with chemical derivatives. By 1916 there was little coal and items that had been taken for granted in summer 1914 such as soap, natural fats, butter, cheese and eggs were almost non-existent. Hoarding, smuggling and the black market drove a wedge through social structures and between the urban and rural populations, as well as the rich and poor.

As a result of the dire state of the German economy and widespread privation, general health deteriorated dramatically. Civilian mortality doubled, then trebled, between 1914 and 1918. Infant mortality doubled in the final eighteen months of the war. Tuberculosis (TB) and the decimating influenza pandemic struck more easily in Germany because of the generally poor state of health.

Ultimately and inevitably, all these conditions combined to destroy the fabric of a formerly orderly and united society and undermined Germany's very legitimacy. The war rent the traditional home asunder.

Above all, the Allied naval blockade cruelly exposed Germany's myths of self-sufficiency and governmental and administrative efficiency. As the demands of the war grew ever greater after the first few months of the conflict, those on the Home Front were forced to fight the burgeoning enemies of social disintegration, hunger, disease and death.

German defeat in the field, and starvation and revolution at home were terrible consequences of the 'great adventure' that all the Kaiser's men and the German people were now paying for. But the casualties at the Front and deaths from privation at home were dwarfed worldwide by the insidious influenza pandemic (known as *la grippe*), which killed an estimated 27 million people globally; two and a half times the number of servicemen and civilians killed as a result of the First World War.

Though the particular strain of the disease had been germinating for years, its virulence was enhanced by the unique set of factors: the unsanitary conditions of life in the trenches; the generally poor diet of millions of people across Europe and the Near East and the ever-increasing crowding of towns and cities worldwide. These all combined in early 1918 and provided the 'Spanish 'flu' with limitless breeding grounds.

The disease ran its course from spring 1918 to the middle of 1919, reaching its peak in the final autumn of the war. Almost 50 per cent of its victims were within the

Reichsarchivzweigstelle Dresden

IV Nr. 101/479/1075

Bei Rückfragen ist diese Bescheinigung beizufügen

Dresden-N15, den 20. August 1934.
Arsenalhauptgebäude, Eingang Tor A, Königsbrücker Straße
Fernruf 54447

Militär-Dienstzeitbescheinigung*)

über den ehem. Grenadier Albert Georg M ü h m e l t ,

geboren am 21. 2. 1897 in S c h a b e n a u - Breslau - Pr.

1. Dienstverhältnisse:
   a) vor dem Kriege: keine.

   b) nach Eintritt der Mobilmachung: 3. 4. 1916 b. 1.Rekr.-D. I.Ers.-Btl. Gren.-Regt. 101 eing.
   17. 8. 1916 z. 1. Komp. Feldr.-D.23.R.D.
   8. 12. 1916 z. 12. " Gren.-Res.-Regt. 100
   16. 11. 1917 z. 5.(Gen.)Kp.II.Ers.-Batl. Gren.-Res.-Rgt.100
   27. 4. 1918 z. 1. Komp. Ers.-Batl. Gren.-Regt. 100
   30. 4. 1918 z. 12. " Gren.-Res.-Regt. 100
   14. 10. 1918 in englische Gefangenschaft geraten.
   Entlassen: 10. Oktober 1919 vom Durchgangslager Hamelburg.

2. Gefechtshandlungen bzw. Aufenthalt im Kriegsgebiet:

(Anordnungsgemäß erfolgt für jedes Jahr nur Angabe einer Kampfhandlung oder eines zweimonatigen Aufenthalts)

1914:
1915:
1916: } 23.8.1916 - 15.3.1917 Stell.-K. im Artois;
1917:
1918: 3.5.- 28.6. Kämpfe zw. Arras und Albert.

3. Beförderungen:

4. Orden: Eisernes Kreuz zweiter Klasse am 31. 10. 1917 verliehen.

5 Bemerkungen: Am 26.9.1917 dch. A.G. am linken Arm verwundet.

Vorstehende Angaben stimmen mit der Kriegs-~~Rangliste~~ Stammrolle Bd. Nr. 101/479/1075 überein.

REICHSARCHIVZWEIGSTELLE DRESDEN

I. A.
[signature]

*) Militärpässe werden bestimmungsgemäß nicht mehr ausgestellt.

Vordr. 86 a

736 34 II D
Din 476 A 4

Service Record of Albert Mühmelt.

(Farley Family Collection)

Albert Mühmelt (back row, right with one cross above his head) as a prisoner of war under British care in November 1918.
(Farley Family Collection)

15–35 age-group. Consequently, thousands of men who had come through the bloody experience of the conflict were struck down by the deadly 'flu in the final weeks of the war, or soon after. On the other hand, thousands of loved ones who had waited stoically for the return of their husband, father, brother or friend were themselves infected and died before seeing their loved ones again. Whether a soldier had fought for God and the King or for the Kaiser believing *Gott mit uns*, it was difficult to believe in a God when this final cruelty in a world already horribly scarred by war took another loved one from a person at this terrible time.

The influenza carried other complications in its wake, such as pneumonia and its debilitating effects. It also exacerbated the effects of other medical problems, leading or contributing to heart disease, tuberculosis, miscarriages and many other ailments. Therefore, it would be impossible to give an entirely accurate total figure of those struck down globally. What is irrefutable is that over 13 million Germans, one in five of the population, suffered from the disease and between 10–15 per cent died in the pandemic period of influenza or similar symptoms.[4]

An estimated 1,808,545, but probably 2 million, German servicemen were killed in action during the First World War, with a further 4,250,000 wounded. The German total of around 6 million battle casualties compare with 5 million French casualties (1,385,000 of whom were killed) and 2,700,000 British/Dominion casualties (around one million dead) on the Western Front (total worldwide of 947,085 dead from total casualties of 3,260,581). This represents 6 million against approximately 8 million casualties overall. Over 1,300,000 German troops were killed in France and Belgium alone. These statistics are remarkable on the Allied side, rather than the lower German casualty bill when compared with the French and BEF total, when one takes into account the fact that the German Army was on the defensive on the Western Front for most of the war and the Allies had to maintain an offensive posture.

Let us never forget that Germany had invaded and occupied most of a neutral country – Belgium – and violated that neutrality in the first instance, as well as invading France. The courage and skill of the BEF and French Army in the late summer and autumn of 1914 prevented the predicted German victory and thereafter the Germans had the advantage of choosing the ground on which they would defend their ill-gotten gains in the West.

The number of American troops killed was 115,660 out of a total casualty figure of 325,876; the Russian Army lost over two million dead and a minimum of a further 5 million wounded between August 1914 and November 1917. However, it should be borne in mind and in context that 80 per cent of those who served in the British and Dominion forces in the First World War survived and, above all, that the Western Allies – i.e. France and Britain supported by her Empire forces – won the war on the ground. The great importance of the USA entering the war in April 1917 and thereafter was the psychological, rather than purely military, factor.

The achievement of the Allies was that they overcame a formidable enemy in the main theatre of war – the Western Front in the First World War. The main theatre of war in the Second World War after 22 June 1941 was undoubtedly the Eastern Front where over 10 million Soviet servicemen died in order to defeat the bulk of the German armed forces by May 1945.

In the early years after 1918, artists and writers predicted that the new, democratic Germany of the Weimar Republic would spring from the ashes of the *Weltkrieg*. But its fragile growth would find little sustenance from a soil poisoned by defeat and humiliation. It would spring up, briefly, but soon be consumed by its crippling economic burden, the failure of a toothless League of Nations, a global financial recession and the growth of extremist ideology, all of which would sink fledgling democracies like Germany across Europe without trace.

Perversely, by 1933, Germany was desperate for a new way, a new faith and a new messiah to revive the Fatherland and make it great once more. National Socialism appeared to provide all three: and most German people were prepared to believe in the new vision. However, under Adolf Hitler, and like the Kaiser's dream a generation before, it was to become a living and bloody nightmare. The 'Führer' would lead the Fatherland into an even deeper abyss than the one into which it fell in 1918.

Gefreiter Adolf Hitler.
(Rudolf Stratz, Weltkrieg)

Appendices

I German Ranks and Equivalents 1914–1918

German Rank	Nominal Command/Equivalent Rank
General Officers	
Generalfeldmarschall	Group of Armies/Field Marshal
Generaloberst	Army/Colonel-General
General der Infanterie/Kavallerie or } General der Artillerie }	Corps/General of Inf/Cav/Arty
Generalleutnant	Division/Lieutenant-General
Generalmajor	Brigade/Major-General
Regimental Officers	
Oberst	Regiment/Colonel
Oberstleutnant	Second-in-Command of Regiment/Lt Col
Major	Battalion/Major
Hauptmann	Captain – Inf, Arty & Engrs
Rittmeister	Captain – Cav, Air service, Train (i.e. logistics units)
Oberleutnant	Lieutenant
Leutnant	Second Lieutenant
Feldwebelleutnant (not commissioned)	Sergeant Major Lieutenant
Offizierstellvertreter	Acting (Probationary) Officer
Non-Commissioned Officers (NCOs)	
Fähnrich	Ensign
Oberfeldwebel*	Regimental Sergeant Major (RSM)
Feldwebel*	Coy Sergeant Major (CSM)
Wachtmeister*	Battery/Squadron CSM
Vizefeldwebel*	Colour Sergeant (Inf, Foot Arty & Engrs)
Vizewachtmeister*	Staff Sergeant (Cav, Field and General Art Logistic units)
Sergeant	Sergeant
Unteroffizier }	Corporal
Oberjäger }	Corporal in Jäger battalion
Obergefreiter	Bombardier (Arty)
Gefreiter	Lance-Bombardier or Lance-Corporal (Inf other arms cf. Arty)
Schütze, Grenadier, Jäger, etc	Private (German title depends on type of Regiment in Inf units)

* = All NCOs marked with * were entitled to wear a sash (*Portepee*) to signify senior NCO rank and were classed as *Portepeeträger* (literally: 'sash-wearers').

Source: General Staff GHQ BEF, *Handbook of the German Army in War: April 1918* (London/Nashville, IWM/Battery Press).

II German Infantry Division Order of Battle (ORBAT) 1914 and 1918

Note

A German infantry division usually consisted of two brigades, each of three regiments. The regiment comprised three battalions, so therefore equated to a British brigade, rather than a regiment. 'Regiment' in the British Army is normally the honorary title of a number of battalions recruited from the same area, for example: 1st, 2nd and 3rd Battalions of the Scots Guards Regiment.

German Infantry Division, 1914 **German Infantry Division, early 1918**

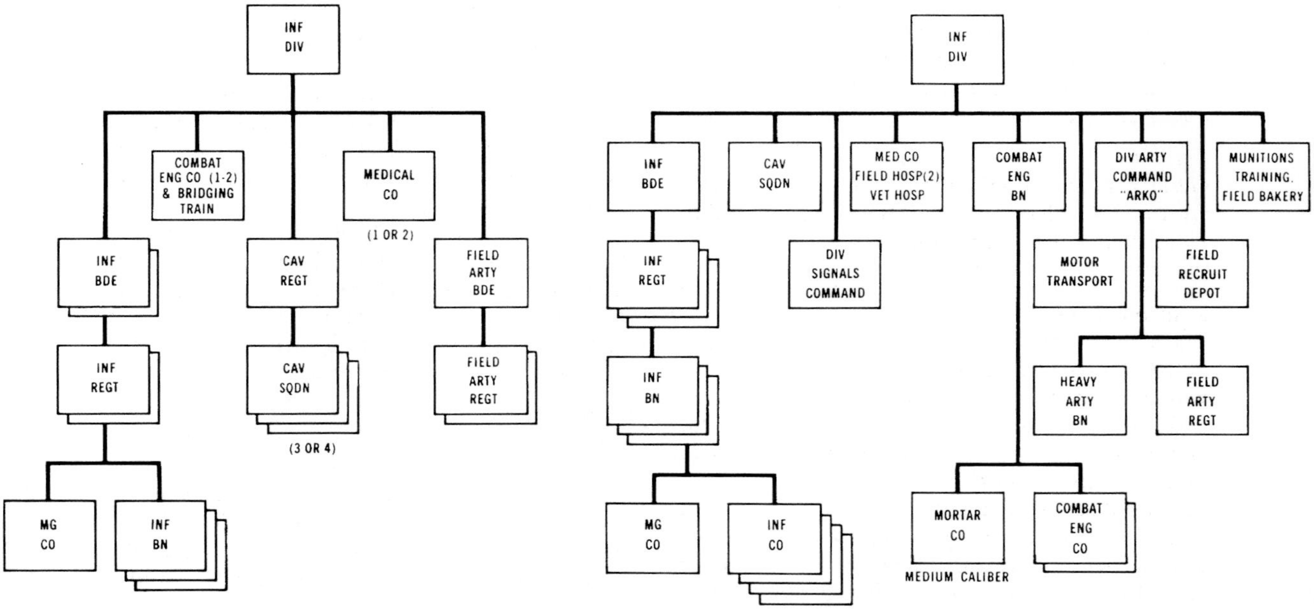

German Infantry Division, 1914 and early 1918.
(Contemporary Diagram)

III German Army Weapons: Characteristics & Ranges 1914–1918

Infantry Weapons

Mauser Gewehr 98/Bayonet 98/05
The standard German rifle throughout the First World War was the bolt-action, high-velocity 7.92mm Mauser-produced *Gewehr* 98. A magazine-fed repeating rifle, in common with the standard British Lee-Enfield SMLE (short magazine Lee-Enfield) and French (*Lebel* 86/93 or *Berthier* 07/15) rifles, it had an effective range of 300 yards for the average infantryman and 500–600 yards as a 'squad' weapon when firing at a mass target.

The German bayonet was the 98/05, which had a fourteen-inch blade.

Snipers
German snipers usually fired the *Gewehr* 98 fitted with a 'X4' telescopic sight. Special ammunition was manufactured, but in the latter part of the war, this was generally unavailable.

Machine Guns
The German Army was issued with the infamous belt-fed MG08 7.92mm medium machine gun with a cyclic rate of fire of 600 rounds per minute and a range of around 2,000 metres. The MG08 and British Maxim or Vickers machine guns were used with great skill throughout the war and have been cited as the main killer on the Western Front. This dubious honour goes hands down to the artillery, which was responsible for almost 60 per cent of the casualties suffered throughout the war, compared with around 30 per cent from machine gun and rifle fire. But the machine gun often held up major attacks and inflicted heavy casualties on both sides.

From 1916 onwards the German infantry, including assault/storm troop detachments, were issued with the belt-fed model MG 08/15 light machine gun, which was designed to match the British Lewis light machine gun as a more portable infantry section weapon in preference to the more cumbersome MG 08. By 1918 there were six MG 08/15s per German infantry company.

The most innovative of the small arms brought into the German arsenal was the magazine-fed, short-muzzled 9mm Bergmann sub-machine gun, which was used extensively by storm troops during the offensives of 1918.

Grenades
Grenades, or 'bombs' as they were popularly known, were for close-quarter fighting and ideal weapons for trench clearing on both sides. The most famous hand grenade of both world wars was the German *Stielhandgranate*, or 'stick-grenade'. Based on a thin metal can-like explosive-filled head, it had a hollow wooden handle for the fuse. The Tommies knew it as a 'potato masher' because of its shape. The characteristic handle helped to give it extra range and accuracy than the British and French equivalent grenades, but it was not as lethal, as it relied more on blast than on fragmentation effect.

The other principal German hand grenade was the *Eiergranate*, or 'egg-grenade', so called because of its shape. Though its range was even greater than that of the stick-grenade, it too had a relatively poor effect unless thrown into a confined space, such as a sap or dugout.

Mortars
The German Army was equipped with light, medium and heavy *Minenwerfer*. Front line units were also armed with the smaller *Granatenwerfer*, or grenade thrower. The 250mm (25cm) heavy mortar had a mortar bomb weighing over 200lb, with an explosive charge of over 103lb and a range of over 500 yards. Its effects were devastating, leaving a huge crater on impact. German mortar rounds were often known as 'Moaning Minnies' on account of the noise that they made when fired. The one advantage of the mortars was that they could be spotted in flight and troops could at least attempt to take evasive action.

Flamethrowers
The Germans had two models in the early part of the war: the *Kleinflammenwerfer*, with a range of 18 metres, carried by one man; and the *Gross-flammenwerfer*, elevated by two men. The light-weight self-igniting *Wex* was used from 1917.

Field Artillery

77mm: 1896 n/A. and F.K. 16 Field Guns
The 77mm *Feldkanone* field gun was the staple field artillery weapon of the German Army and equivalent to the outstanding French quick-firing 75mm *Soixante-Quinze* and British 18-pdr field guns. There were two models, the 1896 n/A (*Feldkanone* 96 n/A. & F.K. 16, *Feldkanone* 1916 pattern). Maximum ranges were between 6,500 and 11,264 yards, depending on type of shell and charge used. It used HE, shrapnel, smoke, 'star' shell flare and gas shells. With its flat trajectory, it was an excellent quick-fire weapon in support of infantry and after 1916 it was utilised as a formidable anti-tank weapon.

10.5cm (105mm): 98/09 Light Field Howitzer
The *leichte Feldhaubitze* 98/09 (l.F.H. 98/09) was based on the 1898 pattern field howitzer, but entirely remodelled and mounted on a shielded recoil carriage. By the end of the war there were three variants; the 98/09 pattern, 1916 version (l.F.H. 16) and the *Krupp* (l.F.H. Kp.). It used HE, shrapnel, smoke, 'star' shell flare and gas shells. Maximum ranges were between 7,655 and 11,210 yards, depending on type of shell and charge used.

Medium and Heavy Guns
The proportion of guns to howitzers in the German foot artillery was approximately 25 to 75 per cent respectively. The guns in most common use were the 10cm (4.1in), 13cm (5.3in), 15cm (5.9in) guns and 24cm (9.4in) naval gun. The calibres of the heavy howitzer batteries were more standardised, comprising the 15cm (5.9in) and 21cm (8.3in) howitzers.

10cm Gun
There were four patterns of the 10cm gun; 10cm gun, 10cm gun '04, 10cm gun '97 and 10cm gun '14. Ammunition used was HE and shrapnel. Maximum ranges varied from 11,264 to 12,249 yards.

13cm Gun
The 13cm gun was a long-range high-velocity, quick-firing (QF) gun. It fired HE and shrapnel and had a maximum range of 15,748 yards for percussion (HE) charge and 15, 311 yards for timed fuse discharge (shrapnel).

15cm Heavy Field Howitzer
Half of the German foot artillery was equipped with the 15cm heavy field howitzer (*schwere Feld Haubitze*, or s.F.H.). There were four variants: original (s.F.H.), 1902 pattern (s.F.H.02), 1913 pattern (s.F.H.13) and Long 1913 pattern (lg. s.F.H.13). It used HE, smoke and gas shells. Maximum ranges were between 6,616 and 9,296 yards, depending on the type of ammunition and howitzer variant fired.

210mm Howitzer (Mortar)
The 210mm/21cm Howitzer or heavy mortar had three patterns: 1902 pattern 21cm *Mörser*, 1910 pattern *Mörser* and the 1917 pattern long mortar, or *lange Mörser*. The 21cm *Mörser* fired HE and gas and had a maximum range of 8,400 and 11,155 yards, depending on type of charge and variant used.

Other Guns
Older patterns of guns, some of huge calibre and range, were used by the German Army during the First World War (including captured guns). The most commonly used were the 9cm field gun, with a maximum range of 7,109 yards; the 12cm heavy gun, with a maximum range of 7,984 yards; the 15cm *Ringkanone* with a maximum range of 8,640 yards and the 15cm 'long gun', with a maximum range of 10,936 yards. Of the largest calibres, the 35.6cm coastal defence and 38cm guns were the most commonly known. The 35.6cm gun had a maximum range of 50,300 yards and the 38cm gun had a maximum range of 46,000 yards.

Aircraft

***Albatros* Series**
A number of variants existed, but chief among these was the *Albatros DIII Vee-Strutter*. The *DIII* was armed with two machine guns, had a speed of 110mph, a ceiling of 18,000 feet and a flight endurance time of over two hours. It was a versatile and formidable fighter and was used by forward combat squadrons, including von Richthofen's. *Albatros DIIIs* had a significant role in inflicting the terrible British RFC losses during 'Bloody April' in 1917.

Fokker Series
Dutch aircraft designer Anthony Fokker produced some of the best German aircraft of the war, most notably the *DVII* and most famously the *Fokker DrI* triplane. The *DVII*, a single-seat biplane, had a ceiling of 15,000 feet and an endurance time of 90 minutes and was armed with two fixed 7.92mm *Spandau* machine guns. It was first deployed with von Richthofen's *Jagdgeschwader (Jasta)* I. It had an 185bhp BMW engine and its design gave it an extraordinary ability to apparently 'hang' in the air where other aircraft would normally stall. The single-seat *Fokker DrI* was designed to counter the threat of the British Sopwith triplane series of

fighters. Armed with two 7.92mm machine guns, it was small, but highly manoeuvrable. Werner Voss scored 10 victories in a *DrI* in September 1917 alone, and Richthofen was flying his famous red *Fokker DrI* when he was shot down and killed on 21 April 1918. The *DVII* and *DrI* followed earlier 'E-Type' single-seater fighters that were brought into service and flown throughout 1915 and 1916.

Junkers Series
The *Junkers DI* was the first all-metal fighter to appear over the Western Front. The *DI* was a single-seater, had a ceiling of around 15,000 feet and could climb to that height more rapidly than virtually any other aircraft. The two-seater *CLI*, a fighter with a dual role as a ground attack aircraft, was introduced in the latter stages of the war and was unable to make the impact that it might have done in greater numbers. The *JI* entered service in 1917 and became a useful close air support aircraft for the infantry, especially during the German spring offensives in 1918.

***Pfalz* Series**
There were a number of *Pfalz* variants, but their principal function was as a dual-roled fighter-scout aircraft. Armed with two 7.92mm machine guns, it was a single-seater with an excellent performance record. The best example of the *Pfalz* range was the *DXII*, with a speed of 180mph and a ceiling of 18,500 feet. The DXII was very sturdily built and this gave it an impressive manoeuvrability that allowed the pilot scope for high altitude patrolling and then steep attack dives that took many Allied pilots by surprise.

Tanks (Armoured Fighting Vehicles/AFVs)

The only tank manufactured by Germany in the First World War was the lumbering A7V. The A7V had a crew of eighteen and was armed with a 57mm gun and six machine guns. It weighed 33 tons and had a maximum cross-country speed of 2–3mph. Only 17 were built and they were of little use to the German Army, whose troops preferred to capture and commandeer British and French tanks where they could, rather than have faith in their own leviathans.

Source: *Handbook of the German Army in War, April 1918.*

IV Selected Biographies

General Erich Ludendorff 1865–1937

Erich Ludendorff was born in Kruszwenia, near Posnan (modern Poland). He was the son of a landowner, but came from a relatively modest background compared with many of his military peers. He was educated at the military school at Gross-Lichterfelde, Berlin, and commissioned into an unglamorous infantry regiment, but quickly established himself as a professional, intelligent and ambitious young officer.

Ludendorff's determination and irrepressible energy marked him out from his contemporaries. General Helmuth von Moltke, the German Army Chief of Staff, who was to command the German Army in 1914, ensured that Ludendorff rose steadily through the ranks.

With the onset of war, Major General Ludendorff played a leading role in the capture of the seemingly impregnable Belgian fort at Liège during the German invasion of the West. For this, he was awarded the *Pour le Mérite*, Prussia's highest military honour. Later in August 1914 he became Chief-of-Staff to Hindenburg on the Eastern Front and assisted in forging the decisive victories against the Russian army in 1914 and 1915.

In August 1916, as the battles of Verdun and the Somme raged on the Western Front, Ludendorff and Hindenburg became the joint heads of the whole German Army. The German casualties of almost a million men in these two battles were so large as to be almost insupportable. Ludendorff and Hindenburg swiftly decided that the only course was to shorten the German line and give up some of the territory held since 1914. In March, they withdrew their hard-pressed forces to the newly prepared defences of the Hindenburg Line, but not without controversy, as Ludendorff was the principal architect of the scorched earth policy that devastated much of the hitherto undamaged territory behind the then German lines.

Despite his undoubted moral courage, Ludendorff had become arrogant, inflexible and prone to panic when military operations did not go according to plan. After the failure of the German offensives in 1918, he became a broken man, and following the further disaster of the Allied attack at Amiens on 8 August he knew that Germany's only practical course was to sue for peace. He was removed from command in October 1918 and replaced by Walter Groener.

Disillusioned by the circumstances of Germany's defeat and his own disgrace, Ludendorff gave his support to a former army corporal, believing that Adolf Hitler's extreme nationalism represented the only way for Germany to regain its honour. Ludendorff took part in Hitler's abortive *putsch* in Munich in November 1923, and was tried for treason, but acquitted. Not until it was too late did he realise that Hitler was about to lead Germany once more into the abyss. Ludendorff died, fearful for his country's future, in 1937.

Field Marshal Paul Ludwig Hans Anton von Beneckendorff und von Hindenburg 1847–1934

Paul von Hindenburg came from a family of the traditional Prussian military aristocracy. A handsome and determined individual as a boy, he became a military cadet, excelled in his peer group and was commissioned at eighteen into the elite Prussian Foot Guards.

He fought with distinction in both the Austro-Prussian and Franco-Prussian wars, and was decorated for bravery in 1870. Following the latter war, he continued to follow a military career and rose steadily through the ranks. Count von Schlieffen, the mastermind behind German strategy in 1914, was due to retire in 1904, and Hindenburg, now a full general himself, was tipped to replace him. However, during the final exercise of the annual military manoeuvres in 1905, he had the misfortune to defeat the Kaiser. Realising that this was not good for his career, Hindenburg resigned. He later wrote: 'My military career had carried me much further than I had dared hope. There was no prospect of war at the time . . . so I applied to retire.'

Although still an active patron of the military, including the Franco-Prussian War Veterans' Association, Hindenburg was frustrated by his inactivity in retirement. But he hardly expected to be recalled for active service when war erupted in August 1914. By the third week in August, General von Moltke, the German Army commander, realised that things were not going well against Russia. He appointed General Ludendorff as the new Chief-of-Staff in East Prussia, with Hindenburg as the commander of the German Eighth Army. Under this new team, with the brilliant staff officer Colonel Hofmann providing the plan, the German Eighth Army trounced two Russian armies at Tannenberg (August 1914) and Hindenburg was given the accolade 'Hero of Tannenberg'. The magnitude of the Russian defeat so early in the war caused psychological damage from which her army never fully recovered.

Hindenburg was promoted to field marshal and became a national icon. Tannenberg also forged the partnership between Hindenburg and Ludendorff, which would oversee Germany's military strategy for the last two years of the First World War. But from early 1917, Hindenburg's influence was diminished as Ludendorff grasped the reins of power. The situation continued until the last month of the war. After the Armistice and Versailles, Hindenburg's credibility remained so high among the ordinary German people that he became President of the Weimar Republic.

He later attempted to limit the burgeoning power of Hitler, whom he disliked intensely, but was forced to make him Chancellor in January 1933. Hindenburg died at 87 in August 1934. He was buried at a newly erected shrine near Tannenberg, the scene of his greatest triumph, with full ceremony. It was an ironic twist of fate that Hitler was the architect of Hindenburg's solemn and respectful funeral ceremony. With Hindenburg's death, Hitler gained absolute power and set Germany on a course that was to prove even more disastrous than that of 1914–18.

General Erich von Falkenhayn 1861–1922

Erich von Falkenhayn was born into an aristocratic but impoverished family, which had a strong military tradition. Thanks to Kaiser Wilhelm's patronage, he enjoyed a rapid rise to military power. The Kaiser had been particularly impressed by Falkenhayn's reports when acting as a liaison officer in China during the Boxer Rebellion of 1900. He succeeded General von Moltke as the German Army's supremo in September 1914. This was just as the Allies brought the German invasion of France to a halt.

Falkenhayn was withdrawn and unpopular, a paradox of ruthlessness and indecision. By early 1916, he had demonstrated both traits. On the one hand, he had restored the German Army's fighting power after its failure to overcome the French and British in the first few weeks of the war. On the other, he had enraged Generals Hindenburg and Ludendorff by his hesitancy on the Eastern Front, halting the German offensive just as a decisive victory seemed within reach. This emotive cocktail would be a significant factor in Falkenhayn's handling of Verdun and the early phases of the Somme campaign, and a major factor in his downfall.

He was forced to resign in August 1916 after the costly failure of Verdun and growing hostility to his leadership. He was replaced by Hindenburg and Ludendorff, who had enjoyed considerable success on the Eastern Front. In September 1916 Romania joined the war on the Allied side and Falkenhayn was sent to crush this new threat, which he did with great ruthlessness. He was then sent to help the Turks recapture Mesopotamia, and tried to do the same in Palestine. Both missions proved abortive.

Falkenhayn spent the last months of the First World War commanding an army in the Baltic State of Lithuania. He died in 1922.

Field Marshal Helmuth Karl Bernhard Graf von Moltke (the Elder) 1800–91

Helmuth von Moltke was born into a well-established Prussian aristocratic family at Parchim, Mecklenburg. His father emigrated to Denmark when he was a small boy and he was educated at the Royal Cadet Corps School in Copenhagen. Although commissioned into the Prussian Army in 1822, he was forced to resign because of ill-health, but was able to return to military duty ten years later, when he joined the Prussian General Staff. He was instrumental in the modernisation of the Turkish Army in the 1830s and became aide-de-camp to the future Kaiser Friedrich III in 1835.

Moltke was appointed chief of the Prussian General Staff on the eve of the Wars of Unification in 1858. He then reorganised the Prussian Army, which had been thoroughly rearmed with modern weaponry. He soon recognised the vital role of railways in the rapid movement of troops and resources to and from the battlefield, which he exploited in the ensuing conflicts.

His strategic planning was instrumental in the run of victories against Denmark (1864), Austria (1866) and, most spectacularly, France (1870–1).

His achievements earned him rich rewards from the Kaiser and from 1871, a grateful fledgling German nation. His triumph at Sedan during the Franco-Prussian War had led to his elevation to both Count (*Graf*) and Field Marshal.

Von Moltke remained chief of the general staff until 1888 and died in 1891. He was succeeded as Chief of the General Staff by Waldersee, Schlieffen and then his own nephew and namesake.

General Helmuth Johannes Ludwig von Moltke (the Younger) 1848–1916

Helmuth von Moltke was born into the same distinguished Prussian military family as Field Marshal von Moltke, who had modernised the Prussian Army prior to the Franco-Prussian War and was the architect of the German Army after 1871. The younger Moltke was his uncle's adjutant in 1882 and later succeeded General von Schlieffen as Chief of the General Staff in 1906. He inherited the Schlieffen Plan for the invasion of France and containment of Russia, which he implemented at the outbreak of war in August 1914.

Moltke soon lost control of the armies under his command and as a result the Schlieffen Plan rapidly unravelled, and any chance of a swift, decisive victory disappeared. The German Army was defeated at the Battle of the Marne (6–12 September 1914). Moltke, an ill and broken man, was removed from command on 14 September and replaced by General von Falkenhayn. He never fully recovered from the trauma of the opening weeks of the war and died in 1916.

Crown Prince Rupprecht of Bavaria 1869–1955

Crown Prince Rupprecht of Bavaria was a rare example of a prince appointed to high responsibilities in the field who demonstrated great talent as a commander throughout the First World War. As the Bavarian Army retained its independence from the remainder of the Prussian-dominated German military establishment, it was particularly appropriate that the largely Bavarian-manned Sixth Army should be commanded by Bavaria's Crown Prince, Rupprecht.

He was promoted Field Marshal and to command of his own Group of Armies after success as GOC Sixth Army in 1914 and 1915. By September 1916, with the succession of Hindenburg and Ludendorff to Supreme Command, he commanded 'Army Group Prince Rupprecht'. Rupprecht's great strength was his determination to speak his mind and censure both Falkenhayn and (especially) Ludendorff, for their poor leadership decisions. He most publicly threatened to resign when Ludendorff ordered a 'scorched earth' policy during the German withdrawal to the *Siegfried Stellung* (Hindenburg Line). Despite leading his Army Group with considerable resolve during the *Kaiserschlacht*, he was one of the first senior German Army commanders to realise that the war was unwinnable and that Ludendorff's plans for victory were doomed. However, he remained loyal to his men and his responsibilities until the end of the war before retiring to private life in Bavaria.

A staunch critic of Hitler – and Ludendorff's support for the Nazi Party in the 1920s – he left Germany during the Second World War and did not return until late 1945. Conversely, he retained an empathy and respect for the British Army and the British people throughout the First World War and beyond. This was perhaps partly because he and his mother Marie Thérèse, who died in 1919, were linked by Jacobite 'succession' to the British throne. Rupprecht died peacefully in 1955.

General Max von Gallwitz 1852–1937

Max von Gallwitz had an impressive and distinguished record of military and combat service. He joined the elite Prussian Guards in 1870 and made his mark as a fearless young officer during the Franco-Prussian war of that year. When war broke out in 1914 he led a Guards Division and was soon promoted to the command of an army.

General Gallwitz was forthright and loyal only to those whom he believed had Germany's best interests at heart. He despised the strategies of the former head of the German Army, General Falkenhayn, and actively supported his removal. He fully endorsed the new command of Hindenburg and Ludendorff, pointing to their successes on the Eastern Front as proof of their genius.

Gallwitz brilliantly routed the Russians in May 1915, where the Tsarist armies 'melted like snow' before the relentless German advance.

In the autumn of 1915 Gallwitz was transferred to Verdun on the Western Front to command 'Army Group Meuse'. Despite his skill as a commander, his Army suffered some 70,000 casualties for an advance of a mere two miles against Verdun in the spring and summer of 1916. But even the German losses at Verdun were to pale against the bloody suffering of the Germans on the Somme later that year, where Gallwitz commanded another Army Group.

Despite the heavy losses he incurred, Gallwitz's reputation remained high. He continued to command on the Western Front, principally against the British, until the German spring 1918 offensive. When this attack failed, he was given his own composite Army Group 'Gallwitz' to defend the vital Meuse-Argonne sector.

Gallwitz's military career ended soon after the Armistice. Though 69 years of age, he went into politics and assisted his mentor Hindenburg in the task of rebuilding Germany under the Weimar Republic. Like Hindenburg, he had no time for Hitler and the Nazi Party, and was convinced that the 'Austrian Corporal' would lead Germany to disaster. Gallwitz spent his final years writing his memoirs and a history of the Prussian Guards, dying two weeks before his 85th birthday, in 1937.

Oswald Boelcke 1891–1916

Oswald Boelcke was the architect of German air tactics and the first national hero as a 'knight of the air'. By the end of 1915, he had shot down ten enemy aircraft and was equally active in the skies over Verdun in early 1916. He was a pioneering air warfare tactician and encapsulated his methods in the ten principles of his *Dikta Boelcke*, which became the professional bible of the German air arm. In July 1916 he was given command of the *Fokker*-equipped *Jasta* II, one of the new dedicated fighter squadrons. Undefeated in the air, he was killed in a freak accident on 16 October 1916 when he collided with a fellow *Jasta* II pilot. Despite his premature death, he remained an inspiration to German airman who continued to regard him as 'the father of air fighting'.

Rittmeister Baron Manfred von Richthofen 1892–1918

Manfred von Richthofen was born in Breslau (now Polish Wroclaw) in 1892, two years before his brother Lothar. He began his military career as a cadet in 1909 before joining the elite Uhlan cavalry regiment as a trainee officer. In August 1914, he was sent to the Eastern Front, but soon found himself on the Western Front where he won the Iron Cross Second Class for courage under fire. In May 1915 he transferred to the German Air Service and returned to the Russian front after qualifying as an observer. In autumn 1915 he trained as a pilot. He qualified in March 1916 and joined *Kampfgruppe* 2 on the Verdun front. Despite another spell in the East in the summer, Richthofen was recruited to the newly formed *Jasta* II under the talented Oswald Boelcke on 1 September 1916. Thereafter, he swiftly established his reputation, was awarded the coveted *Pour le Mérite*, and by July 1917 he was one of the leading air aces on the Western Front.

On 17 July, he escaped death by a whisker when he was shot down and wounded in the head by British FE2s of 20 Sqn RFC. However, by August he was back and claiming more kills. During the German offensives of March and April 1918 his famous 'Flying Circus' (*JG1*) was in the thick of the fighting and he claimed a further seventeen Allied aircraft, bringing his tally to eighty.

But on 21 April 1918, his luck finally ran out and he was shot down, some still argue in controversial circumstances. His body was recovered and he was buried with full military honours at Bertangles British Military Cemetery on the Somme. His brother Lothar survived the war, but was to die tragically in 1922. Von Richthofen's death was a profound shock to both the troops and the German people. He had been a talisman – and many imagined him immortal. The cruel reality of war and the Red Baron's death led to many Germans believing that the war was lost well before the final German offensives petered out in June and July 1918.

Max Immelmann 1890–1916

Max Immelmann was one of the early great air aces and nicknamed the 'Eagle of Lille' after the area of operations in which he flew. Immelmann began as an aerial artillery observer and then moved on to reconnaissance duties. When the *Fokker E1* fighter appeared on the Western Front, Immelmann and the aircraft seemed made for each other. On 1 August 1915 he claimed his first 'kill' in the fighter – a French pilot – and he was awarded the Iron Cross First Class. Like Boelcke, Immelmann was a leading exponent of aerial tactics and he became notorious among Allied pilots for his audacious 'Immelmann Turn', a half loop and roll that put him above any opponent who had attacked his aircraft from the rear. By early 1916 he had claimed fourteen kills and appeared invincible. But his impressive combat record came to an abrupt end on 18 June that year when he was shot down and killed by FE2bs of 25 Sqn RFC shortly before the opening of the Somme offensive.

Werner Voss 1897–1917

Werner Voss began his short but brilliant flying career as an observer during the Somme campaign in the summer of 1916 and by November had qualified as a pilot and joined *Jasta* II. As most of the troops who had fought through the bloody summer and autumn months of the Somme battles took stock through the winter, Voss was hard at work. He shot down his first enemy aircraft, a British BE2c, in November 1916 and by January 1917 his tally had risen to 22 'kills'. In no time he had earned a reputation similar to that of Baron Manfred von Richthofen and seemed destined to match it. This respect was enhanced by still more success during the Nivelle offensive in which he downed several French aircraft. In July 1917 he returned to the Somme in command of *Jasta* X. He was just 20 years of age.

By the third week in September 1917 he had a staggering 48 kills in a mere 10 months at the 'sharp end'. On 23 September, eager to add to his tally, his patrol ran into one of 56 Sqn RFC led by Major James McCudden VC, DSO*, MC*, MM. In the ensuing dogfight, Voss was hit and his aircraft plummeted to the ground. As with the 'Red Baron', Voss was highly respected by friend and foe alike.

V Der Volksbund Deutsche Kriegsgräberfürsorge (German War Graves Maintenance Association)

Soldiers' graves are the greatest reminder to us all of the price of peace; their meaning will remain forever.

Albert Schweitzer

Background

The *Volksbund Deutsche Kriegsgräber-fürsorge*, founded in December 1919, provides a similar service to that of the Commonwealth War Graves Commission by maintaining the German military cemeteries (and the few memorials) worldwide for both world wars, and assisting relatives to find and often visit the graves of their loved ones.

Between 1 August 1914 and 1 January 1915, the German Army suffered 695,000 casualties, of whom 145,000 were killed. At the time, it was a shocking and staggering statistic, for it was five times the total loss incurred during the Franco-Prussian war of 1870–1. By November 1918, 1,930,000 German officers and men were dead, an additional 100,000 officially missing and over five million left crippled or scarred by war. The vast majority of Germany's dead fell or were lost without trace on the Western Front. Over 2,000 German military cemeteries, many with mass-burial sites and memorials to the missing, were dotted across France and Belgium.

After Versailles it was agreed that much of the land occupied by German cemeteries would be handed over to the French and Belgian authorities on the basis that the interred German soldiers were reburied in concentration cemeteries. In 1925 a treaty was signed between Weimar Germany, Belgium and France formalising this arrangement. Until then, the German dead lay scattered in 678 burial places in Belgium and 1,500 cemeteries in France.

Many were exhumed and concentrated in major sites such as Langemarck and Roeselare in Belgium, Fricourt, Vermandovillers and Maissemy in the Somme region and Neuville St Vaast near Vimy Ridge in the Artois region of France.

In 1954 a new convention granted the home authorities more land and the remaining German cemeteries (178 in Belgium and *c.* 500 in France) were transferred to a final total of 26 cemeteries (plus one exclusively for Second World War dead at Recogne-Bastogne) in Belgium and 277 burial places in France. Today, the 27 cemeteries in Belgium contain the remains of 170,000 German officers and men and the 277 French sites represent the last resting place of around 400,000 German dead.

There are German military cemeteries for the dead of both world wars in over eighty countries worldwide.

Gefallen für Deutschland im Weltkrieg

After 1954 the dead from 128 cemeteries were transferred to Langemarck, Vladslo and Menen (Menin). Largely unidentified remains were buried in mass graves, *Kameradengräben*, in these sites, although the record of names that were known from smaller cemeteries and then re-interred here are usually shown on commemorative plaques around the mass burial place. Graves are marked with black metal crosses, black metal plaques fixed to a stone slab, or headstones similar to the British style, but with a flat or inverted 'V' shaped top. A few headstones will be seen in many of the First World War German cemeteries with the 'Star of David' to mark the graves of Jewish soldiers, a perfectly natural parallel with similar markings in British military cemeteries and a difference respected until the advent of the National Socialist era.

Fricourt military cemetery on the Somme is the only German cemetery on or near the British part of the 1916 battlefield, as this was the only site given by Allied authorities for the burial of German dead in this area. The dates shown on the crosses and *Kameradengrab* nominal rolls reflect the heavy fighting here in 1916 and 1918. Given the huge German casualties on the Somme in both campaigns, it seems surprising that a concentration cemetery such as Fricourt does not hold thousands more remains.

Sadly, this mismatch merely highlights the fact that many thousands more were buried where they fell, or were lost during the ebb and flow of battle here. Consequently, their bodies were never recovered and they remain in their 'muddy graves' beneath the former Somme battlefield.

Where an officer or soldier is identified each headstone/grave marker gives name, rank, regiment and dates of birth and death. Unlike in British cemeteries, where every effort is made to bury individual officers and men, there are usually several German dead buried beneath each cross or gravestone, the comrades' grave, which symbolises the spirit of comradeship in death as well as life. Unidentified soldiers, 'known unto God' in English parlance, have a simple inscription, usually either *Unbekannt; Gefallen fur Deutschland* (Unknown; fallen for Germany) or most commonly *Ein Unbekannter Deutscher Soldat* (An unknown German soldier).

The landscaping of each cemetery is generally in stark contrast to those designed by prominent British architects post-1918. In addition to the usual black crosses and plaques, cemeteries tend to have a canopy of trees, normally oak, a traditional German symbol of strength and courage, although others are also used. Some entrances, such as the one at Langemarck in the Ypres salient, have a 'blockhouse' style design, and may have remnants of German bunkers within the site. The overall impression tends to be dark, a sense of brooding and a disquieting feeling of unrest, rather than a reassuring notion of peace as in the British cemeteries.

Respect for the Dead on Either Side of the Wire

During 1914–18, British servicemen who died of wounds in France or Belgium in German captivity were usually buried in German military cemeteries and British units repaid the compliment. Equally, German and British airmen shot down and killed over enemy lines were typically laid to rest in enemy territory with due military respect. The most famous example of such protocol was the interment of Manfred von Richthofen in the British CWGC Cemetery at Bertangles on 22 April 1918, the day after his death.

Therefore, British military and some communal cemeteries contain a number of German graves maintained in the same way as any other burial place in each site. The vast majority of these men were prisoners of war (PoWs) who usually died of wounds and whose bodies were buried and remain undisturbed next to those of British and Dominion soldiers as common victims of war. While Germany was divided, West Germany paid the full maintenance costs of the German graves in British military cemeteries, though the German Democratic Republic (East Germany) did not contribute to the costs at any time in its forty-year history.

Sadly, with few notable exceptions, French cemeteries contain other Allied dead, but no German burials, although the Ossuaries at the French memorial and burial sites at Notre Dame de Lorette (Artois) and Verdun contain the unidentified remains of German and French soldiers killed and intermingled during the horrendous battles fought there in 1914/15 and 1916 respectively. It is a poignant but equally macabre recognition of the mutual sacrifice of French and German troops at both charnel houses during the First World War. American cemeteries are exclusively for American dead.

Care and Maintenance of the German Military Cemeteries

Further improvement, landscaping and continual maintenance began with a programme established by the former West German government in the early 1970s giving students from its own country and later other Western European nations 'working holidays' to France and Belgium to carry out these tasks. This has become a well-established tradition and continues to the present day.

The work in many cemeteries, most notably at Langemarck, was not fully completed until the latter part of the 1980s.

Examples of Main German Military Cemeteries (and Memorials) in Belgium and France[1]

BELGIUM

The four largest German military cemeteries are:

Menen: 'German' end of the Menin Road. 47,864 burials.
Langemarck: Ypres salient. 44,294 burials, of whom 24,916 are interred in the *Kameradengrab*.
Vladslo: Dixmude-Torhout Road. 25,644 burials.
Hooglede: Roeselare-Ostend Road. 8,247 burials.

FRANCE

Main cemeteries for First World War German military dead only are:

Neuville St Vaast/Artois: 36,793 burials plus 8,040 in *Kameradengrab*: 44,833.
St Laurent-Blagny/PdC: 7,069 burials plus 24,870 in *Kameradengrab*: 31,939.
Lens-Sallumines/Pas de Calais (PdC): 8,207 burials plus 7,439 in *Kameradengrab*: 15,646.
Cambrai/Nord: 7,989 burials plus 2,746 in *Kameradengrab*: 10,735.
Vermandovillers/Somme: 9,455 burials plus 13,200 in *Kameradengrab*: 22,655.
Fricourt/Somme: 5,056 burials plus 11,970 in *Kameradengrab*: 17,026.
Rancourt/Somme: 3,930 burials plus 7,492 in *Kameradengrab*: 11,422.
Maissemy/Aisne: 15,478 burials plus 7,814 in *Kameradengrab*: 23,292.
Sissone/Aisne: 10,699 burials plus 3,995 in *Kameradengrab*: 14,694.
Soupir/Aisne: 5,125 burials plus 5,958 in *Kameradengrab*: 11,083.
Servon-Melzicourt/Marne: 3,621 burials plus 6,526 in *Kameradengrab*: 10,147.
Souain/Marne: 2,464 burials plus 11,322 in *Kameradengrab*: 13,786.
St Etienne-à-Arnes/Ardennes: 7,541 burials plus 5,000 in *Kameradengrab*: 12,541.
Consenvoye/Meuse: 8,609 burials plus 2,537 in *Kameradengrab*: 11,146.
Thiaucourt: 8,715 burials plus 72,970 in *Kameradengrab*: 11,685.

German Military Burial Sites in the United Kingdom

Cannock Chase/Staffordshire: 2,143 burials from the First and 2,796 from the Second World War: 4,939.
(There are 111 burials from the Second World War only at St Peter Port, Jersey.)

Volksbund Deutsche Kriegsgräber-fürsorge: Information and Contact Addresses

Volksbund Deutsche Kriegsgräberfürsorge e.V., Werner-Hilpert-Strasse 2, 3500 Kassel, Germany.

References

1 *Volksbund Deutsche Kriegsgräberfürsorge, Schicksal in Zahlen* (Berlin, VDK e.V., 1986). Handbook in German, providing background and locations/statistics of all German war graves of both world wars in over 80 countries worldwide.
2 *Volksbund Deutsche Kriegsgräberfürsorge, Karten und Handbuch der deutschen Krigerfriedhöfe in Frankreich (und Belgien): Deutsche Kriegsgräberstatten im ehemaligen französischen kampfgebiet* (Berlin, VBK, 1931). Maps and handbook of German war cemeteries on the former battlefields of France.

GLOSSARY

Abwehrschlacht	German term for the 'defensive battle'.
Alleyman	British/Dominion nickname for a German soldier (from the French: *Allemagne*).
Anzac	Australian and New Zealand Army Corps (term used generically for all Australian or Kiwi troops).
Arty	Artillery.
Barrage	Artillery bombardment.
Battery	Artillery sub-unit, an equivalent level to that of an infantry company. Commanded by a major in the British/French armies; normally by a captain in the German Army.
Bde/bde	Brigade. A German bde normally consisted of two regiments of three battalions each; a British bde comprised three battalions, an approximate strength of 3,000–5,000 men.
BEF	British Expeditionary Force, abbreviation used throughout the war.
Bn/bn	Battalion. A tactical unit of three or four 'rifle' companies, plus a HQ Coy/Bn HQ. Usual strength was 700–1,000 men.
Bomb	Common term for a hand grenade.
Boche	Derogatory French term for a German and adopted by other Allies. Sometimes spelt 'Bosche'.
Bombardier	Royal Artillery rank equivalent to Corporal.
Box barrage	Artillery barrage used to protect troops carrying out a limited attack, such as a trench raid.
Bunker	Term for well-protected German position, often built of reinforced concrete and designed to provide shelter from artillery fire for HQs, medical stations/posts and forward troop concentrations.
Cable	Telephone land-line, buried to protect it from shell fire whenever time allowed.
Cage	Prisoner of war (PoW) cage: fenced and guarded prisoner holding area close to the front line.
CB	Counter-battery fire: artillery bombardment to destroy or neutralise specific enemy artillery batteries.
C-in-C	Commander-in-Chief.
CO	Commanding officer (usually of a battalion or equivalent).
Company/coy	Company. A tactical sub-unit, an infantry coy consisted of 4 platoons plus coy HQ; a total of 120–50 men.
Corps	(German *Korps*). A formation usually consisting of three or four infantry divisions, with supporting arms such as arty, engineers and logistic units attached.
Creeping barrage	Artillery bombardment designed to protect advancing infantry by extending its range at given intervals to allow attacking infantry to close with the enemy under this 'curtain' of fire, which keeps the enemy's heads down. Introduced by both sides on the Western Front from September 1916, it was an improvement on the more rigid system known as the 'lifting barrage'.
CT	Communication trench: narrow, sometimes covered, trench dug at an angle to a front-line/second-line trench to provide concealed access.
Direct fire	Small-arms, machine-gun, tank and gun fire that is observed by the firer and therefore aimed directly at the target.
Division/Div	Division German: tactical formation of two or three infantry

	regiments or brigades, depending on the operational requirement, with arty, engineers and other supporting arms and services under command. Approximate strength: 12–17,000 men. Allied: tactical formation of three infantry brigades (BEF) or three infantry regiments (French/US), with arty, engineers and other supporting arms and services under command. Approximate strength: 17–20,000 men (exceptionally, US divisions in 1918 were often 25,000 strong).
Dreckfresser	'Mud/dirt eater' – German slang for an infantryman.
Drumfire	Artillery barrage fired by each gun in succession, rather than a salvo (simultaneous firing of the guns). Given its name because of the drum-roll sound of its effect.
Duckboard	Wooden palleted plank used to cover trench floors.
Dugout	Shelter made in the wall of a trench, ranging from a small alcove to large underground rooms.
Ehekruez (Cross of Honour)	President *FM* Paul von Hindenburg established the Cross of Honour shortly before his death in 1934 as a belated remembrance and recognition of 'the imperishable deeds of the German people . . . for all participants as well as for widows and parents of those who fell or died of wounds or as prisoners of war were reported missing and have not since been traced'. It was a bronze cross with two swords passing through it and with '1914–1918' on the reverse side of the medal.
Eiergranate	German egg-shaped grenade.
Eingreif	German independent counter-attack unit, normally used at regimental and divisional level and specifically trained for counter-attack tactics.
Eisen Kreuz (Iron Cross)	*Der Eisen Kreuz*/Iron Cross was introduced by Kaiser Friedrich Wilhelm III in 1813. Its familiar shape was based on a black iron cross, edged with silver and with a spray of oak leaves in the centre. The crown and royal cypher are on the upper arm of the cross and 1813, 1870 or 1914 are emblazoned on the lower arm.
Festung	German term for fortress/ defended locality such as a village.
FM	(General) *Feldmarschall* (German Army)/Field Marshal (BEF).
Feldzug	Military campaign.
Fire trench	Front line trench.
Five-nine	British term for German 5.9in shell.
Flammenwerfer	Flamethrower.
Fritz/Fritzie	BEF term for German troops.
GHQ	General headquarters.
GOC	General, officer commanding (usually brigade/division or above).
Gruppe	German equivalent to a corps or reinforced battle group (*Kampfgruppe*). May be used in context as equivalent of a section or detachment.
Hauptstellung	Main position; main emplacement.
HE	High explosive.
HQ/Hqrs	Headquarters.
Hun	Allied slang for German soldier.
Indirect fire	Artillery, mortar and machine-gun fire, which is not observed by the firers, but predicted or observed and adjusted by forward observation officers.
Interdiction	Long-range artillery fire and aerial bombing to destroy or neutralise enemy lines of communication, troop concentrations and supply dumps, isolating front-line troops from rear areas.
Jerry	German.
Jump-off	To jump off was to begin an attack. Jumping-off positions, or jump-off lines were equivalent to the later term start line (SL) and line of departure (LoD).
Kamerad	German for comrade/friend. Used as a gesture of surrender.
Kameradengrab	Mass grave.
Minenwerfer	German trench mortar: also known as 'Moaning Minnie'.
NCO	Non-commissioned officer, ranks from lance-corporal to

warrant officer class one/ regimental sergeant major.

No-man's-land	Territory between respective front lines.
OC	Officer commanding (a company or equivalent).
ORBAT	Order of battle: a unit or formation's establishment for operations.
OHL	*Oberste Heeresleitung*: German General Headquarters.
Pickelhaube	German helmet, with characteristic spike, worn until 1916.
Pillbox	Reinforced concrete machine-gun or field gun post.
Pioneer	German (military) engineer.
Platoon	(German *Zug*). Infantry sub-unit comprising three or four sections. Section (*Gruppe*) of 8–10 men is the smallest tactical fighting group. Platoon normally commanded by a junior lieutenant in the BEF, but usually an SNCO in the German Army.
Poilu	French infantryman: *poilu* = 'hairy one (on account of moustaches/beards).
Pour le Mérite (Blue Max)	Highest German award for individual gallantry in action. The decoration was based on a Maltese cross in blue enamel edged with gold and four golden between the limbs. On the upper arm of the cross was a letter 'F' in gold surmounted by a crown and on the three other arms *Pour le Mérite*. It was known as the 'Blue Max' by German air aces.
PoW	Prisoner of War.
Redoubt	Strongly fortified position in a trench system, with a labyrinth of tunnels and alternative defensive positions within it.
Regiment	German: three battalions; French and US forces: three battalions; BEF: cavalry unit equivalent to infantry battalion, or honorary title for infantry units, such as 'Hampshire Regiment'.
Register	Confirming fall of artillery or mortar rounds by firing 'trial' shots to observe them and adjust them on to a target.
RFA	Royal Field Artillery.
RFC	Royal Flying Corps.
RGA	Royal Garrison Artillery.
Salient	Bulge in front line that protrudes into enemy territory. The Ypres salient (*Ypern Bogen*) was the most notorious and enduring 'salient' for both sides during the First World War.
Sap	Narrow trench dug at an angle from an existing trench for a number of tasks in no-man's-land. Used for listening/ observation posts, machine-gun and mortar positions, as a covered approach to a dugout or even a covered approach across no-man's-land prior to an attack.
Schützengrab	German for trench.
Sicherheits-besatzung	German front line and main defensive garrison.
SOS	Emergency procedure using telephone, or flares of pre-determined colour (often red) fired by both sides to call down a protective barrage on one or a number of pre-registered target areas to disrupt an enemy attack.
Stalhelm	German steel helmet worn from 1916 on and the archetypal shape for both world wars, known by British and Dominion troops as the 'coal scuttle' or 'Jerry pot' helmet ever since.
Stielhandgranate	Stick grenade; known to British troops as a 'potato masher'.
Stollen	Deep dugout and/or mine tunnel.
Stosstruppen	Local counter-attack troops of a sub-unit within a German division defending the front line.
Strafe	Bombardment or hail of fire, most commonly associated with the actions of fighter pilots of the last eighteen months of the war.
Stunt	A soldier's term for an attack.
Sturmtruppen	German 'storm troops'. Most associated with infiltration and specialist attack troops, their tactics developed in 1916 and especially in the latter part of 1917 and for the German offensives of 1918.
Zero	Zero Day – the day that the attack/offensive starts. Zero Hour – the exact time at which an attack or offensive begins.

NOTES

Chapter One

1 See Herwig, Holger, *The First World War, Germany and Austria-Hungary 1914–1918* (London, Hodder Arnold, 1996), frontispiece.
2 *The Times History of the War*, vol. I, p. 55.
3 Haldane, Lord, *Before the War* (London, Cassell, 1920), p. 117.
4 Tuchmann, Barbara W., *August 1914* (London, Constable, 1962), pp. 30–1.
5 Craig, Gordon A., *Germany 1866–1945* (Oxford, OUP, 1978).
6 Müller, Admiral Georg von, *Regierte der Kaiser?* (Göttingen, Musterschmidt-Verlag, 1959), trans. Savill, Mervyn as *At the Kaiser's Court, the First World War Diaries of Admiral Georg Müller* (London, Macdonald, 1961), pp. 181–2.
7 Reichsarchiv, *Der Weltkrieg: Anlagen zum Ersten Band* (Berlin, E.S. Mittler & Sohn, 1930) esp. Strength and Organisation Tables, pp. 510–30.
8 Ibid.

Chapter Two

1 Old rhyme of the 'German' pikeman; quoted in Hindenburg, FM Paul von, *Out of My Life* (London, Cassell & Co., 1920), p. 205.
2 Jack, Brig Gen James L., DSO, ed. Terraine, John, *General Jack's Diary 1914–1918: The Trench Diary of Brigadier-General J.L. Jack, DSO* (London, Cassell, 1964), p. 23.
3 German veteran interviewed for BBC *Great War Series*, 1963.
4 Ludendorff, Erich, *My War Memories, 1914–1918*, vol. I (London, Hutchinson, 1920), pp. 31–2.
5 Morgan, J.H., *German Atrocities, An Official Investigation* (London, T. Fisher Unwin, 1916), pp. 17–19.
6 For further detailed studies of the atrocities, see: Morgan, *German Atrocities*; Horne, John and Kramer, Alan, *German Atrocities, 1914: A History of Denial* (New Haven and London, Yale University Press, 2001).
7 Quoted in BBC *Great War* series, transmitted 1963, rebroadcast in 2003.
8 Blond, Georges, *The Marne: The Battle that saved Paris and changed the Course of the First World War* (Paris, Presses de la Cité, 1962; London, Prion, 2002), pp. 214–15.
9 Edward Spears, interviewed for BBC *Great War* series, 1963.
10 French GHQ Order of the Day.
11 For a legendary account of the Taxis on the Marne, see Blond, *The Marne*.
12 Jack, *General Jack's Diary*, pp. 51–2.

Chapter Three

1 Falkenhayn, Gen Erich von, *Die Oberste, Heeresleitung, 1914-1916, in ihren, wichtigsten Entschliessungen* (Berlin, Mittler, 1920).
2 Sulzbach, Herbert, *Zwei lebende Mauern*, trans. Thonger, Richard. *With the German Guns: Four Years on the Western Front* (Barnsley, Leo Cooper, 1973, 1998), pp. 36–7.
3 Blücher, Princess Evelyn, *An English Wife in Berlin* (New York, E.P. Dutton, 1920), p. 40.
4 Binding, Rudolf, *Aus dem Kriege*, trans. as *A Fatalist at War* (London, George Allen & Unwin, 1929), pp. 19–20.
5 Falls, Cyril, *The First World War* (London, Longman, 1960).
6 Schwink, Capt Otto, German General Staff, *Die Schlacht an der Yser und bei Ypern im Herbst 1914* (Oldenburg, Gerhard Stalling, 1918), p. xvii.
7 Ibid.
8 Binding, *Aus dem Kriege*, pp. 21–7.
9 Schwink, *Die Schlacht*, p. 126.
10 Hedin, Sven, *With the German Armies in the West* (London, John Lane, 1915), p. 323.

11 Quoted in Terraine, John, *The Great War* (Hutchinson, London, 1965), p. 124.
12 Schwink, *Die Schlacht*, pp. 129–30.
13 Swinton, Maj-Gen Ernest, *Twenty Years After* (London, George Newnes, 1938), vol. I, pp. 107–16.
14 Ashworth, Tony, *Trench Warfare, 1914–1918; the Live and Let Live System* (London, Macmillan/Pan, 1980/2000), p. 33.
15 Sulzbach, *With the German Guns*, p. 37.
16 Ibid.
17 Ashworth, *Trench Warfare*, p. 33.
18 Swinton, *Twenty Years After*, pp. 107–16.

Chapter Four

1 Falkenhayn, *Die Oberste Heeresleitung*, p. 79.
2 Moyer: Lawrence V., *Victory Must Be Ours: Germany in the Great War 1914–1918*, (London, Leo Cooper, 1995), p. 81.
3 Herwig, *The First World War*, pp. 283–4.
4 Sulzbach, *With the German Guns*, pp. 40–1.
5 Marie-Paul Rimbaut, quoted in Ellis, John, *Eye Deep in Hell, The Western Front, 1914–1918* (London, Croom Helm, 1976/1979), pp. 168–9.
6 Heinz, Max (trans. Charles Ashleigh), *Loretto: Sketches of a German War Volunteer* (New York, Horace Liveright, 1930), pp. 72–3.
7 Sulzbach, *With the German Guns*, pp. 41.
8 Heinz, *Loretto*, p. 72.
9 Sulzbach, *With the German Guns*, pp. 50–1.
10 Hauptmann August Stramm, German poet (1874–1915), diary note on 23 February 1915; written near St Quentin, Western Front.
11 Blücher, *An English Wife*, p. 54.
12 Reichsarchiv, *Der Weltkrieg, 1914–1918, Achter Band: (*Berlin, Mittler, 1932).
13 Edmonds, Brig J.E., *British Official History* (*BOH*) (1915), vol. I, p. 177.
14 For a useful study of the nature and use of gas in the First World War, see: Palazzo, Albert, *Seeking Victory on the Western Front: The British Army & Chemical Warfare in World War I* (Lincoln and London, University of Nebraska Press, 2000).
15 *BOH*, 1915, vol. I, p. 192.
16 Falkenhayn, *Die Oberste Heeresleitung*, p. 84.
17 Palazzo, *Seeking Victory*, note 14.
18 Von Müller, Admiral Georg Alexander, *Regierte der Kaiser?*, p. 77.
19 Blücher, *An English Wife*, pp. 50–1.
20 Hierl, *Oberst-Lt* Constantin, *Der Weltkrieg in Umrissen* ('Sketches' of the World War, or the World War in Outline), Vols. I, II & III (Charlottenburg/Berlin, Verlag Offene Worte, from 1921).
21 British soldier interviewed in September 1914, see: Terraine, John, *White Heat: The New Warfare, 1914–1918* (London, Guild, 1982), p. 95.
22 Falkenhayn, Gen Erich von, *General Headquarters 1914–1916 and its critical Decisions* (Hutchinson, 1919), p. 42.
23 Joffre, Marshal Georges, *Memoirs*, ii., pp. 359–60.
24 See *BOH*, 1915, vol. II, p. 178.
25 See *BOH*, 1915, vol. II, p. 177.
26 Regt 26: Part ii, pp. 295–6. See also *BOH*, 1915, vol. II, pp. 180–1.
27 Extract from the diary of a captured German artillery officer.
28 Heinz, *Loretto,* pp. 165–6.
29 Blücher, *An English Wife*, p. 100.
30 Quoted in John Ellis's account of life on the Western Front, *Eye Deep in Hell, The Western Front, 1914–1918* (London, Croom Helm, 1976), p. 68.
31 Walter Rathenau, *Berliner Tageblatt*, newspaper No. 368, 25 December 1915.
32 Blücher, *An English Wife*, p. 100.
33 Von Moser, General, *Das militarish und politisch Wichtigste vom Weltkrieg* (1926) and *BOH*, 1915, vol. I, p. 25.
34 Reichsarchiv, *Der Weltkrieg, 1914–1918, Neunter Band* (Berlin, Mittler, 1933). Note that the casualty figures for the German Army during the war were compiled from formation ration strength and casualty returns that were provided every ten days, or three times a month, compared with British unit daily returns. Consequently, German soldiers who were walking, or slightly wounded would not be included in the casualty lists, as they would have remained

with their unit and on the ration strength and have returned to duty within the ten-day reporting period. It is important to bear this in mind when comparing casualty totals for the respective battles.

Chapter Five

1 Engelke, Gerritt, 'An den Tod', quoted in Cross, Tim, *The Lost Voices of World War I*, (London, Bloomsbury, 1988), p. 83.
2 Falkenhayn, *General Headquarters,* p. 271.
3 Ibid.
4 Operation *Gericht*: Judgment, or execution place.
5 From the diary of a German soldier of the Brandenberg Regiment.
6 'Nous sommes dans un pot de chambre et nous y serons emmerdés!': 'We are in a chamber pot and about to be crapped on!' (General Ducrot, during the Franco-Prussian war).
7 Horne, Alistair, *The Price of Glory: Verdun 1916* (London, Penguin, 1962, 1993), p. 97.
8 Henri Barbusse, quoted in *Eye Deep in Hell,* p. 63.
9 Ellis, *Eye Deep in Hell*, pp. 63–5.
10 Guillaime Apollinaire, 1880–1918. Born to a Polish mother and Italian father, he lived in Paris for most of his life and became a writer, journalist and social commentator. He joined the French Army in 1915 and served at Verdun and Champagne before a near-fatal shrapnel head-wound warranted his discharge in late 1916. He died on 9 November 1918 as a victim not of the war but the 'Spanish 'flu' pandemic.
11 Senger und Etterlin, Gen Frido von, *Neither Fear Nor Hope* (London, MacDonald, 1963), pp. 20–1.

Chapter Six

1 Jack, *General Jack's Diary*, p. 152.
2 Heinz, *Loretto*, p. 73.
3 Original letter and family background: courtesy of Mrs Renate Farley, daughter of Albert Mühlmelt.
4 Blücher, *An English Wife,* pp. 136–7.
5 See *BOH*, 1916, vol. I, p. 317.
6 Rupprecht, Kronprinz von Bayern, *Mein Kriegstagebuch, 1914–1918* (Berlin, Mittler, 1929).
7 Ibid., entry for 14 June 1916.
8 Rupprecht cites the reliable sources and intelligence picture that was building up in his diary throughout June 1916. Falkenhayn, however, makes no reference to these intelligence assessments except that an offensive was expected, though he doubted that the French could mount an attack of any strength because of their preoccupation with Verdun (Falkenhayn, *General Head-quarters,* p. 240). More pointedly, his account of the Somme battle appears written to give the reader the impression that the date and sector were known by him all along; ibid., p. 261.
9 91st Reserve Regiment History, p. 209.
10 Rupprecht, *Kriegestagebach*, entry for 26 June 1916.
11 German Second Army Report to OHL dated 25 June 1916, detailed in Wendt, Hermann, *Verdun 1916* (Berlin, Mittler, 1919), p. 173.
12 *Reserve Regiment No. 119 Regimental History*, part of *Erinnerungsblätter deutsche Regimenter* (German Regimental Recollections) series (Oldenburg, Gerhard Stalling, 1918).
13 See: Reichsarchiv, *Schlachten des Weltkrieges; Somme Nord* (Oldenburg, Stalling, 1919, vol. I); and Gerster, M., *Die Schwaben an der Ancre* (Heilbron, Salzer, 1920).
14 *BOH*, 1916, vol. I, pp. 450–2 for British VIII Corps ('over 14,000') and German casualties of 119th Reserve Regiment (total 292), 121st Reserve Regiment (total 560), both of 26th Reserve Division; and 169th Regiment (total 362) of 52nd Division.
15 Terraine, John, *The True Texture of the Somme* (WFA Occasional Paper, 1991, pp. 1–2.
16 Carrington, Charles E., *Soldier from the Wars Returning* (London, Hutchinson, 1965), p. 120.
17 Gerster, M., *Die Schwaben,* pp. 108–9.
18 Ibid.
19 Müller, *Regierste der Kaiser?*, p. 179.
20 See: *Weltkrieg* (GOH), Band 10, pp. 353–60 and *Somme-Nord*, Vol. I.
21 This incident is an interesting indication of Falkenhayn's character, for he was aware of

the proposal to withdraw but did nothing to prevent it. Though it is possible that he used the retirement as the example on which he based his fateful edict that withdrawal was not an option, it is more likely that his action in removing Grünert and then Pannewitz were spiteful acts after he had been proved wrong about the sector that the Allies had chosen to attack. (See: Rupprecht, *Kriegstagebuch*, entry for 3 July 1916.)

22 General Falkenhayn, *Weltkrieg*, Band 10, p. 355.

23 Pannewitz was also removed from his Corps command by Falkenhayn and replaced by General von Quast on 5 July.

24 A captured copy of Below's Order of the Day is held in FM Sir Douglas Haig's Papers for 4 July 1916.

25 Müller, *Regierte der Kaiser?*, p. 181.

26 In archetypal style, German soldiers were pulled out of the charnel house known already as the 'mill on the Meuse' only to be dropped into a greater mincing machine soon to be equally cursed by German infantrymen as the 'mill on the Somme'.

27 Rupprecht, *Kriegstagebuch*, vol. II, p. 51.

28 General Fritz von Below, GOC German Second Army, Somme Sector 1916, Memorandum January 1917 to OHL, captured document; quoted in Baring, Maurice, *Flying Corps Headquarters 1914–1918* (London, Buchan & Enright, 1920), p. 199.

29 Müller, *Regierste der Kaiser?*, pp. 198–9.

30 Blücher, *An English Wife*, pp. 152–4.

31 Hindenburg, FM Paul von (trans. F.A. Holt), *Out of My Life* (London, Cassell, 1920), p. 217.

32 *Weltkrieg*, Band 11, 1916, Vol. II.

33 See Bischer, Oberstleutnant Alfred, Das 10. *Württembergische Infanterie Regiment Nr. 180 in der Somme Schlacht 1916* (Stuttgart, Uhland'schen Buchdruckerei, 1917), and Hammerton, J.A. and Wilson, H.W., *The Great War, A Standard History of the All-Europe Conflict* (London, Amalgamated Press, 1914–18), vol. VIII, p. 174.

34 Blücher, *An English Wife*, p. 154.

35 Reichsarchiv Monograph, 1928.

36 Carrington, *Soldier From the Wars*, pp. 122–3.

37 *BOH*, *1916*, vol. II, p. xvi.

38 *Weltkrieg*, Band 11, 1916, Vol. II.

39 Quoted in Baring, Maurice, *Flying Corps Headquarters*, p. 121.

Chapter Seven

1 Riebicke, Otto, *Was brauchte der Weltkrieg? Tatsachen und Zahlen aus den deutschen Ringer 1914–1918* (Berlin, Kyffhäuser-Verlag, 1936), p. 78.

2 Herwig, *The First World War*, p. 285

3 Ibid., pp. 291–2.

4 Glaeser, Ernst, quoted in Vincent, Paul, *The Politics of Hunger: The Allied Blockade of Germany 1915–1919* (London, Ohio University Press, 1985), pp. 21–2.

5 *Illustrierte Geschischte der Deutschen Revolution Berlin, 124* (Berlin, 1929); extract from Moyer, Laurence V., *Victory Must be Ours*, p. 174.

Chapter Eight

1 Müller, *Regierte der Kaiser?*, pp. 230–1.

2 Glaeser, Ernst, quoted in Vincent, *Politics of Hunger*, p. 22.

3 Feldman, Gerald D., *Army, Industry and Labour in Germany, 1914–1918* (Princeton, 1966), pp. 270–2.

4 Feldman, *Army, Industry and Labour*, pp. 322–4.

5 Herwig, *The First World War*, pp. 293–6.

6 Blücher, *An English Wife*, p. 166.

7 Ludendorff, *War Memories*, vol. I, pp. 307–8.

8 Jack, *General Jack's Diary*, pp. 200–1.

9 Mangin, General Charles, *Lettres de Guerre, 1914–1918* (Paris, Librairie Arthème Fayard, 1950), pp. 168–9.

Chapter Nine

1 On Arras, see Nicholls, Jonathon, *Cheerful Sacrifice: The Battle of Arras 1917* (London, Leo Cooper, 1990).

2 Blücher, *An English Wife*, p. 167.

3 Brown, Ian, 'Not Glamorous But Effective: the Canadian Corps and the Set-piece Attack, 1917–1918' (London, *Journal of Military History*, No. 58, 1994, pp. 421–44).

4 For the definitive study of the battles for Bullecourt in April and May 1917 and

detailed accounts of the German experience there, see Walker, Jonathan, *The Blood Tub, General Gough and the Battle of Bullecourt, 1917* (Staplehurst, Spellmount, 1998).
5 Ibid., pp. 104–6.
6 Ibid.
7 Named Chemin des Dames in recognition of the fact that it was a favourite riding haunt of King Louis XV's daughters.
8 See *Weltkrieg*, Band 12, pp. 307–8.
9 Ibid., p. 351.
10 Ibid., pp. 403–4.
11 Binding, *Aus dem Kriege*, pp. 158–9.
12 Müller, *Regierte der Kaiser?*, p. 264.
13 *Weltkrieg*, Band 13, pp. 20–30.
14 See Thaer, Albrecht von, *Generalstabsdienst an der Front und in der OHL: Aus Briefen und Tagebuchaufzeichnungen 1915–1919* (Güttingen, Vandenhoeck und Rupprecht, 1958).
15 Walker, *The Blood Tub*, pp. 137–87 for details of 'Second Bullecourt'.
16 Wheeler Bennett, John W., *Brest-Litovsk: The Forgotten Peace, March 1918* (London, Macmillan, 1963), pp. 37–41.

Chapter Ten

1 Füsslein dismissed the threat of large-scale mining and OHL ignored any real danger from mid-May.
2 *Weltkrieg*, Band 12, p. 453.
3 Harington, Maj-Gen Sir Charles, *Plumer of Messines* (London, Murray, 1935), p. 104.
4 Blücher, *An English Wife*, pp. 172–3.
5 Ibid., p. 177.
6 Kuhl, Gen Hermann von, *Flandern 1917*.
7 Blücher, *An English Wife*, pp. 176–7.
8 *Bayerischen Kriegsarchiv*.
9 Bucher, Leutnant Georg, *A German at Third Ypres*; Hammerton, J., *The Great War; I was There*, pp. 1240–2.
10 Ibid.
11 Kuhl, *Flandern 1917*.
12 Philippsen, diary, quoted in Ellis, *Eye Deep in Hell*, p. 165.
13 Ellis, *Eye Deep in Hell*, p. 60.
14 Remarque, Erich Maria, *All Quiet on the Western Front* (London, Putnam, 1929), p. 181; a typical description based on the letters and diaries of German infantrymen 'in the line'.
15 From *Wir Kämpfen in Weltkriege. Feldzugsbriefe under Kriegstagebücher von Front Kämpfer ans dem Material des Reichsarchivs* (Munich, 1929), p. 394.
16 Dix, Otto, *Zum 100te Geburtstag, 1891–1991*, Katalog: National Galerie Stuttgart, 1992, p. 51.
17 *Weltkrieg, Band 13: Die Kriegführung im Sommer und Herbst 1917; und Die Ereignisse ausserhalb der Westfront bis November 1918* (Berlin, Mittler, 1942).
18 Beumelberg, Werner, *Sperrfeuer um Deutschland* (Oldenburg, Stalling, 1929).
19 Lubinski, K., *Collected Memoirs, Accounts and Extracts from the Regimental History of 74th Infantry Regiment*. Liddle Collection, University of Leeds.
20 Kalepky, L., *Personal Memoirs*, held by the Liddle Collection, University of Leeds.
21 Zuckmayer, Carl, *Als wär's ein Stück von Mir. Erinnerungen* (Frankfurt-am-Main, 1969), p. 193.
22 Kuhl, *Flandern 1917*.
23 Blücher, *An English Wife*, pp. 179–80.
24 IWM SS712, BEF GHQ, November 1917. Extracts No. 12 from German Documents and Correspondence: Conditions at the Front and Military Morale (25 November 1917).

Chapter Eleven

1 Ludendorff, *War Memories*, vol. II, p. 479.
2 Ibid., pp. 590–1.
3 *BOH*, 1918, vol. II, p. 64.
4 Ludendorff, *War Memories*, pp. 458–9.
5 *BOH*, 1918, vol. I, pp. 141–2 & Appendix 20.
6 Ibid.
7 Remarque, *All Quiet on the Western Front*, p. 182.
8 Second Army Report dated 16 November 1917; *Weltkrieg*, Band 12.
9 Rupprecht Group of Armies HQ Report for 18 November 1917; *Rupprecht, Kriegstagebuch*; *Weltkrieg*, Band 12.
10 Gruppe Caudry Wng O: *Weltkrieg*, Band 12; *BOH*, 1917, vol. II, p. 49.

11 Obergefreiter Franz Benöhr, *Observations from an intelligence NCO at OHL Spa* (Courtesy of the Liddle Collection, University of Leeds).

12 Kühns, Edwin Valentine (trans: Kühns, Joy), *The Diary of a Young German Soldier, 1917–1918* (London, Avon Books Ltd, 1998), p. 17. Kühns was born on 14 February 1899, hence Valentine, in Kolonie Brinsk, Stralsburg, West Prussia. His family then moved to Thorn (now Torun, Poland) on the River Vistula (Weichsel). He entered teacher training in Thorn, but was then called up, aged 18, in 1917 as a Reservist in the Telephone Section with Inf Regt 141 and 'Division 5'. He served on the Western Front in the Arras-Cambrai sector and was involved in the 'Great Tank Battle' at Cambrai in November/December 1917. After further service throughout 1918, he returned to Thorn and took up teaching as he had planned to do before the war. He died in 1996.

13 See Jones, *War in the Air*, vol. IV, p. 232.

14 FM Haig mentioned this event in later despatches, reporting the heroic exploits of a badly wounded young German artillery officer who had manned his gun alone when all those around him were casualties and knocked out a number of British tanks before he was killed at his gun. The facts are that the German defence of Flesquières was shored up by the courage of German gunners from a number of guns who pulled their 77mm field guns out of their defensive pits to destroy the tanks. Kruger did man his gun alone, but did not destroy the British tank force alone! See Zindler, Oberleutnant E., *Die Tankschlacht bei Cambrai 1917 (Panzer Abwehr der 54th Division am 20ten November 1917)* (Wissen und Wehr, May 1937).

15 Rupprecht, Second Army, Gruppe Caudry and divisional records testify to this 'stunning effect' at the beginning of the British Third Army offensive on 20 November. See also Ludendorff, *War Memories*, vol. II, pp. 494–7.

16 Ludendorff, *War Memories*, p. 494.

17 Kühns, *Diary*, pp. 17–19.

18 Sunrise on 30 November was not until 7.43 a.m.

19 Jünger, Ernst, *In Stahlgewittern* (Berlin, E. Mittler & Sohn, 1920), vol. II, pp. 227–32.

20 Ludendorff, *War Memories*, vol. II, p. 497.

21 Benöhr, *War Memoirs/Observations*, Liddle Collection.

22 Senger und Etterlin, *Neither Fear Nor Hope*, pp. 21–2, Cambrai.

23 Kühns, *Diary*, p. 20.

24 Blücher, *An English Wife*, pp. 182–3.

Chapter Twelve

1 Kühns, *Diary*, p. 27.

2 Feldwebel Max Schultz; quoted in Middlebrook, Martin, *The Kaiser's Battle; 21 March 1918: The First Day of the German Spring Offensive* (London, Penguin, 1978), pp. 121–2.

3 Musketier Willi Raschkow, quoted in Middlebrook, *The Kaiser's Battle*, p. 145.

4 Jünger, *In Stahlgewittern*, pp. 254–5.

5 Ibid., p. 256.

6 Middlebrook, *The Kaiser's Battle*, pp. 331–2.

7 Ibid., pp. 309–22 for detailed analysis and calculation of casualties. I would recommend this as a more accurate picture of the casualties of 21 March 1918 than *Weltkrieg*, vol. 14, or the British official histories (*BOH*).

8 Ibid.

9 *BOH*, 1918, vol. II., p. 464.

10 Müller, *Regierste der Kaiser?*, pp. 343–4.

11 Ibid., p. 344.

12 Awarded to FM Blücher for the timely intervention of the Prussians in support of the Duke of Wellington in the final act of the Battle of Waterloo in June 1815.

13 Terraine, John, *White Heat: The New Warfare 1914–1918* (London, Guild, 1982), p. 286.

14 Kühns, *Diary*, p. 31.

15 Ibid., p. 43.

16 Rupprecht, *Mein Kriegstagebuch*, p. 361.

17 Henriques, J.Q. *The War History of the 1st Bn Queen's Westminster Rifles, 1914–1918* (London, Medici Society, 1923), p. 212.

18 See *Weltkrieg 1914–1918, Vierzehnter Band: Die Kriegführung and der Westen Front, 1918* (Berlin, Mittler, 1944), and *BOH*, 1918, vol II, pp. 52–4.

19 Binding, *Aus dem Kriege*, pp. 209–10.
20 'Regt No. 86' of German 18th Infantry Division: quoted in *BOH*, 1918, vol. II, p. 101.
21 Goes, Hauptmann G., *Der Tag X. Die Grosse Schlacht in Frankreich 21 März–5 April 1918* (Berlin, Kolk, 1920), p. 182.
22 Rupprecht, *Kriegstagebuch*, vol. II, pp. 370–2.
23 Ibid., pp. 371–2.
24 Ludendorff, *War Memories*, vol. II, p. 600.
25 Kuhl, Gen von Hermann, *Entstehung, Durchführung und Zusammenbruch der Offensive von 1918* (Berlin, Deutsche Verlag, 1921), p. 137.
26 Ludendorff, *War Memories*, pp. 600, 602.

Chapter Thirteen

1 *Weltkrieg*, Band 14, 1918.
2 Although these assault divisions were supported by the 44th Reserve and 16th Divisions in the second assault wave, they were also backed up by a further four divisions, namely the 12th, 48th, 240th and 216th Reserve.
3 Quotation taken from captured orders from the German assault units on 9 April.
4 It was reported that the detained German military band was due to play its regiment into Béthune after its fall (*BOH*, 1918, vol. II, pp. 175–6).
5 Rupprecht, *Kriegestagebuch*, p. 375, and also Account from *Die Bayern im grossen Kriege, 1914–1918* (Bavarian Official History).
6 Ludendorff, *War Memories*, vol. II, p. 607.
7 For full details of the circumstances of the Portuguese debacle at Neuve Chapelle and 55th Division's heroic and devastating defence around Givenchy on 9 April 1918, see *BOH*, 1918, vol. II, pp. 156–89.
8 Haig, Despatches.
9 See Kitchen, Martin, *The German Offensives of 1918* (Stroud, Tempus, 2001) as a recent example, and also US 'Historians' especially.
10 *Wissen und Wehr (Knowledge and Truth)*, Berlin, 1924 (see also *BOH*, 1918, vol. II, pp. 462–3).
11 Kabisch, Leut-Gen E., *Ergänzungen zu Streitfragen des Weltkrieges*, p. 426. See also Kabisch, Michael, *Dir Grosse Schlacht in Frankreich im Lenz 1918* (Berlin, Schlegel, 1921) for an excellent general account of the period.
12 *Weltkrieg*, Band 14: 1918, pp. 328–30.
13 Rogerson, Sidney, *The Last of the Ebb* (London, Arthur Barker, 1937).
14 *BOH*, 1918, vol. III, May–July 1918, pp. 48–9.
15 Terraine, John, *The Great War* (London, Hutchinson, 1965), p. 342. See also Kitchen, *The German Offensives*, p. 139.
16 Boraston and Bax, *The Eighth Division in War*, 1914–1918, p. 223.
17 About 50 miles.
18 Binding, *Aus dem Kriege*, p. 234.

Chapter Fourteen

1 German monograph: *Die Katastrophe des 8 August 1918* (Oldenburg, Stalling).
2 See Remarque, *All Quiet on the Western Front*, pp. 183, 185.
3 Jack, *General Jack's Diary*, p. 268.
4 Kühns, *Diary*, pp. 47–8.
5 Jack, *General Jack's Diary*, p. 298.
6 The nine battles listed by Marshal Ferdinand Foch were: Amiens, 8–13 August; Bapaume, 21 August–1 September; Scarpe (Arras), 26 August–3 September; Havrincourt and Epéhy, 12–18 September; Cambrai and the Hindenburg Line, 27 September–5 October; Flanders, with the Belgian Army, 28 September–14 October; Le Cateau, 6–12 October; the Selle, 17–25 October; the Sambre, 1–11 November. French and American offensives complemented these advances between Soissons and the Meuse-Argonne, so that the Allies had all but destroyed any cohesive German resistance by 11 November 1918.

Chapter Fifteen

1 David Fraser, *And We Shall Shock Them.*
2 Herwig, *The First World War*, p. 106.
3 Heinz, Max, *Loretto*, pp. 315–16.
4 By comparison, 30 per cent of the US population, some 20 million, were infected and 3 million (7 per cent) of the British population became victims in the same period.

BIBLIOGRAPHY

Bundesarchiv and German Archive Sources

Note: All the Reichsarchiv *Weltkrieg* vols published by E.S. Mittler und Sohn, Berlin.

Baumgarten-Crusius, Gen-Maj H., *Die Marneschlacht 1914* (Leipzig, Leopold, 1915).

Baumgarten-Crusius, Gen-Maj H., *Deutsche Heereführung im Marne-feldzug 1914* (Berlin, Scherl, 1916).

Bayerischen Kriegsarchiv, *Die Bayern im grossen Kriege, 1914–1918* (Munich, Verlag des Bayerischen Kriegsarchiv, 1928).

Berger, G., *Die 204te Infanterie Division im Weltkrieg 1914–1918* (Stuttgart, Bellser Verlag, 1922).

Beumelburg, Walter, *Flandern 1917: Schlachten des Weltkrieges* (Oldenburg, Stallung, 1928).

Gerster, M., *Die Schwaben and der Ancre* (Schwaben Redoubt): 26th Reserve Divisional History, with emphasis on the Somme campaign 1916) (Berlin, E.S. Mittler & Sohn, 1920).

Lossberg, Gen Fritz von, *Mein Tätigkeit im Weltkriege, 1914–1918* (Berlin, E.S. Mittler und Sohn, 1922).

Reichsarchiv, *Der Weltkrieg, 1914–1918, Anlage zum Ersten Band: Kriegsrüstung und Kriegswirtschaft* (Background to Vol. 1: War Establishment/Armaments and War Economy) (1930).

Reichsarchiv, *Der Weltkrieg, 1914–1918, Erster Band: Das Deutsche Feldeisenbahnwesen – Die Eisenbahnen zu Kriegsbeginn* (Vol. 1: The German Railway Network: The railway (system) at the beginning of the war) (1928).

Reichsarchiv, *Der Weltkrieg, 1914–1918, Zweiter Band: Die Befreiung Ostpreussens (Tannenberg)* (Vol. 2: The Liberation of East Prussia [1914 – Tannenberg]) (1925).

Reichsarchiv, *Der Weltkrieg, 1914–1918, Dritter Band: Der Marne-Feldzug von der Sambre zur Marne* (Vol. 3: The Marne Campaign from the Sambre to the Marne) (1926).

Reichsarchiv, *Der Weltkrieg, 1914–1918, Vierter Band: Der Marne-Feldzug: die Schlacht* (Vol. 4: The Marne Campaign: the battle) (1926).

Reichsarchiv, *Der Weltkrieg, 1914–1918, Fünfter Band: Der Herbst Feldzug 1914 – Im Westen bis zum Stellungskrieg; Im Osten bis zum Rückzug* (Vol. 5: The Autumn Campaign 1914 – in the west until trench warfare; in the east until withdrawal) (1929).

Reichsarchiv, *Der Weltkrieg, 1914–1918, Sechster Band: Der Herbst-Feldzug 1914 – Der Abschluss der Operationen in Westen und Osten* (Vol. 6: The Conclusion of Operations in the West and in the East) (1929).

Reichsarchiv, *Der Weltkrieg, 1914–1918, Siebenter Band: Die Operationen des Jahres 1915 – Die Ereignisse im Winter und Frühjahr* (Vol. 7: Operations in 1915 – the events of the winter and new year) (1931).

Reichsarchiv, *Der Weltkrieg, 1914–1918, Achter Band: Die Operationen des Jahres 1915 – Die Ereignisse im Westen im Früjahr und Sommer, im Osten vom Frujahr bis zum Jahreschluss* (Vol. 8: Operations in 1915 – the events on the Western Front in spring and summer, on the Eastern Front from spring until the end of the year) (1932).

Reichsarchiv, *Der Weltkrieg, 1914–1918, Neunter Band: Die Operationen des Jahres 1915 – Die Ereignisse im Westen und auf dem Balkan vom Sommer bis zum Jahresschluss* (Vol. 9: Operations in 1915 – the events on the Western Front and in the Balkans from summer to the end of the year) (1933).

Reichsarchiv, *Der Weltkrieg, 1914–1918, Zehnter Band: Die Operationen des Jahres 1916: bis zum Wechsel in der Obersten Heeresleitung* (Vol. 10: Operations in 1916: until the change in the High Command) (1936).

Reichsarchiv, *Der Weltkrieg, 1914–1918, Elfter Band: Die Kriegführung im Herbst 1916 und im Winter 1916/1917 – Vom Wechsel in der Obersten Heeresleitung bis zum Entschluss zum Rückzug in die Siegfried Stellung* (Vol. 11: The Conduct of the War in Autumn 1916 and Winter 1916/1917 – from the change of command to the decision to withdraw to the Siegfried Stellung/Hindenburg Line) (1938).

Reichsarchiv, *Der Weltkrieg, 1914–1918, Zwölfter Band: Die Kriegführung im Frühjahr 1917* (Vol. 12: The Conduct of the War in early 1917) (1939).

Reichsarchiv, *Der Weltkrieg, 1914–1918, Dreizehnter Band: Die Kriegführung im Sommer und Herbst 1917 – Die Ereignisse ausserhalb der Westfront bis November 1917* (Vol. 13: The Conduct of the War in Summer and Autumn 1917 and the Events beyond the Western Front (in other theatres of war) until November 1917) (1942).

Reichsarchiv, *Der Weltkrieg, 1914–1918, Vierzehnter Band: Die Kriegführung an der Westfront im Jahre 1918* (Vol. 14: The Conduct of the War on the Western Front in 1918) (1944).

Reichskriegsministerium, Heeressanitätsinspektion, *Sanitätsbericht uber das Deutsche Heer (Deutsches Feld- und Besatzungsheer) im Weltkrieg 1914–1918* (Berlin, von deutscher Kriegsanitätsbericht 1914–1918). Reichsministry reports on German military medical services (in the field and general) 1914–1918 (3 vols, including maps).

Reichsarchiv, *Schlachten des Weltkrieges. Somme-Nord [1916]* (Oldenburg, Stalling, 1920). Two vols.

'Regt. No.' – German Regimental Histories: *Erinnerungs-blätter deutscher Regimenter* (Oldenburg, Gerhard Stalling, various 1918–1930s).

Schwarte, Gen-Lt M., *Der deutsche Landkrieg, Zweite Teil: Vom Früjahr 1915 zum Winter 1916–1917* (Leipzig, Barth, 1920s).

Wellmann, Gen-Lt K., *Mit der 18ten. Reserve-Division in Frankreich (besonderes Pozières Juli–August 1916)* (Hamburg, Berngruber und Hennig, 1920).

Printed Books and Articles: German Source Material

Benöhr, Obergefreiter Franz, *Recollections*, Memoirs of Service with Intelligence Branch of Imperial German HQ (OHL) 1917–1918 (courtesy of the Liddle Collection).

Binding, Rudolf, *Aus dem Kriege*, trans. as *A Fatalist at War* (London, George Allen & Unwin, 1929).

Bloem, Walter, *Vormarsch* (Account of 12th Brandenburg Grenadier Regiment advance to the Aisne, 1914) (Leipzig, Grethlein, 1917).

Blücher, Evelyn, Princess, *An English Wife in Berlin: A Private Memoir of Events, Politics and Daily Life in Germany throughout the War and the Social Revolution in 1918* (New York, E.P. Dutton, 1920).

Brandis, Oberleutnant von, *Die Stürmer von Douaumont* (Berlin, Scherl, 1918).

Bucher, Lt Georg, *I fought on the German Side at Third Ypres.* Extract from Hammerton, Sir John, *The Great War, I was there: Undying Memories of 1914–1918, part 31, pp. 1240–44)* (London, Amalgamated Press, 1939).

Bülow, FM Klaus von, *Mein Bericht zur Marneschlacht 1914* (Berlin, Scherl, 1915).

Cron, Hermann, *Geschischte des Deutschen Heeres im Weltkriege, 1914–1918* (Berlin, Siegesmund, 1937), trans. as *Imperial German Army, 1914–1918; Organisation, Structure, Orders of Battle* (Solihull, Helion, 2002).

Einem, Gen H. von, *Ein Armee Führer erlebt den Weltkrieg* (Leipzig, 1938).

Engelmann, Joachim, *Manstein: Stratege und Trüppenführer Ein Lebensbericht in Bildern* (Friedberg, Podzun-Pallas-Verlag, 1981/82).

Falkenhayn, Gen Erich von, *Die Oberste Heeresleitung 1914–1916 in ihren wichtigsten Entschliessungen* (Berlin, Mittler, 1920), trans. as *General Headquarters, 1914–1916, and its Critical Decisions* (London, Hutchinson, 1921).

Gallwitz, Gen Max von, *Erleben im Westen 1916–1918* (Berlin, Mittler, 1928).

German General Staff, *Die Schlacht an Der Yser und bei Ypern im Herbst 1914*, Oldenburg, Gerhard Stalling, 1918, trans. as *The Battle on the Yser and of Ypres in autumn 1914*, London, Constable, 1919.

Görlitz, Walter, *Deutsche Generalstab 1657–1945*, trans. as *A History of the German General Staff*, Brian Battershaw (New York, Praeger, 1953).

Heinz, Max, trans. Ashleigh, Charles, *Loretto: Sketches of a War Volunteer* (New York, Horace Liveright, 1930).

Hierl, Oberst-Lt Constantin, *Der Weltkrieg in Umrissen* ('Sketches' of the World War, or the World War in Outline), Vols I, II & III (Charlottenburg/Berlin, Verlag 'Offene Worte', 1921 on).

Hindenburg, FM von, trans. Holt, F.A. *Out of My Life* (London, Cassell, 1920).

Hoffmann, Rudolf, *Der Deutsche Soldat – Briefe aus dem Weltkrieg [Vermächtnis]* (Munich, Albert Langen/Georg Müller, 1937). GHI Ref: Sf. 11/117.

Jahr, Dr Christoph, *Gewöhnliche Soldaten: Desertion und Deserteure im Deutschen und Britische Heer 1914–1918* (Normal soldiers: desertion and deserters in the German and British armies 1914–1918) (Göttingen, Vandenhoeck Ruprecht, 1998). GHI Ref: Sf. 10/100.

Jünger, Ernst, *In Stahlgewittern (Storm of Steel)* (Berlin, Mittler, 1920).

Kabisch, Michael, *Die Grosse Schlacht in Frankreich im Lenz 1918* (Berlin, Schlegel, 1921).

Kühl, Gen Hermann von, *Der Weltkrieg 1914–1918*, Vols. I & II (Berlin, Kolk, 1928). (Translation by Col Roderick Macleod DSO, MC, RA).

Kühl, Gen Hermann von, *Entstehung, Durchführung und Zusammenbruch der Offensive von 1918* (Berlin, Deutsche Verlag, 1921).

Kühns, Edwin Valentine, trans. Kühns, Joyce, *The Diary of a Young German Soldier, 1917–1918* (London, Avon, 1998). (Held as pre-published MSS in IWM Department of Documents, Ref: 97/4/1).

Ludendorff, Gen Erich, *My War Memories, 1914–1918, Vol. I: 1914–16, Vol. II: 1917–18* (London, Hutchinson, 1919).

Moser, Gen-Lt Otto von, *Die Württemberger in Weltkriege (1914–1918)*, Württemberg Official History (Stuttgart, Bellsen Verlag, 1925).

Muehlon, Dr Wilhelm, *Dr Muehlon's Diary [Notes written in the early part of the war by an ex-director of Krupps]* (London, Cassell, 1918). GHI Ref: Sf. 10/27a.

Müller, Admiral Georg von, *Regierte der Kaiser?* (Göttingen, Munsterschmidt-Verlag, 1949) trans. as *The Kaiser and His Court: The First World War Diaries of Admiral Georg von Müller* (London, Macdonald, 1961).

Ritter, Gerhardt, *The Schlieffen Plan: Critique of a Myth* (London, Oswald Wolff, 1958). GHI Ref: Sf.10/1815.a.

Rupprecht of Bavaria, Crown Prince, *In Treuefest: Mein Kriegstagebuch (My War Diary)* (Munich, Deutsche National Verlag, 1928).

Schubert-Weller, Christoph, *Kein Schönrer Tod: Die Militarisierung der männlichen Jugend und ihr Einsatz im Ersten Weltkrieg, 1890–1918 (No Finer Death: the militarisation of young men and their experience of the First World War, 1890–1918)* (Weinheim and Munich, Juventa Verlag, 1998). GHI Ref: Sf. 10/140.

Senger und Etterlin, Gen Frido von, *Neither Fear Nor Hope*, London, Macdonald, 1963. (First published as *Krieg in Europa*, Cologne and Berlin, Verlag Kiepenheuer & Witsch, 1960)

Stratz, Rudolf, *Der Weltkrieg, Ein deutsches Volksbuch von dem Weltgeschehen 1914 bis 1918* (A People's Book on World Events of 1914–1918) (Berlin, Verlag Scherl, 1933).

Sulzbach, Herbert, *Zwei lebende Mauern (1935)* trans. by Thonger, Richard, as *With the German Guns: Four Years on the Western Front* (London, Leo Cooper, 1973, 1998).

Tschuppik, Karl, *Ludendorff, die Tragödie des Fachmanns* (Vienna, 1930), trans. by Johnston W.H., as *Ludendorff, The Tragedy of a Specialist* (London, George Allen & Unwin, 1932).
Udet, Ernst, *Ace of the Iron Cross* (London, Newnes, 1937).
Wendt, Hermann, *Verdun 1916* (Berlin, Mittler, 1921).
Werth, German, *Verdun: Die Schlacht und der Mythos (Verdun: The Battle and the Myth)* (Bergisch Gladbach, Gustav Lübbe Verlag, 1979, 1982).
Zuckmayer, Carl, *Der Teufels General (The Devil's General)* (Berlin, Mittler, 1946).

Imperial War Museum, London

Department of Documents: Tactical Pamphlets/Captured and Translated

German Documents

SS135: Instructions for the Training of Infantry Divisions for Offensive Action, August 1917 (Revd April 1918) and The Division in the Attack, November 1918.
SS143: Platoon Training (Evolving Tactics), 1916–1918.
SS151: Notes and Information from Captured Enemy (German) Documents, March 1917 to August 1918.
SS356: Handbook of the German Army in War: January 1917/April 1918 and November 1918.
SS467: Periodical Index of German Divisions, No. 11: At 1 July 1917.
SS473, BEF GHQ, September 1916: Extracts from German Documents and Correspondence (Somme 1916).
SS474, BEF GHQ, September 1916: Reductions in the Scale of German Rations during the Somme Battle (September 1916).
SS478, BEF GHQ, September 1916: Experiences of the IVth German Corps in the Battle of the Somme during July 1916 (translation of German Report dated July 1916).
SS480, BEF GHQ, Lessons Drawn from the Somme Battle by Kampfgruppe (Battle Group) Stein, GOC IVth Reserve Corps Report, October 1916).
SS486, BEF GHQ, Extracts from German Documents dealing with 'Lessons Drawn from the Somme' (October 1916).
IWM SS490, BEF GHQ, German pamphlet on Principles of Trench Warfare (IVth Reserve Corps), dated 19 May 1916.
SS494, BEF GHQ, Extracts: Reports of German Formations employed on the Somme (6th Bavarian Reserve Division, 19 September 1916).
SS515, BEF GHQ, Extracts: German Documents and Correspondence No. 2; Somme 1916.
SS536, BEF GHQ (Intelligence), January 1917: Translation of Report on the Defence of Gommecourt on 1 July 1916 by 55th Reserve Infantry Regiment, 2nd Guards Reserve Division and 'Lessons Learned' by Gen Freiherr von Süsskind, GOC 2nd Guards Reserve Division, July 1916.
SS537, BEF GHQ (pub. March 1917): Summary of Recent Information Regarding the German Army and its Methods, January 1917.
SS540, BEF GHQ: (German) Instructions for Mine Warfare – 1917.
SS544, BEF GHQ, February 1917: Experience of the Recent Fighting at Verdun (signed by Hindenburg, dated December 1916).
SS551: Extracts from Captured German Documents and Correspondence – 1917.
SS553, BEF, GHQ, Issued May 1917: Translation of German Battle Reports: Experience of the German First and Second Army on the Somme (October 1916).
SS553A, BEF GHQ, Issued May 1917: Translation of German Battle Report: The Experience of the German First Army in the Somme Battle (September 1916).
SS555: Vocabulary of German Military Terms and Abbreviations; 1st edn 1917, 2nd edn 1918.

SS567: Diagram Showing Organisation of a German Regimental Defensive Sector: 18 July 1918.

SS574: The Construction of German Defensive Positions; 18 August 1918.

SS600: Organisation of the Infantry Battalion and Normal Formation for the Attack: April 1917.

SS642A: BEF GHQ, May 1918: Historical Notes on the German Divisions engaged on the Western Front up to January 1918.

SS703: Manual of Position Warfare for All Arms, Special Part: The Experience Gained during the English and French Offensives in Spring to October 1917.

SS710, BEF GHQ (November 1917): Translation of Pamphlet/Instructions on new German Tactics (*Brauchitsch*), dated 11 November 1917.

SS712, BEF GHQ, November 1917: Extracts No. 12 from German Documents and Correspondence: Conditions at the Front and Military Morale (25 November 1917).

SS735: BEF GHQ, Translations of Captured German Documents, February to September 1918.

SS745/SS745(2), BEF GHQ, Description of the Siegfried Line – September 1918 (German Second Army).

SS753, BEF GHQ (Intelligence): Change in Discipline and Morale of the German Army, January to September 1918 (7 September 1918).

Other German Documents on 1918: SS737, SS742, SS754, SS757, SS778, SS787.

References CDS 1–20: German Military Engineering, Mines and Trench Warfare; March 1917–November 1918.

German Miscellaneous 13 (Ger Misc 7 (13)): Brigade and Regimental War Diaries and Records 1916–1918.

Military Documents/Papers

Air Ministry (A.I.2.), *Handbook of German Military and Naval Aviation (War), 1914–1918, October 1918* (London, IWM/Battery Press, Impression, 1995).

American Expeditionary Force (AEF), General Staff, Intelligence Section, *Histories of 251 Divisions of the German Army, which participated in the war* (1914–1918) (Washington, USAF HQ, 1919).

Army Quarterly, No. XXIV, *Verdun: Falkenhayn's Strategy*.

Bischer, Oberstleutnant Alfred, *Das 10ten Württemberg Infanterie Regiment Nummer 180 in der Somme Schlacht 1916 (Ovillers/Thiepval)* (Stuttgart, Uhland'schen Buchdruckerei, 1917).

Bruchmüller, Oberst Georg, *Die Artillerie beim Angriff im Stellungskrieg* (Berlin, Mittler, 1926).

Gehre, L., *Die deutsche Kraftverteilung während des Weltkriegs* (Berlin, Mittler, 1914–1919): German Strengths in Divisions on 15th and last days of every month of the war (comparing 'Strength Returns' of BEF/French forces).

General Staff (Intelligence) BEF, Translations of primary German Tactical/Doctrine documents:

– The Attack in Position Warfare, 1 January 1918 (BEF Issue October 1918);

– The Principles of Command in the Defensive Battle in Position Warfare, 1 March 1917 (BEF issue, May 1917):

– The Principles of Command in the Defensive Battle in Position Warfare, 1 September 1917, with amendments on 7 July and 8 August 1918 (translation of text October 1918).

General Staff, War Office, *The German Forces in the Field, 7th Revision, 11 November 1918* (London, IWM/Battery Press, 1995).

General Staff (Intelligence), *Vocabulary of German Military Terms and Abbreviations*, 2nd edn, *July 1918* (London, IWM/Battery Press, 1995).

General Staff (GS BEF), *Handbook of the German Army in War, April 1918* (London, IWM/Battery Press, 1996).

Kerbey, John, *1918 – Year of Victory* (*Army Quarterly and Defence Journal*, vol. 129, no. 2, July 1999, pp. 290–5).

Wynne, G.C., *The Development of the German Defensive Battle in 1917 and its Influence on British Defensive Tactics* (*Army Quarterly*, vol. 34, April 1937).

Printed Books and Articles

Official Histories

Edmonds, Brig-Gen Sir James E., *The Official History of the War: Military Operations in France and Belgium, 1914–1918* (British Official History (*BOH*), HMSO, 1922–49).

Jones, H.A., *The War in the Air: Official History of the Great War 1914–1918* (London, HMSO/Hamish Hamilton, 1928/1969).

Bean, C.E.W, *Official History of Australia in the War of 1914–1918* (Sydney, Angus & Robertson, 1938–1942).

New Zealand, *The Official History of the New Zealand Effort in the Great War, Vol. II: The New Zealanders in France* (Auckland, Whitcombe and Tombs, 1921/1923).

Pétain, Marshal Henri Philippe, *Verdun* (Paris, Payot, 1920).

Books and Articles (General)

Ashworth, Tony, *Trench Warfare, 1914–1918: The Live and Let Live System* (London, Macmillan, 1980).

Asprey, Robert, B., *The German High Command at War: Hindenburg and Ludendorff Conduct World War I* (New York, William Morrow, 1991).

Bailey, Jonathan, *The First World War and the Birth of the Modern Style of Warfare* (Camberley, Strategic and Combat Studies Institute, 1996).

Baring, Maurice, *Flying Corps Headquarters 1914–1918* (London, Buchan & Enright, 1920).

Barnett, Correlli, *The Sword Bearers: Studies in Supreme Command in the First World War* (London, Eyre & Spottiswoode, 1963).

——, *The Great War* (London, Park Lane, 1979, republished 2003 in association with BBC re-transmission of *The Great War* TV series).

Barrie, Alexander, *War Underground* (London, Frederick Muller, 1962).

Blaxland, Gregory, *Amiens: 1918* (London, Frederick Muller, 1968).

Blond, Georges, *The Marne: The Battle that Saved Paris and Changed the Course of the War* (Paris and London, Presses de la Cité, 1962).

Bond, Brian, *War and Society in Europe 1870–1970* (Stroud, Sutton, 1984).

—— *et al.* (British Commission for Military History), *Look to Your Front: Studies in the First World War* (Staplehurst, Spellmount, 1999).

Bridgewater, Patrick, *The German Poets of the First World War* (London & Sydney, Croom Helm, 1985). GHI Ref: Sf.11/130.

Bucholz, Arden, *Moltke, Schlieffen and Prussian War Planning* (New York/Oxford, Berg, 1991). GHI Ref: Sf.10/1816.

Buffetaut, Yves (trans. Bernard Leprêtre), *The 1917 Spring Offensives; Arras, Vimy, le Chemin des Dames* (Paris, Histoire et Collections, 1999).

Cecil, Hugh and Liddle, Peter (eds), *Facing Armageddon: The First World War Experienced* (London, Leo Cooper, 1996).

Churchill, Winston S., *The World Crisis* (London, Butterworth, 1927).

Clemente, Steven, *For King and Kaiser! The Making of the Prussian Army Officer, 1860–1914* (New York/London, Greenwood, 1992). GHI Reference: Sf. 10/820.

Cooper, Bryan, *The Ironclads of Cambrai* (London, Souvenir, 1967).

Cross, Tim, *The Lost Voices of World War I: An International Anthology of Writers, Poets and Playwrights* (London, Bloomsbury, 1988).

Dennis, Peter and Grey, Jeffrey, *Defining 1918 Victory* (Canberra, Australian Army History Unit, Australian Defence Force Academy (ADFA), 1999).

—— *et al.*, *Oxford Companion to Australian Military History* (Oxford, Melbourne, Auckland, New York, OUP, 1995).

Ellis, John, *Eye Deep in Hell: The Western Front 1914–1918* (London, Croom Helm, 1979).
Evans, Martin Marix, *Retreat, Hell! We Just Got Here! The American Expeditionary Force in France 1917–1918* (Oxford, Osprey Military, 1998).
Everest, J.H., *The First Battle of the Tanks* (London, Arthur H. Stockwell, 1943).
Farrar-Hockley, A.H., *The Somme* (London, B. T. Batsford/Pan, 1964/1966).
Foley, Robert, *Alfred von Schlieffen's Military Writings* (London, Frank Cass, 2002).
——, *Institutionalised Innovation: The German Army and the Changing Nature of War 1871–1914* (London, *RUSI Journal*, April 2002).
Fraser, Gen Sir David, *Knight's Cross: A Life of Field Marshal Erwin Rommel* (London, HarperCollins, 1993).
Gibbs, Philip, *The Germans on the Somme* (London, Heinemann, 1917).
——, *From Bapaume to Passchendaele* (London, Heinemann, 1918).
——, *Realities of War* (London, Heinemann, 1920).
Gibot, Jean-Luc and Gorczynski, Philippe (translation by Wendy MacAdam), *Following the Tanks at Cambrai; 20th November – 7th December 1917* (Arras, Imprint, 1999).
Gilbert, Martin, *The First World War* (London, Weidenfeld & Nicolson, 1994).
Goodspeed, Col D.J., *Ludendorff: Soldier; Dictator; Revolutionary* (London, Rupert Hart-Davis, 1966).
Government Pamphlet, *German Prisoners in Great Britain* (Bolton & London, Tillotson, 1917/1918).
Gray, Randal, *Kaiserschlacht 1918: The Final German Offensive* (London, Osprey, 1991).
Griffith, Paddy, *Battle Tactics of the Western Front: The British Army's Art of Attack, 1916–1918* (New Haven and London, Yale University Press, 1994).
Gudmundsson, Bruce I., *Stormtroops Tactic: Innovation in the German Army 1914–1918* (New York, Praeger, 1989).
Haythornthwaite, Philip J., *The World War One Source Book* (London, Cassell, 1992).
Hedin, Sven, *With the German Armies in the West* (London, John Lane, 1915).
Herwig, Holger H., *The First World War: Germany and Austria-Hungary, 1914–1918* (London, Arnold, 1997).
Horne, Alistair, *The Price of Glory: Verdun 1916* (London, Macmillan, 1962 and edns to 1991, Penguin).
Horne, John and Kramer, Alan, *German Atrocities, 1914: A History of Denial* (New Haven and London, Yale University Press, 2001).
Howard, Prof. Michael Eliot, *The Franco-Prussian War: The German Invasion of France, 1870–1871* (London/New York, Macmillan, 1961).
Kitchen, Martin, *The German Offensives of 1918* (Stroud, Tempus, 2001).
Laffargue, Andre, *The Attack in Trench Warfare* (translated for the *US Infantry Journal*, Washington, US Infantry Association, 1916).
Leach, Barry A., *The German General Staff* (London, Ballantine, 1990).
Liddle, Peter (ed.), *Passchendaele in Perspective: The Third Battle of Ypres* (London, Leo Cooper, 1997).
Livesey, Anthony, *The Viking Atlas of World War I* (London, Viking/Penguin, 1994).
Lloyd George, David, *War Memoirs* (London, Nicolson & Watson, 1934).
Lomas, David, *First Ypres 1914: The Graveyard of the Old Contemptibles* (Oxford, Osprey, 1999).
Lupfer, Timothy T., *The Dynamics of Doctrine: The Change in German Tactical Doctrine during the First World War*, Leavenworth Papers No. 4 (Fort Leavenworth, Kansas, US Army Command and General Staff College Combat Studies Institute, 1981).
Macksey, Kenneth, *Why the Germans Lose at War* (London, Greenhill, 1996).
Martin, William, *Verdun 1916: 'They Shall Not Pass'* (Oxford, Osprey, 2001).
McCarthy, Daniel J., *The Prisoner of War in Germany* (London, Skeffington, 1919).
Middlebrook, Martin, *The First Day on the Somme* (London, Allen Lane, 1971).
——, *The Kaiser's Battle, 21 March 1918, the First Day of the German Spring Offensive* (London, Allen Lane, 1978).
—— and Middlebrook, Mary, *The Somme Battlefields, A Comprehensive Guide from Crécy to the Two World Wars* (London, Viking/Penguin, 1991/1994).

Moore, William, *A Wood Called Bourlon: The Cover-up at Cambrai, 1917* (London, Leo Cooper, 1988).
Moreland, A., *The History of the Hun* (120 cartoons) (London, Cecil Palmer & Hayward, 1917).
Morgan, J.H., MA, *German Atrocities, An Official Investigation* (London, T. Fisher Unwin, 1916).
Moyer, Laurence V., *Victory Must be Ours: Germany in the Great War 1914–1918* (London, Leo Cooper, 1995).
Nash, David, *German Infantry 1914–1918* (London, Altmark, 1971).
Nevin, Thomas, *Ernst Jünger and Germany: Into the Abyss 1914–1945* (London, Constable, 1997).
Nicholls, Jonathan, *Cheerful Sacrifice: The Battle of Arras 1917* (London, Leo Cooper, 1990).
O'Connor, Mike, *Airfields and Airmen: Somme* (Barnsley, Leo Cooper Battleground Europe Series, 2002).
Oldham, Peter, *The Hindenburg Line* (London, Leo Cooper, 1995).
——, *Messines Ridge, 1914–1918* (London, Leo Cooper, 1998).
Palazzo, Albert, *Seeking Victory on the Western Front: The British Army and Chemical Warfare in World War I* (Lincoln and London, University of Nebraska Press, 2000).
Palmer, Alan, *The Kaiser: Warlord of the Second Reich* (London, Weidenfeld & Nicolson, 1978).
Parkinson, Roger, *Tormented Warrior: Ludendorff and the Supreme Command* (London, Hodder & Stoughton, 1978).
Paschal, Colonel Rod, *The Defeat of Imperial Germany 1917–1918* (New York, De Capo, 1994).
Passingham, Ian, *Pillars of Fire: The Battle of Messines Ridge, June 1917* (Stroud, Sutton, 1998).
Pershing, General John Joseph, *My Experiences in the World War* (London, Hodder & Stoughton, 1931).
Philpott, William J., *Anglo-French Relations and Strategy on the Western Front, 1914 to 1918* (London/New York, Macmillan, 1996).
Pitt, Barrie, *1918 The Last Act* (London, Cassell, 1962).
Prior, Robin and Wilson, Trevor, *Passchendaele, the Untold Story* (New Haven & London, Yale University Press, 1996).
Remarque, Erich Maria, *All Quiet on the Western Front* (London, Putnam, 1929).
Samuels, Martin, *Doctrine and Dogma: German and British Infantry Tactics in the First World War* (New York, Greenwood, 1992).
Samuels, Martin, *Command or Control? Command, Training and Tactics in the British and German Armies, 1888–1918* (London, Frank Cass, 1996).
Sheffield, Gary, *Forgotten Victory: The First World War, Myths and Realities* (London, Headline, 2001).
Simkins, Peter, *Chronicles of the Great War: The Western Front, 1914–1918* (Godalming, CLB International and Bramley, 1991, 1997).
Sladen, Douglas (ed.), *In Ruhleben: Letters from a Prisoner to his Mother* (London, Hurst & Blackett, 1917).
Spears, Sir Edward, *Prelude to Victory* (London, Cape, 1939).
Steel, Nigel and Hart, Peter, *Tumult in the Clouds: The British Experience of the War in the Air, 1914–1918* (London, Hodder & Stoughton, 1997).
Strachan, Hew, *The First World War, Vol. I: To Arms* (Oxford, OUP, 2001).
Swinton, Maj-Gen Ernest, *Twenty Years After* (London, George Newnes, 1938).
Terraine, John, *Douglas Haig, the Educated Soldier* (London, Hutchinson, 1963).
——, *General Jack's Diary: War on the Western Front 1914–1918* (London, Cassell, 1964).
——, *The Western Front, 1914–1918* (London, Hutchinson, 1964).
——, *The Great War* (London, Hutchinson, 1965).
——, *The Road to Passchendaele: The Flanders Offensive of 1917; A Study in Inevitability* (London, Leo Cooper, 1977).
——, *The Smoke and the Fire: Myths and Anti-Myths of War 1861–1945* (London, Sidgwick & Jackson, 1980).
——, *White Heat: The New Warfare 1914–1918* (London, Guild, 1982).
——, *To Win a War: 1918, The Year of Victory* (London, Macmillan, 1986).

——, *The True Texture of the Somme* (Extract from *The Smoke and the Fire: Myths and Anti-Myths of War, 1861–1945, op. cit.,*) (WFA Occasional Paper published on the occasion of the 75th Anniversary of the Somme campaign, 1991).

Tuchmann, Barbara W., *August 1914* (London, Constable, 1962).

Van der Kiste, John, *Kaiser Wilhelm II: Germany's Last Emperor* (Stroud, Sutton, 1999, 2001).

Van Emden, Richard, *Prisoners of the Kaiser: The Last POWs of the Great War* (Barnsley, Pen & Sword, 2000).

Walker, Jonathan, *The Blood Tub: General Gough and the Battle of Bullecourt* 1917 (Staplehurst, Spellmount, 1998).

Welch, David, *Germany, Propaganda and Total War, 1914–1918; The Sins of Omission* (London, Athlone, 2000). GHI Ref: Sf. 10/165.

Wheeler-Bennett, Sir John, *Hindenburg: The Wooden Titan* (London, Macmillan, 1967).

Wilson, Jean Moorcroft, *Charles Hamilton Sorley: A Biography* (London, Cecil Woolf, 1985).

Woodward, Sir Llewellyn, *The German Withdrawal to the Hindenburg Line: the British Offensive at Arras: Failure of the Nivelle Offensive;* Ch. 18 of *Great Britain & the War of 1914–1918* (London, Methuen, 1964).

Wrigley, Chris J., *Lloyd George* (Oxford, Blackwell, 1992).

Zuber, (Col US Retd) Terence, *The Schlieffen Plan – Fantasy or Catastrophe?* (*History Today*, September 2002, pp. 40–6).

Public Record Office, Kew; Principal References

CAB 23:	War Cabinet Minutes.
WO95:	Operational War Diaries.
WO106:	Directorate of Military Operations Files.
WO153:	Artillery Operational Maps and Operation Orders (Op Os).
WO157:	Directorate of Military Intelligence Files.
WO158:	Operations, BEF.
WO 161/95–100:	Reports on British Prisoners of War (PoWs).
WO256:	Field Marshal Sir Douglas Haig: Diaries/Records, including copies of captured German orders/documents.

INDEX

Italic page numbers indicate an illustration or map.